PHILIP'S RO

DRIVER'S BRITAIN

incamerastock / Alamy

G000298206

www.philips-maps.co.uk

First published in 2006 by Philip's
a division of Octopus Publishing Group Ltd,
Carmelite House, 50 Victoria Embankment
London EC4Y 0DZ
www.octopus-publishing.co.uk
An Hachette UK company
www.hachette.co.uk

Ninth edition 2019
First impression 2019

ISBN 978-1-84907-508-4

Cartography by Philip's
Copyright © 2019 Philip's

This product includes mapping data licensed from
Ordnance Survey®, with the permission of the
Controller of Her Majesty's Stationery Office.
© Crown copyright 2019. All rights reserved.
Licence number 100011710

Information for National Parks, Areas of Outstanding Natural Beauty, National Trails and
Country Parks in Wales supplied by the Countryside Council for Wales.

Information for National Parks, Areas of Outstanding Natural Beauty, National Trails and Country Parks in
England supplied by Natural England. Data for Regional Parks, Long Distance Footpaths and Country Parks in
Scotland provided by Scottish Natural Heritage.

Gaelic name forms used in the Western Isles provided by Comhairle nan Eilean.

Data for the National Nature Reserves in England provided by Natural England. Data for the National Nature
Reserves in Wales provided by Countryside Council for Wales. Darparwyd data'n ymwneud â Gwarchodfeydd
Natur Cenedlaethol Cymru gan Gyngor Cefn Gwlad Cymru.

Information on the location of National Nature Reserves in Scotland was provided by
Scottish Natural Heritage.

Data for National Scenic Areas in Scotland provided by the Scottish Executive Office.
Crown copyright material is reproduced with the permission of the Controller of HMSO and
the Queen's Printer for Scotland. Licence number C02W0003960.

Printed in Malaysia

*Data from Nielsen Total Consumer Market 2016 weeks 1–52

Tourist information

✝ Abbey, cathedral or priory	⌂ House and garden
⌂ Ancient monument	▨ Motor racing circuit
🐟 Aquarium	🏛 Museum
🏛 Art gallery	Ⓟ Picnic area
🦅 Bird collection or aviary	🚂 Preserved railway
🏰 Castle	🏇 Race course
⛪ Church	Roman antiquity
Country park ♈ England and Wales ♈ Scotland	⑂ Safari park
🐴 Farm park	🎡 Theme park
✿ Garden	Tourist information centre 🄸 open all year 🄸 open seasonally
⚓ Historic ship	🐘 Zoo
⌂ House	✦ Other place of interest

Route-finding system

Town names printed in yellow on a green background are those used on Britain's signposts to indicate primary destinations. To find your route quickly and easily, simply follow the signs to the primary destination immediately beyond the place you require.

Below Driving from St Ives to Camborne follow the signs to Redruth, the first primary destination beyond Camborne. These will indicate the most direct main route to the side turning for Camborne.

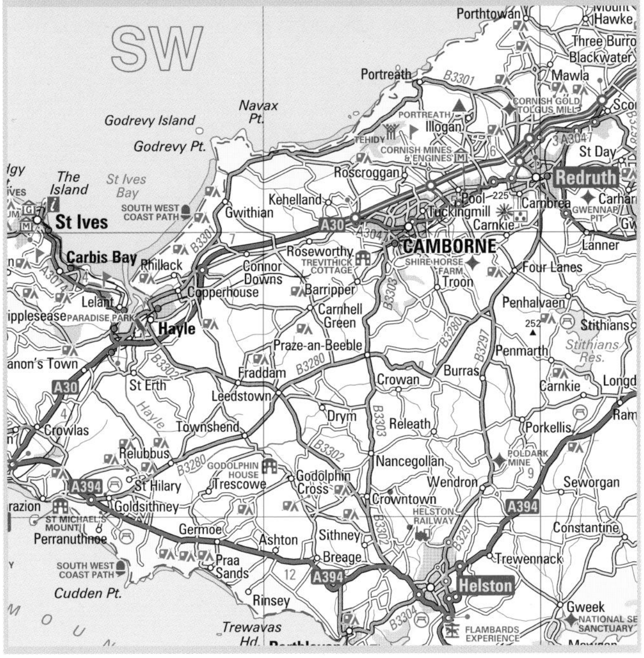

Road map symbols

══M6══	Motorway, toll motorway
④ ⑤	Motorway junction – full, restricted access
Ⓢ Ⓢ	Motorway service area – full, restricted access
═ ═ ═ ═	Motorway under construction
══A453══	Primary route – dual, single carriageway
Ⓢ	Service area, roundabout, multi-level junction
④ ⑤	Numbered junction – full, restricted access
▬ ▬ ▬ ▬	Primary route under construction
	Narrow primary route
Derby	Primary destination
A34	A road – dual, single carriageway
▬ ▬ ▬ ▬	A road under construction, narrow A road
B2135	B road – dual, single carriageway
▬ ▬ ▬ ▬	B road under construction, narrow B road
	Minor road – over 4 metres, under 4 metres wide
─ ─ ─ ─	Minor road with restricted access
─┤2├─	Distance in miles
════	Scenic route
TOLL ←	Toll, steep gradient – arrow points downhill
┤├─┤├	Tunnel
●	National trail – England and Wales
🐾	Long distance footpath – Scotland
●───	Railway with station
─×─┤ ├─●─	Level crossing, tunnel
────	Preserved railway with station
─ · ─ · ─	National boundary
─ · ─ · ─	County / unitary authority boundary
⛴ ⛴	Car ferry, catamaran
⛴ ⛴	Passenger ferry, catamaran
⛴	Hovercraft
CALAIS	Ferry destination
Ferry	Car ferry – river crossing
✈ ✈	Principal airport, other airport
	National park
	Area of Outstanding Natural Beauty – England and Wales **National Scenic Area** – Scotland forest park / regional park / national forest
	Woodland
	Beach
━━━━	Linear antiquity
─ ─ ─ ─	Roman road
⊡ ×1066	Hillfort, battlefield – with date
☼ ♣ ▲795	Viewpoint, nature reserve, spot height – in metres
⚐ ▲ ◉	Golf course, youth hostel, sporting venue
⛺ 🚐 ⛺🚐	Camp site, caravan site, camping and caravan site
🛒 ▲ P&R	Shopping village, park and ride
29	Adjoining page number – road maps

Road map scales

1:265 000 ● 1 cm = 2.65 km ● 1 inch = 4.18 miles

0 2 4 6 8 10 km
0 1 2 3 4 5 6 miles

Parts of Scotland

1:332 000 ● 1cm = 3.32km ● 1 inch = 5.24 miles

0 2 4 6 8 10 12km
0 1 2 3 4 5 6 7 8 miles

Orkney and Shetland Islands

1:400 000 ● 1 cm = 4.00km ● 1 inch = 6.31 miles

0 2 4 6 8 10 12km
0 2 4 6 8miles

Relief

Feet	metres
3000	914
2600	792
2200	671
1800	549
1400	427
1000	305
0	0

Route planning

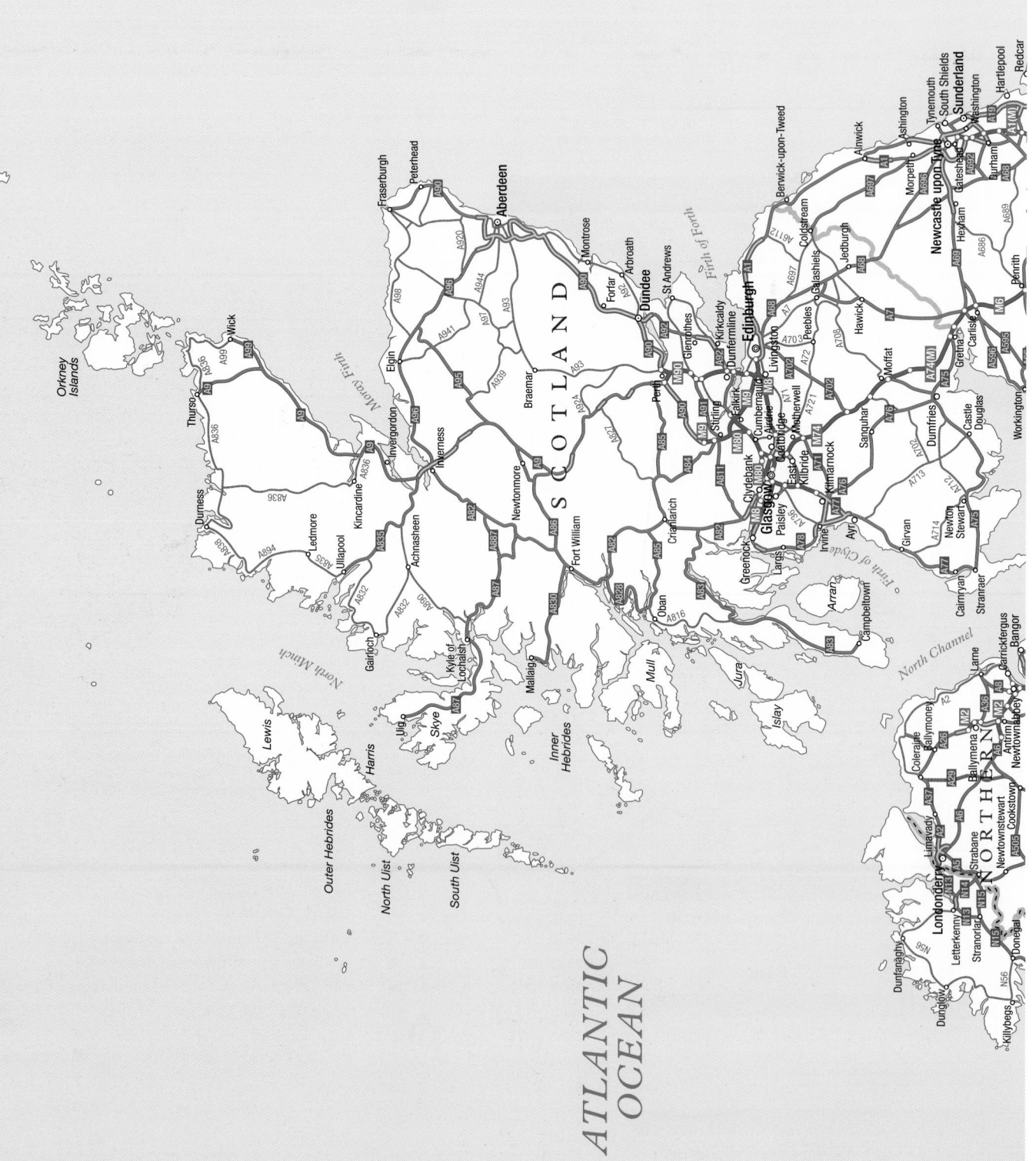
NORTH SEA
ATLANTIC OCEAN
SCOTLAND
NORTHERN
Orkney Islands
Outer Hebrides
Inner Hebrides
Lewis
Harris
North Uist
South Uist
Skye
Mull
Jura
Islay
Arran
North Minch
Moray Firth
Firth of Forth
Firth of Clyde
North Channel
Thurso
Wick
Durness
Ledmore
Ullapool
Kincardine
Invergordon
Elgin
Fraserburgh
Peterhead
Aberdeen
Inverness
Achnasheen
Gairloch
Kyle of Lochalsh
Uig
Mallaig
Fort William
Newtonmore
Braemar
Montrose
Arbroath
Forfar
Dundee
St Andrews
Glenrothes
Kirkcaldy
Dunfermline
Perth
Stirling
Falkirk
Crianlarich
Oban
Campbeltown
Greenock
Largs
Paisley
Glasgow
Clydebank
Cumbernauld
Airdrie
Coatbridge
Motherwell
East Kilbride
Kilmarnock
Irvine
Ayr
Girvan
Cairnryan
Stranraer
Newton Stewart
Edinburgh
Livingston
Peebles
Galashiels
Coldstream
Berwick-upon-Tweed
Jedburgh
Hawick
Moffat
Sanquhar
Dumfries
Castle Douglas
Gretna
Carlisle
Penrith
Workington
Alnwick
Ashington
Morpeth
Hexham
Newcastle upon Tyne
Gateshead
Tynemouth
South Shields
Sunderland
Washington
Durham
Hartlepool
Redcar
Larne
Carrickfergus
Bangor
Ballymoney
Coleraine
Ballymena
Antrim
Newtownabbey
Limavady
Londonderry
Strabane
Newtownstewart
Cookstown
Letterkenny
Stranorlar
Donegal
Dunfanaghy
Dungloe
Killybegs

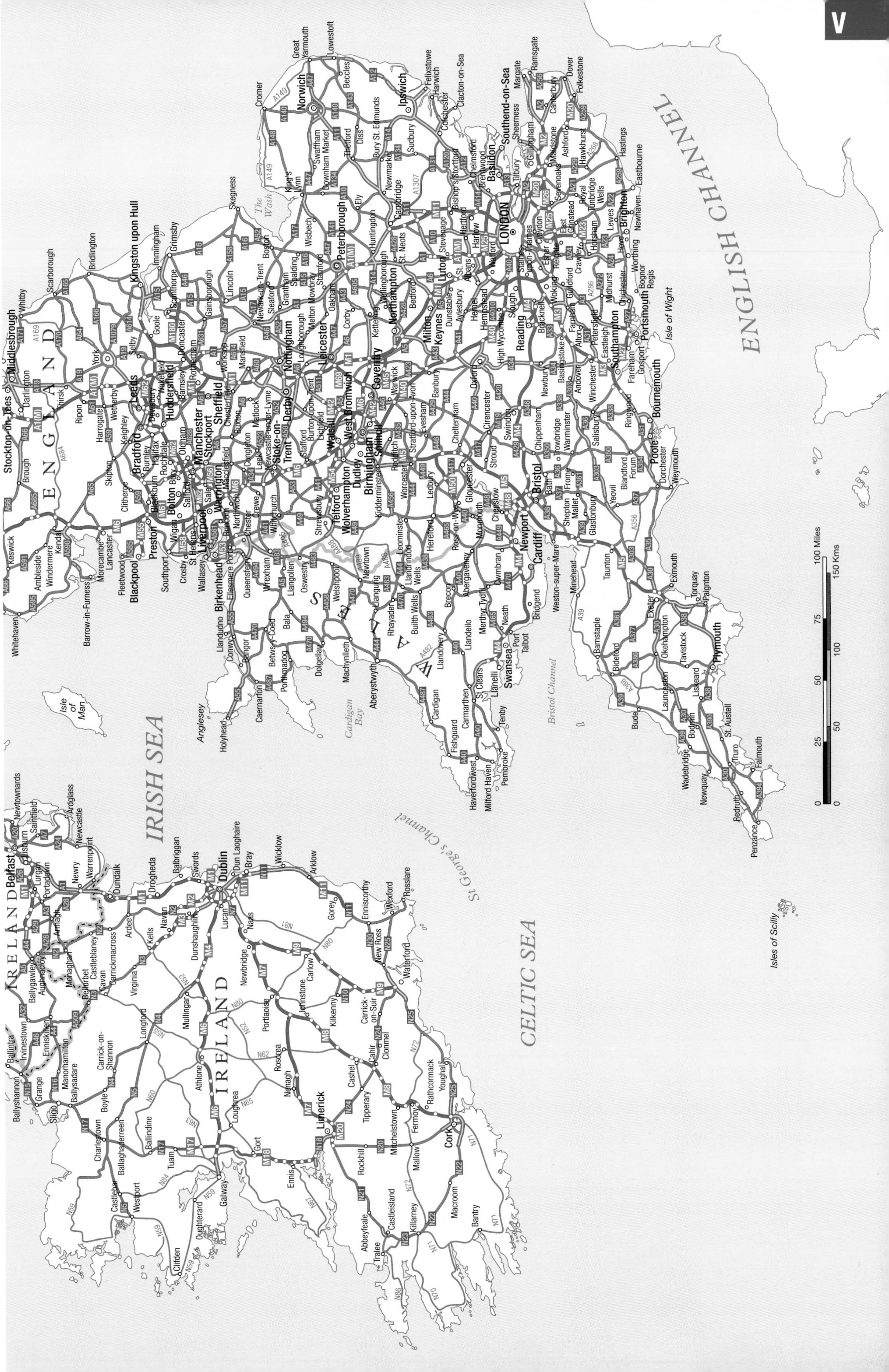

ENGLISH CHANNEL
IRISH SEA
CELTIC SEA
St George's Channel
Bristol Channel
Cardigan Bay
The Wash
Isle of Man
Isle of Wight
Isles of Scilly
Anglesey
ENGLAND
WALES
IRELAND
N. IRELAND
LONDON
Birmingham
Manchester
Liverpool
Leeds
Sheffield
Bristol
Cardiff
Newport
Swansea
Nottingham
Leicester
Coventry
Derby
Stoke-on-Trent
Wolverhampton
Bradford
Kingston upon Hull
Middlesbrough
Stockton-on-Tees
Peterborough
Norwich
Ipswich
Cambridge
Northampton
Milton Keynes
Luton
Reading
Oxford
Southampton
Portsmouth
Brighton
Bournemouth
Poole
Plymouth
Exeter
Basildon
Southend-on-Sea
Blackpool
Preston
Bolton
Warrington
Birkenhead
Huddersfield
Stockport
Walsall
West Bromwich
Dudley
Solihull
Telford
Dublin
Belfast
Cork
Limerick
Galway
Waterford
Wexford
Sligo
Dundalk
Drogheda
Kilkenny
Athlone
Tralee
Killarney
Ennis
Tuam
Westport
Castlebar
Letterkenny
Whitby
Scarborough
Bridlington
York
Lincoln
Skegness
Great Yarmouth
Lowestoft
Cromer
King's Lynn
Colchester
Chelmsford
Margate
Ramsgate
Dover
Folkestone
Canterbury
Hastings
Eastbourne
Worthing
Chichester
Salisbury
Swindon
Gloucester
Cheltenham
Worcester
Hereford
Shrewsbury
Chester
Wrexham
Aberystwyth
Carmarthen
Pembroke
Holyhead
Bangor
Llandudno
Barnstaple
Taunton
Torquay
Penzance
Truro
Falmouth
Newquay
Kendal
Keswick
Whitehaven
Lancaster
0 25 50 75 100 Miles
0 50 100 150 Kms

Borehamwood
Elstree
Aldenham
Rowley Green
Arkley
Ducks Island
Chipping Barnet
New Barnet
East Barnet
Barnet
Underhill
Oakleigh Park
Oak Hill Park
West Watford
Oxhey
Bushey
Watford Heath
Bushey Heath
Caldecote Hill
Merry Hill
Deacons Hill
Barnet Gate
Hyver Hall
Oak Lodge
Totteridge Park
Totteridge
Whetstone
Brunswick Park
Friern Barnet
London Gateway Services
Bury Fm
Brockley Hill Fm
Stanmore Hall
Stanmore Country Park
Bentley Priory
Highwood Hill
Harrow Weald Common
Carpenders Park
South Oxhey
The Kiln
Eastbury
Edgware
Mill Hill
Woodside Park
North Finchley
Colney Hatch
Collegiate School
Canons Park
Harrow Weald
Stanmore
Hatch End
Pinnerwood Park
Pinner Green
Little Stanmore
The Hive London
Burnt Oak
RAF Mus
Allianz Park
Holders Hill
Church End
Finchley
Muswell Hill
East Finchley
Belmont
Colindale
Headstone
Pinner
Wealdstone
Queensbury
Harrow
Greenhill
Kenton
Kingsbury
The Hyde
Hendon
Fortis Green
Hampstead Garden Suburb
Golders Green
Highgate
Eastcote Village
Eastcote
North Harrow
West Harrow
Harrow School
Rayners Lane
Ruislip Manor
Roxeth
Harrow on the Hill
Preston
Fryent Barn Hill
West Hendon
Cool Oak Br
Welsh Harp
Brent Cross
Dollis Hill
Child's Hill
North End
Kenwood Ho
Hampstead Heath
Highgate Cemy
Dartmouth Park
Vale of Health
Parliament Hill
South Harrow
South Ruislip
North Wembley
Wembley
Wembley Park
Neasden
Cricklewood
Hampstead
West Hampstead
Gospel Oak
Ruislip Gardens
Northolt
Sudbury
Tokyngton
Dudden Hill
Conference Centre
Wembley Stadium
Horsenden Hill
Alperton
Church End
Willesden
Willesden Green
Brondesbury
Brondesbury Park
Kilburn
South Hampstead
Camden
Primrose Hill
Jewish Mus
Kent Town
Downe Barns Fm
Perivale
Stonebridge
Harlesden
Kensal Green
Kensal Rise
St John's Wood
ZSL London Zoo
Regent's Park
Greenford
London Motorcycle Mus
Park Royal
Lower Place
College Park
Old Oak Common
West Kilburn
Maida Vale
Westbourne Green
Lisson Grove
Madame Tussauds
British Library
Yeading
North Acton
Kensal Town
North Kensington
Paddington
Linford Christie Stad
HM Prison Wormwood Scrubs
Ealing
West Acton
Bayswater
Royal Academy of Arts
Mayfair
Hayes Town
Hayes
Dormer's Wells
Southall
Hanwell
West Ealing
Ealing Common
Acton
East Acton
Shepherd's Bush
Loftus Road
Notting Hill
Kensington Gardens
Hyde Park
The Serpentine
Kensington Palace
Apsley House
Buckingham Palace
Knightsbridge
Belgravia
Minet
Southall Rly Cent
Norwood Green
Acton Green
South Acton
Bedford Park
Hammersmith
Brook Green
Holland Park
Leighton Ho Museum
Natural History & Science Mus
Kensington
Olympia
West Kensington
Earl's Court
Victoria & Albert Museum
South Kensington
Gunnersbury Park Mus
Gunnersbury
Chiswick
Heston Services
North Hyde
Harlington
Cranford Park
Cranford
Heston
Osterley Park
Osterley
Brentford End
Brentford
Griffin Pk
Steam Mus
Kew Br
Kew
Hogarth's Ho
Chiswick Ho
National Archives
Hammersmith Bridge
Chelsea
Chelsea Physic Gdn
Carlyle's Ho
Battersea Park
Battersea
Spring Grove
Syon House
Royal Botanic Gardens
Wetlands Centre
Craven Cottage
Stamford Bridge
West Brompton
Walham Green
Sands End
Parsons Green
Fulham
Putney Bridge
Clapham Junction
Clapham
Lampton
Hounslow West
Hounslow
Woodlands
Isleworth
Richmond
North Sheen
Mortlake
East Sheen
Grove Park
Barnes
Hatton
North Feltham
Hounslow Heath
Mus of Rugby
Twickenham
St Margarets
East Sheen Common
Roehampton Gate
Grove Ho
Roehampton
Putney
Putney Heath
Wandsworth
Wandsworth Common
West Hill
HM Prison
Southfields
Earlsfield
Whitton
Twickenham Stoop
Marble Hill Ho
Bog Lodge
Richmond Park
White Lodge
Petersham
Ham House
Pen Ponds
Putney Vale
Wimbledon Park
Wimbledon All England Club
Feltham
Hanworth Park
Strawberry Hill
Pembroke Lodge
Ham
Ham Common
Isabella Plantn
Thatched House Lodge
Kingston Vale
Caesar's Camp
Summerstown
Upper Tooting
Lower Feltham
Crane Park Island
Hanworth
Fulwell
Teddington
Warren Fm
Wimbledon Common
Tooting Graveney
Feltham Hill
Sunbury Common
Hampton Hill
Bartons Cott
Warren Ho
Copse Hill
Wimbledon
South Wimbledon
Furzedown
Kempton Park
Hampton
Coombe
Crooked Billet
Collier's Wood
Cottenham Park
Sunbury-on-Thames
Bushy Park
Hampton Wick
Norbiton
Merton
Mitcham
Sunbury Court
Kingston upon Thames
Upper Halliford
Molesey Reservoirs
West Molesey
Hurst Park
Hampton Court Palace
Hampton Court Park
The Cherry Red Records Stad
New Malden
Raynes Park
Cannon Hill
Merton Park
Morden Hall Park
Sunbury Lock
East Molesey
Berrylands
Bushey Mead
Morden
Seething Wells
Motspur Park
West Barnes
Thames Ditton
Queen Elizabeth II Res
Island Barn Res
Surbiton
Old Malden

Scale
1:100 000 • 1cm = 1km • 1 inch = 1.58 miles
0 1 2 3 4 5 km
0 1 2 3 miles

Distance table

John o' Groats
Kyle of Lochalsh
Inverness
Aberdeen
Braemar
Fort William
Dundee
Oban
Edinburgh
Glasgow
Berwick-upon-Tweed
Ayr
Stranraer
Newcastle upon Tyne
Carlisle
York
Kingston upon Hull
Blackpool
Leeds
Manchester
Doncaster
Holyhead
Liverpool
Sheffield
Lincoln
Nottingham
Norwich
Great Yarmouth
Shrewsbury
Leicester
Birmingham
Aberystwyth
Cambridge
Fishguard
Gloucester
Oxford
Harwich
Swansea
Cardiff
Bristol
London
Dover
Southampton
Brighton
Exeter
Bournemouth
Portsmouth
Plymouth
Land's End

How to use this table

Distances are shown in miles and kilometres with estimated journey times in hours and minutes.

For example: the distance between Dover and Fishguard is 331 miles or 533 kilometres with an estimated journey time of 6 hours, 20 minutes.

Estimated driving times are based on an average speed of 60mph on Motorways and 40mph on other roads. Drivers should allow extra time when driving at peak periods or through areas likely to be congested.

	Exeter	Edinburgh	Dundee	Dover
Dundee				523 842 9:10
Edinburgh			56 90 1:30	462 744 8:10
Exeter		450 724 8:00	518 834 9:10	248 399 4:40
Fishguard	230 370 4:30	399 642 7:30	460 740 8:30	331 533 6:20
Fort William	486 782 9:30	560 901 10:20	144 232 3:30	127 204 3:10	596 959 11:00

	Swansea	Stranraer	Southampton	Shrewsbury	Sheffield	Portsmouth	Plymouth	Oxford	Oban	Nottingham	Norwich	Newcastle upon Tyne	Manchester	Liverpool	Lincoln	Leicester	Leeds	Land's End	Kyle of Lochalsh	Kingston upon Hull	John o' Groats	Inverness	Holyhead	Harwich	Great Yarmouth	Gloucester	Glasgow	Fort William	Fishguard	Exeter	Edinburgh	Dundee	Dover	Doncaster	Carlisle	Cardiff	Cambridge	Bristol	Brighton	Braemar	Bournemouth	Blackpool	Birmingham	Berwick-upon-Tweed	Ayr	Aberystwyth	Aberdeen	London
Aberdeen																																																517 832 11:20
Aberystwyth																																															445 716 8:40	211 340 4:40
Ayr																																														317 510 6:10	183 295 4:20	394 634 7:20
Berwick-upon-Tweed																																													134 216 3:00	311 501 6:20	182 293 4:40	352 567 7:30
Birmingham																																												274 441 5:30	289 465 5:30	114 183 2:50	420 676 8:30	117 188 2:50
Blackpool																																											123 198 2:40	181 291 3:50	180 290 3:30	153 246 3:20	308 496 6:20	226 364 4:30
Bournemouth																																										270 435 5:00	147 237 3:10	412 663 7:50	436 702 8:00	207 333 4:30	564 908 10:20	107 172 2:40
Braemar																																									524 843 9:30	281 452 5:20	385 620 7:10	148 238 3:20	143 230 3:00	405 652 7:50	59 95 1:30	482 776 10:30
Brighton																																								534 859 9:40	92 148 2:10	286 460 5:20	163 262 3:20	409 658 7:40	446 718 8:00	253 407 5:10	573 922 10:30	52 84 1:50
Bristol																																							147 237 4:10	477 768 8:40	82 132 2:30	204 328 3:50	81 130 2:00	362 583 6:50	370 595 6:40	125 201 3:00	493 793 9:10	122 196 2:50
Cambridge																																						169 272 3:10	116 187 2:20	438 705 7:50	154 248 3:00	208 335 3:50	100 161 2:10	306 493 5:40	357 575 6:20	214 344 4:20	471 758 10:00	54 87 1:30
Cardiff																																					190 306 3:30	45 72 1:20	182 293 3:40	483 778 8:40	117 188 3:00	209 336 4:00	103 166 2:20	368 592 7:00	382 615 7:00	105 169 2:40	505 813 9:20	157 253 3:20
Carlisle																																				289 465 5:20	264 425 4:40	277 446 5:00	370 596 6:40	196 316 3:50	343 552 6:20	87 140 1:50	196 315 3:50	87 140 2:10	93 150 2:00	224 360 4:30	221 356 4:30	301 484 5:40
Doncaster																																			142 229 3:00	209 336 4:00	116 187 2:10	175 282 3:20	236 380 4:30	310 499 5:40	235 378 4:20	94 151 1:50	94 151 2:00	184 296 3:50	235 378 4:20	176 283 3:40	344 554 6:50	171 275 3:30
Dover																																		242 390 4:30	389 626 7:00	238 383 4:30	125 201 2:30	202 325 3:50	82 132 2:20	553 890 9:50	174 280 4:30	312 502 5:40	194 312 3:50	424 683 7:50	478 769 8:30	297 478 5:50	588 947 10:40	71 114 2:00
Dundee																																	523 842 9:10	275 443 5:00	152 245 3:00	441 710 8:00	406 654 7:10	430 692 7:40	517 832 9:10	52 84 1:20	495 797 8:50	239 385 4:30	349 562 6:20	113 182 2:40	117 188 2:30	376 605 7:10	67 108 1:50	448 721 8:40
Edinburgh																																56 90 1:30	462 744 8:10	219 352 4:00	96 154 2:00	385 620 7:00	345 555 6:10	373 600 6:50	456 734 8:20	91 146 2:10	439 707 8:00	183 295 3:30	292 470 5:30	57 92 1:40	73 117 1:50	320 515 6:20	125 201 3:10	390 628 7:20
Exeter																															450 724 8:00	518 834 9:10	248 399 4:40	251 404 4:30	353 568 6:20	121 195 2:30	249 401 4:30	76 122 1:40	184 296 5:00	550 885 9:40	82 132 2:20	282 454 5:10	157 253 3:10	428 689 7:50	446 718 7:50	201 323 4:10	569 916 10:20	181 291 3:40
Fishguard																														230 370 4:30	399 642 7:30	460 740 8:30	331 533 6:20	247 398 4:50	297 478 5:40	112 180 2:40	270 435 5:10	154 248 3:20	291 468 5:40	493 794 9:10	222 357 4:40	209 336 4:10	170 274 3:40	371 597 7:20	373 600 7:00	56 90 1:30	504 811 10:10	260 418 5:20
Fort William																													486 782 9:30	560 901 10:20	144 232 3:30	127 204 3:10	596 959 11:00	357 575 7:00	206 332 4:30	485 781 9:10	479 771 9:00	486 782 9:10	575 926 10:50	125 201 3:10	539 867 10:10	296 476 6:00	392 631 7:40	190 306 4:40	133 214 3:20	430 692 8:40	149 240 3:50	510 821 9:50
Glasgow																												101 163 2:50	376 605 7:10	449 723 8:00	44 71 1:20	83 134 2:00	488 786 8:40	249 401 4:40	96 154 2:10	385 620 7:00	372 599 6:40	373 600 6:50	468 753 8:30	110 177 2:30	439 707 8:00	183 295 3:40	292 470 5:30	101 163 2:40	33 53 1:10	320 515 6:20	145 233 3:30	397 639 7:30
Gloucester																											346 557 6:10	454 731 8:30	153 246 3:10	111 179 2:10	349 562 6:10	410 660 7:10	191 307 3:30	150 241 2:50	247 398 4:20	56 90 1:20	123 198 2:20	35 56 1:00	159 256 3:10	443 713 8:00	99 159 2:40	174 280 3:10	56 90 1:20	318 512 6:00	330 531 5:50	102 164 2:30	468 753 8:30	109 175 2:30
Great Yarmouth																										225 362 4:40	419 674 8:00	527 848 10:20	366 589 7:20	335 539 6:30	386 621 7:30	484 779 9:00	185 298 4:00	167 269 3:40	320 515 6:20	284 457 5:50	82 132 2:10	275 443 5:40	180 290 4:10	477 768 9:10	240 386 5:00	252 406 5:10	180 290 4:10	345 555 7:00	402 647 7:40	294 473 6:20	517 832 10:50	128 206 3:40
Harwich																									82 132 2:10	196 316 4:00	432 695 8:10	543 874 10:30	337 542 6:40	279 449 5:20	413 665 7:40	469 755 8:40	125 201 2:50	194 312 4:00	336 541 6:20	246 396 5:00	67 108 1:50	217 349 4:30	128 206 3:00	504 811 9:20	187 301 4:00	275 443 5:20	167 269 3:40	372 599 7:20	425 684 8:00	281 452 5:50	535 861 11:20	76 122 2:20
Holyhead																								349 562 7:10	334 538 7:00	191 307 4:00	330 531 6:40	438 705 8:50	167 269 4:00	282 454 5:40	333 536 6:40	394 634 7:30	360 580 7:00	181 291 3:50	231 372 4:50	216 348 5:40	270 435 5:20	206 332 4:30	334 538 6:40	426 686 8:20	288 463 5:50	141 227 3:20	148 238 3:30	311 501 6:30	305 491 6:10	111 179 2:50	439 707 8:40	269 433 5:40
Inverness																							474 763 9:40	569 916 11:00	553 890 11:00	504 811 9:30	166 267 4:00	66 106 1:40	542 872 10:30	618 995 11:30	158 254 3:50	132 212 3:20	622 1001 11:30	383 617 7:30	262 422 5:30	549 884 10:20	505 813 9:30	539 867 10:10	617 993 11:30	75 121 2:00	597 961 11:20	348 560 7:00	458 737 9:00	215 346 5:10	199 320 4:30	486 782 9:40	105 169 2:50	550 885 10:40
John o' Groats																						129 208 3:20	603 970 12:40	693 1116 14:00	677 1090 14:00	628 1011 12:30	295 475 7:10	195 314 5:00	671 1080 13:40	744 1197 14:30	285 459 7:00	259 417 6:30	746 1201 14:40	507 816 10:30	391 629 8:40	680 1094 13:30	630 1014 12:30	668 1075 13:20	741 1193 14:40	202 325 5:00	724 1165 14:20	478 769 10:00	574 924 11:50	342 550 8:10	328 528 7:40	601 967 12:40	232 373 5:50	663 1067 13:30
Kingston upon Hull																					518 834 10:50	394 634 7:50	231 372 4:50	196 316 4:10	207 333 5:20	169 272 3:10	254 409 4:50	369 594 7:20	280 451 5:30	309 497 5:40	234 377 4:30	295 475 5:30	256 412 4:50	47 76 1:10	158 254 3:00	244 393 4:40	139 224 3:10	233 375 4:20	245 394 4:40	327 526 6:10	264 425 5:00	127 204 2:30	134 216 2:50	185 298 3:50	251 404 4:40	223 359 4:40	364 586 7:20	184 296 3:50
Kyle of Lochalsh																				445 716 9:00	189 304 4:40	84 135 2:10	514 827 10:40	611 983 12:10	602 969 12:10	528 850 10:20	179 288 4:40	76 122 1:50	567 913 11:20	628 1011 12:00	216 348 5:20	186 299 4:40	671 1080 12:50	432 695 8:40	275 443 6:10	564 908 11:10	555 893 10:50	552 888 10:50	651 1048 12:40	159 256 4:00	618 995 12:10	372 599 7:50	471 758 9:40	263 423 6:20	212 341 5:10	499 803 10:20	189 304 4:50	586 943 11:40
Land's End																			763 1228 15:10	421 678 8:20	868 1397 17:20	741 1193 14:20	405 652 8:30	390 628 8:00	446 718 9:10	235 378 5:00	573 922 10:50	686 1104 13:20	353 568 7:20	123 198 3:20	574 924 10:50	642 1033 12:00	381 613 7:40	374 602 7:20	477 768 9:10	245 394 5:20	374 602 7:20	200 322 4:40	308 496 7:50	665 1070 12:30	205 330 5:20	405 652 8:00	281 452 6:00	552 888 10:40	570 917 10:50	313 504 6:50	692 1114 13:10	297 478 6:30
Leeds																		405 652 8:00	394 634 8:20	55 89 1:30	487 784 10:20	360 579 7:10	176 283 4:00	223 359 4:30	196 315 4:20	174 280 3:20	215 346 4:10	329 530 6:40	237 381 4:40	270 435 5:00	202 325 4:00	258 415 4:50	260 418 4:50	29 47 0:50	119 192 2:30	232 373 4:20	145 233 2:50	194 312 3:50	260 419 5:00	293 472 5:30	255 410 4:50	72 116 1:40	113 182 2:30	156 251 3:20	212 341 4:00	169 272 3:40	327 526 6:50	189 304 3:50
Leicester																	95 153 2:00	320 515 6:30	500 805 9:50	102 164 2:10	588 947 11:50	461 742 8:50	190 306 4:00	147 237 3:10	140 225 3:20	85 137 1:40	314 505 5:40	422 679 8:00	209 336 4:10	196 315 3:40	296 476 5:20	349 562 6:20	185 298 3:30	74 119 1:30	206 332 3:50	154 248 3:00	68 109 1:20	120 193 2:30	166 267 3:20	389 626 7:00	158 254 3:10	140 225 2:40	39 63 1:10	252 406 5:00	299 481 5:20	153 246 3:20	414 666 7:40	97 156 2:20
Lincoln																51 82 1:20	68 109 1:50	371 597 7:30	476 766 9:40	44 71 1:20	554 892 11:30	427 687 8:30	216 348 4:40	155 249 3:30	128 206 3:20	159 256 3:10	291 468 5:30	399 642 7:50	272 438 5:30	247 398 4:40	258 415 5:00	314 505 5:50	202 325 4:00	39 63 1:10	191 307 3:40	208 335 4:10	85 137 2:20	183 295 3:40	197 317 4:00	357 575 6:40	209 336 4:10	128 206 2:40	90 145 2:10	224 360 4:40	274 441 5:10	199 320 4:20	383 616 7:20	131 211 3:10
Liverpool															129 208 2:50	130 209 2:40	75 121 1:50	361 581 7:20	407 655 8:30	130 209 2:40	511 822 10:40	382 615 7:40	102 164 2:40	265 427 5:20	240 386 5:00	140 225 2:40	216 348 4:10	329 530 6:40	160 257 3:30	237 381 4:30	216 348 4:10	286 460 5:20	299 481 5:30	86 138 1:50	120 193 2:30	169 272 3:20	194 312 3:40	161 259 3:10	272 438 5:10	318 512 6:00	234 377 4:30	49 79 1:20	93 150 2:10	219 352 4:30	213 343 4:10	104 167 2:40	341 549 6:40	202 325 4:10
Manchester														35 56 1:10	84 135 2:00	92 148 2:00	40 64 1:10	361 581 7:20	406 654 8:30	95 153 2:10	500 805 10:30	373 600 7:30	124 200 3:00	228 367 4:40	212 341 4:30	126 203 2:30	215 346 4:10	329 530 6:40	197 317 4:00	236 380 4:20	215 346 4:10	285 459 5:20	276 444 5:10	61 98 1:30	119 192 2:30	183 295 3:40	165 266 3:10	161 259 3:10	257 414 4:50	318 512 6:00	227 365 4:20	48 77 1:20	80 129 2:00	196 315 4:00	212 341 4:00	129 208 3:00	340 547 6:30	185 298 3:50
Newcastle upon Tyne													132 212 2:50	168 270 3:20	159 256 3:20	187 301 3:40	92 148 2:10	498 802 9:40	318 512 7:00	132 212 2:50	395 636 8:50	268 431 5:40	272 438 5:40	308 496 6:00	281 452 5:40	266 428 4:50	148 238 3:10	253 407 5:20	329 529 6:20	364 586 6:30	110 177 2:20	166 267 3:20	358 576 6:30	114 183 2:20	57 92 1:50	325 523 6:00	241 388 4:20	299 481 5:30	352 567 6:30	201 323 4:00	347 558 6:30	129 208 2:40	207 333 4:10	64 103 1:50	149 240 3:00	257 414 5:20	235 378 4:50	286 460 5:40
Norwich												264 425 5:20	185 298 4:30	220 354 4:40	105 169 2:50	119 192 3:20	176 283 3:50	421 678 8:40	582 937 11:50	149 240 4:00	654 1053 13:30	529 852 10:30	311 501 6:40	73 117 2:00	20 32 0:40	204 328 4:10	385 620 9:00	504 811 10:00	343 552 7:00	308 496 6:00	366 589 7:00	422 679 8:00	174 280 3:50	147 237 3:20	289 465 5:40	262 422 5:20	62 100 1:50	252 406 5:10	175 282 4:00	457 735 8:40	214 344 4:40	232 373 4:50	166 267 3:50	328 528 6:40	382 615 7:20	276 444 6:00	496 798 9:40	114 183 3:30
Nottingham											130 209 3:40	157 253 3:10	73 118 1:40	98 158 2:10	35 56 1:10	25 40 0:50	70 113 1:40	345 555 7:00	479 771 9:40	90 145 2:00	557 896 11:30	430 692 8:20	185 298 4:00	150 241 3:20	153 246 3:30	110 177 2:10	293 472 5:30	401 646 7:50	220 354 4:30	221 356 4:10	262 422 4:50	328 528 6:00	205 330 3:50	43 69 1:10	194 312 3:40	172 277 3:20	83 134 1:40	145 233 3:00	193 311 3:50	353 568 6:30	183 295 3:40	111 179 2:20	50 80 1:20	221 356 4:30	274 441 5:10	164 264 3:40	393 633 7:30	122 196 2:40
Oban										390 628 7:30	492 792 9:40	233 375 4:50	307 494 6:00	308 496 6:10	387 623 7:30	419 674 7:50	307 494 6:00	665 1070 12:50	128 206 3:10	346 557 6:40	244 393 6:10	117 188 3:00	427 687 8:30	524 843 10:00	515 829 10:00	441 710 8:10	92 148 2:30	49 79 1:20	481 774 9:10	549 884 10:00	123 198 3:00	117 188 2:50	585 942 10:40	346 557 6:40	188 303 4:00	477 768 9:00	468 753 8:40	465 748 8:40	565 910 10:30	141 227 3:30	530 853 9:50	285 459 5:40	384 618 7:30	180 290 4:20	94 151 2:20	412 663 8:10	178 286 4:20	499 803 9:30
Oxford									462 744 8:30	109 175 2:10	145 233 3:50	260 418 4:50	144 232 2:50	172 277 3:20	137 221 2:50	73 117 1:30	168 270 3:10	274 441 5:40	550 885 10:40	192 309 3:40	656 1056 13:00	532 856 10:00	238 383 4:50	145 233 3:10	200 322 4:20	52 84 1:30	356 573 6:30	472 760 9:00	205 330 4:10	156 251 3:00	372 599 6:40	433 697 7:40	141 227 2:50	145 233 2:40	260 418 4:40	108 174 2:20	83 134 1:40	74 119 1:40	108 174 2:20	465 749 8:20	90 145 2:00	187 301 3:30	64 103 1:30	324 521 6:10	353 568 6:20	154 248 3:20	483 777 8:50	57 92 1:40
Plymouth								199 320 4:00	587 945 11:00	267 430 5:10	343 552 7:00	410 660 7:40	283 455 5:30	283 455 5:30	293 472 5:50	242 389 4:40	316 509 6:00	89 143 2:20	674 1085 13:10	355 571 6:40	790 1271 15:40	664 1069 12:30	328 528 6:40	309 497 6:10	365 588 7:20	157 253 3:20	495 797 9:10	595 958 11:20	264 425 5:30	46 74 1:30	496 798 9:00	552 888 10:00	300 483 5:50	297 478 5:40	399 642 7:20	167 269 3:40	293 472 5:30	122 196 2:50	224 361 6:00	587 945 10:40	128 206 3:30	328 528 6:10	203 327 4:20	474 763 9:00	492 792 9:00	237 382 5:10	615 990 11:20	218 351 4:40
Portsmouth							176 283 4:50	77 124 1:40	545 877 10:00	191 307 3:40	207 333 4:20	337 542 6:10	236 380 4:30	254 409 4:50	201 323 4:00	162 261 3:10	257 414 4:50	259 417 5:40	633 1019 12:10	269 433 5:00	737 1186 14:30	613 987 11:30	311 501 6:10	166 267 3:40	221 356 4:40	119 192 3:00	448 721 8:10	555 893 10:20	251 404 5:00	135 217 2:40	453 729 8:10	514 827 9:00	130 209 2:50	234 377 4:20	348 560 6:10	142 229 3:00	144 232 2:50	97 156 2:10	48 77 1:40	547 881 9:50	52 84 1:30	264 425 4:50	141 227 3:00	401 645 7:30	430 692 7:40	222 357 4:40	560 901 10:10	70 113 2:00
Sheffield						230 370 4:20	283 455 5:30	135 217 2:40	339 546 6:30	37 60 1:00	146 235 3:20	125 201 2:40	38 61 1:00	72 116 1:40	46 74 1:20	62 100 1:20	33 53 1:00	361 581 7:10	427 687 8:40	65 105 1:30	520 837 10:50	393 632 7:40	168 270 3:40	187 301 3:50	166 267 3:40	126 203 2:20	248 399 4:40	348 560 6:50	215 346 4:20	237 381 4:20	235 378 4:20	291 468 5:20	245 394 4:30	18 29 0:40	152 245 3:00	194 312 3:40	120 193 2:20	161 259 3:10	226 364 4:20	320 515 6:00	216 348 4:10	86 138 1:50	76 122 1:50	190 306 4:00	245 394 4:30	159 256 3:30	360 579 6:50	159 256 3:20
Shrewsbury					82 132 2:10	207 333 3:50	225 362 4:40	106 171 2:10	364 586 7:00	93 150 2:00	205 330 4:20	201 323 3:50	69 111 1:40	58 93 1:50	133 214 2:50	84 135 1:40	109 175 2:20	303 488 6:10	451 726 9:00	169 272 3:10	567 912 11:30	438 705 8:20	113 182 2:50	240 386 4:40	225 362 4:40	77 124 1:30	272 438 5:00	382 615 7:20	145 233 3:10	179 288 3:20	274 441 5:00	330 531 6:00	251 404 4:30	109 175 2:10	176 283 3:20	111 179 2:20	159 256 3:00	103 166 2:50	226 364 4:20	371 597 6:50	185 298 3:40	98 158 2:00	45 72 1:20	265 426 5:10	269 433 5:00	77 124 2:10	399 642 7:30	160 258 3:20
Southampton				185 298 4:10	199 320 3:40	21 34 0:50	151 243 4:10	64 103 1:30	530 853 9:40	176 283 3:20	206 332 4:20	324 521 5:50	221 356 4:10	239 385 4:30	204 328 4:00	137 220 2:40	232 373 4:20	228 367 5:00	618 995 12:00	256 412 4:40	723 1164 14:10	598 963 11:10	293 472 5:50	164 264 3:30	220 354 4:40	105 169 2:40	433 697 7:40	541 871 10:00	233 375 4:40	105 169 3:00	438 705 7:50	500 805 8:50	143 230 2:50	209 336 3:50	324 521 5:50	121 195 2:30	148 238 2:50	76 122 2:20	61 98 1:50	532 856 9:30	31 50 1:00	251 404 4:40	128 206 2:40	388 624 7:10	417 671 7:30	201 323 4:10	547 880 10:00	77 124 2:00
Stranraer			445 716 8:20	277 446 5:30	263 423 5:20	461 742 8:40	500 805 9:40	379 610 7:10	148 238 3:40	290 467 5:50	403 649 8:10	158 254 3:40	220 354 4:40	221 356 4:40	298 480 6:00	330 531 6:20	220 354 4:40	585 942 11:30	263 423 6:30	259 417 5:20	379 610 9:00	262 422 6:00	338 544 7:00	410 660 8:10	426 686 8:40	343 552 6:30	84 135 2:30	195 314 4:50	392 631 7:50	454 731 8:30	124 200 3:00	167 269 3:40	496 798 9:10	257 414 5:10	101 163 2:40	390 628 7:30	379 610 7:10	378 608 7:20	475 765 9:00	194 312 4:20	444 715 8:30	188 303 4:00	297 478 6:00	170 274 4:10	51 82 1:20	325 523 6:50	228 367 5:10	402 647 7:50
Swansea		417 671 7:50	161 259 3:00	118 190 2:20	217 349 4:00	182 293 3:30	206 332 4:10	141 227 2:40	506 815 9:20	192 309 3:40	301 485 6:00	347 559 6:20	187 301 3:30	195 314 3:40	233 375 4:30	177 285 3:20	248 399 4:40	285 459 6:00	594 956 11:30	264 425 4:50	696 1120 13:40	572 921 10:40	184 296 4:50	267 430 5:10	329 530 6:30	89 143 1:50	409 658 7:20	496 798 9:20	67 108 1:50	161 259 3:00	412 663 7:20	473 761 8:20	274 441 5:00	232 373 4:10	309 497 5:30	41 66 1:10	227 365 4:10	85 137 1:50	222 357 4:20	505 813 9:00	167 269 3:20	216 348 4:00	119 192 2:30	383 616 7:10	379 610 6:50	73 117 2:00	507 816 9:20	194 312 4:00
York	272 438 5:10	222 357 4:40	258 415 5:10	133 214 2:40	52 84 1:20	278 448 5:10	333 536 6:20	181 291 3:20	309 497 6:00	77 124 1:40	181 291 4:20	84 135 2:20	64 103 1:30	99 159 2:10	75 121 1:50	108 174 2:10	24 39 0:50	411 661 8:00	407 655 8:20	37 60 1:10	479 771 10:10	352 566 7:00	204 328 4:20	228 367 4:40	201 323 4:20	189 304 3:30	217 349 4:10	330 531 6:30	261 420 5:10	287 462 5:10	194 312 3:40	250 402 4:40	282 454 5:10	34 55 1:00	121 195 2:30	244 393 4:40	165 266 3:10	222 357 4:10	275 443 5:10	285 459 5:20	269 433 5:00	96 154 2:00	130 209 2:40	148 238 3:10	214 344 4:00	195 314 4:10	319 513 6:10	207 333 4:10

Supporting

Travel safe – Don't drive tired

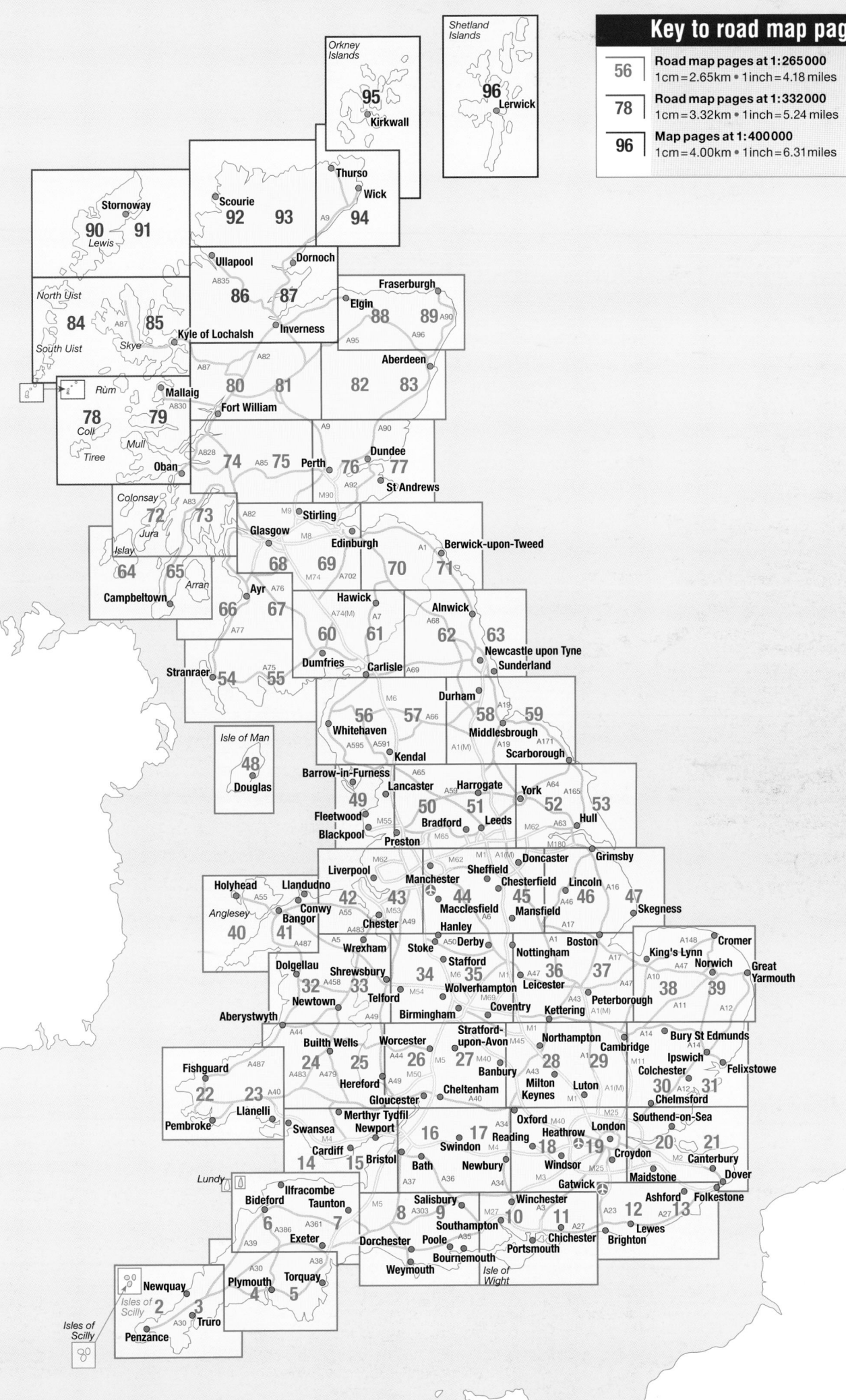

Key to road map pages

56	Road map pages at 1:265000
	1cm = 2.65km • 1inch = 4.18 miles
78	Road map pages at 1:332000
	1cm = 3.32km • 1inch = 5.24 miles
96	Map pages at 1:400000
	1cm = 4.00km • 1inch = 6.31 miles

1   3   2   3   4   5   6

B

Isles of Scilly

SV

2   2

White Island
St Helens
KING CHARLES CASTLE   St Martin's
Bryher   41   New Grimsby   Higher Town
CROMWELL'S CASTLE
Bryher   Tresco
TRESCO ABBEY GARDENS
Samson   BANT'S CARN   Eastern Isles
The Road   Crow Sound
North West Passage   INNISIDGEN CAIRNS
Newford   Maypole
LONGSTONE HERITAGE CEN
B3110   St Mary's
Hugh Town   St MARY'S
Old Town
Crim   GARRISON WALLS
Rocks   1
Broad Sound   Annet   Gugh   PENZANCE
St Agnes   (Mar-Nov)
St Mary's Sound
Smith Sound
St Agnes
Bishop
Rock

8   9

PERRANPORTH
SOUTH WEST
COAST PATH
St Agnes Hd.   Trevellas
St Agnes   Mithian
Goonbell
Porthtowan   Mount Hawke
Three Burrows
Blackwater
SW   Portreath   Illogan   CORNISH GOLD
Godrevy Island   Navax   PORTREATH   & TOLGUS MILL
Godrevy Pt.   Pt.   CORNISH MINES   St Day
The Carracks   Roscroggan   & ENGINES
The   Gwithian   Kehelland   Pool   Redruth
Clodgy   Island   Tuckingmill   Carharrack
Pt.   St Ives Bay   Roseworthy   Carnkie   Gwennap
TATE ST IVES   SOUTH WEST   TREVITHICK   CAMBORNE   Lanner
BARBARA HEPWORTH MUSEUM   COAST PATH   COTTAGE   Four Lanes
St Ives   Gwinear   SHIRE HORSE   Troon   Penhalvaen
Gurnard's   Carbis Bay   Connor Downs   FARM   Carnkie   Longdowns
Head   Zennor   Phillack   Barripper   Carnhell   Stithians
Towednack   247   Copperhouse   Green   Praze-an-Beeble   Penmarth   Res.
Porthmeor   Hayle   Crowan   Burras   Carnkie   Rame
SOUTH WEST   WAYSIDE   Lelant   Carnhell   Longdowns
COAST PATH   FOLK MUSEUM   Nancledra   Crowan
B3306   CHYSAUSTER   Canon's Town   St Erth   Drym   Releath   Porkellis
Morvah   252   ANCIENT VILLAGE   Townshend   GODOLPHIN   Nancegollan
Bojewyan   Newmill   HOUSE   Crowntown   Wendron
Pendeen   Ludgvan   Goldsithney   Tregowe   Constantine
GEEVOR TIN   Higher   Madron   P&R   Gulval   HELSTON   Trewennack
MINE MUSEUM   Boscaswell   Crowlas   RAILWAY
Trewellard   Chyandour   A30   Helubbus   A394
Botallack   Carnyorth   TRENGWAINTON   Marazion   Germoe   Ashton   Sithney   Helston
Cape   B3318   A3071   Heamoor   ST MICHAEL'S   Breage   FLAMBARDS
Cornwall   PENZANCE   MOUNT   Praa   Rinsey   EXPERIENCE
The Brisons   St Just   Newbridge   Penzance   Perranuthnoe   Sands   A394   Gweek   NATIONAL SEAL
BALLOWALL BARROW   Bosavern   SOUTH WEST   Cudden Pt.   Porthleven   The   SANCTUARY
LAND'S END   Kelynack   224 Sancreed   Newlyn   COAST PATH   Loe   Garras   Mawgan
CARN EUNY   Res.   NEWLYN   Trewavas   St Martins
ANCIENT   Tredavoe   ART GALLERY   MOUNT'S   Hd.   TREWARREN
LAND'S   VILLAGE   Paul   Porthleven   FOGOU   Newtown
END   Brane   Lower Drift   Mousehole   BAY   Sands   Gunwalloe   Cross Lanes   Traboe
Whitesand   Crows-   Catchall   St Clement's   Cudden Pt.   Cury   113
Bay   an-wra   B3283   Island   Berepper
Sennen Cove   Kerris   SOUTH WEST   Goonhilly Downs
Longships   8   COAST PATH   Mullion   Penhale   Trelan
Sennen   St Buryan   Trewoofe   St Clement's   THE
LAND'S   B3315   Island   Mullion Cove   LIZARD   Gwenter
END   Polgigga   Lamorna   TREGIFFIAN   Mullion Cove   Gweek   Kuggar
Porthcurno   BURIAL CHAMBER   Mullion Island   Predannack
Treen   Boskenna   Lamorna Cove   Wollas   St   Cadgwith
TELEGRAPH   MINACK OPEN   Vellan Hd.   Ruan   Ruan Minor
MUSEUM   St Levan   AIR THEATRE   Grade
PORTHCURNO   Gwennap Hd.   Runnel   Kynance Cove   SOUTH WEST
Stone   COAST PATH
ISLES OF SCILLY   Lizard   Hot Pt.
(Mar-Nov)   LIZARD
POINT

1

0 1 2 3 4 5 6 miles
0 1 2 3 4 5 6 7 8 9 10km   2   4   3   4   5   6

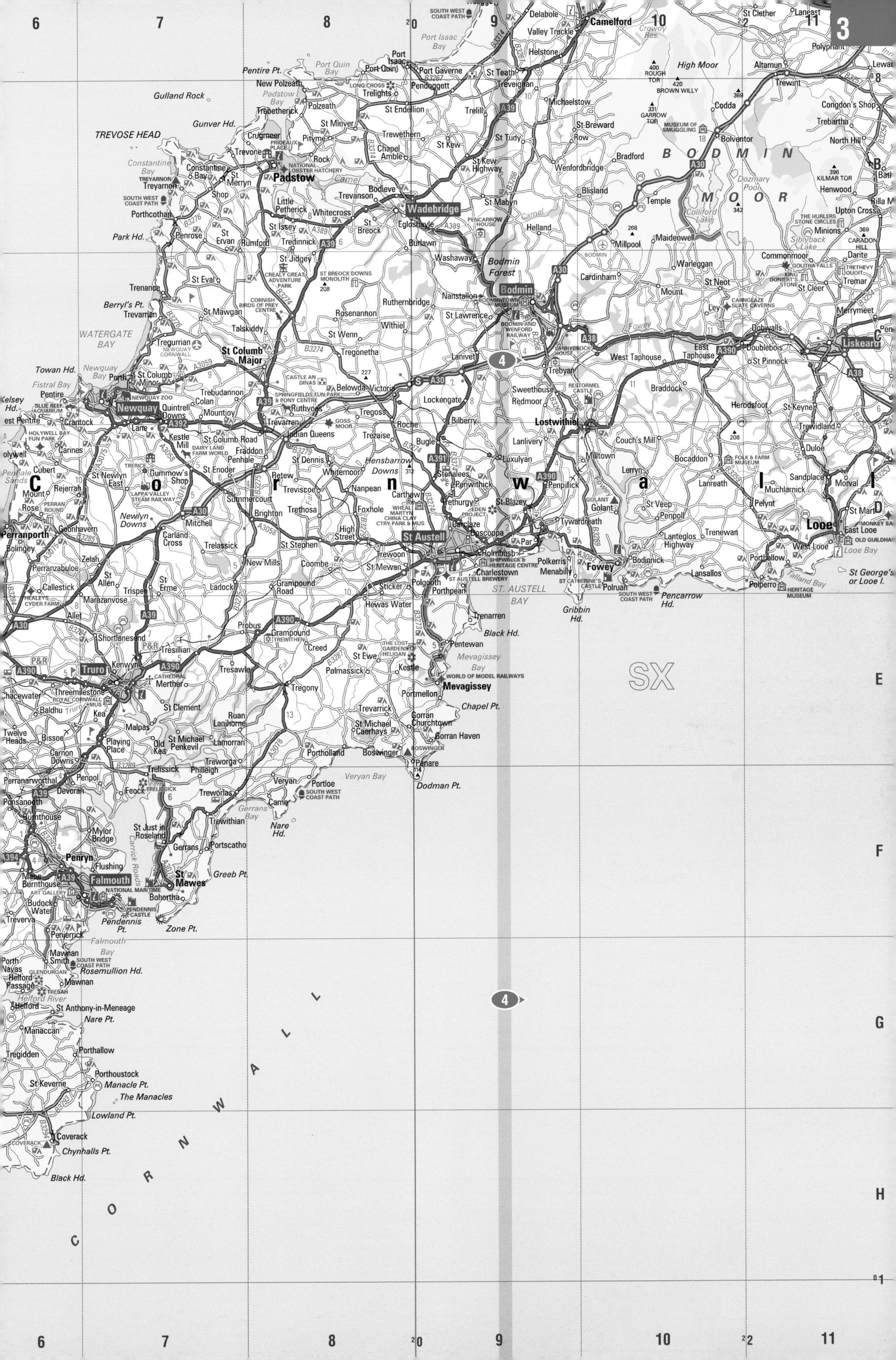

6
7
8
9
10
11
Delabole
Camelford
Valley Truckle
Helstone
Crowdy Res.
St Clether
Laneast
Polyphant
Altarnun
Trewint
High Moor
ROUGH TOR
BROWN WILLY
GARROW TOR
MUSEUM OF SMUGGLING
Codda
Bolventor
Congdon's Shop
Trebartha
North Hill
B O D M I N
M O O R
KILMAR TOR
Henwood
Dozmary Pool
Colliford Lake
Temple
Upton Cross
THE HURLERS STONE CIRCLES
Minions
Siblyback Lake
CARADON HILL
Darite
Commonmoor
GOLITHA FALLS
TRETHEVY QUOIT
KING DONIERT'S STONE
Tremar
St Cleer
Merrymeet
SOUTH WEST COAST PATH
Port Isaac Bay
Port Isaac
Port Quin Bay
Port Quin
Port Gaverne
Pendoggett
Pentire Pt.
New Polzeath
Padstow Bay
LONG CROSS
Trelights
St Endellion
St Teath
Treveighan
Trelill
Michaelstow
St Breward
Row
Gulland Rock
Trebetherick
Polzeath
St Minver
Trewethern
St Tudy
St Kew
Gunver Hd.
TREVOSE HEAD
Crugmeer
Trevone
PRIDEAUX PLACE
Pityme
Chapel Amble
Rock
St Kew Highway
Bradford
Wenfordbridge
Constantine Bay
TREYARNON
Treyarnon
NATIONAL LOBSTER HATCHERY
Padstow
Camel
St Merryn
Shop
Trevanson
Bodieve
Wadebridge
Blisland
St Mabyn
Porthcothan
Little Petherick
Whitecross
Egloshayle
PENCARROW HOUSE
Helland
St Breock
Park Hd.
Penrose
St Ervan
St Issey
Rumford
Tredinnick
Burlawn
Maidenwell
Millpool
BODMIN
St Jidgey
Washaway
Bodmin Forest
Warleggan
CREALY GREAT ADVENTURE PARK
ST BROECK DOWNS MONOLITH
Trenance
St Eval
Cardinham
St Neot
Mount
CORNISH BIRDS OF PREY CENTRE
Berryl's Pt.
Trevarrian
St Mawgan
Rutherbridge
Nanstallon
Bodmin
BODMIN TOWN MUSEUM
CARNGLAZE SLATE CAVERNS
Ley
Rosenannon
St Lawrence
BODMIN AND WENFORD RAILWAY
WATERGATE BAY
Talskiddy
St Wenn
Withiel
Tregurrian
NEWQUAY CORNWALL
St Columb Major
Tregonetha
Lanivet
LANHYDROCK HOUSE
Fowey
Dobwalls
Doublebois
Liskeard
Towan Hd.
Newquay Bay
Fistral Bay
Porth
St Columb Minor
NEWQUAY ZOO
CASTLE AN DINAS
SPRINGFIELDS FUN PARK & PONY CENTRE
Belowda
Victoria
Lockengate
Trebyan
West Taphouse
East Taphouse
St Pinnock
Pentire
Newquay
Trebudannon
Colan
Ruthvoes
Sweethouse
RESTORMEL CASTLE
Redmoor
Braddock
Kelsey Hd.
BLUE REEF AQUARIUM
Crantock
Quintrell Downs
Mountjoy
Trevarren
Tregoss
Roche
Bilberry
Lostwithiel
Herodsfoot
St Keyne
HOLYWELL BAY FUN PARK
Lane
Kestle Mill
DAIRY LAND FARM WORLD
St Columb Road
Indian Queens
GOSS MOOR
Trezaise
Bugle
Lanlivery
Couch's Mill
Trewidland
Holywell
Carines
Fraddon
Penhale
St Dennis
Hensbarrow Downs
Luxulyan
Milltown
Duloe
Penhale Sands
Cubert
TRERICE
Gummow's Shop
St Newlyn East
St Enoder
Whitemoor
Stenalees
Bocaddon
FOLK & FARM MUSEUM
Lerryn
Sandplace
Morval
Mount
Rejerrah
LAPPA VALLEY STEAM RAILWAY
Retew
Treviscoe
Nanpean
Carthew
Penwithick
Penpillick
Lanreath
Muchlarnick
C o r n w a l l
Rose
PERRAN ROUND
Summercourt
WHEAL MARTYN CHINA CLAY CTRY PARK & MUS
Trethurgy
EDEN PROJECT
St Blazey
GOLANT
Golant
St Veep
Penpoll
Pelynt
St Martin
Newlyn Downs
Mitchell
Brighton
Trethosa
Foxhole
Carclaze
Tywardreath
Looe
MONKEY SANCTUARY
East Looe
OLD GUILDHALL
Perranporth
Goonhavern
Carland Cross
High Street
St Austell
Boscoppa
Par
Lanteglos Highway
Trenewan
West Looe
Looe Bay
Bolingey
Zelah
Trelassick
St Stephen
Trewoon
Holmbush
Polkerris
Menabilly
Bodinnick
Fowey
Lansallos
Portnallow
Talland Bay
St George's or Looe I.
Perranzabuloe
St Allen
New Mills
Coombe
St Mewan
Charlestown
SHIPWRECK & HERITAGE CENTRE
ST CATHERINE'S CASTLE
Polruan
Polperro
HERITAGE MUSEUM
Callestick
HEALEYS CYDER FARM
Trispen
St Erme
Ladock
Grampound Road
Sticker
Polgooth
ST AUSTELL BREWERY
Porthpean
ST. AUSTELL BAY
SOUTH WEST COAST PATH
Pencarrow Hd.
Marazanvose
Hewas Water
Gribbin Hd.
Allet
Probus
Grampound
TREWITHEN
Trenarren
Black Hd.
Shortlanesend
P&R
Tresillian
Creed
THE LOST GARDENS OF HELIGAN
Pentewan
Mevagissey Bay
Kenwyn
Truro
Tresawle
St Ewe
Kestle
SX
Merther
CATHEDRAL
Polmassick
WORLD OF MODEL RAILWAYS
Mevagissey
Chacewater
Threemilestone
ROYAL CORNWALL MUS
Fal
Tregony
Portmellon
Baldhu
Kea
St Clement
Chapel Pt.
Ruan Lanihorne
Trevarrick
Gorran Churchtown
Twelve Heads
Bissoe
Malpas
St Michael Caerhays
Gorran Haven
Playing Place
Old Kea
St Michael Penkevil
Lamorran
Carnon Downs
Portholland
Boswinger
BOSWINGER
Treworga
Penare
Perranarworthal
Penpol
Trelissick
Philleigh
Veryan Bay
Devoran
Feock
TRELISSICK
Veryan
Portloe
Dodman Pt.
Ponsanooth
Treworlas
Carne
Gerrans Bay
Burnthouse
Trewithian
Nare Hd.
Mylor Bridge
St Just in Roseland
Carrick Roads
Gerrans
Portscatho
Penryn
Flushing
St Mawes
Greeb Pt.
Mabe Burnthouse
Falmouth
ART GALLERY
NATIONAL MARITIME
Bohortha
Budock Water
PENDENNIS CASTLE
Treverva
Pendennis Pt.
Zone Pt.
Penjerrick
Falmouth Bay
Mawnan Smith
SOUTH WEST COAST PATH
Rosemullion Hd.
Port Navas
GLENDURGAN
Helford Passage
TREBAH
Mawnan
Helford River
Helford
St Anthony-in-Meneage
Nare Pt.
Manaccan
Tregidden
Porthallow
Porthoustock
St Keverne
Manacle Pt.
The Manacles
Lowland Pt.
Coverack
COVERACK
Chynhalls Pt.
Black Hd.
C O R N W A L L
A30
A39
A38
A390
A391
A392
A3058
A3075
A3076
A3078
A3082
A389
A3059
B3266
B3267
B3314
B3274
B3276
B3279
B3275
B3285
B3284
B3287
B3273
B3289
B3268
B3269
B3359
B3254
B3292
B3293
B3294
B3253
B3257
4
B
C
D
E
F
G
H
1

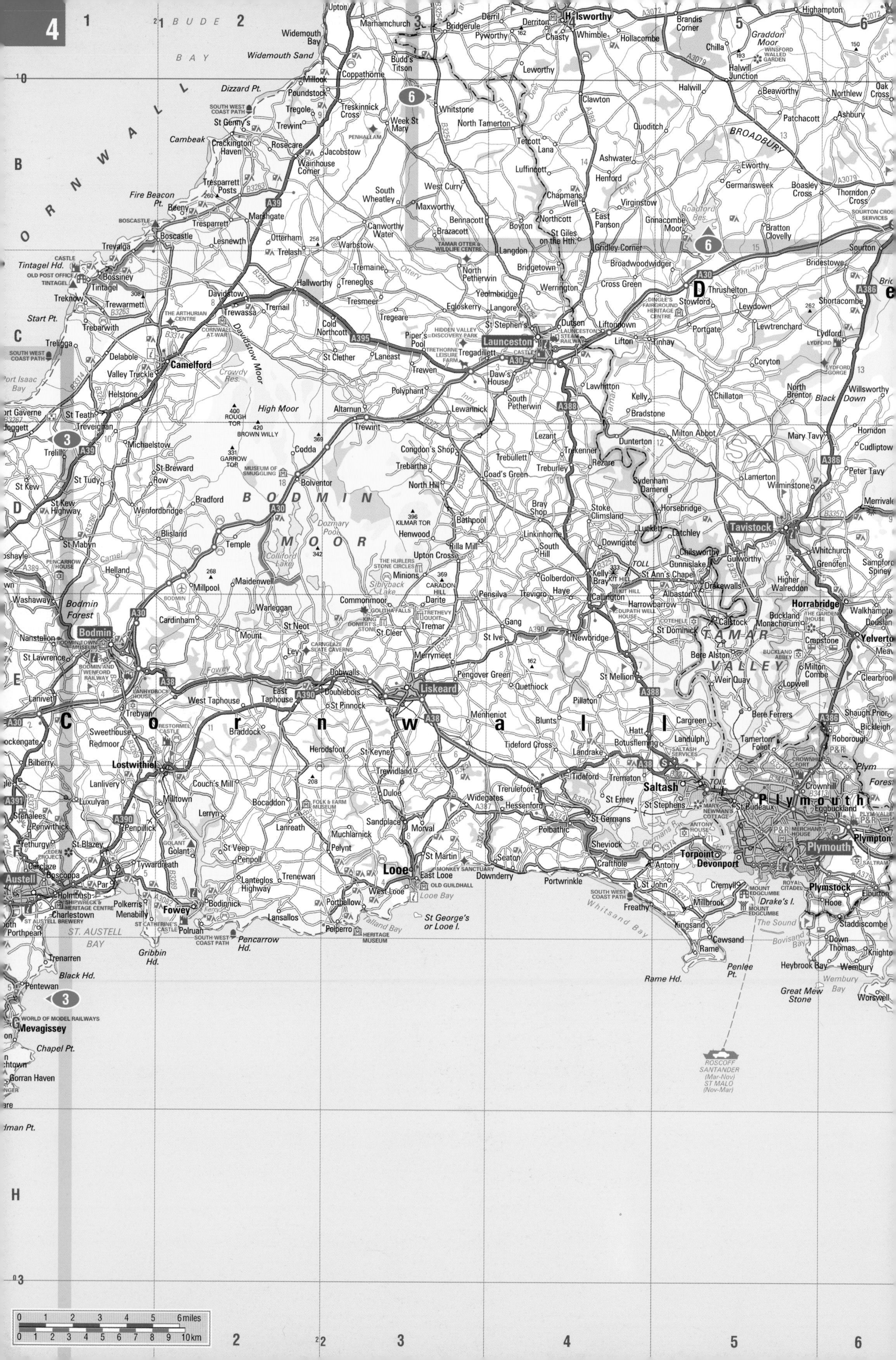
BUDE BAY
Widemouth Sand
Widemouth Bay
CORNWALL
Dizzard Pt.
Cambeak
Fire Beacon Pt.
Boscastle
Tintagel Hd.
Tintagel
Start Pt.
Port Isaac Bay
Camelford
Davidstow Moor
Crowdy Res.
High Moor
ROUGH TOR
BROWN WILLY
Bodmin Moor
Dozmary Pool
Colliford Lake
KILMAR TOR
Bodmin
Bodmin Forest
Launceston
Holsworthy
Tavistock
Liskeard
Lostwithiel
Fowey
Looe
Saltash
Plymouth
Plympton
Plymstock
Devonport
Torpoint
Horrabridge
Yelverton
Mevagissey
Polperro
St. Austell Bay
Austell
Black Hd.
Chapel Pt.
Gorran Haven
Gribbin Hd.
Pencarrow Hd.
Talland Bay
Looe Bay
St George's or Looe I.
Whitsand Bay
Rame Hd.
Penlee Pt.
Drake's I.
The Sound
Bovisand Bay
Heybrook Bay
Great Mew Stone
Wembury Bay
TAMAR VALLEY
BROADBURY
Roadford Res.
Cornwall
D
ROSCOFF SANTANDER (Mar-Nov) ST MALO (Nov-Mar)
A39
A30
A395
A38
A390
A388
A386
A3072
A3079
A387
A374
0 1 2 3 4 5 6 miles
0 1 2 3 4 5 6 7 8 9 10 km

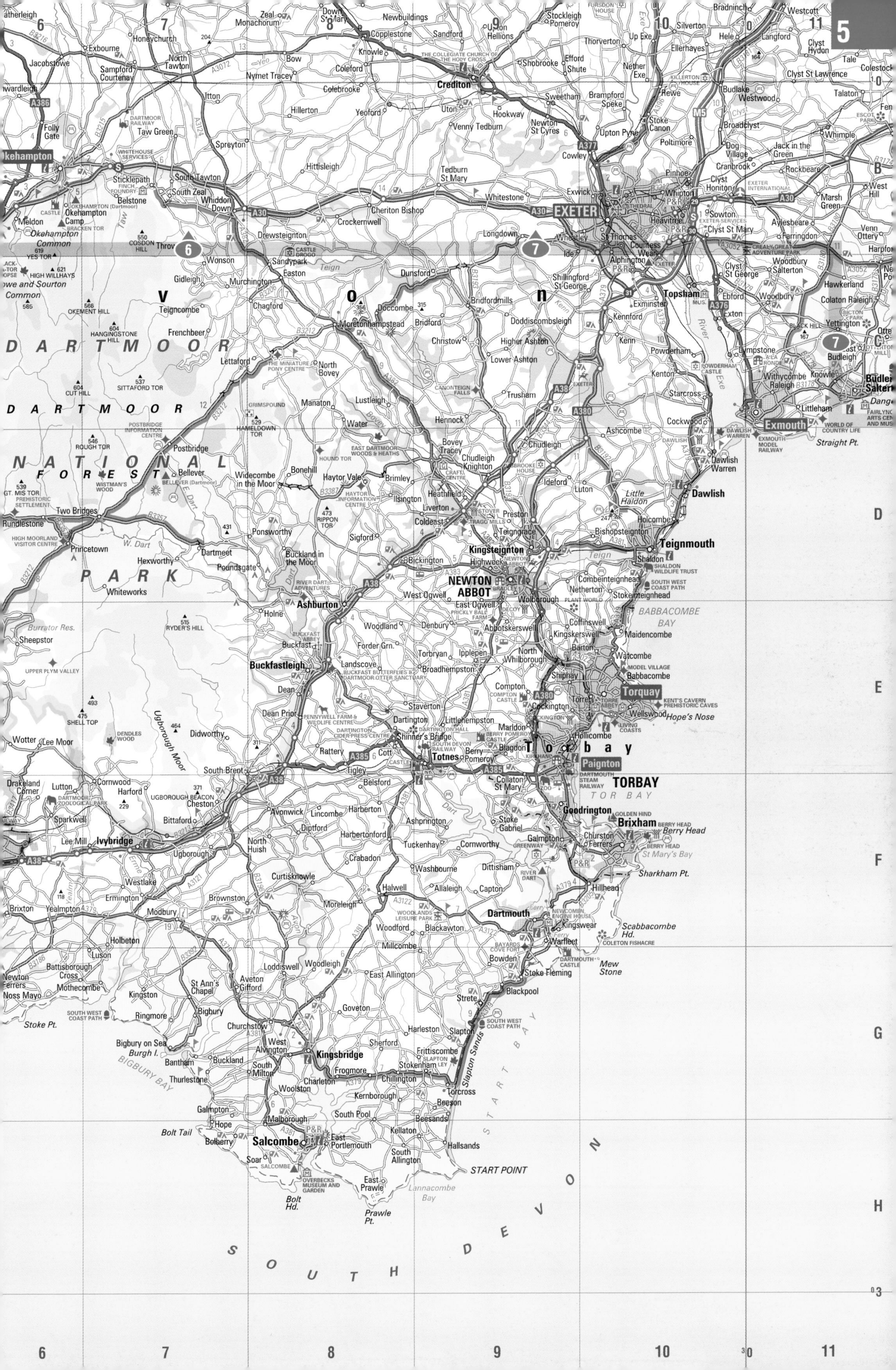

DARTMOOR
DARTMOOR NATIONAL FOREST PARK
DEVON
SOUTH DEVON
TORBAY
Tor bay
EXETER
Okehampton
Exmouth
Torquay
Paignton
Crediton
Copplestone
Newbuildings
Sandford
Bow
Coleford
Colebrooke
Yeoford
Hillerton
North Tawton
Sampford Courtenay
Exbourne
Jacobstowe
Honeychurch
Zeal Monachorum
Down St Mary
Nymet Tracey
Knowle
Itton
Spreyton
Taw Green
Folly Gate
Sticklepath
Belstone
South Tawton
South Zeal
Whiddon Down
Hittisleigh
Tedburn St Mary
Cheriton Bishop
Crockernwell
Drewsteignton
Sandypark
Easton
Murchington
Gidleigh
Chagford
Teigncombe
Frenchbeer
Lettaford
Moretonhampstead
Doccombe
Bridford
Christow
Dunsford
Longdown
Whitestone
Exwick
Ide
Alphington
Countess Wear
St Thomas
Heavitree
Whipton
Pinhoe
Sowton
Clyst St Mary
Clyst Honiton
Topsham
Exminster
Kennford
Kenn
Powderham
Kenton
Starcross
Cockwood
Dawlish Warren
Dawlish
Holcombe
Teignmouth
Shaldon
Bishopsteignton
Lympstone
Woodbury
Woodbury Salterton
Exton
Ebford
Withycombe Raleigh
Littleham
Budleigh Salterton
Knowle
Yettington
Colaton Raleigh
Hawkerland
Aylesbeare
Farringdon
Rockbeare
Marsh Green
Whimple
Broadclyst
Jack in the Green
Cranbrook
Dog Village
Poltimore
Stoke Canon
Rewe
Upton Pyne
Cowley
Newton St Cyres
Sweetham
Brampford Speke
Thorverton
Shobrooke
Efford
Shute
Nether Exe
Up Exe
Silverton
Ellerhayes
Bradninch
Hele
Westcott
Langford
Clyst Hydon
Clyst St Lawrence
Talaton
Budlake
Westwood
Stockleigh Pomeroy
Upton Hellions
Uton
Venny Tedburn
Hookway
Shillingford St George
Bridfordmills
Doddiscombsleigh
Higher Ashton
Lower Ashton
Trusham
Hennock
Chudleigh
Chudleigh Knighton
Bovey Tracey
Lustleigh
Manaton
North Bovey
Water
Haytor Vale
Brimley
Bonehill
Widecombe in the Moor
Ilsington
Heathfield
Liverton
Coldeast
Sigford
Bickington
Kingsteignton
Highweek
Newton Abbot
Preston
Teigngrace
Ideford
Luton
Little Haldon
Ashcombe
Combeinteignhead
Netherton
Stokeinteignhead
Coffinswell
Kingskerswell
Maidencombe
Watcombe
Babbacombe
Barton
Shiphay
Torre
Wellswood
Hope's Nose
Cockington
Hollicombe
Preston
Marldon
Compton
Blagdon
Collaton St Mary
Goodrington
Brixham
Berry Head
Churston Ferrers
Galmpton
Stoke Gabriel
Sharkham Pt.
Hillhead
Kingswear
Dartmouth
Warfleet
Scabbacombe Hd.
Mew Stone
Stoke Fleming
Blackpool
Strete
Slapton
Slapton Sands
Torcross
Beeson
Beesands
Hallsands
Start Point
Start Bay
Kellaton
South Allington
East Prawle
Prawle Pt.
Lannacombe Bay
East Portlemouth
Salcombe
Malborough
Bolt Hd.
Bolt Tail
Soar
Bolberry
Hope
Galmpton
Thurlestone
Bantham
Buckland
South Milton
Woolston
West Alvington
Kingsbridge
Frogmore
Chillington
Stokenham
Frittiscombe
Sherford
Charleton
Kernborough
South Pool
Harleston
Goveton
East Allington
Woodleigh
Loddiswell
Churchstow
Aveton Gifford
Bigbury
Bigbury on Sea
Burgh I.
Bigbury Bay
Ringmore
Kingston
St Ann's Chapel
Mothecombe
Battisborough Cross
Newton Ferrers
Noss Mayo
Stoke Pt.
Holbeton
Luson
Modbury
Yealmpton
Brixton
Ermington
Westlake
Ugborough
Ivybridge
Lee Mill
Sparkwell
Lutton
Drakeland Corner
Cornwood
Harford
Cheston
Bittaford
South Brent
Wotter
Lee Moor
Didworthy
Avonwick
Lincombe
Diptford
North Huish
Harberton
Harbertonford
Ashprington
Tuckenhay
Cornworthy
Dittisham
Washbourne
Allaleigh
Capton
Halwell
Moreleigh
Curtisknowle
Crabadon
Woodford
Blackawton
Millcombe
Bowden
Totnes
Tigley
Belsford
Rattery
Cott
Shinner's Bridge
Dartington
Staverton
Littlehempston
Berry Pomeroy
Dean Prior
Dean
Buckfastleigh
Buckfast
Landscove
Forder Grn.
Woodland
Denbury
Torbryan
Ipplepen
Broadhempston
North Whilborough
Abbotskerswell
East Ogwell
West Ogwell
Wolborough
Ashburton
Holne
Buckland in the Moor
Ponsworthy
Dartmeet
Poundsgate
Hexworthy
Princetown
Two Bridges
Rundlestone
Whiteworks
Sheepstor
Burrator Res.
Postbridge
Bellever
Meldon
Okehampton Camp
Okehampton Common
Throwleigh
Wonson
Yes Tor
High Willhays
Okement Hill
Hangingstone Hill
Cut Hill
Sittaford Tor
Hameldown Tor
Rough Tor
Great Mis Tor
Rippon Tor
Hound Tor
Ryder's Hill
Shell Top
Ugborough Moor
Ugborough Beacon
Cosdon Hill
Babbacombe Bay
Tor Bay
Straight Pt.
St Mary's Bay
Exe
Teign
Dart
Avon
Erme
Yealm
Bovey
Taw
Yeo
Kenn
A30
A38
A380
A381
A382
A383
A385
A386
A3072
A3121
A3122
A376
A377
A379
A3052
M5
B3212
B3357
B3387
B3193
B3192
B3178
B3179
B3180
B3196
B3197
B3205
B3213
B3215
B3216
B3217
B3186
B3344
B3195
6
7
8
9
10
11
B
C
D
E
F
G
H

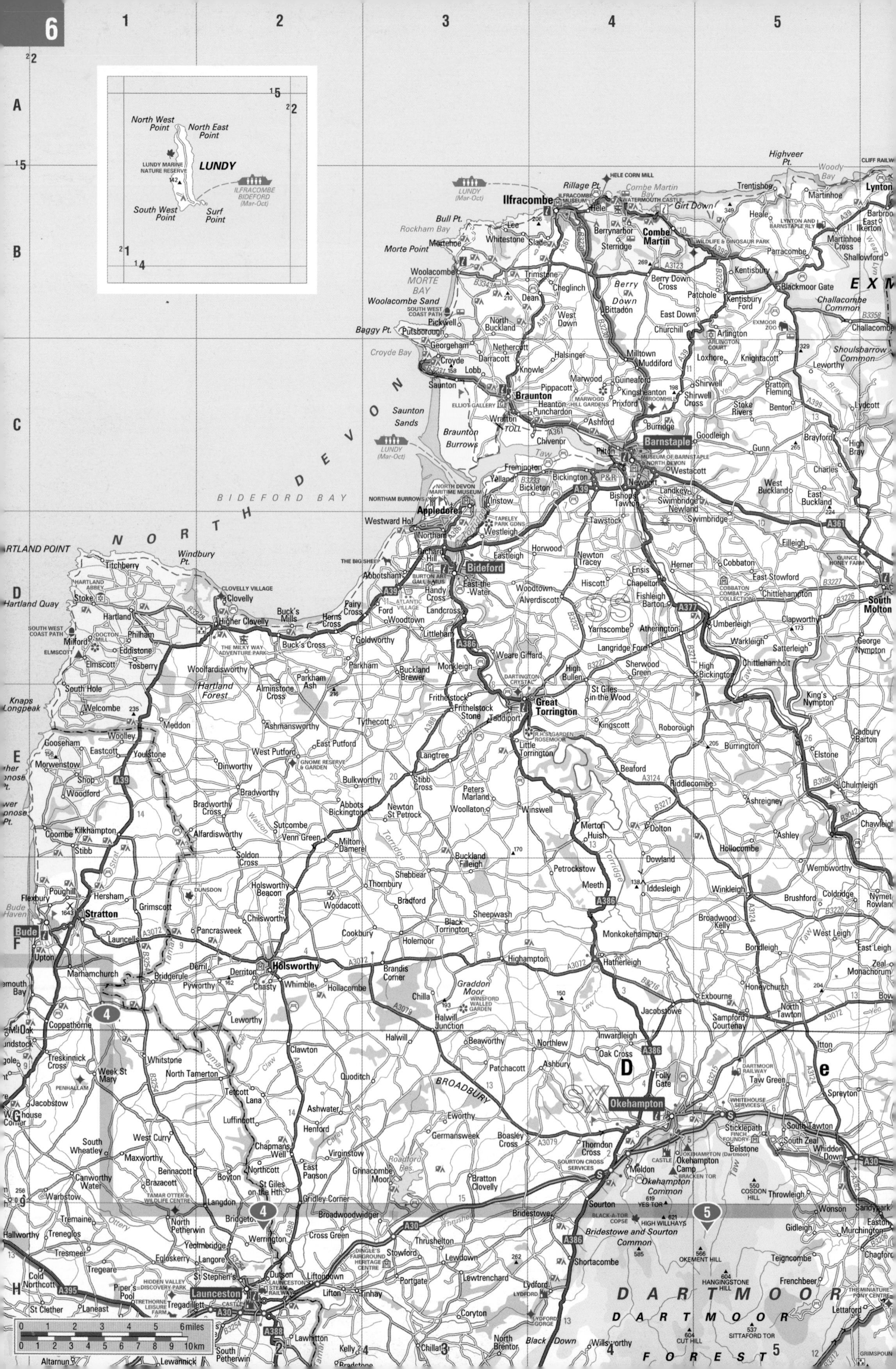
1
2
3
4
5
A
B
C
D
E
F
G
H
North West Point
North East Point
LUNDY
LUNDY MARINE NATURE RESERVE
142
ILFRACOMBE BIDEFORD (Mar-Oct)
South West Point
Surf Point
LUNDY (Mar-Oct)
Highveer Pt.
Woody Bay
CLIFF RAILWAY
Lynton
HELE CORN MILL
Rillage Pt.
Combe Martin Bay
Ilfracombe
ILFRACOMBE MUSEUM
WATERMOUTH CASTLE
Hele
Girt Down
Trentishoe
Martinhoe
Heale
Barbrook
LYNTON AND BARNSTAPLE RLY
Bull Pt.
Rockham Bay
Lee
Whitestone
Slade
Berrynarbor
Combe Martin
WILDLIFE & DINOSAUR PARK
Parracombe
Martinhoe Cross
Shallowford
East Ilkerton
Morte Point
Mortehoe
Sterridge
Woolacombe
MORTE BAY
Trimstone
Cheglinch
Berry Down
Berry Down Cross
Kentisbury
Blackmoor Gate
EXM
Woolacombe Sand
SOUTH WEST COAST PATH
Dean
Bittadon
Patchole
Kentisbury Ford
Challacombe Common
Pickwell
North Buckland
West Down
East Down
EXMOOR ZOO
Challacombe
Baggy Pt.
Putsborough
Churchill
Arlington
ARLINGTON COURT
Croyde Bay
Georgeham
Nethercott
Milltown
Shoulsbarrow Common
Croyde
Darracott
Halsinger
Muddiford
Loxhore
Knightacott
Leworthy
Lobb
Knowle
Saunton
Marwood
Guineaford
Shirwell
Bratton Fleming
Braunton
Pippacott
Kingsheanton
BROOMHILL
Shirwell Cross
ELLIOT GALLERY
MARWOOD HILL GARDENS
Heanton Punchardon
Prixford
Stoke Rivers
Benton
Lydcott
Saunton Sands
Wrafton
TOLL
Ashford
Burridge
Braunton Burrows
Chivenor
Pilton
Barnstaple
Goodleigh
Gunn
Brayford
High Bray
Taw
MUSEUM OF BARNSTAPLE & NORTH DEVON
Fremington
Yelland
Bickington
P&R
Newport
Westacott
Charles
NORTH DEVON MARITIME MUSEUM
Bickleton
Bishops Tawton
Landkey
West Buckland
BIDEFORD BAY
NORTHAM BURROWS
Appledore
Instow
Swimbridge Newland
East Buckland
Westward Ho!
TAPELEY PARK GDNS
Tawstock
Swimbridge
A361
NORTH DEVON
Northam
Westleigh
Filleigh
RTLAND POINT
Windbury Pt.
Orchard Hill
Eastleigh
Horwood
Newton Tracey
Herner
Cobbaton
QUINCEY HONEY FARM
Titchberry
THE BIG SHEEP
Bideford
Ensis
East Stowford
HARTLAND ABBEY
CLOVELLY VILLAGE
Abbotsham
BURTON ART GALLERY & MUS
East-the-Water
Woodtown
Hiscott
Chapelton
COBBATON COMBAT COLLECTION
Chittlehampton
South Molton
Stoke
Clovelly
Handy Cross
Alverdiscott
Fishleigh Barton
Hartland Quay
Hartland
Buck's Mills
Pairy Cross
ATLANTIC VILLAGE
Landcross
A377
Umberleigh
Clapworthy
Higher Clovelly
Horns Cross
Ford
Woodtown
Yarnscombe
Atherington
Philham
SOUTH WEST COAST PATH
DOCTON MILL
Littleham
Warkleigh
George Nympton
Milford
Eddistone
THE MILKY WAY ADVENTURE PARK
Buck's Cross
Goldworthy
Langridge Ford
Satterleigh
ELMSCOTT
Weare Giffard
High Bickington
Elmscott
Tosberry
Parkham
Buckland Brewer
Monkleigh
Sherwood Green
Chittlehamholt
Woolfardisworthy
DARTINGTON CRYSTAL
High Bullen
South Hole
Hartland Forest
Alminstone Cross
Parkham Ash
Frithelstock
St Giles in the Wood
Knaps Longpeak
Welcombe
Frithelstock Stone
Great Torrington
King's Nympton
Taddiport
Meddon
Ashmansworthy
Tythecott
Kingscott
Roborough
Cadbury Barton
Gooseham
Woolley
R.H.S. GARDEN ROSEMOOR
Eastcott
East Putford
Little Torrington
Burrington
Youlstone
West Putford
Langtree
Elstone
Morwenstow
Dinworthy
GNOME RESERVE & GARDEN
Beaford
Shop
Stibb Cross
A3124
Riddlecombe
Chulmleigh
Woodford
Bulkworthy
Peters Marland
Bradworthy
Ashreigney
Bradworthy Cross
Abbots Bickington
Newton St Petrock
Woollaton
Winswell
Waldon
Sutcombe
Merton
Coombe
Kilkhampton
Alfardisworthy
Venn Green
Milton Damerel
Huish
Dolton
Ashley
Chawleigh
Torridge
Soldon Cross
Buckland Filleigh
Dowland
Hollocombe
Stibb
Wembworthy
Petrockstow
Shebbear
Holsworthy Beacon
Thornbury
Meeth
Iddesleigh
Winkleigh
Brushford
Coldridge
Nymet Rowland
Flexbury
Poughill
Hersham
DUNSDON
Bradford
Bude Haven
Stratton
Grimscott
Chilsworthy
Woodacott
Sheepwash
Broadwood Kelly
Bude
Pancrasweek
Cookbury
Black Torrington
Monkokehampton
West Leigh
A3072
Launcells
Holemoor
Bondleigh
East Leigh
Upton
Derril
Holsworthy
Brandis Corner
Highampton
Hatherleigh
Zeal Monachorum
Marhamchurch
Bridgerule
Derriton
Pyworthy
Chasty
Whimble
Hollacombe
Graddon Moor
WINSFORD WALLED GARDEN
emouth Bay
Chilla
150
Exbourne
Honeychurch
Halwill Junction
Jacobstowe
Sampford Courtenay
North Tawton
Coppathorne
Leworthy
Halwill
Beaworthy
Northlew
Inwardleigh
Oak Cross
Itton
Clawton
Whitstone
Ashbury
Treskinnick Cross
Week St Mary
PENHALLAM
North Tamerton
Quoditch
Patchacott
BROADBURY
Folly Gate
DARTMOOR RAILWAY
Taw Green
Spreyton
Jacobstow
Tetcott
Lana
Ashwater
Okehampton
WHITEHOUSE SERVICES
Sticklepath
South Tawton
FINCH FOUNDRY
South Zeal
Belstone
Luffincott
Henford
Ewerthy
Germansweek
Boasley Cross
A3079
Thorndon Cross
Whiddon Down
South Wheatley
West Curry
Maxworthy
Chapmans Well
Virginstow
Roadford Res.
East Panson
Grinacombe Moor
Bratton Clovelly
SOURTON CROSS SERVICES
Meldon
CASTLE
OKEHAMPTON (Dartmoor)
Okehampton Camp
Okehampton Common
BRACKEN TOR
550 COSDON HILL
Throwleigh
Canworthy Water
Bennacott
Brazacott
Boyton
Northcott
Warbstow
TAMAR OTTER & WILDLIFE CENTRE
Langdon
St Giles on the Hth.
Gridley Corner
Sourton
619 YES TOR
Wonson
Sandypark
Tremaine
North Petherwin
Bridgetown
Broadwoodwidger
Bridestowe
BLACK-A-TOR COPSE
HIGH WILLHAYS
Bridestowe and Sourton Common
Gidleigh
Easton
Murchington
Treneglos
Hallworthy
Werrington
Cross Green
Thrushelton
Tresmeer
Yeolmbridge
DINGLE'S FAIRGROUND HERITAGE CENTRE
Stowford
Lewdown
Teigncombe
Chagford
Egloskerry
Langore
Tregeare
St Stephen's
Dutson
Liftondown
Shortacombe
OKEMENT HILL
Lewtrenchard
HANGINGSTONE HILL
Frenchbeer
Cold Northcott
HIDDEN VALLEY DISCOVERY PARK
Launceston
LAUNCESTON STEAM RAILWAY
Lifton
Tinhay
Portgate
Lydford
LYDFORD
THE MINIATURE PONY CENTRE
Piper's Pool
TRETHORNE LEISURE FARM
Tregadillett
CASTLE
DARTMOOR
St Clether
Laneast
Coryton
LYDFORD GORGE
Lettaford
DARTMOOR
CUT HILL
SITTAFORD TOR
Lawhitton
North Brentor
Black Down
Willsworthy
FOREST
South Petherwin
Kelly
Chillaton
Bradstone
Altarnun
Lewannick
GRIMSPOUND
A39
A386
A388
A30
A395
A3072
A3079
A3124
A361
A377
A399
B3227
6miles
10km

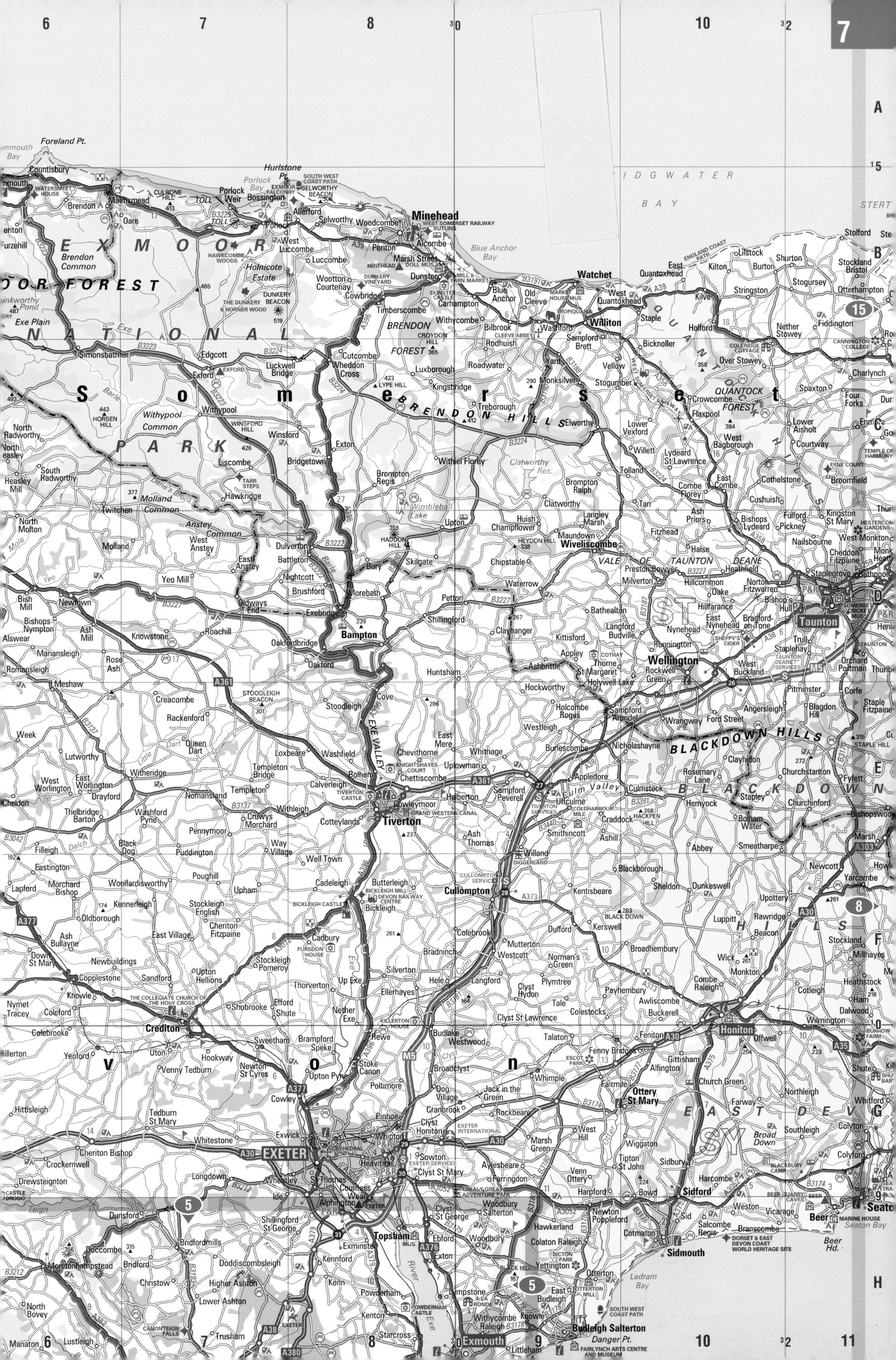
6
7
8
10
A
B
C
D
E
F
G
H
11
Foreland Pt.
Countisbury
Lynmouth
Brendon
Malmsmead
Oare
Porlock Weir
Porlock
Bossington
Hurlstone Pt.
Allerford
Selworthy
Woodcombe
Minehead
WEST SOMERSET RAILWAY
BUTLINS
Alcombe
Periton
Marsh Street
Dunster
DUNSTER CASTLE
Blue Anchor Bay
BRIDGWATER
BAY
STERT
Stolford
Watchet
Williton
West Quantoxhead
Quantoxhead
Kilve
Kilton
Lilstock
Shurton
Stogursey
Stockland Bristol
Otterhampton
Stringston
Holford
Nether Stowey
Fiddington
15
E X M O O R
Brendon Common
HAWKCOMBE WOODS
Holnicote Estate
Luccombe
West Luccombe
Wootton Courtenay
Cowbridge
DUNKERY BEACON
519
THE DUNKERY & HORNER WOOD
FOREST
NATIONAL
PARK
Exe Plain
Pinkworthy Pond
Simonsbath
Timberscombe
Carhampton
Blue Anchor
Old Cleeve
Withycombe
Bilbrook
Washford
CLEEVE ABBEY
TROPIQUARIA
Rodhuish
Sampford Brett
Bicknoller
BRENDON FOREST
CROYDON HILL 365
Edgcott
Exford
Luckwell Bridge
Cutcombe
Wheddon Cross
Luxborough
Kingsbridge
Roadwater
Yard
Monksilver
Stogumber
Vellow
QUANTOCK
Over Stowey
Crowcombe
QUANTOCK FOREST
Flaxpool
Spaxton
Charlynch
Four Forks
Lower Aisholt
S o m e r s e t
BRENDON HILLS
Treborough
Elworthy
Withypool
Withypool Common
HORSEN HILL 443
WINSFORD HILL
Winsford
Exton
Bridgetown
Liscombe
TARR STEPS
Hawkridge
Molland Common
Anstey Common
Dane's Brook
Twitchen
North Radworthy
South Radworthy
North Heasley
Heasley Mill
North Molton
Molland
West Anstey
East Anstey
Dulverton
Battleton
Barle
Brompton Regis
Wimbleball Lake
HADDON HILL
Upton
Withiel Florey
Clatworthy Res.
Clatworthy
Brompton Ralph
Lower Vexford
Willett
Lydeard St Lawrence
Tolland
Combe Florey
East Combe
West Bagborough
Courtway
Cothelstone
Broomfield
Cushuish
Tarr
Ash Priors
Bishops Lydeard
Fulford
Pickney
Kingston St Mary
Huish Champflower
Langley Marsh
Maundown
Wiveliscombe
HEYDON HILL 338
Fitzhead
Halse
Nailsbourne
West Monkton
Cheddon Fitzpaine
Skilgate
Bury
Chipstable
VALE OF TAUNTON DEANE
Preston Bowyer
Heathfield
Milverton
Hillcommon
Oake
Norton Fitzwarren
Staplegrove
Bathpool
Taunton
Hillfarance
Bishop's Hull
Nynehead
East Nynehead
Bradford-on-Tone
SHEPPY'S CIDER
Yeo Mill
Nightcott
Brushford
Morebath
Exebridge
Oldways End
Bampton
Petton
Waterrow
Shillingford
Clayhanger
Bathealton
Langford Budville
Kittisford
Runnington
Wellington
Rockwell Green
Appley
COTHAY
Thorne St Margaret
Ashbrittle
Holywell Lake
West Buckland
Trull
Staplehay
Orchard Portman
Pitminster
Corfe
Bish Mill
Newtown
Bishops Nympton
Ash Mill
Knowstone
Roachill
Oakfordbridge
Oakford
Alswear
Mariansleigh
Romansleigh
Rose Ash
Meshaw
Huntsham
Hockworthy
Holcombe Rogus
Sampford Arundel
Wrangway
Ford Street
Angersleigh
Blagdon Hill
Staple Fitzpaine
Creacombe
Rackenford
STOODLEIGH BEACON
Stoodleigh
Cove
Westleigh
Burlescombe
Nicholashayne
BLACKDOWN HILLS
Clayhidon
Churchstanton
Week
Queen Dart
Loxbeare
Washfield
EXE VALLEY
East Mere
Chevithorne
Whitnage
Uplowman
Appledore
Lutworthy
West Worlington
East Worlington
Drayford
Witheridge
Templeton Bridge
Templeton
Calverleigh
Bolham
KNIGHTSHAYES COURT
Chettiscombe
Tiverton
TIVERTON CASTLE
Cowleymoor
GRAND WESTERN CANAL
Halberton
Sampford Peverell
TIVERTON SERVICES
Uffculme
Culm Valley
Culmstock
Hemyock
Rosemary Lane
Stapley
Churchinford
BLACKDOWN
Bishopswood
Cheldon
Thelbridge Barton
Washford Pyne
Nomansland
Cruwys Morchard
Withleigh
Cotteylands
Ash Thomas
COLDHARBOUR MILL
Craddock
HACKPEN HILL
Ashill
Bolham Water
Smeatharpe
Abbey
Marsh
Pennymoor
Black Dog
Puddington
Way Village
Well Town
Willand
DIGGERLAND
Smithincott
Filleigh
Eastington
Poughill
Woolfardisworthy
Blackborough
Newcott
Yarcombe
Lapford
Morchard Bishop
Upham
Cadeleigh
Butterleigh
BICKLEIGH MILL
DEVON RAILWAY CENTRE
Bickleigh
BICKLEIGH CASTLE
Cullompton
CULLOMPTON SERVICES
Kentisbeare
Sheldon
Dunkeswell
Upottery
Kennerleigh
Oldborough
Stockleigh English
Cheriton Fitzpaine
BLACK DOWN
Dulford
Kerswell
Lupitt
Rawridge
Beacon
HILLS
8
Ash Bullayne
East Village
Cadbury
FURSDON HOUSE
Colebrook
Bradninch
Mutterton
Westcott
Norman's Green
Broadhembury
Wick
Monkton
Stockland
Millhayes
Down St Mary
Copplestone
Newbuildings
Sandford
Upton Hellions
Stockleigh Pomeroy
Silverton
Up Exe
Hele
Langford
Clyst Hydon
Plymtree
Payhembury
Combe Raleigh
Heathstock
Cotleigh
Knowle
Nymet Tracey
Coleford
THE COLLEGIATE CHURCH OF THE HOLY CROSS
Shobrooke
Efford Shute
Thorverton
Ellerhayes
Nether Exe
Tale
Colestocks
Awliscombe
Buckerell
Honiton
Ham
Dalwood
Wilmington
Colebrooke
Crediton
Sweetham
Brampford Speke
Rewe
KILLERTON HOUSE
Budlake
Westwood
Clyst St Lawrence
Talaton
Feniton
Offwell
BURROW FARM
Hillerton
Yeoford
Uton
Hookway
Venny Tedburn
Newton St Cyres
Stoke Canon
Upton Pyne
Broadclyst
ESCOT PARK
Fenny Bridges
Gittisham
Alfington
Shute
Whimple
Poltimore
Dog Village
Jack in the Green
Fairmile
Ottery St Mary
Church Green
Northleigh
Whitford
D e v o n
Hittisleigh
Cowley
Pinhoe
Cranbrook
Rockbeare
Farway
Colyton
Tedburn St Mary
Whitestone
Exwick
Whipton
Clyst Honiton
EXETER INTERNATIONAL
West Hill
Wiggaton
Broad Down
Southleigh
Cheriton Bishop
EXETER
CATHEDRAL
Heavitree
Sowton
EXETER SERVICES
Marsh Green
Tipton St John
Sidbury
BLACKBURY CAMP
Colyford
Crockernwell
Drewsteignton
Longdown
Whetley
St Thomas
Countess Wear
Clyst St Mary
Aylesbeare
Farringdon
Venn Ottery
Harcombe
E A S T D E V
CASTLE DROGO
Teign
5
Ide
Alphington
CREALY GREAT ADVENTURE PARK
Harpford
Bowd
Sidford
BEER QUARRY CAVES
Beer
Seaton
Dunsford
Shillingford St George
Clyst St George
Woodbury Salterton
Hawkerland
Newton Poppleford
Sid
Salcombe Regis
Branscombe
Weston
Vicarage
MARINE HOUSE
Seaton Bay
Bridfordmills
Exminster
Topsham
Ebford
Woodbury
Colaton Raleigh
Cotmaton
Sidmouth
DORSET & EAST DEVON COAST WORLD HERITAGE SITE
Beer Hd.
Doccombe
Bridford
Moretonhampstead
Doddiscombsleigh
Kennford
Exton
BICTON PARK
Yettington
Otterton
OTTERTON MILL
Ladram Bay
Christow
Higher Ashton
Lower Ashton
Kenn
Powderham
POWDERHAM CASTLE
Lympstone
A LA RONDE
Withycombe Raleigh
Knowle
East Budleigh
SOUTH WEST COAST PATH
North Bovey
Kenton
CANONTEIGN FALLS
Trusham
Starcross
Exmouth
Littleham
Budleigh Salterton
Danger Pt.
FAIRLYNCH ARTS CENTRE AND MUSEUM
Manaton
Lustleigh
BLACK HILL
A39
A396
A358
A361
A38
A30
A35
A373
A377
A380
A379
A376
A3052
A375
A303
M5
B3224
B3223
B3227
B3222
B3191
B3188
B3137
B3042
B3212
B3181
B3174
B3177
B3180
B3178
B3179
B3391
B3440
B3170

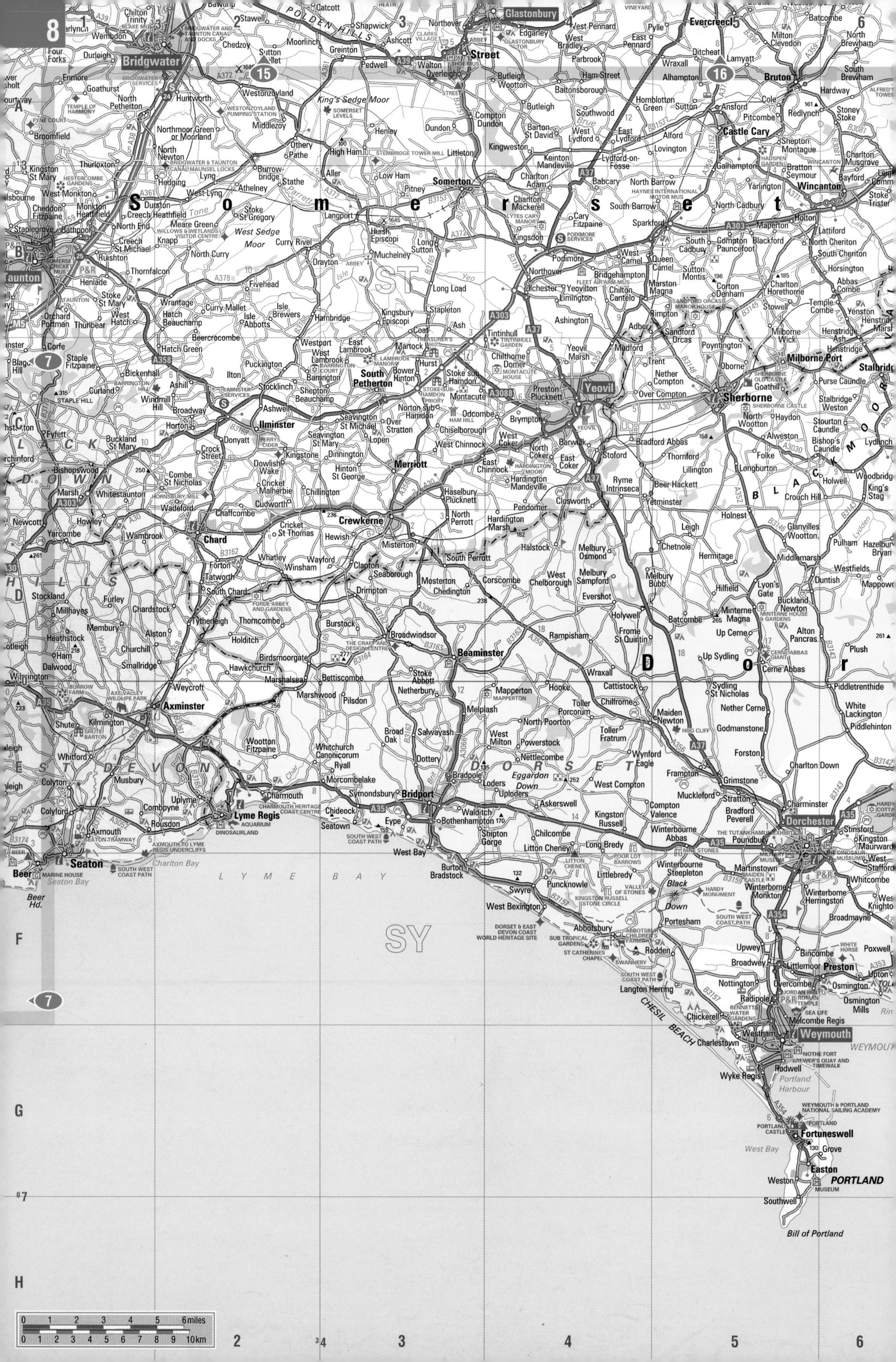
Glastonbury
Bridgwater
Street
Somerton
Langport
Ilminster
Chard
Crewkerne
South Petherton
Yeovil
Sherborne
Castle Cary
Bruton
Wincanton
Milborne Port
Taunton
Axminster
Lyme Regis
Seaton
Beer
Bridport
Beaminster
Merriott
Dorchester
Weymouth
Fortuneswell
Evercreech
Somerset
Dorset
Devon
POLDEN HILLS
King's Sedge Moor
West Sedge Moor
BLACKMOOR
BLACKDOWN HILLS
EAST DEVON
LYME BAY
Charlton Bay
Seaton Bay
Beer Hd.
CHESIL BEACH
Portland Harbour
West Bay
PORTLAND
Bill of Portland
Eggardon Down
Black Down
Chilton Trinity
Wembdon
Durleigh
Four Forks
Enmore
Goathurst
North Petherton
Huntworth
Chedzoy
Sutton Mallet
Westonzoyland
Middlezoy
Othery
Pathe
Stawell
Moorlinch
Shapwick
Ashcott
Catcott
Greinton
Pedwell
Walton
Overleigh
Northover
Edgarley
West Pennard
East Pennard
West Bradley
Parbrook
Pylle
Wraxall
Ditcheat
Lamyatt
Alhampton
Ham Street
Batcombe
Milton Clevedon
North Brewham
South Brewham
Butleigh Wootton
Butleigh
Baltonsborough
Hornblotton Green
Southwood
Compton Dundon
Dundon
Henley
High Ham
Low Ham
Aller
Littleton
Kingweston
Barton St David
West Lydford
East Lydford
Alford
Lovington
Ansford
Cole
Pitcombe
Redlynch
Hardway
Stoney Stoke
Shepton Montague
Charlton Musgrove
Bayford
Galhampton
Brattom Seymour
Yarlington
North Cadbury
Keinton Mandeville
Lydford-on-Fosse
Charlton Adam
Charlton Mackerell
Babcary
North Barrow
South Barrow
Sparkford
Cary Fitzpaine
Kingsdon
Podimore
Maperton
Holton
Lattiford
North Cheriton
South Cheriton
Horsington
Abbas Combe
Templecombe
Henstridge
Stalbridge
Purse Caundle
Stalbridge Weston
Kingston St Mary
Cheddon Fitzpaine
West Monkton
Monkton Heathfield
Staplegrove
Bathpool
Creech Heathfield
Creech St Michael
Ruishton
Thurloxton
Durston
Hedging
North Newton
Northmoor Green or Moorland
Burrowbridge
Athelney
West Lyng
Lyng
Stathe
Stoke St Gregory
Meare Green
North End
Knapp
North Curry
Curry Rivel
Huish Episcopi
Muchelney
Long Sutton
Pitney
Drayton
Thornfalcon
Henlade
Stoke St Mary
West Hatch
Orchard Portman
Thurlbear
Fivehead
Wrantage
Hatch Beauchamp
Curry Mallet
Isle Brewers
Isle Abbotts
Beercrocombe
Hatch Green
Hambridge
Kingsbury Episcopi
Long Load
Stapleton
Ash
Coat
Martock
Hurst
Stoke sub Hamdon
Tintinhull
Chilthorne Domer
Montacute
Odcombe
Brympton
Preston Plucknett
Ilchester
Northover
Yeovilton
Limington
West Camel
Queen Camel
Marston Magna
Chilton Cantelo
Bridgehampton
Sutton Montis
Corton Denham
Charlton Horethorne
Stowell
Milborne Wick
Rimpton
Adber
Sandford Orcas
Poyntington
Oborne
Trent
Mudford
Nether Compton
Over Compton
Ashington
Yeovil Marsh
Corfe
Staple Fitzpaine
Blagdon Hill
Bickenhall
Curland
Ashill
Windmill Hill
Broadway
Puckington
Ilton
Stocklinch
Ashwell
Shepton Beauchamp
Barrington
West Lambrook
East Lambrook
Westport
Bower Hinton
Norton sub Hamdon
Seavington St Michael
Seavington St Mary
Over Stratton
Lopen
Chiselborough
West Chinnock
West Coker
East Chinnock
North Coker
East Coker
Barwick
Stoford
Bradford Abbas
Thornford
Yetminster
Beer Hackett
Ryme Intrinseca
Closworth
Hardington Mandeville
Pendomer
Hardington Marsh
North Wootton
Haydon
Alweston
Folke
Longburton
Lillington
Stourton Caundle
Bishop's Caundle
Holwell
Lydlinch
King's Stag
Woodbridge
Crouch Hill
Holnest
Glanvilles Wootton
Pulham
Hazelbury Bryan
Middlemarsh
Westfields
Dunstish
Mappowder
Buckland Newton
Lyon's Gate
Minterne Magna
Batcombe
Hermitage
Leigh
Chetnole
Melbury Osmond
Melbury Sampford
Melbury Bubb
Evershot
Holywell
Frome St Quintin
Rampisham
Cattistock
Chilfrome
Maiden Newton
Toller Porcorum
Toller Fratrum
Wynford Eagle
Frampton
Grimstone
Stratton
Bradford Peverell
Charminster
Stinsford
Kingston Maurward
West Stafford
Whitcombe
Winterborne Herringston
Broadmayne
Knighton
Poxwell
Preston
Upton
Osmington
Osmington Mills
Bincombe
Littlemoor
Overcombe
Radipole
Melcombe Regis
Westham
Rodwell
Wyke Regis
Charlestown
Chickerell
Nottington
Broadwey
Upwey
Portesham
Winterborne Steepleton
Winterborne Monkton
Martinstown
Poundbury
Winterbourne Abbas
Compton Valence
Muckleford
West Compton
Long Bredy
Littlebredy
Kingston Russell
Askerswell
Litton Cheney
Puncknowle
Chilcombe
Swyre
West Bexington
Abbotsbury
Rodden
Langton Herring
Shipton Gorge
Uploders
Loders
Bradpole
Walditch
Bothenhampton
Burton Bradstock
West Bay
Eype
Chideock
Seatown
Symondsbury
Morcombelake
Charmouth
Whitchurch Canonicorum
Ryall
Wootton Fitzpaine
Uplyme
Combpyne
Rousdon
Axmouth
Colyford
Colyton
Musbury
Whitford
Shute
Kilmington
Weycroft
Hawkchurch
Marshalsea
Birdsmoorgate
Bettiscombe
Marshwood
Pilsdon
Broad Oak
Salwayash
Netherbury
Stoke Abbott
Broadwindsor
Burstock
Drimpton
Mosterton
Chedington
Corscombe
West Chelborough
Halstock
South Perrott
North Perrott
Haselbury Plucknett
Misterton
Seaborough
Clapton
Wayford
Winsham
Whatley
Hewish
Cricket St Thomas
Chaffcombe
Cudworth
Chillington
Cricket Malherbie
Hinton St George
Dinnington
Kingstone
Dowlish Wake
Donyatt
Crock Street
Combe St Nicholas
Wadeford
Whitestaunton
Horton
Buckland St Mary
Bishopswood
Marsh
Howley
Newcott
Yarcombe
Wambrook
Forton
Tatworth
South Chard
Chardstock
Tytherleigh
Thorncombe
Holditch
Alston
Churchill
Smallridge
Membury
Furley
Stockland
Millhayes
Heathstock
Dalwood
Wilmington
Fyfett
Mapperton
Hooke
North Poorton
West Milton
Powerstock
Nettlecombe
Melplash
Dottery
Bridport
Sydling St Nicholas
Up Sydling
Up Cerne
Cerne Abbas
Nether Cerne
Godmanstone
Forston
Charlton Down
Alton Pancras
Plush
Piddletrenthide
White Lackington
Piddlehinton
Grove
Easton
Weston
Southwell
A39
A361
A372
A37
A303
A378
A358
A30
A3088
A356
A35
A352
A354
A353
A3066
A3052
A371
A359
A3030
B3151
B3153
B3165
B3168
B3162
B3163
B3164
B3157
B3159
B3143
B3145
B3148
B3146
B3081
B3153
B3174
B3172
B3261
B3167
M5
15
16
7
SY
ST
0 1 2 3 4 5 6 miles
0 1 2 3 4 5 6 7 8 9 10 km
A B C D E F G H
1 2 3 4 5 6

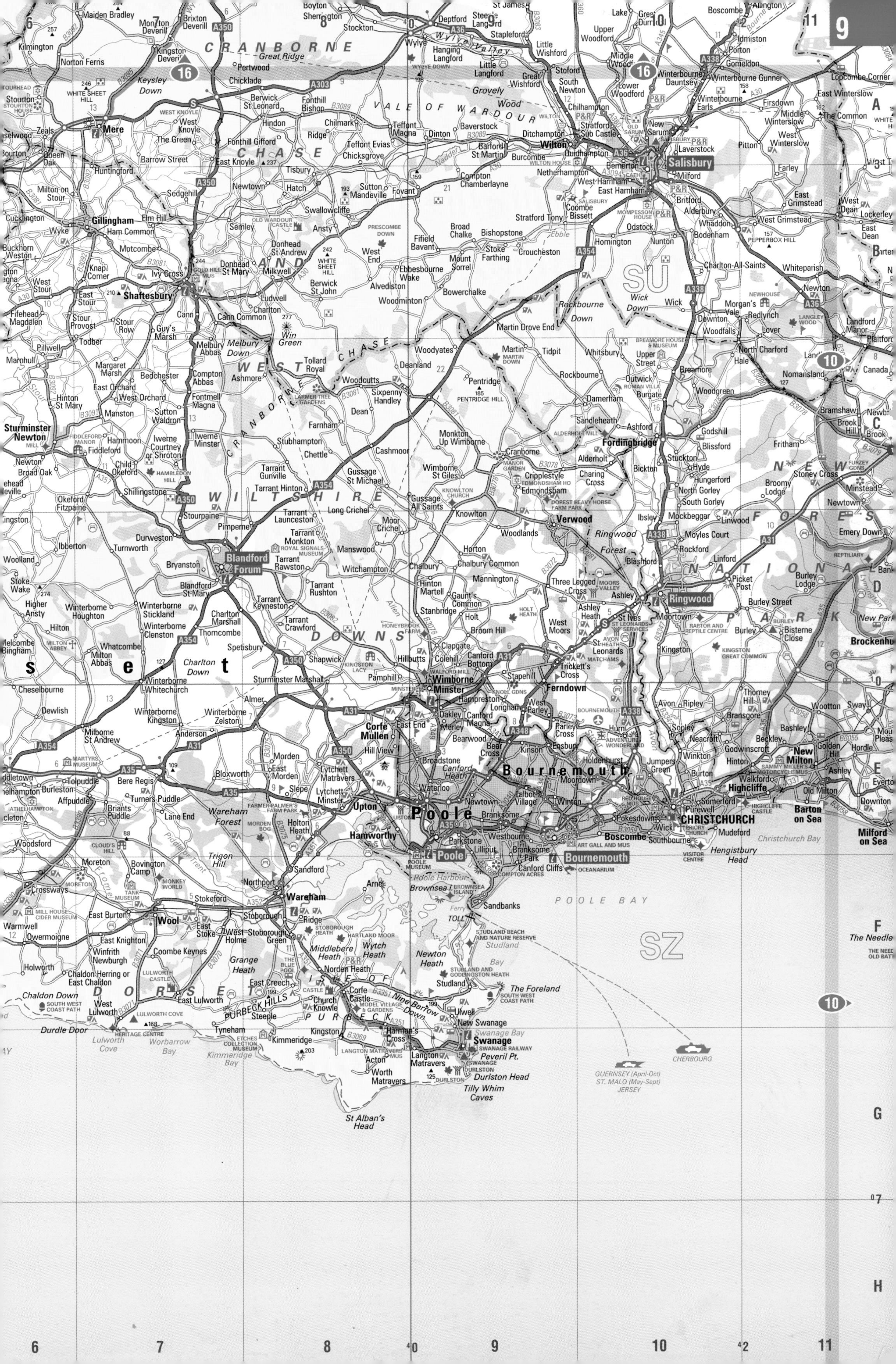

CRANBORNE
CHASE
Great Ridge
Keysley Down
VALE OF WARDOUR
Grovely Wood
WEST CHASE
CRANBORNE
WILTSHIRE
DOWNS
Maiden Bradley
Monkton Deverill
Brixton Deverill
Kingston Deverill
Kilmington
Norton Ferris
Pertwood
Chicklade
Stourton
Zeals
Mere
West Knoyle
The Green
Fonthill Gifford
Fonthill Bishop
Berwick St Leonard
Hindon
Chilmark
Teffont Magna
Teffont Evias
Chicksgrove
Dinton
Baverstock
Barford St Martin
Burcombe
Ditchampton
Wilton
Tisbury
East Knoyle
Barrow Street
Huntingford
Milton on Stour
Gillingham
Ham Common
Motcombe
Sedgehill
Semley
Donhead St Andrew
Donhead St Mary
Ansty
Swallowcliffe
Sutton Mandeville
Fovant
Compton Chamberlayne
Hatch
Newtown
Cucklington
Wyke
Buckhorn Weston
Kington Magna
Knap Corner
Shaftesbury
Ivy Cross
East Stour
West Stour
Fifehead Magdalen
Stour Provost
Stour Row
Todber
Guy's Marsh
Cann
Cann Common
Charlton
Ludwell
Berwick St John
Alvediston
Ebbesbourne Wake
West End
Fifield Bavant
Broad Chalke
Bishopstone
Mount Sorrel
Stoke Farthing
Croucheston
Bowerchalke
Woodminton
Win Green
Melbury Abbas
Melbury Down
Compton Abbas
Ashmore
Tollard Royal
Woodcutts
Sixpenny Handley
Deanland
Woodyates
Dean
Farnham
Pillwell
Marnhull
Margaret Marsh
Bedchester
East Orchard
West Orchard
Fontmell Magna
Sutton Waldron
Hinton St Mary
Manston
Sturminster Newton
Fiddleford
Hammoon
Iwerne Courtney or Shroton
Iwerne Minster
Child Okeford
Shillingstone
Okeford Fitzpaine
Newton
Broad Oak
Stubhampton
Chettle
Tarrant Gunville
Tarrant Hinton
Cashmoor
Gussage St Michael
Gussage All Saints
Long Crichel
Moor Crichel
Tarrant Launceston
Tarrant Monkton
Stourpaine
Pimperne
Durweston
Turnworth
Ibberton
Woolland
Bryanston
Blandford Forum
Blandford St Mary
Tarrant Rawston
Tarrant Keyneston
Tarrant Rushton
Tarrant Crawford
Manswood
Witchampton
Stoke Wake
Higher Ansty
Winterborne Houghton
Winterborne Stickland
Winterborne Clenston
Charlton Marshall
Thorncombe
Spetisbury
Hilton
Melcombe Bingham
Whatcombe
Milton Abbas
Charlton Down
Winterborne Whitechurch
Cheselbourne
Dewlish
Winterborne Kingston
Winterborne Zelston
Almer
Sturminster Marshall
Shapwick
Anderson
Milborne St Andrew
Tolpuddle
Bere Regis
Burleston
Affpuddle
Turners Puddle
Briants Puddle
Bloxworth
Morden
East Morden
Slepe
Lytchett Matravers
Lytchett Minster
Woodsford
Moreton
Bovington Camp
Wareham Forest
Trigon Hill
Lane End
Holton Heath
Sandford
Northport
Wareham
Crossways
Stokeford
Wool
East Burton
East Stoke
West Holme
Stoborough
Stoborough Green
Ridge
Warmwell
Owermoigne
East Knighton
Winfrith Newburgh
Coombe Keynes
Holworth
Chaldon Herring or East Chaldon
Grange Heath
Middlebere Heath
Wytch Heath
Norden Heath
East Lulworth
East Creech
Chaldon Down
West Lulworth
Durdle Door
Lulworth Cove
Worbarrow Bay
Tyneham
Steeple
Kimmeridge
Kimmeridge Bay
PURBECK HILLS
ISLE OF PURBECK
Church Knowle
Corfe Castle
Kingston
Harman's Cross
Nine Barrow Down
Acton
Worth Matravers
Langton Matravers
St Alban's Head
Swanage
Swanage Bay
Peveril Pt.
Durlston Head
Tilly Whim Caves
New Swanage
Ulwell
Studland
Studland Bay
The Foreland
Newton Heath
Sandbanks
Brownsea Island
Arne
Poole Harbour
Hamworthy
Poole
Upton
Corfe Mullen
Hill View
East End
Broadstone
Canford Heath
Waterloo
Newtown
Parkstone
Lilliput
Branksome
Branksome Park
Canford Cliffs
Westbourne
Talbot Village
Bournemouth
Boscombe
Southbourne
Pokesdown
Moordown
Winton
Kinson
Bear Cross
Bearwood
Merley
Oakley
Canford Magna
Hampreston
Longham
Wimborne Minster
Colehill
Pamphill
Hillbutts
Clapgate
Canford Bottom
Stapehill
West Parley
Parley Cross
Ensbury
Holdenhurst
Hurn
Ferndown
Trickett's Cross
St Leonards
St Ives
West Moors
Ashley Heath
Three Legged Cross
Woodlands
Verwood
Horton
Chalbury
Chalbury Common
Mannington
Hinton Martell
Stanbridge
Gaunt's Common
Holt
Broom Hill
Knowlton
Wimborne St Giles
Monkton Up Wimborne
Cranborne
Cripplestyle
Edmondsham
Alderholt
Charing Cross
Pentridge
Martin
Martin Drove End
Tidpit
Whitsbury
Rockbourne
Rockbourne Down
Damerham
Sandleheath
Fordingbridge
Ashford
Bickton
Upper Street
Outwick
Burgate
Breamore
Woodgreen
Godshill
Blissford
Stuckton
Hyde
Hungerford
North Gorley
South Gorley
Mockbeggar
Ibsley
Moyles Court
Rockford
Linwood
Blashford
Ringwood Forest
Ringwood
Ashley
Moortown
Kingston
Avon
Ripley
Sopley
Neacroft
Winkton
Jumpers Green
Burton
Christchurch
Purewell
Mudeford
Somerford
Highcliffe
Walkford
Hinton
Bransgore
Thorney Hill
Godwinscroft
Beckley
Bashley
Wootton
New Milton
Barton on Sea
Milford on Sea
Old Milton
Ashley
Golden Hill
Hordle
Downton
Everton
Sway
Christchurch Bay
Hengistbury Head
POOLE BAY
Burley
Burley Street
Burley Lodge
Bisterne Close
Picket Post
Linford
Emery Down
Minstead
Stoney Cross
Newtown
Broomy Lodge
Fritham
Brook
Bramshaw
Nomansland
Canada
Landford Manor
Plaitford
Redlynch
Lover
Hale
North Charford
Woodfalls
Morgan's Vale
Downton
Wick
Wick Down
Newton
Whiteparish
Charlton-All-Saints
Nunton
Odstock
Bodenham
Whaddon
Alderbury
Britford
Homington
Coombe Bissett
Stratford Tony
East Harnham
West Harnham
Netherhampton
Bemerton
Quidhampton
Salisbury
Milford
Laverstock
Stratford sub Castle
Old Sarum
New Sarum
Chilhampton
South Newton
Stoford
Great Wishford
Little Langford
Hanging Langford
Steeple Langford
Stapleford
Little Wishford
Wylye
Wylye Valley
Deptford
Stockton
Sherrington
Boyton
Upper Woodford
Middle Woodford
Lower Woodford
Lake
Great Durnford
Boscombe
Allington
Idmiston
Porton
Gomeldon
Winterbourne Dauntsey
Winterbourne Gunner
Winterbourne Earls
Firsdown
Middle Winterslow
West Winterslow
East Winterslow
The Common
Lopcombe Corner
Pitton
Farley
East Grimstead
West Grimstead
West Dean
Lockerley
East Dean
Pepperbox Hill
Brockenhurst
The Needles
NEW FOREST NATIONAL PARK
SU
SZ
CHERBOURG
GUERNSEY (April-Oct)
ST. MALO (May-Sept)
JERSEY
A303
A350
A36
A30
A354
A338
A31
A35
A348
A351
A352
16
10

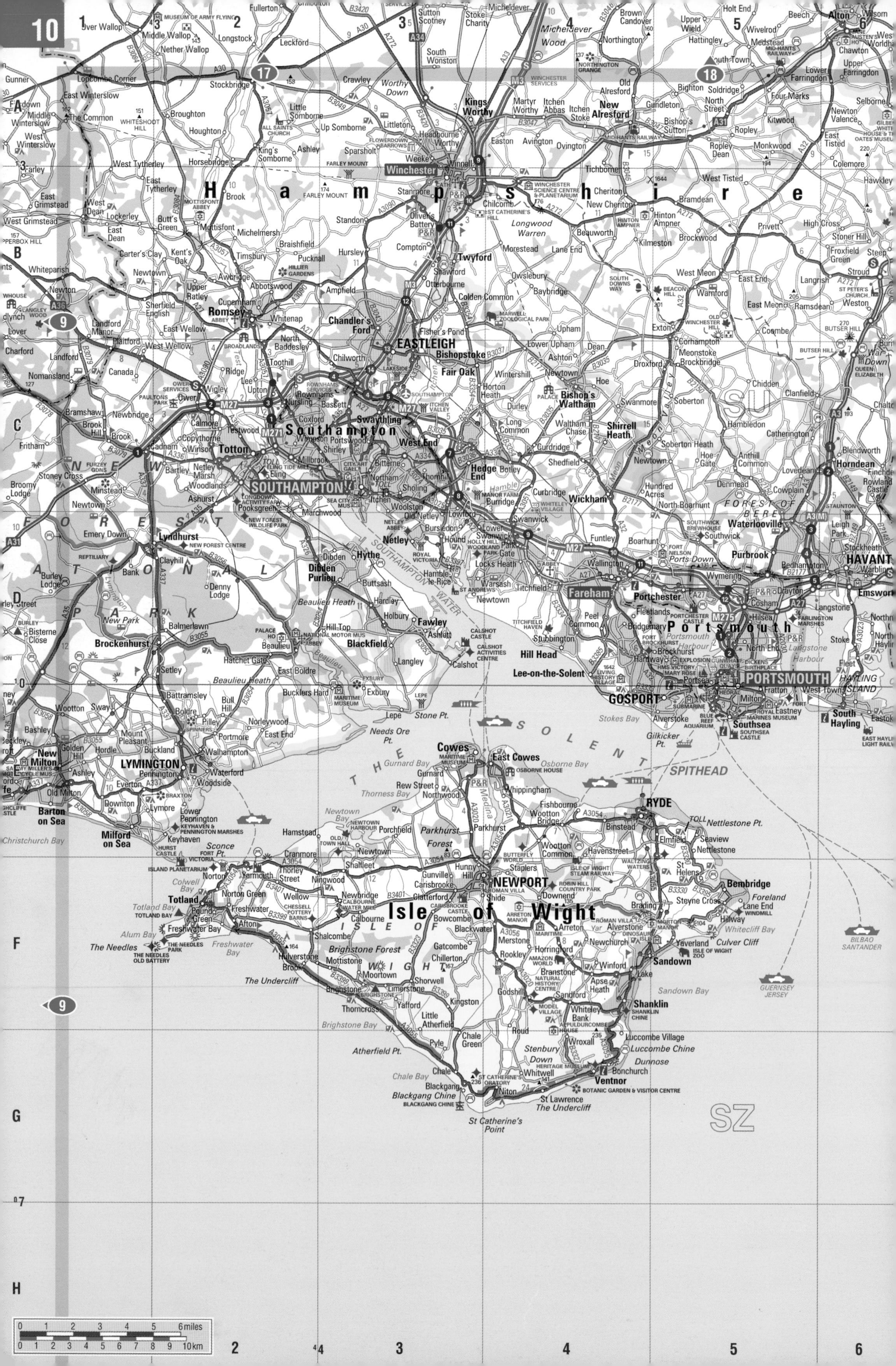
Hampshire
Isle of Wight
New Forest National Park
Southampton
SOUTHAMPTON
Winchester
EASTLEIGH
Portsmouth
PORTSMOUTH
GOSPORT
HAVANT
Fareham
LYMINGTON
NEWPORT
RYDE
Romsey
Totton
Hythe
Fawley
Lyndhurst
Brockenhurst
New Milton
Barton on Sea
Milford on Sea
Cowes
East Cowes
Yarmouth
Totland
Freshwater
Sandown
Shanklin
Ventnor
Bembridge
Alton
Alresford
New Alresford
Stockbridge
Kings Worthy
Twyford
Bishop's Waltham
Wickham
Waterlooville
Horndean
Hedge End
West End
Netley
Dibden Purlieu
Blackfield
Lee-on-the-Solent
Hill Head
Portchester
Southsea
South Hayling
Hayling Island
Emsworth
Chandler's Ford
Bishopstoke
Fair Oak
Marchwood
Ashurst
Minstead
Cadnam
Beaulieu
Exbury
East Boldre
Sway
Bransgore
Ashley
Hordle
Everton
Keyhaven
Pennington
Lower Pennington
Lymore
Downton
Old Milton
Mottistone
Brighstone
Shorwell
Chale
Niton
Whitwell
Wroxall
Godshill
Arreton
Brading
Bonchurch
St Lawrence
Carisbrooke
Gurnard
Northwood
Wootton Bridge
Fishbourne
Binstead
Seaview
St Helens
Lake
Shalfleet
Calbourne
Newbridge
Wellow
Thorley
Solent
The Solent
Spithead
Southampton Water
Beaulieu Heath
Portsmouth Harbour
Langstone Harbour
Christchurch Bay
Needs Ore Pt.
Stone Pt.
Calshot
Gilkicker Pt.
Stokes Bay
Osborne Bay
Gurnard Bay
Thorness Bay
Newtown Bay
Colwell Bay
Totland Bay
Alum Bay
The Needles
Freshwater Bay
Brighstone Bay
Chale Bay
Atherfield Pt.
St Catherine's Point
Blackgang
Blackgang Chine
The Undercliff
Luccombe Village
Luccombe Chine
Dunnose
Sandown Bay
Culver Cliff
Whitecliff Bay
Foreland
Nettlestone Pt.
Parkhurst Forest
Brighstone Forest
Longwood Warren
Micheldever Wood
Forest of Bere
Ports Down
M3
M27
M271
M275
A27
A31
A32
A33
A34
A35
A36
A337
A3(M)
SU
SZ
BILBAO SANTANDER
GUERNSEY JERSEY
0 1 2 3 4 5 6 miles
0 1 2 3 4 5 6 7 8 9 10 km

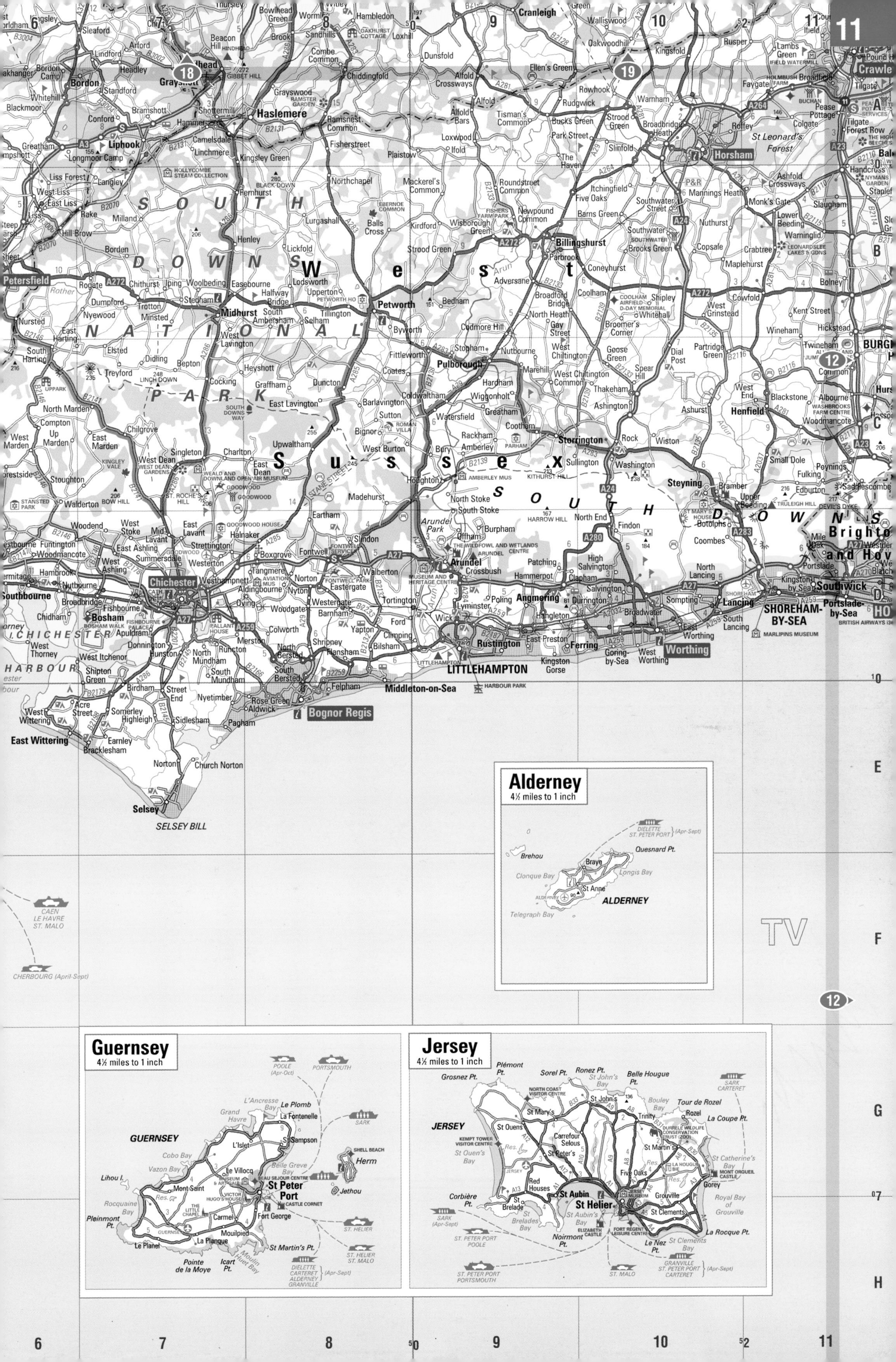
Haslemere
Liphook
Bordon
Grayshott
Hindhead
Petersfield
Midhurst
Petworth
Pulborough
Billingshurst
Horsham
Cranleigh
Crawley
Storrington
Steyning
Henfield
Arundel
Chichester
Bosham
Littlehampton
Rustington
Angmering
Worthing
Lancing
Shoreham-by-Sea
Southwick
Portslade-by-Sea
Brighton and Hove
Bognor Regis
Middleton-on-Sea
Selsey
Selsey Bill
East Wittering
Emsworth
Southbourne
Chichester Harbour
South Downs National Park
West Sussex
South Downs
Alderney
4½ miles to 1 inch
Braye
St Anne
Quesnard Pt.
Longis Bay
Clonque Bay
Telegraph Bay
Brehou
Guernsey
4½ miles to 1 inch
St Peter Port
St Sampson
L'Islet
Le Villocq
Mont Saint
Fort George
Herm
Jethou
Sark
Pleinmont Pt.
Le Planel
La Planque
Icart Pt.
Jersey
4½ miles to 1 inch
St Helier
St Aubin
St Ouens
St Mary's
St John's
St Martin's
St Clements
Gorey
Rozel
Grouville
Trinity
Five Oaks
Red Houses
Corbière Pt.
Grosnez Pt.
Plémont Pt.
La Rocque Pt.
Noirmont Pt.
Caen
Le Havre
St. Malo
Cherbourg (April-Sept)
TV

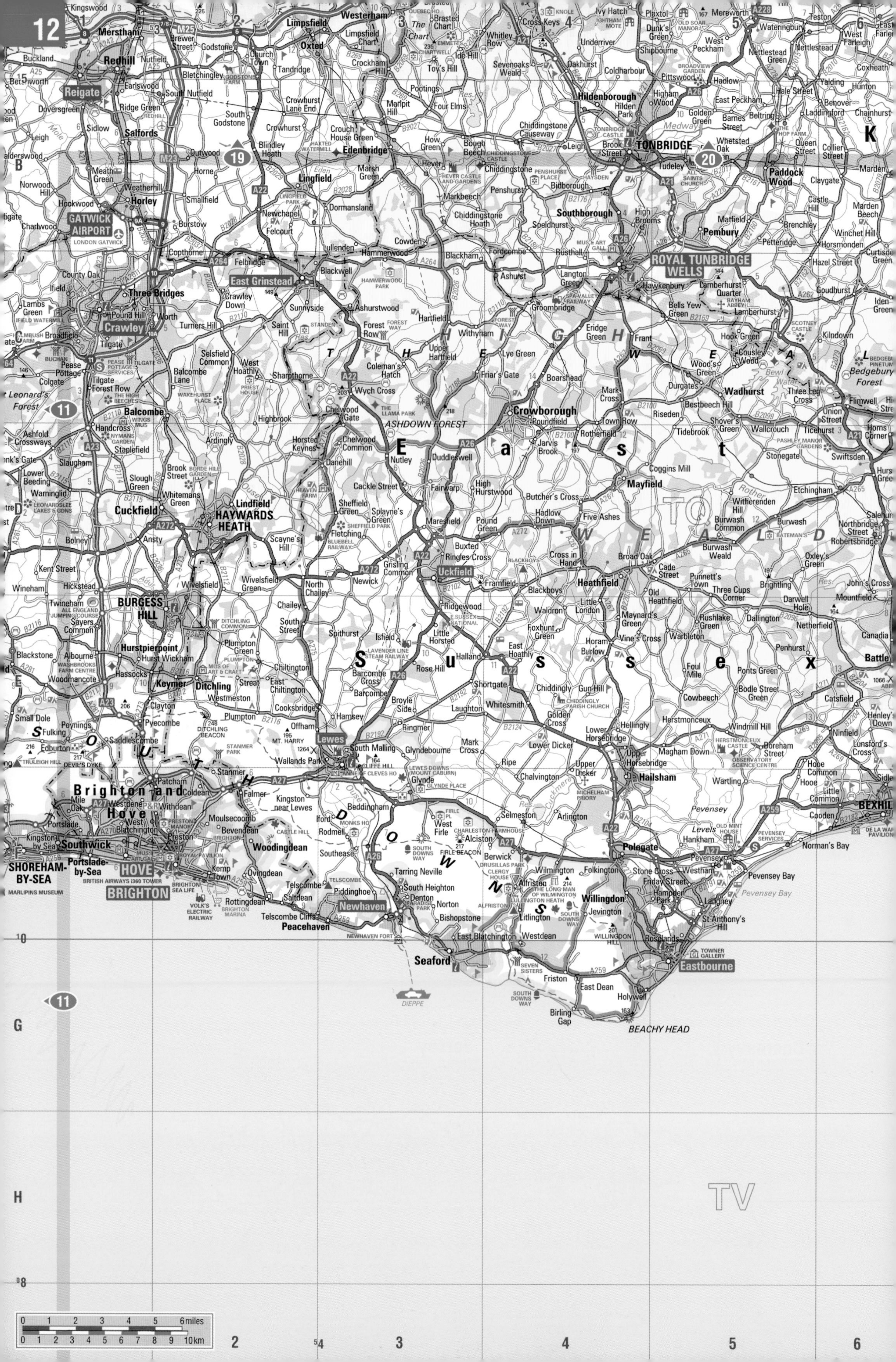

Kingswood
Merstham
Redhill
Reigate
Limpsfield
Oxted
Westerham
Brasted
Ivy Hatch
Plaxtol
Mereworth
Teston
Wateringbury
West Farleigh
Godstone
Bletchingley
Nutfield
South Nutfield
Earlswood
Salfords
Horley
GATWICK AIRPORT
Crawley
Three Bridges
East Grinstead
Lingfield
Edenbridge
Hever
Chiddingstone
Penshurst
Leigh
Hildenborough
TONBRIDGE
Tudeley
Paddock Wood
Southborough
ROYAL TUNBRIDGE WELLS
Pembury
Matfield
Brenchley
Horsmonden
Goudhurst
Lamberhurst
Frant
Wadhurst
Ticehurst
Flimwell
Crowborough
Forest Row
Wych Cross
ASHDOWN FOREST
Nutley
Mayfield
Heathfield
Uckfield
Maresfield
Buxted
Framfield
Fletching
Newick
Haywards Heath
Lindfield
Cuckfield
Balcombe
Handcross
BURGESS HILL
Hurstpierpoint
Hassocks
Keymer
Ditchling
Lewes
Brighton and Hove
HOVE
BRIGHTON
SHOREHAM-BY-SEA
Southwick
Portslade
Woodingdean
Rottingdean
Saltdean
Peacehaven
Newhaven
Seaford
Alfriston
Polegate
Willingdon
Hailsham
Herstmonceux
Pevensey
Pevensey Bay
Eastbourne
BEACHY HEAD
Birling Gap
Friston
East Dean
Burwash
Etchingham
Robertsbridge
Battle
BEXHILL
Norman's Bay
HIGH WEALD
East Sussex
SOUTH DOWNS
TQ
TV
DIEPPE
19
20
11
0 1 2 3 4 5 6 miles
0 1 2 3 4 5 6 7 8 9 10 km

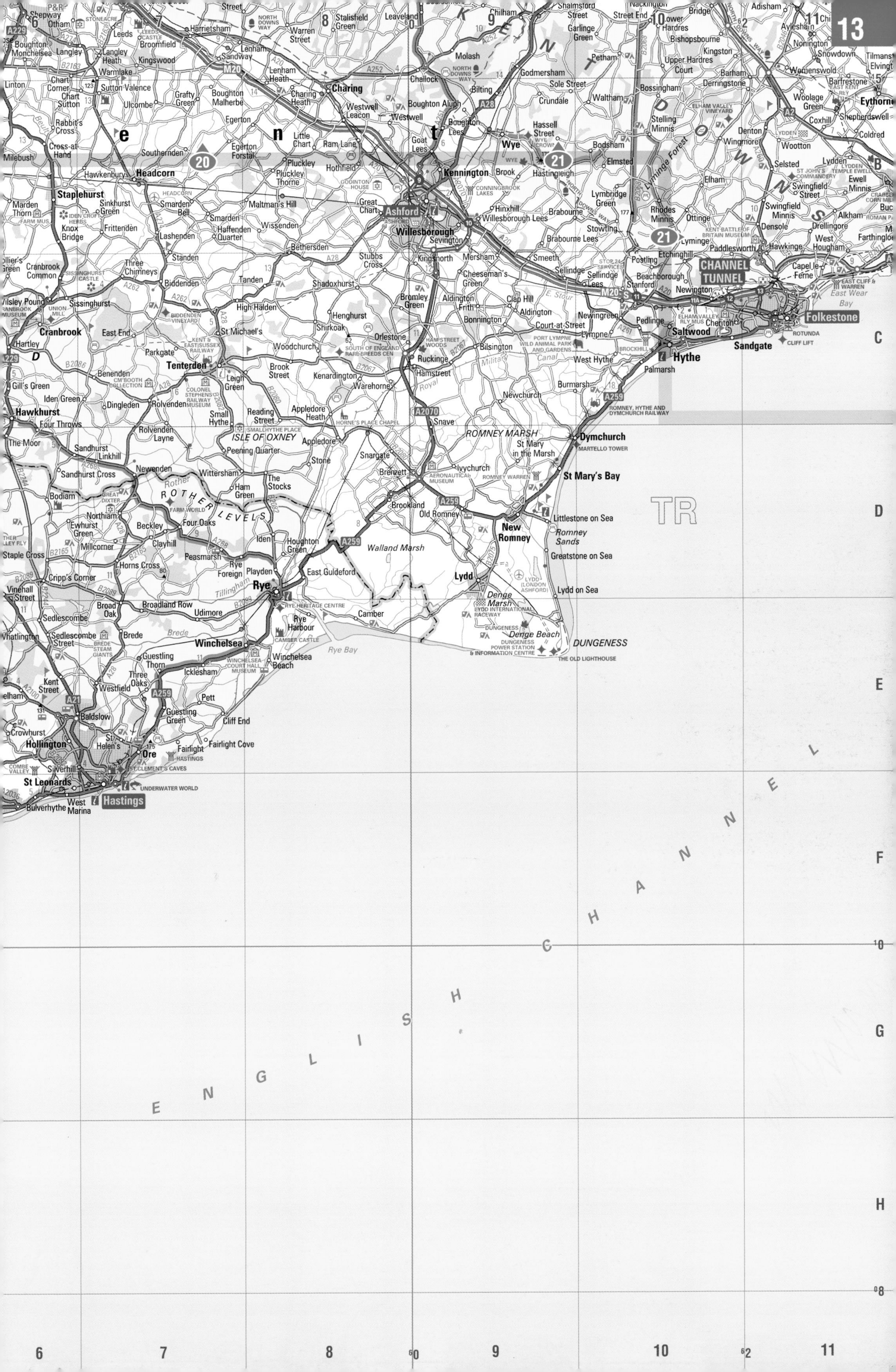
KENT DOWNS
Shepway
Otham
Harrietsham
Leeds
Lenham
Warren Street
Stalisfield Green
Leaveland
Chilham
Shalmsford Street
Street End
Lower Hardres
Bridge
Adisham
Aylesham
Boughton Monchelsea
Langley
Langley Heath
Broomfield
Kingswood
Sandway
Molash
Garlinge Green
Petham
Bishopsbourne
Kingston
Nonington
Snowdown
Upper Hardres Court
Barham
Womenswold
Linton
Chart Corner
Warmlake
Sutton Valence
Chart Sutton
Ulcombe
Grafty Green
Boughton Malherbe
Lenham Heath
Charing Heath
Charing
Challock
Godmersham
Sole Street
Bossingham
Derringstone
Barfrestone
Eythorne
Westwell Leacon
Westwell
Boughton Aluph
Bilting
Crundale
Waltham
Woolage Green
Coxhill
Shepherdswell
Rabbit's Cross
Egerton
Little Chart
Ram Lane
Goat Lees
Boughton Lees
Hassell Street
Wye
Stelling Minnis
Denton
Wingmore
Wootton
Coldred
Cross-at-Hand
Milebush
Southernden
Egerton Forstal
Pluckley
Pluckley Thorne
Hothfield
Kennington
Brook
Hastingleigh
Bodsham
Elmsted
Lyminge Forest
Selsted
Lydden
Ewell Minnis
Hawkenbury
Headcorn
Staplehurst
Smarden Bell
Maltman's Hill
Great Chart
Ashford
Conningbrook Lakes
Hinxhill
Willesborough Lees
Brabourne
Lymbridge Green
Rhodes Minnis
Ottinge
Elham
Swingfield Street
Swingfield Minnis
Alkham
Marden Thorn
Sinkhurst Green
Knox Bridge
Frittenden
Smarden
Haffenden Quarter
Wissenden
Willesborough
Sevington
Stowting
Brabourne Lees
Lyminge
Densole
Drellingore
West Hougham
Farthingloe
Lashenden
Bethersden
Stubbs Cross
Kingsnorth
Mersham
Smeeth
Postling
Etchinghill
Paddlesworth
Hawkinge
Capel le Ferne
Cranbrook Common
Three Chimneys
Standen
Tanden
Shadoxhurst
Cheeseman's Green
Sellindge
Sellindge Lees
Beachborough
Stanford
Newington
CHANNEL TUNNEL
Biddenden
High Halden
Bromley Green
Aldington Frith
Clap Hill
Aldington
Bonnington
Newingreen
Pedlinge
Cheriton
Folkestone
Sissinghurst
Cranbrook
East End
St Michael's
Henghurst
Shirkoak
Orlestone
Court-at-Street
Lympne
Saltwood
Hythe
Sandgate
Hartley
Parkgate
Tenterden
Woodchurch
Ruckinge
Bilsington
West Hythe
Palmarsh
Gill's Green
Benenden
Leigh Green
Brook Street
Kenardington
Warehorne
Hamstreet
Burmarsh
Iden Green
Dingleden
Rolvenden
Reading Street
Small Hythe
Appledore Heath
Newchurch
Hawkhurst
Four Throws
Rolvenden Layne
ISLE OF OXNEY
Appledore
Snave
ROMNEY MARSH
Dymchurch
The Moor
Sandhurst
Linkhurst
Peening Quarter
Stone
Snargate
St Mary in the Marsh
Sandhurst Cross
Newenden
Wittersham
Ham Green
The Stocks
Brenzett
Ivychurch
St Mary's Bay
Bodiam
ROTHER LEVELS
Brookland
Old Romney
Littlestone on Sea
TR
Northiam
Ewhurst Green
Beckley
Four Oaks
Iden
Houghton Green
Walland Marsh
New Romney
Romney Sands
Millcorner
Clayhill
Staple Cross
Horns Cross
Peasmarsh
Rye Foreign
Playden
East Guldeford
Greatstone on Sea
Cripp's Corner
Rye
Lydd
Lydd on Sea
Denge Marsh
Vinehall Street
Broad Oak
Broadland Row
Udimore
Camber
Sedlescombe
Rye Harbour
Brede
Winchelsea
Rye Bay
Winchelsea Beach
Denge Beach
DUNGENESS
Sedlescombe Street
Guestling Thorn
Icklesham
Three Oaks
Westfield
Kent Street
Pett
Baldslow
Guestling Green
Cliff End
Crowhurst
Hollington
St Helen's
Ore
Fairlight
Fairlight Cove
Silverhill
St Leonards
West Marina
Hastings
Bulverhythe
ENGLISH CHANNEL
6
7
8
9
10
11
C
D
E
F
G
H

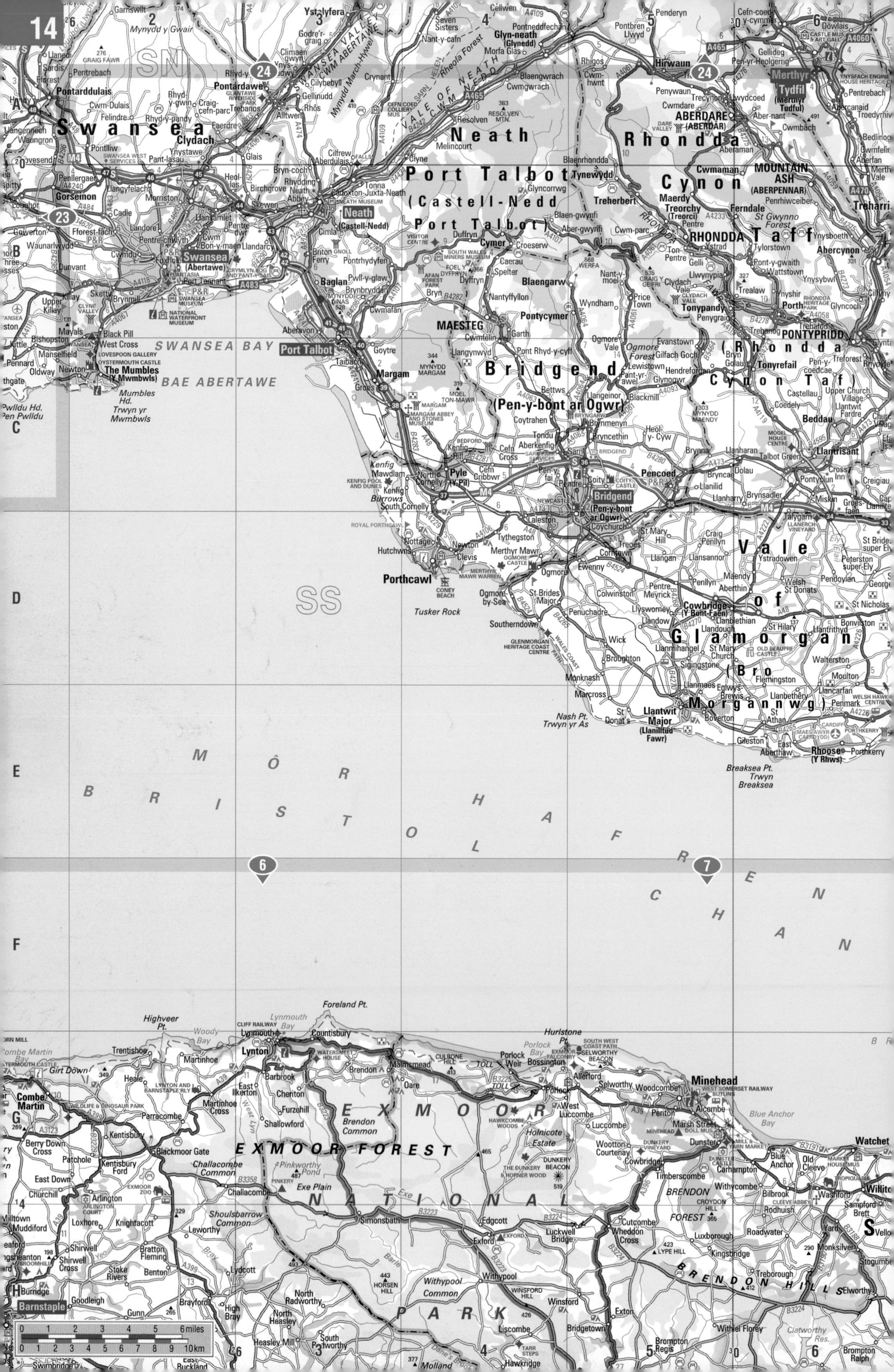
SN
SS
Swansea
Neath
Port Talbot
(Castell-Nedd Port Talbot)
Rhondda Cynon Taff
(Rhondda Cynon Taf)
Bridgend
(Pen-y-bont ar Ogwr)
Vale of Glamorgan
(Bro Morgannwg)
SWANSEA BAY
BAE ABERTAWE
BRISTOL CHANNEL
MÔR HAFREN
EXMOOR
EXMOOR FOREST
EXMOOR NATIONAL PARK
BRENDON HILLS
Swansea (Abertawe)
Neath (Castell-Nedd)
Port Talbot
Bridgend (Pen-y-bont ar Ogwr)
Merthyr Tydfil (Merthyr Tudful)
Barnstaple
Pontarddulais
Gorseinon
Clydach
Pontardawe
Ystalyfera
Glyn-neath (Glynedd)
Hirwaun
ABERDARE (ABERDAR)
MOUNTAIN ASH (ABERPENNAR)
PONTYPRIDD
Porth
Tonypandy
Treorchy (Treorci)
Maerdy
Ferndale
Llantrisant
Beddau
Talbot Green
Pencoed
Maesteg
Pontycymer
Blaengarw
Pyle (Y Pîl)
Porthcawl
Cowbridge (Y Bont-Faen)
Llantwit Major (Llanilltud Fawr)
Rhoose (Y Rhws)
The Mumbles (Y Mwmbwls)
Mumbles Hd. Trwyn yr Mwmbwls
Tusker Rock
Nash Pt. Trwyn yr As
Breaksea Pt. Trwyn Breaksea
Foreland Pt.
Highveer Pt.
Hurlstone Pt.
Lynton
Lynmouth
Combe Martin
Minehead
Porlock
Dunster
Watchet
Simonsbath
Exford
Withypool
Dulverton
A48
A465
A4109
A4061
A4107
A4063
A4119
A473
A4222
A39
A396
B3223
B3224
M4
24
23
6
7
0 1 2 3 4 5 6 miles
0 1 2 3 4 5 6 7 8 9 10km

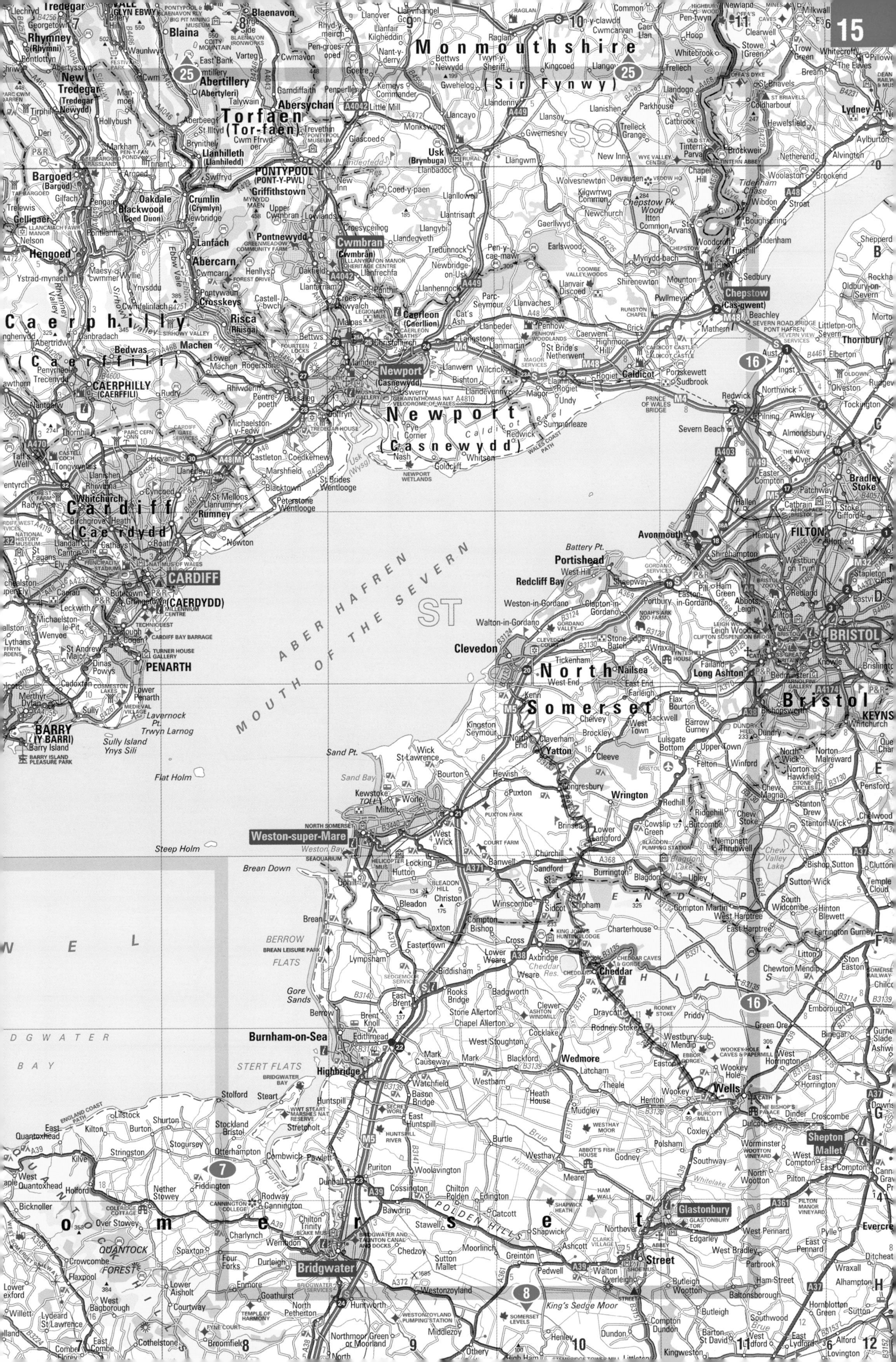
Monmouthshire
(Sir Fynwy)
Torfaen
(Tor-faen)
Caerphilly
(Caerffili)
Newport
(Casnewydd)
Cardiff
(Caerdydd)
North
Somerset
Bristol
Somerset
ABER HAFREN
MOUTH OF THE SEVERN
BRIDGWATER
BAY
Tredegar
Rhymney
(Rhymni)
New
Tredegar
Blaina
Blaenavon
Abertillery
(Abertyleri)
Abersychan
Bargoed
(Bargod)
Blackwood
(Coed Duon)
Oakdale
Crumlin
(Crymlyn)
PONTYPOOL
(PONT-Y-PWL)
Griffithstown
Pontnewydd
Cwmbran
(Cwmbrân)
Usk
(Brynbuga)
Hengoed
Gelligaer
Abercarn
Risca
(Rhisga)
Crosskeys
Caerleon
(Caerllion)
Bedwas
Machen
CAERPHILLY
(CAERFFILI)
Newport
(Casnewydd)
Chepstow
(Cas-gwent)
Caldicot
Lydney
Thornbury
CARDIFF
(CAERDYDD)
PENARTH
BARRY
(Y BARRI)
Barry Island
Sully Island
Ynys Sili
Lavernock
Pt.
Trwyn Larnog
Flat Holm
Steep Holm
Portishead
Battery Pt.
Redcliff Bay
Clevedon
Nailsea
Avonmouth
FILTON
BRISTOL
Long Ashton
KEYNSHAM
Yatton
Wrington
Congresbury
Weston-super-Mare
Sand Pt.
Sand Bay
Brean Down
Cheddar
Axbridge
Burnham-on-Sea
Highbridge
Wedmore
Wells
Shepton
Mallet
Glastonbury
Street
Bridgwater
Stolford
QUANTOCK
FOREST
POLDEN HILLS
King's Sedge Moor
BERROW
FLATS
STERT FLATS
Gore
Sands
M4
M48
M5
M49
M32
A48
A449
A4042
A38
A39
A37
A371
A370
A369
A403
25
16
7
8

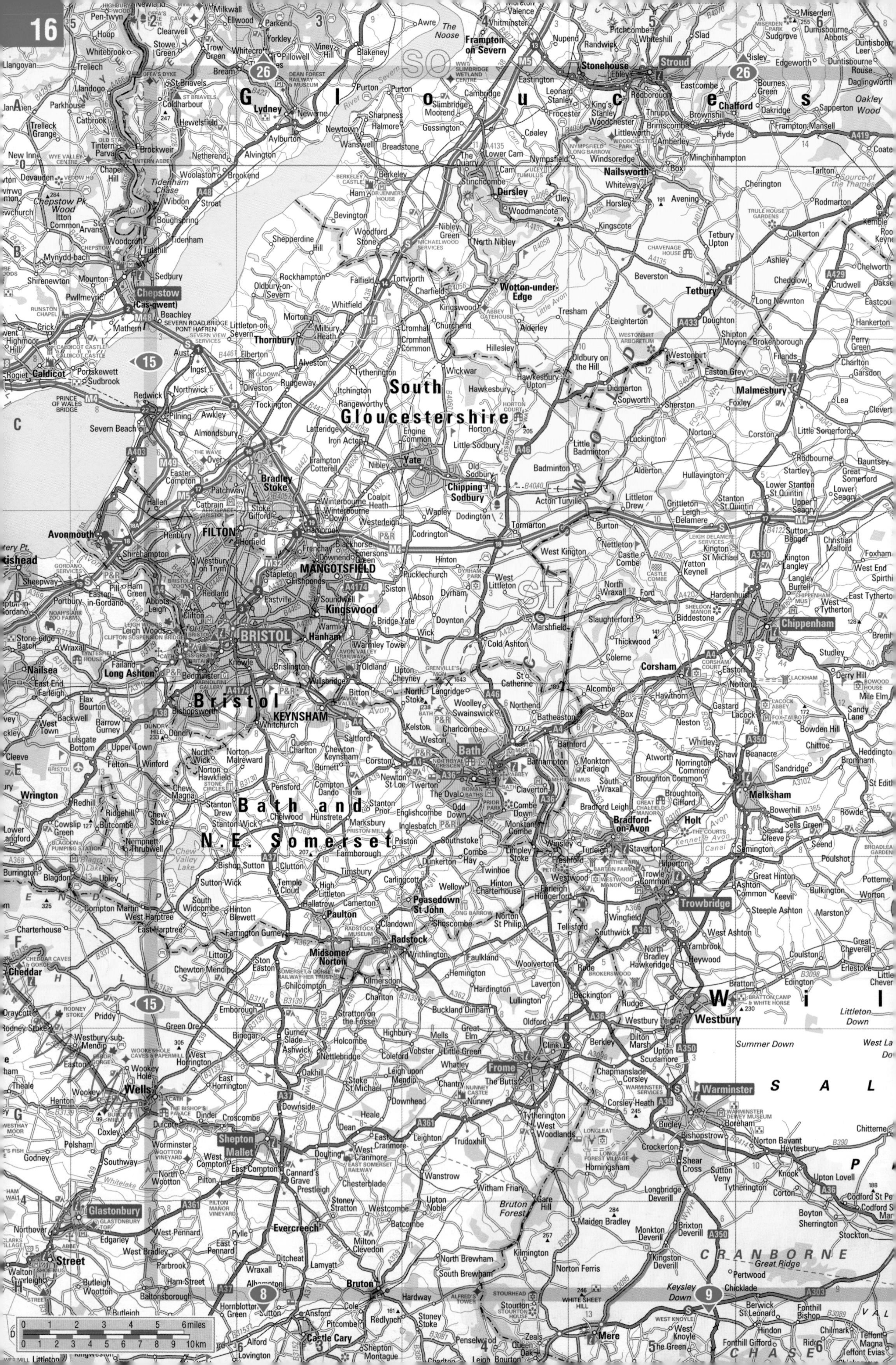
Gloucestershire
South Gloucestershire
Bristol
Bath and N.E. Somerset
Wiltshire
SALISBURY PLAIN
CRANBORNE CHASE
COTSWOLDS
Stroud
Stonehouse
Frampton on Severn
Lydney
Chepstow (Cas-gwent)
Caldicot
Dursley
Nailsworth
Tetbury
Wotton-under-Edge
Thornbury
Malmesbury
Yate
Chipping Sodbury
Bradley Stoke
Filton
Avonmouth
Mangotsfield
Kingswood
BRISTOL
Keynsham
Bath
Chippenham
Corsham
Melksham
Bradford-on-Avon
Trowbridge
Westbury
Warminster
Frome
Radstock
Midsomer Norton
Wells
Shepton Mallet
Glastonbury
Street
Bruton
Castle Cary
Mere
Nailsea
Long Ashton
Portishead
Wrington
Cheddar
Clevedon
Severn Beach
Portskewett
River Severn
The Noose
Chew Valley Lake
Blagdon Lake
Kennet & Avon Canal
Summer Down
Great Ridge
Bruton Forest
M4
M5
M48
M49
M32
A4
A36
A37
A38
A46
A350
A361
A303
15
26
8
9
0 1 2 3 4 5 6 miles
0 1 2 3 4 5 6 7 8 9 10 km

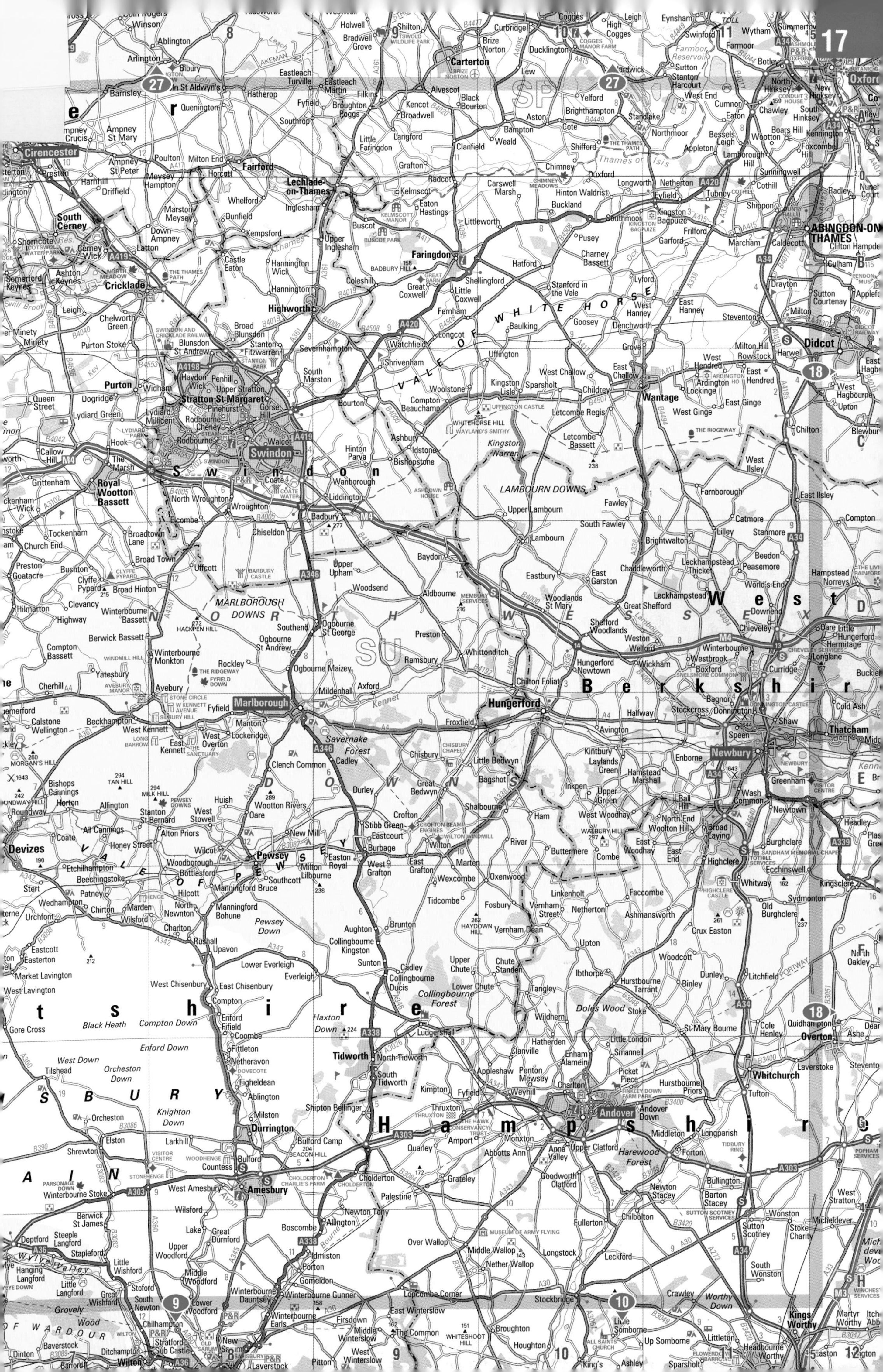
Winson
Ablington
Arlington
Bibury
Barnsley
St Aldwyn's
Quenington
Hatherop
Eastleach Turville
Eastleach Martin
Fyfield
Southrop
Filkins
Broughton Poggs
Holwell
Bradwell Grove
Shilton
Carterton
Brize Norton
Curbridge
Ducklington
Alvescot
Kencot
Broadwell
Black Bourton
Clanfield
Bampton
Weald
Aston
Cote
Yelford
Brighthampton
Standlake
Northmoor
Eynsham
Swinford
Wytham
Farmoor
Botley
Oxford
North Hinksey
Chawley
South Hinksey
Boars Hill
Wootton
Kennington
Cumnor
Eaton
Bessels Leigh
Appleton
Stanton Harcourt
Sutton
West End
Cirencester
Preston
Harnhill
Driffield
Ampney Crucis
Ampney St Mary
Ampney St Peter
Poulton
Milton End
Fairford
Meysey Hampton
Lechlade-on-Thames
Inglesham
Kelmscot
Eaton Hastings
Buscot
Faringdon
Little Faringdon
Langford
Grafton
Radcot
Littleworth
Carswell Marsh
Buckland
Hinton Waldrist
Longworth
Duxford
Chimney
Shifford
Fyfield
Kingston Bagpuize
Southmoor
Tubney
Netherton
Cothill
Shippon
Frilford
Garford
Marcham
Abingdon-on-Thames
Radley
Culham
Drayton
Sutton Courtenay
Steventon
Milton
Didcot
Harwell
Milton Hill
Rowstock
South Cerney
Cerney Wick
Ashton Keynes
Somerford Keynes
Cricklade
Latton
Down Ampney
Marston Meysey
Dunfield
Kempsford
Whelford
Castle Eaton
Hannington Wick
Hannington
Highworth
Coleshill
Great Coxwell
Little Coxwell
Shellingford
Hatford
Pusey
Charney Bassett
Stanford in the Vale
Lyford
West Hanney
East Hanney
Denchworth
Goosey
Baulking
Fernham
Longcot
Watchfield
Shrivenham
Uffington
Woolstone
Kingston Lisle
Sparsholt
West Challow
East Challow
Childrey
Wantage
Ardington
Lockinge
East Hendred
West Hendred
East Ginge
West Ginge
Letcombe Regis
Letcombe Bassett
Chilton
Blewbury
Upton
West Hagbourne
VALE OF WHITE HORSE
Leigh
Minety
Purton Stoke
Purton
Chelworth Green
Broad Blunsdon
Blunsdon St Andrew
Stanton Fitzwarren
Sevenhampton
South Marston
Bourton
Compton Beauchamp
Ashbury
Idstone
Bishopstone
Hinton Parva
Wanborough
Liddington
Badbury
Chiseldon
Swindon
Stratton St Margaret
Upper Stratton
Haydon Wick
Penhill
Pinehurst
Gorse Hill
Rodbourne
Walcot
Lydiard Millicent
Lydiard Green
Queen Street
Dogridge
Hook
Callow Hill
The Marsh
Royal Wootton Bassett
Grittenham
North Wroughton
Wroughton
Elcombe
Coate
Tockenham
Church End
Broadtown Lane
Broad Town
Bushton
Preston
Goatacre
Clyffe Pypard
Broad Hinton
Uffcott
Hilmarton
Clevancy
Highway
Winterbourne Bassett
MARLBOROUGH DOWNS
Hackpen Hill
Compton Bassett
Berwick Bassett
Winterbourne Monkton
Yatesbury
Avebury
Cherhill
Calstone Wellington
Beckhampton
West Kennett
East Kennett
West Overton
Lockeridge
Fyfield
Marlborough
Manton
Ogbourne St George
Ogbourne St Andrew
Ogbourne Maizey
Southend
Upper Upham
Woodsend
Aldbourne
Baydon
Preston
Ramsbury
Whittonditch
Axford
Mildenhall
Rockley
LAMBOURN DOWNS
Kingston Warren
Upper Lambourn
Lambourn
Eastbury
East Garston
Woodlands St Mary
Great Shefford
Shefford Woodlands
Weston
Welford
Fawley
South Fawley
Brightwalton
Chaddleworth
Leckhampstead Thicket
Leckhampstead
Farnborough
West Ilsley
East Ilsley
Lilley
Catmore
Stanmore
Compton
Beedon
Peasemore
World's End
Downend
Chieveley
Hampstead Norreys
Hermitage
Curridge
Winterbourne
Westbrook
Boxford
Wickham
Hungerford Newtown
Chilton Foliat
Hungerford
Froxfield
Halfway
Stockcross
Bagnor
Donnington
Speen
Shaw
Newbury
Thatcham
Cold Ash
Avington
Kintbury
Laylands Green
Enborne
Hamstead Marshall
Greenham
Inkpen
Upper Green
West Woodhay
Wash Common
Ball Hill
North End
Woolton Hill
Broad Laying
East Woodhay
East End
Highclere
Newtown
Burghclere
Headley
Kingsclere
Ecchinswell
Sydmonton
Old Burghclere
Whitway
Berkshire
West Berkshire
Savernake Forest
Cadley
Clench Common
Durley
Chisbury
Little Bedwyn
Great Bedwyn
Bagshot
Shalbourne
Crofton
Stibb Green
Eastcourt
Burbage
Wilton
Ham
Rivar
Buttermere
Combe
Marten
Oxenwood
Wexcombe
Tidcombe
Fosbury
Vernham Street
Vernham Dean
Linkenholt
Netherton
Faccombe
Ashmansworth
Crux Easton
Upton
Ibthorpe
Hurstbourne Tarrant
Woodcott
Dunley
Binley
Litchfield
North Oakley
Devizes
Bishops Cannings
Horton
Roundway
Coate
All Cannings
Allington
Stanton St Bernard
Alton Priors
Huish
West Stowell
Oare
Wootton Rivers
New Mill
Honey Street
Wilcot
Pewsey
Milton Lilbourne
Easton Royal
West Grafton
East Grafton
Woodborough
Bottlesford
Southcott
Manningford Bruce
Manningford Bohune
Etchilhampton
Beechingstoke
Patney
Marden
Chirton
Wilsford
Hilcott
North Newnton
Wedhampton
Urchfont
Stert
Charlton
Rushall
Upavon
Pewsey Down
Eastcott
Easterton
Market Lavington
West Lavington
VALE OF PEWSEY
Lower Everleigh
Everleigh
West Chisenbury
East Chisenbury
Compton
Enford
Fifield
Coombe
Fittleton
Netheravon
Figheldean
Ablington
Milston
Durrington
Larkhill
Bulford
Bulford Camp
Countess
Amesbury
West Amesbury
Wilsford
Lake
Great Durnford
Upper Woodford
Middle Woodford
Lower Woodford
Salisbury Plain
Black Heath
Compton Down
Enford Down
West Down
Orcheston Down
Tilshead
Orcheston
Knighton Down
Elston
Shrewton
Winterbourne Stoke
Berwick St James
Steeple Langford
Stapleford
Deptford
Hanging Langford
Little Langford
Little Wishford
Great Wishford
Wylye Valley
Grovely Wood
South Newton
Stoford
Chilhampton
Stratford sub Castle
Wilton
Ditchampton
Baverstock
Dinton
Barford
Aughton
Collingbourne Kingston
Brunton
Sunton
Cadley
Collingbourne Ducis
Collingbourne Forest
Haxton Down
Ludgershall
Tidworth
North Tidworth
South Tidworth
Shipton Bellinger
Kimpton
Fyfield
Thruxton
Amport
Quarley
Monxton
Abbotts Ann
Grateley
Cholderton
Palestine
Newton Tony
Allington
Boscombe
Idmiston
Porton
Gomeldon
Winterbourne Dauntsey
Winterbourne Gunner
Winterbourne Earls
Firsdown
Middle Winterslow
West Winterslow
The Common
East Winterslow
Lopcombe Corner
Pitton
Laverstock
Old Sarum
Upper Chute
Chute Standen
Lower Chute
Tangley
Wildhern
Doles Wood
Hatherden
Clanville
Appleshaw
Penton Mewsey
Weyhill
Enham Alamein
Charlton
Andover
Anna Valley
Upper Clatford
Goodworth Clatford
Little London
Smannell
Picket Piece
Hurstbourne Priors
Andover Down
Middleton
Longparish
Forton
Harewood Forest
St Mary Bourne
Stoke
Cole Henley
Quidhampton
Overton
Whitchurch
Laverstoke
Tufton
Bullington
Barton Stacey
Newton Stacey
Chilbolton
Wonston
Sutton Scotney
Micheldever
Stoke Charity
South Wonston
West Stratton
Fullerton
Over Wallop
Middle Wallop
Nether Wallop
Longstock
Leckford
Stockbridge
Crawley
Worthy Down
Kings Worthy
Headbourne Worthy
Martyr Worthy
Littleton
Up Somborne
Little Somborne
Broughton
Houghton
Ashley
King's Somborne
Sparsholt
Hampshire
M4
A4
A34
A303
A338
A346
A417
A419
A420
A36
A30
A345
A343
A339

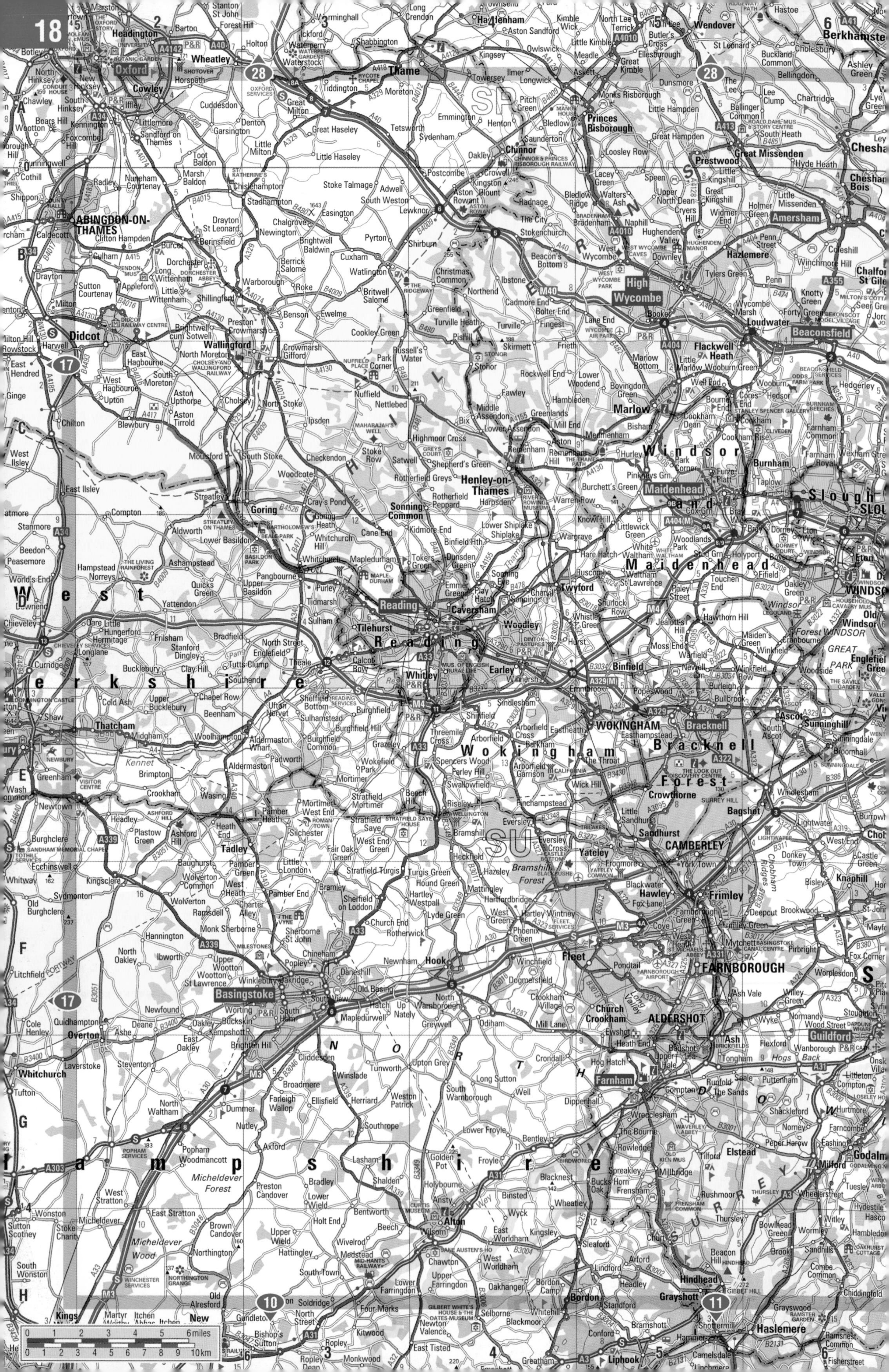

Headington
Oxford
Wheatley
Cowley
Thame
Haddenham
Wendover
Berkhamsted
Princes Risborough
Great Missenden
Chesham
Amersham
Chinnor
Stokenchurch
High Wycombe
Beaconsfield
Marlow
Maidenhead
Slough
Windsor
Eton
ABINGDON-ON-THAMES
Didcot
Wallingford
Goring
Pangbourne
Reading
Tilehurst
Caversham
Woodley
Henley-on-Thames
Twyford
Sonning Common
Wokingham
Bracknell
Ascot
Sunninghill
Thatcham
Newbury
Tadley
Crowthorne
Sandhurst
Camberley
Yateley
Frimley
Fleet
Hook
FARNBOROUGH
ALDERSHOT
Basingstoke
Overton
Whitchurch
Farnham
Alton
Bordon
Grayshott
Hindhead
Haslemere
Guildford
Godalming
Milford
Liphook
West Berkshire
Maidenhead and Windsor
Wokingham
Bracknell Forest
Hampshire
Surrey
North Downs
Chiltern Hills
SP
SU
M4
M40
M3
A34
A33
A30
A31
A339
A303
A329(M)
A404(M)
0 1 2 3 4 5 6 miles
0 1 2 3 4 5 6 7 8 9 10 km

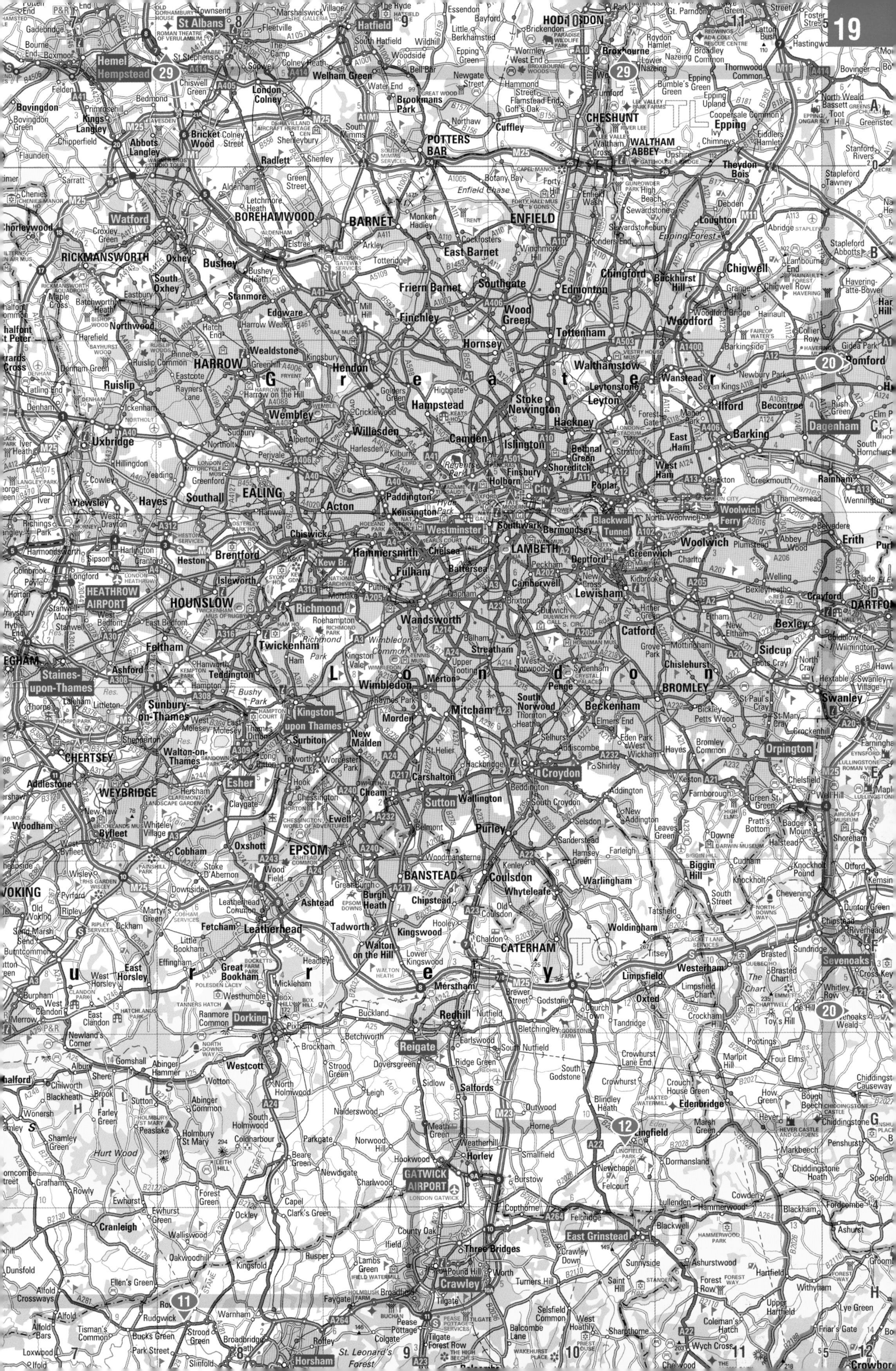
St Albans
Hatfield
Hemel Hempstead
Hoddesdon
Broxbourne
Harlow
Watford
Borehamwood
Barnet
Enfield
Cheshunt
Waltham Abbey
Epping
Potters Bar
Rickmansworth
Harrow
Chingford
Loughton
Chigwell
Woodford
Romford
Wembley
Hampstead
Camden
Islington
Hackney
Ilford
Barking
Dagenham
Uxbridge
Ealing
Southall
Hayes
Acton
Paddington
Westminster
City
Lambeth
Woolwich
Erith
Dartford
Heathrow Airport
Hounslow
Richmond
Brentford
Hammersmith
Fulham
Chelsea
Wandsworth
Lewisham
Bexley
Egham
Staines-upon-Thames
Twickenham
Kingston upon Thames
Wimbledon
Croydon
Bromley
Orpington
Swanley
Chertsey
Weybridge
Esher
Epsom
Sutton
Purley
Woking
Leatherhead
Banstead
Coulsdon
Caterham
Sevenoaks
Dorking
Reigate
Redhill
Westerham
Oxted
Edenbridge
Lingfield
Horley
Gatwick Airport
East Grinstead
Crawley
Cranleigh
Horsham
Crowborough
Greater London
Surrey
M25
M1
M11
M20
M23
M3
M4
M40
Thames

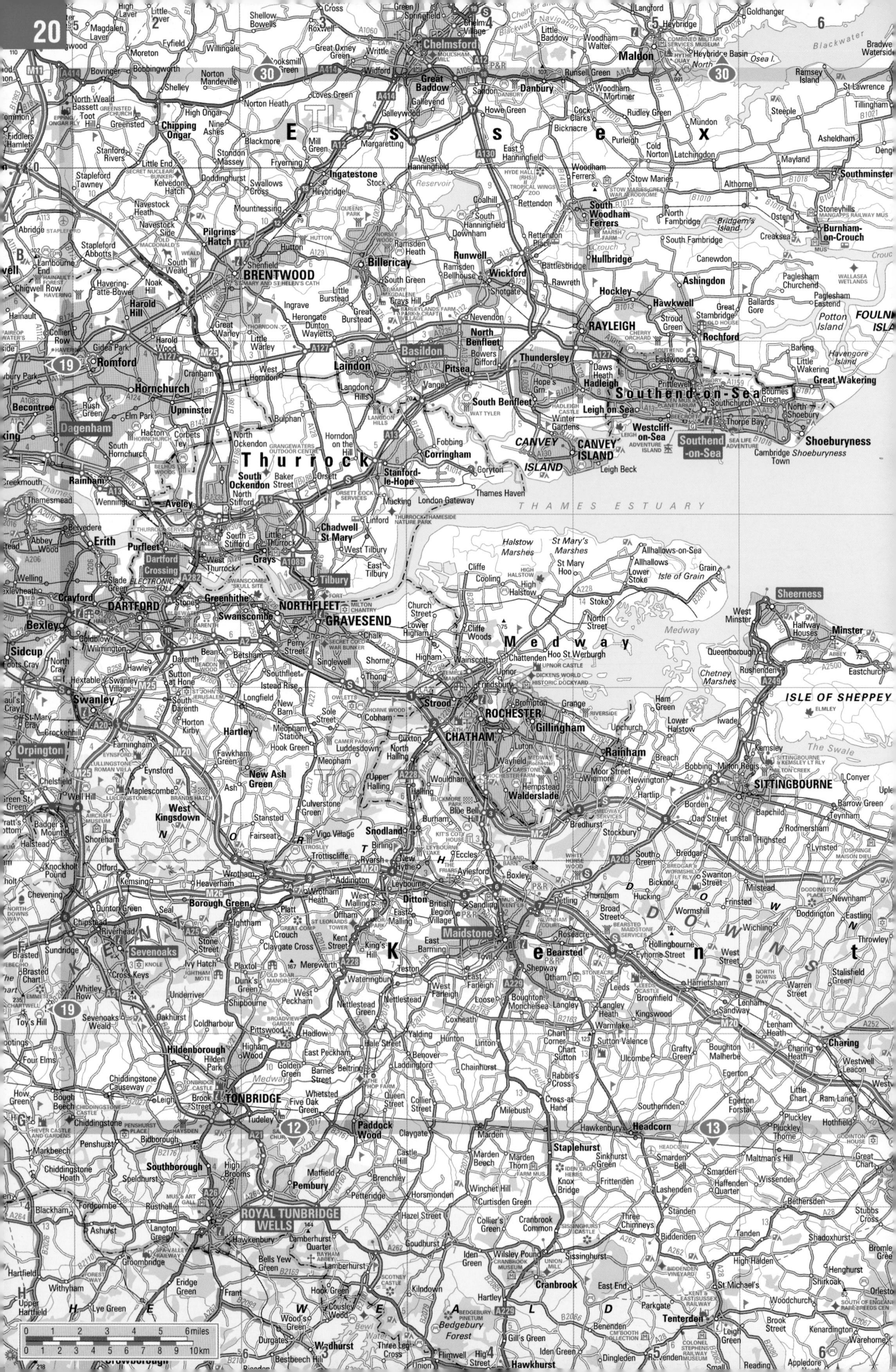
Essex
Kent
Medway
Thurrock
Chelmsford
Maldon
Great Baddow
Danbury
Chipping Ongar
Ingatestone
Billericay
BRENTWOOD
Wickford
South Woodham Ferrers
Burnham-on-Crouch
Southminster
Hullbridge
Hockley
RAYLEIGH
Rochford
Ashingdon
Hawkwell
Basildon
Laindon
Pitsea
North Benfleet
South Benfleet
Thundersley
Hadleigh
Leigh on Sea
Westcliff-on-Sea
Southend-on-Sea
Shoeburyness
Great Wakering
CANVEY ISLAND
Romford
Hornchurch
Upminster
Dagenham
Becontree
Harold Hill
Rainham
Corringham
Stanford-le-Hope
South Ockendon
Aveley
Grays
Tilbury
Purfleet
Dartford Crossing
Erith
Bexley
Sidcup
Crayford
DARTFORD
Swanscombe
Greenhithe
NORTHFLEET
GRAVESEND
Swanley
Orpington
Strood
ROCHESTER
CHATHAM
Gillingham
Rainham
Walderslade
Sheerness
Minster
ISLE OF SHEPPEY
SITTINGBOURNE
Snodland
Maidstone
Bearsted
Sevenoaks
Borough Green
West Malling
Ditton
Aylesford
Paddock Wood
TONBRIDGE
Hildenborough
Southborough
ROYAL TUNBRIDGE WELLS
Pembury
Headcorn
Staplehurst
Marden
Cranbrook
Charing
Tenterden
Wadhurst
Hawkhurst
Bedgebury Forest
THAMES ESTUARY
Medway
Isle of Grain
Halstow Marshes
St Mary's Marshes
Potton Island
Foulness Island
Blackwater
The Swale
NORTH DOWNS
WEALD
0 1 2 3 4 5 6 miles
0 1 2 3 4 5 6 7 8 9 10 km

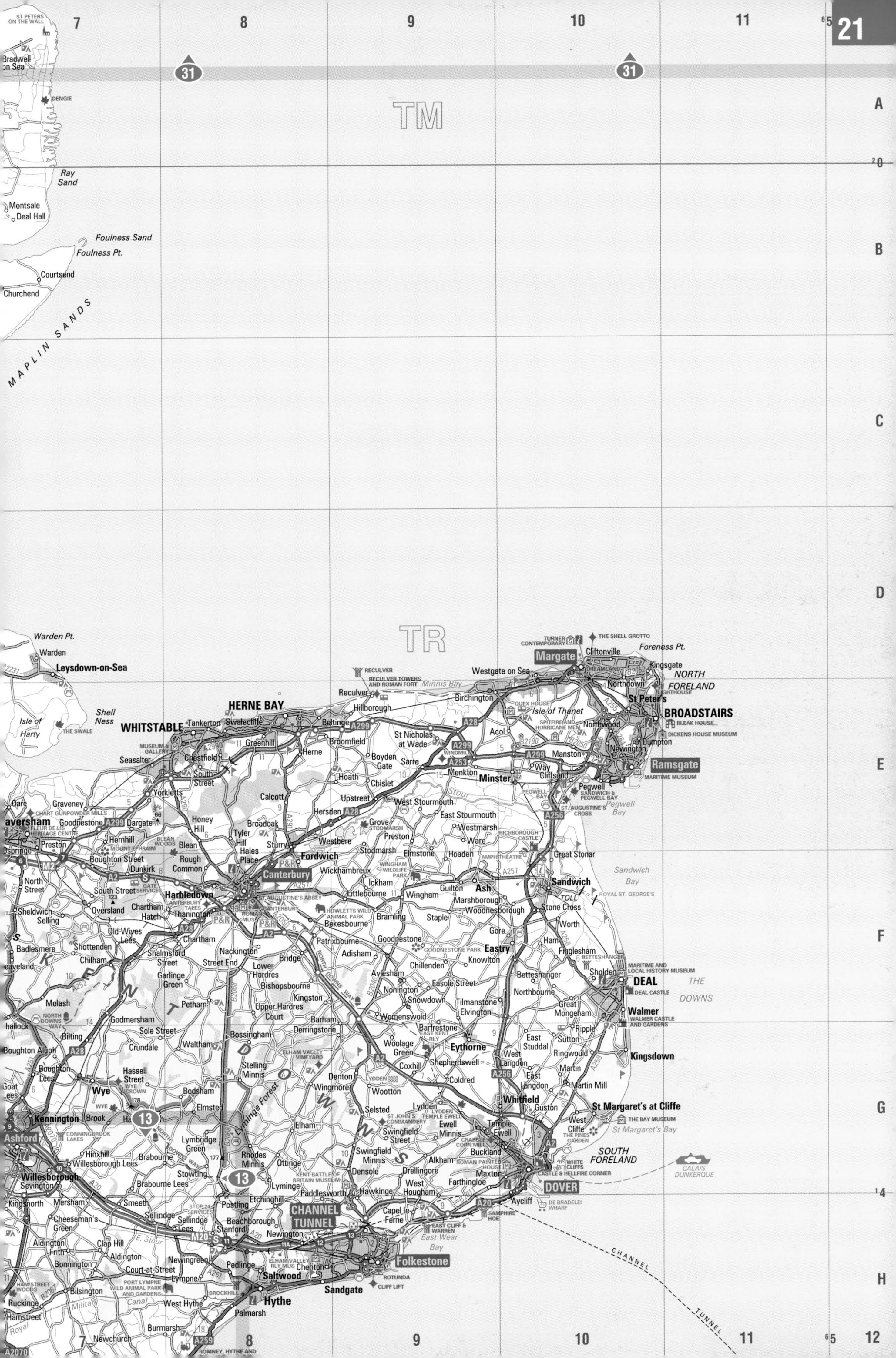
TM
TR
ST PETERS ON THE WALL
Bradwell on Sea
DENGIE
Ray Sand
Montsale
Deal Hall
Foulness Sand
Foulness Pt.
Courtsend
Churchend
MAPLIN SANDS
Warden Pt.
Warden
Leysdown-on-Sea
Isle of Harty
THE SWALE
Shell Ness
WHITSTABLE
Tankerton
Swalecliffe
HERNE BAY
Seasalter
Chestfield
Greenhill
Herne
South Street
Yorkletts
Graveney
Oare
Faversham
Goodnestone
Dargate
Hernhill
Preston
Boughton Street
Dunkirk
Honey Hill
Blean
Rough Common
Tyler Hill
Hales Place
Broadoak
Calcott
Sturry
Fordwich
Canterbury
Harbledown
Thanington
Chartham Hatch
Chartham
Oversland
Selling
Sheldwich
North Street
South Street
Old Wives Lees
Badlesmere
Shottenden
Chilham
Shalmsford Street
Garlinge Green
Nackington
Street End
Lower Hardres
Bishopsbourne
Bridge
Petham
Molash
Godmersham
Bilting
Sole Street
Crundale
Waltham
Bossingham
Upper Hardres Court
Kingston
Barham
Derringstone
Stelling Minnis
Boughton Aluph
Boughton Lees
Hassell Street
Wye
Bodsham
Elmsted
Kennington
Brook
Ashford
Willesborough
Willesborough Lees
Hinxhill
Brabourne
Brabourne Lees
Lymbridge Green
Stowting
Sevington
Mersham
Kingsnorth
Cheeseman's Green
Smeeth
Sellindge
Aldington
Aldington Frith
Clap Hill
Bonnington
Newingreen
Court-at-Street
Lympne
Bilsington
Ruckinge
Hamstreet
West Hythe
Burmarsh
Newchurch
Hythe
Palmarsh
Saltwood
Sandgate
Folkestone
Cheriton
Newington
Pedlinge
Postling
Etchinghill
Lyminge
Rhodes Minnis
Ottinge
Paddlesworth
Hawkinge
Densole
Swingfield Minnis
Swingfield Street
Elham
Selsted
Denton
Wingmore
Wootton
Lydden
Coxhill
Shepherdswell
Coldred
Eythorne
Woolage Green
Womenswold
Barfrestone
Nonington
Snowdown
Aylesham
Adisham
Patrixbourne
Bekesbourne
Littlebourne
Ickham
Wickhambreux
Stodmarsh
Westbere
Hersden
Upstreet
Chislet
Hoath
Boyden Gate
Broomfield
Beltinge
Hillborough
Reculver
Minnis Bay
Birchington
Westgate on Sea
Margate
Cliftonville
Foreness Pt.
Kingsgate
NORTH FORELAND
Northdown
St Peter's
BROADSTAIRS
Dumpton
Northwood
Newington
Manston
Ramsgate
Isle of Thanet
Acol
St Nicholas at Wade
Sarre
Monkton
Minster
Cliffsend
Pegwell
Pegwell Bay
West Stourmouth
East Stourmouth
Westmarsh
Ware
Grove
Preston
Elmstone
Hoaden
Wingham
Bramling
Guilton
Ash
Marshborough
Woodnesborough
Staple
Goodnestone
Chillenden
Knowlton
Eastry
Gore
Sandwich
Sandwich Bay
Great Stonar
Stone Cross
Worth
Ham
Finglesham
Betteshanger
Northbourne
Sholden
DEAL
THE DOWNS
Walmer
Great Mongeham
Ripple
Sutton
Tilmanstone
Elvington
East Studdal
Ringwould
Kingsdown
West Langdon
East Langdon
Martin
Martin Mill
Whitfield
Guston
St Margaret's at Cliffe
St Margaret's Bay
West Cliffe
SOUTH FORELAND
Temple Ewell
Ewell Minnis
Buckland
Alkham
Drellingore
West Hougham
Maxton
Farthingloe
DOVER
Aycliff
Capel le Ferne
East Wear Bay
CHANNEL TUNNEL
CALAIS DUNKERQUE
Stour
E. Stour
Royal Military Canal
Lyminge Forest
NORTH DOWNS WAY
KENT
DOWNS

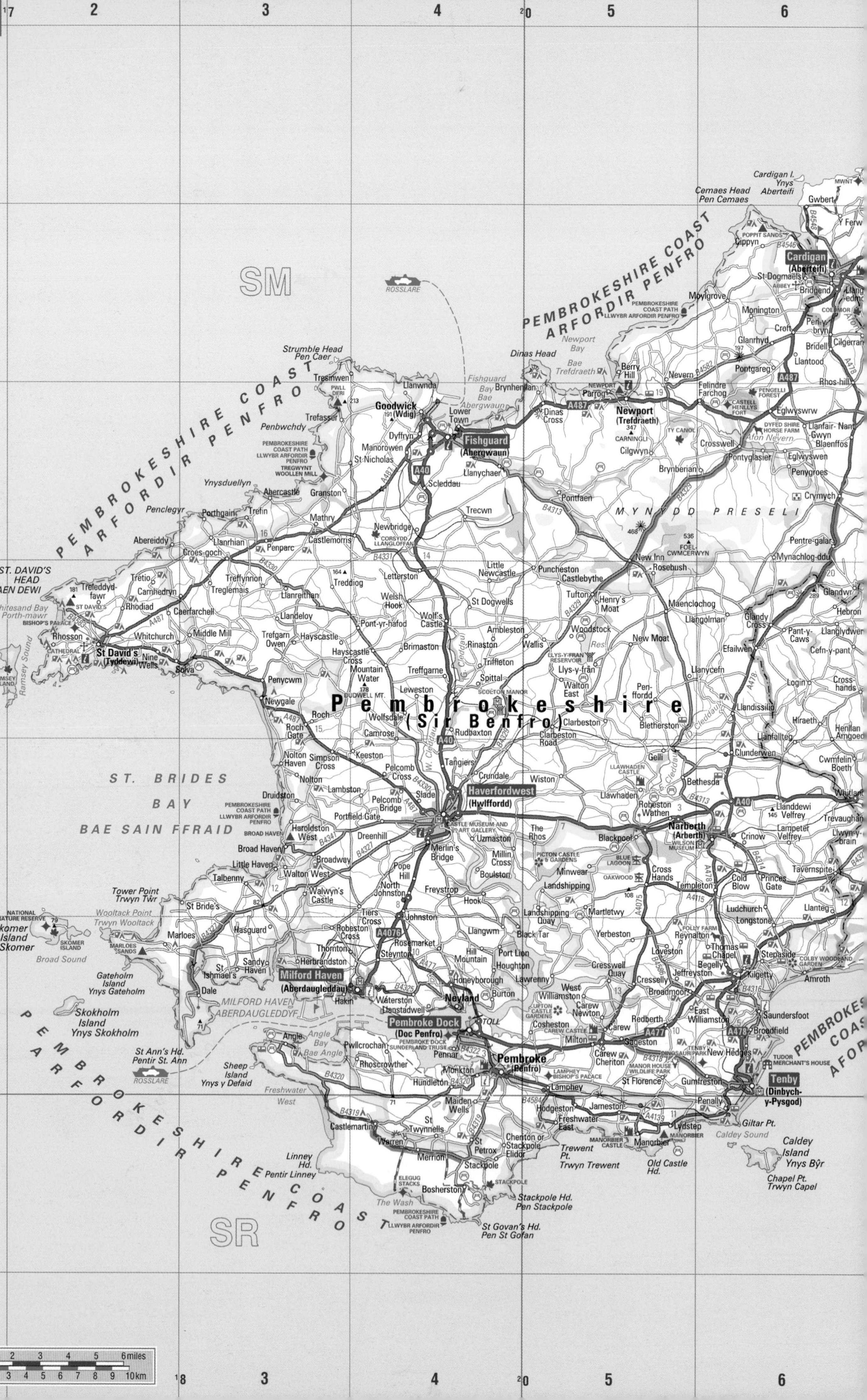
SM
SR
Pembrokeshire
(Sir Benfro)
PEMBROKESHIRE COAST
ARFORDIR PENFRO
MYNYDD PRESELI
ST. BRIDES BAY
BAE SAIN FFRAID
ROSSLARE
Cardigan I.
Ynys Aberteifi
Cemaes Head
Pen Cemaes
Gwbert
Y Ferwig
Cardigan
(Aberteifi)
Poppit Sands
Cippyn
St Dogmaels
Bridgend
Llangoedmor
Moylgrove
Monington
Croft
Pen-y-bryn
Cilgerran
Glanrhyd
Bridell
Pontgareg
Llantood
Newport Bay
Dinas Head
Bae Trefdraeth
Berry Hill
Nevern
Felindre Farchog
Castell Henllys Fort
Pengelli Forest
Rhos-hill
Eglwyswrw
Newport
(Trefdraeth)
Parrog
Carningli
Cilgwyn
Ty Canol
Crosswell
Dyfed Shire Horse Farm
Afon Nevern
Llanfair-Nant-Gwyn
Blaenffos
Pontyglasier
Eglwyswen
Penygroes
Crymych
Brynberian
Pontfaen
Foel Cwmcerwyn
Pentre-galar
Mynachlog-ddu
New Inn
Rosebush
Strumble Head
Pen Caer
Tresinwen
Pwll Deri
Goodwick
(Wdig)
Llanwnda
Fishguard Bay
Bae Abergwaun
Lower Town
Brynhenllan
Dinas Cross
Fishguard
(Abergwaun)
Trefasser
Penbwchdy
Dyffryn
Manorowen
St Nicholas
Llanychaer
Scleddau
Tregwynt Woollen Mill
Ynysduellyn
Abercastle
Granston
Trecwn
Penclegyr
Porthgain
Trefin
Mathry
Newbridge
Corsydd Llangloffan
Abereiddy
Llanrhian
Penparc
Castlemorris
Croes-goch
Treffynnon
Treddiog
Letterston
Little Newcastle
Puncheston
Castlebythe
Tufton
Henry's Moat
Maenclochog
St. David's Head
Penmaen Dewi
Treleddyd-fawr
Tretio
Carnhedryn
Treglemais
Llanreithan
Welsh Hook
Wolf's Castle
St Dogwells
Llangolman
Glandy Cross
Glandwr
Hebron
Whitesand Bay
Porth-mawr
Bishop's Palace
Rhodiad
Caerfarchell
Llandeloy
Pont-yr-hafod
Ambleston
Woodstock
New Moat
Pant-y-Caws
Llanglydwen
Cefn-y-pant
Ramsey Island
Ynys Dewi
Ramsey Sound
Rhosson
Cathedral
St David's
(Tyddewi)
Whitchurch
Middle Mill
Nine Wells
Solva
Trefgarn Owen
Hayscastle
Hayscastle Cross
Mountain Water
Brimaston
Rinaston
Wallis
Llys-y-frân Reservoir
Llys-y-frân
Efailwen
Treffgarne
Triffleton
Spittal
Walton East
Llanycefn
Login
Cross-hands
Penycwm
Newgale
Dudwell Mt.
Leweston
Penffordd
Roch
Roch Gate
Wolfsdale
Camrose
Rudbaxton
Clarbeston
Clarbeston Road
Bletherston
Llandissilio
Hiraeth
Llanfallteg
Henllan Amgoed
Nolton Haven
Simpson Cross
Keeston
Pelcomb Cross
Tangiers
Crundale
Wiston
Gelli
Clunderwen
Cwmfelin Boeth
Nolton
Lambston
Llawhaden Castle
Bethesda
Druidston
Pelcomb Bridge
Slade
Haverfordwest
(Hwlffordd)
Llawhaden
Robeston Wathen
Whitland
Llanddewi Velfrey
Portfield Gate
Broad Haven
Haroldston West
Dreenhill
Castle Museum and Art Gallery
The Rhos
Uzmaston
Blackpool
Narberth
(Arberth)
Wilson Museum
Crinow
Lampeter Velfrey
Trevaughan
Llwyn-y-brain
Merlin's Bridge
Millin Cross
Picton Castle & Gardens
Blue Lagoon
Oakwood
Cross Hands
Templeton
Cold Blow
Princes Gate
Tavernspite
Little Haven
Broadway
Walton West
Talbenny
Pope Hill
Boulston
Minwear
Landshipping
Tower Point
Trwyn Twr
Walwyn's Castle
North Johnston
Freystrop
Hook
Martletwy
Ludchurch
Longstone
Llanteg
National Nature Reserve
Wooltack Point
Trwyn Woolteck
St Bride's
Tiers Cross
Johnston
Landshipping Quay
Black Tar
Yerbeston
Folly Farm
Reynalton
Skomer Island
Ynys Skomer
Marloes
Hasguard
Robeston Cross
Rosemarket
Llangwm
Loveston
Thomas Chapel
Stepaside
Colby Woodland Garden
Marloes Sands
Broad Sound
Thornton
Herbrandston
Steynton
Hill Mountain
Port Lion
Houghton
Cresswell Quay
Begelly
Amroth
Gateholm Island
Ynys Gateholm
St Ishmael's
Sandy Haven
Milford Haven
(Aberdaugleddau)
Honeyborough
Lawrenny
Jeffreyston
Cresselly
Kilgetty
Dale
Waterston
Neyland
Burton
West Williamston
Broadmoor
Milford Haven
Aberdaugleddyf
Hakin
Llanstadwell
Upton Castle Gardens
Carew Newton
East Williamston
Saundersfoot
Skokholm Island
Ynys Skokholm
Pembroke Dock
(Doc Penfro)
Toll
Cosheston
Carew Castle
Redberth
Broadfield
Angle
Angle Bay
Bae Angle
Pwllcrochan
Pembroke Dock Sunderland Trust
Milton
Carew
Sageston
Tenby Dinosaur Park
New Hedges
Tudor Merchant's House
St Ann's Hd.
Pentir St. Ann
Rhoscrowther
Pennar
Pembroke
(Penfro)
Carew Cheriton
Manor House Wildlife Park
Sheep Island
Ynys y Defaid
Hundleton
Monkton
Lamphey Bishop's Palace
St Florence
Gumfreston
Tenby
(Dinbych-y-Pysgod)
Freshwater West
Lamphey
Maiden Wells
Hodgeston
Jameston
Penally
Giltar Pt.
Castlemartin
St Twynnells
Freshwater East
Lydstep
Caldey Sound
Warren
St Petrox
Cheriton or Stackpole Elidor
Trewent Pt.
Trwyn Trewent
Manorbier Castle
Manorbier
Old Castle Hd.
Caldey Island
Ynys Bŷr
Linney Hd.
Pentir Linney
Merrion
Stackpole
Chapel Pt.
Trwyn Capel
Elegug Stacks
Bosherston
Stackpole Hd.
Pen Stackpole
The Wash
Pembrokeshire Coast Path
Llwybr Arfordir Penfro
St Govan's Hd.
Pen St Gofan
A40
A487
A477
A478
A4076
B4313
B4329
B4330
B4331
B4320
B4319
B4322
B4327
B4341
B4325
B4584
B4582
B4546
B4548
0 1 2 3 4 5 6 miles
0 1 2 3 4 5 6 7 8 9 10 km
A
B
C
D
E
F
G
H
2
3
4
5
6

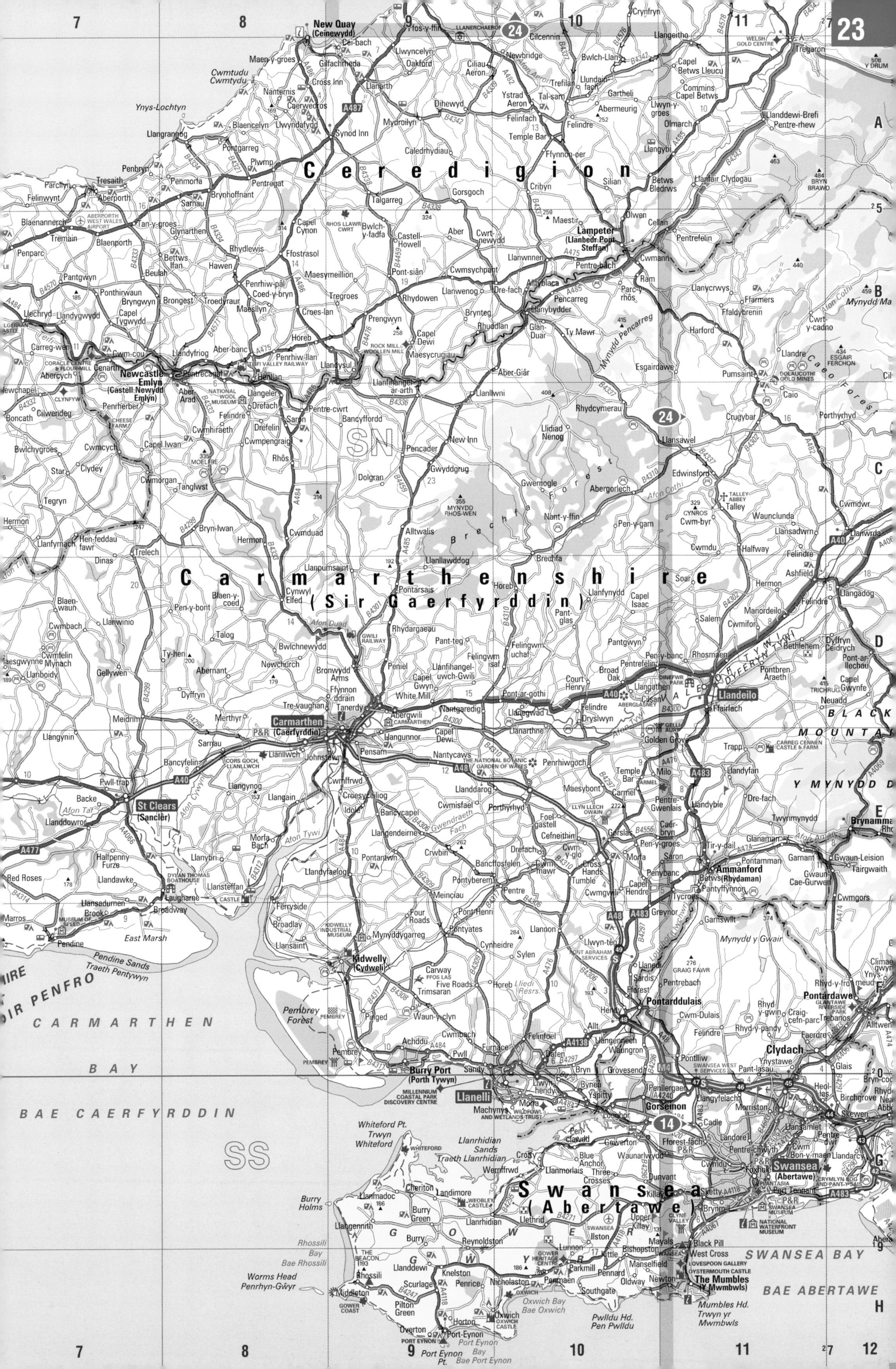
Ceredigion
Carmarthenshire
(Sir Gaerfyrddin)
Swansea
(Abertawe)
CARMARTHEN
BAY
BAE CAERFYRDDIN
SWANSEA BAY
BAE ABERTAWE
SIR PENFRO
SN
SS
New Quay
(Ceinewydd)
Cei-bach
Maen-y-groes
Gilfachrheda
Cross Inn
Llanarth
Oakford
Llwyncelyn
Ffos-y-ffin
Cilcennin
Cwmtudu
Cwmtydu
Ynys-Lochtyn
Nanternis
Caerwedros
Llwyndafydd
Blaencelyn
Llangrannog
Synod Inn
Mydroilyn
Dihewyd
Ciliau Aeron
Newbridge
Ystrad Aeron
Felinfach
Temple Bar
Trefilan
Tal-sarn
Llundain-fach
Bwlch-Llan
Llangeitho
Capel Betws Lleucu
Commins Capel Betws
Gartheli
Abermeurig
Llwyn-y-groes
Olmarch
Felindre
Llangybi
Tregaron
Llanddewi-Brefi
Pentre-rhew
Ffynnon-oer
Cribyn
Silian
Betws Bledrws
Llanfair Clydogau
Caledrhydiau
Pontgarreg
Plwmp
Penbryn
Tresaith
Parcllyn
Aberporth
Penmorfa
Pentregat
Brynhoffnant
Sarnau
Felinwynt
Blaenannerch
Tan-y-groes
Glynarthen
Tremain
Blaenporth
Penparc
Rhydlewis
Bettws Ifan
Hawen
Beulah
Pantgwyn
Capel Cynon
Talgarreg
Bwlch-y-fadfa
Gorsgoch
Castell-Howell
Aber
Cwrt-newydd
Maestir
Lampeter
(Llanbedr Pont Steffan)
Olwen
Cellan
Pentrefelin
Cwmann
Fostrasol
Maesymeillion
Pont-siân
Cwmsychpant
Llanwnnen
Pentre-bach
Ram
Parc-y-rhôs
Llanycrwys
Ffarmers
Ffaldybrenin
Penthirwaun
Bryngwyn
Brongest
Troedyraur
Penrhiw-pâl
Coed-y-bryn
Maesllyn
Tregroes
Rhydowen
Llanwenog
Dre-fach
Alltyblaca
Pencarreg
Llanybydder
Mynydd Pencarreg
Capel Tygwydd
Llechryd
Llandygwydd
Croes-lan
Prengwyn
Capel Dewi
Brynteg
Rhuddlan
Glan-Duar
Ty Mawr
Harford
Cwrt-y-cadno
Carreg-wen
Cwm-cou
Llandyfriog
Aber-banc
Horeb
Penrhiw-llan
Llandysul
Maesycrugiau
Esgairdawe
Pumsaint
Caio
Caeo Forest
Llandre
Cenarth
Abercych
Newcastle Emlyn
(Castell Newydd Emlyn)
Pentrecagal
Henllan
Llangeler
Drefach
Aber-Arad
Felindre
Llanfihangel-ar-arth
Aber-Giâr
Llanllwni
Rhydcymerau
Crugybar
Porthyrhyd
Boncath
Cilwendeg
Penrherber
Cwmhiraeth
Pentre-cwrt
Saron
Bancyffordd
Llidiad Nenog
Llansawel
Bwlchygroes
Cwmcych
Capel Iwan
Cwmpengraig
Drefelin
Pencader
New Inn
Rhôs
Edwinsford
Star
Clydey
Cwmorgan
Tanglwst
Dolgran
Gwyddgrug
Gwernogle
Abergorlech
Talley
Cwm-byr
Waunclunda
Tegryn
Mynydd Rhos-Wen
Brechfa Forest
Nant-y-ffin
Pen-y-garn
Cwmdu
Llansadwrn
Hermon
Llanfyrnach
Hen-feddau fawr
Bryn-Iwan
Cwmduad
Alltwalis
Halfway
Dinas
Trelech
Llanpumsaint
Llanllawddog
Brechfa
Soar
Felindre
Ashfield
Llangadog
Blaen-y-coed
Cynwyl Elfed
Pontarsais
Horeb
Llanfynydd
Capel Isaac
Blaen-waun
Pen-y-bont
Pant-glas
Manordeilo
Cwmbach
Llanwinio
Afon Duad
Salem
Cwmifor
Talog
Rhydargaeau
Pant-teg
Pantgwyn
Dyffryn Ceidrych
Bethlehem
Cwmfelin Mynach
Ty-hen
Bwlchnewydd
Felingwm uchaf
Pen-y-banc
Rhosmaen
Pont-ar-llechau
Llanboidy
Gellywen
Abernant
Newchurch
Felingwm isaf
Pentrefelin
Dyffryn Tywi
Llanfihangel-uwch-Gwili
Capel Gwyn
Peniel
Broad Oak
Court Henry
Llangathen
Llandeilo
Pontbren Araeth
Capel Gwynfe
Dyffryn
Bronwydd Arms
Ffynnon ddrain
White Mill
Pont-ar-gothi
Felindre
Dryslwyn
Ffairfach
Neuadd
Black Mountain
Tre-vaughan
Tanerdy
Abergwili
Nantgaredig
Llanegwad
Meidrim
Merthyr
Carmarthen
(Caerfyrddin)
Llangunnor
Capel Dewi
Llanarthne
Golden Grove
Trapp
Carreg Cennen Castle & Farm
Llangynin
Sarnau
Llanllwch
Johnstown
Pensarn
Nantycaws
Penrhiwgoch
Temple Bar
Milo
Y Mynydd Du
Bancyfelin
Pwll-trap
St Clears
(Sanclêr)
Llangynog
Cwmffrwd
Llanddarog
Maesybont
Carmel
Llandyfan
Backe
Afon Taf
Llanddowror
Llangain
Croesyceiliog
Idole
Bancycapel
Cwmisfael
Porthyrhyd
Foel-gastell
Cefneithin
Pentre-Gwenlais
Llandybie
Dre-fach
Twynmynydd
Brynamman
Llangendeirne
Gwendraeth Fach
Crwbin
Gorslas
Caer-bryn
Glanaman
Garnant
Gwaun-Leision
Tairgwaith
Halfpenny Furze
Llanybri
Morfa Bach
Pontantwn
Drefach
Cwm-y-glo
Cross Hands
Pen-y-groes
Tir-y-dail
Pontamman
Ammanford
Betws (Rhydaman)
Pantyffynnon
Gwaun-Cae-Gurwen
Red Roses
Llandawke
Llansteffan
Llandyfaelog
Bancffosfelen
Cwm-mawr
Tumble
Morfa
Saron
Penybanc
Capel Hendre
Cwmgwili
Tycroes
Cwmgors
Marros
Llansadurnen
Brook
Laugharne
Broadway
Ferryside
Meinciau
Pontyberem
Pentre
Greynor
Garnswllt
Mynydd y Gwair
Pendine
East Marsh
Pendine Sands
Traeth Pentywyn
Broadlay
Four Roads
Pont-Henri
Pontyates
Llannon
Llansaint
Mynyddygarreg
Cynheidre
Llwyn-teg
Sylen
Kidwelly
(Cydweli)
Carway
Five Roads
Trimsaran
Horeb
Lliedi Resrs.
Llanedi
Sardis
Fforest
Pontrebach
Pontarddulais
Pontardawe
Rhyd-y-fro
Pembrey Forest
Pinged
Waun-y-clyn
Hendy
Cwm-Dulais
Rhyd-y-gwin
Craig-cefn-parc
Trebanos
Alltwen
Rhyd-y-pandy
Felindre
Achddu
Cwmbach
Pembrey
Pwll
Furnace
Felinfoel
Allt
Llangennech
Waungron
Pontlliw
Clydach
Ynystawe
Pant-lasau
Glais
Burry Port
(Porth Tywyn)
Millennium Coastal Park Discovery Centre
Sandy
Llanelli
Dafen
Bryn
Llwynhendy
Bynea
Yspitty
Grovesend
Penllergaer
Gorseinon
Llangyfelach
Morriston
Heol-las
Birchgrove
Skewen
Machynys
Morfa
Loughor
Cadle
Llansamlet
Whiteford Pt.
Trwyn Whiteford
Llanrhidian Sands
Traeth Llanrhidian
Crofty
Penclawdd
Gowerton
Waunarlwydd
Fforest-fach
Landore
Pentre-chwyth
Cwm
Bon-y-maen
Llandarcy
Weobley Castle
Wernffrwd
Llanmorlais
Blue Anchor
Three Crosses
Dunvant
Cwmdu
Foxhole
Swansea
(Abertawe)
Port Tennant
Cheriton
Landimore
Llanmadoc
Burry Holms
Burry Green
Llanrhidian
Llethrid
Upper Killay
Killay
Sketty
Brynmill
National Waterfront Museum
Llangennith
Gower
Burry
Reynoldston
Ilston
Mayals
Black Pill
Rhossili Bay
Bae Rhossili
The Beacon
Rhossili
Llanddewi
Knelston
Lunnon
Parkmill
Kittle
Bishopston
West Cross
Worms Head
Penrhyn-Gŵyr
Scurlage
Penrice
Nicholaston
Penmaen
Pennard
Mansel field
Oldway
Newton
Lovespoon Gallery
Oystermouth Castle
The Mumbles
(Y Mwmbwls)
Middleton
Pilton Green
Southgate
Oxwich Bay
Bae Oxwich
Oxwich
Horton
Mumbles Hd.
Trwyn yr Mwmbwls
Pwlldu Hd.
Pen Pwlldu
Overton
Port-Eynon
Port Eynon Pt.
Port Eynon Bay
Bae Port Eynon
A487
A486
A475
A485
A484
A40
A48
A483
A477
A4066
A4138
A4067
A4118
A4069
A474
A482
B4342
B4338
B4337
B4343
B4333
B4334
B4299
B4298
B4301
B4310
B4300
B4302
B4306
B4308
B4309
B4317
B4312
B4311
B4297
B4295
B4271
B4247
B4296
B4556
B4570
B4332
B4314
B4459
B4476
M4
24
14
7
8
9
10
11
12
A
B
C
D
E
F
G
H

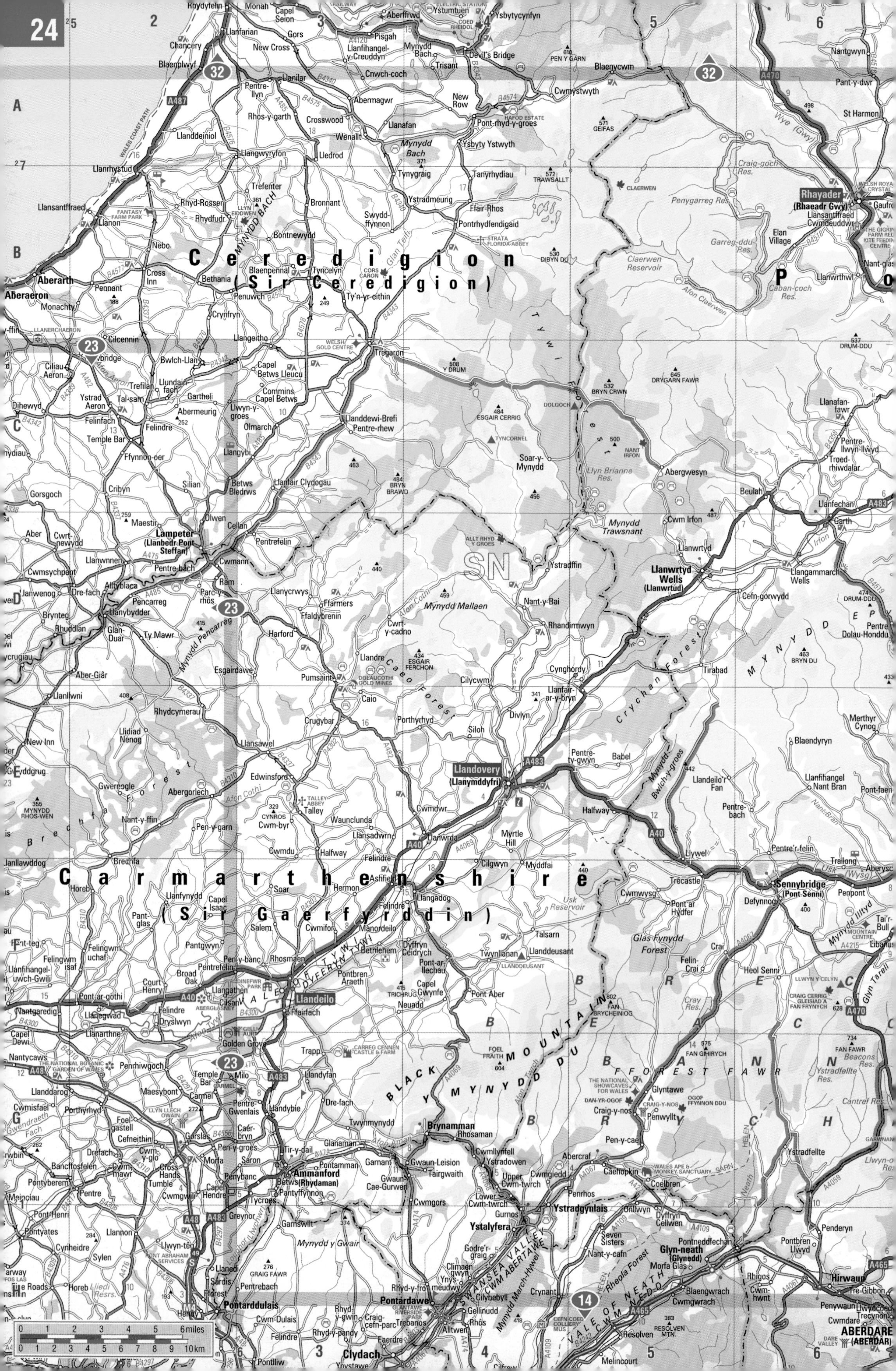
Ceredigion
(Sir Ceredigion)
Carmarthenshire
(Sir Gaerfyrddin)
SN
Aberaeron
Aberarth
Llanrhystud
Llansantffraed
Llanon
Chancery
Blaenplwyf
Llanfarian
Rhydyfelin
Capel Seion
Gors
New Cross
Pisgah
Aberffrwd
Ystumtuen
Ysbytycynfyn
Devil's Bridge
Trisant
Mynydd Bach
Llanfihangel-y-Creuddyn
Llanilar
Cnwch-coch
Abermagwr
New Row
Cwmystwyth
Blaenycwm
Pont-rhyd-y-groes
Hafod Estate
Llanafan
Crosswood
Wenallt
Ysbyty Ystwyth
Pentre-llyn
Rhos-y-garth
Llanddeiniol
Llangwyryfon
Lledrod
Tynygraig
Tanyrhydiau
Trefenter
Rhyd-Rosser
Rhydfudr
Mynydd Bach
Llyn Eiddwen
Fantasy Farm Park
Bronnant
Swydd-ffynnon
Ystradmeurig
Ffair-Rhos
Pontrhydfendigaid
Strata Florida Abbey
Nebo
Bontnewydd
Blaenpennal
Tyncelyn
Cors Caron
Glan Teifi
Cross Inn
Bethania
Penuwch
Ty'n-yr-eithin
Pennant
Monachty
Llanerchaeron
Cilcennin
Cynfryn
Llangeitho
Welsh Gold Centre
Tregaron
Bwlch-Llan
Capel Betws Lleucu
Commins Capel Betws
Ciliau Aeron
Trefilan
Llundain-fach
Ystrad Aeron
Tal-sarn
Gartheli
Abermeurig
Dihewyd
Felinfach
Felindre
Temple Bar
Llwyn-y-groes
Olmarch
Llanddewi-Brefi
Pentre-rhew
Llangybi
Ffynnon-oer
Silian
Betws Bledrws
Llanfair Clydogau
Cribyn
Gorsgoch
Maestir
Lampeter
(Llanbedr Pont Steffan)
Olwen
Cellan
Pentrefelin
Cwmann
Aber
Cwrt-newydd
Llanwnnen
Pentre-bach
Cwmsychpant
Alltyblaca
Dre-fach
Llanwenog
Pencarreg
Llanybydder
Parc-y-rhôs
Ram
Brynteg
Rhuddlan
Glan-Duar
Ty Mawr
Mynydd Pencarreg
Harford
Ffarmers
Ffaldybrenin
Llanycrwys
Cwrt-y-cadno
Mynydd Mallaen
Afon Cothi
Aber-Giâr
Esgairdawe
Llanllwni
Rhydcymerau
Llandre
Pumsaint
Dolaucothi Gold Mines
Caio
Caeo Forest
Esgair Fechon
Cilycwm
Rhandirmwyn
Nant-y-Bai
Ystradffin
Allt Rhyd y Groes
Cynghordy
Llanfair-ar-y-bryn
Porthyrhyd
Siloh
Divlyn
Crugybar
New Inn
Llidiad Nenog
Llansawel
Edwinsford
Talley
Talley Abbey
Cynros
Cwm-byr
Abergorlech
Gwernogle
Brechfa Forest
Nant-y-ffin
Pen-y-garn
Mynydd Rhos-wen
Wauncłunda
Llansadwrn
Cwmdu
Halfway
Brechfa
Llanllawddog
Llandovery
(Llanymddyfri)
Cwmdwr
Llanwrda
Myrtle Hill
Cilgwyn
Myddfai
Felindre
Ashfield
Hermon
Soar
Horeb
Llanfynydd
Capel Isaac
Pant-glas
Salem
Cwmifor
Manordeilo
Llangadog
Pantgwyn
Felingwm uchaf
Felingwm isaf
Llanfihangel-uwch-Gwili
Pen-y-banc
Rhosmaen
Bethlehem
Dyffryn Ceidrych
Pont-ar-llechau
Pentrefelin
Broad Oak
Court Henry
Pont-ar-gothi
Llangathen
Dinefwr Park
Cilsan
Vale of Tywi
Dyffryn Tywi
Llandeilo
Aberglasney
Llanegwad
Nantgaredig
Felindre
Dryslwyn
Ffairfach
Pontbren Araeth
Trichrug
Capel Gwynfe
Pont Aber
Neuadd
Llanarthne
Golden Grove
Gelli Aur
Capel Dewi
Nantycaws
The National Botanic Garden of Wales
Penrhiwgoch
Trapp
Carreg Cennen Castle & Farm
Temple Bar
Milo
Llandyfan
Carmel
Maesybont
Llanddarog
Porthyrhyd
Llyn Llech Owain
Pentre-Gwenlais
Llandybie
Dre-fach
Cwmisfael
Foel gastell
Gwendraeth Fach
Cefneithin
Gorslas
Caer-bryn
Tycroes
Twynmynydd
Black Mountain
Y Mynydd Du
Foel Fraith
Fan Brycheiniog
Usk Reservoir
Brynamman
Rhosaman
Glanaman
Afon Aman
Garnant
Gwaun-Leision
Tairgwaith
Gwaun-Cae-Gurwen
Cwmgors
Tir-y-dail
Ammanford
(Rhydaman)
Betws
Pontamman
Pantyffynnon
Penygroes
Saron
Penybanc
Capel Hendre
Drefach
Cwm-y-glo
Cross Hands
Morfa
Bancffosfelen
Cwmmawr
Tumble
Cwmgwili
Pontyberem
Pentre
Pont Henri
Pontyates
Llannon
Greynor
Garnswllt
Mynydd y Gwair
Llwyn-teg
Pont Abraham Services
Cynheidre
Sylen
Llanedi
Sardis
Pentrebach
Graig Fawr
Forest
Pontarddulais
Hendy
Lliedi Resrs.
Five Roads
Cwm-Dulais
Felindre
Rhyd-y-pandy
Craig-cefn-parc
Rhyd-y-gwin
Clydach
Ynystawe
Faerdre
Trebanos
Pontardawe
Glantawe Riverside Park
Alltwen
Rhôs
Gellinudd
Clilybebyll
Rhyd-y-fro
Ynysmeudwy
Godre'r-graig
Ystalyfera
Swansea Valley
Cwm Abertawe
Mynydd March-Hywel
Crynant
Cwmllynfell
Ystradowen
Upper Cwm-twrch
Lower Cwm-twrch
Gurnos
Ystradgynlais
Cwmgiedd
Penrhos
Abercraf
Caehopkin
Wales Ape & Monkey Sanctuary
Coelbren
Onllwyn
Dyffryn Cellwen
Seven Sisters
Nant-y-cafn
Pen-y-cae
Craig-y-nos
Dan-yr-Ogof
The National Showcaves for Wales
Glyntawe
Penwyllt
Ogof Ffynnon Ddu
Fforest Fawr
Brecon Beacons
Fan Gihirych
Cray Res.
Crai
Felin-Crai
Glas Fynydd Forest
Heol Senni
Llwyn y Celyn
Craig Cerrig Gleisiad a Fan-Frynych
Fan Fawr
Beacons Res.
Ystradfellte Res.
Cantref Res.
Ystradfellte
Llwyn-on
Garwnant
Glyn-neath
(Glynedd)
Pontneddfechan
Morfa Glas
Rheola Forest
Blaengwrach
Cwmgwrach
Vale of Neath
Cwm Nedd
Resolven
Resolven Mtn.
Melincourt
Cefn Coed Colliery Mus.
Rhigos
Cwm-hwnt
Penderyn
Pontbren Llwyd
Hirwaun
Tre-Gibbon
Penywaun
Llwydcoed
Trecynon
Cwmdare
Dare Valley
ABERDARE
(ABERDÂR)
Glyn Tarell
Libanus
Tai'r-Bull
Mountain Centre
Mynydd Illtyd
Penpont
Defynnog
Sennybridge
(Pont Senni)
Trallong
Aberyscir
Usk (Wysg)
Trecastle
Cwmwysg
Pont ar Hydfer
Talsarn
Llanddeusant
Twynllanan
Llywel
Halfway
Pentre'r-felin
Pentre-bach
Llandeilo'r Fan
Llanfihangel Nant Bran
Pont-faen
Blaendyryn
Merthyr Cynog
Mynydd Bwlch-y-groes
Babel
Pentre-ty-gwyn
Crychan Forest
Tirabad
Mynydd Epynt
Bryn Du
Dolau-Honddu
Pentre
Drum-ddu
Cefn-gorwydd
Llangammarch Wells
Llanwrtyd Wells
(Llanwrtud)
Llanwrtyd
Cwm Irfon
Mynydd Trawsnant
Llyn Brianne Res.
Soar-y-Mynydd
Abergwesyn
Nant Irfon
Beulah
Garth
Llanfechan
Irfon
Troed-rhiwdalar
Pentre-llwyn-llwyd
Llanafan-fawr
Drygarn Fawr
Bryn Crwn
Dolgoch
Tywi Forest
Esgair Cerrig
Tyncornel
Bryn Brawd
Y Drum
Drum-ddu
Claerwen
Claerwen Reservoir
Afon Claerwen
Caban-coch Res.
Garreg-ddu Res.
Penygarreg Res.
Craig-goch Res.
Elan Village
Llanwrthwl
Nant-glas
Rhayader
(Rhaeadr Gwy)
Llansantffraed Cwmdeuddwr
Gaufron
Welsh Royal Crystal
The Gigrin Farm Red Kite Feeding Centre
Wye (Gwy)
St Harmon
Pant-y-dwr
Nantgwyn
Geifas
Trawsallt
Dibyn Du
Pen y Garn
Coed Rheidol
Electric Station
Wales Coast Path
0 1 2 3 4 5 6 miles
0 1 2 3 4 5 6 7 8 9 10 km

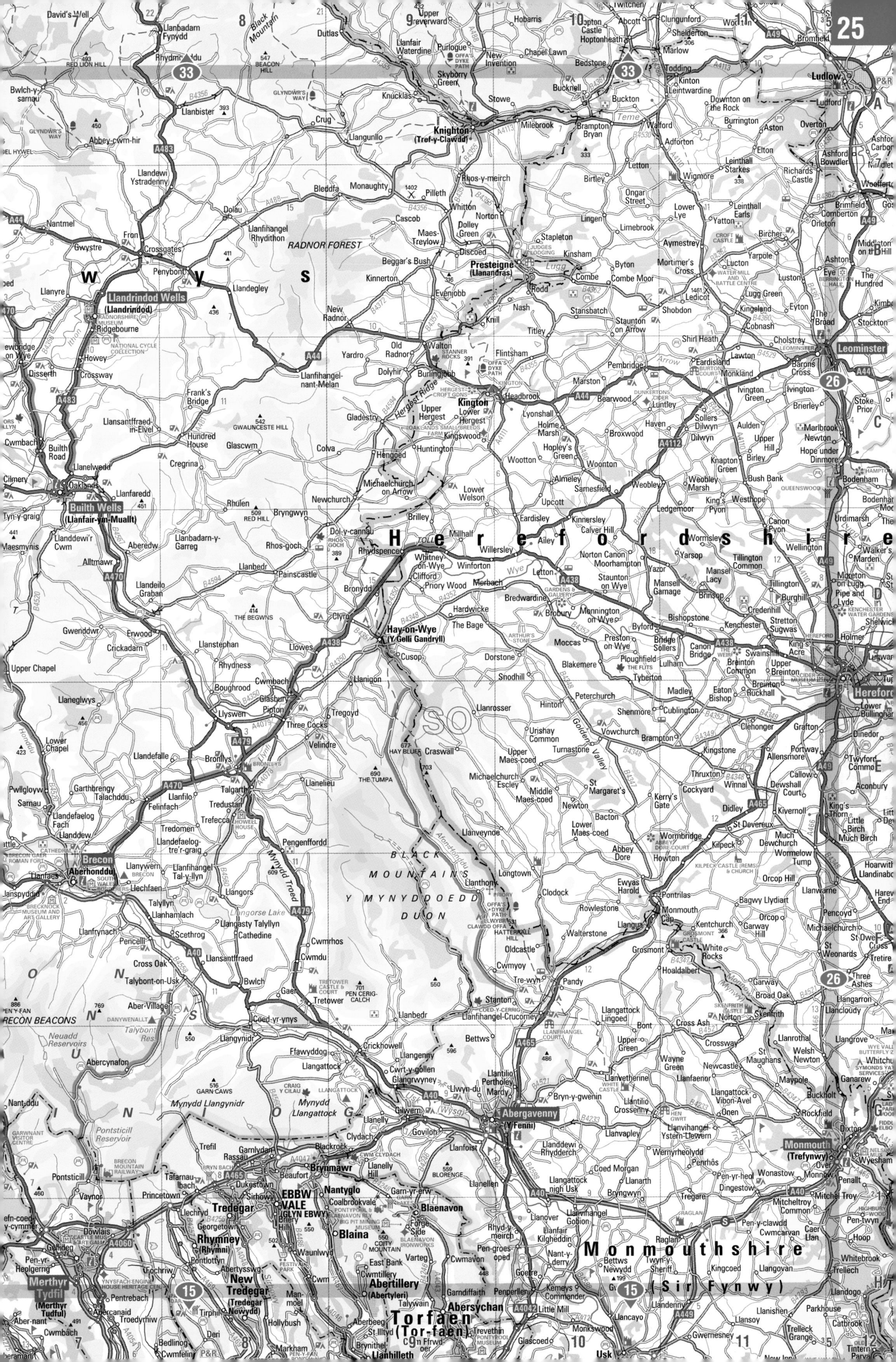
Llanbadarn Fynydd
Black Mountain
Upper Treverward
Hobarris
Clungunford
Knighton (Tref-y-Clawdd)
Ludlow
Llanbister
Abbey-cwm-hir
Llandewi Ystradenny
Bleddfa
Monaughty
Pilleth
Whitton
Presteigne (Llanandras)
Radnor Forest
Wigmore
Leintwardine
Nantmel
Crossgates
Penybont
Llandrindod Wells (Llandrindod)
Llandegley
New Radnor
Kington
Leominster
Builth Wells (Llanfair-ym-Muallt)
Newchurch
Eardisley
Weobley
Hay-on-Wye (Y Gelli Gandryll)
Herefordshire
Hereford
Clyro
Talgarth
Brecon (Aberhonddu)
Black Mountains
Y Mynydd Doedd Duon
Pontrilas
Longtown
Llanthony
Crickhowell
Abergavenny (Y Fenni)
Monmouth (Trefynwy)
Brecon Beacons
Merthyr Tydfil (Merthyr Tudful)
Tredegar
Ebbw Vale (Glyn Ebwy)
Brynmawr
Blaenavon
Blaina
Abertillery (Abertyleri)
Torfaen (Tor-faen)
Monmouthshire (Sir Fynwy)
Raglan
Usk
Rhymney (Rhymni)
New Tredegar (Tredegar Newydd)
Abersychan
Pontypool
Hergest Ridge
Golden Valley
Mynydd Troed
Mynydd Llangatwg
Mynydd Llangynidr
Pontsticill Reservoir
Talybont Reservoir
Llangorse Lake
Ross
SO
A44
A438
A470
A479
A40
A465
A49
A4113
A480
A4112
A466
33
26
15

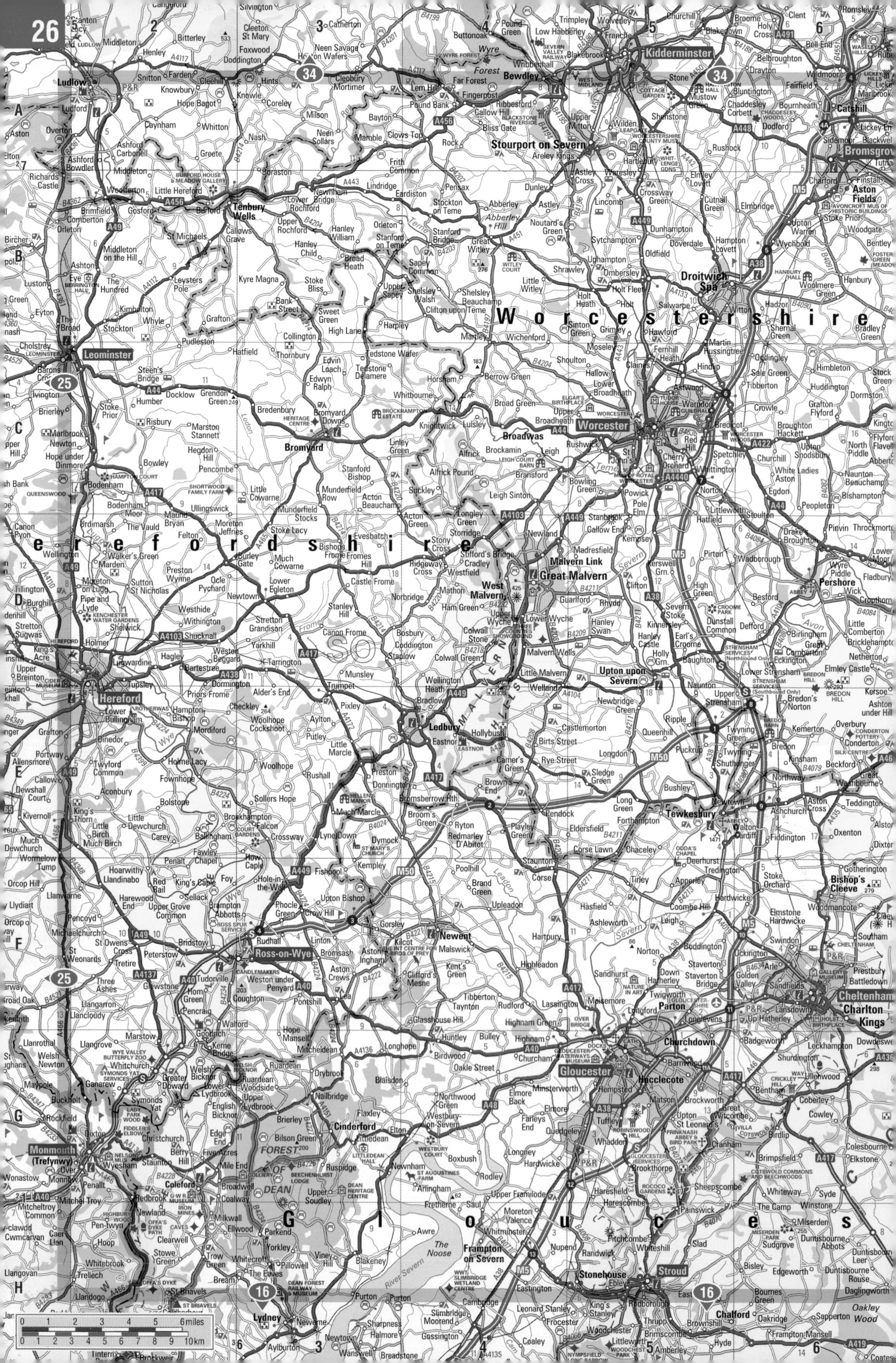

Ludlow
Kidderminster
Bewdley
Stourport on Severn
Bromsgrove
Catshill
Droitwich Spa
Worcestershire
Leominster
Tenbury Wells
Bromyard
Worcester
Great Malvern
West Malvern
Malvern Wells
Herefordshire
Hereford
Ledbury
Upton upon Severn
Pershore
Tewkesbury
Ross-on-Wye
Newent
Bishop's Cleeve
Cheltenham
Charlton Kings
Monmouth
(Trefynwy)
Coleford
Cinderford
Gloucester
Hucclecote
Churchdown
Gloucestershire
Frampton on Severn
Stonehouse
Stroud
Chalford
Lydney

0 1 2 3 4 5 6 miles
0 1 2 3 4 5 6 7 8 9 10km

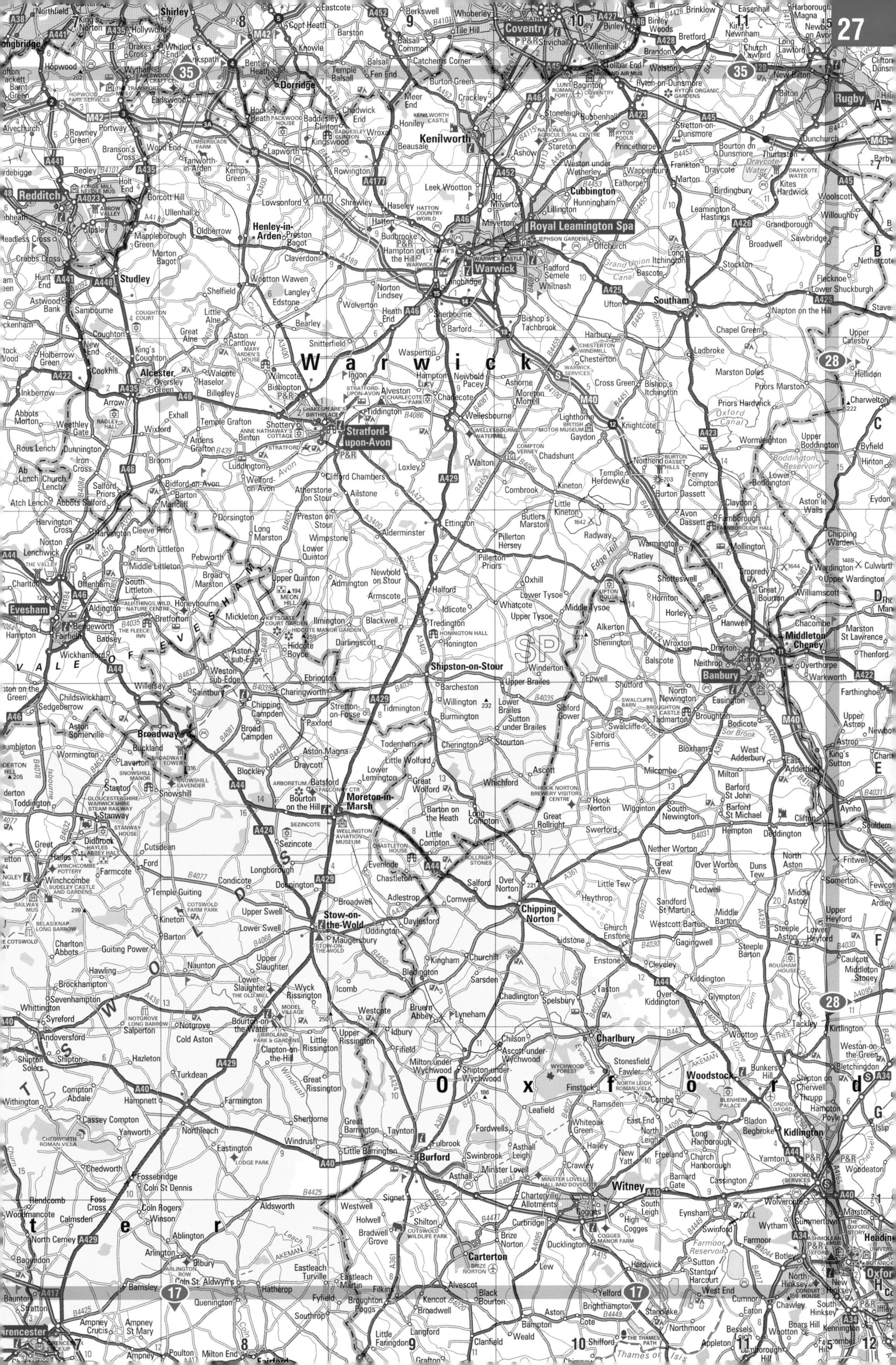
Warwick
Oxford
Vale of Evesham
Cotswolds
Coventry
Kenilworth
Royal Leamington Spa
Warwick
Stratford-upon-Avon
Rugby
Redditch
Evesham
Banbury
Southam
Henley-in-Arden
Studley
Alcester
Shipston-on-Stour
Chipping Campden
Broadway
Moreton-in-Marsh
Stow-on-the-Wold
Chipping Norton
Charlbury
Woodstock
Kidlington
Witney
Burford
Carterton
Cirencester
Winchcombe
Middleton Cheney
Shirley
Dorridge
Knowle
Solihull
Hockley Heath
Lapworth
Wellesbourne
Kineton
Gaydon
Cubbington
Whitnash
Bishop's Tachbrook
Ettington
Tredington
Bourton-on-the-Water
Northleach
Fairford
Eynsham
Botley
Cumnor
Standlake
Bampton
Shifford
Ducklington
Minster Lovell
Finstock
Enstone
Hook Norton
Deddington
Adderbury
Bloxham
Long Compton
Little Compton
Mickleton
Ilmington
Honington
Snowshill
Stanway
Guiting Power
Naunton
Andoversford
Shipton
Chedworth
Bibury
Coln St Aldwyn's
Lechlade
Kingham
Bledington
Milton-under-Wychwood
Shipton-under-Wychwood
Ascott-under-Wychwood
Chadlington
Spelsbury
Stonesfield
Bladon
Begbroke
Yarnton
Cassington
Wolvercote
Summertown
Marston
Headington
Kennington
Appleton
Northmoor
Clanfield
Alvescot
Black Bourton
Brize Norton
Curbridge
Langford
Filkins
Kencot
Broadwell
Southrop
Quenington
Barnsley
Ampney Crucis
Ampney St Mary
Poulton
Hatherop
Eastleach Turville
Westwell
Holwell
Shilton
Signet
Asthall
Swinbrook
Fulbrook
Taynton
Great Barrington
Little Barrington
Windrush
Sherborne
Farmington
Hampnett
Turkdean
Hazleton
Salperton
Notgrove
Cold Aston
Lower Slaughter
Upper Slaughter
Wyck Rissington
Little Rissington
Great Rissington
Upper Rissington
Clapton-on-the-Hill
Icomb
Westcote
Idbury
Fifield
Bruern Abbey
Lyneham
Sarsden
Churchill
Daylesford
Oddington
Adlestrop
Cornwell
Salford
Over Norton
Chastleton
Evenlode
Longborough
Donnington
Broadwell
Condicote
Temple Guiting
Kineton
Barton
Lower Swell
Upper Swell
Sezincote
Bourton on the Hill
Batsford
Draycott
Blockley
Aston Magna
Paxford
Broad Campden
Ebrington
Charingworth
Willersey
Saintbury
Weston-sub-Edge
Aston-sub-Edge
Hidcote Boyce
Darlingscott
Blackwell
Armscote
Halford
Idlicote
Whatcote
Oxhill
Pillerton Priors
Pillerton Hersey
Butlers Marston
Radway
Ratley
Warmington
Shotteswell
Hornton
Horley
Hanwell
Wroxton
Drayton
Alkerton
Shenington
Balscote
Epwell
Shutford
North Newington
Broughton
Tadmarton
Swalcliffe
Sibford Gower
Sibford Ferris
Winderton
Upper Brailes
Lower Brailes
Sutton under Brailes
Stourton
Cherington
Burmington
Willington
Barcheston
Tidmington
Todenham
Little Wolford
Great Wolford
Lower Lemington
Barton on the Heath
Whichford
Ascott
Great Rollright
Swerford
Wigginton
South Newington
Milcombe
Barford St John
Barford St Michael
Hempton
Clifton
Aynho
Souldern
Fritwell
Somerton
North Aston
Middle Aston
Steeple Aston
Lower Heyford
Upper Heyford
Caulcott
Middleton Stoney
Kirtlington
Tackley
Wootton
Glympton
Kiddington
Over Kiddington
Gagingwell
Westcott Barton
Middle Barton
Steeple Barton
Sandford St Martin
Ledwell
Over Worton
Duns Tew
Great Tew
Little Tew
Nether Worton
Heythrop
Church Enstone
Lidstone
Cleveley
Taston
Fawler
Ramsden
Leafield
Fordwells
Asthall Leigh
Crawley
Hailey
New Yatt
North Leigh
East End
Freeland
Long Hanborough
Church Hanborough
Combe
South Leigh
High Cogges
Cogges
Barnard Gate
Hardwick
Sutton
Stanton Harcourt
West End
Yelford
Brighthampton
Aston
Cote
Lew
Chimney
Northfield
King's Norton
Longbridge
Hopwood
Barnt Green
Alvechurch
Rowney Green
Beoley
Holt End
Ipsley
Headless Cross
Crabbs Cross
Hunt End
Astwood Bank
Sambourne
Coughton
New End
Holberrow Green
Inkberrow
Abbots Morton
Arrow
Weethley Gate
Rous Lench
Dunnington
Iron Cross
Ab Lench
Church Lench
Atch Lench
Abbots Salford
Salford Priors
Harvington
Norton
Lenchwick
Charlton
Offenham
Aldington
Bengeworth
Hampton
Fairfield
Badsey
Wickhamford
Childswickham
Sedgeberrow
Aston Somerville
Wormington
Dumbleton
Toddington
Didbrook
Greet
Hailes
Ford
Farmcote
Charlton Abbots
Hawling
Brockhampton
Sevenhampton
Whittington
Syreford
Compton Abdale
Withington
Cassey Compton
Yanworth
Eastington
Fossebridge
Coln St Dennis
Coln Rogers
Winson
Aldsworth
Ablington
Arlington
Rendcomb
Woodmancote
Calmsden
North Cerney
Bagendon
Baunton
Stratton
Foss Cross
Hollywood
Drakes Cross
Wythall
Earlswood
Portway
Branson's Cross
Wood End
Tanworth-in-Arden
Kemps Green
Gorcott Hill
Ullenhall
Oldberrow
Mappleborough Green
Morton Bagot
Preston Bagot
Claverdon
Wootton Wawen
Langley
Edstone
Shelfield
Little Alne
Great Alne
Aston Cantlow
Bearley
Snitterfield
Wolverton
Norton Lindsey
Heath End
Sherbourne
Barford
Wasperton
Hampton Lucy
Charlecote
Alveston
Tiddington
Ingon
Wilmcote
Bishopton
Shottery
Binton
Temple Grafton
Ardens Grafton
Exhall
Wixford
Haselor
Walcote
Billesley
Oversley Green
Kings Coughton
Broom
Bidford-on-Avon
Barton
Marlcliff
Cleeve Prior
Dorsington
Welford-on-Avon
Luddington
Long Marston
Pebworth
Broad Marston
Honeybourne
Bretforton
Upper Quinton
Lower Quinton
Admington
Newbold on Stour
Preston on Stour
Atherstone on Stour
Alderminster
Clifford Chambers
Ailstone
Loxley
Walton
Wimpstone
Newbold Pacey
Ashorne
Moreton Morrell
Combrook
Little Kineton
Chadshunt
Lighthorne
Knightcote
Burton Dassett
Fenny Compton
Avon Dassett
Farnborough
Mollington
Claydon
Cropredy
Great Bourton
Williamscott
Wardington
Upper Wardington
Chacombe
Marston St Lawrence
Thenford
Overthorpe
Warkworth
Farthinghoe
Newbottle
King's Sutton
Charlton
Upper Astrop
Astrop
Nethercote
Flecknoe
Lower Shuckburgh
Napton on the Hill
Stave
Upper Catesby
Hellidon
Charwelton
Byfield
Hinton
Eydon
Chipping Warden
Aston le Walls
Upper Boddington
Lower Boddington
Priors Hardwick
Priors Marston
Marston Doles
Wormleighton
Ladbroke
Chapel Green
Harbury
Chesterton
Bishop's Itchington
Cross Green
Itchington
Bascote
Ufton
Long Itchington
Stockton
Broadwell
Sawbridge
Grandborough
Leamington Hastings
Birdingbury
Marton
Frankton
Draycote
Wappenbury
Eathorpe
Hunningham
Weston under Wetherley
Princethorpe
Stretton-on-Dunsmore
Bourton on Dunsmore
Thurlaston
Dunchurch
Kites Hardwick
Woolscott
Willoughby
Barby
Clifton
New Bilton
Bilton
Church Lawford
Long Lawford
King's Newnham
Brandon
Bretford
Wolston
Ryton-on-Dunsmore
Binley
Binley Woods
Brinklow
Easenhall
Harborough Magna
Newbold on Avon
Willenhall
Stivichall
Baginton
Tollbar End
Stoneleigh
Bubbenhall
Stareton
Ashow
Whoberley
Tile Hill
Berkswell
Balsall Common
Temple Balsall
Fen End
Burton Green
Crackley
Meer End
Chadwick End
Honiley
Beausale
Wroxall
Baddesley Clinton
Kingswood
Rowington
Shrewley
Haseley
Hatton
Budbrooke
Hampton on the Hill
Leek Wootton
Old Milverton
Milverton
Lillington
Offchurch
Radford Semele
Longbridge
Bentley Heath
Copt Heath
Eastcote
Barston
Catchems Corner
Balsall
Whitlock's End
Grand Union Canal
Oxford Canal
Edge Hill
Draycote Water
Farmoor Reservoir
Boddington Reservoir
Thames or Isis
SP
M40
M42
M45
M5
A46
A44
A429
A40
A34
A361
A422
A423
A425
A452
A435
A3400
A424
A436
A4260
A4095
A415
A417
A44
35
17
28

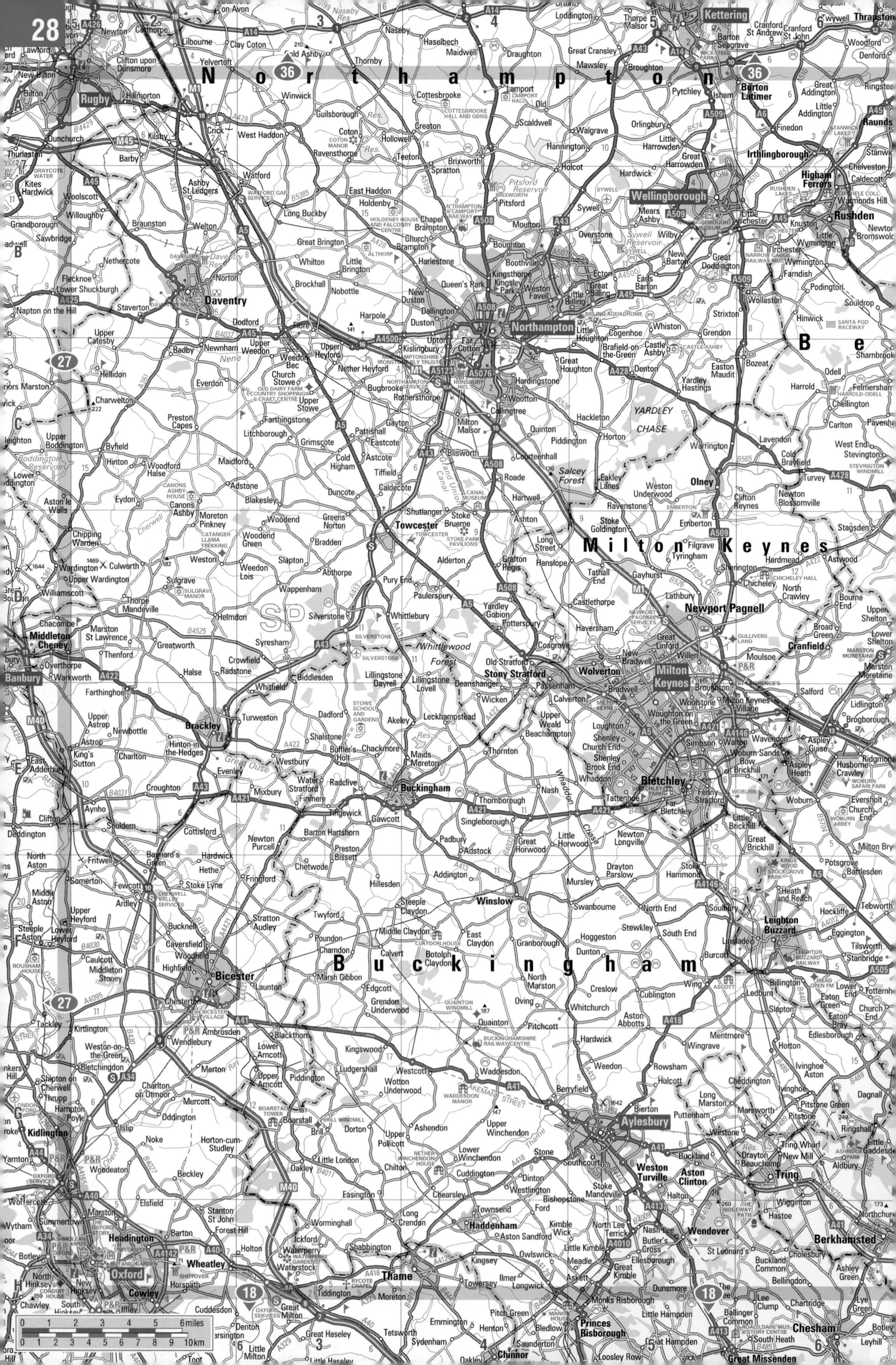
Northampton
Milton Keynes
Buckingham
Rugby
Kettering
Burton Latimer
Wellingborough
Irthlingborough
Higham Ferrers
Rushden
Raunds
Daventry
Northampton
Towcester
Olney
Newport Pagnell
Stony Stratford
Wolverton
Milton Keynes
Bletchley
Brackley
Buckingham
Banbury
Middleton Cheney
Winslow
Leighton Buzzard
Bicester
Aylesbury
Tring
Wendover
Berkhamsted
Thame
Haddenham
Princes Risborough
Chesham
Great Missenden
Chinnor
Oxford
Headington
Wheatley
Cowley
Kidlington
Cranfield
Salcey Forest
Whittlewood Forest
Yardley Chase
Silverstone
0 1 2 3 4 5 6 miles
0 1 2 3 4 5 6 7 8 9 10 km

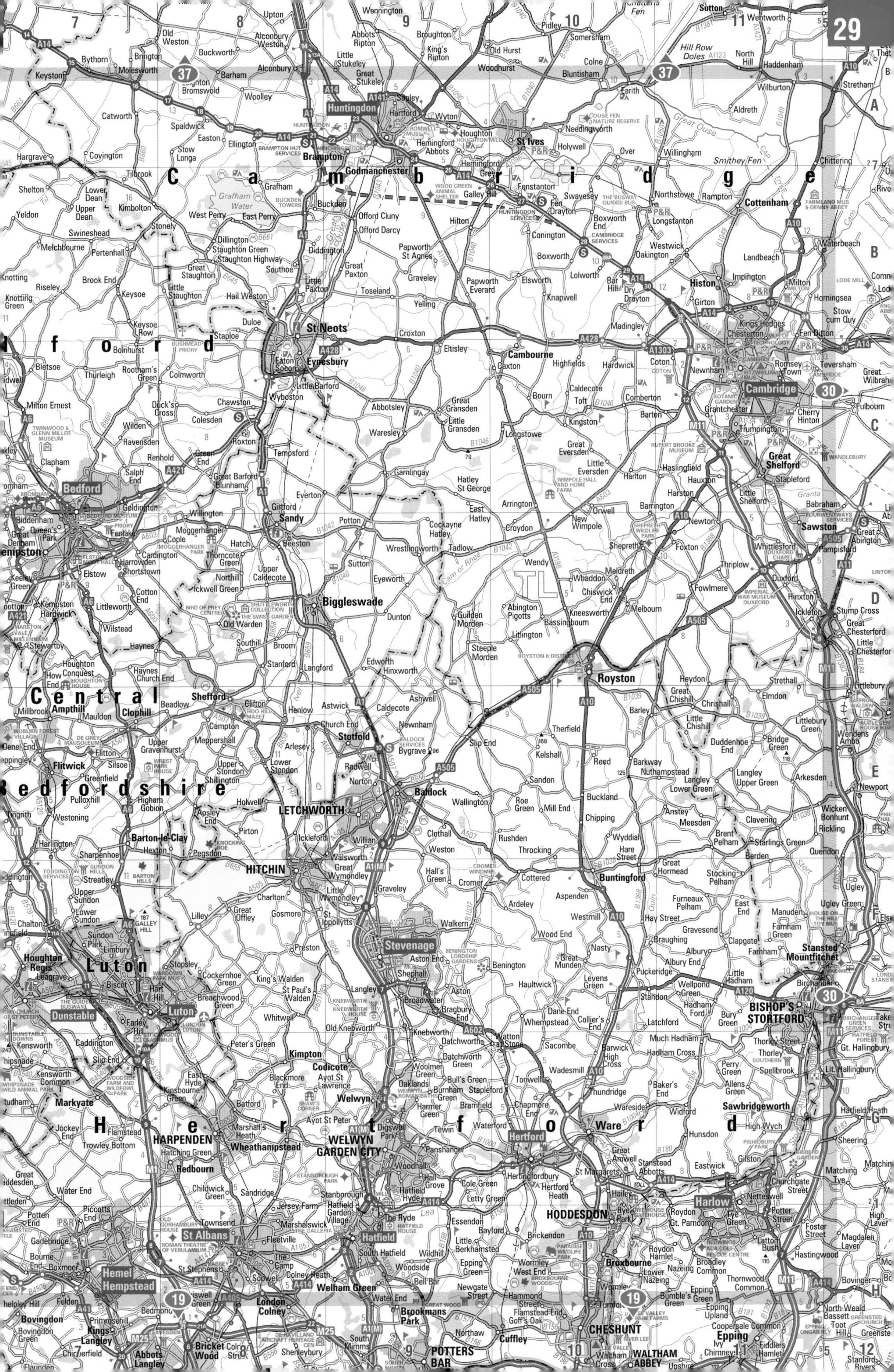
Cambridge
Bedford
Central Bedfordshire
Hertford
Huntingdon
St Neots
St Ives
Godmanchester
Brampton
Buckden
Cottenham
Histon
Cambourne
Royston
Sandy
Biggleswade
Shefford
Stotfold
Baldock
LETCHWORTH
HITCHIN
Stevenage
Luton
Dunstable
HARPENDEN
St Albans
Hemel Hempstead
WELWYN GARDEN CITY
Welwyn
Hatfield
Ware
HODDESDON
Harlow
BISHOP'S STORTFORD
Sawbridgeworth
Stansted Mountfitchet
Buntingford
Sawston
Great Shelford
Flitwick
Ampthill
Kempston
Barton-le-Clay
Wheathampstead
Redbourn
Welham Green
London Colney
Brookmans Park
POTTERS BAR
CHESHUNT
WALTHAM ABBEY
Epping
Broxbourne
Waterbeach
Longstanton
Papworth Everard
Gamlingay
Potton
Bassingbourn
Melbourn
Duxford
Great Chesterford
Grafham Water
Eynesbury
Eaton Socon
Kings Langley
Abbots Langley
Bricket Wood
Markyate
Houghton Regis
Toddington
Clophill
Henlow
Arlesey
Knebworth
Codicote
Kimpton
Stanstead Abbotts
Great Amwell
A14
A1
A1(M)
A428
A505
A10
A120
A414
A6
A421
A603
A602
M1
M11
M25
37
30
19
TL

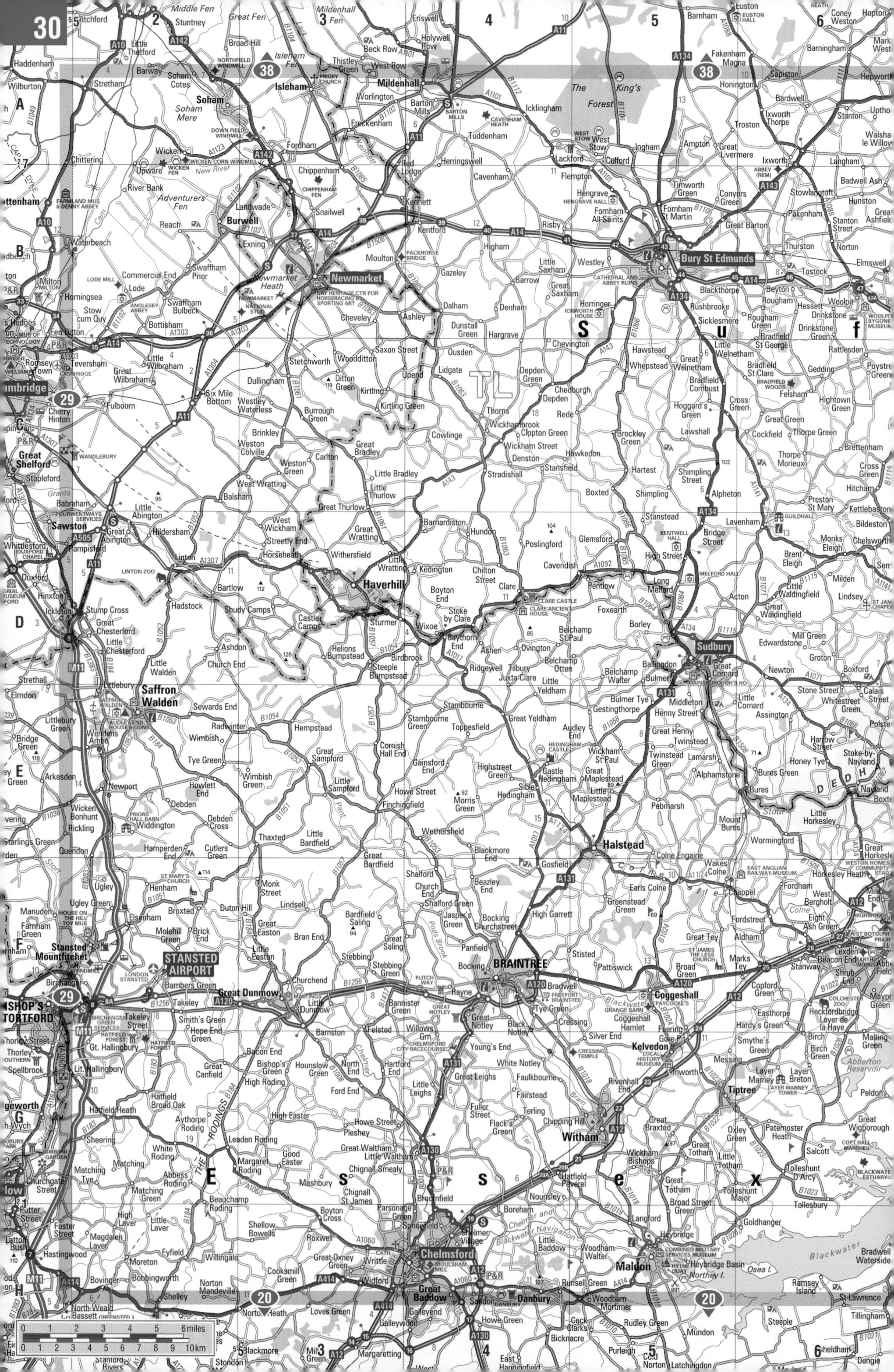
Middle Fen
Great Fen
Mildenhall Fen
Isleham Fen
Soham
Soham Mere
Isleham
Mildenhall
The King's Forest
Barton Mills
Icklingham
Wicken
Burwell
Fordham
Chippenham
Kennett
Red Lodge
Kentford
Herringswell
Cavenham
Tuddenham
Risby
Higham
West Stow
Culford
Ingham
Ampton
Great Livermere
Ixworth
Fornham All Saints
Fornham St Martin
Bury St Edmunds
Great Barton
Newmarket
Newmarket Heath
Exning
Swaffham Prior
Swaffham Bulbeck
Bottisham
Stow cum Quy
Horningsea
Waterbeach
Milton
Fen Ditton
Teversham
Cambridge
Great Wilbraham
Little Wilbraham
Fulbourn
Six Mile Bottom
Cherry Hinton
Great Shelford
Stapleford
Sawston
Pampisford
Babraham
Great Abington
Little Abington
Hildersham
Linton
Whittlesford
Duxford
Hinxton
Ickleton
Stump Cross
Great Chesterford
Little Chesterford
Saffron Walden
Littlebury
Wendens Ambo
Newport
Arkesden
Widdington
Quendon
Rickling
Ugley
Ugley Green
Manuden
Stansted Mountfitchet
Stansted Airport
Bishop's Stortford
Takeley
Great Dunmow
Little Dunmow
Thaxted
Great Bardfield
Finchingfield
Wethersfield
Haverhill
Withersfield
Kedington
Sturmer
Clare
Stoke by Clare
Cavendish
Long Melford
Glemsford
Lavenham
Sudbury
Great Cornard
Hadleigh
Boxford
Nayland
Stoke-by-Nayland
Bures
Halstead
Castle Hedingham
Sible Hedingham
Great Yeldham
Gosfield
Earls Colne
Coggeshall
Kelvedon
Braintree
Bocking
Rayne
Great Notley
Black Notley
Witham
Tiptree
Maldon
Heybridge
Danbury
Great Baddow
Chelmsford
Broomfield
Writtle
Felsted
Great Waltham
Little Waltham
Pleshey
High Easter
Good Easter
Leaden Roding
Hatfield Heath
Hatfield Broad Oak
Sheering
Matching
Harlow
Hastingwood
North Weald Bassett
Chipping Ongar
Blackmore
Margaretting
Galleywood
Woodham Mortimer
Purleigh
Latchingdon
Tollesbury
Tolleshunt D'Arcy
Goldhanger
Osea I.
Northey I.
Blackwater
Abberton Reservoir
Layer de la Haye
Copford Green
Stanway
Lexden
Marks Tey
Wormingford
Dedham
Great Horkesley
Boxted
West Bergholt
Fordham
Stour
Colne
Chelmer
Pant
Blackwater
Suffolk
Essex
TL
A14
A11
A10
A142
A134
A143
A1307
A505
A120
A12
A130
A131
A414
A1060
M11
6 miles
10 km

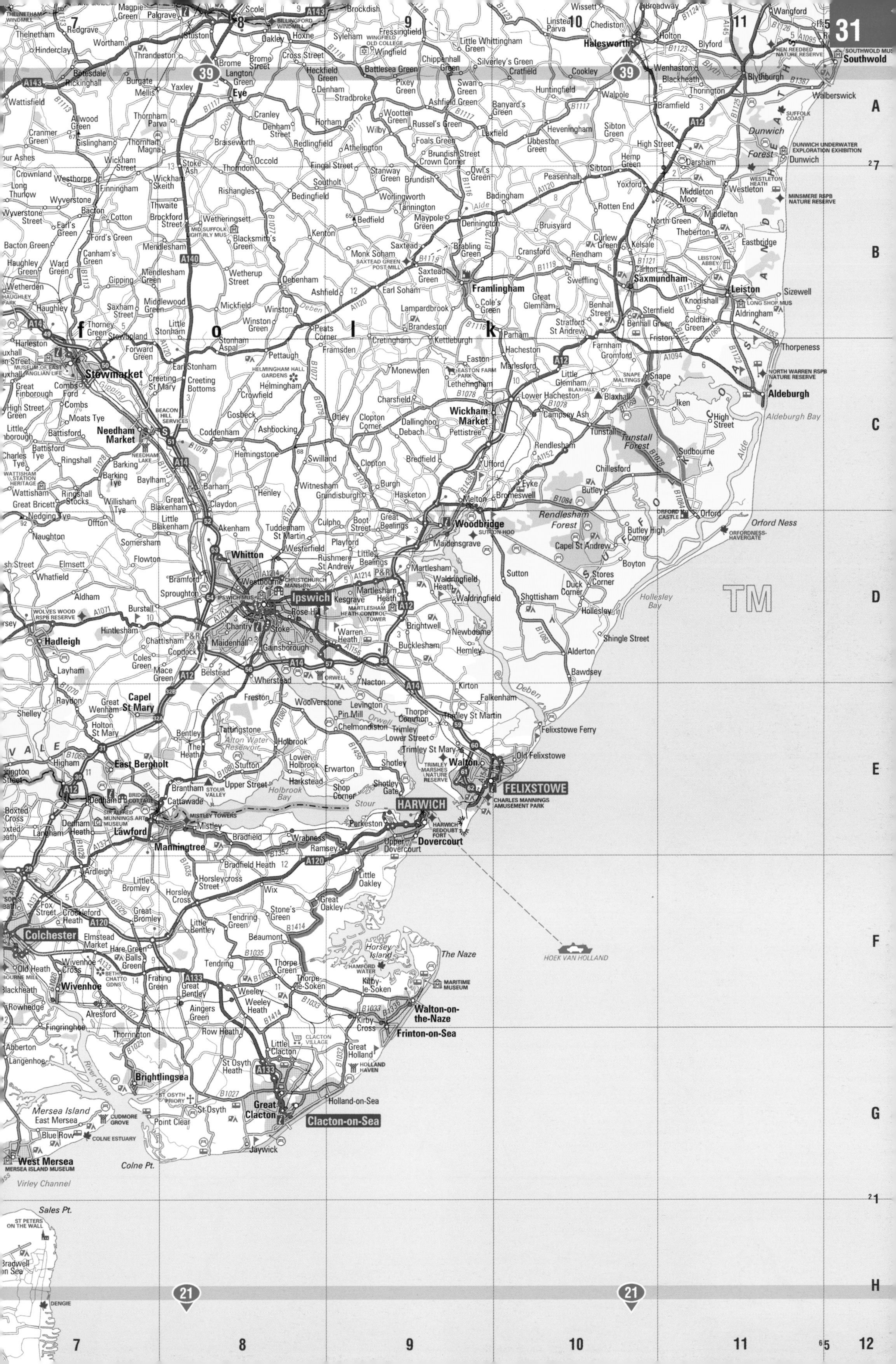

7
8
9
10
11
12
A
B
C
D
E
F
G
H
39
21
TM
Scole
Brockdish
Wissett
Broadway
Wangford
Halesworth
Southwold
Walberswick
Blythburgh
Dunwich
DUNWICH UNDERWATER EXPLORATION EXHIBITION
SUFFOLK COAST
Westleton
MINSMERE RSPB NATURE RESERVE
Eastbridge
Sizewell
Leiston
LONG SHOP MUS
LEISTON ABBEY
Aldringham
Thorpeness
NORTH WARREN RSPB NATURE RESERVE
Aldeburgh
Aldeburgh Bay
Snape
SNAPE MALTINGS
Saxmundham
Yoxford
Peasenhall
Sibton
Framlingham
Dennington
Laxfield
Fressingfield
Hoxne
Eye
Diss
Mellis
Botesdale
Rickinghall
Thelnetham
Redgrave
Wortham
Palgrave
Stradbroke
Wingfield
Debenham
Earl Soham
Saxtead Green
SAXTEAD GREEN POST MILL
Stowmarket
MUSEUM OF EAST ANGLIAN LIFE
Needham Market
NEEDHAM LAKE
Stowupland
Haughley
Combs
Great Finborough
Battisford
Ringshall
Barking
Wattisham
Great Bricett
Nedging Tye
Naughton
Somersham
Hadleigh
WOLVES WOOD RSPB RESERVE
Aldham
Hintlesham
Chattisham
Layham
Raydon
Shelley
Capel St Mary
Great Wenham
Holton St Mary
Higham
East Bergholt
Dedham
Stratford St Mary
Langham
Lawford
Manningtree
Mistley
MISTLEY TOWERS
Bradfield
Wrabness
Ramsey
Dovercourt
Upper Dovercourt
Parkeston
HARWICH
HARWICH REDOUBT FORT
Harkstead
Shotley
Shotley Gate
Erwarton
Holbrook
Stutton
Brantham
Cattawade
Tattingstone
Alton Water Reservoir
Holbrook Bay
Stour
Orwell
Chelmondiston
Pin Mill
Woolverstone
Freston
Wherstead
Belstead
Ipswich
IPSWICH MUS
CHRISTCHURCH MANSION
Whitton
Westbourne
Rose Hill
Chantry
Maidenhall
Stoke
Gainsborough
Rushmere St Andrew
Kesgrave
Martlesham
Martlesham Heath
MARTLESHAM HEATH CONTROL TOWER
Warren Heath
Brightwell
Bucklesham
Nacton
Levington
Kirton
Falkenham
Trimley St Martin
Trimley St Mary
Walton
TRIMLEY MARSHES NATURE RESERVE
FELIXSTOWE
Old Felixstowe
Felixstowe Ferry
CHARLES MANNINGS AMUSEMENT PARK
Woodbridge
Melton
SUTTON HOO
Sutton
Shottisham
Bawdsey
Alderton
Hollesley
Hollesley Bay
Shingle Street
Boyton
Butley
Chillesford
Rendlesham Forest
Capel St Andrew
Orford
ORFORD CASTLE
Orford Ness
ORFORDNESS-HAVERGATE
Sudbourne
Iken
Tunstall Forest
Tunstall
Campsey Ash
Wickham Market
Ufford
Eyke
Rendlesham
Marlesford
Parham
Hacheston
Easton
EASTON FARM PARK
Letheringham
Grundisburgh
Witnesham
Otley
Helmingham
HELMINGHAM HALL GARDENS
Claydon
Barham
Great Blakenham
Bramford
Sproughton
Copdock
Burstall
HOEK VAN HOLLAND
Colchester
Ardleigh
Wivenhoe
Elmstead Market
BETH CHATTO GDNS
Alresford
Brightlingsea
Thorrington
Great Bentley
Weeley
Thorpe-le-Soken
Tendring
Great Oakley
Little Oakley
Beaumont
Horsey Island
HAMFORD WATER
The Naze
Kirby-le-Soken
Walton-on-the-Naze
MARITIME MUSEUM
Frinton-on-Sea
Kirby Cross
Great Holland
HOLLAND HAVEN
Holland-on-Sea
Clacton-on-Sea
Great Clacton
Little Clacton
CLACTON VILLAGE
St Osyth
ST OSYTH PRIORY
Point Clear
Jaywick
Mersea Island
East Mersea
West Mersea
MERSEA ISLAND MUSEUM
CUDMORE GROVE
COLNE ESTUARY
Colne Pt.
River Colne
Virley Channel
Sales Pt.
ST PETERS ON THE WALL
Bradwell on Sea
DENGIE
A12
A14
A140
A143
A144
A1120
A137
A120
A133
A1071
A1214
A1156
A1152
A1094
B1078
B1079
B1077
B1119
B1116
B1084
B1083
B1069
B1121
B1122
B1125
B1035
B1033
B1027
B1029
B1414
B1032
B1456
B1080
B1070
B1068
B1352

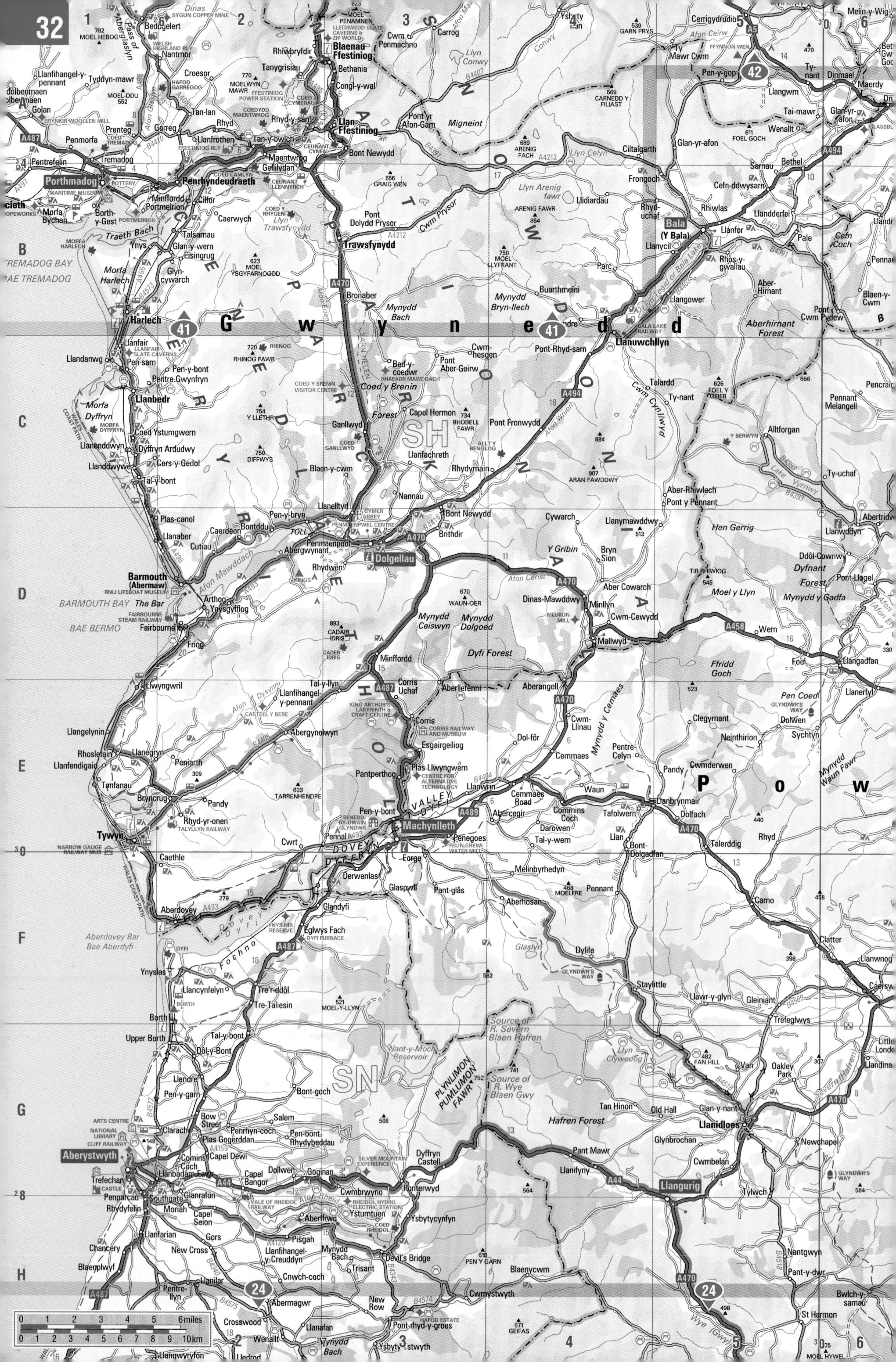
Beddgelert
Pass of Aberglaslyn
782 MOEL HEBOG
Nantmor
Rhiwbryfdir
Blaenau Ffestiniog
Cwm Penmachno
Carrog
Llyn Conwy
Ysbyty Ifan
539 GARN PRYS
Cerrigydrudion
Melin-y-Wig
Llanfihangel-y-pennant
Tyddyn-mawr
Croesor
Tanygrisiau
Bethania
Congl-y-wal
HAFOD GARREGOG
FFESTINIOG POWER STATION
770 MOELWYN MAWR
MOEL-DDU 552
Golan
BRYNKIR WOOLLEN MILL
Tan-lan
Rhyd
Rhyd-y-sarn
Llan Ffestiniog
Pont yr Afon-Gam
Migneint
669 CARNEDD Y FILIAST
Ty Mawr Cwm
Pen-y-gop
Llangwm
Tai-mawr
Glan-yr-afon
Maerdy
Dinmael
Ty-nant
Penmorfa
Prenteg
Garreg
Llanfrothen
Tan-y-bwlch
Wenallt
611 FOEL GOCH
Pentrefelin
Tremadog
Maentwrog
Gellilydan
Bont Newydd
689 ARENIG FACH
Llyn Celyn
Ciltalgarth
Glan-yr-afon
Porthmadog
Penrhyndeudraeth
556 GRAIG WEN
Frongoch
Sarnau
Bethel
Cefn-ddwysarn
Minffordd
Portmeirion
Cilfor
Llyn Arenig fawr
Llidiardau
Morfa Bychan
Borth-y-Gest
Caerwych
Llyn Trawsfynydd
Pont Dolydd Prysor
Cwm Prysor
ARENIG FAWR 854
Rhyd-uchaf
Rhiwlas
Llandderfel
Traeth Bach
Talsarnau
Bala (Y Bala)
Llanfor
Pale
Cefn Coch
TREMADOG BAY
BAE TREMADOG
Ynys
Glan-y-wern
Eisingrug
Trawsfynydd
750 MOEL LLYFRANT
Llanycil
Rhos-y-gwaliau
623 MOEL YSGYFARNOGOD
Morfa Harlech
Glyn-cywarch
Parc
Bronaber
Mynydd Bach
Mynydd Bryn-llech
Buarthmeini
Aber-Hirnant
Blaen-y-Cwm
Llangower
Harlech
Gwynedd
Llanuwchllyn
Pont Cwm Pydew
Aberhirnant Forest
Llanfair
720 RHINOG
RHINOG FAWR
Cwm-hesgen
Pont-Rhyd-sarn
Llandanwg
Pen-sarn
Pen-y-bont
Pentre Gwynfryn
Bed-y-coedwr
Pont Aber-Geirw
Talardd
Ty-nant
626 FOEL Y GEIFR
Pencraig
Llanbedr
COED Y BRENIN VISITOR CENTRE
Coed y Brenin Forest
Cwm Cynllwyd
Pennant Melangell
Morfa Dyffryn
754 Y LLETHR
Capel Hermon
734 RHOBELL FAWR
Pont Fronwydd
Afon Wnion
Ganllwyd
SH
Alltforgan
Coed Ystumgwern
Llanenddwyn
Dyffryn Ardudwy
Cors-y-Gedol
750 DIFFWYS
Llanfachreth
ALLT Y BENGLOG
884
Y BERWYN
Llanddwywe
Tal-y-bont
Blaen-y-cwm
Rhydymain
907 ARAN FAWDDWY
Ty-uchaf
Lake Vyrnwy
Nannau
Aber-Rhiwlech
Pont y Pennant
Plas-canol
Pen-y-bryn
Llanelltyd
CYMER ABBEY
Bont Newydd
Cywarch
Llanymawddwy
Hen Gerrig
Abertridwr
Llanaber
Caerdeon
Bontddu
Cutiau
Penmaenpool
Brithdir
513
Llanwddyn
Abergwynant
Dolgellau
Y Gribin
Bryn Sion
Ddôl-Cownwy
Barmouth (Abermaw)
RNLI LIFEBOAT MUSEUM
Rhydwen
Afon Mawddach
Afon Cerist
TIR RHIWIOG 545
Dyfnant Forest
Pont-Llogel
Aber Cowarch
BARMOUTH BAY
The Bar
Arthog
Ynysgyffylog
670 WAUN-OER
Dinas-Mawddwy
Minllyn
Moel y Llyn
Mynydd y Gadfa
FAIRBOURNE STEAM RAILWAY
MEIRION MILL
Cwm-Cewydd
BAE BERMO
Fairbourne
893 CADAIR IDRIS
Mynydd Ceiswyn
Mynydd Dolgoed
Wern
Mallwyd
Friog
CADER IDRIS
Dyfi Forest
Foel
Llangadfan
Ffridd Goch
Minffordd
Llwyngwril
Tal-y-llyn
Corris Uchaf
Aberllefenni
Aberangell
523
Pen Coed
Llanerfyl
Llanfihangel-y-pennant
KING ARTHUR'S LABYRINTH & CRAFT CENTRE
CASTELL Y BERE
Afon Dysynni
Corris
CORRIS RAILWAY AND MUSEUM
Cwm-Llinau
Mynydd y Cemaes
Clegyrnant
GLYNDWR'S WAY
Dolwen
Llangelynin
Abergynolwyn
Dol-fôr
Neinthirion
Sychtyn
Rhoslefain
Llanegryn
Esgairgeiliog
Pentre-Celyn
Llanfendigaid
Peniarth
Plas Llwyngwern
Cemmaes
Pandy
Cwmderwen
Mynydd Waun Fawr
Tonfanau
309
Pantperthog
CENTRE FOR ALTERNATIVE TECHNOLOGY
Llanwrin
Waun
Powys
633 TARRENHENDRE
DYFI VALLEY
Cemmaes Road
Llanbrynmair
Bryncrug
Pandy
Pen-y-bont
Machynlleth
Abercegir
Commins Coch
Tafolwern
Dolfach
440
Rhyd-yr-onen
TALYLLYN RAILWAY
SENEDD-DY-OWAIN GLYNDWR
Darowen
Tywyn
NARROW GAUGE RAILWAY MUS
Cwrt
Pennal
DOVEY DYFI
Penegoes
FELIN CREWI WATER MILL
Llan
Tal-y-wern
Bont-Dolgadfan
Talerddig
Rhyd
Caethle
Forge
Derwenlas
Melinbyrhedyn
13
Glaspwll
Pant-glâs
468 MOELFRE
Pennant
279
Aberhosan
Carno
458
WALES COAST PATH
Aberdovey
Glandyfi
YNYS HIR RESERVE
Eglwys Fach
DYFI FURNACE
Aberdovey Bar
Bae Aberdyfi
Fochno
Glaslyn
Dylife
Clatter
DYFI
Ynyslas
582
GLYNDWR'S WAY
398
Llanwnog
Llancynfelyn
Tre'r-ddôl
Staylittle
Llawr-y-glyn
Gleiniant
Caersws
Tre-Taliesin
521 MOEL-Y-LLYN
BORTH
Borth
Source of R. Severn Blaen Hafren
Trefeglwys
Upper Borth
Tal-y-bont
Dôl-y-Bont
Nant-y-Moch Reservoir
Llyn Clywedog
482 FAN HILL
Van
Oakley Park
Little London
Llandinam
Llandre
PLYNLIMON PUMLUMON FAWR
741
752
Source of R. Wye Blaen Gwy
Pen-y-garn
SN
Bont-goch
Severn (Hafren)
Tan Hinon
Old Hall
Glan-y-nant
ARTS CENTRE
NATIONAL LIBRARY
CLIFF RAILWAY
Bow Street
Salem
506
Hafren Forest
Llanidloes
Clarach
Penrhyn-coch
Pen-bont Rhydybeddau
Glynbrochan
Newchapel
Aberystwyth
Plas Gogerddan
SILVER MOUNTAIN EXPERIENCE
Dyffryn Castell
Pant Mawr
Comins Coch
Capel Dewi
Cwmbelan
Trefechan
Llanbadarn Fawr
Capel Bangor
Dollwen
Goginan
Llanifyny
GLYNDWR'S WAY
CASTLE
Penparcau
Southgate
Glanrafon
Cwmbrwyno
Ponterwyd
564
Llangurig
Tylwch
584
Rhydyfelin
Moriah
VALE OF RHEIDOL RAILWAY
Afon Rheidol
RHEIDOL HYDRO ELECTRIC STATION
Capel Seion
Ystumtuen
Aberffrwd
CWM RHEIDOL
Ysbytycynfyn
Llanfarian
Gors
Chancery
New Cross
Pisgah
Llanfihangel-y-Creuddyn
Mynydd Bach
Devil's Bridge
610 PEN Y GARN
Nantgwyn
Blaenplwyf
Trisant
Blaenycwm
Pant-y-dwr
Cnwch-coch
Llanilar
Pentre-llyn
Abermagwr
New Row
Cwmystwyth
HAFOD ESTATE
Bwlch-y-sarnau
498
St Harmon
Crosswood
Llanafan
Pont-rhyd-y-groes
571 GEIFAS
Wye (Gwy)
Wenallt
Mynydd Bach
Ysbyty Ystwyth
MOEL HYWEL
Llangwyryfon
Lledrod
0 1 2 3 4 5 6 miles
0 1 2 3 4 5 6 7 8 9 10km

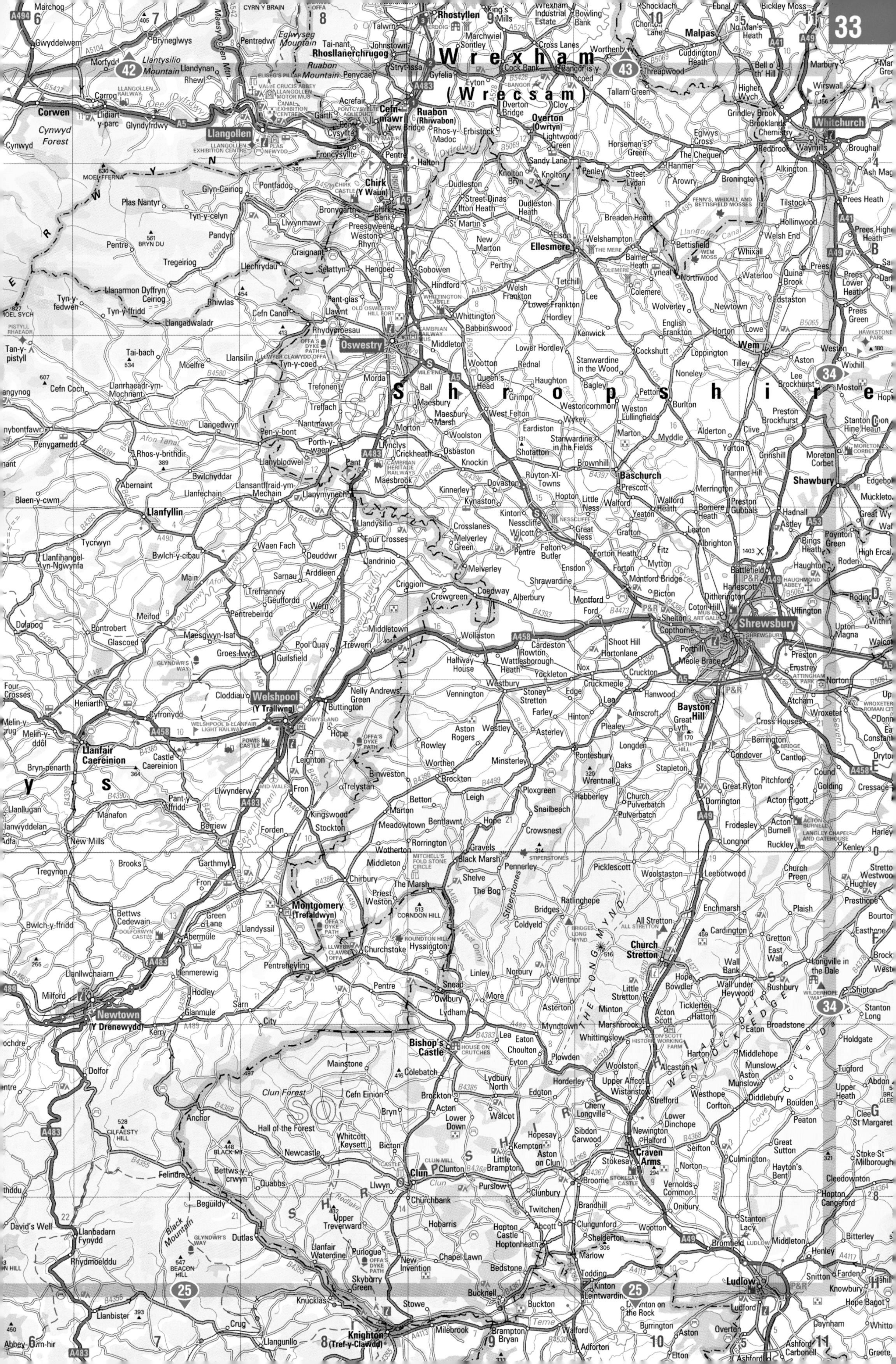
Wrexham
(Wrecsam)
Shropshire
Marchog
Rhostyllen
Wrexham Industrial Estate
Bowling Bank
Shocklach
Malpas
Bickley Moss
Corwen
Cynwyd Forest
Llangollen
Rhosllanerchrugog
Ruabon (Rhiwabon)
Cefn-mawr
Overton (Owrtyn)
Bangor-is-y-coed
Threapwood
Whitchurch
Chirk (Y Waun)
Glyn-Ceiriog
Llanarmon Dyffryn Ceiriog
Ellesmere
Welshampton
Wem
Oswestry
Whittington
Gobowen
Tan-y-pistyll
Llanrhaeadr-ym-Mochnant
Llansilin
Trefonen
Morda
Baschurch
Prees
Shawbury
Llanfyllin
Llansantffraid-ym-Mechain
Llanymynech
Four Crosses
Nesscliffe
Shrewsbury
Battlefield
Uffington
Welshpool (Y Trallwng)
Llanfair Caereinion
Pontesbury
Minsterley
Westbury
Bayston Hill
Condover
Dorrington
Atcham
Cressage
Berriew
Montgomery (Trefaldwyn)
Chirbury
Church Stretton
All Stretton
Stiperstones
Long Mynd
Wenlock Edge
Newtown (Y Drenewydd)
Kerry
Bishop's Castle
Clun Forest
Clun
Craven Arms
Stokesay Castle
Church Stretton
Knighton (Tref-y-Clawdd)
Ludlow
Bromfield
Leintwardine
Llanbister
Abbey-cwm-hir
Brampton Bryan
A5
A483
A458
A49
A41
A495
A488
A489
A4113
42
43
34
25

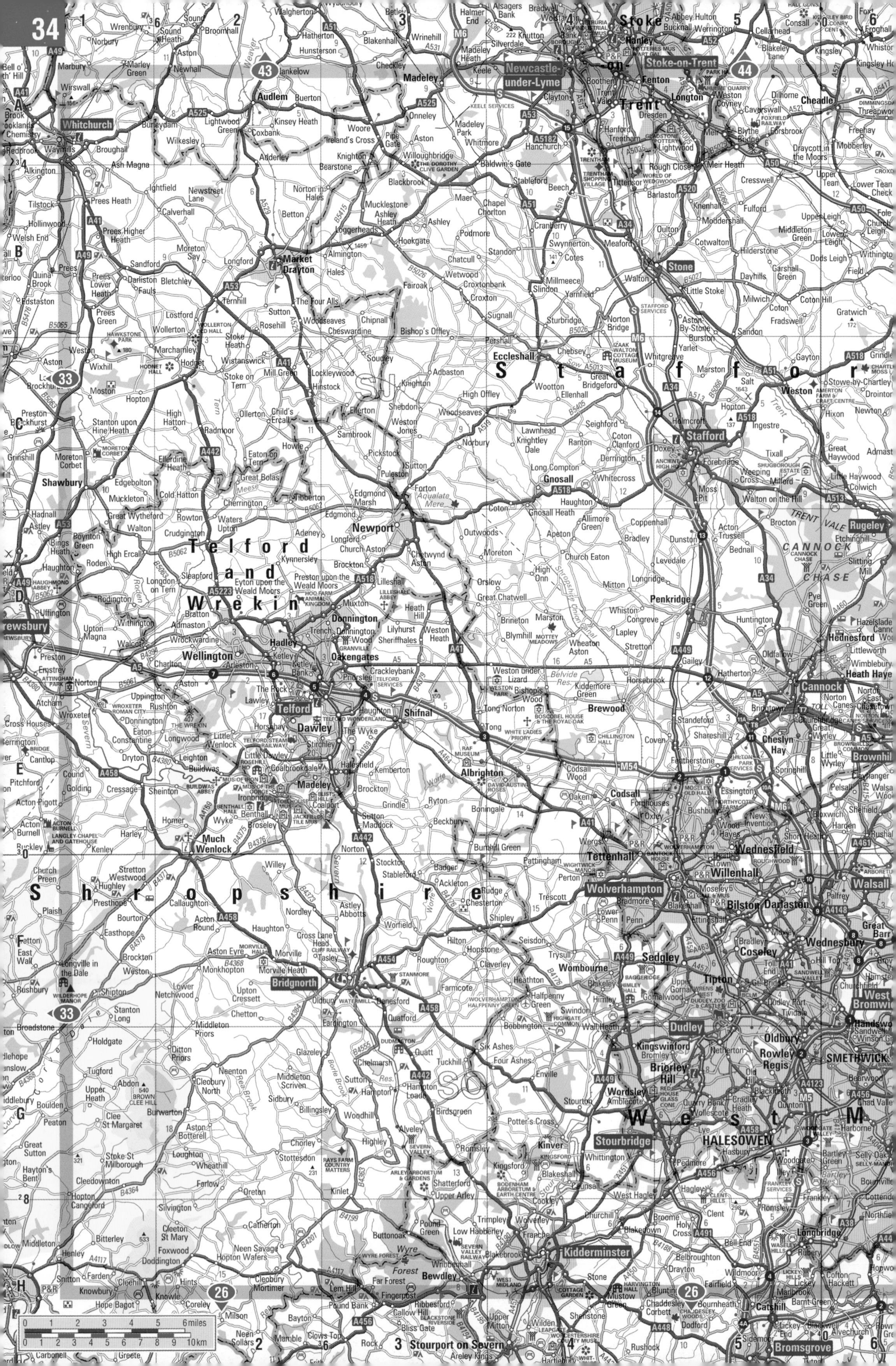

Whitchurch
Market Drayton
Newcastle-under-Lyme
Stoke-on-Trent
Stoke
Hanley
Fenton
Longton
Trent
Stone
Eccleshall
Stafford
Staffordshire
Rugeley
Cannock
Cannock Chase
Newport
Telford and Wrekin
Wellington
Hadley
Oakengates
Donnington
Telford
Dawley
Madeley
Shifnal
Albrighton
Codsall
Tettenhall
Wolverhampton
Willenhall
Wednesfield
Bilston
Darlaston
Walsall
Wednesbury
Sedgley
Coseley
Tipton
Dudley
Oldbury
Smethwick
Rowley Regis
Brierley Hill
Kingswinford
Stourbridge
Halesowen
West Midlands
Wombourne
Kinver
Kidderminster
Bewdley
Stourport on Severn
Bromsgrove
Bridgnorth
Much Wenlock
Shropshire
Shrewsbury
Shawbury
Audlem
Gnosall
Penkridge
Brewood
Cheslyn Hay
Hednesford
Cheadle
Madeley
Catshill
Longbridge
Wyre Forest
M6
M54
M5
A5
A41
A49
A442
A449
A458
A34
A51
A50
A53
0 1 2 3 4 5 6 miles
0 1 2 3 4 5 6 7 8 9 10 km

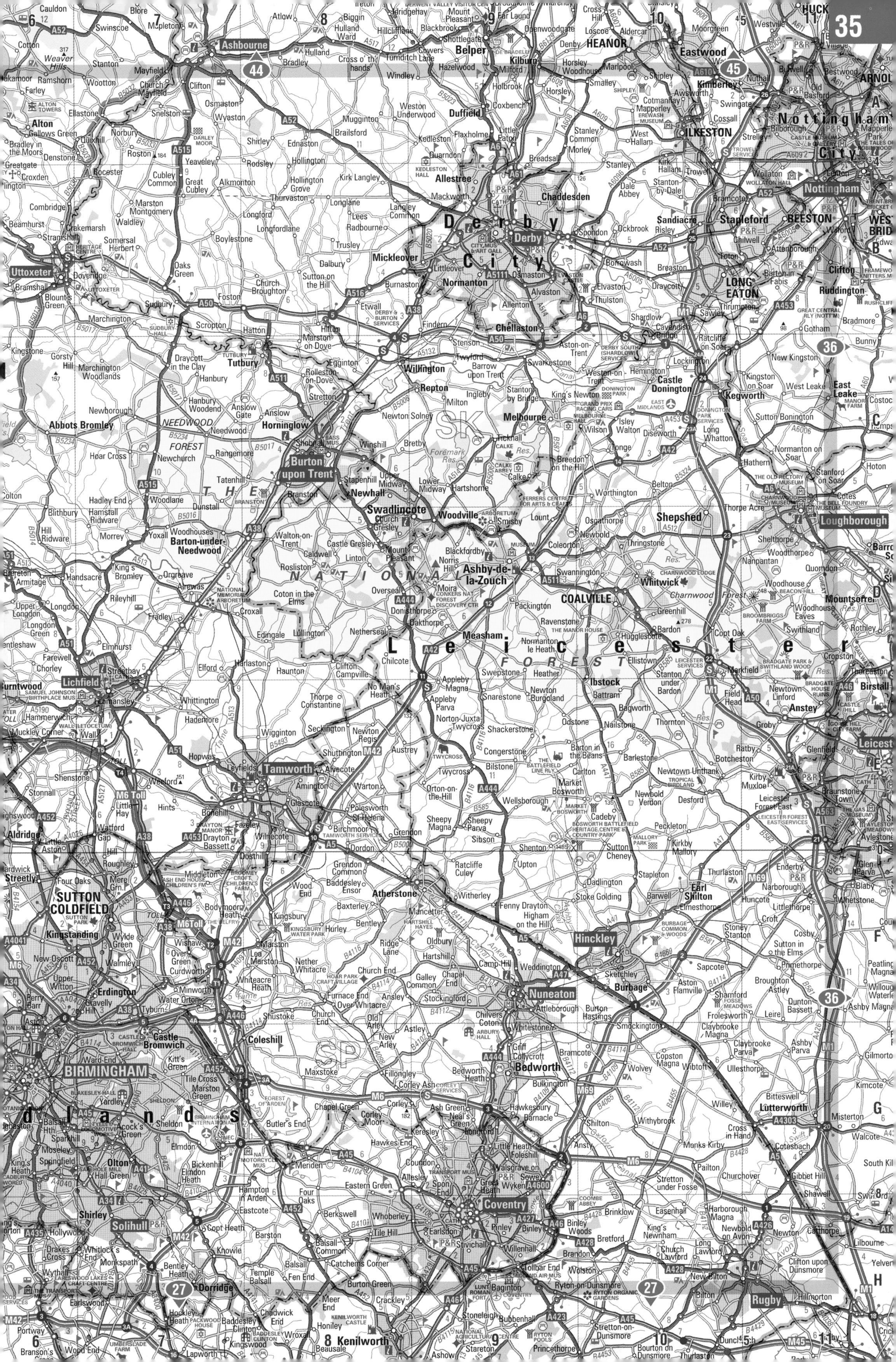
Ashbourne
44
45
Belper
HEANOR
Eastwood
Kimberley
ARNOLD
Duffield
ILKESTON
Nottingham City
Nottingham
Allestree
Chaddesden
Derby City
Derby
Stapleford
BEESTON
Uttoxeter
Mickleover
Sandiacre
Normanton
LONG EATON
Clifton
Ruddington
Chellaston
Castle Donington
36
Tutbury
Kegworth
Repton
Melbourne
Abbots Bromley
Horninglow
Burton upon Trent
Newhall
Swadlincote
Woodville
Shepshed
Loughborough
Barton-under-Needwood
Ashby-de-la-Zouch
COALVILLE
Whitwick
Mountsorrel
NATIONAL FOREST
Measham
Leicester
Lichfield
Ibstock
Birstall
Tamworth
Anstey
Leicester
Market Bosworth
Atherstone
Earl Shilton
SUTTON COLDFIELD
Hinckley
Nuneaton
Burbage
Erdington
Castle Bromwich
Coleshill
Bedworth
BIRMINGHAM
Lutterworth
Coventry
Solihull
Shirley
27
Rugby
Kenilworth

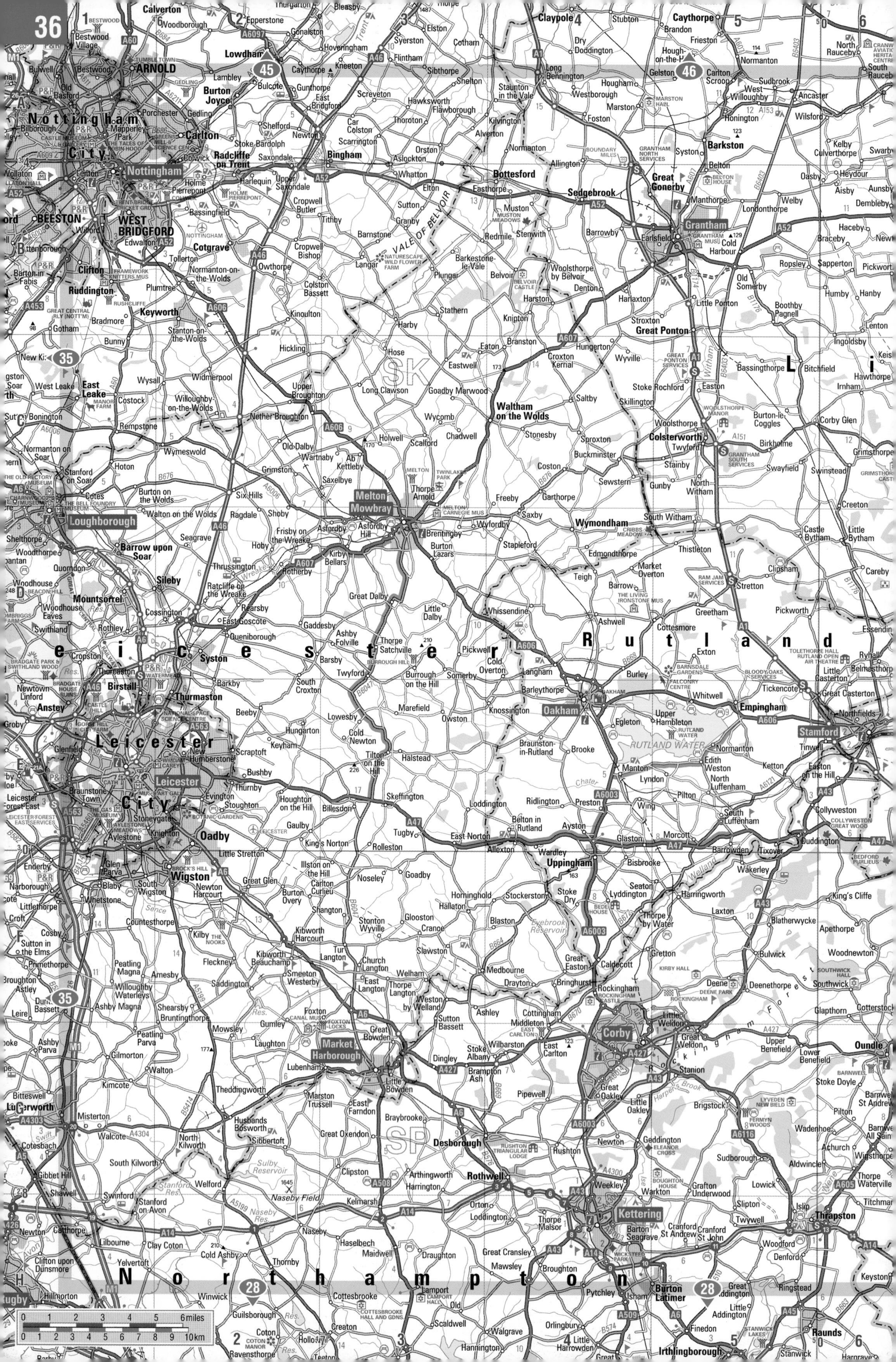
Nottingham
City
Nottingham
ARNOLD
BEESTON
WEST BRIDGFORD
Calverton
Woodborough
Epperstone
Lowdham
Bestwood Village
Bulwell
Burton Joyce
Carlton
Gedling
Radcliffe on Trent
Bingham
Cotgrave
Ruddington
Clifton
Keyworth
Edwalton
Claypole
Long Bennington
Caythorpe
Grantham
Great Gonerby
Sedgebrook
Bottesford
Barrowby
Great Ponton
Colsterworth
Little Ponton
Ancaster
Barkston
Belton
VALE OF BELVOIR
Belvoir
Woolsthorpe by Belvoir
Harby
Stathern
Waltham on the Wolds
Long Clawson
Upper Broughton
East Leake
Loughborough
Barrow upon Soar
Sileby
Mountsorrel
Quorndon
Melton Mowbray
Asfordby
Wymondham
South Witham
Leicester
Leicester City
Birstall
Syston
Thurmaston
Anstey
Oadby
Wigston
Rutland
Oakham
Uppingham
RUTLAND WATER
Empingham
Stamford
Cottesmore
Exton
Greetham
Stretton
Langham
Whissendine
Lincolnshire
Market Harborough
Great Bowden
Lubenham
Husbands Bosworth
Lutterworth
Corby
Kettering
Desborough
Rothwell
Burton Latimer
Thrapston
Oundle
Irthlingborough
Raunds
Rugby
Northampton
Naseby
Broughton Astley
Kibworth Harcourt
Kibworth Beauchamp
Hallaton
Medbourne
Rockingham
Great Oakley
Geddington
Brigstock
Rockingham Forest
SK
SP
Welland
Wreake
Soar
Trent
Witham
Chater
Eyebrook Reservoir
Sulby Reservoir
Naseby Field
45
46
35
28
A1
A6
A14
A43
A46
A47
A52
A606
A607
A6003
M1
0 1 2 3 4 5 6 miles
0 1 2 3 4 5 6 7 8 9 10 km

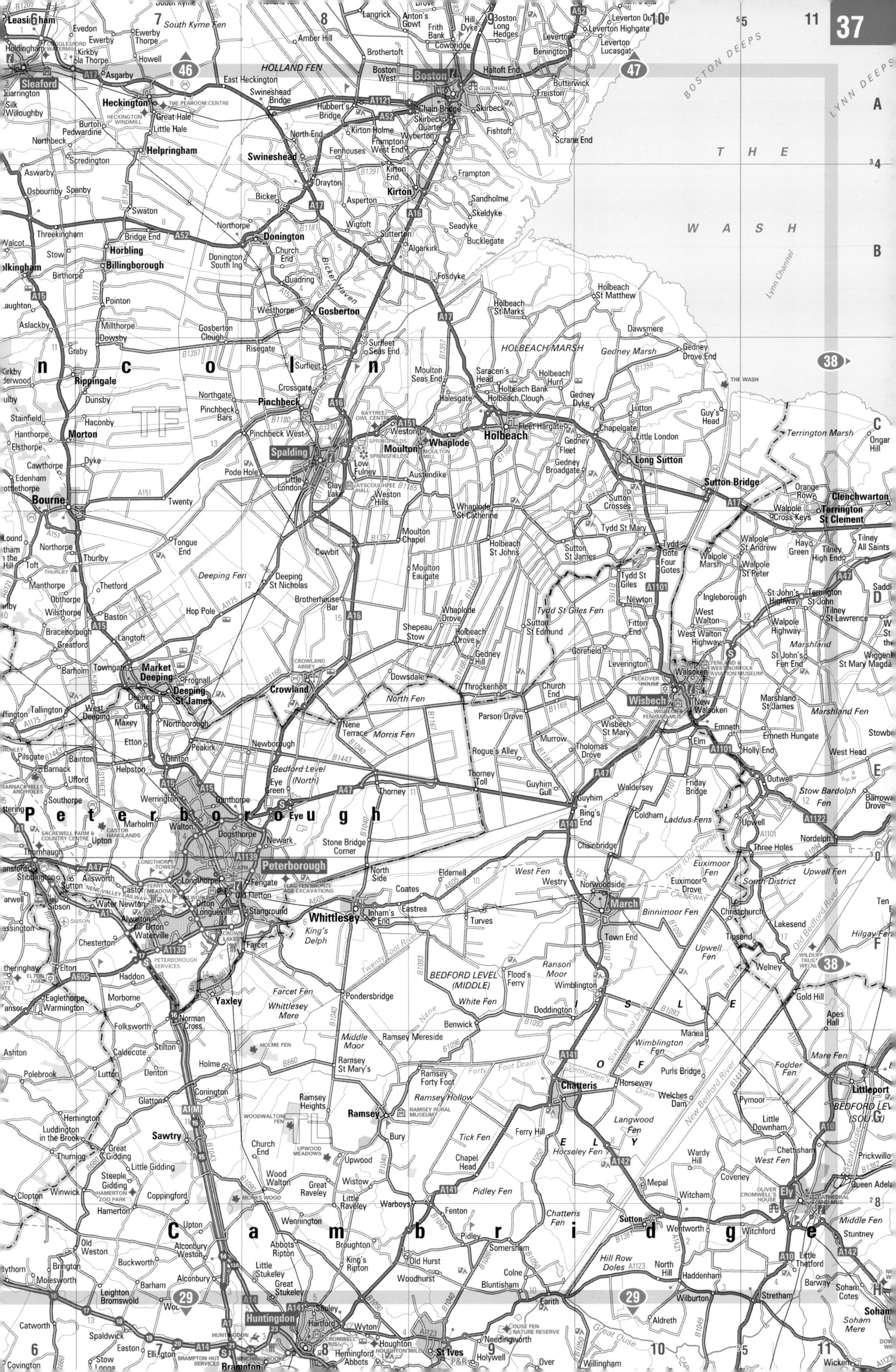
Sleaford
Heckington
Helpringham
Swineshead
Boston
Kirton
Donington
Horbling
Billingborough
Gosberton
Pinchbeck
Spalding
Moulton
Whaplode
Holbeach
Long Sutton
Sutton Bridge
Terrington St Clement
Clenchwarton
Bourne
Rippingale
Morton
Market Deeping
Deeping St James
Crowland
Wisbech
Peterborough
Whittlesey
March
Yaxley
Sawtry
Ramsey
Chatteris
Littleport
Ely
Sutton
Huntingdon
St Ives
Brampton
THE WASH
BOSTON DEEPS
LYNN DEEPS
Lynn Channel
HOLLAND FEN
HOLBEACH MARSH
Gedney Marsh
Terrington Marsh
Deeping Fen
North Fen
Morris Fen
Bedford Level (North)
BEDFORD LEVEL (MIDDLE)
BEDFORD LEVEL (SOUTH)
Tydd St Giles Fen
Marshland Fen
Upwell Fen
Hilgay Fen
Farcet Fen
Whittlesey Mere
Ramsey Hollow
Pidley Fen
Chatteris Fen
South Kyme Fen
Lincoln
Peterborough
Cambridge
ISLE OF ELY
TF
TL
46
47
38
29
A17
A52
A16
A15
A151
A1101
A47
A141
A142
A10
A605
A1139
A1(M)
A1
A14
A1123
A1122
Old Bedford River
New Bedford River
Great Ouse
Nene

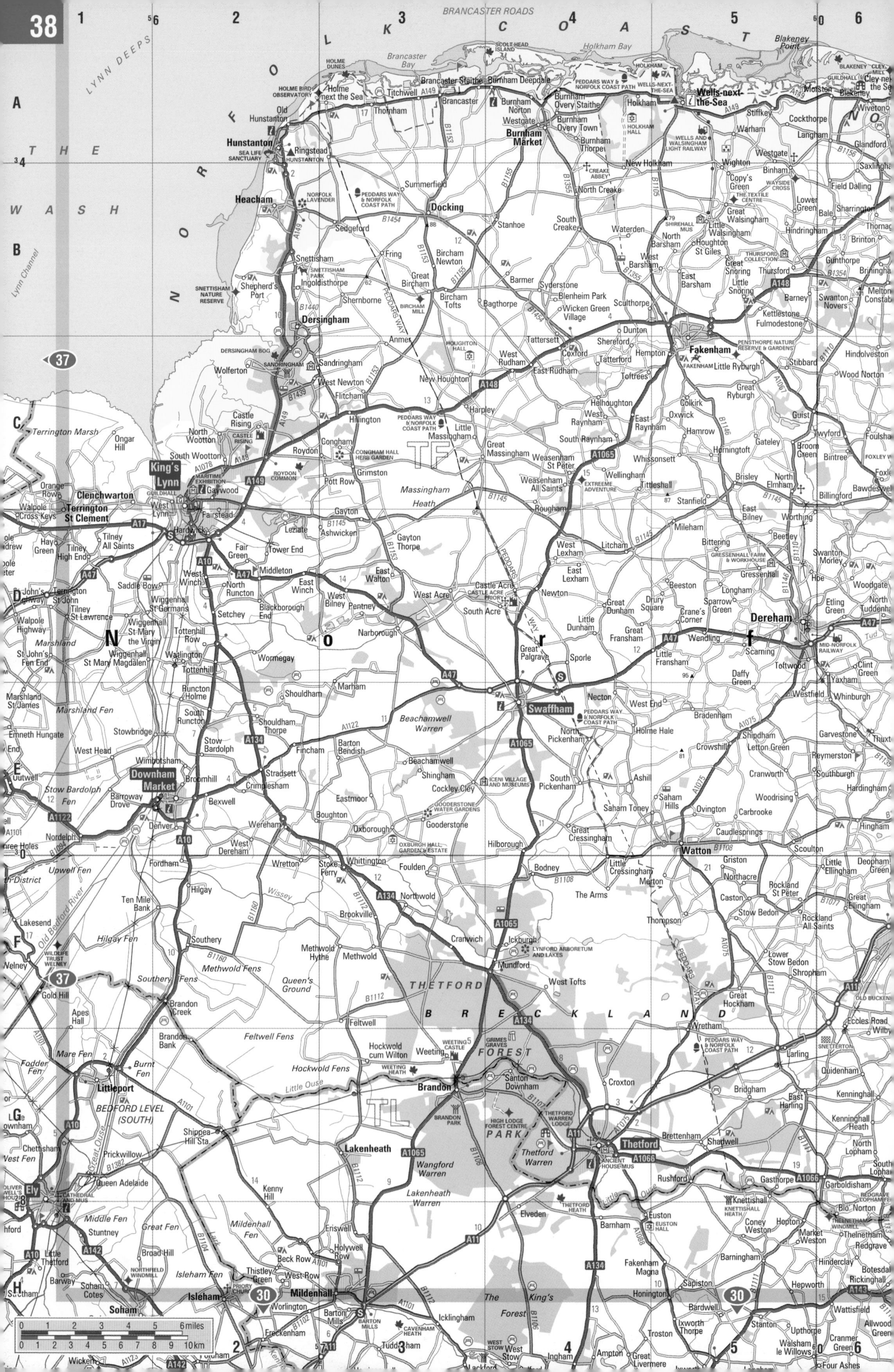
BRANCASTER ROADS
NORFOLK COAST
LYNN DEEPS
THE WASH
Lynn Channel
Holkham Bay
Blakeney Point
Brancaster Bay
SCOLT HEAD ISLAND
HOLME DUNES
HOLME BIRD OBSERVATORY
Holme next the Sea
Titchwell
Brancaster Staithe
Burnham Deepdale
Brancaster
Thornham
Old Hunstanton
Hunstanton
SEA LIFE SANCTUARY
Ringstead
Burnham Norton
Westgate
Burnham Market
Burnham Overy Staithe
Burnham Overy Town
Burnham Thorpe
PEDDARS WAY & NORFOLK COAST PATH
HOLKHAM
WELLS-NEXT-THE-SEA
Holkham
HOLKHAM HALL
Wells-next-the-Sea
WELLS AND WALSINGHAM LIGHT RAILWAY
Stiffkey
Warham
Cockthorpe
Langham
Morston
Blakeney
Wiveton
Cley next the Sea
Glandford
Saxlingham
Binham
Field Dalling
Westgate
Wighton
New Holkham
CREAKE ABBEY
North Creake
Copy's Green
WAYSIDE CROSS
THE TEXTILE CENTRE
Great Walsingham
Little Walsingham
SHIREHALL MUS
Houghton St Giles
Hindringham
Lower Green
Bale
Sharrington
Brinton
Thornage
Gunthorpe
Briningham
Heacham
NORFOLK LAVENDER
PEDDARS WAY & NORFOLK COAST PATH
Summerfield
Docking
Sedgeford
Stanhoe
South Creake
Waterden
North Barsham
West Barsham
East Barsham
THURSFORD COLLECTION
Thursford
Great Snoring
Little Snoring
Barney
Swanton Novers
Melton Constable
Snettisham
SNETTISHAM PARK
Fring
Bircham Newton
Great Bircham
Barmer
Syderstone
Blenheim Park
SNETTISHAM NATURE RESERVE
Shepherd's Port
Ingoldisthorpe
Shernborne
BIRCHAM MILL
Bircham Tofts
Bagthorpe
Wicken Green Village
Sculthorpe
Kettlestone
Fulmodestone
Dersingham
PEDDARS WAY
Anmer
HOUGHTON HALL
West Rudham
Tattersett
Coxford
East Rudham
Dunton
Shereford
Tatterford
Hempton
Fakenham
PENSTHORPE NATURE RESERVE & GARDENS
FAKENHAM
Little Ryburgh
Stibbard
Hindolveston
Wood Norton
DERSINGHAM BOG
SANDRINGHAM
Sandringham
Wolferton
West Newton
Flitcham
New Houghton
Toftrees
Helhoughton
Colkirk
Great Ryburgh
Guist
Terrington Marsh
Ongar Hill
Castle Rising
CASTLE RISING
North Wootton
South Wootton
Hillington
Harpley
Little Massingham
West Raynham
East Raynham
Oxwick
Hamrow
South Raynham
Twyford
Foulsham
Congham
CONGHAM HALL HERB GARDEN
Roydon
ROYDON COMMON
Great Massingham
Weasenham St Peter
Whissonsett
Horningtoft
Gateley
Broom Green
Bintree
FOXLEY WOOD
King's Lynn
MARITIME EXHIBITION
GUILDHALL
Gaywood
Grimston
Pott Row
Massingham Heath
Weasenham All Saints
EXTREME ADVENTURE
Wellingham
Tittleshall
Brisley
North Elmham
Bawdeswell
Foxley
Orange Row
Clenchwarton
Walpole Cross Keys
Terrington St Clement
West Lynn
Fairstead
Gayton
Leziate
Ashwicken
Rougham
Stanfield
Billingford
Worthing
East Bilney
Tilney All Saints
Tilney High End
Hay Green
Hardwick
Fair Green
Tower End
Gayton Thorpe
West Lexham
Litcham
Mileham
Bittering
Beetley
Swanton Morley
GRESSENHALL FARM & WORKHOUSE
Gressenhall
Hoe
Woodgate
East Lexham
Middleton
East Walton
East Winch
West Winch
North Runcton
Saddle Bow
Wiggenhall St Germans
Terrington St John
St John's Highway
Tilney St Lawrence
Walpole Highway
West Bilney
Pentney
West Acre
CASTLE ACRE PRIORY
Castle Acre
Newton
Beeston
Longham
Etling Green
North Tuddenham
South Acre
Great Dunham
Drury Square
Sparrow Green
Crane's Corner
Dereham
Setchey
Blackborough End
Wiggenhall St Mary the Virgin
Tottenhill Row
Marshland
Narborough
Little Dunham
Great Fransham
Wendling
MID-NORFOLK RAILWAY
St John's Fen End
Wiggenhall St Mary Magdalen
Watlington
Tottenhill
Wormegay
Great Palgrave
Sporle
Little Fransham
Scarning
Toftwood
Clint Green
Yaxham
Daffy Green
Marshland St James
Runcton Holme
Shouldham
Marham
Swaffham
Necton
West End
Westfield
Whinburgh
Marshland Fen
South Runcton
Shouldham Thorpe
Beachamwell Warren
Bradenham
North Pickenham
Holme Hale
Emneth Hungate
Stowbridge
West Head
Stow Bardolph
Fincham
Barton Bendish
Shipdham
Letton Green
Garvestone
Thuxton
Crowshill
Reymerston
Wimbotsham
Beachamwell
Shingham
Cockley Cley
ICENI VILLAGE AND MUSEUMS
South Pickenham
Ashill
Cranworth
Southburgh
Outwell
Stow Bardolph Fen
Downham Market
Broomhill
Stradsett
Crimplesham
Hardingham
Barroway Drove
Bexwell
Eastmoor
GOODERSTONE WATER GARDENS
Saham Hills
Saham Toney
Woodrising
Nordelph
Denver
Wereham
Boughton
Gooderstone
Ovington
Carbrooke
Great Cressingham
Caudlesprings
Hingham
Three Holes
West Dereham
Oxborough
OXBURGH HALL, GARDEN & ESTATE
Hilborough
Watton
Scoulton
Upwell Fen
Fordham
Wretton
Stoke Ferry
Whittington
Foulden
Bodney
Little Cressingham
Griston
Little Ellingham
Deopham Green
Hilgay
Merton
Northacre
Rockland St Peter
Wissey
Northwold
The Arms
Caston
Great Ellingham
Ten Mile Bank
Stow Bedon
Rockland All Saints
Brookville
Thompson
Lakesend
Old Bedford River
Cranwich
Ickburgh
LYNFORD ARBORETUM AND LAKES
Southery
Hilgay Fen
Methwold Hythe
Methwold
Lower Stow Bedon
WILDLIFE TRUST WELNEY
Welney
Methwold Fens
Mundford
Shropham
Queen's Ground
THETFORD
West Tofts
Gold Hill
Southery Fens
BRECKLAND
Brandon Creek
Great Hockham
OLD BUCKENHAM
Apes Hall
Feltwell
Eccles Road
Wilby
Feltwell Fens
GRIMES GRAVES
Wretham
PEDDARS WAY & NORFOLK COAST PATH
SNETTERTON
Brandon Bank
Mare Fen
Hockwold cum Wilton
Weeting
WEETING CASTLE
FOREST
Larling
Fodder Fen
Burnt Fen
Hockwold Fens
WEETING HEATH
Quidenham
Littleport
Little Ouse
Brandon
Santon Downham
Croxton
Bridgham
Kenninghall
BEDFORD LEVEL (SOUTH)
East Harling
BRANDON PARK
HIGH LODGE FOREST CENTRE
THETFORD WARREN LODGE
Kenninghall Heath
Little Downham
Shippea Hill Sta.
PARK
Brettenham
Shadwell
North Lopham
Chettisham
Prickwillow
Lakenheath
Thetford Warren
Thetford
ANCIENT HOUSE MUS
South Lopham
Great Ouse
Wangford Warren
Rushford
Gasthorpe
Garboldisham
Ely
CATHEDRAL AND MUS
OLIVER CROMWELL'S HOUSE
Queen Adelaide
Kenny Hill
Lakenheath Warren
Knettishall
KNETTISHALL HEATH
Redgrave
Blo' Norton
THELNETHAM WINDMILL
Middle Fen
Great Fen
Mildenhall Fen
Elveden
THETFORD HEATH
Barnham
Euston
EUSTON HALL
Coney Weston
Hopton
Market Weston
Thelnetham
Stuntney
Broad Hill
Eriswell
Holywell Row
Beck Row
Fakenham Magna
Barningham
Hinderclay
Little Thetford
Lark
NORTHFIELD WINDMILL
Isleham Fen
Thistley Green
West Row
Sapiston
Hepworth
Botesdale
Rickinghall
Barway
Soham Cotes
PRIORY CHURCH
Isleham
Mildenhall
The King's Forest
Honington
Bardwell
Wattisfield
Soham
Worlington
Barton Mills
BARTON MILLS
Icklingham
Ixworth Thorpe
Stanton
Upthorpe
Allwood Green
CAVENHAM HEATH
Troston
Walsham le Willows
Cranmer Green
Freckenham
Tuddenham
West Stow
Ingham
Ampton
Great Livermere
Four Ashes
Wicken
0 1 2 3 4 5 6 miles
0 1 2 3 4 5 6 7 8 9 10km

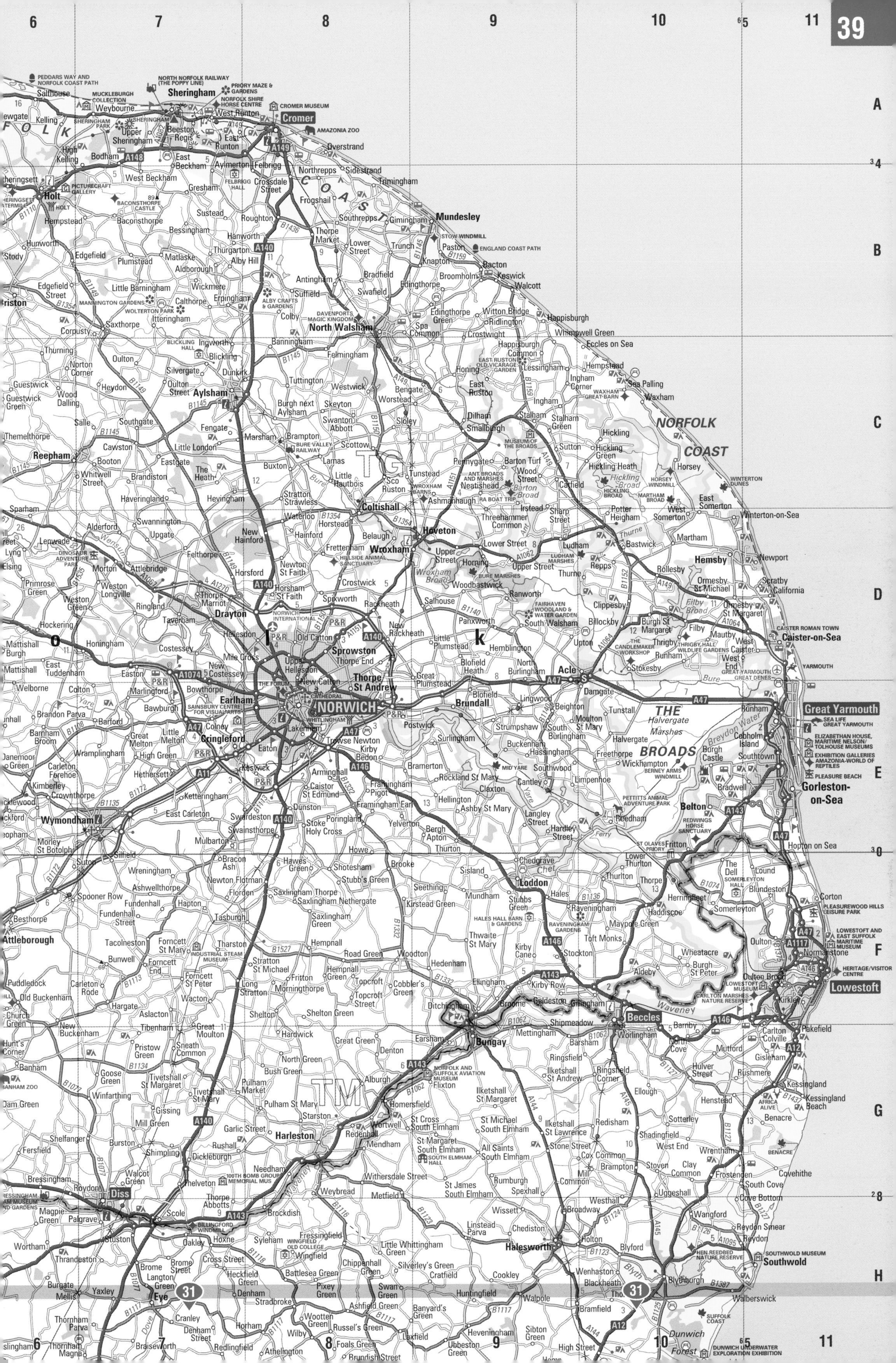
NORWICH
Great Yarmouth
Lowestoft
Cromer
Sheringham
Holt
Aylsham
North Walsham
Mundesley
Wroxham
Hoveton
Coltishall
Acle
Caister-on-Sea
Gorleston-on-Sea
Beccles
Bungay
Harleston
Diss
Eye
Halesworth
Southwold
Wymondham
Attleborough
Reepham
Drayton
Loddon
NORFOLK COAST
THE BROADS
Halvergate Marshes
TG
TM
A47
A11
A140
A146
A143
A149
A12
A1074
A1151
A148
A144
A145
A1062
A1064
A1117
A1270
31

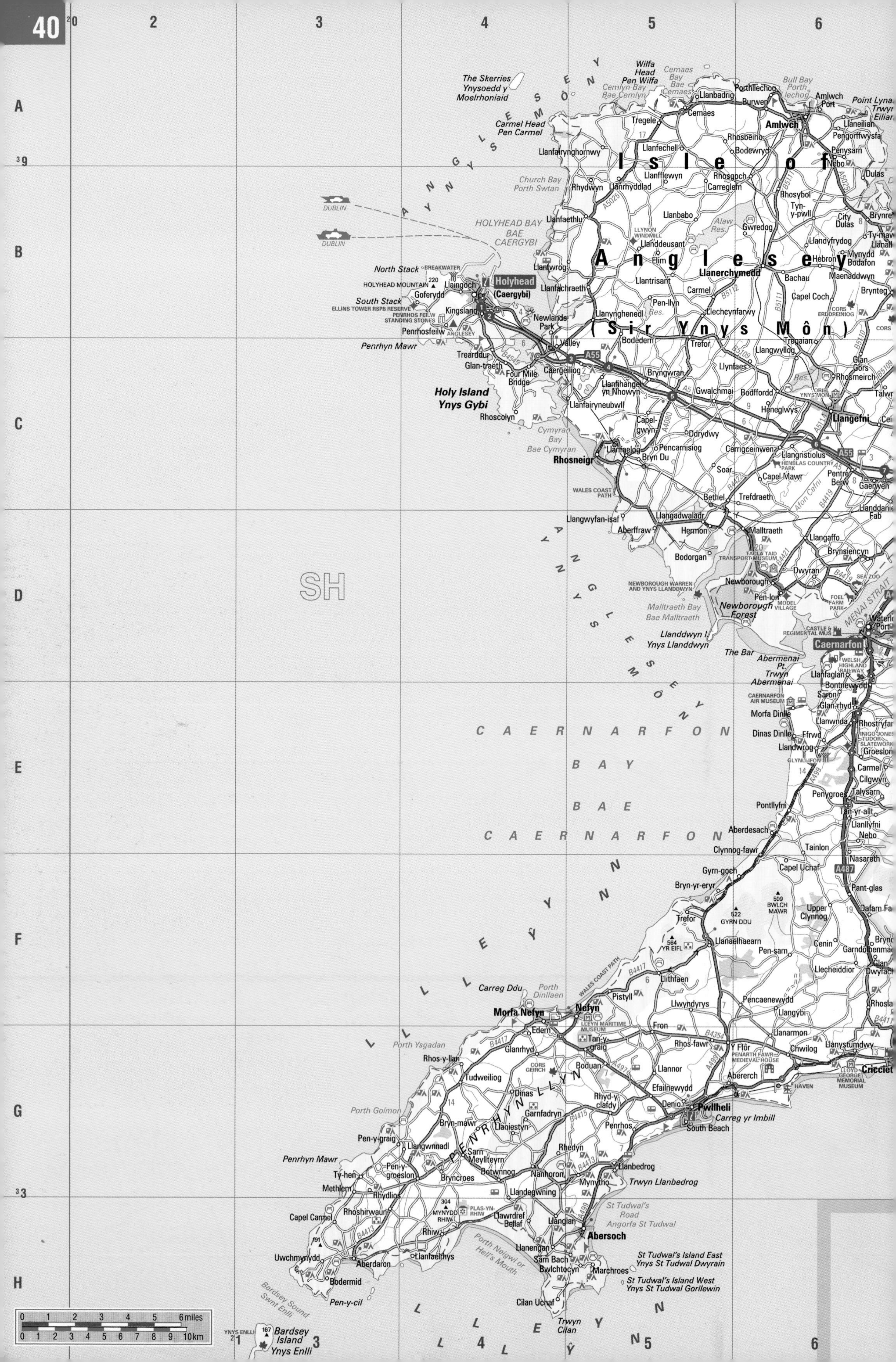

2
3
4
5
6
A
B
C
D
E
F
G
H
SH
The Skerries
Ynysoedd y Moelrhoniaid
Carmel Head
Pen Carmel
Wylfa Head
Pen Wylfa
Cemaes Bay
Bae Cemaes
Cemlyn Bay
Bae Cemlyn
Bull Bay
Porth Llechog
Llanbadrig
Porthllechog
Burwen
Cemaes
Amlwch Port
Amlwch
Point Lynas
Trwyn Eilian
Llaneilian
Pengorffwysfa
Tregele
Llanfechell
Rhosbeirio
Bodewryd
Penysarn
Nebo
Llanfairynghornwy
Isle of Anglesey
Llanfflewyn
Rhosgoch
Carreglefn
Dulas
Church Bay
Porth Swtan
Rhydwyn
Llanrhyddlad
Rhosybol
Tyn-y-pwll
City Dulas
Brynrefail
DUBLIN
Llanfaethlu
Llanbabo
Alaw Res.
Gwredog
HOLYHEAD BAY
BAE CAERGYBI
LLYNON WINDMILL
Llanddeusant
Llandyfrydog
Mynydd Bodafon
North Stack
BREAKWATER
Llanfwrog
Elim
Hebron
Maenaddwyn
HOLYHEAD MOUNTAIN
220
Llaingoch
Holyhead
(Caergybi)
Llanfachraeth
Llantrisant
Llanerchymedd
Bachau
Brynteg
Goferydd
Carmel
Capel Coch
South Stack
ELLINS TOWER RSPB RESERVE
PENRHOS FEILW STANDING STONES
Kingsland
Newlands Park
Pen-llyn
Llanynghenedl
Cefni Res.
Llechcynfarwy
CORS ERDDREINIOG
Penrhosfeilw
Anglesey
(Sir Ynys Môn)
Tregaian
CORS
Penrhyn Mawr
Valley
Bodedern
Trefor
Llangwyllog
Trearddur
Glan-traeth
Four Mile Bridge
Caergeiliog
Llynfaes
Glan Gors
Rhosmeirch
Holy Island
Ynys Gybi
Llanfihangel yn Nhowyn
Bryngwran
Gwalchmai
Bodffordd
ORIEL YNYS MÔN
Talwrn
Llanfairyneubwll
Heneglwys
Llangefni
Rhoscolyn
Capel-gwyn
Ddrydwy
Cymyran Bay
Bae Cymyran
Llanfaelog
Pencarnisiog
Cerrigceinwen
Llangristiolus
HENBLAS COUNTRY PARK
Rhosneigr
Bryn Du
Soar
Capel Mawr
Pentre Berw
Gaerwen
WALES COAST PATH
Bethel
Trefdraeth
Afon Cefni
Llanddaniel Fab
Llangwyfan-isaf
Llangadwaladr
Aberffraw
Hermon
Malltraeth
Llangaffo
Bodorgan
TACLA TAID TRANSPORT MUSEUM
Brynsiencyn
Dwyran
SEA ZOO
NEWBOROUGH WARREN AND YNYS LLANDDWYN
Newborough
Pen-lon
MODEL VILLAGE
FOEL FARM PARK
MENAI STRAIT
Malltraeth Bay
Bae Malltraeth
Newborough Forest
Waterloo Port
CASTLE & REGIMENTAL MUS
Llanddwyn I.
Ynys Llanddwyn
Caernarfon
The Bar
Abermenai Pt.
Trwyn Abermenai
WELSH HIGHLAND RAILWAY
Llanfaglan
Bontnewydd
CAERNARFON AIR MUSEUM
Saron
Glan-rhyd
Morfa Dinlle
Llanwnda
Rhostryfan
CAERNARFON BAY
BAE CAERNARFON
Dinas Dinlle
Ffrwd
INIGO JONES TUDOR SLATEWORKS
Llandwrog
Groeslon
GLYNLLIFON
Carmel
Cilgwyn
Penygroes
Talysarn
Pontllyfni
Tan-yr-allt
Llanllyfni
Aberdesach
Nebo
Clynnog-fawr
Tainlon
Nasareth
Capel Uchaf
Gyrn-goch
Bryn-yr-eryr
509 BWLCH MAWR
Pant-glas
522 GYRN DDU
Upper Clynnog
Dafarn Faig
Trefor
564 YR EIFL
Llanaelhaearn
Cenin
Bryncir
Garndolbenmaen
Pen-sarn
Llecheiddior
Dwyfach
Llithfaen
Carreg Ddu
Porth Dinllaen
Pistyll
Llwyndyrys
Pencaenewydd
Nefyn
Morfa Nefyn
Rhoslan
LLEYN MARITIME MUSEUM
Llangybi
Edern
Fron
Porth Ysgadan
Llanarmon
Tan-y-graig
Rhos-fawr
Y Ffôr
Chwilog
Llanystumdwy
Glanrhyd
PENARTH FAWR MEDIEVAL HOUSE
Rhos-y-llan
CORS GEIRCH
Boduan
Llannor
Criccieth
LLOYD GEORGE MEMORIAL MUSEUM
Aberech
HAVEN
Tudweiliog
Efailnewydd
Dinas
Rhyd-y-clafdy
Denio
Pwllheli
Porth Golmon
Garnfadryn
Carreg yr Imbill
Bryn-mawr
South Beach
PENRHYN LLYN
LLEYN
Llaniestyn
Penrhos
Pen-y-graig
Llangwnnadl
Rhedyn
Penrhyn Mawr
Sarn Meyllteyrn
Llanbedrog
Pen-y-groeslon
Botwnnog
Nanhoron
Mynytho
Trwyn Llanbedrog
Ty-hen
Bryncroes
Methlem
Rhydlios
304 MYNYDD RHIW
Llandegwning
St Tudwal's Road
Angorfa St Tudwal
PLAS-YN-RHIW
Capel Carmel
Rhoshirwaun
Llawrdref Bellaf
Llangian
Rhiw
Abersoch
191
Porth Neigwl or Hell's Mouth
Llanengan
Uwchmynydd
Aberdaron
Llanfaelrhys
Sarn Bach
St Tudwal's Island East
Ynys St Tudwal Dwyrain
Bwlchtocyn
Marchroes
Bodermid
St Tudwal's Island West
Ynys St Tudwal Gorllewin
Bardsey Sound
Swnt Enlli
Pen-y-cil
Cilan Uchaf
Trwyn Cilan
YNYS ENLLI
167
Bardsey Island
Ynys Enlli
0 1 2 3 4 5 6 miles
0 1 2 3 4 5 6 7 8 9 10 km
A55
A5
A5025
B5112
B5111
B5109
B5110
A5114
A4080
B4422
B4419
B4421
B4545
A4087
A499
A487
B4417
B4354
A497
B4415
B4413
A4413

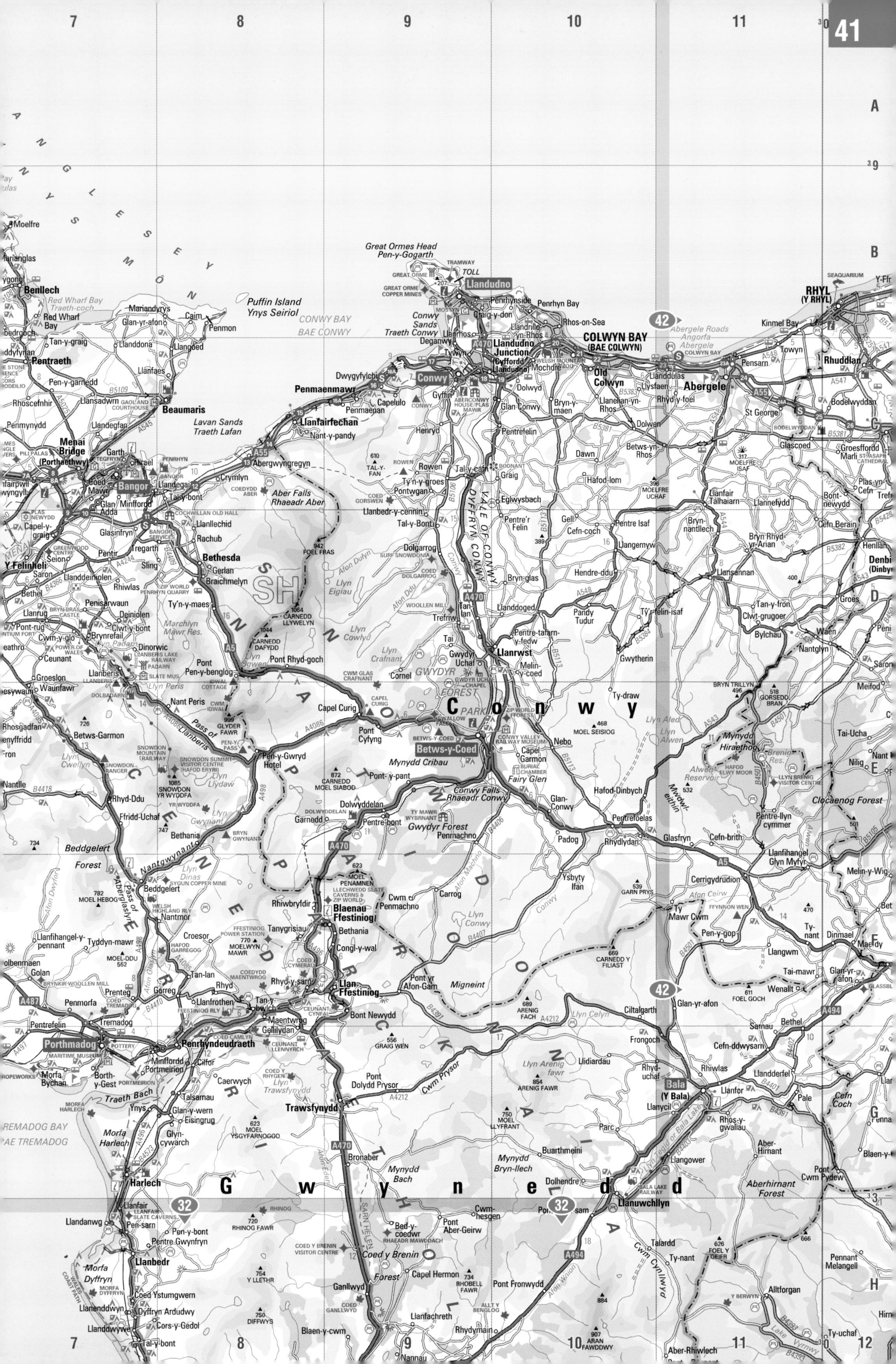
7
8
9
10
11
12
A
B
C
D
E
F
G
H
ANGLESEY
MÔN
Great Ormes Head
Pen-y-Gogarth
Llandudno
Puffin Island
Ynys Seiriol
CONWY BAY
BAE CONWY
Conwy Sands
Traeth Conwy
Penrhyn Bay
Rhos-on-Sea
COLWYN BAY
(BAE COLWYN)
Llandudno Junction
(Cyffordd Llandudno)
Deganwy
Conwy
Abergele
Old Colwyn
Llanddulas
Abergele Roads
Angorfa Abergele
RHYL
(Y RHYL)
Kinmel Bay
Towyn
Pensarn
Rhuddlan
St George
Bodelwyddan
Benllech
Red Wharf Bay
Traeth-coch
Pentraeth
Beaumaris
Menai Bridge
(Porthaethwy)
Bangor
Penmon
Llanfairfechan
Penmaenmawr
Dwygyfylchi
Lavan Sands
Traeth Lafan
Aber Falls
Rhaeadr Aber
Abergwyngregyn
Bethesda
Tal-y-Bont
Y Felinheli
Llanrwst
Trefriw
Betws-y-Coed
Capel Curig
Llanberis
Pass of Llanberis
Nant Peris
Snowdon
Yr Wyddfa
Beddgelert
Beddgelert Forest
Nantgwynant
Dolwyddelan
Blaenau Ffestiniog
Llan Ffestiniog
Tanygrisiau
Maentwrog
Penrhyndeudraeth
Porthmadog
Tremadog
Minffordd
Portmeirion
Traeth Bach
Harlech
Morfa Harlech
TREMADOG BAY
BAE TREMADOG
Llanbedr
Trawsfynydd
Bronaber
Coed y Brenin
Ganllwyd
Gwydyr Forest
Conwy
Gwynedd
SNOWDONIA
PARC CENEDLAETHOL ERYRI
Vale of Conwy
Dyffryn Conwy
Mynydd Hiraethog
Llyn Brenig
Alwen Reservoir
Clocaenog Forest
Cerrigydrudion
Llyn Celyn
Bala
(Y Bala)
Llyn Tegid or Bala Lake
Llanuwchllyn
Aberhirnant Forest
Llanfor
Denbigh
(Dinbych)
Mynydd Bach
Mynydd Bryn-llech
Pont Fronwydd
Migneint
A5
A55
A470
A494
A487
A496
A4212
A4086
A543
A548
A547
A544
42
32
SH

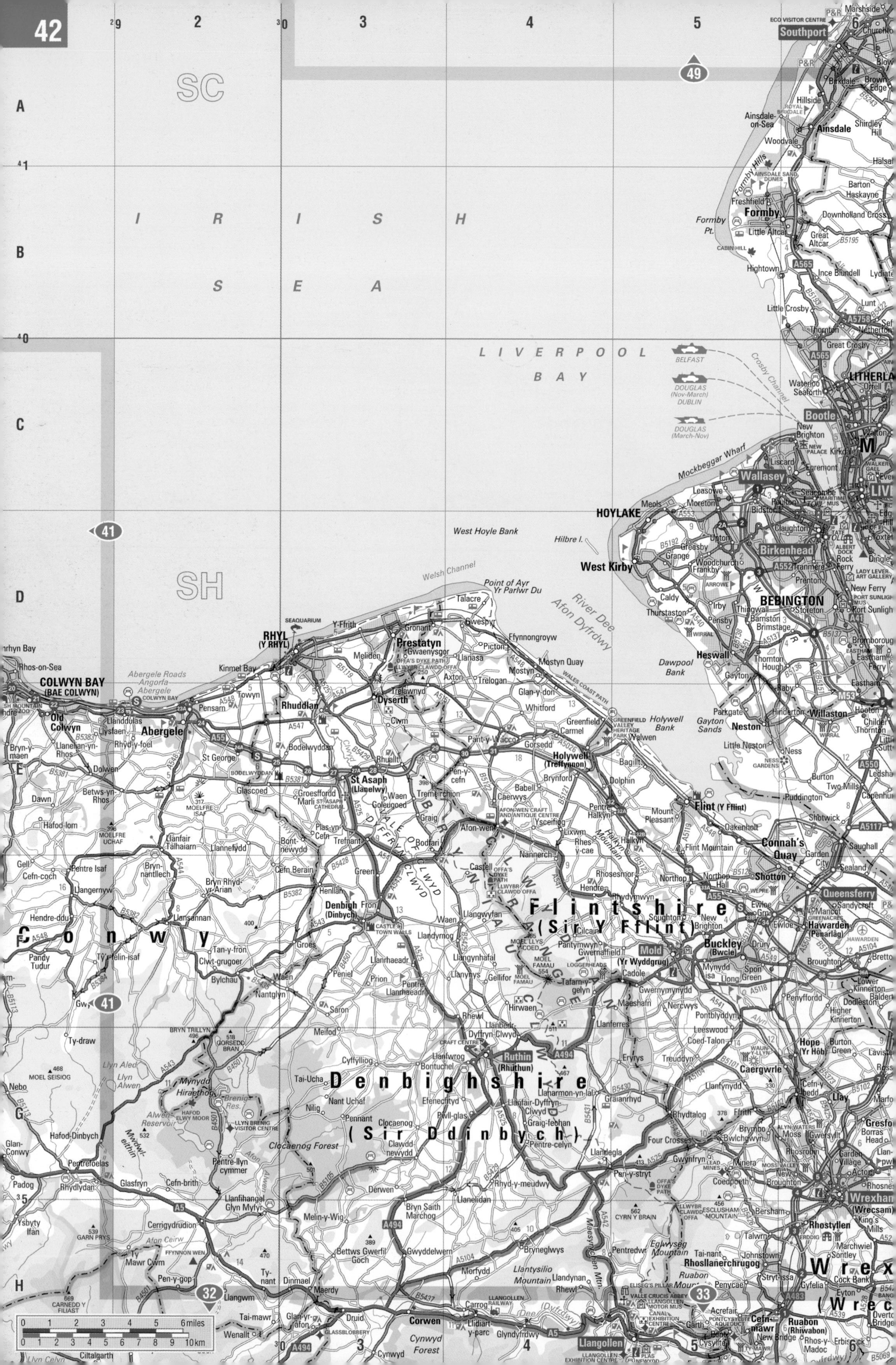
IRISH SEA
LIVERPOOL BAY
SC
SH
Southport
Ainsdale
Formby
Crosby
Bootle
Wallasey
HOYLAKE
West Kirby
Birkenhead
BEBINGTON
Heswall
Neston
Ellesmere Port
Connah's Quay
Queensferry
Flint (Y Fflint)
Holywell (Treffynnon)
Prestatyn
RHYL (Y RHYL)
Rhuddlan
St Asaph (Llanelwy)
Denbigh (Dinbych)
Ruthin (Rhuthun)
Mold (Yr Wyddgrug)
Buckley (Bwcle)
Hawarden (Penarlâg)
Caergwrle
Wrexham (Wrecsam)
Ruabon (Rhiwabon)
Llangollen
Corwen
COLWYN BAY (BAE COLWYN)
Abergele
Old Colwyn
Conwy
Flintshire (Sir Y Fflint)
Denbighshire (Sir Ddinbych)
West Hoyle Bank
Hilbre I.
Point of Ayr Yr Parlwr Du
River Dee Afon Dyfrdwy
Welsh Channel
Mockbeggar Wharf
Crosby Channel
Dawpool Bank
Holywell Bank
Gayton Sands
Formby Pt.
Clocaenog Forest
Alwen Reservoir
Llyn Brenig
Cynwyd Forest
BELFAST
DOUGLAS (Nov-March) DUBLIN
DOUGLAS (March-Nov)
0 1 2 3 4 5 6 miles
0 1 2 3 4 5 6 7 8 9 10 km
49
41
32
33

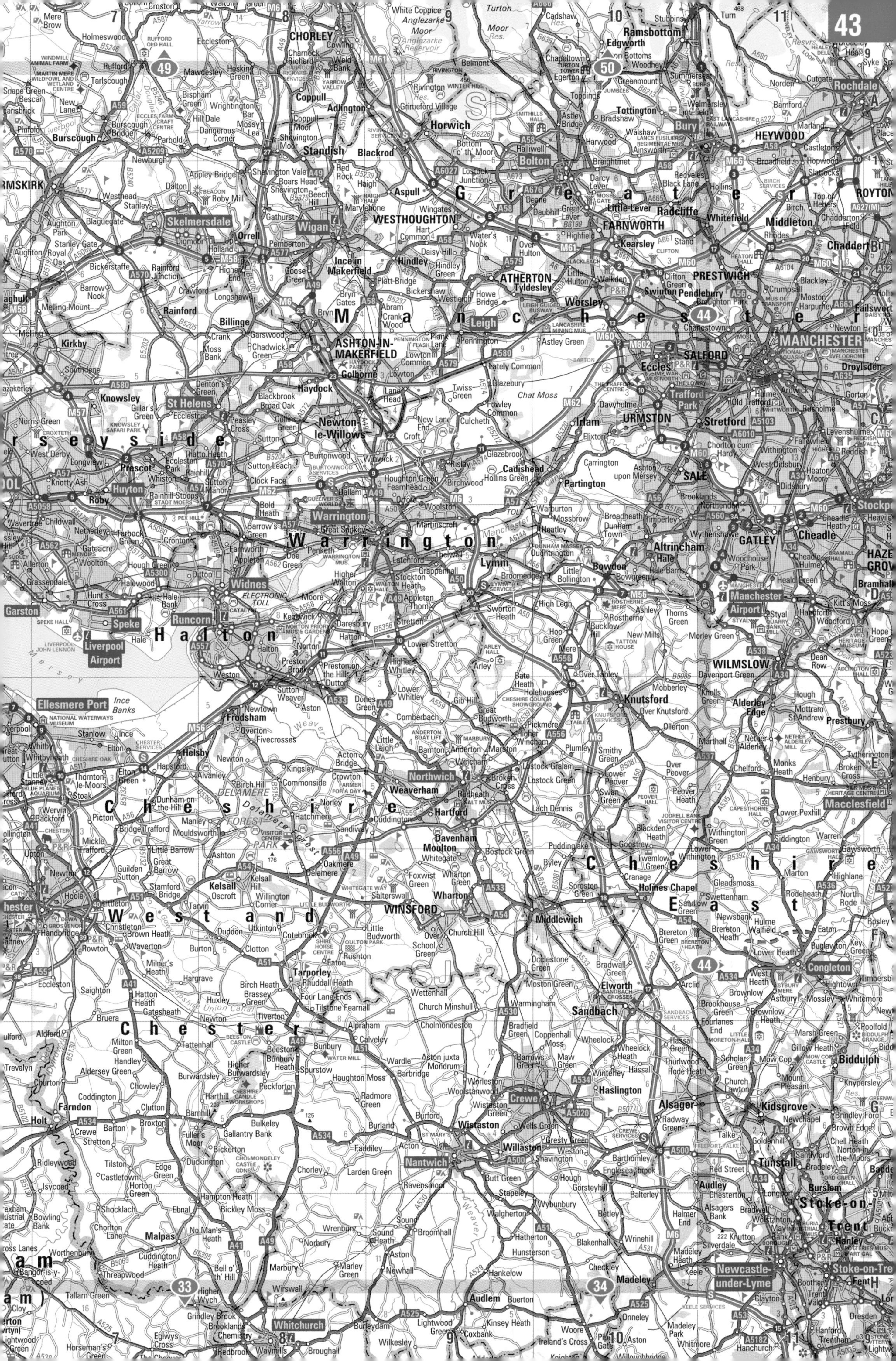

CHORLEY
Ramsbottom
Edgworth
Rochdale
HEYWOOD
ROYTON
Bury
Skelmersdale
Wigan
Standish
Horwich
Bolton
WESTHOUGHTON
FARNWORTH
Radcliffe
Middleton
PRESTWICH
Whitefield
Chadderton
Orrell
Ince in Makerfield
Hindley
ATHERTON
Tyldesley
Worsley
Swinton
Pendlebury
Leigh
Greater Manchester
ASHTON-IN-MAKERFIELD
Golborne
Haydock
Kirkby
Knowsley
St Helens
Newton-le-Willows
Eccles
SALFORD
MANCHESTER
Droylsden
Trafford Park
URMSTON
Irlam
Stretford
SALE
Partington
Cadishead
Merseyside
Prescot
Huyton
Roby
Warrington
Altrincham
GATLEY
Cheadle
Lymm
Widnes
Runcorn
Halton
Speke
Garston
Liverpool Airport
Manchester Airport
WILMSLOW
Knutsford
Ellesmere Port
Frodsham
Helsby
Northwich
Weaverham
Hartford
Cheshire West and Chester
Cheshire East
Macclesfield
WINSFORD
Middlewich
Holmes Chapel
Congleton
Tarporley
Sandbach
Alsager
Crewe
Kidsgrove
Biddulph
Tunstall
Nantwich
Farndon
Holt
Malpas
Audley
Burslem
Stoke-on-Trent
Hanley
Newcastle-under-Lyme
Madeley
Audlem
Whitchurch

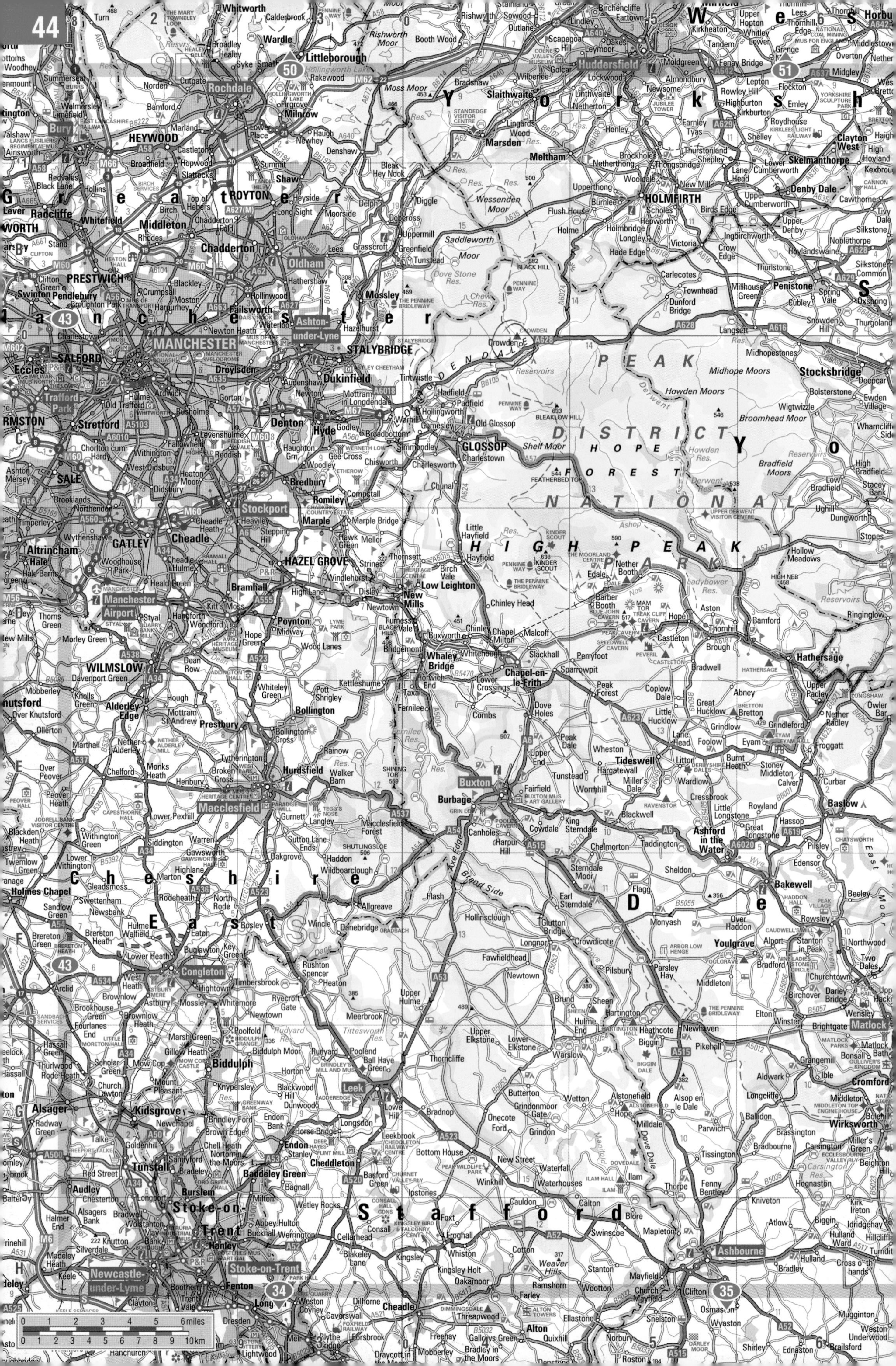
Greater Manchester
West Yorkshire
South Yorkshire
Derbyshire
East Cheshire
Staffordshire
PEAK DISTRICT NATIONAL PARK
HOPE FOREST
HIGH PEAK
MANCHESTER
SALFORD
Trafford Park
Manchester Airport
Stockport
Oldham
Rochdale
Bury
Ashton-under-Lyne
Huddersfield
Macclesfield
Congleton
Buxton
Leek
Stoke-on-Trent
Newcastle-under-Lyme
Ashbourne
Matlock
Whitworth
Littleborough
Wardle
Milnrow
HEYWOOD
ROYTON
Shaw
Middleton
Chadderton
Radcliffe
Whitefield
PRESTWICH
Swinton
Pendlebury
Eccles
Stretford
Sale
Altrincham
Hale
GATLEY
Cheadle
HAZEL GROVE
Bramhall
Poynton
Wilmslow
Alderley Edge
Knutsford
Prestbury
Bollington
Denton
Hyde
Dukinfield
STALYBRIDGE
Droylsden
Mossley
Glossop
Hadfield
Marple
Romiley
Bredbury
New Mills
Whaley Bridge
Chapel-en-le-Frith
Hayfield
Edale
Castleton
Hathersage
Tideswell
Bakewell
Baslow
Ashford in the Water
Youlgrave
Hartington
Longnor
Biddulph
Kidsgrove
Alsager
Tunstall
Burslem
Hanley
Fenton
Longton
Cheadle
Alton
Holmfirth
Marsden
Meltham
Slaithwaite
Penistone
Stocksbridge
Denby Dale
Skelmanthorpe
Wirksworth
Cromford
Holmes Chapel
Sandbach
Audley
Ladybower Res.
Howden Moors
Bleaklow Hill
Kinder Scout
Saddleworth Moor
Wessenden Moor
Dove Dale
Weaver Hills
Axe Edge
0 1 2 3 4 5 6 miles
0 1 2 3 4 5 6 7 8 9 10km

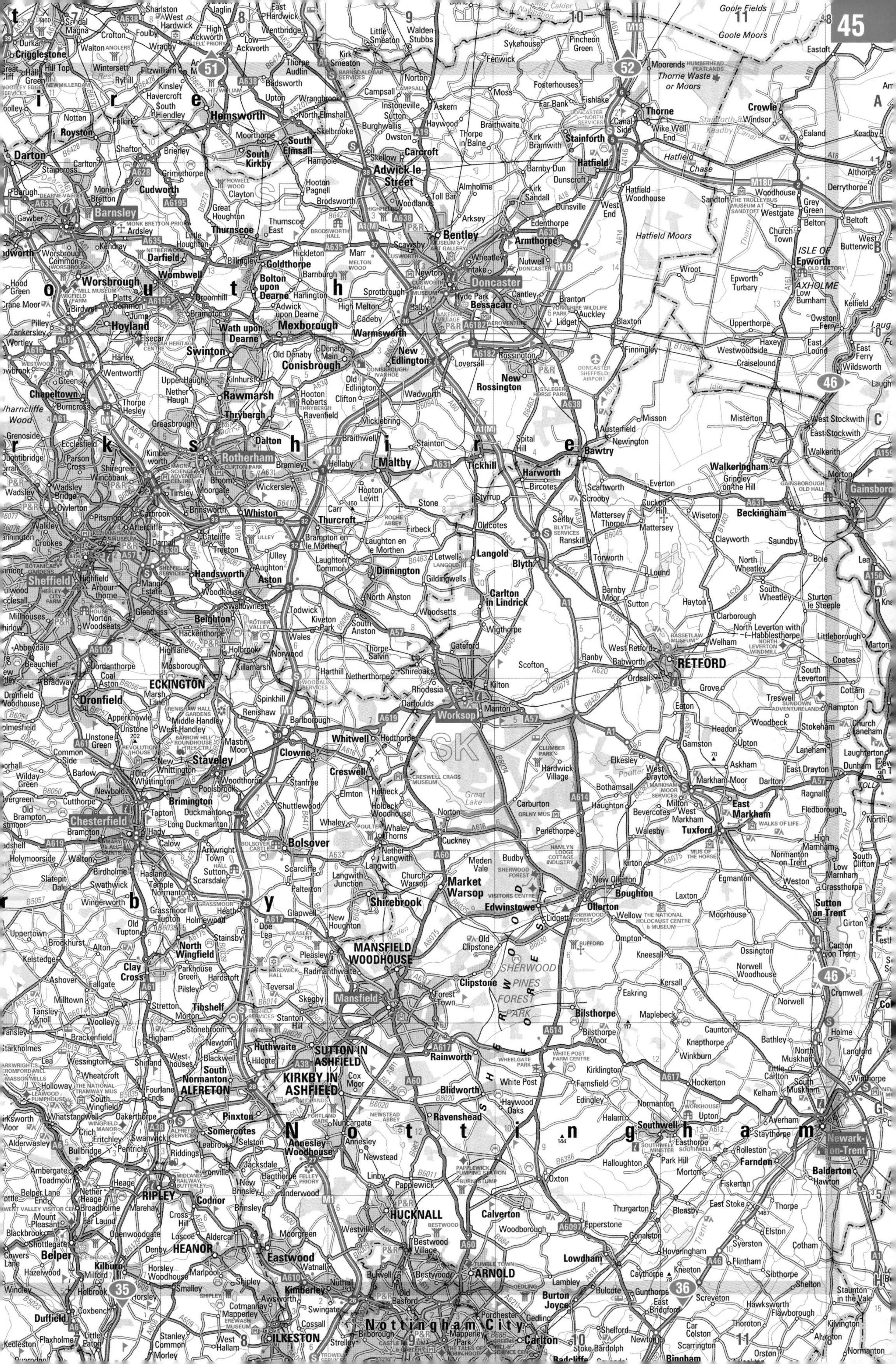
Barnsley
Doncaster
Rotherham
Sheffield
Chesterfield
Worksop
Mansfield
RETFORD
Hemsworth
Cudworth
Royston
Darton
Hoyland
Wombwell
Darfield
Thurnscoe
South Elmsall
South Kirkby
Adwick le Street
Bentley
Armthorpe
Bessacarr
Mexborough
Conisbrough
Swinton
Rawmarsh
Thrybergh
Maltby
Tickhill
Harworth
Bawtry
Thorne
Hatfield
Stainforth
Crowle
Epworth
ISLE OF AXHOLME
Edlington
New Rossington
Dinnington
Langold
Blyth
Carlton in Lindrick
Handsworth
Aston
Beighton
ECKINGTON
Dronfield
Staveley
Clowne
Bolsover
Shirebrook
Market Warsop
MANSFIELD WOODHOUSE
Edwinstowe
Ollerton
Boughton
Tuxford
East Markham
Sutton on Trent
Clay Cross
North Wingfield
Tibshelf
Huthwaite
SUTTON IN ASHFIELD
KIRKBY IN ASHFIELD
ALFRETON
Somercotes
RIPLEY
HEANOR
Belper
Eastwood
HUCKNALL
ARNOLD
Calverton
Lowdham
Southwell
Newark-on-Trent
Balderton
Carlton
ILKESTON
Kimberley
Nottingham City
Bingham
Sherwood Forest
South Yorkshire
Nottingham
Derby

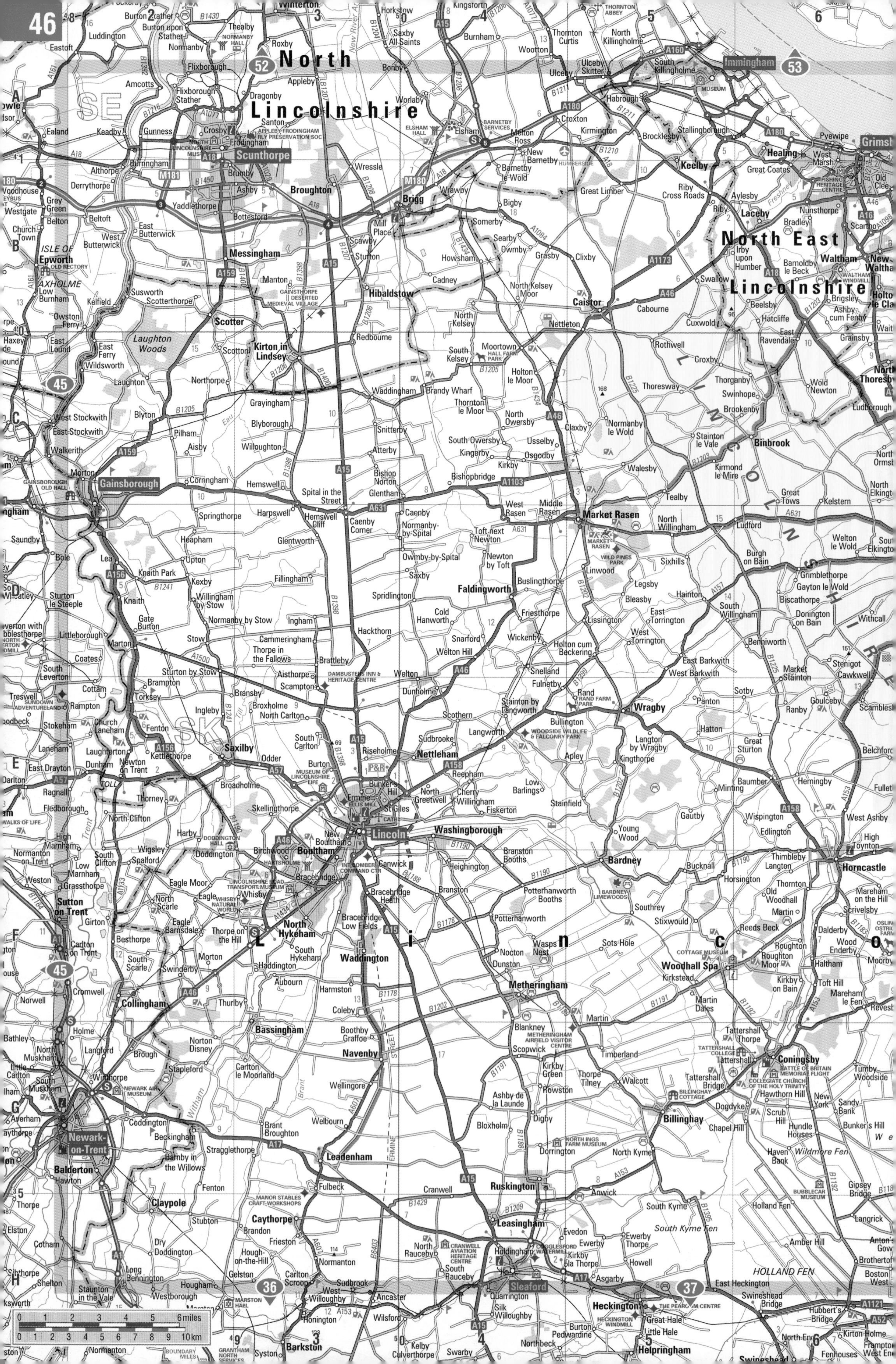
North Lincolnshire
North East Lincolnshire
Lincolnshire
Scunthorpe
Immingham
Grimsby
Gainsborough
Lincoln
Newark-on-Trent
Sleaford
Market Rasen
Brigg
Caistor
Horncastle
Woodhall Spa
Coningsby
Wragby
Epworth
Isle of Axholme
Winterton
Burton upon Stather
Normanby
Flixborough
Amcotts
Roxby
Appleby
Thealby
Luddington
Eastoft
Crosby
Gunness
Keadby
Althorpe
Burringham
Bottesford
Yaddlethorpe
Ashby
Brumby
Frodingham
Broughton
Wressle
Messingham
East Butterwick
West Butterwick
Belton
Haxey
Owston Ferry
Kirton in Lindsey
Scotter
Scotton
Laughton Woods
Laughton
Blyton
Northorpe
Redbourne
Hibaldstow
Scawby
Sturton
Cadney
Howsham
North Kelsey
South Kelsey
Moortown
Nettleton
Holton le Moor
Thornton le Moor
Waddingham
Brandy Wharf
Grayingham
Blyborough
Willoughton
Snitterby
Atterby
Bishop Norton
Glentham
Hemswell
Harpswell
Spital in the Street
Hemswell Cliff
Caenby Corner
Caenby
Normanby-by-Spital
Owmby-by-Spital
Saxby
Spridlington
Hackthorn
Welton
Dunholme
Scothern
Sudbrooke
Nettleham
Riseholme
Burton
Scampton
Aisthorpe
Brattleby
Cammeringham
Ingham
Fillingham
Glentworth
Heapham
Springthorpe
Corringham
Upton
Kexby
Willingham by Stow
Normanby by Stow
Stow
Sturton by Stow
Marton
Gate Burton
Knaith
Knaith Park
Lea
Morton
Walkerith
East Stockwith
West Stockwith
Pilham
Aisby
Sturton le Steeple
Littleborough
Saundby
Bole
North Leverton
South Leverton
Coates
Cottam
Rampton
Treswell
Stokeham
Laneham
Church Laneham
Torksey
Brampton
Fenton
Kettlethorpe
Laughterton
Newton on Trent
Dunham
East Drayton
Ragnall
Fledborough
High Marnham
Low Marnham
Normanton on Trent
South Clifton
North Clifton
Harby
Thorney
Broadholme
Saxilby
Ingleby
Bransby
Broxholme
North Carlton
South Carlton
Odder
Skellingthorpe
Doddington
Wigsley
Spalford
Eagle Moor
Eagle
North Scarle
Eagle Barnsdale
Whisby
Thorpe on the Hill
Birchwood
Boultham
New Boultham
Bracebridge
Bracebridge Heath
Bracebridge Low Fields
North Hykeham
South Hykeham
Waddington
Canwick
Washingborough
Heighington
Branston
Branston Booths
Potterhanworth
Potterhanworth Booths
Nocton
Dunston
Wasps Nest
Metheringham
Blankney
Scopwick
Kirkby Green
Martin
Timberland
Walcott
Thorpe Tilney
Billinghay
Dogdyke
Tattershall
Tattershall Bridge
Tattershall Thorpe
Kirkstead
Martin Dales
Bardney
Southrey
Stixwould
Bucknall
Horsington
Gautby
Minting
Baumber
Wispington
Edlington
Thimbleby
Langton
Thornton
Old Woodhall
Martin
Roughton
Roughton Moor
Kirkby on Bain
Haltham
Tumby
Tumby Woodside
New York
Sandy Bank
Chapel Hill
Langrick
Holland Fen
Amber Hill
Brothertoft
South Kyme
South Kyme Fen
Ewerby
Ewerby Thorpe
Evedon
Howell
Kirkby la Thorpe
Asgarby
Heckington
Great Hale
Little Hale
Helpringham
East Heckington
Swineshead Bridge
Hubbert's Bridge
Quarrington
Silk Willoughby
Holdingham
Leasingham
Ruskington
Anwick
North Kyme
Dorrington
Digby
Rowston
Bloxholm
Ashby de la Launde
Cranwell
North Rauceby
South Rauceby
Wilsford
Ancaster
Sudbrook
West Willoughby
Honington
Barkston
Syston
Normanton
Carlton Scroop
Hough-on-the-Hill
Gelston
Brandon
Caythorpe
Frieston
Fulbeck
Leadenham
Welbourn
Wellingore
Navenby
Boothby Graffoe
Coleby
Harmston
Bassingham
Aubourn
Haddington
Thurlby
Norton Disney
Carlton le Moorland
Stapleford
Brant Broughton
Stragglethorpe
Beckingham
Barnby in the Willows
Fenton
Claypole
Stubton
Dry Doddington
Long Bennington
Westborough
Hougham
Balderton
Hawton
Coddington
Winthorpe
Langford
Holme
North Muskham
South Muskham
Collingham
Brough
Besthorpe
South Scarle
Girton
Sutton on Trent
Carlton on Trent
Cromwell
Norwell
Swinderby
Morton
Thorpe
Elston
Cotham
Shelton
Staunton in the Vale
Brigsley
Waltham
Holton le Clay
Laceby
Aylesby
Healing
Great Coates
Keelby
Riby
Stallingborough
Habrough
Brocklesby
Kirmington
Croxton
Ulceby
Ulceby Skitter
Thornton Curtis
Wootton
North Killingholme
South Killingholme
Burnham
Barrow
Horkstow
Saxby All Saints
Bonby
Worlaby
Elsham
Melton Ross
New Barnetby
Barnetby le Wold
Wrawby
Bigby
Somerby
Searby
Owmby
Grasby
Clixby
North Kelsey Moor
Great Limber
Riby Cross Roads
Irby upon Humber
Barnoldby le Beck
Swallow
Cabourne
Cuxwold
Rothwell
Thoresway
Croxby
Thorganby
Swinhope
Brookenby
Binbrook
Stainton le Vale
Kirmond le Mire
Normanby le Wold
Claxby
Usselby
Osgodby
Kirkby
Kingerby
South Owersby
North Owersby
Bishopbridge
West Rasen
Middle Rasen
Toft next Newton
Newton by Toft
Faldingworth
Buslingthorpe
Friesthorpe
Linwood
Lissington
Wickenby
Snarford
Cold Hanworth
Welton Hill
Holton cum Beckering
Snelland
Fulnetby
Rand
Stainton by Langworth
Langworth
Bullington
Apley
Reepham
Cherry Willingham
Fiskerton
Low Barlings
Stainfield
Young Wood
North Greetwell
Langton by Wragby
Kingthorpe
Panton
Hatton
East Barkwith
West Barkwith
East Torrington
West Torrington
Legsby
Bleasby
Sixhills
Hainton
North Willingham
Walesby
Tealby
Ludford
Great Tows
Burgh on Bain
South Willingham
Benniworth
Market Stainton
Sotby
Great Sturton
Ranby
Hemingby
Donington on Bain
Gayton le Wold
Grimblethorpe
Biscathorpe
Welton le Wold
Kelstern
Stenigot
Cawkwell
Goulceby
Belchford
West Ashby
High Toynton
Mareham on the Hill
Scrivelsby
Dalderby
Wood Enderby
Moorby
Toft Hill
Mareham le Fen
Revesby
Hawthorn Hill
Scrub Hill
Hundle Houses
Haven Bank
Wildmore Fen
Gipsey Bridge
Bunker's Hill
Holland Fen
Boston West
Kirton Holme
East Ravendale
Hatcliffe
Beelsby
Ashby cum Fenby
Wold Newton
Ludborough
North Thoresby
Great Limber
Healing
Pyewipe
West Marsh
Nunsthorpe
Bradley
Scartho
Old Clee
Helpringham
Swaton
Northbeck
Burton Pedwardine
Kelby
Culverthorpe
Swarby
North Ings Farm Museum
Cottage Museum
Bubblecar Museum
Marston Hall
Manor Stables Craft Workshops
Cranwell Aviation Heritage Centre
Cogglesford Watermill
The Pearoom Centre
Heckington Windmill
Battle of Britain Memorial Flight
Collegiate Church of the Holy Trinity
Billinghay Cottage
Tattershall College
Metheringham Airfield Visitor Centre
Bardney Limewoods
Woodside Wildlife & Falconry Park
Rand Farm Park
Wild Pines Park
Hall Farm Park
Dambusters Inn & Heritage Centre
Museum of Lincolnshire Life
Int. Bomber Command Ctr
Lincolnshire Road Transport Museum
Whisby Natural World
Doddington Hall
Hartsholme
Newark Air Museum
Gainsborough Old Hall
Sundown Adventureland
Gainsthorpe Deserted Medieval Village
Elsham Hall
Barnetby Services
Normanby Hall
Appleby Frodingham Rly Preservation Soc
North Lincolnshire Museum
Old Rectory
Thornton Abbey
Humberside
Waltham Windmill
Fishing Heritage Centre
Grantham North Services
52
53
45
36
37
0 1 2 3 4 5 6 miles
0 1 2 3 4 5 6 7 8 9 10 km

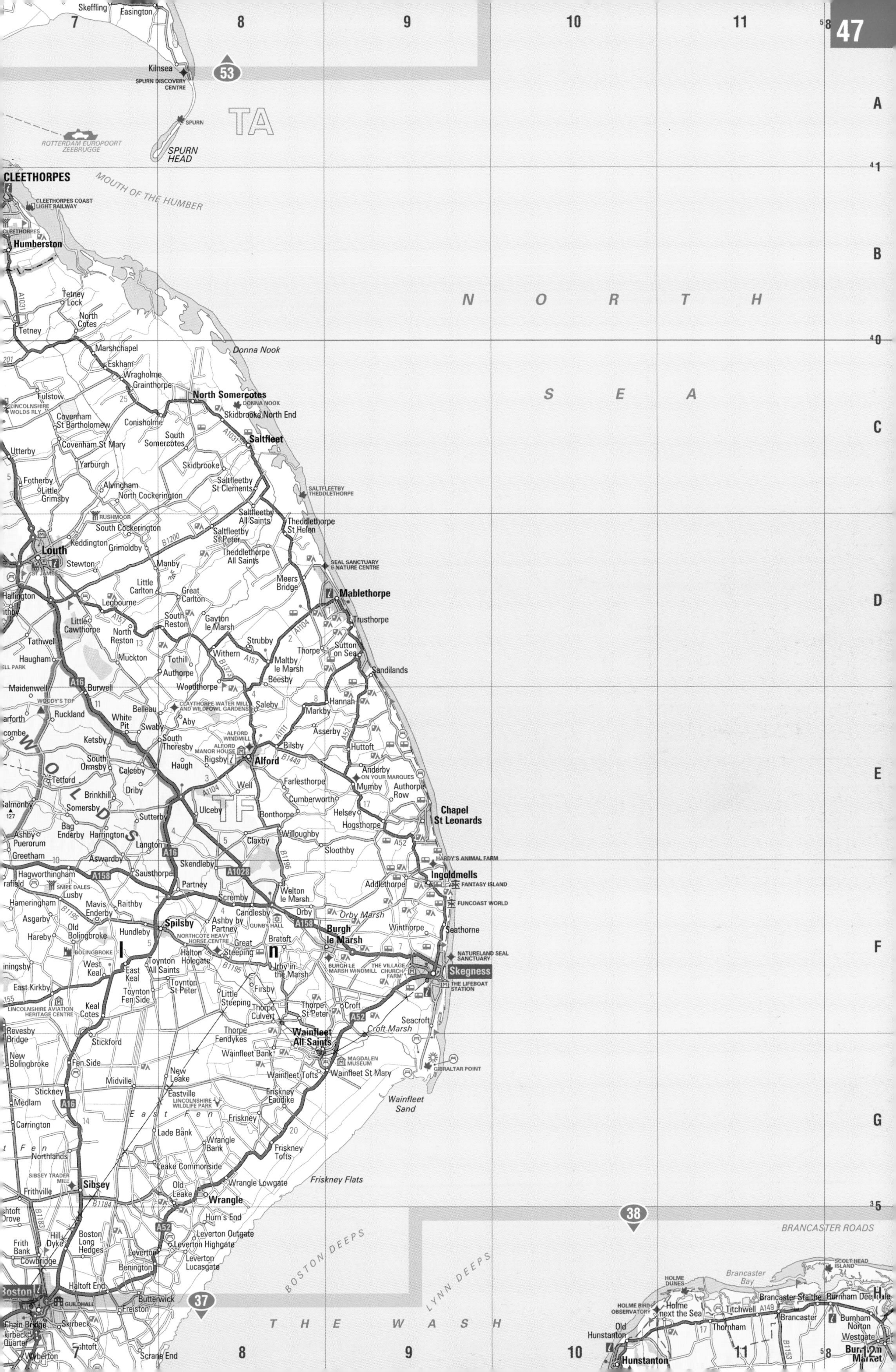
Skeffling
Easington
Kilnsea
SPURN DISCOVERY CENTRE
SPURN
SPURN HEAD
TA
ROTTERDAM EUROPOORT ZEEBRUGGE
CLEETHORPES
MOUTH OF THE HUMBER
CLEETHORPES COAST LIGHT RAILWAY
Humberston
Tetney Lock
North Cotes
Tetney
Marshchapel
Donna Nook
Eskham
Wragholme
Grainthorpe
Fulstow
LINCOLNSHIRE WOLDS RLY
North Somercotes
DONNA NOOK
Skidbrooke North End
Covenham St Bartholomew
Conisholme
South Somercotes
Saltfleet
Utterby
Covenham St Mary
Yarburgh
Skidbrooke
Fotherby
Little Grimsby
Alvingham
North Cockerington
Saltfleetby St Clements
SALTFLEETBY THEDDLETHORPE
RUSHMOOR
South Cockerington
Saltfleetby All Saints
Theddlethorpe St Helen
Saltfleetby St Peter
Keddington
Grimoldby
Louth
ST JAMES
Stewton
Manby
Theddlethorpe All Saints
SEAL SANCTUARY & NATURE CENTRE
Little Carlton
Great Carlton
Meers Bridge
Mablethorpe
Hallington
Legbourne
South Reston
Gayton le Marsh
Trusthorpe
Little Cawthorpe
North Reston
Tathwell
Strubby
Sutton on Sea
Haugham
Muckton
Tothill
Withern
Maltby le Marsh
Thorpe
Sandilands
Authorpe
Beesby
Maidenwell
Burwell
Woodthorpe
WOODY'S TOP
Hannah
Ruckland
Belleau
CLAYTHORPE WATER MILL AND WILDFOWL GARDENS
Saleby
Markby
White Pit
Swaby
Aby
Asserby
ALFORD WINDMILL
Ketsby
South Thoresby
ALFORD MANOR HOUSE
Bilsby
Huttoft
South Ormsby
Calceby
Haugh
Rigsby
Alford
Anderby
Tetford
ON YOUR MARQUES
Mumby
Driby
Well
Farlesthorpe
Authorpe Row
Brinkhill
Salmonby
Somersby
Ulceby
Cumberworth
TF
Bonthorpe
Helsey
Chapel St Leonards
Sutterby
Hogsthorpe
Ashby Puerorum
Bag Enderby
Harrington
Langton
Claxby
Willoughby
Sloothby
Greetham
Aswardby
HARDY'S ANIMAL FARM
Hagworthingham
Skendleby
Sausthorpe
Ingoldmells
SNIPE DALES
Lusby
Partney
Welton le Marsh
Addlethorpe
FANTASY ISLAND
Hameringham
Mavis Enderby
Raithby
Scremby
FUNCOAST WORLD
Asgarby
Candlesby
Orby
Orby Marsh
Old Bolingbroke
Spilsby
Ashby by Partney
GUNBY HALL
Burgh le Marsh
Winthorpe
Seathorne
Hareby
Hundleby
NORTHCOTE HEAVY HORSE CENTRE
Bratoft
BOLINGBROKE
Halton Holegate
Great Steeping
NATURELAND SEAL SANCTUARY
West Keal
East Keal
Toynton All Saints
Irby in the Marsh
BURGH LE MARSH WINDMILL
THE VILLAGE CHURCH FARM
Skegness
THE LIFEBOAT STATION
East Kirkby
Toynton Fen Side
Toynton St Peter
Firsby
LINCOLNSHIRE AVIATION HERITAGE CENTRE
Keal Cotes
Little Steeping
Thorpe Culvert
Thorpe St Peter
Croft
Revesby Bridge
Stickford
Thorpe Fendykes
Wainfleet All Saints
Seacroft
Croft Marsh
New Bolingbroke
Fen Side
Wainfleet Bank
MAGDALEN MUSEUM
GIBRALTAR POINT
Midville
New Leake
Wainfleet Tofts
Wainfleet St Mary
Stickney
Eastville
Medlam
LINCOLNSHIRE WILDLIFE PARK
Friskney Eaudike
Wainfleet Sand
East Fen
Carrington
Lade Bank
Friskney
Northlands
Wrangle Bank
Friskney Tofts
Leake Commonside
SIBSEY TRADER MILL
Sibsey
Old Leake
Wrangle Lowgate
Friskney Flats
Frithville
Wrangle
Hurn's End
Frith Bank
Hill Dyke
Boston Long Hedges
Leverton Outgate
Leverton Highgate
Leverton
Cowbridge
Leverton Lucasgate
Benington
BOSTON DEEPS
LYNN DEEPS
Boston
Haltoft End
GUILDHALL
Butterwick
Freiston
Skirbeck
Chain Bridge
Skirbeck Quarter
Wyberton
Fishtoft
Scrane End
THE WASH
NORTH SEA
BRANCASTER ROADS
Brancaster Bay
SCOLT HEAD ISLAND
HOLME DUNES
HOLME BIRD OBSERVATORY
Holme next the Sea
Brancaster Staithe
Burnham Deepdale
Titchwell
Brancaster
Burnham Norton
Old Hunstanton
Thornham
Westgate
Hunstanton
Burnham Market
A1031
A16
A157
A1104
A52
A1111
B1449
B1373
A158
A1028
B1196
B1195
B1200
B1184
B1183
A149
B1153
53
37
38
7
8
9
10
11
A
B
C
D
E
F
G
H

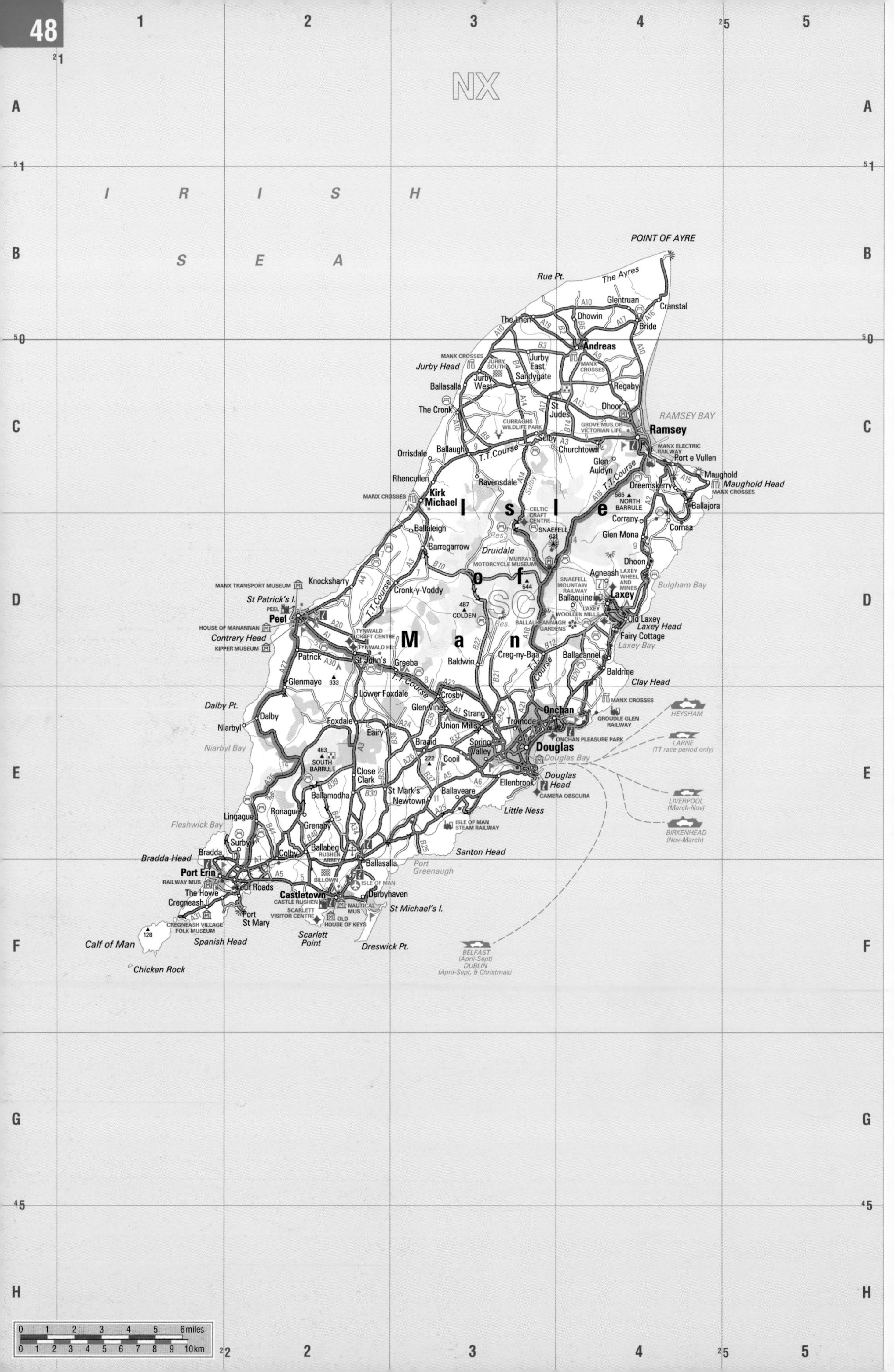
NX
IRISH SEA
Isle of Man
SC
POINT OF AYRE
The Ayres
Rue Pt.
Glentruan
Cranstal
Bride
The Lhen
Dhowin
Andreas
MANX CROSSES
Jurby Head
JURBY SOUTH
Jurby East
Jurby West
Sandygate
Ballasalla
Regaby
The Cronk
St Judes
Dhoor
CURRAGHS WILDLIFE PARK
GROVE MUS OF VICTORIAN LIFE
RAMSEY BAY
Ramsey
Orrisdale
Ballaugh
T.T. Course
Sulby
Churchtown
MANX ELECTRIC RAILWAY
Port e Vullen
Glen Auldyn
Maughold
Maughold Head
Rhencullen
Ravensdale
Dreemskerry
MANX CROSSES
Kirk Michael
565 NORTH BARRULE
Ballajora
CELTIC CRAFT CENTRE
Corrany
Cornaa
Ballaleigh
SNAEFELL 621
Glen Mona
Barregarrow
Druidale
Dhoon
MURRAYS MOTORCYCLE MUSEUM
Agneash
LAXEY WHEEL AND MINES
MANX TRANSPORT MUSEUM
Knocksharry
544
SNAEFELL MOUNTAIN RAILWAY
Bulgham Bay
Cronk-y-Voddy
Laxey
St Patrick's I.
Ballaquine
PEEL
487 COLDEN
LAXEY WOOLLEN MILLS
Peel
BALLALHEANNAGH GARDENS
Old Laxey
HOUSE OF MANANNAN
TYNWALD CRAFT CENTRE
Laxey Head
Contrary Head
Fairy Cottage
KIPPER MUSEUM
TYNWALD HILL
Laxey Bay
Creg-ny-Baa
Ballacannel
Patrick
St John's
Greeba
Baldwin
333
Baldrine
Glenmaye
Clay Head
Lower Foxdale
Crosby
MANX CROSSES
HEYSHAM
Dalby Pt.
Glen Vine
Strang
Onchan
GROUDLE GLEN RAILWAY
Dalby
Niarbyl
Foxdale
Union Mills
Tromode
ONCHAN PLEASURE PARK
LARNE (TT race period only)
Eairy
Braaid
Spring Valley
Douglas
Niarbyl Bay
483 SOUTH BARRULE
222
Cooil
Douglas Bay
Close Clark
Douglas Head
Ellenbrook
CAMERA OBSCURA
Ballamodha
St Mark's
Newtown
Ballaveare
LIVERPOOL (March-Nov)
Ronague
Little Ness
Lingague
Fleshwick Bay
Grenaby
ISLE OF MAN STEAM RAILWAY
BIRKENHEAD (Nov-March)
Surby
Ballabeg
RUSHEN ABBEY
Santon Head
Bradda Head
Bradda
Colby
Ballasalla
Port Greenaugh
Port Erin
RAILWAY MUS
Four Roads
BILLOWN
ISLE OF MAN
The Howe
Castletown
CASTLE RUSHEN
Derbyhaven
Cregneash
SCARLETT VISITOR CENTRE
NAUTICAL MUS
St Michael's I.
Port St Mary
OLD HOUSE OF KEYS
CREGNEASH VILLAGE FOLK MUSEUM
128
Scarlett Point
Calf of Man
Spanish Head
Dreswick Pt.
BELFAST (April-Sept)
DUBLIN (April-Sept, & Christmas)
Chicken Rock
A10 A19 B2 B6 A17 A16 B3 A9 B4 A14 A13 A17 B7 B9 B14 A3 A15 A14 A18 A2 A4 A3 B10 A20 A1 A30 B22 B12 A27 A23 B21 A22 A21 B20 A24 B35 B36 B32 A5 A25 B37 A6 A36 B39 B30 A34 B41 B40 B44 B25 A31 A5
0 1 2 3 4 5 6 miles
0 1 2 3 4 5 6 7 8 9 10 km

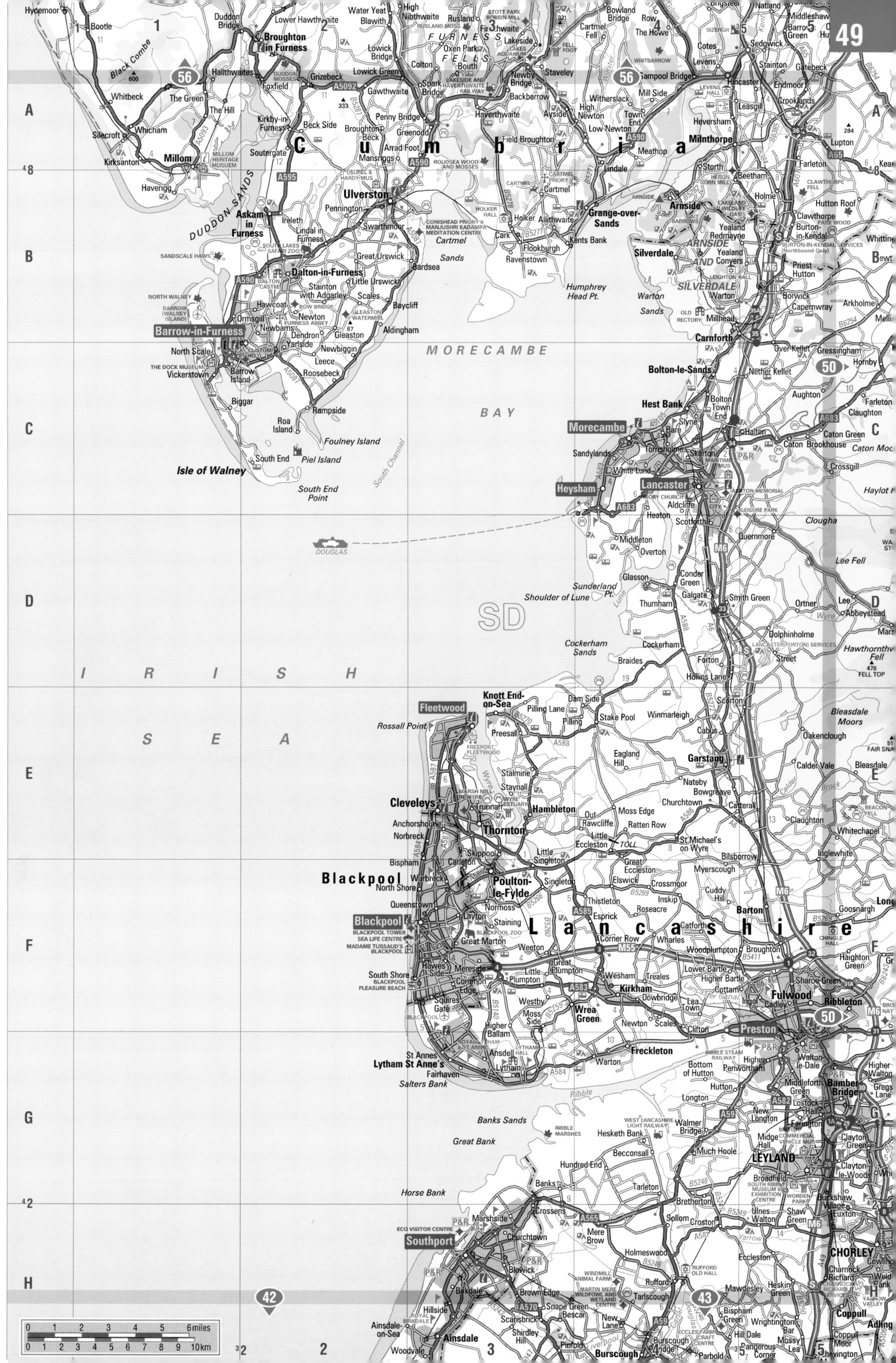
Cumbria
Lancashire
IRISH SEA
MORECAMBE BAY
SD
DUDDON SANDS
FURNESS FELLS
ARNSIDE AND SILVERDALE
Hycemoor
Bootle
Black Combe
600
Whitbeck
The Green
The Hill
Whicham
Silecroft
Kirksanton
Millom
MILLOM HERITAGE MUSEUM
Haverigg
Duddon Bridge
Broughton in Furness
Lower Hawthwaite
Hallthwaites
Foxfield
DUDDON MOSSES
Grizebeck
Kirkby-in-Furness
Beck Side
Soutergate
Water Yeat
Blawith
High Nibthwaite
Rusland
RUSLAND MOSS
STOTT PARK BOBBIN MILL
Finsthwaite
Lakeside
LAKES AQUARIUM
Oxen Park
Colton
Lowick Bridge
Lowick Green
Gawthwaite
Penny Bridge
Broughton Beck
Greenodd
Arrad Foot
Mansriggs
Spark Bridge
Bouth
LAKESIDE AND HAVERTHWAITE RAILWAY
Haverthwaite
Newby Bridge
Backbarrow
Staveley
FELL FOOT
Ayside
High Newton
Witherslack
Low Newton
Town End
Bowland Bridge
The Howe
Cartmel Fell
WHITBARROW
Sampool Bridge
Mill Side
Meathop
Lindale
Field Broughton
ROUDSEA WOOD AND MOSSES
LAUREL & HARDY MUS
Ulverston
Pennington
CONISHEAD PRIORY & MANJUSHRI KADAMPA MEDITATION CENTRE
Swarthmoor
Great Urswick
Little Urswick
Bardsea
Cartmel Sands
CARTMEL PRIORY
Cartmel
HOLKER HALL
Holker
Allithwaite
Grange-over-Sands
Kents Bank
Cark
Flookburgh
Ravenstown
Humphrey Head Pt.
Askam in Furness
Ireleth
Lindal in Furness
SOUTH LAKES SAFARI ZOO
SANDSCALE HAWS
Dalton-in-Furness
DALTON CASTLE
Stainton with Adgarley
Scales
Baycliff
NORTH WALNEY
BARROW (WALNEY ISLAND)
Hawcoat
BOW BRIDGE
Ormsgill
Newton
FURNESS ABBEY
Newbarns
GLEASTON WATERMILL
Gleaston
Dendron
Aldingham
Barrow-in-Furness
North Scale
THE DOCK MUSEUM
Vickerstown
Barrow Island
Yarlside
Newbiggin
Leece
Roosebeck
Biggar
Rampside
Roa Island
Foulney Island
Piel Island
South End
Isle of Walney
South End Point
South Channel
DOUGLAS
Natland
Middleshaw
Barrows Green
SIZERGH
Sedgwick
Cotes
Levens
LEVENS HALL
Stainton
Gatebeck
Hincaster
Endmoor
Crooklands
Leasgill
Heversham
Milnthorpe
Lupton
Farleton
Storth
HERON CORN MILL
Beetham
CLAWTHORPE FELL
Holme
Hutton Roof
Arnside
LAKELAND WILDLIFE OASIS
Clawthorpe
Burton-in-Kendal
BURTON-IN-KENDAL SERVICES (Northbound Only)
Yealand Redmayne
Silverdale
Yealand Conyers
LEIGHTON HALL
Priest Hutton
Warton
Warton Sands
Borwick
Capernwray
Arkholme
Whittington
OLD RECTORY
Millhead
Carnforth
Over Kellet
Gressingham
Hornby
Nether Kellet
Bolton-le-Sands
Aughton
Farleton
Claughton
Hest Bank
Bolton Town End
Slyne
Halton
Caton Green
Caton
Brookhouse
Morecambe
Bare
Torrisholme
Skerton
Sandylands
White Lund
Crossgill
Heysham
Lancaster
ASHTON MEMORIAL
PRIORY CHURCH
Aldcliffe
LEISURE PARK
Heaton
Scotforth
Clougha
Quernmore
Middleton
Overton
Lee Fell
Glasson
Conder Green
Sunderland Pt.
Shoulder of Lune
Galgate
Thurnham
Smith Green
Ortner
Lee
Abbeystead
Dolphinholme
LANCASTER (FORTON) SERVICES
Cockerham Sands
Cockerham
Hawthornthwaite Fell
Street
FELL TOP
Braides
Forton
Hollins Lane
Knott End-on-Sea
Fleetwood
Rossall Point
Pilling Lane
Dam Side
Pilling
Stake Pool
Winmarleigh
Scorton
Bleasdale Moors
Preesall
FREEPORT FLEETWOOD
Cabus
Oakenclough
Eagland Hill
Garstang
Calder Vale
Bleasdale
Stalmine
Staynall
Nateby
Bowgreave
Churchtown
Cleveleys
MARSH MILL-IN-WYRE
WYRE ESTUARY
Trunnah
Hambleton
Out Rawcliffe
Moss Edge
Ratten Row
Catterall
Claughton
Whitechapel
Anchorsholme
Thornton
Little Eccleston
TOLL
St Michael's on Wyre
Norbreck
Bispham
Carleton
Skippool
Little Singleton
Great Eccleston
Bilsborrow
Inglewhite
Blackpool
North Shore
Warbreck
Poulton-le-Fylde
Singleton
Elswick
Myerscough
Crossmoor
Inskip
Cuddy Hill
Queenstown
Normoss
Thistleton
Roseacre
Barton
Goosnargh
Layton
Staining
BLACKPOOL ZOO
Esprick
BLACKPOOL TOWER
SEA LIFE CENTRE
MADAME TUSSAUD'S BLACKPOOL
Great Marton
Corner Row
Catforth
Wharles
Woodplumpton
Broughton
Haighton Green
Weeton
South Shore
BLACKPOOL PLEASURE BEACH
Hawes Side
Mereside
Great Plumpton
Little Plumpton
Common Edge
Wesham
Treales
Lower Bartle
Higher Bartle
Cottam
Sharoe Green
Kirkham
Dowbridge
Ingol
Fulwood
Cadley
Ribbleton
Squires Gate
Westby
Moss Side
Wrea Green
Lea Town
Newton
Scales
Clifton
Preston
Higher Ballam
ROYAL LYTHAM ST ANNES
Ansdell
LYTHAM HALL
Freckleton
RIBBLE STEAM RAILWAY
St Annes
Lytham St Anne's
Lytham
Fairhaven
Warton
Salters Bank
Penwortham
Walton-le-Dale
Bottom of Hutton
Hutton
Middleforth Green
Bamber Bridge
Higher Walton
Gregson Lane
Ribble
Longton
Lostock Hall
New Longton
Farington
Banks Sands
RIBBLE MARSHES
WEST LANCASHIRE LIGHT RAILWAY
Hesketh Bank
Walmer Bridge
Great Bank
Becconsall
Much Hoole
COMMERCIAL VEHICLE MUS
Midge Hall
Clayton Green
LEYLAND
Clayton-le-Woods
Hundred End
Banks
Tarleton
Broadfield
SOUTH RIBBLE MUSEUM & EXHIBITION CENTRE
WORDEN PARK
Horse Bank
Bretherton
Buckshaw Village
Euxton
Crossens
Sollom
Croston
Ulnes Walton
Shaw Green
ECO VISITOR CENTRE
Marshside
Mere Brow
Southport
Churchtown
Holmeswood
Eccleston
CHORLEY
Cowling
RUFFORD OLD HALL
WINDMILL ANIMAL FARM
Blowick
Rufford
Charnock Richard
MARTIN MERE WILDFOWL AND WETLAND CENTRE
Tarlscough
Mawdesley
Heskin Green
Birkdale
Brown Edge
Snape Green
Bescar
Bispham Green
Wrightington Bar
Coppull
Hillside
ROYAL BIRKDALE
Scarisbrick
New Lane
Hill Dale
Mossy Lea
Adlington
Ainsdale-on-Sea
Shirdley Hill
ECCLES FARM CRAFT CENTRE
Burscough Bridge
Dangerous Corner
Coppull Moor
Woodvale
Ainsdale
Pinfold
Burscough
Parbold
Shevington
A595
A5092
A590
A5093
A5087
B5281
B5278
B5277
B5271
A65
A6
B6254
B6384
B6385
A6070
M6
A683
A589
A5105
A588
B5272
A587
A584
A585
A586
B5269
B5266
B5260
B5411
M55
A583
B5259
B5140
A582
A59
B5248
B5249
A581
B5246
A565
A570
A49
56
50
42
43
1
2
3
4
5
A
B
C
D
E
F
G
H
0 1 2 3 4 5 6 miles
0 1 2 3 4 5 6 7 8 9 10 km

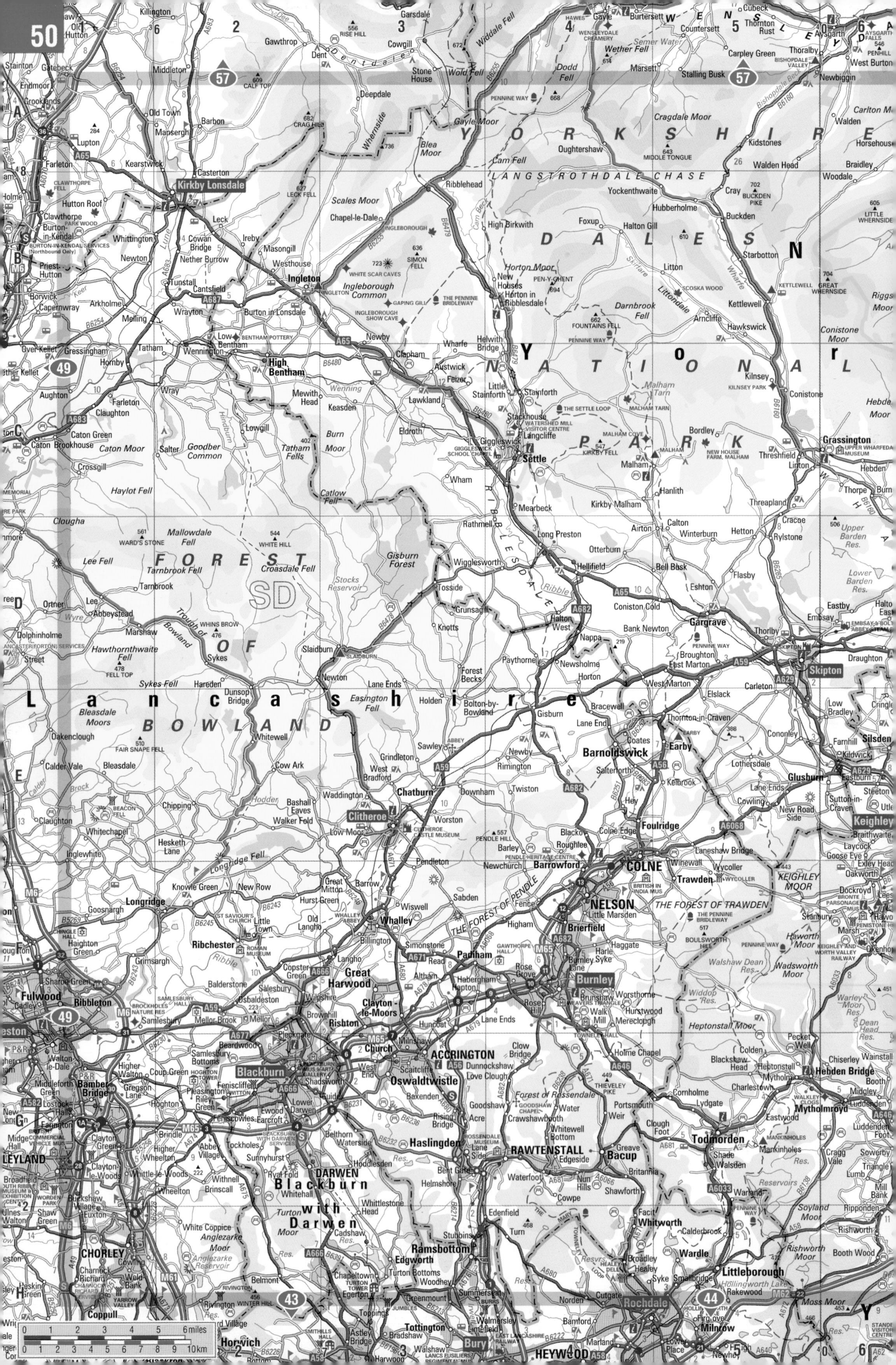

Killington
Garsdale
Gawthrop
Dent
Dentdale
Cowgill
RISE HILL
Widdale Fell
Hawes
Gayle
Burtersett
Countersett
Thornton Rust
Aysgarth
Semer Water
WENSLEYDALE CREAMERY
Wether Fell
Carpley Green
Thoralby
Middleton
CALF TOP
Stone House
Wold Fell
Dodd Fell
Marsett
Stalling Busk
BISHOPDALE VALLEY
Newbiggin
West Burton
Deepdale
PENNINE WAY
Old Town
Barbon
Mansergh
CRAG HILL
Whernside
Blea Moor
Gayle Moor
Cragdale Moor
Walden
Carlton Moor
YORKSHIRE
Kidstones
Horsehouse
Lupton
Kearstwick
Farleton
Casterton
Cam Fell
Oughtershaw
MIDDLE TONGUE
Walden Head
Braidley
Woodale
LANGSTROTHDALE CHASE
Kirkby Lonsdale
CLAWTHORPE FELL
LECK FELL
Ribblehead
Yockenthwaite
Cray
BUCKDEN PIKE
LITTLE WHERNSIDE
Hutton Roof
Scales Moor
Hubberholme
Buckden
Clawthorpe
PARK WOOD
Burton-in-Kendal
Leck
Chapel-le-Dale
High Birkwith
Foxup
Halton Gill
BURTON-IN-KENDAL SERVICES (Northbound Only)
Whittington
Cowan Bridge
Ireby
INGLEBOROUGH
DALES
Masongill
Starbotton
Nether Burrow
SIMON FELL
Newton
Westhouse
Priest Hutton
WHITE SCAR CAVES
Horton Moor
PEN-Y-GHENT
Litton
Ingleton
Ingleborough Common
New Houses
Horton in Ribblesdale
SCOSKA WOOD
Kettlewell
GREAT WHERNSIDE
Borwick
Tunstall
Cantsfield
GAPING GILL
THE PENNINE BRIDLEWAY
Darnbrook Fell
Littondale
Riggs Moor
Capernwray
Arkholme
Wrayton
Burton in Lonsdale
INGLEBOROUGH SHOW CAVE
Arncliffe
Hawkswick
Melling
FOUNTAINS FELL
Conistone Moor
Low Bentham
BENTHAM POTTERY
Newby
Over Kellet
Gressingham
Tatham
Wennington
Clapham
Wharfe
Helwith Bridge
Hornby
High Bentham
Austwick
NATIONAL
Feizor
Malham Tarn
Kilnsey
KILNSEY PARK
Conistone
Aughton
Farleton
Wray
Mewith Head
Wenning
Lawkland
Little Stainforth
Stainforth
THE SETTLE LOOP
MALHAM TARN
Hebden Moor
Claughton
Keasden
Stackhouse
WATERSHED MILL VISITOR CENTRE
Caton Green
Lowgill
Eldroth
Bordley
Caton
Brookhouse
Caton Moor
Salter
Goodber Common
Tatham Fells
Burn Moor
Giggleswick
GIGGLESWICK SCHOOL CHAPEL
Langcliffe
MALHAM COVE
PARK
KIRKBY FELL
Malham
NEW HOUSE FARM, MALHAM
Threshfield
Grassington
UPPER WHARFEDALE MUSEUM
Linton
Hebden
Crossgill
Settle
Wham
Hanlith
Haylot Fell
Catlow Fell
Thorpe
Burn
Mearbeck
Kirkby Malham
Threapland
Clougha
Rathmell
Airton
Calton
Winterburn
Hetton
Cracoe
Rylstone
Upper Barden Res.
WARD'S STONE
Mallowdale Fell
WHITE HILL
Long Preston
Otterburn
Lee Fell
FOREST
Tarnbrook Fell
Croasdale Fell
Gisburn Forest
Wigglesworth
Hellifield
Bell Busk
Flasby
Lower Barden Res.
Tarnbrook
SD
Stocks Reservoir
Tosside
RIBBLESDALE
Ribble
Eshton
Ortner
Lee
Grunsagill
Coniston Cold
Eastby
Abbeystead
Wyre
Trough of Bowland
WHINS BROW
Knotts
Halton West
Gargrave
Embsay
Marshaw
Bank Newton
Thorlby
EMBSAY & BOLTON ABBEY STEAM RLY
Dolphinholme
Nappa
PENNINE WAY
LANCASTER (FORTON) SERVICES
Hawthornthwaite Fell
OF
Slaidburn
Paythorne
Broughton
Draughton
Street
FELL TOP
Sykes
Newsholme
East Marton
Skipton
Sykes Fell
Hareden
Newton
Lane Ends
Forest Becks
Horton
West Marton
Carleton
Lancashire
Dunsop Bridge
Easington Fell
Holden
Bolton-by-Bowland
Bracewell
Elslack
Low Bradley
Cringles
Bleasdale Moors
BOWLAND
Gisburn
Lane End
Thornton-in-Craven
Silsden
Oakenclough
Whitewell
ABBEY
Coates
EARBY
Cononley
Farnhill
Kildwick
FAIR SNAPE FELL
Sawley
Newby
Barnoldswick
Earby
Grindleton
Rimington
Salterforth
Lothersdale
Glusburn
Eastburn
Calder Vale
Bleasdale
Cow Ark
West Bradford
Kelbrook
Lane Ends
Steeton
Twiston
Chatburn
Downham
Hey
Cowling
Sutton-in-Craven
Chipping
BEACON FELL
Waddington
Bashall Eaves
Hodder
New Road Side
Keighley
Claughton
Clitheroe
Worston
Foulridge
Whitechapel
Walker Fold
Low Moor
CLITHEROE CASTLE MUSEUM
PENDLE HILL
Blacko
Colne Edge
Braithwaite
Laycock
Hesketh Lane
Barley
Roughlee
Laneshaw Bridge
Goose Eye
Inglewhite
Longridge Fell
Pendleton
Newchurch
PENDLE HERITAGE CENTRE
Barrowford
Colne
Winewall
Wycoller
Exley Head
KEIGHLEY MOOR
Oakworth
Great Mitton
Barrow
BRITISH IN INDIA MUS
Trawden
Knowle Green
New Row
Longridge
Goosnargh
Hurst Green
Sabden
THE FOREST OF PENDLE
Nelson
Little Marsden
THE FOREST OF TRAWDEN
Dockroyd
BRONTE PARSONAGE MUS
ST SAVIOUR'S CHURCH
Little Town
Old Langho
WHALLEY ABBEY
Wiswell
Whalley
Fence
Higham
Brierfield
THE PENNINE BRIDLEWAY
Stanbury
Haworth
Ribchester
ROMAN MUSEUM
Billington
Simonstone
GAWTHORPE HALL
Haggate
BOULSWORTH HILL
Haworth Moor
KEIGHLEY AND WORTH VALLEY RAILWAY
Oxenhope
Haighton Green
Grimsargh
Langho
Read
Padiham
Harle Syke
Burnley Lane
Walshaw Dean Res.
Wadsworth Moor
Copster Green
Great Harwood
Altham
Habergham
Rose Grove
Burnley
Sharoe Green
Balderstone
Salesbury
Hapton
Widdop Res.
Fulwood
Ribbleton
SAMLESBURY HALL
Osbaldeston
Wilpshire
Clayton-le-Moors
Rose Hill
Brunshaw
Worsthorne
Hurstwood
Warley Moor Res.
BROCKHOLES NATURE RES
Mellor Brook
Mellor
Brownhill
Rishton
Huncoat
Lane Ends
WEAVERS TRIANGLE
Walk Mill
Mereclough
Heptonstall Moor
Dean Head Res.
Samlesbury
Pleckgate
Milnshaw
TOWNELEY HALL
Pecket Well
Walton-le-Dale
Beardwood
Church
ACCRINGTON
Clow Bridge
Holme Chapel
Colden
Blackshaw Head
Heptonstall
Chiserley
Wainstalls
Samlesbury Bottoms
Blackburn
MUSEUM & ART GALLERY
West End
Scaitcliffe
Dunnockshaw
Love Clough
THIEVELEY PIKE
Mytholm
Hebden Bridge
Booth
Higher Walton
Coup Green
HOGHTON TOWER
Feniscliffe
Shadsworth
Oswaldtwistle
Middleforth
Bamber Bridge
Lostock Hall
Gregson Lane
Pleasington
WITTON
Riley Green
Guide
Lower Darwen
Baxenden
Goodshaw
Forest of Rossendale
GOODSHAW CHAPEL
Water
Portsmouth
Cornholme
Charlestown
Lydgate
Midgley
WALKLEY CLOGS
Luddenden
Mytholmroyd
Farington
Hoghton
Feniscowles
Ewood
Earcroft
Rising Bridge
Acre
Crawshawbooth
Weir
Clough Foot
Eastwood
Luddenden Foot
COMMERCIAL VEHICLE MUS
Clayton Green
Brindle
Belthorn
Waterside
Haslingden
ROSSENDALE MUSEUM
Whitewell Bottom
RAWTENSTALL
Bacup
Greave
Todmorden
MANKINHOLES
Higher Wheelton
Abbey Village
BLACKBURN WITH DARWEN SERVICES
Tockholes
Lane Side
Shade
Walsden
Mankinholes
Cragg Vale
Sowerby
LEYLAND
Clayton-le-Woods
Whittle-le-Woods
Sunnyhurst
Hoddlesden
Bent Gate
Edgeside
Britannia
Triangle
Broadfield
SOUTH RIBBLE MUSEUM & EXHIBITION CENTRE
Ryal Fold
DARWEN
Blackburn with Darwen
Waterfoot
Nun Hills
Shawforth
Reservoirs
Lumb
WORDEN PARK
Withnell
Brinscall
Wheelton
Helmshore
Whitehall
Whittlestone Head
Cowpe
Warland
Mill Bank
Buckshaw Village
Euxton
Shaw Green
Turton Moor
Edenfield
Facit
Whitworth
PENNINE WAY
Soyland Moor
Ripponden
Walton
White Coppice
Anglezarke Moor
Cadshaw
Stubbins
Turn
Calderbrook
Rishworth
CHORLEY
Cowling
Anglezarke Reservoir
Ramsbottom
Edgworth
Broadley
Healey
Wardle
Rishworth Moor
Booth Wood
Charnock Richard
CHARNOCK RICHARD SERVICES
Weld Bank
Chapeltown
TURTON TOWER
Turton Bottoms
Woodhey
HEALEY DELL
Syke
Smallbridge
Littleborough
Hollingworth Lake
Rakewood
Heskin Green
Belmont
YARROW VALLEY
RIVINGTON
WINTER HILL
Egerton
Greenmount
Summerseat
Norden
Cutgate
Rochdale
Moss Moor
Coppull
Rivington
Toppings
JUMBLES
BURRS
Bamford
Firgrove
Milnrow
Hill End
Astley Bridge
SMITHILLS HALL
Bradshaw
Tottington
Walmersley
Limefield
EAST LANCASHIRE RAILWAY
Newhey
Horwich
Walshaw
Bury
HEYWOOD
Marland
Lower Place
0 1 2 3 4 5 6 miles
0 1 2 3 4 5 6 7 8 9 10 km

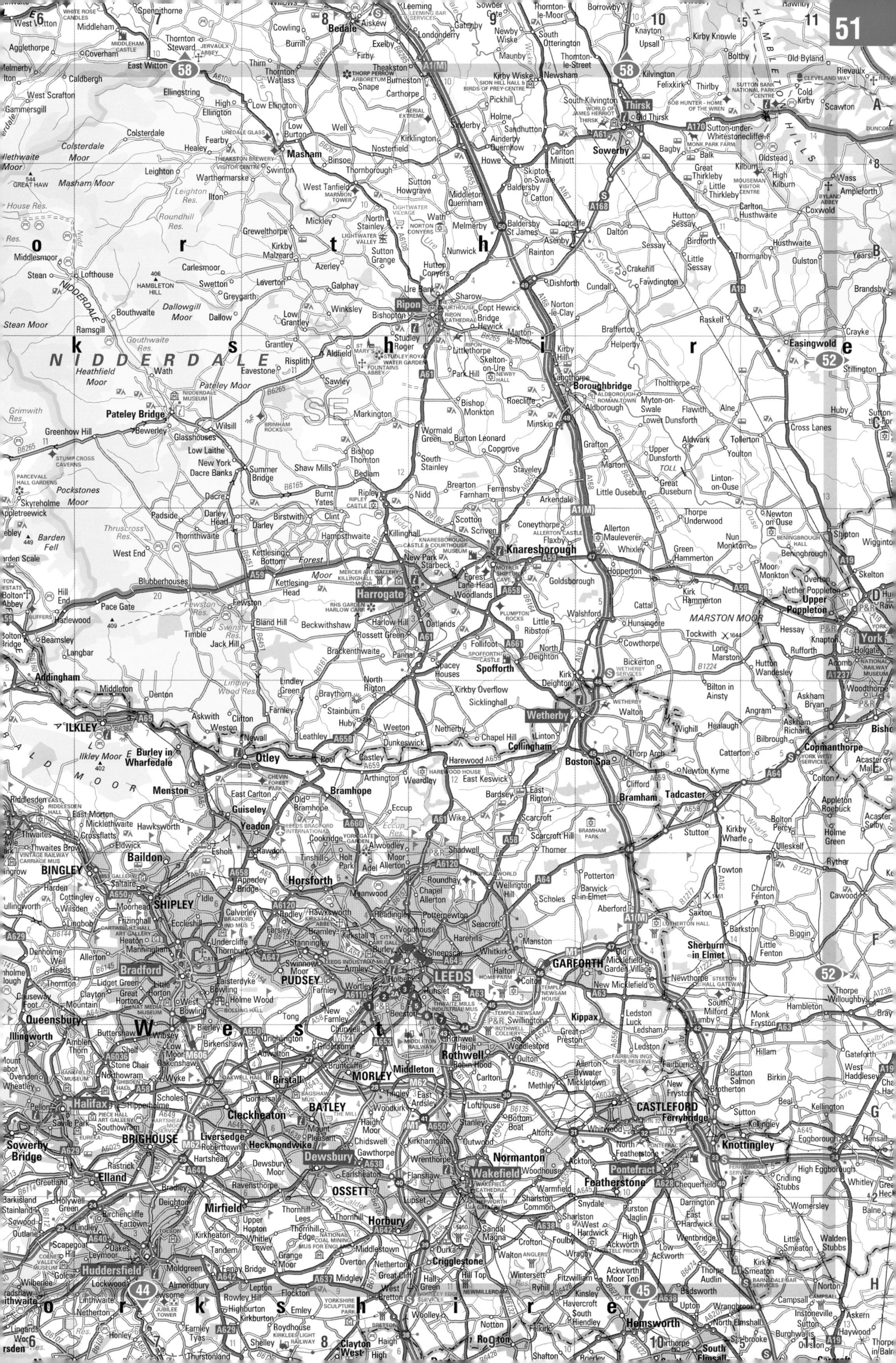
Bedale
Thirsk
Sowerby
Masham
Ripon
NIDDERDALE
Pateley Bridge
Boroughbridge
Easingwold
Knaresborough
Harrogate
MARSTON MOOR
York
Wetherby
ILKLEY
Otley
Burley in Wharfedale
Menston
Guiseley
Yeadon
Baildon
BINGLEY
SHIPLEY
Bradford
Horsforth
LEEDS
PUDSEY
GARFORTH
Tadcaster
Sherburn in Elmet
Queensbury
Halifax
BRIGHOUSE
Cleckheaton
BATLEY
MORLEY
Rothwell
Dewsbury
OSSETT
Wakefield
Normanton
CASTLEFORD
Pontefract
Knottingley
Featherstone
Huddersfield
Elland
Mirfield
Horbury
Crigglestone
Hemsworth
West Yorkshire
North Yorkshire
HAMBLETON HILLS
Ilkley Moor

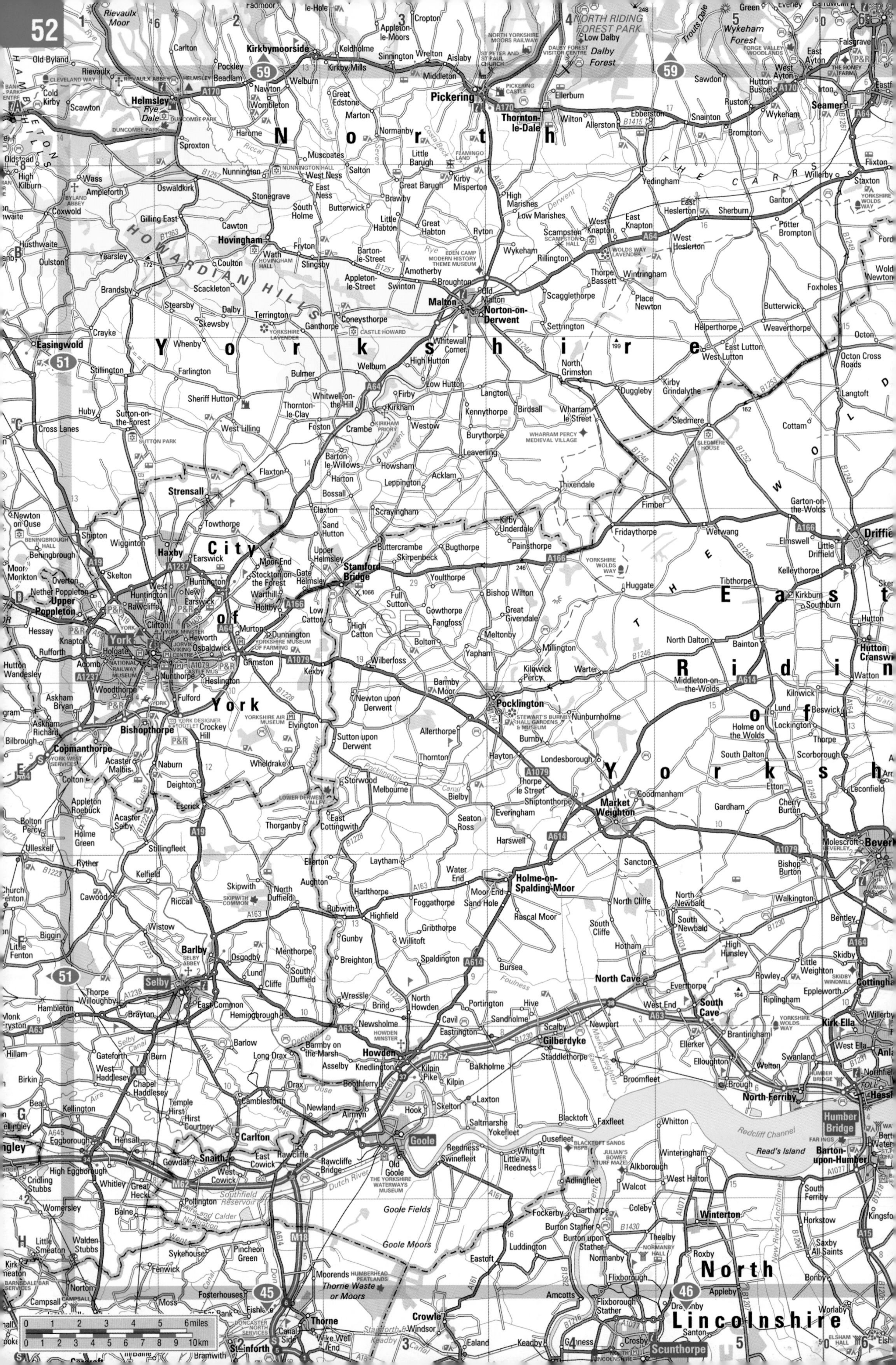
Rievaulx Moor
Fadmoor
le-Hole
Cropton
Appleton-le-Moors
NORTH RIDING FOREST PARK
NORTH YORKSHIRE MOORS RAILWAY
Low Dalby
DALBY FOREST VISITOR CENTRE
Dalby Forest
Trouts Dale
Wykeham Forest
Green
Everley
FORGE VALLEY WOODLANDS
Falsgrave
East Ayton
West Ayton
THE HONEY FARM
Carlton
Kirkbymoorside
Keldholme
Sinnington
Wrelton
Aislaby
Middleton
ST PETER AND ST PAUL CHURCH
Old Byland
Pockley
Beadlam
Kirkby Mills
Rievaulx
CLEVELAND WAY
RIEVAULX ABBEY
HELMSLEY
Nawton
Welburn
Pickering
PICKERING CASTLE
Ellerburn
Sawdon
Hutton Buscel
Irton
Cold Kirby
Scawton
Helmsley
Rye Dale
DUNCOMBE PARK
Wombleton
Great Edstone
Thornton-le-Dale
Wilton
Allerston
Ebberston
Snainton
Ruston
Wykeham
Seamer
Marton
Normanby
Harome
North
Brompton
HAMBLETON HILLS
Oldstead
Sproxton
Riccal
Muscoates
Little Barugh
FLAMINGO LAND
THE CARRS
Willerby
Flixton
High Kilburn
Wass
Nunnington
NUNNINGTON HALL
West Ness
Salton
Kirby Misperton
Great Barugh
Yedingham
Staxton
Ampleforth
BYLAND ABBEY
Oswaldkirk
Stonegrave
East Ness
High Marishes
Derwent
Ganton
East Heslerton
Sherburn
YORKSHIRE WOLDS WAY
Coxwold
South Holme
Butterwick
Brawby
Low Marishes
Gilling East
Cawton
Little Habton
Great Habton
Scampston
SCAMPSTON HALL
West Knapton
East Knapton
Potter Brompton
Husthwaite
HOWARDIAN HILLS
Hovingham
Fryton
Ryton
Wykeham
West Heslerton
Yearsley
Wath
HOVINGHAM HALL
Barton-le-Street
Rye
EDEN CAMP MODERN HISTORY THEME MUSEUM
Rillington
WOLDS WAY LAVENDER
Oulston
Coulston
Slingsby
Amotherby
Thorpe Bassett
Wintringham
Brandsby
Scackleton
Appleton-le-Street
Swinton
Broughton
Old Malton
Foxholes
Malton
Norton-on-Derwent
Scagglethorpe
Place Newton
Stearsby
Dalby
Terrington
Coneysthorpe
Butterwick
Skewsby
Settrington
Helperthorpe
Weaverthorpe
Octon
Crayke
YORKSHIRE LAVENDER
Ganthorpe
CASTLE HOWARD
Easingwold
Whenby
Whitewall Corner
North Yorkshire
High Hutton
North Grimston
East Lutton
West Lutton
Octon Cross Roads
Stillington
Farlington
Welburn
Bulmer
Low Hutton
Langton
Kirby Grindalythe
Duggleby
Langtoft
Sheriff Hutton
Whitwell-on-the-Hill
Thornton-le-Clay
Firby
Kirkham
Kennythorpe
Birdsall
Wharram le Street
Huby
Sutton-on-the-Forest
KIRKHAM PRIORY
Crambe
Westow
Sledmere
Cottam
Cross Lanes
SUTTON PARK
West Lilling
Foston
Burythorpe
WHARRAM PERCY MEDIEVAL VILLAGE
SLEDMERE HOUSE
Barton le Willows
Howsham
Leavening
Harton
Leppington
Acklam
Thixendale
Flaxton
Strensall
Bossall
Claxton
Scrayingham
Fimber
Garton-on-the-Wolds
Newton on Ouse
BENINGBROUGH HALL
Sand Hutton
Kirby Underdale
Towthorpe
Fridaythorpe
Wetwang
Driffield
Shipton
Wigginton
Buttercrambe
Bugthorpe
Elmswell
Little Driffield
Beningbrough
Haxby
City of York
Upper Helmsley
Painsthorpe
Earswick
Moor End
Skirpenbeck
YORKSHIRE WOLDS WAY
Moor Monkton
Skelton
Stamford Bridge
Youlthorpe
Kelleythorpe
Overton
Huntington
Stockton on the Forest
Gate Helmsley
Tibthorpe
Nether Poppleton
West Huntington
New Earswick
Warthill
Huggate
Upper Poppleton
Rawcliffe
Holtby
Full Sutton
Bishop Wilton
Kirkburn
Southburn
Clifton
Low Catton
Gowthorpe
Great Givendale
Hessay
YORK MINSTER
Murton
Fangfoss
Hutton
Knapton
York
Heworth
Dunnington
YORKSHIRE MUSEUM OF FARMING
High Catton
SE
Meltonby
North Dalton
Bainton
Rufforth
Holgate
JORVIK VIKING CENTRE
Osbaldwick
Bolton
Yapham
Millington
Hutton Cranswick
Acomb
NATIONAL RAILWAY MUSEUM
CASTLE MUS
Grimston
Kexby
Wilberfoss
Hutton Wandesley
Nunthorpe
Heslington
Warter
Kilnwick Percy
East Riding
Middleton-on-the-Wolds
Watton
Woodthorpe
Barmby Moor
Askham Bryan
Fulford
Newton upon Derwent
Pocklington
Kilnwick
Askham Richard
YORK DESIGNER OUTLET
YORKSHIRE AIR MUSEUM
Elvington
STEWART'S BURNBY HALL GARDENS & MUSEUM
Nunburnholme
Lund
Beswick
Bilbrough
Bishopthorpe
Crockey Hill
Sutton upon Derwent
Allerthorpe
Burnby
Holme on the Wolds
Lockington
Copmanthorpe
YORK WEST SERVICES
Thorpe
Acaster Malbis
Naburn
Thornton
Hayton
Londesborough
South Dalton
Scorborough
of Yorksh
Colton
Deighton
Wheldrake
Storwood
Melbourne
Pocklington Canal
Bielby
Thorpe le Street
Shiptonthorpe
Goodmanham
Etton
Leconfield
Appleton Roebuck
Escrick
LOWER DERWENT VALLEY
East Cottingwith
Seaton Ross
Everingham
Market Weighton
Gardham
Cherry Burton
Bolton Percy
Acaster Selby
Thorganby
Holme Green
Stillingfleet
Harswell
Molescroft
BEVERLEY
Beverley
Ulleskelf
Ellerton
Laytham
Sancton
Bishop Burton
Ryther
Kelfield
Water End
Aughton
Holme-on-Spalding-Moor
Church Fenton
Cawood
Skipwith
SKIPWITH COMMON
North Duffield
Harlthorpe
Moor End
Sand Hole
Foggathorpe
North Cliffe
North Newbald
Walkington
Riccall
Bubwith
Highfield
Rascal Moor
South Newbald
Bentley
Wistow
Gribthorpe
South Cliffe
Biggin
Gunby
Willitoft
Hotham
High Hunsley
Skidby
Little Fenton
Barlby
SELBY ABBEY
Osgodby
Menthorpe
Breighton
Spaldington
Bursea
Little Weighton
SKIDBY WINDMILL
Selby
Lund
Cliffe
South Duffield
Foulness
North Cave
Everthorpe
Rowley
Eppleworth
Cottingham
Thorpe Willoughby
Wressle
Brind
North Howden
Portington
Hive
West End
South Cave
Riplingham
Hambleton
East Common
Hemingbrough
Sandholme
Newport
Brayton
Newsholme
HOWDEN MINSTER
Cavil
Eastrington
Scalby
Gilberdyke
Market Weighton Canal
YORKSHIRE WOLDS WAY
Kirk Ella
Monk Fryston
Selby Canal
Derwent
Barlow
Barmby on the Marsh
Brantingham
Willerby
Hillam
Gateforth
Burn
Long Drax
Howden
Staddlethorpe
Ellerker
West Ella
Anlaby
West Haddlesey
Asselby
Knedlington
Kilpin Pike
Kilpin
Balkholme
Broomfleet
Elloughton
Swanland
Chapel Haddlesey
Ouse
Drax
Boothferry
Brough
Welton
HUMBER BRIDGE
Hessle
Birkin
Temple Hirst
Camblesforth
Skelton
North Ferriby
Aire
Newland
Laxton
Beal
Kellington
Hirst Courtney
Airmyn
Hook
Saltmarshe
Blacktoft
Faxfleet
Whitton
Redcliff Channel
Humber Bridge
Eggborough
Hensall
Carlton
Goole
Yokefleet
Ousefleet
BLACKTOFT SANDS RSPB
JULIAN'S BOWER (TURF MAZE)
Winteringham
Read's Island
FAR INGS
Barton-upon-Humber
Snaith
East Cowick
Rawcliffe
Reedness
Whitgift
Little Reedness
Alkborough
West Halton
High Eggborough
Gowdall
West Cowick
Rawcliffe Bridge
Old Goole
THE YORKSHIRE WATERWAYS MUSEUM
Swinefleet
Adlingfleet
South Ferriby
Cridling Stubbs
Whitley
Great Heck
Dutch River
Walcot
Winterton
Kingsforth
Womersley
Pollington
Southfield Reservoir
Goole Fields
Fockerby
Garthorpe
Coleby
New River Ancholme
Balne
Aire and Calder Navigation
Burton Stather
Burton upon Stather
Thealby
Horkstow
Little Smeaton
Walden Stubbs
Went
Goole Moors
Luddington
NORMANBY HALL
Saxby All Saints
Kirk Smeaton
Sykehouse
Pincheon Green
Normanby
Roxby
BARNSDALE BAR SERVICES
Norton
Fenwick
Canal
Eastoft
Flixborough
North
Bonby
Moorends
HUMBERHEAD PEATLANDS
Thorne Waste or Moors
Amcotts
Appleby
Campsall
Fosterhouses
Fishlake
Flixborough Stather
Dragonby
Moss
Worlaby
Lincolnshire
Thorne
Crowle
Canal Side
Stainforth & Keadby Canal
Windsor
DONCASTER NORTH SERVICES
Stainforth
Wike Well End
Ealand
Keadby
Gunness
Crosby
Scunthorpe
Santon
ELSHAM HALL
Bramwith
0 1 2 3 4 5 6 miles
0 1 2 3 4 5 6 7 8 9 10km

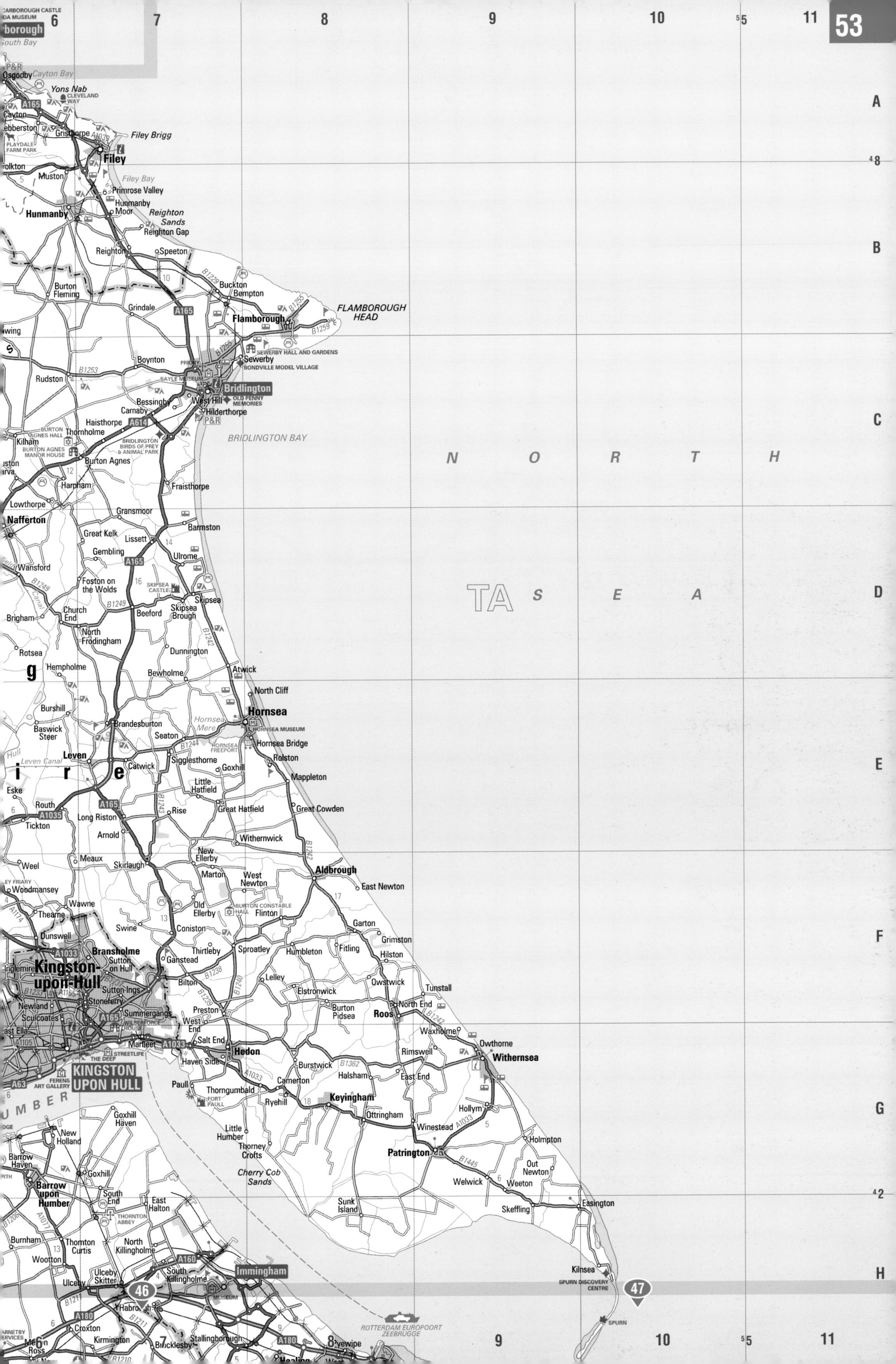
SCARBOROUGH CASTLE
SEA LIFE MUSEUM
Scarborough
South Bay
P&R
Osgodby
Cayton Bay
Yons Nab
CLEVELAND WAY
A165
Cayton
Lebberston
Gristhorpe
A1039
Filey Brigg
PLAYDALE FARM PARK
Filey
Folkton
Muston
Filey Bay
Primrose Valley
Hunmanby
Hunmanby Moor
Reighton Sands
Reighton Gap
Reighton
Speeton
B1229
Buckton
Bempton
Burton Fleming
B1255
FLAMBOROUGH HEAD
Grindale
A165
Flamborough
B1259
Boynton
SEWERBY HALL AND GARDENS
Sewerby
BONDVILLE MODEL VILLAGE
PRIORY
B1253
Rudston
BAYLE MUSEUM
Bridlington
Bessingby
West Hill
OLD PENNY MEMORIES
Carnaby
Hilderthorpe
Haisthorpe
A614
BURTON AGNES HALL
Thornholme
BRIDLINGTON BIRDS OF PREY & ANIMAL PARK
Kilham
BURTON AGNES MANOR HOUSE
BRIDLINGTON BAY
Burton Agnes
N O R T H
Harpham
Fraisthorpe
Lowthorpe
Gransmoor
Nafferton
Barmston
Great Kelk
Lissett
Gembling
A165
Ulrome
Wansford
B1249
Foston on the Wolds
SKIPSEA CASTLE
Skipsea
TA
S E A
B1249
Church End
Beeford
Skipsea Brough
Brigham
North Frodingham
B1242
Rotsea
Dunnington
Hempholme
Bewholme
Atwick
North Cliff
Burshill
Hornsea Mere
Hornsea
Brandesburton
HORNSEA MUSEUM
Baswick Steer
Seaton
B1244
HORNSEA FREEPORT
Hornsea Bridge
Hull
Leven Canal
Leven
Catwick
Sigglesthorne
Goxhill
Rolston
Mappleton
Little Hatfield
Eske
A165
B1243
Great Hatfield
Great Cowden
Routh
A1035
Long Riston
Rise
Tickton
Arnold
Withernwick
B1242
New Ellerby
Meaux
Skirlaugh
Weel
Aldbrough
Marton
West Newton
East Newton
Woodmansey
Wawne
Old Ellerby
BURTON CONSTABLE HALL
Flinton
Thearne
A1174
Swine
Coniston
Garton
Dunswell
Grimston
Thirtleby
Sproatley
Fitling
Bransholme
Humbleton
Hilston
A1033
Sutton on Hull
Ganstead
Kingston-upon-Hull
B1238
Inglemire
Bilton
Lelley
Owstwick
Tunstall
B1233
A1165
Sutton-Ings
B1240
Elstronwick
Stoneferry
B1239
North End
Newland
Burton Pidsea
Roos
Preston
B1242
Sculcoates
A165
Summergangs
Waxholme
WILBERFORCE HOUSE
West End
Owthorne
East Ella
A1105
Marfleet
A1033
Salt End
Hedon
Rimswell
Withernsea
THE DEEP
STREETLIFE
Haven Side
B1362
Burstwick
Halsham
East End
A63
FERENS ART GALLERY
KINGSTON UPON HULL
Paull
A1033
Camerton
Thorngumbald
FORT PAULL
Ryehill
Keyingham
Hollym
HUMBER
Goxhill Haven
Ottringham
Winestead
A1033
Little Humber
Holmpton
New Holland
Thorney Crofts
Patrington
Barrow Haven
B1445
Out Newton
Goxhill
Cherry Cob Sands
Welwick
Weeton
Barrow upon Humber
South End
Sunk Island
Skeffling
Easington
East Halton
THORNTON ABBEY
A1077
B1206
Burnham
Thornton Curtis
North Killingholme
Wootton
A160
Immingham
Kilnsea
Ulceby
Ulceby Skitter
South Killingholme
SPURN DISCOVERY CENTRE
46
47
MUSEUM
B1211
A180
Habrough
B1211
ROTTERDAM EUROPOORT
ZEEBRUGGE
SPURN
Croxton
Kirmington
Brocklesby
Stallingborough
A180
Keelby
Healing
Ross
B1210

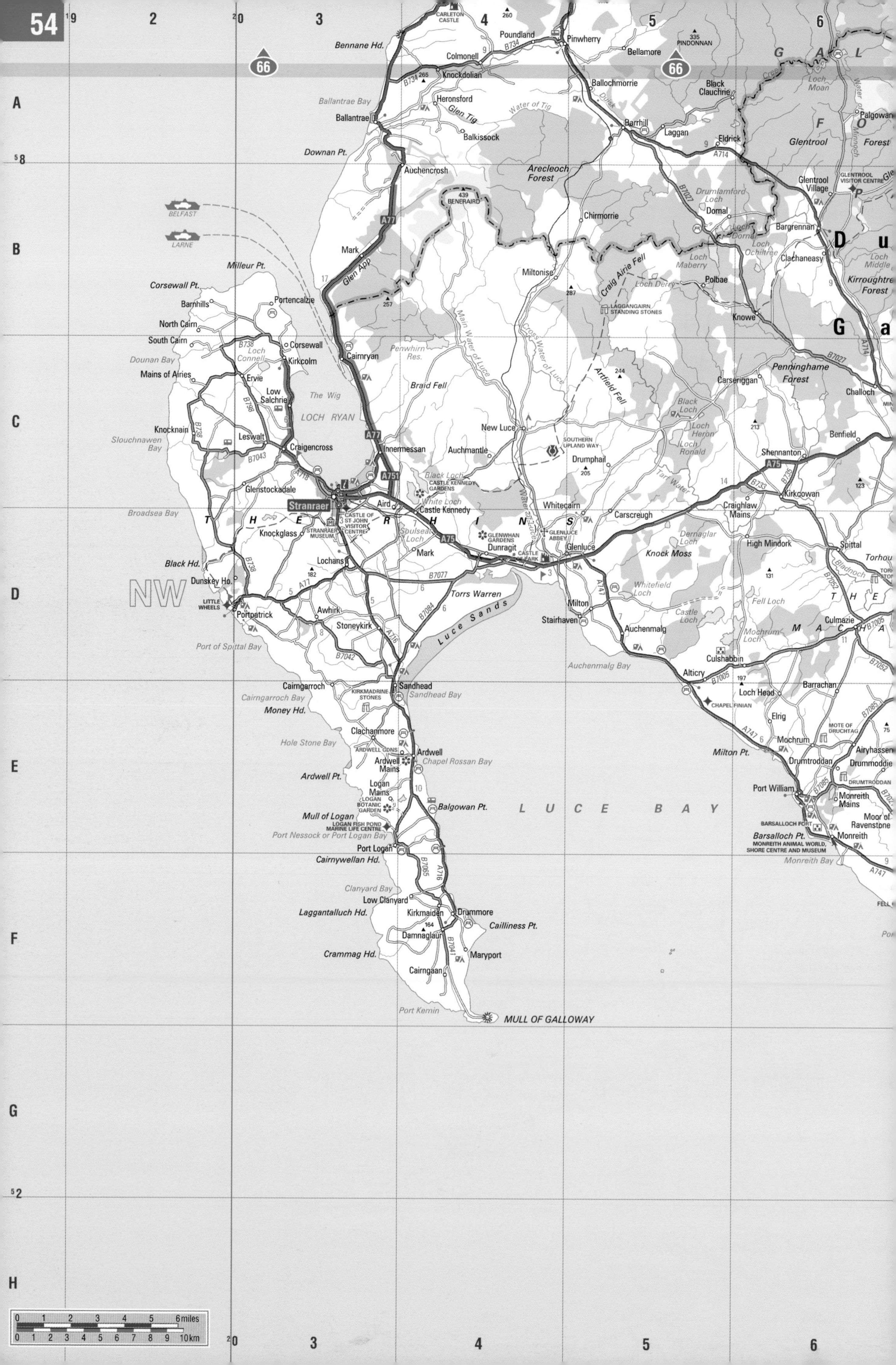

66
Bennane Hd.
Carleton Castle
Poundland
Pinwherry
Bellamore
335 Pindonnan
Colmonell
Knockdolian
Ballochmorrie
Black Clauchrie
Ballantrae Bay
Heronsford
Glen Tig
Water of Tig
Ballantrae
Balkissock
Barrhill
Laggan
Eldrick
Glentrool
Glentrool Village
Glentrool Visitor Centre
Forest
Loch Moan
Palgowan
Downan Pt.
Auchencrosh
Arecleoch Forest
Drumlamford Loch
439 Beneraird
Chirmorrie
Dornal
Bargrennan
Loch Dornal
Loch Ochiltree
Loch Maberry
Clachaneasy
Loch Middle
Kirroughtree Forest
Belfast
Larne
Mark
Glen App
Milleur Pt.
Miltonise
Craig Airie Fell
Loch Derry
Polbae
Corsewall Pt.
Portencalzie
Barnhills
Laggangairn Standing Stones
Knowe
North Cairn
South Cairn
Corsewall
Loch Connell
Kirkcolm
Cairnryan
Penwhirn Res.
Dounan Bay
Mains of Airies
Ervie
Braid Fell
Main Water of Luce
Cross Water of Luce
Artfield Fell
Carseriggan
Penninghame Forest
Challoch
Low Salchrie
The Wig
Loch Ryan
Black Loch
Knocknain
Slouchnawen Bay
Leswalt
New Luce
Southern Upland Way
Loch Heron
Loch Ronald
Benfield
Craigencross
Innermessan
Auchmantle
Drumphail
Shennanton
Glenstockadale
Castle Kennedy Gardens
White Loch
Tarf Water
Kirkcowan
Stranraer
Aird
Castle Kennedy
Whitecairn
Carscreugh
Craighlaw Mains
Broadsea Bay
Castle of St John Visitor Centre
Stranraer Museum
Knockglass
Soulseat Loch
Glenwhan Gardens
Glenluce Abbey
Dernaglar Loch
High Mindork
Spittal
Torhouse
The Rhins
Knock Moss
Mark
Dunragit
Castle of Park
Glenluce
Lochans
Black Hd.
Torrs Warren
Whitefield Loch
Dunskey Ho.
NW
Little Wheels
Portpatrick
Awhirk
Luce Sands
Milton
Stairhaven
Fell Loch
Stoneykirk
Auchenmalg
Castle Loch
Mochrum Loch
The Machars
Culmazie
Port of Spittal Bay
Bladnoch
Culshabbin
Auchenmalg Bay
Cairngarroch
Sandhead
Alticry
Loch Head
Barrachan
Cairngarroch Bay
Kirkmadrine Stones
Sandhead Bay
Chapel Finian
Money Hd.
Elrig
Mote of Druchtag
Clachanmore
Hole Stone Bay
Ardwell Gdns
Ardwell
Ardwell Mains
Chapel Rossan Bay
Milton Pt.
Mochrum
Airyhassen
Drumtroddan
Drummoddie
Ardwell Pt.
Logan Mains
Logan Botanic Garden
Balgowan Pt.
Luce Bay
Port William
Monreith Mains
Mull of Logan
Logan Fish Pond Marine Life Centre
Port Nessock or Port Logan Bay
Barsalloch Fort
Moor of Ravenstone
Port Logan
Barsalloch Pt.
Monreith
Monreith Animal World, Shore Centre and Museum
Cairnywellan Hd.
Monreith Bay
Clanyard Bay
Low Clanyard
Laggantalluch Hd.
Kirkmaiden
Drummore
Cailliness Pt.
Damnaglaur
Crammag Hd.
Maryport
Cairngaan
Port Kemin
Mull of Galloway
A77
A751
A75
A714
A747
A716
B7027
B7077
B7084
B7042
B7043
B738
B798
B734
B733
B735
B7052
B7005
B7085
B7065
B7041
0 1 2 3 4 5 6 miles
0 1 2 3 4 5 6 7 8 9 10 km

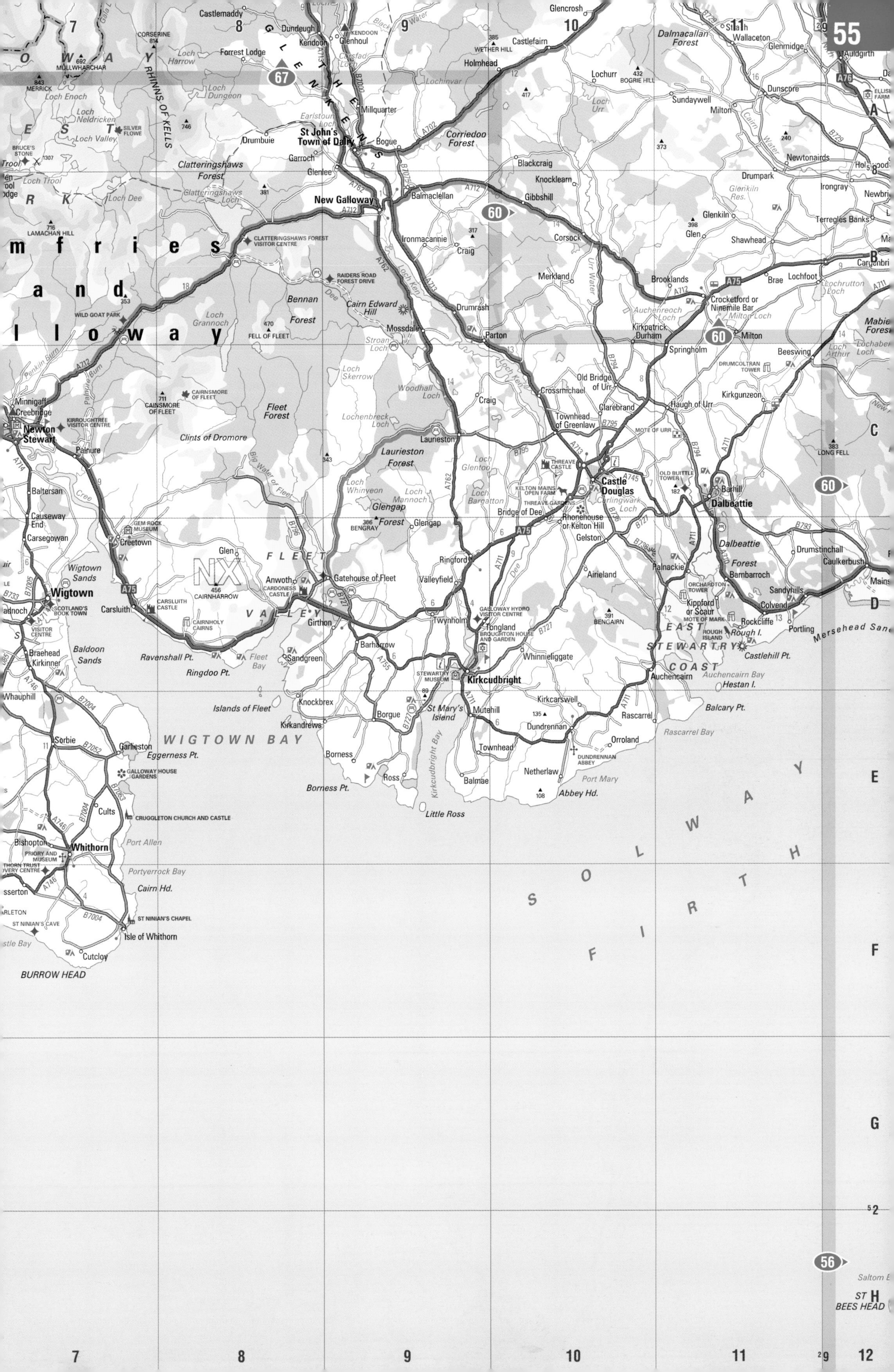

7
8
9
10
11
12
Castlemaddy
Dundeugh
Kendoon
Glenhoul
Glencrosh
Dalmacallan Forest
Wallaceton
Glenmidge
Auldgirth
CORSERINE 814
MULLWHARCHAR 692
MERRICK 843
Forrest Lodge
Loch Harrow
GLENKENS
WETHER HILL 385
Castlefairn
Holmhead
Lochurr
BOGRIE HILL 432
Dunscore
Loch Enoch
Loch Dungeon
RHINNS OF KELLS
Millquarter
Sundaywell
Milton
Loch Neldricken
SILVER FLOWE
Loch Valley
Earlstoun Loch
St John's Town of Dalry
Corriedoo Forest
Drumbuie
Bogue
BRUCE'S STONE
Garroch
Blackcraig
Newtonairds
Clatteringshaws Forest
Glenlee
Knocklearn
Drumpark
Irongray
Loch Trool
Clatteringshaws Loch
Loch Dee
New Galloway
Balmaclellan
Gibbshill
Glenkiln Res.
Glenkiln
Newbridge
LAMACHAN HILL 716
Ironmacannie
Craig
Corsock
Glen
Shawhead
Terregles Banks
Dumfries and Galloway
CLATTERINGSHAWS FOREST VISITOR CENTRE
RAIDERS ROAD FOREST DRIVE
Merkland
Brooklands
Brae
Lochfoot
Cargenbridge
Urr Water
Lochrutton Loch
WILD GOAT PARK
Bennan Forest
Cairn Edward Hill
Drumrash
Crocketford or Ninemile Bar
Loch Grannoch
FELL OF FLEET 470
Mossdale
Auchenreoch Loch
Kirkpatrick Durham
Milton Loch
Mabie Forest
Parton
Stroan Loch
Springholm
Milton
Beeswing
Loch Arthur
Lochaber Loch
Loch Skerrow
DRUMCOLTRAN TOWER
Minnigaff
Creebridge
CAIRNSMORE OF FLEET
CAINSMORE OF FLEET 711
Woodhall Loch
Loch Ken
Craig
Crossmichael
Old Bridge of Urr
Haugh of Urr
Kirkgunzeon
Newton Stewart
KIRROUGHTREE VISITOR CENTRE
Fleet Forest
Lochenbreck Loch
Clarebrand
Townhead of Greenlaw
Palnure
Clints of Dromore
Laurieston
MOTE OF URR
LONG FELL 383
Laurieston Forest
Loch Glentoo
THREAVE CASTLE
Castle Douglas
Baltersan
Loch Whinyeon
Loch Mannoch
KELTON MAINS OPEN FARM
OLD BUITTLE TOWER
Barhill
Glengap Forest
Loch Bargatton
THREAVE GARDENS
Carlingwark Loch
Dalbeattie
Causeway End
BENGRAY 366
Glengap
Bridge of Dee
Rhonehouse or Kelton Hill
Carsegowan
GEM ROCK MUSEUM
Creetown
Gelston
Dalbeattie Forest
Drumstinchall
Caulkerbush
Wigtown Sands
Glen
FLEET
Ringford
Palnackie
Bambarroch
Wigtown
NX
Anwoth
CARDONESS CASTLE
Gatehouse of Fleet
Valleyfield
Airieland
ORCHARDTON TOWER
Sandyhills
Mains
SCOTLAND'S BOOK TOWN
Carsluith
CARSLUITH CASTLE
CAIRNHARROW 456
Kippford or Scaur
Colvend
VISITOR CENTRE
CAIRNHOLY CAIRNS
VALLEY
Girthon
Twynholm
GALLOWAY HYDRO VISITOR CENTRE
Tongland
BROUGHTON HOUSE AND GARDEN
BENGAIRN 391
MOTE OF MARK
Rockcliffe
Portling
Mersehead Sands
ROUGH ISLAND
Rough I.
EAST STEWARTRY COAST
Castlehill Pt.
Braehead
Kirkinner
Baldoon Sands
Ravenshall Pt.
Fleet Bay
Sandgreen
Barharrow
Whinnieliggate
Auchencairn
Auchencairn Bay
Ringdoo Pt.
STEWARTRY MUSEUM
Kirkcudbright
Hestan I.
Whauphill
Islands of Fleet
Knockbrex
St Mary's Isle
Kirkcaswell
Balcary Pt.
Kirkandrews
Borgue
Mutehill
Dundrennan
Rascarrel
Sorbie
WIGTOWN BAY
Garlieston
Eggerness Pt.
Borness
Kirkcudbright Bay
Townhead
DUNDRENNAN ABBEY
Orroland
Rascarrel Bay
GALLOWAY HOUSE GARDENS
Ross
Netherlaw
Balmae
Port Mary
Borness Pt.
Abbey Hd.
Cults
CRUGGLETON CHURCH AND CASTLE
Little Ross
Bishopton
Whithorn
PRIORY AND MUSEUM
Port Allen
Portyerrock Bay
Cairn Hd.
ST NINIAN'S CHAPEL
ST NINIAN'S CAVE
Isle of Whithorn
Cutcloy
BURROW HEAD
SOLWAY FIRTH
A
B
C
D
E
F
G
H
Saltom Bay
ST BEES HEAD

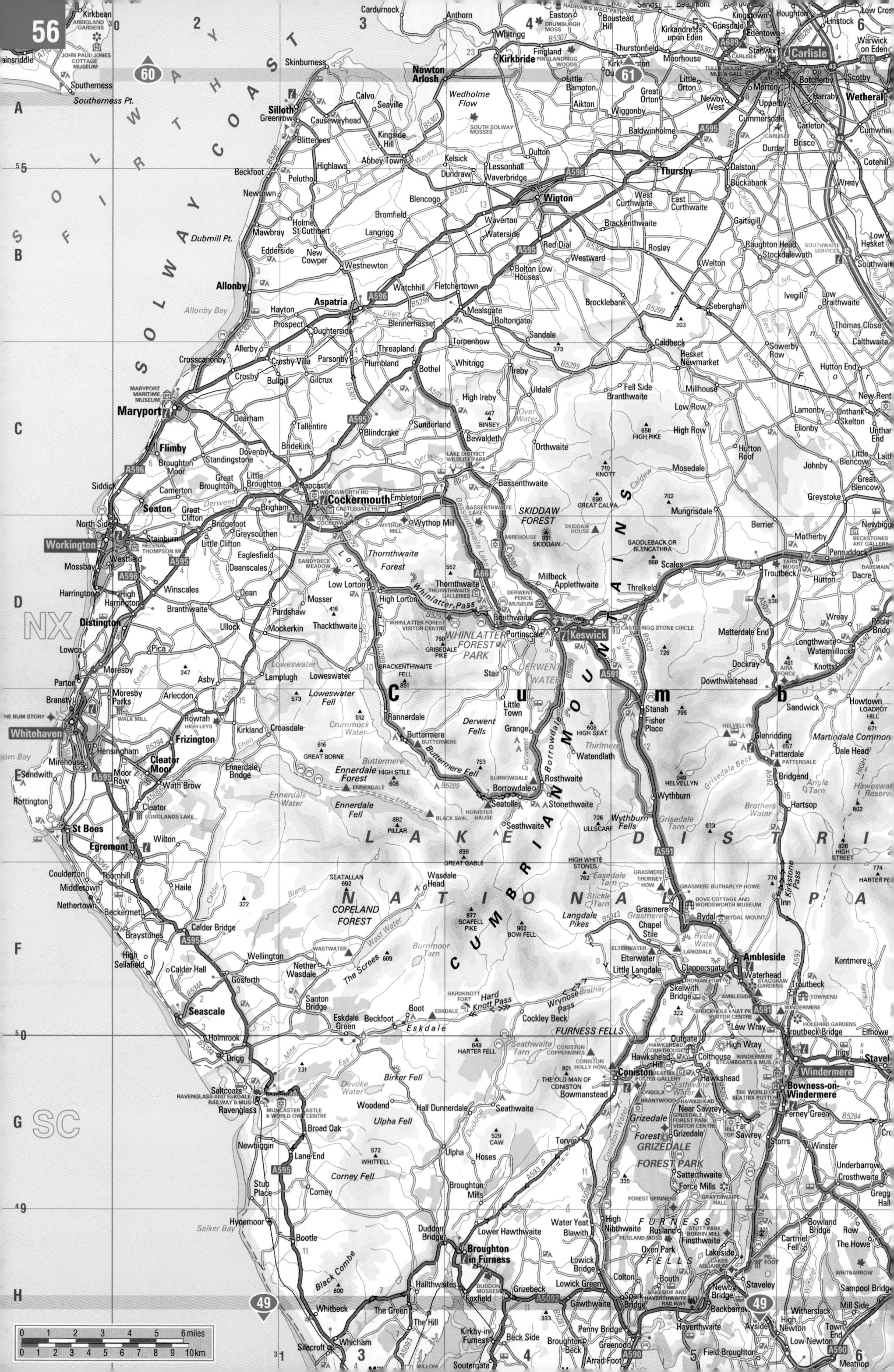
SOLWAY FIRTH COAST
Southerness Pt.
Silloth
Allonby
Allonby Bay
Dubmill Pt.
Maryport
Workington
Whitehaven
St Bees
Egremont
Seascale
Ravenglass
Selker Bay
Carlisle
Wigton
Thursby
Aspatria
Cockermouth
Keswick
Kirkbride
Newton Arlosh
Wedholme Flow
SKIDDAW FOREST
Skiddaw
Thornthwaite Forest
Whinlatter Pass
WHINLATTER FOREST PARK
Derwent Water
Derwent Fells
Borrowdale
Buttermere
Crummock Water
Loweswater
Ennerdale Water
Ennerdale Forest
Ennerdale Fell
LAKE DISTRICT NATIONAL PARK
CUMBRIAN MOUNTAINS
Cumbria
Helvellyn
Thirlmere
Ullswater
Grasmere
Ambleside
Windermere
Bowness-on-Windermere
Coniston
Grizedale Forest
GRIZEDALE FOREST PARK
FURNESS FELLS
Scafell Pike
Great Gable
Pillar
Bow Fell
Langdale Pikes
Wast Water
The Screes
Copeland Forest
Eskdale
Hard Knott Pass
Wrynose Pass
Seathwaite Tarn
Devoke Water
Birker Fell
Ulpha Fell
Corney Fell
Black Combe
Broughton in Furness
Kirkstone Pass
Penrith
Dacre
NX
SC
60
61
49
0 1 2 3 4 5 6 miles
0 1 2 3 4 5 6 7 8 9 10 km

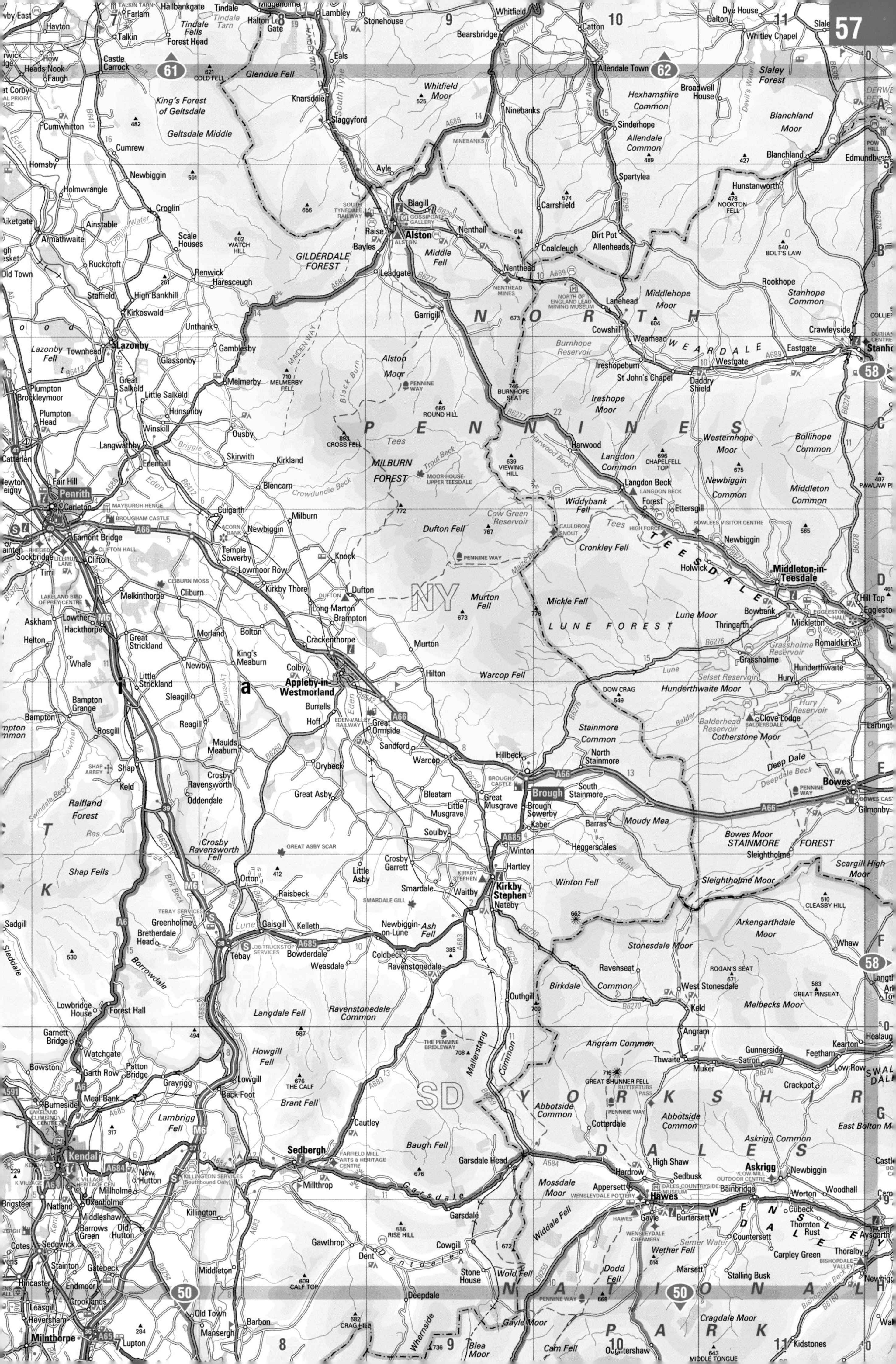

Talkin Tarn
Farlam
Hallbankgate
Tindale
Midgeholme
Lambley
Stonehouse
Whitfield
Catton
Dye House
Dalton
Whitley Chapel
Slaley
Hayton
Tindale Fells
Tindale Tarn
Halton Lea Gate
Talkin
Forest Head
Bearsbridge
How
Heads Nook
Faugh
Castle Carrock
Gelt
621 COLD FELL
Glendue Fell
Eals
Allendale Town
Slaley Forest
Broadwell House
Hexhamshire Common
Whitfield Moor
525
Knarsdale
South Tyne
Great Corby
King's Forest of Geltsdale
482
Geltsdale Middle
Slaggyford
A686
Ninebanks
Sinderhope
Blanchland Moor
Allendale Common
489
Blanchland
427
Edmundbyers
Cumwhitton
Cumrew
Eden
Hornsby
Newbiggin
591
Holmwrangle
Ayle
NINEBANKS
Spartylea
Hunstanworth
478 NOOKTON FELL
Croglin
656
SOUTH TYNEDALE RAILWAY
Blagill
GOSSIPGATE GALLERY
574 Carrshield
Aiketgate
Ainstable
Croglin Water
Armathwaite
Scale Houses
602 WATCH HILL
Raise
Alston
Nenthall
614
Coalcleugh
Dirt Pot
Allenheads
540 BOLT'S LAW
Ruckcroft
GILDERDALE FOREST
Bayles
Middle Fell
Nenthead
NENTHEAD MINES
NORTH OF ENGLAND LEAD MINING MUSEUM
Rookhope
Stanhope Common
Old Town
Renwick
Haresceugh
261
Leadgate
A689
Middlehope Moor
Staffield
High Bankhill
Kirkoswald
Garrigill
673
Lanehead
604
Unthank
NORTH
Cowshill
Wearhead
Crawleyside
Stanhope
Lazonby Fell
Townhead
Lazonby
Gamblesby
Glassonby
MAIDEN WAY
Alston Moor
Burnhope Reservoir
WEARDALE
Eastgate
Westgate
Ireshopeburn
St John's Chapel
Daddry Shield
Plumpton
Brockleymoor
Great Salkeld
Melmerby
710 MELMERBY FELL
PENNINE WAY
746 BURNHOPE SEAT
Ireshope Moor
Plumpton Head
Little Salkeld
Hunsonby
685 ROUND HILL
Black Burn
Winskill
Ousby
893 CROSS FELL
PENNINES
Harwood
Westernhope Moor
Bollihope Common
Langwathby
Briggle Beck
Skirwith
Kirkland
Tees
MILBURN FOREST
Trout Beck
639 VIEWING HILL
Harwood Beck
Langdon Common
696 CHAPELFELL TOP
675
Catterlen
Edenhall
Blencarn
MOOR HOUSE-UPPER TEESDALE
Langdon Beck
LANGDON BECK
Newbiggin Common
Middleton Common
487 PAWLAW PIKE
Newton Reigny
Fair Hill
Penrith
Crowdundle Beck
Widdybank Fell
Forest
Ettersgill
Carleton
MAYBURGH HENGE
Culgaith
772
Milburn
Cow Green Reservoir
BROUGHAM CASTLE
ACORN BANK
Newbiggin
Dufton Fell
767
CAULDRON SNOUT
HIGH FORCE
BOWLEES VISITOR CENTRE
Eamont Bridge
A66
Temple Sowerby
Cronkley Fell
Newbiggin
565
Sockbridge
Clifton
CLIFTON HALL
Knock
PENNINE WAY
Maize Beck
TEESDALE
Tirril
Lowmoor Row
Holwick
Middleton-in-Teesdale
CLIBURN MOSS
Cliburn
Kirkby Thore
DUFTON
Dufton
NY
Murton Fell
Mickle Fell
Lune Moor
LAKELAND BIRD OF PREY CENTRE
Melkinthorpe
Long Marton
Brampton
673
776
LUNE FOREST
Bowbank
Thringarth
Mickleton
EGGLESTONE HALL
Eggleston
Hill Top
Askham
Lowther
Hackthorpe
M6
Helton
Great Strickland
Morland
Bolton
Crackenthorpe
Murton
B6276
Grassholme Reservoir
Romaldkirk
Whale
King's Meaburn
Newby
Colby
Appleby-in-Westmorland
Hilton
Warcop Fell
Lune
Grassholme
Hunderthwaite
Little Strickland
Selset Reservoir
Hury
Bampton Grange
Bampton
Sleagill
Lyvennet
Burrells
DOW CRAG 549
Hunderthwaite Moor
Hury Reservoir
Hoff
Reagill
EDEN VALLEY RAILWAY
Great Ormside
Balder
Balderhead Reservoir
Clove Lodge
BALDERSDALE
Cotherstone Moor
Lartington
Rosgill
Maulds Meaburn
Sandford
Stainmore Common
Lowther
Warcop
Hillbeck
North Stainmore
Deep Dale
Deepdale Beck
SHAP ABBEY
Shap
Drybeck
Crosby Ravensworth
BROUGH CASTLE
Brough
South Stainmore
PENNINE WAY
Bowes
BOWES CASTLE
Keld
Oddendale
Great Asby
Bleatarn
Great Musgrave
Brough Sowerby
A66
Gilmonby
Ralfland Forest
Swindale Beck
Little Musgrave
Kaber
Barras
Moudy Mea
Res.
Soulby
Bowes Moor
STAINMORE
FOREST
Crosby Ravensworth Fell
GREAT ASBY SCAR
Winton
Heggerscales
Belah
Sleightholme
Hartley
Scargill High Moor
Shap Fells
412
Orton
Little Asby
Crosby Garrett
KIRKBY STEPHEN
Kirkby Stephen
Winton Fell
Sleightholme Moor
Birk Beck
Raisbeck
Smardale
Waitby
Nateby
510 CLEASBY HILL
TEBAY SERVICES
SMARDALE GILL
662
Arkengarthdale Moor
Sadgill
Greenholme
Bretherdale Head
Lune
Gaisgill
Kelleth
Newbiggin-on-Lune
Ash Fell
Tebay
J38 TRUCKSTOP SERVICES
A685
Bowderdale
Coldbeck
385
Stonesdale Moor
Whaw
530
Borrowdale
Weasdale
Ravenstonedale
Ravenseat
ROGAN'S SEAT 671
Sleddale
Birkdale
Common
West Stonesdale
583 GREAT PINSEAT
Langthwaite
Lowbridge House
Forest Hall
Langdale Fell
Ravenstonedale Common
Outhgill
709
B6270
Keld
Melbecks Moor
Garnett Bridge
494
587
THE PENNINE BRIDLEWAY
708
Mallerstang
Common
Angram
Angram Common
Thwaite
Gunnerside
Kearton
Healaugh
Watchgate
Howgill Fell
Muker
Satron
Feetham
Low Row
Swaledale
Bowston
Garth Row
Patton Bridge
Lowgill
676 THE CALF
716 GREAT SHUNNER FELL
BUTTERTUBS PASS
Crackpot
Grayrigg
SD
YORKSHIRE
Burneside
Meal Bank
Beck Foot
Brant Fell
Abbotside Common
PENNINE WAY
Abbotside Common
LAKELAND CLIMBING CENTRE
Lambrigg Fell
317
Cautley
Cotterdale
Askrigg Common
East Bolton Moor
Kendal
Sedbergh
FARFIELD MILL ARTS & HERITAGE CENTRE
Baugh Fell
Garsdale Head
A684
DALES
Askrigg
Newbiggin
Castle Bolton
229
A684
New Hutton
KILLINGTON SERVICES (Southbound Only)
676
Hardrow
High Shaw
LOW MILL OUTDOOR CENTRE
Woodhall
Carperby
K VILLAGE HERITAGE CEN
Millholme
Millthrop
Garsdale
Mossdale Moor
WENSLEYDALE POTTERY
Appersett
Sedbusk
DALES COUNTRYSIDE MUSEUM
Hawes
Bainbridge
Worton
Oxenholme
Natland
Middleshaw
Dee
Killington
Garsdale
Gayle
Burtersett
WENSLEYDALE
Cubeck
Thornton Rust
Aysgarth
Brigsteer
Barrows Green
Old Hutton
556 RISE HILL
Cowgill
672
Widdale Fell
HAWES
WENSLEYDALE CREAMERY
Countersett
Semer Water
Carpley Green
Thoralby
Cotes
Sedgwick
Gawthrop
Dent
Dentdale
Wether Fell
614
BISHOPDALE VALLEY
Stainton
Gatebeck
Stone House
Wold Fell
Dodd Fell
Marsett
Stalling Busk
Newbiggin
Hincaster
Endmoor
Middleton
609 CALF TOP
Deepdale
NATIONAL
PENNINE WAY
668
Bishopdale Beck
Leasgill
Crooklands
Old Town
Heversham
682 CRAG HILL
Gayle Moor
Cragdale Moor
Milnthorpe
A65
284
Lupton
Mansergh
Barbon
Whernside
736
Blea Moor
Cam Fell
Oughtershaw
PARK
643 MIDDLE TONGUE
Kidstones
61
62
58
50
7
8
9
10
11

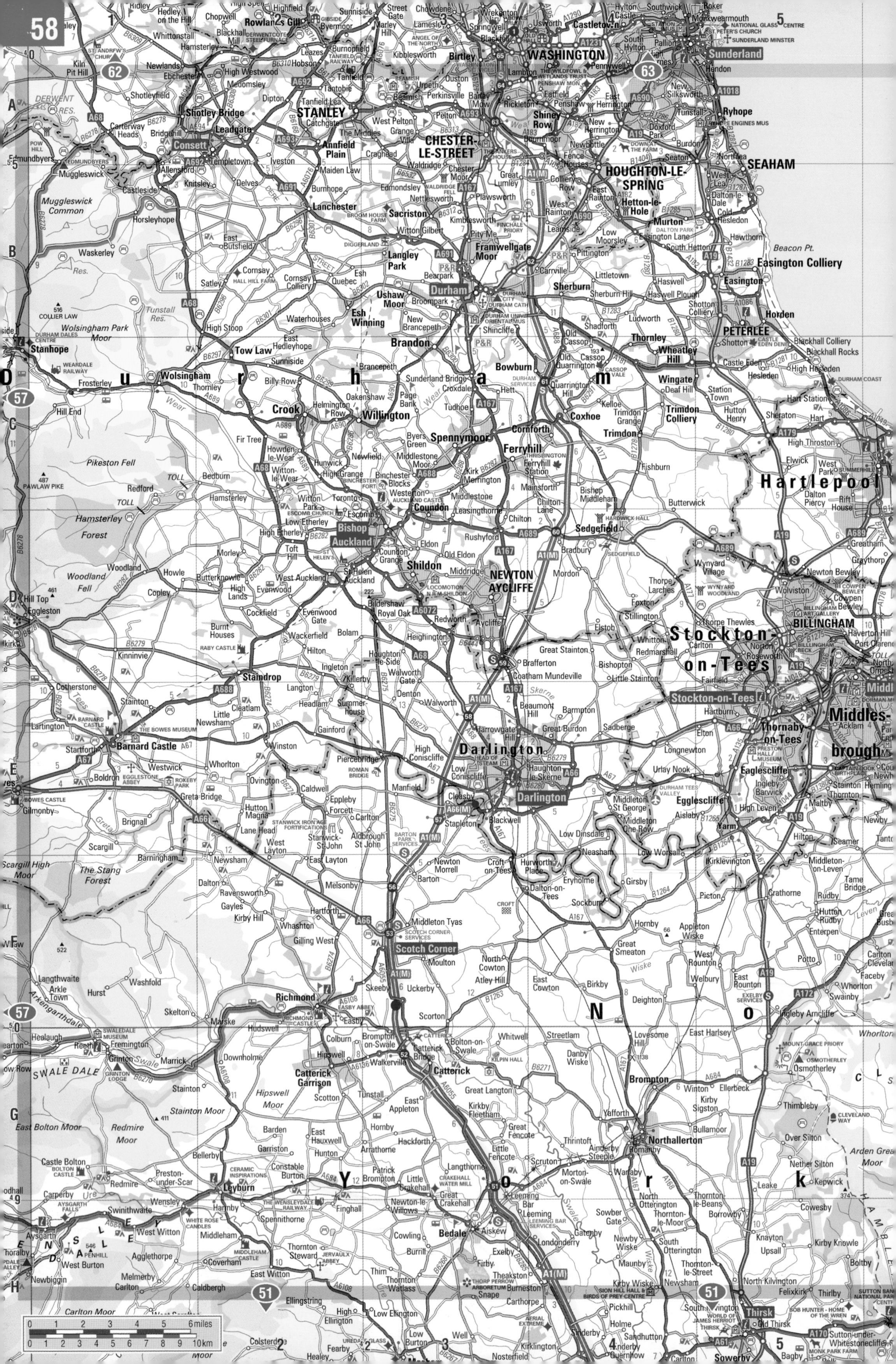
Durham
North Yorkshire
WASHINGTON
Sunderland
STANLEY
CHESTER-LE-STREET
Consett
HOUGHTON-LE-SPRING
SEAHAM
Lanchester
Sacriston
Framwellgate Moor
Durham
Easington Colliery
Easington
Horden
PETERLEE
Stanhope
Wolsingham
Tow Law
Crook
Willington
Brandon
Bowburn
Spennymoor
Ferryhill
Cornforth
Coxhoe
Trimdon
Hartlepool
Bishop Auckland
Shildon
NEWTON AYCLIFFE
Sedgefield
Stockton-on-Tees
BILLINGHAM
Middlesbrough
Thornaby-on-Tees
Eaglescliffe
Yarm
Darlington
Staindrop
Barnard Castle
Greta Bridge
Richmond
Scotch Corner
Catterick
Catterick Garrison
Northallerton
Brompton
Bedale
Leyburn
Thirsk
Hamsterley Forest
Wolsingham Park Moor
Muggleswick Common
Pikeston Fell
Woodland Fell
Barningham Moor
The Stang Forest
SWALE DALE
Hipswell Moor
Redmire Moor
Arden Great Moor
Beacon Pt.
Carlton Moor
0 1 2 3 4 5 6 miles
0 1 2 3 4 5 6 7 8 9 10 km
57
62
63
51

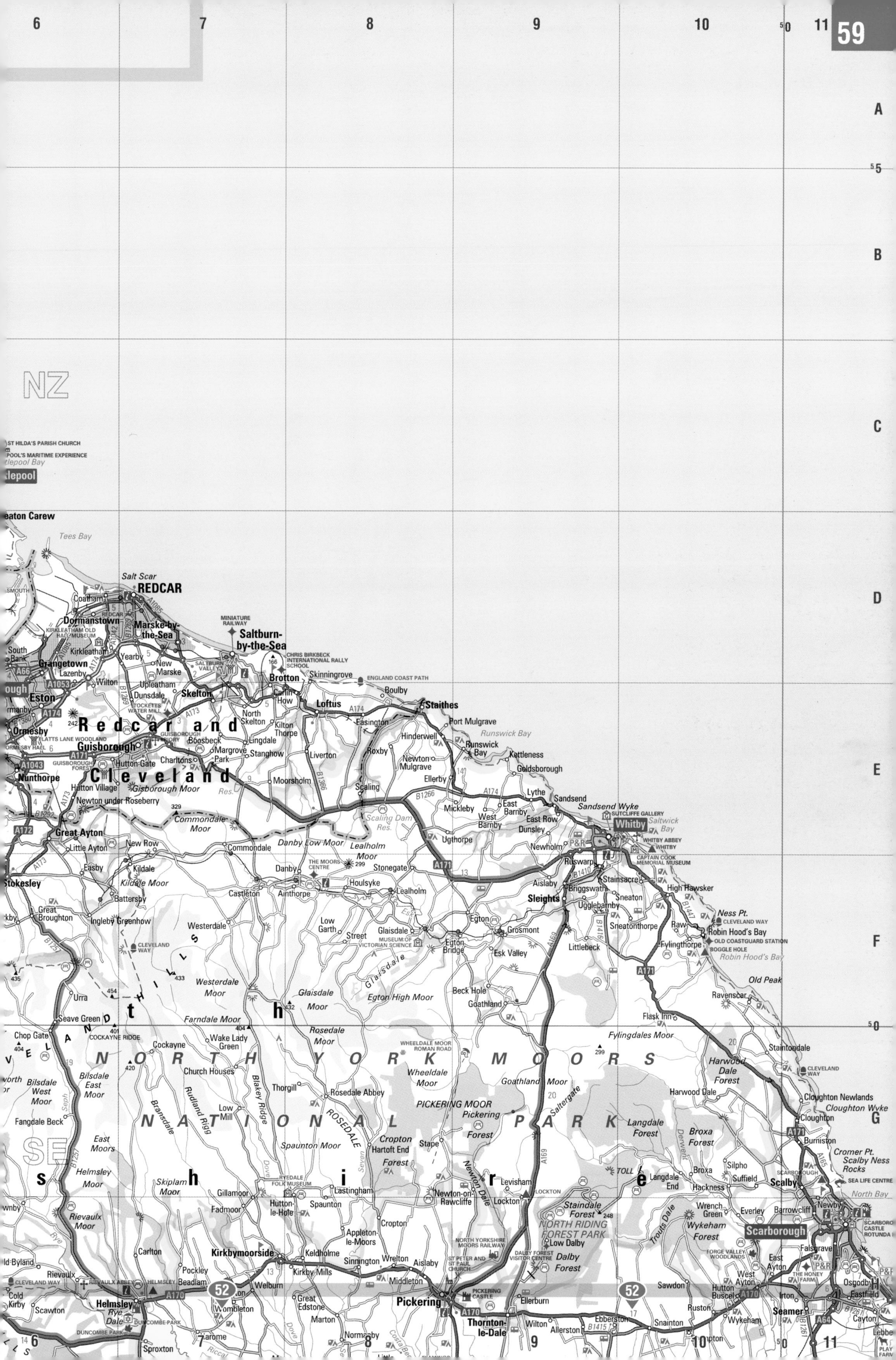

NZ
SE
Tees Bay
Salt Scar
REDCAR
Coatham
Dormanstown
Marske-by-the-Sea
KIRKLEATHAM OLD HALL MUSEUM
Kirkleatham
MINIATURE RAILWAY
Saltburn-by-the-Sea
CHRIS BIRKBECK INTERNATIONAL RALLY SCHOOL
South Bank
Grangetown
Yearby
New Marske
SALTBURN VALLEY
Lazenby
Wilton
Upleatham
Brotton
Skinningrove
ENGLAND COAST PATH
Boulby
Eston
Dunsdale
Skelton
Carlin How
Loftus
Staithes
TOCKETTS WATER MILL
North Skelton
Kilton Thorpe
Easington
Port Mulgrave
Runswick Bay
Redcar and Cleveland
Ormesby
GUISBOROUGH PRIORY
Boosbeck
Lingdale
Hinderwell
Runswick Bay
Kettleness
Guisborough
FLATTS LANE WOODLAND
ORMESBY HALL
Margrove Park
Stanghow
Liverton
Roxby
Newton Mulgrave
Goldsborough
GUISBOROUGH FOREST
Hutton Gate
Charltons
Nunthorpe
Moorsholm
Ellerby
Hutton Village
Gisborough Moor
Scaling
Lythe
Sandsend
Sandsend Wyke
SUTCLIFFE GALLERY
Newton under Roseberry
Mickleby
East Barnby
West Barnby
East Row
Dunsley
Whitby
Saltwick Bay
WHITBY ABBEY
Commondale Moor
Scaling Dam Res.
Great Ayton
Little Ayton
New Row
Commondale
Danby Low Moor
Lealholm Moor
Ugthorpe
Newholm
CAPTAIN COOK MEMORIAL MUSEUM
Easby
Kildale
Kildale Moor
Danby
THE MOORS CENTRE
Stonegate
Ruswarp
Stainsacre
Stokesley
Castleton
Ainthorpe
Houlsyke
Lealholm
Aislaby
Briggswath
High Hawsker
Battersby
Sleights
Sneaton
Great Broughton
Ingleby Greenhow
Westerdale
Low Garth
Street
Glaisdale
Egton
Grosmont
Ugglebarnby
Sneatonthorpe
Raw
Ness Pt.
CLEVELAND WAY
Robin Hood's Bay
OLD COASTGUARD STATION
BOGGLE HOLE
MUSEUM OF VICTORIAN SCIENCE
Egton Bridge
Esk Valley
Fylingthorpe
Littlebeck
Robin Hood's Bay
CLEVELAND WAY
Glaisdale
Westerdale Moor
Glaisdale Moor
Egton High Moor
Beck Hole
Goathland
Old Peak
Ravenscar
Urra
Seave Green
CLEVELAND HILLS
Farndale Moor
Flask Inn
Fylingdales Moor
Chop Gate
COCKAYNE RIDGE
Wake Lady Green
Rosedale Moor
WHEELDALE MOOR ROMAN ROAD
Staintondale
Cockayne
NORTH YORK MOORS NATIONAL PARK
Church Houses
Bilsdale East Moor
Bilsdale West Moor
Wheeldale Moor
Goathland Moor
Harwood Dale Forest
CLEVELAND WAY
Thorgill
Rosedale Abbey
Harwood Dale
Cloughton Newlands
Cloughton Wyke
Fangdale Beck
Low Mill
Rudland Rigg
Blakey Ridge
Bransdale
ROSEDALE
PICKERING MOOR
Pickering Forest
Saltergate
Langdale Forest
Cloughton
Broxa Forest
Burniston
Cromer Pt.
Scalby Ness Rocks
East Moors
Spaunton Moor
Crompton
Hartoft End
Forest
Stape
Helmsley Moor
Skiplam Moor
RYEDALE FOLK MUSEUM
Lastingham
Newton Dale
Levisham
TOLL
Langdale End
Broxa
Hackness
Silpho
Suffield
Scalby
SEA LIFE CENTRE
North Bay
Gillamoor
Fadmoor
Hutton-le-Hole
Spaunton
Newton-on-Rawcliffe
Lockton
LOCKTON
Staindale Forest
NORTH RIDING FOREST PARK
Trouts Dale
Wrench Green
Wykeham Forest
Everley
Barrowcliff
Newby
Scarborough
SCARBOROUGH CASTLE
ROTUNDA
Rievaulx Moor
Cropton
Appleton-le-Moors
NORTH YORKSHIRE MOORS RAILWAY
Low Dalby
DALBY FOREST VISITOR CENTRE
Dalby Forest
FORGE VALLEY WOODLANDS
Falsgrave
Carlton
Kirkbymoorside
Keldholme
Sinnington
Wrelton
Aislaby
ST PETER AND ST PAUL CHURCH
East Ayton
Old Byland
Rievaulx
Pockley
Kirkby Mills
Middleton
West Ayton
THE HONEY FARM
Osgodby
CLEVELAND WAY
RIEVAULX ABBEY
HELMSLEY
Beadlam
Welburn
PICKERING CASTLE
Sawdon
Hutton Buscel
Irton
Eastfield
Cold Kirby
Scawton
Helmsley
Rye Dale
DUNCOMBE PARK
Wombleton
Great Edstone
Pickering
Ellerburn
Ruston
Seamer
Cayton
Marton
Thornton-le-Dale
Wilton
Allerston
Ebberston
Snainton
Wykeham
Normanby
Nunnington
Sproxton
DUNCOMBE PARK
Lebberston
ST HILDA'S PARISH CHURCH
Tees Bay
Seaton Carew
A174
A171
A169
A170
A1085
A1053
A1043
A172
A173
A66
A64
A165
B1366
B1266
B1416
B1447
B1415
B1257
B1257
52
6
7
8
9
10
11
A
B
C
D
E
F
G

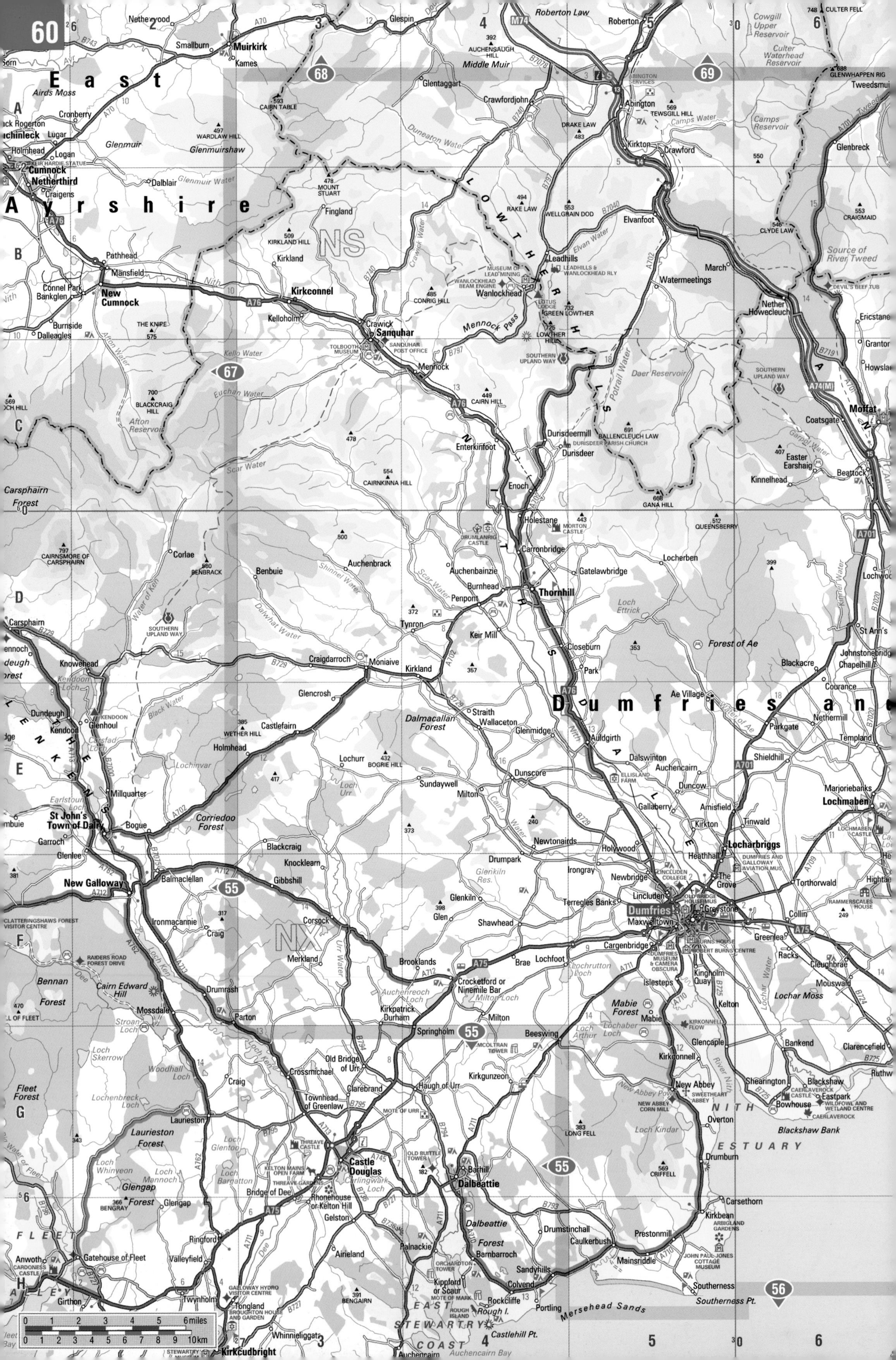
East Ayrshire
Dumfries and
Netherwood
Muirkirk
Smallburn
Kames
Glespin
Roberton Law
Roberton
Cowgill Upper Reservoir
Culter Waterhead Reservoir
CULTER FELL
GLENWHAPPEN RIG
Tweedsmuir
392 AUCHENSAUGH HILL
Middle Muir
68
69
ABINGTON SERVICES
Abington
TEWSGILL HILL
Camps Water
Camps Reservoir
Glentaggart
Crawfordjohn
593 CAIRN TABLE
Airds Moss
Cronberry
497 WARDLAW HILL
DRAKE LAW
Duneaton Water
Kirkton
Crawford
Glenbreck
Auchinleck
Lugar
Glenmuir
Glenmuirshaw
Holmhead
Logan
KEIR HARDIE STATUE
Cumnock
Netherthird
Dalblair
Glenmuir Water
478 MOUNT STUART
494 RAKE LAW
553 WELLGRAIN DOD
Elvanfoot
546 CLYDE LAW
553 CRAIGMAID
Fingland
LOWTHER HILLS
509 KIRKLAND HILL
NS
Kirkland
Leadhills
LEADHILLS & WANLOCKHEAD RLY
MUSEUM OF LEAD MINING
Elvan Water
Source of River Tweed
Pathhead
Mansfield
March
Watermeetings
Connel Park
Bankglen
New Cumnock
Nith
Kirkconnel
Kelloholm
485 CONRIG HILL
WANLOCKHEAD BEAM ENGINE
Wanlockhead
LOTUS LODGE
732 GREEN LOWTHER
DEVIL'S BEEF TUB
Nether Howecleuch
Ericstane
Burnside
Dalleagles
THE KNIPE 575
Afton Water
Crawick
Sanquhar
TOLBOOTH MUSEUM
SANQUHAR POST OFFICE
Mennock Pass
725 LOWTHER HILL
SOUTHERN UPLAND WAY
Potrail Water
Daer Reservoir
Grantor
Howslа
Kello Water
67
Mennock
Euchan Water
700 BLACKCRAIG HILL
Afton Reservoir
449 CAIRN HILL
Moffat
Coatsgate
Durisdeermill
DURISDEER PARISH CHURCH
Durisdeer
691 BALLENCLEUCH LAW
Enterkinfoot
478
Scar Water
554 CAIRNKINNA HILL
Enoch
Easter Earshaig
Garpol Water
Kinnelhead
Beattock
668 GANA HILL
Carsphairn Forest
Holestane
443 MORTON CASTLE
512 QUEENSBERRY
797 CAIRNSMORE OF CARSPHAIRN
Corlae
580 BENBRACK
500
DRUMLANRIG CASTLE
Carronbridge
Locherben
Benbuie
Auchenbrack
Shinnel Water
Auchenbainzie
Gatelawbridge
399
Lochwood
Water of Ken
Burnhead
Penpont
Thornhill
Loch Ettrick
Dalwhat Water
372
Tynron
Carsphairn
SOUTHERN UPLAND WAY
Keir Mill
Closeburn
353
Forest of Ae
St Ann's
Knowehead
Kendoon Loch
Craigdarroch
Moniaive
Kirkland
357
Park
Blackacre
Johnstonebridge
Chapelhill
Courance
Glencrosh
Straith
Wallaceton
Ae Village
Water of Ae
Nethermill
Parkgate
Templand
Dundeugh
Kendoon
Glenhoul
Black Water
385 WETHER HILL
Castlefairn
Dalmacallan Forest
Glenmidge
Auldgirth
Holmhead
Lochinvar
Lochurr
432 BOGRIE HILL
417
Dalswinton
Auchencairn
Shieldhill
Sundaywell
Dunscore
ELLISLAND FARM
Duncow
Millquarter
Earlstoun Loch
St John's Town of Dalry
Corriedoo Forest
Milton
Cairn Water
240
Gallaberry
Amisfield
Tinwald
Marjoriebanks
Lochmaben
LOCHMABEN CASTLE
Bogue
373
Newtonairds
Kirkton
Garroch
Glenlee
Blackcraig
Drumpark
Holywood
Heathhall
Locharbriggs
381
Knocklearn
Glenkiln Res.
Irongray
Newbridge
LINCLUDEN COLLEGE
The Grove
DUMFRIES AND GALLOWAY AVIATION MUS
Torthorwald
Hightae
New Galloway
Balmaclellan
55
Gibbshill
Glenkiln
Lincluden
OLD BRIDGE HOUSE MUS
Dumfries
Greystone
RAMMERSCALES HOUSE
CLATTERINGSHAWS FOREST VISITOR CENTRE
Ironmacannie
317 Craig
398 Glen
Corsock
Shawhead
Terregles Banks
Maxwelltown
Collin
249
NX
Urr Water
BURNS HOUSE
ROBERT BURNS CENTRE
Greenlea
RAIDERS ROAD FOREST DRIVE
Merkland
Cargenbridge
DUMFRIES MUSEUM & CAMERA OBSCURA
Racks
Cleughbrae
Bennan Forest
Cairn Edward Hill
Brooklands
Brae
Lochfoot
Lochrutton Loch
Kingholm Quay
Loch Ken
Drumrash
Auchenreoch Loch
Crocketford or Ninemile Bar
Milton Loch
Isleсteps
Mouswald
470
FELL OF FLEET
Mossdale
Stroan Loch
Parton
Kirkpatrick Durham
Milton
Mabie Forest
Mabie
Lochar Moss
KIRKCONNELL FLOW
Kelton
Loch Skerrow
Springholm
MCOLTRAN TOWER
Beeswing
Loch Arthur
Lochaber Loch
Glencaple
Bankend
Clarencefield
Woodhall Loch
Old Bridge of Urr
Crossmichael
Haugh of Urr
Kirkgunzeon
Kirkconnell
Fleet Forest
Craig
Clarebrand
New Abbey Pow
New Abbey
SWEETHEART ABBEY
River Nith
Shearington
Blackshaw
CAERLAVEROCK CASTLE
Eastpark
Bowhouse
CAERLAVEROCK
WILDFOWL AND WETLAND CENTRE
Ruthw
Lochenbreck Loch
Townhead of Greenlaw
MOTE OF URR
NEW ABBEY CORN MILL
Overton
NITH ESTUARY
Blackshaw Bank
Laurieston
Laurieston Forest
383 LONG FELL
Loch Kindar
343
Loch Glentoo
THREAVE CASTLE
Castle Douglas
KELTON MAINS OPEN FARM
THREAVE GARDENS
Carlingwark Loch
OLD BUITTLE TOWER
182
Barhill
Dalbeattie
569 CRIFFELL
Drumburn
Loch Whinyeon
Loch Mannoch
Glengap Forest
Loch Bargatton
Bridge of Dee
Rhonehouse or Kelton Hill
366 BENGRAY
Glengap
Carsethorn
Gelston
Drumstinchall
Kirkbean
ARBIGLAND GARDENS
FLEET
Ringford
Dalbeattie Forest
Caulkerbush
Prestonmill
Palnackie
Airieland
Mainsriddle
JOHN PAUL JONES COTTAGE MUSEUM
Anwoth
CARDONESS CASTLE
Gatehouse of Fleet
Valleyfield
ORCHARDTON TOWER
Barnbarroch
Sandyhills
Colvend
Southerness
Southerness Pt.
56
Kippford or Scaur
MOTE OF MARK
ROUGH ISLAND
Rough I.
Rockcliffe
Portling
Mersehead Sands
GALLOWAY HYDRO VISITOR CENTRE
Tongland
BROUGHTON HOUSE AND GARDEN
391 BENGAIRN
EAST STEWARTRY COAST
Castlehill Pt.
Girthon
Twynholm
Whinnieliggate
Kirkcudbright
STEWARTRY MUSEUM
Auchencairn
Auchencairn Bay
0 1 2 3 4 5 6 miles
0 1 2 3 4 5 6 7 8 9 10 km
A
B
C
D
E
F
G
H
2
3
4
5
6
M74
A70
A76
A702
A712
A75
A762
A713
A711
A710
A701
A709
A725
A724
A745
A74(M)
B740
B797
B7040
B729
B7000
B7075
B794
B795
B736
B727
B721
B793
B725
B7020
B719
B743
B741

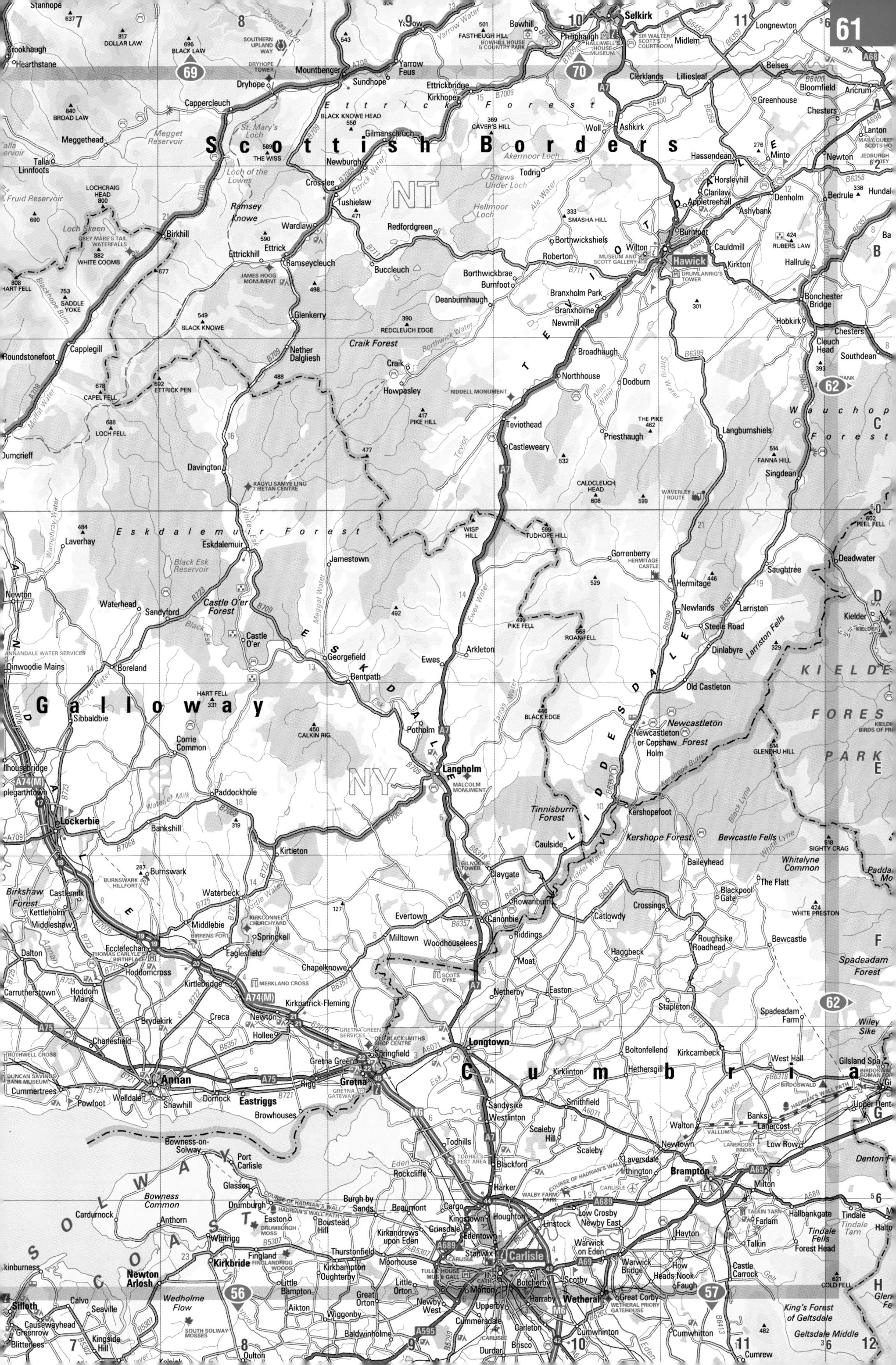
Scottish Borders
Galloway
Cumbria
Ettrick Forest
Eskdalemuir Forest
Craik Forest
Castle O'er Forest
Kielder Forest Park
Wauchope Forest
Kershope Forest
Newcastleton Forest
Tinnisburn Forest
Spadeadam Forest
Solway Coast
Teviotdale
Eskdale
Liddesdale
Annandale
NT
NY
Selkirk
Hawick
Langholm
Lockerbie
Annan
Gretna
Longtown
Carlisle
Brampton
Newcastleton or Copshaw Holm
Ecclefechan
Eastriggs
Kirkbride
Silloth
Wetheral
Yarrow
Mountbenger
Dryhope
Cappercleuch
Tushielaw
Ettrick
Ettrickbridge
Ramseycleuch
Eskdalemuir
Bentpath
Canonbie
Kirkpatrick-Fleming
Denholm
Ancrum
Bonchester Bridge
Saughtree
Kielder
Bewcastle
Gilsland Spa
Dumfries and Galloway
St. Mary's Loch
Megget Reservoir
Loch Skeen
Grey Mare's Tail Waterfalls
White Coomb
Hart Fell
Ettrick Pen
Black Knowe
Pike Hill
Hermitage Castle
Drumlanrig's Tower
Museum and Scott Gallery
Kagyu Samye Ling Tibetan Centre
Malcolm Monument
Scots Dyke
Gretna Green
Hadrian's Wall Path
Course of Hadrian's Wall
Lanercost Priory
Birdoswald
Carlisle Airport
Talkin Tarn
Castle Carrock
King's Forest of Geltsdale
Geltsdale Middle
A7
A74(M)
A75
A69
A689
A6071
A595
M6
B709
B7009
B711
B6357
B6318
B6399
62
69
70
56
57

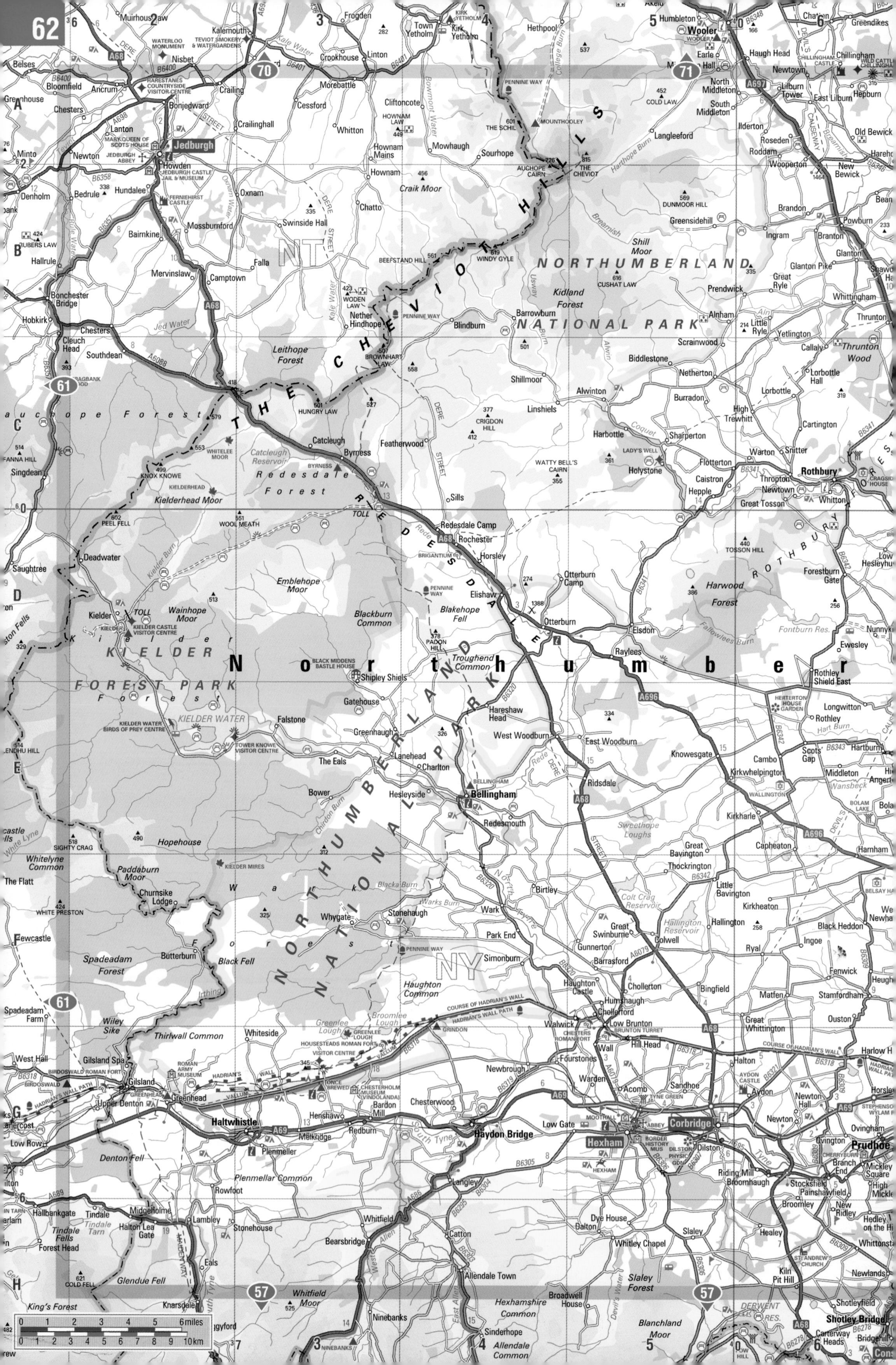
70
71
61
57
THE CHEVIOT HILLS
NORTHUMBERLAND NATIONAL PARK
Northumberland
NORTHUMBERLAND NATIONAL PARK
KIELDER FOREST PARK
Kielder Forest
Wark Forest
Redesdale Forest
REDESDALE
ROTHBURY FOREST
NT
NY
Muirhouselaw
Kalemouth
WATERLOO MONUMENT
TEVIOT SMOKERY & WATERGARDENS
Nisbet
Frogden
Town Yetholm
Kirk Yetholm
Hethpool
Humbleton
Wooler
Chatton
Greendikes
Belses
Bloomfield
Ancrum
HARESTANES COUNTRYSIDE VISITOR CENTRE
Crailing
Crookhouse
Linton
Morebattle
Earle
Hall
Haugh Head
Chillingham
CHILLINGHAM CASTLE
Newtown
Greenhouse
Chesters
Bonjedward
Crailinghall
Cessford
Cliftoncote
North Middleton
South Middleton
Lilburn Tower
East Lilburn
Hepburn
Lanton
MARY QUEEN OF SCOTS HOUSE
Jedburgh
JEDBURGH ABBEY
Howden
JEDBURGH CASTLE JAIL & MUSEUM
Minto
Newton
Whitton
HOWNAM LAW
Hownam Mains
Mowhaugh
Sourhope
THE SCHIL
MOUNTHOOLEY
COLD LAW
Langleeford
Ilderton
Roseden
Roddam
Wooperton
Old Bewick
New Bewick
Denholm
Bedrule
Hundalee
FERNIEHIRST CASTLE
Oxnam
Hownam
Craik Moor
AUCHOPE CAIRN
THE CHEVIOT
DUNMOOR HILL
Brandon
Powburn
Bairnkine
Mossburnford
Swinside Hall
Chatto
Greensidehill
Ingram
Branton
RUBERS LAW
Hallrule
Mervinslaw
Falla
Camptown
BEEFSTAND HILL
WINDY GYLE
Shill Moor
Glanton
Glanton Pike
Great Ryle
CUSHAT LAW
Bonchester Bridge
WODEN LAW
Kidland Forest
Prendwick
Whittingham
Hobkirk
Chesters
Cleuch Head
Southdean
Nether Hindhope
PENNINE WAY
Blindburn
Barrowburn
Alnham
Little Ryle
Yetlington
Thrunton
Callaly
Thrunton Wood
Leithope Forest
BROWNHART LAW
Scrainwood
Biddlestone
Netherton
Lorbottle Hall
Lorbottle
Shillmoor
Alwinton
Burradon
High Trewhitt
HUNGRY LAW
CRIGDON HILL
Linshiels
Cartington
Harbottle
Sharperton
Catcleugh
Catcleugh Reservoir
Byrness
Featherwood
LADY'S WELL
Holystone
Warton
Snitter
Rothbury
Flotterton
Caistron
Thropton
Newtown
Hepple
Great Tosson
Whitton
WHITELEE MOOR
KNOX KNOWE
KIELDERHEAD
Kielderhead Moor
WATTY BELL'S CAIRN
Singdean
Sills
PEEL FELL
WOOL MEATH
TOLL
Redesdale Camp
Rochester
BRIGANTIUM
Horsley
TOSSON HILL
Harwood Forest
Forestburn Gate
Deadwater
Saughtree
Emblehope Moor
Otterburn Camp
Elishaw
Blakehope Fell
Otterburn
Elsdon
Fontburn Res.
Ewesley
Kielder
Wainhope Moor
KIELDER CASTLE VISITOR CENTRE
Blackburn Common
PADON HILL
Troughend Common
Raylees
Rothley Shield East
BLACK MIDDENS BASTLE HOUSE
Shipley Shiels
Gatehouse
Hareshaw Head
HERTERTON HOUSE GARDEN
Longwitton
Rothley
KIELDER WATER
KIELDER WATER BIRDS OF PREY CENTRE
Falstone
Greenhaugh
TOWER KNOWE VISITOR CENTRE
West Woodburn
East Woodburn
Knowesgate
Cambo
Scots' Gap
Hartburn
The Eals
Lanehead
Charlton
Ridsdale
Kirkwhelpington
Middleton
WALLINGTON
Bower
Hesleyside
Bellingham
Redesmouth
Sweethope Loughs
Kirkharle
SIGHTY CRAG
Hopehouse
Great Bavington
Capheaton
Harnham
Whitelyne Common
The Flatt
Paddaburn Moor
KIELDER MIRES
Thockrington
Little Bavington
Birtley
Churnsike Lodge
WHITE PRESTON
Blacka Burn
Wark
Colt Crag Reservoir
Kirkheaton
Whygate
Stonehaugh
Hallington
Hallington Reservoir
Black Heddon
Bewcastle
Great Swinburne
Colwell
Ingoe
Spadeadam Forest
Butterburn
Black Fell
Park End
Gunnerton
Barrasford
Ryal
Simonburn
Haughton Common
Haughton Castle
Chollerton
Bingfield
Fenwick
Stamfordham
Matfen
Spadeadam Farm
COURSE OF HADRIAN'S WALL
HADRIAN'S WALL PATH
Humshaugh
Chollerford
Wiley Sike
Greenlee Lough
Broomlee Lough
GRINDON
Walwick
Low Brunton
BRUNTON TURRET
CHESTERS ROMAN FORT
Great Whittington
Ouston
Thirlwall Common
Whiteside
HOUSESTEADS ROMAN FORT
VISITOR CENTRE
Hill Head
Fourstones
Wall
Halton
Harlow Hill
West Hall
Gilsland Spa
BIRDOSWALD ROMAN FORT
ROMAN ARMY MUSEUM
ONCE BREWED
CHESTERHOLM MUSEUM (VINDOLANDA)
Newbrough
Warden
AYDON CASTLE
Aydon
Gilsland
Greenhead
Upper Denton
Bardon Mill
Chesterwood
Acomb
Sandhoe
TYNE GREEN
Newton Hall
Henshaw
Haltwhistle
Melkridge
Redburn
Haydon Bridge
Low Gate
Hexham
ABBEY
Corbridge
Newton
Ovingham
Prudhoe
Low Row
Plenmeller
BORDER HISTORY MUS
Dilston
DILSTON PHYSIC GDN
Ovington
Cherryburn
Denton Fell
Plenmellar Common
Riding Mill
Broomhaugh
Branch End
Mickley Square
Langley
Stocksfield
Painshawfield
Rowfoot
Broomley
New Ridley
Hallbankgate
Tindale
Midgeholme
Halton Lea Gate
Lambley
Stonehouse
Whitfield
Catton
Dye House
Dalton
Slaley
Hedley on the Hill
Healey
Tindale Fells
Tindale Tarn
Forest Head
Bearsbridge
Whitley Chapel
Whittonstall
ST ANDREW'S CHURCH
COLD FELL
Glendue Fell
Eals
Allendale Town
Kiln Pit Hill
Newlands
Slaley Forest
Whitfield Moor
Hexhamshire Common
Broadwell House
Shotleyfield
King's Forest
Knarsdale
Ninebanks
DERWENT RES.
Shotley Bridge
Blanchland Moor
Carterway Heads
Sinderhope
Allendale Common
NINEBANKS
A68
A69
A696
A697
A6088
A689
A686
A6079
B6318
B6320
B6341
B6342
B6343
B6306
B6305
B6304
B6295
B6309
B6321
B6319
B6401
B6400
B6358
B6357
B6348
B6346
B6278
B6295
DERE STREET
DEVIL'S CAUSEWAY
MAIDEN WAY
0 1 2 3 4 5 6 miles
0 1 2 3 4 5 6 7 8 9 10 km

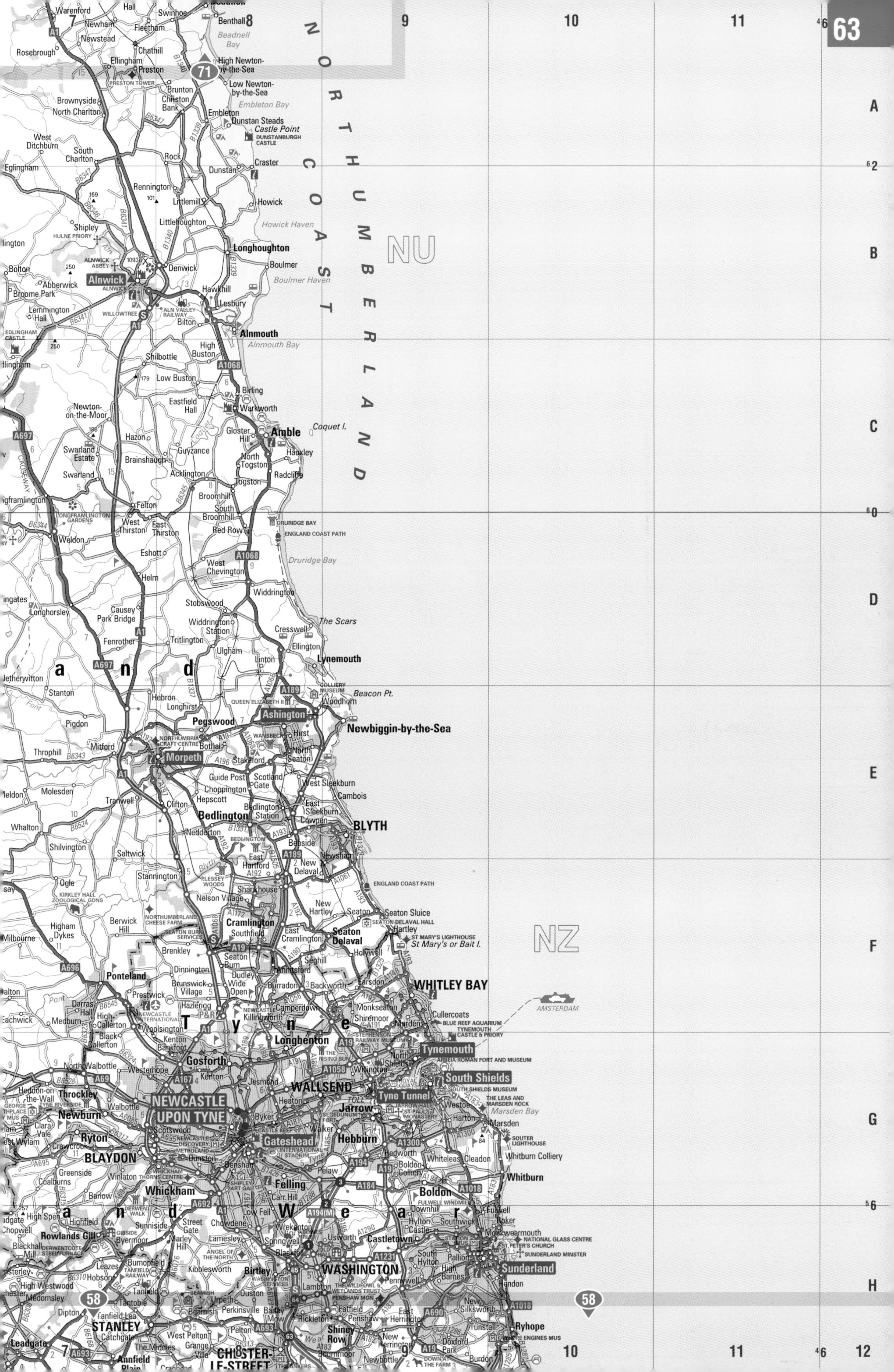
NORTHUMBERLAND COAST
NU
NZ
Warenford
Hall
Swinhoe
Benthall
Beadnell Bay
Newham
Fleetham
Newstead
Chathill
Rosebrough
Ellingham
Preston
PRESTON TOWER
High Newton-by-the-Sea
Low Newton-by-the-Sea
Brunton
Christon Bank
Embleton Bay
Brownyside
North Charlton
Embleton
Dunstan Steads
Castle Point
DUNSTANBURGH CASTLE
West Ditchburn
South Charlton
Rock
Craster
Eglingham
Dunstan
Rennington
Littlemill
Howick
Howick Haven
Shipley
HULNE PRIORY
Littlehoughton
Longhoughton
Boulmer
Boulmer Haven
ALNWICK ABBEY
Denwick
Bolton
Abberwick
Alnwick
ALNWICK
Hawkhill
Broome Park
Lesbury
Lemmington Hall
WILLOWTREE
ALN VALLEY RAILWAY
Bilton
Alnmouth
Alnmouth Bay
EDLINGHAM CASTLE
High Buston
Shilbottle
Low Buston
Birling
Newton-on-the-Moor
Eastfield Hall
Warkworth
Coquet I.
Amble
Gloster Hill
Hauxley
Hazon
Swarland Estate
Guyzance
Brainshaugh
North Togston
Swarland
Acklington
Radcliffe
Togston
Broomhill
South Broomhill
Felton
LONGFRAMLINGTON GARDENS
West Thirston
East Thirston
Red Row
Weldon
DRURIDGE BAY
ENGLAND COAST PATH
Eshott
Druridge Bay
West Chevington
Helm
Widdrington
Longhorsley
Causey Park Bridge
Stobswood
Widdrington Station
The Scars
Cresswell
Fenrother
Tritlington
Ellington
Ulgham
Lynemouth
Linton
COLLIERY MUSEUM
Beacon Pt.
Stanton
Hebron
Longhirst
QUEEN ELIZABETH II
Woodhorn
Ashington
Pigdon
Pegswood
Newbiggin-by-the-Sea
NORTHUMBRIA CRAFT CENTRE
WANSBECK
Hirst
Bothal
Mitford
Throphill
Morpeth
North Seaton
Stakeford
Guide Post
Scotland Gate
West Sleekburn
Choppington
Cambois
Molesden
Tranwell
Clifton
Hepscott
Bedlington Station
East Sleekburn
Bedlington
Cowpen
BLYTH
Whalton
Nedderton
BEDLINGTON
Bebside
Shilvington
Saltwick
East Hartford
Newsham
Stannington
New Delaval
Ogle
PLESSEY WOODS
ENGLAND COAST PATH
KIRKLEY HALL ZOOLOGICAL GDNS
Nelson Village
Shankhouse
New Hartley
Seaton
Seaton Sluice
Berwick Hill
NORTHUMBERLAND CHEESE FARM
Cramlington
Seaton Delaval
DELAVAL HALL
Higham Dykes
SEATON BURN SERVICES
Southfield
East Cramlington
Hartley
ST MARY'S LIGHTHOUSE
St Mary's or Bait I.
Milbourne
Brenkley
Seaton Burn
Seghill
Holywell
Dinnington
Annitsford
WHITLEY BAY
Ponteland
Dudley
Earsdon
Brunswick Village
Wide Open
Burradon
Backworth
Prestwick
AMSTERDAM
Darras Hall
High Callerton
NEWCASTLE INTERNATIONAL
Hazlerigg
Camperdown
Monkseaton
Cullercoats
Medburn
Woolsington
Killingworth
Shiremoor
Marden
BLUE REEF AQUARIUM
TYNEMOUTH CASTLE & PRIORY
Black Callerton
Kenton Bankfoot
Longbenton
STEPHENSON RAILWAY MUSEUM
Tynemouth
North Walbottle
Gosforth
North Shields
ARBEIA ROMAN FORT AND MUSEUM
Westerhope
Kenton
Jesmond
WALLSEND
Willington
South Shields
Heddon-on-the-Wall
Throckley
NEWCASTLE UPON TYNE
Walbottle
Heaton
Tyne Tunnel
SOUTH SHIELDS MUSEUM
Newburn
Byker
Jarrow
Westoe
THE LEAS AND MARSDEN ROCK
Marsden Bay
Clara Vale
Scotswood
SEGEDUNUM
ST PAUL'S MONASTERY
Harton
Marsden
Ryton
Crawcrook
DISCOVERY
Gateshead
Hebburn
SOUTER LIGHTHOUSE
BLAYDON
Dunston
INTERNATIONAL STADIUM
Hedworth
Whiteleas
Cleadon
Whitburn Colliery
Greenside
Winlaton
THORNS CENTRE
Bensham
Pelaw
Boldon Colliery
Whitburn
Coalburns
Whickham
SHIPLEY ART GALLERY
Felling
Boldon
Barlow
Carr Hill
FULWELL WINDMILL
Fulwell
High Spen
Highfield
Sunniside
Street Gate
Chowdene
Low Fell
Wrekenton
Downhill
Hylton Castle
Southwick
Roker
Rowlands Gill
GIBSIDE
Byermoor
Marley Hill
Lamesley
Springwell
Usworth
Castletown
Monkwearmouth
NATIONAL GLASS CENTRE
ST PETER'S CHURCH
SUNDERLAND MINSTER
Blackhall Mill
DERWENTCOTE STEEL FURNACE
ANGEL OF THE NORTH
Blackfell
South Hylton
Pallion
Burnopfield
TANFIELD RAILWAY
Kibblesworth
Birtley
WASHINGTON
Sunderland
Leazes
Hobson
High Barnes
Hendon
High Westwood
Medomsley
Tanfield
Lambton
WASHINGTON SERVICES
THE WILDFOWL & WETLANDS TRUST
PENSHAW MONUMENT
Pennywell
Tantobie
BEAMISH
Urpeth
Ouston
New Silksworth
Dipton
Tanfield Lea
Beamish
Perkinsville
Bailey Mow
Rickleton
Fatfield
Penshaw
East Herrington
Tunstall
Ryhope
STANLEY
Catchgate
West Pelton
Pelton
Shiney Row
New Herrington
Doxford Park
RYHOPE ENGINES MUS
Leadgate
The Middles
Grange Villa
CHESTER-LE-STREET
Bournmoor
Newbottle
DOWN AT THE FARM
Burdon
Annfield Plain
Craghead
58
71
A1
A697
A1068
A189
A19
A69
A167
A184
A194(M)
A1300
A1018
A692
A693
A1231
A690
A183
A193
A192
A696
A695
B1340
B1339
B6347
B6341
B6343
B6524
B1337
A
B
C
D
E
F
G
H
2
0
6
7
8
9
10
11
12

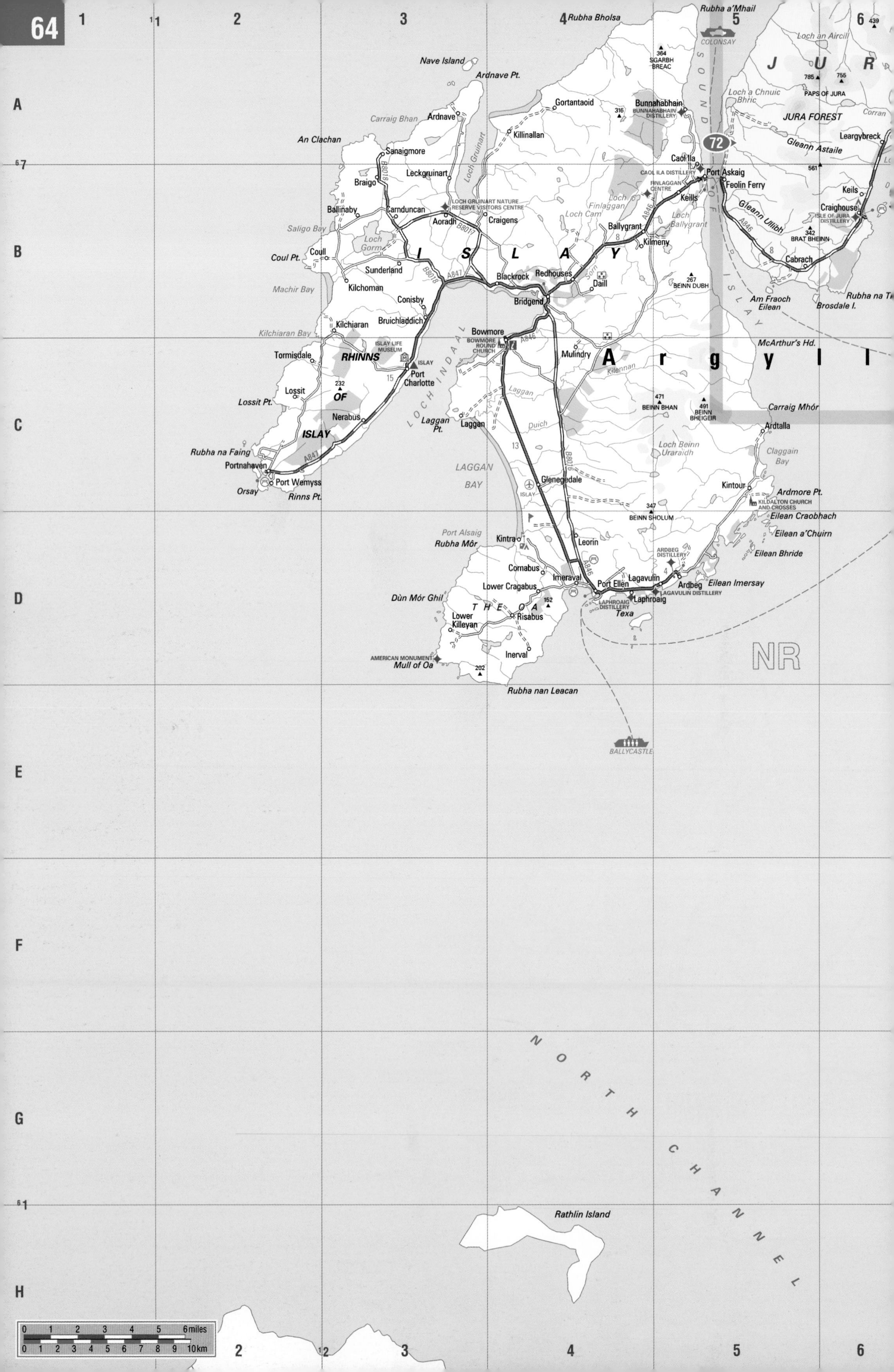

Rubha a'Mhail
Rubha Bholsa
COLONSAY
Loch an Aircil
JURA
PAPS OF JURA
JURA FOREST
Corran
Leargybreck
Gleann Astaile
Loch a Chnuic Bhric
364 SGARBH BREAC
SOUND OF ISLAY
Nave Island
Ardnave Pt.
Ardnave
Carraig Bhan
An Clachan
Gortantaoid
Bunnahabhain
BUNNAHABHAIN DISTILLERY
Killinallan
Loch Gruinart
Sanaigmore
Braigo
Leckgruinart
Caol Ila
CAOL ILA DISTILLERY
Port Askaig
Feolin Ferry
FINLAGGAN CENTRE
Loch Finlaggan
Keills
Craighouse
ISLE OF JURA DISTILLERY
LOCH GRUINART NATURE RESERVE VISITORS CENTRE
Ballinaby
Carnduncan
Aoradh
Craigens
Loch Cam
Ballygrant
Loch Ballygrant
Kilmeny
Gleann Ullibh
342 BRAT BHEINN
Cabrach
Saligo Bay
Loch Gorm
Coull
Coul Pt.
I S L A Y
Sunderland
Blackrock
Redhouses
Daill
267 BEINN DUBH
Kilchoman
Machir Bay
Conisby
Bridgend
Am Fraoch Eilean
Brosdale I.
Rubha na T
Kilchiaran
Kilchiaran Bay
Bruichladdich
Bowmore
BOWMORE ROUND CHURCH
Mulindry
McArthur's Hd.
Tormisdale
RHINNS
ISLAY LIFE MUSEUM
ISLAY
Port Charlotte
LOCH INDAAL
Argyll
Kilennan
Laggan
471 BEINN BHAN
491 BEINN BHEIGEIR
232
Lossit
OF
Lossit Pt.
Carraig Mhór
Nerabus
ISLAY
Laggan Pt.
Duich
Ardtalla
Loch Beinn Uraraidh
Claggain Bay
Rubha na Faing
Portnahaven
Port Wemyss
Orsay
Rinns Pt.
LAGGAN BAY
Glenegedale
Kintour
Ardmore Pt.
KILDALTON CHURCH AND CROSSES
347 BEINN SHOLUM
Eilean Craobhach
Port Alsaig
Rubha Mór
Kintra
Leorin
Eilean a'Chuirn
ARDBEG DISTILLERY
Eilean Bhride
Cornabus
Imeraval
Lagavulin
Ardbeg
Eilean Imersay
Lower Cragabus
Port Ellen
LAGAVULIN DISTILLERY
Dùn Mór Ghil
THE OA
152
Laphroaig
LAPHROAIG DISTILLERY
Texa
Lower Killeyan
Risabus
AMERICAN MONUMENT
Mull of Oa
Inerval
202
Rubha nan Leacan
NR
BALLYCASTLE
NORTH CHANNEL
Rathlin Island
0 1 2 3 4 5 6 miles
0 1 2 3 4 5 6 7 8 9 10 km

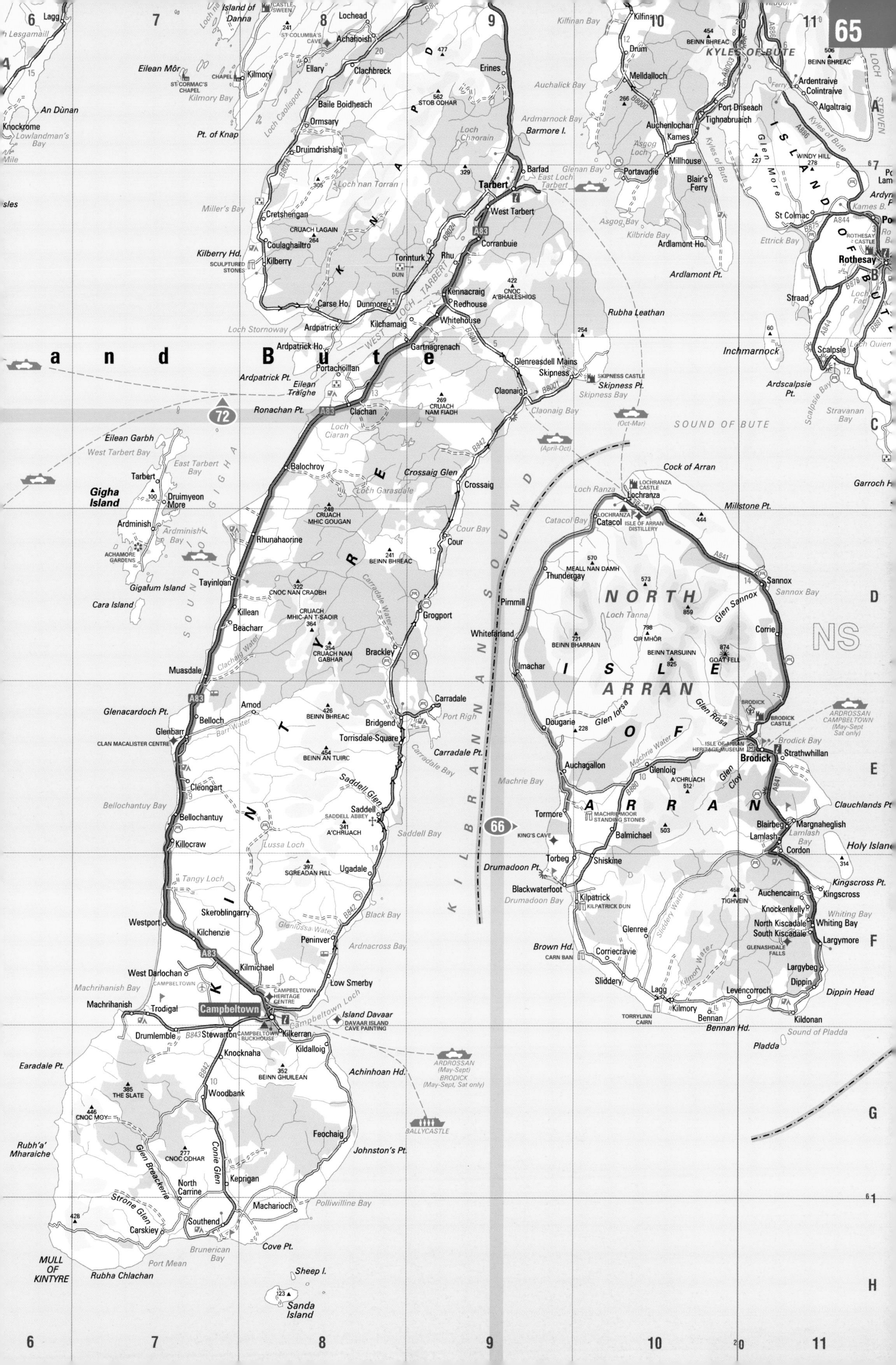
Lagg
Island of Danna
Lochead
Achahoish
St Columba's Cave
Eilean Mòr
St Cormac's Chapel
Kilmory
Kilmory Bay
Ellary
Clachbreck
An Dùnan
Knockrome
Lowlandman's Bay
Pt. of Knap
Loch Caolisport
Baile Boidheach
Ormsary
Stob Odhar
Erines
Druimdrishaig
Loch Chaorain
Loch nan Torran
Barmore I.
Barfad
Tarbert
West Tarbert
Miller's Bay
Cretshengan
Cruach Lagain
Coulaghailtro
Kilberry Hd.
Sculptured Stones
Kilberry
Torinturk
Dun
Rhu
Corranbuie
Kennacraig
Redhouse
Cnoc A'Bhaileshios
Carse Ho.
Dunmore
Kilchamaig
West Loch Tarbert
Whitehouse
Ardpatrick
Loch Stornoway
Ardpatrick Ho.
Gartnagrenach
Portachoillan
Ardpatrick Pt.
Eilean Traighe
and Bute
Glenreasdell Mains
Skipness
Skipness Castle
Skipness Pt.
Skipness Bay
Claonaig
Claonaig Bay
Ronachan Pt.
Clachan
Cruach nam Fiadh
72
Loch Ciaran
Eilean Garbh
West Tarbert Bay
East Tarbert Bay
Balochroy
Crossaig Glen
Crossaig
Tarbert
Gigha Island
Druimyeon More
Loch Garasdale
Cruach Mhic Gougan
Ardminish
Ardminish Bay
Achamore Gardens
Rhunahaorine
Cour Bay
Cour
Beinn Bhreac
Gigalum Island
Tayinloan
Cnoc nan Craobh
Carradale Water
Cara Island
Killean
Cruach Mhic-an t-Saoir
Grogport
Beacharr
Cruach nan Gabhar
Brackley
Clachaig Water
Muasdale
Amod
Carradale
Port Righ
Glenacardoch Pt.
Belloch
Beinn Bhreac
Bridgend
Glenbarr
Barr Water
Clan Macalister Centre
Torrisdale Square
Beinn an Tuirc
Carradale Pt.
Carradale Bay
Cleongart
Saddell Glen
Saddell
Saddell Abbey
A'Chruach
Bellochantuy Bay
Bellochantuy
Saddell Bay
Killocraw
Lussa Loch
Sgreadan Hill
Ugadale
Tangy Loch
Skeroblingarry
Black Bay
Westport
Kilchenzie
Glenlussa Water
Peninver
Ardnacross Bay
West Darlochan
Kilmichael
Low Smerby
Machrihanish Bay
Campbeltown
Campbeltown Heritage Centre
Machrihanish
Trodigal
Campbeltown Loch
Island Davaar
Davaar Island Cave Painting
Drumlemble
Stewarton
Campbeltown Buckhouse
Kilkerran
Knocknaha
Kildalloig
Earadale Pt.
Beinn Ghuilean
Achinhoan Hd.
Ardrossan (May-Sept)
Brodick (May-Sept, Sat only)
The Slate
Woodbank
Cnoc Moy
Ballycastle
Rubh'a' Mharaiche
Feochaig
Cnoc Odhar
Glen Breackerie
Conie Glen
Johnston's Pt.
North Carrine
Kepirigan
Strone Glen
Machariocch
Polliwilline Bay
Carskiey
Southend
Cove Pt.
Brunerican Bay
Mull of Kintyre
Port Mean
Rubha Chlachan
Sheep I.
Sanda Island
Kintyre
Knapdale
Kilfinan Bay
Kilfinan
Drum
Beinn Bhreac
Kyles of Bute
Melldalloch
Auchalick Bay
Ardentraive
Colintraive
Port Driseach
Tighnabruaich
Algaltraig
Ardmarnock Bay
Auchenlochan
Kames
Asgog Loch
Millhouse
Glen More
Windy Hill
Island of Bute
Portavadie
Glenan Bay
East Loch Tarbert
Blair's Ferry
Asgog Bay
St Colmac
Kames B.
Kilbride Bay
Ardlamont Ho.
Ettrick Bay
Rothesay Castle
Rothesay
Ardlamont Pt.
Straad
Rubha Leathan
Inchmarnock
Scalpsie
Loch Quien
Ardscalpsie Pt.
Scalpsie Bay
Stravanan Bay
(Oct-Mar)
(April-Oct)
Sound of Bute
Cock of Arran
Lochranza Castle
Loch Ranza
Lochranza
Millstone Pt.
Catacol Bay
Catacol
Isle of Arran Distillery
Kilbrannan Sound
Meall nan Damh
Thundergay
North
Sannox
Sannox Bay
Pirnmill
Loch Tanna
Glen Sannox
Cir Mhòr
Corrie
Whitefarland
Beinn Bharrain
Beinn Tarsuinn
Goat Fell
Imachar
Isle of Arran
Glen Iorsa
Glen Rosa
Brodick Castle
Ardrossan
Campbeltown (May-Sept Sat only)
Dougarie
Brodick Bay
Isle of Arran Heritage Museum
Strathwhillan
Brodick
Auchagallon
Machrie Water
Glenloig
Glen Cloy
Machrie Bay
A'Chruach
Clauchlands Pt.
Tormore
Machrie Moor Standing Stones
66
King's Cave
Balmichael
Blairbeg
Margnaheglish
Lamlash
Lamlash Bay
Holy Island
Cordon
Torbeg
Shiskine
Drumadoon Pt.
Kingscross Pt.
Blackwaterfoot
Kilpatrick
Kilpatrick Dun
Auchencairn
Kingscross
Drumadoon Bay
Tighvein
Sliddery Water
Knockenkelly
Whiting Bay
North Kiscadale
South Kiscadale
Glenree
Brown Hd.
Carn Ban
Glenashdale Falls
Largymore
Corriecravie
Kilmory Water
Largybeg
Sliddery
Lagg
Levencorroch
Dippin
Dippin Head
Kilmory
Torrylinn Cairn
Bennan
Bennan Hd.
Kildonan
Sound of Pladda
Pladda
NS
A83
B8024
B8001
B842
B843
A841
B880
A844
A886
B875
B878
B881
A8003
B8000
6
7
8
9
10
11
A
B
C
D
E
F
G
H

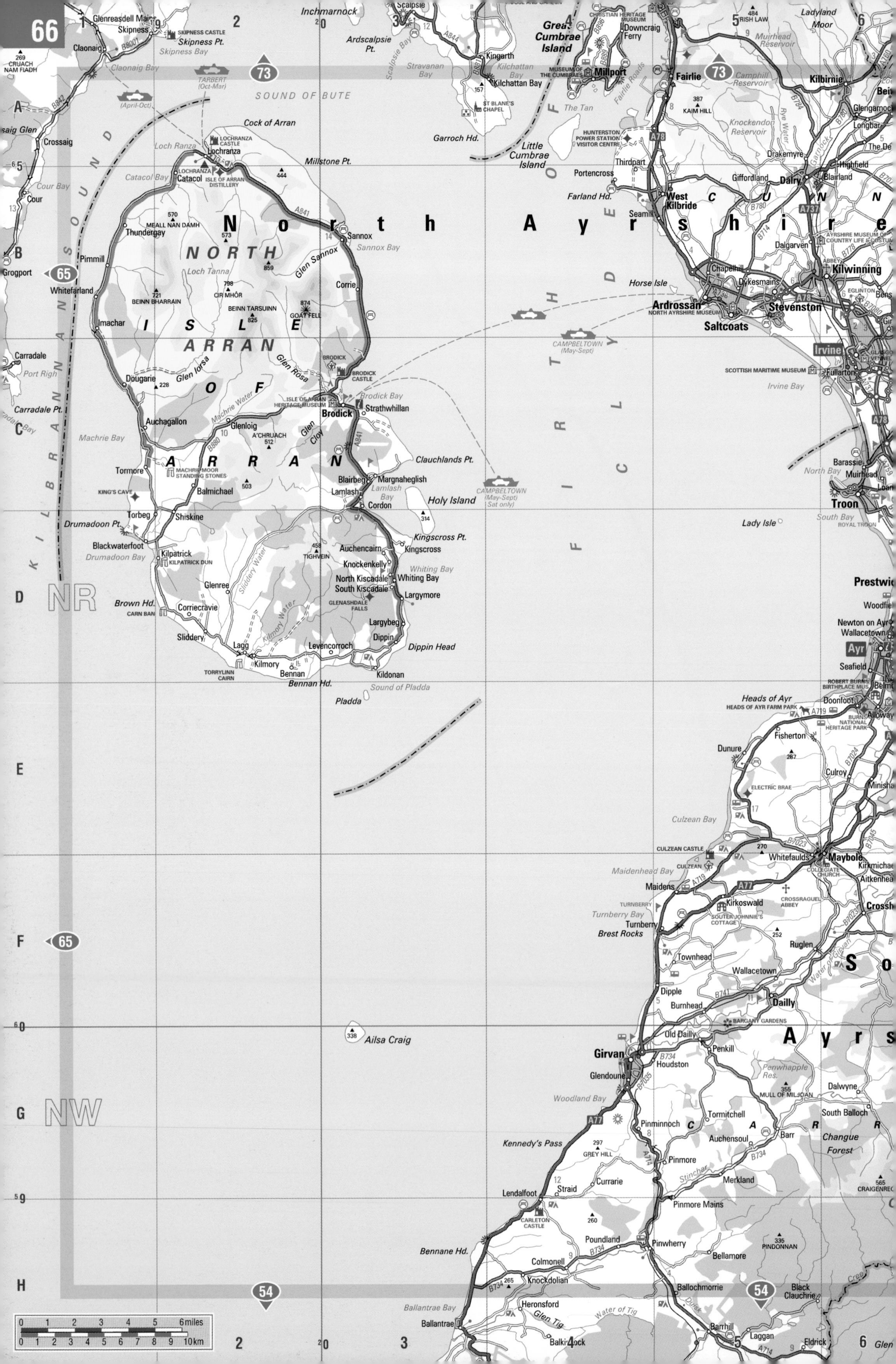
North Ayrshire
ISLE OF ARRAN
NORTH ARRAN
ARRAN
FIRTH OF CLYDE
KILBRANNAN SOUND
SOUND OF BUTE
CUNNINGHAME
CARRICK
South Ayrshire
NR
NW
Glenreasdell Mains
Skipness
Skipness Castle
Skipness Pt.
Skipness Bay
Claonaig
Claonaig Bay
Tarbert (Oct-Mar)
(April-Oct)
Inchmarnock
Ardscalpsie Pt.
Scalpsie Bay
Stravanan Bay
Kingarth
Kilchattan Bay
St Blane's Chapel
Garroch Hd.
Great Cumbrae Island
Christian Heritage Museum
Downcraig Ferry
Millport
Museum of the Cumbraes
Little Cumbrae Island
The Tan
Fairlie Roads
Fairlie
Camphill Reservoir
Kaim Hill
Knockendon Reservoir
Kilbirnie
Glengarnock
Longbar
Drakemyre
Highfield
Blairland
Dalry
Giffordland
Hunterston Power Station Visitor Centre
Thirdpart
Portencross
Farland Hd.
Seamill
West Kilbride
Ayrshire Museum of Country Life & Costume
Dalgarven
Kilwinning
Chapelhill
Dykesmains
Horse Isle
Ardrossan
North Ayrshire Museum
Saltcoats
Stevenston
Eglinton
Irvine
Scottish Maritime Museum
Fullarton
Irvine Bay
Campbeltown (May-Sept)
Campbeltown (May-Sept) Sat only
Barassie
North Bay
Muirhead
Troon
Lady Isle
South Bay
Royal Troon
Prestwick
Newton on Ayr
Wallacetown
Ayr
Seafield
Robert Burns Birthplace Mus.
Doonfoot
Alloway
Heads of Ayr
Heads of Ayr Farm Park
Burns National Heritage Park
Fisherton
Dunure
Culroy
Electric Brae
Culzean Bay
Culzean Castle
Culzean
Whitefaulds
Maybole
Collegiate Church
Kirkmichael
Aitkenhead
Maidenhead Bay
Maidens
Crossraguel Abbey
Kirkoswald
Souter Johnnie's Cottage
Turnberry
Turnberry Bay
Brest Rocks
Ruglen
Townhead
Wallacetown
Water of Girvan
Dipple
Burnhead
Dailly
Old Dailly
Bargany Gardens
Girvan
Houdston
Penkill
Glendoune
Penwhapple Res.
Mull of Miljoan
Dalwyne
Woodland Bay
Pinminnoch
Tormitchell
Auchensoul
Barr
South Balloch
Changue Forest
Kennedy's Pass
Grey Hill
Pinmore
Stinchar
Merkland
Craigenreoch
Lendalfoot
Straid
Currarie
Pinmore Mains
Carleton Castle
Poundland
Pindonnan
Bennane Hd.
Pinwherry
Bellamore
Colmonell
Knockdolian
Ballochmorrie
Black Clauchrie
Ballantrae Bay
Heronsford
Glen Tig
Water of Tig
Ballantrae
Balkissock
Barrhill
Laggan
Eldrick
Duisk
Cock of Arran
Lochranza Castle
Lochranza
Millstone Pt.
Catacol Bay
Catacol
Isle of Arran Distillery
Meall nan Damh
Thundergay
Sannox
Sannox Bay
Glen Sannox
Pimmill
Loch Tanna
Whitefarland
Beinn Bharrain
Cir Mhòr
Corrie
Beinn Tarsuinn
Goat Fell
Imachar
Glen Rosa
Brodick Castle
Brodick
Glen Iorsa
Dougarie
Brodick Bay
Isle of Arran Heritage Museum
Strathwhillan
Machrie Water
Auchagallon
Glenloig
A'Chruach
Glen Cloy
Machrie Bay
Clauchlands Pt.
Tormore
Machrie Moor Standing Stones
Blairbeg
Margnaheglish
Lamlash
Lamlash Bay
Balmichael
Holy Island
King's Cave
Cordon
Torbeg
Shiskine
Drumadoon Pt.
Kingscross Pt.
Blackwaterfoot
Drumadoon Bay
Tighvein
Auchencairn
Kingscross
Kilpatrick
Kilpatrick Dun
Sliddery Water
Knockenkelly
Whiting Bay
Glenree
North Kiscadale
South Kiscadale
Largymore
Brown Hd.
Carn Ban
Corriecravie
Glenashdale Falls
Kilmory Water
Largybeg
Dippin
Sliddery
Dippin Head
Lagg
Levencorroch
Kilmory
Torrylinn Cairn
Bennan
Kildonan
Bennan Hd.
Sound of Pladda
Pladda
Ailsa Craig
Carradale
Port Righ
Carradale Pt.
Crossaig
Cour Bay
Cour
Grogport
Cruach nam Fiadh
A841
A78
A737
A77
A719
A714
B734
B741
B7023
B7024
B842
B8001
B880
0 1 2 3 4 5 6 miles
0 1 2 3 4 5 6 7 8 9 10 km

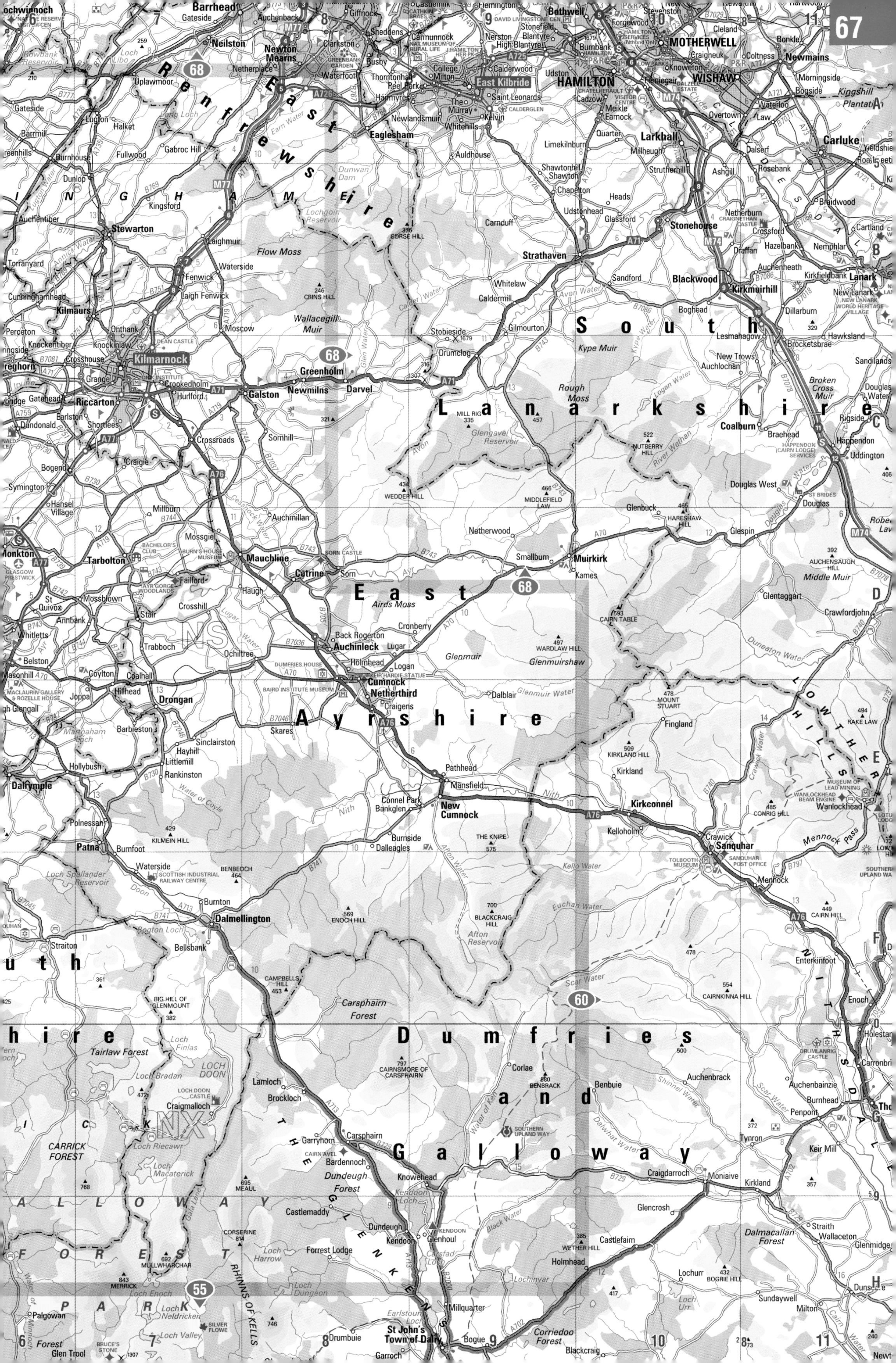
Barrhead
Gateside
Neilston
Auchenback
Giffnock
Newton Mearns
Netherplace
Clarkston
Busby
Sheddens
Carmunnock
Thorntonhall
Peel Park
Waterfoot
College Milton
East Kilbride
Calderwood
Nerston
High Blantyre
Stonefield
Blantyre
Bothwell
Burnbank
HAMILTON
MOTHERWELL
WISHAW
Cleland
Bonkle
Newmains
Coltness
Craigneuk
Knoweton
Ferniegair
Udston
Cadzow
Meikle Earnock
Saint Leonards
The Murray
Kelvin
Whitehills
Newlandsmuir
Eaglesham
Auldhouse
Quarter
Larkhall
Millheugh
Limekilnburn
Shawtonhill
Shawton
Chapelton
Strutherhill
Ashgill
Dalserf
Rosebank
Carluke
Morningside
Bogside
Kingshill
Waterloo
Law
Overtown
Uplawmoor
Gateside
Lugton
Halket
Barrmill
Burnhouse
Fullwood
Gabroc Hill
Dunlop
Kingsford
Stewarton
Auchentiber
Torranyard
Laighmuir
Waterside
Fenwick
Laigh Fenwick
Cunninghamhead
Kilmaurs
Perceton
Knockentiber
Onthank
Knockinlaw
Crosshouse
Kilmarnock
Grange
Crookedholm
Hurlford
Riccarton
Earlston
Shortlees
Gatehead
Dundonald
Moscow
Galston
Newmilns
Greenholm
Darvel
Crossroads
Sornhill
Craigie
Bogend
Symington
Hansel Village
Millburn
Auchmillan
Mossgiel
Mauchline
Catrine
Sorn
Tarbolton
Failford
Monkton
St Quivox
Mossblown
Annbank
Whitletts
Stair
Haugh
Crosshill
Trabboch
Ochiltree
Back Rogerton
Auchinleck
Lugar
Cronberry
Holmhead
Logan
Cumnock
Netherthird
Craigens
Belston
Coylton
Coalhall
Masonhill
Joppa
Hillhead
Drongan
Barbieston
Skares
Sinclairston
Hayhill
Littlemill
Rankinston
Hollybush
Dalrymple
Polnessan
Patna
Burnfoot
Waterside
Burnton
Dalmellington
Bellsbank
Straiton
Pathhead
Mansfield
Connel Park
Bankglen
New Cumnock
Burnside
Dalleagles
Carnduff
Udstonhead
Heads
Glassford
Stonehouse
Strathaven
Whitelaw
Caldermill
Gilmourton
Sandford
Blackwood
Kirkmuirhill
Boghead
Stobieside
Drumclog
Lesmahagow
Brocketsbrae
New Trows
Auchlochan
Coalburn
Braehead
Happendon
Uddington
Douglas West
Douglas
Glenbuck
Glespin
Netherwood
Smallburn
Muirkirk
Kames
Dalblair
Fingland
Kirkland
Kirkconnel
Kelloholm
Crawick
Sanquhar
Mennock
Glentaggart
Crawfordjohn
Wanlockhead
Enterkinfoot
Enoch
Holestane
Carronbridge
Auchenbainzie
Penpont
Burnhead
Tynron
Keir Mill
Kirkland
Moniaive
Craigdarroch
Glencrosh
Auchenbrack
Benbuie
Corlae
Castlefairn
Holmhead
Lochurr
Sundaywell
Milton
Dunscore
Straith
Wallaceton
Glenmidge
Blackcraig
Carsphairn
Garryhorn
Bardennoch
Knowehead
Lamloch
Brockloch
Craigmalloch
Castlemaddy
Dundeugh
Kendoon
Glenhoul
Forrest Lodge
Millquarter
St John's Town of Dalry
Drumbuie
Garroch
Bogue
Palgowan
Glen Trool
Crossford
Hazelbank
Nemphlar
Braidwood
Netherburn
Auchenheath
Kirkfieldbank
Lanark
New Lanark
Dillarburn
Hawksland
Sandilands
Flow Moss
Wallacegill Muir
Kype Muir
Rough Moss
Airds Moss
Glenmuir
Glenmuirshaw
Middle Muir
Broken Cross Muir
Carsphairn Forest
Tairlaw Forest
Carrick Forest
Dundeugh Forest
Dalmacallan Forest
Corriedoo Forest
Renfrewshire
East Renfrewshire
South Lanarkshire
East Ayrshire
Dumfries and Galloway
Lowther Hills
Clydesdale
Nithsdale
The Glenkens
Rhinns of Kells
Galloway Forest Park
CORSE HILL 376
CRINS HILL 246
MILL RIG 335
WEDDER HILL 434
MIDDLEFIELD LAW 466
NUTBERRY HILL 522
HARESHAW HILL 465
CAIRN TABLE 593
WARDLAW HILL 497
AUCHENSAUGH HILL 392
MOUNT STUART 478
KIRKLAND HILL 509
RAKE LAW 494
CONRIG HILL 485
KILMEIN HILL 429
BENBEOCH 464
ENOCH HILL 569
THE KNIPE 575
BLACKCRAIG HILL 700
CAIRN HILL 449
CAIRNKINNA HILL 554
CAMPBELLS HILL 453
BIG HILL OF GLENMOUNT 382
CAIRNSMORE OF CARSPHAIRN 797
BENBRACK 580
MEAUL 695
CORSERINE 814
MULLWHARCHAR 692
MERRICK 843
WETHER HILL 385
BOGRIE HILL 432
Loch Doon
Loch Bradan
Loch Riecawr
Loch Finlas
Afton Reservoir
Glengavel Reservoir
Lochgoin Reservoir
Dunwan Dam
Loch Spallander Reservoir
Kendoon Loch
Carsfad Loch
Earlstoun Loch
Lochinvar
Loch Dungeon
Loch Harrow
Loch Enoch
Loch Neldricken
Loch Valley
Loch Macaterick
Loch Urr
Water of Coyle
Nith
Afton Water
Kello Water
Euchan Water
Scar Water
Shinnel Water
Dalwhat Water
Black Water
Water of Ken
Duneaton Water
Douglas Water
Glenmuir Water
Lugar Water
Cessnock Water
Avon Water
Calder Water
Glen Water
Logan Water
Kype Water
River Nethan
Mennock Pass
SCOTTISH INDUSTRIAL RAILWAY CENTRE
DUMFRIES HOUSE
BAIRD INSTITUTE MUSEUM
KEIR HARDIE STATUE
BURNS HOUSE MUSEUM
BACHELOR'S CLUB
AYR GORGE WOODLANDS
SORN CASTLE
DEAN CASTLE
DICK INSTITUTE
TOLBOOTH MUSEUM
SANQUHAR POST OFFICE
MUSEUM OF LEAD MINING
WANLOCKHEAD BEAM ENGINE
DRUMLANRIG CASTLE
LOCH DOON CASTLE
SOUTHERN UPLAND WAY
CAIRN AVEL
KENDOON
CHATELHERAULT
CALDERGLEN
NEW LANARK WORLD HERITAGE VILLAGE
CRAIGNETHAN CASTLE
HAPPENDON (CAIRN LODGE) SERVICES
ST BRIDES
GREENBANK GARDEN
NAT. MUSEUM OF RURAL LIFE
DAVID LIVINGSTONE CEN
HAMILTON SERVICES
SILVER FLOWE
BRUCE'S STONE
M77
M74
A71
A76
A70
A77
A713
A726
A725
A723
A72
A73
A702
A719
A735
A736
B743
B741
B729
B7046
B7036
B7078
68
60
55
NS
NX

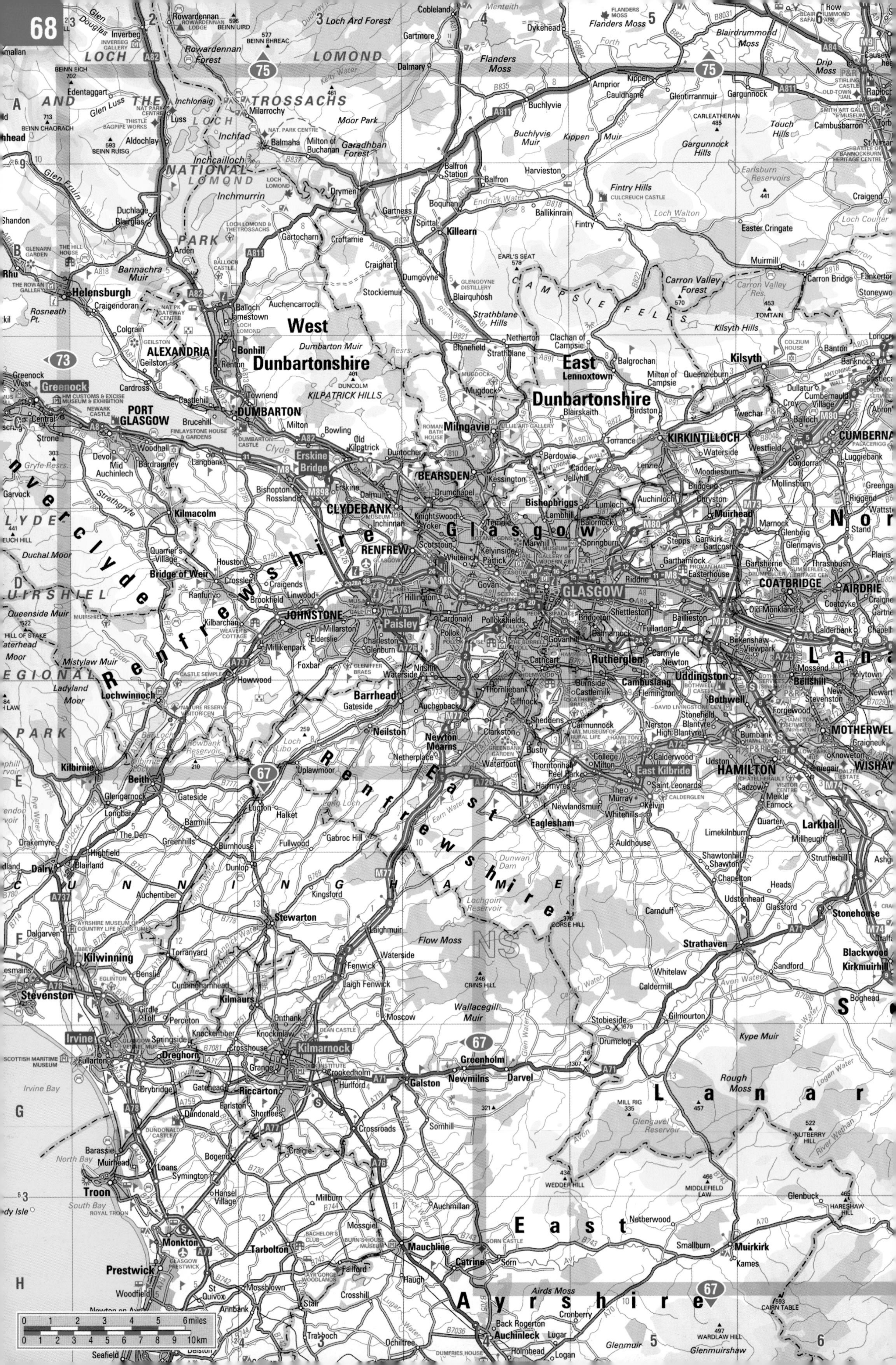
LOCH LOMOND AND THE TROSSACHS NATIONAL PARK
West Dunbartonshire
East Dunbartonshire
Inverclyde
Renfrewshire
East Renfrewshire
Glasgow
NORTH AYRSHIRE
CUNNINGHAME
EAST AYRSHIRE
LANARK
CLYDE MUIRSHIEL REGIONAL PARK
Lanar
East
Ayrshire
Nor
Lana
S
NS
Glen Douglas
Inverbeg
Rowardennan
Rowardennan Lodge
Rowardennan Forest
Beinn Uird
Beinn Bhreac
Loch Ard Forest
Cobleland
Menteith
Gartmore
Dalmary
Flanders Moss
Dykehead
Forth
Blairdrummond Moss
Blair Drummond Safari Park
Drip Moss
Causewayhead
Kippen
Arnprior
Cauldhame
Glentirranmuir
Gargunnock
Stirling Castle
Raploch
Cambusbarron
Touch Hills
Carleatheran
Gargunnock Hills
St Ninians
Bannockburn Heritage Centre
Earlsburn Reservoirs
Craigend
Loch Coulter
Easter Cringate
Loch Walton
Fintry Hills
Culcreuch Castle
Fintry
Ballikinrain
Harviestoun
Buchlyvie
Buchlyvie Muir
Muir
Balfron
Balfron Station
Endrick Water
Boquhan
Killearn
Spittal
Gartness
Drymen
Croftamie
Gartocharn
Milarrochy
Balmaha
Milton of Buchanan
Garadhban Forest
Moor Park
Inchcailloch
Inchmurrin
Inchfad
Inchlonaig
Luss
Glen Luss
Edentaggart
Beinn Eich
Beinn Chaorach
Beinn Ruisg
Aldochlay
Glen Fruin
Duchlage
Blairglas
Arden
Bannachra Muir
Glenarn Garden
The Hill House
Rhu
Helensburgh
Craigendoran
Rosneath Pt.
Balloch
Balloch Castle
Jamestown
Auchencarroch
Bonhill
Renton
Alexandria
Geilston
Colgrain
Cardross
Dumbarton
Dumbarton Castle
Dumbarton Muir
Duncolm
Kilpatrick Hills
Townend
Castlehill
Brucehill
Milton
Bowling
Old Kilpatrick
Duntocher
Erskine Bridge
Erskine
Greenock
Port Glasgow
Newark Castle
Finlaystone House & Gardens
Langbank
Woodhall
Bardrainney
Devol
Mid Auchinlech
Strone
Gryfe Resrs.
Strathgryfe
Garvock
Kilmacolm
Duchal Moor
Quarrier's Village
Bridge of Weir
Houston
Crosslee
Ranfurly
Craigends
Brookfield
Linwood
Kilbarchan
Weaver's Cottage
Johnstone
Millarston
Elderslie
Paisley
Milliken Park
Howwood
Castle Semple
Lochwinnoch
Ladyland Moor
Mistylaw Muir
Hill of Stake
Queenside Muir
Muirshiel
Kilbirnie
Beith
Glengarnock
Longbar
Gateside
Barrmill
The Den
Drakemyre
Highfield
Blairland
Dalry
Auchentiber
Greenhills
Burnhouse
Dunlop
Lugton
Halket
Uplawmoor
Neilston
Barrhead
Gateside
Foxbar
Glenburn
Charleston
Gleniffer Braes
Waterside
Nitshill
Auchenback
Newton Mearns
Netherplace
Clarkston
Busby
Thorntonhall
Waterfoot
Eaglesham
Peel Park
Hairmyres
Newlandsmuir
East Kilbride
College Milton
Calderwood
Saint Leonards
The Murray
Whitehills
Kelvin
Calderglen
Auldhouse
Dunwan Dam
Lochgoin Reservoir
Corse Hill
Flow Moss
Crins Hill
Wallacegill Muir
Gabroc Hill
Fullwood
Kingsford
Stewarton
Laighmuir
Waterside
Fenwick
Laigh Fenwick
Moscow
Onthank
Knockinlaw
Kilmaurs
Cunninghamhead
Torranyard
Bensley
Kilwinning
Dalgarven
Stevenston
Girdle Toll
Perceton
Knockentiber
Crosshouse
Springside
Dreghorn
Irvine
Scottish Maritime Museum
Fullarton
Irvine Bay
Kilmarnock
Dean Castle
Grange
Crookedholm
Hurlford
Galston
Newmilns
Greenholm
Darvel
Riccarton
Gatehead
Drybridge
Earlston
Shortlees
Dundonald
Dundonald Castle
Crossroads
Craigie
Sornhill
Barassie
North Bay
Muirhead
Loans
Symington
Bogend
Troon
South Bay
Royal Troon
Hansel Village
Millburn
Auchmillan
Mossgiel
Mauchline
Burns House Museum
Tarbolton
Bachelor's Club
Failford
Sorn
Sorn Castle
Catrine
Haugh
Monkton
Prestwick
Glasgow Prestwick
Woodfield
St Quivox
Mossblown
Stair
Annbank
Crosshill
Trabboch
Ochiltree
Auchinleck
Back Rogerton
Cronberry
Lugar
Logan
Holmhead
Dumfries House
Airds Moss
Glenmuir
Wardlaw Hill
Glenmuirshaw
Cairn Table
Muirkirk
Kames
Smallburn
Netherwood
Middlefield Law
Wedder Hill
Glengavel Reservoir
Mill Rig
Rough Moss
Kype Muir
Drumclog
Stobieside
Gilmourton
Caldermill
Whitelaw
Avon Water
Strathaven
Sandford
Boghead
Glenbuck
Hareshaw Hill
Nutberry Hill
River Wellan
Blackwood
Kirkmuirhill
Stonehouse
Glassford
Udstonhead
Heads
Carnduff
Chapelton
Shawtonhill
Shawton
Limekilnburn
Quarter
Larkhall
Millheugh
Strutherhill
Ashgill
Meikle Earnock
Cadzow
Hamilton
Chatelherault
Udston
Burnbank
Bothwell
Bothwell Castle
Uddingston
Stonefield
Blantyre
High Blantyre
Nerston
David Livingstone Centre
Calderbank
Holytown
Bellshill
Mossend
New Stevenston
Newarthill
Forgewood
Motherwell
Craigneuk
Knowetop
Wishaw
Ferniegair
Coatbridge
Airdrie
Coatdyke
Gartsherrie
Thrashbush
Glenmavis
Glenboig
Marnock
Gartcosh
Garnkirk
Stepps
Muirhead
Chryston
Bridgend
Moodiesburn
Mollinsburn
Riggend
Greengairs
Stand
Plains
Easterhouse
Garthamlock
Provan Hall
Drumpellier
Old Monkland
Baillieston
Birkenshaw
Viewpark
Carmyle
Newton
Fullarton
Shettleston
Riddrie
Cambuslang
Flemington
Rutherglen
Bridgeton
Dalmarnock
Castlemilk
Burnside
Cathkin Braes
Carmunnock
Cathcart
Thornliebank
Giffnock
Sheddens
Govanhill
Pollokshields
Pollok
Cardonald
Hillington
Crookston
Govan
Partick
Kelvinside
Maryhill
Whiteinch
Scotstoun
Yoker
Knightswood
Drumchapel
Bearsden
Milngavie
Kessington
Bardowie
Cadder
Jellyhill
Bishopbriggs
Lambhill
Balornock
Springburn
Lumloch
Auchinloch
Lenzie
Kirkintilloch
Waterside
Torrance
Blairskaith
Birdston
Twechar
Westfield
Condorrat
Luggiebank
Cumbernauld
Cumbernauld Village
Balloch
Dullatur
Croy
Kilsyth
Queenzieburn
Banknock
Banton
Colzium House
Kilsyth Hills
Tomtain
Carron Valley Forest
Carron Valley Res.
Carron Bridge
Fankerton
Stoneywood
Muirmill
Milton of Campsie
Lennoxtown
Balgrochan
Clachan of Campsie
Campsie Fells
Earl's Seat
Strathblane
Strathblane Hills
Netherton
Blanefield
Mugdock
Mugdock Country Park
Glengoyne Distillery
Blairquhosh
Dumgoyne
Craighat
Stockiemuir
Clydebank
Dalmuir
Inchinnan
Renfrew
Bishopton
Rossland
Glasgow Airport
Glasgow Botanic Gdns
Gallery of Modern Art
Hunterian Art Gallery
Glasgow Science Centre
People's Palace
Burrell Collection
Pollok House
Hampden Park
National Museum of Rural Life
Hamilton Services
Bothwell Services
Summerlee Heritage Centre
Roman Bath House
Lillie Art Gallery
Antonine Wall
HM Customs & Excise Museum & Exhibition
Ayrshire Museum of Country Life & Costume
Eglinton
Dick Institute
Nature Reserve Visitor Centre
Rowbank Reservoir
Barr Loch
Long Loch
Loch Libo
Earn Water
Blane Water
Annick Water
Glen Water
Logan Water
Kype Water
Cessnock Water
Lugar Water
Calder Water
Rye Water
River Avon
Ayr
Clyde
M8
M9
M73
M74
M77
M80
M898
A82
A84
A811
A81
A809
A8
A726
A725
A736
A737
A760
A761
A71
A73
A76
A77
A78
A70
A719
A723
A726
B8031
B822
B835
B837
B818
B802
B7081
B7086
B743
B744
B751
B769
B778
B7036
75
73
67
0 1 2 3 4 5 6 miles
0 1 2 3 4 5 6 7 8 9 10 km

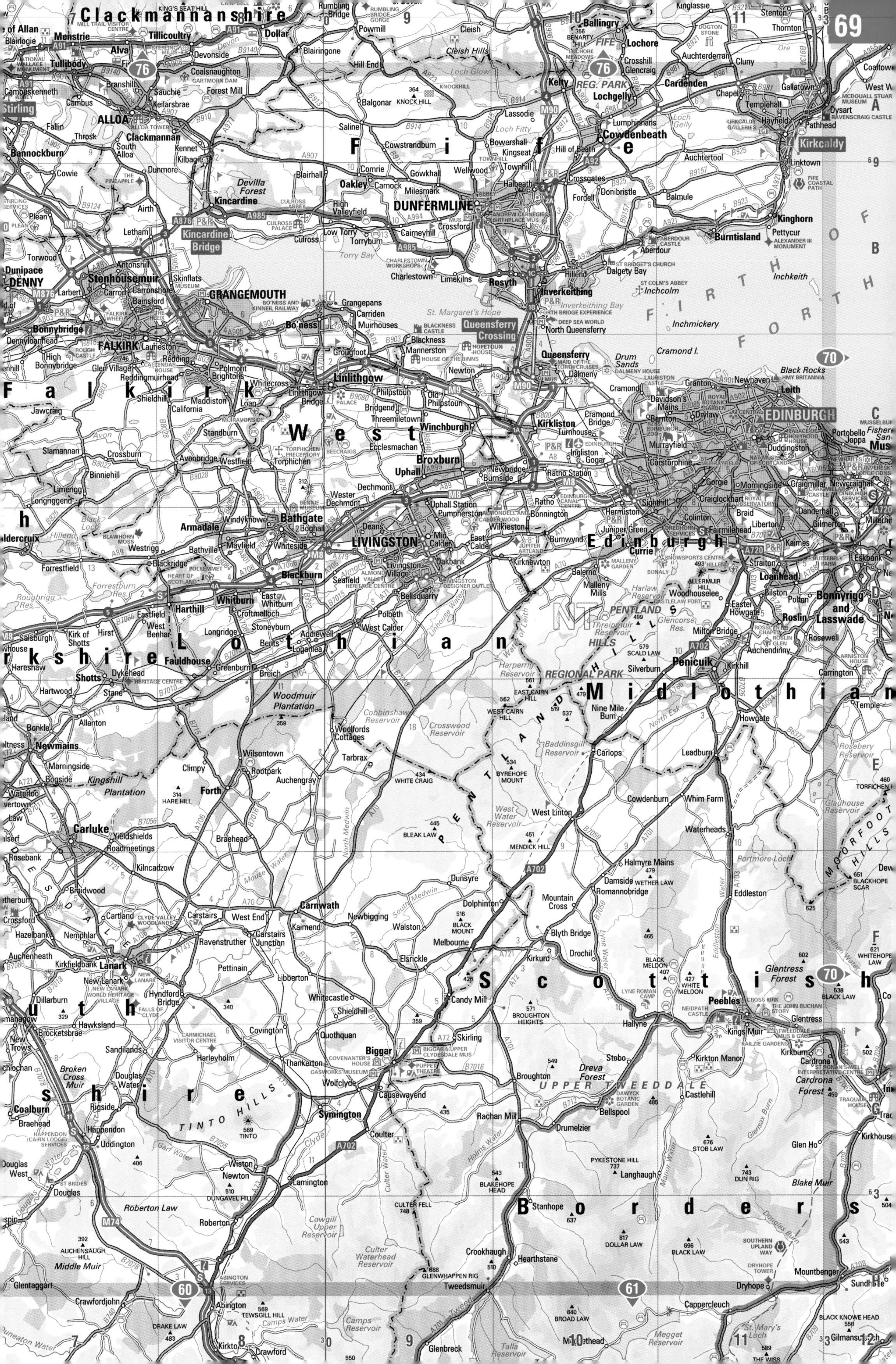

Clackmannanshire
Menstrie
Alva
Tillicoultry
Dollar
Tullibody
Cambuskenneth
Stirling
Alloa
Clackmannan
Bannockburn
Kincardine
Kincardine Bridge
Airth
Dunipace
Denny
Stenhousemuir
Larbert
Grangemouth
Bonnybridge
Falkirk
Polmont
Bo'ness
Linlithgow
Falkirk
West Lothian
Armadale
Bathgate
Livingston
Whitburn
Harthill
Fauldhouse
Shotts
Broxburn
Uphall
Winchburgh
Kirkliston
Queensferry
Queensferry Crossing
North Queensferry
Inverkeithing
Rosyth
Dunfermline
Fife
Kelty
Lochgelly
Cowdenbeath
Cardenden
Kirkcaldy
Kinghorn
Burntisland
Aberdour
Dalgety Bay
Firth of Forth
Inchkeith
Inchcolm
Inchmickery
Cramond I.
Leith
Edinburgh
Portobello
Musselburgh
Dalkeith
Loanhead
Bonnyrigg and Lasswade
Roslin
Penicuik
Pentland Hills Regional Park
Midlothian
Currie
Balerno
West Calder
Carlops
West Linton
Leadburn
Eddleston
Peebles
Innerleithen
Carluke
Lanark
Forth
Carnwath
Carstairs
Biggar
Tinto Hills
Upper Tweeddale
Scottish Borders
Lanarkshire
Douglas
Abington
Tweedsmuir
Crawford
Broughton
Dreva Forest
Glentress Forest
Cardrona Forest
Moorfoot Hills
Culter Fell
Talla Reservoir
Megget Reservoir
Cappercleuch
Mountbenger

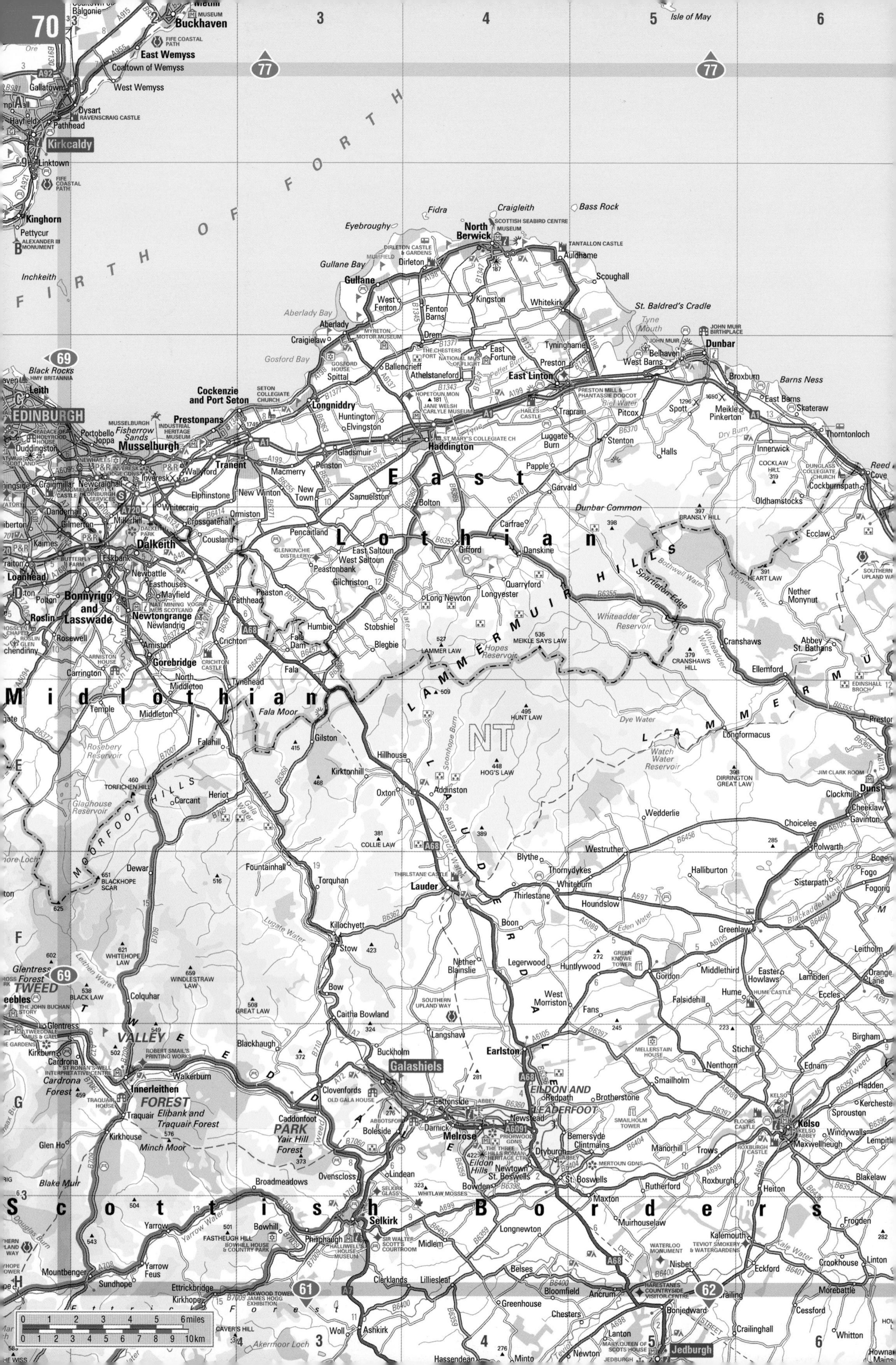

3
4
5
6
77
77
69
69
61
62
Isle of May
Buckhaven
East Wemyss
Coaltown of Wemyss
West Wemyss
FIFE COASTAL PATH
Gallatown
Dysart
RAVENSCRAIG CASTLE
Pathhead
Hayfield
Kirkcaldy
Linktown
Kinghorn
Pettycur
ALEXANDER III MONUMENT
Inchkeith
FIRTH OF FORTH
Fidra
Craigleith
Bass Rock
Eyebroughy
North Berwick
SCOTTISH SEABIRD CENTRE
TANTALLON CASTLE
Auldhame
DIRLETON CASTLE & GARDENS
Dirleton
Gullane Bay
Gullane
Scoughall
West Fenton
Fenton Barns
Kingston
Whitekirk
St. Baldred's Cradle
Aberlady Bay
Aberlady
Craigielaw
MYRETON MOTOR MUSEUM
Drem
Tyne Mouth
JOHN MUIR BIRTHPLACE
Dunbar
Gosford Bay
THE CHESTERS FORT
NATIONAL MUS OF FLIGHT
East Fortune
Tyninghame
Belhaven
West Barns
GOSFORD HOUSE
Ballencrieff
Athelstaneford
Spittal
Preston
East Linton
Broxburn
Barns Ness
Black Rocks
HMY BRITANNIA
Leith
EDINBURGH
Cockenzie and Port Seton
SETON COLLEGIATE CHURCH
Longniddry
HOPETOUN MON
JANE WELSH CARLYLE MUSEUM
PRESTON MILL & PHANTASSIE DOOCOT
HAILES CASTLE
Traprain
Pitcox
Spott
Meikle Pinkerton
East Barns
Skateraw
Prestonpans
Huntington
Elvington
Haddington
ST. MARY'S COLLEGIATE CH
Luggate Burn
Stenton
Thorntonloch
Portobello
Joppa
Musselburgh
Fisherrow Sands
Duddingston
Gladsmuir
Penston
Halls
Innerwick
COCKLAW HILL
DUNGLASS COLLEGIATE CHURCH
Reed Cove
Cockburnspath
Craigmillar
Newcraighall
Inveresk
Wallyford
Tranent
Macmerry
Papple
Garvald
Oldhamstocks
Danderhall
Elphinstone
New Winton
New Town
Samuelston
East Lothian
Bolton
Dunbar Common
BRANSLY HILL
Gilmerton
Millerhill
Whitecraig
Ormiston
Crossgatehall
Carfrae
Ecclaw
Kaimes
Dalkeith
Cousland
Pencaitland
GLENKINCHIE DISTILLERY
East Saltoun
West Saltoun
Gifford
Danskine
Eskbank
Peastonbank
Loanhead
Newbattle
Easthouses
Mayfield
Gilchriston
Quarryford
HEART LAW
SOUTHERN UPLAND WAY
Bonnyrigg and Lasswade
Newtongrange
Newlandrig
Pathhead
Peaston
Long Newton
Longyester
LAMMERMUIR HILLS
Spartleton Edge
Bothwell Water
Nether Monynut
Polton
Roslin
Rosewell
Arniston
Crichton
Humbie
Fala Dam
Stobshiel
Blegbie
Whiteadder Reservoir
Cranshaws
Abbey St. Bathans
CRICHTON CASTLE
LAMMER LAW
MEIKLE SAYS LAW
Hopes Reservoir
CRANSHAWS HILL
Carrington
Gorebridge
North Middleton
Tynehead
Fala
Ellemford
EDINSHALL BROCH
Midlothian
Temple
Middleton
Fala Moor
HUNT LAW
Dye Water
Preston
Longformacus
Gilston
Hillhouse
NT
Watch Water Reservoir
Rosebery Reservoir
Falahill
Kirktonhill
HOG'S LAW
DIRRINGTON GREAT LAW
JIM CLARK ROOM
TORFICHEN HILL
Carcant
Heriot
Oxton
Addinston
Clockmill
Duns
MOORFOOT HILLS
Gladhouse Reservoir
Wedderlie
Cheeklaw
Choicelee
Gavinton
COLLIE LAW
Westruther
Polwarth
Dewar
Fountainhall
Blythe
Thornydykes
Halliburton
Bogen
BLACKHOPE SCAR
Torquhan
THIRLSTANE CASTLE
Lauder
Whiteburn
Thirlestane
Houndslow
Sisterpath
Fogo
Fogorig
Killochyett
Boon
Blackadder Water
Eden Water
Greenlaw
Stow
WHITEHOPE LAW
Nether Blainslie
Legerwood
Huntlywood
GREEN KNOWE TOWER
Gordon
Middlethird
Leitholm
Glentress Forest
TWEED
WINDLESTRAW LAW
BLACK LAW
Easter Howlaws
Lambden
Orange Lane
Peebles
THE JOHN BUCHAN STORY
Colquhar
Bow
SOUTHERN UPLAND WAY
West Morriston
Hume
HUME CASTLE
Eccles
GREAT LAW
Falsidehill
Glentress
TWEEDDALE MUS & GALL
Caitha Bowland
Fans
Kirkburn
VALLEY
Blackhaugh
Langshaw
MELLERSTAIN HOUSE
Stichill
Birgham
Cardrona
ROBERT SMAIL'S PRINTING WORKS
Buckholm
Earlston
Nenthorn
Ednam
ST RONAN'S WELL INTERPRETATIVE CENTRE
Walkerburn
Galashiels
Smailholm
Hadden
Cardrona Forest
Innerleithen
Clovenfords
OLD GALA HOUSE
EILDON AND LEADERFOOT
Redpath
Brotherstone
Kerchester
TRAQUAIR HOUSE
FOREST
Traquair
Elibank and Traquair Forest
Caddonfoot
ABBOTSFORD
Gattonside
ABBEY
Newstead
SMAILHOLM TOWER
FLOORS CASTLE
Kelso
KELSO ABBEY
Sprouston
Kirkhouse
PARK
Yair Hill Forest
Boleside
Darnick
Melrose
PRIORWOOD GDNS
THE THREE HILLS ROMAN HERITAGE CTR
Bemersyde
Clintmains
Dryburgh
Windywalls
Maxwellheugh
Glen Ho
Minch Moor
Eildon Hills
Newtown St. Boswells
MERTOUN GDNS
Manorhill
Trows
ROXBURGH CASTLE
Lempitla
Blake Muir
Broadmeadows
Ovenscloss
Lindean
SELKIRK GLASS
WHITLAW MOSSES
Bowden
St. Boswells
Rutherford
Roxburgh
Heiton
Blakelaw
Scottish Borders
Maxton
Muirhouselaw
Selkirk
Yarrow
Yarrow Water
FASTHEUGH HILL
BOWHILL HOUSE & COUNTRY PARK
Bowhill
Philiphaugh
HALLIWELL'S HOUSE MUSEUM
SIR WALTER SCOTT'S COURTROOM
Midlem
Longnewton
Frogden
Kalemouth
TEVIOT SMOKERY & WATERGARDENS
WATERLOO MONUMENT
Nisbet
Kale Water
Crookhouse
Linton
Mountbenger
Yarrow Feus
Sundhope
Douglas Burn
Ettrickbridge
Kirkhope
AIKWOOD TOWER JAMES HOGG EXHIBITION
Clerklands
Lilliesleaf
Belses
Bloomfield
Ancrum
HARESTANES COUNTRYSIDE VISITOR CENTRE
Eckford
Morebattle
Greenhouse
Chesters
Bonjedward
Cessford
Crailinghall
Ettrick Forest
CAVER'S HILL
Akermoor Loch
Woll
Ashkirk
Hassendean
Minto
Newton
Lanton
MARY QUEEN OF SCOTS HOUSE
JEDBURGH
Jedburgh
Whitton
Hownam Mains
0 1 2 3 4 5 6 miles
0 1 2 3 4 5 6 7 8 9 10 km

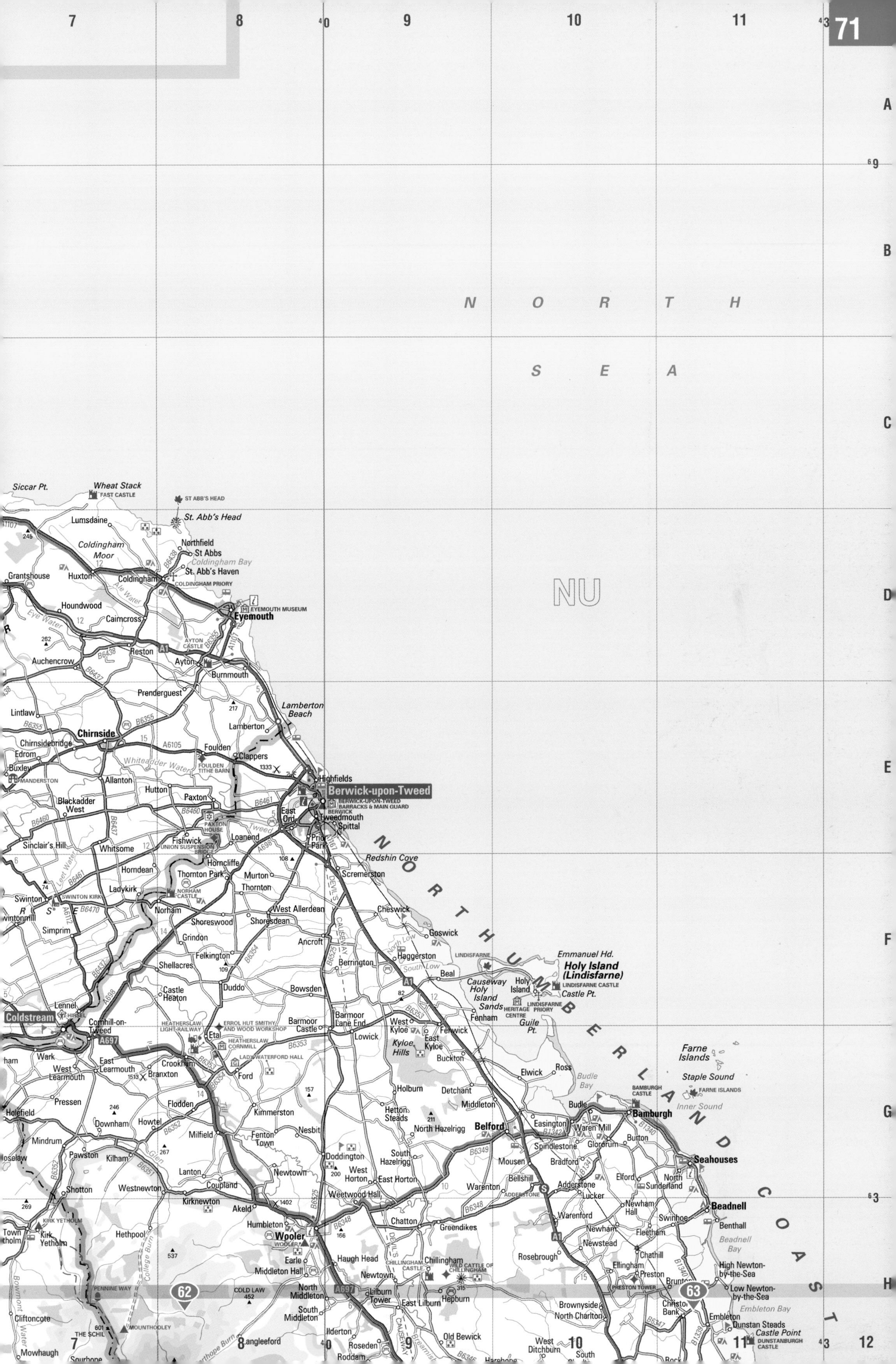
NORTH SEA
NU
NORTHUMBERLAND COAST
Siccar Pt.
Wheat Stack
FAST CASTLE
ST ABB'S HEAD
St. Abb's Head
Lumsdaine
Coldingham Moor
Northfield
St Abbs
Coldingham Bay
St. Abb's Haven
Grantshouse
Huxton
Coldingham
COLDINGHAM PRIORY
Ale Water
Houndwood
Eye Water
Cairncross
EYEMOUTH MUSEUM
Eyemouth
AYTON CASTLE
Reston
Auchencrow
Ayton
Burnmouth
Prenderguest
Lamberton Beach
Lamberton
Linthaw
Chirnside
Chirnsidebridge
Edrom
Foulden
Clappers
Whiteadder Water
FOULDEN TITHE BARN
Buxley
MANDERSTON
Allanton
Highfields
Berwick-upon-Tweed
BERWICK-UPON-TWEED BARRACKS & MAIN GUARD
Hutton
Paxton
Blackadder West
East Ord
Tweedmouth
Spittal
PAXTON HOUSE
Tweed
Sinclair's Hill
Whitsome
Fishwick
UNION SUSPENSION BRIDGE
Loanend
Prior Park
Redshin Cove
Horndean
Horncliffe
Thornton Park
Murton
Scremerston
Ladykirk
NORHAM CASTLE
Thornton
Swinton
SWINTON KIRK
Norham
West Allerdean
Cheswick
Simprim
Shoreswood
Shoresdean
Goswick
Grindon
Ancroft
Felkington
Haggerston
LINDISFARNE
Emmanuel Hd.
Holy Island (Lindisfarne)
Berrington
Beal
Shellacres
Castle Heaton
Duddo
Bowsden
Causeway
Holy Island Sands
Holy Island
LINDISFARNE CASTLE
Castle Pt.
LINDISFARNE PRIORY
HERITAGE CENTRE
Fenham
Guile Pt.
Lennel
Coldstream
HIRSEL
Cornhill-on-Tweed
HEATHERSLAW LIGHT RAILWAY
ERROL HUT SMITHY AND WOOD WORKSHOP
Etal
HEATHERSLAW CORNMILL
Barmoor Castle
Barmoor Lane End
Lowick
West Kyloe
East Kyloe
Kyloe Hills
Fenwick
Buckton
Farne Islands
Wark
West Learmouth
East Learmouth
LADY WATERFORD HALL
Crookham
Branxton
Ford
Elwick
Ross
Budle Bay
Staple Sound
FARNE ISLANDS
BAMBURGH CASTLE
Inner Sound
Pressen
Holburn
Detchant
Middleton
Budle
Bamburgh
Holefield
Downham
Flodden
Kimmerston
Hetton Steads
North Hazelrigg
Belford
Easington
Waren Mill
Mindrum
Howtel
Milfield
Fenton Town
Nesbit
Spindlestone
Glororum
Burton
Seahouses
Pawston
Kilham
Glen
Doddington
South Hazelrigg
Mousen
Bradford
Elford
North Sunderland
Lanton
Coupland
Newtown
West Horton
East Horton
Warenton
Bellshill
Adderstone
ADDERSTONE
Lucker
Shotton
Westnewton
Kirknewton
Akeld
Wetwood Hall
Newham Hall
Swinhoe
Beadnell
KIRK YETHOLM
Kirk Yetholm
Town Yetholm
Hethpool
Humbleton
Wooler
WOOLER
Chatton
Greendikes
Warenford
Benthall
Newham
Fleetham
Beadnell Bay
Newstead
College Burn
Earle
Haugh Head
CHILLINGHAM CASTLE
Chillingham
WILD CATTLE OF CHILLINGHAM
Rosebrough
Chathill
Middleton Hall
Newtown
Ellingham
Preston
High Newton-by-the-Sea
Bowmont Water
PENNINE WAY
COLD LAW
North Middleton
Lilburn Tower
Hepburn
PRESTON TOWER
Brunton
Low Newton-by-the-Sea
East Lilburn
Brownyside
North Charlton
Christon Bank
Embleton Bay
Cliftoncote
South Middleton
Embleton
Dunstan Steads
Castle Point
THE SCHIL
MOUNTHOOLEY
Langleeford
Ilderton
Roseden
Old Bewick
West Ditchburn
South
DUNSTANBURGH CASTLE
Mowhaugh
Sourhope
Roddam
Harehope
DEVIL'S CAUSEWAY
A1
A697
A698
A6105
A1107
B6438
B6437
B6355
B6460
B6461
B6470
B6437
B6354
B6353
B6352
B6351
B6525
B6348
B6349
B1342
B1341
B1340
B6347
B1339
62
63
7
8
9
10
11
12
A
B
C
D
E
F
G
H

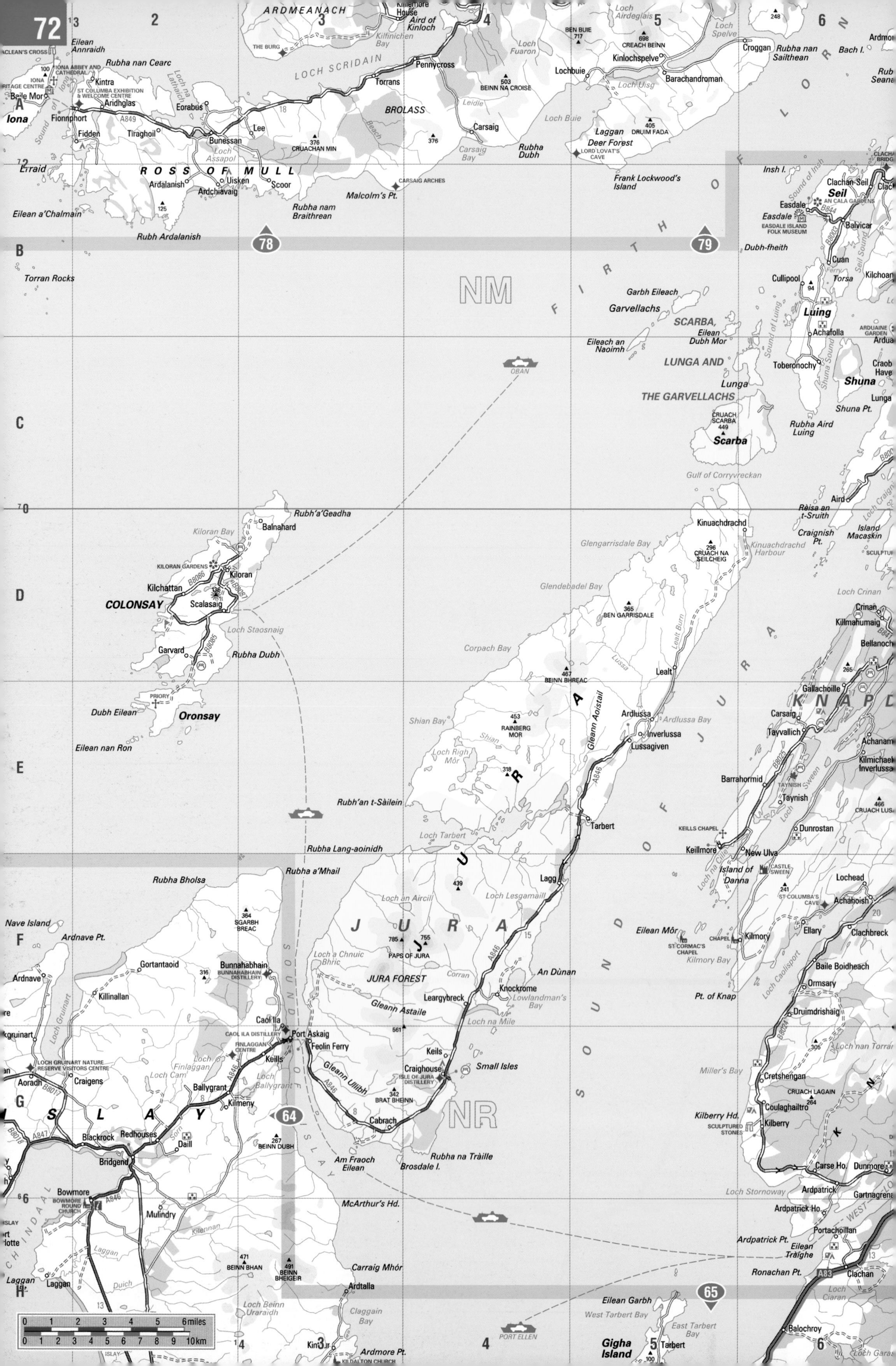
ARDMEANACH
Killiemore House
Aird of Kinloch
Kilfinichen Bay
THE BURG
LOCH SCRIDAIN
Pennycross
Torrans
Loch Airdeglais
BEN BUIE 717
698 CREACH BEINN
Loch Fuaron
Kinlochspelve
Loch Spelve
Croggan
Rubha nan Sailthean
Bach I.
Ardmor
Lochbuie
Barachandroman
Loch Uisg
503 BEINN NA CROISE
BROLASS
Leidle
Loch Buie
Laggan Deer Forest
405 DRUIM FADA
LORD LOVAT'S CAVE
Carsaig
Carsaig Bay
Rubha Dubh
376 CRUACHAN MIN
376
Eilean Annraidh
CLEAN'S CROSS
Rubha nan Cearc
IONA ABBEY AND CATHEDRAL
IONA HERITAGE CENTRE
Kintra
ST COLUMBA EXHIBITION & WELCOME CENTRE
Baile Mor
Iona
Aridhglas
Fionnphort
Fidden
Tiraghoil
Eorabus
Lee
Bunessan
A849
Loch na Lathaich
Sound of Iona
Erraid
ROSS OF MULL
Loch Assapol
Ardalanish
Uisken
Ardchiavaig
Scoor
CARSAIG ARCHES
Malcolm's Pt.
Frank Lockwood's Island
Rubha nam Braithrean
Eilean a'Chalmain
125
Rubh Ardalanish
78
79
Insh I.
Sound of Insh
Clachan-Seil
Seil
AN CALA GARDENS
Easdale
EASDALE ISLAND FOLK MUSEUM
Balvicar
B844
B8003
Dubh-fheith
Cuan
Seil Sound
Kilchoan
Torran Rocks
NM
FIRTH OF LORN
Garbh Eileach
Garvellachs
Cullipool
94
Torsa
Luing
SCARBA, Eilean Dubh Mor
Eileach an Naoimh
Achafolla
ARDUAINE GARDEN
Sound of Luing
OBAN
LUNGA AND
Lunga
THE GARVELLACHS
Toberonochy
Shuna Sound
Shuna
Lunga
Shuna Pt.
CRUACH SCARBA 449
Scarba
Rubha Aird Luing
Gulf of Corryvreckan
Aird
Rèisa an t-Sruith
Craignish Pt.
Island Macaskin
Loch Craignish
Rubh'a'Geadha
Balnahard
Kiloran Bay
KILORAN GARDENS
Kiloran
B8086
B8087
Kilchattan
COLONSAY
Scalasaig
Loch Staosnaig
B8085
Garvard
Rubha Dubh
PRIORY
Dubh Eilean
Oronsay
Eilean nan Ron
Kinuachdrachd
Kinuachdrachd Harbour
Glengarrisdale Bay
296 CRUACH NA SEILCHEIG
Glendebadel Bay
365 BEN GARRISDALE
Loch Crinan
Crinan
Kilmahumaig
Bellanoch
Corpach Bay
Lealt Burn
Lussa
Lealt
467 BEINN BHREAC
Gleann Aoistail
Ardlussa
Ardlussa Bay
Inverlussa
Lussagiven
Shian Bay
453 RAINBERG MOR
Shian
Loch Righ Mòr
318
A846
265
Gallachoille
KNAPDALE
Carsaig
Tayvallich
B8025
Achanamara
Kilmichael Inverlussa
Barrahormid
TAYNISH
Taynish
Loch Sween
466 CRUACH LUSACH
Rubh'an t-Sàilein
Tarbert
KEILLS CHAPEL
Keillmore
Dunrostan
New Ulva
Loch Tarbert
Rubha Lang-aoinidh
Rubha a'Mhail
Rubha Bholsa
Lagg
439
Loch Lesgamaill
Loch an Aircill
CASTLE SWEEN
Island of Danna
Loch na Cille
Lochhead
241 ST COLUMBA'S CAVE
Achahoish
364 SGARBH BREAC
JURA
785
755
PAPS OF JURA
Loch a Chnuic Bhric
Eilean Mòr
ST CORMAC'S CHAPEL
CHAPEL
Kilmory
Kilmory Bay
Ellary
Clachbreck
Nave Island
Ardnave Pt.
Gortantaoid
316
Bunnahabhain
BUNNAHABHAIN DISTILLERY
JURA FOREST
Corran
An Dùnan
Knockrome
Lowlandman's Bay
Baile Boidheach
Loch Caolisport
Ormsary
Pt. of Knap
Ardnave
Killinallan
Loch Gruinart
Leargybreck
Gleann Astaile
Loch na Mile
Druimdrishaig
SOUND OF JURA
Caol Ila
CAOL ILA DISTILLERY
FINLAGGAN CENTRE
Port Askaig
Feolin Ferry
561
Keils
306
Loch nan Torran
LOCH GRUINART NATURE RESERVE VISITORS CENTRE
Loch Finlaggan
Keills
Craighouse
ISLE OF JURA DISTILLERY
Small Isles
Miller's Bay
Cretshengan
Aoradh
Craigens
Loch Cam
Loch Ballygrant
Gleann Ullibh
342 BRAT BHEINN
CRUACH LAGAIN 264
Ballygrant
A846
Kilmeny
64
NR
Coulaghailtro
Kilberry Hd.
SCULPTURED STONES
Kilberry
ISLAY
B8018
A847
Blackrock
Redhouses
Daill
267 BEINN DUBH
Cabrach
Am Fraoch Eilean
Rubha na Tràille
Brosdale I.
Bridgend
Carse Ho.
Dunmore
Bowmore
BOWMORE ROUND CHURCH
A846
Loch Stornoway
Ardpatrick
Gartnagrenach
McArthur's Hd.
SOUND OF ISLAY
Mulindry
LOCH INDAAL
Ardpatrick Ho.
WEST LOCH TARBERT
Portachoillan
Laggan
471 BEINN BHAN
491 BEINN BHEIGEIR
Carraig Mhór
Ardpatrick Pt.
Eilean Traighe
Ronachan Pt.
A83
Clachan
Laggan
Duich
Ardtalla
65
Eilean Garbh
West Tarbert Bay
Loch Beinn Uraraidh
Claggain Bay
PORT ELLEN
East Tarbert Bay
Loch Ciaran
Balochroy
Gigha Island
Tarbert
100
Kintour
Ardmore Pt.
KILDALTON CHURCH
0 1 2 3 4 5 6 miles
0 1 2 3 4 5 6 7 8 9 10 km

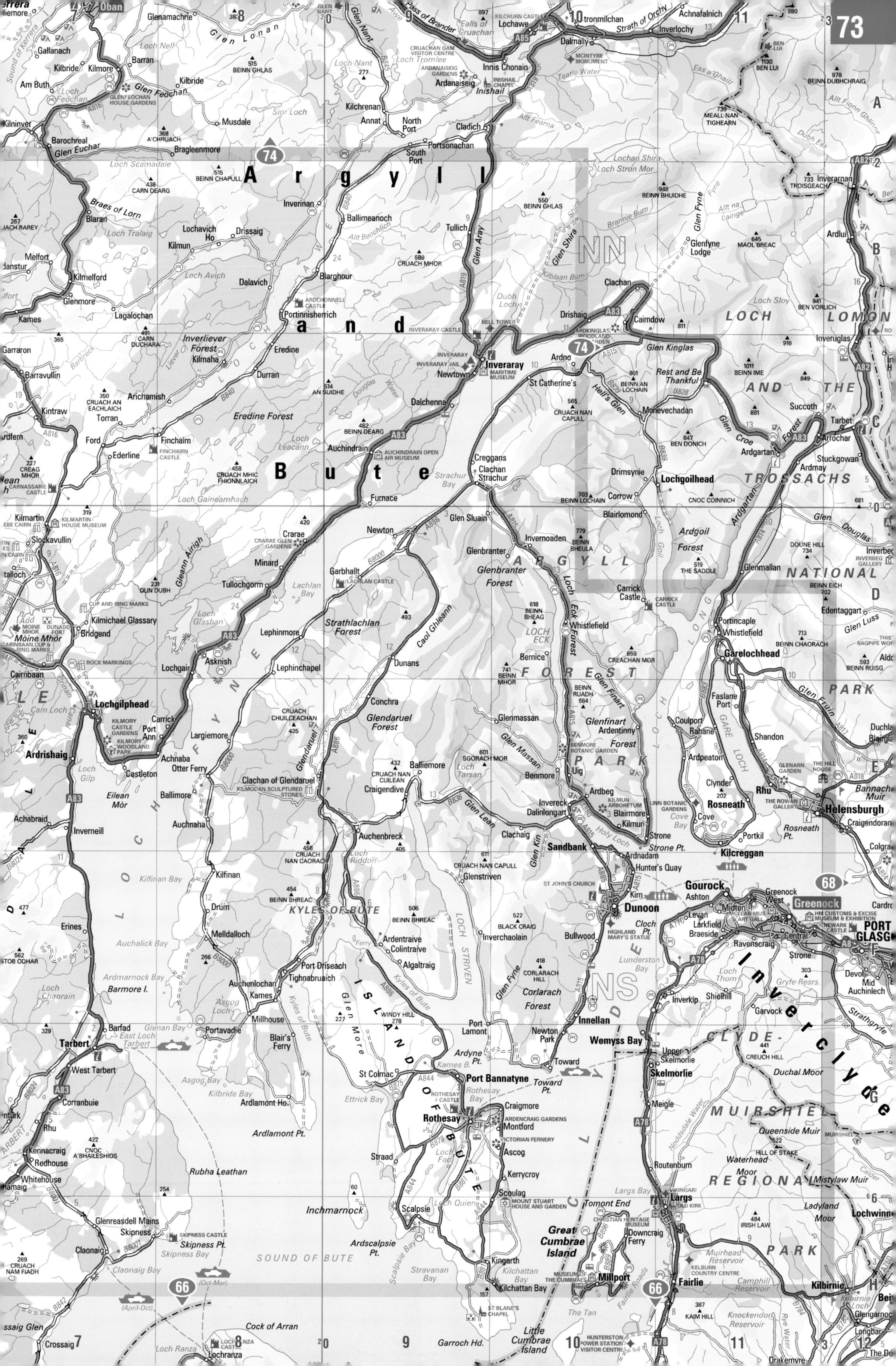
Oban
Glen Lonan
Glenamachrie
Gallanach
Kilbride
Kilmore
Barran
Am Buth
Glen Feochan
Kilninver
Barochreal
Glen Euchar
Bragleenmore
Musdale
Pass of Brander
Falls of Cruachan
Lochawe
Kilchurn Castle
Dalmally
Strath of Orchy
Inverlochy
Achnafalnich
Ben Lui
Innis Chonain
Ardanaiseig
Inishail
Kilchrenan
Annat
North Port
Cladich
Portsonachan
South Port
Argyll
and
Bute
Braes of Lorn
Blarau
Loch Tralaig
Lochavich
Kilmun
Drissaig
Inverinan
Ballimeanoch
Melfort
Kilmelford
Glenmore
Kames
Lagalochan
Dalavich
Blarghour
Portinnisherrich
Inverliever Forest
Kilmaha
Eredine
Durran
Arichamish
Eredine Forest
Barravullin
Kintraw
Torran
Ford
Ederline
Finchairn
Kilmartin
Slockavullin
Kilmichael Glassary
Bridgend
Moine Mhor
Cairnbaan
Lochgilphead
Ardrishaig
Achabraid
Inverneill
Erines
Barmore I.
Barfad
Tarbert
West Tarbert
Corranbuie
Rhu
Kennacraig
Redhouse
Whitehouse
Glenreasdell Mains
Skipness
Skipness Pt.
Claonaig
Crossaig
Lochranza
Cock of Arran
Sound of Bute
Inchmarnock
Ardscalpsie Pt.
Scalpsie
Kingarth
Kilchattan Bay
Garroch Hd.
Little Cumbrae Island
Great Cumbrae Island
Millport
Fairlie
Largs
Skelmorlie
Wemyss Bay
Inverkip
Gourock
Greenock
Port Glasgow
Inverclyde
Kilmacolm
Helensburgh
Rhu
Rosneath
Kilcreggan
Garelochhead
Whistlefield
Portincaple
Arrochar
Tarbet
Ardlui
Inverarnan
Loch Lomond and the Trossachs National Park
Succoth
Ardgartan
Lochgoilhead
Carrick Castle
Drimsynie
Ardgoil Forest
Inveraray
Newtown
Dalchenna
Auchindrain
Furnace
Crarae
Minard
Tullochgorm
Lochgair
Asknish
Strachur
Creggans
St Catherine's
Cairndow
Ardno
Glen Kinglas
Rest and Be Thankful
Glen Croe
Glen Fyne
Glenfyne Lodge
Clachan
Glen Shira
Glen Aray
Tullich
Glen Sluain
Newton
Garbhallt
Strathlachlan Forest
Lephinmore
Lephinchapel
Invernoaden
Glenbranter
Glenbranter Forest
Argyll Forest Park
Loch Eck
Whistlefield
Glenfinart
Ardentinny
Benmore
Dunans
Conchra
Glendaruel Forest
Clachan of Glendaruel
Largiemore
Otter Ferry
Ballimore
Auchnaha
Kilfinan
Drum
Melldalloch
Auchenlochan
Kames
Tighnabruaich
Port Driseach
Portavadie
Millhouse
Blair's Ferry
Ardlamont Pt.
Kyles of Bute
Colintraive
Ardentraive
Auchenbreck
Craigendive
Glenstriven
Loch Striven
Inverchaolain
Corlarach Forest
Port Lamont
Toward
Innellan
Dunoon
Kirn
Hunter's Quay
Sandbank
Ardnadam
Holy Loch
Kilmun
Strone
Clachaig
Island of Bute
Port Bannatyne
Rothesay
Craigmore
Montford
Ascog
Kerrycroy
Scoulag
St Colmac
Straad
Muirshiel Regional Park
Kilbirnie
Lochwinnoch

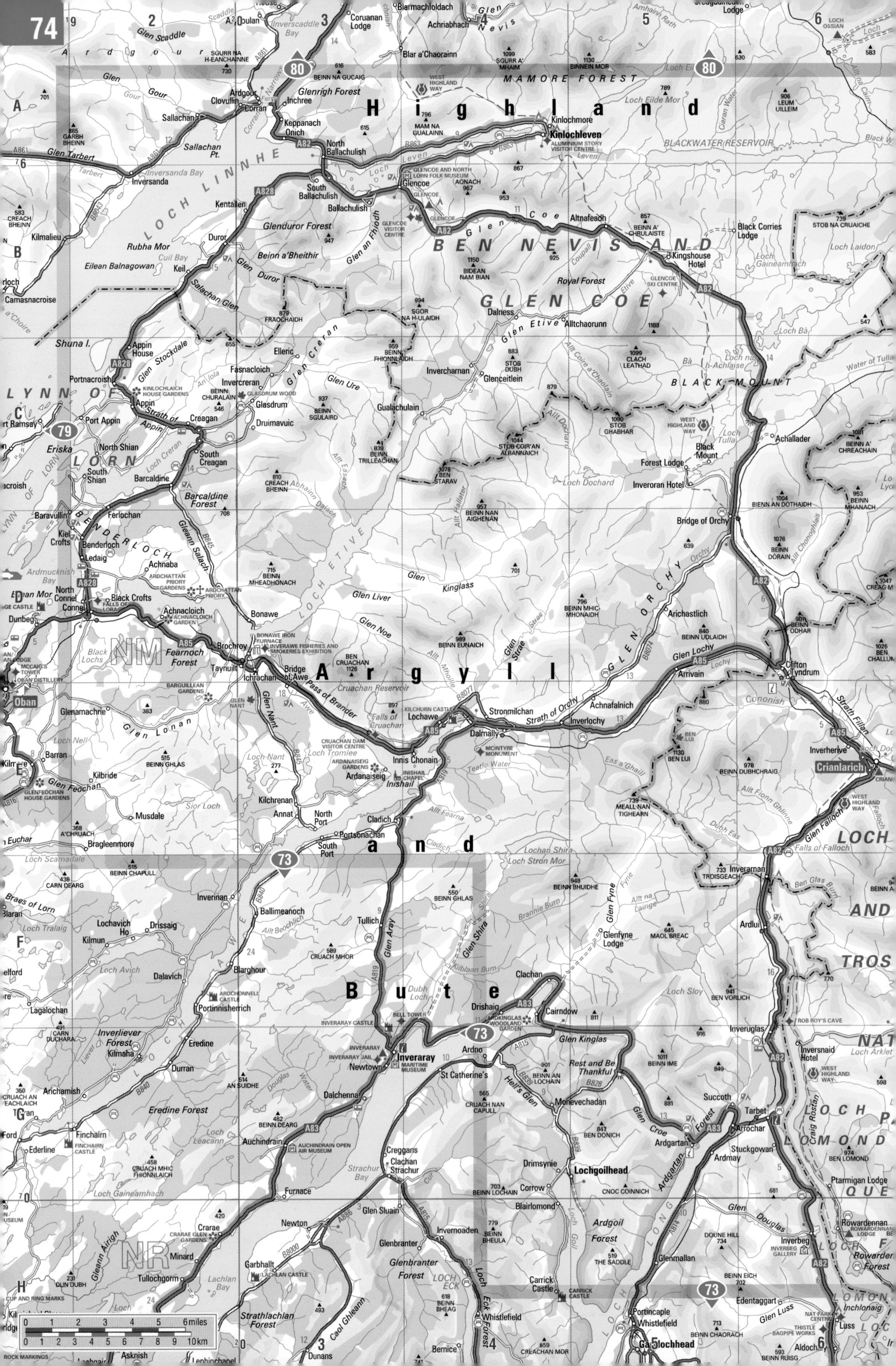
Highland
Argyll and Bute
BEN NEVIS AND GLEN COE
MAMORE FOREST
BLACK MOUNT
BLACKWATER RESERVOIR
LOCH LINNHE
LOCH ETIVE
GLEN ORCHY
Ardgour
Glen Scaddle
Glen Gour
Glen Tarbert
Inversanda
Kentallen
Duror
Glenduror Forest
Beinn a'Bheithir
Rubha Mor
Eilean Balnagowan
Keil
Camasnacroise
Shuna I.
Appin House
Glen Stockdale
Portnacroish
Appin
Port Appin
Eriska
North Shian
LORN
South Shian
Barcaldine
Barcaldine Forest
Benderloch
Ledaig
North Connel
Connel
Dunbeg
Oban
Black Crofts
Achnacloich
Bonawe
Taynuilt
Brochroy
Fearnoch Forest
Ichrachan
Bridge of Awe
Pass of Brander
Cruachan Reservoir
Glen Nant
Glen Lonan
Glenamachrie
Barran
Kilbride
Glen Feochan
Musdale
Bragleenmore
Corran
Clovullin
Sallachan
Onich
Keppanach
Inchree
Glenrigh Forest
North Ballachulish
South Ballachulish
Ballachulish
Glencoe
Kinlochleven
Kinlochmore
Blar a'Chaorainn
Achriabhach
Glen Nevis
Coruanan Lodge
Altnafeadh
Kingshouse Hotel
Black Corries Lodge
Royal Forest
Dalness
Glen Etive
Alltchaorunn
Invercharnan
Glenceitlein
Gualachulain
Elleric
Fasnacloich
Invercreran
Glen Creran
Glasdrum
Creagan
South Creagan
Druimavuic
Glen Ure
Forest Lodge
Inveroran Hotel
Bridge of Orchy
Achallader
Loch Tulla
Loch Dochard
Glen Kinglass
Glen Liver
Glen Noe
Glen Strae
Arichastlich
Glen Lochy
Tyndrum
Clifton
Arrivain
Achnafalnich
Inverlochy
Stronmilchan
Strath of Orchy
Dalmally
Lochawe
Falls of Cruachan
Innis Chonain
Ardanaiseig
Inishail
Kilchrenan
Annat
North Port
Cladich
Portsonachan
South Port
Strath Fillan
Inverherive
Crianlarich
Glen Falloch
Falls of Falloch
Inverarnan
Ardlui
LOCH LOMOND
Inveruglas
Inversnaid Hotel
Tarbet
Arrochar
Succoth
Ardgartan
Ardmay
Stuckgowan
Ptarmigan Lodge
Rowardennan
Inverbeg
Glen Douglas
Edentaggart
Luss
Inchlonaig
Aldochlay
Glen Luss
Garelochhead
Whistlefield
Portincaple
Glenmallan
Loch Long
Carrick Castle
Ardgoil Forest
Lochgoilhead
Drimsynie
Corrow
Blairlomond
Monevechadan
Rest and Be Thankful
Glen Kinglas
Glen Croe
Hell's Glen
Cairndow
Clachan
Drishaig
Glen Fyne
Glenfyne Lodge
Glen Shira
Glen Aray
Tullich
Inveraray
Newtown
Ardno
St Catherine's
Dalchenna
Auchindrain
Creggans
Strachur
Furnace
Glen Sluain
Newton
Invernoaden
Glenbranter
Glenbranter Forest
Loch Eck
Whistlefield
Bernice
Crarae
Minard
Garbhallt
Lachlan Bay
Tullochgorm
Strathlachlan Forest
Dunans
Asknish
Inverinan
Ballimeanoch
Lochavich
Drissaig
Kilmun
Dalavich
Blarghour
Portinnisherrich
Inverliever Forest
Kilmaha
Eredine
Durran
Eredine Forest
Arichamish
Finchairn
Ederline
Lagalochan
Braes of Lorn
Loch Avich
Loch Awe
0 1 2 3 4 5 6 miles
0 1 2 3 4 5 6 7 8 9 10 km

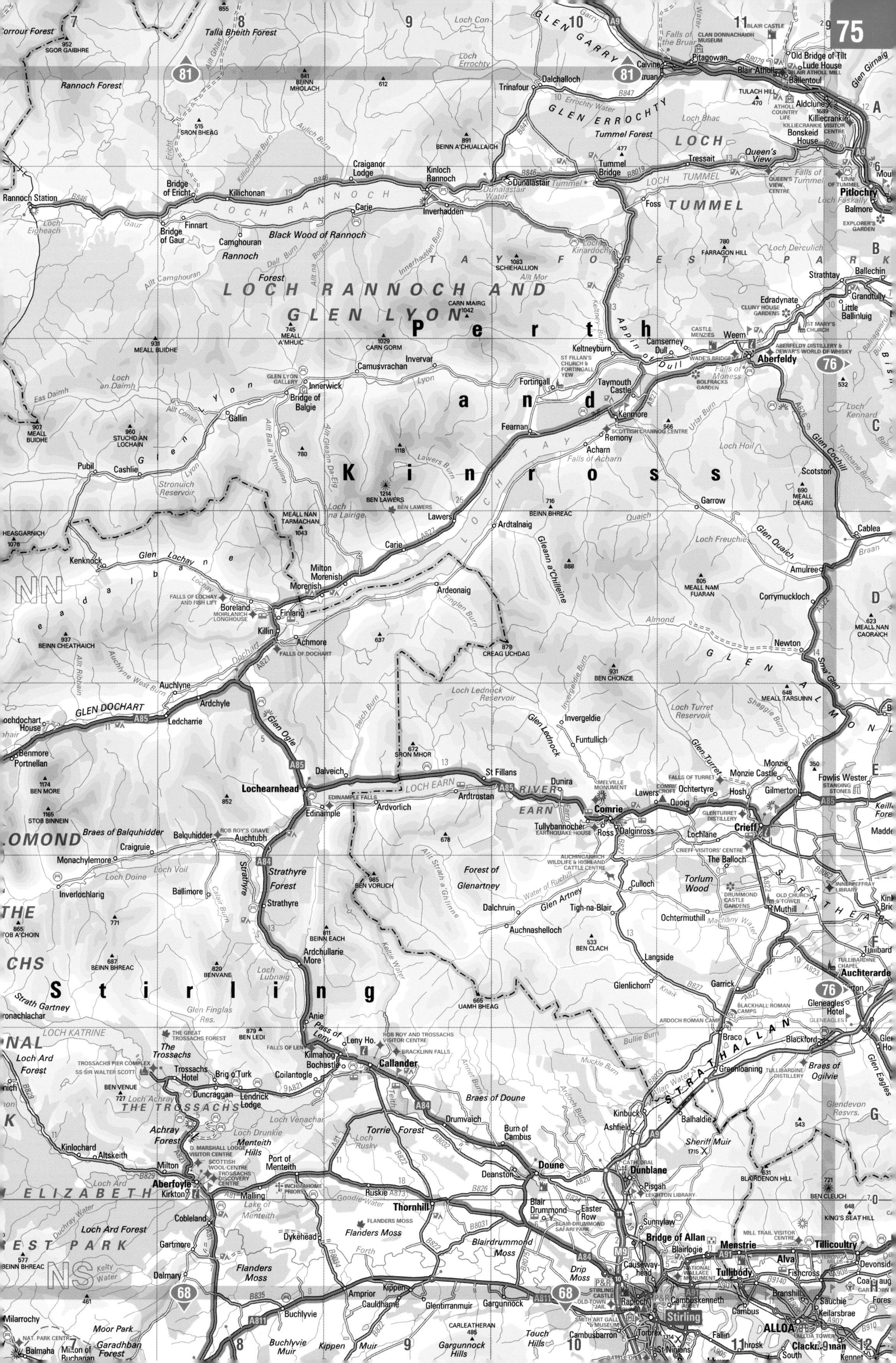
Corrour Forest
952 SGOR GAIBHRE
Talla Bheith Forest
Loch Con
GLEN GARRY
Falls of the Bruar
CLAN DONNACHAIDH MUSEUM
BLAIR CASTLE
81
Rannoch Forest
841 BEINN MHOLACH
612
Loch Errochty
Dalchalloch
Trinafour
Calvine
Pitagowan
Blair Atholl
Old Bridge of Tilt
Lude House
BLAIR ATHOLL MILL
Bailentoul
Glen Girnaig
TULACH HILL
470
ATHOLL COUNTRY LIFE
Aldclune
1689
Killiecrankie
KILLIECRANKIE VISITOR CENTRE
Bonskeid House
GLEN ERROCHTY
Errochty Water
Tummel Forest
Loch Bhac
LOCH
515 SRON BHEAG
Aulich Burn
891 BEINN A'CHUALLAICH
477
Queen's View
QUEEN'S VIEW CENTRE
Tressait
Falls of Tummel
LINN OF TUMMEL
Pitlochry
Craiganor Lodge
Kinloch Rannoch
Dunalastair
Dunalastair Water
Tummel Bridge
LOCH TUMMEL
Bridge of Ericht
Killichonan
Rannoch Station
Loch Eigheach
LOCH RANNOCH
Carie
Inverhadden
Foss
TUMMEL
Loch Faskally
Balmore
EXPLORER'S GARDEN
Bridge of Gaur
Finnart
Camghouran
Black Wood of Rannoch
Rannoch
Forest
Loch Kinardochy
780 FARRAGON HILL
Loch Derculich
1083 SCHIEHALLION
TAY FOREST PARK
Strathtay
Ballechin
Grandtully
Allt Camghouran
Dall Burn
Allt Mor
LOCH RANNOCH AND
GLEN LYON
CARN MAIRG 1042
Perth
Edradynate
CLUNY HOUSE GARDENS
Little Ballinluig
931 MEALL BUIDHE
745 MEALL A'MHUIC
1029 CARN GORM
Camusvrachan
Invervar
Keltneyburn
Camserney
Dull
CASTLE MENZIES
Weem
ST MARY'S CHURCH
ABERFELDY DISTILLERY & DEWAR'S WORLD OF WHISKY
Aberfeldy
WADE'S BRIDGE
Appin of Dull
76
532
Loch an Daimh
GLEN LYON GALLERY
Innerwick
ST FILLAN'S CHURCH & FORTINGALL YEW
Fortingall
Taymouth Castle
Falls of Moness
BOLFRACKS GARDEN
Eas Daimh
Bridge of Balgie
and
Kenmore
SCOTTISH CRANNOG CENTRE
Urlar Burn
Loch Kennard
907 MEALL BUIDHE
960 STUCHD AN LOCHAIN
Gallin
Fearnan
566
Remony
Acharn
Falls of Acharn
Glen Cochill
Loch Hoil
Tombane Burn
Pubil
Cashlie
780
1118
Lawers Burn
Kinross
Scotston
Stronuich Reservoir
690 MEALL DEARG
1214 BEN LAWERS
Garrow
HEASGARNICH 1076
MEALL NAN TARMACHAN 1043
Loch na Lairige
Lawers
716 BEINN BHREAC
Quaich
Cablea
Kenknock
Glen Lochay
Carie
LOCH TAY
Ardtalnaig
Loch Freuchie
Glen Quaich
Braan
888
Gleann a' Chilleine
Amulree
NN
Milton Morenish
Morenish
805 MEALL NAM FUARAN
Corrymuckloch
FALLS OF LOCHAY AND FISH LIFT
Boreland
MOIRLANICH LONGHOUSE
Finlarig
Ardeonaig
Finglen Burn
D
Killin
Achmore
637
Almond
623 MEALL NAN CAORAICH
937 BEINN CHEATHAICH
FALLS OF DOCHART
879 CREAG UCHDAG
Newton
GLEN ALMOND
Allt Ribhain
Auchlyne West Burn
Auchlyne
931 BEN CHONZIE
Sma' Glen
Loch Lednock Reservoir
648 MEALL TARSUINN
Ardchyle
Glen Ogle
Beich Burn
Invergeldie Burn
Loch Turret Reservoir
Shaggie Burn
GLEN DOCHART
Ledcharrie
Glen Lednock
Invergeldie
Glen Turret
Lochdochart House
Funtullich
Benmore
Portnellan
672 SRON MHOR
Monzie
Monzie Castle
350
Fowlis Wester
1174 BEN MORE
Dalveich
St Fillans
Dunira
MELVILLE MONUMENT
FALLS OF TURRET
STANDING STONES
Lochearnhead
LOCH EARN
Ardtrostan
RIVER EARN
COMRIE CROFT
Lawers
Ochtertyre
Hosh
Gilmerton
1165 STOB BINNEIN
852
EDINAMPLE FALLS
Edinample
Ardvorlich
Comrie
Quoig
GLENTURRET DISTILLERY
Crieff
Braes of Balquhidder
ROB ROY'S GRAVE
Balquhidder
Auchtubh
678
Tullybannocher
EARTHQUAKE HOUSE
Ross
Dalginross
Lochlane
CRIEFF VISITORS' CENTRE
LOMOND
Craigruie
Monachylemore
Loch Doine
Loch Voil
Strathyre
Strathyre Forest
Allt Strath a' Ghlinne
AUCHINGARRICH WILDLIFE & HIGHLAND CATTLE CENTRE
Forest of Glenartney
Water of Ruchill
The Balloch
Culloch
Torlum Wood
STRATHEARN
INNERPEFFRAY LIBRARY
Inverlochlarig
Ballimore
Calair Burn
985 BEN VORLICH
Glen Artney
DRUMMOND CASTLE GARDENS
OLD CHURCH & TOWER
Muthill
THE
771
Strathyre
Dalchruin
Tigh-na-Blair
Ochtermuthill
Machany Water
865 STOB A'CHOIN
811 BEINN EACH
Keltie Water
Auchnashelloch
533 BEN CLACH
CHS
687 BEINN BHREAC
820 BENVANE
Ardchullarie More
Langside
TULLIBARDINE CHAPEL
Auchterarder
Tullibardine
Stirling
Loch Lubnaig
665 UAMH BHEAG
Glenlichorn
Knaik
Garrick
Strath Gartney
Glen Finglas Res.
BLACKHALL ROMAN CAMPS
Gleneagles Hotel
GLENEAGLES
ARDOCH ROMAN CAMP
NAL
LOCH KATRINE
THE GREAT TROSSACHS FOREST
879 BEN LEDI
Anie
Pass of Leny
ROB ROY AND TROSSACHS VISITOR CENTRE
Leny Ho.
BRACKLINN FALLS
Bullie Burn
Braco
STRATHALLAN
Blackford
Glen Eagles
Loch Ard Forest
The Trossachs
FALLS OF LENY
Kilmahog
Bochastle
Callander
Muckle Burn
Greenloaning
TULLIBARDINE DISTILLERY
Braes of Ogilvie
TROSSACHS PIER COMPLEX
SS SIR WALTER SCOTT
Trossachs Hotel
Brig o' Turk
Coilantogle
Annet Burn
BEN VENUE
727
Loch Achray
Duncraggan
Lendrick Lodge
Teith
Braes of Doune
Ardoch Burn
Allan Water
Glendevon Resvrs.
THE TROSSACHS
Loch Venachar
Drumvaich
Kinbuck
Balhaldie
Achray Forest
Loch Drunkie
Menteith Hills
Torrie Forest
Loch Rusky
Burn of Cambus
Ashfield
543
Kinlochard
Altskeith
D. MARSHALL LODGE VISITOR CENTRE
SCOTTISH WOOL CENTRE
TROSSACHS DISCOVERY CENTRE
Port of Menteith
Sheriff Muir
1715
Milton
Aberfoyle
Loch Ard
Kirkton
INCHMAHOME PRIORY
Doune
Deanston
CATHEDRAL
Dunblane
Pisgah
LEIGHTON LIBRARY
631 BLAIRDENON HILL
721 BEN CLEUCH
ELIZABETH
Malling
Goodie Water
Ruskie
Thornhill
Blair Drummond
Easter Row
BLAIR DRUMMOND SAFARI PARK
648 KING'S SEAT HILL
Duchray Water
Lake of Menteith
Cobleland
FLANDERS MOSS
Flanders Moss
Sunnylaw
MILL TRAIL VISITOR CENTRE
Loch Ard Forest
Gartmore
Dykehead
Blairdrummond Moss
Bridge of Allan
Blairlogie
Menstrie
Tillicoultry
EST PARK
577 BEINN BHREAC
NS
Kelty Water
Dalmary
Flanders Moss
Forth
Drip Moss
Causewayhead
NATIONAL WALLACE MONUMENT
Tullibody
Alva
Fishcross
Devonside
68
461
Amprior
Kippen
Gauldhame
Glentirranmuir
Gargunnock
STIRLING CASTLE
OLD TOWN JAIL
Raploch
Cambuskenneth
Cambus
Branshill
Sauchie
Keilarsbrae
Coalsnaughton
Milarrochy
Moor Park
Buchlyvie
CARLEATHERAN 485
Gargunnock Hills
Touch Hills
SMITH ART GALLERY & MUSEUM
Stirling
ALLOA
ALLOA TOWER
NAT. PARK CENTRE
Balmaha
Milton of Buchanan
Garadhban Forest
Buchlyvie Muir
Kippen Muir
Cambusbarron
Torbrex
1314
St Ninians
Fallin
Clackmannan
Kennet
South
A9
A85
A84
A827
A826
A822
A823
A821
A81
A873
A811
A91
A907
A908
M9
B846
B847
B8019
B8079
B827
B8033
B8032
B822
B826
B824
B8031
B8075
B835
B829
B8062
B9140
B910
A B C D E F G H
7 8 9 10 11 12

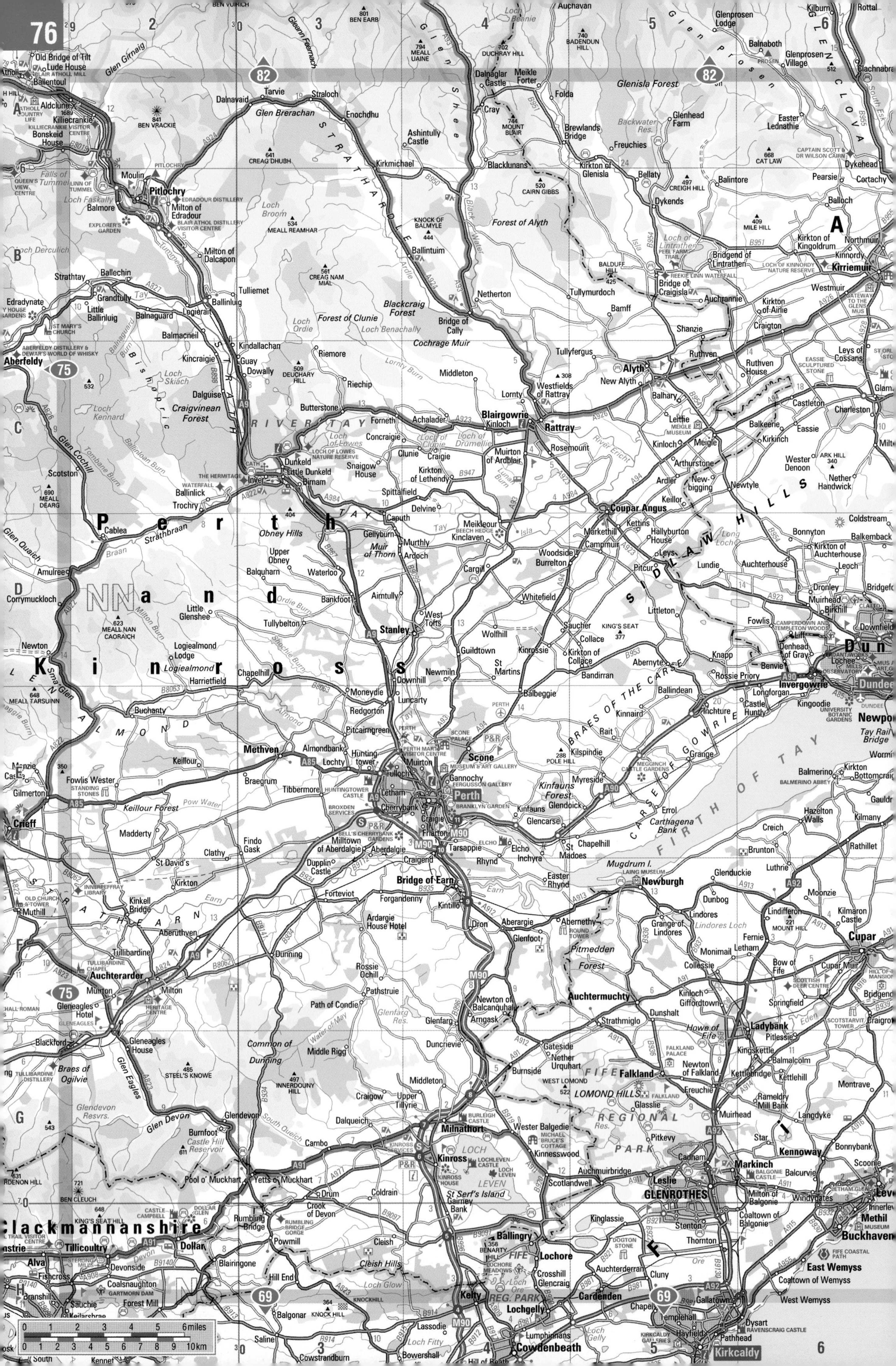
Ben Vuirich
801 Ben Earb
Gleann Fearnach
Glen Shee
Loch Beanie
Auchavan
740 Badendun Hill
Glen Prosen
Glenprosen Lodge
Kilburn
Rottal
Glen Clova
Old Bridge of Tilt
Lude House
Blair Atholl
Glen Girnaig
794 Meall Uaine
702 Duchray Hill
82
Dalnaglar Castle
Meikle Forter
Folda
Glenisla Forest
Balnaboth
Glenprosen Village
Clachnabrae
Ballentoul
Tarvie
Straloch
Dalnavaid
Glen Brerachan
Enochdhu
Cray
744 Mount Blair
Brewlands Bridge
Backwater Res.
Glenhead Farm
Easter Lednathie
Killiecrankie
Aldclune
841 Ben Vrackie
Ashintully Castle
Freuchies
Bonskeid House
641 Creag Dhubh
Strathardle
Kirkmichael
Blacklunans
Kirkton of Glenisla
668 Cat Law
Captain Scott & Dr Wilson Cairn
Dykehead
Cortachy
Pearsie
Falls of Tummel
Queen's View Centre
Linn of Tummel
Moulin
Pitlochry
Loch Faskally
Balmore
Milton of Edradour
Edradour Distillery
Blair Athol Distillery Visitor Centre
Explorer's Garden
Loch Broom
534 Meall Reamhar
520 Cairn Gibbs
Bellaty
497 Creigh Hill
Balintore
Balloch
Dykends
409 Mile Hill
Knock of Balmyle 444
Forest of Alyth
Black Water
Loch Derculich
Milton of Dalcapon
Ballintuim
Loch of Lintrathen
Peel Farm Trail
Bridgend of Lintrathen
Loch of Kinnordy Nature Reserve
Kirkton of Kingoldrum
Northmuir
Kinnordy
Kirriemuir
Balduff Hill 425
Reekie Linn Waterfall
Bridge of Craigisla
Strathtay
Ballechin
561 Creag nam Mial
Tulliemet
Netherton
Tullymurdoch
Westmuir
Auchrannie
Kirkton of Airlie
Gateway to the Glens Mus
Edradynate
Grandtully
Little Ballinlug
Balnaguard
Logierait
Ballinluig
Blackcraig Forest
Forest of Clunie
Loch Ordie
Loch Benachally
Bridge of Cally
Bamff
Craigton
St Mary's Church
Balmacneil
Kindallachan
Cochrage Muir
Shanzie
Aberfeldy Distillery & Dewar's World of Whisky
Aberfeldy
75
Bishopric
Loch Skiach
Kincraigie
Guay
Dowally
509 Deuchary Hill
Riemore
Riechip
Middleton
Tullyfergus
Alyth
Ruthven
Ruthven House
Eassie Sculptured Stone
Leys of Cossans
New Alyth
Westfields of Rattray
308
Lornty
Dalguise
Craigvinean Forest
Loch Kennard
Butterstone
Forneth
Achalader
Blairgowrie
Kinloch
Rattray
Balhary
Leitfie
Meigle Museum
Castleton
Charleston
Glen Cochill
River Tay
Loch of Lowes
Loch of Lowes Nature Reserve
Concraigie
Loch of Clunie
Loch of Drumellie
Clunie
Craigie
Muirton of Ardblair
Rosemount
River Ericht
Kinloch
Meigle
Balkeerie
Eassie
Kirkinch
Scotston
The Hermitage
Inver
Dunkeld
Little Dunkeld
Birnam
Snaigow House
Kirkton of Lethendy
Arthurstone
Ardler
New-bigging
Newtyle
Wester Denoon
Ark Hill 340
Nether Handwick
690 Meall Dearg
Waterfall
Ballinlick
Trochry
Spittalfield
Delvine
Keillor
Coupar Angus
Sidlaw Hills
Coldstream
Perth and Kinross
Cablea
Strathbraan
Obney Hills
Caputh
Gellyburn
Muir of Thorn
Murthly
Ardoch
Meikleour
Beech Hedge
Kinclaven
Markethill
Kettins
Campmuir
Hallyburton House
Long Loch
Bonnyton
Kirkton of Auchterhouse
Balkemback
Glen Quaich
Amulree
Braan
Upper Obney
Balquharn
Waterloo
Cargill
Woodside
Burrelton
Leys
Pitcur
Lundie
Auchterhouse
Leoch
Corrymuckloch
623 Meall nan Caoraich
Little Glenshee
Bankfoot
Airntully
Whitefield
Dronley
Muirhead
Birkhill
Clatto
Bridgefoot
Tullybelton
Stanley
West Tofts
Littleton
Saucher
King's Seat 377
Collace
Fowlis
Camperdown and Templeton Woods
Downfield
Newton
Logiealmond Lodge
Logiealmond
Wolfhill
Guildtown
Kinrossie
Kirkton of Collace
Abernyte
Knapp
Denhead of Gray
Liff
Verdant Works
Dundee
Chapelhill
Harrietfield
St Martins
Newmiln
Bandirran
Rossie Priory
Benvie
Lochee
Mills Observatory
648 Meall Tarsuinn
Moneydie
Downhill
Luncarty
Balbeggie
Braes of the Carse
Ballindean
Invergowrie
Longforgan
Castle Huntly
Kingoodie
Dundee Airport
University Botanic Gardens
Newport
Glen Almond
Buchanty
Redgorton
Pitcairngreen
Kinnaird
Inchture
Rait
Tay Rail Bridge
Wormit
Methven
Almondbank
Hunting tower
Scone Palace
Scone
Perth Mart Visitor Centre
Kilspindie
288 Pole Hill
Grange
Carse of Gowrie
Firth of Tay
Balmerino
Kirkton
Bottomcraig
Balmerino Abbey
Menzie
350
Keillour
Lochty
Muirton
Museum & Art Gallery
Megginch Castle Gardens
Fowlis Wester
Standing Stones
Braegrum
Tibbermore
Huntingtower Castle
Tulloch
Letham
Gannochy
Fergusson Gallery
Perth
Kinfauns Forest
Myreside
Gauldry
Gilmerton
Pow Water
Broxden Services
Cherrybank
Branklyn Garden
Kinfauns
Glendoick
Errol
Hazelton Walls
Kilmany
Crieff
Keillour Forest
Madderty
Craigie
Friarton
Glencarse
Carthagena Bank
Creich
Bell's Cherrybank Gardens
Findo Gask
Clathy
Milltown of Aberdalgie
Aberdalgie
Tarsappie
Elcho
Inchyra
St Madoes
Chapelhill
Brunton
Rathillet
St David's
Dupplin Castle
Craigend
Rhynd
Mugdrum I.
Luthrie
Kirkton
Innerpeffray Library
Bridge of Earn
Easter Rhynd
Laing Museum
Newburgh
Glenduckie
Old Church & Tower
Muthill
Kinkell Bridge
Strathearn
Forteviot
Forgandenny
Kintillo
Dunbog
Moonzie
Aberuthven
Ardargie House Hotel
Dron
Aberargie
Abernethy Round Tower
Grange of Lindores
Lindores
Lindores Loch
Lindifferon
221 Mount Hill
Kilmaron Castle
Tullibardine
Tullibardine Chapel
Dunning
Glenfoot
Pitmedden Forest
Monimail
Fernie
Letham
Cupar
Auchterarder
Milton
Rossie Ochill
Collessie
Bow of Fife
Cupar Muir
Hill of Tarvit Mansion
Muirton
Gleneagles Hotel
Heritage Centre
Pathstruie
Newton of Balcanquhal
Auchtermuchty
Kinloch
Scottish Deer Centre
Bridgend
Path of Condie
Glenfarg Res.
Glenfarg
Arngask
Dunshalt
Giffordtown
Springfield
Scotstarvit Tower
Craigrothie
Blackford
Water of May
Strathmiglo
Howe of Fife
Ladybank
Gleneagles House
Common of Dunning
Middle Rigg
Duncrievie
Gateside
Nether Urquhart
Falkland Palace
Newton of Falkland
Kingskettle
Pitlessie
Balmalcolm
Tullibardine Distillery
Braes of Ogilvie
Glen Eagles
485 Steel's Knowe
497 Innerdouny Hill
Middleton
Burnside
Fife
Falkland
Freuchie
Kettlebridge
Kettlehill
Montrave
West Lomond 522
Lomond Hills
Rameldry Mill Bank
Glendevon Resvrs.
Craigow
Upper Tillyrie
Burleigh Castle
Milnathort
Wester Balgedie
Glasslie
Regional Park
Muirhead
Langdyke
Glen Devon
Glendevon
Dalqueich
Michael Bruce's Cottage
Pitkevy
Star
Kennoway
Bonnybank
543
Burnfoot
Castle Hill Reservoir
611
Carnbo
Kinross Services
Kinross
Lochleven Castle
Kinnesswood
Cadham
Markinch
Balgonie Castle
Balcurvie
Scoonie
Pool o' Muckhart
Yetts o' Muckhart
A977
Loch Leven
Kinross House
Auchmuirbridge
Scotlandwell
Leslie
Glenrothes
Milton of Balgonie
Windygates
Letham Glen
Leven
721 Ben Cleuch
Drum
Coldrain
St Serf's Island
Gairney Bank
Innerleven
Methil
Buckhaven
Clackmannanshire
King's Seat Hill
Castle Campbell
Dollar Glen
Crook of Devon
Rumbling Bridge
Rumbling Bridge Gorge
Kinglassie
Coaltown of Balgonie
Stenton
Thornton
Fife Coastal Path
Tillicoultry
Dollar
Ballingry
356 Benarty Hill
Lochore Meadows
Lochore
Dogton Stone
Powmill
Cleish
East Wemyss
Alva
Devonside
Blairingone
Cleish Hills
Crosshill
Glencraig
Auchterderran
Cluny
Coaltown of Wemyss
Fishcross
Coalsnaughton
Gartmorn Dam
Hill End
Loch Glow
Knockhill
Kelty
Reg. Park
Cardenden
69
Gallatown
West Wemyss
Sauchie
Forest Mill
364 Knock Hill
Lochgelly
Chapel
Templehall
Dysart
Ravenscraig Castle
Balgonar
Lassodie
Lumphinnans
Loch Gelly
Hayfield
Pathhead
Saline
Loch Fitty
Cowdenbeath
Kirkcaldy Galleries
Kirkcaldy
Bowershall
Cowstrandburn
Kennet
Hill of Beath
0 1 2 3 4 5 6 miles
0 1 2 3 4 5 6 7 8 9 10 km

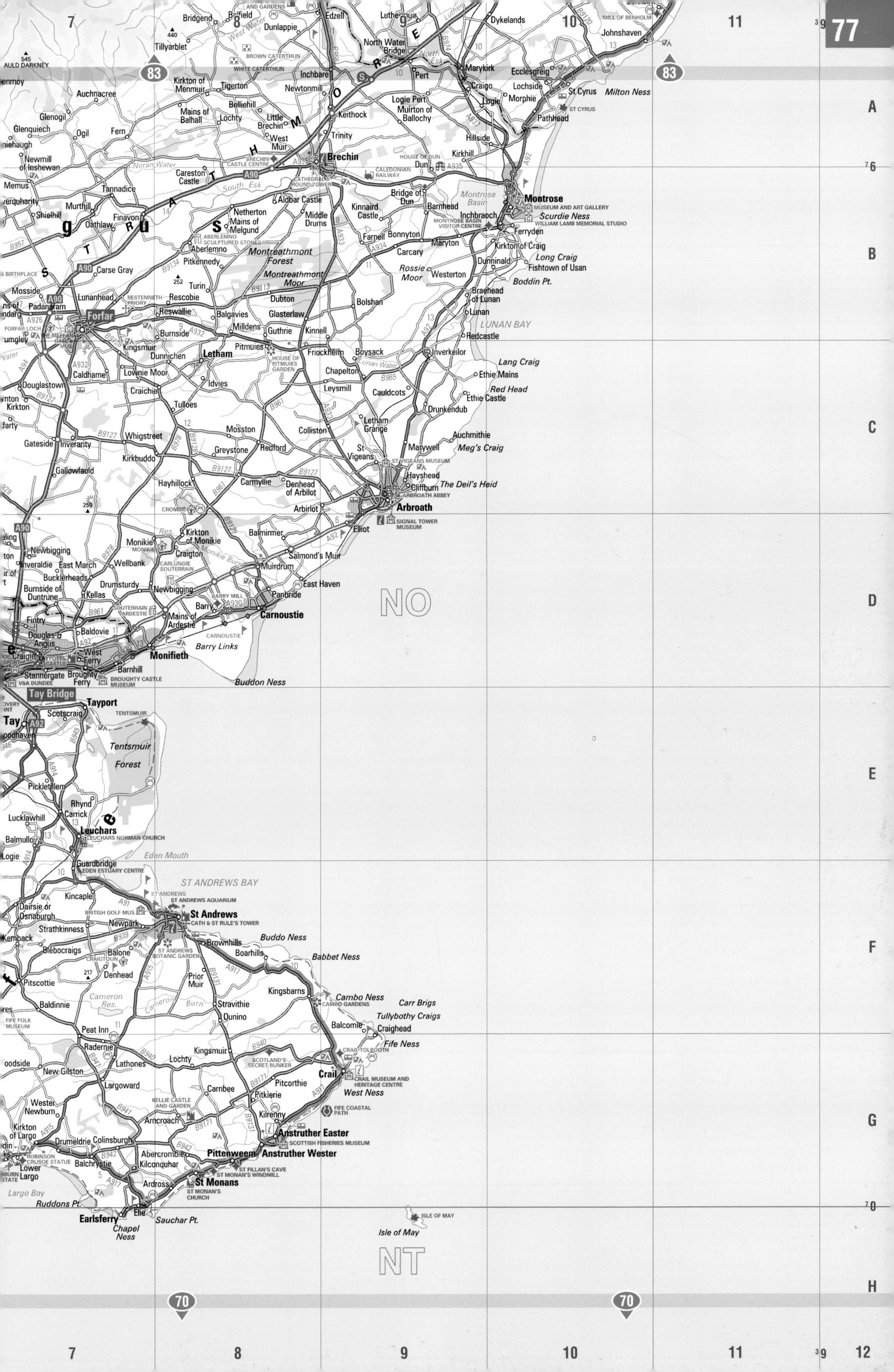
7
8
9
10
11
12
A
B
C
D
E
F
G
H
83
70
NO
NT
Edzell
Dykelands
Johnshaven
MILL OF BENHOLM
Bridgend
Balfield
Dunlappie
Luthermuir
North Water Bridge
Tillyarblet
AULD DARKNEY
BROWN CATERTHUN
WHITE CATERTHUN
Inchbare
Pert
Marykirk
Ecclesgreig
Kirkton of Menmuir
Tigerton
Newtonmill
Craigo
Lochside
St Cyrus
Milton Ness
Auchnacree
Logie Pert
Logie
Morphie
ST CYRUS
Bellichill
Muirton of Ballochy
Keithock
Pathhead
Glenogil
Mains of Balhall
Lochty
Little Brechin
Glenquiech
Ogil
Fern
West Muir
Trinity
Hillside
Kirkhill
Newmill of Inshewan
Brechin
HOUSE OF DUN
Dun
BRECHIN CASTLE CENTRE
CALEDONIAN RAILWAY
Noran Water
Careston Castle
Memus
Tannadice
South Esk
CATHEDRAL & ROUND TOWER
Montrose Basin
Bridge of Dun
Montrose
MUSEUM AND ART GALLERY
Scurdie Ness
WILLIAM LAMB MEMORIAL STUDIO
Murthill
Netherton
Aldbar Castle
Kinnaird Castle
Barnhead
Inchbraoch
MONTROSE BASIN VISITOR CENTRE
Ferryden
Shielhill
Oathlaw
Finavon
Mains of Melgund
Middle Drums
Farnell
Bonnyton
Maryton
Kirkton of Craig
ABERLEMNO SCULPTURED STONES
Aberlemno
Montreathmont Forest
Carcary
Long Craig
Fishtown of Usan
Dunninald
Carse Gray
Pitkennedy
Rossie Moor
Westerton
Montreathmont Moor
Boddin Pt.
Turin
Mosside
Lunanhead
RESTENNETH PRIORY
Rescobie
Dubton
Braehead of Lunan
Padanaram
Bolshan
Forfar
Reswallie
Balgavies
Glasterlaw
Lunan
LUNAN BAY
FORFAR LOCH
Milldens
Guthrie
Kinnell
Redcastle
Burnside
Kingsmuir
Pitmuies
HOUSE OF PITMUIES GARDEN
Friockheim
Boysack
Inverkeilor
Dunnichen
Letham
Lunan Water
Chapelton
Lang Craig
Ethie Mains
Caldhame
Lownie Moor
Leysmill
Cauldcots
Red Head
Ethie Castle
Douglastown
Craichie
Idvies
Kirkton
Tulloes
Drunkendub
Letham Grange
Colliston
Auchmithie
Meg's Craig
Gateside
Inverarity
Whigstreet
Mosston
Marywell
Greystone
Redford
St Vigeans
ST VIGEANS MUSEUM
Kirkbuddo
Gallowfauld
Hayshead
Hayhillock
Carmyllie
Denhead of Arbilot
Cliffburn
The Deil's Heid
ARBROATH ABBEY
Arbirlot
Arbroath
SIGNAL TOWER MUSEUM
CROMBIE
Elliot
Kirkton of Monikie
Balmirmer
Monikie
Craigton
Salmond's Muir
Newbigging
Inveraldie
East March
Wellbank
CARLUNGIE SOUTERRAIN
Monikie Burn
Muirdrum
Bucklerheads
Drumsturdy
East Haven
Burnside of Duntrune
Kellas
BARRY MILL
Panbride
SOUTERRAIN ARDESTIE
Barry
Carnoustie
Fintry
Baldovie
Mains of Ardestie
Douglas & Angus
CARNOUSTIE
Barry Links
Craigie
West Ferry
Monifieth
Barnhill
Stannergate
Broughty Ferry
BROUGHTY CASTLE MUSEUM
V&A DUNDEE
Buddon Ness
Tay Bridge
Tayport
TENTSMUIR
Tay
Scotscraig
Tentsmuir Forest
Pickletillem
Rhynd
Carrick
Lucklawhill
Leuchars
LEUCHARS NORMAN CHURCH
Balmullo
Logie
Eden Mouth
Guardbridge
EDEN ESTUARY CENTRE
ST ANDREWS BAY
ST ANDREWS
ST ANDREWS AQUARIUM
Kincaple
Dairsie or Osnaburgh
BRITISH GOLF MUS
St Andrews
CATH & ST RULE'S TOWER
Strathkinness
Newpark
Buddo Ness
Kemback
Brownhills
Blebocraigs
Balone
ST ANDREWS BOTANIC GARDEN
Boarhills
Babbet Ness
CRAIGTOUN
Denhead
Prior Muir
Pitscottie
Kingsbarns
Cameron Res.
Cambo Ness
CAMBO GARDENS
Carr Brigs
Baldinnie
Stravithie
Dunino
Tullybothy Craigs
FIFE FOLK MUSEUM
Balcomie
Craighead
Peat Inn
Fife Ness
Radernie
Kingsmuir
CRAIL TOLBOOTH
Lathones
Lochty
SCOTLAND'S SECRET BUNKER
New Gilston
Crail
CRAIL MUSEUM AND HERITAGE CENTRE
Largoward
Pitcorthie
West Ness
Carnbee
Pitkierie
Wester Newburn
KELLIE CASTLE AND GARDEN
FIFE COASTAL PATH
Kilrenny
Arncroach
Kirkton of Largo
Anstruther Easter
Drumeldrie
Colinsburgh
SCOTTISH FISHERIES MUSEUM
ROBINSON CRUSOE STATUE
Abercrombie
Pittenweem
Anstruther Wester
Balchrystie
Kilconquhar
ST FILLAN'S CAVE
ST MONAN'S WINDMILL
Lower Largo
Ardross
St Monans
ST MONAN'S CHURCH
Largo Bay
Ruddons Pt.
Earlsferry
Elie
Sauchar Pt.
Chapel Ness
ISLE OF MAY
Isle of May
STRATHMORE
STRUAN
A90
A92
A94
A926
A932
A933
A934
A935
A930
A91
A915
A917
A914
A937
B961
B965
B9127
B9128
B9134
B9113
B974
B966
B957
B945
B939
B940
B941
B942
B9131
B9171

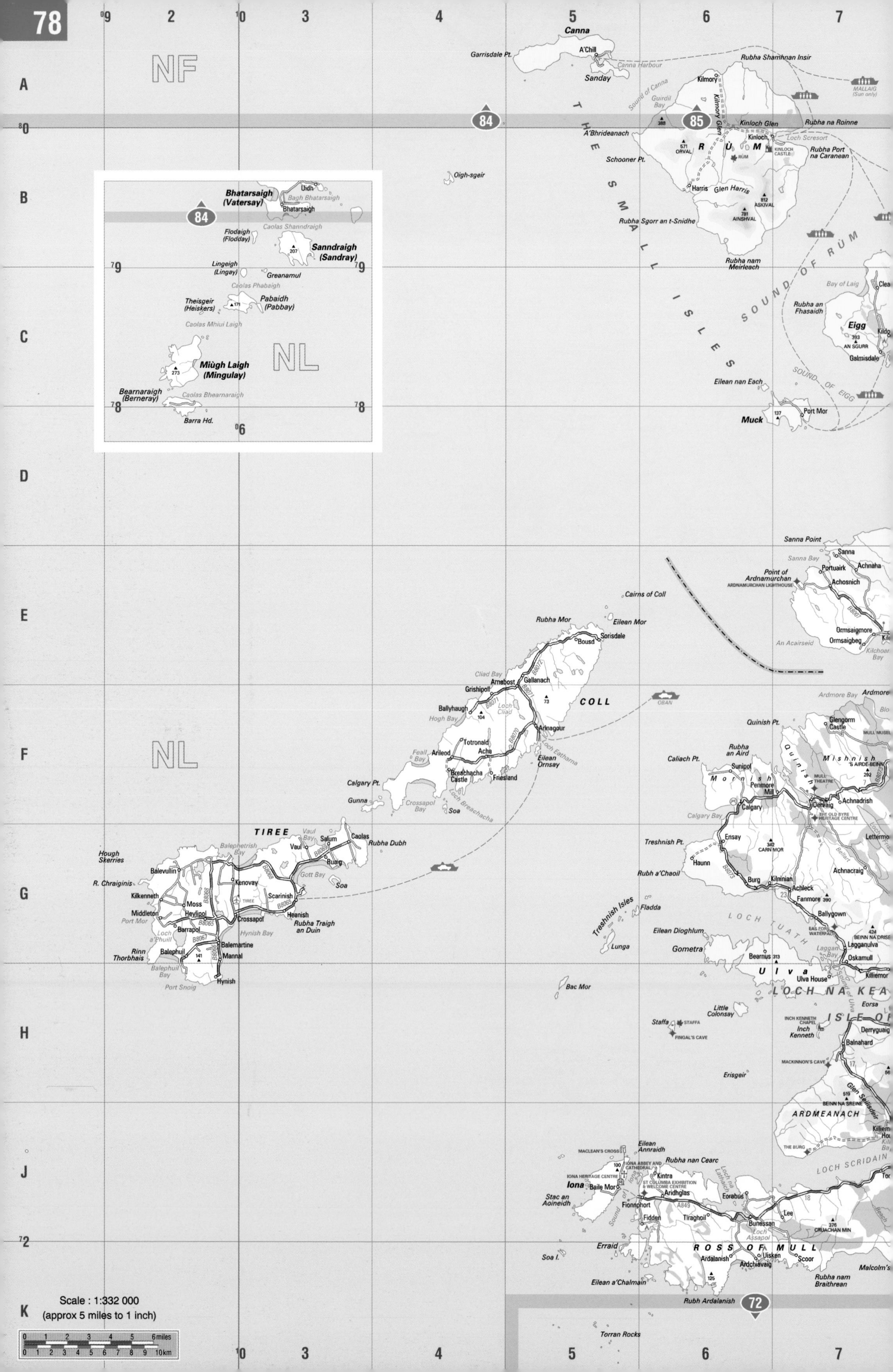
NF
NL
NL
84
85
84
72
Canna
A'Chill
Garrisdale Pt.
Canna Harbour
Sanday
Rubha Shamhnan Insir
Kilmory
Sound of Canna
Guirdil Bay
MALLAIG (Sun only)
Kilmory Glen
Kinloch Glen
Rubha na Roinne
A'Bhrideanach
Kinloch
Loch Scresort
KINLOCH CASTLE
Rubha Port na Caranean
571 ORVAL
RÙM
Schooner Pt.
Oigh-sgeir
Harris
Glen Harris
812 ASKIVAL
781 AINSHVAL
Rubha Sgorr an t-Snidhe
Rubha nam Meirleach
THE SMALL ISLES
SOUND OF RÙM
Bay of Laig
Rubha an Fhasaidh
Eigg
393 AN SGURR
Galmisdale
SOUND OF EIGG
Eilean nan Each
Muck
137
Port Mor
Bhatarsaigh (Vatersay)
Uidh
Bagh Bhatarsaigh
Bhatarsaigh
Flodaigh (Flodday)
Caolas Shanndraigh
Sanndraigh (Sandray)
207
Lingeigh (Lingay)
Greanamul
Caolas Phabaigh
Theisgeir (Heiskers)
171
Pabaidh (Pabbay)
Caolas Mhiui Laigh
Miùgh Laigh (Mingulay)
273
Bearnaraigh (Berneray)
Caolas Bhearnaraigh
Barra Hd.
Sanna Point
Sanna Bay
Sanna
Portuairk
Achnaha
Point of Ardnamurchan
ARDNAMURCHAN LIGHTHOUSE
Achosnich
B8007
Ormsaigmore
Ormsaigbeg
An Acairseid
Kilchoan Bay
Cairns of Coll
Rubha Mor
Eilean Mor
Bousd
Sorisdale
Cliad Bay
Arnabost
Gallanach
Grishipoll
B8072
B8071
Ballyhaugh
Hogh Bay
104
Loch Cliad
73
COLL
OBAN
Arinagour
B8070
Totronald
Feall Bay
Arileod
Acha
Loch Eatharna
Eilean Ornsay
Breachacha Castle
Friesland
Calgary Pt.
Gunna
Crossapol Bay
Soa
Loch Breachacha
Ardmore Bay
Ardmore
Quinish Pt.
Glengorm Castle
MULL MUSEUM
Rubha an Aird
Caliach Pt.
Sunipol
Mornish
Quinish
Mishnish
S AIRDE-BEINN
292
Penmore Mill
MULL THEATRE
Dervaig
Achnadrish
Calgary
Calgary Bay
THE OLD BYRE HERITAGE CENTRE
Lettermore
TIREE
Vaul Bay
Salum
Caolas
Rubha Dubh
Vaul
B8069
Balephetrish Bay
Ruaig
Hough Skerries
Balevullin
B8068
Kenovay
Gott Bay
Soa
R. Chraiginis
Kilkenneth
Moss
TIREE
Scarinish
Middleton
Heylipol
B8065
Heanish
Port Mor
Crossapol
Rubha Traigh an Duin
Barrapol
Hynish Bay
Loch a'Phuill
B8067
Rinn Thorbhais
Balephuil
141
Balemartine
Mannal
Balephuil Bay
Hynish
Port Snoig
Treshnish Pt.
Ensay
342 CARN MOR
Haunn
B8073
Bellart
Achnacraig
Rubh a'Chaoil
Burg
Kilninian
Achleck
Fanmore
390
Treshnish Isles
Fladda
LOCH TUATH
Ballygown
EAS FORS WATERFALL
424 BEINN NA DRISE
Eilean Dioghlum
Lunga
Gometra
Laggan Bay
Lagganulva
Bearnus
313
Oskamull
Ulva
Ulva House
Sound of Ulva
Killiemor
Bac Mor
LOCH NA KEAL
Little Colonsay
Eorsa
Staffa
STAFFA
FINGAL'S CAVE
INCH KENNETH CHAPEL
Inch Kenneth
ISLE OF
Derryguaig
Balnahard
MACKINNON'S CAVE
Erisgeir
519 BEINN NA SREINE
Glen Seilisdeir
ARDMEANACH
Killiemor
THE BURG
MACLEAN'S CROSS
Eilean Annraidh
IONA ABBEY AND CATHEDRAL
Rubha nan Cearc
100
IONA HERITAGE CENTRE
Kintra
Loch na Lathaich
ST COLUMBA EXHIBITION & WELCOME CENTRE
LOCH SCRIDAIN
Iona
Baile Mor
Aridhglas
Eorabus
Stac an Aoineidh
Sound of Iona
Fionnphort
A849
Lee
Fidden
Tiraghoil
Bunessan
376 CRUACHAN MIN
Loch Assapol
Erraid
ROSS OF MULL
Soa I.
Ardalanish
Uisken
Ardchiavaig
Scoor
Malcolm's
125
Eilean a'Chalmain
Rubha nam Braithrean
Rubh Ardalanish
Torran Rocks
Scale : 1:332 000
(approx 5 miles to 1 inch)
0 1 2 3 4 5 6 miles
0 1 2 3 4 5 6 7 8 9 10 km
A
B
C
D
E
F
G
H
J
K
2
3
4
5
6
7

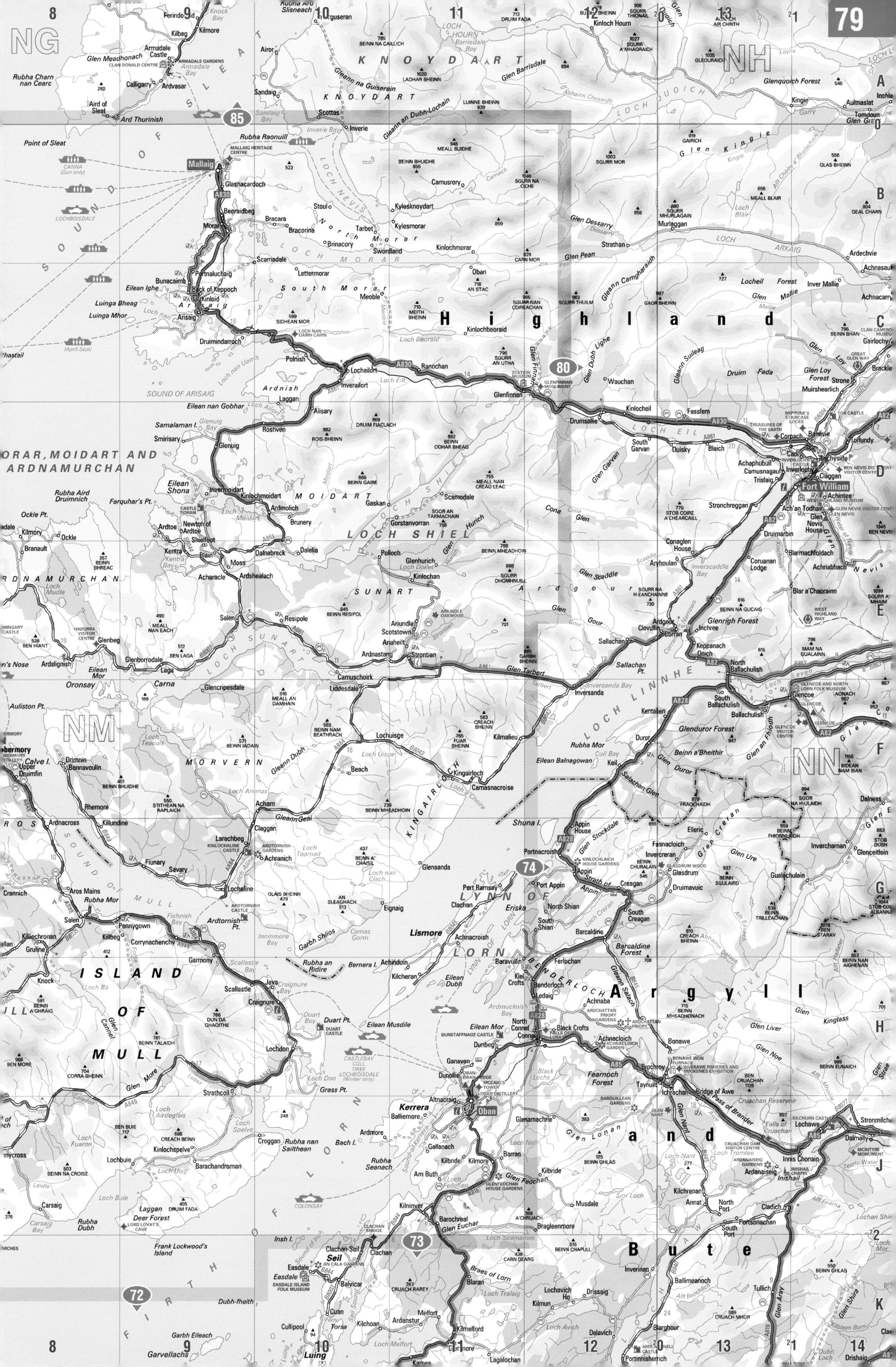

NG
NH
NM
NN
Knoydart
Highland
Argyll and Bute
Moidart
Sunart
Morvern
Ardgour
Island of Mull
Lismore
Kerrera
Seil
Luing
Mallaig
Fort William
Oban
Sound of Sleat
Sound of Arisaig
Sound of Mull
Firth of Lorn
Lynn of Lorn
Loch Nevis
Loch Morar
Loch Shiel
Loch Sunart
Loch Linnhe
Loch Eil
Loch Arkaig
Loch Quoich
Loch Etive
Loch Awe
Loch Leven
Loch Hourn
Loch Teacuis
Loch Aline
Loch Creran
Loch Feochan
Loch Spelve
Loch Buie
Loch Uisg
Glen Finnan
Glen Dessarry
Glen Pean
Glen Kingie
Glen Barrisdale
Glen Tarbert
Glen Scaddle
Glen Gour
Glen Duror
Glen Creran
Glen Ure
Glen Etive
Glen Orchy
Glen Lonan
Glen Euchar
Glen More
Glen Nevis
Glen Loy
Glen Mallie
Glen Garry
Glen Coe
Glencoe
Armadale Castle
Ardvasar
Kilbeg
Kilmore
Inverie
Airor
Sandaig
Scottas
Morar
Arisaig
Glenfinnan
Lochailort
Glenuig
Kinlochmoidart
Acharacle
Salen
Strontian
Kingairloch
Camasnacroise
Lochaline
Drimnin
Tobermory
Craignure
Lochdon
Duart Castle
Corran
Ardgour
Inversanda
Onich
North Ballachulish
South Ballachulish
Kentallen
Duror
Portnacroish
Appin
Port Appin
Creagan
Barcaldine
Benderloch
Connel
North Connel
Dunbeg
Taynuilt
Bonawe
Dalmally
Lochawe
Kilchrenan
Portsonachan
Cladich
Kilninver
Clachan-Seil
Easdale
Cullipool
Kilmelford
Melfort
Ardanstur
Arduaine
Corpach
Banavie
Caol
Inverlochy
Claggan
Achintee
Gairlochy
Achnacarry
Kinlochleven
Inverie Bay
Camusnagaul
Kinlocheil
Fassfern
Drumsallie
Kilchoan
Kinlochspelve
Lochbuie
Carsaig
Strathcoil
Gruline
Knock
Killiechronan
Pennygown
Fishnish Bay
Ardtornish Castle
Rubha an Ridire
Bernera I.
Eilean Musdile
Shuna I.
Eriska
Insh I.
Garvellachs
Dubh-fheith
Point of Sleat
Ard Thurinish
Rubha Raonuill
Eilean Shona
Ardnamurchan
A830
A861
A82
A828
A85
A816
A849
A884
B8043
B845
B840
B8077
B8007
B8044
85
80
74
73
72

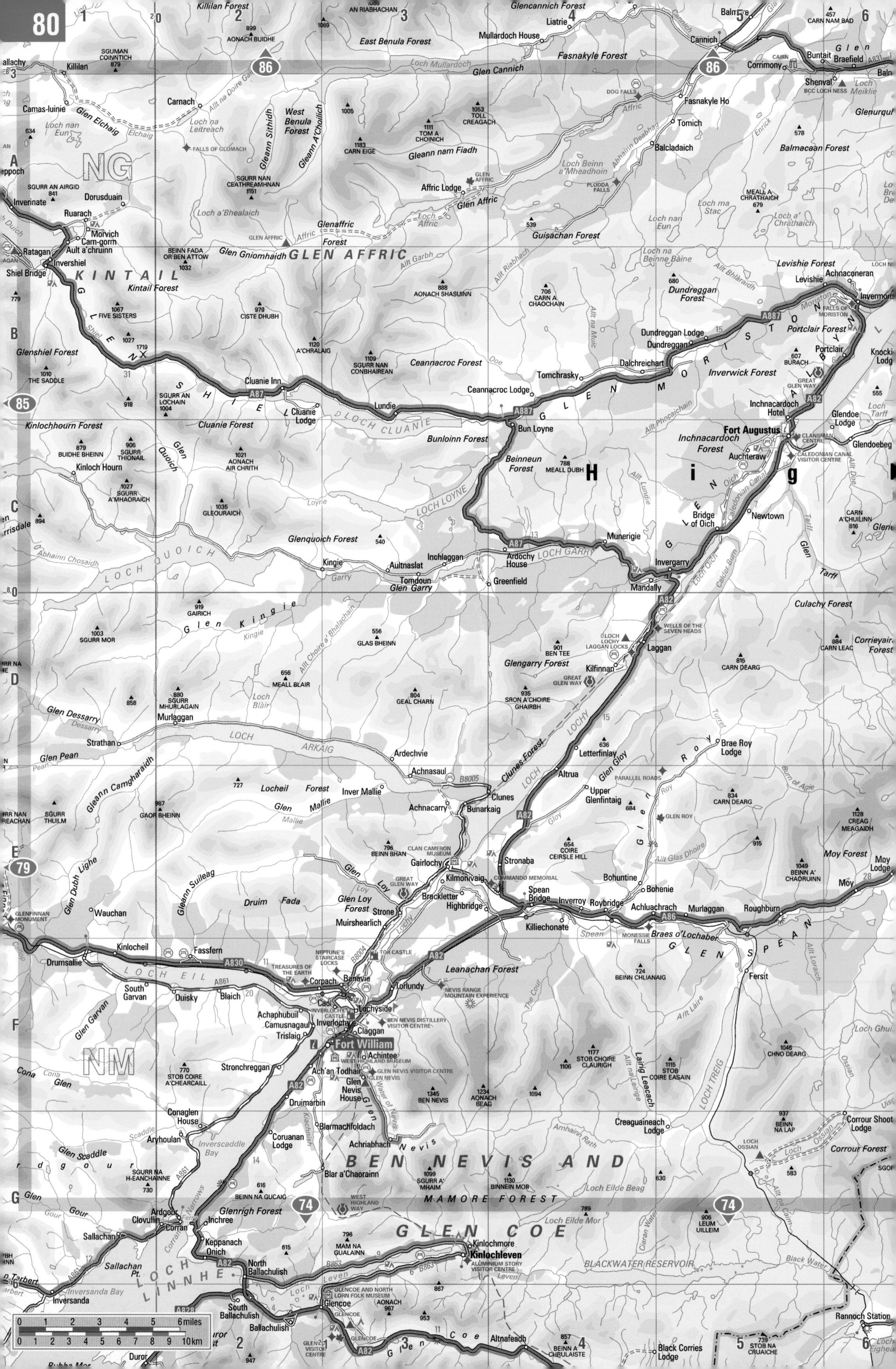

Killilan Forest
AN RIABHACHAN
Glencannich Forest
AONACH BUIDHE
East Benula Forest
Mullardoch House
Liatrie
Cannich
CARN NAM BAD
86
Loch Mullardoch
Glen Cannich
Fasnakyle Forest
Killilan
SGUMAN COINNTICH
Buntait
Glen Braefield
Corrimony
Shenval
BCC LOCH NESS
Loch Meiklie
Glenurquhart
Carnach
Camas-luinie
Glen Elchaig
Loch nan Eun
Loch na Leitreach
FALLS OF GLOMACH
Gleann Sithidh
West Benula Forest
Gleann A'Choilich
TOLL CREAGACH
TOM A CHOINICH
CARN EIGE
Gleann nam Fiadh
DOG FALLS
Affric
Fasnakyle Ho
Tomich
Abhainn Deabhag
Balcladaich
Balmacaan Forest
NG
SGURR AN AIRGID
Dorusduain
Inverinate
SGURR NAN CEATHREAMHNAN
GLEN AFFRIC
Affric Lodge
Glen Affric
Loch Beinn a'Mheadhoin
PLODDA FALLS
MEALL A CHRATHAICH
Loch ma Stac
Loch a'Chrathaich
Ruarach
Morvich
Carn-gorm
Ault a'chruinn
Ratagan
Invershiel
Shiel Bridge
Loch a'Bhealaich
Glenaffric Forest
Loch Affric
Guisachan Forest
Loch nan Eun
BEINN FADA OR BEN ATTOW
Glen Gniomhaidh
Allt Garbh
Loch na Beinne Bàine
Levishie Forest
Achnaconeran
Levishie
Invermoriston
KINTAIL
Kintail Forest
AONACH SHASUINN
CARN A CHAOCHAIN
Dundreggan Forest
FIVE SISTERS
CISTE DHUBH
A'CHRALAIG
SGURR NAN CONBHAIREAN
Ceannacroc Forest
Dundreggan Lodge
Dundreggan
Dalchreichart
FALLS OF MORISTON
Portclair Forest
Portclair
BURACH
Glenshiel Forest
THE SADDLE
Cluanie Inn
Tomchrasky
Ceannacroc Lodge
Inverwick Forest
GREAT GLEN WAY
Glen Moriston
SGURR AN LOCHAIN
Cluanie Lodge
Lundie
Loch Cluanie
Bun Loyne
Inchnacardoch Hotel
Glendoe Lodge
Glendoebeg
Kinlochhourn Forest
Cluanie Forest
Bunloinn Forest
Fort Augustus
Inchnacardoch Forest
CLANSMAN CENTRE
CALEDONIAN CANAL VISITOR CENTRE
BUIDHE BHEINN
SGURR THIONAIL
Glen Quoich
AONACH AIR CHRITH
Beinneun Forest
MEALL DUBH
Auchteraw
Kinloch Hourn
SGURR A'MHAORAICH
GLEOURAICH
Loch Loyne
Bridge of Oich
Newtown
CARN A'CHUILINN
Glenquoich Forest
A87
Munerigie
Abhainn Chosaidh
Loch Quoich
Kingie
Aultnaslat
Inchlaggan
Ardochy House
Loch Garry
Invergarry
Glen Tarff
Tomdoun
Glen Garry
Greenfield
Mandally
Culachy Forest
GAIRICH
Glen Kingie
SGURR MOR
GLAS BHEINN
WELLS OF THE SEVEN HEADS
LOCH LOCHY
LAGGAN LOCKS
BEN TEE
Laggan
CARN LEAC
Corrieyairack Forest
Glengarry Forest
Kilfinnan
CARN DEARG
MEALL BLAIR
GEAL CHARN
SRON A'CHOIRE GHAIRBH
SGURR MHURLAGAIN
Loch Blàir
Glen Dessarry
Murlaggan
Strathan
Loch Arkaig
Letterfinlay
Brae Roy Lodge
Glen Pean
Ardechvie
Achnasaul
Clunes Forest
Altrua
Glen Gloy
Glen Roy
PARALLEL ROADS
Gleann Camgharaidh
Locheil Forest
Inver Mallie
Clunes
Upper Glenfintaig
CARN DEARG
Glen Mallie
Achnacarry
Bunarkaig
GLEN ROY
SGURR THUILM
GAOR BHEINN
CREAG MEAGAIDH
Moy Forest
BEINN BHAN
CLAN CAMERON MUSEUM
Gairlochy
Stronaba
COIRE CEIRSLE HILL
Allt Glas Dhoire
BEINN A' CHAORUINN
Moy Lodge
Moy
Glen Dubh Lighe
Gleann Suileag
Glen Loy
Kilmonivaig
COMMANDO MEMORIAL
Bohuntine
Bohenie
Druim Fada
Glen Loy Forest
Brackletter
Highbridge
Spean Bridge
Inverroy
Roybridge
Achluachrach
Murlaggan
Roughburn
GLENFINNAN MONUMENT
Wauchan
Strone
Muirshearlich
Killiechonate
MONESSIE FALLS
Braes o'Lochaber
Glen Spean
Kinlocheil
Fassfern
Drumsallie
TREASURES OF THE EARTH
NEPTUNE'S STAIRCASE LOCKS
TOR CASTLE
Leanachan Forest
Loch Eil
Corpach
Banavie
BEINN CHLIANAIG
Fersit
South Garvan
Duisky
Blaich
Torlundy
NEVIS RANGE MOUNTAIN EXPERIENCE
Achaphubuil
INVERLOCHY CASTLE
Lochyside
BEN NEVIS DISTILLERY VISITOR CENTRE
Glen Garvan
Camusnagaul
Inverlochy
Claggan
Trislaig
Fort William
WEST HIGHLAND MUSEUM
Achintee
NM
STOB CHOIRE CLAURIGH
Lairig Leacach
STOB COIRE EASAIN
CHNO DEARG
Loch Treig
Stronchreggan
Ach'an Todhair
GLEN NEVIS VISITOR CENTRE
Cona Glen
STOB COIRE A'CHEARCAILL
Glen Nevis House
BEN NEVIS
AONACH BEAG
Druimarbin
Glen Nevis
Water of Nevis
Conaglen House
Blarmachfoldach
Creaguaineach Lodge
BEINN NA LAP
Corrour Shooting Lodge
Aryhoulan
Inverscaddle Bay
Coruanan Lodge
Achriabhach
LOCH OSSIAN
Loch Ossian
Corrour Forest
Glen Scaddle
BEN NEVIS AND
MAMORE FOREST
Blar a'Chaorainn
SGURR A' MHAIM
BINNEIN MOR
Loch Eilde Beag
SGURR NA H-EANCHAINNE
Corran Narrows
BEINN NA GUCAIG
74
WEST HIGHLAND WAY
Glen Gour
Ardgour
Clovullin
Corran
Inchree
Glenrigh Forest
Loch Eilde Mor
LEUM UILLEIM
Sallachan
Keppanach
Onich
GLEN COE
MAM NA GUALAINN
Kinlochmore
Kinlochleven
ALUMINIUM STORY VISITOR CENTRE
Sallachan Pt.
Loch Linnhe
A82
North Ballachulish
BLACKWATER RESERVOIR
Black Water
Inversanda Bay
Inversanda
Loch Leven
GLENCOE AND NORTH LORN FOLK MUSEUM
AONACH
Glencoe
Ballachulish
South Ballachulish
Rannoch Station
GLENCOE VISITOR CENTRE
Glen Coe
Altnafeadh
BEINN A CHRULAISTE
Black Corries Lodge
STOB NA CRUAICHE
0 1 2 3 4 5 6 miles
0 1 2 3 4 5 6 7 8 9 10 km

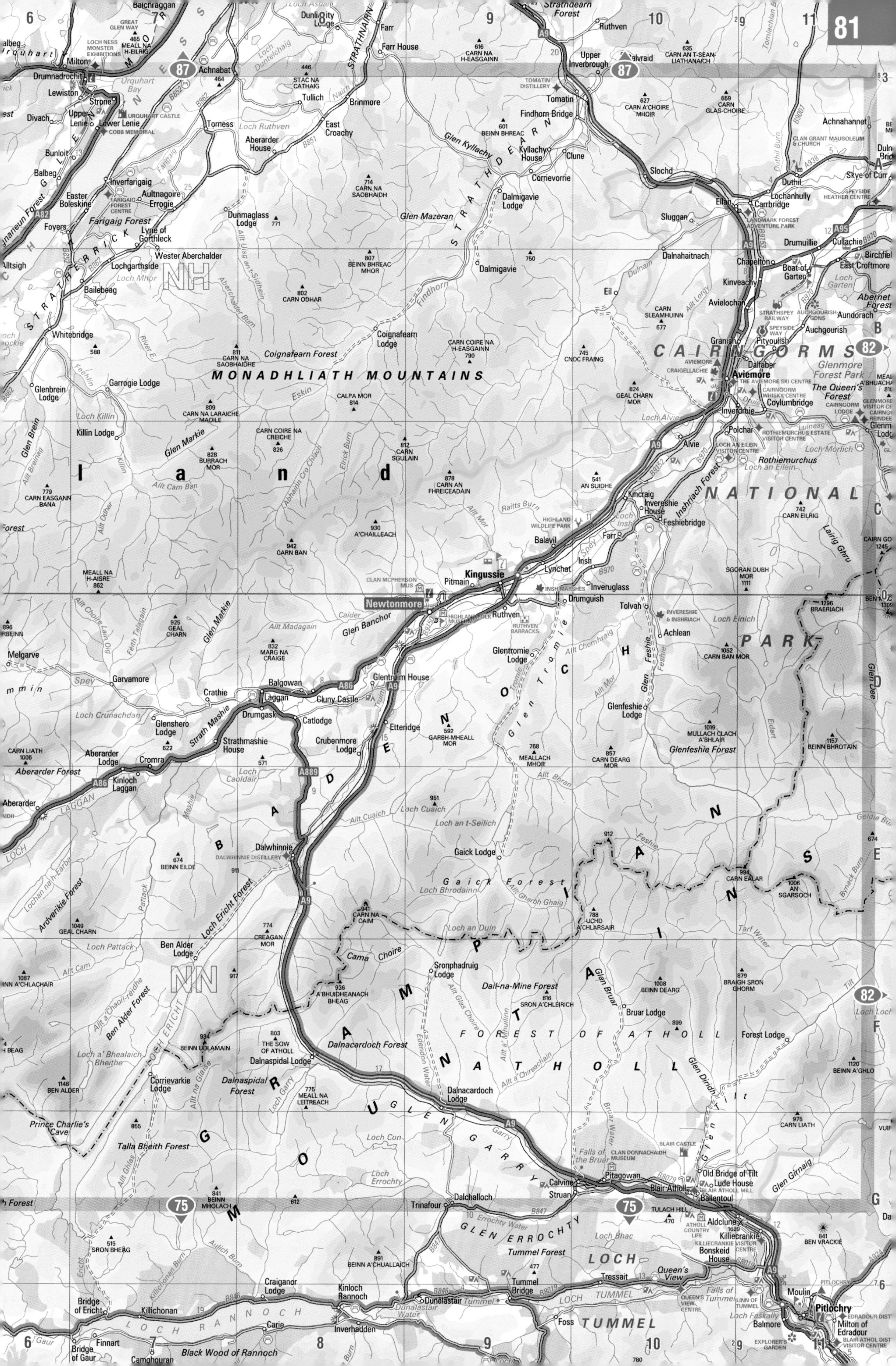

Balchraggan
Dunlichity Lodge
Strathdearn Forest
Ruthven
Farr
Farr House
616 CARN NA H-EASGAINN
635 CARN AN T-SEAN-LIATHANAICH
Upper Inverbrough
Calvraid
87
GREAT GLEN WAY
LOCH NESS MONSTER EXHIBITIONS
465 MEALL NA H-EILRIG
Urquhart
Milton
Drumnadrochit
Achnabat
464
446 STAC NA CATHAIG
Loch Duntelchaig
STRATHNAIRN
TOMATIN DISTILLERY
Tomatin
627 CARN A'CHOIRE MHOIR
659 CARN GLAS-CHOIRE
Lewiston
Strone
Urquhart Bay
URQUHART CASTLE
Upper Lenie
Lower Lenie
COBB MEMORIAL
Divach
Tullich
Brinmore
Torness
Loch Ruthven
East Croachy
Aberarder House
601 BEINN BHREAC
Findhorn Bridge
Glen Kyllachy
Kyllachy House
Clune
STRATHDEARN
Achnahannet
CLAN GRANT MAUSOLEUM & CHURCH
Bunloit
Balbeg
Inverfarigaig
FARIGAIG FOREST CENTRE
Aultnagoire
Errogie
Easter Boleskine
714 CARN NA SAOBHAIDH
Corrievorrie
Dalmigavie Lodge
Slochd
Duthil
Lochanhully
Carrbridge
Skye of Curr
SPEYSIDE HEATHER CENTRE
Ellan
LANDMARK FOREST ADVENTURE PARK
Farigaig Forest
Foyers
Lyne of Gorthleck
Dunmaglass Lodge
771
Glen Mazeran
Sluggan
Drumuillie
Cullachie
Wester Aberchalder
Alltsigh
Lochgarthside
Loch Mhor
NH
Allt Uisg an t-Sidhein
807 BEINN BHREAC MHOR
750
Dalmigavie
Dalnahaitnach
Chapelton
Boat of Garten
Birchfield
East Croftmore
Loch Garten
Bailebeag
802 CARN ODHAR
Eil
Dulnain
Kinveachy
Avielochan
Abernethy Forest
Aundorach
STRATHERRICK
Whitebridge
588
Findhorn
Coignafearn Lodge
CARN SLEAMHUINN
677
STRATHSPEY RAILWAY
AUCHGOURISH GDNS
Auchgourish
SPEYSIDE WAY
Pityoulish
811 CARN NA SAOBHAIDHE
Coignafearn Forest
CARN COIRE NA H-EASGAINN
790
745 CNOC FRAING
CAIRNGORMS
Granish
AVIEMORE
82
Glenmore Forest Park
Dalfaber
CRAIGELLACHIE
Aviemore
THE AVIEMORE SKI CENTRE
MONADHLIATH MOUNTAINS
Glenbrein Lodge
Garrogie Lodge
Eskin
CALPA MOR 814
824 GEAL CHARN MOR
CAIRNGORM WHISKY CENTRE
Coylumbridge
The Queen's Forest
Loch Killin
809 CARN NA LARAICHE MAOILE
Inverdruie
CAIRNGORM LODGE
Killin Lodge
CARN COIRE NA CREICHE
826
812 CARN SGULAIN
Loch Alvie
Polchar
ROTHIEMURCHUS ESTATE VISITOR CENTRE
Glen Brein
Glen Markie
828 BURRACH MOR
Alvie
LOCH AN EILEIN VISITOR CENTRE
Loch Morlich
Rothiemurchus
Loch an Eilein
Highland
878 CARN AN FHREICEADAIN
541 AN SUIDHE
779 CARN EASGANN BANA
Allt Cam Ban
Kincraig
Inveshie House
Inshriach Forest
NATIONAL
742 CARN EILRIG
Raitts Burn
HIGHLAND WILDLIFE PARK
Loch Insh
Feshiebridge
930 A'CHAILLEACH
Lairig Ghru
Forest
942 CARN BAN
Balavil
Farr
CAIRN GORM 1245
Insh
MEALL NA H-AISRE 862
CLAN MCPHERSON MUS
Pitmain
Kingussie
Lynchat
B970
SGORAN DUBH MOR 1111
INSH MARSHES
Inveruglass
Newtonmore
Drumguish
Tolvah
1296 BRAERIACH
BEN MACDUI 1309
Calder
HIGHLAND FOLK MUSEUM
Ruthven
RUTHVEN BARRACKS
INVERESHIE & INSHRIACH
Loch Einich
896
925 GEAL CHARN
Allt Madagain
Glen Banchor
Achlean
PARK
832 MARG NA CRAIGE
Glentromie Lodge
Allt Chomhraig
1052 CARN BAN MOR
Glen Dee
Melgarve
Spey
Garvamore
Balgowan
Glentruim House
A86
A9
Glen Feshie
Crathie
Laggan
Cluny Castle
Glen Tromie
Loch Crunachdan
Drumgask
Catlodge
Glenshero Lodge
Etteridge
Glenfeshie Lodge
Strath Mashie
Crubenmore Lodge
592 GARBH-MHEALL MOR
1019 MULLACH CLACH A'BHLAIR
Eidart
CARN LIATH 1006
Strathmashie House
622
571
768 MEALLACH MHOR
857 CARN DEARG MOR
Glenfeshie Forest
1157 BEINN BHROTAIN
Aberarder Lodge
Cromra
Aberarder Forest
Loch Caoldair
A889
Allt Bhran
Kinloch Laggan
A86
Aberarder
LAGGAN
951
Loch Cuaich
Allt Cuaich
Loch an t-Seilich
Geldie Burn
LOCH
912
Feshie
674
674 BEINN EILDE
Dalwhinnie
DALWHINNIE DISTILLERY
911
Gaick Lodge
994 CARN EALAR
1006 AN SGARSOCH
Bynack Burn
Ardverikie Forest
Loch Ericht Forest
Gaick Forest
Loch Bhrodainn
Allt Gharbh Ghaig
941 CARN NA CAIM
788 UCHD A'CHLARSAIR
Loch an Duin
1049 GEAL CHARN
774 CREAGAN MOR
Tarf Water
Loch Pattack
Ben Alder Lodge
Cama Choire
Sronphadruig Lodge
Glen Bruar
879 BRAIGH SRON GHORM
1087
NN
917
936 A'BHUIDHEANACH BHEAG
Dail-na-Mine Forest
816 SRON A'CHLEIRICH
1008 BEINN DEARG
Allt a'Chaoil-reidhe
Ben Alder Forest
LOCH ERICHT
Allt Glas Choire
Bruar Lodge
899
Loch Loch
934 BEINN UDLAMAIN
803 THE SOW OF ATHOLL
Dalnacardoch Forest
Edendon Water
FOREST OF ATHOLL
Forest Lodge
Loch a' Bhealaich Bheithe
Dalnaspidal Lodge
Allt a' Mhuilinn
Allt a' Chireachain
Glen Diridh
1120 BEINN A'GHLO
1148 BEN ALDER
Corrievarkie Lodge
Dalnaspidal Forest
Allt na Glaise
775 MEALL NA LEITREACH
Loch Garry
Dalnacardoch Lodge
GLEN GARRY
Tilt
Prince Charlie's Cave
855
975 CARN LIATH
Talla Bheith Forest
Loch Con
BLAIR CASTLE
Falls of the Bruar
CLAN DONNACHAIDH MUSEUM
Glen Tilt
Bruar Water
Loch Errochty
Calvine
Pitagowan
Blair Atholl
Old Bridge of Tilt
Lude House
Glen Girnaig
841 BEINN MHOLACH
612
Struan
BLAIR ATHOLL MILL
Ballentoul
75
Trinafour
Dalchalloch
B847
Errochty Water
TULACH HILL 470
ATHOLL COUNTRY LIFE
Aldclune
Killiecrankie
KILLIECRANKIE VISITOR CENTRE
841 BEN VRACKIE
GLEN ERROCHTY
Loch Bhac
Bonskeid House
515 SRON BHEAG
Aulich Burn
Tummel Forest
891 BEINN A'CHUALLAICH
477
LOCH
Queen's View
QUEEN'S VIEW CENTRE
Craiganor Lodge
Kinloch Rannoch
Tummel Bridge
Tressait
Falls of Tummel
LINN OF TUMMEL
PITLOCHRY
Moulin
Pitlochry
EDRADOUR DISTILLERY
Bridge of Ericht
Killichonan
LOCH RANNOCH
Dunalastair
Dunalastair Water
LOCH TUMMEL
Loch Faskally
Balmore
Milton of Edradour
BLAIR ATHOLL DISTILLERY VISITOR CENTRE
Carie
Inverhadden
Foss
TUMMEL
Finnart
Bridge of Gaur
Black Wood of Rannoch
EXPLORER'S GARDEN
Camghouran
780

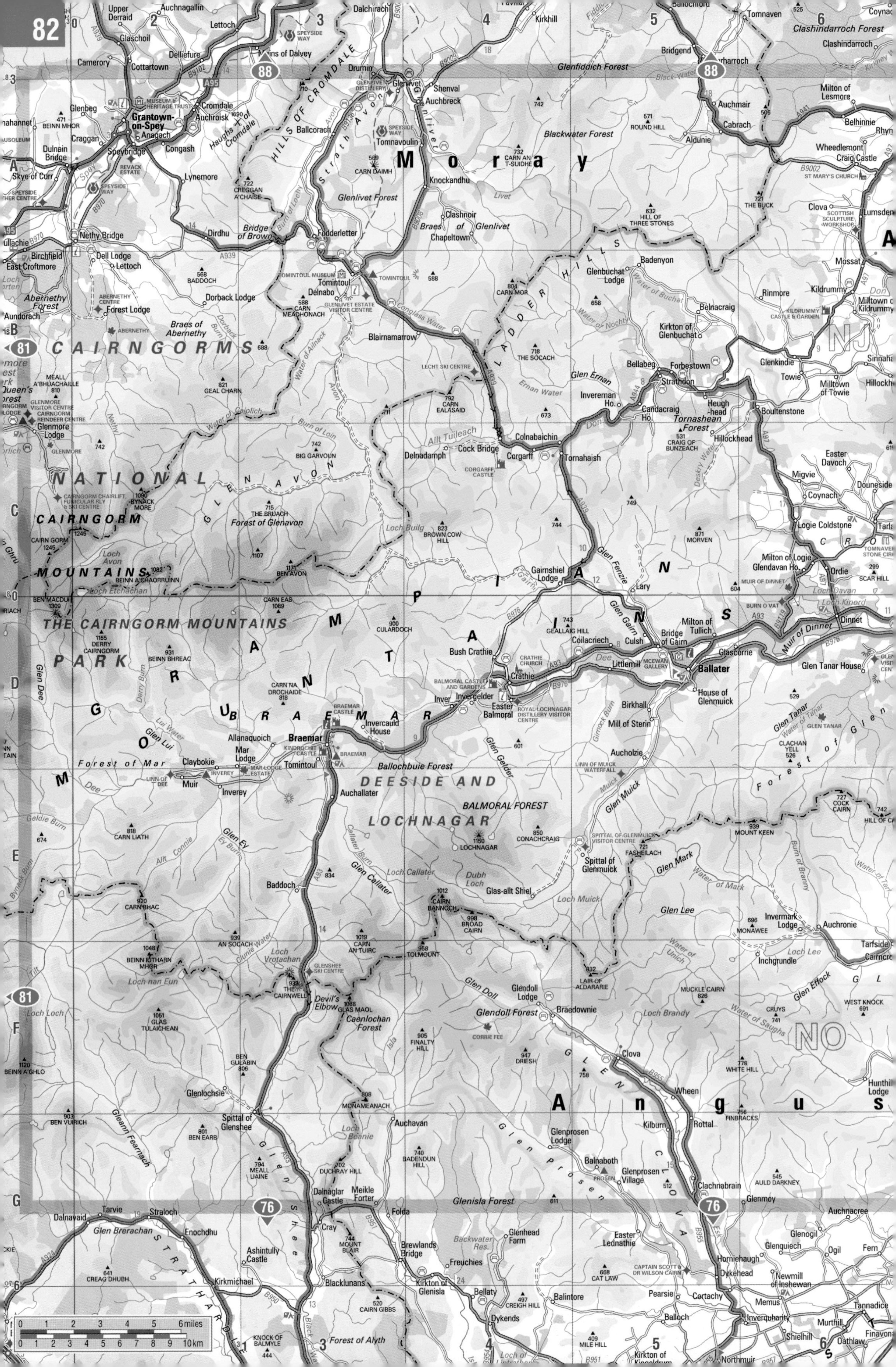
Moray
CAIRNGORMS
NATIONAL PARK
CAIRNGORM MOUNTAINS
THE CAIRNGORM MOUNTAINS
GRAMPIAN MOUNTAINS
DEESIDE AND LOCHNAGAR
Angus
Grantown-on-Spey
Nethy Bridge
Tomintoul
Glenlivet
Tomnavoulin
Cock Bridge
Corgarff
Strathdon
Bellabeg
Ballater
Braemar
Crathie
Balmoral Castle and Gardens
Bridge of Gairn
Dinnet
Glenmore Lodge
Spittal of Glenshee
Glenshee Ski Centre
The Cairnwell
Devil's Elbow
Clova
Glen Clova
Glen Prosen
Glenisla Forest
Forest of Alyth
Kirkmichael
Blacklunans
Glen Doll
Braedownie
Lochnagar
Loch Muick
Spittal of Glenmuick
Glen Tanar House
Mount Keen
Lecht Ski Centre
Ladder Hills
Hills of Cromdale
Glenlivet Forest
Blackwater Forest
Glenfiddich Forest
Clashindarroch Forest
Abernethy Forest
Forest of Mar
Ballochbuie Forest
Balmoral Forest
Caenlochan Forest
Glendoll Forest
Ben Macdui 1309
Cairn Gorm 1245
Ben Avon 1171
Beinn a' Ghlo 1120
Glas Maol 1068
88
81
76
NO
NJ
0 1 2 3 4 5 6 miles
0 1 2 3 4 5 6 7 8 9 10 km

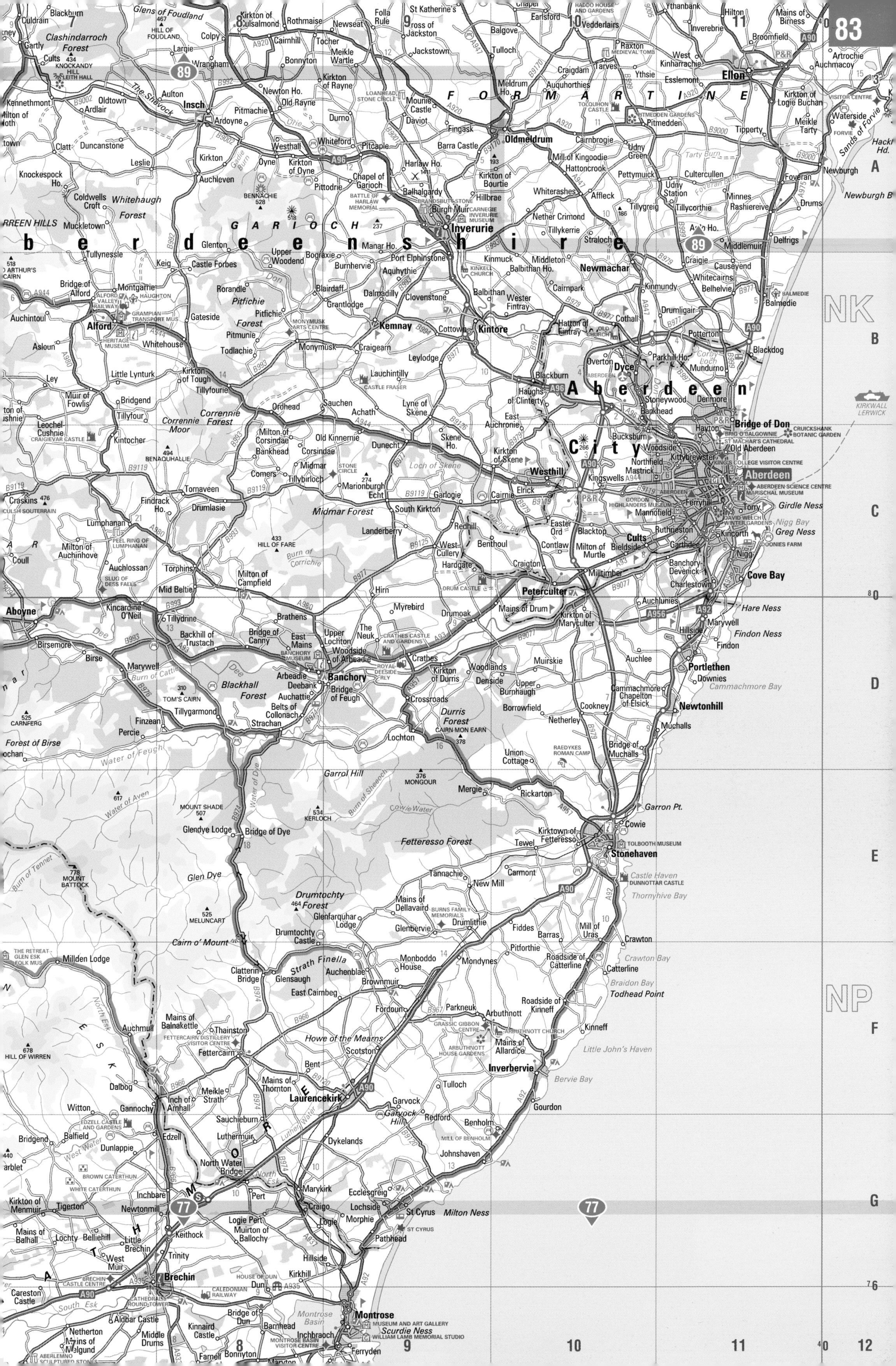

Glens of Foudland
Blackhurn
Culdrain
Gartly
Clashindarroch Forest
Cults
KNOCKANDY HILL
LEITH HALL
HILL OF FOUDLAND
Largie
Wrangham
Kirkton of Culsalmond
Rothmaise
Colpy
Cairnhill
Tocher
Newseat
Folla Rule
St Katherine's
Cross of Jackston
Jackstown
Meikle Wartle
Bonnyton
Kirkton of Rayne
Newton Ho.
Old Rayne
LOANHEAD STONE CIRCLE
Mounie Castle
Daviot
Durno
Balgove
Tulloch
Earlsford
Vedderlairs
HADDO HOUSE AND GARDENS
Ythanbank
Hilton
Mains of Birness
Broomfield
Raxton
MEDIEVAL TOMB
West Kinharrachie
Inverebrie
Ythsie
Esslemont
Ellon
Artrochie
Auchmacoy
Tarves
Craigdam
Auquhorthies
Meldrum Ho.
F O R M A R T I N E
TOLQUHON CASTLE
PITMEDDEN GARDENS
Pitmedden
Kirkton of Logie Buchan
VISITOR CENTRE
Waterside
FORVIE
Sands of Forvie
Meikle Tarty
Tipperty
Hackley Hd.
Kennethmont
Oldtown
Ardlair
Aulton
The Shevock
Insch
Pitmachie
Ardoyne
Whiteford
Pitcaple
Fingask
Oldmeldrum
Barra Castle
Cairnbrogie
Udny Green
Mill of Kingoodie
Hattoncrook
Pettymuick
Cultercullen
Newburgh
Newburgh Bar
Foveran
Udny Station
Minnes
Tarty Burn
Foveran Burn
Tillycorthie
Rashiereive
Drums
Clatt
Duncanstone
Leslie
Kirkton
Oyne
Westhall
Kirkton of Oyne
Harlaw Ho.
Chapel of Garioch
Pittodrie
Balhalgardy
Knockespock Ho.
Auchleven
BENNACHIE
Kirkton of Bourtie
Hillbrae
Whiterashes
Affleck
Tillygreig
BATTLE OF HARLAW MEMORIAL
BRANDSBUTT STONE
CARNEGIE INVERURIE MUSEUM
Burgh Muir
Inverurie
Nether Crimond
Tillykerrie
Coldwells Croft
Whitehaugh Forest
Muckletown
CORREEN HILLS
G A R I O C H
Auchorthies
Middlemuir
Delfrigs
Straloch
A b e r d e e n s h i r e
Glenton
Manar Ho.
Upper Woodend
Bograxie
Port Elphinstone
Kinmuck
Middleton
Newmachar
Craigie
Causeyend
Tullynessle
Keig
Castle Forbes
Burnhervie
Aquhythie
KINKELL CHURCH
Balbithan Ho.
Whitecairns
Belhelvie
Balmedie
BALMEDIE
Bridge of Alford
ALFORD VALLEY RAILWAY
Montgarrie
HAUGHTON
GRAMPIAN TRANSPORT MUS
Rorandle
Pitfichie Forest
Blairdaff
Dalmadilly
Clovenstone
Balbithan
Wester Fintray
Cairnpark
Kinmundy
Drumligair
Auchintoul
Alford
HERITAGE MUSEUM
Gateside
Grantlodge
Pitfichie
MONYMUSK ARTS CENTRE
Kemnay
Cottown
Kintore
Hatton of Fintray
OLD CHURCH
Cothall
Potterton
Blackdog
NK
Asloun
Whitehouse
Pitmunie
Todlachie
Monymusk
Craigearn
Leylodge
Overton
Dyce
Parkhill Ho.
Corby Loch
Mundurno
Ley
Little Lynturk
Kirkton of Tough
Tillyfourie
Lauchintilly
CASTLE FRASER
Blackburn
Haughs of Clinterty
Aberdeen City
Stoneywood
Denmore
Bankhead
KIRKWALL LERWICK
Muir of Fowlis
Bridgend
Tillyfour
Ordhead
Sauchen
Achath
Lyne of Skene
East Auchronie
Bridge of Don
Hayton
BRIG O' BALGOWNIE
CRUICKSHANK BOTANIC GARDEN
ST MACHAR'S CATHEDRAL
Old Aberdeen
Leochel Cushnie
CRAIGIEVAR CASTLE
Correnie Moor
Corrennie Forest
Milton of Corsindae
Old Kinnernie
Dunecht
Skene Ho.
Bucksburn
Woodside
Kittybrewster
KING'S COLLEGE VISITOR CENTRE
Kintocher
BENAQUHALLIE
Bankhead
Corsindae
Midmar
STONE CIRCLE
Loch of Skene
Kirkton of Skene
Westhill
Northfield
Mastrick
Aberdeen
Comers
Tillybirloch
Marionburgh
Echt
Garlogie
Cairnie
Elrick
Kingswells
ABERDEEN SCIENCE CENTRE
MARISCHAL MUSEUM
Craskins
CULSH SOUTERRAIN
Tornaveen
Drumlasie
Findrack Ho.
Midmar Forest
South Kirkton
GORDON HIGHLANDERS MUSEUM
Mannofield
Ferryhill
Torry
Girdle Ness
Lumphanan
PEEL RING OF LUMPHANAN
Landerberry
Redhill
Benthoul
Easter Ord
Blacktop
Ruthrieston
DAVID WELCH WINTER GARDENS
Nigg Bay
Greg Ness
Kincorth
Milton of Auchinhove
Coull
Auchlossan
SLUG OF DESS FALLS
HILL OF FARE
Burn of Corrichie
West Cullery
Hardgate
Contlaw
Milton of Murtle
Cults
Bieldside
Garthdee
DOONIES FARM
Nigg
Torphins
Mid Beltie
Milton of Campfield
Hirn
DRUM CASTLE
Craigton
Milltimber
Peterculter
Banchory Devenick
Charlestown
Cove Bay
Aboyne
Kincardine O'Neil
Tillydrine
Myrebird
Drumoak
Mains of Drum
Kirkton of Maryculter
Auchlunies
Hare Ness
Marywell
Findon Ness
Hillside
Findon
Birsemore
Backhill of Trustach
Bridge of Canny
Brathens
Upper Lochton
The Neuk
CRATHES CASTLE AND GARDENS
East Mains
BANCHORY MUSEUM
Woodside of Arbeadie
Crathes
ROYAL DEESIDE RLY
Auchlee
Portlethen
Birse
Marywell
Burn of Cattie
Dee
Blackhall Forest
TOM'S CAIRN
Arbeadie
Deebank
Banchory
Bridge of Feugh
Auchattie
Belts of Collonach
Kirkton of Durris
Woodlands
Denside
Muirskie
Upper Burnhaugh
Downies
Cammachmore Bay
Cammachmore
Chapelton of Elsick
Newtonhill
CARNFERG
Finzean
Tillygarmond
Strachan
Crossroads
Durris Forest
CAIRN MON EARN
Borrowfield
Netherley
Cookney
Muchalls
Percie
Forest of Birse
Water of Feugh
Lochton
RAEDYKES ROMAN CAMP
Bridge of Muchalls
Union Cottage
Garrol Hill
MONGOUR
Burn of Sheeoch
Mergie
Rickarton
Water of Aven
MOUNT SHADE
Water of Dye
KERLOCH
Cowie Water
Garron Pt.
Cowie
Glendye Lodge
Bridge of Dye
Fetteresso Forest
Kirktown of Fetteresso
Tewel
TOLBOOTH MUSEUM
Stonehaven
Burn of Tennet
MOUNT BATTOCK
Glen Dye
Tannachie
New Mill
Carmont
Castle Haven
DUNNOTTAR CASTLE
Thornyhive Bay
Drumtochty Forest
Mains of Dellavaird
BURNS FAMILY MEMORIALS
Glenbervie
Drumlithie
Fiddes
Barras
Mill of Uras
MELUNCART
Glenfarquhar Lodge
Cairn o' Mount
Drumtochty Castle
Pitforthie
Crawton
THE RETREAT GLEN ESK FOLK MUS
Millden Lodge
Strath Finella
Monboddo House
Mondynes
Roadside of Catterline
Crawton Bay
Catterline
Clatterin Bridge
Glensaugh
Auchenblae
Brownmuir
East Cairnbeg
Braidon Bay
Todhead Point
NP
North Esk
Fordoun
Parkneuk
Arbuthnott
Roadside of Kinneff
GRASSIC GIBBON CENTRE
ARBUTHNOTT CHURCH
Kinneff
Mains of Balnakettle
Thainston
Auchmull
FETTERCAIRN DISTILLERY VISITOR CENTRE
Howe of the Mearns
ARBUTHNOTT HOUSE GARDENS
Mains of Allardice
HILL OF WIRREN
Fettercairn
Scotston
Little John's Haven
Inverbervie
Bent
Bervie Bay
Dalbog
Meikle Strath
Mains of Thornton
Laurencekirk
Tulloch
Witton
Gannochy
Inch of Arnhall
Garvock
Garvock Hill
Gourdon
EDZELL CASTLE AND GARDENS
Sauchieburn
Redford
Benholm
Bridgend
Balfield
Edzell
Luthermuir
Luther Water
Dykelands
MILL OF BENHOLM
West Water
Dunlappie
Johnshaven
BROWN CATERTHUN
North Water Bridge
WHITE CATERTHUN
Marykirk
Ecclesgreig
Inchbare
Pert
Lochside
Kirkton of Menmuir
Tigerton
Newtonmill
Craigo
St Cyrus
Milton Ness
Logie Pert
Morphie
Mains of Balhall
Lochty
Belliehill
Keithock
Muirton of Ballochy
Logie
ST CYRUS
Little Brechin
Pathhead
West Muir
Trinity
Hillside
BRECHIN CASTLE CENTRE
Brechin
HOUSE OF DUN
Kirkhill
Dun
CALEDONIAN RAILWAY
Careston Castle
CATHEDRAL ROUND TOWER
South Esk
Montrose Basin
Bridge of Dun
Montrose
MUSEUM AND ART GALLERY
Aldbar Castle
Scurdie Ness
Netherton
Kinnaird Castle
Middle Drums
Barnhead
WILLIAM LAMB MEMORIAL STUDIO
Mains of Melgund
Inchbraoch
MONTROSE BASIN VISITOR CENTRE
ABERLEMNO SCULPTURED STONES
Farnell
Bonnyton
Ferryden
7
8
9
10
11
12
A
B
C
D
E
F
G

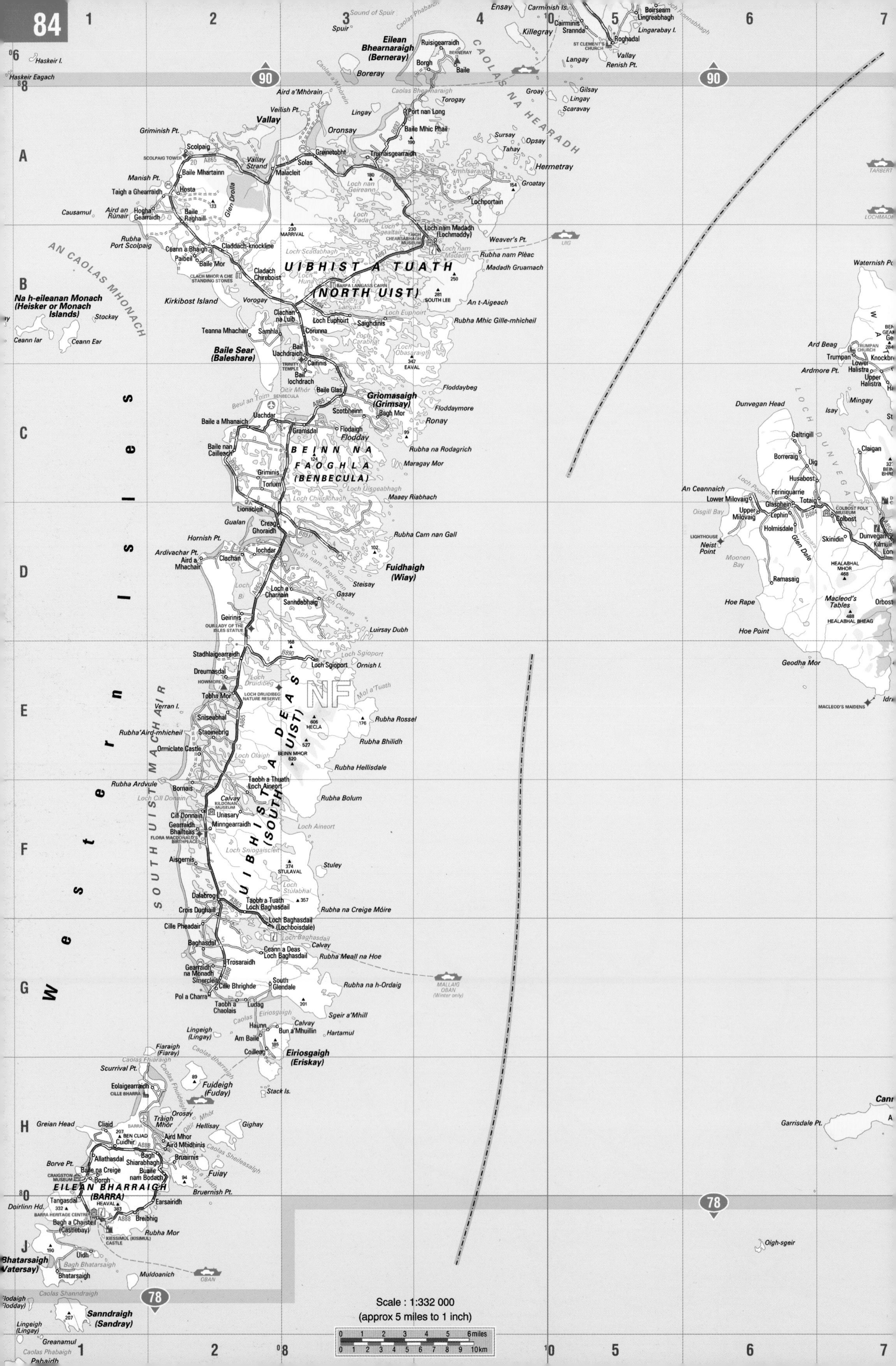

Eilean Bhearnaraigh (Berneray)
Ruisigearraidh
Borgh
Baile
Boreray
Lingay
Pabbay
Oronsay
Vallay
Griminish Pt.
Scolpaig
Scolpaig Tower
Vallay Strand
Malacleit
Solas
Greinetobht
Port nan Long
Baile Mhic Phail
Trumaisgearraidh
Loch nan Geireann
Baile Mhartainn
Manish Pt.
Taigh a Ghearraidh
Hosta
Glen Drolla
Causamul
Aird an Runair
Hogha Gearraidh
Baile Raghaill
Rubha Port Scolpaig
Ceann a Bhaigh
Paibeil
Baile Mor
Claddach-knockline
Clach Mhor a Che Standing Stones
Cladach Chireboist
Marrival
Loch Scadabhagh
Loch Fada
Loch Sgealtair
Taigh Chearsabhagh Museum
Loch nam Madadh (Lochmaddy)
Loch Amhlasaigh
Lochportain
Hermetray
Groatay
Weaver's Pt.
Rubha nam Plèac
Madadh Gruamach
UIBHIST A TUATH (NORTH UIST)
Loch Hunn
Barpa Langass Cairn
Loch Langais
South Lee
An t-Aigeach
Rubha Mhic Gille-mhicheil
AN CAOLAS MHONACH
Na h-eileanan Monach (Heisker or Monach Islands)
Stockay
Ceann Iar
Ceann Ear
Kirkibost Island
Vorogay
Clachan na Luib
Loch Euphoirt
Saighdinis
Corunna
Loch Carabhat
Loch Obasaraigh
Eaval
Teanna Mhachair
Samhla
Baile Sear (Baleshare)
Bail Uachdraich
Trinity Temple
Cairinis
Bail Iochdrach
Oitir Mhòr
Baile Glas
Griomasaigh (Grimsay)
Floddaybeg
Floddaymore
Beul an Toim
Benbecula
Uachdar
Scotbheinn
Bagh Mor
Ronay
Baile a Mhanaich
Gramsdal
Flodaigh
Flodday
Rubha na Rodagrich
Baile nan Cailleach
BEINN NA FAOGHLA (BENBECULA)
Maragay Mor
Griminis
Torlum
Loch Uisgeabhagh
Loch Chiurabhagh
Maaey Riabhach
Lionacleit
Gualan
Creag Ghoraidh
Rubha Cam nan Gall
Hornish Pt.
Ardivachar Pt.
Aird a Mhachair
Clachan
Iochdar
Bagh nam Faoilean
Fuidhaigh (Wiay)
Loch Bi
Loch a Charnain
Sanndabhaig
Steisay
Gasay
Loch Carnan
Geirinis
Our Lady of the Isles Statue
Luirsay Dubh
Stadhlaigearraidh
Loch Sgioport
Ornish I.
Dreumasdal
Howmore
Loch Druidibeg
Loch Druidibeg Nature Reserve
NF
Mol a' Tuath
Tobha Mor
Verran I.
Sniseabhal
Hecla
Rubha Rossel
Rubha'Aird-mhicheil
Staoinebrig
Rubha Bhilidh
Ormiclate Castle
Beinn Mhor
Loch Olaigh
Rubha Hellisdale
Rubha Ardvule
Bornais
Taobh a Thuath Loch Aineort
Loch Cill Donnain
Calvay
Kildonan Museum
Rubha Bolum
Cill Donnain
Unasary
Gearraidh Bhailteas
Minngearraidh
Loch Aineort
Flora MacDonald's Birthplace
UIBHIST A DEAS (SOUTH UIST)
Loch Sniogaiscleit
Aisgernis
Stuley
Stulaval
Loch Stulabhal
SOUTH UIST MACHAIR
Dalabrog
Taobh a Tuath Loch Baghasdail
Rubha na Creige Móire
Crois Dughaill
Loch Baghasdail (Lochboisdale)
Cille Pheadair
Baghasdal
Ceann a Deas Loch Baghasdail
Rubha Meall na Hoe
Trosaraidh
Gearraidh na Monadh
Smercleit
Cille Bhrighde
South Glendale
Rubha na h-Ordaig
Mallaig Oban (Winter only)
Pol a Charra
Taobh a Chaolais
Ludag
Caolas Eiriosgeigh
Sgeir a'Mhill
Lingeigh (Lingay)
Haunn
Bun a'Mhuillin
Calvay
Hartamul
Am Baile
Coilleag
Eiriosgaigh (Eriskay)
Fiaraigh (Fiaray)
Caolas Fhiaraigh
Scurrival Pt.
Fuideigh (Fuday)
Eolaigearraidh
Cille Bharra
Stack Is.
Orosay
Greian Head
Cliaid
Traigh Mhor
Hellisay
Gighay
Ben Cliad
Cuidhir
Aird Mhor
Aird Mhidhinis
Caolas Sheileasaigh
Allathasdal
Bagh
Shiarabhagh
Buaile nam Bodach
Bruairnis
Fuiay
Borve Pt.
Baile na Creige
Craigston Museum
Borgh
EILEAN BHARRAIGH (BARRA)
Bruernish Pt.
Tangasdal
Heaval
Earsairidh
Doirlinn Hd.
Barra Heritage Centre
Breibhig
Bagh a Chaisteil (Castlebay)
Kiessimul (Kisimul) Castle
Rubha Mor
Bhatarsaigh (Vatersay)
Uidh
Bagh Bhatarsaigh
Bhatarsaigh
Muldoanich
Oban
Caolas Shanndraigh
Flodaigh (Flodday)
Sanndraigh (Sandray)
Lingeigh (Lingay)
Greanamul
Caolas Phabaidh
Pabaidh
Sound of Spuir
Spuir
Caolas Phabaidh
Ensay
Carminish Is.
Killegray
Cairminis
Srannda
St Clement's Church
Boirseam
Lingreabhagh
Lingarabay I.
Roghadal
Langay
Vallay
Renish Pt.
Caolas Bhearnaraigh
Torogay
Groay
Gilsay
Lingay
Scaravay
CAOLAS NA HEARADH
Sursay
Opsay
Tahay
Aird a'Mhòrain
Veilish Pt.
Uig
Tarbert
Lochmaddy
Waternish Pen.
Ard Beag
Trumpan
Trumpan Church
Lower Halistra
Upper Halistra
Knockbreck
Ardmore Pt.
Mingay
Isay
Dunvegan Head
Loch Dunvegan
Galtrigill
Borreraig
Uig
Claigan
Husabost
An Ceannaich
Loch Pooltiel
Lower Milovaig
Feriniquarrie
Glasphein
Totaig
Colbost Folk Museum
Colbost
Oisgill Bay
Upper Milovaig
Lephin
Holmisdale
Glen Dale
Skinidin
Dunvegan
Kilmuir
Lighthouse
Neist Point
Moonen Bay
Healabhal Mhor
Ramasaig
Hoe Rape
Macleod's Tables
Healabhal Bheag
Orbost
Hoe Point
Geodha Mor
Macleod's Maidens
Idrigill
Canna
Garrisdale Pt.
Oigh-sgeir
Western Isles
90
78
A
B
C
D
E
F
G
H
J
1
2
3
4
5
6
7
Scale : 1:332 000
(approx 5 miles to 1 inch)
0 1 2 3 4 5 6 miles
0 1 2 3 4 5 6 7 8 9 10km

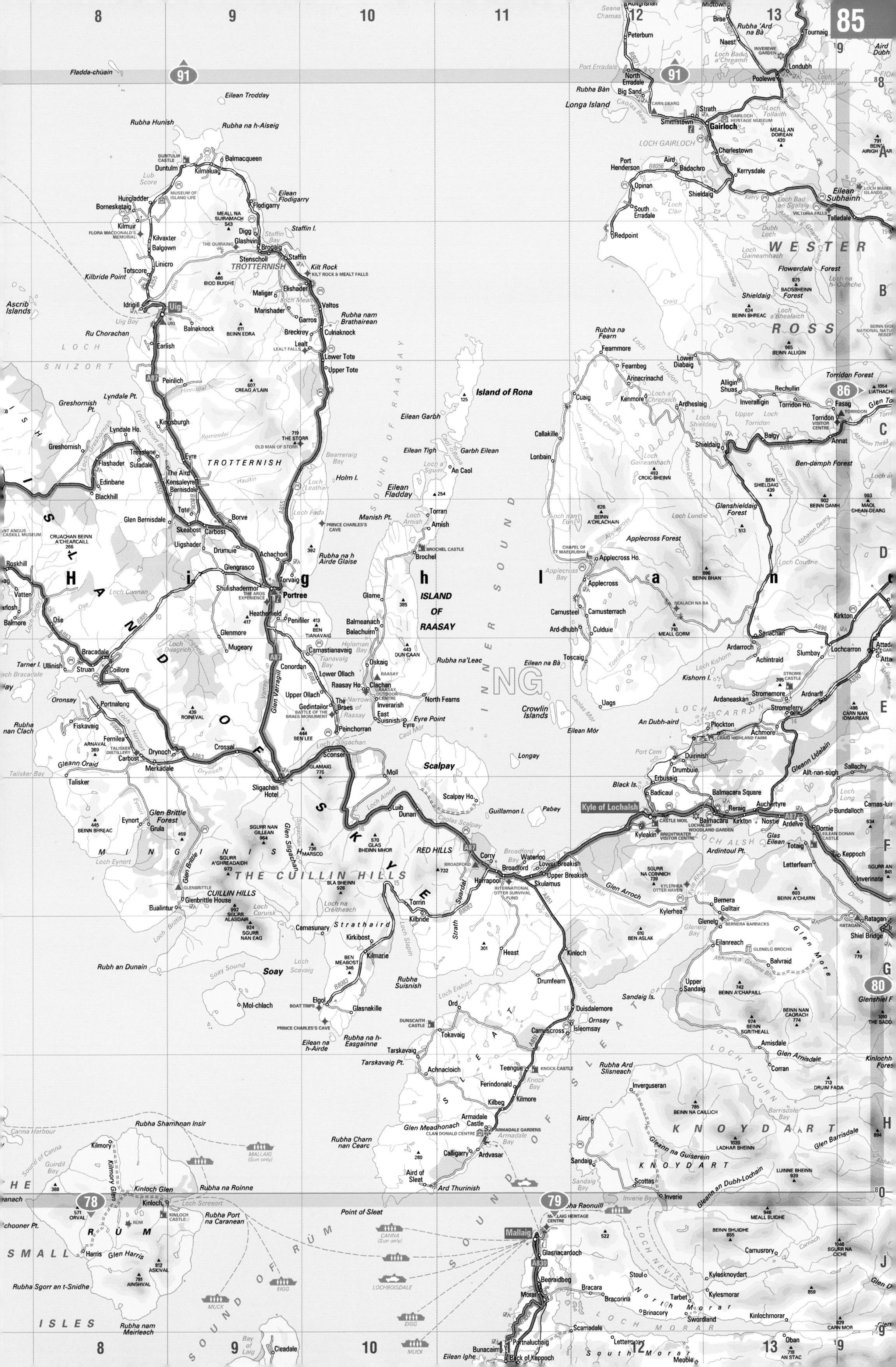
8
9
10
11
12
13
91
Fladda-chùain
Eilean Trodday
Rubha Hunish
Rubha na h-Aiseig
Duntulm Castle
Duntulm
Kilmaluag
Balmacqueen
Lub Score
Hungladder
Borneskeitaig
Museum of Island Life
Eilean Flodigarry
Flodigarry
Meall na Suiramach
543
Kilmuir
Flora Macdonald's Memorial
Kilvaxter
Balgown
Digg
Glashvin
Staffin Bay
Staffin I.
The Quiraing
Brogaig
Staffin
Stenscholl
Trotternish
Linicro
Totscore
Kilbride Point
466
Biod Buidhe
Kilt Rock
Kilt Rock & Mealt Falls
Elishader
Maligar
Loch Mealt
Valtos
Marishader
Garros
Rubha nam Brathairean
Ascrib Islands
Idrigill
Uig
Uig Bay
Ru Chorachan
Balnaknock
611
Beinn Edra
Breckrey
Culnaknock
Lealt
Lealt Falls
Earlish
Loch Snizort
Lower Tote
Upper Tote
A87
Peinlich
607
Creag a' Lain
Greshornish Pt.
Lyndale Pt.
Lyndale Ho.
Kingsburgh
Romesdal
719
The Storr
Old Man of Storr
Greshornish
Treaslane
Suladale
Flashader
Eyre
Trotternish
Bearreraig Bay
The Aird
Kensaleyre
Bernisdale
Edinbane
Blackhill
Haultin
Loch Leathan
Tote
Loch Fada
Borve
Glen Bernisdale
Skeabost
Carbost
Prince Charles's Cave
Cruachan Beinn a' Chearcaill
266
Uigshader
Drumuie
Achachork
392
Rubha na h Airde Glaise
Roskhill
Vatten
Glengrasco
Torvaig
Shulishadermor
The Aros Experience
Portree
Loch Connan
Ose
Heatherfield
417
Penifiler
413
Ben Tianavaig
Balmore
B885
Glenmore
Mugeary
Loch Duagrich
Camastianavaig
Tianavaig Bay
Bracadale
Tarner I.
Ullinish
Struan
Coillore
Conordan
Lower Ollach
Oronsay
Portnalong
439
Roineval
Upper Ollach
Gedintailor
Battle of the Braes Monument
The Braes
Fiskavaig
Rubha nan Clach
Fernilea
Arnaval
369
Talisker Distillery
Carbost
Drynoch
Crossal
444
Ben Lee
Peinchorran
Loch Sligachan
Gleann Oraid
Talisker Bay
Talisker
Merkadale
Sligachan Hotel
Sconser
Glamaig
775
Glen Brittle Forest
445
Beinn Bhreac
Eynort
Grula
459
Sgurr nan Gillean
964
Glen Sligachan
570
Glas Bheinn Mhor
736
Marsco
Loch Eynort
Sgurr a' Ghreadaidh
973
The Cuillin Hills
Bla Bheinn
928
Glenbrittle
Cuillin Hills
Glenbrittle House
Bualintur
992
Sgurr Alasdair
924
Sgurr nan Eag
Loch Coruisk
Loch na Creitheach
Camasunary
Strathaird
Kirkibost
Rubh an Dunain
Soay Sound
Soay
Loch Scavaig
Ben Meabost
346
Kilmarie
Mol-chlach
Elgol
Boat Trips
Glasnakille
Prince Charles's Cave
Eilean na h-Airde
Rubha na h-Easgainne
Skye
Island of Skye
Sound of Raasay
Island of Rona
125
Eilean Garbh
Eilean Tigh
Garbh Eilean
An Caol
Holm I.
Eilean Fladday
254
Torran
Manish Pt.
Arnish
Brochel Castle
Brochel
Island of Raasay
Glame
385
Balmeanach
Balachuim
Holoman Bay
443
Dun Caan
Oskaig
Raasay
Clachan
Raasay Outdoor Centre
Raasay Ho.
Inverarish
East Suisnish
Eyre
Eyre Point
North Fearns
Rubha na' Leac
Caol Mòr
Moll
Scalpay
Scalpay Ho.
Loch Ainort
Luib
Dunan
Caolas Scalpay
Red Hills
Corry
Broadford
Broadford Bay
732
Harrapool
International Otter Survival Fund
Torrin
Kilbride
Strath Suardal
B8083
Loch Slapin
301
Heast
Rubha Suisnish
Loch Eishort
Ord
Dunscaith Castle
Tokavaig
Tarskavaig
Tarskavaig Pt.
Achnacloich
Sleat
Teangue
Knock Castle
Knock Bay
Ferindonald
Kilbeg
Kilmore
Armadale Castle
Armadale Gardens
Clan Donald Centre
Armadale Bay
Glen Meadhonach
Rubha Charn nan Cearc
280
Calligarry
Ardvasar
Aird of Sleat
Ard Thurinish
Point of Sleat
Inner Sound
Guillamon I.
Pabay
Longay
Crowlin Islands
Eilean Mòr
Eilean na Bà
Waterloo
Lower Breakish
Upper Breakish
Skulamus
A851
Kinloch
Drumfearn
Loch na Dal
Duisdalemore
Isleornsay
Camuscross
Ornsay
Sound of Sleat
Rubha Ard Slisneach
Seana Chamas
Aultgrishan
Midtown
Peterburn
Brae
Rubha 'Ard na Bà
Naast
Inverewe Garden
Loch Bad a' Chreamh
Tournaig
Londubh
Aird Dubh
Poolewe
Port Erradale
North Erradale
Rubha Bàn
Big Sand
Longa Island
Caolas Beag
Carn Dearg
Strath
Gairloch Heritage Museum
Smithstown
Gairloch
Loch Tollaidh
Meall an Doirean
420
Loch Gairloch
Charlestown
791
Beinn Airigh Char
Port Henderson
Aird
B8056
Badachro
Kerrysdale
Opinan
Shieldaig
Eilean Subhainn
Loch Maree Islands
South Erradale
Loch Clàir
Loch Bad an Sgalaig
Victoria Falls
Talladale
Redpoint
Wester Ross
Loch Gaineamhach
Flowerdale Forest
875
Baosbheinn
Shieldaig Forest
Craig
624
Beinn Bhreac
Loch a' Bhealaich
Beinn Eighe National Nature Reserve
Rubha na Fearn
Fearnmore
Fearnbeg
Loch Torridon
Arinacrinachd
Lower Diabaig
985
Beinn Alligin
Torridon Forest
1054
Liathach
Cuaig
Kenmore
Alligin Shuas
Inverallgin
Rechullin
Torridon Ho.
86
Fasag
Ardheslaig
Upper Loch Torridon
Torridon Visitor Centre
Callakille
Loch Shieldaig
Balgy
A896
Annat
Lonbain
Shieldaig
Loch Gaineamhach
493
Croic-Bheinn
Ben-damph Forest
Ben Shieldaig
439
902
Beinn Damh
993
Maol Chean-dearg
626
Beinn a' Chlachain
Glenshieldaig Forest
Loch Lundie
513
Applecross Forest
Chapel of St Maelrubha
Applecross Ho.
896
Beinn Bhan
Applecross Bay
Applecross
Bealach na Bà
Camusteel
Camusterrach
Ard-dhubh
Culduie
710
Meall Gorm
Sanachan
Kirkton
Ardarroch
Achintraid
Slumbay
Lochcarron
Toscaig
Loch Kishorn
Kishorn I.
Strome Castle
395
Uags
Ardaneaskan
Stromemore
Ardnarff
Strome Ferry
486
Carn nan Iomairean
Loch Carron
An Dubh-aird
Plockton
Craig Highland Farm
Achmore
Port Cam
Duirinish
Drumbuie
Gleann Udalain
Allt-nan-sugh
Sallachy
Black Is.
Erbusaig
Badicaul
Balmacara Square
Kyle of Lochalsh
Castle Moil
Lochalsh Woodland Garden
Balmacara
Reraig
Kirkton
Auchertyre
Nostie
Ardelve
Bundalloch
Camas-luinie
Kyleakin
Brightwater Visitor Centre
Loch Alsh
Glas Eilean
Eilean Donan Castle
Dornie
Totaig
Ardintoul Pt.
Keppoch
Letterfearn
Sgurr na Coinnich
739
Kylerhea Otter Haven
Glen Arroch
Kyle Rhea
Kylerhea
603
Beinn a' Chuirn
Invertinate
Loch Duich
Bernera
Galltair
Bernera Barracks
Glenelg
Glenelg Bay
Ratagan
Shiel Bridge
610
Ben Aslak
Eilanreach
Glenelg Brochs
Glen More
Balvraid
779
Sandaig Is.
Upper Sandaig
742
Beinn a' Chapaill
80
Glenshiel Forest
974
Beinn Sgritheall
Beinn nan Caorach
774
1010
The Saddle
Arnisdale
Glen Arnisdale
Corran
Loch Hourn
Kinlochhourn Forest
713
Druim Fada
Inverguseran
785
Beinn na Caillich
Barrisdale Bay
Airor
Knoydart
1020
Ladhar Bheinn
Glen Barrisdale
894
Gleann na Guiserein
Sandaig
Sandaig Bay
Luinne Bheinn
939
Scottas
Inverie
Inverie Bay
Gleann an Dubh-Lochain
946
Meall Buidhe
Beinn Bhuidhe
855
Camusrory
Carnach
1040
Sgurr na Ciche
Loch Nevis
Rubha Raonuill
79
Mallaig Heritage Centre
Mallaig
522
Glasnacardoch
A830
Stoul
Kylesknoydart
Kylesmorar
859
Beoraidbeg
Bracara
Bracorina
Tarbet
North Morar
Morar
Brinacory
Swordland
Kinlochmorar
829
Carn Mòr
Scamadale
Letterm...
Portnaluchaig
South Morar
Oban
718
An Stac
Meoble
Bunacaimb
Back of Keppoch
Eilean Ighe
Canna Harbour
Rubha Shamhnan Insir
Sound of Canna
Guirdil Bay
Kilmory
388
Kilmory Glen
Kinloch Glen
Rubha na Roinne
Mallaig (Sun only)
78
571
Orval
Kinloch
Loch Scresort
Kinloch Castle
Rubha Port na Caranean
Rùm
Schooner Pt.
Small Isles
Harris
Glen Harris
812
Askival
781
Ainshval
Rubha Sgorr an t-Snidhe
Rubha nam Meirleach
Sound of Rùm
Canna (Sun only)
Lochboisdale
Eigg
Muck
Bay of Laig
Cleadale
Isle of Skye
NG
A
B
C
D
E
F
G
H
J

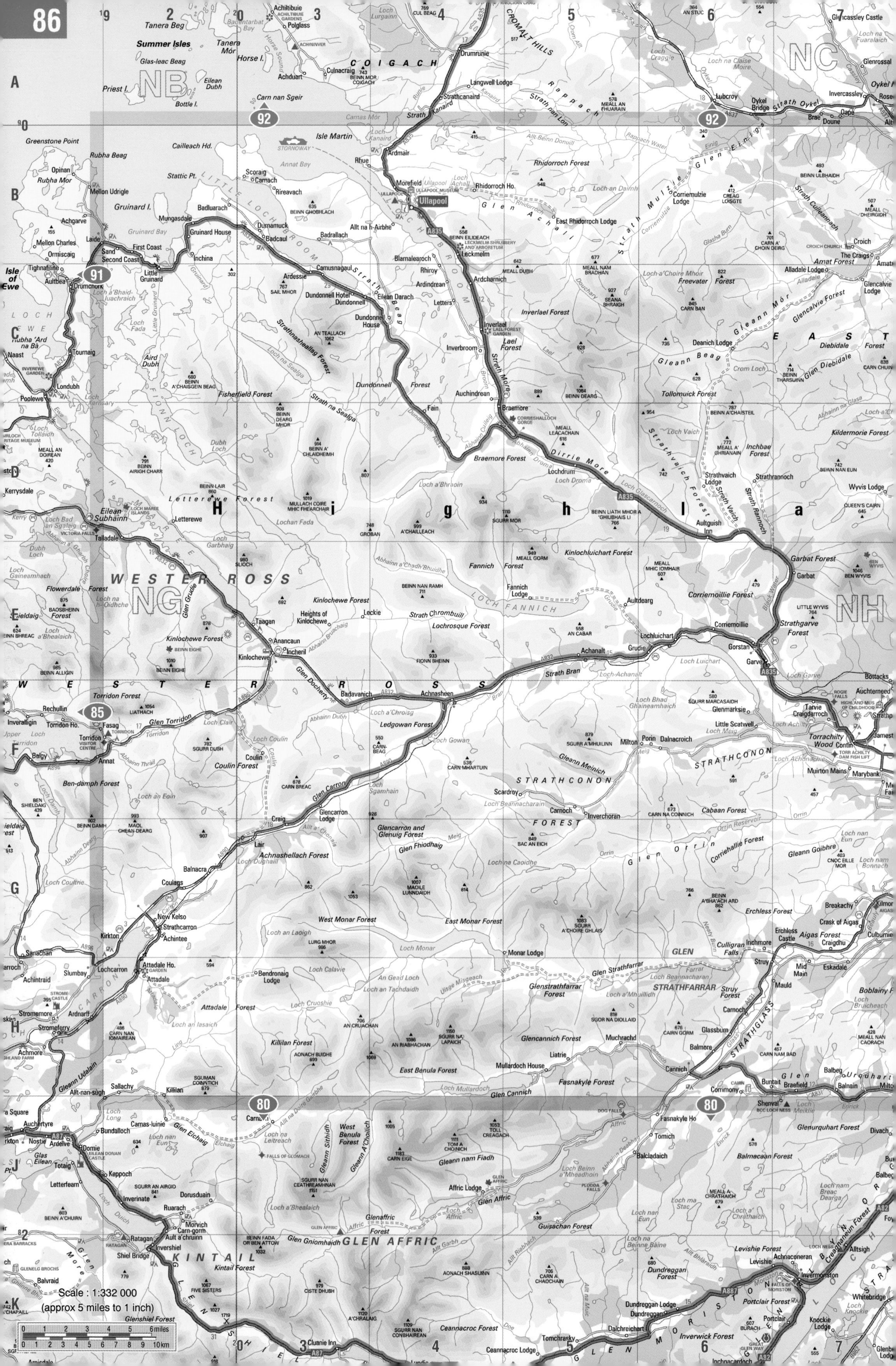
Summer Isles
Tanera Beg
Tanera Mór
Horse I.
Glas-leac Beag
Priest I.
NB
Eilean Dubh
Bottle I.
Achiltibuie
Polglass
Achduart
Culnacraig
COIGACH
Carn nan Sgeir
92
Drumrunie
CROMALT HILLS
Langwell Lodge
Strathcanaird
Rappach
Strath nan Lon
Lubcroy
Oykel Bridge
Strath Oykel
Invercassley
NC
Glencassley Castle
Glenrossal
Greenstone Point
Rubha Beag
Opinan
Rubha Mor
Mellon Udrigle
Gruinard I.
Achgarve
Mellon Charles
Ormiscaig
Laide
Sand
Second Coast
First Coast
Gruinard House
Mungasdale
Badluarach
Isle Martin
Cailleach Hd.
Stattic Pt.
Scoraig
Carnach
Rireavach
Annat Bay
Ardmair
Rhue
Morefield
Ullapool
Rhidorroch Forest
Rhidorroch Ho.
Glen Achall
East Rhidorroch Lodge
Strath Mulzie
Corriemulzie Lodge
Glen Einig
Strath Cuileannach
Croich
The Craigs
Amat Forest
Alladale Lodge
Glencalvie Lodge
Glencalvie Forest
Isle of Ewe
Tighnafiline
Aultbea
Drumchork
91
Little Gruinard
Inchina
Dundonnell
Badcaul
Badrallach
Camusnagaul
Ardessie
Dundonnell Hotel
Eilean Darach
Dundonnell House
Strath Beag
Leckmelm
Ardcharnich
Blarnalearoch
Rhiroy
Ardindrean
Letters
Inverlael
Inverlael Forest
Freevater Forest
Deanich Lodge
Gleann Mór
Gleann Beag
EAST
Diebidale
Tournaig
Inverewe Garden
Londubh
Poolewe
Aird Dubh
Loch Fada
Strathnasheallag Forest
An Teallach
Fisherfield Forest
Strath na Sealga
Dundonnell Forest
Inverbroom
Lael Forest
Strath More
Auchindrean
Braemore
Fain
Beinn Dearg
Tollomuick Forest
Kildermorie Forest
Loch Maree
Letterewe Forest
Braemore Forest
Dirrie More
Lochdrum
Strathvaich Forest
Strathvaich Lodge
Strath Rannoch
Strathrannoch
Wyvis Lodge
Kerrysdale
Eilean Subhainn
Talladale
Letterewe
Lochan Fada
H
i
g
h
l
a
Aultguish Inn
Fannich Forest
Kinlochluichart Forest
Loch Fannich
Fannich Lodge
Garbat Forest
Garbat
Ben Wyvis
WESTER ROSS
NG
Flowerdale Forest
Kinlochewe Forest
Heights of Kinlochewe
Leckie
Strath Chrombuill
Lochrosque Forest
Taagan
Anancaun
Kinlochewe
Incheril
Glen Docherty
Corriemoillie Forest
Aultdearg
Corriemoillie
Lochluichart
Grudie
Achanalt
Strath Bran
Gorstan
Garve
Strathgarve Forest
NH
Little Wyvis
WESTER ROSS
Torridon Forest
Rechullin
Inveralligin
Torridon Ho.
85
Fasag
Torridon
Glen Torridon
Badavanich
Achnasheen
Ledgowan Forest
Glenmarksie
Little Scatwell
Loch Meig
Milton
Porin
Dalnacroich
Tarvie
Craigdarroch
Torrachilty Wood
Contin
Balgy
Annat
Coulin
Coulin Forest
Ben-damph Forest
Glen Carron
STRATHCONON
Gleann Meinich
Scardroy
Carnoch
Inverchoran
FOREST
Muirton Mains
Marybank
Craig
Glencarron Lodge
Glencarron and Glenuig Forest
Glen Fhiodhaig
Lair
Achnashellach Forest
Glen Orrin
Corriehallie Forest
Cabaan Forest
Gleann Goibhre
Balnacra
Coulags
New Kelso
Strathcarron
Achintee
Kirkton
Sanachan
Achintraid
Slumbay
Lochcarron
Attadale Ho.
Attadale
West Monar Forest
East Monar Forest
Loch Monar
Monar Lodge
Erchless Forest
Erchless Castle
Aigas Forest
Crask of Aigas
Breakachy
Culligran Falls
Inchmore
Struy
Mid Main
Eskadale
GLEN
Glen Strathfarrar
Glenstrathfarrar Forest
STRATHFARRAR
Struy Forest
Bendronaig Lodge
Attadale Forest
Stromemore
Ardnarff
Stromeferry
Achmore
Killilan Forest
Glencannich Forest
Muchrachd
Mullardoch House
Liatrie
Glassburn
Carnoch
Balmore
Cannich
STRATHGLASS
Mauld
Boblainy Forest
East Benula Forest
Fasnakyle Forest
Glen Cannich
Gleann Udalain
Allt-nan-sugh
Sallachy
Killilan
Balbeg
Buntait
Braefield
Glen Urquhart
Balnain
Corrimony
80
Shenval
Auchertyre
Nostie
Ardelve
Dornie
Eilean Donan Castle
Totaig
Camas-luinie
Glen Elchaig
Bundalloch
West Benula Forest
Fasnakyle Ho
Tomich
Balcladaich
Glenurquhart Forest
Divach
Balmacaan Forest
Keppoch
Letterfearn
Inverinate
Dorusduain
Ruarach
Morvich
Carn-gorm
Ault a'chruinn
Gleann nam Fiadh
Affric Lodge
Glen Affric
Glenaffric Forest
GLEN AFFRIC
Guisachan Forest
Plodda Falls
Ratagan
Invershiel
Shiel Bridge
KINTAIL
Kintail Forest
Five Sisters
Glen Shiel
Levishie Forest
Levishie
Achnaconeran
Invermoriston
Dundreggan Forest
Dundreggan Lodge
Dundreggan
Portclair Forest
Portclair
Inverwick Forest
Glen Moriston
Dalchreichart
Tomchrasky
Ceannacroc Forest
Ceannacroc Lodge
Cluanie Inn
Whitebridge
Knockie Lodge
Glenelg Brochs
Balvraid
Glenshiel Forest
Scale : 1:332 000
(approx 5 miles to 1 inch)
0 1 2 3 4 5 6 miles
0 1 2 3 4 5 6 7 8 9 10 km

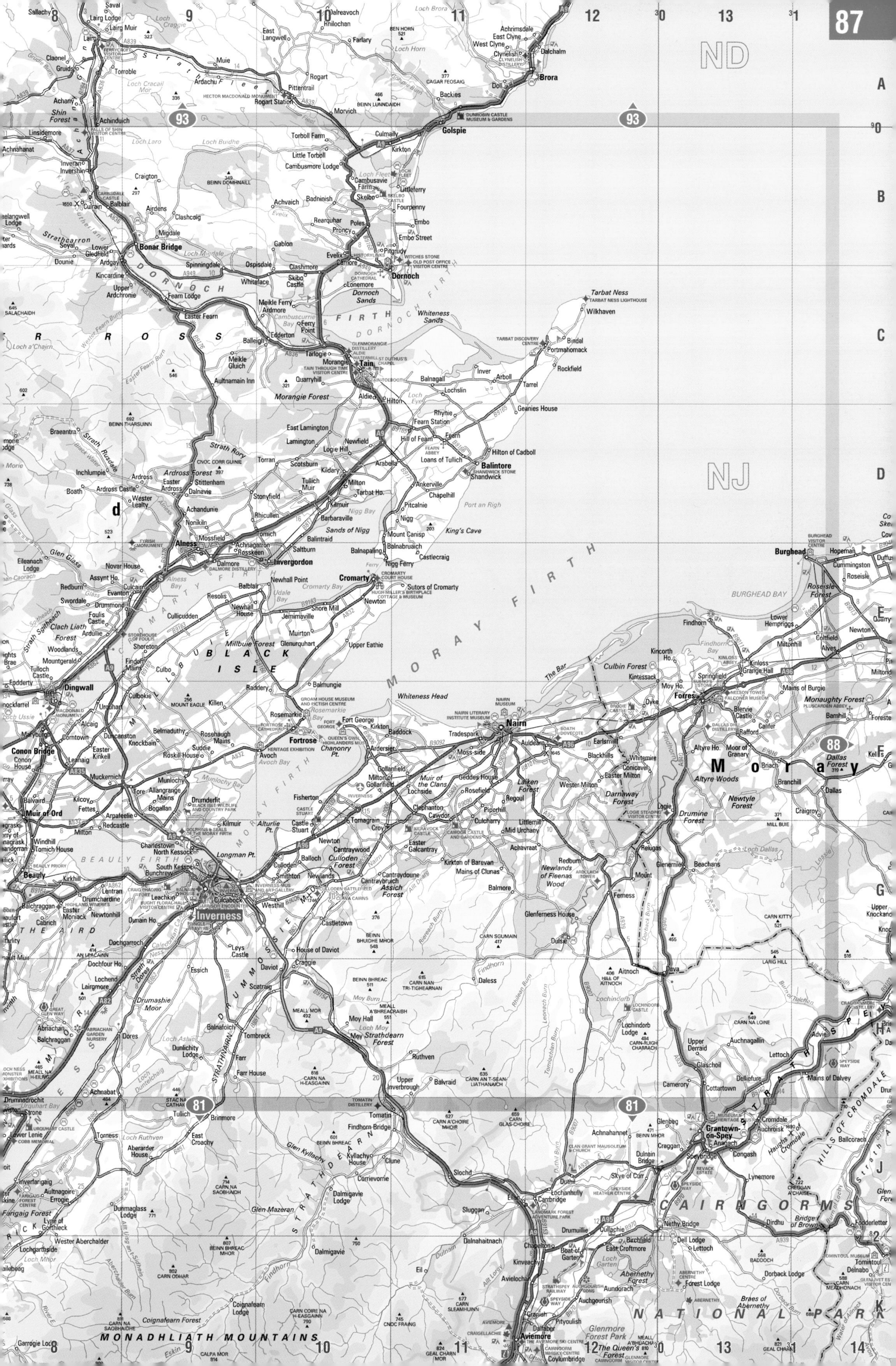
ND
NJ
Brora
Golspie
Dornoch
DORNOCH FIRTH
Bonar Bridge
Tain
Tarbat Ness
Portmahomack
ROSS
Balintore
Invergordon
Alness
Cromarty
CROMARTY FIRTH
MORAY FIRTH
BLACK ISLE
Dingwall
Conon Bridge
Fortrose
Muir of Ord
Beauly
BEAULY FIRTH
Inverness
Nairn
Forres
Burghead
BURGHEAD BAY
Moray
Culbin Forest
Kinloss
Findhorn
Cawdor
Culloden Forest
Strathdearn Forest
Grantown-on-Spey
Carrbridge
Aviemore
Boat of Garten
Nethy Bridge
Tomintoul
CAIRNGORMS NATIONAL PARK
MONADHLIATH MOUNTAINS
DRUMMOSSIE
THE AIRD
Dalwhinnie
Tomatin
Slochd
Dulnain Bridge
Cromdale
HILLS OF CROMDALE
Lochindorb
Ferness
Dallas
Dava
Whiteness Head
Sands of Nigg
Dornoch Sands
Morangie Forest
Strath Rory
Glen Glass
Strathcarron
Glen Mazeran
Glen Kyllachy
Glenmore Forest Park
Abernethy Forest
Coignafearn Forest
Loch Ruthven
Loch Fleet
Strath Fleet
93
81
88
A9
A96
A95
A939
A949
A836
A835
A862
A832
B9176

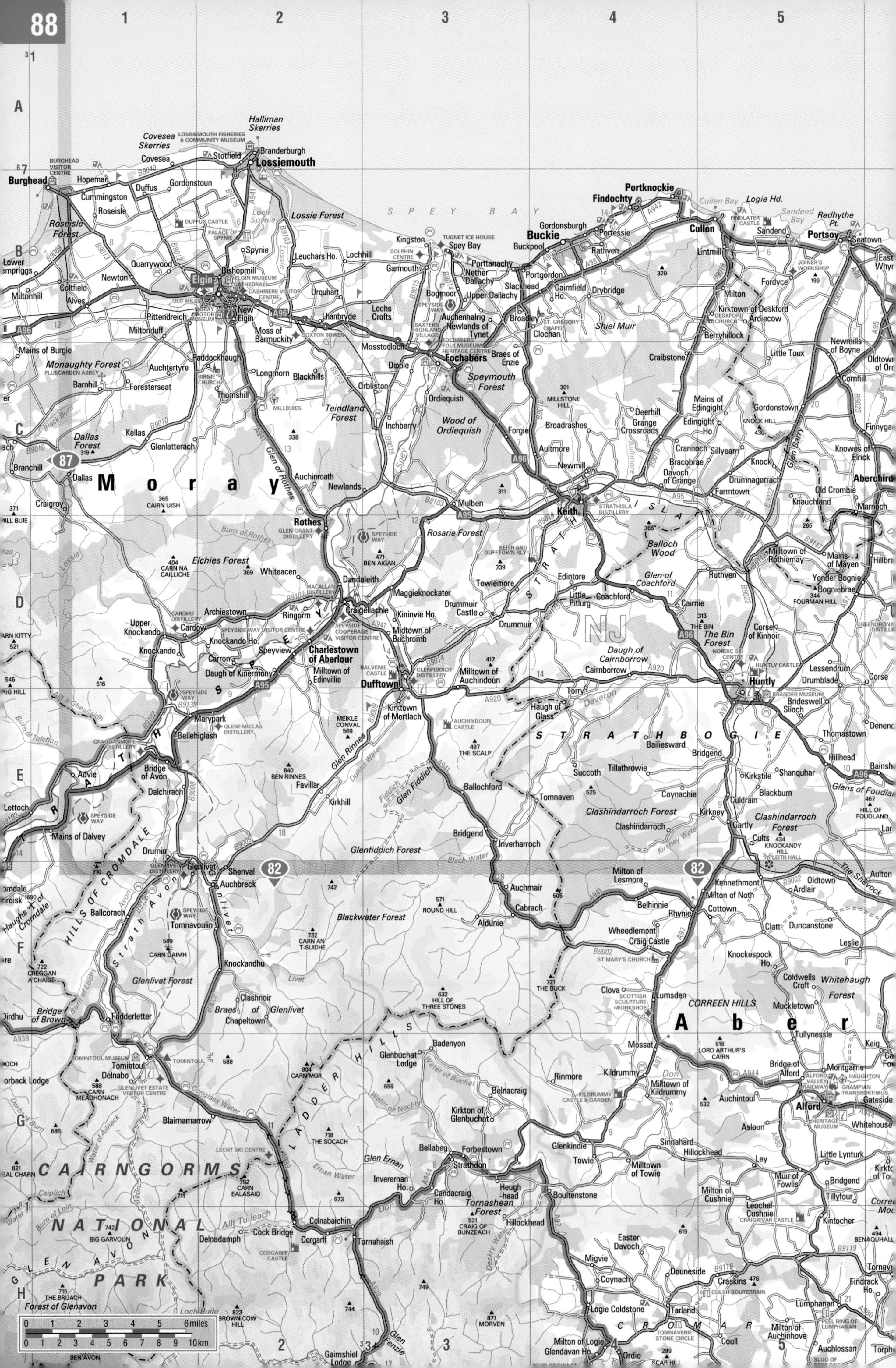
1
2
3
4
5
A
B
C
D
E
F
G
H
Halliman Skerries
Covesea Skerries
LOSSIEMOUTH FISHERIES & COMMUNITY MUSEUM
Branderburgh
Lossiemouth
Stotfield
Covesea
BURGHEAD VISITOR CENTRE
Burghead
Hopeman
Duffus
Gordonstoun
Cummingston
Roseisle
Roseisle Forest
DUFFUS CASTLE
PALACE OF SPYNIE
Loch Spynie
Lossie Forest
Spynie
Quarrywood
Bishopmill
Elgin
ELGIN MUSEUM
CATHEDRAL
CASHMERE VISITOR CENTRE
OLD MILLS
MORAY MOTOR MUSEUM
New Elgin
Newton
Coltfield
Alves
Miltonhill
Lower Hempriggs
Pittendreich
Miltonduff
Moss of Barmuckity
COXTON TOWER
Mains of Burgie
Monaughty Forest
PLUSCARDEN ABBEY
Paddockhaugh
Auchtertyre
BIRNIE CHURCH
Barnhill
Foresterseat
Thomshill
Longmorn
Blackhills
MILLBUIES
Kellas
Dallas Forest
Glenlatterach
Branchill
Dallas
87
Moray
Craigroy
MILL BUIE
365 CAIRN UISH
Glen of Rothes
Rothes
GLEN GRANT DISTILLERY
Burn of Rothes
404 CARN NA CAILLICHE
Elchies Forest
Whiteacen
MACALLAN DISTILLERY
CARDHU DISTILLERY
Archiestown
Upper Knockando
Cardow
Knockando Ho.
Knockando
Carron
Daugh of Kinermony
Speyview
Ringorm
Charlestown of Aberlour
SPEYSIDE COOPERAGE VISITOR CENTRE
Craigellachie
Dandaleith
SPEYSIDE WAY
Marypark
Bellehiglash
GLENFARCLAS DISTILLERY
CRAGGANMORE DISTILLERY
Advie
Bridge of Avon
Dalchirach
Lettoch
Mains of Dalvey
Drumin
GLENLIVET DISTILLERY
Glenlivet
Shenval
Auchbreck
82
HILLS OF CROMDALE
Haughs of Cromdale
Ballcorach
Tomnavoulin
CARN DAIMH
722 CREGGAN A'CHAISE
Strath Avon
Knockandhu
Glenlivet Forest
Clashnoir
Braes of Glenlivet
Chapeltown
Bridge of Brown
Fodderletter
Tomintoul
TOMINTOUL MUSEUM
Delnabo
588 CARN MEADHONACH
GLENLIVET ESTATE VISITOR CENTRE
Conglass Water
Blairnamarrow
LECHT SKI CENTRE
CAIRNGORMS
NATIONAL
PARK
GLEN AVON
742 BIG GARVOUN
792 CARN EALASAID
Delnadamph
Cock Bridge
Allt Tuileach
Corgarff
CORGARFF CASTLE
Colnabaichin
Tornahaish
715 THE BRUACH
Forest of Glenavon
823 BROWN COW HILL
BEN AVON
Gairnshiel Lodge
Glen Fenzie
LADDER HILLS
Carn Mor
718 THE SOCACH
Glenbuchat Lodge
Badenyon
Water of Buchat
Kirkton of Glenbuchat
Belnacraig
Glen Ernan
Invererman Ho.
Bellabeg
Strathdon
Forbestown
Candacraig Ho.
Heugh-head
Tornashean Forest
531 CRAIG OF BUNZEACH
Hillockhead
Boultenstone
Deskry Water
871 MORVEN
SPEY BAY
Kingston
TUGNET ICE HOUSE
Spey Bay
DOLPHIN CENTRE
Garmouth
Leuchars Ho.
Lochhill
Urquhart
Lochs Crofts
Lhanbryde
Porttanachy
Nether Dallachy
Upper Dallachy
Bogmoor
Auchenhalrig
Newlands of Tynet
BAXTERS HIGHLAND VILLAGE
FOCHABERS FOLK MUSEUM & HERITAGE CENTRE
Mosstodloch
Fochabers
Braes of Enzie
Dipple
Speymouth Forest
Orbliston
Teindland Forest
Ordiequish
Wood of Ordiequish
Inchberry
Auchinroath
Newlands
Mulben
SPEYSIDE WAY
471 BEN AIGAN
Rosarie Forest
Maggieknockater
Kininvie Ho.
Midtown of Buchromb
Drummuir Castle
Drummuir
Towiemore
BALVENIE CASTLE
Milltown of Edinvillie
GLENFIDDICH DISTILLERY
Dufftown
Milltown of Auchindoun
Kirktown of Mortlach
MEIKLE CONVAL
AUCHINDOUN CASTLE
487 THE SCALP
840 BEN RINNES
Glen Rinnes
Favillar
Kirkhill
Glen Fiddich
Ballochford
Bridgend
Inverharroch
Glenfiddich Forest
Black Water
Auchmair
Cabrach
Aldunie
571 ROUND HILL
Blackwater Forest
732 CARN AN T-SUIDHE
632 HILL OF THREE STONES
Livet
Buckie
Gordonsburgh
Findochty
Portknockie
Portessie
Buckpool
Rathven
Portgordon
Slackhead
Cairnfield Ho.
Drybridge
Broadley
Clochan
ST. GREGORY'S CHAPEL
Shiel Muir
301 MILLSTONE HILL
Deerhill
Grange Crossroads
Broadrashes
Forgie
Aultmore
Newmill
Keith
STRATHISLA DISTILLERY
KEITH AND DUFFTOWN RLY
STRATH ISLA
Edintore
Little Pitlurg
Coachford
Glen of Coachford
Balloch Wood
NJ
Daugh of Cairnborrow
Cairnborrow
Torry
Haugh of Glass
Deveron
STRATHBOGIE
Bailiesward
Bridgend
Succoth
Tillathrowie
Tomnaven
Coynachie
Clashindarroch Forest
Clashindarroch
Kirkney Water
Milton of Lesmore
Belhinnie
Rhynie
Wheedlemont
Craig Castle
ST MARY'S CHURCH
721 THE BUCK
Clova
SCOTTISH SCULPTURE WORKSHOP
Lumsden
CORREEN HILLS
Aber
Mossat
518 LORD ARTHUR'S CAIRN
Kildrummy
KILDRUMMY CASTLE & GARDEN
Milltown of Kildrummy
Don
Rinmore
Glenkindie
Towie
Milltown of Towie
Sinnahard
Hillockhead
Easter Davoch
Migvie
Coynach
Douneside
Logie Coldstone
Tarland
TOMNAVERIE STONE CIRCLE
CROMAR
Milton of Logie
Glendavan Ho.
Ordie
299 SCAR HILL
Coull
Cullen
Cullen Bay
Logie Hd.
FINDLATER CASTLE
Sandend
Sandend Bay
Redhythe Pt.
Portsoy
Seatown
Lintmill
JOINER'S WORKSHOP
Fordyce
Milton
Kirktown of Deskford
DESKFORD CHURCH
Ardiecow
Berryhillock
Craibstone
Little Toux
Newmills of Boyne
Cornhill
Mains of Edingight
Edingight Ho.
Gordonstown
KNOCK HILL
Crannoch
Sillyearn
Bracobrae
Davoch of Grange
Knock
Glen Barry
Drumnagorrach
Farmtown
Knowes of Elrick
Aberchirder
Old Crombie
Knauchland
Marnoch
Milltown of Rothiemay
Mains of Mayen
Yonder Bognie
Bogniebrae
344 FOURMAN HILL
Ruthven
Cairnie
313 THE BIN
The Bin Forest
NORDIC SKI CENTRE
Corse of Kinnoir
HUNTLY CASTLE
Huntly
BRANDER MUSEUM
Lessendrum
Drumblade
Brideswell
Slioch
Thomastown
Hillhead
Kirkstile
Shanquhar
Blackburn
Culdrain
Gartly
Clashindarroch Forest
Cults
434 KNOCKANDY HILL
LEITH HALL
467 HILL OF FOULAND
Glens of Foudland
The Shevock
Kennethmont
Milton of Noth
Oldtown
Ardlair
Cottown
Clatt
Duncanstone
Leslie
Knockespock Ho.
Coldwells Croft
Whitehaugh Forest
Muckletown
Tullynessle
Keig
Bridge of Alford
Montgarrie
ALFORD VALLEY RAILWAY
GRAMPIAN TRANSPORT MUS.
HAUGHTON
Alford
HERITAGE MUSEUM
Gateside
Whitehouse
Auchintoul
Asloun
Little Lynturk
Ley
Muir of Fowlis
Bridgend
Milton of Cushnie
Tillyfour
Leochel-Cushnie
CRAIGIEVAR CASTLE
Kintocher
494 BENAQUHALLIE
Craskins
CULSH SOUTERRAIN
Findrack Ho.
Lumphanan
PEEL RING OF LUMPHANAN
Milton of Auchinhove
Auchlossan
Tornaveen
0 1 2 3 4 5 6 miles
0 1 2 3 4 5 6 7 8 9 10 km

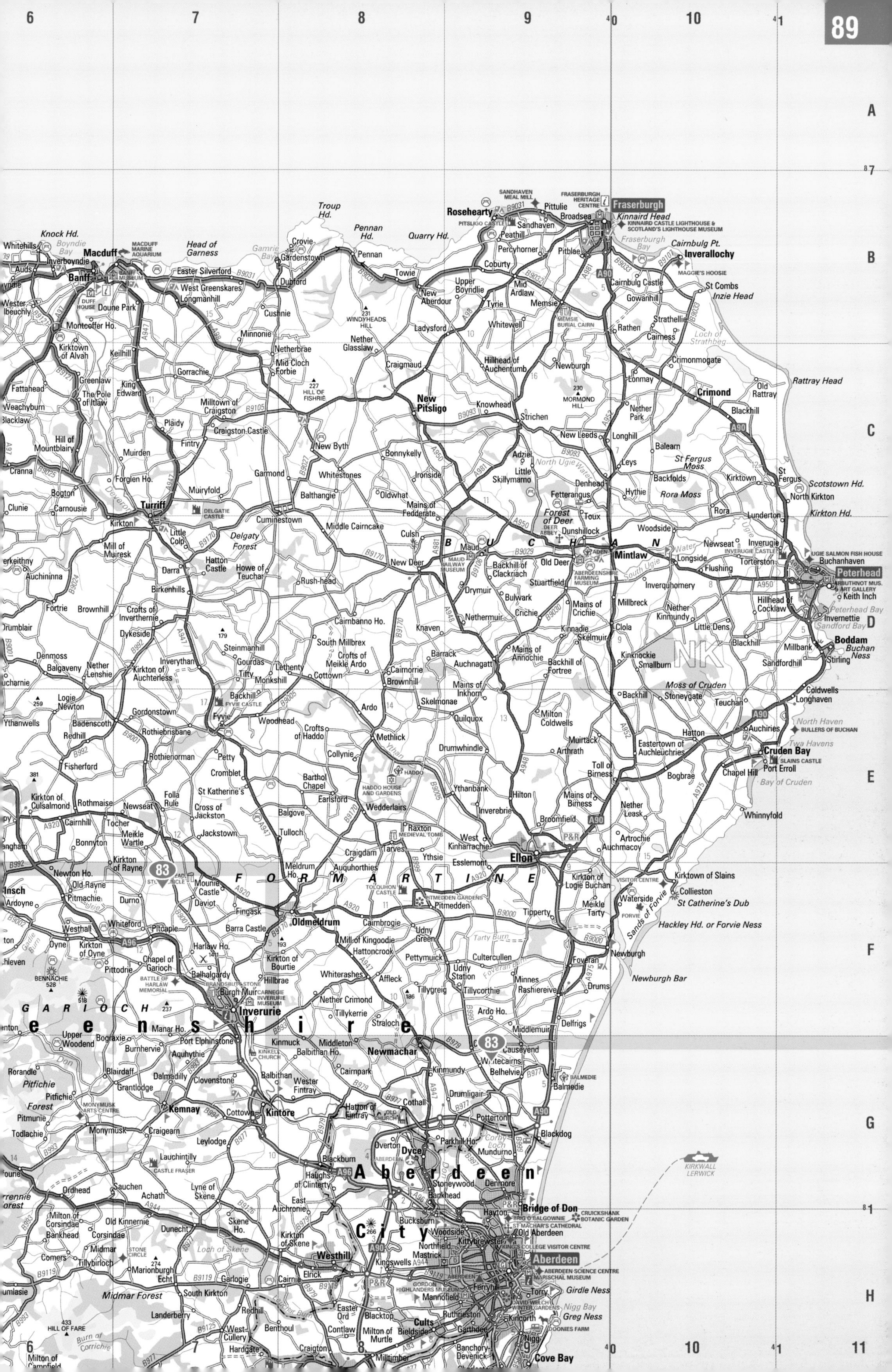
6
7
8
9
10
11
A
B
C
D
E
F
G
H
Fraserburgh
Kinnaird Head
KINNAIRD CASTLE LIGHTHOUSE & SCOTLAND'S LIGHTHOUSE MUSEUM
FRASERBURGH HERITAGE CENTRE
SANDHAVEN MEAL MILL
Rosehearty
Pittulie
Sandhaven
Broadsea
PITSLIGO CASTLE
Peathill
Percyhorner
Pitblae
Fraserburgh Bay
Cairnbulg Pt.
Inverallochy
MAGGIE'S HOOSIE
Cairnbulg Castle
Gowanhill
St Combs
Inzie Head
Troup Hd.
Pennan Hd.
Quarry Hd.
Knock Hd.
Head of Garness
Gamrie Bay
Boyndie Bay
Whitehills
Macduff
MACDUFF MARINE AQUARIUM
Inverboyndie
Banff
BANFF MUSEUM
DUFF HOUSE
Doune Park
Crovie
Gardenstown
Pennan
Towie
Easter Silverford
West Greenskares
Longmanhill
Dubford
New Aberdour
Upper Boyndie
Coburty
Mid Ardlaw
Tyrie
Memsie
MEMSIE BURIAL CAIRN
Whitewell
Ladysford
Rathen
Strathellie
Cairness
Loch of Strathbeg
Cushnie
WINDYHEADS HILL
Nether Glasslaw
Minnonie
Netherbrae
Mid Cloch Forbie
Craigmaud
Hillhead of Auchentumb
Newburgh
Crimonmogate
Lonmay
Crimond
Old Rattray
Rattray Head
Montcoffer Ho.
Kirktown of Alvah
Keilhill
King Edward
Gorrachie
HILL OF FISHRIE
New Pitsligo
Knowhead
Strichen
MORMOND HILL
Nether Park
Blackhill
Greenlaw
The Pole of Itlaw
Fattahead
Weachyburn
Blacklaw
Milltown of Craigston
Plaidy
Craigston Castle
Fintry
New Byth
Bonnykelly
New Leeds
Longhill
Balearn
Hill of Mountblairy
Muirden
Adziel
North Ugie Water
St Fergus Moss
Leys
St Fergus
Scotstown Hd.
Cranna
Forglen Ho.
Garmond
Whitestones
Ironside
Little Skillymarno
Denhead
Backfolds
Kirktown
Bogton
Muiryfold
Balthangie
Oldwhat
Mains of Fedderate
Fetterangus
Hythie
Rora Moss
North Kirkton
Clunie
Carnousie
Turriff
DELGATIE CASTLE
Cuminestown
Middle Cairncake
Forest of Deer
DEER ABBEY
Toux
Dunshillock
Rora
Lunderton
Kirkton Hd.
Kirkton
Little Colp
Delgaty Forest
Culsh
Woodside
Newseat
Inverugie
INVERUGIE CASTLE
UGIE SALMON FISH HOUSE
Buchanhaven
Peterhead
Mill of Muiresk
Hatton Castle
Darra
Howe of Teuchar
New Deer
Maud
MAUD RAILWAY MUSEUM
Backhill of Clackriach
Old Deer
ADEN
ABERDEENSHIRE FARMING MUSEUM
Mintlaw
Longside
Torterston
Flushing
ARBUTHNOT MUS. & ART GALLERY
Keith Inch
Auchininna
Birkenhills
Rush-head
Drymuir
Stuartfield
Inverquhomery
Fortrie
Brownhill
Crofts of Inverthernie
Bulwark
Crichie
Mains of Crichie
Millbreck
Nether Kinmundy
Hillhead of Cocklaw
Peterhead Bay
Dumblair
Cairnbanno Ho.
Knaven
Nethermuir
Kinnadie
Clola
Little Dens
Sandford Bay
Dykeside
Steinmanhill
South Millbrex
Crofts of Meikle Ardo
Skelmuir
Blackhill
Boddam
Millbank
Buchan Ness
Denmoss
Balgaveny
Nether Lenshie
Inverythan
Gourdas
Tifty
Monkshill
Lethenty
Cottown
Barrack
Cairnorrie
Auchnagatt
Mains of Annochie
Backhill of Fortree
Kinknockie
Smallburn
Sandfordhill
Stirling
Kirkton of Auchterless
Brownhill
Mains of Inkhorn
Moss of Cruden
Coldwells
Longhaven
Logie Newton
Backhill
FYVIE CASTLE
Skelmonae
Quilquox
Stoneygate
Teuchan
Ythanwells
Gordonstown
Fyvie
Woodhead
Ardo
Milton Coldwells
Badenscoth
Rothiebrisbane
Crofts of Haddo
Methlick
Muirtack
Arthrath
Hatton
Auchiries
North Haven
BULLERS OF BUCHAN
Redhill
Rothienorman
Petty
Collynie
Drumwhindle
Eastertown of Auchleuchries
Twa Havens
Cruden Bay
SLAINS CASTLE
Port Erroll
Fisherford
Cromblet
HADDO
Toll of Birness
Bogbrae
Chapel Hill
Bay of Cruden
St Katherine's
Barthol Chapel
HADDO HOUSE AND GARDENS
Ythanbank
Hilton
Kirkton of Culsalmond
Rothmaise
Newseat
Folla Rule
Cross of Jackston
Earlsford
Wedderlairs
Inverebrie
Mains of Birness
Nether Leask
Whinnyfold
Cairnhill
Tocher
Balgove
Broomfield
Meikle Wartle
Jackstown
Tulloch
Raxton
MEDIEVAL TOMB
West Kinharrachie
Artrochie
Auchmacoy
Bonnyton
Kirkton of Rayne
Craigdam
Tarves
Ythsie
Ellon
Newton Ho.
Old Rayne
Meldrum Ho.
Auquhorthies
Esslemont
Kirkton of Logie Buchan
Kirktown of Slains
VISITOR CENTRE
Collieston
Insch
Pitmachie
Mounie Castle
Daviot
F O R M A R T I N E
TOLQUHON CASTLE
PITMEDDEN GARDENS
Pitmedden
Waterside
St Catherine's Dub
Ardoyne
Durno
Fingask
Oldmeldrum
Cairnbrogie
Tipperty
Meikle Tarty
FORVIE
Sands of Forvie
Hackley Hd. or Forvie Ness
Westhall
Whiteford
Pitcaple
Barra Castle
Udny Green
Tarty Burn
Oyne
Kirkton of Oyne
Harlaw Ho.
Mill of Kingoodie
Hattoncrook
Pettymuick
Culterculllen
Foveran
Newburgh
Chapel of Garioch
Pittodrie
Balhalgardy
Kirkton of Bourtie
Whiterashes
Affleck
Udny Station
Minnes
Foveran Burn
Drums
Newburgh Bar
BENNACHIE
BATTLE OF HARLAW MEMORIAL
BRANDSBUTT STONE
Hillbrae
Tillygreig
Tillycorthie
Rashierieve
Burgh Muir
CARNEGIE INVERURIE MUSEUM
Nether Crimond
G A R I O C H
Inverurie
Tillykerrie
Ardo Ho.
Delfrigs
e e n s h i r e
Manar Ho.
Straloch
Middlemuir
Upper Woodend
Bograxie
Port Elphinstone
KINKELL CHURCH
Kinmuck
Middleton
Balbithan Ho.
Newmachar
Causeyend
Whitecairns
Burnhervie
Aquhythie
Belhelvie
Rorandle
Pitfichie
Blairdaff
Dalmadilly
Clovenstone
Balbithan
Wester Fintray
Cairnpark
Kinmundy
BALMEDIE
Balmedie
Pitfichie Forest
Grantlodge
Drumligair
MONYMUSK ARTS CENTRE
Kemnay
Cottown
Kintore
Hatton of Fintray
OLD CHURCH
Cothall
Pitmunie
Potterton
Todlachie
Monymusk
Craigearn
Leylodge
Overton
Dyce
Parkhill Ho.
Corby Loch
Blackdog
Mundurno
Lauchintilly
CASTLE FRASER
Blackburn
ABERDEEN
A b e r d e e n
KIRKWALL LERWICK
Haughs of Clinterty
Stoneywood
Denmore
Sauchen
Ordhead
Achath
Lyne of Skene
East Auchronie
Bankhead
Bridge of Don
CRUICKSHANK BOTANIC GARDEN
Hayton
BRIG O' BALGOWNIE
ST MACHAR'S CATHEDRAL
Old Aberdeen
Milton of Corsindae
Old Kinnernie
Dunecht
Skene Ho.
Bucksburn
Corsindae
Bankhead
C i t y
Woodside
Kittybrewster
KING'S COLLEGE VISITOR CENTRE
Loch of Skene
Kirkton of Skene
Northfield
Mastrick
Aberdeen
ABERDEEN SCIENCE CENTRE
MARISCHAL MUSEUM
Comers
Midmar
STONE CIRCLE
Tillybirloch
Marionburgh
Echt
Westhill
Kingswells
Garlogie
Elrick
Cairnie
GORDON HIGHLANDERS MUSEUM
Ferryhill
Torry
Girdle Ness
Midmar Forest
South Kirkton
Mannofield
DAVID WELCH WINTER GARDENS
Nigg Bay
Greg Ness
Landerberry
Redhill
Easter Ord
Blacktop
Ruthrieston
Kincorth
DOONIES FARM
HILL OF FARE
West Cullery
Benthoul
Contlaw
Milton of Murtle
Cults
Bieldside
Garthdee
Nigg
Burn of Corrichie
Hardgate
Craigton
Millimber
Banchory-Devenick
Cove Bay
Milton of Campfield
Aberdeenshire
A90
A98
A97
A947
A96
A920
A952
A950
A948
A981
A975
A944
A93
B9031
B9032
B9033
B9105
B9093
B9027
B9170
B9029
B9030
B9005
B9000
B999
B977
B979
B9119
B9125
B9001
B992
B9002
B993
B9126
83
P&R

⁰6

⁹6

⁹0

⁸8

A

B

C

D

E

F

G

H

J

1 2 3 4 ⁰ 5 6 7

NA

Na h-Eileanan Flannach

St. Kilda

NA

CNOC GLAS
376 *Soay*
*Loch a'
Ghlinne* *ST KILDA* *Boreray*
584

CONACHAIR
576
MULLACH BI ST KILDA
358
*Bàgh a'
Bhaile* *St Kilda or Hirta
(Hiort)*
Dun

NF

⁰1

⁹0

⁰1

*Siabost bho Thu
Shawbost Norse Mill
Siabost bho Dheas*
Bàgh Dhail Beag *Po
Shiat*
GEARRANNAN
BLACKHOUSE VILLAGE
GARENIN *Dail Beag*
Na Gearrannan
Borghastan *Dail Mòr*
Carlabhagh
Loch Chàrlabhaigh
Campay
DUN CARLOWAY BROCH
Floday *Little
Bernera* *Cirbhig*
Harsgeir *Crothair* *Little
Charlabhaigh*
IRON AGE HOUSE
An Galan Uigeach *Tobson* NORSE
MILL
AN CAOLAS *Pabay
Mòr* *Tolastadh a Chaolais*
Aird Uig *Vacsay* BERNERA
*Bàgh
Fhabhaig* *Cliobh* *Bhaltos* **Great Bernera**
Timsgearraidh 205 *Miabhig* *Riof* *Vuia
Mòr* *Tacleit* *Breaclet* *Keava*
Cradhlastadh *Circebost* *Barraglom* *Duh
Barraglom* *Breascleit*
Ard More Mangersta *Càrnais* *Uigen* *Cairisiadar* *Loch Ròg* *Floday* *Tobhtarol* *Calanais* CALANAIS VISITOR
CENTRE
Mangurstadh *Eadar Dha
Fhadhail* SUAINAVAL
429 *Geisiadar* *Crulabhig* *Vuia Beag* CALANAIS STANDING
STONES CALANAIS SMALL
STONE CIRCLES
Aird Fenish *Einacleite* 256 *Gearraidh
na h-Aibhne*
Linsiadar
Aird Brenish 574
MEALISVAL *Giosla* *Loch Ròg* *Loch
Tungabhat* B8011
Islibhig *Loch
Grunabhat* *Giosla* 19 B8011 *Loch Lacab*
Breanais *Loch
Chaolartan* *Loch Fuaroil* *Loch Airigh
na h-Airde*
Mealasta Island *Loch Cro
Croisdaig* 397
BEINN MHEADHONACH *Loch
Morsgail* *Loch
Strandabhat*
*Ceann
Tarabhaigh* A859 *Airidh
Bhruai*
Kearstay *Bràighe
Mòr* MORSGAIL
Forest *Aird an
Troim*
308 *Loch
Beinniseabhat*
Scarp *Loch
a' Ghlinne* *Loch
Bòdabhat* *Loch Langabhat*
Gaisgeir *Loch Tealasbhaigh* *Loch
Réasort*
Huisinis 489 **SOUTH LEWIS,** STULAVAL *Aline Lodge* 572
BEINN M
Hushinish Pt. *Tirga Mòr* 679 659 *Aird a' Mhulaidh* *Seaforth I.*
Gobhaig *Abhainn Suidhe* ULLAVAL 17
Horsanish *Arda Mòra* *Forest of Harris* USGNAVAL
MORE
729 CLISHAM
799 *Maraig* 449
Taransay Glorigs *Soay Mòr* *Cliasmol* **HARRIS AND** *Loch
Sìphoirt*
Soay Beag 13 CEANN A TUATH NA
HEARADH
Miabhag *Bun Abhainn
Eadarra* 559 *Reinigeadal*
OLD WHALING STATION
*Camus an
t-suithean* **NORTH UIST** *Aird Asaig* *Lochan
Lacasdail* 3
Tarasaigh 436 *Isay* *Loch Trollamarig*
(Taransay) BEN LUSKENTYRE
Paible 99 *Losgaintir* *Tairbeart* *Urgha*
Rubha Sgeirigin 467 *(Tarbert)* *Carragraich*
LUSKENTYRE
BEACH *Caolas Scalpaigh*
Caolas Tharasaigh *South Harris
Forest* A859 *Loch Ceann
Dibig* *Sgeotasaigh* *Camach*
Seilebost *Miabhag* *Rudha Cra*
Toe Head *Borve Lodge* 23 *Loch
an
Tairbeart* *Scalpay*
Burgh A859 *Drinisiadar* *Eil
Coppay SCARISTA
STANDING STONE **NA HEARADH** *Plocrapol Pt.* *Sca*
CHAIPAVAL *Sgarasta Mhòr* **(HARRIS)** *Kennacley* *Plocfapol*
365 386 *Aird Mhighe* *Greosabhagh* *Leac a Li* *Scadabhagh*
Shillay *Liceasto* *Cluthal*
Little Shillay 398 *Rubha
Bhocaig*
BLEAVAL *Geocrab* *Caolas
Stocinis*
Sound of Shillay *Rubha'an Teampuill* *Loch Langabhat* *Beacrabhaic*
Brenish Pt. *Taobh Tuath* *Stockinish I.*
196 SEALLAM *Aird
Mhighe* *Manais*
Pabaidh *Fleoideabhagh*
(Pabbay) *An t-Ob (Leverburgh)* *Cuidhtinis* UIG
Quinish *Fionnsbhagh*
Ensay *Bòrsam* *Loch Fionnsbhagh*
NF *Sound of Spuir* ROINEABAL *Lingreabhagh*
Carminnis Is. *Lingarabay I.*
Spuir *Killegray* *Cairninis* *Srannda* *Roghadal*
ST CLEMENT'S
CHURCH *Valley*
*Eilean
Bhearnaraigh* *Ruisigearraidh* *Langay* *Renish Pt.*
(Berneray) BERNERAY
Haskeir I. *Borgh* *Baile* *Groay* *Gilsay*
Boreray *Scaraay*
Haskeir Eagach **84** *Aird a'Mhòrain* *Caolas Bheàrnaraigh* **84**
Veilish Pt. *Torogay* *Lingay*
Griminish Pt. **Vallay** *Scaravay*
Port nan Long *Hermetray*
*Vallay
Strand* *Oronsay* *Baile Mhic Phàil*
Scolpaig 180
20 A865 *Solas* *Trumaisgearraidh*
Baile Mhàrtainn *Malacleit* **NA HEARADH**
Sursay *Opsay*
Tahay *Hermetray*

Scale : 1:332 000
(approx 5 miles to 1 inch)

0 1 2 3 4 5 6miles
0 1 2 3 4 5 6 7 8 9 10km

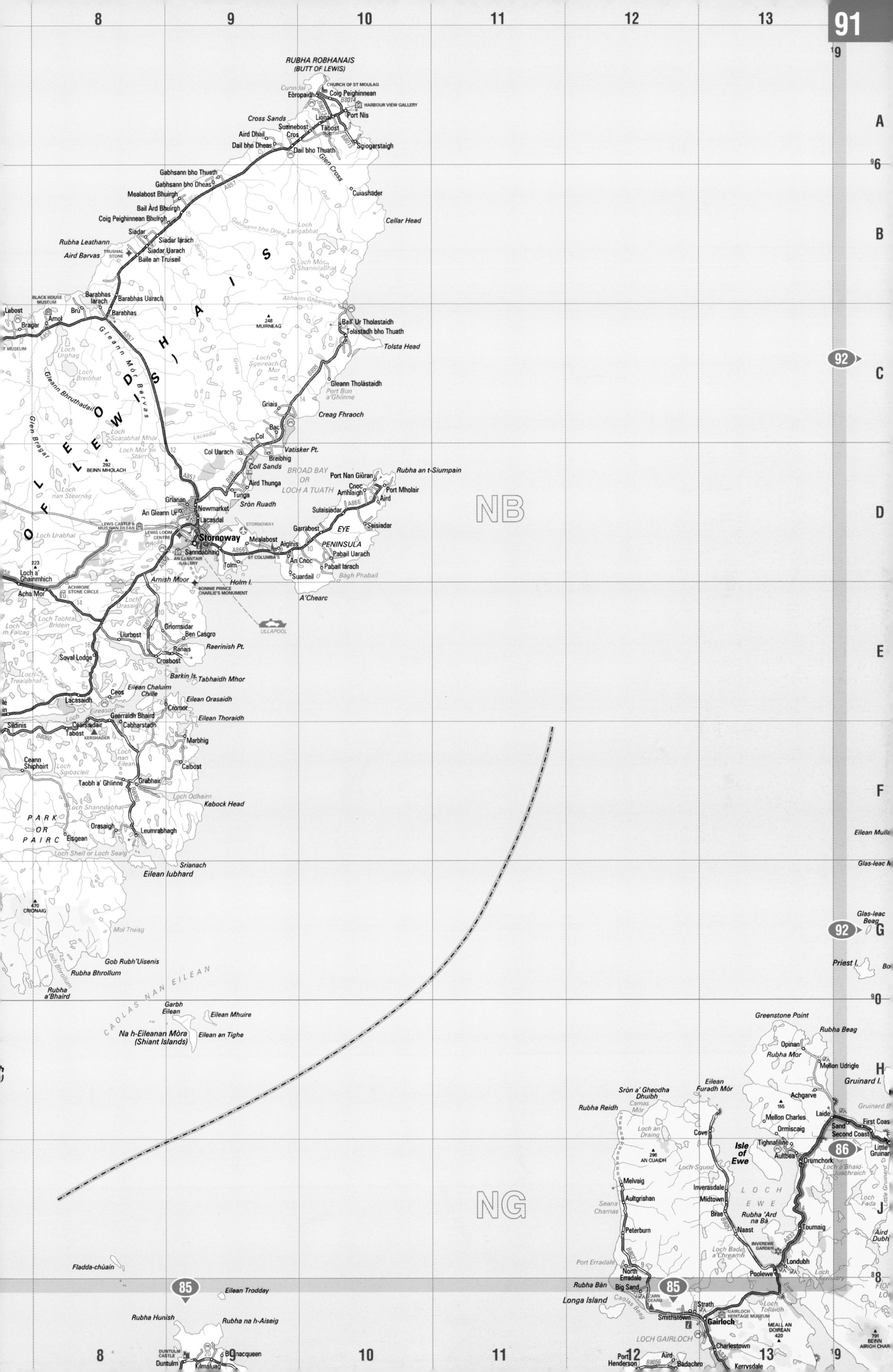
8
9
10
11
12
13
RUBHA ROBHANAIS
(BUTT OF LEWIS)
Cunndal
Eòropaidh
CHURCH OF ST MOULAG
Coig Peighinnean
HARBOUR VIEW GALLERY
Lional
Port Nis
Cross Sands
Suainebost
Tàbost
Aird Dhail
Cros
Dail bho Dheas
Dail bho Thuath
Sgiogarstaigh
Glen Cross
Gabhsann bho Thuath
Gabhsann bho Dheas
Mealabost Bhuirgh
Cuiashader
Bail Àrd Bhuirgh
Coig Peighinnean Bhuirgh
Cellar Head
Siadar
Rubha Leathann
Siadar Iarach
Aird Barvas
TRUSHAL STONE
Siadar Uarach
Baile an Truiseil
BLACK HOUSE MUSEUM
Barabhas Iarach
Barabhas Uarach
Labost
Brù
Barabhas
Arnol
Bragar
248 MUIRNEAG
Bail' Ur Tholastaidh
Tolastadh bho Thuath
Tolsta Head
Gleann Mòr Barvas
Gleann Tholàstaidh
Gleann Bhruthadail
Griais
Creag Fhraoch
Glen Bragar
Col
Bac
Col Uarach
Vatisker Pt.
Breibhig
Coll Sands
292 BEINN MHOLACH
BROAD BAY OR LOCH A TUATH
Port Nan Giùran
Rubha an t-Siumpain
Aird Thunga
Cnoc
Amhlaigh
Port Mholair
Aird
Tunga
Griànan
Sròn Ruadh
NB
An Gleann Ur
Newmarket
Sulaisiadar
Lacasdal
LEWIS CASTLE & MUS NAN EILEAN
LEWIS LOOM CENTRE
STORNOWAY
Garrabost
EYE
Seisiadar
Stornoway
Mealabost
Aiginis
PENINSULA
Sanndabhaig
AN LANNTAIR GALLERY
ST COLUMBA'S
An Cnoc
Pabail Uarach
Tolm
Pabail Iarach
Bàgh Phabail
Suardail
223
Loch a' Ghainmhich
Arnish Moor
Holm I.
Acha Mor
ACHMORE STONE CIRCLE
BONNIE PRINCE CHARLIE'S MONUMENT
A'Chearc
ULLAPOOL
Griomsidar
Liurbost
Ben Casgro
Raerinish Pt.
Ranais
Crosbost
Soval Lodge
Barkin Is.
Tabhaidh Mhor
Eilean Chaluim Chille
Ceos
Lacasaidh
Eilean Orasaidh
Cromor
Eilean Thoraidh
Sildinis
Cearsiadair
Geerraidh Bhaird
Cabharstadh
Tabost
KERSHADER
Marbhig
Ceann Shiphoirt
Calbost
Taobh a' Ghlinne
Grabhair
Kebock Head
PARK OR PAIRC
Orasaigh
Eisgean
Leumrabhagh
Loch Shell or Loch Sealg
Srianach
Eilean Iubhard
470 CRIONAIG
Mol Truisg
Gob Rubh' Uisenis
Rubha Bhrollum
Rubha a'Bhaird
CAOLAS NAN EILEAN
Garbh Eilean
Eilean Mhuire
Na h-Eileanan Mòra (Shiant Islands)
Eilean an Tighe
NG
Eilean Mulla
Glas-leac M
Glas-leac Beag
92
Priest I.
Greenstone Point
Rubha Beag
Opinan
Rubha Mor
Mellon Udrigle
Gruinard I.
Sròn a' Gheodha Dhuibh
Eilean Furadh Mór
Rubha Reidh
Achgarve
Laide
First Coast
Mellon Charles
Sand
Second Coast
Ormiscaig
Cove
296 AN CUAIDH
Isle of Ewe
Tighnafiline
Aultbea
Drumchork
86
Little Gruinard
Melvaig
Inverasdale
LOCH EWE
Aultgrishan
Midtown
Brae
Rubha 'Ard na Bà
Tournaig
Naast
Peterburn
INVEREWE GARDEN
Port Erradale
Londubh
North Erradale
Poolewe
Fladda-chùain
Rubha Bàn
Big Sand
85
Eilean Trodday
Longa Island
Strath
Rubha Hunish
Rubha na h-Aiseig
Smithstown
Gairloch
GAIRLOCH HERITAGE MUSEUM
MEALL AN DOIREAN 420
LOCH GAIRLOCH
791 BEINN AIRIGH CHAR
DUNTULM CASTLE
Duntulm
Kilmaluag
Port Henderson
Aird
Badachro
Charlestown
Kerrysdale
A
B
C
D
E
F
G
H
J

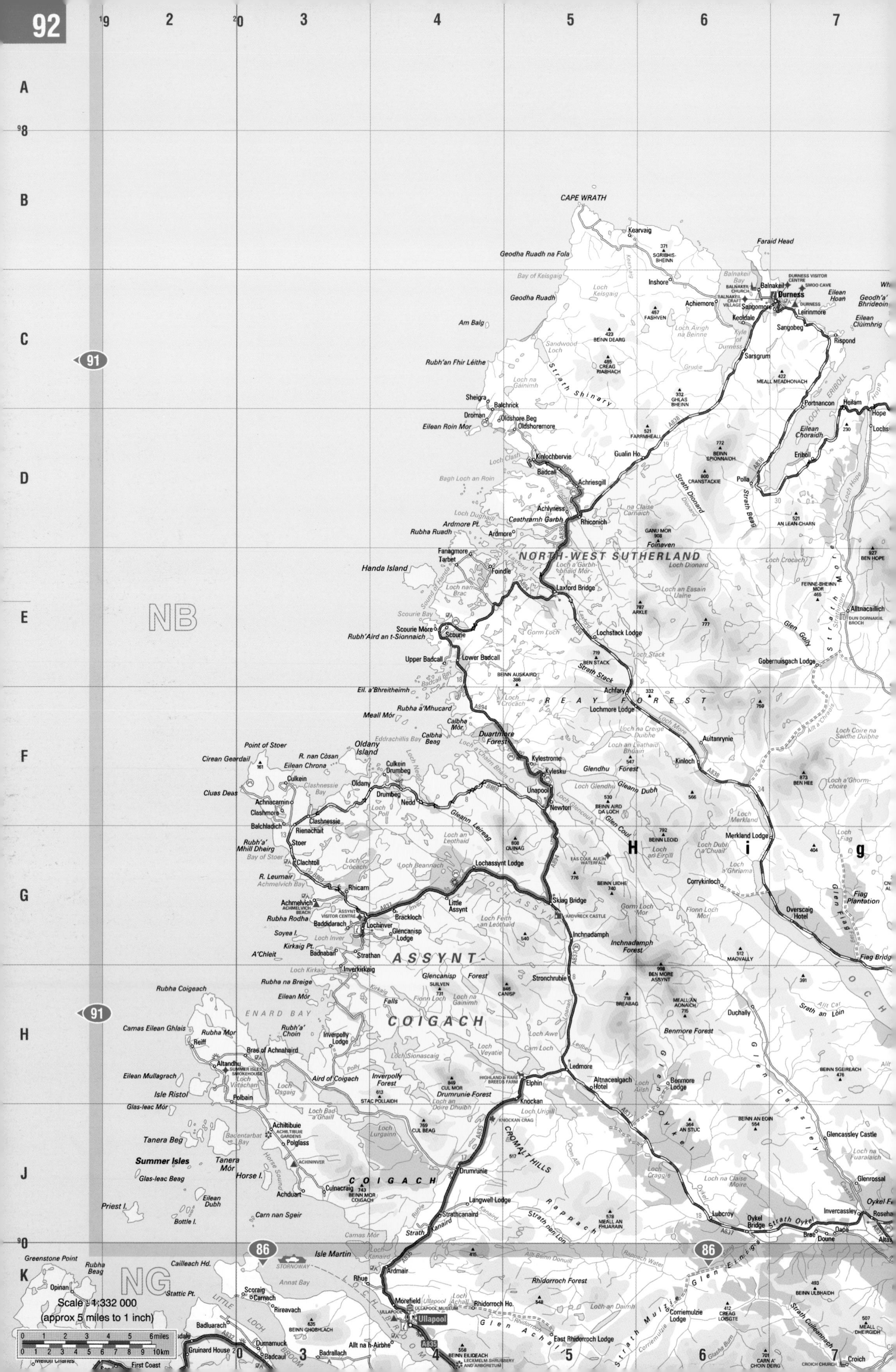
CAPE WRATH
Kearvaig
371 SGRIBHIS-BHEINN
Faraid Head
Geodha Ruadh na Fola
Bay of Keisgaig
Balnakeil Bay
Inshore
Loch Keisgaig
BALNAKEIL CHURCH
BALNAKEIL CRAFT VILLAGE
Balnakeil
DURNESS VISITOR CENTRE
SMOO CAVE
Durness
Eilean Hoan
Geodh'a' Bhrideoin
Geodha Ruadh
Achiemore
457 FASHVEN
Sangomore
Keoldale
Leirinmore
Eilean Clùimhrig
Loch Airigh na Beinne
Kyle of Durness
Sangobeg
Am Balg
Rispond
423 BEINN DEARG
Sandwood Loch
Sarsgrum
Rubh'an Fhir Léithe
485 CREAG RIABHACH
Grudie
422 MEALL MEADHONACH
Loch na Gainimh
Strath Shinary
332 GHLAS BHEINN
LOCH ERIBOLL
Portnancon
Heilam
Hope
Sheigra
Balchrick
Droman
Oldshore Beg
Oldshoremore
Eilean Roin Mor
521 FARRMHEALL
772 BEINN SPIONNAIDH
Eilean Choraidh
230
Loch Clash
Kinlochbervie
Gualin Ho.
Eriboll
Badcall
Achriesgill
Bagh Loch an Roin
800 CRANSTACKIE
Strath Dionard
Strath Beag
Polla
Loch Hope
Loch Dughaill
Achlyness
L. na Claise Carnaich
521 AN LEAN-CHARN
Ardmore Pt.
Ceathramh Garbh
Rhiconich
Rubha Ruadh
Ardmore
GANU MOR 908
Foinaven
927 BEN HOPE
Fanagmore
Tarbet
NORTH-WEST SUTHERLAND
Loch Crocach
Loch Dionard
Handa Island
Foindle
Loch a' Garbh-bhaid Mór
Loch Laxford
Sound of Handa
Laxford Bridge
Loch an Easain Uaine
FEINNE-BHEINN MOR 465
Loch nam Brac
Scourie Bay
787 ARKLE
777
Alltnacaillich
DUN DORNAIGIL BROCH
Scourie More
Scourie
Rubh'Aird an t-Sionnaich
Gorm Loch
Lochstack Lodge
Glen Golly
Upper Badcall
Lower Badcall
719 BEN STACK
Loch Stack
Strath Stack
Gobernuisgach Lodge
Badcall Bay
BEINN AUSKAIRD 386
Eil. a'Bhreitheimh
Achfary
332
REAY FOREST
Loch Crocach
Lochmore Lodge
759
Rubha a'Mhucard
Meall Mór
Calbha Mór
Loch More
Eddrachillis Bay
Calbha Beag
Duartmore Forest
Loch na Creige Duibhe
Aultanrynie
Loch Coire na Saidhe Duibhe
Point of Stoer
Oldany Island
Loch an Leathaid Bhuain
Allt a' Chraois
Cirean Geardail
R. nan Còsan
Kylestrome
Kinloch
Eilean Chrona
161
Culkein Drumbeg
Loch a' Chàirn Bhàin
Kylesku
Forest
Glendhu
873 BEN HEE
Loch a' Ghorm-choire
Culkein
Clashnessie Bay
Oldany
Loch Nedd
Unapool
Loch Glendhu
Gleann Dubh
Cluas Deas
Drumbeg
Nedd
B869
Newton
530 BEINN AIRD DA LOCH
566
Achnacarnin
Clashmore
Loch Poll
Loch Glencoul
Glen Coul
Loch Merkland
Balchladich
Clashnessie
Gleann Leireag
792 BEINN LEOID
Merkland Lodge
Loch Fiag
Rubh'a' Mhill Dheirg
Rienachait
Loch an Leothaid
808 QUINAG
Loch an Eircill
Loch Dubh a'Chuail
404
Stoer
Bay of Stoer
Clachtoll
Loch Cròcach
Loch Beannach
Lochassynt Lodge
EAS COUL AULIN WATERFALL
Loch a'Ghriama
Fiag Plantation
R. Leumair
Achmelvich Bay
776
Corrykinloch
Rhicarn
LOCH ASSYNT
BEINN UIDHE 740
Skiag Bridge
Glen Fiag
Achmelvich
ACHMELVICH BEACH
ASSYNT VISITOR CENTRE
Little Assynt
Gorm Loch Mor
Fionn Loch Mor
Overscaig Hotel
Rubha Rodha
Brackloch
ARDVRECK CASTLE
Baddidarach
Lochinver
Glencanisp Lodge
Loch Feith an Leòthaid
Inchnadamph
Soyea I.
Loch Inver
540
Inchnadamph Forest
Kirkaig Pt.
Strathan
512 MAOVALLY
Fiag Bridge
A'Chleit
Badnaban
ASSYNT-
Loch Kirkaig
998 BEN MORE ASSYNT
Inverkirkaig
Glencanisp
Forest
Stronchrubie
391
LOCH SHIN
Rubha na Breige
846 CANISP
731 SULVEN
Rubha Coigeach
Eilean Mór
Fionn Loch
Loch na Gainimh
718 BREABAG
MEALL AN AONAICH 715
Allt Cat
Strath an Loin
Falls
ENARD BAY
Rubh'a' Choin
COIGACH
Duchally
Camas Eilean Ghlais
Rubha Mor
Reiff
Inverpolly Lodge
Loch Awe
Benmore Forest
Brae of Achnahaird
Loch Veyatie
Cam Loch
Altandhu
SUMMER ISLES SMOKEHOUSE
Loch Sionascaig
Ledmore
Glen Oykel
Glen Cassley
Eilean Mullagrach
Loch Vatachan
Aird of Coigach
Inverpolly Forest
849 CUL MOR
HIGHLAND RARE BREEDS FARM
Elphin
Altnacealgach Hotel
Loch Ailsh
Benmore Lodge
BEINN SGEIREACH 476
Isle Ristol
Polbain
Loch Osgaig
613 STAC POLLAIDH
Drumrunie Forest
Knockan
Loch an Doire Dhuibh
Loch Urigill
Glas-leac Mór
Loch Bad a'Ghaill
KNOCKAN CRAG
769 CUL BEAG
364 AN STUC
BEINN AN EOIN 554
Achiltibuie
ACHILTIBUIE GARDENS
Badentarbat Bay
Tanera Beg
Polglass
Loch Lurgainn
CROMALT HILLS
Glencassley Castle
Summer Isles
Tanera Mór
ACHININVER
517
Loch na Fuaralaich
Horse Sound
Horse I.
Glas-leac Beag
Drumrunie
COIGACH
Loch Craggie
Glenrossal
Achduart
Culnacraig
743 BEINN MOR COIGACH
Loch na Claise Moire
Eilean Dubh
Langwell Lodge
Priest I.
Rappach
Lubcroy
Oykel Bridge
Strath Oykel
Invercassley
Carn nan Sgeir
Strathcanaird
578 MEALL AN FHUARAIN
Rosehall
Bottle I.
Strath Kanaird
Strath nan Lon
Brae
Doune
Altass
Camas Mór
Greenstone Point
Isle Martin
Rubha Beag
Cailleach Hd.
STORNOWAY
Allt Bean Donuill
Rappach Water
Glen Einig
Opinan
Annat Bay
Ardmair
Rhue
Rhidorroch Forest
493 BEINN ULBHAIDH
Stattic Pt.
Scoraig
Carnach
Morefield
Ullapool
Loch Achall
Rhidorroch Ho.
Loch an Daimh
Strath Mulzie
Corriemulzie Lodge
412 CREAG LOISGTE
Strath Cuileannach
Rireavach
LITTLE LOCH BROOM
ULLAPOOL MUSEUM
548
Badluarach
635 BEINN GHOBHLACH
Glen Achall
East Rhidorroch Lodge
507 MEALL DHEIRGIDH
Dundonnell
Dumnamuck
Gruinard House
Badcall
Badrallach
Allt na h-Airbhe
558 BEINN EILIDEACH
LECKMELM SHRUBBERY AND ARBORETUM
LOCH BROOM
Glasha Burn
701 CARN A' CHOIN DEIRG
CROICH CHURCH
Croich
Mellon Charles
First Coast
NB
NG
91
86
Scale 1:332 000
(approx 5 miles to 1 inch)
0 1 2 3 4 5 6 miles
0 1 2 3 4 5 6 7 8 9 10km

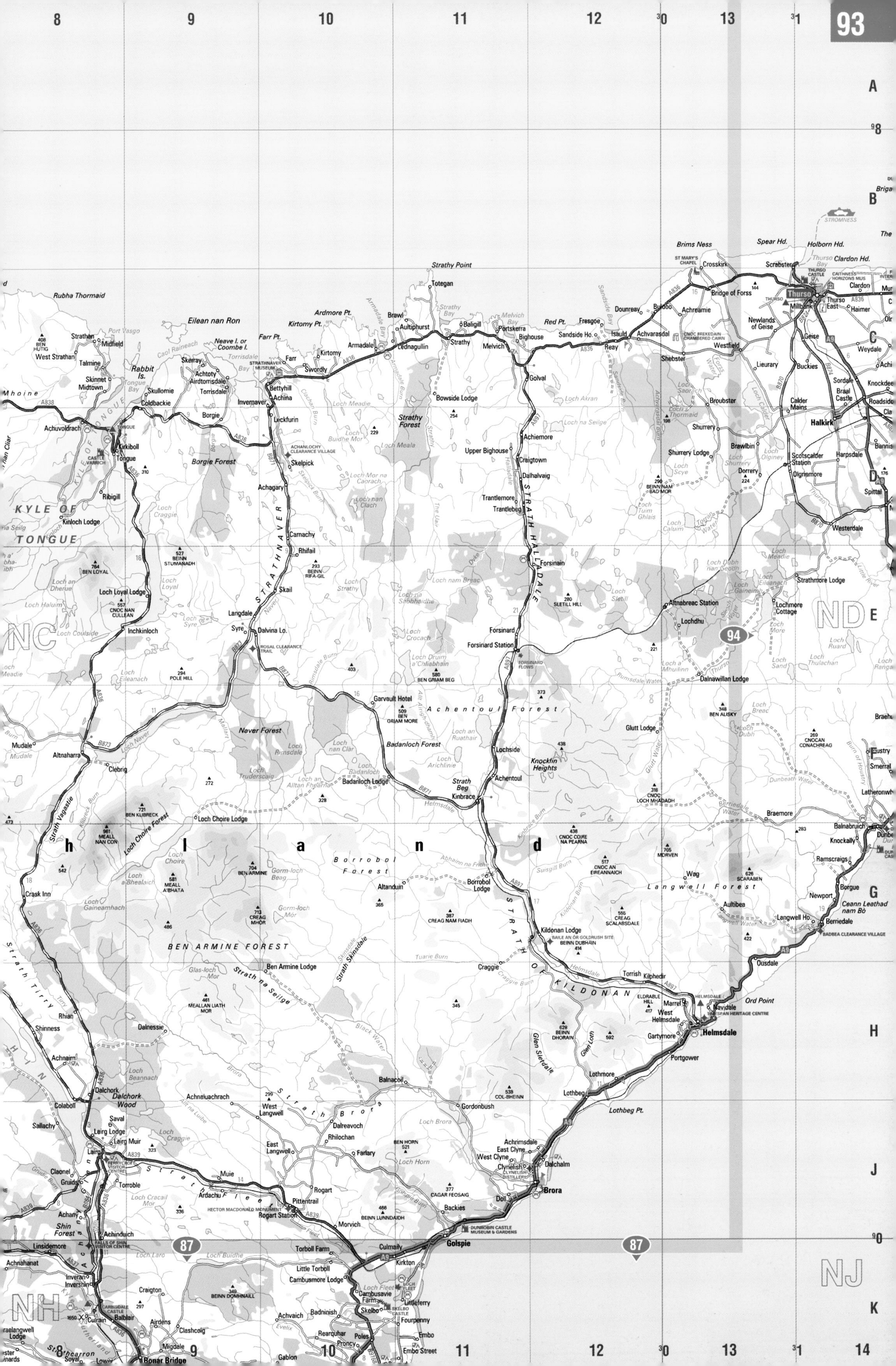

Strathy Point
Totegan
Rubha Thormaid
Eilean nan Ron
Ardmore Pt.
Kirtomy Pt.
Port Vasgo
Strathan
Midfield
West Strathan
Talmine
Skinnet
Midtown
Rabbit Is.
Tongue Bay
Skullomie
Coldbackie
Skerray
Neave I. or Coombe I.
Achtoty
Airdtorrisdale
Torrisdale
Borgie
Farr Pt.
Farr
Swordly
Kirtomy
Armadale
Armadale Bay
Brawl
Aultiphurst
Lednagullin
Strathy Bay
Strathy
Baligill
Melvich Bay
Portskerra
Melvich
Bighouse
Red Pt.
Fresgoe
Sandside Ho.
Sandside Bay
Isauld
Reay
Dounreay
Buldoo
Achvarasdal
Achreamie
Brims Ness
St Mary's Chapel
Crosskirk
Bridge of Forss
Spear Hd.
Holborn Hd.
Scrabster
Thurso Bay
Clardon Hd.
Thurso
Thurso Castle
Caithness Horizons Mus
Thurso East
Millbank
Clardon
Haimer
Stromness
Newlands of Geise
Geise
Weydale
Westfield
Shebster
Cnoc Freiceadain Chambered Cairn
Lieurary
Buckies
Sordale
Knockdee
Braal Castle
Roadside
Calder Mains
Halkirk
Broubster
Loch Calder
Loch Saorach
Loch Thormaid
Shurrery
Shurrery Lodge
Brawlbin
Scotscalder Station
Harpsdale
Dorrery
Olgrinmore
Spittal
Bannis
Westerdale
Beinn nam Bad Mor
Loch Tuim Ghlais
Loch Caluim
Golval
Loch Akran
Loch na Seilge
Achiemore
Upper Bighouse
Craigtown
Dalhalvaig
Trantlemore
Trantlebeg
Strath Halladale
Forsinain
Bowside Lodge
Strathy Forest
Loch Meala
Loch Buidhe Mor
Loch Meadie
Loch Mor na Caorach
Loch nan Clach
Loch nam Breac
Loch na Sabbhaidhe
Loch Strathy
Loch Crocach
Loch Druim a'Chliabhain
Ben Griam Beg
Forsinard
Forsinard Station
Forsinard Flows
Sletill Hill
Loch Sletill
Loch Dubh nan Geodh
Altnabreac Station
Lochdhu
Loch Gaineimh
Loch Eileanach
Loch Meadie
Strathmore Lodge
Lochmore Cottage
Loch More
Loch Ruard
Loch Thulachan
Loch Sand
Loch a' Mhuilinn
Rumsdale Water
Dalnawillan Lodge
Ben Alisky
Glutt Lodge
Glutt Water
Loch Breac
Loch Dubh
Cnocan Conachreag
Smerral
Dunbeath Water
Latheronwheel
Cnoc Loch Mhadadh
Berriedale Water
Braemore
Balnabruich
Dunbeath
Knockally
Ramscraigs
Morven
Wag
Langwell Forest
Scaraben
Borgue
Newport
Aultibea
Ceann Leathad nam Bò
Langwell Ho.
Berriedale
Badbea Clearance Village
Ousdale
Ord Point
Navidale
Timespan Heritage Centre
Helmsdale
Eldrable Hill
Marrel
West Helmsdale
Gartymore
Portgower
Kilphedir
Torrish
Kildonan Lodge
Baile an Or Goldrush Site
Beinn Dubhain
Strath of Kildonan
Craggie
Creag Scalabsdale
Cnoc an Eireannaich
Cnoc Coire na Pearna
Suisgill Burn
Kinbrace Burn
Beinn Dhorain
Glen Loth
Glen Sletdale
Lothmore
Lothbeg
Lothbeg Pt.
Col-Bheinn
Gordonbush
Loch Brora
Achrimsdale
East Clyne
West Clyne
Clynelish
Clynelish Distillery
Dalchalm
Brora
Doll
Cagar Feosaig
Ben Horn
Loch Horn
Backies
Dunrobin Castle Museum & Gardens
Golspie
Culmaily
Kirkton
Loch Fleet
Littleferry
Cambusavie Farm
Skelbo
Skelbo Castle
Fourpenny
Embo
Embo Street
Poles
Proncy
Rearquhar
Badninish
Achvaich
Evelix
Cambusmore Lodge
Little Torboll
Torboll Farm
Loch Buidhe
Beinn Domhnaill
Morvich
Beinn Lunndaidh
Hector Macdonald Monument
Rogart Station
Pittentrail
Rogart
Fleet
Strath Fleet
Muie
Ardachu
Loch Cracail Mor
Torroble
Lairg
Ferrycroft Visitor Centre
Lairg Lodge
Lairg Muir
Saval
Dalchork
Dalchork Wood
Loch Craggie
Colaboll
Sallachy
Achnairn
Shinness
Loch Shin
Rhian
Strath Tirry
Crask Inn
Loch Beannach
Dalnessie
Achnaluachrach
West Langwell
East Langwell
Strath Brora
Dalreavoch
Rhilochan
Farlary
Balnacoil
Black Water
Meallan Liath Mor
Strath na Seilge
Ben Armine Lodge
Ben Armine Forest
Glas-loch Mor
Creag Mhor
Gorm-loch Mor
Gorm-loch Beag
Ben Armine
Meall a' Bhata
Loch a' Bhealaich
Loch Gaineamhach
Loch Choire
Loch Choire Forest
Loch Choire Lodge
Meall nan Con
Ben Klibreck
Strath Vagastie
Altnaharra
Mudale
Clebrig
Loch Naver
Never Forest
Loch Rimsdale
Loch Truderscaig
Loch nan Clàr
Loch Badanloch
Loch an Alltan Fhearna
Badanloch Lodge
Badanloch Forest
Garvault Hotel
Ben Griam More
Achentoul Forest
Loch an Ruathair
Loch Arichlinie
Lochside
Achentoul
Knockfin Heights
Strath Beg
Kinbrace
Borrobol Forest
Borrobol Lodge
Altanduin
Creag nam Fiadh
Abhainn na Frithe
Tuarie Burn
Strath Skinsdale
Highland
Kyle of Tongue
Tongue
Kirkiboll
Castle Varrich
Achuvoldrach
Ribigill
Kinloch Lodge
Loch Craggie
Ben Loyal
Loch an Dherue
Loch Loyal
Loch Loyal Lodge
Cnoc nan Cullean
Loch Haluim
Inchkinloch
Loch Coulside
Beinn Stumanadh
Borgie Forest
Bettyhill
Strathnaver Museum
Achina
Invernaver
Leckfurin
Achanlochy Clearance Village
Skelpick
Achagary
Carnachy
Rhifail
Beinn Rifa-gil
Skail
Strathnaver
Langdale
Syre
Dalvina Lo.
Rosal Clearance Trail
Loch Syre
Pole Hill
Loch Eileanach
Linsidemore
Falls of Shin Visitor Centre
Achinduich
Shin Forest
Achany
Gruids
Claonel
Achnahanat
Inveran
Invershin
Carbisdale Castle
Culrain
Balblair
Craigton
Airdens
Clashcoig
Migdale
Bonar Bridge
Gablon
Soyal
Spinningdale
NC
ND
NH
NJ
A9
A836
A838
A897
A839
B871
B873
B874
B870

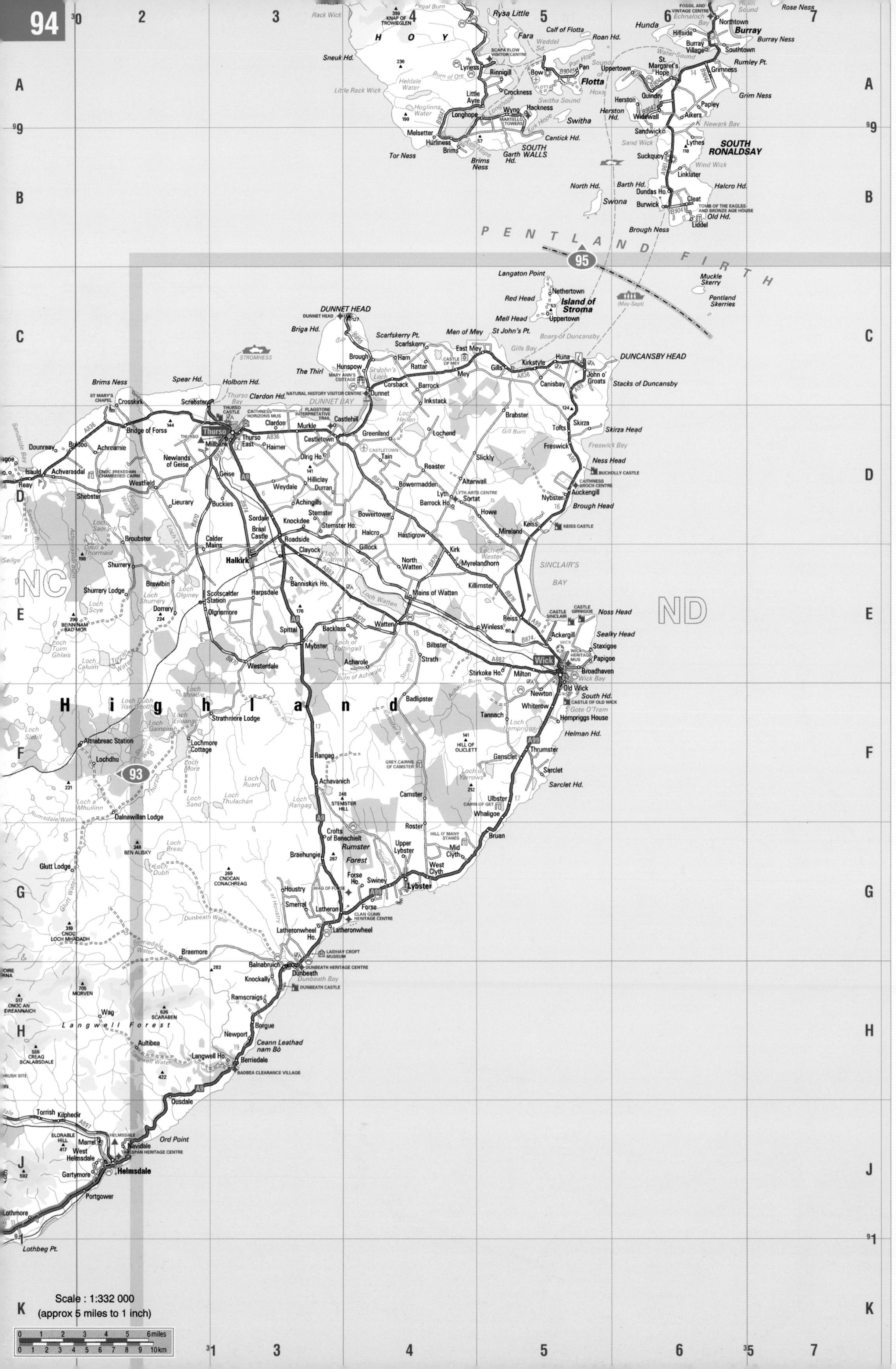
HOY
Rack Wick
399 KNAP OF TROWIEGLEN
Pegal Burn
Rysa Little
Fara
Calf of Flotta
Roan Hd.
Sneuk Hd.
Lyness
Rinnigill
SCAPA FLOW VISITOR CENTRE
Weddel Sd.
Bow
B9045
Pan
Pan Hope
Sound of Hoxa
Flotta
Uppertown
Little Rack Wick
Heldale Water
Burn of Ore
Little Ayre
Crockness
Hoglinns Water
Longhope
Wyng
Hackness
MARTELLO TOWERS
Switha Sound
Switha
Melsetter
Hurliness
Brims
Brims Ness
Aith Hope
Kirk Hope
SOUTH WALLS
Garth Hd.
Cantick Hd.
Tor Ness
Hunda
Echnaloch Bay
FOSSIL AND VINTAGE CENTRE
Northtown
Burray
Hillside
Burray Village
Southtown
Rose Ness
Burray Ness
Rumley Pt.
Water Sound
St. Margaret's Hope
Grimness
Grim Ness
Herston
Herston Hd.
Quindry
Widewall
Papley
Aikers
Newark Bay
Sandwick
Sand Wick
Lythes
Suckquoy
SOUTH RONALDSAY
Wind Wick
Linklater
North Hd.
Barth Hd.
Dundas Ho.
Halcro Hd.
Swona
Burwick
Cleat
TOMB OF THE EAGLES AND BRONZE AGE HOUSE
Old Hd.
Liddel
Brough Ness
PENTLAND FIRTH
95
Langaton Point
Muckle Skerry
Pentland Skerries
Red Head
Nethertown
Island of Stroma
Mell Head
Uppertown
DUNNET HEAD
Briga Hd.
Scarfskerry Pt.
Scarfskerry
Men of Mey
St John's Pt.
Boars of Duncansby
Gills Bay
East Mey
CASTLE OF MEY
Brough
Ham
Rattar
Gills
Kirkstyle
Huna
DUNCANSBY HEAD
John o' Groats
Canisbay
Stacks of Duncansby
STROMNESS
The Thirl
Hunspow
St John's Loch
MARY ANN'S COTTAGE
Corsback
Barrock
Mey
Brims Ness
Spear Hd.
Holborn Hd.
Thurso Bay
Clardon Hd.
NATURAL HISTORY VISITOR CENTRE
Dunnet
DUNNET BAY
Inkstack
ST MARY'S CHAPEL
Crosskirk
Scrabster
THURSO CASTLE
CAITHNESS HORIZONS MUS
FLAGSTONE INTERPRETATIVE TRAIL
Castlehill
Brabster
Skirza
Tofts
Skirza Head
Sandside Bay
Bridge of Forss
Thurso
Clardon
Murkle
Greenland
Loch Heilen
Lochend
Gill Burn
Dounreay
Buldoo
Achreamie
Newlands of Geise
Millbank
Thurso East
Haimer
Castletown
CASTLETOWN
Freswick
Freswick Bay
Isauld
Achvarasdal
CNOC FREKEDAIN CHAMBERED CAIRN
Olrig Ho.
Tain
Slickly
Ness Head
BUCHOLLY CASTLE
Reay
Westfield
Geise
Hilliclay
Durran
Reaster
Alterwall
CAITHNESS BROCH CENTRE
Auckengill
Shebster
Weydale
Bowermadden
Lyth
LYTH ARTS CENTRE
Sortat
Nybster
Brough Head
Lieurary
Buckies
Achingills
Barrock Ho.
Howe
Loch Saorach
Stemster
Bowertower
Keiss
KEISS CASTLE
Sordale
Knockdee
Stemster Ho.
Mireland
Broubster
Braal Castle
Halcro
Hastigrow
Calder Mains
Loch Calder
Roadside
Gillock
Loch Tuim Thormaid
Clayock
Loch Scarmclate
Kirk
Loch of Wester
SINCLAIR'S BAY
Shurrery
Halkirk
North Watten
Myrelandhorn
NC
Brawlbin
Banniskirk Ho.
Shurrery Lodge
Loch Olginey
Killimster
Scotscalder Station
Harpsdale
Loch Shurrery
Mains of Watten
Loch Watten
ND
Loch Scye
Dorrery
Olgrinmore
CASTLE SINCLAIR
CASTLE GIRNIGOE
Noss Head
BEINN NAM BAD MOR
Spittal
Backlass
Watten
Winless
Reiss
Ackergill
Sealky Head
Loch Tuim Ghlais
Loch of Toftingall
Bilbster
Mybster
WICK HERITAGE MUS
Staxigoe
Papigoe
Loch Caluim
Torrish Water
Westerdale
Acharole
Strath
Stirkoke Ho.
Milton
Wick
Broadhaven
Wick Bay
Burn of Acharole
Old Wick
Loch Meadie
Highland
Loch Dubh nan Geodh
Badlipster
Achairn Burn
Newton
South Hd.
CASTLE OF OLD WICK
Gote O'Tram
Whiterow
Hempriggs House
Loch Eileanach
Strathmore Lodge
Tannach
Loch Hempriggs
Loch Gaineimh
Little River
Helman Hd.
Loch Sletill
Altnabreac Station
Lochmore Cottage
HILL OF OLICLETT
Thrumster
Rangag
Gansclet
GREY CAIRNS OF CAMSTER
Sarclet
Lochdhu
93
Loch More
Loch Ruard
Loch of Yarrows
Achavanich
Sarclet Hd.
Loch Thulachan
STEMSTER HILL
Camster
CAIRN OF GET
Loch a' Mhuilinn
Loch Sand
Loch Rangag
Ulbster
Whaligoe
Rumsdale Water
Dalnawillan Lodge
Crofts of Benachielt
Roster
HILL O' MANY STANES
Bruan
BEN ALISKY
Loch Breac
Braehungie
Rumster Forest
Upper Lybster
Mid Clyth
Glutt Lodge
Loch Dubh
CNOCAN CONACHREAG
Burn of Houstry
Forse Ho.
Swiney
West Clyth
Lybster
Houstry
WAG OF FORSE
Forse
Glutt Water
Smerral
Latheron
CLAN GUNN HERITAGE CENTRE
Dunbeath Water
CNOC LOCH MHADADH
Latheronwheel Ho.
Latheronwheel
LAIDHAY CROFT MUSEUM
Berriedale Water
Braemore
Balnabruich
Dunbeath
DUNBEATH HERITAGE CENTRE
Dunbeath Bay
Knockally
DUNBEATH CASTLE
MORVEN
Ramscraigs
CNOC AN EIREANNAICH
Wag
SCARABEN
Langwell Forest
Borgue
CREAG SCALABSDALE
Aultibea
Newport
Ceann Leathad nam Bò
Langwell Ho.
Berriedale
Langwell Water
BADBEA CLEARANCE VILLAGE
Ousdale
Torrish
Kilphedir
Ord Point
ELDRABLE HILL
Marrel
HELMSDALE
Navidale
West Helmsdale
TIMESPAN HERITAGE CENTRE
Gartymore
Helmsdale
Portgower
Lothmore
Lothbeg Pt.
Scale : 1:332 000
(approx 5 miles to 1 inch)
0 1 2 3 4 5 6 miles
0 1 2 3 4 5 6 7 8 9 10 km

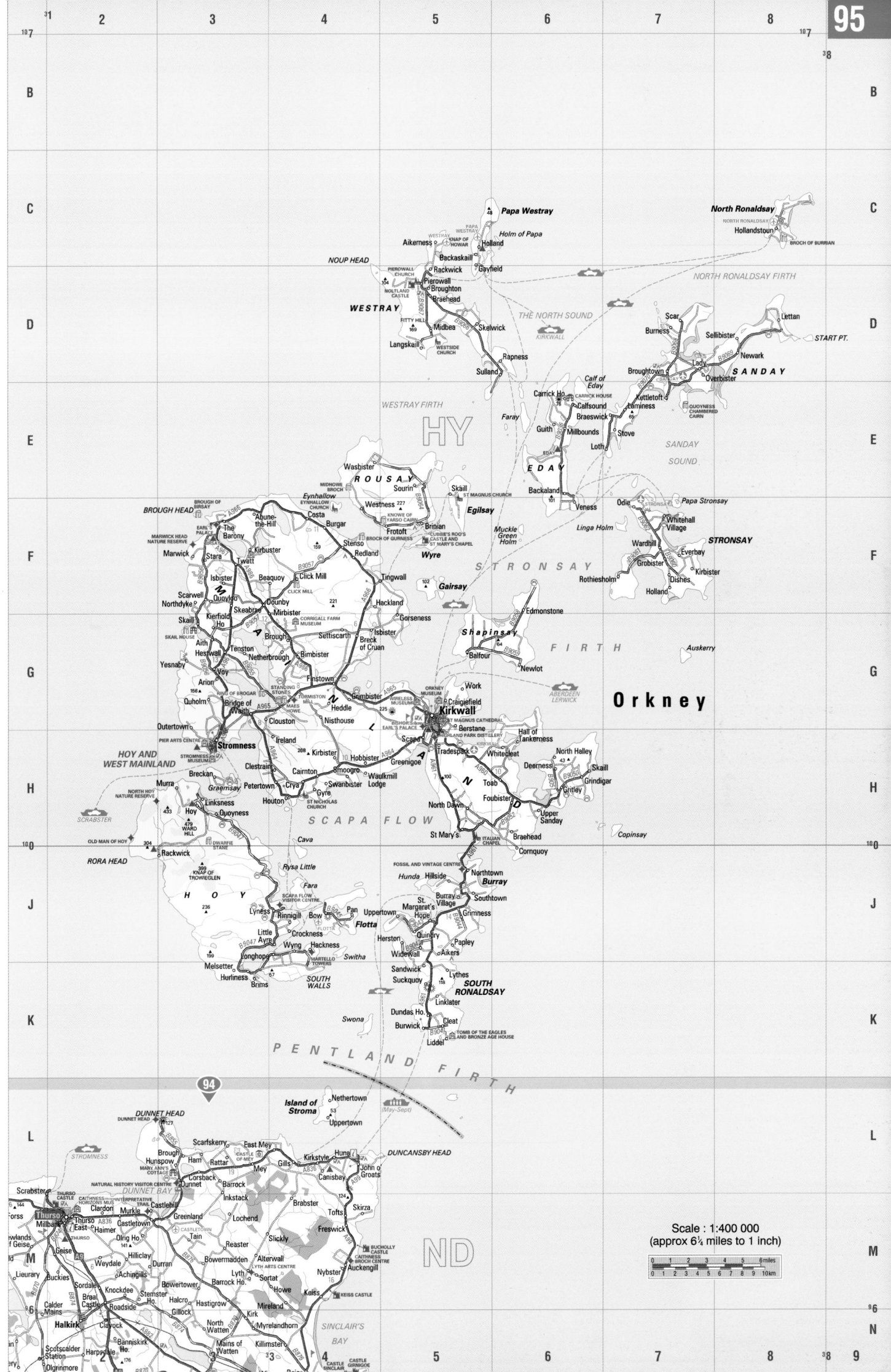
Papa Westray
Holm of Papa
North Ronaldsay
Hollandstoun
BROCH OF BURRIAN
NORTH RONALDSAY FIRTH
Aikerness
KNAP OF HOWAR
Holland
Backaskaill
Gayfield
NOUP HEAD
Rackwick
PIEROWALL CHURCH
Pierowall
Broughton
NOLTLAND CASTLE
Braehead
WESTRAY
FITTY HILL
Midbea
Skelwick
Langskaill
WESTSIDE CHURCH
Rapness
Sulland
THE NORTH SOUND
KIRKWALL
Scar
Burness
Sellibister
Lettan
START PT.
Newark
Lady
Broughtown
Overbister
SANDAY
Calf of Eday
Carrick Ho.
CARRICK HOUSE
Kettletoft
Calfsound
Laminess
QUOYNESS CHAMBERED CAIRN
WESTRAY FIRTH
HY
Faray
Braeswick
Guith
Millbounds
Stove
Loth
SANDAY SOUND
EDAY
Wasbister
ROUSAY
MIDHOWE BROCH
Sourin
Skaill
ST MAGNUS CHURCH
Egilsay
Backaland
Veness
Odie
Papa Stronsay
Eynhallow
EYNHALLOW CHURCH
Westness
KNOWE OF YARSO CAIRN
Whitehall Village
BROUGH HEAD
BROUGH OF BIRSAY
Costa
Abune-the-Hill
Burgar
Frotoft
Brinian
CUBBIE ROO'S CASTLE AND ST MARY'S CHAPEL
Muckle Green Holm
Linga Holm
EARL'S PALACE
The Barony
Kirbuster
Stenso
BROCH OF GURNESS
Wardhill
STRONSAY
MARWICK HEAD NATURE RESERVE
Marwick
Stara
Twatt
Redland
Wyre
Everbay
STRONSAY
Grobister
Kirbister
Isbister
Beaquoy
Click Mill
CLICK MILL
Tingwall
Rothiesholm
Dishes
Gairsay
Holland
Scarwell
Northdyke
Quoylo
Dounby
Hackland
Edmonstone
Skeabrae
Mirbister
Kierfiold Ho
CORRIGALL FARM MUSEUM
Gorseness
Skaill
SKAILL HOUSE
Isbister
Shapinsay
Settiscarth
Breck of Cruan
Aith
Brough
Hestwall
Tenston
Netherbrough
Bimbister
FIRTH
Auskerry
Balfour
Yesnaby
Voy
Newlot
Finstown
Arion
RING OF BRODGAR
STANDING STONES
Work
ABERDEEN LERWICK
Quholm
Grimbister
ORKNEY MUSEUM
Bridge of Waith
TORMISTON MILL
MAES HOWE
WIRELESS MUSEUM
Craigiefield
Orkney
Heddle
Kirkwall
Clouston
Nisthouse
ST MAGNUS CATHEDRAL
BISHOP'S & EARL'S PALACE
Berstane
Outertown
HIGHLAND PARK DISTILLERY
Hall of Tankerness
PIER ARTS CENTRE
Ireland
Scapa
Stromness
Tradespark
HOY AND WEST MAINLAND
Kirbister
Hobbister
Whitecleat
North Halley
STROMNESS MUSEUM
Greenigoe
Skaill
Deerness
Clestrain
Grindigar
Breckan
Cairnton
Smoogro
Waulkmill Lodge
Graemsay
Murra
Petertown
Crya
Swanbister
Toab
Gritley
NORTH HOY NATURE RESERVE
Houton
Gyre
Foubister
Linksness
ST NICHOLAS CHURCH
North Dawn
Upper Sanday
SCRABSTER
Hoy
Quoyness
SCAPA FLOW
WARD HILL
St Mary's
Braehead
ITALIAN CHAPEL
Copinsay
OLD MAN OF HOY
DWARFIE STANE
Cava
Cornquoy
Rackwick
RORA HEAD
KNAP OF TROWIEGLEN
Rysa Little
FOSSIL AND VINTAGE CENTRE
Northtown
Burray
Hunda
Hillside
Fara
HOY
SCAPA FLOW VISITOR CENTRE
Burray Village
Southtown
St. Margaret's Hope
Lyness
Rinnigill
Bow
Pan
Uppertown
Grimness
Flotta
Little Ayre
Crockness
Herston
Quindry
Papley
Wyng
Hackness
Widewall
Aikers
Switha
Longhope
MARTELLO TOWERS
Melsetter
Sandwick
Hurliness
Lythes
Suckquoy
Brims
SOUTH WALLS
SOUTH RONALDSAY
Linklater
Dundas Ho.
Swona
Cleat
Burwick
TOMB OF THE EAGLES AND BRONZE AGE HOUSE
Liddel
PENTLAND FIRTH
94
Nethertown
Island of Stroma
(May-Sept)
Uppertown
DUNNET HEAD
DUNCANSBY HEAD
Scarfskerry
East Mey
STROMNESS
Brough
Ham
Rattar
CASTLE OF MEY
Gills
Kirkstyle
Huna
Hunspow
Mey
Canisbay
John o' Groats
MARY ANN'S COTTAGE
Corsback
Dunnet
NATURAL HISTORY VISITOR CENTRE
DUNNET BAY
Barrock
Scrabster
THURSO CASTLE
CAITHNESS HORIZONS MUS
INTERPRETATIVE TRAIL CENTRE
Inkstack
Brabster
Skirza
Thurso
Clardon
Murkle
Castlehill
Tofts
Forss
Millbank
East
Haimer
Castletown
Greenland
Lochend
Freswick
CASTLETOWN
Tain
Slickly
Geise
Olrig Ho.
Reaster
ND
BUCHOLLY CASTLE
CAITHNESS BROCH CENTRE
Hillclay
Durran
Bowermadden
Alterwall
Auckengill
Weydale
Achingills
LYTH ARTS CENTRE
Lieurary
Buckies
Lyth
Sortat
Nybster
Sordale
Knockdee
Stemster Ho.
Barrock Ho.
Bowertower
Howe
Keiss
KEISS CASTLE
Calder Mains
Braal Castle
Roadside
Halcro
Hastigrow
Gillock
Mireland
Halkirk
Clayock
North Watten
Kirk
Myrelandhorn
SINCLAIR'S BAY
Scotscalder Station
Harpsdale
Bannskirk Ho.
Mains of Watten
Killimster
Olgrinmore
CASTLE SINCLAIR
CASTLE GIRNIGOE
Scale : 1:400 000
(approx 6¼ miles to 1 inch)
0 1 2 3 4 5 6 miles
0 1 2 3 4 5 6 7 8 9 10km

B **HO** **HP** B

C C

Shetland

D D

E E

F F

G G

H H

J **HT** J

Fair Isle

HZ

K **HU** K

L L

M M

Scale : 1:400 000
(approx 6¼ miles to 1 inch)

0   6 miles
0   10km

N N

Town plan symbols

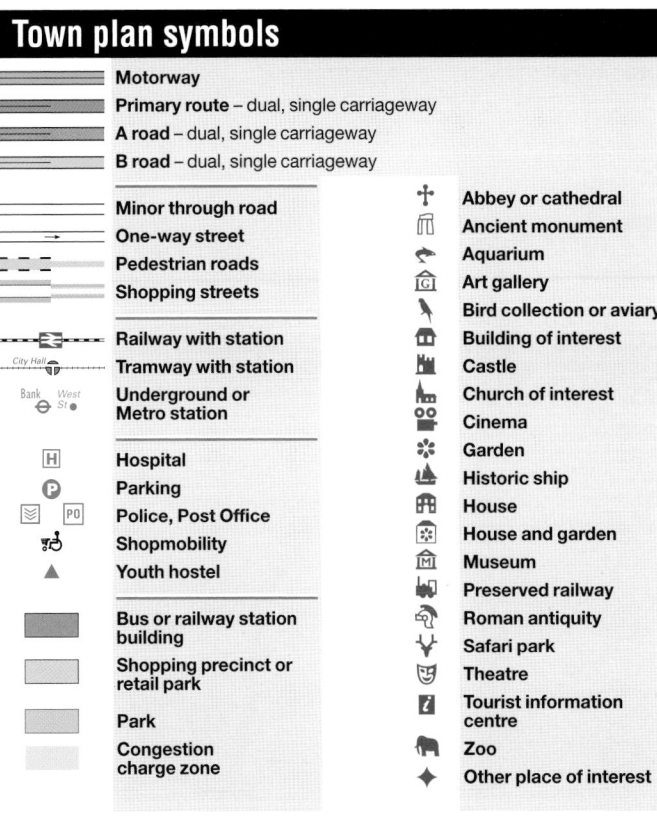

Motorway	
Primary route – dual, single carriageway	
A road – dual, single carriageway	
B road – dual, single carriageway	

Minor through road
One-way street
Pedestrian roads
Shopping streets

Railway with station
Tramway with station
Underground or
Metro station

H Hospital
P Parking
Police, Post Office
Shopmobility
Youth hostel

Bus or railway station
building

Shopping precinct or
retail park

Park

Congestion
charge zone

Abbey or cathedral
Ancient monument
Aquarium
Art gallery
Bird collection or aviary
Building of interest
Castle
Church of interest
Cinema
Garden
Historic ship
House
House and garden
Museum
Preserved railway
Roman antiquity
Safari park
Theatre
Tourist information
centre
Zoo
Other place of interest

Aberdeen

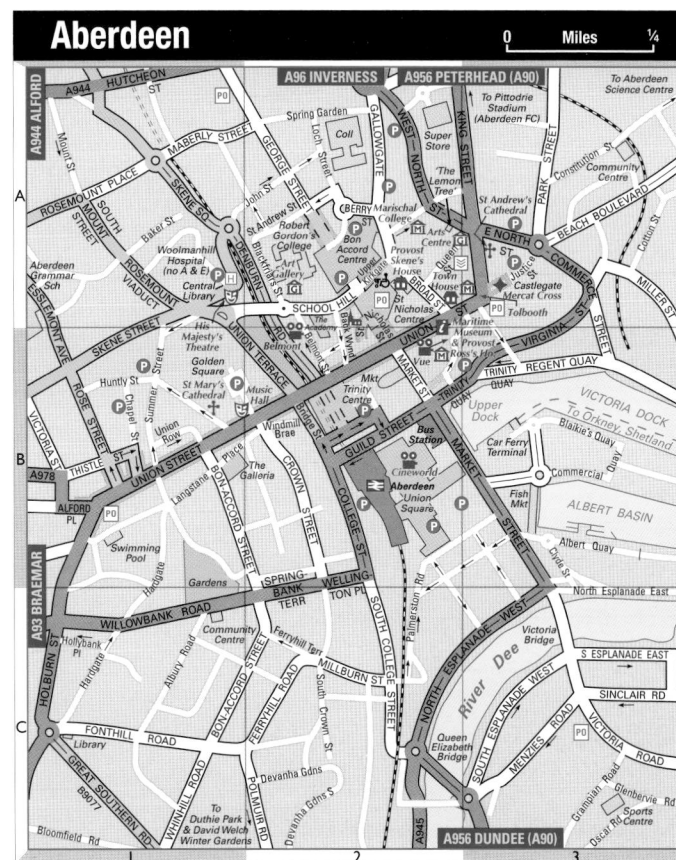

Bath

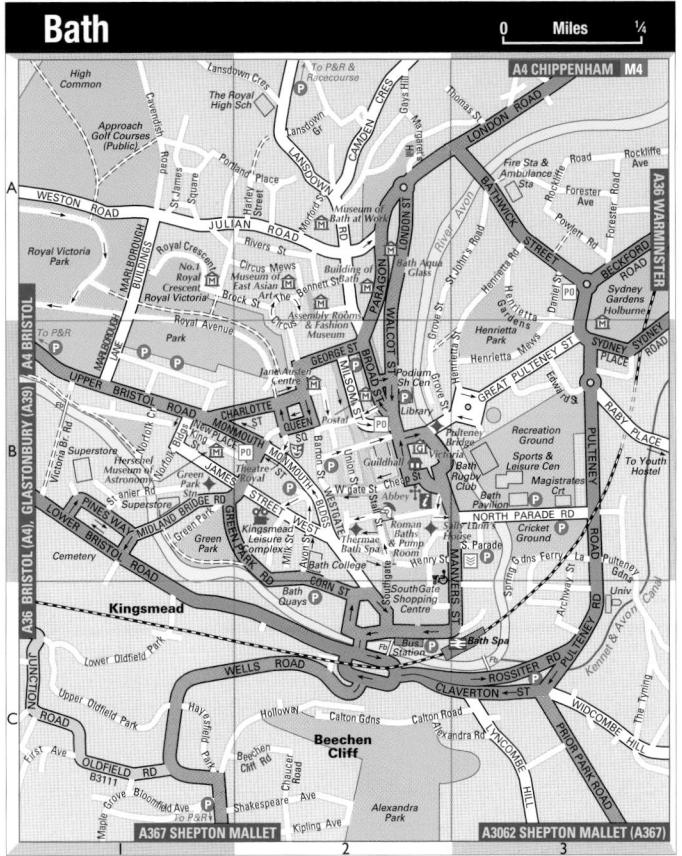

Blackpool

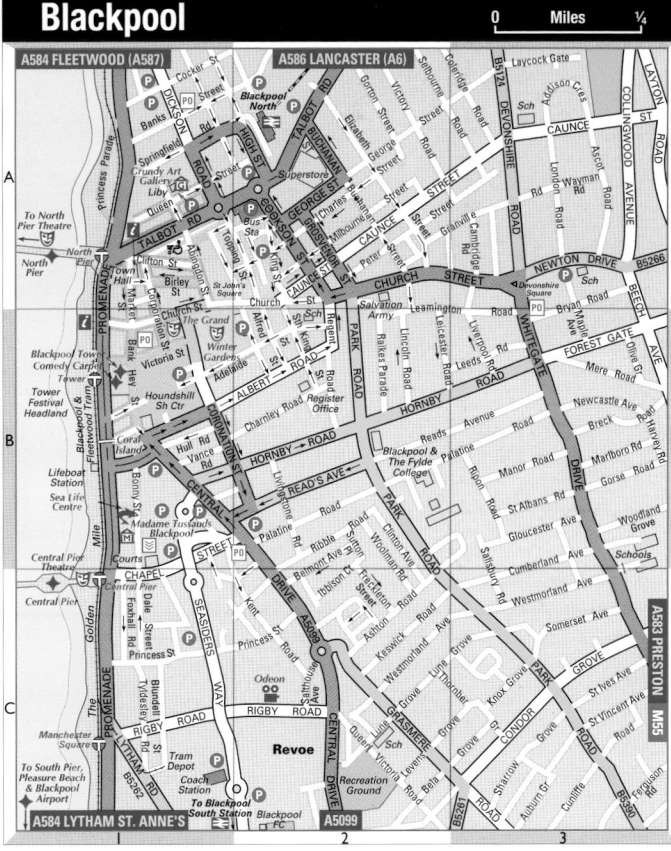

Birmingham

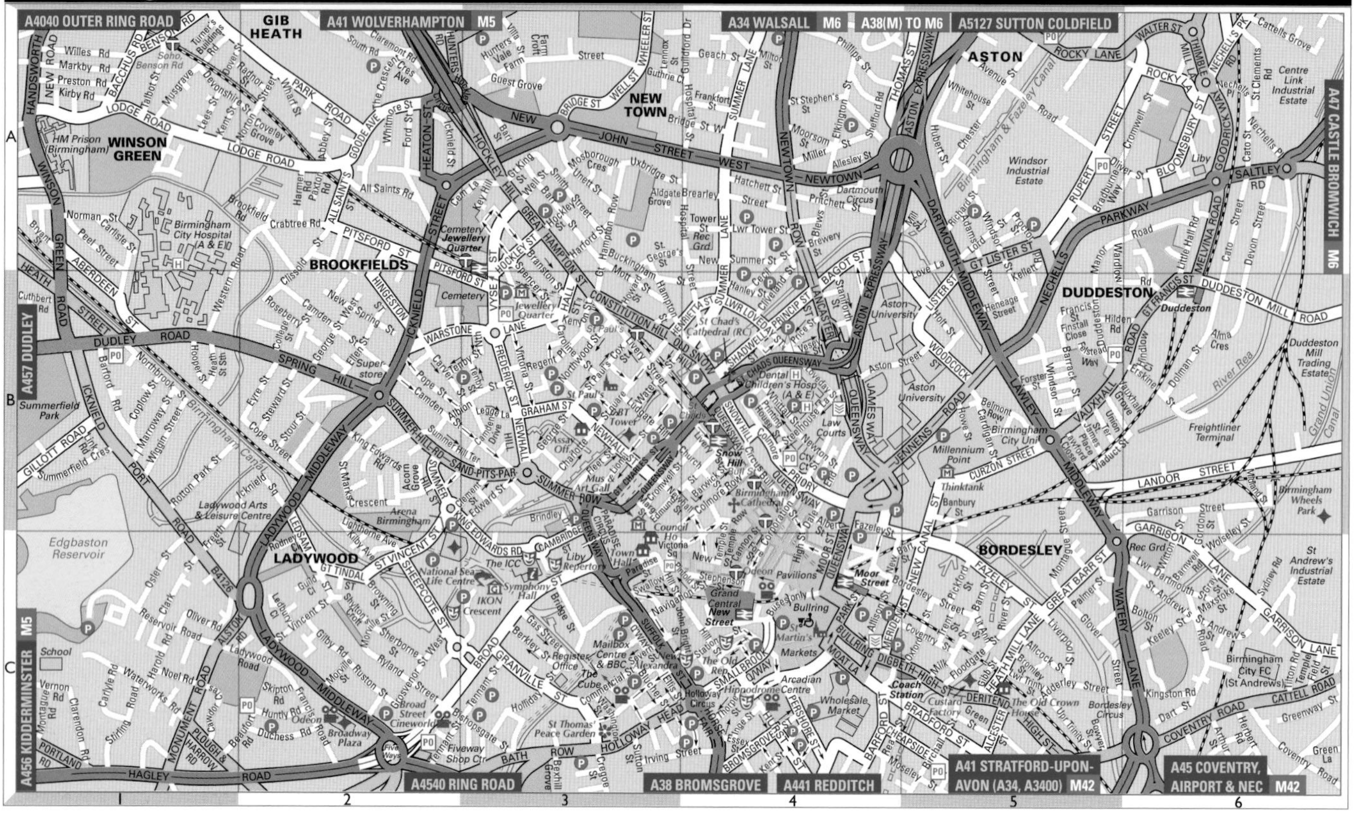
0 Miles ¼
A4040 OUTER RING ROAD
A41 WOLVERHAMPTON M5
A34 WALSALL M6
A38(M) TO M6
A5127 SUTTON COLDFIELD
A47 CASTLE BROMWICH M6
A457 DUDLEY
A456 KIDDERMINSTER M5
A4540 RING ROAD
A38 BROMSGROVE
A441 REDDITCH
A41 STRATFORD-UPON-AVON (A34, A3400) M42
A45 COVENTRY, AIRPORT & NEC M42
GIB HEATH
NEW TOWN
ASTON
WINSON GREEN
HM Prison Birmingham
Birmingham City Hospital (A & E)
BROOKFIELDS
DUDDESTON
Windsor Industrial Estate
Centre Link Industrial Estate
Aston University
Birmingham Children's Hosp (A & E)
Millennium Point
Thinktank
Freightliner Terminal
Duddeston Mill Trading Estate
Birmingham Wheels Park
LADYWOOD
Ladywood Arts & Leisure Centre
Edgbaston Reservoir
Summerfield Park
Arena Birmingham
National Sea Life Centre
The ICC
Symphony Hall
IKON
St Chad's Cathedral (RC)
St Philip's Cathedral
Snow Hill
Moor Street
New Street
Grand Central
Bullring
Markets
Arcadian Centre
Hippodrome
Coach Station
Wholesale Market
The Mailbox Centre & BBC
The Cube
St Thomas' Peace Garden
Broadway Plaza
BORDESLEY
St Andrew's Industrial Estate
Birmingham City FC (St Andrews)
Kingston Rd
HAGLEY ROAD
PORTLAND RD
CONSTITUTION HILL
SUMMER ROW
BROAD ST
DIGBETH HIGH ST
DERITEND
CURZON STREET
LANDOR STREET
COVENTRY ROAD
CATTELL ROAD
GARRISON LANE
SALTLEY RD
DUDDESTON MILL ROAD
NECHELLS
LAWLEY MIDDLEWAY
DARTMOUTH MIDDLEWAY
ASTON EXPRESSWAY
LADYWOOD MIDDLEWAY
SPRING HILL
DUDLEY ROAD
LODGE ROAD
PARK ROAD
JOHN STREET WEST
NEWTOWN
QUEENSWAY
WATERY LANE
River Rea
Grand Union Canal
Birmingham & Fazeley Canal
Birmingham Canal
1 2 3 4 5 6
A B C

Bournemouth

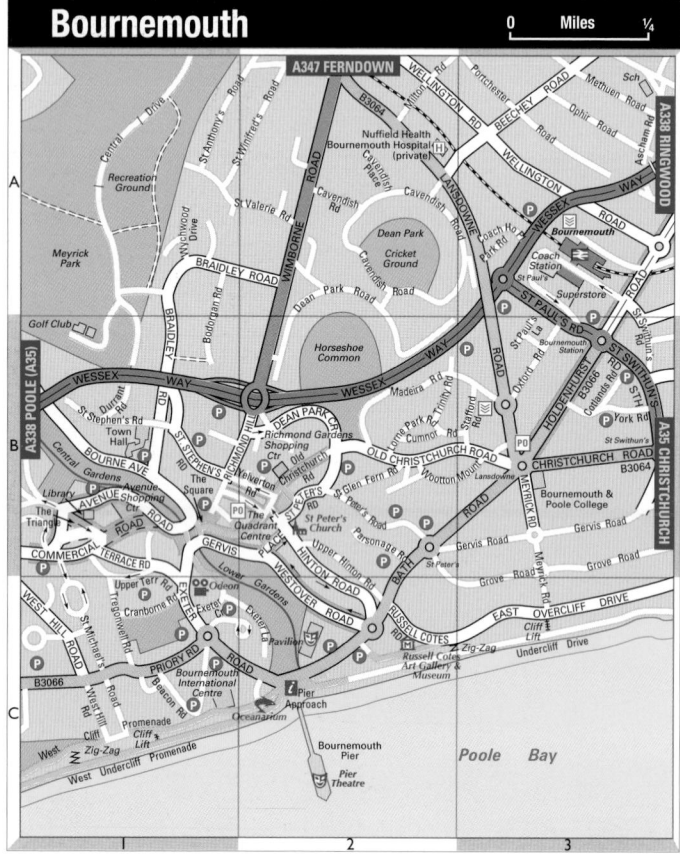
0 Miles ¼
A347 FERNDOWN
A338 RINGWOOD
A338 POOLE (A35)
A35 CHRISTCHURCH
Recreation Ground
Meyrick Park
Golf Club
Nuffield Health Bournemouth Hospital (private)
Dean Park Cricket Ground
Horseshoe Common
WESSEX WAY
WIMBORNE ROAD
BRAIDLEY ROAD
Coach Station
Bournemouth
Superstore
ST PAUL'S RD
HOLDENHURST RD
CHRISTCHURCH ROAD
Richmond Gardens Shopping Ctr
Town Hall
Central Gardens
Library
The Triangle
The Square
St Peter's Church
The Quadrant Centre
Bournemouth & Poole College
Lansdowne
Odeon
Pavilion
Bournemouth International Centre
Pier Approach
Oceanarium
Bournemouth Pier
Pier Theatre
Russell Cotes Art Gallery & Museum
EAST OVERCLIFF DRIVE
Undercliff Drive
Cliff Lift
Zig-Zag
West Undercliff Promenade
Poole Bay
B3064
B3066
1 2 3
A B C

Bradford

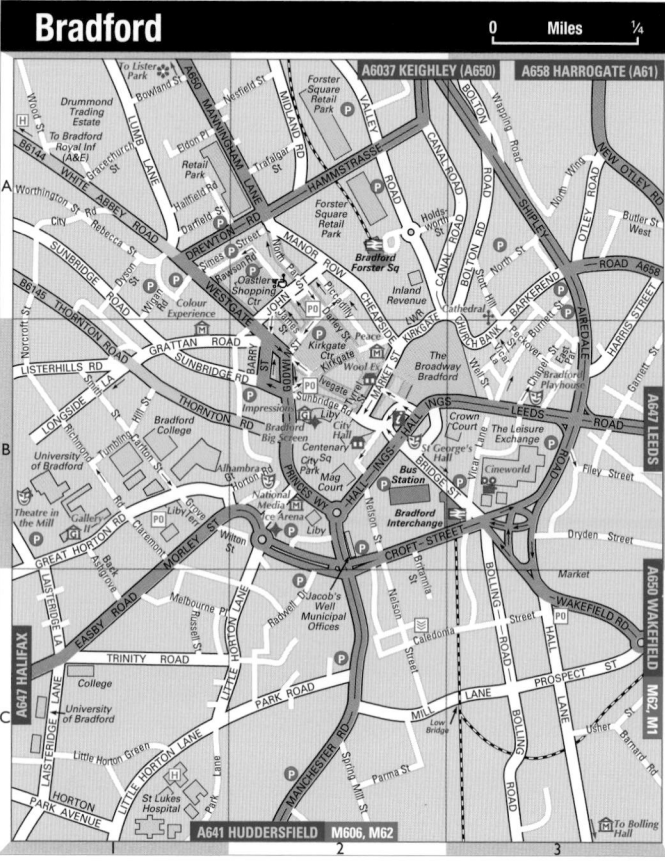
0 Miles ¼
A6037 KEIGHLEY (A650)
A658 HARROGATE (A61)
A647 LEEDS
A650 WAKEFIELD M62, M1
A647 HALIFAX
A641 HUDDERSFIELD M606, M62
To Lister Park
Drummond Trading Estate
To Bradford Royal Inf (A&E)
Forster Square Retail Park
Bradford Forster Sq
Inland Revenue
Cathedral
Oastler Shopping Ctr
Kirkgate Ctr
Colour Experience
Bradford College
University of Bradford
Theatre in the Mill
Alhambra
National Media Museum
Ice Arena
City Hall
Centenary Sq
Bus Station
Bradford Interchange
The Broadway Bradford
Crown Court
The Leisure Exchange
Cineworld
St George's Hall
Bradford Playhouse
Jacob's Well Municipal Offices
St Lukes Hospital
To Bolling Hall
HAMMSTRASSE
MANNINGHAM LANE
WHITE ABBEY ROAD
THORNTON ROAD
SUNBRIDGE RD
GREAT HORTON RD
MORLEY ST
CROFT STREET
WAKEFIELD RD
MANCHESTER RD
PARK ROAD
TRINITY ROAD
MILL LANE
LEEDS ROAD
HARRIS STREET
BARKEREND ROAD
SHIPLEY AIREDALE ROAD
CANAL ROAD
1 2 3
A B C

Bristol

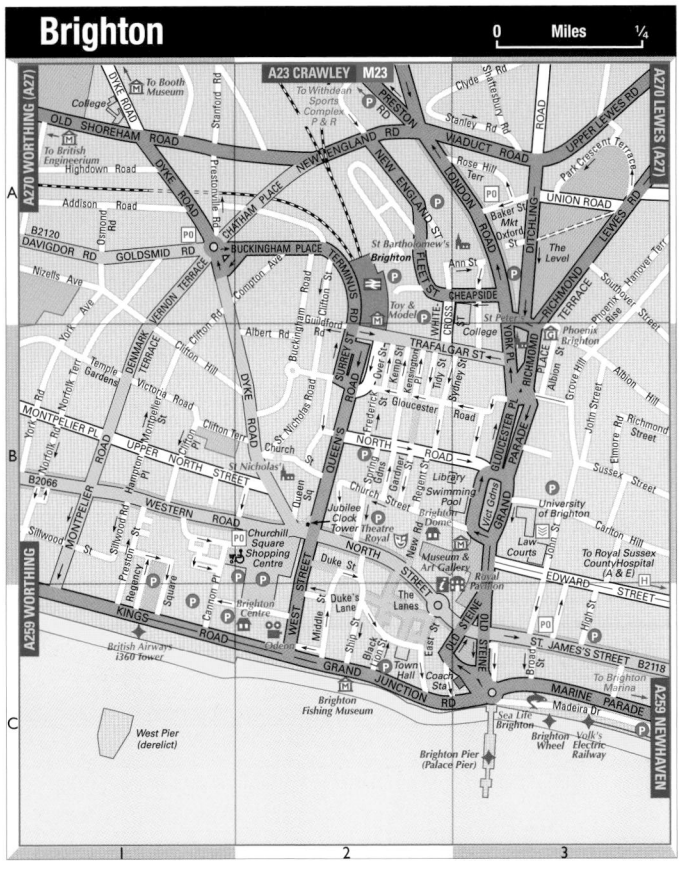

Brighton

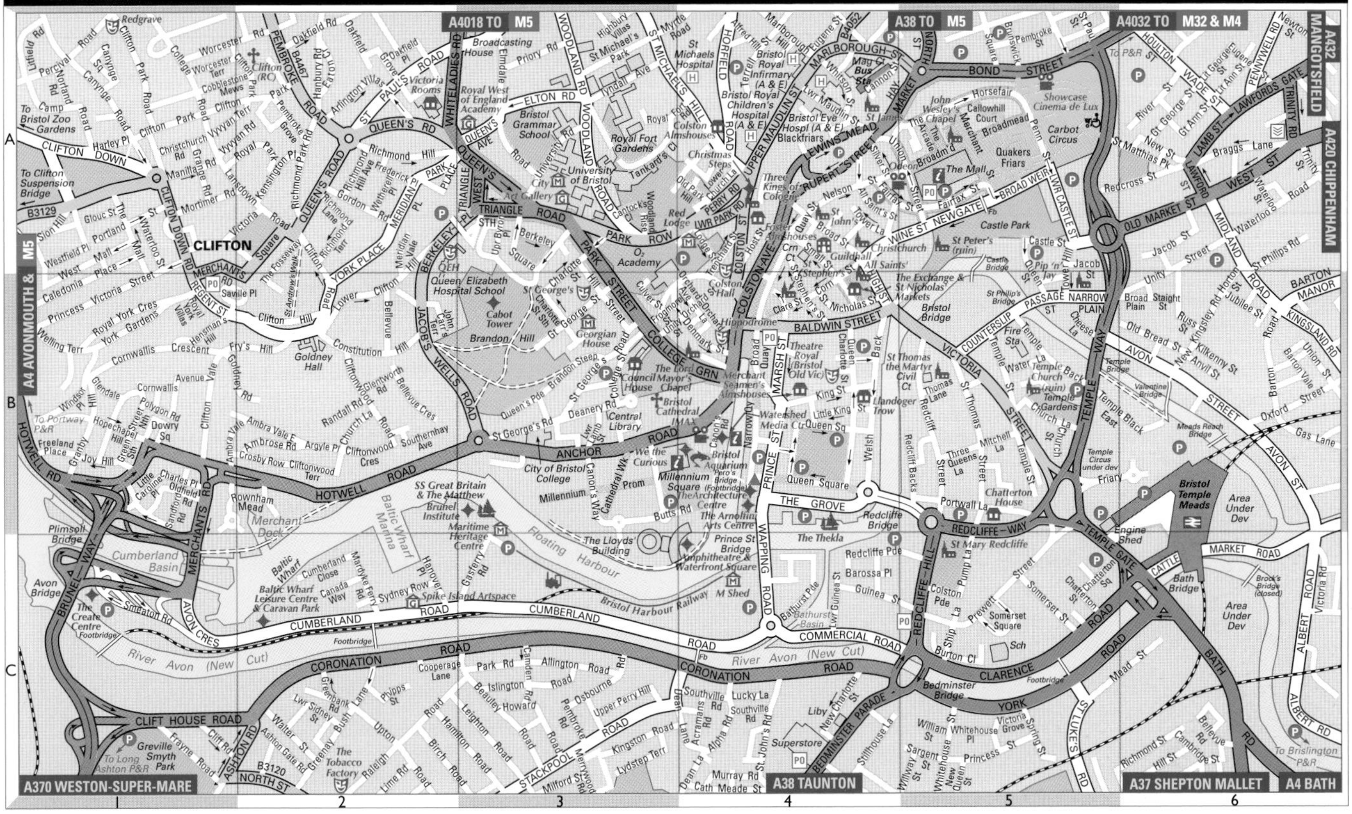

Cambridge

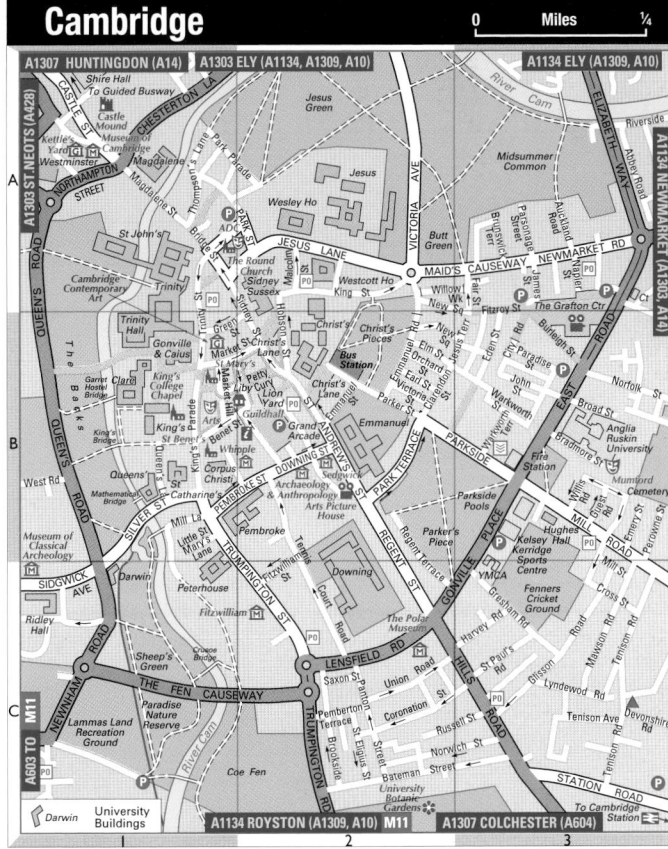

Canterbury

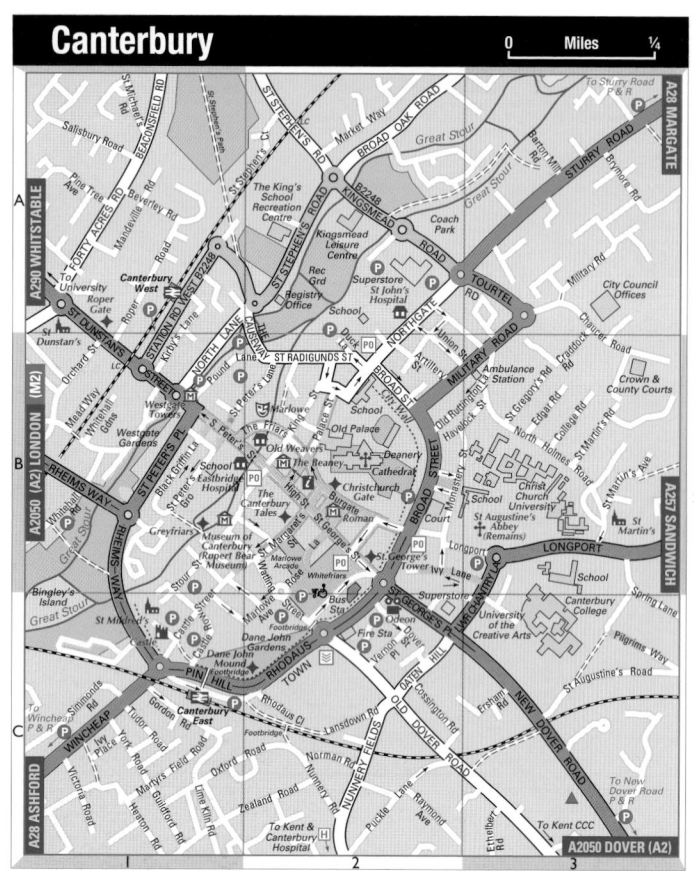

Cardiff / Caerdydd

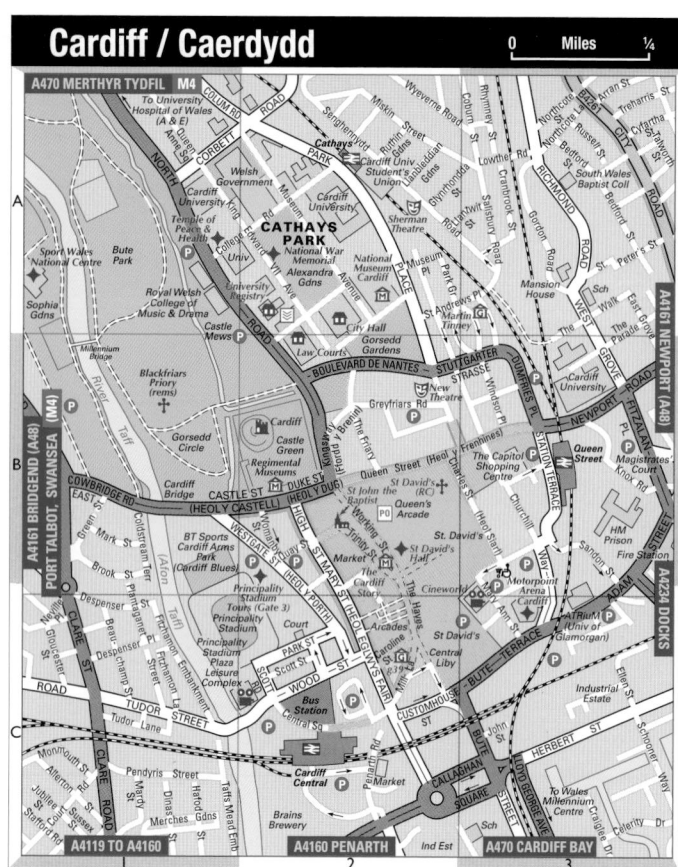

Cheltenham

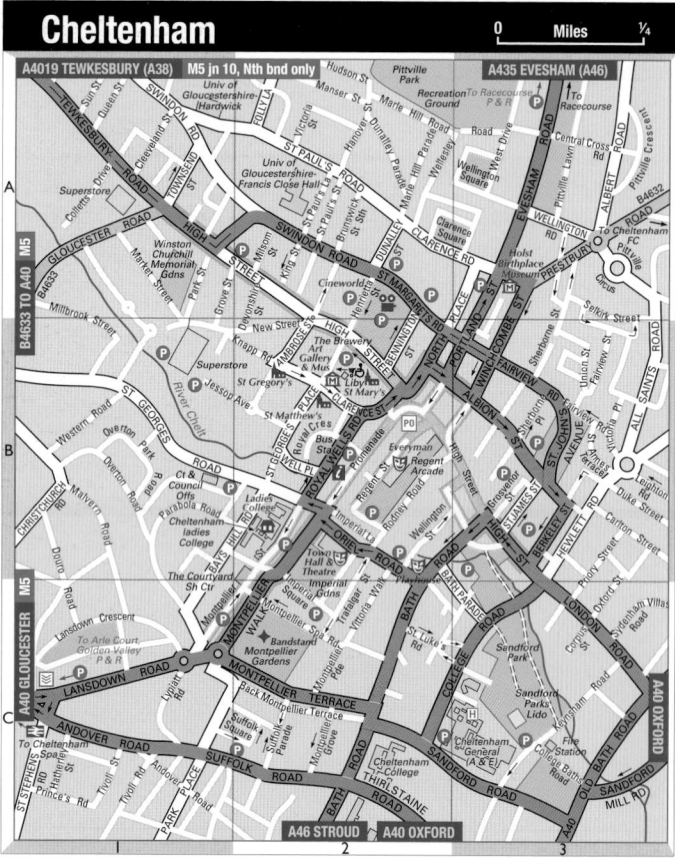

Chester

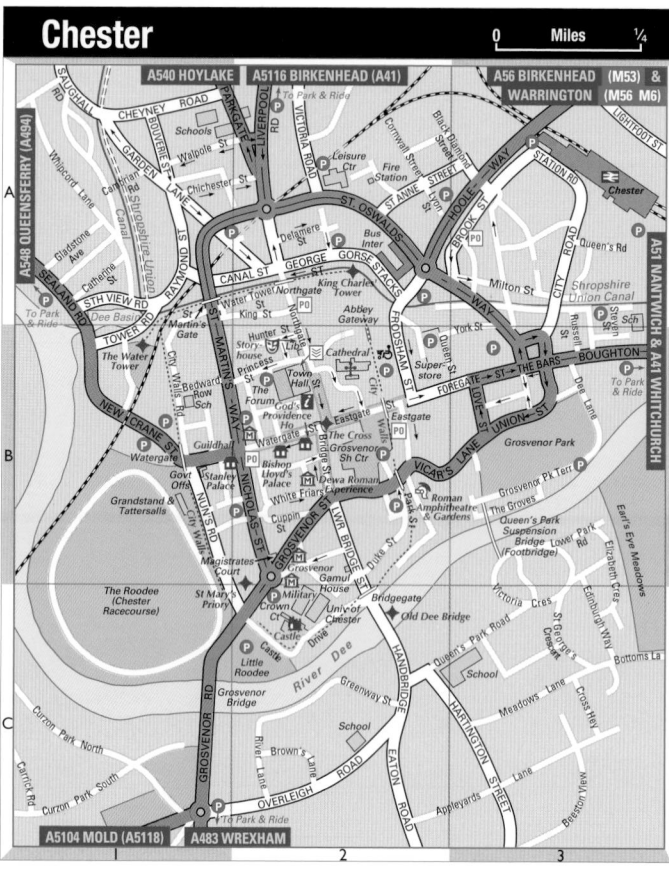

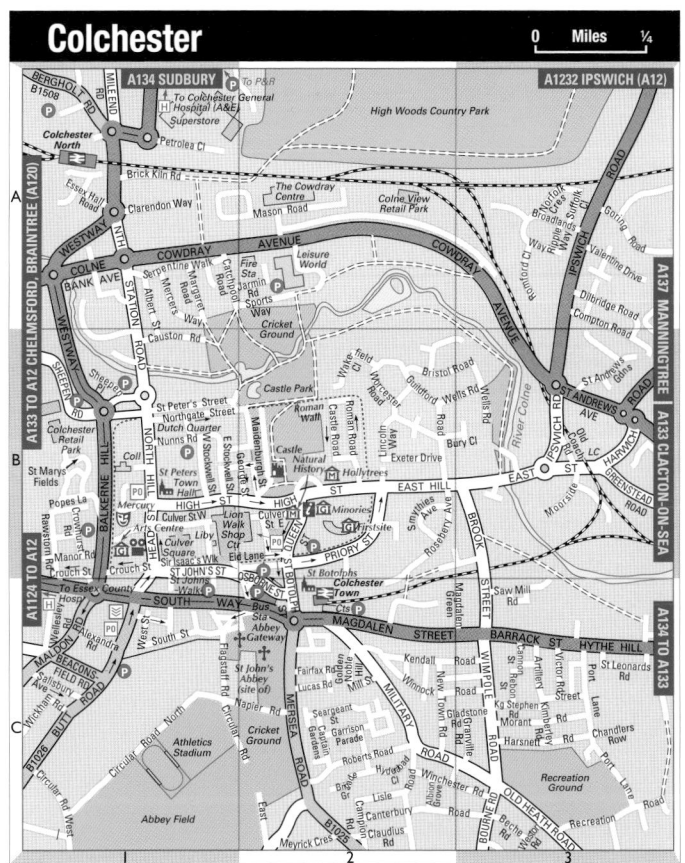

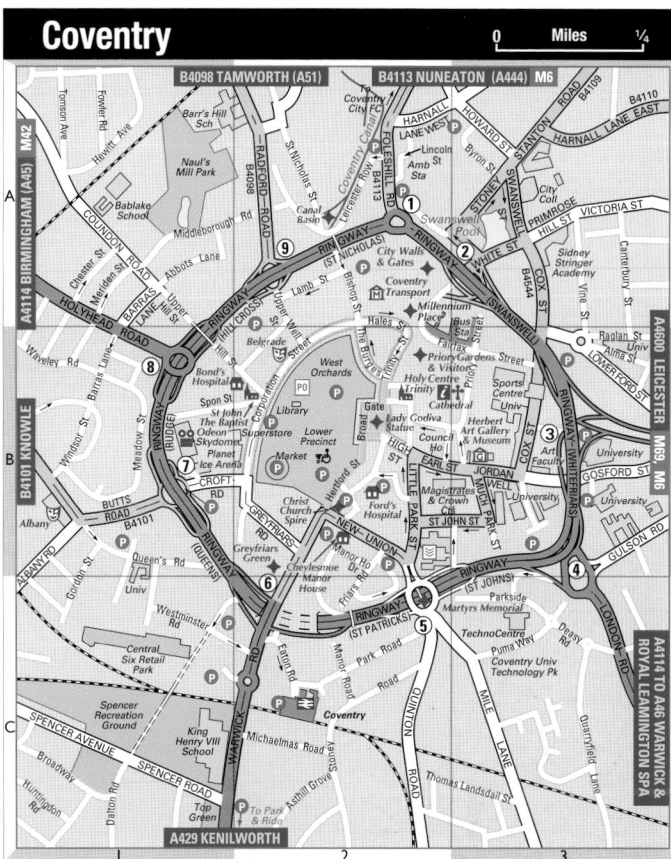

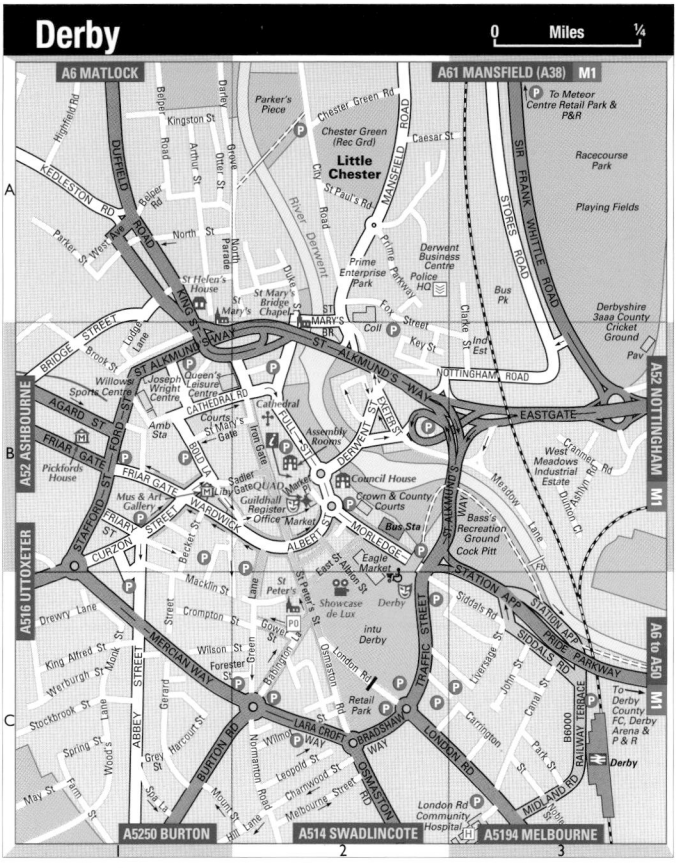

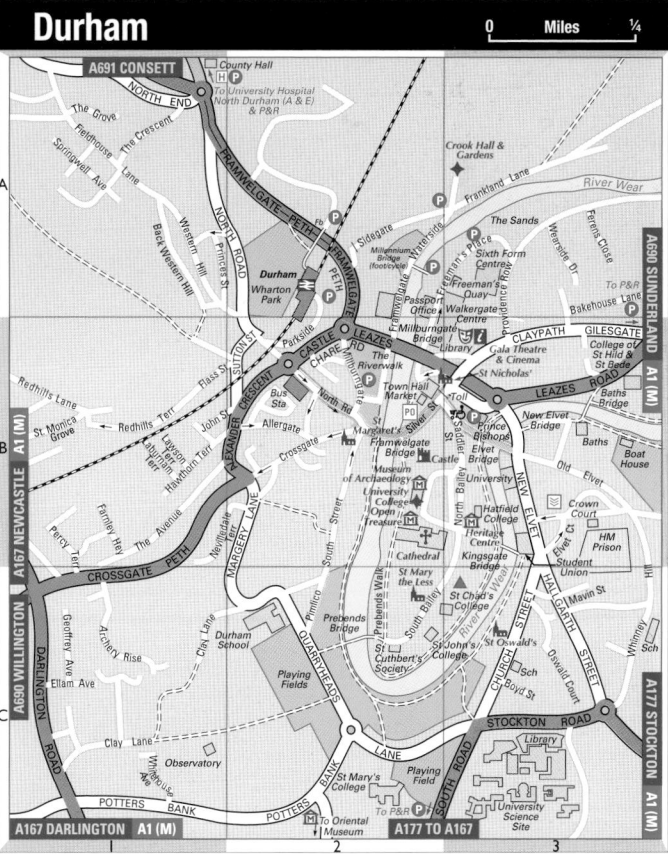

Edinburgh

0 Miles ¼

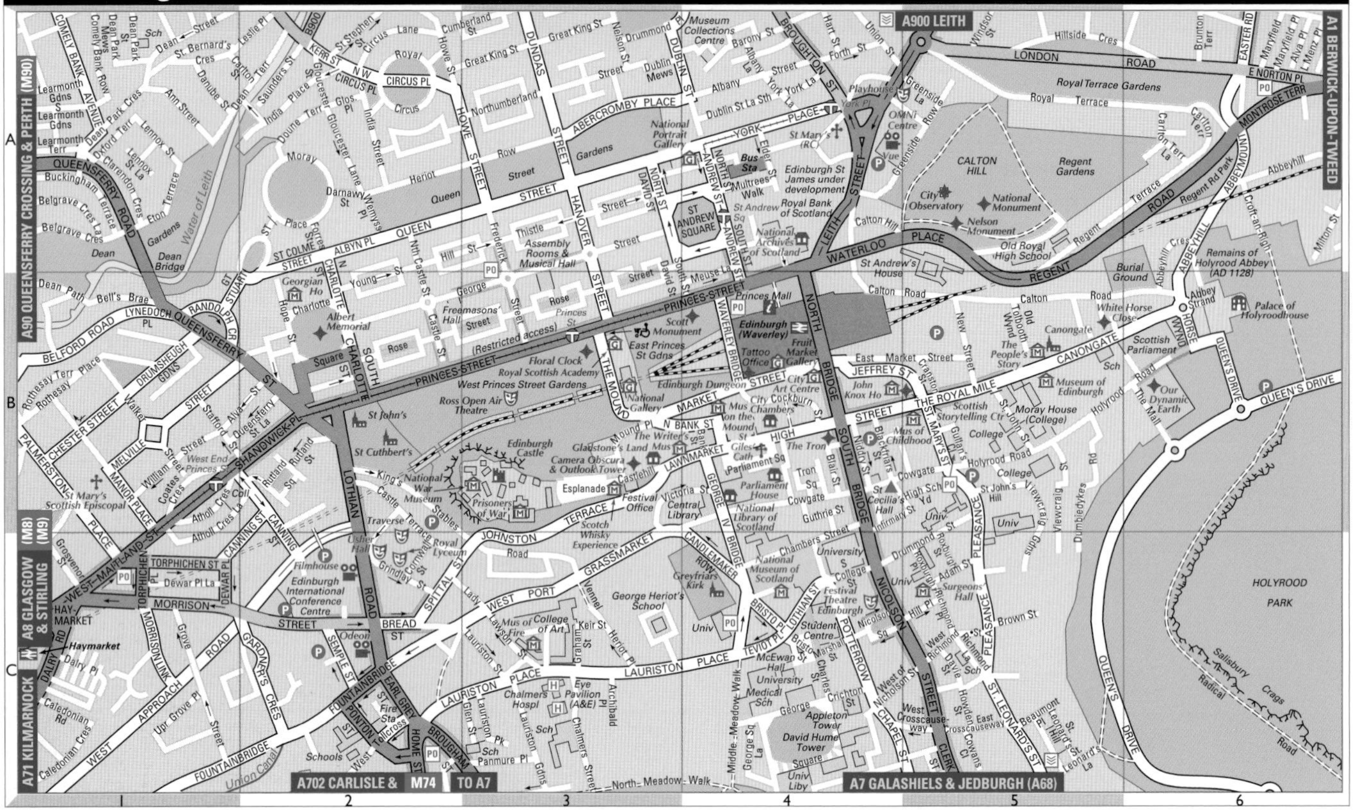

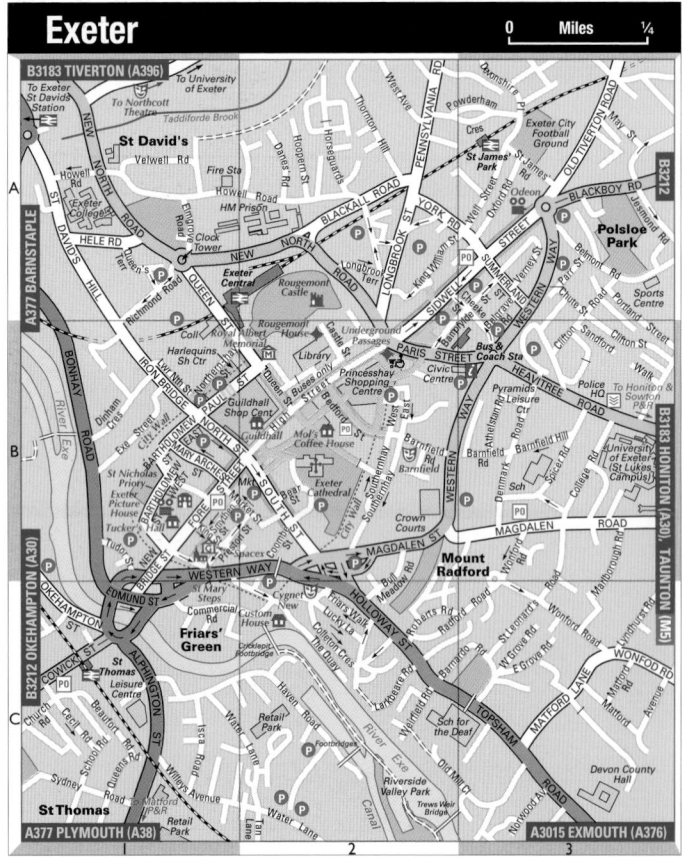

Exeter

0 Miles ¼

Gloucester

0 Miles ¼

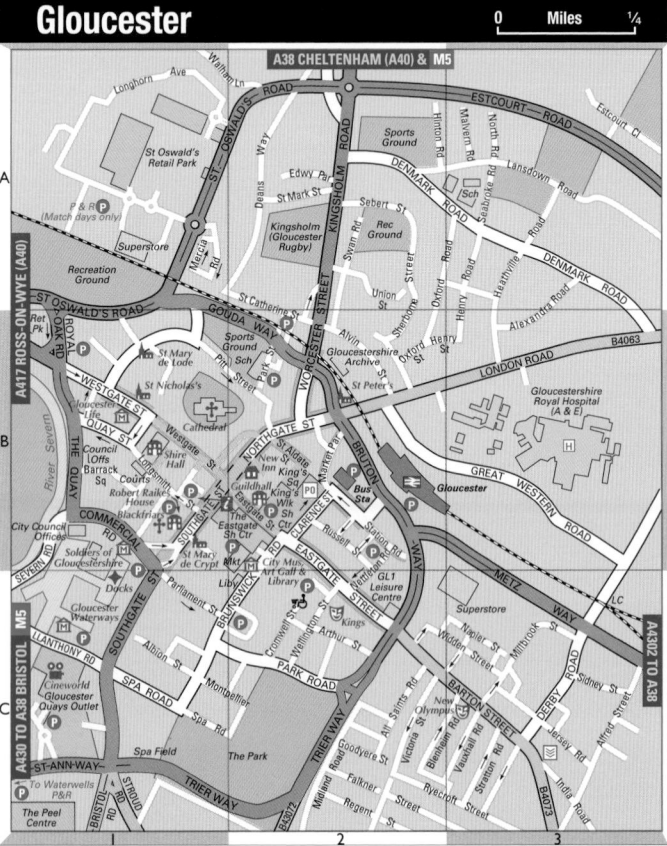

Glasgow

0 Miles ¼

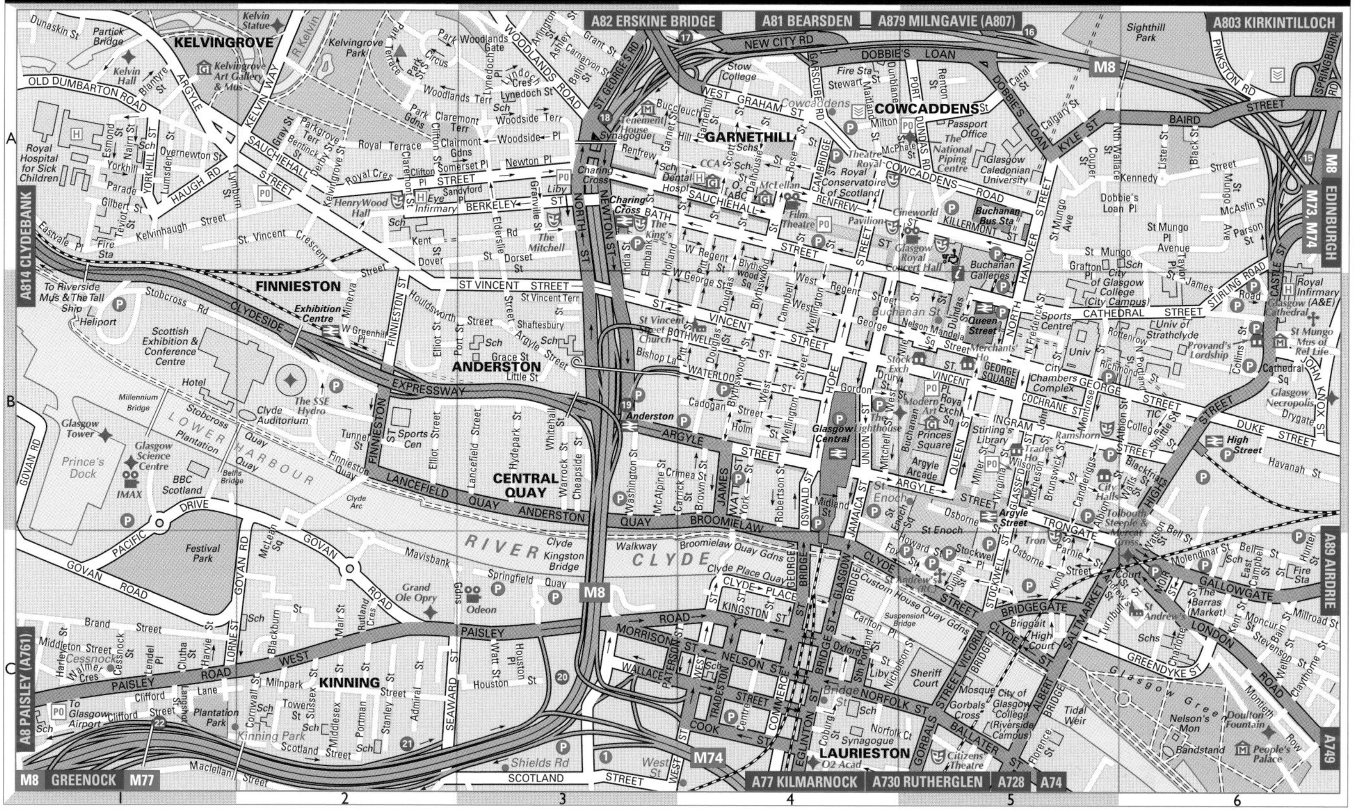
A82 ERSKINE BRIDGE
A81 BEARSDEN
A879 MILNGAVIE (A807)
A803 KIRKINTILLOCH
M8 EDINBURGH
M73, M74
A89 AIRDRIE
A749
A814 CLYDEBANK
A8 PAISLEY (A761)
M8 GREENOCK M77
A77 KILMARNOCK
A730 RUTHERGLEN
A728
A74
KELVINGROVE
COWCADDENS
GARNETHILL
FINNIESTON
ANDERSTON
CENTRAL QUAY
KINNING
LAURIESTON
RIVER CLYDE
Glasgow Central
Queen Street
High Street
Argyle Street
Anderston
Charing Cross
Exhibition Centre
Prince's Dock
Festival Park
Glasgow Green
Sighthill Park
Glasgow Necropolis
Kinning Park

Hull

0 Miles ¼

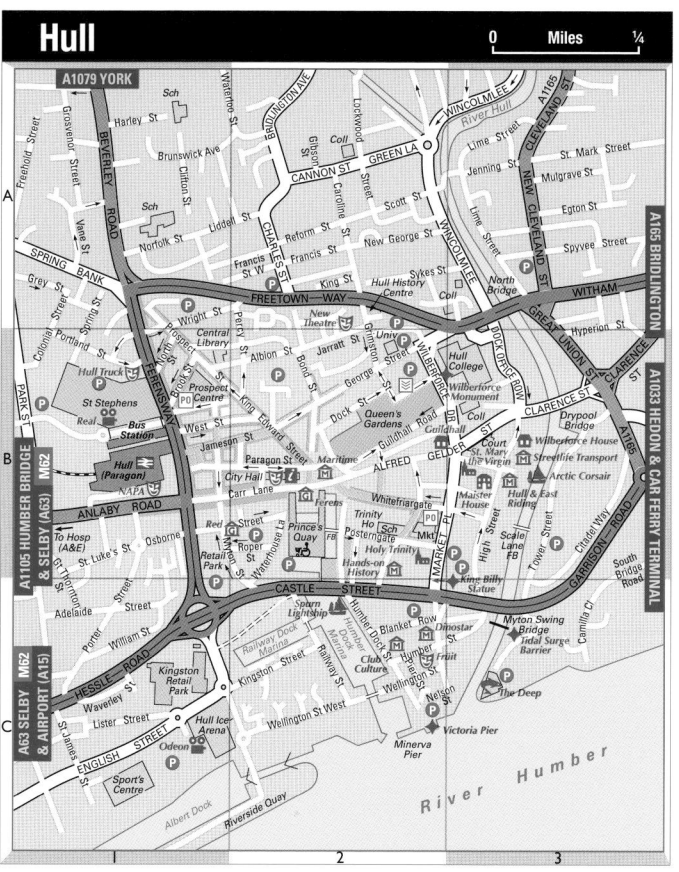
A1079 YORK
A165 BRIDLINGTON
A1033 HEDON & CAR FERRY TERMINAL
A1105 HUMBER BRIDGE & SELBY (A63) M62
A63 SELBY M62 & AIRPORT (A15)
FREETOWN WAY
CASTLE STREET
ANLABY ROAD
Hull (Paragon)
Queen's Gardens
River Hull
River Humber
Victoria Pier
Minerva Pier
Albert Dock
Humber Dock Marina
Railway Dock Marina
The Deep

Ipswich

0 Miles ¼

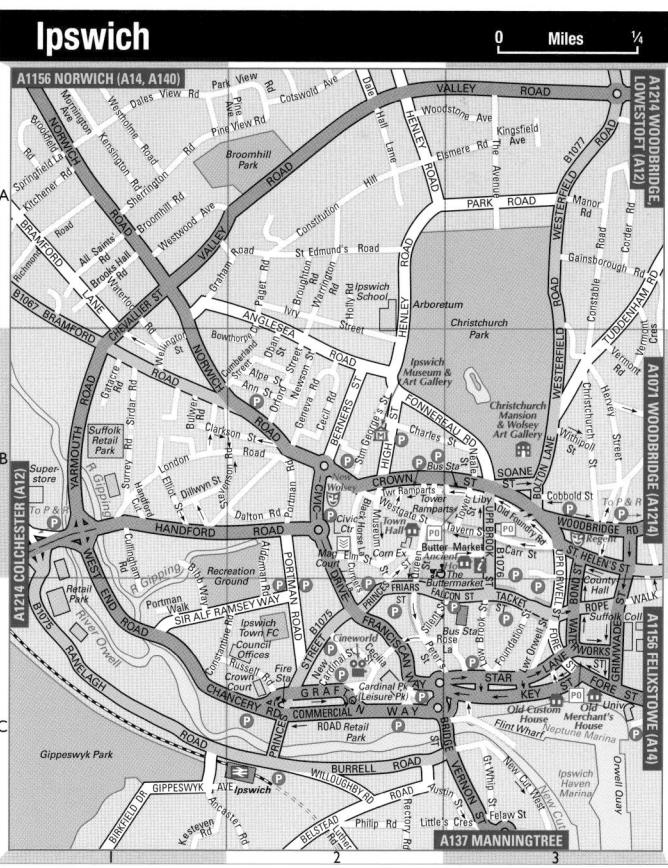
A1156 NORWICH (A14, A140)
A1214 WOODBRIDGE LOWESTOFT (A12)
A1071 WOODBRIDGE (A1214)
A1156 FELIXSTOWE (A14)
A1214 COLCHESTER (A12)
A137 MANNINGTREE
Christchurch Park
Arboretum
Broomhill Park
Gippeswyk Park
Ipswich
River Orwell
R Gipping
Ipswich Town FC
Ipswich Haven Marina
Neptune Marina
Recreation Ground

REGENT'S PARK
REGENT'S PARK
SOMERS TOWN
Euston
St. Pancras International
King's Cross St Pancras
BLOOMSBURY
FITZROVIA
SOHO
MAYFAIR
ST. JAMES'S
WESTMINSTER
HYDE PARK
GREEN PARK
ST. JAMES'S PARK
Buckingham Palace
Buckingham Palace Gardens
British Museum
British Library
University College
University of London
University of Westminster
Wallace Collection
Piccadilly Circus
Cambridge Circus
Oxford Circus
Charing Cross
Victoria
Westminster Abbey
Houses of Parliament
London Eye Millennium Pier
London Aquarium
Royal Opera House
National Gallery
National Portrait Gall
Belgrave Square
Grosvenor Square
Berkeley Square
Bedford Square
Russell Square
Soho Square
Leicester Square
Trafalgar Square
Covent Garden
Marble Arch
Hyde Park Corner
Wellington Arch
Queen Victoria Memorial
Speakers Corner
Westminster Bridge
Lambeth Bridge
OXFORD STREET
REGENT STREET
PICCADILLY
EUSTON ROAD
MARYLEBONE ROAD
PARK LANE
BAKER ST
GOWER STREET
TOTTENHAM COURT ROAD
CHARING CROSS ROAD
SHAFTESBURY AVENUE
STRAND
WHITEHALL
VICTORIA STREET
BUCKINGHAM PALACE ROAD
GROSVENOR PLACE
KNIGHTSBRIDGE
SLOANE STREET
EMBANKMENT
HIGH HOLBORN
KINGSWAY
Miles
0
1/2

Congestion Charging Zone

London Docklands

0 Miles 1

106

Leeds page 51 • **Leicester** page 36 • **Lincoln** page 46

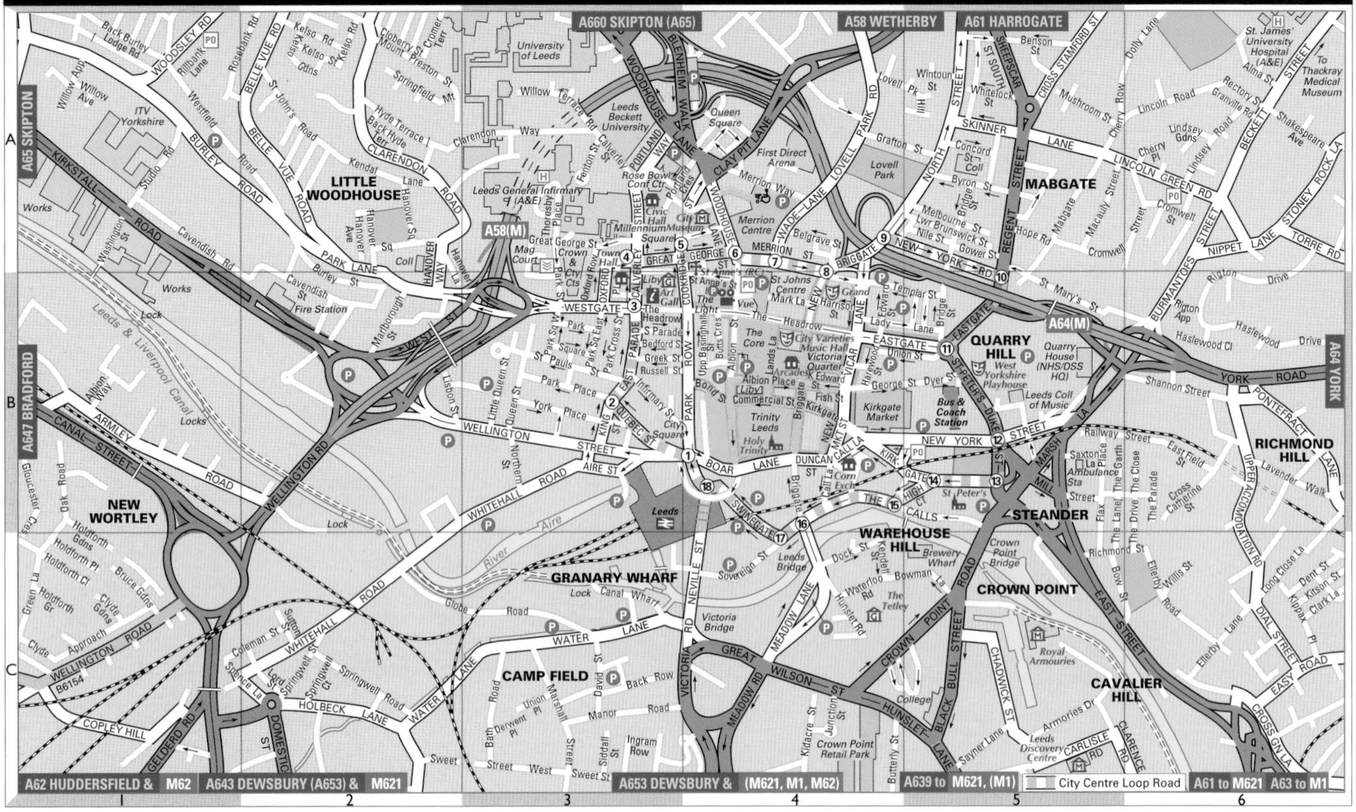

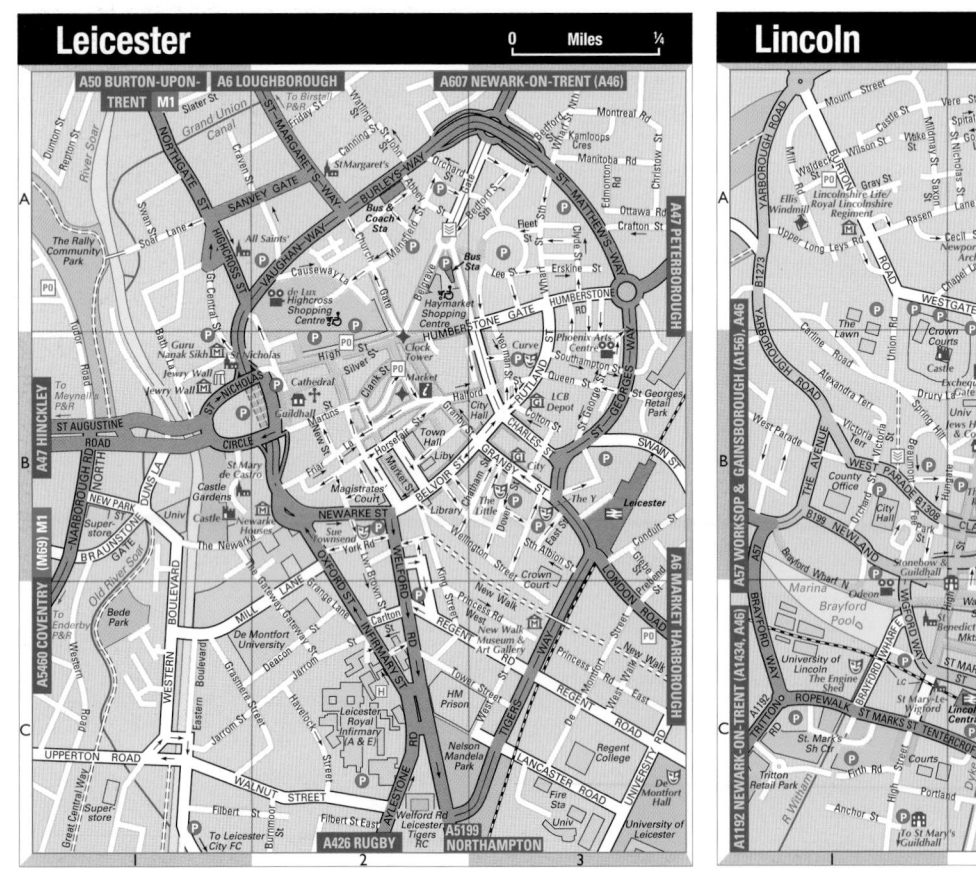

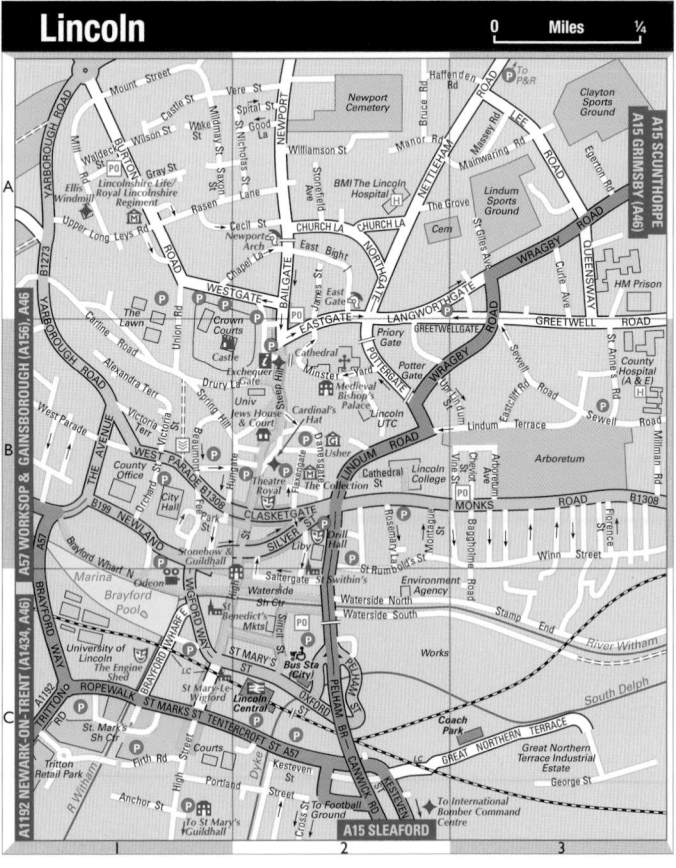

Liverpool

0   Miles   ¼

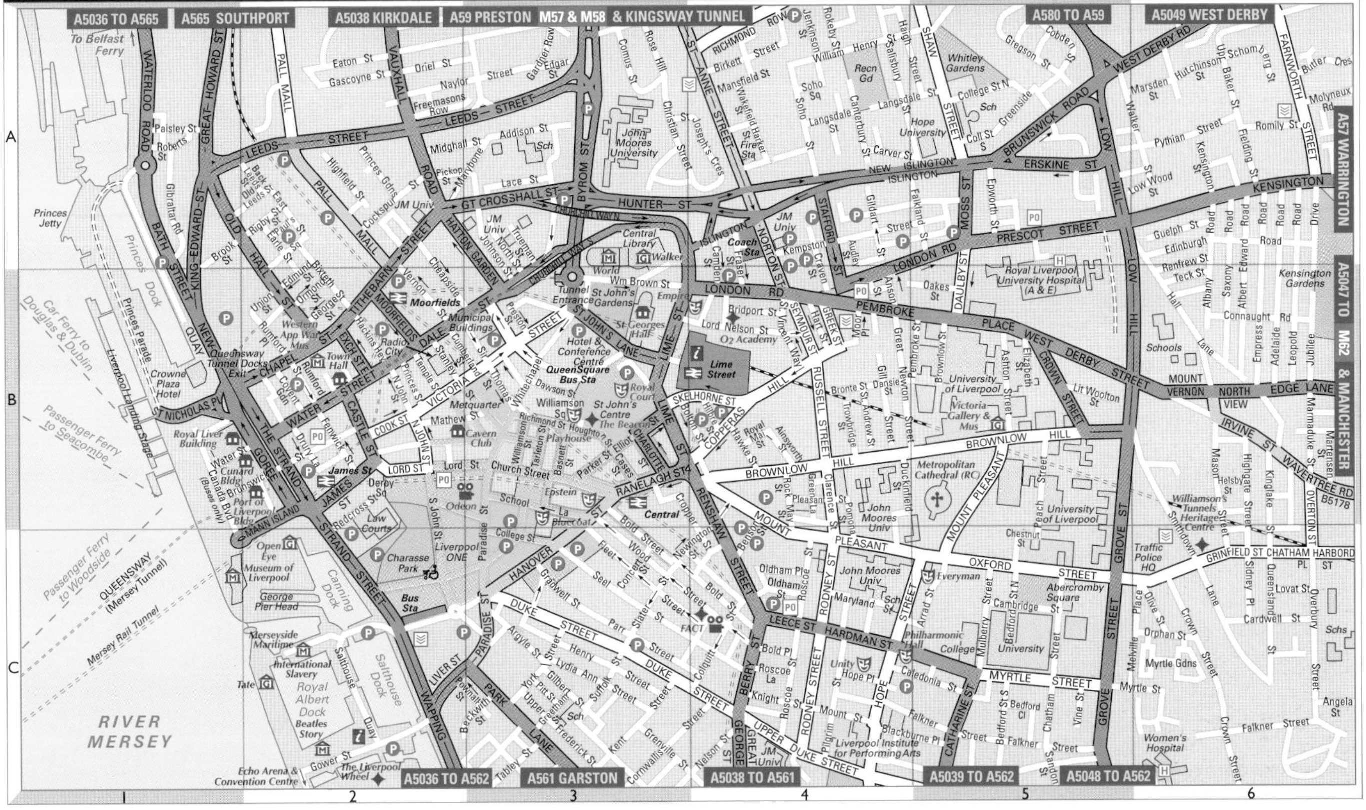

A5036 TO A565 | A565 SOUTHPORT | A5038 KIRKDALE | A59 PRESTON | M57 & M58 & KINGSWAY TUNNEL | A580 TO A59 | A5049 WEST DERBY

A5036 TO A562 | A561 GARSTON | A5038 TO A561 | A5039 TO A562 | A5048 TO A562

A57 WARRINGTON | A5047 | M62 & MANCHESTER

RIVER MERSEY

Manchester

0   Miles   ¼

A6042 TO A56 | A56 BURY | A665 TO A56 | A664 ROCHDALE | A62 OLDHAM

A56 ALTRINCHAM | A6144 STRETFORD | A5103 MANCHESTER AIRPORT (M56) | A34 CONGLETON | A6 STOCKPORT | A57 DENTON

A6 PRESTON | M6 | A57 WARRINGTON | M602 | A5065 TO A56 | M60 | A635 ASHTON-u-Lyne | A62 DROYLSDEN

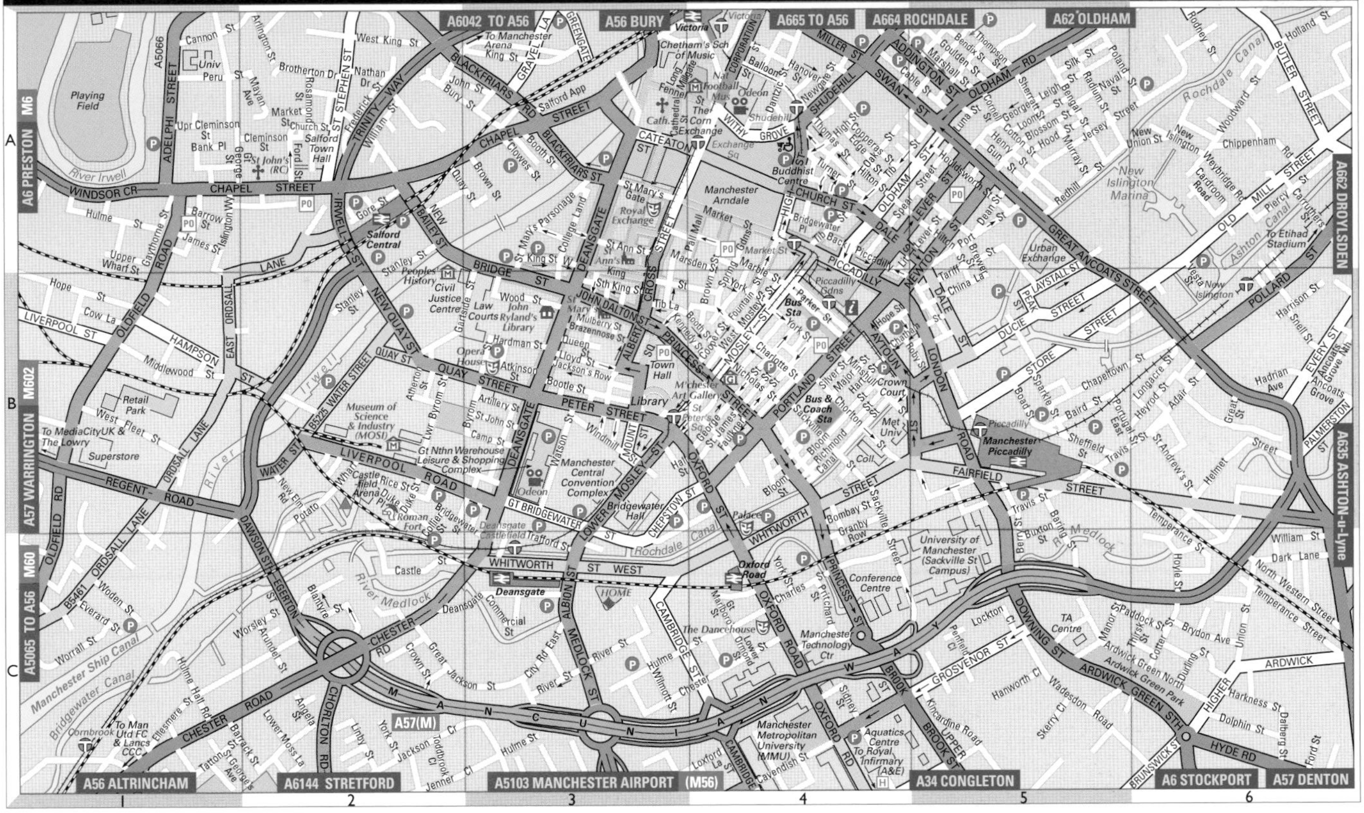

Middlesbrough

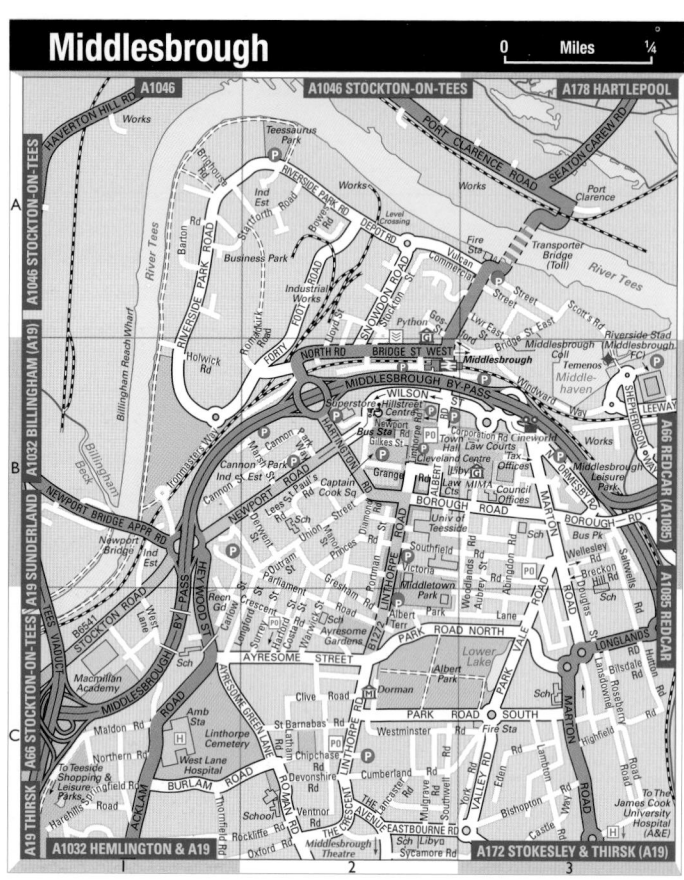

Newcastle upon Tyne

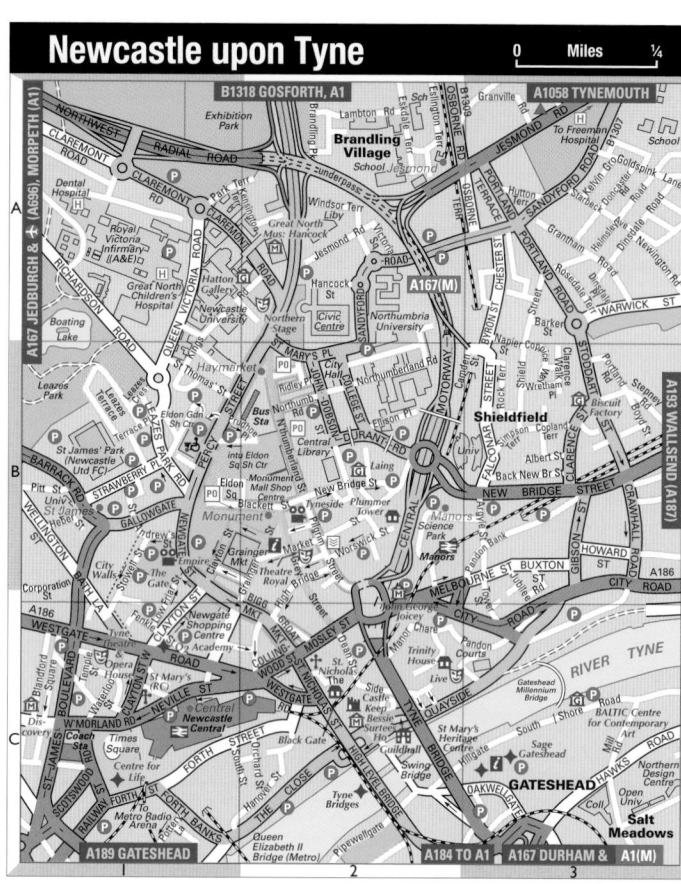

Northampton

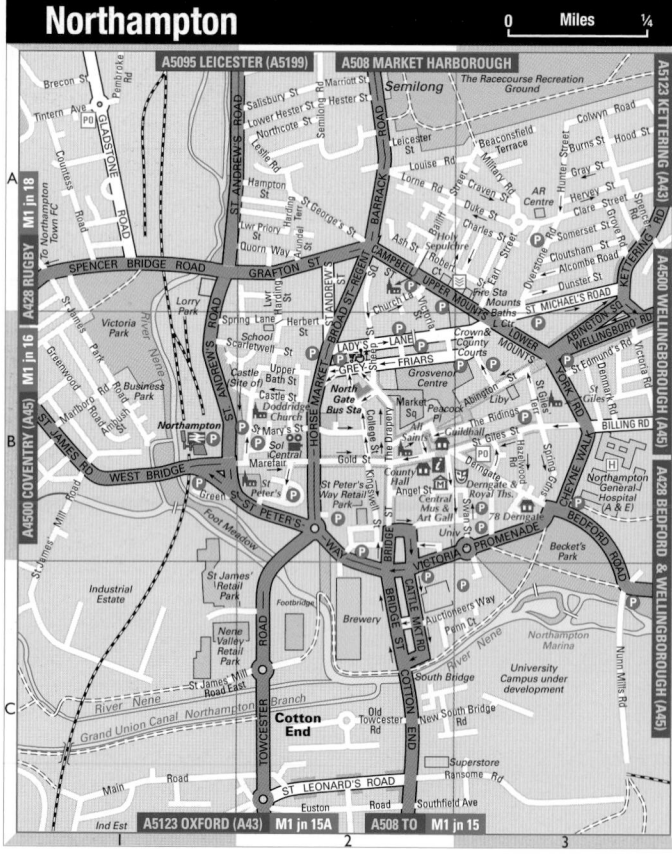

Norwich

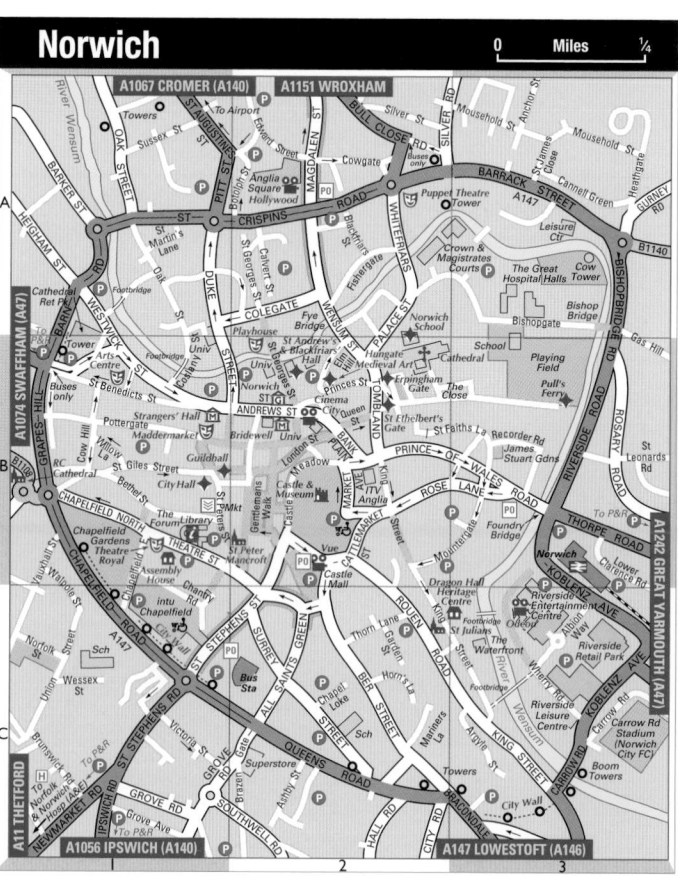

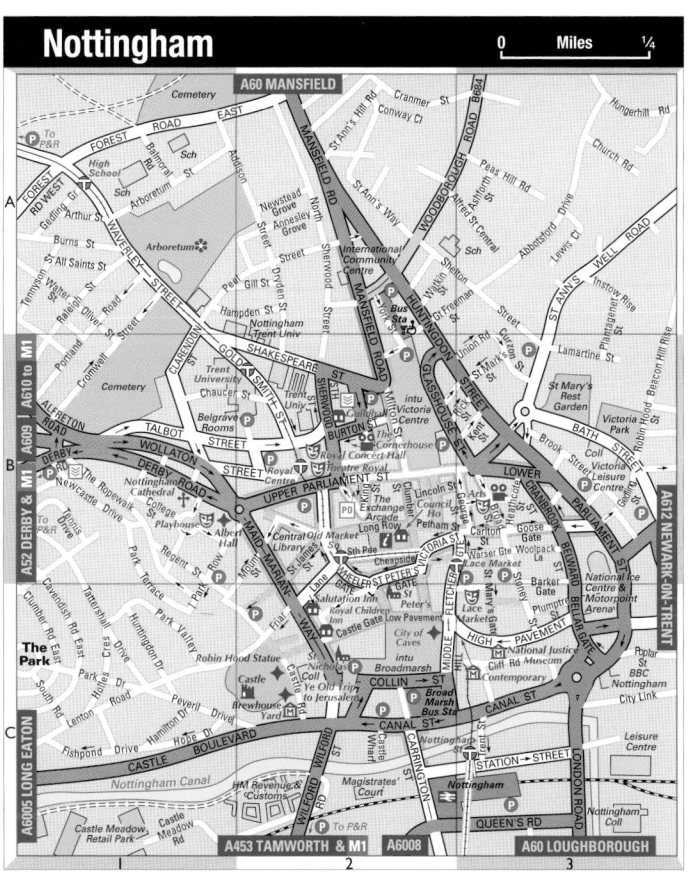

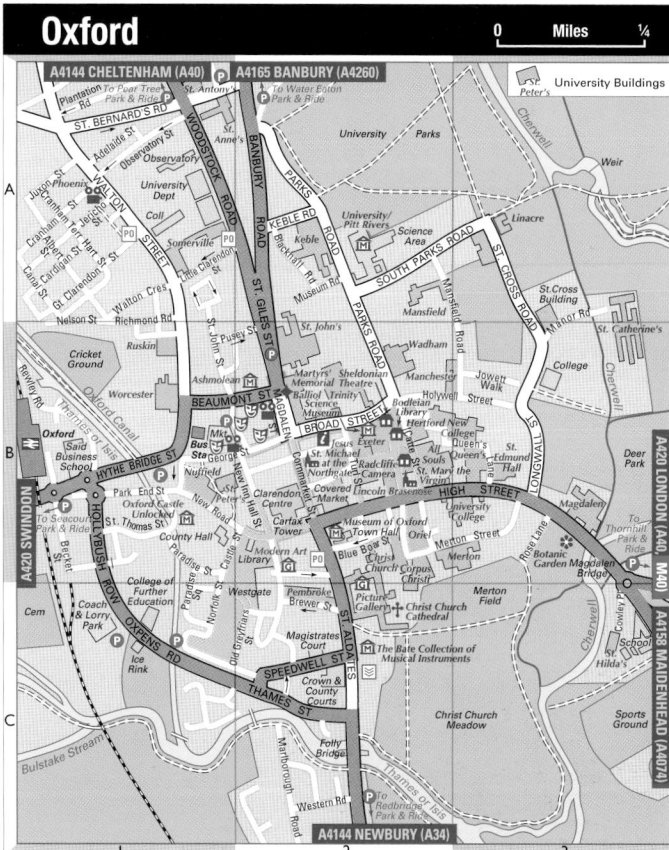

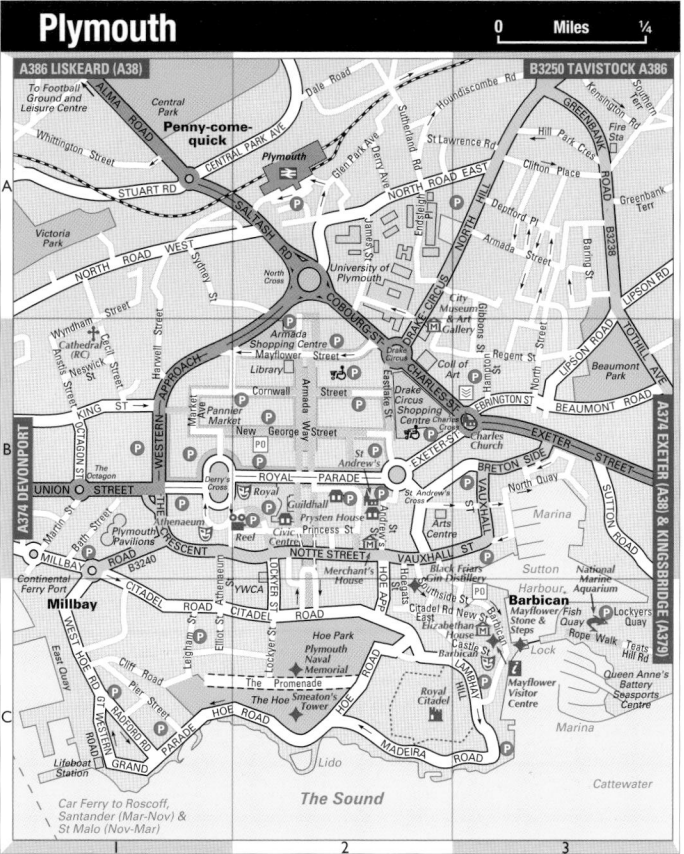

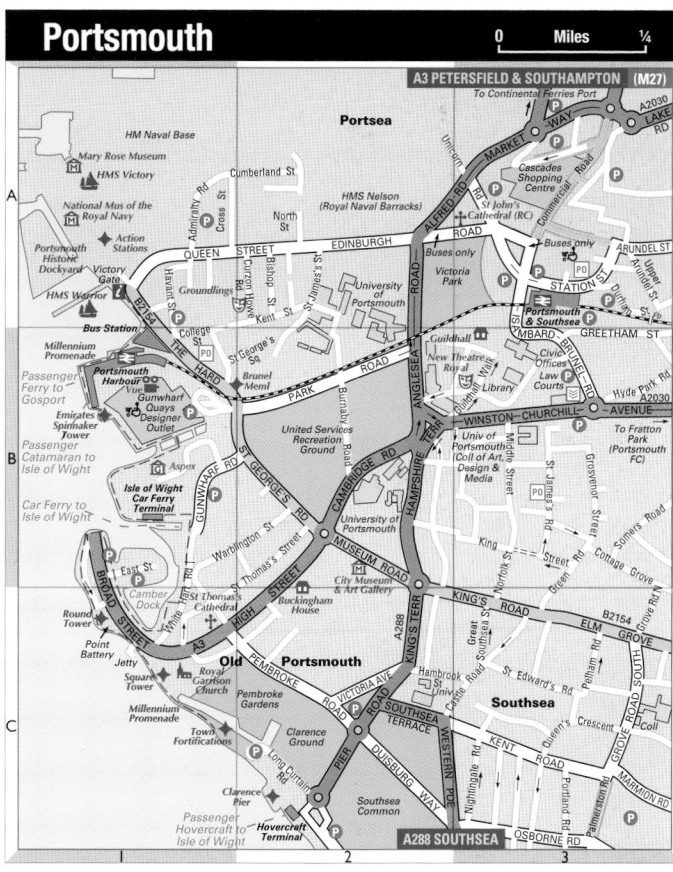

Reading

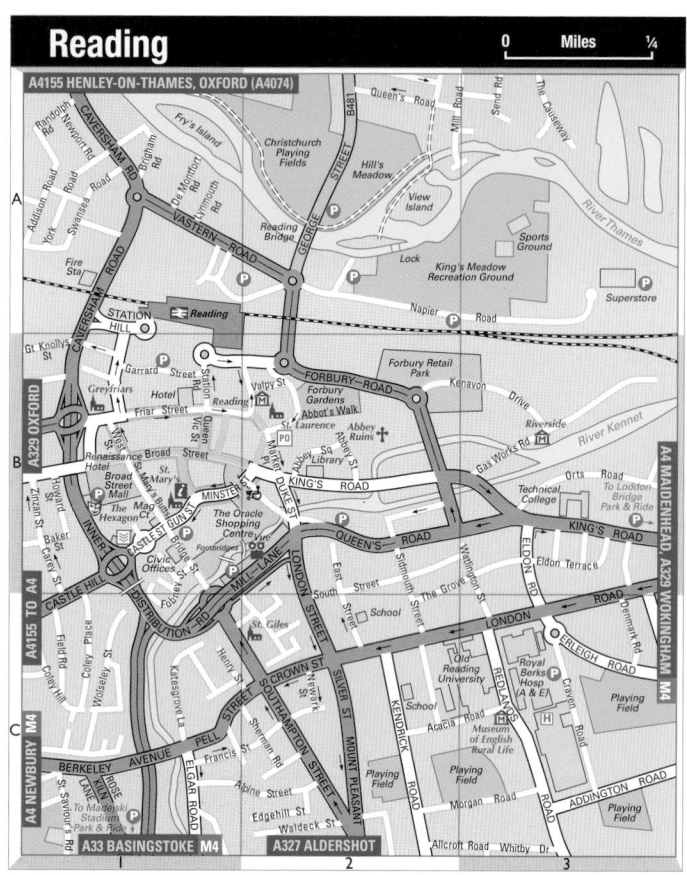
0 Miles ¼
A4155 HENLEY-ON-THAMES, OXFORD (A4074)
A329 OXFORD
A4155 TO A4
A4 NEWBURY M4
A33 BASINGSTOKE M4
A327 ALDERSHOT
A4 MAIDENHEAD, A329 WOKINGHAM M4
Reading
Christchurch Playing Fields
Hill's Meadow
View Island
Sports Ground
King's Meadow Recreation Ground
River Thames
Superstore
Forbury Retail Park
Forbury Gardens
Abbot's Walk
Abbey Ruins
River Kennet
Technical College
To Loddon Bridge Park & Ride
The Oracle Shopping Centre
Civic Offices
Old Reading University
Royal Berks Hosp (A&E)
Museum of English Rural Life
Playing Field
To Madejski Stadium Park & Ride
CAVERSHAM RD
VASTERN ROAD
NAPIER ROAD
FORBURY ROAD
KING'S ROAD
QUEEN'S ROAD
LONDON ROAD
LONDON STREET
SOUTHAMPTON STREET
SILVER ST
MOUNT PLEASANT
CASTLE HILL
INNER DISTRIBUTION RD
BERKELEY AVENUE
ELGAR ROAD
ADDINGTON ROAD
KENDRICK RD
REDLANDS RD
ELDON RD
ERLEIGH ROAD
CROWN ST
PELL STREET
MILL LANE
DUKE ST
MINSTER ST
Broad Street
Friar Street
Station Hill
Gas Works Rd
Kenavon Drive
Watlington St
Sidmouth St
Eldon Terrace
Denmark Rd
Craven Road
Acacia Road
Morgan Road
Allcroft Road
Whitby Dr
Waldeck St
Edgehill St
Alpine Street
Francis St
Sherman Rd
Katesgrove La
Coley Place
Field Rd
Baker St
Howard St
Zinzan St
St. Giles
St. Laurence
St. Mary's
Greyfriars
Renaissance Hotel
Broad Street Mall
The Hexagon
Fire Sta
Lock
Reading Bridge
Queen's Road
Mill Road
Send Rd
The Causeway
Fry's Island
De Montfort Rd
Lynmouth Rd
Swansea Road
Addison Road
Randolph Rd
Newport Rd
Brigham Rd

Salisbury

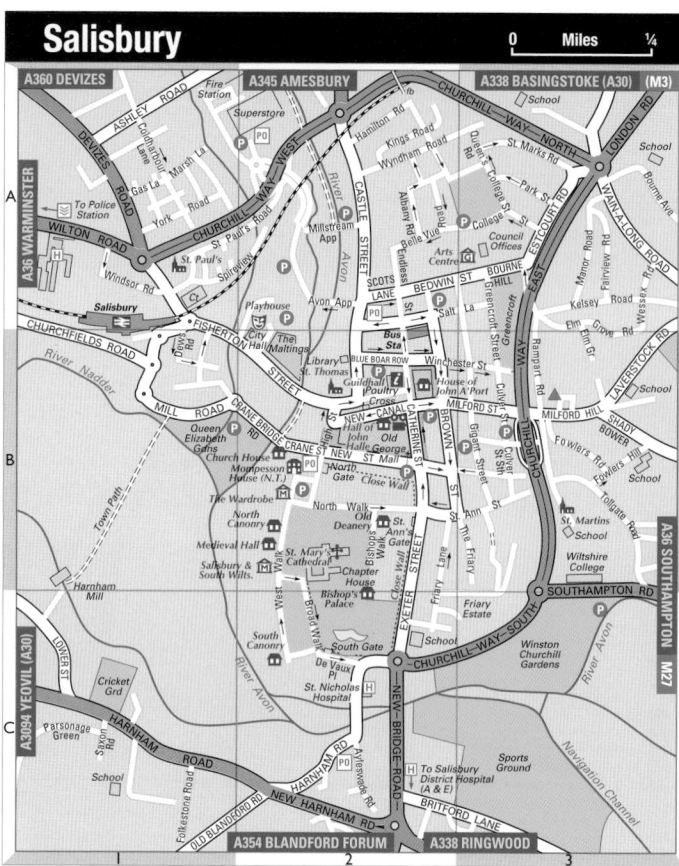
0 Miles ¼
A360 DEVIZES
A345 AMESBURY
A338 BASINGSTOKE (A30) (M3)
A36 WARMINSTER
A3094 YEOVIL (A30)
A354 BLANDFORD FORUM
A338 RINGWOOD
A36 SOUTHAMPTON M27
Salisbury
CHURCHILL WAY NORTH
CHURCHILL WAY WEST
CHURCHILL WAY EAST
CHURCHILL WAY SOUTH
WILTON ROAD
DEVIZES ROAD
ASHLEY ROAD
CASTLE STREET
FISHERTON STREET
CHURCHFIELDS ROAD
MILL ROAD
CRANE BRIDGE RD
CRANE ST
NEW ST
NEW CANAL
MILFORD ST
SCOTS LANE
BEDWIN ST
BOURNE HILL
ESTCOURT RD
WAIN-A-LONG ROAD
LONDON RD
EXETER STREET
NEW BRIDGE ROAD
HARNHAM ROAD
NEW HARNHAM RD
HARNHAM RD
OLD BLANDFORD RD
BRITFORD LANE
SOUTHAMPTON RD
LAVERSTOCK RD
MILFORD HILL
SHADY BOWER
CATHERINE ST
BROWN ST
Fire Station
Superstore
To Police Station
St. Paul's
Playhouse
City Hall
The Maltings
Library
Guildhall
Poultry Cross
Bus Sta
House of John A'Port
Hall of John Halle
Old George
Queen Elizabeth Gdns
Church House
Mompesson House (N.T.)
The Wardrobe
North Canonry
Medieval Hall
Salisbury & South Wilts. Mus.
St. Mary's Cathedral
Chapter House
Bishop's Palace
South Canonry
South Gate
St. Nicholas Hospital
Harnham Mill
Cricket Grd
Parsonage Green
School
Council Offices
Arts Centre
St. Thomas
St. Martins
Wiltshire College
Friary Estate
Winston Churchill Gardens
Sports Ground
To Salisbury District Hospital (A & E)
Millstream App
River Nadder
River Avon
Town Path
Navigation Channel
Folkestone Road
Kings Road
Wyndham Road
Hamilton Rd
St. Marks Rd
Manor Road
Kelsey Road
Fowlers Rd
Tollgate Road

Scarborough

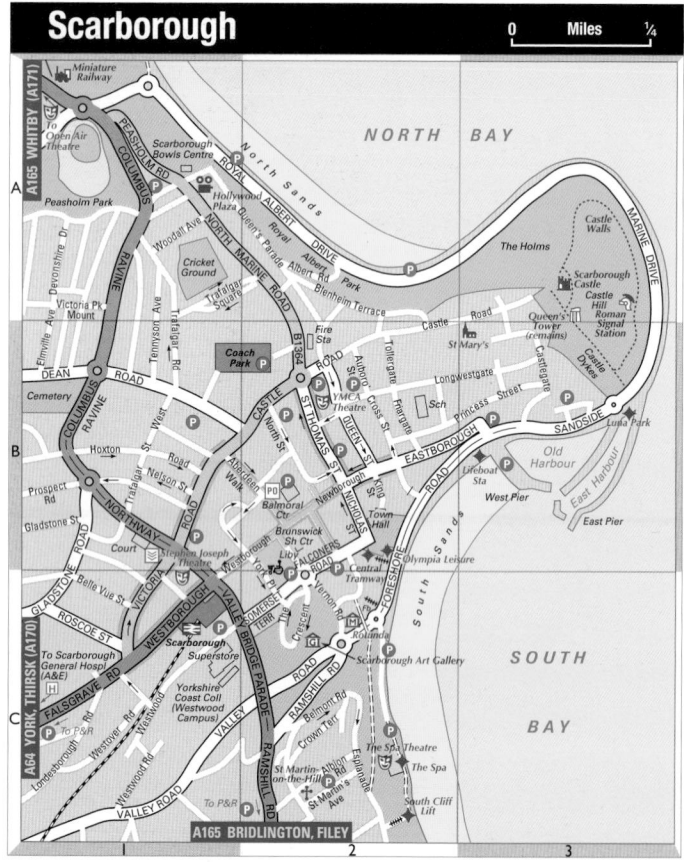
0 Miles ¼
A165 WHITBY (A171)
A64 YORK, THIRSK (A170)
A165 BRIDLINGTON, FILEY
NORTH BAY
SOUTH BAY
North Sands
South Sands
Miniature Railway
To Open Air Theatre
Peasholm Park
Scarborough Bowls Centre
Hollywood Plaza
Cricket Ground
Trafalgar Square
Victoria Pk Mount
Coach Park
Cemetery
The Holms
Castle Walls
Scarborough Castle
Castle Hill Roman Signal Station
Queen's Tower (remains)
Castle Dykes
St Mary's
Fire Sta
YMCA Theatre
Balmoral Ctr
Brunswick Sh Ctr
Stephen Joseph Theatre
Town Hall
Central Tramway
Olympia Leisure
Lifeboat Sta
Old Harbour
East Harbour
West Pier
East Pier
Luna Park
Rotunda
Scarborough Art Gallery
Scarborough
Superstore
Yorkshire Coast Coll (Westwood Campus)
To Scarborough General Hospl (A&E)
The Spa Theatre
The Spa
South Cliff Lift
St Martin-on-the-Hill
To P&R
PEASHOLM RD
COLUMBUS RAVINE
ROYAL ALBERT DRIVE
NORTH MARINE ROAD
MARINE DRIVE
DEAN ROAD
CASTLE ROAD
ST THOMAS ST
QUEEN ST
EASTBOROUGH
SANDSIDE
FORESHORE ROAD
NORTHWAY
WESTBOROUGH
VALLEY BRIDGE PARADE
VICTORIA RD
FALSGRAVE RD
GLADSTONE ROAD
ROSCOE ST
VALLEY ROAD
VALLEY
RAMSHILL RD
FALCONERS RD
SOMERSET TERR
Castle Road
Princess Street
Longwestgate
Blenheim Terrace
Queen's Parade
Woodall Ave
Tennyson Ave
Devonshire Dr
Elmville Ave
Hoxton Road
Prospect Rd
Gladstone St
Belle Vue St
Westover Rd
Londesborough Rd
Crown Terr
Belmont Rd
Esplanade

Southampton

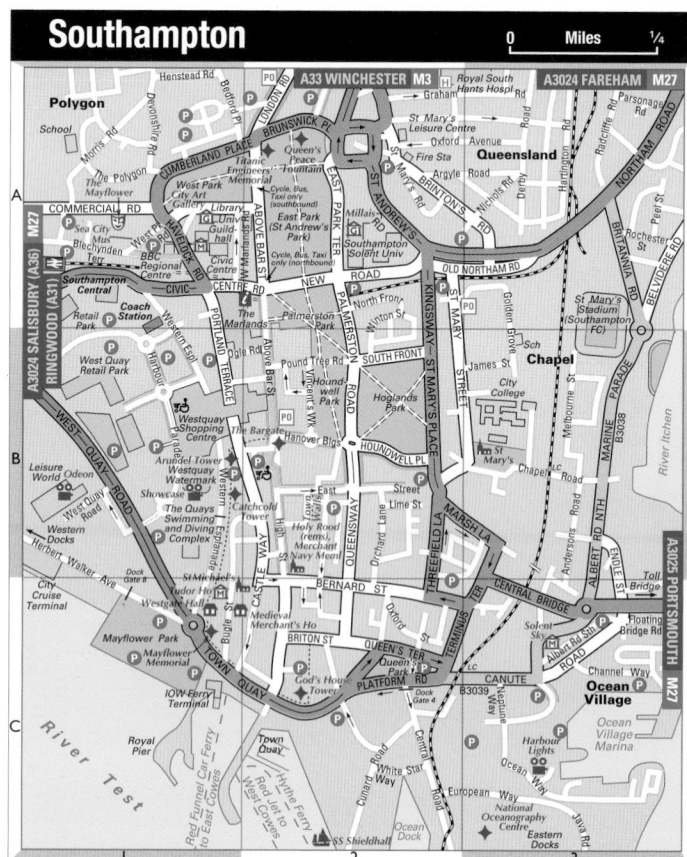
0 Miles ¼
A33 WINCHESTER M3
A3024 FAREHAM M27
M27 A3024 SALISBURY (A36) RINGWOOD (A31)
A3025 PORTSMOUTH M27
Polygon
Queensland
Chapel
Ocean Village
River Test
River Itchen
Royal South Hants Hospl
St Mary's Leisure Centre
The Polygon
The Mayflower
West Park
City Art Gallery
Library
Titanic Engineers' Memorial
Queen's Peace Fountain
East Park (St Andrew's Park)
Southampton Solent Univ
Sea City Mus
BBC Regional Centre
Southampton Central
Coach Station
Retail Park
West Quay Retail Park
Civic Centre
Guild-hall
The Marlands
Palmerston Park
Houndwell Park
Hoglands Park
Westquay Shopping Centre
Westquay Watermark
Arundel Tower
The Bargate
Leisure World
Odeon
Western Docks
City Cruise Terminal
The Quays Swimming and Diving Complex
Catchcold Tower
Holy Rood (rems), Merchant Navy Meml
Tudor Ho
St Michael's
Westgate Hall
Medieval Merchant's Ho
Mayflower Park
Mayflower Memorial
God's House Tower
IOW Ferry Terminal
Royal Pier
Town Quay
Red Funnel Car Ferry to East Cowes
Red Jet to West Cowes
Hythe Ferry
SS Shieldhall
Ocean Dock
White Star Way
National Oceanography Centre
Eastern Docks
Harbour Lights
Ocean Village Marina
St Mary's Stadium (Southampton FC)
City College
St Mary's
Solent Sky
Floating Bridge Rd
Toll Bridge
CUMBERLAND PLACE
BRUNSWICK PL
LONDON RD
COMMERCIAL RD
CIVIC CENTRE RD
NEW ROAD
ABOVE BAR ST
EAST PARK TER
ST ANDREW'S RD
BRINTON'S RD
NORTHAM RD
OLD NORTHAM RD
KINGSWAY
ST MARY'S PLACE
ST MARY STREET
PALMERSTON ROAD
PORTLAND TERRACE
SOUTH FRONT
HOUNDWELL PL
QUEENSWAY
THREEFIELD LA
MARSH LA
BERNARD ST
BRITON ST
CASTLE WAY
WEST QUAY ROAD
TOWN QUAY
PLATFORM RD
QUEEN'S TER
TERMINUS TER
CENTRAL BRIDGE
CANUTE RD
MARINE PARADE
ALBERT RD NTH
BRITANNIA RD
BELVIDERE RD
HAVELOCK RD
Henstead Rd
Bedford Pl
Devonshire Rd
Morris Rd
Graham Rd
Oxford Avenue
Argyle Road
Nichols Rd
Derby Rd
Golden Grove
James St
Melbourne St
Chapel Rd
Andersons Rd
East Street
Lime St
Orchard Lane
Oxford St
Pound Tree Rd
Hanover Blgs
Western Esplanade
Herbert Walker Ave
Central Rd
Cunard Rd
European Way
Channel Way
Neptune Way
Ocean Way
Java Rd
Parsonage Rd
Radcliffe Rd
Peel St
Rochester St

Sheffield

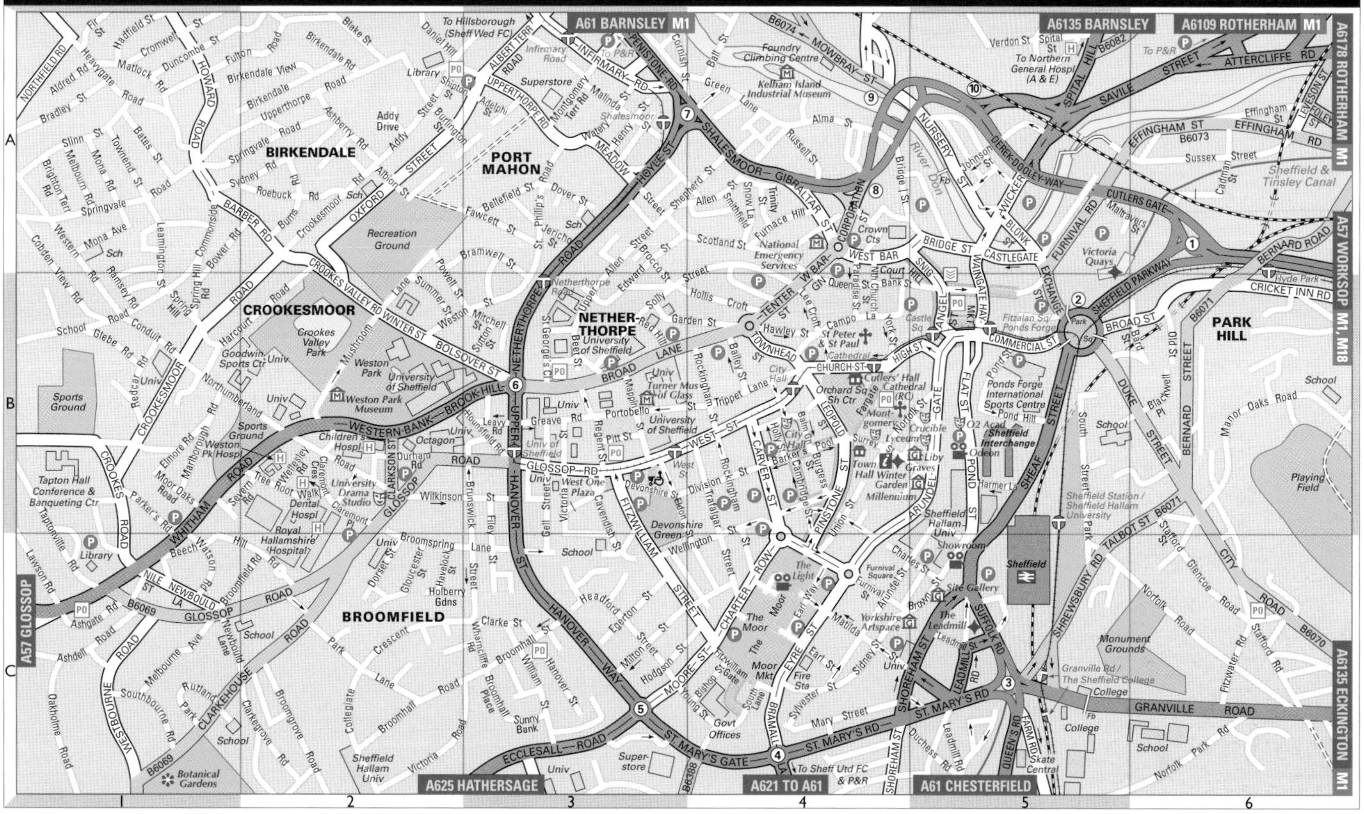

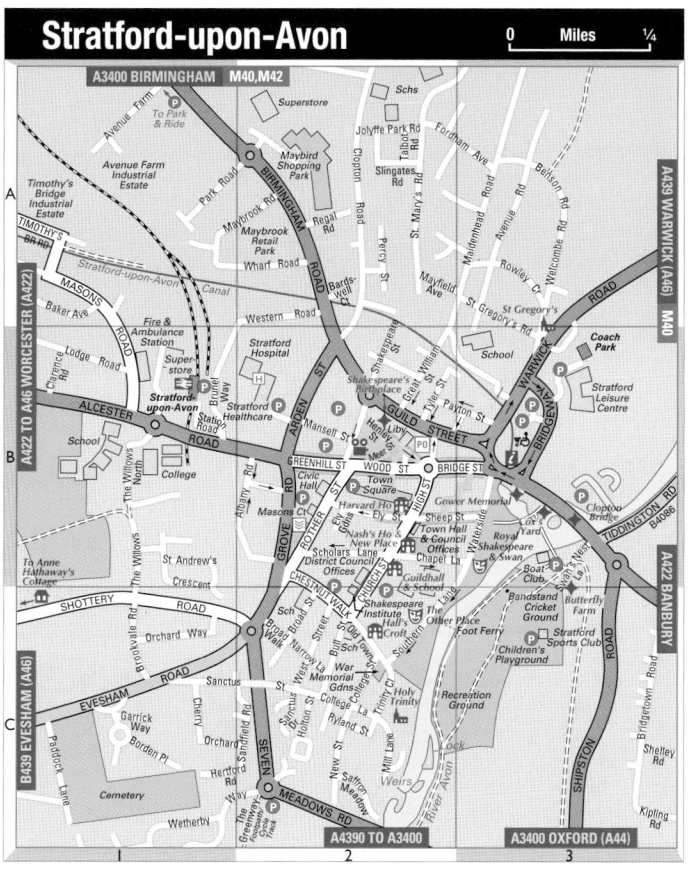

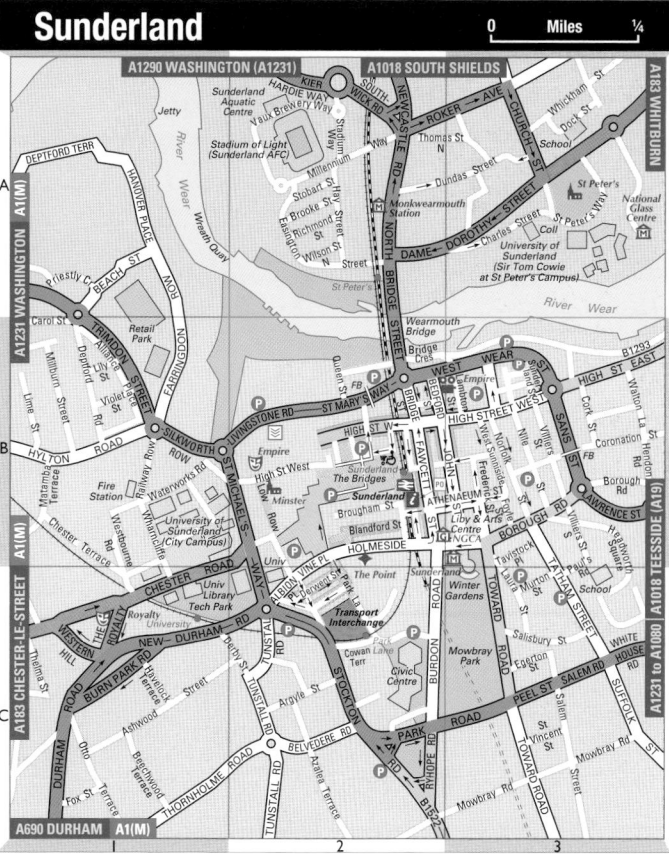

Swansea / Abertawe

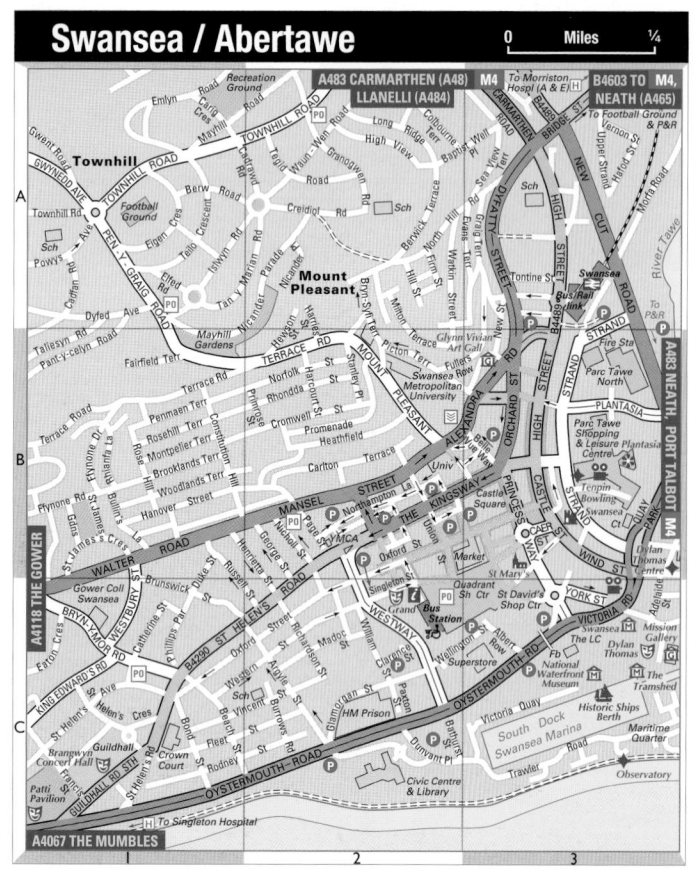

Winchester

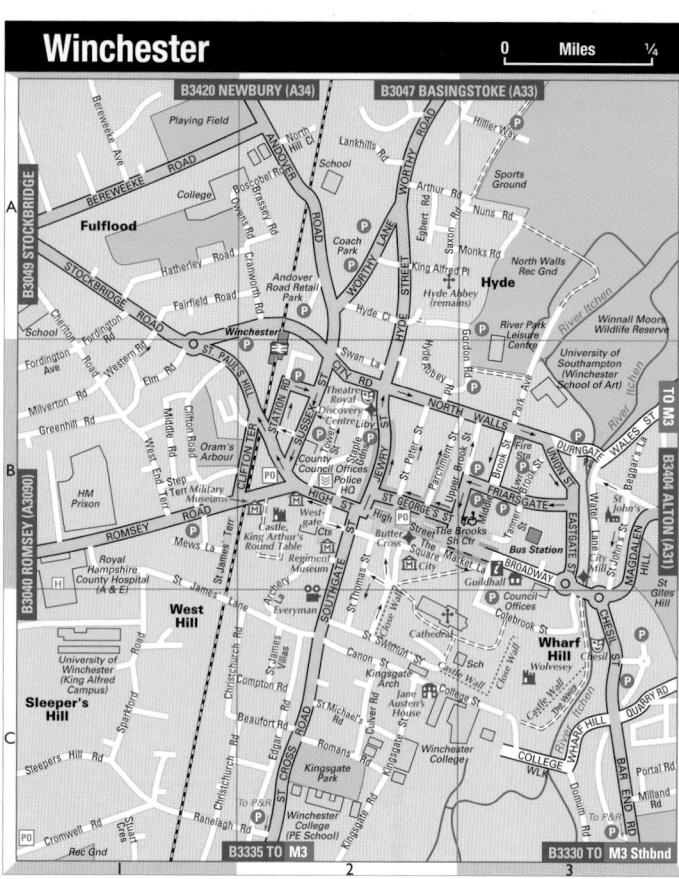

Worcester

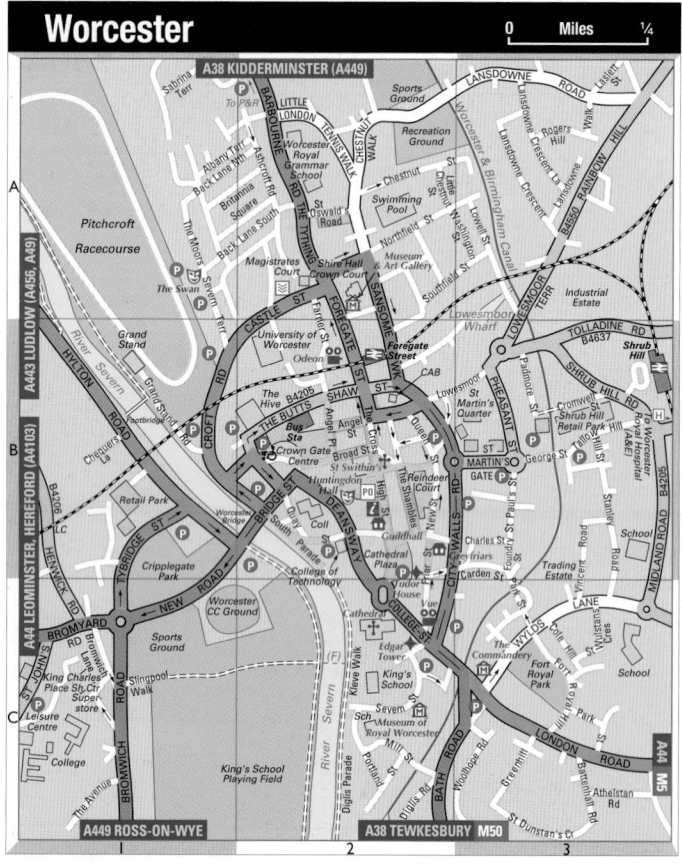

York

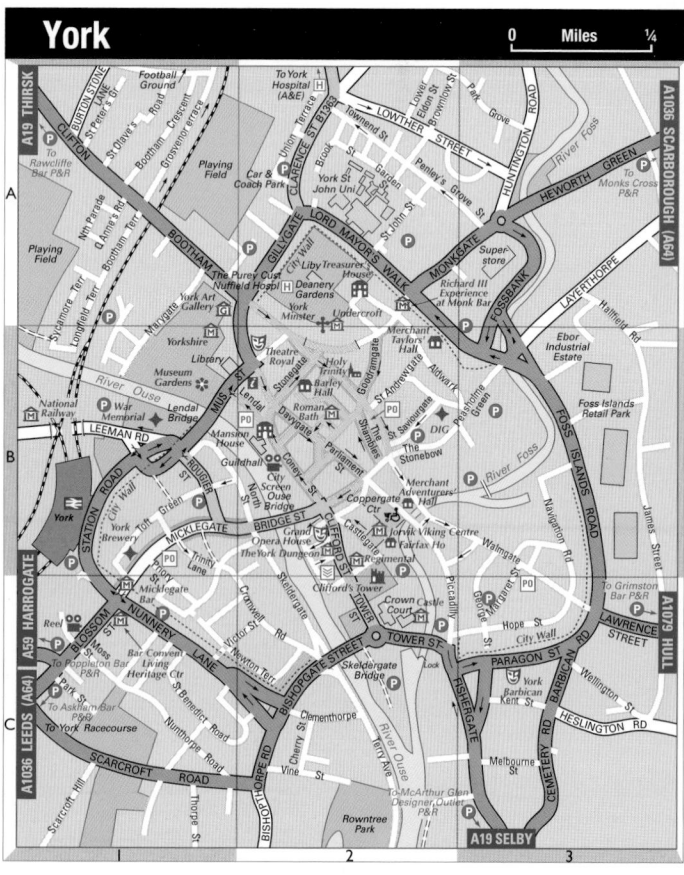

Abbreviations used in the index

Aberdeen	**Aberdeen City**	E Loth	**East Lothian**
Aberds	**Aberdeenshire**	E Renf	**East Renfrewshire**
Ald	**Alderney**	E Sus	**East Sussex**
Anglesey	**Isle of Anglesey**	E Yorks	**East Riding of Yorkshire**
Angus	**Angus**	Edin	**City of Edinburgh**
Argyll	**Argyll and Bute**	Essex	**Essex**
Bath	**Bath and North East**	Falk	**Falkirk**
	Somerset	Fife	**Fife**
Bedford	**Bedford**	Flint	**Flintshire**
Bl Gwent	**Blaenau Gwent**	Glasgow	**City of Glasgow**
Blackburn	**Blackburn with Darwen**	Glos	**Gloucestershire**
Blackpool	**Blackpool**	Gtr Man	**Greater Manchester**
Bmouth	**Bournemouth**	Guern	**Guernsey**
Borders	**Scottish Borders**	Gwyn	**Gwynedd**
Brack	**Bracknell**	Halton	**Halton**
Bridgend	**Bridgend**	Hants	**Hampshire**
Brighton	**City of Brighton and**	Hereford	**Herefordshire**
	Hove	Herts	**Hertfordshire**
Bristol	**City and County of**	Highld	**Highland**
	Bristol	Hrtlpl	**Hartlepool**
Bucks	**Buckinghamshire**	Hull	**Hull**
C Beds	**Central Bedfordshire**	IoM	**Isle of Man**
Caerph	**Caerphilly**	IoW	**Isle of Wight**
Cambs	**Cambridgeshire**	Invclyd	**Inverclyde**
Cardiff	**Cardiff**	Jersey	**Jersey**
Carms	**Carmarthenshire**	Kent	**Kent**
Ceredig	**Ceredigion**	Lancs	**Lancashire**
Ches E	**Cheshire East**	Leicester	**City of Leicester**
Ches W	**Cheshire West and**	Leics	**Leicestershire**
	Chester	Lincs	**Lincolnshire**
Clack	**Clackmannanshire**	London	**Greater London**
Conwy	**Conwy**	Luton	**Luton**
Corn	**Cornwall**	M Keynes	**Milton Keynes**
Cumb	**Cumbria**	M Tydf	**Merthyr Tydfil**
Darl	**Darlington**	Mbro	**Middlesbrough**
Denb	**Denbighshire**	Medway	**Medway**
Derby	**City of Derby**	Mers	**Merseyside**
Derbys	**Derbyshire**	Midloth	**Midlothian**
Devon	**Devon**	Mon	**Monmouthshire**
Dorset	**Dorset**	Moray	**Moray**
Dumfries	**Dumfries and Galloway**	N Ayrs	**North Ayrshire**
Dundee	**Dundee City**	N Lincs	**North Lincolnshire**
Durham	**Durham**	N Lanark	**North Lanarkshire**
E Ayrs	**East Ayrshire**	N Som	**North Somerset**
E Dunb	**East Dunbartonshire**	N Yorks	**North Yorkshire**

NE Lincs	**North East Lincolnshire**	Soton	**Southampton**
Neath	**Neath Port Talbot**	Staffs	**Staffordshire**
Newport	**City and County of**	Southend	**Southend-on-Sea**
	Newport	Stirling	**Stirling**
Norf	**Norfolk**	Stockton	**Stockton-on-Tees**
Northants	**Northamptonshire**	Stoke	**Stoke-on-Trent**
Northumb	**Northumberland**	Suff	**Suffolk**
Nottingham	**City of Nottingham**	Sur	**Surrey**
Notts	**Nottinghamshire**	Swansea	**Swansea**
Orkney	**Orkney**	Swindon	**Swindon**
Oxon	**Oxfordshire**	T&W	**Tyne and Wear**
Pboro	**Peterborough**	Telford	**Telford and Wrekin**
Pembs	**Pembrokeshire**	Thurrock	**Thurrock**
Perth	**Perth and Kinross**	Torbay	**Torbay**
Plym	**Plymouth**	Torf	**Torfaen**
Poole	**Poole**	V Glam	**The Vale of Glamorgan**
Powys	**Powys**	W Berks	**West Berkshire**
Ptsmth	**Portsmouth**	W Dunb	**West Dunbartonshire**
Reading	**Reading**	W Isles	**Western Isles**
Redcar	**Redcar and Cleveland**	W Loth	**West Lothian**
Renfs	**Renfrewshire**	W Mid	**West Midlands**
Rhondda	**Rhondda Cynon Taff**	W Sus	**West Sussex**
Rutland	**Rutland**	W Yorks	**West Yorkshire**
S Ayrs	**South Ayrshire**	Warks	**Warwickshire**
S Glos	**South Gloucestershire**	Warr	**Warrington**
S Lanark	**South Lanarkshire**	Wilts	**Wiltshire**
S Yorks	**South Yorkshire**	Windsor	**Windsor and**
Scilly	**Scilly**		**Maidenhead**
Shetland	**Shetland**	Wokingham	**Wokingham**
Shrops	**Shropshire**	Worcs	**Worcestershire**
Slough	**Slough**	Wrex	**Wrexham**
Som	**Somerset**	York	**City of York**

How to use the index

Example

Trudoxhill Som   **16** G4

— grid square
— page number
— county or unitary authority

Index to road maps of Britain

A

Ab Kettleby Leics	36 C3	Aberdalgie Perth	76 E3
Ab Lench Worcs	27 C7	Aberdare =	
Abbas Combe Som	8 B6	Aberdâr Rhondda	14 A5
Abberley Worcs	26 B4	Aberdaron Gwyn	40 H3
Abberton Essex	31 G7	Aberdaugleddau =	
Abberton Worcs	26 C6	Milford Haven Pembs	22 F4
Abberwick Northumb	63 B7	Aberdeen Aberdeen	83 C11

Anstruther Easter Fife		77 G8

Anstruther Wester Fife 77 G8
Ansty Hants 18 G4
Ansty W Sus 12 D1
Ansty Warks 35 G9
Ansty Wilts 9 B8
Anthill Common Hants 10 C5
Anthorn Cumb 61 H7
Antingham Norf 39 B8
Anton's Gowt Lincs 46 H6
Antonshill Falk 69 B7
Antony Corn 4 F4
Anwick Lincs 46 G5
Anwoth Dumfries 55 D8
Aoradh Argyll 64 B3
Apes Hall Cambs 38 F1
Apethorpe Northants 36 F6
Apeton Staffs 34 D4
Apley Lincs 46 E5
Apperknowle Derbys 45 E7
Apperley Glos 26 F5
Apperley Bridge W Yorks 51 F7
Appersett N Yorks 57 G10
Appin Argyll 74 C2
Appin House Argyll 74 C2
Appleby N Lincs 46 A3
Appleby-in-Westmorland Cumb 57 D8
Appleby Magna Leics 35 E9
Appleby Parva Leics 35 E9
Applecross Highld 85 D12
Applecross Ho. Highld 85 D12
Appledore Devon 6 C3
Appledore Devon 7 E9
Appledore Kent 13 D8
Appledore Heath Kent 13 C8
Appleford Oxon 18 B2
Applegarthtown Dumfries 61 E7
Appleshaw Hants 17 G10
Applethwaite Cumb 56 D4
Appleton Halton 43 D8
Appleton Oxon 17 A11
Appleton-le-Moors N Yorks 59 H8
Appleton-le-Street N Yorks 52 B3
Appleton Roebuck N Yorks 52 E1
Appleton Thorn Warr 43 D9
Appleton Wiske N Yorks 58 F4
Appletreehall Borders 61 B11
Appletreewick N Yorks 51 C6
Appley Som 7 D9
Appley Bridge Lancs 43 B8
Apse Heath IoW 10 F4
Apsley End C Beds 29 E8
Apuldram W Sus 11 D7
Aquhythie Aberds 83 B9
Arabella Highld 87 D11
Arbeadie Aberds 83 D8
Arberth = Narberth Pembs 22 E6
Arbirlot Angus 77 C9
Arboll Highld 87 C11
Arborfield Wokingham 18 E4
Arborfield Cross Wokingham 18 E4
Arborfield Garrison Wokingham 18 E4
Arbour-thorne S Yorks 45 D7
Arbroath Angus 77 C9
Arbuthnott Aberds 83 F9
Archiestown Moray 88 D2
Arclid Ches E 43 F10
Ard-dhubh Highld 85 D12
Ardachu Highld 93 J9
Ardalanish Argyll 78 K6
Ardanaiseig Argyll 74 E3
Ardaneaskan Highld 85 E13
Ardanstur Argyll 73 B7
Ardargie House Hotel Perth 76 F3
Ardarroch Highld 85 E13
Ardbeg Argyll 64 D5
Ardbeg Argyll 73 E10
Ardcharnich Highld 86 C4
Ardchiavaig Argyll 78 K6
Ardchullarie More Stirling 75 F8
Ardchyle Stirling 75 E8
Arddleen Powys 33 D8
Ardechvie Highld 80 D3
Ardeley Herts 29 F10
Ardelve Highld 85 F13
Arden Argyll 68 B2
Ardens Grafton Warks 27 C8
Ardentinny Argyll 73 E10
Ardentraive Argyll 73 F9
Ardeonaig Stirling 75 D9
Ardersier Highld 87 F10
Ardessie Highld 86 C3
Ardfern Argyll 73 C7
Ardgartan Argyll 74 G5
Ardgay Highld 87 B8
Ardgour Highld 74 A3
Ardheslaig Highld 85 C12
Ardiecow Moray 88 B5
Ardindrean Highld 86 C4
Ardingly W Sus 12 D2
Ardington Oxon 17 C11
Ardlair Aberds 83 A7
Ardlamont Ho. Argyll 73 G8
Ardleigh Essex 31 F7
Ardler Perth 76 C5
Ardley Oxon 28 F2
Ardlui Argyll 74 F6
Ardlussa Argyll 72 E5
Ardmair Highld 86 B4
Ardmay Argyll 74 G5
Ardminish Argyll 65 D7
Ardmolich Highld 79 D10
Ardmore Argyll 79 J10
Ardmore Highld 87 C10
Ardmore Highld 92 D5
Ardnacross Argyll 79 G8
Ardnadam Argyll 73 F10
Ardnagrask Highld 87 G8
Ardnarff Highld 85 E13
Ardnastang Highld 79 E11
Ardnave Argyll 64 A3
Ardno Argyll 73 C10
Ardo Aberds 89 E8
Ardo Ho. Aberds 89 F9
Ardoch Perth 76 D3
Ardochy House Highld 80 C4
Ardoyne Aberds 83 A8
Ardpatrick Argyll 72 G6
Ardpatrick Ho. Argyll 72 H6
Ardpeaton Argyll 73 E11
Ardrishaig Argyll 73 E7
Ardross Fife 77 G8
Ardross Highld 87 D9
Ardross Castle Highld 87 D9
Ardrossan N Ayrs 66 B5
Ardshealach Highld 79 E9
Ardsley S Yorks 45 B7
Ardslignish Highld 79 E8
Ardtalla Argyll 64 C5
Ardtalnaig Perth 75 D10
Ardtoe Highld 79 D9
Ardtrostan Perth 75 E9
Arduaine Argyll 72 B6
Ardullie Highld 87 E8
Ardvasar Highld 85 H11
Ardvorlich Perth 75 E9
Ardwell Dumfries 54 E4
Ardwell Mains Dumfries 54 E4
Ardwick Gtr Man 44 C2
Areley Kings Worcs 26 A5
Arford Hants 18 H5
Argoed Caerph 15 B7
Argoed Powys 24 B6
Arichamish Argyll 73 C8
Arichastlich Argyll 74 D5
Aridhglas Argyll 78 J6
Arileod Argyll 78 F4
Arinacrinachd Highld 85 C12
Arinagour Argyll 78 F5
Arion Orkney 95 G3
Arisaig Highld 79 C9
Ariundle Highld 79 E11
Arkendale N Yorks 51 C9
Arkesden Essex 29 E11
Arkholme Lancs 50 B1
Arkle Town N Yorks 58 F1
Arkleton Dumfries 61 D9
Arkley London 19 B9
Arksey S Yorks 45 B9
Arkwright Town Derbys 45 E8
Arle Glos 26 F6
Arlecdon Cumb 56 E2
Arlesey C Beds 29 E8
Arleston Telford 34 D2
Arley Ches E 43 D9
Arlingham Glos 26 G4
Arlington Devon 6 B5
Arlington E Sus 12 F4
Arlington Glos 27 H8
Armadale Highld 93 C10
Armadale W Loth 69 D8
Armadale Castle Highld 85 H11
Armathwaite Cumb 57 B7
Arminghall Norf 39 E8
Armitage Staffs 35 D6
Armley W Yorks 51 F8
Armscote Warks 27 D9
Armthorpe S Yorks 45 B10
Arnabost Argyll 78 F5
Arncliffe N Yorks 50 B5
Arncroach Fife 77 G8
Arne Dorset 9 F8
Arnesby Leics 36 F2
Arngask Perth 76 F4
Arnisdale Highld 85 G13
Arnish Highld 85 D10
Arniston Engine Midloth 70 D2
Arnol W Isles 91 C8
Arnold E Yorks 53 E7
Arnold Notts 45 H9
Arnprior Stirling 68 A5
Arnside Cumb 49 B4
Aros Mains Argyll 79 G8
Arowry Wrex 33 B10
Arpafeelie Highld 87 F9
Arrad Foot Cumb 49 A3
Arram E Yorks 52 E6
Arrathorne N Yorks 58 G3
Arreton IoW 10 F4
Arrington Cambs 29 C10
Arrivain Argyll 74 D5
Arrochar Argyll 74 G5
Arrow Warks 27 C7
Arthington W Yorks 51 E8
Arthingworth Northants 36 G3
Arthog Gwyn 32 D2
Arthrath Aberds 89 E9
Arthurstone Perth 76 C5
Artrochie Aberds 89 E10
Arundel W Sus 11 D9
Aryhoulan Highld 80 G2
Asby Cumb 56 D2
Ascog Argyll 73 G10
Ascot Windsor 18 E6
Ascott Warks 27 E10
Ascott-under-Wychwood Oxon 27 G10
Asenby N Yorks 51 B9
Asfordby Leics 36 D3
Asfordby Hill Leics 36 D3
Asgarby Lincs 46 H5
Asgarby Lincs 47 F7
Ash Kent 20 E2
Ash Kent 21 F9
Ash Som 8 B3
Ash Sur 18 F5
Ash Bullayne Devon 7 F6
Ash Green Warks 35 G9
Ash Magna Shrops 34 B1
Ash Mill Devon 7 D6
Ash Priors Som 7 D10
Ash Street Suff 31 D7
Ash Thomas Devon 7 E9
Ash Vale Sur 18 F5
Ashampstead W Berks 18 D2
Ashbocking Suff 31 C8
Ashbourne Derbys 44 H5
Ashbrittle Som 7 D9
Ashburton Devon 5 E8
Ashbury Devon 6 G4
Ashbury Oxon 17 C9
Ashby N Lincs 46 B3
Ashby by Partney Lincs 47 F8
Ashby cum Fenby NE Lincs 46 B6
Ashby de la Launde Lincs 46 G4
Ashby-de-la-Zouch Leics 35 D9
Ashby Folville Leics 36 D3
Ashby Magna Leics 36 F1
Ashby Parva Leics 35 G11
Ashby Puerorum Lincs 47 E7
Ashby St Ledgers Northants 28 B2
Ashby St Mary Norf 39 E9
Ashchurch Glos 26 E6
Ashcombe Devon 5 D10
Ashcott Som 15 H10
Ashdon Essex 30 D2
Ashe Hants 18 G2
Asheldham Essex 20 A6
Ashen Essex 30 D4
Ashendon Bucks 28 G4
Ashfield Carms 24 F4
Ashfield Stirling 75 G10
Ashfield Suff 31 B9
Ashfield Green Suff 31 A9
Ashfold Crossways W Sus 11 B11
Ashford Devon 6 C4
Ashford Hants 9 C10
Ashford Kent 13 B9
Ashford Sur 19 D7
Ashford Bowdler Shrops 26 A2
Ashford Carbonell Shrops 26 A2
Ashford Hill Hants 18 E2
Ashford in the Water Derbys 44 F5
Ashgill S Lanark 68 F6
Ashill Devon 7 E9
Ashill Norf 38 E4
Ashill Som 8 C2
Ashingdon Essex 20 B5
Ashington Northumb 63 E8
Ashington Som 8 B4
Ashington W Sus 11 C10
Ashintully Castle Perth 76 A4
Ashkirk Borders 61 A10
Ashlett Hants 10 D3
Ashleworth Glos 26 F5
Ashley Cambs 30 B3
Ashley Ches E 43 D10
Ashley Devon 6 E5
Ashley Dorset 9 D10
Ashley Glos 16 B6
Ashley Hants 10 E2
Ashley Hants 10 E1
Ashley Northants 36 F3
Ashley Staffs 34 B3
Ashley Green Bucks 28 H6
Ashley Heath Dorset 9 D10
Ashley Heath Staffs 34 B3
Ashmanhaugh Norf 39 C9
Ashmansworth Hants 17 F11
Ashmansworthy Devon 6 E2
Ashmore Dorset 9 C8
Ashorne Warks 27 C10
Ashover Derbys 45 F7
Ashow Warks 27 A10
Ashprington Devon 5 F9
Ashreigney Devon 6 E5
Ashtead Sur 19 F8
Ashton Ches W 43 F8
Ashton Corn 2 G5
Ashton Hants 10 C4
Ashton Hereford 26 B2
Ashton Invclyd 73 F11
Ashton Northants 28 D4
Ashton Northants 37 G6
Ashton Common Wilts 16 F5
Ashton-In-Makerfield Gtr Man 43 C8
Ashton Keynes Wilts 17 B7
Ashton under Hill Worcs 26 E6
Ashton-under-Lyne Gtr Man 44 C3
Ashton upon Mersey Gtr Man 43 C10
Ashurst Hants 10 C2
Ashurst Kent 12 C4
Ashurst W Sus 11 C10
Ashurstwood W Sus 12 C3
Ashwater Devon 6 G2
Ashwell Herts 29 E9
Ashwell Rutland 36 D4
Ashwell Som 8 C2
Ashwellthorpe Norf 39 F7
Ashwick Som 16 G3
Ashwicken Norf 38 D3
Ashybank Borders 61 B11
Askam in Furness Cumb 49 B2
Askern S Yorks 45 A9
Askerswell Dorset 8 E4
Askett Bucks 28 H5
Askham Cumb 57 D7
Askham Notts 45 E11
Askham Bryan York 52 E1
Askham Richard York 51 E11
Asknish Argyll 73 D8
Askrigg N Yorks 57 G11
Askwith N Yorks 51 E7
Aslackby Lincs 37 B6
Aslacton Norf 39 F7
Aslockton Notts 36 B3
Asloun Aberds 83 B7
Aspatria Cumb 56 B3
Aspenden Herts 29 F10
Asperton Lincs 37 B8
Aspley Guise C Beds 28 E6
Aspley Heath C Beds 28 E6
Aspull Gtr Man 43 B9
Asselby E Yorks 52 G3
Asserby Lincs 47 E8
Assington Suff 30 E6
Assynt Ho. Highld 87 E8
Astbury Ches E 44 F2
Astcote Northants 28 C3
Asterley Shrops 33 E9
Asterton Shrops 33 F9
Asthall Oxon 27 G9
Asthall Leigh Oxon 27 G10
Astley Shrops 33 D11
Astley Warks 35 G9
Astley Worcs 26 B4
Astley Abbotts Shrops 34 F3
Astley Bridge Gtr Man 43 A10
Astley Cross Worcs 26 B5
Astley Green Gtr Man 43 C10
Aston Ches E 43 H9
Aston Ches W 43 E8
Aston Derbys 44 D5
Aston Hereford 25 A11
Aston Herts 29 F9
Aston Oxon 17 A10
Aston S Yorks 45 D8
Aston Shrops 33 C11
Aston Staffs 34 A3
Aston Telford 34 E2
Aston W Mid 35 G6
Aston Wokingham 18 C4
Aston Abbotts Bucks 28 F5
Aston Botterell Shrops 34 G2
Aston-By-Stone Staffs 34 B5
Aston Cantlow Warks 27 C8
Aston Clinton Bucks 28 G5
Aston Crews Hereford 26 F3
Aston Cross Glos 26 E6
Aston End Herts 29 F9
Aston Eyre Shrops 34 F2
Aston Fields Worcs 26 B6
Aston Flamville Leics 35 F10
Aston Ingham Hereford 26 F3
Aston juxta Mondrum Ches E 43 G9
Aston le Walls Northants 27 C11
Aston Magna Glos 27 E8
Aston Munslow Shrops 33 G11
Aston on Clun Shrops 33 G9
Aston-on-Trent Derbys 35 C10
Aston Rogers Shrops 33 E9
Aston Rowant Oxon 18 B4
Aston Sandford Bucks 28 H4
Aston Somerville Worcs 27 E7
Aston Subedge Glos 27 D8
Aston Tirrold Oxon 18 C2
Aston Upthorpe Oxon 18 C2
Astrop Northants 28 E2
Astwick C Beds 29 E9
Astwood M Keynes 28 D6
Astwood Worcs 26 C5
Astwood Bank Worcs 27 B7
Aswarby Lincs 37 B6
Aswardby Lincs 47 E7
Atch Lench Worcs 27 C7
Atcham Shrops 33 E11
Athelhampton Dorset 9 E6
Athelington Suff 31 A9
Athelney Som 8 B2
Athelstaneford E Loth 70 C4
Atherington Devon 6 D4
Atherstone Warks 35 F9
Atherstone on Stour Warks 27 C9
Atherton Gtr Man 43 B9
Atley Hill N Yorks 58 F3
Atlow Derbys 44 H6
Attadale Highld 86 H2
Attadale Ho. Highld 86 H2
Attenborough Notts 35 B11
Atterby Lincs 46 C3
Attercliffe S Yorks 45 D7
Attleborough Norf 38 F6
Attleborough Warks 35 F9
Attlebridge Norf 39 D7
Atwick E Yorks 53 D7
Atworth Wilts 16 E5
Aubourn Lincs 46 F3
Auchagallon N Ayrs 66 C1
Auchallater Aberds 82 E3
Aucharnie Aberds 89 D6
Auchattie Aberds 83 D8
Auchavan Angus 82 G3
Auchbreck Moray 82 A4
Auchenback E Renf 68 E4
Auchenbainzie Dumfries 60 D4
Auchenblae Aberds 83 F9
Auchenbrack Dumfries 60 D3
Auchenbreck Argyll 73 E9
Auchencairn Dumfries 55 D10
Auchencairn Dumfries 60 E5
Auchencairn N Ayrs 66 D3
Auchencrosh S Ayrs 54 B4
Auchencrow Borders 71 D7
Auchendinny Midloth 69 D11
Auchengray S Lanark 69 E8
Auchenhalrig Moray 88 B3
Auchenheath S Lanark 69 F7
Auchenlochan Argyll 73 F8
Auchenmalg Dumfries 54 D5
Auchensoul S Ayrs 66 G5
Auchentiber N Ayrs 67 B6
Auchertyre Highld 85 F13
Auchgourish Highld 81 B11
Auchincarroch W Dunb 68 B3
Auchindrain Argyll 73 C9
Auchindrean Highld 86 C4
Auchininna Aberds 89 D6
Auchinleck E Ayrs 67 D8
Auchinloch N Lanark 68 C5
Auchinroath Moray 88 C2
Auchintoul Aberds 83 B7
Auchiries Aberds 89 E10
Auchlee Aberds 83 D10
Auchleven Aberds 83 A8
Auchlochan S Lanark 69 G7
Auchlossan Aberds 83 C7
Auchlunies Aberds 83 D10
Auchlyne Stirling 75 E8
Auchmacoy Aberds 89 E9
Auchmair Moray 82 A5
Auchmantle Dumfries 54 C4
Auchmillan E Ayrs 67 D8
Auchmithie Angus 77 C9
Auchmuirbridge Fife 76 G5
Auchmull Angus 83 F7
Auchnacree Angus 77 A7
Auchnagallin Highld 87 H13
Auchnagatt Aberds 89 D9
Auchnaha Argyll 73 E8
Auchnashelloch Perth 75 F10
Aucholzie Aberds 82 D5
Auchrannie Angus 76 B5
Auchroisk Highld 82 A2
Auchronie Angus 82 E6
Auchterarder Perth 76 F2
Auchteraw Highld 80 C5
Auchterderran Fife 76 H5
Auchterhouse Angus 76 D6
Auchtermuchty Fife 76 F5
Auchterneed Highld 86 F7
Auchtertool Fife 69 A11
Auchtertyre Moray 88 C1
Auchtubh Stirling 75 E8
Auckengill Highld 94 D5
Auckley S Yorks 45 B10
Audenshaw Gtr Man 44 C3
Audlem Ches E 34 A2
Audley Staffs 43 G10
Audley End Essex 30 E5
Auds Aberds 89 B6
Aughton E Yorks 52 F3
Aughton Lancs 43 B6
Aughton Lancs 50 C1
Aughton S Yorks 45 D8
Aughton Wilts 17 F9
Aughton Park Lancs 43 B7
Auldearn Highld 87 F12
Aulden Hereford 25 C11
Auldgirth Dumfries 60 E5
Auldhame E Loth 70 B4
Auldhouse S Lanark 68 E5
Ault a'chruinn Highld 80 A1
Aultanrynie Highld 92 F6
Aultbea Highld 91 J13
Aultdearg Highld 86 E5
Aultgrishan Highld 91 J12
Aultguish Inn Highld 86 D6
Aultibea Highld 93 G13
Aultiphurst Highld 93 C11
Aultmore Moray 88 C4
Aultnagoire Highld 81 A7
Aultnamain Inn Highld 87 C9
Aultnaslat Highld 80 C3
Aulton Aberds 83 A8
Aundorach Highld 82 B1
Aunsby Lincs 36 B6
Auquhorthies Aberds 89 F8
Aust S Glos 16 C2
Austendike Lincs 37 C8
Austerfield S Yorks 45 C10
Austrey Warks 35 E8
Austwick N Yorks 50 C3
Authorpe Lincs 47 D8
Authorpe Row Lincs 47 E9
Avebury Wilts 17 E8
Aveley Thurrock 20 C2
Avening Glos 16 B5
Averham Notts 45 G11
Aveton Gifford Devon 5 G7
Avielochan Highld 81 B11
Aviemore Highld 81 B10
Avington Hants 10 A4
Avington W Berks 17 E10
Avoch Highld 87 F10
Avon Hants 9 E10
Avon Dassett Warks 27 D11
Avonbridge Falk 69 C8
Avonmouth Bristol 15 D11
Avonwick Devon 5 F8
Awbridge Hants 10 B2
Awhirk Dumfries 54 D3
Awkley S Glos 16 C2
Awliscombe Devon 7 F10
Awre Glos 26 H4
Awsworth Notts 35 A10
Axbridge Som 15 F10
Axford Hants 18 G3
Axford Wilts 17 D9
Axminster Devon 8 E1
Axmouth Devon 8 E1
Axton Flint 42 D4
Aycliff Kent 21 G10
Aycliffe Durham 58 D3
Aydon Northumb 62 G6
Aylburton Glos 16 A3
Ayle Northumb 57 B9
Aylesbeare Devon 7 G9
Aylesbury Bucks 28 G5
Aylesby NE Lincs 46 B6
Aylesford Kent 20 F4
Aylesham Kent 21 F9
Aylestone Leicester 36 E1
Aylmerton Norf 39 B7
Aylsham Norf 39 C7
Aylton Hereford 26 E3
Aymestrey Hereford 25 B11
Aynho Northants 28 E2
Ayot St Lawrence Herts 29 G8
Ayot St Peter Herts 29 G9
Ayr S Ayrs 66 D6
Aysgarth N Yorks 58 H1
Ayside Cumb 49 A3
Ayston Rutland 36 E4
Aythorpe Roding Essex 30 G2
Ayton Borders 71 D8
Aywick Shetland 96 E7
Azerley N Yorks 51 B8

B

Babbacombe Torbay 5 E10
Babbinswood Shrops 33 B9
Babcary Som 8 B4
Babel Carms 24 E5
Babell Flint 42 E4
Babraham Cambs 30 C2
Babworth Notts 45 D10
Bac W Isles 91 C9
Bachau Anglesey 40 B6
Back of Keppoch Highld 79 C9
Back Rogerton E Ayrs 67 D8
Backaland Orkney 95 E6
Backaskaill Orkney 95 C5
Backbarrow Cumb 49 A3
Backe Carms 23 E7
Backfolds Aberds 89 C10
Backford Ches W 43 E7
Backford Cross Ches W 43 E6
Backhill Aberds 89 E10
Backhill Aberds 89 E7
Backhill of Clackriach Aberds 89 D9
Backhill of Fortree Aberds 89 D9
Backhill of Trustach Aberds 83 D8
Backies Highld 93 J11
Backlass Highld 94 E4
Backwell N Som 15 E10
Backworth T&W 63 F9
Bacon End Essex 30 G3
Baconsthorpe Norf 39 B7
Bacton Hereford 25 E10
Bacton Norf 39 B9
Bacton Suff 31 B7
Bacton Green Suff 31 B7
Bacup Lancs 50 G4
Badachro Highld 85 A12
Badanloch Lodge Highld 93 F10
Badavanich Highld 86 F4
Badbury Swindon 17 C8
Badby Northants 28 C2
Badcall Highld 92 D5
Badcaul Highld 86 B3
Baddeley Green Stoke 44 G3
Baddesley Clinton Warks 27 A9
Baddesley Ensor Warks 35 F8
Baddidarach Highld 92 G3
Baddoch Aberds 82 E3
Baddock Highld 87 F10
Badenscoth Aberds 89 E7
Badenyon Aberds 82 B5
Badger Shrops 34 F3
Badger's Mount Kent 19 E11
Badgeworth Glos 26 G6
Badgworth Som 15 F9
Badicaul Highld 85 F12
Badingham Suff 31 B10
Badlesmere Kent 21 F7
Badlipster Highld 94 F4
Badluarach Highld 86 B2
Badminton S Glos 16 C5
Badnaban Highld 92 G3
Badninish Highld 87 B10
Badrallach Highld 86 B3
Badsey Worcs 27 D7
Badshot Lea Sur 18 G5
Badsworth W Yorks 45 A8
Badwell Ash Suff 30 B6
Bae Colwyn = Colwyn Bay Conwy 41 C10
Bag Enderby Lincs 47 E7
Bagby N Yorks 51 A10
Bagendon Glos 27 H7
Bagh a Chaisteil = Castlebay W Isles 84 J1
Bagh Mor W Isles 84 C3
Bagh Shiarabhagh W Isles 84 H2
Baghasdal W Isles 84 G2
Bagillt Flint 42 E5
Baginton Warks 27 A10
Baglan Neath 14 B3
Bagley Shrops 33 C10
Bagnall Staffs 44 G3
Bagnor W Berks 17 E11
Bagshot Sur 18 E6
Bagshot Wilts 17 E10
Bagthorpe Norf 38 B3
Bagthorpe Notts 45 G8
Bagworth Leics 35 E10
Bagwy Llydiart Hereford 25 F11
Bail Àrd Bhuirgh W Isles 91 B9
Bail' Iochdrach W Isles 84 C3
Bail Uachdraich W Isles 84 B3
Bail' Ur Tholastaidh W Isles 91 C10
Baildon W Yorks 51 F7
Baile W Isles 90 J4
Baile a Mhanaich W Isles 84 C2
Baile Ailein W Isles 91 E7
Baile an Truiseil W Isles 91 B8
Baile Boidheach Argyll 72 F6
Baile Glas W Isles 84 C3
Baile Mhartainn W Isles 84 A2
Baile Mhic Phail W Isles 84 A3
Baile Mor Argyll 78 J5
Baile Mor W Isles 84 B2
Baile na Creige W Isles 84 H1
Baile nan Cailleach W Isles 84 C2
Baile Raghaill W Isles 84 A2
Bailebeag Highld 81 B7
Baileyhead Cumb 61 F11
Bailiesward Aberds 88 E4
Baillieston Glasgow 68 D5
Bainbridge N Yorks 57 G11
Bainsford Falk 69 B7
Bainshole Aberds 88 E6
Bainton E Yorks 52 D5
Bainton Pboro 37 E6
Bairnkine Borders 62 B2
Baker Street Thurrock 20 C3
Baker's End Herts 29 G10
Bakewell Derbys 44 F6
Bala = Y Bala Gwyn 32 B5
Balachuirn Highld 85 D10
Balavil Highld 81 C9
Balbeg Highld 81 A6
Balbeg Highld 86 H7
Balbeggie Perth 76 E4
Balbithan Aberds 83 B9
Balbithan Ho. Aberds 83 B10
Balblair Highld 87 B8
Balblair Highld 87 E10
Balby S Yorks 45 B9
Balchladich Highld 92 F3
Balchraggan Highld 87 G8
Balchraggan Highld 87 H8
Balchrick Highld 92 D4
Balchrystie Fife 77 G7
Balcladaich Highld 80 A4
Balcombe W Sus 12 C2
Balcombe Lane W Sus 12 C2
Balcomie Fife 77 F9
Balcurvie Fife 76 G6
Baldersby N Yorks 51 B9
Baldersby St James N Yorks 51 B9
Balderstone Lancs 50 F2
Balderton Ches W 42 F6
Balderton Notts 46 G2
Baldhu Corn 3 E6
Baldinnie Fife 77 F7
Baldock Herts 29 E9
Baldovie Dundee 77 D7
Baldrine IoM 48 D4
Baldslow E Sus 13 E6
Baldwin IoM 48 D3
Baldwinholme Cumb 56 A5
Baldwin's Gate Staffs 34 A3
Bale Norf 38 B6
Balearn Aberds 89 C10
Balemartine Argyll 78 G2
Balephuil Argyll 78 G2
Balerno Edin 69 D10
Balevullin Argyll 78 G2
Balfield Angus 83 G7
Balfour Orkney 95 G5
Balfron Stirling 68 B4
Balfron Station Stirling 68 B4
Balgaveny Aberds 89 D6
Balgavies Angus 77 B8
Balgonar Fife 69 A9
Balgove Aberds 89 E8
Balgowan Highld 81 D8
Balgown Highld 85 B8
Balgrochan E Dunb 68 C5
Balgy Highld 85 C13
Balhaldie Stirling 75 G11
Balhalgardy Aberds 83 A9
Balham London 19 D9
Balhary Perth 76 C5
Baliasta Shetland 96 C8
Baligill Highld 93 C11
Balintore Angus 76 B5
Balintore Highld 87 D11
Balintraid Highld 87 D10
Balk N Yorks 51 A10
Balkeerie Angus 76 C6
Balkemback Angus 76 D6
Balkholme E Yorks 52 G3
Balkissock S Ayrs 54 A4
Ball Shrops 33 C9
Ball Haye Green Staffs 44 G3
Ball Hill Hants 17 E11
Ballabeg IoM 48 E2
Ballacannel IoM 48 D4
Ballachulish Highld 74 B3
Ballajora IoM 48 C4
Ballaleigh IoM 48 D3
Ballamodha IoM 48 E2
Ballantrae S Ayrs 54 A3
Ballaquine IoM 48 D4
Ballards Gore Essex 20 B6
Ballasalla IoM 48 C3
Ballasalla IoM 48 E2
Ballater Aberds 82 D5
Ballaugh IoM 48 C3
Ballaveare IoM 48 E3
Ballcorach Moray 82 A3
Ballechin Perth 76 B2
Balleigh Highld 87 C10
Ballencrieff E Loth 70 C3
Ballentoul Perth 81 G10
Ballidon Derbys 44 G6
Balliemore Argyll 73 E9
Balliemore Argyll 79 J11
Ballikinrain Stirling 68 B4
Ballimeanoch Argyll 73 B9
Ballimore Argyll 73 E8
Ballimore Stirling 75 F8
Ballinaby Argyll 64 B3
Ballindean Perth 76 E5
Ballingdon Suff 30 D5
Ballinger Common Bucks 18 A6
Ballingham Hereford 26 E2
Ballingry Fife 76 H4
Ballinlick Perth 76 C2
Ballinluig Perth 76 B2
Ballintuim Perth 76 B4
Balloch Angus 76 B6
Balloch Highld 87 G10
Balloch N Lanark 68 C6
Balloch W Dunb 68 B2
Ballochan Aberds 83 D7
Ballochford Moray 88 E3
Ballochmorrie S Ayrs 54 A5
Balls Cross W Sus 11 B8
Balls Green Essex 31 F7
Ballygown Argyll 78 G7
Ballygrant Argyll 64 B4
Ballyhaugh Argyll 78 F4
Balmacara Highld 85 F13
Balmacara Square Highld 85 F13
Balmaclellan Dumfries 55 B9
Balmacneil Perth 76 B2
Balmacqueen Highld 85 A9
Balmae Dumfries 55 E9
Balmaha Stirling 68 A3
Balmalcolm Fife 76 G6
Balmeanach Highld 85 D10
Balmedie Aberds 83 B11
Balmer Heath Shrops 33 B10
Balmerino Fife 76 E6
Balmerlawn Hants 10 D2
Balmichael N Ayrs 66 C2
Balmirmer Angus 77 D8
Balmore Highld 85 D7
Balmore Highld 86 H6
Balmore Highld 87 G11
Balmore Perth 76 B2
Balmule Fife 69 B11
Balmullo Fife 77 E7
Balmungie Highld 87 F10
Balnaboth Angus 82 G5
Balnabruaich Highld 87 E10
Balnabruich Highld 94 H3
Balnacoil Highld 93 H11
Balnacra Highld 86 G2
Balnafoich Highld 87 H9
Balnagall Highld 87 C11
Balnaguard Perth 76 B2
Balnahard Argyll 72 D3
Balnahard Argyll 78 H7
Balnain Highld 86 H7
Balnakeil Highld 92 C6
Balnaknock Highld 85 B9
Balnapaling Highld 87 E10
Balne N Yorks 52 H1
Balochroy Argyll 65 C8
Balone Fife 77 F7
Balornock Glasgow 68 D5
Balquharn Perth 76 D3
Balquhidder Stirling 75 E8
Balsall W Mid 35 H8
Balsall Common W Mid 35 H8
Balsall Hth. W Mid 35 G6
Balscott Oxon 27 D10
Balsham Cambs 30 C2
Baltasound Shetland 96 C8
Balterley Staffs 43 G10
Baltersan Dumfries 55 C7
Balthangie Aberds 89 C8
Baltonsborough Som 8 A4
Balvaird Highld 87 F8
Balvicar Argyll 72 B6
Balvraid Highld 85 G13
Balvraid Highld 87 H11
Bamber Bridge Lancs 50 G1
Bambers Green Essex 30 F2
Bamburgh Northumb 71 G10
Bamff Perth 76 B5
Bamford Derbys 44 D6
Bamford Gtr Man 44 A2
Bampton Cumb 57 E7
Bampton Devon 7 D8
Bampton Oxon 17 A10
Bampton Grange Cumb 57 E7
Banavie Highld 80 F3
Banbury Oxon 27 D11
Bancffosfelen Carms 23 E9
Banchory Aberds 83 D8
Banchory-Devenick Aberds 83 C11
Bancycapel Carms 23 E9
Bancyfelin Carms 23 E8
Bancyffordd Carms 23 C9
Bandirran Perth 76 D5
Banff Aberds 89 B6
Bangor Gwyn 41 C7
Bangor-is-y-coed Wrex 43 H6
Banham Norf 39 G6
Bank Hants 10 D1
Bank Newton N Yorks 50 D5
Bank Street Worcs 26 B3
Bankend Dumfries 60 G6
Bankfoot Perth 76 D3
Bankglen E Ayrs 67 E9
Bankhead Aberdeen 83 B10
Bankhead Aberds 83 C8
Banknock Falk 68 C6
Banks Cumb 61 G11
Banks Lancs 49 G3
Bankshill Dumfries 61 E7
Banningham Norf 39 C8
Banniskirk Ho. Highld 94 E3
Bannister Green Essex 30 F3
Bannockburn Stirling 69 A7
Banstead Sur 19 F9
Bantham Devon 5 G7
Banton N Lanark 68 C6
Banwell N Som 15 F9
Banyard's Green Suff 31 A9
Bapchild Kent 20 E6
Bar Hill Cambs 29 B10
Barabhas W Isles 91 C8
Barabhas Iarach W Isles 91 C8
Barabhas Uarach W Isles 91 B8
Barachandroman Argyll 79 J9
Barassie S Ayrs 67 C6
Baravullin Argyll 79 H11
Barbaraville Highld 87 D10
Barber Booth Derbys 44 D5
Barbieston S Ayrs 67 E7
Barbon Cumb 50 A2
Barbridge Ches E 43 G9
Barbrook Devon 6 B6
Barby Northants 28 A2
Barcaldine Argyll 74 C2
Barcheston Warks 27 E9
Barcombe E Sus 12 E3
Barcombe Cross E Sus 12 E3
Barden N Yorks 58 G2
Barden Scale N Yorks 51 D6
Bardennoch Dumfries 67 G8
Bardfield Saling Essex 30 F3
Bardister Shetland 96 F5
Bardney Lincs 46 F5
Bardon Leics 35 D10
Bardon Mill Northumb 62 G3
Bardowie E Dunb 68 C4
Bardrainney Invclyd 68 C2
Bardsea Cumb 49 B3
Bardsey W Yorks 51 E9
Bardwell Suff 30 A6
Bare Lancs 49 C4
Barfad Argyll 73 G7
Barford Norf 39 E7
Barford Warks 27 B9
Barford St John Oxon 27 E11
Barford St Martin Wilts 9 A9
Barford St Michael Oxon 27 E11
Barfrestone Kent 21 F9
Bargod = Bargoed Caerph 15 B7
Bargoed = Bargod Caerph 15 B7
Bargrennan Dumfries 54 B6
Barham Cambs 37 H7
Barham Kent 21 F9
Barham Suff 31 C8
Barharrow Dumfries 55 D9
Barhill Dumfries 55 C11
Barholm Lincs 37 D6
Barkby Leics 36 E2
Barkestone-le-Vale Leics 36 B3
Barkham Wokingham 18 E4
Barking London 19 C11
Barking Suff 31 C7
Barking Tye Suff 31 C7
Barkingside London 19 C11
Barkisland W Yorks 51 H6
Barkston Lincs 36 A5
Barkston N Yorks 51 F10
Barkway Herts 29 E10
Barlaston Staffs 34 B4
Barlavington W Sus 11 C8
Barlborough Derbys 45 E8
Barlby N Yorks 52 F2
Barlestone Leics 35 E10
Barley Herts 29 E10
Barley Lancs 50 E4
Barley Mow T&W 58 A3
Barleythorpe Rutland 36 E4
Barling Essex 20 C6
Barlow Derbys 45 E7
Barlow N Yorks 52 G2
Barlow T&W 63 G7
Barmby Moor E Yorks 52 E3
Barmby on the Marsh E Yorks 52 G2
Barmer Norf 38 B4
Barmoor Castle Northumb 71 G8
Barmoor Lane End Northumb 71 G9
Barmouth = Abermaw Gwyn 32 D2
Barmpton Darl 58 E4
Barmston E Yorks 53 D7
Barnack Pboro 37 E6
Barnacle Warks 35 G9
Barnard Castle Durham 58 E1
Barnard Gate Oxon 27 G11
Barnardiston Suff 30 D4
Barnbarroch Dumfries 55 D11
Barnburgh S Yorks 45 B8
Barnby Suff 39 G10
Barnby Dun S Yorks 45 B10
Barnby in the Willows Notts 46 G2
Barnby Moor Notts 45 D10
Barnes Street Kent 20 G3
Barnet London 19 B9
Barnetby le Wold N Lincs 46 B4
Barney Norf 38 B5
Barnham Suff 38 H4
Barnham W Sus 11 D8
Barnham Broom Norf 39 E6
Barnhead Angus 77 B9
Barnhill Ches W 43 G7
Barnhill Dundee 77 D7
Barnhill Moray 88 C1
Barnhills Dumfries 54 B2
Barningham Durham 58 E1
Barningham Suff 38 H5
Barnoldby le Beck NE Lincs 46 B6
Barnoldswick Lancs 50 E4
Barns Green W Sus 11 B10
Barnsley Glos 27 H7
Barnsley S Yorks 45 B7
Barnstaple Devon 6 C4
Barnston Essex 30 G3
Barnston Mers 42 D5
Barnstone Notts 36 B3
Barnt Green Worcs 27 A7
Barnton Ches W 43 E9
Barnton Edin 69 C10
Barnwell All Saints Northants 36 G6
Barnwell St Andrew Northants 36 G6
Barnwood Glos 26 G5
Barochreal Argyll 79 J11
Barons Cross Hereford 25 C11
Barr S Ayrs 66 G5
Barra Castle Aberds 83 A9
Barrachan Dumfries 54 E6
Barrack Aberds 89 D8
Barraglom W Isles 90 D6
Barrahormid Argyll 72 E6
Barran Argyll 79 J11
Barrapol Argyll 78 G2
Barras Aberds 83 E10
Barras Cumb 57 E10
Barrasford Northumb 62 F5
Barravullin Argyll 73 C7
Barregarrow IoM 48 D3
Barrhead E Renf 68 E3
Barrhill S Ayrs 54 A5
Barrington Cambs 29 D10
Barrington Som 8 C2
Barripper Corn 2 F5
Barrmill N Ayrs 67 A6
Barrock Highld 94 C4
Barrock Ho. Highld 94 D4
Barrow Lancs 50 F3
Barrow Rutland 36 D4
Barrow Suff 30 B4
Barrow Green Kent 20 E6
Barrow Gurney N Som 15 E11
Barrow Haven N Lincs 53 G6
Barrow-in-Furness Cumb 49 C2
Barrow Island Cumb 49 C1
Barrow Nook Lancs 43 B7
Barrow Street Wilts 9 A7
Barrow upon Humber N Lincs 53 G6
Barrow upon Soar Leics 36 D1
Barrow upon Trent Derbys 35 C9
Barroway Drove Norf 38 E1
Barrowburn Northumb 62 B4
Barrowby Lincs 36 B4
Barrowcliff N Yorks 59 H11
Barrowden Rutland 36 E5
Barrowford Lancs 50 F4
Barrows Green Ches E 43 G9
Barrows Green Cumb 57 H7
Barrow's Green Mers 43 D8
Barry Angus 77 D8
Barry = Y Barri V Glam 15 E7
Barry Island V Glam 15 E7
Barsby Leics 36 D2
Barsham Suff 39 G9
Barston W Mid 35 H8
Bartestree Hereford 26 D2
Barthol Chapel Aberds 89 E8
Barthomley Ches E 43 G10
Bartley Hants 10 C2
Bartley Green W Mid 34 G6
Bartlow Cambs 30 D2
Barton Cambs 29 C11
Barton Ches W 43 G7
Barton Glos 27 F8
Barton Lancs 42 B6
Barton Lancs 49 F5
Barton N Yorks 58 F3
Barton Oxon 28 H2
Barton Torbay 5 E10
Barton Warks 27 C8
Barton Bendish Norf 38 E3
Barton Hartshorn Bucks 28 E3
Barton in Fabis Notts 35 B11
Barton in the Beans Leics 35 E9
Barton-le-Clay C Beds 29 E7
Barton-le-Street N Yorks 52 B3
Barton-le-Willows N Yorks 52 C3
Barton Mills Suff 30 A4
Barton on Sea Hants 9 E11
Barton on the Heath Warks 27 E9
Barton St David Som 8 A4
Barton Seagrave Northants 36 H4
Barton Stacey Hants 17 G11
Barton Turf Norf 39 C9
Barton-under-Needwood Staffs 35 D7
Barton-upon-Humber N Lincs 52 G6
Barton Waterside N Lincs 52 G6
Barugh S Yorks 45 B7
Barway Cambs 37 H11
Barwell Leics 35 F10
Barwick Herts 29 G10
Barwick Som 8 C4
Barwick in Elmet W Yorks 51 F9
Baschurch Shrops 33 C10
Bascote Warks 27 B11
Basford Green Staffs 44 G3
Bashall Eaves Lancs 50 E2
Bashley Hants 9 E11
Basildon Essex 20 C4
Basingstoke Hants 18 F3
Baslow Derbys 44 E6
Bason Bridge Som 15 G9
Bassaleg Newport 15 C8
Bassenthwaite Cumb 56 C4
Bassett Soton 10 C3
Bassingbourn Cambs 29 D10
Bassingfield Notts 36 B2
Bassingham Lincs 46 F3
Bassingthorpe Lincs 36 C5
Basta Shetland 96 D7
Baston Lincs 37 D7
Bastwick Norf 39 D10
Baswick Steer E Yorks 53 E6
Batchworth Heath Herts 19 B7
Batcombe Dorset 8 D5
Batcombe Som 16 H3
Bate Heath Ches E 43 E9
Batford Herts 29 G8
Bath Bath 16 E4
Bathampton Bath 16 E4
Bathealton Som 7 D9
Batheaston Bath 16 E4
Bathford Bath 16 E4
Bathgate W Loth 69 D8
Bathley Notts 45 G11
Bathpool Corn 4 D3
Bathpool Som 8 B1
Bathville W Loth 69 D8
Batley W Yorks 51 G8
Batsford Glos 27 E8
Battersby N Yorks 59 F6
Battersea London 19 D9
Battisborough Cross Devon 5 G6
Battisford Suff 31 C7
Battisford Tye Suff 31 C7
Battle E Sus 12 E6
Battle Powys 25 E7
Battledown Glos 26 F6
Battlefield Shrops 33 D11
Battlesbridge Essex 20 B4
Battlesden C Beds 28 F6
Battlesea Green Suff 39 H8
Battleton Som 7 D8
Battram Leics 35 E10
Battramsley Hants 10 E2
Baughton Worcs 26 D5
Baughurst Hants 18 F2
Baulking Oxon 17 B10
Baumber Lincs 46 E6
Baunton Glos 17 A7
Baverstock Wilts 9 A9
Bawburgh Norf 39 E7
Bawdeswell Norf 39 C6
Bawdrip Som 15 H9
Bawdsey Suff 31 D10
Bawtry S Yorks 45 C10
Baxenden Lancs 50 G3
Baxterley Warks 35 F8
Baybridge Hants 10 B4

Baycliff Cumb 49 B2
Baydon Wilts 17 D9
Bayford Herts 29 H10
Bayford Som 8 B6
Bayles Cumb 57 B9
Baylham Suff 31 C8
Baynard's Green Oxon 28 F2
Bayston Hill Shrops 33 E10
Baythorn End Essex 30 D4
Bayton Worcs 26 A3
Beach Highld 79 F10
Beachampton Bucks 28 E4
Beachamwell Norf 38 E3
Beachans Moray 87 G13
Beacharr Argyll 65 D7
Beachborough Kent 21 H8
Beachley Glos 16 B2
Beacon Devon 7 F10
Beacon End Essex 30 F6
Beacon Hill Sur 18 H5
Beacon's Bottom Bucks 18 B4
Beaconsfield Bucks 18 C6
Beacrabhaic W Isles 90 H6
Beadlam N Yorks 52 A2
Beadlow C Beds 29 E8
Beadnell Northumb 71 H11
Beaford Devon 6 E4
Beal N Yorks 51 G11
Beal Northumb 71 F9
Beamhurst Staffs 35 B6
Beaminster Dorset 8 D3
Beamish Durham 58 A3
Beamsley N Yorks 51 D6
Bean Kent 20 D2
Beanacre Wilts 16 E6
Beanley Northumb 62 B6
Beaquoy Orkney 95 F4
Bear Cross Bmouth 9 E9
Beardwood Blackburn 50 G2
Beare Green Sur 19 G8
Bearley Warks 27 B8
Bearnus Argyll 78 G6
Bearpark Durham 58 B3
Bearsbridge Northumb 62 H3
Bearsden E Dunb 68 C4
Bearsted Kent 20 F4
Bearstone Shrops 34 B3
Bearwood Hereford 25 C10
Bearwood Poole 9 E9
Bearwood W Mid 34 G6
Beattock Dumfries 60 C6
Beauchamp Roding Essex 30 G2
Beauchief S Yorks 45 D7
Beaufort Bl Gwent 25 G8
Beaufort Castle Highld 87 G8
Beaulieu Hants 10 D2
Beauly Highld 87 G8
Beaumaris Anglesey 41 C8
Beaumont Cumb 61 H9
Beaumont Essex 31 F8
Beaumont Hill Darl 58 E3
Beausale Warks 27 A9
Beauworth Hants 10 B4
Beaworthy Devon 6 G3
Beazley End Essex 30 F4
Bebington Mers 42 D6
Bebside Northumb 63 E8
Beccles Suff 39 F10
Becconsall Lancs 49 G4
Beck Foot Cumb 57 G8
Beck Hole N Yorks 59 F9
Beck Row Suff 38 H2
Beck Side Cumb 49 A2
Beckbury Shrops 34 E3
Beckenham London 19 E10
Beckermet Cumb 56 F2
Beckfoot Cumb 56 B2
Beckfoot Cumb 56 F3
Beckford Worcs 26 E6
Beckhampton Wilts 17 E7
Beckingham Lincs 46 G2
Beckingham Notts 45 D11
Beckington Som 16 F5
Beckley E Sus 13 D7
Beckley Hants 9 E11
Beckley Oxon 28 G2
Beckton London 19 C11
Beckwithshaw N Yorks 51 D8
Becontree London 19 C11
Bed-y-coedwr Gwyn 32 C3
Bedale N Yorks 58 H3
Bedburn Durham 58 C2
Bedchester Dorset 9 C7
Beddau Rhondda 14 C6
Beddgelert Gwyn 41 F7
Beddingham E Sus 12 F3
Beddington London 19 E10
Bedfield Suff 31 B9
Bedford Bedford 29 C7
Bedham W Sus 11 B9
Bedhampton Hants 10 D6
Bedingfield Suff 31 B8
Bedlam N Yorks 51 C8
Bedlington Northumb 63 E8
Bedlington Station Northumb 63 E8
Bedlinog M Tydf 14 A6
Bedminster Bristol 16 D2
Bedmond Herts 19 A7
Bednall Staffs 34 D5
Bedrule Borders 62 B2
Bedstone Shrops 33 H9
Bedwas Caerph 15 C7
Bedworth Warks 35 G9
Bedworth Heath Warks 35 G9
Beeby Leics 36 E2
Beech Hants 18 H3
Beech Staffs 34 B4
Beech Hill Gtr Man 43 B8
Beech Hill W Berks 18 E3
Beechingstoke Wilts 17 F7
Beedon W Berks 17 D11
Beeford E Yorks 53 D7
Beeley Derbys 44 F6
Beelsby NE Lincs 46 B6
Beenham W Berks 18 E2
Beeny Corn 4 B2
Beer Devon 7 H11
Beer Hackett Dorset 8 C4
Beercrocombe Som 8 B2
Beesands Devon 5 G9
Beesby Lincs 47 D8
Beeson Devon 5 G9
Beeston C Beds 29 D8
Beeston Ches W 43 G8
Beeston Norf 38 D5
Beeston Notts 35 B11
Beeston W Yorks 51 F8
Beeston Regis Norf 39 A7
Beeswing Dumfries 55 C11
Beetham Cumb 49 B4
Beetley Norf 38 D5
Begbroke Oxon 27 G11
Begelly Pembs 22 F6
Beggar's Bush Powys 25 B9
Beguildy Powys 33 H7
Beighton Norf 39 E9
Beighton S Yorks 45 D8
Beighton Hill Derbys 44 G6
Beith N Ayrs 66 A6
Bekesbourne Kent 21 F8
Belaugh Norf 39 D8
Belbroughton Worcs 34 H5
Belchamp Otten Essex 30 D5
Belchamp St Paul Essex 30 D4
Belchamp Walter Essex 30 D5
Belchford Lincs 46 E6
Belford Northumb 71 G10
Belhaven E Loth 70 C5
Belhelvie Aberds 83 B11
Belhinnie Aberds 82 A6
Bell Bar Herts 29 H9
Bell Busk N Yorks 50 D5
Bell End Worcs 34 H5
Bell o' th' Hill Ches W 43 H8
Bellabeg Aberds 82 B5
Bellamore S Ayrs 66 H5
Bellanoch Argyll 72 D6
Bellaty Angus 76 B5
Belleau Lincs 47 E8
Bellehiglash Moray 88 E1
Bellerby N Yorks 58 G2
Bellever Devon 5 D7
Belliehill Angus 77 A8
Bellingdon Bucks 28 H6
Bellingham Northumb 62 E4
Belloch Argyll 65 E7
Bellochantuy Argyll 65 E7
Bells Yew Green E Sus 12 C5
Bellsbank E Ayrs 67 F7
Bellshill N Lanark 68 D6
Bellshill Northumb 71 G10
Bellspool Borders 69 G10
Bellsquarry W Loth 69 D9
Belmaduthy Highld 87 F9
Belmesthorpe Rutland 36 D6
Belmont Blackburn 50 H2
Belmont London 19 E9
Belmont S Ayrs 66 D6
Belmont Shetland 96 C7
Belnacraig Aberds 82 B5
Belowda Corn 3 C8
Belper Derbys 45 H7
Belper Lane End Derbys 45 H7
Belsay Northumb 63 F7
Belses Borders 70 H4
Belsford Devon 5 F8
Belstead Suff 31 D8
Belston S Ayrs 67 D6
Belstone Devon 6 G5
Belthorn Blackburn 50 G3
Beltinge Kent 21 E8
Beltoft N Lincs 46 B2
Belton Leics 35 C10
Belton Lincs 36 B5
Belton N Lincs 45 B11
Belton Norf 39 E10
Belton in Rutland Rutland 36 E4
Beltring Kent 20 G3
Belts of Collonach Aberds 83 D8
Belvedere London 19 D11
Belvoir Leics 36 B4
Bembridge IoW 10 F5
Bemersyde Borders 70 G4
Bemerton Wilts 9 A10
Bempton E Yorks 53 B7
Ben Alder Lodge Highld 81 F7
Ben Armine Lodge Highld 93 H10
Ben Casgro W Isles 91 E9
Benacre Suff 39 G11
Benbuie Dumfries 60 D3
Benderloch Argyll 74 D2
Bendronaig Lodge Highld 86 H3
Benenden Kent 13 C7
Benfield Dumfries 54 C6
Bengate Norf 39 C9
Bengeworth Worcs 27 D7
Benhall Green Suff 31 B10
Benhall Street Suff 31 B10
Benholm Aberds 83 G10
Beningbrough N Yorks 51 D11
Benington Herts 29 F9
Benington Lincs 47 H7
Benllech Anglesey 41 B7
Benmore Argyll 73 E10
Benmore Stirling 75 E7
Benmore Lodge Highld 92 H6
Bennacott Corn 6 G1
Bennan N Ayrs 66 D2
Benniworth Lincs 46 D6
Benover Kent 20 G4
Bensham T&W 63 G8
Benslie N Ayrs 66 B6
Benson Oxon 18 B3
Bent Aberds 83 F8
Bent Gate Lancs 50 H3
Benthall Northumb 71 H11
Benthall Shrops 34 E2
Bentham Glos 26 G6
Benthoul Aberdeen 83 C10
Bentlawnt Shrops 33 E9
Bentley E Yorks 52 F6
Bentley Hants 18 G4
Bentley S Yorks 45 B9
Bentley Suff 31 E8
Bentley Warks 35 F8
Bentley Worcs 26 B6
Bentley Heath W Mid 35 H7
Benton Devon 6 C5
Bentpath Dumfries 61 D9
Bents W Loth 69 D8
Bentworth Hants 18 G3
Benvie Dundee 76 D6
Benwick Cambs 37 F9
Beoley Worcs 27 B7
Beoraidbeg Highld 79 B9
Bepton W Sus 11 C7
Berden Essex 29 F11
Bere Alston Devon 4 E5
Bere Ferrers Devon 4 E5
Bere Regis Dorset 9 E7
Berepper Corn 2 G5
Bergh Apton Norf 39 E9
Berinsfield Oxon 18 B2
Berkeley Glos 16 B3
Berkhamsted Herts 28 H6
Berkley Som 16 G5
Berkswell W Mid 35 H8
Bermondsey London 19 D10
Bernera Highld 85 F13
Bernice Argyll 73 D10
Bernisdale Highld 85 C9
Berrick Salome Oxon 18 B3
Berriedale Highld 94 H3
Berrier Cumb 56 D5
Berriew Powys 33 E7
Berrington Northumb 71 F9
Berrington Shrops 33 E11
Berrow Som 15 F9
Berrow Green Worcs 26 C4
Berry Down Cross Devon 6 B4
Berry Hill Glos 26 G2
Berry Hill Pembs 22 B5
Berry Pomeroy Devon 5 E9
Berryhillock Moray 88 B5
Berrynarbor Devon 6 B4
Bersham Wrex 42 H6
Berstane Orkney 95 G5
Berwick E Sus 12 F4
Berwick Bassett Wilts 17 D7
Berwick Hill Northumb 63 F7
Berwick St James Wilts 17 H7
Berwick St John Wilts 9 B8
Berwick St Leonard Wilts 9 A8
Berwick-upon-Tweed Northumb 71 E8
Bescar Lancs 43 A6
Besford Worcs 26 D6
Bessacarr S Yorks 45 B10
Bessels Leigh Oxon 17 A11
Bessingby E Yorks 53 C7
Bessingham Norf 39 B7
Bestbeech Hill E Sus 12 C5
Besthorpe Norf 39 F6
Besthorpe Notts 46 F2
Bestwood Nottingham 36 A1
Bestwood Village Notts 45 H9
Beswick E Yorks 52 E6
Betchworth Sur 19 G9
Bethania Ceredig 24 B2
Bethania Gwyn 41 E8
Bethania Gwyn 41 F9
Bethel Anglesey 40 C5
Bethel Gwyn 32 B5
Bethel Gwyn 41 D7
Bethersden Kent 13 B8
Bethesda Gwyn 41 D8
Bethesda Pembs 22 E5
Bethlehem Carms 24 F3
Bethnal Green London 19 C10
Betley Staffs 43 H10
Betsham Kent 20 D3
Betteshanger Kent 21 F10
Bettiscombe Dorset 8 E2
Bettisfield Wrex 33 B10
Betton Shrops 33 E9
Betton Shrops 34 B2
Bettws Bridgend 14 C5
Bettws Mon 25 G9
Bettws Newport 15 B8
Bettws Cedewain Powys 33 F7
Bettws Gwerfil Goch Denb 42 H3
Bettws Ifan Ceredig 23 B8
Bettws Newydd Mon 25 H10
Bettws-y-crwyn Shrops 33 G8
Bettyhill Highld 93 C10
Betws Carms 24 G3
Betws Bledrws Ceredig 23 A10
Betws-Garmon Gwyn 41 E7
Betws-y-Coed Conwy 41 E9
Betws-yn-Rhos Conwy 42 E2
Beulah Ceredig 23 B7
Beulah Powys 24 C6
Bevendean Brighton 12 F2
Bevercotes Notts 45 E10
Beverley E Yorks 52 F6
Beverston Glos 16 B5
Bevington Glos 16 B3
Bewaldeth Cumb 56 C4
Bewcastle Cumb 61 F11
Bewdley Worcs 34 H3
Bewerley N Yorks 51 C7
Bewholme E Yorks 53 D7
Bexhill E Sus 12 F6
Bexley London 19 D11
Bexleyheath London 19 D11
Bexwell Norf 38 E2
Beyton Suff 30 B6
Bhaltos W Isles 90 D5
Bhatarsaigh W Isles 84 J1
Bibury Glos 27 H8
Bicester Oxon 28 F2
Bickenhall Som 8 C1
Bickenhill W Mid 35 G7
Bicker Lincs 37 B8
Bickershaw Gtr Man 43 B9
Bickerstaffe Lancs 43 B7
Bickerton Ches E 43 G8
Bickerton N Yorks 51 D10
Bickington Devon 5 D8
Bickington Devon 6 C4
Bickleigh Devon 4 E6
Bickleigh Devon 7 F8
Bickleton Devon 6 C4
Bickley London 19 E11
Bickley Moss Ches W 43 H8
Bicknacre Essex 20 A4
Bicknoller Som 7 C10
Bicknor Kent 20 F5
Bickton Hants 9 C10
Bicton Shrops 33 D10
Bicton Shrops 33 G8
Bidborough Kent 12 B4
Biddenden Kent 13 C7
Biddenham Bedford 29 D7
Biddestone Wilts 16 D5
Biddisham Som 15 F9
Biddlesden Bucks 28 D3
Biddlestone Northumb 62 C5
Biddulph Staffs 44 G2
Biddulph Moor Staffs 44 G3
Bideford Devon 6 D3
Bidford-on-Avon Warks 27 C8
Bidston Mers 42 C5
Bielby E Yorks 52 E3
Bieldside Aberdeen 83 C10
Bierley IoW 10 G4
Bierley W Yorks 51 F7
Bierton Bucks 28 G5
Big Sand Highld 85 A12
Bigbury Devon 5 G7
Bigbury on Sea Devon 5 G7
Bigby Lincs 46 B4
Biggar Cumb 49 C1
Biggar S Lanark 69 G9
Biggin Derbys 44 G5
Biggin Derbys 44 H6
Biggin N Yorks 51 F11
Biggin Hill London 19 F11
Biggings Shetland 96 G3
Biggleswade C Beds 29 D8
Bighouse Highld 93 C11
Bighton Hants 10 A5
Bignor W Sus 11 C8
Bigton Shetland 96 L5
Bilberry Corn 3 C9
Bilborough Nottingham 35 A11
Bilbrook Som 7 B9
Bilbrough N Yorks 51 E11
Bilbster Highld 94 E4
Bildershaw Durham 58 D3
Bildeston Suff 30 D6
Billericay Essex 20 B3
Billesdon Leics 36 E3
Billesley Warks 27 C8
Billingborough Lincs 37 B7
Billinge Mers 43 B8
Billingford Norf 38 C6
Billingham Stockton 58 D5
Billinghay Lincs 46 G5
Billingley S Yorks 45 B8
Billingshurst W Sus 11 B9
Billingsley Shrops 34 G3
Billington C Beds 28 F6
Billington Lancs 50 F3
Billockby Norf 39 D10
Billy Row Durham 58 C2
Bilsborrow Lancs 49 F5
Bilsby Lincs 47 E8
Bilsham W Sus 11 D8
Bilsington Kent 13 C9
Bilson Green Glos 26 G3
Bilsthorpe Notts 45 F10
Bilsthorpe Moor Notts 45 G10
Bilston Midloth 69 D11
Bilston W Mid 34 F5
Bilstone Leics 35 E9
Bilting Kent 21 G7
Bilton E Yorks 53 F7
Bilton Northumb 63 B8
Bilton Warks 27 A11
Bilton in Ainsty N Yorks 51 E10
Bimbister Orkney 95 G4
Binbrook Lincs 46 C6
Binchester Blocks Durham 58 C3
Bincombe Dorset 8 F5
Bindal Highld 87 C12
Binegar Som 16 G3
Binfield Brack 18 D5
Binfield Hth. Oxon 18 D4
Bingfield Northumb 62 F5
Bingham Notts 36 B3
Bingley W Yorks 51 F7
Bings Heath Shrops 33 D11
Binham Norf 38 B5
Binley Hants 17 F11
Binley W Mid 35 H9
Binley Woods Warks 35 H9
Binniehill Falk 69 C7
Binsoe N Yorks 51 B8
Binstead IoW 10 E4
Binsted Hants 18 G4
Binton Warks 27 C8
Bintree Norf 38 C6
Binweston Shrops 33 E9
Birch Essex 30 G6
Birch Gtr Man 44 B2
Birch Green Essex 30 G6
Birch Heath Ches W 43 F8
Birch Hill Ches W 43 E8
Birch Vale Derbys 44 D4
Bircham Newton Norf 38 B3
Bircham Tofts Norf 38 B3
Birchanger Essex 30 F2
Birchencliffe W Yorks 51 H7
Bircher Hereford 25 B11
Birchgrove Cardiff 15 D7
Birchgrove Swansea 14 B3
Birchington Kent 21 E9
Birchmoor Warks 35 E8
Birchover Derbys 44 F6
Birchwood Lincs 46 F3
Birchwood Warr 43 C9
Bircotes Notts 45 C10
Birdbrook Essex 30 D4
Birdforth N Yorks 51 B10
Birdham W Sus 11 E7
Birdholme Derbys 45 F7
Birdingbury Warks 27 B11
Birdlip Glos 26 G6
Birds Edge W Yorks 44 B6
Birdsall N Yorks 52 C4
Birdsgreen Shrops 34 G3
Birdsmoor Gate Dorset 8 D2
Birdston E Dunb 68 C5
Birdwell S Yorks 45 B7
Birdwood Glos 26 G4
Birgham Borders 70 G6
Birkby N Yorks 58 F4
Birkdale Mers 49 H3
Birkenhead Mers 42 D6
Birkenhills Aberds 89 D7
Birkenshaw N Lanark 68 D5
Birkenshaw W Yorks 51 G8
Birkhall Aberds 82 D5
Birkhill Angus 76 D6
Birkhill Borders 61 B8
Birkholme Lincs 36 C5
Birkin N Yorks 51 G11
Birley Hereford 25 C11
Birling Kent 20 E3
Birling Northumb 63 C8
Birling Gap E Sus 12 G4
Birlingham Worcs 26 D6
Birmingham W Mid 35 G6
Birnam Perth 76 C3
Birse Aberds 83 D7
Birsemore Aberds 83 D7
Birstall Leics 36 E1
Birstall W Yorks 51 G8
Birstwith N Yorks 51 D8
Birthorpe Lincs 37 B7
Birtley Hereford 25 B10
Birtley Northumb 62 F4
Birtley T&W 63 H8
Birts Street Worcs 26 E4
Bisbrooke Rutland 36 F4
Biscathorpe Lincs 46 D6
Biscot Luton 29 F7
Bish Mill Devon 7 D6
Bisham Windsor 18 C5
Bishampton Worcs 26 C6
Bishop Auckland Durham 58 D3
Bishop Burton E Yorks 52 F5
Bishop Middleham Durham 58 C4
Bishop Monkton N Yorks 51 C9
Bishop Norton Lincs 46 C3
Bishop Sutton Bath 16 F2
Bishop Thornton N Yorks 51 C8
Bishop Wilton E Yorks 52 D3
Bishopbridge Lincs 46 C4
Bishopbriggs E Dunb 68 D5
Bishopmill Moray 88 B2
Bishops Cannings Wilts 17 E7
Bishop's Castle Shrops 33 G9
Bishop's Caundle Dorset 8 C5
Bishop's Cleeve Glos 26 F6
Bishops Frome Hereford 26 D3
Bishop's Green Essex 30 G3
Bishop's Hull Som 7 D11
Bishop's Itchington Warks 27 C10
Bishops Lydeard Som 7 D10
Bishops Nympton Devon 7 D6
Bishop's Offley Staffs 34 C3
Bishop's Stortford Herts 29 F11
Bishop's Sutton Hants 10 A5
Bishop's Tachbrook Warks 27 B10
Bishops Tawton Devon 6 C4
Bishop's Waltham Hants 10 C4
Bishop's Wood Staffs 34 E4
Bishopsbourne Kent 21 F8
Bishopsteignton Devon 5 D10
Bishopstoke Hants 10 C3
Bishopston Swansea 23 H10
Bishopstone Bucks 28 G5
Bishopstone E Sus 12 F3
Bishopstone Hereford 25 D11
Bishopstone Swindon 17 C9
Bishopstone Wilts 9 B9
Bishopstrow Wilts 16 G5
Bishopswood Som 8 C1
Bishopsworth Bristol 16 E2
Bishopthorpe York 52 E1
Bishopton Darl 58 D4
Bishopton Dumfries 55 E7
Bishopton N Yorks 51 B9
Bishopton Renfs 68 C3
Bishopton Warks 27 C8
Bishton Newport 15 C9
Bisley Glos 26 H6
Bisley Sur 18 F6
Bispham Blackpool 49 E3
Bispham Green Lancs 43 A7
Bissoe Corn 3 E6
Bisterne Close Hants 9 D11
Bitchfield Lincs 36 C5
Bittadon Devon 6 B4
Bittaford Devon 5 F7
Bittering Norf 38 D5
Bitterley Shrops 34 H1
Bitterne Soton 10 C3
Bitteswell Leics 35 G11
Bitton S Glos 16 E3
Bix Oxon 18 C4
Bixter Shetland 96 H5
Blaby Leics 36 F1
Black Bourton Oxon 17 A9
Black Callerton T&W 63 G7
Black Clauchrie S Ayrs 54 A5
Black Corries Lodge Highld 74 B5
Black Crofts Argyll 74 D2
Black Dog Devon 7 F7
Black Heddon Northumb 62 F6
Black Lane Gtr Man 43 B10
Black Marsh Shrops 33 F9
Black Mount Argyll 74 C5
Black Notley Essex 30 F4
Black Pill Swansea 14 B2
Black Tar Pembs 22 F4
Black Torrington Devon 6 F3
Blackacre Dumfries 60 D6
Blackadder West Borders 71 E7
Blackawton Devon 5 F9
Blackborough Devon 7 F9
Blackborough End Norf 38 D2
Blackboys E Sus 12 D4
Blackbrook Derbys 45 H7
Blackbrook Mers 43 C8
Blackbrook Staffs 34 B3
Blackburn Aberds 83 B10
Blackburn Aberds 88 E5
Blackburn Blackburn 50 G2
Blackburn W Loth 69 D8
Blackcraig Dumfries 60 E3
Blackden Heath Ches E 43 E10
Blackdog Aberds 83 B11
Blackfell T&W 63 H8
Blackfield Hants 10 D3
Blackford Cumb 61 G9
Blackford Perth 75 G11
Blackford Som 8 B5
Blackford Som 15 G10
Blackfordby Leics 35 D9
Blackgang IoW 10 G3
Blackhall Colliery Durham 58 C5
Blackhall Mill T&W 63 H7
Blackhall Rocks Durham 58 C5
Blackham E Sus 12 C3
Blackhaugh Borders 70 G3
Blackheath Essex 31 F7
Blackheath Suff 31 A11
Blackheath Sur 19 G7
Blackheath W Mid 34 G5
Blackhill Aberds 89 C10
Blackhill Aberds 89 D10
Blackhill Highld 85 C8
Blackhills Highld 87 F12
Blackhills Moray 88 C2
Blackhorse S Glos 16 D3
Blackland Wilts 17 E7
Blacklaw Aberds 89 C6
Blackley Gtr Man 44 B2
Blacklunans Perth 76 A4
Blackmill Bridgend 14 C5
Blackmoor Hants 11 A6
Blackmoor Gate Devon 6 B5
Blackmore Essex 20 A3
Blackmore End Essex 30 E4
Blackmore End Herts 29 G8
Blackness Falk 69 C9
Blacknest Hants 18 G4
Blacko Lancs 50 E4
Blackpool Blackpool 49 F3
Blackpool Devon 5 G9
Blackpool Pembs 22 E5
Blackpool Gate Cumb 61 F11
Blackridge W Loth 69 D7
Blackrock Argyll 64 B4
Blackrock Mon 25 G9
Blackrod Gtr Man 43 A9
Blackshaw Dumfries 60 G6
Blackshaw Head W Yorks 50 G5
Blacksmith's Green Suff 31 B8
Blackstone W Sus 11 C11
Blackthorn Oxon 28 G3
Blackthorpe Suff 30 B6
Blacktoft E Yorks 52 G4
Blacktop Aberdeen 83 C10
Blacktown Newport 15 C8
Blackwall Tunnel London 19 C10
Blackwater Corn 2 E6
Blackwater Hants 18 F5
Blackwater IoW 10 F4
Blackwaterfoot N Ayrs 66 D1
Blackwell Darl 58 E3
Blackwell Derbys 44 E5
Blackwell Derbys 45 G8
Blackwell W Sus 12 C2
Blackwell Warks 27 D9
Blackwell Worcs 26 A6
Blackwood = Coed Duon Caerph 15 B7
Blackwood S Lanark 68 F6
Blackwood Hill Staffs 44 G3
Blacon Ches W 43 F6
Bladnoch Dumfries 55 D7
Bladon Oxon 27 G11
Blaen-gwynfi Neath 14 B4
Blaen-waun Carms 23 D7
Blaen-y-coed Carms 23 D8
Blaen-y-Cwm Denb 32 B6
Blaen-y-cwm Gwyn 32 C3
Blaen-y-cwm Powys 33 C6
Blaenannerch Ceredig 23 B7
Blaenau Ffestiniog Gwyn 41 F9
Blaenavon Torf 25 H9
Blaencelyn Ceredig 23 A8
Blaendyryn Powys 24 E6
Blaenffos Pembs 22 C6
Blaengarw Bridgend 14 B5
Blaengwrach Neath 24 H5
Blaenpennal Ceredig 24 B3
Blaenplwyf Ceredig 32 H1
Blaenporth Ceredig 23 B7
Blaenrhondda Rhondda 14 A5
Blaenycwm Ceredig 32 H4
Blagdon N Som 15 F11
Blagdon Torbay 5 E9
Blagdon Hill Som 7 E11
Blagill Cumb 57 B9
Blaguegate Lancs 43 B7
Blaich Highld 80 F2
Blain Highld 79 E9
Blaina Bl Gwent 25 H9
Blair Atholl Perth 81 G10
Blair Drummond Stirling 75 H10
Blairbeg N Ayrs 66 C3
Blairdaff Aberds 83 B8
Blairglas Argyll 68 B2
Blairgowrie Perth 76 C4
Blairhall Fife 69 B9
Blairingone Perth 76 H2
Blairland N Ayrs 66 B6
Blairlogie Stirling 75 H11
Blairlomond Argyll 74 H4
Blairmore Argyll 73 E10
Blairnamarrow Moray 82 B4
Blairquhosh Stirling 68 B4
Blair's Ferry Argyll 73 G8
Blairskaith E Dunb 68 C4
Blaisdon Glos 26 G4
Blakebrook Worcs 34 H4
Blakedown Worcs 34 H4
Blakelaw Borders 70 G6
Blakeley Staffs 34 F4
Blakeley Lane Staffs 44 H3
Blakemere Hereford 25 D10
Blakeney Glos 26 H3
Blakeney Norf 38 A6
Blakenhall Ches E 43 H10
Blakenhall W Mid 34 F5
Blakeshall Worcs 34 G4
Blakesley Northants 28 C3
Blanchland Northumb 57 A11
Bland Hill N Yorks 51 D8
Blandford Forum Dorset 9 D7
Blandford St Mary Dorset 9 D7
Blanefield Stirling 68 C4
Blankney Lincs 46 F4
Blantyre S Lanark 68 E5
Blar a'Chaorainn Highld 80 G3
Blaran Argyll 73 B7
Blarghour Argyll 73 B8
Blarmachfoldach Highld 80 G2
Blarnalearoch Highld 86 B4
Blashford Hants 9 D10
Blaston Leics 36 F4
Blatherwycke Northants 36 F5
Blawith Cumb 56 H4
Blaxhall Suff 31 C10
Blaxton S Yorks 45 B10
Blaydon T&W 63 G7
Bleadon N Som 15 F9
Bleak Hey Nook Gtr Man 44 B4
Blean Kent 21 E8
Bleasby Lincs 46 D5
Bleasby Notts 45 H11
Bleasdale Lancs 50 E1
Bleatarn Cumb 57 E9
Blebocraigs Fife 77 F7
Bleddfa Powys 25 B9
Bledington Glos 27 F9
Bledlow Bucks 18 A4
Bledlow Ridge Bucks 18 B4
Blegbie E Loth 70 D3
Blencarn Cumb 57 C8
Blencogo Cumb 56 B3
Blendworth Hants 10 C6
Blenheim Park Norf 38 B4
Blennerhasset Cumb 56 B3
Blervie Castle Moray 87 F13
Bletchingdon Oxon 28 G2
Bletchingley Sur 19 F10
Bletchley M Keynes 28 E5
Bletchley Shrops 34 B2
Bletherston Pembs 22 D5
Bletsoe Bedford 29 C7
Blewbury Oxon 18 C2
Blickling Norf 39 C7
Blidworth Notts 45 G9
Blindburn Northumb 62 B4
Blindcrake Cumb 56 C3
Blindley Heath Sur 19 G10
Blisland Corn 4 D2
Bliss Gate Worcs 26 A4
Blissford Hants 9 C10
Blisworth Northants 28 C4
Blithbury Staffs 35 C6
Blitterlees Cumb 56 A3
Blo' Norton Norf 38 H6
Blockley Glos 27 E8
Blofield Norf 39 E9
Blofield Heath Norf 39 D9
Bloomfield Borders 61 A11
Blore Staffs 44 H5
Blount's Green Staffs 35 B6
Blowick Mers 49 H3
Bloxham Oxon 27 E11
Bloxholm Lincs 46 G4
Bloxwich W Mid 34 E5
Bloxworth Dorset 9 E7
Blubberhouses N Yorks 51 D7
Blue Anchor Som 7 B9
Blue Anchor Swansea 23 G10
Blue Row Essex 31 G7
Blundeston Suff 39 F11
Blunham C Beds 29 C8
Blunsdon St Andrew Swindon 17 C8
Bluntington Worcs 26 A5
Bluntisham Cambs 29 A10
Blunts Corn 4 E4
Blyborough Lincs 46 C3
Blyford Suff 39 H10
Blymhill Staffs 34 D4
Blyth Northumb 63 E9
Blyth Notts 45 D10
Blyth Bridge Borders 69 F10
Blythburgh Suff 39 H10
Blythe Borders 70 F4
Blythe Bridge Staffs 34 A5
Blyton Lincs 46 C2
Boarhills Fife 77 F8
Boarhunt Hants 10 D5
Boars Head Gtr Man 43 B8
Boars Hill Oxon 17 A11
Boarshead E Sus 12 C4
Boarstall Bucks 28 G3
Boasley Cross Devon 6 G3
Boat of Garten Highld 81 B11
Boath Highld 87 D8
Bobbing Kent 20 E5
Bobbington Staffs 34 F4
Bobbingworth Essex 30 H2
Bocaddon Corn 4 F2
Bochastle Stirling 75 G9
Bocking Essex 30 F4
Bocking Churchstreet Essex 30 F4
Boddam Aberds 89 D11
Boddam Shetland 96 M5
Boddington Glos 26 F5
Bodedern Anglesey 40 B5
Bodelwyddan Denb 42 E3
Bodenham Hereford 26 C2
Bodenham Wilts 9 B10
Bodenham Moor Hereford 26 C2
Bodermid Gwyn 40 H3
Bodewryd Anglesey 40 A5
Bodfari Denb 42 E3
Bodffordd Anglesey 40 C6
Bodham Norf 39 A7
Bodiam E Sus 13 D6
Bodicote Oxon 27 E11
Bodieve Corn 3 B8
Bodinnick Corn 4 F2
Bodle Street Green E Sus 12 E5
Bodmin Corn 4 E1
Bodney Norf 38 F4
Bodorgan Anglesey 40 D5
Bodsham Kent 21 G8
Boduan Gwyn 40 G5
Bodymoor Heath Warks 35 F7
Bogallan Highld 87 F9
Bogbrae Aberds 89 E10
Bogend Borders 70 F6
Bogend S Ayrs 67 C6
Boghall W Loth 69 D8
Boghead S Lanark 68 F6
Bogmoor Moray 88 B3
Bogniebrae Aberds 88 D5
Bognor Regis W Sus 11 E8
Bograxie Aberds 83 B9
Bogside N Lanark 69 E7
Bogton Aberds 89 C6
Bogue Dumfries 55 A9
Bohenie Highld 80 E4
Bohortha Corn 3 F7
Bohuntine Highld 80 E4
Boirseam W Isles 90 J5
Bojewyan Corn 2 F2
Bolam Durham 58 D2
Bolam Northumb 62 E6
Bolberry Devon 5 H7
Bold Heath Mers 43 D8
Boldon T&W 63 G9
Boldon Colliery T&W 63 G9
Boldre Hants 10 E2
Boldron Durham 58 E1
Bole Notts 45 D11
Bolehill Derbys 44 G6
Boleside Borders 70 G3
Bolham Devon 7 E8
Bolham Water Devon 7 E10
Bolingey Corn 3 D6
Bollington Ches E 44 E3
Bollington Cross Ches E 44 E3
Bolney W Sus 12 D1
Bolnhurst Bedford 29 C7
Bolshan Angus 77 B9
Bolsover Derbys 45 E8
Bolsterstone S Yorks 44 C6
Bolstone Hereford 26 E2
Boltby N Yorks 58 H5
Bolter End Bucks 18 B4
Bolton Cumb 57 D8
Bolton E Loth 70 C4
Bolton E Yorks 52 D3
Bolton Gtr Man 43 B10
Bolton Northumb 63 B7
Bolton Abbey N Yorks 51 D6
Bolton Bridge N Yorks 51 D6
Bolton-by-Bowland Lancs 50 E3
Bolton-le-Sands Lancs 49 C4
Bolton Low Houses Cumb 56 B4
Bolton-on-Swale N Yorks 58 G3
Bolton Percy N Yorks 51 E11
Bolton Town End Lancs 49 C4
Bolton upon Dearne S Yorks 45 B8
Boltonfellend Cumb 61 G10
Boltongate Cumb 56 B4
Bolventor Corn 4 D2
Bomere Heath Shrops 33 D10
Bon-y-maen Swansea 14 B2
Bonar Bridge Highld 87 B9
Bonawe Argyll 74 D3
Bonby N Lincs 52 H6
Boncath Pembs 23 C7
Bonchester Bridge Borders 61 B11
Bonchurch IoW 10 G4
Bondleigh Devon 6 F5
Bonehill Devon 5 D8
Bonehill Staffs 35 E7
Bo'ness Falk 69 B8
Bonhill W Dunb 68 C2
Boningale Shrops 34 E4
Bonjedward Borders 62 A2
Bonkle N Lanark 69 E7
Bonnavoulin Highld 79 F8
Bonnington Edin 69 D10
Bonnington Kent 13 C9
Bonnybank Fife 76 G6
Bonnybridge Falk 69 B7
Bonnykelly Aberds 89 C8
Bonnyrigg and Lasswade Midloth 70 D2
Bonnyton Aberds 89 E6
Bonnyton Angus 76 D6
Bonnyton Angus 77 B9
Bonsall Derbys 44 G6
Bonskeid House Perth 75 A11
Bont Mon 25 G10
Bont-Dolgadfan Powys 32 E4
Bont-goch Ceredig 32 G2
Bont-newydd Conwy 42 E3
Bont Newydd Gwyn 32 C3
Bont Newydd Gwyn 41 F9
Bontddu Gwyn 32 D2
Bonthorpe Lincs 47 E8
Bontnewydd Ceredig 24 B3
Bontnewydd Gwyn 40 E6
Bontuchel Denb 42 G3
Bonvilston V Glam 14 D6
Booker Bucks 18 B5
Boon Borders 70 F4
Boosbeck Redcar 59 E7
Boot Cumb 56 F3
Boot Street Suff 31 D9
Booth W Yorks 50 G6
Booth Wood W Yorks 50 H6
Boothby Graffoe Lincs 46 G3
Boothby Pagnell Lincs 36 B5
Boothen Stoke 34 A4
Boothferry E Yorks 52 G3
Boothville Northants 28 B4
Bootle Cumb 56 H3
Bootle Mers 42 C6
Booton Norf 39 C7
Boquhan Stirling 68 B4
Boraston Shrops 26 A3
Borden Kent 20 E5
Borden W Sus 11 B7
Bordley N Yorks 50 C5
Bordon Hants 18 H5
Bordon Camp Hants 18 H4
Boreham Essex 30 H4
Boreham Wilts 16 G5
Boreham Street E Sus 12 E5
Borehamwood Herts 19 B8
Boreland Dumfries 61 D7
Boreland Stirling 75 D8
Borgh W Isles 84 H1
Borgh W Isles 90 J4
Borghastan W Isles 90 C7
Borgie Highld 93 D9
Borgue Dumfries 55 E9
Borgue Highld 94 H3
Borley Essex 30 D5
Bornais W Isles 84 F2
Bornesketaig Highld 85 A8
Borness Dumfries 55 E9
Borough Green Kent 20 F3
Boroughbridge N Yorks 51 C9
Borras Head Wrex 42 G6
Borreraig Highld 84 C6
Borrobol Lodge Highld 93 G11
Borrowash Derbys 35 B10
Borrowby N Yorks 58 H5
Borrowdale Cumb 56 E4
Borrowfield Aberds 83 D10
Borth Ceredig 32 F2
Borth-y-Gest Gwyn 41 G7
Borthwickbrae Borders 61 B10
Borthwickshiels Borders 61 B10
Borve Highld 85 D9
Borve Lodge W Isles 90 H5
Borwick Lancs 49 B5
Bosavern Corn 2 F2
Bosbury Hereford 26 D3
Boscastle Corn 4 B2
Boscombe Bmouth 9 E10
Boscombe Wilts 17 H9
Boscoppa Corn 3 D9
Bosham W Sus 11 D7
Bosherston Pembs 22 G4
Boskenna Corn 2 G3
Bosley Ches E 44 F3
Bossall N Yorks 52 C3
Bossiney Corn 4 C1
Bossingham Kent 21 G8
Bossington Som 7 B7
Bostock Green Ches W 43 F9
Boston Lincs 37 A9
Boston Long Hedges Lincs 47 H7
Boston Spa W Yorks 51 E10
Boston West Lincs 46 H6
Boswinger Corn 3 E8
Botallack Corn 2 F2
Botany Bay London 19 B9
Botcherby Cumb 61 H10
Botcheston Leics 35 E10
Botesdale Suff 38 H6
Bothal Northumb 63 E8
Bothamsall Notts 45 E10
Bothel Cumb 56 C3
Bothenhampton Dorset 8 E3
Bothwell S Lanark 68 E6
Botley Bucks 18 A6
Botley Hants 10 C4
Botley Oxon 27 H11
Botolph Claydon Bucks 28 F4
Botolphs W Sus 11 D10
Bottacks Highld 86 E7
Bottesford Leics 36 B4
Bottesford N Lincs 46 B2
Bottisham Cambs 30 B2
Bottlesford Wilts 17 F8
Bottom Boat W Yorks 51 G9
Bottom House Staffs 44 G4
Bottom o' th' Moor Gtr Man 43 A9
Bottom of Hutton Lancs 49 G4
Bottomcraig Fife 76 E6
Botusfleming Corn 4 E5
Botwnnog Gwyn 40 G4
Bough Beech Kent 19 G11
Boughrood Powys 25 E8
Boughspring Glos 16 B2
Boughton Norf 38 E2
Boughton Northants 28 B4
Boughton Notts 45 F10
Boughton Aluph Kent 21 G7
Boughton Lees Kent 21 G7
Boughton Malherbe Kent 20 G5
Boughton Monchelsea Kent 20 F4
Boughton Street Kent 21 F7
Boulby Redcar 59 E8
Boulden Shrops 33 G11
Boulmer Northumb 63 B8
Boulston Pembs 22 E4
Boultenstone Aberds 82 B6
Boultham Lincs 46 F3
Bourn Cambs 29 C10
Bourne Lincs 37 C6
Bourne End Bucks 18 C5
Bourne End C Beds 28 D6
Bourne End Herts 29 H7
Bournemouth Bmouth 9 E9
Bournes Green Glos 16 A6
Bournes Green Southend 20 C6
Bournheath Worcs 26 A6
Bournmoor Durham 58 A4
Bournville W Mid 34 G6
Bourton Dorset 9 A6
Bourton N Som 15 E9
Bourton Oxon 17 C9
Bourton Shrops 34 F1
Bourton on Dunsmore Warks 27 A11
Bourton on the Hill Glos 27 E8
Bourton-on-the-Water Glos 27 F8
Bousd Argyll 78 E5
Boustead Hill Cumb 61 H8
Bouth Cumb 56 H5
Bouthwaite N Yorks 51 B7
Boveney Bucks 18 D6
Boverton V Glam 14 E5
Bovey Tracey Devon 5 D9
Bovingdon Herts 19 A7
Bovingdon Green Bucks 18 C5
Bovingdon Green Herts 19 A7
Bovinger Essex 30 H2
Bovington Camp Dorset 9 F7
Bow Borders 70 F3
Bow Devon 6 F6
Bow Orkney 95 J4
Bow Brickhill M Keynes 28 E6
Bow of Fife Fife 76 F6
Bow Street Ceredig 32 G2
Bowbank Durham 57 D11
Bowburn Durham 58 C4
Bowcombe IoW 10 F3
Bowd Devon 7 G10
Bowden Borders 70 G4
Bowden Devon 5 G9
Bowden Hill Wilts 16 E6
Bowderdale Cumb 57 F8
Bowdon Gtr Man 43 D10
Bower Northumb 62 E3
Bower Hinton Som 8 C3
Bowerchalke Wilts 9 B9
Bowerhill Wilts 16 E6
Bowermadden Highld 94 D4
Bowers Gifford Essex 20 C4
Bowershall Fife 69 A9
Bowertower Highld 94 D4
Bowes Durham 57 E11
Bowgreave Lancs 49 E4
Bowgreen Gtr Man 43 D10
Bowhill Borders 70 H3
Bowhouse Dumfries 60 G6
Bowland Bridge Cumb 56 H6
Bowley Hereford 26 C2
Bowlhead Green Sur 18 H6
Bowling W Dunb 68 C3
Bowling W Yorks 51 F7
Bowling Bank Wrex 43 H6
Bowling Green Worcs 26 C5
Bowmanstead Cumb 56 G5
Bowmore Argyll 64 C4
Bowness-on-Solway Cumb 61 G8
Bowness-on-Windermere Cumb 56 G6
Bowsden Northumb 71 F8
Bowside Lodge Highld 93 C11
Bowston Cumb 57 G6
Bowthorpe Norf 39 E7
Box Glos 16 A5
Box Wilts 16 E5
Box End Bedford 29 D7
Boxbush Glos 26 G4
Boxford Suff 30 D6
Boxford W Berks 17 D11
Boxgrove W Sus 11 D8
Boxley Kent 20 F4
Boxmoor Herts 29 H7
Boxted Essex 30 E6
Boxted Suff 30 C5
Boxted Cross Essex 31 E7
Boxted Heath Essex 31 E7
Boxworth Cambs 29 B10
Boxworth End Cambs 29 B10
Boyden Gate Kent 21 E9
Boylestone Derbys 35 B7
Boyndie Aberds 89 B6
Boynton E Yorks 53 C7
Boysack Angus 77 C9
Boyton Corn 6 G2
Boyton Suff 31 D10
Boyton Wilts 16 H6
Boyton Cross Essex 30 H3
Boyton End Suff 30 D4
Bozeat Northants 28 C6
Braaid IoM 48 E3
Braal Castle Highld 94 D3
Brabling Green Suff 31 B9
Brabourne Kent 13 B9
Brabourne Lees Kent 13 B9
Brabster Highld 94 D5
Bracadale Highld 85 E8
Bracara Highld 79 B10
Braceborough Lincs 37 D6
Bracebridge Lincs 46 F3
Bracebridge Heath Lincs 46 F3
Bracebridge Low Fields Lincs 46 F3
Braceby Lincs 36 B6
Bracewell Lancs 50 E4
Brackenfield Derbys 45 G7
Brackenthwaite Cumb 56 B4
Brackenthwaite N Yorks 51 D8
Bracklesham W Sus 11 E7
Brackletter Highld 80 E3
Brackley Argyll 65 D8
Brackley Northants 28 E2
Brackloch Highld 92 G4
Bracknell Brack 18 E5
Braco Perth 75 G11
Bracobrae Moray 88 C5
Bracon Ash Norf 39 F7
Bracorina Highld 79 B10
Bradbourne Derbys 44 G6
Bradbury Durham 58 D4

Bradda IoM 48 F1
Bradden Northants 28 D3
Braddock Corn 4 E2
Bradeley Stoke 44 G2
Bradenham Bucks 18 B5
Bradenham Norf 38 E5
Bradenstoke Wilts 17 D7
Bradfield Essex 31 E8
Bradfield Norf 39 B8
Bradfield W Berks 18 D3
Bradfield Combust Suff 30 C5
Bradfield Green Ches E 43 G9
Bradfield Heath Essex 31 F8
Bradfield St Clare Suff 30 C6
Bradfield St George Suff 30 B6
Bradford Corn 4 D2
Bradford Derbys 44 F6
Bradford Devon 6 F3
Bradford Northumb 71 G10
Bradford W Yorks 51 F7
Bradford Abbas Dorset 8 C4
Bradford Leigh Wilts 16 E5
Bradford-on-Avon Wilts 16 E5
Bradford-on-Tone Som 7 D10
Bradford Peverell Dorset 8 E5
Brading IoW 10 F5
Bradley Derbys 44 H6
Bradley Hants 18 G3
Bradley NE Lincs 46 B6
Bradley Staffs 34 D4
Bradley W Mid 34 F5
Bradley W Yorks 51 G7
Bradley Green Worcs 26 B6
Bradley in the Moors Staffs 35 A6
Bradley Stoke S Glos 16 C3
Bradlow Hereford 26 E4
Bradmore Notts 36 B1
Bradmore W Mid 34 F4
Bradninch Devon 7 F9
Bradnop Staffs 44 G4
Bradpole Dorset 8 E3
Bradshaw Gtr Man 43 A10
Bradshaw W Yorks 44 A4
Bradstone Devon 4 C4
Bradwall Green Ches E 43 F10
Bradway S Yorks 45 D7
Bradwell Derbys 44 D5
Bradwell Essex 30 F5
Bradwell M Keynes 28 E5
Bradwell Norf 39 E11
Bradwell Staffs 44 H2
Bradwell Grove Oxon 27 H9
Bradwell on Sea Essex 31 H7
Bradwell Waterside Essex 30 H6
Bradworthy Devon 6 E2
Bradworthy Cross Devon 6 E2
Brae Dumfries 60 F4
Brae Highld 91 J13
Brae Highld 92 J7
Brae Shetland 96 G5
Brae of Achnahaird Highld 92 H3
Brae Roy Lodge Highld 80 D5
Braeantra Highld 87 D8
Braedownie Angus 82 F4
Braefield Highld 86 H7
Braegrum Perth 76 E3
Braehead Dumfries 55 D7
Braehead Orkney 95 D5
Braehead Orkney 95 H6
Braehead S Lanark 69 E8
Braehead S Lanark 69 G7
Braehead of Lunan Angus 77 B9
Braehoulland Shetland 96 F4
Braehungie Highld 94 G3
Braelangwell Lodge Highld 87 B8
Braemar Aberds 82 D3
Braemore Highld 86 D4
Braemore Highld 94 G2
Braes of Enzie Moray 88 C3
Braeside Invclyd 73 F11
Braeswick Orkney 95 E7
Braewick Shetland 96 H5
Brafferton Darl 58 D3
Brafferton N Yorks 51 B10
Brafield-on-the-Green Northants 28 C5
Bragar W Isles 91 C7
Bragbury End Herts 29 F9
Bragleenmore Argyll 74 E2
Braichmelyn Gwyn 41 D8
Braid Edin 69 D11
Braides Lancs 49 D4
Braidley N Yorks 50 A6
Braidwood S Lanark 69 F7
Braigo Argyll 64 B3
Brailsford Derbys 35 A8
Brainshaugh Northumb 63 C8
Braintree Essex 30 F4
Braiseworth Suff 31 A8
Braishfield Hants 10 B2
Braithwaite Cumb 56 D4
Braithwaite S Yorks 45 A10
Braithwaite W Yorks 50 E6
Braithwell S Yorks 45 C9
Bramber W Sus 11 C10
Bramcote Notts 35 B11
Bramcote Warks 35 G10
Bramdean Hants 10 B5
Bramerton Norf 39 E8
Bramfield Herts 29 G9
Bramfield Suff 31 A10
Bramford Suff 31 D8
Bramhall Gtr Man 44 D2
Bramham W Yorks 51 E10
Bramhope W Yorks 51 E8
Bramley Hants 18 F3
Bramley S Yorks 45 C8
Bramley Sur 19 G7
Bramley W Yorks 51 F8
Bramling Kent 21 F9
Brampford Speke Devon 7 G8
Brampton Cambs 29 A9
Brampton Cumb 57 D8
Brampton Cumb 61 G11
Brampton Derbys 45 E7
Brampton Hereford 25 E11
Brampton Lincs 46 E2
Brampton Norf 39 C8
Brampton S Yorks 45 B8
Brampton Suff 39 G10
Brampton Abbotts Hereford 26 F3
Brampton Ash Northants 36 G3
Brampton Bryan Hereford 25 A10
Brampton en le Morthen S Yorks 45 D8
Bramshall Staffs 35 B6
Bramshaw Hants 10 C1
Bramshill Hants 18 E4
Bramshott Hants 11 A7
Bran End Essex 30 F3
Branault Highld 79 E8
Brancaster Norf 38 A3
Brancaster Staithe Norf 38 A3
Brancepeth Durham 58 C3
Branch End Northumb 62 G6
Branchill Moray 87 F13
Brand Green Glos 26 F4
Branderburgh Moray 88 A2
Brandesburton E Yorks 53 E7
Brandeston Suff 31 B9
Brandhill Shrops 33 H10
Brandis Corner Devon 6 F3
Brandiston Norf 39 C7
Brandon Durham 58 C3
Brandon Lincs 46 H3
Brandon Northumb 62 B6
Brandon Suff 38 G3
Brandon Warks 35 H10
Brandon Bank Cambs 38 G2
Brandon Creek Norf 38 F2
Brandon Parva Norf 39 E6
Brandsby N Yorks 52 B1
Brandy Wharf Lincs 46 C4
Brane Corn 2 G3
Branksome Poole 9 E9
Branksome Park Poole 9 E9
Bransby Lincs 46 E2
Branscombe Devon 7 H10
Bransford Worcs 26 C4
Bransgore Hants 9 E10
Branshill Clack 69 A7
Bransholme Hull 53 F7
Branson's Cross Worcs 27 A7
Branston Leics 36 C4
Branston Lincs 46 F4
Branston Staffs 35 C8
Branston Booths Lincs 46 F4
Branstone IoW 10 F4
Bransty Cumb 56 E1
Brant Broughton Lincs 46 G3
Brantham Suff 31 E8
Branthwaite Cumb 56 C4
Branthwaite Cumb 56 D2
Brantingham E Yorks 52 G5
Branton Northumb 62 B6
Branton S Yorks 45 B10
Branxholm Park Borders 61 B10
Branxholme Borders 61 B10
Branxton Northumb 71 G7
Brassey Green Ches W 43 F8
Brassington Derbys 44 G6
Brasted Kent 19 F11
Brasted Chart Kent 19 F11
Brathens Aberds 83 D8
Bratoft Lincs 47 F8
Brattleby Lincs 46 D3
Bratton Telford 34 D2
Bratton Wilts 16 F6
Bratton Clovelly Devon 6 G3
Bratton Fleming Devon 6 C5
Bratton Seymour Som 8 B5
Braughing Herts 29 F10
Braunston Northants 28 B2
Braunston-in-Rutland Rutland 36 E4
Braunstone Town Leicester 36 E1
Braunton Devon 6 C3
Brawby N Yorks 52 B3
Brawl Highld 93 C11
Brawlbin Highld 94 E2
Bray Windsor 18 D6
Bray Shop Corn 4 D4
Bray Wick Windsor 18 D5
Braybrooke Northants 36 G3
Braye Ald 11
Brayford Devon 6 C5
Braystones Cumb 56 F2
Braythorn N Yorks 51 E8
Brayton N Yorks 52 F2
Brazacott Corn 6 G1
Breach Kent 20 E5
Breachacha Castle Argyll 78 F4
Breachwood Green Herts 29 F8
Breacleit W Isles 90 D6
Breaden Heath Shrops 33 B10
Breadsall Derbys 35 B9
Breadstone Glos 16 A4
Breage Corn 2 G5
Breakachy Highld 86 G7
Bream Glos 26 H3
Breamore Hants 9 C10
Brean Som 15 F8
Breanais W Isles 90 E4
Brearton N Yorks 51 C9
Breascleit W Isles 90 D7
Breaston Derbys 35 B10
Brechfa Carms 23 C10
Brechin Angus 77 A8
Breck of Cruan Orkney 95 G4
Breckan Orkney 95 H3
Breckrey Highld 85 B10
Brecon = Aberhonddu Powys 25 F7
Bredbury Gtr Man 44 C3
Brede E Sus 13 E7
Bredenbury Hereford 26 C3
Bredfield Suff 31 C9
Bredgar Kent 20 E5
Bredhurst Kent 20 E4
Bredicot Worcs 26 C6
Bredon Worcs 26 E6
Bredon's Norton Worcs 26 E6
Bredwardine Hereford 25 D10
Breedon on the Hill Leics 35 C10
Breibhig W Isles 84 J1
Breibhig W Isles 91 D9
Breich W Loth 69 D8
Breightmet Gtr Man 43 B10
Breighton E Yorks 52 F3
Breinton Hereford 25 E11
Breinton Common Hereford 25 D11
Breiwick Shetland 96 J6
Bremhill Wilts 16 D6
Bremirehoull Shetland 96 L6
Brenchley Kent 12 B5
Brendon Devon 7 B6
Brenkley T&W 63 F8
Brent Eleigh Suff 30 D6
Brent Knoll Som 15 F9
Brent Pelham Herts 29 E11
Brentford London 19 D8
Brentingby Leics 36 D3
Brentwood Essex 20 B2
Brenzett Kent 13 D9
Brereton Staffs 35 D6
Brereton Green Ches E 43 F10
Brereton Heath Ches E 44 F2
Bressingham Norf 39 G6
Bretby Derbys 35 C8
Bretford Warks 35 H10
Bretforton Worcs 27 D7
Bretherdale Head Cumb 57 F7
Bretherton Lancs 49 G4
Brettabister Shetland 96 H6
Brettenham Norf 38 G5
Brettenham Suff 30 C6
Bretton Derbys 44 E6
Bretton Flint 42 F6
Brewer Street Sur 19 F10
Brewlands Bridge Angus 76 A4
Brewood Staffs 34 E4
Briach Moray 87 F13
Briants Puddle Dorset 9 E7
Brick End Essex 30 F2
Brickendon Herts 29 H10
Bricket Wood Herts 19 A8
Bricklehampton Worcs 26 D6
Bride IoM 48 B4
Bridekirk Cumb 56 C3
Bridell Pembs 22 B6
Bridestowe Devon 4 C6
Brideswell Aberds 88 E5
Bridford Devon 5 C9
Bridfordmills Devon 5 C9
Bridge Kent 21 F8
Bridge End Lincs 37 B7
Bridge Green Essex 29 E11
Bridge Hewick N Yorks 51 B9
Bridge of Alford Aberds 83 B7
Bridge of Allan Stirling 75 H10
Bridge of Avon Moray 88 E1
Bridge of Awe Argyll 74 E3
Bridge of Balgie Perth 75 C8
Bridge of Cally Perth 76 B4
Bridge of Canny Aberds 83 D8
Bridge of Craigisla Angus 76 B5
Bridge of Dee Dumfries 55 D10
Bridge of Don Aberdeen 83 B11
Bridge of Dun Angus 77 B9
Bridge of Dye Aberds 83 E8
Bridge of Earn Perth 76 F4
Bridge of Ericht Perth 75 B8
Bridge of Feugh Aberds 83 D9
Bridge of Forss Highld 93 C13
Bridge of Gairn Aberds 82 D5
Bridge of Gaur Perth 75 B8
Bridge of Muchalls Aberds 83 D10
Bridge of Oich Highld 80 C5
Bridge of Orchy Argyll 74 D5
Bridge of Waith Orkney 95 G3
Bridge of Walls Shetland 96 H4
Bridge of Weir Renfs 68 D2
Bridge Sollers Hereford 25 D11
Bridge Street Suff 30 D5
Bridge Trafford Ches W 43 E7
Bridge Yate S Glos 16 D3
Bridgefoot Angus 76 D6
Bridgefoot Cumb 56 D2
Bridgehampton Som 8 B4
Bridgehill Durham 58 A1
Bridgemary Hants 10 D4
Bridgemont Derbys 44 D4
Bridgend Aberds 83 B7
Bridgend Aberds 88 E5
Bridgend Angus 83 G7
Bridgend Argyll 64 B4
Bridgend Argyll 65 E8
Bridgend Argyll 73 D7
Bridgend = Pen-y-bont ar Ogwr Bridgend 14 D5
Bridgend Cumb 56 E5
Bridgend Fife 76 F6
Bridgend Moray 88 E3
Bridgend N Lanark 68 C5
Bridgend Pembs 22 B6
Bridgend W Loth 69 C9
Bridgend of Lintrathen Angus 76 B5
Bridgerule Devon 6 F1
Bridges Shrops 33 F9
Bridgeton Glasgow 68 D5
Bridgetown Corn 4 C4
Bridgetown Som 7 C8
Bridgham Norf 38 G5
Bridgnorth Shrops 34 F3
Bridgtown Staffs 34 E5
Bridgwater Som 15 H9
Bridlington E Yorks 53 C7
Bridport Dorset 8 E3
Bridstow Hereford 26 F2
Brierfield Lancs 50 F4
Brierley Glos 26 G3
Brierley Hereford 25 C11
Brierley S Yorks 45 A8
Brierley Hill W Mid 34 G5
Briery Hill Bl Gwent 25 H8
Brig o'Turk Stirling 75 G8
Brigg N Lincs 46 B4
Briggswath N Yorks 59 F9
Brigham Cumb 56 C2
Brigham E Yorks 53 D6
Brighouse W Yorks 51 G7
Brighstone IoW 10 F3
Brightgate Derbys 44 G6
Brighthampton Oxon 17 A10
Brightling E Sus 12 D5
Brightlingsea Essex 31 G7
Brighton Brighton 12 F2
Brighton Corn 3 D8
Brighton Hill Hants 18 G3
Brightons Falk 69 C8
Brightwalton W Berks 17 D11
Brightwell Suff 31 D9
Brightwell Baldwin Oxon 18 B3
Brightwell cum Sotwell Oxon 18 B2
Brignall Durham 58 E1
Brigsley NE Lincs 46 B6
Brigsteer Cumb 57 H6
Brigstock Northants 36 G5
Brill Bucks 28 G3
Brilley Hereford 25 D9
Brimaston Pembs 22 D4
Brimfield Hereford 26 B2
Brimington Derbys 45 E8
Brimley Devon 5 D8
Brimpsfield Glos 26 G6
Brimpton W Berks 18 E2
Brims Orkney 95 K3
Brimscombe Glos 16 A5
Brimstage Mers 42 D6
Brinacory Highld 79 B10
Brind E Yorks 52 F3
Brindister Shetland 96 H4
Brindister Shetland 96 K6
Brindle Lancs 50 G2
Brindley Ford Stoke 44 G2
Brineton Staffs 34 D4
Bringhurst Leics 36 F4
Brington Cambs 37 H6
Brinian Orkney 95 F5
Briningham Norf 38 B6
Brinkhill Lincs 47 E7
Brinkley Cambs 30 C3
Brinklow Warks 35 H10
Brinkworth Wilts 17 C7
Brinmore Highld 81 A8
Brinscall Lancs 50 G2
Brinsea N Som 15 E10
Brinsley Notts 45 H8
Brinsop Hereford 25 D11
Brinsworth S Yorks 45 D8
Brinton Norf 38 B6
Brisco Cumb 56 A6
Brisley Norf 38 C5
Brislington Bristol 16 D3
Bristol Bristol 16 D2
Briston Norf 39 B6
Britannia Lancs 50 G4
Britford Wilts 9 B10
Brithdir Gwyn 32 D3
British Legion Village Kent 20 F4
Briton Ferry Neath 14 B3
Britwell Salome Oxon 18 B3
Brixham Torbay 5 F10
Brixton Devon 5 F6
Brixton London 19 D10
Brixton Deverill Wilts 16 H5
Brixworth Northants 28 A4
Brize Norton Oxon 27 H10
Broad Blunsdon Swindon 17 B8
Broad Campden Glos 27 E8
Broad Chalke Wilts 9 B9
Broad Green C Beds 28 D6
Broad Green Essex 30 F5
Broad Green Worcs 26 C4
Broad Haven Pembs 22 E3
Broad Heath Worcs 26 B3
Broad Hill Cambs 38 H1
Broad Hinton Wilts 17 D8
Broad Laying Hants 17 E11
Broad Marston Worcs 27 D8
Broad Oak Carms 23 D10
Broad Oak Cumb 56 G3
Broad Oak Dorset 8 E3
Broad Oak Dorset 9 C6
Broad Oak E Sus 12 D5
Broad Oak E Sus 13 E7
Broad Oak Hereford 25 F11
Broad Oak Mers 43 C8
Broad Street Kent 20 F5
Broad Street Green Essex 30 H5
Broad Town Wilts 17 D7
Broadbottom Gtr Man 44 C3
Broadbridge W Sus 11 D7
Broadbridge Heath W Sus 11 A10
Broadclyst Devon 7 G8
Broadfield Gtr Man 44 A2
Broadfield Lancs 49 G5
Broadfield Pembs 22 F6
Broadfield W Sus 12 C1
Broadford Highld 85 F11
Broadford Bridge W Sus 11 B9
Broadhaugh Borders 61 C10
Broadhaven Highld 94 E5
Broadheath Gtr Man 43 D10
Broadhembury Devon 7 F10
Broadhempston Devon 5 E9
Broadholme Derbys 45 H7
Broadholme Lincs 46 E2
Broadland Row E Sus 13 E7
Broadlay Carms 23 F8
Broadley Lancs 50 H4
Broadley Moray 88 B3
Broadley Common Essex 29 H11
Broadmayne Dorset 8 F6
Broadmeadows Borders 70 G3
Broadmere Hants 18 G3
Broadmoor Pembs 22 F5
Broadoak Kent 21 E8
Broadrashes Moray 88 C4
Broadsea Aberds 89 B9
Broadstairs Kent 21 E10
Broadstone Poole 9 E9
Broadstone Shrops 33 G11
Broadtown Lane Wilts 17 D7
Broadwas Worcs 26 C4
Broadwater Herts 29 F9
Broadwater W Sus 11 D10
Broadway Carms 23 F7
Broadway Pembs 22 E3
Broadway Som 8 C2
Broadway Suff 39 H9
Broadway Worcs 27 E7
Broadwell Glos 26 G2
Broadwell Glos 27 F9
Broadwell Oxon 17 A9
Broadwell Warks 27 B11
Broadwell House Northumb 57 A11
Broadwey Dorset 8 F5
Broadwindsor Dorset 8 D3
Broadwood Kelly Devon 6 F5
Broadwoodwidger Devon 4 C5
Brobury Hereford 25 D10
Brochel Highld 85 D10
Brochloch Dumfries 67 G8
Brochroy Argyll 74 D3
Brockamin Worcs 26 C4
Brockbridge Hants 10 C5
Brockdam Northumb 63 A7
Brockdish Norf 39 H8
Brockenhurst Hants 10 D2
Brocketsbrae S Lanark 69 G7
Brockford Street Suff 31 B8
Brockhall Northants 28 B3
Brockham Sur 19 G8
Brockhampton Glos 27 F7
Brockhampton Hereford 26 E2
Brockholes W Yorks 44 A5
Brockhurst Derbys 45 F7
Brockhurst Hants 10 D5
Brocklebank Cumb 56 B5
Brocklesby Lincs 46 A5
Brockley N Som 15 E10
Brockley Green Suff 30 C5
Brockleymoor Cumb 57 C6
Brockton Shrops 33 E9
Brockton Shrops 33 G9
Brockton Shrops 34 E3
Brockton Shrops 34 F1
Brockton Telford 34 D3
Brockweir Glos 15 A11
Brockwood Hants 10 B5
Brockworth Glos 26 G5
Brocton Staffs 34 D5
Brodick N Ayrs 66 C3
Brodsworth S Yorks 45 B9
Brogaig Highld 85 B9
Brogborough C Beds 28 E6
Broken Cross Ches E 44 E2
Broken Cross Ches W 43 E9
Brokenborough Wilts 16 C6
Bromborough Mers 42 D6
Brome Suff 39 H7
Brome Street Suff 39 H7
Bromeswell Suff 31 C10
Bromfield Cumb 56 B3
Bromfield Shrops 33 H10
Bromham Bedford 29 C7
Bromham Wilts 16 E6
Bromley London 19 E11
Bromley W Mid 34 G5
Bromley Common London 19 E11
Bromley Green Kent 13 C8
Brompton Medway 20 E4
Brompton N Yorks 52 A5
Brompton N Yorks 58 G4
Brompton-on-Swale N Yorks 58 G3
Brompton Ralph Som 7 C9
Brompton Regis Som 7 C8
Bromsash Hereford 26 F3
Bromsberrow Hth. Glos 26 E4
Bromsgrove Worcs 26 A6
Bromyard Hereford 26 C3
Bromyard Downs Hereford 26 C3
Bronaber Gwyn 41 G9
Brongest Ceredig 23 B8
Bronington Wrex 33 B10
Bronllys Powys 25 E8
Bronnant Ceredig 24 B3
Bronwydd Arms Carms 23 D9
Bronydd Powys 25 D9
Bronygarth Shrops 33 B8
Brook Carms 23 F7
Brook Hants 10 B2
Brook Hants 10 C1
Brook IoW 10 F2
Brook Kent 13 B9
Brook Sur 18 H6
Brook Sur 19 G7
Brook End Bedford 29 B7
Brook Hill Hants 10 C1
Brook Street Kent 13 C8
Brook Street Kent 20 G2
Brook Street W Sus 12 D2
Brooke Norf 39 F8
Brooke Rutland 36 E4
Brookenby Lincs 46 C6
Brookend Glos 16 B2
Brookfield Renfs 68 D3
Brookhouse Lancs 49 C5
Brookhouse Green Ches E 44 F2
Brookland Kent 13 D8
Brooklands Dumfries 60 F4
Brooklands Gtr Man 43 C10
Brooklands Shrops 33 A11
Brookmans Park Herts 19 A9
Brooks Powys 33 F7
Brooks Green W Sus 11 B10
Brookthorpe Glos 26 G5
Brookville Norf 38 F3
Brookwood Sur 18 F6
Broom C Beds 29 D8
Broom S Yorks 45 C8
Broom Warks 27 C7
Broom Worcs 34 H5
Broom Green Norf 38 C5
Broom Hill Dorset 9 D9
Broome Norf 39 F9
Broome Shrops 33 G10
Broome Park Northumb 63 B7
Broomedge Warr 43 D10
Broomer's Corner W Sus 11 B10
Broomfield Aberds 89 E9
Broomfield Essex 30 G4
Broomfield Kent 20 F5
Broomfield Kent 21 E8
Broomfield Som 7 C11
Broomfleet E Yorks 52 G4
Broomhall Ches E 43 H9
Broomhall Windsor 18 E6
Broomhaugh Northumb 62 G6
Broomhill Norf 38 E2
Broomhill Northumb 63 C8
Broomhill S Yorks 45 B8
Broomholm Norf 39 B9
Broomley Northumb 62 G6
Broompark Durham 58 B3
Broom's Green Glos 26 E4
Broomy Lodge Hants 9 C11
Brora Highld 93 J12
Broseley Shrops 34 E2
Brotherhouse Bar Lincs 37 D8
Brotherstone Borders 70 G5
Brothertoft Lincs 46 H6
Brotherton N Yorks 51 G10
Brotton Redcar 59 E7
Broubster Highld 93 C13
Brough Cumb 57 E9
Brough Derbys 44 D5
Brough E Yorks 52 G5
Brough Highld 94 C4
Brough Notts 46 G2
Brough Orkney 95 G4
Brough Shetland 96 F7
Brough Shetland 96 F6
Brough Shetland 96 G7
Brough Shetland 96 H6
Brough Shetland 96 J7
Brough Lodge Shetland 96 D7
Brough Sowerby Cumb 57 E9
Broughall Shrops 34 A1
Broughton Borders 69 G10
Broughton Cambs 37 H8
Broughton Flint 42 F6
Broughton Hants 10 A2
Broughton Lancs 49 F5
Broughton M Keynes 28 D5
Broughton N Lincs 46 B3
Broughton N Yorks 50 D5
Broughton N Yorks 52 B3
Broughton Northants 36 H4
Broughton Orkney 95 D5
Broughton Oxon 27 E11
Broughton V Glam 14 D5
Broughton Astley Leics 35 F11
Broughton Beck Cumb 49 A2
Broughton Common Wilts 16 E5
Broughton Gifford Wilts 16 E5
Broughton Hackett Worcs 26 C6
Broughton in Furness Cumb 56 H4
Broughton Mills Cumb 56 G4
Broughton Moor Cumb 56 C2
Broughton Park Gtr Man 44 B2
Broughton Poggs Oxon 17 A9
Broughtown Orkney 95 D7
Broughty Ferry Dundee 77 D7
Browhouses Dumfries 61 G8
Browland Shetland 96 H4
Brown Candover Hants 18 H2
Brown Edge Lancs 42 A6
Brown Edge Staffs 44 G3
Brown Heath Ches W 43 F7
Brownhill Aberds 89 D8
Brownhill Aberds 89 D6
Brownhill Blackburn 50 F2
Brownhill Shrops 33 C10
Brownhills Fife 77 F8
Brownhills W Mid 34 E6
Brownlow Ches E 44 F2
Brownlow Heath Ches E 44 F2
Brownmuir Aberds 83 F9
Brown's End Glos 26 E4
Brownshill Glos 16 A5
Brownston Devon 5 F7
Brownyside Northumb 63 A7
Broxa N Yorks 59 G10
Broxbourne Herts 29 H10
Broxburn E Loth 70 C5
Broxburn W Loth 69 C9
Broxholme Lincs 46 E3
Broxted Essex 30 F2
Broxton Ches W 43 G7
Broxwood Hereford 25 C10
Broyle Side E Sus 12 E3
Brù W Isles 91 C8
Bruairnis W Isles 84 H2
Bruan Highld 94 G5
Bruar Lodge Perth 81 F10
Brucehill W Dunb 68 C2
Bruera Ches W 43 F7
Bruern Abbey Oxon 27 F9
Bruichladdich Argyll 64 B3
Bruisyard Suff 31 B10
Brumby N Lincs 46 B2
Brund Staffs 44 F5
Brundall Norf 39 E9
Brundish Suff 31 B9
Brundish Street Suff 31 A9
Brunery Highld 79 D10
Brunshaw Lancs 50 F4
Brunswick Village T&W 63 F8
Bruntcliffe W Yorks 51 G8
Bruntingthorpe Leics 36 F2
Brunton Fife 76 E6
Brunton Northumb 63 A8
Brunton Wilts 17 F9
Brushford Devon 6 F5
Brushford Som 7 D8
Bruton Som 8 A5
Bryanston Dorset 9 D7
Brydekirk Dumfries 61 F7
Bryher Scilly 2 C2
Brymbo Wrex 42 G5
Brympton Som 8 C4
Bryn Carms 23 F10
Bryn Gtr Man 43 B8
Bryn Neath 14 B4
Bryn Shrops 33 G8
Bryn-coch Neath 14 B3
Bryn Du Anglesey 40 C5
Bryn Gates Gtr Man 43 B8
Bryn-glas Conwy 41 D10
Bryn Golau Rhondda 14 C5
Bryn-Iwan Carms 23 C8
Bryn-mawr Gwyn 40 G4
Bryn-nantllech Conwy 42 F2
Bryn-penarth Powys 33 E7
Bryn Rhyd-yr-Arian Conwy 42 F2
Bryn Saith Marchog Denb 42 G3
Bryn Sion Gwyn 32 D4
Bryn-y-gwenin Mon 25 G10
Bryn-y-maen Conwy 41 C10
Bryn-yr-eryr Gwyn 40 F5
Brynamman Carms 24 G4
Brynberian Pembs 22 C6
Brynbryddan Neath 14 B3
Brynbuga = Usk Mon 15 A9
Bryncae Rhondda 14 C5
Bryncethin Bridgend 14 C5
Bryncir Gwyn 40 F6
Bryncroes Gwyn 40 G4
Bryncrug Gwyn 32 E2
Bryneglwys Denb 42 H4
Brynford Flint 42 E4
Bryngwran Anglesey 40 C5
Bryngwyn Ceredig 23 B7
Bryngwyn Mon 25 H10
Bryngwyn Powys 25 D8
Brynhenllan Pembs 22 C5
Brynhoffnant Ceredig 23 A8
Brynithel Bl Gwent 15 A8
Brynmawr Bl Gwent 25 G8
Brynmenyn Bridgend 14 C5
Brynmill Swansea 14 B2
Brynna Rhondda 14 C5
Brynrefail Anglesey 40 B6
Brynrefail Gwyn 41 D7
Brynsadler Rhondda 14 C6
Brynsiencyn Anglesey 40 D6
Brynteg Anglesey 40 B6
Brynteg Ceredig 23 B9
Buaile nam Bodach W Isles 84 H2
Bualintur Highld 85 F9
Buarthmeini Gwyn 41 G10
Bubbenhall Warks 27 A10
Bubwith E Yorks 52 F3
Buccleuch Borders 61 B9
Buchanhaven Aberds 89 D11
Buchanty Perth 76 E2
Buchlyvie Stirling 68 A4
Buckabank Cumb 56 B5
Buckden Cambs 29 B8
Buckden N Yorks 50 B5
Buckenham Norf 39 E9
Buckerell Devon 7 F10
Buckfast Devon 5 E8
Buckfastleigh Devon 5 E8
Buckhaven Fife 76 H6
Buckholm Borders 70 G3
Buckholt Mon 26 G2
Buckhorn Weston Dorset 9 B6
Buckhurst Hill Essex 19 B11
Buckie Moray 88 B4
Buckies Highld 94 D3
Buckingham Bucks 28 E3
Buckland Bucks 28 G5
Buckland Devon 5 G7
Buckland Glos 27 E7
Buckland Hants 10 E2
Buckland Herts 29 E10
Buckland Kent 21 G10
Buckland Oxon 17 B10
Buckland Sur 19 F9
Buckland Brewer Devon 6 D3
Buckland Common Bucks 28 H6
Buckland Dinham Som 16 F4
Buckland Filleigh Devon 6 F3
Buckland in the Moor Devon 5 D8
Buckland Monachorum Devon 4 E5
Buckland Newton Dorset 8 D5
Buckland St Mary Som 8 C1
Bucklebury W Berks 18 D2
Bucklegate Lincs 37 B9
Bucklerheads Angus 77 D7
Bucklers Hard Hants 10 E3
Bucklesham Suff 31 D9
Buckley = Bwcle Flint 42 F5
Bucklow Hill Ches E 43 D10
Buckminster Leics 36 C4
Bucknall Lincs 46 F5
Bucknall Stoke 44 H3
Bucknell Oxon 28 F2
Bucknell Shrops 25 A10
Buckpool Moray 88 B4
Buck's Cross Devon 6 D2
Bucks Green W Sus 11 A9
Bucks Horn Oak Hants 18 G5
Buck's Mills Devon 6 D2
Bucksburn Aberdeen 83 C10
Buckshaw Village Lancs 50 G1
Buckskin Hants 18 F3
Buckton E Yorks 53 B7
Buckton Hereford 25 A10
Buckton Northumb 71 G9
Buckworth Cambs 37 H7
Budbrooke Warks 27 B9
Budby Notts 45 F10
Budd's Titson Corn 4 A3
Bude Corn 6 F1
Budlake Devon 7 G8
Budle Northumb 71 G10
Budleigh Salterton Devon 7 H9
Budock Water Corn 3 F6
Buerton Ches E 34 A2
Buffler's Holt Bucks 28 E3
Bugbrooke Northants 28 C3
Buglawton Ches E 44 F2
Bugle Corn 3 D9
Bugley Wilts 16 G5
Bugthorpe E Yorks 52 D3
Buildwas Shrops 34 E2
Builth Road Powys 25 C7
Builth Wells = Llanfair-ym-Muallt Powys 25 C7
Buirgh W Isles 90 H5
Bulby Lincs 37 C6
Bulcote Notts 36 A2
Buldoo Highld 93 C12
Bulford Wilts 17 G8
Bulford Camp Wilts 17 G8
Bulkeley Ches E 43 G8
Bulkington Warks 35 G9
Bulkington Wilts 16 F6
Bulkworthy Devon 6 E2
Bull Hill Hants 10 E2
Bullamoor N Yorks 58 G4
Bullbridge Derbys 45 G7
Bullbrook Brack 18 E5
Bulley Glos 26 G4
Bullgill Cumb 56 C2
Bullington Hants 17 G11
Bullington Lincs 46 E4
Bull's Green Herts 29 G9
Bullwood Argyll 73 F10
Bulmer Essex 30 D5
Bulmer N Yorks 52 C2
Bulmer Tye Essex 30 E5
Bulphan Thurrock 20 C3
Bulverhythe E Sus 13 F6
Bulwark Aberds 89 D9
Bulwell Nottingham 45 H9
Bulwick Northants 36 F5
Bumble's Green Essex 29 H11
Bun Abhainn Eadarra W Isles 90 G6
Bun a'Mhuillin W Isles 84 G2
Bun Loyne Highld 80 C4
Bunacaimb Highld 79 C9
Bunarkaig Highld 80 E3
Bunbury Ches E 43 G8
Bunbury Heath Ches E 43 G8
Bunchrew Highld 87 G9
Bundalloch Highld 85 F13
Buness Shetland 96 C8
Bunessan Argyll 78 J6
Bungay Suff 39 G9
Bunker's Hill Lincs 46 E3
Bunker's Hill Lincs 46 G6
Bunkers Hill Oxon 27 G11
Bunloit Highld 81 A7
Bunnahabhain Argyll 64 A5
Bunny Notts 36 C1
Buntait Highld 86 H6
Buntingford Herts 29 F10
Bunwell Norf 39 F7
Burbage Derbys 44 E4
Burbage Leics 35 F10
Burbage Wilts 17 E9
Burchett's Green Windsor 18 C5
Burcombe Wilts 9 A9
Burcot Oxon 18 B2
Burcott Bucks 28 F5
Burdon T&W 58 A4
Bures Suff 30 E6
Bures Green Suff 30 E6
Burford Ches E 43 G9
Burford Oxon 27 G9
Burford Shrops 26 B2
Burg Argyll 78 G6
Burgar Orkney 95 F4
Burgate Hants 9 C10
Burgate Suff 39 H6
Burgess Hill W Sus 12 E2
Burgh Suff 31 C9
Burgh by Sands Cumb 61 H9
Burgh Castle Norf 39 E10
Burgh Heath Sur 19 F9
Burgh le Marsh Lincs 47 F9
Burgh Muir Aberds 83 A9
Burgh next Aylsham Norf 39 C8
Burgh on Bain Lincs 46 D6
Burgh St Margaret Norf 39 D10
Burgh St Peter Norf 39 F10
Burghclere Hants 17 E11
Burghead Moray 87 E14
Burghfield W Berks 18 E3
Burghfield Common W Berks 18 E3
Burghfield Hill W Berks 18 E3
Burghill Hereford 25 D11
Burghwallis S Yorks 45 A9
Burham Kent 20 E4
Buriton Hants 10 B6
Burland Ches E 43 G9
Burlawn Corn 3 B8
Burleigh Brack 18 E5
Burlescombe Devon 7 E9
Burleston Dorset 9 E6
Burley Hants 9 D11
Burley Rutland 36 D4
Burley W Yorks 51 F8
Burley Gate Hereford 26 D2
Burley in Wharfedale W Yorks 51 E7
Burley Lodge Hants 9 D11
Burley Street Hants 9 D11
Burleydam Ches E 34 A2
Burlingjobb Powys 25 C9
Burlow E Sus 12 E4
Burlton Shrops 33 C10
Burmarsh Kent 13 C9
Burmington Warks 27 E9
Burn N Yorks 52 G1
Burn of Cambus Stirling 75 G10
Burnaston Derbys 35 B8
Burnbank S Lanark 68 E6
Burnby E Yorks 52 E4
Burncross S Yorks 45 C7
Burneside Cumb 57 G7
Burness Orkney 95 D7
Burneston N Yorks 58 H4
Burnett Bath 16 E3
Burnfoot Borders 61 B11
Burnfoot Borders 61 B10
Burnfoot E Ayrs 67 F7
Burnfoot Perth 76 G2
Burnham Bucks 18 C6
Burnham N Lincs 53 H6
Burnham Deepdale Norf 38 A4
Burnham Green Herts 29 G9
Burnham Market Norf 38 A4
Burnham Norton Norf 38 A4
Burnham-on-Crouch Essex 20 B6
Burnham-on-Sea Som 15 G9
Burnham Overy Staithe Norf 38 A4
Burnham Overy Town Norf 38 A4
Burnham Thorpe Norf 38 A4
Burnhead Dumfries 60 D4
Burnhead S Ayrs 66 F5
Burnhervie Aberds 83 B9
Burnhill Green Staffs 34 E3
Burnhope Durham 58 B2
Burnhouse N Ayrs 67 A6
Burniston N Yorks 59 G11
Burnlee W Yorks 44 B5
Burnley Lancs 50 F4
Burnley Lane Lancs 50 F4
Burnmouth Borders 71 D8
Burnopfield Durham 63 H7
Burnsall N Yorks 50 C6
Burnside Angus 77 B8
Burnside E Ayrs 67 E8
Burnside Fife 76 G4
Burnside S Lanark 68 D5
Burnside Shetland 96 F4
Burnside W Loth 69 C9
Burnside of Duntrune Angus 77 D7
Burnswark Dumfries 61 F7
Burnt Heath Derbys 44 E6
Burnt Houses Durham 58 D2
Burnt Yates N Yorks 51 C8
Burntcommon Sur 19 F7
Burnthouse Corn 3 F6
Burntisland Fife 69 B11
Burnton E Ayrs 67 F7
Burntwood Staffs 35 E6
Burnwynd Edin 69 D10
Burpham Sur 19 F7
Burpham W Sus 11 D9
Burradon Northumb 62 C5
Burradon T&W 63 F8
Burrafirth Shetland 96 B8
Burraland Shetland 96 F5
Burraland Shetland 96 J4
Burras Corn 2 F5
Burravoe Shetland 96 F7
Burravoe Shetland 96 G5
Burray Village Orkney 95 J5
Burrells Cumb 57 E8
Burrelton Perth 76 D5
Burridge Devon 6 C4
Burridge Hants 10 C4
Burrill N Yorks 58 H3
Burringham N Lincs 46 B2
Burrington Devon 6 E5
Burrington Hereford 25 A11
Burrington N Som 15 F10
Burrough Green Cambs 30 C3
Burrough on the Hill Leics 36 D3
Burrow-bridge Som 8 B2
Burrowhill Sur 18 E6
Burry Swansea 23 G9
Burry Green Swansea 23 G9
Burry Port = Porth Tywyn Carms 23 F9
Burscough Lancs 43 A7
Burscough Bridge Lancs 43 A7
Bursea E Yorks 52 F4
Burshill E Yorks 53 E6
Bursledon Hants 10 D3
Burslem Stoke 44 H2
Burstall Suff 31 D7
Burstock Dorset 8 D3
Burston Norf 39 G7
Burston Staffs 34 B5
Burstow Sur 12 B2
Burstwick E Yorks 53 G8
Burtersett N Yorks 57 H10
Burtle Som 15 G9
Burton Ches W 43 E6
Burton Ches W 43 F8
Burton Dorset 9 E10
Burton Lincs 46 E3
Burton Northumb 71 G10
Burton Pembs 22 F4
Burton Som 7 B10
Burton Wilts 16 D5
Burton Agnes E Yorks 53 C7
Burton Bradstock Dorset 8 F3
Burton Dassett Warks 27 C10
Burton Fleming E Yorks 53 B6
Burton Green W Mid 35 H8
Burton Green Wrex 42 G6
Burton Hastings Warks 35 F10
Burton-in-Kendal Cumb 49 B5
Burton in Lonsdale N Yorks 50 B2
Burton Joyce Notts 36 A2
Burton Latimer Northants 28 A6
Burton Lazars Leics 36 D3
Burton-le-Coggles Lincs 36 C5
Burton Leonard N Yorks 51 C9
Burton on the Wolds Leics 36 C1
Burton Overy Leics 36 F2
Burton Pedwardine Lincs 37 A7
Burton Pidsea E Yorks 53 F8
Burton Salmon N Yorks 51 G10
Burton Stather N Lincs 52 H4
Burton upon Stather N Lincs 52 H4
Burton upon Trent Staffs 35 C8
Burtonwood Warr 43 C8
Burwardsley Ches W 43 G8
Burwarton Shrops 34 G2
Burwash E Sus 12 D5
Burwash Common E Sus 12 D5
Burwash Weald E Sus 12 D5
Burwell Cambs 30 B2
Burwell Lincs 47 E7
Burwen Anglesey 40 A6
Burwick Orkney 95 K5
Bury Cambs 37 G8
Bury Gtr Man 44 A2
Bury Som 7 D8
Bury W Sus 11 C9
Bury Green Herts 29 F11
Bury St Edmunds Suff 30 B5
Burythorpe N Yorks 52 C3
Busby E Renf 68 E4
Buscot Oxon 17 B9
Bush Bank Hereford 25 C11
Bush Crathie Aberds 82 D4
Bush Green Norf 39 G8
Bushbury W Mid 34 E5
Bushby Leics 36 E2
Bushey Herts 19 B8
Bushey Heath Herts 19 B8
Bushley Worcs 26 E5
Bushton Wilts 17 D7
Buslingthorpe Lincs 46 D4
Busta Shetland 96 G5
Butcher's Cross E Sus 12 D4
Butcombe N Som 15 E11
Butetown Cardiff 15 D7
Butleigh Som 8 A4
Butleigh Wootton Som 15 H11
Butler's Cross Bucks 28 H5
Butler's End Warks 35 G8
Butlers Marston Warks 27 C11
Butley Suff 31 C10
Butley High Corner Suff 31 D10
Butt Green Ches E 43 G9
Butterburn Cumb 62 F2
Buttercrambe N Yorks 52 D3
Butterknowle Durham 58 D2
Butterleigh Devon 7 F8
Buttermere Cumb 56 E3
Buttermere Wilts 17 E10
Buttershaw W Yorks 51 G7
Butterstone Perth 76 C3
Butterton Staffs 44 G4
Butterwick Durham 58 D4
Butterwick Lincs 47 H7
Butterwick N Yorks 52 B3
Butterwick N Yorks 52 B5
Buttington Powys 33 E8
Buttonoak Worcs 34 H3
Butt's Green Hants 10 B2
Buttsash Hants 10 D3
Buxhall Suff 31 C7
Buxhall Fen Street Suff 31 C7
Buxley Borders 71 E7
Buxted E Sus 12 D3
Buxton Derbys 44 E4
Buxton Norf 39 C8
Buxworth Derbys 44 D4
Bwcle = Buckley Flint 42 F5
Bwlch Powys 25 F8
Bwlch-Llan Ceredig 23 A10
Bwlch-y-cibau Powys 33 D7
Bwlch-y-fadfa Ceredig 23 B9
Bwlch-y-ffridd Powys 33 F6
Bwlch-y-sarnau Powys 25 A7
Bwlchgwyn Wrex 42 G5
Bwlchnewydd Carms 23 D8
Bwlchtocyn Gwyn 40 H5

Bwl–Chu 117

Bwlchyddar Powys 33 C7
Bwlchygroes Pembs 23 C7
Byermoor T&W 63 H7
Byers Green Durham 58 C3
Byfield Northants 28 C2
Byfleet Sur 19 E7
Byford Hereford 25 D10
Bygrave Herts 29 E9
Byker T&W 63 G8
Bylchau Conwy 42 F2
Byley Ches W 43 F10
Bynea Carms 23 G10
Byrness Northumb 62 C3
Bythorn Cambs 37 H6
Byton Hereford 25 B10
Byworth W Sus 11 B8

C

Cabharstadh W Isles 91 E8
Cablea Perth 76 D2
Cabourne Lincs 46 B5
Cabrach Argyll 72 G3
Cabrach Moray 82 A5
Cabrich Highld 87 G8
Cabus Lancs 49 E4
Cackle Street E Sus 12 D3
Cadbury Devon 7 F8
Cadbury Barton Devon 6 E5
Cadder E Dunb 68 C5
Caddington C Beds 29 G7
Caddonfoot Borders 70 G3
Cade Street E Sus 12 D5
Cadeby Leics 35 E10
Cadeby S Yorks 45 B9
Cadeleigh Devon 7 F8
Cadgwith Corn 2 H6
Cadham Fife 76 G5
Cadishead Gtr Man 43 C10
Cadle Swansea 14 B2
Cadley Lancs 49 F5
Cadley Wilts 17 E9
Cadley Wilts 17 F9
Cadmore End Bucks 18 B4
Cadnam Hants 10 C1
Cadney N Lincs 46 B4
Cadole Flint 42 F5
Cadoxton V Glam 15 E7
Cadoxton-Juxta-Neath Neath 14 B3
Cadshaw Blackburn 50 H3
Cadzow S Lanark 68 E6
Caeathro Gwyn 41 D7
Caehopkin Powys 24 G5
Caenby Lincs 46 D4
Caenby Corner Lincs 46 D3
Caér-bryn Carms 23 E10
Caer Llan Mon 25 H11
Caerau Bridgend 14 B4
Caerau Cardiff 15 D7
Caerdeon Gwyn 32 D2
Caerdydd = Cardiff Cardiff 15 D7
Caerfarchell Pembs 22 D2
Caerffili = Caerphilly Caerph 15 C7
Caerfyrddin = Carmarthen Carms 23 D9
Caergeiliog Anglesey 40 C5
Caergwrle Flint 42 G6
Caergybi = Holyhead Anglesey 40 B4
Caerleon = Caerllion Newport 15 B9
Caerllion = Caerleon Newport 15 B9
Caernarfon Gwyn 40 D6
Caerphilly = Caerffili Caerph 15 C7
Caersws Powys 32 F6
Caerwedros Ceredig 23 A8
Caerwent Mon 15 B10
Caerwych Gwyn 41 G8
Caerwys Flint 42 E4
Caethle Gwyn 32 F2
Caim Anglesey 41 B8
Caio Carms 24 E3
Cairinis W Isles 84 B3
Cairisiadar W Isles 90 D5
Cairminis W Isles 90 J5
Cairnbaan Argyll 73 D7
Cairnbanno Ho. Aberds 89 D8
Cairnborrow Aberds 88 D4
Cairnbrogie Aberds 89 F8
Cairnbulg Castle Aberds 89 B10
Cairncross Angus 82 F6
Cairncross Borders 71 D7
Cairndow Argyll 74 F4
Cairness Aberds 89 B10
Cairneyhill Fife 69 B9
Cairnfield Ho. Moray 88 B4
Cairngaan Dumfries 54 F4
Cairngarroch Dumfries 54 E3
Cairnhill Aberds 89 E6
Cairnie Aberds 83 C10
Cairnie Aberds 88 D4
Cairnorrie Aberds 89 D8
Cairnpark Aberds 83 B10
Cairnryan Dumfries 54 C3
Cairnton Orkney 95 H4
Caister-on-Sea Norf 39 D11
Caistor Lincs 46 B5
Caistor St Edmund Norf 39 E8
Caistron Northumb 62 C5
Caitha Bowland Borders 70 F3
Calais Street Suff 30 E6
Calanais W Isles 90 D7
Calbost W Isles 91 F9
Calbourne IoW 10 F3
Calceby Lincs 47 E7
Calcot Row W Berks 18 D3
Calcott Kent 21 E8
Caldback Shetland 96 C8
Caldbeck Cumb 56 C5
Caldbergh N Yorks 58 H1
Caldecote Cambs 29 C10
Caldecote Cambs 37 G7
Caldecote Herts 29 E9
Caldecote Northants 28 C3
Caldecott Northants 28 B6
Caldecott Oxon 17 B11
Caldecott Rutland 36 F4
Calder Bridge Cumb 56 F2
Calder Hall Cumb 56 F2
Calder Mains Highld 94 E2
Calder Vale Lancs 49 E5
Calderbank N Lanark 68 D6
Calderbrook Gtr Man 50 H5
Caldercruix N Lanark 69 D7
Caldermill S Lanark 68 F5
Calderwood S Lanark 68 E5
Caldhame Angus 77 C7
Caldicot Mon 15 C10
Caldwell Derbys 35 D8
Caldwell N Yorks 58 E2
Caldy Mers 42 D5
Caledrhydiau Ceredig 23 A9
Calfsound Orkney 95 E6
Calgary Argyll 78 F6
Califer Moray 87 F13
California Falk 69 C8
California Norf 39 D11
Calke Derbys 35 C9
Callakille Highld 85 C11
Callaly Northumb 62 C6
Callander Stirling 75 G9
Callaughton Shrops 34 F2
Callestick Corn 3 D6
Calligarry Highld 85 H11
Callington Corn 4 E4
Callow Hereford 25 E11
Callow End Worcs 26 D5
Callow Hill Wilts 17 C7
Callow Hill Worcs 26 A4
Callows Grave Worcs 26 B2
Calmore Hants 10 C2
Calmsden Glos 27 H7
Calne Wilts 17 D7
Calow Derbys 45 E8
Calshot Hants 10 D3
Calstock Corn 4 E5
Calstone Wellington Wilts 17 E7
Calthorpe Norf 39 B7
Calthwaite Cumb 56 B6
Calton N Yorks 50 D5
Calton Staffs 44 G5
Calveley Ches E 43 G8
Calver Derbys 44 E6
Calver Hill Hereford 25 D10
Calverhall Shrops 34 B2
Calverleigh Devon 7 E8
Calverley W Yorks 51 F8
Calvert Bucks 28 F3
Calverton M Keynes 28 E4
Calverton Notts 45 H10
Calvine Perth 81 G10
Calvo Cumb 56 A3
Cam Glos 16 B4
Camas-luinie Highld 80 A1
Camasnacroise Highld 79 F11
Camastianavaig Highld 85 E10
Camasunary Highld 85 G10
Camault Muir Highld 87 G8
Camb Shetland 96 D7
Camber E Sus 13 E8
Camberley Sur 18 E5
Camberwell London 19 D10
Camblesforth N Yorks 52 G2
Cambo Northumb 62 E6
Cambois Northumb 63 E9
Camborne Corn 2 E5
Cambourne Cambs 29 C10
Cambridge Cambs 29 C11
Cambridge Glos 16 A4
Cambridge Town Southend 20 C6
Cambus Clack 69 A7
Cambusavie Farm Highld 87 B10
Cambusbarron Stirling 68 A6
Cambuskenneth Stirling 69 A7
Cambuslang S Lanark 68 D5
Cambusmore Lodge Highld 87 B10
Camden London 19 C9
Camelford Corn 4 C2
Camelsdale Sur 11 A7
Camerory Highld 87 H13
Camer's Green Worcs 26 E4
Camerton Bath 16 F3
Camerton Cumb 56 C2
Camerton E Yorks 53 G8
Camghouran Perth 75 B8
Cammachmore Aberds 83 D11
Cammeringham Lincs 46 D3
Camore Highld 87 B10
Camp Hill Warks 35 F9
Campbeltown Argyll 65 F8
Camperdown T&W 63 F8
Campmuir Perth 76 D5
Campsall S Yorks 45 A9
Campsey Ash Suff 31 C10
Campton C Beds 29 E8
Camptown Borders 62 B2
Camrose Pembs 22 D4
Camserney Perth 75 C11
Camster Highld 94 F4
Camuschoirk Highld 79 E10
Camuscross Highld 85 G11
Camusnagaul Highld 80 F2
Camusnagaul Highld 86 C3
Camusrory Highld 79 B11
Camusteel Highld 85 D12
Camusterrach Highld 85 D12
Camusvrachan Perth 75 C9
Canada Hants 10 C1
Canadia E Sus 12 E6
Canal Side S Yorks 45 A10
Candacraig Ho. Aberds 82 B5
Candlesby Lincs 47 F8
Candy Mill S Lanark 69 F9
Cane End Oxon 18 D3
Canewdon Essex 20 B5
Canford Bottom Dorset 9 D9
Canford Cliffs Poole 9 F9
Canford Magna Poole 9 E9
Canham's Green Suff 31 B7
Canholes Derbys 44 E4
Canisbay Highld 94 C5
Cann Dorset 9 B7
Cann Common Dorset 9 B7
Cannard's Grave Som 16 G3
Cannich Highld 86 H6
Cannington Som 15 H8
Cannock Staffs 34 E5
Cannock Wood Staffs 34 D6
Canon Bridge Hereford 25 D11
Canon Frome Hereford 26 D3
Canon Pyon Hereford 25 D11
Canonbie Dumfries 61 F9
Canons Ashby Northants 28 C2
Canonstown Corn 2 F4
Canterbury Kent 21 F8
Cantley Norf 39 E9
Cantley S Yorks 45 B10
Cantlop Shrops 33 E11
Canton Cardiff 15 D7
Cantraybruich Highld 87 G10
Cantraydoune Highld 87 G10
Cantraywood Highld 87 G10
Cantsfield Lancs 50 B2
Canvey Island Essex 20 C4
Canwick Lincs 46 F3
Canworthy Water Corn 4 B3
Caol Highld 80 F3
Caol Ila Argyll 64 A5
Caolas Argyll 78 G3
Caolas Scalpaigh W Isles 90 H7
Caolas Stocinis W Isles 90 H6
Capel Sur 19 G8
Capel Bangor Ceredig 32 G2
Capel Betws Lleucu Ceredig 24 C3
Capel Carmel Gwyn 40 H3
Capel Coch Anglesey 40 B6
Capel Curig Conwy 41 E9
Capel Cynon Ceredig 23 B8
Capel Dewi Carms 23 D9
Capel Dewi Ceredig 23 B9
Capel Dewi Ceredig 32 G2
Capel Garmon Conwy 41 E10
Capel-gwyn Anglesey 40 C5
Capel Gwyn Carms 23 D9
Capel Gwynfe Carms 24 F4
Capel Hendre Carms 23 E10
Capel Hermon Gwyn 32 C3
Capel Isaac Carms 23 D10
Capel Iwan Carms 23 C7
Capel le Ferne Kent 21 H9
Capel Llanilltern Cardiff 14 C6
Capel Mawr Anglesey 40 C6
Capel St Andrew Suff 31 D10
Capel St Mary Suff 31 E7
Capel Seion Ceredig 32 H2
Capel Tygwydd Ceredig 23 B7
Capel Uchaf Gwyn 40 F6
Capel-y-graig Gwyn 41 D7
Capelulo Conwy 41 C9
Capenhurst Ches W 42 E6
Capernwray Lancs 49 B5
Capheaton Northumb 62 E6
Cappercleuch Borders 61 A8
Capplegill Dumfries 61 C7
Capton Devon 5 F9
Caputh Perth 76 D3
Car Colston Notts 36 A3
Carbis Bay Corn 2 F4
Carbost Highld 85 D9
Carbost Highld 85 E8
Carbrook S Yorks 45 D7
Carbrooke Norf 38 E5
Carburton Notts 45 E10
Carcant Borders 70 E2
Carcary Angus 77 B9
Carclaze Corn 3 D9
Carcroft S Yorks 45 A9
Cardenden Fife 69 A11
Cardeston Shrops 33 D9
Cardiff = Caerdydd Cardiff 15 D7
Cardigan = Aberteifi Ceredig 22 B6
Cardington Bedford 29 D7
Cardington Shrops 33 F11
Cardinham Corn 4 E2
Cardonald Glasgow 68 D4
Cardow Moray 88 D1
Cardrona Borders 70 G2
Cardross Argyll 68 C2
Cardurnock Cumb 61 H7
Careby Lincs 36 D6
Careston Castle Angus 77 B8
Carew Pembs 22 F5
Carew Cheriton Pembs 22 F5
Carew Newton Pembs 22 F5
Carey Hereford 26 E2
Carfrae E Loth 70 D4
Cargenbridge Dumfries 60 F5
Cargill Perth 76 D4
Cargo Cumb 61 H9
Cargreen Corn 4 E5
Carham Northumb 71 G7
Carhampton Som 7 B9
Carharrack Corn 2 E6
Carie Perth 75 B9
Carie Perth 75 D9
Carines Corn 3 D6
Carisbrooke IoW 10 F3
Cark Cumb 49 B3
Carlabhagh W Isles 90 C7
Carland Cross Corn 3 D7
Carlby Lincs 37 D6
Carlecotes S Yorks 44 B5
Carlesmoor N Yorks 51 B7
Carleton Cumb 56 A6
Carleton Cumb 57 D7
Carleton Lancs 49 F3
Carleton N Yorks 50 E5
Carleton Forehoe Norf 39 E6
Carleton Rode Norf 39 F7
Carlin How Redcar 59 E8
Carlingcott Bath 16 F3
Carlisle Cumb 61 H10
Carlops Borders 69 E10
Carlton Bedford 28 C6
Carlton Cambs 30 C3
Carlton Leics 35 E9
Carlton N Yorks 51 A6
Carlton N Yorks 52 G2
Carlton N Yorks 58 E2
Carlton N Yorks 59 H7
Carlton Notts 36 A2
Carlton S Yorks 45 A7
Carlton Stockton 58 D4
Carlton Suff 31 B10
Carlton W Yorks 51 G9
Carlton Colville Suff 39 G11
Carlton Curlieu Leics 36 F2
Carlton Husthwaite N Yorks 51 B10
Carlton in Cleveland N Yorks 58 F6
Carlton in Lindrick Notts 45 D9
Carlton le Moorland Lincs 46 G3
Carlton Miniott N Yorks 51 A9
Carlton on Trent Notts 45 F11
Carlton Scroop Lincs 36 A5
Carluke S Lanark 69 E7
Carmarthen = Caerfyrddin Carms 23 D9
Carmel Anglesey 40 B5
Carmel Carms 23 E10
Carmel Flint 42 E4
Carmel Guern 11
Carmel Gwyn 40 E6
Carmont Aberds 83 E10
Carmunnock Glasgow 68 E5
Carmyle Glasgow 68 D5
Carmyllie Angus 77 C8
Carn-gorm Highld 80 A1
Carnaby E Yorks 53 C7
Carnach Highld 80 A2
Carnach Highld 86 B3
Carnach W Isles 90 H7
Carnachy Highld 93 D10
Càrnais W Isles 90 D5
Carnbee Fife 77 G8
Carnbo Perth 76 G3
Carnbrea Corn 2 E5
Carnduff S Lanark 68 F5
Carnduncan Argyll 64 B3
Carne Corn 3 F8
Carnforth Lancs 49 B4
Carnhedryn Pembs 22 D3
Carnhell Green Corn 2 F5
Carnkie Corn 2 F5
Carnkie Corn 2 F6
Carno Powys 32 F5
Carnoch Highld 86 F5
Carnoch Highld 86 H6
Carnock Fife 69 B9
Carnon Downs Corn 3 E6
Carnousie Aberds 89 C6
Carnoustie Angus 77 D8
Carnwath S Lanark 69 F8
Carnyorth Corn 2 F2
Carperby N Yorks 58 H1
Carpley Green N Yorks 57 H11
Carr S Yorks 45 C9
Carr Hill T&W 63 G8
Carradale Argyll 65 E9
Carragraich W Isles 90 H6
Carrbridge Highld 81 A11
Carrefour Selous Jersey 11
Carreg-wen Pembs 23 B7
Carreglefn Anglesey 40 B5
Carrick Argyll 73 E8
Carrick Fife 77 E7
Carrick Castle Argyll 73 D10
Carrick Ho. Orkney 95 E6
Carriden Falk 69 B9
Carrington Gtr Man 43 C10
Carrington Lincs 47 G7
Carrington Midloth 70 D2
Carrog Conwy 41 F9
Carrog Denb 33 A7
Carron Falk 69 B7
Carron Moray 88 D2
Carron Bridge Stirling 68 B6
Carronbridge Dumfries 60 D4
Carronshore Falk 69 B7
Carrshield Northumb 57 B10
Carrutherstown Dumfries 61 F7
Carrville Durham 58 B4
Carsaig Argyll 72 E6
Carsaig Argyll 79 J8
Carscreugh Dumfries 54 D5
Carse Gray Angus 77 B7
Carse Ho. Argyll 72 G6
Carsegowan Dumfries 55 D7
Carseriggan Dumfries 54 C6
Carsethorn Dumfries 60 H5
Carshalton London 19 E9
Carsington Derbys 44 G6
Carskiey Argyll 65 H7
Carsluith Dumfries 55 D7
Carsphairn Dumfries 67 G8
Carstairs S Lanark 69 F8
Carstairs Junction S Lanark 69 F8
Carswell Marsh Oxon 17 B10
Carter's Clay Hants 10 B2
Carterton Oxon 27 H9
Carterway Heads Northumb 58 A1
Carthew Corn 3 D9
Carthorpe N Yorks 51 A9
Cartington Northumb 62 C6
Cartland S Lanark 69 F7
Cartmel Cumb 49 B3
Cartmel Fell Cumb 56 H6
Carway Carms 23 F9
Cary Fitzpaine Som 8 B4
Cas-gwent = Chepstow Mon 15 B11
Cascob Powys 25 B9
Cashlie Perth 75 C7
Cashmoor Dorset 9 C8
Casnewydd = Newport Newport 15 C9
Cassey Compton Glos 27 G7
Cassington Oxon 27 G11
Cassop Durham 58 C4
Castell Denb 42 F4
Castell-Howell Ceredig 23 B9
Castell-Nedd = Neath Neath 14 B3
Castell Newydd Emlyn = Newcastle Emlyn Carms 23 B8
Castell-y-bwch Torf 15 B8
Castellau Rhondda 14 C6
Casterton Cumb 50 B2
Castle Acre Norf 38 D4
Castle Ashby Northants 28 C5
Castle Bolton N Yorks 58 G1
Castle Bromwich W Mid 35 G7
Castle Bytham Lincs 36 D5
Castle Caereinion Powys 33 E7
Castle Camps Cambs 30 D3
Castle Carrock Cumb 61 H11
Castle Cary Som 8 A5
Castle Combe Wilts 16 D5
Castle Donington Leics 35 C10
Castle Douglas Dumfries 55 C10
Castle Eaton Swindon 17 B8
Castle Eden Durham 58 C5
Castle Forbes Aberds 83 B8
Castle Frome Hereford 26 D3
Castle Green Sur 18 E6
Castle Gresley Derbys 35 D8
Castle Heaton Northumb 71 F8
Castle Hedingham Essex 30 E4
Castle Hill Kent 12 B5
Castle Huntly Perth 76 E6
Castle Kennedy Dumfries 54 D4
Castle O'er Dumfries 61 D8
Castle Pulverbatch Shrops 33 E10
Castle Rising Norf 38 C2
Castle Stuart Highld 87 G10
Castlebay = Bagh a Chaisteil W Isles 84 J1
Castlebythe Pembs 22 D5
Castlecary N Lanark 68 C6
Castlecraig Highld 87 E11
Castlefairn Dumfries 60 E3
Castleford W Yorks 51 G10
Castlehill Borders 69 G11
Castlehill Highld 94 D3
Castlehill W Dunb 68 C2
Castlemaddy Dumfries 67 H8
Castlemartin Pembs 22 G4
Castlemilk Dumfries 61 F7
Castlemilk Glasgow 68 E5
Castlemorris Pembs 22 C4
Castlemorton Worcs 26 E4
Castleside Durham 58 B1
Castlethorpe M Keynes 28 D5
Castleton Angus 76 C6
Castleton Argyll 73 E7
Castleton Derbys 44 D5
Castleton Gtr Man 44 A2
Castleton N Yorks 59 F7
Castleton Newport 15 C8
Castletown Ches W 43 G7
Castletown Highld 87 G10
Castletown Highld 94 D3
Castletown IoM 48 F2
Castletown T&W 63 H9
Castleweary Borders 61 C10
Castley N Yorks 51 E8
Caston Norf 38 F5
Castor Pboro 37 F7
Catacol N Ayrs 66 B2
Catbrain S Glos 16 C2
Catbrook Mon 15 A11
Catchall Corn 2 G3
Catchems Corner W Mid 35 H8
Catchgate Durham 58 A2
Catcleugh Northumb 62 C3
Catcliffe S Yorks 45 D8
Catcott Som 15 H9
Caterham Sur 19 F10
Catfield Norf 39 C9
Catfirth Shetland 96 H6
Catford London 19 D10
Catforth Lancs 49 F4
Cathays Cardiff 15 D7
Cathcart Glasgow 68 D4
Cathedine Powys 25 F8
Catherington Hants 10 C5
Catherton Shrops 34 H2
Catlodge Highld 81 D8
Catlowdy Cumb 61 F10
Catmore W Berks 17 C11
Caton Lancs 49 C5
Caton Green Lancs 49 C5
Catrine E Ayrs 67 D8
Cat's Ash Newport 15 B9
Catsfield E Sus 12 E6
Catshill Worcs 26 A6
Cattal N Yorks 51 D10
Cattawade Suff 31 E8
Catterall Lancs 49 E4
Catterick N Yorks 58 G3
Catterick Bridge N Yorks 58 G3
Catterick Garrison N Yorks 58 G2
Catterlen Cumb 57 C6
Catterline Aberds 83 F10
Catterton N Yorks 51 E11
Catthorpe Leics 36 H1
Cattistock Dorset 8 E4
Catton N Yorks 51 B9
Catton Northumb 62 H4
Catwick E Yorks 53 E7
Catworth Cambs 29 A7
Caudlesprings Norf 38 E5
Caulcott Oxon 28 F2
Cauldcots Angus 77 C9
Cauldhame Stirling 68 A5
Cauldmill Borders 61 B11
Cauldon Staffs 44 H4
Caulkerbush Dumfries 60 H5
Caulside Dumfries 61 E10
Caunsall Worcs 34 G4
Caunton Notts 45 G11
Causeway End Dumfries 55 C7
Causeway Foot W Yorks 51 F6
Causeway-head Stirling 75 H10
Causewayend S Lanark 69 G9
Causewayhead Cumb 56 A3
Causey Park Bridge Northumb 63 D7
Causeyend Aberds 83 B11
Cautley Cumb 57 G8
Cavendish Suff 30 D5
Cavendish Bridge Leics 35 C10
Cavenham Suff 30 B4
Caversfield Oxon 28 F2
Caversham Reading 18 D4
Caverswall Staffs 34 A5
Cavil E Yorks 52 F3
Cawdor Highld 87 F11
Cawkwell Lincs 46 E6
Cawood N Yorks 52 F1
Cawsand Corn 4 F5
Cawston Norf 39 C7
Cawthorne S Yorks 44 B6
Cawthorpe Lincs 37 C6
Cawton N Yorks 52 B2
Caxton Cambs 29 C10
Caynham Shrops 26 A2
Caythorpe Lincs 46 H3
Caythorpe Notts 45 H10
Cayton N Yorks 53 A6
Ceann a Bhaigh W Isles 84 B2
Ceann a Deas Loch Baghasdail W Isles 84 G2
Ceann Shiphoirt W Isles 91 F7
Ceann Tarabhaigh W Isles 90 F7
Ceannacroc Lodge Highld 80 B4
Cearsiadair W Isles 91 E8
Cefn Berain Conwy 42 F2
Cefn-brith Conwy 42 G2
Cefn Canol Powys 33 B8
Cefn-coch Conwy 41 D10
Cefn Coch Powys 33 C7
Cefn-coed-y-cymmer M Tydf 25 H7
Cefn Cribbwr Bridgend 14 C4
Cefn Cross Bridgend 14 C4
Cefn-ddwysarn Gwyn 32 B5
Cefn Einion Shrops 33 G8
Cefn-gorwydd Powys 24 D6
Cefn-mawr Wrex 33 A8
Cefn-y-bedd Flint 42 G6
Cefn-y-pant Carms 22 D6
Cefneithin Carms 23 E10
Cei-bach Ceredig 23 A9
Ceinewydd = New Quay Ceredig 23 A8
Ceint Anglesey 40 C6
Cellan Ceredig 24 D3
Cellarhead Staffs 44 H3
Cemaes Anglesey 40 A5
Cemmaes Powys 32 E4
Cemmaes Road Powys 32 E4
Cenarth Carms 23 B7
Cenin Gwyn 40 F6
Central Invclyd 73 F11
Ceos W Isles 91 E8
Ceres Fife 77 F7
Cerne Abbas Dorset 8 D5
Cerney Wick Glos 17 B7
Cerrigceinwen Anglesey 40 C6
Cerrigydrudion Conwy 42 H2
Cessford Borders 62 A3
Ceunant Gwyn 41 D7
Chaceley Glos 26 E5
Chacewater Corn 3 E6
Chackmore Bucks 28 E3
Chacombe Northants 27 D11
Chad Valley W Mid 34 G6
Chadderton Gtr Man 44 B3
Chadderton Fold Gtr Man 44 B2
Chaddesden Derby 35 B9
Chaddesley Corbett Worcs 26 A5
Chaddleworth W Berks 17 D11
Chadlington Oxon 27 F10
Chadshunt Warks 27 C10
Chadwell Leics 36 C3
Chadwell St Mary Thurrock 20 D3
Chadwick End W Mid 27 A9
Chadwick Green Mers 43 C8
Chaffcombe Som 8 C2
Chagford Devon 5 C8
Chailey E Sus 12 E2
Chain Bridge Lincs 37 A9
Chainbridge Cambs 37 E10
Chainhurst Kent 20 G4
Chalbury Dorset 9 D9
Chalbury Common Dorset 9 D9
Chaldon Sur 19 F10
Chaldon Herring Dorset 9 F6
Chale IoW 10 G3
Chale Green IoW 10 G3
Chalfont Common Bucks 19 B7
Chalfont St Giles Bucks 18 B6
Chalfont St Peter Bucks 19 B7
Chalford Glos 16 A5
Chalgrove Oxon 18 B3
Chalk Kent 20 D3
Challacombe Devon 6 B5
Challoch Dumfries 54 C6
Challock Kent 21 F7
Chalton C Beds 29 F7
Chalton Hants 10 C6
Chalvington E Sus 12 F4
Chancery Ceredig 32 H1
Chandler's Ford Hants 10 B3
Channel Tunnel Kent 21 H8
Channerwick Shetland 96 L6
Chantry Som 16 G4
Chantry Suff 31 D8
Chapel Fife 69 A11
Chapel Allerton Som 15 F10
Chapel Allerton W Yorks 51 F9
Chapel Amble Corn 3 B8
Chapel Brampton Northants 28 B4
Chapel Chorlton Staffs 34 B4
Chapel-en-le-Frith Derbys 44 D4
Chapel End Warks 35 F9
Chapel Green Warks 27 B11
Chapel Green Warks 35 G8
Chapel Haddlesey N Yorks 52 G1
Chapel Head Cambs 37 G9
Chapel Hill Aberds 89 E10
Chapel Hill Lincs 46 G6
Chapel Hill Mon 15 B11
Chapel Hill N Yorks 51 E9
Chapel Lawn Shrops 33 H9
Chapel-le-Dale N Yorks 50 B3
Chapel Milton Derbys 44 D4
Chapel of Garioch Aberds 83 A9
Chapel Row W Berks 18 E2
Chapel St Leonards Lincs 47 E9
Chapel Stile Cumb 56 F5
Chapelgate Lincs 37 C10
Chapelhall N Lanark 68 D6
Chapelhill Dumfries 60 D6
Chapelhill Highld 87 D11
Chapelhill N Ayrs 66 B5
Chapelhill Perth 76 D3
Chapelhill Perth 76 E5
Chapelknowe Dumfries 61 F9
Chapelton Angus 77 C9
Chapelton Devon 6 D4
Chapelton Highld 81 B11
Chapelton S Lanark 68 F5
Chapeltown Blackburn 50 H3
Chapeltown Moray 82 A4
Chapeltown S Yorks 45 C7
Chapmans Well Devon 6 G2
Chapmanslade Wilts 16 G5
Chapmore End Herts 29 G10
Chappel Essex 30 F5
Chard Som 8 D2
Chardstock Devon 8 D2
Charfield S Glos 16 B4
Charford Worcs 26 B6
Charing Kent 20 G6
Charing Cross Dorset 9 C10
Charing Heath Kent 20 G6
Charingworth Glos 27 E9
Charlbury Oxon 27 G10
Charlcombe Bath 16 E4
Charlecote Warks 27 C9
Charles Devon 6 C5
Charles Tye Suff 31 C7
Charlesfield Dumfries 61 G7
Charleston Angus 76 C6
Charleston Renfs 68 D3
Charlestown Aberdeen 83 C11
Charlestown Corn 3 D9
Charlestown Derbys 44 C4
Charlestown Dorset 8 G5
Charlestown Fife 69 B9
Charlestown Gtr Man 44 B2
Charlestown Highld 85 A13
Charlestown Highld 87 G9
Charlestown W Yorks 50 G5
Charlestown of Aberlour Moray 88 D2
Charlesworth Derbys 44 C4
Charleton Devon 5 G8
Charlton Hants 17 G10
Charlton Herts 29 F8
Charlton London 19 D11
Charlton Northants 28 E2
Charlton Northumb 62 E4
Charlton Som 16 F3
Charlton Telford 34 D1
Charlton W Sus 11 C7
Charlton Wilts 9 B8
Charlton Wilts 16 C6
Charlton Wilts 17 F8
Charlton Worcs 27 D7
Charlton Abbots Glos 27 F7
Charlton Adam Som 8 B4
Charlton-All-Saints Wilts 9 B10
Charlton Down Dorset 8 E5
Charlton Horethorne Som 8 B5
Charlton Kings Glos 26 F6
Charlton Mackerell Som 8 B4
Charlton Marshall Dorset 9 D7
Charlton Musgrove Som 8 B6
Charlton on Otmoor Oxon 28 G2
Charltons Redcar 59 E7
Charlwood Sur 19 G9
Charlynch Som 7 C11
Charminster Dorset 8 E5
Charmouth Dorset 8 E2
Charndon Bucks 28 F3
Charney Bassett Oxon 17 B10
Charnock Richard Lancs 50 H1
Charsfield Suff 31 C9
Chart Corner Kent 20 F4
Chart Sutton Kent 20 G5
Charter Alley Hants 18 F2
Charterhouse Som 15 F10
Charterville Allotments Oxon 27 G10
Chartham Kent 21 F8
Chartham Hatch Kent 21 F8
Chartridge Bucks 18 A6
Charvil Wokingham 18 D4
Charwelton Northants 28 C2
Chasetown Staffs 34 E6
Chastleton Oxon 27 F9
Chasty Devon 6 F2
Chatburn Lancs 50 E3
Chatcull Staffs 34 B3
Chatham Medway 20 E4
Chathill Northumb 71 H10
Chattenden Medway 20 D4
Chatteris Cambs 37 G9
Chattisham Suff 31 D7
Chatto Borders 62 B3
Chatton Northumb 71 H9
Chawleigh Devon 7 E6
Chawley Oxon 17 A11
Chawston Bedford 29 C8
Chawton Hants 18 H4
Cheadle Gtr Man 44 D2
Cheadle Staffs 34 A6
Cheadle Heath Gtr Man 44 D2
Cheadle Hulme Gtr Man 44 D2
Cheam London 19 E9
Cheapside Sur 19 F7
Chearsley Bucks 28 G4
Chebsey Staffs 34 C4
Checkendon Oxon 18 C3
Checkley Ches E 43 H10
Checkley Hereford 26 E2
Checkley Staffs 34 B6
Chedburgh Suff 30 C4
Cheddar Som 15 F10
Cheddington Bucks 28 G6
Cheddleton Staffs 44 G3
Cheddon Fitzpaine Som 8 B1
Chedglow Wilts 16 B6
Chedgrave Norf 39 F9
Chedington Dorset 8 D3
Chediston Suff 39 H9
Chedworth Glos 27 G7
Chedzoy Som 15 H9
Cheeklaw Borders 70 E6
Cheeseman's Green Kent 13 C9
Cheglinch Devon 6 B4
Cheldon Devon 7 E6
Chelford Ches E 44 E2
Chell Heath Stoke 44 G2
Chellaston Derby 35 B9
Chellington Bedford 28 C6
Chelmarsh Shrops 34 G3
Chelmer Village Essex 30 H4
Chelmondiston Suff 31 E9
Chelmorton Derbys 44 F5
Chelmsford Essex 30 H4
Chelsea London 19 D9
Chelsfield London 19 E11
Chelsworth Suff 30 D6
Cheltenham Glos 26 F6
Chelveston Northants 28 B6
Chelvey N Som 15 E10
Chelwood Bath 16 E3
Chelwood Common E Sus 12 D3
Chelwood Gate E Sus 12 D3
Chelworth Wilts 16 B6
Chelworth Green Wilts 17 B7
Chemistry Shrops 33 A11
Chenies Bucks 19 B7
Cheny Longville Shrops 33 G10
Chepstow = Cas-gwent Mon 15 B11
Chequerfield W Yorks 51 G10
Cherhill Wilts 17 D7
Cherington Glos 16 B6
Cherington Warks 27 E9
Cheriton Devon 7 B6
Cheriton Hants 10 B4
Cheriton Kent 21 H8
Cheriton Swansea 23 G9
Cheriton Bishop Devon 7 G6
Cheriton Fitzpaine Devon 7 F7
Cheriton or Stackpole Elidor Pembs 22 G4
Cherrington Telford 34 C2
Cherry Burton E Yorks 52 E5
Cherry Hinton Cambs 29 C11
Cherry Orchard Worcs 26 C5
Cherry Willingham Lincs 46 E4
Cherrybank Perth 76 E4
Chertsey Sur 19 E7
Cheselbourne Dorset 9 E6
Chesham Bucks 18 A6
Chesham Bois Bucks 18 B6
Cheshunt Herts 19 A10
Cheslyn Hay Staffs 34 E5
Chessington London 19 E8
Chester Ches W 43 F7
Chester-Le-Street Durham 58 A3
Chester Moor Durham 58 B3
Chesterblade Som 16 G3
Chesterfield Derbys 45 E7
Chesters Borders 62 A2
Chesters Borders 62 B2
Chesterton Cambs 29 B11
Chesterton Cambs 37 F7
Chesterton Glos 17 A7
Chesterton Oxon 28 F2
Chesterton Shrops 34 F3
Chesterton Staffs 44 H2
Chesterton Warks 27 C10
Chesterwood Northumb 62 G4
Chestfield Kent 21 E8
Cheston Devon 5 F7
Cheswardine Shrops 34 C3
Cheswick Northumb 71 F9
Chetnole Dorset 8 D5
Chettiscombe Devon 7 E8
Chettisham Cambs 37 G11
Chettle Dorset 9 C8
Chetton Shrops 34 F2
Chetwode Bucks 28 F3
Chetwynd Aston Telford 34 D3
Cheveley Cambs 30 B3
Chevening Kent 19 F11
Chevington Suff 30 C4
Chevithorne Devon 7 E8
Chew Magna Bath 16 E2
Chew Stoke Bath 16 E2
Chewton Keynsham Bath 16 E3
Chewton Mendip Som 16 F2
Chicheley M Keynes 28 D6
Chichester W Sus 11 D7
Chickerell Dorset 8 F5
Chicklade Wilts 9 A8
Chicksgrove Wilts 9 A8
Chidden Hants 10 C5
Chiddingfold Sur 18 H6
Chiddingly E Sus 12 E4
Chiddingstone Kent 19 G11
Chiddingstone Causeway Kent 20 G2
Chiddingstone Hoath Kent 12 B3
Chideock Dorset 8 E3
Chidham W Sus 11 D6
Chidswell W Yorks 51 G8
Chieveley W Berks 17 D11
Chignall St James Essex 30 H3
Chignall Smealy Essex 30 G3
Chigwell Essex 19 B11
Chigwell Row Essex 19 B11
Chilbolton Hants 17 H10
Chilcomb Hants 10 B4
Chilcombe Dorset 8 E4
Chilcompton Som 16 F3
Chilcote Leics 35 D8
Child Okeford Dorset 9 C7
Childer Thornton Ches W 42 E6
Childrey Oxon 17 C10
Child's Ercall Shrops 34 C2
Childswickham Worcs 27 E7
Childwall Mers 43 D7
Childwick Green Herts 29 G8
Chilfrome Dorset 8 E4
Chilgrove W Sus 11 C7
Chilham Kent 21 F7
Chilhampton Wilts 9 A9
Chilla Devon 6 F3
Chillaton Devon 4 C5
Chillenden Kent 21 F9
Chillerton IoW 10 F3
Chillesford Suff 31 C10
Chillingham Northumb 71 H9
Chillington Devon 5 G8
Chillington Som 8 C2
Chilmark Wilts 9 A8
Chilson Oxon 27 G10
Chilsworthy Corn 4 D5
Chilsworthy Devon 6 F2
Chilthorne Domer Som 8 C4
Chiltington E Sus 12 E2
Chilton Bucks 28 G3
Chilton Durham 58 D3
Chilton Oxon 17 C11
Chilton Cantelo Som 8 B4
Chilton Foliat Wilts 17 D10
Chilton Lane Durham 58 C4
Chilton Polden Som 15 H9
Chilton Street Suff 30 D4
Chilton Trinity Som 15 H8
Chilvers Coton Warks 35 F9
Chilwell Notts 35 B11
Chilworth Hants 10 C3
Chilworth Sur 19 G7
Chimney Oxon 17 A10
Chineham Hants 18 F3
Chingford London 19 B10
Chinley Derbys 44 D4
Chinley Head Derbys 44 D4
Chinnor Oxon 18 A4
Chipnall Shrops 34 B3
Chippenhall Green Suff 39 H8
Chippenham Cambs 30 B3
Chippenham Wilts 16 D6
Chipperfield Herts 19 A7
Chipping Herts 29 E10
Chipping Lancs 50 E2
Chipping Campden Glos 27 E8
Chipping Hill Essex 30 G5
Chipping Norton Oxon 27 F10
Chipping Ongar Essex 20 A2
Chipping Sodbury S Glos 16 C4
Chipping Warden Northants 27 D11
Chipstable Som 7 D9
Chipstead Kent 19 F11
Chipstead Sur 19 F9
Chirbury Shrops 33 F8
Chirk = Y Waun Wrex 33 B8
Chirk Bank Shrops 33 B8
Chirmorrie S Ayrs 54 B5
Chirnside Borders 71 E7
Chirnsidebridge Borders 71 E7
Chirton Wilts 17 F7
Chisbury Wilts 17 E9
Chiselborough Som 8 C3
Chiseldon Swindon 17 D8
Chiserley W Yorks 50 G6
Chislehampton Oxon 18 B2
Chislehurst London 19 D11
Chislet Kent 21 E9
Chiswell Green Herts 19 A8
Chiswick London 19 D9
Chiswick End Cambs 29 D10
Chisworth Derbys 44 C3
Chithurst W Sus 11 B7
Chittering Cambs 29 A11
Chitterne Wilts 16 G6
Chittlehamholt Devon 6 D5
Chittlehampton Devon 6 D5
Chittoe Wilts 16 E6
Chivenor Devon 6 C4
Chobham Sur 18 E6
Choicelee Borders 70 E6
Cholderton Wilts 17 G9
Cholesbury Bucks 28 H6
Chollerford Northumb 62 F5
Chollerton Northumb 62 F5
Cholmondeston Ches E 43 F9
Cholsey Oxon 18 C2
Cholstrey Hereford 25 C11
Chop Gate N Yorks 59 G6
Choppington Northumb 63 E8
Chopwell T&W 63 H7
Chorley Ches E 43 G8
Chorley Lancs 50 H1
Chorley Shrops 34 G2
Chorley Staffs 35 D6
Chorleywood Herts 19 B7
Chorlton cum Hardy Gtr Man 44 C2
Chorlton Lane Ches W 43 H7
Choulton Shrops 33 G9
Chowdene T&W 63 H8
Chowley Ches W 43 G7
Chrishall Essex 29 E11
Christchurch Cambs 37 F10
Christchurch Dorset 9 E10
Christchurch Glos 26 G2
Christchurch Newport 15 C9
Christian Malford Wilts 16 D6
Christleton Ches W 43 F7
Christmas Common Oxon 18 B4
Christon N Som 15 F9
Christon Bank Northumb 63 A8
Christow Devon 5 C9
Chryston N Lanark 68 C5
Chudleigh Devon 5 D9
Chudleigh Knighton Devon 5 D9
Chulmleigh Devon 6 E5
Chunal Derbys 44 C4
Church Lancs 50 G3
Church Aston Telford 34 D3
Church Brampton Northants 28 B4
Church Broughton Derbys 35 B8
Church Crookham Hants 18 F5
Church Eaton Staffs 34 D4
Church End C Beds 28 E6
Church End C Beds 28 F6
Church End C Beds 29 E8
Church End Cambs 37 E9
Church End Cambs 37 G8
Church End E Yorks 53 D6
Church End Essex 30 D2
Church End Essex 30 F4
Church End Hants 18 F3
Church End Lincs 37 B8
Church End Warks 35 F8
Church End Wilts 17 D7
Church Enstone Oxon 27 F10
Church Fenton N Yorks 51 F11
Church Green Devon 7 G10
Church Green Norf 39 F6
Church Gresley Derbys 35 D8
Church Hanborough Oxon 27 G11
Church Hill Ches W 43 F9
Church Houses N Yorks 59 G7
Church Knowle Dorset 9 F8
Church Laneham Notts 46 E2
Church Langton Leics 36 F3
Church Lawford Warks 35 H10
Church Lawton Ches E 44 G2
Church Leigh Staffs 34 B6
Church Lench Worcs 27 C7
Church Mayfield Staffs 35 A7
Church Minshull Ches E 43 F9
Church Norton W Sus 11 E7
Church Preen Shrops 33 F11
Church Pulverbatch Shrops 33 E10
Church Stoke Powys 33 F8
Church Stowe Northants 28 C3
Church Street Kent 20 D4
Church Stretton Shrops 33 F10
Church Town N Lincs 45 B11
Church Town Sur 19 F10
Church Village Rhondda 14 C6
Church Warsop Notts 45 F9
Churcham Glos 26 G4
Churchbank Shrops 33 H8
Churchbridge Staffs 34 E5
Churchdown Glos 26 G5
Churchend Essex 21 B7
Churchend Essex 30 F3
Churchend S Glos 16 B4
Churchfield W Mid 34 F6
Churchgate Street Essex 29 G11
Churchill Devon 6 B4
Churchill Devon 8 D2

Churchill N Som 15 F10
Churchill Oxon 27 F9
Churchill Worcs 26 C6
Churchill Worcs 34 H4
Churchinford Som 7 E11
Churchover Warks 35 G11
Churchstanton Som 7 E10
Churchstow Devon 5 G8
Churchtown Derbys 44 F6
Churchtown IoM 48 C4
Churchtown Lancs 49 E4
Churchtown Mers 49 H3
Churnsike Lodge Northumb 62 F2
Churston Ferrers Torbay 5 F10
Churt Sur 18 H5
Churton Ches W 43 G7
Churwell W Yorks 51 G8
Chute Standen Wilts 17 F10
Chwilog Gwyn 40 G6
Chyandour Corn 2 F3
Cilan Uchaf Gwyn 40 H4
Cilcain Flint 42 F4
Cilcennin Ceredig 24 B2
Cilfor Gwyn 41 G8
Cilfrew Neath 14 A3
Cilfynydd Rhondda 14 B6
Cilgerran Pembs 22 B6
Cilgwyn Carms 24 F4
Cilgwyn Gwyn 40 E6
Cilgwyn Pembs 22 C5
Ciliau Aeron Ceredig 23 A9
Cill Donnain W Isles 84 F2
Cille Bhrighde W Isles 84 G2
Cille Pheadair W Isles 84 G2
Cilmery Powys 25 C7
Cilsan Carms 23 D10
Ciltalgarth Gwyn 41 F10
Cilwendeg Pembs 23 C7
Cilybebyll Neath 14 A3
Cilycwm Carms 24 E4
Cimla Neath 14 B3
Cinderford Glos 26 G3
Cippyn Pembs 22 B6
Circebost W Isles 90 D6
Cirencester Glos 17 A7
Ciribhig W Isles 90 C6
City London 19 C10
City Powys 33 G8
City Dulas Anglesey 40 B6
Clachaig Argyll 73 E10
Clachan Argyll 72 B6
Clachan Argyll 72 H6
Clachan Argyll 74 F4
Clachan Argyll 79 G11
Clachan Highld 85 E10
Clachan W Isles 84 D2
Clachan na Luib W Isles 84 B3
Clachan of Campsie E Dunb 68 C5
Clachan of Glendaruel Argyll 73 E8
Clachan-Seil Argyll 72 B6
Clachan Strachur Argyll 73 C9
Clachaneasy Dumfries 54 B6
Clachanmore Dumfries 54 E3
Clachbreck Argyll 72 F6
Clachnabrain Angus 82 G5
Clachtoll Highld 92 G3
Clackmannan Clack 69 A8
Clacton-on-Sea Essex 31 G8
Cladach Chireboist W Isles 84 B2
Claddach-knockline W Isles 84 B2
Cladich Argyll 74 E3
Claggan Highld 79 G9
Claggan Highld 80 F3
Claigan Highld 84 C7
Claines Worcs 26 C5
Clandown Bath 16 F3
Clanfield Hants 10 C5
Clanfield Oxon 17 A9
Clanville Hants 17 G10
Claonaig Argyll 73 H7
Claonel Highld 93 J8
Clap Hill Kent 13 C9
Clapgate Dorset 9 D9
Clapgate Herts 29 F11
Clapham Bedford 29 C7
Clapham London 19 D9
Clapham N Yorks 50 C3
Clapham W Sus 11 D9
Clappers Borders 71 E8
Clappersgate Cumb 56 F5
Clapton Som 8 D3
Clapton-in-Gordano N Som 15 D10
Clapton-on-the-Hill Glos 27 G8
Clapworthy Devon 6 D5
Clara Vale T&W 63 G7
Clarach Ceredig 32 G2
Clarbeston Pembs 22 D5
Clarbeston Road Pembs 22 D5
Clarborough Notts 45 D11
Clardon Highld 94 D3
Clare Suff 30 D4
Clarebrand Dumfries 55 C10
Clarencefield Dumfries 60 G6
Clarilaw Borders 61 B11
Clark's Green Sur 19 H8
Clarkston E Renf 68 E4
Clashandorran Highld 87 G8
Clashcoig Highld 87 B9
Clashindarroch Aberds 88 E4
Clashmore Highld 87 C10
Clashmore Highld 92 F3
Clashnessie Highld 92 F3
Clashnoir Moray 82 A4
Clate Shetland 96 G7
Clathy Perth 76 F2
Clatt Aberds 83 A7
Clatter Powys 32 F5
Clatterford IoW 10 F3
Clatterin Bridge Aberds 83 F8
Clatworthy Som 7 C9
Claughton Lancs 49 E5
Claughton Lancs 50 C1
Claughton Mers 42 D6
Claverdon Warks 27 B8
Claverham N Som 15 E10
Clavering Essex 29 E11
Claverley Shrops 34 F3
Claverton Bath 16 E4
Clawdd-newydd Denb 42 G3
Clawthorpe Cumb 49 B5
Clawton Devon 6 G2
Claxby Lincs 46 C5
Claxby Lincs 47 E8
Claxton NYorks 52 C2
Claxton Norf 39 E9
Clay Common Suff 39 G10
Clay Coton Northants 36 H1
Clay Cross Derbys 45 F7
Clay Hill W Berks 18 D2
Clay Lake Lincs 37 C8
Claybokie Aberds 82 D2
Claybrooke Magna Leics 35 G10
Claybrooke Parva Leics 35 G10
Claydon Oxon 27 C11
Claydon Suff 31 C8
Claygate Dumfries 61 F9
Claygate Kent 12 B6
Claygate Sur 19 E8
Claygate Cross Kent 20 F3
Clayhanger Devon 7 D9
Clayhanger W Mid 34 E6
Clayhidon Devon 7 E10
Clayhill E Sus 13 D7
Clayhill Hants 10 D2
Clayock Highld 94 E3
Claypole Lincs 46 H2
Clayton S Yorks 45 B8
Clayton Staffs 34 A4
Clayton W Sus 12 E1
Clayton W Yorks 51 F7
Clayton Green Lancs 50 G1
Clayton-le-Moors Lancs 50 F3
Clayton-le-Woods Lancs 50 G1
Clayton West W Yorks 44 A6
Clayworth Notts 45 D11
Cleadale Highld 78 C7
Cleadon T&W 63 G9
Clearbrook Devon 4 E6
Clearwell Glos 26 H2
Cleasby N Yorks 58 E3
Cleat Orkney 95 K5
Cleatlam Durham 58 E2
Cleator Cumb 56 E2
Cleator Moor Cumb 56 E2
Clebrig Highld 93 F8
Cleckheaton W Yorks 51 G7
Clee St Margaret Shrops 34 G1
Cleedownton Shrops 34 G1
Cleehill Shrops 34 H1
Cleethorpes NE Lincs 47 B7
Cleeton St Mary Shrops 34 H2
Cleeve N Som 15 E10
Cleeve Hill Glos 26 F6
Cleeve Prior Worcs 27 D7
Clegyrnant Powys 32 E5
Clehonger Hereford 25 E11
Cleish Perth 76 H3
Cleland N Lanark 69 E7
Clench Common Wilts 17 E8
Clenchwarton Norf 38 C1
Clent Worcs 34 H5
Cleobury Mortimer Shrops 34 H2
Cleobury North Shrops 34 G2
Cleongart Argyll 65 E7
Clephanton Highld 87 F11
Clerklands Borders 61 A11
Clestrain Orkney 95 H4
Cleuch Head Borders 61 B11
Cleughbrae Dumfries 60 F6
Clevancy Wilts 17 D7
Clevedon N Som 15 D10
Cleveley Oxon 27 F10
Cleveleys Lancs 49 E3
Cleverton Wilts 16 C6
Clevis Bridgend 14 D4
Clewer Som 15 F10
Cley next the Sea Norf 38 A6
Cliaid W Isles 84 H1
Cliasmol W Isles 90 G5
Cliburn Cumb 57 D7
Click Mill Orkney 95 F4
Cliddesden Hants 18 G3
Cliff End E Sus 13 E7
Cliffburn Angus 77 C9
Cliffe Medway 20 D4
Cliffe N Yorks 52 F2
Cliffe Woods Medway 20 D4
Clifford Hereford 25 D9
Clifford W Yorks 51 E10
Clifford Chambers Warks 27 C8
Clifford's Mesne Glos 26 F4
Cliffsend Kent 21 E10
Clifton Bristol 16 D2
Clifton C Beds 29 E8
Clifton Cumb 57 D7
Clifton Derbys 35 A7
Clifton Lancs 49 F4
Clifton N Yorks 51 E7
Clifton Northumb 63 E8
Clifton Nottingham 36 B1
Clifton Oxon 27 E11
Clifton S Yorks 45 C9
Clifton Stirling 74 D6
Clifton Worcs 26 D5
Clifton York 52 D1
Clifton Campville Staffs 35 D8
Clifton Green Gtr Man 43 B10
Clifton Hampden Oxon 18 B2
Clifton Reynes M Keynes 28 C6
Clifton upon Dunsmore Warks 35 H11
Clifton upon Teme Worcs 26 B4
Cliftoncote Borders 62 A4
Cliftonville Kent 21 D10
Climaen gwyn Neath 24 H4
Climping W Sus 11 D9
Climpy S Lanark 69 E8
Clink Som 16 G4
Clint N Yorks 51 D8
Clint Green Norf 38 D6
Clintmains Borders 70 G5
Cliobh W Isles 90 D5
Clippesby Norf 39 D10
Clipsham Rutland 36 D5
Clipston Northants 36 G3
Clipstone Notts 45 F9
Clitheroe Lancs 50 E3
Cliuthar W Isles 90 H6
Clive Shrops 33 C11
Clivocast Shetland 96 C8
Clixby Lincs 46 B5
Clocaenog Denb 42 G3
Clochan Moray 88 B4
Clock Face Mers 43 C8
Clockmill Borders 70 E6
Cloddiau Powys 33 E8
Clodock Hereford 25 F10
Clola Aberds 89 D10
Clophill C Beds 29 E7
Clopton Northants 37 G6
Clopton Suff 31 C9
Clopton Corner Suff 31 C9
Clopton Green Suff 30 C4
Close Clark IoM 48 E2
Closeburn Dumfries 60 D4
Closworth Som 8 C4
Clothall Herts 29 E9
Clotton Ches W 43 F8
Clough Foot W Yorks 50 G5
Cloughton N Yorks 59 G11
Cloughton Newlands N Yorks 59 G11
Clousta Shetland 96 H5
Clouston Orkney 95 G3
Clova Aberds 82 A6
Clova Angus 82 F5
Clove Lodge Durham 57 E11
Clovelly Devon 6 D2
Clovenfords Borders 70 G3
Clovenstone Aberds 83 B9
Clovullin Highld 74 A3
Clow Bridge Lancs 50 G4
Clowne Derbys 45 E8
Clows Top Worcs 26 A4
Cloy Wrex 33 A9
Cluanie Inn Highld 80 B2
Cluanie Lodge Highld 80 B2
Clun Shrops 33 G9
Clunbury Shrops 33 G9
Clunderwen Carms 22 E6
Clune Highld 81 A9
Clunes Highld 80 E4
Clungunford Shrops 33 H9
Clunie Aberds 89 C6
Clunie Perth 76 C4
Clunton Shrops 33 G9
Cluny Fife 76 H5
Cluny Castle Highld 81 D8
Clutton Bath 16 F3
Clutton Ches W 43 G7
Clwt-grugoer Conwy 42 F2
Clwt-y-bont Gwyn 41 D7
Clydach Mon 25 G9
Clydach Swansea 14 A2
Clydach Vale Rhondda 14 B5
Clydebank W Dunb 68 C3
Clydey Pembs 23 C7
Clyffe Pypard Wilts 17 D7
Clynder Argyll 73 E11
Clyne Neath 14 A4
Clynelish Highld 93 J11
Clynnog-fawr Gwyn 40 E6
Clyro Powys 25 D9
Clyst Honiton Devon 7 G8
Clyst Hydon Devon 7 F9
Clyst St George Devon 5 C10
Clyst St Lawrence Devon 7 F9
Clyst St Mary Devon 7 G8
Cnoc Amhlaigh W Isles 91 D10
Cnwch-coch Ceredig 32 H2
Coachford Aberds 88 D4
Coad's Green Corn 4 D3
Coal Aston Derbys 45 E7
Coalbrookdale Telford 34 E2
Coalbrookvale Bl Gwent 25 H8
Coalburn S Lanark 69 G7
Coalburns T&W 63 G7
Coalcleugh Northumb 57 B10
Coaley Glos 16 A4
Coalhall E Ayrs 67 E7
Coalhill Essex 20 B4
Coalpit Heath S Glos 16 C3
Coalport Telford 34 E2
Coalsnaughton Clack 76 H2
Coaltown of Balgonie Fife 76 H5
Coaltown of Wemyss Fife 76 H6
Coalville Leics 35 D10
Coalway Glos 26 G2
Coat Som 8 B3
Coatbridge N Lanark 68 D6
Coatdyke N Lanark 68 D6
Coate Swindon 17 C8
Coate Wilts 17 E7
Coates Cambs 37 F9
Coates Glos 16 A6
Coates Lancs 50 E4
Coates Notts 46 D2
Coates W Sus 11 C8
Coatham Redcar 59 D6
Coatham Mundeville Darl 58 D3
Coatsgate Dumfries 60 C6
Cobbaton Devon 6 D5
Cobbler's Green Norf 39 F8
Coberley Glos 26 G6
Cobham Kent 20 E3
Cobham Sur 19 E8
Cobholm Island Norf 39 E11
Cobleland Stirling 75 H8
Cobnash Hereford 25 B11
Coburty Aberds 89 B9
Cock Bank Wrex 42 H6
Cock Bridge Aberds 82 C4
Cock Clarks Essex 20 A5
Cockayne N Yorks 59 G7
Cockayne Hatley Cambs 29 D9
Cockburnspath Borders 70 C6
Cockenzie and Port Seton E Loth 70 C3
Cockerham Lancs 49 D4
Cockermouth Cumb 56 C3
Cockernhoe Green Herts 29 F8
Cockfield Durham 58 D2
Cockfield Suff 30 C6
Cockfosters London 19 B9
Cocking W Sus 11 C7
Cockington Torbay 5 E9
Cocklake Som 15 G10
Cockley Beck Cumb 56 F4
Cockley Cley Norf 38 E3
Cockshutt Shrops 33 C10
Cockthorpe Norf 38 A5
Cockwood Devon 5 C10
Cockyard Hereford 25 E11
Codda Corn 4 D2
Coddenham Suff 31 C8
Coddington Ches W 43 G7
Coddington Hereford 26 D4
Coddington Notts 46 G2
Codford St Mary Wilts 16 H6
Codford St Peter Wilts 16 H6
Codicote Herts 29 G9
Codmore Hill W Sus 11 B9
Codnor Derbys 45 H8
Codrington S Glos 16 D4
Codsall Staffs 34 E4
Codsall Wood Staffs 34 E4
Coed Duon = Blackwood Caerph 15 B7
Coed Mawr Gwyn 41 C7
Coed Morgan Mon 25 G10
Coed-Talon Flint 42 G5
Coed-y-bryn Ceredig 23 B8
Coed-y-paen Mon 15 B9
Coed-yr-ynys Powys 25 F8
Coed Ystumgwern Gwyn 32 C1
Coedely Rhondda 14 C6
Coedkernew Newport 15 C8
Coedpoeth Wrex 42 G5
Coedway Powys 33 D9
Coelbren Powys 24 G5
Coffinswell Devon 5 E9
Cofton Hackett Worcs 34 H6
Cogan V Glam 15 D7
Cogenhoe Northants 28 B5
Cogges Oxon 27 H10
Coggeshall Essex 30 F5
Coggeshall Hamlet Essex 30 F5
Coggins Mill E Sus 12 D4
Coig Peighinnean W Isles 91 A10
Coig Peighinnean Bhuirgh W Isles 91 B9
Coignafearn Lodge Highld 81 B8
Coilacriech Aberds 82 D5
Coilantogle Stirling 75 G8
Coilleag W Isles 84 G2
Coillore Highld 85 E8
Coity Bridgend 14 C5
Col W Isles 91 C9
Col Uarach W Isles 91 D9
Colaboll Highld 93 H8
Colan Corn 3 C7
Colaton Raleigh Devon 7 H9
Colbost Highld 84 D7
Colburn N Yorks 58 G2
Colby Cumb 57 D8
Colby IoM 48 E2
Colby Norf 39 B8
Colchester Essex 31 F7
Colcot V Glam 15 E7
Cold Ash W Berks 18 E2
Cold Ashby Northants 36 H2
Cold Ashton S Glos 16 D4
Cold Aston Glos 27 G8
Cold Blow Pembs 22 E6
Cold Brayfield M Keynes 28 C6
Cold Hanworth Lincs 46 D4
Cold Harbour Lincs 36 B5
Cold Hatton Telford 34 C2
Cold Hesledon Durham 58 B5
Cold Higham Northants 28 C3
Cold Kirby N Yorks 51 A11
Cold Newton Leics 36 E3
Cold Northcott Corn 4 C3
Cold Norton Essex 20 A5
Cold Overton Leics 36 D4
Coldbackie Highld 93 D9
Coldbeck Cumb 57 F9
Coldblow London 20 D2
Coldean Brighton 12 F2
Coldeast Devon 5 D9
Colden W Yorks 50 G5
Colden Common Hants 10 B3
Coldfair Green Suff 31 B11
Coldham Cambs 37 E10
Coldharbour Glos 16 A2
Coldharbour Kent 20 F2
Coldharbour Sur 19 G8
Coldingham Borders 71 D8
Coldrain Perth 76 G3
Coldred Kent 21 G9
Coldridge Devon 6 F5
Coldstream Angus 76 D6
Coldstream Borders 71 G7
Coldwaltham W Sus 11 C9
Coldwells Aberds 89 D11
Coldwells Croft Aberds 83 A7
Coldyeld Shrops 33 F9
Cole Som 8 A5
Cole Green Herts 29 G9
Cole Henley Hants 17 F11
Colebatch Shrops 33 G9
Colebrook Devon 7 F9
Colebrooke Devon 7 G6
Coleby Lincs 46 F3
Coleby N Lincs 52 H4
Coleford Devon 7 F6
Coleford Glos 26 G2
Coleford Som 16 G3
Colehill Dorset 9 D9
Coleman's Hatch E Sus 12 C3
Colemere Shrops 33 B10
Colemore Hants 10 A6
Coleorton Leics 35 D10
Colerne Wilts 16 D5
Cole's Green Suff 31 B9
Coles Green Suff 31 D7
Colesbourne Glos 26 G6
Colesden Bedford 29 C8
Coleshill Bucks 18 B6
Coleshill Oxon 17 B9
Coleshill Warks 35 G8
Colestocks Devon 7 F9
Colgate W Sus 11 A11
Colgrain Argyll 68 B2
Colinsburgh Fife 77 G7
Colinton Edin 69 D11
Colintraive Argyll 73 F9
Colkirk Norf 38 C5
Collace Perth 76 D5
Collafirth Shetland 96 G6
Collaton St Mary Torbay 5 F9
College Milton S Lanark 68 E5
Collessie Fife 76 F5
Collier Row London 20 B2
Collier Street Kent 20 G4
Collier's End Herts 29 F10
Collier's Green Kent 13 C6
Colliery Row T&W 58 B4
Collieston Aberds 89 F10
Collin Dumfries 60 F6
Collingbourne Ducis Wilts 17 F9
Collingbourne Kingston Wilts 17 F9
Collingham Notts 46 F2
Collingham W Yorks 51 E9
Collington Hereford 26 B3
Collingtree Northants 28 C4
Collins Green Warr 43 C8
Colliston Angus 77 C9
Collycroft Warks 35 G9
Collynie Aberds 89 E8
Collyweston Northants 36 E5
Colmonell S Ayrs 66 H4
Colmworth Bedford 29 C8
Coln Rogers Glos 27 H7
Coln St Aldwyn's Glos 27 H8
Coln St Dennis Glos 27 G7
Colnabaichin Aberds 82 C4
Colnbrook Slough 19 D7
Colne Cambs 37 H9
Colne Lancs 50 E4
Colne Edge Lancs 50 E4
Colne Engaine Essex 30 E5
Colney Norf 39 E7
Colney Heath Herts 29 H9
Colney Street Herts 19 A8
Colpy Aberds 89 E6
Colquhar Borders 70 F2
Colsterdale N Yorks 51 A7
Colsterworth Lincs 36 C5
Colston Bassett Notts 36 B2
Coltfield Moray 87 E14
Colthouse Cumb 56 G5
Coltishall Norf 39 D8
Coltness N Lanark 69 E7
Colton Cumb 56 H5
Colton N Yorks 51 E11
Colton Norf 39 E7
Colton Staffs 35 C6
Colton W Yorks 51 F9
Colva Powys 25 C9
Colvend Dumfries 55 D11
Colvister Shetland 96 D7
Colwall Green Hereford 26 D4
Colwall Stone Hereford 26 D4
Colwell Northumb 62 F5
Colwich Staffs 34 C6
Colwick Notts 36 A2
Colwinston V Glam 14 D5
Colworth W Sus 11 D8
Colwyn Bay = Bae Colwyn Conwy 41 C10
Colyford Devon 8 E1
Colyton Devon 8 E1
Combe Hereford 25 B10
Combe Oxon 27 G11
Combe W Berks 17 E10
Combe Common Sur 18 H6
Combe Down Bath 16 E4
Combe Florey Som 7 C10
Combe Hay Bath 16 F4
Combe Martin Devon 6 B4
Combe Moor Hereford 25 B10
Combe Raleigh Devon 7 F10
Combe St Nicholas Som 8 C2
Combeinteignhead Devon 5 D10
Comberbach Ches W 43 E9
Comberton Cambs 29 C10
Comberton Hereford 25 B11
Combpyne Devon 8 E1
Combridge Staffs 35 B6
Combrook Warks 27 C10
Combs Derbys 44 E4
Combs Suff 31 C7
Combs Ford Suff 31 C7
Combwich Som 15 G8
Comers Aberds 83 C8
Comins Coch Ceredig 32 G2
Commercial End Cambs 30 B2
Commins Capel Betws Ceredig 24 C3
Commins Coch Powys 32 E4
Common Edge Blackpool 49 F3
Common Side Derbys 45 E7
Commondale N Yorks 59 E7
Commonmoor Corn 4 E3
Commonside Ches W 43 E8
Compstall Gtr Man 44 C3
Compton Devon 5 E9
Compton Hants 10 B3
Compton Sur 18 G5
Compton Sur 18 G6
Compton W Berks 18 D2
Compton W Sus 11 C6
Compton Wilts 17 F8
Compton Abbas Dorset 9 C7
Compton Abdale Glos 27 G7
Compton Bassett Wilts 17 D7
Compton Beauchamp Oxon 17 C9
Compton Bishop Som 15 F9
Compton Chamberlayne Wilts 9 B9
Compton Dando Bath 16 E3
Compton Dundon Som 8 A3
Compton Martin Bath 15 F11
Compton Pauncefoot Som 8 B5
Compton Valence Dorset 8 E4
Comrie Fife 69 B9
Comrie Perth 75 E10
Conaglen House Highld 80 G2
Conchra Argyll 73 E9
Concraigie Perth 76 C4
Conder Green Lancs 49 D4
Conderton Worcs 26 E6
Condicote Glos 27 F8
Condorrat N Lanark 68 C6
Condover Shrops 33 E10
Coney Weston Suff 38 H5
Coneyhurst W Sus 11 B10
Coneysthorpe N Yorks 52 B3
Coneythorpe N Yorks 51 D9
Conford Hants 11 A7
Congash Highld 82 A2
Congdon's Shop Corn 4 D3
Congerstone Leics 35 E9
Congham Norf 38 C3
Congl-y-wal Gwyn 41 F9
Congleton Ches E 44 F2
Congresbury N Som 15 E10
Congreve Staffs 34 D5
Conicavel Moray 87 F12
Coningsby Lincs 46 G6
Conington Cambs 29 B10
Conington Cambs 37 G7
Conisbrough S Yorks 45 C9
Conisby Argyll 64 B3
Conisholme Lincs 47 C8
Coniston Cumb 56 G5
Coniston E Yorks 53 F7
Coniston Cold N Yorks 50 D5
Conistone N Yorks 50 C5
Connah's Quay Flint 42 F5
Connel Argyll 74 D2
Connel Park E Ayrs 67 E9
Connor Downs Corn 2 F4
Conon Bridge Highld 87 F8
Conon House Highld 87 F8
Cononley N Yorks 50 E5
Conordan Highld 85 E10
Consall Staffs 44 H3
Consett Durham 58 A2
Constable Burton N Yorks 58 G2
Constantine Corn 2 G6
Constantine Bay Corn 3 B7
Contin Highld 86 F7
Contlaw Aberdeen 83 C10
Conwy Conwy 41 C9
Conyer Kent 20 E6
Conyers Green Suff 30 B5
Cooden E Sus 12 F6
Cooil IoM 48 E3
Cookbury Devon 6 F3
Cookham Windsor 18 C5
Cookham Dean Windsor 18 C5
Cookham Rise Windsor 18 C5
Cookhill Worcs 27 C7
Cookley Suff 39 H9
Cookley Worcs 34 G4
Cookley Green Oxon 18 B3
Cookney Aberds 83 D10
Cookridge W Yorks 51 E8
Cooksbridge E Sus 12 E3
Cooksmill Green Essex 30 H3
Coolham W Sus 11 B10
Cooling Medway 20 D4
Coombe Corn 3 D8
Coombe Corn 6 E1
Coombe Hants 10 B5
Coombe Wilts 17 F8
Coombe Bissett Wilts 9 B10
Coombe Hill Glos 26 F5
Coombe Keynes Dorset 9 F7
Coombes W Sus 11 D10
Coopersale Common Essex 19 A11
Cootham W Sus 11 C9
Copdock Suff 31 D8
Copford Green Essex 30 F6
Copgrove N Yorks 51 C9
Copister Shetland 96 F6
Cople Bedford 29 D8
Copley Durham 58 D1
Coplow Dale Derbys 44 E5
Copmanthorpe York 52 E1
Coppathorne Corn 4 A3
Coppenhall Staffs 34 D5
Coppenhall Moss Ches E 43 G10
Copperhouse Corn 2 F4
Coppingford Cambs 37 G7
Copplestone Devon 7 F6
Coppull Lancs 43 A8
Coppull Moor Lancs 43 A8
Copsale W Sus 11 B10
Copster Green Lancs 50 F2
Copston Magna Warks 35 G10
Copt Heath W Mid 35 H7
Copt Hewick N Yorks 51 B9
Copt Oak Leics 35 D10
Copthorne Shrops 33 D10
Copthorne Sur 12 C2
Copy's Green Norf 38 B5
Copythorne Hants 10 C2
Corbets Tey London 20 C2
Corbridge Northumb 62 G5
Corby Northants 36 G4
Corby Glen Lincs 36 C5
Cordon N Ayrs 66 C3
Coreley Shrops 26 A3
Cores End Bucks 18 C6
Corfe Som 7 E11
Corfe Castle Dorset 9 F8
Corfe Mullen Dorset 9 E8
Corfton Shrops 33 G10
Corgarff Aberds 82 C4
Corhampton Hants 10 B5
Corlae Dumfries 67 G9
Corley Warks 35 G9
Corley Ash Warks 35 G8
Corley Moor Warks 35 G8
Cornaa IoM 48 D4
Cornabus Argyll 64 D4
Cornel Conwy 41 D9
Corner Row Lancs 49 F4
Corney Cumb 56 G3
Cornforth Durham 58 C4
Cornhill Aberds 88 C5
Cornhill-on-Tweed Northumb 71 G7
Cornholme W Yorks 50 G5
Cornish Hall End Essex 30 E3
Cornquoy Orkney 95 J6
Cornsay Durham 58 B2
Cornsay Colliery Durham 58 B2
Corntown Highld 87 F8
Corntown V Glam 14 D5
Cornwell Oxon 27 F9
Cornwood Devon 5 F7
Cornworthy Devon 5 F9
Corpach Highld 80 F2
Corpusty Norf 39 B7
Corran Highld 74 A3
Corran Highld 85 H13
Corranbuie Argyll 73 G7
Corrany IoM 48 D4
Corrie N Ayrs 66 B3
Corrie Common Dumfries 61 E8
Corriecravie N Ayrs 66 D2
Corriemoillie Highld 86 E6
Corriemulzie Lodge Highld 86 B6
Corrievarkie Lodge Perth 81 F7
Corrievorrie Highld 81 A9
Corrimony Highld 86 H6
Corringham Lincs 46 C2
Corringham Thurrock 20 C4
Corris Gwyn 32 E3
Corris Uchaf Gwyn 32 E3
Corrour Shooting Lodge Highld 80 G6
Corrow Argyll 74 G4
Corry Highld 85 F11
Corry of Ardnagrask Highld 87 G8
Corrykinloch Highld 92 G6
Corrymuckloch Perth 75 D11
Corrynachenchy Argyll 79 G9
Cors-y-Gedol Gwyn 32 C1
Corsback Highld 94 C4
Corscombe Dorset 8 D4
Corse Aberds 88 D6
Corse Glos 26 F4
Corse Lawn Worcs 26 E5
Corse of Kinnoir Aberds 88 D5
Corsewall Dumfries 54 C3
Corsham Wilts 16 D5
Corsindae Aberds 83 C8
Corsley Wilts 16 G5
Corsley Heath Wilts 16 G5
Corsock Dumfries 60 F3
Corston Bath 16 E3
Corston Wilts 16 C6
Corstorphine Edin 69 C10
Cortachy Angus 76 B6
Corton Suff 39 F11
Corton Wilts 16 G6
Corton Denham Som 8 B5
Coruanan Lodge Highld 80 G2
Corunna W Isles 84 B3
Corwen Denb 33 A6
Coryton Devon 4 C5
Coryton Thurrock 20 C4
Cosby Leics 35 F11
Coseley W Mid 34 F5
Cosgrove Northants 28 D4
Cosham Ptsmth 10 D5
Cosheston Pembs 22 F5
Cossall Notts 35 A10
Cossington Leics 36 D2
Cossington Som 15 G9
Costa Orkney 95 F4
Costessey Norf 39 D7
Costock Notts 36 C1
Coston Leics 36 C4
Cote Oxon 17 A10
Cotebrook Ches W 43 F8
Cotehill Cumb 56 A6
Cotes Cumb 57 H6
Cotes Leics 36 C1
Cotes Staffs 34 B4
Cotesbach Leics 35 G11
Cotgrave Notts 36 B2
Cothall Aberds 83 B10
Cotham Notts 45 H11
Cothelstone Som 7 C10
Cotherstone Durham 58 E1
Cothill Oxon 17 B11
Cotleigh Devon 7 F11
Cotmanhay Derbys 35 A10
Cotmaton Devon 7 H10
Coton Cambs 29 C11
Coton Northants 28 A3
Coton Staffs 34 B5
Coton Staffs 34 C4
Coton Clanford Staffs 34 C4
Coton Hill Shrops 33 D10
Coton Hill Staffs 34 B5
Coton in the Elms Derbys 35 D8
Cott Devon 5 E8
Cottam E Yorks 52 C5
Cottam Lancs 49 F5
Cottam Notts 46 E2
Cottartown Highld 87 H13
Cottenham Cambs 29 B11
Cotterdale N Yorks 57 G10
Cottered Herts 29 F10
Cotteridge W Mid 34 H6
Cotterstock Northants 36 F6
Cottesbrooke Northants 28 A4
Cottesmore Rutland 36 D5
Cotteylands Devon 7 E8
Cottingham E Yorks 52 F6
Cottingham Northants 36 F4
Cottingley W Yorks 51 F7
Cottisford Oxon 28 E2
Cotton Staffs 44 H4
Cotton Suff 31 B7
Cotton End Bedford 29 D7
Cottown Aberds 83 A7
Cottown Aberds 83 B9
Cottown Aberds 89 D8
Cotwalton Staffs 34 B5
Couch's Mill Corn 4 F2
Coughton Hereford 26 F2
Coughton Warks 27 B7
Coulaghailtro Argyll 72 G6
Coulags Highld 86 G2
Coulby Newham Mbro 58 E6
Coulderton Cumb 56 F1
Coulin Highld 86 F3
Coull Aberds 83 C7
Coull Argyll 64 B3
Coulport Argyll 73 E11
Coulsdon London 19 F9
Coulston Wilts 16 F6
Coulter S Lanark 69 G9
Coulton N Yorks 52 B2
Cound Shrops 34 E1
Coundon Durham 58 D3
Coundon W Mid 35 G9
Coundon Grange Durham 58 D3
Countersett N Yorks 57 H11
Countess Wilts 17 G8
Countess Wear Devon 5 C10
Countesthorpe Leics 36 F1
Countisbury Devon 7 B6
County Oak W Sus 12 C1
Coup Green Lancs 50 G1
Coupar Angus Perth 76 C5
Coupland Northumb 71 G8
Cour Argyll 65 D9
Courance Dumfries 60 D6
Court-at-Street Kent 13 C9
Court Henry Carms 23 D10
Courteenhall Northants 28 C4
Courtsend Essex 21 B7
Courtway Som 7 C11
Cousland Midloth 70 D2
Cousley Wood E Sus 12 C5
Cove Argyll 73 E11
Cove Borders 70 C6
Cove Devon 7 E8
Cove Hants 18 F5
Cove Highld 91 H13
Cove Bay Aberdeen 83 C11
Cove Bottom Suff 39 H10
Covehithe Suff 39 G11
Coven Staffs 34 E5
Coveney Cambs 37 G10
Covenham St Bartholomew Lincs 47 C7
Covenham St Mary Lincs 47 C7
Coventry W Mid 35 H9
Coverack Corn 3 H6
Coverham N Yorks 58 H2
Covesea Moray 88 A1
Covington Cambs 29 A7
Covington S Lanark 69 G8
Cow Ark Lancs 50 E2
Cowan Bridge Lancs 50 B2
Cowbeech E Sus 12 E5
Cowbit Lincs 37 D8
Cowbridge Lincs 47 H7
Cowbridge Som 7 B8
Cowbridge = Y Bont-Faen V Glam 14 D5
Cowdale Derbys 44 E4
Cowden Kent 12 B3
Cowdenbeath Fife 69 A10
Cowdenburn Borders 69 E11
Cowers Lane Derbys 45 H7
Cowes IoW 10 E3
Cowesby N Yorks 58 H5
Cowfold W Sus 11 B11
Cowgill Cumb 57 H9
Cowie Aberds 83 E10
Cowie Stirling 69 B7
Cowley Devon 7 G8
Cowley Glos 26 G6
Cowley London 19 C7
Cowley Oxon 18 A2
Cowleymoor Devon 7 E8
Cowling Lancs 50 H1
Cowling N Yorks 50 E5
Cowling N Yorks 58 H3
Cowlinge Suff 30 C4
Cowpe Lancs 50 G4
Cowpen Northumb 63 E8
Cowpen Bewley Stockton 58 D5
Cowplain Hants 10 C5
Cowshill Durham 57 B10
Cowslip Green N Som 15 E10
Cowstrandburn Fife 69 A9
Cowthorpe N Yorks 51 D10
Cox Common Suff 39 G9
Cox Green Windsor 18 D5
Cox Moor Notts 45 G9
Coxbank Ches E 34 A2
Coxbench Derbys 35 A9
Coxford Norf 38 C4
Coxford Soton 10 C2
Coxheath Kent 20 F4
Coxhill Kent 21 G9
Coxhoe Durham 58 C4
Coxley Som 15 G11
Coxwold N Yorks 51 B11
Coychurch Bridgend 14 D5
Coylton S Ayrs 67 D7
Coylumbridge Highld 81 B11
Coynach Aberds 82 C6
Coynachie Aberds 88 E4
Coytrahen Bridgend 14 C4
Crabadon Devon 5 F8
Crabbs Cross Worcs 27 B7
Crabtree W Sus 11 B11
Crackenthorpe Cumb 57 D8
Crackington Haven Corn 4 B2
Crackley Warks 27 A9
Crackleybank Shrops 34 D3
Crackpot N Yorks 57 G11
Cracoe N Yorks 50 C5
Craddock Devon 7 E9
Cradhlastadh W Isles 90 D5
Cradley Hereford 26 D4
Cradley Heath W Mid 34 G5
Crafthole Corn 4 F4
Cragg Vale W Yorks 50 G6
Craggan Highld 82 A2
Craggie Highld 87 H10
Craggie Highld 93 H11
Craghead Durham 58 A3
Crai Powys 24 F5
Craibstone Moray 88 C4
Craichie Angus 77 C8
Craig Dumfries 55 B9
Craig Dumfries 55 C9
Craig Highld 86 G3
Craig Castle Aberds 82 A6
Craig-cefn-parc Swansea 14 A2
Craig Penllyn V Glam 14 D5
Craig-y-don Conwy 41 B9
Craig-y-nos Powys 24 G5
Craiganor Lodge Perth 75 B9
Craigdam Aberds 89 E8
Craigdarroch Dumfries 60 D3
Craigdarroch Highld 86 F7
Craigdhu Highld 86 G7
Craigearn Aberds 83 B9
Craigellachie Moray 88 D2
Craigencross Dumfries 54 C3
Craigend Perth 76 E4
Craigend Stirling 68 B6
Craigendive Argyll 73 E9
Craigendoran Argyll 68 B2
Craigends Renfs 68 D3
Craigens Argyll 64 B3
Craigens E Ayrs 67 E8
Craighat Stirling 68 B3
Craighead Fife 77 G9
Craighlaw Mains Dumfries 54 C6
Craighouse Argyll 72 G4
Craigie Aberds 83 B11
Craigie Dundee 77 D7
Craigie Perth 76 C4
Craigie Perth 76 E4
Craigie S Ayrs 67 C7
Craigiefield Orkney 95 G5
Craigielaw E Loth 70 C3
Craiglockhart Edin 69 C11
Craigmalloch E Ayrs 67 G7
Craigmaud Aberds 89 C8
Craigmillar Edin 69 C11
Craigmore Argyll 73 G10
Craignant Shrops 33 B8
Craigneuk N Lanark 68 D6
Craigneuk N Lanark 68 E6
Craignure Argyll 79 H10
Craigo Angus 77 A9
Craigow Perth 76 G3
Craigrothie Fife 76 F6
Craigroy Moray 87 F14
Craigruie Stirling 75 E7
Craigston Castle Aberds 89 C7
Craigton Aberdeen 83 C10
Craigton Angus 76 B6
Craigton Angus 77 D8
Craigton Highld 87 B9
Craigtown Highld 93 D11
Craik Borders 61 C9
Crail Fife 77 G9
Crailing Borders 62 A2
Crailinghall Borders 62 A2
Craiselound N Lincs 45 C11
Crakehill N Yorks 51 B10
Crakemarsh Staffs 35 B6
Crambe N Yorks 52 C3
Cramlington Northumb 63 F8
Cramond Edin 69 C10
Cramond Bridge Edin 69 C10
Cranage Ches E 43 F10
Cranberry Staffs 34 B4
Cranborne Dorset 9 C9
Cranbourne Brack 18 D6
Cranbrook Devon 7 G9
Cranbrook Kent 13 C6
Cranbrook Common Kent 13 C6
Crane Moor S Yorks 45 B7
Crane's Corner Norf 38 D5
Cranfield C Beds 28 D6
Cranford London 19 D8
Cranford St Andrew Northants 36 H5
Cranford St John Northants 36 H5
Cranham Glos 26 G5
Cranham London 20 C2
Crank Mers 43 C8
Crank Wood Gtr Man 43 B9
Cranleigh Sur 19 H7
Cranley Suff 31 A8
Cranmer Green Suff 31 A7
Cranmore IoW 10 F2
Cranna Aberds 89 C6
Crannich Argyll 79 G8
Crannoch Moray 88 C4
Cranoe Leics 36 F3
Cransford Suff 31 B10
Cranshaws Borders 70 D5
Cranstal IoM 48 B4
Crantock Corn 3 C6
Cranwell Lincs 46 H4
Cranwich Norf 38 F3
Cranworth Norf 38 E5
Craobh Haven Argyll 72 C6
Crapstone Devon 4 E6
Crarae Argyll 73 D8
Crask Inn Highld 93 G8
Crask of Aigas Highld 86 G7
Craskins Aberds 83 C7
Craster Northumb 63 B8
Craswall Hereford 25 E9
Cratfield Suff 39 H9
Crathes Aberds 83 D9
Crathie Aberds 82 D4
Crathie Highld 81 D7
Crathorne N Yorks 58 F5
Craven Arms Shrops 33 G10
Crawcrook T&W 63 G7
Crawford Lancs 43 B7
Crawford S Lanark 60 A5
Crawfordjohn S Lanark 60 A4
Crawick Dumfries 60 B3
Crawley Hants 10 A3
Crawley Oxon 27 G10
Crawley W Sus 12 C1
Crawley Down W Sus 12 C2
Crawleyside Durham 57 B11
Crawshawbooth Lancs 50 G4
Crawton Aberds 83 F10
Cray N Yorks 50 B5
Cray Perth 76 A4
Crayford London 20 D2
Crayke N Yorks 52 B1
Crays Hill Essex 20 B4
Cray's Pond Oxon 18 C3
Creacombe Devon 7 E7
Creag Ghoraidh W Isles 84 D2
Creagan Argyll 74 C2
Creaguaineach Lodge Highld 80 G5
Creaksea Essex 20 B6
Creaton Northants 28 A4
Creca Dumfries 61 F8
Credenhill Hereford 25 D11
Crediton Devon 7 F7
Creebridge Dumfries 55 C7
Creech Heathfield Som 8 B1
Creech St Michael Som 8 B1
Creed Corn 3 E8
Creekmouth London 19 C11
Creeting Bottoms Suff 31 C8
Creeting St Mary Suff 31 C7
Creeton Lincs 36 C6
Creetown Dumfries 55 D7
Creg-ny-Baa IoM 48 D3
Creggans Argyll 73 C9
Cregneash IoM 48 F1
Cregrina Powys 25 C8
Creich Fife 76 E6
Creigiau Cardiff 14 C6
Cremyll Corn 4 F5
Creslow Bucks 28 F5
Cressage Shrops 34 E1
Cressbrook Derbys 44 E5
Cresselly Pembs 22 F5
Cressing Essex 30 F4
Cresswell Northumb 63 D8
Cresswell Staffs 34 B5
Cresswell Quay Pembs 22 F5
Creswell Derbys 45 E9
Cretingham Suff 31 B9
Cretshengan Argyll 72 G6
Crewe Ches E 43 G10
Crewe Ches W 43 G7
Crewgreen Powys 33 D9
Crewkerne Som 8 D3
Crianlarich Stirling 74 E6
Cribyn Ceredig 23 A10
Criccieth Gwyn 40 G6
Crich Derbys 45 G7
Crichie Aberds 89 D9
Crichton Midloth 70 D2
Crick Mon 15 B10
Crick Northants 28 A2
Crickadarn Powys 25 D7
Cricket Malherbie Som 8 C2
Cricket St Thomas Som 8 D2
Crickheath Shrops 33 C8
Crickhowell Powys 25 G9
Cricklade Wilts 17 B8
Cricklewood London 19 C9
Cridling Stubbs N Yorks 51 G11
Crieff Perth 75 E11
Criggion Powys 33 D8
Crigglestone W Yorks 51 H9
Crimond Aberds 89 C10
Crimonmogate Aberds 89 C10
Crimplesham Norf 38 E2
Crinan Argyll 72 D6
Cringleford Norf 39 E7
Cringles W Yorks 50 E6
Crinow Pembs 22 E6
Cripplesease Corn 2 F4
Cripplestyle Dorset 9 C9
Cripp's Corner E Sus 13 D6
Croasdale Cumb 56 E2
Crock Street Som 8 C2
Crockenhill Kent 20 E2
Crockernwell Devon 7 G6
Crockerton Wilts 16 G5
Crocketford or Ninemile Bar Dumfries 60 F4
Crockey Hill York 52 E2
Crockham Hill Kent 19 F11
Crockleford Heath Essex 31 F7
Crockness Orkney 95 J4
Croes-goch Pembs 22 C3
Croes-lan Ceredig 23 B8

Croes-y-mwyalch Torf 15 B9
Croeserw Neath 14 B4
Croesor Gwyn 41 F8
Croesyceiliog Carms 23 E9
Croesyceiliog Torf 15 B9
Croesywaun Gwyn 41 E7
Croft Leics 35 F11
Croft Lincs 47 F9
Croft Pembs 22 B6
Croft Warr 43 C9
Croft-on-Tees N Yorks 58 F3
Croftamie Stirling 68 B3
Croftmalloch W Loth 69 D8
Crofton W Yorks 51 H9
Crofton Wilts 17 E9
Crofts of Benachielt Highld 94 G3
Crofts of Haddo Aberds 89 E8
Crofts of Inverthernie Aberds 89 D7
Crofts of Meikle Ardo Aberds 89 D8
Crofty Swansea 23 G10
Croggan Argyll 79 J10
Croglin Cumb 57 B7
Croich Highld 86 B7
Crois Dughaill W Isles 84 F2
Cromarty Highld 87 E10
Cromblet Aberds 89 E7
Cromdale Highld 82 A2
Cromer Herts 29 F9
Cromer Norf 39 A8
Cromford Derbys 44 G6
Cromhall S Glos 16 B3
Cromhall Common S Glos 16 C3
Cromor W Isles 91 E9
Cromra Highld 81 D7
Cromwell Notts 45 F11
Cronberry E Ayrs 67 D9
Crondall Hants 18 G4
Cronk-y-Voddy IoM 48 D3
Cronton Mers 43 D7
Crook Cumb 56 G6
Crook Durham 58 C2
Crook of Devon Perth 76 G3
Crookedholm E Ayrs 67 C7
Crookes S Yorks 45 D7
Crookham Northumb 71 G8
Crookham W Berks 18 E2
Crookham Village Hants 18 F4
Crookhaugh Borders 69 H10
Crookhouse Borders 70 H6
Crooklands Cumb 49 A5
Cropredy Oxon 27 D11
Cropston Leics 36 D1
Cropthorne Worcs 26 D6
Cropton N Yorks 59 H8
Cropwell Bishop Notts 36 B2
Cropwell Butler Notts 36 B2
Cros W Isles 91 A10
Crosbost W Isles 91 E8
Crosby Cumb 56 C2
Crosby IoM 48 E3
Crosby N Lincs 46 A2
Crosby Garrett Cumb 57 F9
Crosby Ravensworth Cumb 57 E8
Crosby Villa Cumb 56 C2
Croscombe Som 16 G2
Cross Som 15 F10
Cross Ash Mon 25 G11
Cross-at-Hand Kent 20 G4
Cross Green Devon 4 C4
Cross Green Suff 30 C6
Cross Green Suff 30 C5
Cross Green Warks 27 C10
Cross-hands Carms 22 D6
Cross Hands Carms 23 E10
Cross Hands Pembs 22 E5
Cross Hill Derbys 45 H8
Cross Houses Shrops 33 E11
Cross in Hand E Sus 12 D4
Cross in Hand Leics 35 G11
Cross Inn Ceredig 23 A8
Cross Inn Ceredig 24 B2
Cross Inn Rhondda 14 C6
Cross Keys Kent 20 F2
Cross Lane Head Shrops 34 F3
Cross Lanes Corn 2 G5
Cross Lanes N Yorks 51 C11
Cross Lanes Wrex 43 H6
Cross o' th' hands Derbys 44 H6
Cross Oak Powys 25 F8
Cross of Jackston Aberds 89 E7
Cross Street Suff 39 H7
Cross Trickett's Dorset 9 D9
Crossaig Argyll 65 C9
Crossal Highld 85 E9
Crossapol Argyll 78 G2
Crossburn Falk 69 C7
Crossbush W Sus 11 D9
Crosscanonby Cumb 56 C2
Crossdale Street Norf 39 B8
Crossens Mers 49 H3
Crossflatts W Yorks 51 E7
Crossford Fife 69 B9
Crossford S Lanark 69 F7
Crossgate Lincs 37 C8
Crossgatehall E Loth 70 D2
Crossgates Fife 69 B10
Crossgates Powys 25 B7
Crossgill Lancs 50 C1
Crosshill E Ayrs 67 D7
Crosshill Fife 76 H4
Crosshill S Ayrs 66 F6
Crosshouse E Ayrs 67 C6
Crossings Cumb 61 F11
Crosskeys Caerph 15 B8
Crosskirk Highld 93 B13
Crosslanes Shrops 33 D9
Crosslee Borders 61 B9
Crosslee Renfs 68 D3
Crossmichael Dumfries 55 C10
Crossmoor Lancs 49 F4
Crossroads Aberds 83 D9
Crossroads E Ayrs 67 C7
Crossway Hereford 26 E3
Crossway Mon 25 G11
Crossway Powys 25 C7
Crossway Green Worcs 26 B5
Crossways Dorset 9 F6
Crosswell Pembs 22 C6
Crosswood Ceredig 24 A3
Crosthwaite Cumb 56 G6
Croston Lancs 49 H4
Crostwick Norf 39 D8
Crostwight Norf 39 C9
Crothair W Isles 90 D6
Crouch Kent 20 F3
Crouch Hill Dorset 8 C6
Crouch House Green Kent 19 G11
Croucheston Wilts 9 B9
Croughton Northants 28 E2
Crovie Aberds 89 B8
Crow Edge S Yorks 44 B5
Crow Hill Hereford 26 F3
Crowan Corn 2 F5
Crowborough E Sus 12 C4
Crowcombe Som 7 C10
Crowdecote Derbys 44 F5
Crowden Derbys 44 C4
Crowell Oxon 18 B4
Crowfield Northants 28 D3
Crowfield Suff 31 C8
Crowhurst E Sus 13 E6
Crowhurst Sur 19 G10
Crowhurst Lane End Sur 19 G10
Crowland Lincs 37 D8
Crowlas Corn 2 F4
Crowle N Lincs 45 A11
Crowle Worcs 26 C6
Crowmarsh Gifford Oxon 18 C3
Crown Corner Suff 31 A9
Crownhill Plym 4 F5
Crownland Suff 31 B7
Crownthorpe Norf 39 E6
Crowntown Corn 2 F5
Crows-an-wra Corn 2 G2
Crowshill Norf 38 E5
Crowsnest Shrops 33 E9
Crowthorne Brack 18 E5
Crowton Ches W 43 E8
Croxall Staffs 35 D7
Croxby Lincs 46 C5
Croxdale Durham 58 C3
Croxden Staffs 35 B6
Croxley Green Herts 19 B7
Croxton Cambs 29 B9
Croxton N Lincs 46 A4
Croxton Norf 38 G4
Croxton Staffs 34 B3
Croxton Kerrial Leics 36 C4
Croxtonbank Staffs 34 B3
Croy Highld 87 G10
Croy N Lanark 68 C6
Croyde Devon 6 C3
Croydon Cambs 29 D10
Croydon London 19 E10
Crubenmore Lodge Highld 81 D8
Cruckmeole Shrops 33 E10
Cruckton Shrops 33 D10
Cruden Bay Aberds 89 E10
Crudgington Telford 34 D2
Crudwell Wilts 16 B6
Crug Powys 25 A8
Crugmeer Corn 3 B8
Crugybar Carms 24 E3
Crulabhig W Isles 90 D6
Crumlin = Crymlyn Caerph 15 B8
Crumpsall Gtr Man 44 B2
Crundale Kent 21 G7
Crundale Pembs 22 E4
Cruwys Morchard Devon 7 E7
Crux Easton Hants 17 F11
Crwbin Carms 23 E9
Crya Orkney 95 H4
Cryers Hill Bucks 18 B5
Crymlyn = Crumlin Caerph 15 B8
Crymlyn Gwyn 41 C8
Crymych Pembs 22 C6
Crynant Neath 14 A3
Crynfryn Ceredig 24 B2
Cuaig Highld 85 C12
Cuan Argyll 72 B6
Cubbington Warks 27 B10
Cubeck N Yorks 57 H11
Cubert Corn 3 D6
Cubley S Yorks 44 B6
Cubley Common Derbys 35 B7
Cublington Bucks 28 F5
Cublington Hereford 25 E11
Cuckfield W Sus 12 D2
Cucklington Som 9 B6
Cuckney Notts 45 E9
Cuckoo Hill Notts 45 C11
Cuddesdon Oxon 18 A3
Cuddington Bucks 28 G4
Cuddington Ches W 43 E9
Cuddington Heath Ches W 43 H7
Cuddy Hill Lancs 49 F4
Cudham London 19 F11
Cudliptown Devon 4 D6
Cudworth S Yorks 45 B7
Cudworth Som 8 C2
Cuffley Herts 19 A10
Cuiashader W Isles 91 B10
Cuidhir W Isles 84 H1
Cuidhtinis W Isles 90 J5
Culbo Highld 87 E9
Culbokie Highld 87 F9
Culburnie Highld 86 G7
Culcabock Highld 87 G9
Culcairn Highld 87 E9
Culcharry Highld 87 F11
Culcheth Warr 43 C9
Culdrain Aberds 88 E5
Culduie Highld 85 D12
Culford Suff 30 A5
Culgaith Cumb 57 D8
Culham Oxon 18 B2
Culkein Highld 92 F3
Culkein Drumbeg Highld 92 F4
Culkerton Glos 16 B6
Cullachie Highld 81 A11
Cullen Moray 88 B5
Cullercoats T&W 63 F9
Cullicudden Highld 87 E9
Cullingworth W Yorks 51 F6
Cullipool Argyll 72 B6
Cullivoe Shetland 96 C7
Culloch Perth 75 F10
Culloden Highld 87 G10
Cullompton Devon 7 F9
Culmaily Highld 87 B11
Culmazie Dumfries 54 D6
Culmington Shrops 33 G10
Culmstock Devon 7 E10
Culnacraig Highld 92 J3
Culnaknock Highld 85 B10
Culpho Suff 31 D9
Culrain Highld 87 B8
Culross Fife 69 B8
Culroy S Ayrs 66 E6
Culsh Aberds 82 D5
Culsh Aberds 89 D8
Culshabbin Dumfries 54 D6
Culswick Shetland 96 J4
Cultercullen Aberds 89 F9
Cults Aberdeen 83 C10
Cults Aberds 88 E5
Cults Dumfries 55 E7
Culverstone Green Kent 20 E3
Culverthorpe Lincs 36 A6
Culworth Northants 28 D2
Culzie Lodge Highld 87 D8
Cumbernauld N Lanark 68 C6
Cumbernauld Village N Lanark 68 C6
Cumberworth Lincs 47 E9
Cuminestown Aberds 89 C8
Cumlewick Shetland 96 L6
Cummersdale Cumb 56 A5
Cummertrees Dumfries 61 G7
Cummingston Moray 88 B1
Cumnock E Ayrs 67 D8
Cumnor Oxon 17 A11
Cumrew Cumb 57 A7
Cumwhinton Cumb 56 A6
Cumwhitton Cumb 57 A7
Cundall N Yorks 51 B10
Cunninghamhead N Ayrs 67 B6
Cunnister Shetland 96 D7
Cupar Fife 76 F6
Cupar Muir Fife 76 F6
Cupernham Hants 10 B2
Curbar Derbys 44 E6
Curbridge Hants 10 C4
Curbridge Oxon 27 H10
Curdridge Hants 10 C4
Curdworth Warks 35 F7
Curland Som 8 C1
Curlew Green Suff 31 B10
Currarie S Ayrs 66 G4
Curridge W Berks 17 D11
Currie Edin 69 D10
Curry Mallet Som 8 B2
Curry Rivel Som 8 B2
Curtisden Green Kent 12 B6
Curtisknowle Devon 5 F8
Cury Corn 2 G5
Cushnie Aberds 89 B7
Cushuish Som 7 C10
Cusop Hereford 25 D9
Cutcloy Dumfries 55 F7
Cutcombe Som 7 C8
Cutgate Gtr Man 44 A2
Cutiau Gwyn 32 D2
Cutlers Green Essex 30 E2
Cutnall Green Worcs 26 B5
Cutsdean Glos 27 E7
Cutthorpe Derbys 45 E7
Cutts Shetland 96 K6
Cuxham Oxon 18 B3
Cuxton Medway 20 E4
Cuxwold Lincs 46 B5
Cwm Bl Gwent 25 H8
Cwm Denb 42 E3
Cwm Swansea 14 B2
Cwm-byr Carms 24 E3
Cwm-Cewydd Gwyn 32 D4
Cwm-cou Ceredig 23 B7
Cwm-Dulais Swansea 14 A2
Cwm-felin-fach Caerph 15 B7
Cwm Ffrwd-oer Torf 15 A8
Cwm-hesgen Gwyn 32 C3
Cwm-hwnt Rhondda 24 H6
Cwm Irfon Powys 24 D5
Cwm-Llinau Powys 32 E4
Cwm-mawr Carms 23 E10
Cwm-parc Rhondda 14 B5
Cwm Penmachno Conwy 41 F9
Cwm-y-glo Carms 23 E10
Cwm-y-glo Gwyn 41 D7
Cwmafan Neath 14 B3
Cwmaman Rhondda 14 B6
Cwmann Carms 23 B10
Cwmavon Torf 25 H9
Cwmbach Carms 23 D7
Cwmbach Carms 23 F9
Cwmbach Powys 25 C7
Cwmbach Powys 25 E8
Cwmbâch Rhondda 14 A6
Cwmbelan Powys 32 G5
Cwmbrân = Cwmbran Torf 15 B8
Cwmbran = Cwmbrân Torf 15 B8
Cwmbrwyno Ceredig 32 G3
Cwmcarn Caerph 15 B8
Cwmcarvan Mon 25 H11
Cwmcych Carms 23 C7
Cwmdare Rhondda 14 A5
Cwmderwen Powys 32 E5
Cwmdu Carms 24 E3
Cwmdu Powys 25 F8
Cwmdu Swansea 14 B2
Cwmduad Carms 23 C8
Cwmdwr Carms 24 E4
Cwmfelin Bridgend 14 C4
Cwmfelin M Tydf 14 A6
Cwmfelin Boeth Carms 22 E6
Cwmfelin Mynach Carms 23 D7
Cwmffrwd Carms 23 E9
Cwmgiedd Powys 24 G4
Cwmgors Neath 24 G4
Cwmgwili Carms 23 E10
Cwmgwrach Neath 14 A4
Cwmhiraeth Carms 23 C8
Cwmifor Carms 24 F3
Cwmisfael Carms 23 E9
Cwmllynfell Neath 24 G4
Cwmorgan Pembs 23 C7
Cwmpengraig Carms 23 C8
Cwmrhos Powys 25 F8
Cwmsychpant Ceredig 23 B9
Cwmtillery Bl Gwent 25 H9
Cwmwysg Powys 24 F5
Cwmyoy Mon 25 F9
Cwmystwyth Ceredig 24 A4
Cwrt Gwyn 32 E2
Cwrt-newydd Ceredig 23 B9
Cwrt-y-cadno Carms 24 D3
Cwrt-y-gollen Powys 25 G9
Cydweli = Kidwelly Carms 23 F9
Cyffordd Llandudno = Llandudno Junction Conwy 41 C9
Cyffylliog Denb 42 G3
Cyfronydd Powys 33 E7
Cymer Neath 14 B4
Cyncoed Cardiff 15 C7
Cynghordy Carms 24 D5
Cynheidre Carms 23 F9
Cynwyd Denb 33 A6
Cynwyl Elfed Carms 23 D8
Cywarch Gwyn 32 D4

D

Dacre Cumb 56 D6
Dacre N Yorks 51 C7
Dacre Banks N Yorks 51 C7
Daddry Shield Durham 57 C10
Dadford Bucks 28 E3
Dadlington Leics 35 F10
Dafarn Faig Gwyn 40 F6
Dafen Carms 23 F10
Daffy Green Norf 38 E5
Dagenham London 19 C11
Daglingworth Glos 26 H6
Dagnall Bucks 28 G6
Dail Beag W Isles 90 C7
Dail bho Dheas W Isles 91 A9
Dail bho Thuath W Isles 91 A9
Dail Mor W Isles 90 C7
Daill Argyll 64 B4
Dailly S Ayrs 66 F5
Dairsie or Osnaburgh Fife 77 F7
Daisy Hill Gtr Man 43 B9
Dalabrog W Isles 84 F2
Dalavich Argyll 73 B8
Dalbeattie Dumfries 55 C11
Dalblair E Ayrs 67 E9
Dalbog Angus 83 F7
Dalbury Derbys 35 B8
Dalby IoM 48 E2
Dalby N Yorks 52 B2
Dalchalloch Perth 75 A10
Dalchalm Highld 93 J12
Dalchenna Argyll 73 C9
Dalchirach Moray 88 E1
Dalchork Highld 93 H8
Dalchreichart Highld 80 B4
Dalchruin Perth 75 F10
Dalderby Lincs 46 F6
Dale Pembs 22 F3
Dale Abbey Derbys 35 B10
Dale Head Cumb 56 E6
Dale of Walls Shetland 96 H3
Dalelia Highld 79 E10
Daless Highld 87 H11
Dalfaber Highld 81 B11
Dalgarven N Ayrs 66 B5
Dalgety Bay Fife 69 B10
Dalginross Perth 75 E10
Dalguise Perth 76 C2
Dalhalvaig Highld 93 D11
Dalham Suff 30 B4
Dalinlongart Argyll 73 E10
Dalkeith Midloth 70 D2
Dallam Warr 43 C8
Dallas Moray 87 F14
Dalleagles E Ayrs 67 E8
Dallinghoo Suff 31 C9
Dallington E Sus 12 E5
Dallington Northants 28 B4
Dallow N Yorks 51 B7
Dalmadilly Aberds 83 B9
Dalmally Argyll 74 E4
Dalmarnock Glasgow 68 D5
Dalmary Stirling 75 H8
Dalmellington E Ayrs 67 F7
Dalmeny Edin 69 C10
Dalmigavie Highld 81 B9
Dalmigavie Lodge Highld 81 A9
Dalmore Highld 87 E9
Dalmuir W Dunb 68 C3
Dalnabreck Highld 79 E9
Dalnacardoch Lodge Perth 81 F9
Dalnacroich Highld 86 F6
Dalnaglar Castle Perth 76 A4
Dalnahaitnach Highld 81 A10
Dalnaspidal Lodge Perth 81 F8
Dalnavaid Perth 76 A3
Dalnavie Highld 87 D9
Dalnawillan Lodge Highld 93 E13
Dalness Highld 74 B4
Dalnessie Highld 93 H9
Dalqueich Perth 76 G3
Dalreavoch Highld 93 J10
Dalry N Ayrs 66 B5
Dalrymple E Ayrs 67 E6
Dalserf S Lanark 69 E7
Dalston Cumb 56 A5
Dalswinton Dumfries 60 E5
Dalton Dumfries 61 F7
Dalton Lancs 43 B7
Dalton N Yorks 51 B10
Dalton N Yorks 58 F2
Dalton Northumb 62 H5
Dalton Northumb 63 F7
Dalton S Yorks 45 C8
Dalton-in-Furness Cumb 49 B2
Dalton-le-Dale Durham 58 B5
Dalton-on-Tees N Yorks 58 F3
Dalton Piercy Hrtlpl 58 C5
Dalveich Stirling 75 E9
Dalvina Lo. Highld 93 E9
Dalwhinnie Highld 81 E8
Dalwood Devon 8 D1
Dalwyne S Ayrs 66 G6
Dam Green Norf 39 G6
Dam Side Lancs 49 E4
Damerham Hants 9 C10
Damgate Norf 39 E10
Damnaglaur Dumfries 54 F4
Damside Borders 69 F10
Danbury Essex 30 H4
Danby N Yorks 59 F8
Danby Wiske N Yorks 58 G4
Dandaleith Moray 88 D2
Danderhall Midloth 70 D2
Dane End Herts 29 F10
Danebridge Ches E 44 F3
Danehill E Sus 12 D3
Danemoor Green Norf 39 E6
Danesford Shrops 34 F3
Daneshill Hants 18 F3
Dangerous Corner Lancs 43 A8
Danskine E Loth 70 D4
Darcy Lever Gtr Man 43 B10
Darenth Kent 20 D2
Daresbury Halton 43 D8
Darfield S Yorks 45 B8
Darfoulds Notts 45 E9
Dargate Kent 21 E7
Darite Corn 4 E3
Darlaston W Mid 34 F5
Darley N Yorks 51 D8
Darley Bridge Derbys 44 F6
Darley Head N Yorks 51 D7
Darlingscott Warks 27 D9
Darlington Darl 58 E3
Darliston Shrops 34 B1
Darlton Notts 45 E11
Darnall S Yorks 45 D7
Darnick Borders 70 G4
Darowen Powys 32 E4
Darra Aberds 89 D7
Darracott Devon 6 C3
Darras Hall Northumb 63 F7
Darrington W Yorks 51 G10
Darsham Suff 31 B11
Dartford Kent 20 D2
Dartford Crossing Kent 20 D2
Dartington Devon 5 E8
Dartmeet Devon 5 D7
Dartmouth Devon 5 F9
Darton S Yorks 45 B7
Darvel E Ayrs 68 G4
Darwell Hole E Sus 12 E5
Darwen Blackburn 50 G2
Datchet Windsor 18 D6
Datchworth Herts 29 G9
Datchworth Green Herts 29 G9
Daubhill Gtr Man 43 B10
Daugh of Kinermony Moray 88 D2
Dauntsey Wilts 16 C6
Dava Moray 87 H13
Davenham Ches W 43 E9
Davenport Green Ches E 44 E2
Daventry Northants 28 B2
David's Well Powys 33 H6
Davidson's Mains Edin 69 C11
Davidstow Corn 4 C2
Davington Dumfries 61 C8
Daviot Aberds 83 A9
Daviot Highld 87 H10
Davoch of Grange Moray 88 C4
Davyhulme Gtr Man 43 C10
Dawley Telford 34 E2
Dawlish Devon 5 D10
Dawlish Warren Devon 5 D10
Dawn Conwy 41 C10
Daws Heath Essex 20 C5
Daw's House Corn 4 C4
Dawsmere Lincs 37 B10
Dayhills Staffs 34 B5
Daylesford Glos 27 F9
Ddôl-Cownwy Powys 32 D6
Ddrydwy Anglesey 40 C5
Deadwater Northumb 62 D2
Deaf Hill Durham 58 C4
Deal Kent 21 F10
Deal Hall Essex 21 B7
Dean Cumb 56 D2
Dean Devon 5 E8
Dean Devon 6 B4
Dean Dorset 9 C8
Dean Hants 10 C4
Dean Som 16 G3
Dean Prior Devon 5 E8
Dean Row Ches E 44 D2
Deanburnhaugh Borders 61 B9
Deane Gtr Man 43 B9
Deane Hants 18 F2
Deanich Lodge Highld 86 C6
Deanland Dorset 9 C8
Deans W Loth 69 D9
Deanscales Cumb 56 D2
Deanshanger Northants 28 E4
Deanston Stirling 75 G10
Dearham Cumb 56 C2
Debach Suff 31 C9
Debden Essex 19 B11
Debden Essex 30 E2
Debden Cross Essex 30 E2
Debenham Suff 31 B8
Dechmont W Loth 69 C9
Deddington Oxon 27 E11
Dedham Essex 31 E7
Dedham Heath Essex 31 E7
Deebank Aberds 83 D8
Deene Northants 36 F5
Deenethorpe Northants 36 F5
Deepcar S Yorks 44 C6
Deepcut Sur 18 F6
Deepdale Cumb 50 A3
Deeping Gate Lincs 37 E7
Deeping St James Lincs 37 E7
Deeping St Nicholas Lincs 37 D8
Deerhill Moray 88 C4
Deerhurst Glos 26 F5
Deerness Orkney 95 H6
Defford Worcs 26 D6
Defynnog Powys 24 F6
Deganwy Conwy 41 C9
Deighton N Yorks 58 F4
Deighton W Yorks 51 H7
Deighton York 52 E2
Deiniolen Gwyn 41 D7
Delabole Corn 4 C1
Delamere Ches W 43 F8
Delfrigs Aberds 89 F9
Dell Lodge Highld 82 B2
Delliefure Highld 87 H13
Delnabo Moray 82 B3
Delnadamph Aberds 82 C4
Delph Gtr Man 44 B3
Delves Durham 58 B2
Delvine Perth 76 C4
Dembleby Lincs 36 B6
Denaby Main S Yorks 45 C8
Denbigh = Dinbych Denb 42 F3
Denbury Devon 5 E9
Denby Derbys 45 H7
Denby Dale W Yorks 44 B6
Denchworth Oxon 17 B10
Dendron Cumb 49 B2
Denel End C Beds 29 E7
Denend Aberds 88 E6
Denford Northants 36 H5
Dengie Essex 20 A6
Denham Bucks 19 C7
Denham Suff 30 B4
Denham Suff 31 A8
Denham Street Suff 31 A8
Denhead Aberds 89 C9
Denhead Fife 77 F7
Denhead of Arbilot Angus 77 C8
Denhead of Gray Dundee 76 D6
Denholm Borders 61 B11
Denholme W Yorks 51 F6
Denholme Clough W Yorks 51 F6
Denio Gwyn 40 G5
Denmead Hants 10 C5
Denmore Aberdeen 83 B11
Denmoss Aberds 89 D6
Dennington Suff 31 B9
Denny Falk 69 B7
Denny Lodge Hants 10 D2
Dennyloanhead Falk 69 B7
Denshaw Gtr Man 44 A3
Denside Aberds 83 D10
Densole Kent 21 G9
Denston Suff 30 C4
Denstone Staffs 35 A7
Dent Cumb 57 H9
Denton Cambs 37 G7
Denton Darl 58 E3
Denton E Sus 12 F3
Denton Gtr Man 44 C3
Denton Kent 21 G9
Denton Lincs 36 B4
Denton N Yorks 51 E7
Denton Norf 39 G8
Denton Northants 28 C5
Denton Oxon 18 A2
Denton's Green Mers 43 C7
Denver Norf 38 E2
Denwick Northumb 63 B8
Deopham Norf 39 E6
Deopham Green Norf 38 F6
Depden Suff 30 C4
Depden Green Suff 30 C4
Deptford London 19 D10
Deptford Wilts 17 H7
Derby Derby 35 B9
Derbyhaven IoM 48 F2
Dereham Norf 38 D5
Deri Caerph 15 A7
Derril Devon 6 F2
Derringstone Kent 21 G9
Derrington Staffs 34 C4
Derriton Devon 6 F2
Derry Hill Wilts 16 D6
Derryguaig Argyll 78 H7
Derrythorpe N Lincs 46 B2
Dersingham Norf 38 B2
Dervaig Argyll 78 F7
Derwen Denb 42 G3
Derwenlas Powys 32 F3
Desborough Northants 36 G4
Desford Leics 35 E10
Detchant Northumb 71 G9
Detling Kent 20 F4
Deuddwr Powys 33 D8
Devauden Mon 15 B10
Devil's Bridge Ceredig 32 H3
Devizes Wilts 17 E7
Devol Invclyd 68 C2
Devonport Plym 4 F5
Devonside Clack 76 H2
Devoran Corn 3 F6
Dewar Borders 70 F2
Dewlish Dorset 9 E6
Dewsbury W Yorks 51 G8
Dewsbury Moor W Yorks 51 G8
Dewshall Court Hereford 25 E11
Dhoon IoM 48 D4
Dhoor IoM 48 C4
Dhowin IoM 48 B4
Dial Post W Sus 11 C10
Dibden Hants 10 D3
Dibden Purlieu Hants 10 D3
Dickleburgh Norf 39 G7
Didbrook Glos 27 E7
Didcot Oxon 18 C2
Diddington Cambs 29 B8
Diddlebury Shrops 33 G11
Didley Hereford 25 E11
Didling W Sus 11 C7
Didmarton Glos 16 C5
Didsbury Gtr Man 44 C2
Didworthy Devon 5 E7
Digby Lincs 46 G4
Digg Highld 85 B9
Diggle Gtr Man 44 B4
Digmoor Lancs 43 B7
Digswell Park Herts 29 G9
Dihewyd Ceredig 23 A9
Dilham Norf 39 C9
Dilhorne Staffs 34 A5
Dillarburn S Lanark 69 F7
Dillington Cambs 29 B8
Dilston Northumb 62 G5
Dilton Marsh Wilts 16 G5
Dilwyn Hereford 25 C11
Dinas Carms 23 C7
Dinas Gwyn 40 G4
Dinas Cross Pembs 22 C5
Dinas Dinlle Gwyn 40 E6
Dinas-Mawddwy Gwyn 32 D4
Dinas Powys V Glam 15 D7
Dinbych = Denbigh Denb 42 F3
Dinbych-y-Pysgod = Tenby Pembs 22 F6
Dinder Som 16 G2
Dinedor Hereford 26 E2
Dingestow Mon 25 G11
Dingle Mers 42 D6
Dingleden Kent 13 C7
Dingley Northants 36 G3
Dingwall Highld 87 F8
Dinlabyre Borders 61 D11
Dinmael Conwy 32 A6
Dinnet Aberds 82 D6
Dinnington S Yorks 45 D9
Dinnington Som 8 C3
Dinnington T&W 63 F8
Dinorwic Gwyn 41 D7
Dinton Bucks 28 G4
Dinton Wilts 9 A9
Dinwoodie Mains Dumfries 61 D7
Dinworthy Devon 6 E2
Dippen N Ayrs 66 D3
Dippenhall Sur 18 G5
Dipple Moray 88 C3
Dipple S Ayrs 66 F5
Diptford Devon 5 F8
Dipton Durham 58 A2
Dirdhu Highld 82 A2
Dirleton E Loth 70 B4
Dirt Pot Northumb 57 B10
Discoed Powys 25 B9
Diseworth Leics 35 C10
Dishes Orkney 95 F7
Dishforth N Yorks 51 B9
Disley Ches E 44 D3
Diss Norf 39 H7
Disserth Powys 25 C7
Distington Cumb 56 D2
Ditchampton Wilts 9 A9
Ditcheat Som 16 H3
Ditchingham Norf 39 F9
Ditchling E Sus 12 E2
Ditherington Shrops 33 D11
Dittisham Devon 5 F9
Ditton Halton 43 D7
Ditton Kent 20 F4
Ditton Green Cambs 30 C3
Ditton Priors Shrops 34 G2
Divach Highld 81 A6
Divlyn Carms 24 E4
Dixton Glos 26 E6
Dixton Mon 26 G2
Dobcross Gtr Man 44 B3
Dobwalls Corn 4 E3
Doc Penfro = Pembroke Dock Pembs 22 F4
Doccombe Devon 5 C8
Dochfour Ho. Highld 87 H9
Dochgarroch Highld 87 G9
Docking Norf 38 B3
Docklow Hereford 26 C2
Dockray Cumb 56 D5
Dockroyd W Yorks 50 F6
Dodburn Borders 61 C10
Doddinghurst Essex 20 B2
Doddington Cambs 37 F9
Doddington Kent 20 F6
Doddington Lincs 46 E3
Doddington Northumb 71 G8
Doddington Shrops 34 H2
Doddiscombsleigh Devon 5 C9
Dodford Northants 28 B3
Dodford Worcs 26 A6
Dodington S Glos 16 C4
Dodleston Ches W 42 F6
Dods Leigh Staffs 34 B6
Dodworth S Yorks 45 B7
Doe Green Warr 43 D8
Doe Lea Derbys 45 F8
Dog Village Devon 7 G8
Dogdyke Lincs 46 G6
Dogmersfield Hants 18 F4
Dogridge Wilts 17 C7
Dogsthorpe Pboro 37 E7
Dol-fôr Powys 32 E4
Dôl-y-Bont Ceredig 32 G2
Dol-y-cannau Powys 25 D9
Dolanog Powys 33 D6
Dolau Powys 25 B8
Dolau Rhondda 14 C5
Dolbenmaen Gwyn 41 F7
Dolfach Powys 32 E5
Dolfor Powys 33 G7
Dolgarrog Conwy 41 D9
Dolgellau Gwyn 32 D3
Dolgran Carms 23 C9
Dolhendre Gwyn 41 G10
Doll Highld 93 J11
Dollar Clack 76 H2
Dolley Green Powys 25 B9
Dollwen Ceredig 32 G2
Dolphin Flint 42 E4
Dolphinholme Lancs 49 D5
Dolphinton S Lanark 69 F10
Dolton Devon 6 E4
Dolwen Conwy 41 C10
Dolwen Powys 32 E5
Dolwyd Conwy 41 C10
Dolwyddelan Conwy 41 E9
Dolyhir Powys 25 C9
Doncaster S Yorks 45 B9
Dones Green Ches W 43 E9
Donhead St Andrew Wilts 9 B8
Donhead St Mary Wilts 9 B8
Donibristle Fife 69 B10
Donington Lincs 37 B8
Donington on Bain Lincs 46 D6
Donington South Ing Lincs 37 B8
Donisthorpe Leics 35 D9
Donkey Town Sur 18 E6
Donnington Glos 27 F8
Donnington Hereford 26 E4
Donnington Shrops 34 E1
Donnington Telford 34 D3
Donnington W Berks 17 E11
Donnington W Sus 11 D7
Donnington Wood Telford 34 D3
Donyatt Som 8 C2
Doonfoot S Ayrs 66 E6
Dorback Lodge Highld 82 B2
Dorchester Dorset 8 E5
Dorchester Oxon 18 B2
Dordon Warks 35 E8
Dore S Yorks 45 D7
Dores Highld 87 H8
Dorking Sur 19 G8
Dormansland Sur 12 B3
Dormanstown Redcar 59 D6
Dormington Hereford 26 D2
Dormston Worcs 26 C6
Dornal S Ayrs 54 B5
Dorney Bucks 18 D6
Dornie Highld 85 F13
Dornoch Highld 87 C10
Dornock Dumfries 61 G8
Dorrery Highld 94 E2
Dorridge W Mid 35 H7
Dorrington Lincs 46 G4
Dorrington Shrops 33 E10
Dorsington Warks 27 D8
Dorstone Hereford 25 D10
Dorton Bucks 28 G3
Dorusduain Highld 80 A1
Dosthill Staffs 35 F8
Dottery Dorset 8 E3
Doublebois Corn 4 E2
Dougarie N Ayrs 66 C1
Doughton Glos 16 B5
Douglas IoM 48 E3
Douglas S Lanark 69 G7
Douglas & Angus Dundee 77 D7
Douglas Water S Lanark 69 G7
Douglas West S Lanark 69 G7
Douglastown Angus 77 C7
Doulting Som 16 G3
Dounby Orkney 95 F3
Doune Highld 92 J7
Doune Stirling 75 G10
Doune Park Aberds 89 B7
Douneside Aberds 82 C6
Dounie Highld 87 B8
Dounreay Highld 93 C12
Dousland Devon 4 E6
Dovaston Shrops 33 C9
Dove Holes Derbys 44 E4
Dovenby Cumb 56 C2
Dover Kent 21 G10
Dovercourt Essex 31 E9
Doverdale Worcs 26 B5
Doveridge Derbys 35 B7
Doversgreen Sur 19 G9
Dowally Perth 76 C3
Dowbridge Lancs 49 F4
Dowdeswell Glos 26 G6
Dowlais M Tydf 25 H7
Dowland Devon 6 E4
Dowlish Wake Som 8 C2
Down Ampney Glos 17 B8
Down Hatherley Glos 26 F5
Down St Mary Devon 7 F6
Down Thomas Devon 4 F6
Downcraig Ferry N Ayrs 73 H10
Downderry Corn 4 F4
Downe London 19 E11
Downend IoW 10 F4
Downend S Glos 16 D3
Downend W Berks 17 D11
Downfield Dundee 76 D6
Downgate Corn 4 D4
Downham Essex 20 B4
Downham Lancs 50 E3
Downham Northumb 71 G7
Downham Market Norf 38 E2
Downhead Som 16 G3
Downhill Perth 76 D3
Downhill T&W 63 H9
Downholland Cross Lancs 42 B6
Downholme N Yorks 58 G2
Downies Aberds 83 D11
Downley Bucks 18 B5
Downside Som 16 G3
Downside Sur 19 F8
Downton Hants 10 E1
Downton Wilts 9 B10
Downton on the Rock Hereford 25 A11
Dowsby Lincs 37 C7
Dowsdale Lincs 37 D8
Dowthwaitehead Cumb 56 D5
Doxey Staffs 34 C5
Doxford Northumb 63 A7
Doxford Park T&W 58 A4
Doynton S Glos 16 D4
Draffan S Lanark 68 F6
Dragonby N Lincs 46 A3
Drakeland Corner Devon 5 F6
Drakemyre N Ayrs 66 A5
Drake's Broughton Worcs 26 D6
Drakes Cross Worcs 35 H6
Drakewalls Corn 4 D5
Draughton N Yorks 50 D6
Draughton Northants 36 H3
Drax N Yorks 52 G2
Draycote Warks 27 A11
Draycott Derbys 35 B10
Draycott Glos 27 E8
Draycott Som 15 F10
Draycott in the Clay Staffs 35 C7
Draycott in the Moors Staffs 34 A5
Drayford Devon 7 E6
Drayton Leics 36 F4
Drayton Lincs 37 B8
Drayton Norf 39 D7
Drayton Oxon 17 B11
Drayton Oxon 27 D11
Drayton Ptsmth 10 D5
Drayton Som 8 B3
Drayton Worcs 34 H5
Drayton Bassett Staffs 35 E7
Drayton Beauchamp Bucks 28 G6
Drayton Parslow Bucks 28 F5
Drayton St Leonard Oxon 18 B1
Dre-fach Carms 24 G3
Dre-fach Ceredig 23 B10
Drebley N Yorks 51 D6
Dreemskerry IoM 48 C4
Dreenhill Pembs 22 E4
Drefach Carms 23 C8
Drefach Carms 23 E10
Drefelin Carms 23 C8
Dreghorn N Ayrs 67 C6
Drellingore Kent 21 G9
Drem E Loth 70 C4
Dresden Stoke 34 A5
Dreumasdal W Isles 84 E2
Drewsteignton Devon 7 G6
Driby Lincs 47 E7
Driffield E Yorks 52 D6
Driffield Glos 17 B7
Drigg Cumb 56 G2
Drighlington W Yorks 51 G8
Drimnin Highld 79 F8
Drimpton Dorset 8 D3
Drimsynie Argyll 74 G4
Drinisiadar W Isles 90 H6
Drinkstone Suff 30 B6
Drinkstone Green Suff 30 B6
Drishaig Argyll 74 F4
Drissaig Argyll 73 B8
Drochil Borders 69 F10
Drointon Staffs 34 C6
Droitwich Spa Worcs 26 B5
Droman Highld 92 D4
Dron Perth 76 F4
Dronfield Derbys 45 E7
Dronfield Woodhouse Derbys 45 E7
Drongan E Ayrs 67 E7
Dronley Angus 76 D6
Droxford Hants 10 C5
Droylsden Gtr Man 44 C3
Druid Denb 32 A6
Druidston Pembs 22 E3
Druimarbin Highld 80 F2
Druimavuic Argyll 74 C3
Druimdrishaig Argyll 72 F6
Druimindarroch Highld 79 C9
Druimyeon More Argyll 65 C7
Drum Argyll 73 F8
Drum Perth 76 G3
Drumbeg Highld 92 F4
Drumblade Aberds 88 D5
Drumblair Aberds 89 D6
Drumbuie Dumfries 55 A8
Drumbuie Highld 85 E12
Drumburgh Cumb 61 H8
Drumburn Dumfries 60 G5
Drumchapel Glasgow 68 C4
Drumchardine Highld 87 G8
Drumchork Highld 91 J13
Drumclog S Lanark 68 G5
Drumderfit Highld 87 F9
Drumeldrie Fife 77 G7
Drumelzier Borders 69 G10
Drumfearn Highld 85 G11
Drumgask Highld 81 D8
Drumgley Angus 77 B7
Drumguish Highld 81 D9
Drumin Moray 88 E1
Drumlasie Aberds 83 C8
Drumlemble Argyll 65 G7
Drumligair Aberds 83 B11
Drumlithie Aberds 83 E9
Drummoddie Dumfries 54 E6
Drummond Highld 87 E9
Drummore Dumfries 54 F4
Drummuir Moray 88 D3
Drummuir Castle Moray 88 D3
Drumnadrochit Highld 81 A7
Drumnagorrach Moray 88 C5
Drumoak Aberds 83 D9
Drumpark Dumfries 60 E4
Drumphail Dumfries 54 C5
Drumrash Dumfries 55 B9
Drumrunie Highld 92 J4
Drums Aberds 89 F9
Drumsallie Highld 80 F1
Drumstinchall Dumfries 55 D11
Drumsturdy Angus 77 D7
Drumtochty Castle Aberds 83 F8
Drumtroddan Dumfries 54 E6
Drumuie Highld 85 D9
Drumuillie Highld 81 A11
Drumvaich Stirling 75 G9
Drumwhindle Aberds 89 E9
Drunkendub Angus 77 C9
Drury Flint 42 F5
Drury Square Norf 38 D5
Dry Doddington Lincs 46 H2
Dry Drayton Cambs 29 B10
Drybeck Cumb 57 E8
Drybridge Moray 88 B4
Drybridge N Ayrs 67 C6
Drybrook Glos 26 G3
Dryburgh Borders 70 G4
Dryhope Borders 61 A8
Drylaw Edin 69 C11
Drym Corn 2 F5
Drymen Stirling 68 B3
Drymuir Aberds 89 D9
Drynoch Highld 85 E9
Dryslwyn Carms 23 D10
Dryton Shrops 34 E1
Dubford Aberds 89 B8
Dubton Angus 77 B8
Duchally Highld 92 H6
Duchlage Argyll 68 B2
Duck Corner Suff 31 D10
Duckington Ches W 43 G7
Ducklington Oxon 27 H10
Duckmanton Derbys 45 E8
Duck's Cross Bedford 29 C8
Duddenhoe End Essex 29 E11
Duddingston Edin 69 C11
Duddington Northants 36 E5
Duddleswell E Sus 12 D3
Duddo Northumb 71 F8
Duddon Ches W 43 F8
Duddon Bridge Cumb 56 H4
Dudleston Shrops 33 B9
Dudleston Heath Shrops 33 B9
Dudley T&W 63 F8
Dudley W Mid 34 F5
Dudley Port W Mid 34 F5
Duffield Derbys 35 A9
Duffryn Neath 14 B4
Duffryn Newport 15 C8
Dufftown Moray 88 E3
Duffus Moray 88 B1
Dufton Cumb 57 D8
Duggleby N Yorks 52 C4
Duirinish Highld 85 E12
Duisdalemore Highld 85 G12
Duisky Highld 80 F2
Dukestown Bl Gwent 25 G8
Dukinfield Gtr Man 44 C3
Dulas Anglesey 40 B6
Dulcote Som 16 G2
Dulford Devon 7 F9
Dull Perth 75 C11
Dullatur N Lanark 68 C6
Dullingham Cambs 30 C3
Dulnain Bridge Highld 82 A1
Duloe Bedford 29 B8
Duloe Corn 4 F3
Dulsie Highld 87 G12
Dulverton Som 7 D8
Dulwich London 19 D10
Dumbarton W Dunb 68 C2
Dumbleton Glos 27 E7
Dumcrieff Dumfries 61 C7
Dumfries Dumfries 60 F5
Dumgoyne Stirling 68 B4
Dummer Hants 18 G2
Dumpford W Sus 11 B7
Dumpton Kent 21 E10
Dun Angus 77 B9
Dun Charlabhaigh W Isles 90 C6
Dunain Ho. Highld 87 G9
Dunalastair Perth 75 B10
Dunan Highld 85 F10
Dunans Argyll 73 D9
Dunball Som 15 G9
Dunbar E Loth 70 C5
Dunbeath Highld 94 H3
Dunbeg Argyll 79 H11
Dunblane Stirling 75 G10
Dunbog Fife 76 F5
Duncanston Highld 87 F8
Duncanstone Aberds 83 A7
Dunchurch Warks 27 A11
Duncote Northants 28 C3
Duncow Dumfries 60 E5
Duncraggan Stirling 75 G8
Duncrievie Perth 76 G4
Duncton W Sus 11 C8
Dundas Ho. Orkney 95 K5
Dundee Dundee 77 D7
Dundeugh Dumfries 67 H8
Dundon Som 8 A3
Dundonald S Ayrs 67 C6

Dundonnell Highld 86 C3
Dundonnell Hotel Highld 86 C3
Dundonnell House Highld 86 C4
Dundraw Cumb 56 B4
Dundreggan Highld 80 B5
Dundreggan Lodge Highld 80 B5
Dundrennan Dumfries 55 E10
Dundry N Som 16 E2
Dunecht Aberds 83 C9
Dunfermline Fife 69 B9
Dunfield Glos 17 B8
Dunford Bridge S Yorks 44 B5
Dungworth S Yorks 44 D6
Dunham Notts 46 E2
Dunham-on-the-Hill Ches W 43 E7
Dunham Town Gtr Man 43 D10
Dunhampton Worcs 26 B5
Dunholme Lincs 46 E4
Dunino Fife 77 F8
Dunipace Falk 69 B7
Dunira Perth 75 E10
Dunkeld Perth 76 C3
Dunkerton Bath 16 F4
Dunkeswell Devon 7 F10
Dunkeswick N Yorks 51 E9
Dunkirk Kent 21 F7
Dunkirk Norf 39 C8
Dunk's Green Kent 20 F3
Dunlappie Angus 83 G7
Dunley Hants 17 F11
Dunley Worcs 26 B4
Dunlichity Lodge Highld 87 H9
Dunlop E Ayrs 67 B7
Dunmaglass Lodge Highld 81 A7
Dunmore Argyll 72 G6
Dunmore Falk 69 B7
Dunnet Highld 94 C4
Dunnichen Angus 77 C8
Dunninald Angus 77 B10
Dunning Perth 76 F3
Dunnington E Yorks 53 D7
Dunnington Warks 27 C7
Dunnington York 52 D2
Dunnockshaw Lancs 50 G4
Dunollie Argyll 79 H11
Dunoon Argyll 73 F10
Dunragit Dumfries 54 D4
Dunrostan Argyll 72 E6
Duns Borders 70 E6
Duns Tew Oxon 27 F11
Dunsby Lincs 37 C7
Dunscore Dumfries 60 E4
Dunscroft S Yorks 45 B10
Dunsdale Redcar 59 E7
Dunsden Green Oxon 18 D4
Dunsfold Sur 19 H7
Dunsford Devon 5 C9
Dunshalt Fife 76 F5
Dunshillock Aberds 89 D9
Dunskey Ho. Dumfries 54 D3
Dunsley N Yorks 59 E9
Dunsmore Bucks 28 H5
Dunsop Bridge Lancs 50 D2
Dunstable C Beds 29 F7
Dunstall Staffs 35 C7
Dunstall Common Worcs 26 D5
Dunstall Green Suff 30 B4
Dunstan Northumb 63 B8
Dunstan Steads Northumb 63 A8
Dunster Som 7 B8
Dunston Lincs 46 F4
Dunston Norf 39 E8
Dunston Staffs 34 D5
Dunston T&W 63 G8
Dunsville S Yorks 45 B10
Dunswell E Yorks 53 F6
Dunsyre S Lanark 69 F9
Dunterton Devon 4 D4
Duntisbourne Abbots Glos 26 H6
Duntisbourne Leer Glos 26 H6
Duntisbourne Rouse Glos 26 H6
Duntish Dorset 8 D5
Duntocher W Dunb 68 C3
Dunton Bucks 28 F5
Dunton C Beds 29 D9
Dunton Norf 38 B4
Dunton Bassett Leics 35 F11
Dunton Green Kent 20 F2
Dunton Wayletts Essex 20 B3
Duntulm Highld 85 A9
Dunure S Ayrs 66 E5
Dunvant Swansea 23 G10
Dunvegan Highld 84 D7
Dunwich Suff 31 A11
Dunwood Staffs 44 G3
Dupplin Castle Perth 76 F3
Durdar Cumb 56 A6
Durgates E Sus 12 C5
Durham Durham 58 B3
Durisdeer Dumfries 60 C4
Durisdeermill Dumfries 60 C4
Durkar W Yorks 51 H9
Durleigh Som 15 H8
Durley Hants 10 C4
Durley Wilts 17 E9
Durnamuck Highld 86 B3
Durness Highld 92 C7
Durno Aberds 83 A9
Duror Highld 74 B2
Durran Argyll 73 C8
Durran Highld 94 D3
Durrington W Sus 11 D10
Durrington Wilts 17 G8
Dursley Glos 16 B4
Durston Som 8 B1
Durweston Dorset 9 D7
Dury Shetland 96 G6
Duston Northants 28 B4
Duthil Highld 81 A11
Dutlas Powys 33 H8
Duton Hill Essex 30 F3
Dutson Corn 4 C4
Dutton Ches W 43 E8
Duxford Cambs 29 D11
Duxford Oxon 17 B10
Dwygyfylchi Conwy 41 C9
Dwyran Anglesey 40 D6
Dyce Aberdeen 83 B10
Dye House Northumb 62 H5
Dyffryn Bridgend 14 B4
Dyffryn Carms 23 D8
Dyffryn Pembs 22 C4
Dyffryn Ardudwy Gwyn 32 C1
Dyffryn Castell Ceredig 32 G3
Dyffryn Ceidrych Carms 24 F4
Dyffryn Cellwen Neath 24 H5
Dyke Lincs 37 C7
Dyke Moray 87 F12
Dykehead Angus 76 A6
Dykehead N Lanark 69 E7
Dykehead Stirling 75 H8
Dykelands Aberds 83 G9
Dykends Angus 76 B5
Dykeside Aberds 89 D7
Dykesmains N Ayrs 66 B5
Dylife Powys 32 F4
Dymchurch Kent 13 D9
Dymock Glos 26 E4
Dyrham S Glos 16 D4
Dysart Fife 70 A2
Dyserth Denb 42 E3

E

Eachwick Northumb 63 F7
Eadar Dha Fhadhail W Isles 90 D5
Eagland Hill Lancs 49 E4
Eagle Lincs 46 F2
Eagle Barnsdale Lincs 46 F2
Eagle Moor Lincs 46 F2
Eaglescliffe Stockton 58 E5
Eaglesfield Cumb 56 D2
Eaglesfield Dumfries 61 F8
Eaglesham E Renf 68 E4
Eaglethorpe Northants 37 F6
Eairy IoM 48 E2
Eakley Lanes M Keynes 28 C5
Eakring Notts 45 F10
Ealand N Lincs 45 A11
Ealing London 19 C8
Eals Northumb 62 H2
Eamont Bridge Cumb 57 D7
Earby Lancs 50 E5
Earcroft Blackburn 50 G2
Eardington Shrops 34 F3
Eardisland Hereford 25 C11
Eardisley Hereford 25 D10
Eardiston Shrops 33 C9
Eardiston Worcs 26 B3
Earith Cambs 29 A10
Earl Shilton Leics 35 F10
Earl Soham Suff 31 B9
Earl Sterndale Derbys 44 F4
Earl Stonham Suff 31 C8
Earle Northumb 71 H8
Earley Wokingham 18 D4
Earlham Norf 39 E8
Earlish Highld 85 B8
Earls Barton Northants 28 B5
Earls Colne Essex 30 F5
Earl's Croome Worcs 26 D5
Earl's Green Suff 31 B7
Earlsdon W Mid 35 H9
Earlsferry Fife 77 H7
Earlsfield Lincs 36 B5
Earlsford Aberds 89 E8
Earlsheaton W Yorks 51 G8
Earlsmill Moray 87 F12
Earlston Borders 70 G4
Earlston E Ayrs 67 C7
Earlswood Mon 15 B10
Earlswood Sur 19 G9
Earlswood Warks 27 A8
Earnley W Sus 11 E7
Earsairidh W Isles 84 J2
Earsdon T&W 63 F9
Earsham Norf 39 G9
Earswick York 52 D2
Eartham W Sus 11 D8
Easby N Yorks 58 F2
Easby N Yorks 59 F6
Easdale Argyll 72 B6
Easebourne W Sus 11 B7
Easenhall Warks 35 H10
Eashing Sur 18 G6
Easington Bucks 28 G3
Easington Durham 58 B5
Easington E Yorks 53 H9
Easington Northumb 71 G10
Easington Oxon 18 B3
Easington Oxon 27 E11
Easington Redcar 59 E8
Easington Colliery Durham 58 B5
Easington Lane T&W 58 B4
Easingwold N Yorks 51 C11
Easole Street Kent 21 F9
Eassie Angus 76 C6
East Aberthaw V Glam 14 E6
East Adderbury Oxon 27 E11
East Allington Devon 5 G8
East Anstey Devon 7 D7
East Appleton N Yorks 58 G3
East Ardsley W Yorks 51 G9
East Ashling W Sus 11 D7
East Auchronie Aberds 83 C10
East Ayton N Yorks 59 H10
East Bank Bl Gwent 25 H9
East Barkwith Lincs 46 D5
East Barming Kent 20 F4
East Barnby N Yorks 59 E9
East Barnet London 19 B9
East Barns E Loth 70 C6
East Barsham Norf 38 B5
East Beckham Norf 39 B7
East Bedfont London 19 D7
East Bergholt Suff 31 E7
East Bilney Norf 38 D5
East Blatchington E Sus 12 F3
East Boldre Hants 10 D2
East Brent Som 15 F9
East Bridgford Notts 36 A2
East Buckland Devon 6 C5
East Budleigh Devon 7 H9
East Burrafirth Shetland 96 H5
East Burton Dorset 9 F7
East Butsfield Durham 58 B2
East Butterwick N Lincs 46 B2
East Cairnbeg Aberds 83 F9
East Calder W Loth 69 D9
East Carleton Norf 39 E7
East Carlton Northants 36 G4
East Carlton W Yorks 51 E8
East Chaldon Dorset 9 F6
East Challow Oxon 17 C10
East Chiltington E Sus 12 E2
East Chinnock Som 8 C3
East Chisenbury Wilts 17 F8
East Clandon Sur 19 F7
East Claydon Bucks 28 F4
East Clyne Highld 93 J12
East Coker Som 8 C4
East Combe Som 7 C10
East Common N Yorks 52 F2
East Compton Som 16 G3
East Cottingwith E Yorks 52 E3
East Cowes IoW 10 E4
East Cowick E Yorks 52 G2
East Cowton N Yorks 58 F4
East Cramlington Northumb 63 F8
East Cranmore Som 16 G3
East Creech Dorset 9 F8
East Croachy Highld 81 A8
East Croftmore Highld 81 B11
East Curthwaite Cumb 56 B5
East Dean E Sus 12 G4
East Dean Hants 10 B1
East Dean W Sus 11 C8
East Down Devon 6 B5
East Drayton Notts 45 E11
East Ella Hull 53 G6
East End Dorset 9 E8
East End E Yorks 53 G8
East End Hants 10 B5
East End Hants 10 E2
East End Hants 17 E11
East End Herts 29 F11
East End Kent 13 C7
East End N Som 15 D10
East End Oxon 27 G10
East Farleigh Kent 20 F4
East Farndon Northants 36 G3
East Ferry Lincs 46 C2
East Fortune E Loth 70 C4
East Garston W Berks 17 D10
East Ginge Oxon 17 C11
East Goscote Leics 36 D2
East Grafton Wilts 17 E9
East Grimstead Wilts 9 B11
East Grinstead W Sus 12 C2
East Guldeford E Sus 13 D8
East Haddon Northants 28 B3
East Hagbourne Oxon 18 C2
East Halton N Lincs 53 H7
East Ham London 19 C11
East Hanney Oxon 17 B11
East Hanningfield Essex 20 A4
East Hardwick W Yorks 51 H10
East Harling Norf 38 G5
East Harlsey N Yorks 58 G5
East Harnham Wilts 9 B10
East Harptree Bath 16 F2
East Hartford Northumb 63 F8
East Harting W Sus 11 C6
East Hatley Cambs 29 C9
East Hauxwell N Yorks 58 G2
East Haven Angus 77 D8
East Heckington Lincs 37 A7
East Hedleyhope Durham 58 B2
East Hendred Oxon 17 C11
East Herrington T&W 58 A4
East Heslerton N Yorks 52 B5
East Hoathly E Sus 12 E4
East Horrington Som 16 G2
East Horsley Sur 19 F7
East Horton Northumb 71 G9
East Huntspill Som 15 G9
East Hyde C Beds 29 G8
East Ilkerton Devon 6 B6
East Ilsley W Berks 17 C11
East Keal Lincs 47 F7
East Kennett Wilts 17 E8
East Keswick W Yorks 51 E9
East Kilbride S Lanark 68 E5
East Kirkby Lincs 47 F7
East Knapton N Yorks 52 B4
East Knighton Dorset 9 F7
East Knoyle Wilts 9 A7
East Kyloe Northumb 71 G9
East Lambrook Som 8 C3
East Lamington Highld 87 D10
East Langdon Kent 21 G10
East Langton Leics 36 F3
East Langwell Highld 93 J10
East Lavant W Sus 11 D7
East Lavington W Sus 11 C8
East Layton N Yorks 58 F2
East Leake Notts 36 C1
East Learmouth Northumb 71 G7
East Leigh Devon 6 F5
East Lexham Norf 38 D4
East Lilburn Northumb 62 A6
East Linton E Loth 70 C4
East Liss Hants 11 B6
East Looe Corn 4 F3
East Lound N Lincs 45 C11
East Lulworth Dorset 9 F7
East Lutton N Yorks 52 C5
East Lydford Som 8 A4
East Mains Aberds 83 D8
East Malling Kent 20 F4
East March Angus 77 D7
East Marden W Sus 11 C7
East Markham Notts 45 E11
East Marton N Yorks 50 D5
East Meon Hants 10 B5
East Mere Devon 7 E8
East Mersea Essex 31 G7
East Mey Highld 94 C5
East Molesey Sur 19 E8
East Morden Dorset 9 E8
East Morton W Yorks 51 E6
East Ness N Yorks 52 B2
East Newton E Yorks 53 F8
East Norton Leics 36 E3
East Nynehead Som 7 D10
East Oakley Hants 18 F2
East Ogwell Devon 5 D9
East Orchard Dorset 9 C7
East Ord Northumb 71 E8
East Panson Devon 6 G2
East Peckham Kent 20 G3
East Pennard Som 16 H2
East Perry Cambs 29 B8
East Portlemouth Devon 5 H8
East Prawle Devon 5 H8
East Preston W Sus 11 D9
East Putford Devon 6 E2
East Quantoxhead Som 7 B10
East Rainton T&W 58 B4
East Ravendale NE Lincs 46 C6
East Raynham Norf 38 C4
East Rhidorroch Lodge Highld 86 B5
East Rigton W Yorks 51 E9
East Rounton N Yorks 58 F5
East Row N Yorks 59 E9
East Rudham Norf 38 C4
East Runton Norf 39 A7
East Ruston Norf 39 C9
East Saltoun E Loth 70 D3
East Sleekburn Northumb 63 E8
East Somerton Norf 39 D10
East Stockwith Lincs 45 C11
East Stoke Dorset 9 F7
East Stoke Notts 45 H11
East Stour Dorset 9 B7
East Stourmouth Kent 21 E9
East Stowford Devon 6 D5
East Stratton Hants 18 H2
East Studdal Kent 21 G10
East Suisnish Highld 85 E10
East Taphouse Corn 4 E2
East-the-Water Devon 6 D3
East Thirston Northumb 63 D7
East Tilbury Thurrock 20 D3
East Tisted Hants 10 A6
East Torrington Lincs 46 D5
East Tuddenham Norf 39 D6
East Tytherley Hants 10 B1
East Tytherton Wilts 16 D6
East Village Devon 7 F7
East Wall Shrops 33 F11
East Walton Norf 38 D3
East Wellow Hants 10 B2
East Wemyss Fife 76 H6
East Whitburn W Loth 69 D8
East Williamston Pembs 22 F5
East Winch Norf 38 D2
East Winterslow Wilts 9 A11
East Wittering W Sus 11 E6
East Witton N Yorks 58 H2
East Woodburn Northumb 62 E5
East Woodhay Hants 17 E11
East Worldham Hants 18 H4
East Worlington Devon 7 E6
East Worthing W Sus 11 D10
Eastbourne E Sus 12 G5
Eastbridge Suff 31 B11
Eastburn W Yorks 50 E6
Eastbury London 19 B7
Eastbury W Berks 17 D10
Eastby N Yorks 50 D6
Eastchurch Kent 20 D6
Eastcombe Glos 16 A5
Eastcote London 19 C8
Eastcote Northants 28 C3
Eastcote W Mid 35 H7
Eastcott Corn 6 E1
Eastcott Wilts 17 F7
Eastcourt Wilts 16 B6
Eastcourt Wilts 17 E9
Easter Ardross Highld 87 D9
Easter Balmoral Aberds 82 D4
Easter Boleskine Highld 81 A7
Easter Compton S Glos 16 C2
Easter Cringate Stirling 68 B6
Easter Davoch Aberds 82 C6
Easter Earshaig Dumfries 60 C6
Easter Fearn Highld 87 C9
Easter Galcantray Highld 87 G11
Easter Howgate Midloth 69 D11
Easter Howlaws Borders 70 F6
Easter Kinkell Highld 87 F8
Easter Lednathie Angus 76 A6
Easter Milton Highld 87 F12
Easter Moniack Highld 87 G8
Easter Ord Aberdeen 83 C10
Easter Quarff Shetland 96 K6
Easter Rhynd Perth 76 F4
Easter Row Stirling 75 H10
Easter Silverford Aberds 89 B7
Easter Skeld Shetland 96 J5
Easter Whyntie Aberds 88 B6
Eastergate W Sus 11 D8
Easterhouse Glasgow 68 D5
Eastern Green W Mid 35 G8
Easterton Wilts 17 F7
Eastertown Som 15 F9
Eastertown of Auchleuchries Aberds 89 E10
Eastfield N Lanark 69 D7
Eastfield N Yorks 52 A6
Eastfield Hall Northumb 63 C8
Eastgate Durham 57 C11
Eastgate Norf 39 C7
Eastham Mers 42 D6
Eastham Ferry Mers 42 D6
Easthampstead Brack 18 E5
Eastheath Wokingham 18 E5
Easthope Shrops 34 F1
Easthorpe Essex 30 F6
Easthorpe Leics 36 B4
Easthorpe Notts 45 G11
Easthouses Midloth 70 D2
Eastington Devon 7 F6
Eastington Glos 26 H4
Eastington Glos 27 G8
Eastleach Martin Glos 27 H9
Eastleach Turville Glos 27 H8
Eastleigh Devon 6 D3
Eastleigh Hants 10 C3
Eastling Kent 20 F6
Eastmoor Derbys 45 E7
Eastmoor Norf 38 E3
Eastney Ptsmth 10 E5
Eastnor Hereford 26 E4
Eastoft N Lincs 52 H4
Eastoke Hants 10 E6
Easton Cambs 29 A8
Easton Cumb 61 F10
Easton Cumb 61 H8
Easton Devon 5 C8
Easton Dorset 8 G5
Easton Hants 10 A4
Easton Lincs 36 C5
Easton Norf 39 D7
Easton Som 15 G11
Easton Suff 31 C9
Easton Wilts 16 D5
Easton Grey Wilts 16 C5
Easton-in-Gordano N Som 15 D11
Easton Maudit Northants 28 C5
Easton on the Hill Northants 36 E6
Easton Royal Wilts 17 E9
Eastpark Dumfries 60 G6
Eastrea Cambs 37 F8
Eastriggs Dumfries 61 G8
Eastrington E Yorks 52 G3
Eastry Kent 21 F10
Eastville Bristol 16 D3
Eastville Lincs 47 G8
Eastwell Leics 36 C3
Eastwick Herts 29 G11
Eastwick Shetland 96 F5
Eastwood Notts 45 H8
Eastwood Southend 20 C5
Eastwood W Yorks 50 G5
Eathorpe Warks 27 B10
Eaton Ches E 44 F2
Eaton Ches W 43 F8
Eaton Leics 36 C3
Eaton Norf 39 E8
Eaton Notts 45 E11
Eaton Oxon 17 A11
Eaton Shrops 33 G9
Eaton Shrops 33 G11
Eaton Bishop Hereford 25 E11
Eaton Bray C Beds 28 F6
Eaton Constantine Shrops 34 E1
Eaton Green C Beds 28 F6
Eaton Hastings Oxon 17 B9
Eaton on Tern Shrops 34 C2
Eaton Socon Cambs 29 C8
Eavestone N Yorks 51 C8
Ebberston N Yorks 52 A4
Ebbesbourne Wake Wilts 9 B8
Ebbw Vale = Glyn Ebwy Bl Gwent 25 H8
Ebchester Durham 63 H7
Ebford Devon 5 C10
Ebley Glos 26 H5
Ebnal Ches W 43 H7
Ebrington Glos 27 D8
Ecchinswell Hants 17 F11
Ecclaw Borders 70 D6
Ecclefechan Dumfries 61 F7
Eccles Borders 70 F6
Eccles Gtr Man 43 C10
Eccles Kent 20 E4
Eccles on Sea Norf 39 C10
Eccles Road Norf 38 F6
Ecclesall S Yorks 45 D7
Ecclesfield S Yorks 45 C7
Ecclesgreig Aberds 83 G9
Eccleshall Staffs 34 C4
Eccleshill W Yorks 51 F7
Ecclesmachan W Loth 69 C9
Eccleston Ches W 43 F7
Eccleston Lancs 49 H5
Eccleston Mers 43 C7
Eccleston Park Mers 43 C7
Eccup W Yorks 51 E8
Echt Aberds 83 C9
Eckford Borders 70 H6
Eckington Derbys 45 E8
Eckington Worcs 26 D6
Ecton Northants 28 B5
Edale Derbys 44 D5
Edburton W Sus 11 C11
Edderside Cumb 56 B2
Edderton Highld 87 C10
Eddistone Devon 6 D1
Eddleston Borders 69 F11
Eden Park London 19 E10
Edenbridge Kent 19 G11
Edenfield Lancs 50 H3
Edenhall Cumb 57 C7
Edenham Lincs 37 C6
Edensor Derbys 44 F6
Edentaggart Argyll 68 A2
Edenthorpe S Yorks 45 B10
Edentown Cumb 61 H9
Ederline Argyll 73 C7
Edern Gwyn 40 G4
Edgarley Som 15 H11
Edgbaston W Mid 35 G6
Edgcott Bucks 28 F3
Edgcott Som 7 C7
Edge Shrops 33 E9
Edge End Glos 26 G2
Edge Green Ches W 43 G7
Edge Hill Mers 42 C6
Edgebolton Shrops 34 C1
Edgefield Norf 39 B6
Edgefield Street Norf 39 B6
Edgeside Lancs 50 G4
Edgeworth Glos 26 H6
Edgmond Telford 34 D3
Edgmond Marsh Telford 34 C3
Edgton Shrops 33 G9
Edgware London 19 B8
Edgworth Blackburn 50 H3
Edinample Stirling 75 E8
Edinbane Highld 85 C8
Edinburgh Edin 69 C11
Edingale Staffs 35 D8
Edingight Ho. Moray 88 C5
Edingley Notts 45 G10
Edingthorpe Norf 39 B9
Edingthorpe Green Norf 39 B9
Edington Som 15 H9
Edington Wilts 16 F6
Edintore Moray 88 D4
Edith Weston Rutland 36 E5
Edithmead Som 15 G9
Edlesborough Bucks 28 G6
Edlingham Northumb 63 C7
Edlington Lincs 46 E6
Edmondsham Dorset 9 C9
Edmondsley Durham 58 B3
Edmondthorpe Leics 36 D4
Edmonstone Orkney 95 F6
Edmonton London 19 B10
Edmundbyers Durham 58 A1
Ednam Borders 70 G6
Ednaston Derbys 35 A8
Edradynate Perth 75 B11
Edrom Borders 71 E7
Edstaston Shrops 33 B11
Edstone Warks 27 B8
Edvin Loach Hereford 26 C3
Edwalton Notts 36 B1
Edwardstone Suff 30 D6
Edwinsford Carms 24 E3
Edwinstowe Notts 45 F10
Edworth C Beds 29 D9
Edwyn Ralph Hereford 26 C3
Edzell Angus 83 G7
Efail Isaf Rhondda 14 C6
Efailnewydd Gwyn 40 G5
Efailwen Carms 22 D6
Efenechtyd Denb 42 G4
Effingham Sur 19 F8
Effirth Shetland 96 H5
Efford Devon 7 F7
Egdon Worcs 26 C6
Egerton Gtr Man 43 A10
Egerton Kent 20 G6
Egerton Forstal Kent 20 G5
Eggborough N Yorks 52 G1
Eggbuckland Plym 4 F6
Eggington C Beds 28 F6
Egginton Derbys 35 C8
Egglescliffe Stockton 58 E5
Eggleston Durham 57 D11
Egham Sur 19 D7
Egleton Rutland 36 E4
Eglingham Northumb 63 B7
Egloshayle Corn 3 B8
Egloskerry Corn 4 C3
Eglwys-Brewis V Glam 14 E6
Eglwys Cross Wrex 33 A10
Eglwys Fach Ceredig 32 F2
Eglwysbach Conwy 41 C10
Eglwyswen Pembs 22 C6
Eglwyswrw Pembs 22 C6
Egmanton Notts 45 F11
Egremont Cumb 56 E2
Egremont Mers 42 C6
Egton N Yorks 59 F9
Egton Bridge N Yorks 59 F9
Eight Ash Green Essex 30 F6
Eignaig Highld 79 G10
Eil Highld 81 B10
Eilanreach Highld 85 G13
Eilean Darach Highld 86 C4
Eileanach Lodge Highld 87 E8
Einacleite W Isles 90 E6
Eisgean W Isles 91 F8
Eisingrug Gwyn 41 G8
Elan Village Powys 24 B6
Elberton S Glos 16 C3
Elburton Plym 4 F6
Elcho Perth 76 E4
Elcombe Swindon 17 C8
Eldernell Cambs 37 F9
Eldersfield Worcs 26 E5
Elderslie Renfs 68 D3
Eldon Durham 58 D3
Eldrick S Ayrs 54 A5
Eldroth N Yorks 50 C3
Eldwick W Yorks 51 E7
Elfhowe Cumb 56 G6
Elford Northumb 71 G10
Elford Staffs 35 D7
Elgin Moray 88 B2
Elgol Highld 85 G10
Elham Kent 21 G8
Elie Fife 77 G7
Elim Anglesey 40 B5
Eling Hants 10 C2
Elishader Highld 85 B10
Elishaw Northumb 62 D4
Elkesley Notts 45 E10
Elkstone Glos 26 G6
Ellan Highld 81 A10
Elland W Yorks 51 G7
Ellary Argyll 72 F6
Ellastone Staffs 35 A7
Ellemford Borders 70 D6
Ellenbrook IoM 48 E3
Ellenhall Staffs 34 C4
Ellen's Green Sur 19 H7
Ellerbeck N Yorks 58 G5
Ellerburn N Yorks 52 A4
Ellerby N Yorks 59 E8
Ellerdine Heath Telford 34 C2
Ellerhayes Devon 7 F8
Elleric Argyll 74 C3
Ellerker E Yorks 52 G5
Ellerton E Yorks 52 F3
Ellerton Shrops 34 C3
Ellesborough Bucks 28 H5
Ellesmere Shrops 33 B10
Ellesmere Port Ches W 43 E7
Ellingham Norf 39 F9
Ellingham Northumb 71 H10
Ellingstring N Yorks 51 A7
Ellington Cambs 29 A8
Ellington Northumb 63 D8
Elliot Angus 77 D9
Ellisfield Hants 18 G3
Ellistown Leics 35 D10
Ellon Aberds 89 E9
Ellonby Cumb 56 C6
Ellough Suff 39 G10
Elloughton E Yorks 52 G5
Ellwood Glos 26 H2
Elm Cambs 37 E10
Elm Hill Dorset 9 B7
Elm Park London 20 C2
Elmbridge Worcs 26 B6
Elmdon Essex 29 E11
Elmdon W Mid 35 G7
Elmdon Heath W Mid 35 G7
Elmers End London 19 E10
Elmesthorpe Leics 35 F10
Elmfield IoW 10 E5
Elmhurst Staffs 35 D7
Elmley Castle Worcs 26 D6
Elmley Lovett Worcs 26 B5
Elmore Glos 26 G4
Elmore Back Glos 26 G4
Elmscott Devon 6 D1
Elmsett Suff 31 D7
Elmstead Market Essex 31 F7
Elmsted Kent 13 B10
Elmstone Kent 21 E9
Elmstone Hardwicke Glos 26 F6
Elmswell E Yorks 52 D5
Elmswell Suff 30 B6
Elmton Derbys 45 E9
Elphin Highld 92 H5
Elphinstone E Loth 70 C2
Elrick Aberds 83 C10
Elrig Dumfries 54 E6
Elsdon Northumb 62 D5
Elsecar S Yorks 45 C7
Elsenham Essex 30 F2
Elsfield Oxon 28 G2
Elsham N Lincs 46 A4
Elsing Norf 39 D6
Elslack N Yorks 50 E5
Elson Shrops 33 B9
Elsrickle S Lanark 69 F9
Elstead Sur 18 G6
Elsted W Sus 11 C7
Elsthorpe Lincs 37 C6
Elstob Durham 58 D4
Elston Notts 45 H11
Elston Wilts 17 G7
Elstone Devon 6 E5
Elstow Bedford 29 D7
Elstree Herts 19 B8
Elstronwick E Yorks 53 F8
Elswick Lancs 49 F4
Elsworth Cambs 29 B10
Elterwater Cumb 56 F5
Eltham London 19 D11
Eltisley Cambs 29 C9
Elton Cambs 37 F6
Elton Ches W 43 E7
Elton Derbys 44 F6
Elton Glos 26 G4
Elton Hereford 25 A11
Elton Notts 36 B3
Elton Stockton 58 E5
Elton Green Ches W 43 E7
Elvanfoot S Lanark 60 B5
Elvaston Derbys 35 B10
Elveden Suff 38 H4
Elvingston E Loth 70 C3
Elvington Kent 21 F9
Elvington York 52 E2
Elwick Hrtlpl 58 C5
Elwick Northumb 71 G10
Elworth Ches E 43 F10
Elworthy Som 7 C9
Ely Cambs 37 G11
Ely Cardiff 15 D7
Emberton M Keynes 28 D5
Embleton Cumb 56 C3
Embleton Northumb 63 A8
Embo Highld 87 B11
Embo Street Highld 87 B11
Emborough Som 16 F3
Embsay N Yorks 50 D6
Emersons Green S Glos 16 D3
Emery Down Hants 10 D1
Emmbrook Wokingham 18 E4
Emmer Green Reading 18 D4
Emmington Oxon 18 A4
Emneth Norf 37 E10
Emneth Hungate Norf 37 E11
Empingham Rutland 36 E5
Empshott Hants 11 A6
Emstrey Shrops 33 D11
Emsworth Hants 10 D6
Enborne W Berks 17 E11
Enchmarsh Shrops 33 F11
Enderby Leics 35 F11
Endmoor Cumb 49 A5
Endon Staffs 44 G3
Endon Bank Staffs 44 G3
Enfield London 19 B10
Enfield Wash London 19 B10
Enford Wilts 17 F8
Engamoor Shetland 96 H4
Engine Common S Glos 16 C3
Englefield W Berks 18 D3
Englefield Green Sur 18 D6
Englesea-brook Ches E 43 G10
English Bicknor Glos 26 G2
English Frankton Shrops 33 C10
Englishcombe Bath 16 E4
Enham Alamein Hants 17 G10
Enmore Som 8 A1
Ennerdale Bridge Cumb 56 E2
Enoch Dumfries 60 C4
Enochdhu Perth 76 A3
Ensay Argyll 78 G6
Ensbury Bmouth 9 E9
Ensdon Shrops 33 D10
Ensis Devon 6 D4
Enstone Oxon 27 F10
Enterkinfoot Dumfries 60 C4
Enterpen N Yorks 58 F5
Enville Staffs 34 G4
Eolaigearraidh W Isles 84 H2
Eorabus Argyll 78 J6
Eòropaidh W Isles 91 A10
Epperstone Notts 45 H10
Epping Essex 19 A11
Epping Green Essex 29 H11
Epping Green Herts 29 H9
Epping Upland Essex 19 A11
Eppleby N Yorks 58 E2
Eppleworth E Yorks 52 F6
Epsom Sur 19 E9
Epwell Oxon 27 D10
Epworth N Lincs 45 B11
Epworth Turbary N Lincs 45 B11
Erbistock Wrex 33 A9
Erbusaig Highld 85 F12
Erchless Castle Highld 86 G7
Erdington W Mid 35 F7
Eredine Argyll 73 C8
Eriboll Highld 92 D7
Ericstane Dumfries 60 B6
Eridge Green E Sus 12 C4
Erines Argyll 73 F7
Eriswell Suff 38 H3
Erith London 20 D2
Erlestoke Wilts 16 F6
Ermine Lincs 46 E3
Ermington Devon 5 F7
Erpingham Norf 39 B7
Errogie Highld 81 A7
Errol Perth 76 E5
Erskine Renfs 68 C3
Erskine Bridge Renfs 68 C3
Ervie Dumfries 54 C3
Erwarton Suff 31 E9
Erwood Powys 25 D7
Eryholme N Yorks 58 F4
Eryrys Denb 42 G5
Escomb Durham 58 D2
Escrick N Yorks 52 E2
Esgairdawe Carms 24 D3
Esgairgeiliog Powys 32 E3
Esh Durham 58 B2
Esh Winning Durham 58 B2
Esher Sur 19 E8
Esholt W Yorks 51 E7
Eshott Northumb 63 D8
Eshton N Yorks 50 D5
Esk Valley N Yorks 59 F9
Eskadale Highld 86 H7
Eskbank Midloth 70 D2
Eskdale Green Cumb 56 F3
Eskdalemuir Dumfries 61 D8
Eske E Yorks 53 E6
Eskham Lincs 47 C7
Esprick Lancs 49 F4
Essendine Rutland 36 D6
Essendon Herts 29 H9
Essich Highld 87 H9
Essington Staffs 34 E5
Esslemont Aberds 89 F9
Eston Redcar 59 E6
Eswick Shetland 96 H6
Etal Northumb 71 G8
Etchilhampton Wilts 17 E7
Etchingham E Sus 12 D6
Etchinghill Kent 21 H8
Etchinghill Staffs 34 D6
Ethie Castle Angus 77 C9
Ethie Mains Angus 77 C9
Etling Green Norf 38 D6
Eton Windsor 18 D6
Eton Wick Windsor 18 D6
Etteridge Highld 81 D8
Ettersgill Durham 57 D10
Ettingshall W Mid 34 F5
Ettington Warks 27 D9
Etton E Yorks 52 E5
Etton Pboro 37 E7
Ettrick Borders 61 B8
Ettrickbridge Borders 61 A9
Ettrickhill Borders 61 B8
Etwall Derbys 35 B8
Euston Suff 38 H4
Euximoor Drove Cambs 37 F10
Euxton Lancs 50 H1
Evanstown Bridgend 14 C5
Evanton Highld 87 E9
Evedon Lincs 46 H4
Evelix Highld 87 B10
Evenjobb Powys 25 B9
Evenley Northants 28 E2
Evenlode Glos 27 F9
Evenwood Durham 58 D2
Evenwood Gate Durham 58 D2
Everbay Orkney 95 F7
Evercreech Som 16 H3
Everdon Northants 28 C2
Everingham E Yorks 52 E4
Everleigh Wilts 17 F9
Everley N Yorks 59 H10
Eversholt C Beds 28 E6
Evershot Dorset 8 D4
Eversley Hants 18 E4
Eversley Cross Hants 18 E4
Everthorpe E Yorks 52 F5
Everton C Beds 29 C9
Everton Hants 10 E1
Everton Mers 42 C6
Everton Notts 45 C10
Evertown Dumfries 61 F9
Evesbatch Hereford 26 D3
Evesham Worcs 27 D7
Evington Leicester 36 E2
Ewden Village S Yorks 44 C6
Ewell Sur 19 E9
Ewell Minnis Kent 21 G9
Ewelme Oxon 18 B3
Ewen Glos 17 B7
Ewenny V Glam 14 D5
Ewerby Lincs 46 H5
Ewerby Thorpe Lincs 46 H5
Ewes Dumfries 61 D9
Ewesley Northumb 62 D6
Ewhurst Sur 19 G7
Ewhurst Green E Sus 13 D6
Ewhurst Green Sur 19 H7
Ewloe Flint 42 F6
Ewloe Green Flint 42 F5
Ewood Blackburn 50 G2
Eworthy Devon 6 G3
Ewshot Hants 18 G5
Ewyas Harold Hereford 25 F10
Exbourne Devon 6 F5
Exbury Hants 10 E3
Exebridge Devon 7 D8
Exelby N Yorks 58 H3
Exeter Devon 7 G8
Exford Som 7 C7
Exhall Warks 27 C8
Exley Head W Yorks 50 F6
Exminster Devon 5 C10
Exmouth Devon 5 C11
Exnaboe Shetland 96 M5
Exning Suff 30 B3
Exton Devon 5 C10
Exton Hants 10 B5
Exton Rutland 36 D5
Exton Som 7 C8
Exwick Devon 7 G8
Eyam Derbys 44 E6
Eydon Northants 28 C2
Eye Hereford 25 B11
Eye Pboro 37 E8
Eye Suff 31 A8
Eye Green Pboro 37 E8
Eyemouth Borders 71 D8
Eyeworth C Beds 29 D9
Eyhorne Street Kent 20 F5
Eyke Suff 31 C10
Eynesbury Cambs 29 C8
Eynort Highld 85 F8
Eynsford Kent 20 E2
Eynsham Oxon 27 H11
Eype Dorset 8 E3
Eyre Highld 85 C9
Eyre Highld 85 E10
Eythorne Kent 21 G9
Eyton Hereford 25 B11
Eyton Shrops 33 G9
Eyton Wrex 33 A9
Eyton upon the Weald Moors Telford 34 D2

F

Faccombe Hants 17 F10
Faceby N Yorks 58 F5
Facit Lancs 50 H4
Faddiley Ches E 43 G8
Fadmoor N Yorks 59 H7
Faerdre Swansea 14 A2
Failand N Som 15 D11
Failford S Ayrs 67 D7
Failsworth Gtr Man 44 B2
Fain Highld 86 D4
Fair Green Norf 38 D2
Fair Hill Cumb 57 C7
Fair Oak Hants 10 C3
Fair Oak Green Hants 18 E3
Fairbourne Gwyn 32 D2
Fairburn N Yorks 51 G10
Fairfield Derbys 44 E4
Fairfield Stockton 58 E5
Fairfield Worcs 27 D7
Fairfield Worcs 34 H5
Fairford Glos 17 A8
Fairhaven Lancs 49 G3
Fairlie N Ayrs 73 H11
Fairlight E Sus 13 E7
Fairlight Cove E Sus 13 E7
Fairmile Devon 7 G9
Fairmilehead Edin 69 D11
Fairoak Staffs 34 B3
Fairseat Kent 20 E3
Fairstead Essex 30 G4
Fairstead Norf 38 C2
Fairwarp E Sus 12 D3
Fairy Cottage IoM 48 D4
Fairy Cross Devon 6 D3
Fakenham Norf 38 C5
Fakenham Magna Suff 38 H5
Fala Midloth 70 D3
Fala Dam Midloth 70 D3
Falahill Borders 70 E2
Falcon Hereford 26 E3
Faldingworth Lincs 46 D4
Falfield S Glos 16 B3
Falkenham Suff 31 E9
Falkirk Falk 69 C7
Falkland Fife 76 G5
Falla Borders 62 B3
Fallgate Derbys 45 F7
Fallin Stirling 69 A7
Fallowfield Gtr Man 44 C2
Fallsidehill Borders 70 F5
Falmer E Sus 12 F2
Falmouth Corn 3 F7
Falsgrave N Yorks 59 H11
Falstone Northumb 62 E3
Fanagmore Highld 92 E4
Fangdale Beck N Yorks 59 G6
Fangfoss E Yorks 52 D3
Fankerton Falk 68 B6
Fanmore Argyll 78 G7
Fannich Lodge Highld 86 E5
Fans Borders 70 F5
Far Bank S Yorks 45 A10
Far Bletchley M Keynes 28 E5
Far Cotton Northants 28 C4
Far Forest Worcs 26 A4
Far Laund Derbys 45 H7
Far Sawrey Cumb 56 G5
Farcet Cambs 37 F8
Farden Shrops 34 H1
Fareham Hants 10 D4
Farewell Staffs 35 D6
Farforth Lincs 47 E7
Faringdon Oxon 17 B9
Farington Lancs 49 G5
Farlam Cumb 61 H11
Farlary Highld 93 J10
Farleigh N Som 15 E10
Farleigh Sur 19 E10
Farleigh Hungerford Som 16 F5
Farleigh Wallop Hants 18 G3
Farlesthorpe Lincs 47 E8
Farleton Cumb 49 A5
Farleton Lancs 50 C1
Farley Shrops 33 E9
Farley Staffs 35 A6
Farley Wilts 9 B11
Farley Green Sur 19 G7
Farley Hill Luton 29 F7
Farley Hill Wokingham 18 E4
Farleys End Glos 26 G4
Farlington N Yorks 52 C2
Farlow Shrops 34 G2
Farmborough Bath 16 E3
Farmcote Glos 27 F7
Farmcote Shrops 34 F3
Farmington Glos 27 G8
Farmoor Oxon 27 H11
Farmtown Moray 88 C5
Farnborough Hants 18 F5
Farnborough London 19 E11
Farnborough W Berks 17 C11
Farnborough Warks 27 D11
Farnborough Green Hants 18 F5
Farncombe Sur 18 G6
Farndish Bedford 28 B6
Farndon Ches W 43 G7
Farndon Notts 45 G11
Farnell Angus 77 B9
Farnham Dorset 9 C8
Farnham Essex 29 F11
Farnham N Yorks 51 C9
Farnham Suff 31 B10
Farnham Sur 18 G5
Farnham Common Bucks 18 C6
Farnham Green Essex 29 F11
Farnham Royal Bucks 18 C6
Farnhill N Yorks 50 E6
Farningham Kent 20 E2
Farnley N Yorks 51 E8
Farnley W Yorks 51 F8
Farnley Tyas W Yorks 44 A5
Farnsfield Notts 45 G10
Farnworth Gtr Man 43 B10
Farnworth Halton 43 D8
Farr Highld 81 C10
Farr Highld 87 H9
Farr Highld 93 C10
Farr House Highld 87 H9
Farringdon Devon 7 G9
Farrington Gurney Bath 16 F3
Farsley W Yorks 51 F8
Farthinghoe Northants 28 E2
Farthingloe Kent 21 G9
Farthingstone Northants 28 C3
Fartown W Yorks 51 H7
Farway Devon 7 G10
Fasag Highld 85 C13
Fascadale Highld 79 D8
Faslane Port Argyll 73 E11
Fasnacloich Argyll 74 C3
Fasnakyle Ho Highld 80 A5
Fassfern Highld 80 F2
Fatfield T&W 58 A4
Fattahead Aberds 89 C6
Faugh Cumb 57 A7
Fauldhouse W Loth 69 D8
Faulkbourne Essex 30 G4
Faulkland Som 16 F4

Fauls Shrops 34 B1
Faversham Kent 21 E7
Favillar Moray 88 E2
Fawdington N Yorks 51 B10
Fawfieldhead Staffs 44 F4
Fawkham Green Kent 20 E2
Fawler Oxon 27 G10
Fawley Bucks 18 C4
Fawley Hants 10 D3
Fawley W Berks 17 C10
Fawley Chapel Hereford 26 F2
Faxfleet E Yorks 52 G4
Faygate W Sus 11 A11
Fazakerley Mers 43 C6
Fazeley Staffs 35 E8
Fearby N Yorks 51 A7
Fearn Highld 87 D11
Fearn Lodge Highld 87 C9
Fearn Station Highld 87 D11
Fearnan Perth 75 C10
Fearnbeg Highld 85 C12
Fearnhead Warr 43 C9
Fearnmore Highld 85 B12
Featherstone Staffs 34 E5
Featherstone W Yorks 51 G10
Featherwood Northumb 62 C4
Feckenham Worcs 27 B7
Feering Essex 30 F5
Feetham N Yorks 57 G11
Feizor N Yorks 50 C3
Felbridge Sur 12 C2
Felbrigg Norf 39 B8
Felcourt Sur 12 B2
Felden Herts 19 A7
Felin-Crai Powys 24 F5
Felindre Carms 23 C8
Felindre Carms 23 D10
Felindre Carms 24 E3
Felindre Carms 24 F4
Felindre Ceredig 23 A10
Felindre Powys 33 G7
Felindre Swansea 14 A2
Felindre Farchog Pembs 22 C6
Felinfach Ceredig 23 A10
Felinfach Powys 25 E7
Felinfoel Carms 23 F10
Felingwm isaf Carms 23 D10
Felingwm uchaf Carms 23 D10
Felinwynt Ceredig 23 A7
Felixkirk N Yorks 51 A10
Felixstowe Suff 31 E9
Felixstowe Ferry Suff 31 E10
Felkington Northumb 71 F8
Felkirk W Yorks 45 A7
Fell Side Cumb 56 C5
Felling T&W 63 G8
Felmersham Bedford 28 C6
Felmingham Norf 39 C8
Felpham W Sus 11 E8
Felsham Suff 30 C6
Felsted Essex 30 F3
Feltham London 19 D8
Felthorpe Norf 39 D7
Felton Hereford 26 D2
Felton N Som 15 E11
Felton Northumb 63 C7
Felton Butler Shrops 33 D9
Feltwell Norf 38 F3
Fen Ditton Cambs 29 B11
Fen Drayton Cambs 29 B10
Fen End W Mid 35 H8
Fen Side Lincs 47 G7
Fenay Bridge W Yorks 51 H7
Fence Lancs 50 F4
Fence Houses T&W 58 A4
Fengate Norf 39 C7
Fengate Pboro 37 F8
Fenham Northumb 71 F9
Fenhouses Lincs 37 A8
Feniscliffe Blackburn 50 G2
Feniscowles Blackburn 50 G2
Feniton Devon 7 G10
Fenlake Bedford 29 D7
Fenny Bentley Derbys 44 G5
Fenny Bridges Devon 7 G10
Fenny Compton Warks 27 C11
Fenny Drayton Leics 35 F9
Fenny Stratford M Keynes 28 E5
Fenrother Northumb 63 D7
Fenstanton Cambs 29 B10
Fenton Cambs 37 H9
Fenton Lincs 46 E2
Fenton Lincs 46 G2
Fenton Stoke 34 A4
Fenton Barns E Loth 70 B4
Fenton Town Northumb 71 G8
Fenwick E Ayrs 67 B7
Fenwick Northumb 62 F6
Fenwick Northumb 71 F9
Fenwick S Yorks 52 H1
Feochaig Argyll 65 G8
Feock Corn 3 F7
Feolin Ferry Argyll 72 G3
Ferindonald Highld 85 H11
Feriniquarrie Highld 84 C6
Ferlochan Argyll 74 C2
Fern Angus 77 A7
Ferndale Rhondda 14 B6
Ferndown Dorset 9 D9
Ferness Highld 87 G12
Ferney Green Cumb 56 G6
Fernham Oxon 17 B9
Fernhill Heath Worcs 26 C5
Fernhurst W Sus 11 B7
Fernie Fife 76 F6
Ferniegair S Lanark 68 E6
Fernilea Highld 85 E8
Fernilee Derbys 44 E4
Ferrensby N Yorks 51 C9
Ferring W Sus 11 D9
Ferry Hill Cambs 37 G9
Ferry Point Highld 87 C10
Ferrybridge W Yorks 51 G10
Ferryden Angus 77 B10
Ferryhill Aberdeen 83 C11
Ferryhill Durham 58 C3
Ferryhill Station Durham 58 C4
Ferryside Carms 23 E8
Fersfield Norf 39 G6
Fersit Highld 80 F5
Ferwig Ceredig 22 B6
Feshiebridge Highld 81 C10
Fetcham Sur 19 F8
Fetterangus Aberds 89 C9
Fettercairn Aberds 83 F8
Fettes Highld 87 F8
Fewcott Oxon 28 F2
Fewston N Yorks 51 D7
Ffair-Rhos Ceredig 24 B4
Ffairfach Carms 24 F3
Ffaldybrenin Carms 24 D3
Ffarmers Carms 24 D3
Ffawyddog Powys 25 G9
Fforest Carms 23 F10
Fforest-fâch Swansea 14 B2
Ffos-y-ffin Ceredig 24 B1
Ffostrasol Ceredig 23 B8
Ffridd-Uchaf Gwyn 41 E7
Ffrith Wrex 42 G5
Ffrwd Gwyn 40 E6
Ffynnon ddrain Carms 23 D9
Ffynnon-oer Ceredig 23 A10
Ffynnongroyw Flint 42 D4
Fidden Argyll 78 J6
Fiddes Aberds 83 E10
Fiddington Glos 26 E6
Fiddington Som 7 B11
Fiddleford Dorset 9 C7
Fiddlers Hamlet Essex 19 A11
Field Staffs 34 B6
Field Broughton Cumb 49 A3
Field Dalling Norf 38 B6
Field Head Leics 35 E10
Fifehead Magdalen Dorset 9 B6
Fifehead Neville Dorset 9 C6
Fifield Oxon 27 G9
Fifield Wilts 17 F8
Fifield Windsor 18 D6
Fifield Bavant Wilts 9 B9
Figheldean Wilts 17 G8
Filands Wilts 16 C6
Filby Norf 39 D10
Filey N Yorks 53 A7
Filgrave M Keynes 28 D5
Filkins Oxon 17 A9
Filleigh Devon 6 D5
Filleigh Devon 7 E6
Fillingham Lincs 46 D3
Fillongley Warks 35 G8
Filton S Glos 16 D3
Fimber E Yorks 52 C4
Finavon Angus 77 B7
Finchairn Argyll 73 C8
Fincham Norf 38 E2
Finchampstead Wokingham 18 E4
Finchdean Hants 10 C6
Finchingfield Essex 30 E3
Finchley London 19 B9
Findern Derbys 35 B9
Findhorn Moray 87 E13
Findhorn Bridge Highld 81 A10
Findo Gask Perth 76 E3
Findochty Moray 88 B4
Findon Aberds 83 D11
Findon W Sus 11 D10
Findon Mains Highld 87 E9
Findrack Ho. Aberds 83 C8
Finedon Northants 28 A6
Fingal Street Suff 31 B9
Fingask Aberds 83 A9
Fingerpost Worcs 26 A4
Fingest Bucks 18 B4
Finghall N Yorks 58 H2
Fingland Cumb 61 H8
Fingland Dumfries 60 B3
Finglesham Kent 21 F10
Fingringhoe Essex 31 F7
Finlarig Stirling 75 D8
Finmere Oxon 28 E3
Finnart Perth 75 B8
Finningham Suff 31 B7
Finningley S Yorks 45 C10
Finnygaud Aberds 88 C5
Finsbury London 19 C10
Finstall Worcs 26 B6
Finsthwaite Cumb 56 H5
Finstock Oxon 27 G10
Finstown Orkney 95 G4
Fintry Aberds 89 C7
Fintry Dundee 77 D7
Fintry Stirling 68 B5
Finzean Aberds 83 D8
Fionnphort Argyll 78 J6
Fionnsbhagh W Isles 90 J5
Fir Tree Durham 58 C2
Firbeck S Yorks 45 D9
Firby N Yorks 52 C3
Firby N Yorks 58 H3
Firgrove Gtr Man 44 A3
Firsby Lincs 47 F8
Firsdown Wilts 9 A11
First Coast Highld 86 B2
Fishbourne IoW 10 E4
Fishbourne W Sus 11 D7
Fishburn Durham 58 C4
Fishcross Clack 75 H11
Fisher Place Cumb 56 E5
Fisherford Aberds 89 E6
Fisher's Pond Hants 10 B3
Fisherstreet W Sus 11 A8
Fisherton Highld 87 F10
Fisherton S Ayrs 66 E5
Fishguard = Abergwaun Pembs 22 C4
Fishlake S Yorks 45 A10
Fishleigh Barton Devon 6 D4
Fishponds Bristol 16 D3
Fishpool Glos 26 F3
Fishtoft Lincs 37 A9
Fishtoft Drove Lincs 47 H7
Fishtown of Usan Angus 77 B10
Fishwick Borders 71 E8
Fiskavaig Highld 85 E8
Fiskerton Lincs 46 E4
Fiskerton Notts 45 G11
Fitling E Yorks 53 F8
Fittleton Wilts 17 G8
Fittleworth W Sus 11 C9
Fitton End Cambs 37 D10
Fitz Shrops 33 D10
Fitzhead Som 7 D10
Fitzwilliam W Yorks 51 H10
Fiunary Highld 79 G9
Five Acres Glos 26 G2
Five Ashes E Sus 12 D4
Five Oak Green Kent 20 G3
Five Oaks Jersey 11
Five Oaks W Sus 11 B9
Five Roads Carms 23 F9
Fivecrosses Ches W 43 E8
Fivehead Som 8 B2
Flack's Green Essex 30 G4
Flackwell Heath Bucks 18 C5
Fladbury Worcs 26 D6
Fladdabister Shetland 96 K6
Flagg Derbys 44 F5
Flamborough E Yorks 53 B8
Flamstead Herts 29 G7
Flamstead End Herts 19 A10
Flansham W Sus 11 D8
Flanshaw W Yorks 51 G9
Flasby N Yorks 50 D5
Flash Staffs 44 F4
Flashader Highld 85 C8
Flask Inn N Yorks 59 F10
Flaunden Herts 19 A7
Flawborough Notts 36 A3
Flawith N Yorks 51 C10
Flax Bourton N Som 15 E11
Flaxby N Yorks 51 D9
Flaxholme Derbys 35 A9
Flaxley Glos 26 G3
Flaxpool Som 7 C10
Flaxton N Yorks 52 C2
Fleckney Leics 36 F2
Flecknoe Warks 28 B2
Fledborough Notts 46 E2
Fleet Hants 10 D6
Fleet Hants 18 F5
Fleet Lincs 37 C9
Fleet Hargate Lincs 37 C9
Fleetham Northumb 71 H10
Fleetlands Hants 10 D4
Fleetville Herts 29 H8
Fleetwood Lancs 49 E3
Flemingston V Glam 14 D6
Flemington S Lanark 68 E5
Flempton Suff 30 B5
Fleoideabhagh W Isles 90 J5
Fletchertown Cumb 56 B4
Fletching E Sus 12 D3
Flexbury Corn 6 F1
Flexford Sur 18 G6
Flimby Cumb 56 C2
Flimwell E Sus 12 C6
Flint = Y Fflint Flint 42 E5
Flint Mountain Flint 42 E5
Flintham Notts 45 H11
Flinton E Yorks 53 F8
Flintsham Hereford 25 C10
Flitcham Norf 38 C3
Flitton C Beds 29 E7
Flitwick C Beds 29 E7
Flixborough N Lincs 52 H4
Flixborough Stather N Lincs 46 A2
Flixton Gtr Man 43 C10
Flixton N Yorks 52 B6
Flixton Suff 39 G9
Flockton W Yorks 44 A6
Flodaigh W Isles 84 C3
Flodden Northumb 71 G8
Flodigarry Highld 85 A9
Flood's Ferry Cambs 37 F9
Flookburgh Cumb 49 B3
Florden Norf 39 F7
Flore Northants 28 B3
Flotterton Northumb 62 C5
Flowton Suff 31 D7
Flush House W Yorks 44 B5
Flushing Aberds 89 D10
Flushing Corn 3 F7
Flyford Flavell Worcs 26 C6
Foals Green Suff 31 A9
Fobbing Thurrock 20 C4
Fochabers Moray 88 C3
Fochriw Caerph 25 H8
Fockerby N Lincs 52 H4
Fodderletter Moray 82 A3
Fodderty Highld 87 F8
Foel Powys 32 D5
Foel-gastell Carms 23 E10
Foffarty Angus 77 C7
Foggathorpe E Yorks 52 F3
Fogo Borders 70 F6
Fogorig Borders 70 F6
Foindle Highld 92 E4
Folda Angus 76 A4
Fole Staffs 34 B6
Foleshill W Mid 35 G9
Folke Dorset 8 C5
Folkestone Kent 21 H9
Folkingham Lincs 37 B6
Folkington E Sus 12 F4
Folksworth Cambs 37 G7
Folkton N Yorks 53 B6
Folla Rule Aberds 89 E7
Follifoot N Yorks 51 D9
Folly Gate Devon 6 G4
Fonthill Bishop Wilts 9 A8
Fonthill Gifford Wilts 9 A8
Fontmell Magna Dorset 9 C7
Fontwell W Sus 11 D8
Foolow Derbys 44 E5
Foots Cray London 19 D11
Forbestown Aberds 82 B5
Force Mills Cumb 56 G5
Forcett N Yorks 58 E2
Ford Argyll 73 C7
Ford Bucks 28 H4
Ford Devon 6 D3
Ford Glos 27 F7
Ford Northumb 71 G8
Ford Shrops 33 D10
Ford Staffs 44 G4
Ford W Sus 11 D9
Ford Wilts 16 D5
Ford End Essex 30 G3
Ford Street Som 7 E10
Fordcombe Kent 12 B4
Fordell Fife 69 B10
Forden Powys 33 E8
Forder Green Devon 5 E8
Fordham Cambs 30 A3
Fordham Essex 30 F6
Fordham Norf 38 F2
Fordhouses W Mid 34 E5
Fordingbridge Hants 9 C10
Fordon E Yorks 52 B6
Fordoun Aberds 83 F9
Ford's Green Suff 31 B7
Fordstreet Essex 30 F6
Fordwells Oxon 27 G10
Fordwich Kent 21 F8
Fordyce Aberds 88 B5
Forebridge Staffs 34 C5
Forest Durham 57 C10
Forest Becks Lancs 50 D3
Forest Gate London 19 C11
Forest Green Sur 19 G8
Forest Hall Cumb 57 F7
Forest Head Cumb 61 H11
Forest Hill Oxon 28 H2
Forest Lane Head N Yorks 51 D9
Forest Lodge Argyll 74 C5
Forest Lodge Highld 82 B2
Forest Lodge Perth 81 F11
Forest Mill Clack 69 A8
Forest Row E Sus 12 C3
Forest Town Notts 45 F9
Forestburn Gate Northumb 62 D6
Foresterseat Moray 88 C1
Forestside W Sus 11 C6
Forfar Angus 77 B7
Forgandenny Perth 76 F3
Forge Powys 32 F3
Forge Side Torf 25 H9
Forgewood N Lanark 68 E6
Forgie Moray 88 C3
Forglen Ho. Aberds 89 C6
Formby Mers 42 B6
Forncett End Norf 39 F7
Forncett St Mary Norf 39 F7
Forncett St Peter Norf 39 F7
Forneth Perth 76 C3
Fornham All Saints Suff 30 B5
Fornham St Martin Suff 30 B5
Forres Moray 87 F13
Forrest Lodge Dumfries 67 H8
Forrestfield N Lanark 69 D7
Forsbrook Staffs 34 A5
Forse Highld 94 G4
Forse Ho. Highld 94 G4
Forsinain Highld 93 E12
Forsinard Highld 93 E11
Forsinard Station Highld 93 E11
Forston Dorset 8 E5
Fort Augustus Highld 80 C5
Fort George Guern 11
Fort George Highld 87 F10
Fort William Highld 80 F3
Forteviot Perth 76 F3
Forth S Lanark 69 E8
Forth Road Bridge Edin 69 C10
Forthampton Glos 26 E5
Fortingall Perth 75 C10
Forton Hants 17 G11
Forton Lancs 49 D4
Forton Shrops 33 D10
Forton Som 8 D2
Forton Staffs 34 C3
Forton Heath Shrops 33 D10
Fortrie Aberds 89 D6
Fortrose Highld 87 F10
Fortuneswell Dorset 8 G5
Forty Green Bucks 18 B6
Forty Hill London 19 B10
Forward Green Suff 31 C7
Fosbury Wilts 17 F10
Fosdyke Lincs 37 B9
Foss Perth 75 B10
Foss Cross Glos 27 H7
Fossebridge Glos 27 G7
Foster Street Essex 29 H11
Fosterhouses S Yorks 45 A10
Foston Derbys 35 B7
Foston Lincs 36 A4
Foston N Yorks 52 C2
Foston on the Wolds E Yorks 53 D7
Fotherby Lincs 47 C7
Fotheringhay Northants 37 F6
Foubister Orkney 95 H6
Foul Mile E Sus 12 E5
Foulby W Yorks 51 H9
Foulden Borders 71 E8
Foulden Norf 38 F3
Foulis Castle Highld 87 E8
Foulridge Lancs 50 E4
Foulsham Norf 38 C6
Fountainhall Borders 70 F3
Four Ashes Staffs 34 G4
Four Ashes Suff 31 A7
Four Crosses Powys 33 D8
Four Crosses Powys 33 E6
Four Crosses Wrex 42 G5
Four Elms Kent 19 G11
Four Forks Som 7 C11
Four Gotes Cambs 37 D10
Four Lane Ends Ches W 43 F8
Four Lanes Corn 2 F5
Four Marks Hants 10 A5
Four Mile Bridge Anglesey 40 C4
Four Oaks E Sus 13 D7
Four Oaks W Mid 35 F7
Four Oaks W Mid 35 G8
Four Roads Carms 23 F9
Four Roads IoM 48 F2
Four Throws Kent 13 D6
Fourlane Ends Derbys 45 G7
Fourlanes End Ches E 44 G2
Fourpenny Highld 87 B11
Fourstones Northumb 62 G4
Fovant Wilts 9 B9
Foveran Aberds 89 F9
Fowey Corn 4 F2
Fowley Common Warr 43 C9
Fowlis Angus 76 D6
Fowlis Wester Perth 76 E2
Fowlmere Cambs 29 D11
Fownhope Hereford 26 E2
Fox Corner Sur 18 F6
Fox Lane Hants 18 F5
Fox Street Essex 31 F7
Foxbar Renfs 68 D3
Foxcombe Hill Oxon 17 A11
Foxdale IoM 48 E2
Foxearth Essex 30 D5
Foxfield Cumb 56 H4
Foxham Wilts 16 D6
Foxhole Corn 3 D8
Foxhole Swansea 14 B2
Foxholes N Yorks 52 B6
Foxhunt Green E Sus 12 E4
Foxley Norf 38 C6
Foxley Wilts 16 C5
Foxt Staffs 44 H4
Foxton Cambs 29 D11
Foxton Durham 58 D4
Foxton Leics 36 F3
Foxup N Yorks 50 B4
Foxwist Green Ches W 43 F9
Foxwood Shrops 34 H2
Foy Hereford 26 F2
Foyers Highld 81 A6
Fraddam Corn 2 F4
Fraddon Corn 3 D8
Fradley Staffs 35 D7
Fradswell Staffs 34 B5
Fraisthorpe E Yorks 53 C7
Framfield E Sus 12 D3
Framingham Earl Norf 39 E8
Framingham Pigot Norf 39 E8
Framlingham Suff 31 B9
Frampton Dorset 8 E5
Frampton Lincs 37 B9
Frampton Cotterell S Glos 16 C3
Frampton Mansell Glos 16 A6
Frampton on Severn Glos 26 H4
Frampton West End Lincs 37 A8
Framsden Suff 31 C8
Framwellgate Moor Durham 58 B3
Franche Worcs 34 H4
Frankby Mers 42 D5
Frankley Worcs 34 G5
Frank's Bridge Powys 25 C8
Frankton Warks 27 A11
Frant E Sus 12 C4
Fraserburgh Aberds 89 B9
Frating Green Essex 31 F7
Fratton Ptsmth 10 E5
Freathy Corn 4 F4
Freckenham Suff 30 A3
Freckleton Lancs 49 G4
Freeby Leics 36 C4
Freehay Staffs 34 A6
Freeland Oxon 27 G11
Freester Shetland 96 H6
Freethorpe Norf 39 E10
Freiston Lincs 37 A9
Fremington Devon 6 C4
Fremington N Yorks 58 G1
Frenchay S Glos 16 D3
Frenchbeer Devon 5 C7
Frenich Stirling 75 G7
Frensham Sur 18 G5
Fresgoe Highld 93 C12
Freshfield Mers 42 B5
Freshford Bath 16 E4
Freshwater IoW 10 F2
Freshwater Bay IoW 10 F2
Freshwater East Pembs 22 G5
Fressingfield Suff 39 H8
Freston Suff 31 E8
Freswick Highld 94 D5
Fretherne Glos 26 H4
Frettenham Norf 39 D8
Freuchie Fife 76 G5
Freuchies Angus 76 A5
Freystrop Pembs 22 E4
Friar's Gate E Sus 12 C3
Friarton Perth 76 E4
Friday Bridge Cambs 37 E10
Friday Street E Sus 12 F5
Fridaythorpe E Yorks 52 D4
Friern Barnet London 19 B9
Friesland Argyll 78 F4
Friesthorpe Lincs 46 D4
Frieston Lincs 46 H3
Frieth Bucks 18 B4
Frilford Oxon 17 B11
Frilsham W Berks 18 D2
Frimley Sur 18 F5
Frimley Green Sur 18 F5
Frindsbury Medway 20 D4
Fring Norf 38 B3
Fringford Oxon 28 F3
Frinsted Kent 20 F5
Frinton-on-Sea Essex 31 F9
Friockheim Angus 77 C8
Friog Gwyn 32 D2
Frisby on the Wreake Leics 36 D2
Friskney Lincs 47 G8
Friskney Eaudike Lincs 47 G8
Friskney Tofts Lincs 47 G8
Friston E Sus 12 G4
Friston Suff 31 B11
Fritchley Derbys 45 G7
Frith Bank Lincs 47 H7
Frith Common Worcs 26 B3
Fritham Hants 9 C11
Frithelstock Devon 6 E3
Frithelstock Stone Devon 6 E3
Frithville Lincs 47 G7
Frittenden Kent 13 B7
Frittiscombe Devon 5 G9
Fritton Norf 39 E10
Fritton Norf 39 F8
Fritwell Oxon 28 F2
Frizinghall W Yorks 51 F7
Frizington Cumb 56 E2
Frocester Glos 16 A4
Frodesley Shrops 33 E11
Frodingham N Lincs 46 A2
Frodsham Ches W 43 E8
Frogden Borders 70 H6
Froggatt Derbys 44 E6
Froghall Staffs 44 H4
Frogmore Devon 5 G8
Frogmore Hants 18 F5
Frognall Lincs 37 D7
Frogshail Norf 39 B8
Frolesworth Leics 35 F11
Frome Som 16 G4
Frome St Quintin Dorset 8 D4
Fromes Hill Hereford 26 D3
Fron Denb 42 F3
Fron Gwyn 40 G5
Fron Gwyn 41 E7
Fron Powys 25 B7
Fron Powys 33 E8
Fron Powys 33 F7
Froncysyllte Wrex 33 A8
Frongoch Gwyn 32 B5
Frostenden Suff 39 G10
Frosterley Durham 58 C1
Frotoft Orkney 95 F5
Froxfield Wilts 17 E9
Froxfield Green Hants 10 B6
Froyle Hants 18 G4
Fryerning Essex 20 A3
Fryton N Yorks 52 B2
Fulbeck Lincs 46 G3
Fulbourn Cambs 30 C2
Fulbrook Oxon 27 G9
Fulford Som 7 D11
Fulford Staffs 34 B5
Fulford York 52 E2
Fulham London 19 D9
Fulking W Sus 11 C11
Full Sutton E Yorks 52 D3
Fullarton Glasgow 68 D5
Fullarton N Ayrs 66 C6
Fuller Street Essex 30 G4
Fuller's Moor Ches W 43 G7
Fullerton Hants 17 H10
Fulletby Lincs 46 E6
Fullwood E Ayrs 67 A7
Fulmer Bucks 18 C6
Fulmodestone Norf 38 B5
Fulnetby Lincs 46 E4
Fulstow Lincs 47 C7
Fulwell T&W 63 H9
Fulwood Lancs 49 F5
Fulwood S Yorks 45 D7
Fundenhall Norf 39 F7
Fundenhall Street Norf 39 F7
Funtington W Sus 11 D6
Funtley Hants 10 D4
Funtullich Perth 75 E10
Funzie Shetland 96 D8
Furley Devon 8 D1
Furnace Argyll 73 C9
Furnace Carms 23 F10
Furnace End Warks 35 F8
Furneaux Pelham Herts 29 F11
Furness Vale Derbys 44 D4
Furze Platt Windsor 18 C5
Furzehill Devon 7 B6
Fyfett Som 7 E11
Fyfield Essex 30 H2
Fyfield Glos 17 A9
Fyfield Hants 17 G9
Fyfield Oxon 17 B11
Fyfield Wilts 17 E8
Fylingthorpe N Yorks 59 F10
Fyvie Aberds 89 E7

G

Gabhsann bho Dheas W Isles 91 B9
Gabhsann bho Thuath W Isles 91 B9
Gablon Highld 87 B10
Gabroc Hill E Ayrs 67 A7
Gaddesby Leics 36 D2
Gadebridge Herts 29 H7
Gaer Powys 25 F8
Gaerllwyd Mon 15 B10
Gaerwen Anglesey 40 C6
Gagingwell Oxon 27 F11
Gaick Lodge Highld 81 E9
Gailey Staffs 34 D5
Gainford Durham 58 E2
Gainsborough Lincs 46 C2
Gainsborough Suff 31 D8
Gainsford End Essex 30 E4
Gairloch Highld 85 A13
Gairlochy Highld 80 E3
Gairney Bank Perth 76 H4
Gairnshiel Lodge Aberds 82 C4
Gaisgill Cumb 57 F8
Gaitsgill Cumb 56 B5
Galashiels Borders 70 G3
Galgate Lancs 49 D4
Galhampton Som 8 B5
Gallaberry Dumfries 60 E5
Gallachoille Argyll 72 E6
Gallanach Argyll 78 E5
Gallanach Argyll 79 J11
Gallantry Bank Ches E 43 G8
Gallatown Fife 69 A11
Galley Common Warks 35 F9
Galley Hill Cambs 29 B10
Galleyend Essex 20 A4
Galleywood Essex 20 A4
Gallin Perth 75 C8
Gallowfauld Angus 77 C7
Gallows Green Staffs 35 A6
Galltair Highld 85 F13
Galmisdale Highld 78 C7
Galmpton Devon 5 G7
Galmpton Torbay 5 F9
Galphay N Yorks 51 B8
Galston E Ayrs 67 C8
Galtrigill Highld 84 C6
Gamblesby Cumb 57 C8
Gamesley Derbys 44 C4
Gamlingay Cambs 29 C9
Gammersgill N Yorks 51 A6
Gamston Notts 45 E11
Ganarew Hereford 26 G2
Ganavan Argyll 79 H11
Gang Corn 4 E4
Ganllwyd Gwyn 32 C3
Gannochy Angus 83 F7
Gannochy Perth 76 E4
Gansclet Highld 94 F5
Ganstead E Yorks 53 F7
Ganthorpe N Yorks 52 B2
Ganton N Yorks 52 B5
Garbat Highld 86 E7
Garbhallt Argyll 73 D9
Garboldisham Norf 38 G6
Garden City Flint 42 F6
Garden Village W Yorks 51 F10
Garden Village Wrex 42 G6
Gardenstown Aberds 89 B7
Garderhouse Shetland 96 J5
Gardham E Yorks 52 E5
Gardin Shetland 96 G6
Gare Hill Som 16 G4
Garelochhead Argyll 73 D11
Garford Oxon 17 B11
Garforth W Yorks 51 F10
Gargrave N Yorks 50 D5
Gargunnock Stirling 68 A6
Garlic Street Norf 39 G8
Garlieston Dumfries 55 E7
Garlinge Green Kent 21 F8
Garlogie Aberds 83 C9
Garmond Aberds 89 C8
Garmony Argyll 79 G9
Garmouth Moray 88 B3
Garn-yr-erw Torf 25 G9
Garnant Carms 24 G3
Garndiffaith Torf 15 A8
Garndolbenmaen Gwyn 40 F6
Garnedd Conwy 41 E9
Garnett Bridge Cumb 57 G7
Garnfadryn Gwyn 40 G4
Garnkirk N Lanark 68 D5
Garnlydan Bl Gwent 25 G8
Garnswllt Swansea 24 H3
Garrabost W Isles 91 D10
Garraron Argyll 73 C7
Garras Corn 2 G6
Garreg Gwyn 41 F8
Garrick Perth 75 F11
Garrigill Cumb 57 B9
Garriston N Yorks 58 G2
Garroch Dumfries 67 H8
Garrogie Lodge Highld 81 B7
Garros Highld 85 B9
Garrow Perth 75 C11
Garryhorn Dumfries 67 G8
Garsdale Cumb 57 H9
Garsdale Head Cumb 57 G9
Garsdon Wilts 16 C6
Garshall Green Staffs 34 B5
Garsington Oxon 18 A2
Garstang Lancs 49 E4
Garston Mers 43 D7
Garswood Mers 43 C8
Gartcosh N Lanark 68 D5
Garth Bridgend 14 B4
Garth Gwyn 41 C7
Garth Powys 24 D6
Garth Shetland 96 H4
Garth Wrex 33 A8
Garth Row Cumb 57 G7
Garthamlock Glasgow 68 D5
Garthbrengy Powys 25 E7
Garthdee Aberdeen 83 C11
Gartheli Ceredig 23 A10
Garthmyl Powys 33 F7
Garthorpe Leics 36 C4
Garthorpe N Lincs 52 H4
Gartly Aberds 88 E5
Gartmore Stirling 75 H8
Gartnagrenach Argyll 72 H6
Gartness N Lanark 68 D6
Gartness Stirling 68 B4
Gartocharn W Dunb 68 B3
Garton E Yorks 53 F8
Garton-on-the-Wolds E Yorks 52 D5
Gartsherrie N Lanark 68 D6
Gartymore Highld 93 H13
Garvald E Loth 70 C4
Garvamore Highld 81 D7
Garvard Argyll 72 D2
Garvault Hotel Highld 93 F10
Garve Highld 86 E6
Garvestone Norf 38 E6
Garvock Aberds 83 F9
Garvock Invclyd 73 F11
Garway Hereford 25 F11
Garway Hill Hereford 25 F11
Gaskan Highld 79 D10
Gastard Wilts 16 E5
Gasthorpe Norf 38 G5
Gatcombe IoW 10 F3
Gate Burton Lincs 46 D2
Gate Helmsley N Yorks 52 D2
Gateacre Mers 43 D7
Gatebeck Cumb 57 H7
Gateford Notts 45 D9
Gateforth N Yorks 52 G1
Gatehead E Ayrs 67 C6
Gatehouse Northumb 62 E3
Gatehouse of Fleet Dumfries 55 D9
Gatelawbridge Dumfries 60 D5
Gateley Norf 38 C5
Gatenby N Yorks 58 H4
Gateshead T&W 63 G8
Gatesheath Ches W 43 F7
Gateside Aberds 83 B8
Gateside Angus 77 C7
Gateside E Renf 68 E3
Gateside Fife 76 G4
Gateside N Ayrs 67 A6
Gathurst Gtr Man 43 B8
Gatley Gtr Man 44 D2
Gattonside Borders 70 G4
Gatwick Airport W Sus 12 B1
Gaufron Powys 24 B6
Gaulby Leics 36 E2
Gauldry Fife 76 E6
Gaunt's Common Dorset 9 D9
Gautby Lincs 46 E5
Gavinton Borders 70 E6
Gawber S Yorks 45 B7
Gawcott Bucks 28 E3
Gawsworth Ches E 44 F2
Gawthorpe W Yorks 51 G8
Gawthrop Cumb 57 H8
Gawthwaite Cumb 49 A2
Gay Street W Sus 11 B9
Gaydon Warks 27 C10
Gayfield Orkney 95 C5
Gayhurst M Keynes 28 D5
Gayle N Yorks 57 H10
Gayles N Yorks 58 F2
Gayton Mers 42 D5
Gayton Norf 38 D3
Gayton Northants 28 C4
Gayton Staffs 34 C5
Gayton le Marsh Lincs 47 D8
Gayton le Wold Lincs 46 D6
Gayton Thorpe Norf 38 D3
Gaywood Norf 38 C2
Gazeley Suff 30 B4
Geanies House Highld 87 D11
Gearraidh Bhailteas W Isles 84 F2
Gearraidh Bhaird W Isles 91 E8
Gearraidh na h-Aibhne W Isles 90 D7
Gearraidh na Monadh W Isles 84 G2
Geary Highld 84 B7
Geddes House Highld 87 F11
Gedding Suff 30 C6
Geddington Northants 36 G4
Gedintailor Highld 85 E10
Gedling Notts 36 A2
Gedney Lincs 37 C10
Gedney Broadgate Lincs 37 C10
Gedney Drove End Lincs 37 C10
Gedney Dyke Lincs 37 C10
Gedney Hill Lincs 37 D9
Gee Cross Gtr Man 44 C3
Geilston Argyll 68 C2
Geirinis W Isles 84 D2
Geise Highld 94 D3
Geisiadar W Isles 90 D6
Geldeston Norf 39 F9
Gell Conwy 41 D10
Gelli Pembs 22 E5
Gelli Rhondda 14 B5
Gellideg M Tydf 25 H7
Gellifor Denb 42 F4
Gelligaer Caerph 15 B7
Gellilydan Gwyn 41 G8
Gellinudd Neath 14 A3
Gellyburn Perth 76 D3
Gellywen Carms 23 D7
Gelston Dumfries 55 D10
Gelston Lincs 36 A5
Gembling E Yorks 53 D7
Gentleshaw Staffs 35 D6
Geocrab W Isles 90 H6
George Green Bucks 19 C7
George Nympton Devon 6 D6
Georgefield Dumfries 61 D8
Georgeham Devon 6 C3
Georgetown Bl Gwent 25 H8
Gerlan Gwyn 41 D8
Germansweek Devon 6 G3
Germoe Corn 2 G4
Gerrans Corn 3 F7
Gerrards Cross Bucks 19 C7
Gestingthorpe Essex 30 E5
Geuffordd Powys 33 D8
Gib Hill Ches W 43 E9
Gibbet Hill Warks 35 G11
Gibbshill Dumfries 60 F3
Gidea Park London 20 C2
Gidleigh Devon 5 C7
Giffnock E Renf 68 E4
Gifford E Loth 70 D4
Giffordland N Ayrs 66 B5
Giffordtown Fife 76 F5
Giggleswick N Yorks 50 C4
Gilberdyke E Yorks 52 G4
Gilchriston E Loth 70 D3
Gilcrux Cumb 56 C3
Gildersome W Yorks 51 G8
Gildingwells S Yorks 45 D9
Gileston V Glam 14 E6
Gilfach Caerph 15 B7
Gilfach Goch Rhondda 14 C5
Gilfachrheda Ceredig 23 A9
Gillamoor N Yorks 59 H7
Gillar's Green Mers 43 C7
Gillen Highld 84 C7
Gilling East N Yorks 52 B2
Gilling West N Yorks 58 F2
Gillingham Dorset 9 B7
Gillingham Medway 20 E4
Gillingham Norf 39 F10
Gillock Highld 94 E4
Gillow Heath Staffs 44 G2
Gills Highld 94 C5
Gill's Green Kent 13 C6
Gilmanscleuch Borders 61 A9
Gilmerton Edin 69 D11
Gilmerton Perth 75 E11
Gilmonby Durham 57 E11
Gilmorton Leics 36 G1
Gilmourton S Lanark 68 F5
Gilsland Northumb 62 G2
Gilsland Spa Cumb 62 G2
Gilston Borders 70 E3
Gilston Herts 29 G11
Gilwern Mon 25 G9
Gimingham Norf 39 B8
Giosla W Isles 90 E6
Gipping Suff 31 B7
Gipsey Bridge Lincs 46 H6
Girdle Toll N Ayrs 66 B6
Girlsta Shetland 96 H6
Girsby N Yorks 58 F4
Girtford C Beds 29 C8
Girthon Dumfries 55 D9
Girton Cambs 29 B11
Girton Notts 46 F2
Girvan S Ayrs 66 G4
Gisburn Lancs 50 E4
Gisleham Suff 39 G11
Gislingham Suff 31 A7
Gissing Norf 39 G7
Gittisham Devon 7 G10
Gladestry Powys 25 C9
Gladsmuir E Loth 70 C3
Glais Swansea 14 A3
Glaisdale N Yorks 59 F8
Glame Highld 85 D10
Glamis Angus 76 C6
Glan Adda Gwyn 41 C7
Glan Conwy Conwy 41 D10
Glan-Conwy Conwy 41 E10
Glan-Duar Carms 23 B10
Glan-Dwyfach Gwyn 40 F6
Glan Gors Anglesey 40 C6
Glan-rhyd Gwyn 40 E6
Glan-traeth Anglesey 40 C4
Glan-y-don Flint 42 E4
Glan-y-nant Powys 32 G5
Glan-y-wern Gwyn 41 G8
Glan-yr-afon Anglesey 41 B8
Glan-yr-afon Gwyn 32 A5
Glan-yr-afon Gwyn 32 A6
Glanaman Carms 24 G3
Glandford Norf 38 A6
Glandwr Pembs 22 D6
Glandy Cross Carms 22 D6
Glandyfi Ceredig 32 F2
Glangrwyney Powys 25 G9
Glanmule Powys 33 F7
Glanrafon Ceredig 32 G2
Glanrhyd Gwyn 40 G4
Glanrhyd Pembs 22 B6
Glanton Northumb 62 B6
Glanton Pike Northumb 62 B6
Glanvilles Wootton Dorset 8 D5
Glapthorn Northants 36 F6
Glapwell Derbys 45 F8
Glas-allt Shiel Aberds 82 E4
Glasbury Powys 25 E8
Glaschoil Highld 87 H13
Glascoed Denb 42 E2
Glascoed Mon 15 A9
Glascoed Powys 33 D7
Glascorrie Aberds 82 D5
Glascote Staffs 35 E8
Glascwm Powys 25 C8
Glasdrum Argyll 74 C3
Glasfryn Conwy 42 G2
Glasgow Glasgow 68 D4
Glashvin Highld 85 B9
Glasinfryn Gwyn 41 D7
Glasnacardoch Highld 79 B9
Glasnakille Highld 85 G10
Glasphein Highld 84 D6
Glaspwll Powys 32 F3
Glassburn Highld 86 H6
Glasserton Dumfries 55 F7
Glassford S Lanark 68 F6
Glasshouse Hill Glos 26 F4
Glasshouses N Yorks 51 C7
Glasslie Fife 76 G5
Glasson Cumb 61 G8
Glasson Lancs 49 D4
Glassonby Cumb 57 C7
Glasterlaw Angus 77 B8
Glaston Rutland 36 E4
Glastonbury Som 15 H11
Glatton Cambs 37 G7
Glazebrook Warr 43 C9
Glazebury Warr 43 C9
Glazeley Shrops 34 G3
Gleadless S Yorks 45 D7
Gleadsmoss Ches E 44 F2
Gleann Tholàstaidh W Isles 91 C10
Gleaston Cumb 49 B2
Gleiniant Powys 32 F5
Glemsford Suff 30 D5
Glen Dumfries 55 D8
Glen Dumfries 60 F4
Glen Auldyn IoM 48 C4
Glen Bernisdale Highld 85 D9
Glen Ho Borders 69 G11
Glen Mona IoM 48 D4
Glen Nevis House Highld 80 F3
Glen Parva Leics 36 F1
Glen Sluain Argyll 73 D9
Glen Tanar House Aberds 82 D6
Glen Trool Lodge Dumfries 55 A7
Glen Village Falk 69 C7
Glen Vine IoM 48 E3
Glenamachrie Argyll 74 E2
Glenbarr Argyll 65 E7
Glenbeg Highld 79 E8
Glenbeg Highld 82 A2
Glenbervie Aberds 83 E9
Glenboig N Lanark 68 D6
Glenborrodale Highld 79 E9
Glenbranter Argyll 73 D10
Glenbreck Borders 60 A6
Glenbrein Lodge Highld 81 B6
Glenbrittle House Highld 85 F9
Glenbuchat Lodge Aberds 82 B5
Glenbuck E Ayrs 68 H6
Glenburn Renfs 68 D3
Glencalvie Lodge Highld 86 C7
Glencanisp Lodge Highld 92 G4
Glencaple Dumfries 60 G5
Glencarron Lodge Highld 86 F3
Glencarse Perth 76 E4
Glencassley Castle Highld 92 J7
Glenceitlein Highld 74 C4
Glencoe Highld 74 B3
Glencraig Fife 76 H4
Glencripesdale Highld 79 F9
Glencrosh Dumfries 60 E3
Glendavan Ho. Aberds 82 C6
Glendevon Perth 76 G2
Glendoe Lodge Highld 80 C6
Glendoebeg Highld 80 C6
Glendoick Perth 76 E5
Glendoll Lodge Angus 82 F4
Glendoune S Ayrs 66 G4
Glenduckie Fife 76 F5
Glendye Lodge Aberds 83 E8
Gleneagles Hotel Perth 76 F2
Gleneagles House Perth 76 G2
Glenegedale Argyll 64 C4
Glenelg Highld 85 G13
Glenernie Moray 87 G13
Glenfarg Perth 76 F4
Glenfarquhar Lodge Aberds 83 E9
Glenferness House Highld 87 G12
Glenfeshie Lodge Highld 81 D10
Glenfield Leics 35 E11
Glenfinnan Highld 79 C11
Glenfoot Perth 76 F4
Glenfyne Lodge Argyll 74 F5
Glengap Dumfries 55 D9
Glengarnock N Ayrs 66 A6
Glengorm Castle Argyll 78 F7
Glengrasco Highld 85 D9
Glenhead Farm Angus 76 A5
Glenhoul Dumfries 67 H9
Glenhurich Highld 79 E11
Glenkerry Borders 61 B8
Glenkiln Dumfries 60 F4
Glenkindie Aberds 82 B6
Glenlatterach Moray 88 C1
Glenlee Dumfries 55 A9
Glenlichorn Perth 75 F10
Glenlivet Moray 82 A3
Glenlochsie Perth 82 F2
Glenloig N Ayrs 66 C2
Glenluce Dumfries 54 D5
Glenmallan Argyll 74 H5
Glenmarksie Highld 86 F6
Glenmassan Argyll 73 E10
Glenmavis N Lanark 68 D6
Glenmaye IoM 48 E2
Glenmidge Dumfries 60 E4
Glenmore Argyll 73 B7
Glenmore Highld 85 D9
Glenmore Lodge Highld 82 C1
Glenmoy Angus 77 A7
Glenogil Angus 77 A7
Glenprosen Lodge Angus 82 G4
Glenprosen Village Angus 82 G5
Glenquiech Angus 77 A7
Glenreasdell Mains Argyll 73 H7
Glenree N Ayrs 66 D2
Glenridding Cumb 56 E5
Glenrossal Highld 92 J7
Glenrothes Fife 76 G5
Glensanda Highld 79 G11
Glensaugh Aberds 83 F8
Glenshero Lodge Highld 81 D7
Glenstockadale Dumfries 54 C3
Glenstriven Argyll 73 F9
Glentaggart S Lanark 69 H7
Glentham Lincs 46 C4
Glentirranmuir Stirling 68 A5
Glenton Aberds 83 A8
Glentress Borders 69 G11
Glentromie Lodge Highld 81 D9
Glentrool Village Dumfries 54 B6
Glentruan IoM 48 B4
Glentruim House Highld 81 D8
Glentworth Lincs 46 D3
Glenuig Highld 79 D9
Glenurquhart Highld 87 E10
Glespin S Lanark 69 H7
Gletness Shetland 96 H6
Glewstone Hereford 26 F2
Glinton Pboro 37 E7
Glooston Leics 36 F3
Glororum Northumb 71 G10
Glossop Derbys 44 C4
Gloster Hill Northumb 63 C8
Gloucester Glos 26 G5
Gloup Shetland 96 C7
Glusburn N Yorks 50 E6
Glutt Lodge Highld 93 F12
Glutton Bridge Staffs 44 F4
Glympton Oxon 27 F11
Glyn-Ceiriog Wrex 33 B8
Glyn-cywarch Gwyn 41 G8
Glyn Ebwy = Ebbw Vale Bl Gwent 25 H8
Glyn-neath = Glynedd Neath 24 H5
Glynarthen Ceredig 23 B8
Glynbrochan Powys 32 G5
Glyncoch Rhondda 14 B6
Glyncorrwg Neath 14 B4
Glynde E Sus 12 F3

Glyndebourne E Sus 12 E3
Glyndyfrdwy Denb 33 A7
Glynedd = Glyn-neath Neath 24 H5
Glynogwr Bridgend 14 C5
Glyntaff Rhondda 14 C6
Glyntawe Powys 24 G5
Gnosall Staffs 34 C4
Gnosall Heath Staffs 34 C4
Goadby Leics 36 F3
Goadby Marwood Leics 36 C3
Goat Lees Kent 21 G7
Goatacre Wilts 17 D7
Goathill Dorset 8 C5
Goathland N Yorks 59 F9
Goathurst Som 8 A1
Gobernuisgach Lodge Highld 92 E7
Gobhaig W Isles 90 G5
Gobowen Shrops 33 B9
Godalming Sur 18 G6
Godley Gtr Man 44 C3
Godmanchester Cambs 29 A9
Godmanstone Dorset 8 E5
Godmersham Kent 21 F7
Godney Som 15 G10
Godolphin Cross Corn 2 F5
Godre'r-graig Neath 24 H4
Godshill Hants 9 C10
Godshill IoW 10 F4
Godstone Sur 19 F10
Godwinscroft Hants 9 E10
Goetre Mon 25 H10
Goferydd Anglesey 40 B4
Goff's Oak Herts 19 A10
Gogar Edin 69 C10
Goginan Ceredig 32 G2
Golan Gwyn 41 F7
Golant Corn 4 F2
Golberdon Corn 4 D4
Golborne Gtr Man 43 C9
Golcar W Yorks 51 H7
Gold Hill Norf 37 F11
Goldcliff Newport 15 C9
Golden Cross E Sus 12 E4
Golden Green Kent 20 G3
Golden Grove Carms 23 E10
Golden Hill Hants 10 E1
Golden Pot Hants 18 G4
Golden Valley Glos 26 F6
Goldenhill Stoke 44 G2
Golders Green London 19 C9
Goldhanger Essex 30 H6
Golding Shrops 33 E11
Goldington Bedford 29 C7
Goldsborough N Yorks 51 D9
Goldsborough N Yorks 59 E9
Goldsithney Corn 2 F4
Goldsworthy Devon 6 D2
Goldthorpe S Yorks 45 B8
Gollanfield Highld 87 F11
Golspie Highld 93 J11
Golval Highld 93 C11
Gomeldon Wilts 17 H8
Gomersal W Yorks 51 G8
Gomshall Sur 19 G7
Gonalston Notts 45 H10
Gonfirth Shetland 96 G5
Good Easter Essex 30 G3
Gooderstone Norf 38 E3
Goodleigh Devon 6 C5
Goodmanham E Yorks 52 E4
Goodnestone Kent 21 E7
Goodnestone Kent 21 F9
Goodrich Hereford 26 G2
Goodrington Torbay 5 F9
Goodshaw Lancs 50 G4
Goodwick = Wdig Pembs 22 C4
Goodworth Clatford Hants 17 G10
Goole E Yorks 52 G3
Goonbell Corn 2 E6
Goonhavern Corn 3 D6
Goose Eye W Yorks 50 E6
Goose Green Gtr Man 43 B8
Goose Green Norf 39 G7
Goose Green W Sus 11 C10
Gooseham Corn 6 E1
Goosey Oxon 17 B10
Goosnargh Lancs 50 F1
Goostrey Ches E 43 E10
Gorcott Hill Warks 27 B7
Gord Shetland 96 L6
Gordon Borders 70 F5
Gordonbush Highld 93 J11
Gordonsburgh Moray 88 B4
Gordonstoun Moray 88 B1
Gordonstown Aberds 88 C5
Gordonstown Aberds 89 E7
Gore Kent 21 F10
Gore Cross Wilts 17 F7
Gore Pit Essex 30 G5
Gorebridge Midloth 70 D2
Gorefield Cambs 37 D10
Gorey Jersey 11
Gorgie Edin 69 C11
Goring Oxon 18 C3
Goring-by-Sea W Sus 11 D10
Goring Heath Oxon 18 D3
Gorleston-on-Sea Norf 39 E11
Gornalwood W Mid 34 F5
Gorrachie Aberds 89 C7
Gorran Churchtown Corn 3 E8
Gorran Haven Corn 3 E9
Gorrenberry Borders 61 D10
Gors Ceredig 32 H2
Gorse Hill Swindon 17 C8
Gorsedd Flint 42 E4
Gorseinon Swansea 23 G10
Gorseness Orkney 95 G5
Gorsgoch Ceredig 23 A9
Gorslas Carms 23 E10
Gorsley Glos 26 F3
Gorstan Highld 86 E6
Gorstanvorran Highld 79 D11
Gorsteyhill Staffs 43 G10
Gorsty Hill Staffs 35 C7
Gortantaoid Argyll 64 A4
Gorton Gtr Man 44 C2
Gosbeck Suff 31 C8
Gosberton Lincs 37 B8
Gosberton Clough Lincs 37 C7
Gosfield Essex 30 F4
Gosford Hereford 26 B2
Gosforth Cumb 56 F2
Gosforth T&W 63 G8
Gosmore Herts 29 F8
Gosport Hants 10 E5
Gossabrough Shetland 96 E7
Gossington Glos 16 A4
Goswick Northumb 71 F9
Gotham Notts 35 B11
Gotherington Glos 26 F6
Gott Shetland 96 J6
Goudhurst Kent 12 C6
Goulceby Lincs 46 E6
Gourdas Aberds 89 D7
Gourdon Aberds 83 F10
Gourock Invclyd 73 F11
Govan Glasgow 68 D4
Govanhill Glasgow 68 D4
Goveton Devon 5 G8
Govilon Mon 25 G9
Gowanhill Aberds 89 B10
Gowdall E Yorks 52 G2
Gowerton Swansea 23 G10
Gowkhall Fife 69 B9
Gowthorpe E Yorks 52 D3
Goxhill E Yorks 53 E7
Goxhill N Lincs 53 G7
Goxhill Haven N Lincs 53 G7
Goytre Neath 14 C3
Grabhair W Isles 91 F8
Graby Lincs 37 C6
Grade Corn 2 H6
Graffham W Sus 11 C8
Grafham Cambs 29 B8
Grafham Sur 19 G7
Grafton Hereford 25 E11
Grafton N Yorks 51 C10
Grafton Oxon 17 A9
Grafton Shrops 33 D10
Grafton Worcs 26 B2
Grafton Flyford Worcs 26 C6
Grafton Regis Northants 28 D4
Grafton Underwood Northants 36 G5
Grafty Green Kent 20 G5
Graianrhyd Denb 42 G5
Graig Conwy 41 C10
Graig Denb 42 E3
Graig-fechan Denb 42 G4
Grain Medway 20 D5
Grainsby Lincs 46 C6
Grainthorpe Lincs 47 C7
Grampound Corn 3 E8
Grampound Road Corn 3 D8
Gramsdal W Isles 84 C3
Granborough Bucks 28 F4
Granby Notts 36 B3
Grandborough Warks 27 B11
Grandtully Perth 76 B2
Grange Cumb 56 E4
Grange E Ayrs 67 C7
Grange Medway 20 E4
Grange Mers 42 D5
Grange Perth 76 E5
Grange Crossroads Moray 88 C4
Grange Hall Moray 87 E13
Grange Hill Essex 19 B11
Grange Moor W Yorks 51 H8
Grange of Lindores Fife 76 F5
Grange-over-Sands Cumb 49 B4
Grange Villa Durham 58 A3
Grangemill Derbys 44 G6
Grangemouth Falk 69 B8
Grangepans Falk 69 B9
Grangetown Cardiff 15 D7
Grangetown Redcar 59 D6
Granish Highld 81 B11
Gransmoor E Yorks 53 D7
Granston Pembs 22 C3
Grantchester Cambs 29 C11
Grantham Lincs 36 B5
Grantley N Yorks 51 C8
Grantlodge Aberds 83 B9
Granton Dumfries 60 C6
Granton Edin 69 C11
Grantown-on-Spey Highld 82 A2
Grantshouse Borders 71 D7
Grappenhall Warr 43 D9
Grasby Lincs 46 B4
Grasmere Cumb 56 F5
Grasscroft Gtr Man 44 B3
Grassendale Mers 43 D6
Grassholme Durham 57 D11
Grassington N Yorks 50 C6
Grassmoor Derbys 45 F8
Grassthorpe Notts 45 F11
Grateley Hants 17 G9
Gratwich Staffs 34 B6
Graveley Cambs 29 B9
Graveley Herts 29 F9
Gravelly Hill W Mid 35 F7
Gravels Shrops 33 E9
Graven Shetland 96 F6
Graveney Kent 21 E7
Gravesend Herts 29 F11
Gravesend Kent 20 D3
Grayingham Lincs 46 C3
Grayrigg Cumb 57 G7
Grays Thurrock 20 D3
Grayshott Hants 18 H5
Grayswood Sur 11 A8
Graythorp Hrtlpl 58 D6
Grazeley Wokingham 18 E3
Greasbrough S Yorks 45 C8
Greasby Mers 42 D5
Great Abington Cambs 30 D2
Great Addington Northants 28 A6
Great Alne Warks 27 C8
Great Altcar Lancs 42 B6
Great Amwell Herts 29 G10
Great Asby Cumb 57 E8
Great Ashfield Suff 30 B6
Great Ayton N Yorks 59 E6
Great Baddow Essex 20 A4
Great Bardfield Essex 30 E3
Great Barford Bedford 29 C8
Great Barr W Mid 34 F6
Great Barrington Glos 27 G9
Great Barrow Ches W 43 F7
Great Barton Suff 30 B5
Great Barugh N Yorks 52 B3
Great Bavington Northumb 62 E5
Great Bealings Suff 31 D9
Great Bedwyn Wilts 17 E9
Great Bentley Essex 31 F8
Great Billing Northants 28 B5
Great Bircham Norf 38 B3
Great Blakenham Suff 31 C8
Great Blencow Cumb 56 C6
Great Bolas Telford 34 C2
Great Bookham Sur 19 F8
Great Bourton Oxon 27 D11
Great Bowden Leics 36 G3
Great Bradley Suff 30 C3
Great Braxted Essex 30 G5
Great Bricett Suff 31 C7
Great Brickhill Bucks 28 E6
Great Bridge W Mid 34 F5
Great Bridgeford Staffs 34 C4
Great Brington Northants 28 B3
Great Bromley Essex 31 F7
Great Broughton Cumb 56 C2
Great Broughton N Yorks 59 F6
Great Budworth Ches W 43 E9
Great Burdon Darl 58 E4
Great Burgh Sur 19 F9
Great Burstead Essex 20 B3
Great Busby N Yorks 58 F6
Great Canfield Essex 30 G2
Great Carlton Lincs 47 D8
Great Casterton Rutland 36 E6
Great Chart Kent 13 B8
Great Chatwell Staffs 34 D3
Great Chesterford Essex 30 D2
Great Cheverell Wilts 16 F6
Great Chishill Cambs 29 E11
Great Clacton Essex 31 G8
Great Cliff W Yorks 51 H9
Great Clifton Cumb 56 D2
Great Coates NE Lincs 46 B6
Great Comberton Worcs 26 D6
Great Corby Cumb 56 A6
Great Cornard Suff 30 D5
Great Cowden E Yorks 53 E8
Great Coxwell Oxon 17 B9
Great Crakehall N Yorks 58 G3
Great Cransley Northants 36 H4
Great Cressingham Norf 38 E4
Great Crosby Mers 42 C6
Great Cubley Derbys 35 B7
Great Dalby Leics 36 D3
Great Denham Bedford 29 D7
Great Doddington Northants 28 B5
Great Dunham Norf 38 D4
Great Dunmow Essex 30 F3
Great Durnford Wilts 17 H8
Great Easton Essex 30 F3
Great Easton Leics 36 F4
Great Eccleston Lancs 49 E4
Great Edstone N Yorks 52 A3
Great Ellingham Norf 38 F6
Great Elm Som 16 G4
Great Eversden Cambs 29 C10
Great Fencote N Yorks 58 G3
Great Finborough Suff 31 C7
Great Fransham Norf 38 D4
Great Gaddesden Herts 29 G7
Great Gidding Cambs 37 G7
Great Givendale E Yorks 52 D4
Great Glemham Suff 31 B10
Great Glen Leics 36 F2
Great Gonerby Lincs 36 B4
Great Gransden Cambs 29 C9
Great Green Norf 39 G8
Great Green Suff 30 C6
Great Habton N Yorks 52 B3
Great Hale Lincs 37 A7
Great Hallingbury Essex 30 G2
Great Hampden Bucks 18 A5
Great Harrowden Northants 28 A5
Great Harwood Lancs 50 F3
Great Haseley Oxon 18 A3
Great Hatfield E Yorks 53 E7
Great Haywood Staffs 34 C6
Great Heath W Mid 35 G9
Great Heck N Yorks 52 G1
Great Henny Essex 30 E5
Great Hinton Wilts 16 F6
Great Hockham Norf 38 F5
Great Holland Essex 31 G9
Great Horkesley Essex 30 E6
Great Hormead Herts 29 F10
Great Horton W Yorks 51 F7
Great Horwood Bucks 28 E4
Great Houghton Northants 28 C4
Great Houghton S Yorks 45 B8
Great Hucklow Derbys 44 E5
Great Kelk E Yorks 53 D7
Great Kimble Bucks 28 H5
Great Kingshill Bucks 18 B5
Great Langton N Yorks 58 G3
Great Leighs Essex 30 G4
Great Lever Gtr Man 43 B10
Great Limber Lincs 46 B5
Great Linford M Keynes 28 D5
Great Livermere Suff 30 A5
Great Longstone Derbys 44 E6
Great Lumley Durham 58 B3
Great Lyth Shrops 33 E10
Great Malvern Worcs 26 D4
Great Maplestead Essex 30 E5
Great Marton Blackpool 49 F3
Great Massingham Norf 38 C3
Great Melton Norf 39 E7
Great Milton Oxon 18 A3
Great Missenden Bucks 18 A5
Great Mitton Lancs 50 F3
Great Mongeham Kent 21 F10
Great Moulton Norf 39 F7
Great Munden Herts 29 F10
Great Musgrave Cumb 57 E9
Great Ness Shrops 33 D9
Great Notley Essex 30 F4
Great Oakley Essex 31 F8
Great Oakley Northants 36 G4
Great Offley Herts 29 F8
Great Ormside Cumb 57 E9
Great Orton Cumb 56 A5
Great Ouseburn N Yorks 51 C10
Great Oxendon Northants 36 G3
Great Oxney Green Essex 30 H3
Great Palgrave Norf 38 D4
Great Parndon Essex 29 H11
Great Paxton Cambs 29 B9
Great Plumpton Lancs 49 F3
Great Plumstead Norf 39 D9
Great Ponton Lincs 36 B5
Great Preston W Yorks 51 G10
Great Raveley Cambs 37 G8
Great Rissington Glos 27 G8
Great Rollright Oxon 27 E10
Great Ryburgh Norf 38 C5
Great Ryle Northumb 62 B6
Great Ryton Shrops 33 E10
Great Saling Essex 30 F4
Great Salkeld Cumb 57 C7
Great Sampford Essex 30 E3
Great Sankey Warr 43 D8
Great Saxham Suff 30 B4
Great Shefford W Berks 17 D10
Great Shelford Cambs 29 C11
Great Smeaton N Yorks 58 F4
Great Snoring Norf 38 B5
Great Somerford Wilts 16 C6
Great Stainton Darl 58 D4
Great Stambridge Essex 20 B5
Great Staughton Cambs 29 B8
Great Steeping Lincs 47 F8
Great Stonar Kent 21 F10
Great Strickland Cumb 57 D7
Great Stukeley Cambs 29 A9
Great Sturton Lincs 46 E6
Great Sutton Ches W 43 E6
Great Sutton Shrops 33 G11
Great Swinburne Northumb 62 F5
Great Tew Oxon 27 F10
Great Tey Essex 30 F5
Great Thurkleby N Yorks 51 B10
Great Thurlow Suff 30 C3
Great Torrington Devon 6 E3
Great Tosson Northumb 62 C6
Great Totham Essex 30 G5
Great Totham Essex 30 G5
Great Tows Lincs 46 C6
Great Urswick Cumb 49 B2
Great Wakering Essex 20 C6
Great Waldingfield Suff 30 D6
Great Walsingham Norf 38 B5
Great Waltham Essex 30 G3
Great Warley Essex 20 B2
Great Washbourne Glos 26 E6
Great Weldon Northants 36 G5
Great Welnetham Suff 30 C5
Great Wenham Suff 31 E7
Great Whittington Northumb 62 F6
Great Wigborough Essex 30 G6
Great Wilbraham Cambs 30 C2
Great Wishford Wilts 17 H7
Great Witcombe Glos 26 G6
Great Witley Worcs 26 B4
Great Wolford Warks 27 E9
Great Wratting Suff 30 D3
Great Wymondley Herts 29 F9
Great Wyrley Staffs 34 E5
Great Wytheford Shrops 34 D1
Great Yarmouth Norf 39 E11
Great Yeldham Essex 30 E4
Greater Doward Hereford 26 G2
Greatford Lincs 37 D6
Greatgate Staffs 35 A6
Greatham Hants 11 A6
Greatham Hrtlpl 58 D5
Greatham W Sus 11 C9
Greatstone on Sea Kent 13 D9
Greatworth Northants 28 D2
Greave Lancs 50 G4
Greeba IoM 48 D3
Green Denb 42 F3
Green End Bedford 29 C8
Green Hammerton N Yorks 51 D10
Green Lane Powys 33 F7
Green Ore Som 16 F2
Green St Green London 19 E11
Green Street Herts 19 B8
Greenbank Shetland 96 C7
Greenburn W Loth 69 D8
Greendikes Northumb 71 H9
Greenfield C Beds 29 E7
Greenfield Flint 42 E4
Greenfield Gtr Man 44 B3
Greenfield Highld 80 C4
Greenfield Oxon 18 B4
Greenford London 19 C8
Greengairs N Lanark 68 C6
Greenham W Berks 17 E11
Greenhaugh Northumb 62 E3
Greenhead Northumb 62 G2
Greenhill Falk 69 C7
Greenhill Kent 21 E8
Greenhill Leics 35 D10
Greenhill London 19 C8
Greenhills N Ayrs 67 A6
Greenhithe Kent 20 D2
Greenholm E Ayrs 67 C8
Greenholme Cumb 57 F7
Greenhouse Borders 61 A11
Greenhow Hill N Yorks 51 C7
Greenigoe Orkney 95 H5
Greenland Highld 94 D4
Greenlands Bucks 18 C4
Greenlaw Aberds 89 C6
Greenlaw Borders 70 F6
Greenlea Dumfries 60 F6
Greenloaning Perth 75 G11
Greenmount Gtr Man 43 A10
Greenmow Shetland 96 L6
Greenock Invclyd 73 F11
Greenock West Invclyd 73 F11
Greenodd Cumb 49 A3
Greenrow Cumb 56 A3
Greens Norton Northants 28 D3
Greenside T&W 63 G7
Greensidehill Northumb 62 B5
Greenstead Green Essex 30 F5
Greensted Essex 20 A2
Greenwich London 19 D10
Greet Glos 27 E7
Greete Shrops 26 A2
Greetham Lincs 47 E7
Greetham Rutland 36 D5
Greetland W Yorks 51 G6
Gregg Hall Cumb 56 G6
Gregson Lane Lancs 50 G1
Greinetobht W Isles 84 A3
Greinton Som 15 H10
Gremista Shetland 96 J6
Grenaby IoM 48 E2
Grendon Northants 28 B5
Grendon Warks 35 E8
Grendon Common Warks 35 F8
Grendon Green Hereford 26 C2
Grendon Underwood Bucks 28 F3
Grenofen Devon 4 D5
Grenoside S Yorks 45 C7
Greosabhagh W Isles 90 H6
Gresford Wrex 42 G6
Gresham Norf 39 B7
Greshornish Highld 85 C8
Gressenhall Norf 38 D5
Gressingham Lancs 50 C1
Gresty Green Ches E 43 G10
Greta Bridge Durham 58 E1
Gretna Dumfries 61 G9
Gretna Green Dumfries 61 G9
Gretton Glos 27 E7
Gretton Northants 36 F4
Gretton Shrops 33 F11
Grewelthorpe N Yorks 51 B8
Grey Green N Lincs 45 B11
Greygarth N Yorks 51 B7
Greynor Carms 23 F10
Greysouthen Cumb 56 D2
Greystoke Cumb 56 C6
Greystone Angus 77 C8
Greystone Dumfries 60 F5
Greywell Hants 18 F4
Griais W Isles 91 C9
Grianan W Isles 91 D9
Gribthorpe E Yorks 52 F3
Gridley Corner Devon 6 G2
Griff Warks 35 G9
Griffithstown Torf 15 B8
Grimbister Orkney 95 G4
Grimblethorpe Lincs 46 D6
Grimeford Village Lancs 43 A9
Grimethorpe S Yorks 45 B8
Griminis W Isles 84 C2
Grimister Shetland 96 D6
Grimley Worcs 26 B5
Grimness Orkney 95 J5
Grimoldby Lincs 47 D7
Grimpo Shrops 33 C9
Grimsargh Lancs 50 F1
Grimsbury Oxon 27 D11
Grimsby NE Lincs 46 A6
Grimscote Northants 28 C3
Grimscott Corn 6 F1
Grimsthorpe Lincs 36 C6
Grimston E Yorks 53 F8
Grimston Leics 36 C2
Grimston Norf 38 C3
Grimston York 52 D2
Grimstone Dorset 8 E5
Grinacombe Moor Devon 6 G3
Grindale E Yorks 53 B7
Grindigar Orkney 95 H6
Grindiscol Shetland 96 K6
Grindle Shrops 34 E3
Grindleford Derbys 44 E6
Grindleton Lancs 50 E3
Grindley Staffs 34 C6
Grindley Brook Shrops 33 A11
Grindlow Derbys 44 E5
Grindon Northumb 71 F8
Grindon Staffs 44 G4
Grindonmoor Gate Staffs 44 G4
Gringley on the Hill Notts 45 C11
Grinsdale Cumb 61 H9
Grinshill Shrops 33 C11
Grinton N Yorks 58 G1
Griomsidar W Isles 91 E8
Grishipoll Argyll 78 F4
Grisling Common E Sus 12 D3
Gristhorpe N Yorks 53 A6
Griston Norf 38 F5
Gritley Orkney 95 H6
Grittenham Wilts 17 C7
Grittleton Wilts 16 C5
Grizebeck Cumb 49 A2
Grizedale Cumb 56 G5
Grobister Orkney 95 F7
Groby Leics 35 E11
Groes Conwy 42 F3
Groes Neath 14 C3
Groes-faen Rhondda 14 C6
Groes-lwyd Powys 33 D8
Groesffordd Marli Denb 42 E3
Groeslon Gwyn 40 E6
Groeslon Gwyn 41 D7
Grogport Argyll 65 D9
Gromford Suff 31 C10
Gronant Flint 42 D3
Groombridge E Sus 12 C4
Grosmont Mon 25 F11
Grosmont N Yorks 59 F9
Groton Suff 30 D6
Grougfoot Falk 69 C9
Grouville Jersey 11
Grove Dorset 8 G6
Grove Kent 21 E9
Grove Notts 45 E11
Grove Oxon 17 B11
Grove Park London 19 D11
Grove Vale W Mid 34 F6
Grovesend Swansea 23 F10
Grudie Highld 86 E6
Gruids Highld 93 J8
Gruinard House Highld 86 B2
Grula Highld 85 F8
Gruline Argyll 79 G8
Grunasound Shetland 96 K5
Grundisburgh Suff 31 C9
Grunsagill Lancs 50 D3
Gruting Shetland 96 J4
Grutness Shetland 96 N6
Gualachulain Highld 74 C4
Gualin Ho. Highld 92 D6
Guardbridge Fife 77 F7
Guarlford Worcs 26 D5
Guay Perth 76 C3
Guestling Green E Sus 13 E7
Guestling Thorn E Sus 13 E7
Guestwick Norf 39 C6
Guestwick Green Norf 39 C6
Guide Blackburn 50 G3
Guide Post Northumb 63 E8
Guilden Morden Cambs 29 D9
Guilden Sutton Ches W 43 F7
Guildford Sur 18 G6
Guildtown Perth 76 D4
Guilsborough Northants 28 A3
Guilsfield Powys 33 D8
Guilton Kent 21 F9
Guineaford Devon 6 C4
Guisborough Redcar 59 E7
Guiseley W Yorks 51 E7
Guist Norf 38 C5
Guith Orkney 95 E6
Guiting Power Glos 27 F7
Gulberwick Shetland 96 K6
Gullane E Loth 70 B3
Gulval Corn 2 F3
Gulworthy Devon 4 D5
Gumfreston Pembs 22 F6
Gumley Leics 36 F2
Gummow's Shop Corn 3 D7
Gun Hill E Sus 12 E4
Gunby E Yorks 52 F3
Gunby Lincs 36 C5
Gundleton Hants 10 A5
Gunn Devon 6 C5
Gunnerside N Yorks 57 G11
Gunnerton Northumb 62 F5
Gunness N Lincs 46 A2
Gunnislake Corn 4 D5
Gunnista Shetland 96 J7
Gunthorpe Norf 38 B6
Gunthorpe Notts 36 A2
Gunthorpe Pboro 37 E7
Gunville IoW 10 F3
Gunwalloe Corn 2 G5
Gurnard IoW 10 E3
Gurnett Ches E 44 E3
Gurney Slade Som 16 G3
Gurnos Powys 24 H4
Gussage All Saints Dorset 9 C9
Gussage St Michael Dorset 9 C8
Guston Kent 21 G10
Gutcher Shetland 96 D7
Guthrie Angus 77 B8
Guyhirn Cambs 37 E9
Guyhirn Gull Cambs 37 E9
Guy's Head Lincs 37 C10
Guy's Marsh Dorset 9 B7
Guyzance Northumb 63 C8
Gwaenysgor Flint 42 D3
Gwalchmai Anglesey 40 C5
Gwaun-Cae-Gurwen Neath 24 G4
Gwaun-Leision Neath 24 G4
Gwbert Ceredig 22 B6
Gweek Corn 2 G6
Gwehelog Mon 15 A9
Gwenddwr Powys 25 D7
Gwennap Corn 2 F6
Gwenter Corn 2 H6
Gwernaffield Flint 42 F5
Gwernesney Mon 15 A10
Gwernogle Carms 23 C10
Gwernymynydd Flint 42 F5
Gwersyllt Wrex 42 G6
Gwespyr Flint 42 D4
Gwithian Corn 2 E4
Gwredog Anglesey 40 B6
Gwyddelwern Denb 42 H3
Gwyddgrug Carms 23 C9
Gwydyr Uchaf Conwy 41 D9
Gwynfryn Wrex 42 G5
Gwystre Powys 25 B7
Gwytherin Conwy 41 D10
Gyfelia Wrex 42 H6
Gyffin Conwy 41 C9
Gyre Orkney 95 H4
Gyrn-goch Gwyn 40 F6

H

Habberley Shrops 33 E9
Habergham Lancs 50 F4
Habrough NE Lincs 46 A5
Haceby Lincs 36 B6
Hacheston Suff 31 C10
Hackbridge London 19 E9
Hackenthorpe S Yorks 45 D8
Hackford Norf 39 E6
Hackforth N Yorks 58 G3
Hackland Orkney 95 F4
Hackleton Northants 28 C5
Hackness N Yorks 59 G10
Hackness Orkney 95 J4
Hackney London 19 C10
Hackthorn Lincs 46 D3
Hackthorpe Cumb 57 D7
Haconby Lincs 37 C7
Hacton London 20 C2
Hadden Borders 70 G6
Haddenham Bucks 28 H4
Haddenham Cambs 37 H10
Haddington E Loth 70 C4
Haddington Lincs 46 F3
Haddiscoe Norf 39 F10
Haddon Cambs 37 F7
Haddon Ches E 44 F3
Hade Edge W Yorks 44 B5
Hademore Staffs 35 E7
Hadfield Derbys 44 C4
Hadham Cross Herts 29 G11
Hadham Ford Herts 29 F11
Hadleigh Essex 20 C5
Hadleigh Suff 31 D7
Hadley Telford 34 D2
Hadley End Staffs 35 C7
Hadlow Kent 20 G3
Hadlow Down E Sus 12 D4
Hadnall Shrops 33 D11
Hadstock Essex 30 D2
Hady Derbys 45 E7
Hadzor Worcs 26 B6
Haffenden Quarter Kent 13 B7
Hafod-Dinbych Conwy 41 E10
Hafod-Iom Conwy 41 C10
Haggate Lancs 50 F4
Haggbeck Cumb 61 F10
Haggerston Northumb 71 F9
Haggrister Shetland 96 F5
Hagley Hereford 26 D2
Hagley Worcs 34 G5
Hagworthingham Lincs 47 F7
Haigh Gtr Man 43 B9
Haigh S Yorks 44 A6
Haigh Moor W Yorks 51 G8
Haighton Green Lancs 50 F1
Hail Weston Cambs 29 B8
Haile Cumb 56 F2
Hailes Glos 27 E7
Hailey Herts 29 G10
Hailey Oxon 27 G10
Hailsham E Sus 12 F4
Haimer Highld 94 D3
Hainault London 19 B11
Hainford Norf 39 D8
Hainton Lincs 46 D5
Hairmyres S Lanark 68 E5
Haisthorpe E Yorks 53 C7
Hakin Pembs 22 F3
Halam Notts 45 G10
Halbeath Fife 69 B10
Halberton Devon 7 E9
Halcro Highld 94 D4
Hale Gtr Man 43 D10
Hale Halton 43 D7
Hale Hants 9 C10
Hale Bank Halton 43 D7
Hale Street Kent 20 G3
Halebarns Gtr Man 43 D10
Hales Norf 39 F9
Hales Staffs 34 B3
Hales Place Kent 21 F8
Halesfield Telford 34 E3
Halesgate Lincs 37 C9
Halesowen W Mid 34 G5
Halesworth Suff 39 H9
Halewood Mers 43 D7
Halford Shrops 33 G10
Halford Warks 27 D9
Halfpenny Furze Carms 23 E7
Halfpenny Green Staffs 34 F4
Halfway Carms 24 E3
Halfway Carms 24 E5
Halfway W Berks 17 E11
Halfway Bridge W Sus 11 B8
Halfway House Shrops 33 D9
Halfway Houses Kent 20 D6
Halifax W Yorks 51 G6
Halket E Ayrs 67 A7
Halkirk Highld 94 E3
Halkyn Flint 42 E5
Hall Dunnerdale Cumb 56 G4
Hall Green W Mid 35 G7
Hall Green W Yorks 51 H9
Hall Grove Herts 29 G9
Hall of Tankerness Orkney 95 H6
Hall of the Forest Shrops 33 G8
Halland E Sus 12 E3
Hallaton Leics 36 F3
Hallatrow Bath 16 F3
Hallbankgate Cumb 61 H11
Hallen S Glos 15 C11
Halliburton Borders 70 F5
Hallin Highld 84 C7
Halling Medway 20 E4
Hallington Lincs 47 D7
Hallington Northumb 62 F5
Halliwell Gtr Man 43 A10
Halloughton Notts 45 G10
Hallow Worcs 26 C5
Hallrule Borders 61 B11
Halls E Loth 70 C5
Hall's Green Herts 29 F9
Hallsands Devon 5 H9
Hallthwaites Cumb 56 H3
Hallworthy Corn 4 C2
Hallyburton House Perth 76 D5
Hallyne Borders 69 F10
Halmer End Staffs 43 H10
Halmore Glos 16 A3
Halmyre Mains Borders 69 F10
Halnaker W Sus 11 D8
Halsall Lancs 42 A6
Halse Northants 28 D2
Halse Som 7 D10
Halsetown Corn 2 F4
Halsham E Yorks 53 G8
Halsinger Devon 6 C4
Halstead Essex 30 E5
Halstead Kent 19 E11
Halstead Leics 36 E3
Halstock Dorset 8 D4
Haltham Lincs 46 F6
Haltoft End Lincs 47 H7
Halton Bucks 28 G5
Halton Halton 43 D8
Halton Lancs 49 C5
Halton Northumb 62 G5
Halton W Yorks 51 F9
Halton Wrex 33 B9
Halton East N Yorks 50 D6
Halton Gill N Yorks 50 B4
Halton Holegate Lincs 47 F8
Halton Lea Gate Northumb 62 H2
Halton West N Yorks 50 D4
Haltwhistle Northumb 62 G3
Halvergate Norf 39 E10
Halwell Devon 5 F8
Halwill Devon 6 G3
Halwill Junction Devon 6 F3
Ham Devon 7 F11
Ham Glos 16 B3
Ham Highld 94 C4
Ham Kent 21 F10
Ham London 19 D8
Ham Shetland 96 K1
Ham Wilts 17 E10
Ham Common Dorset 9 B7
Ham Green Hereford 26 D4
Ham Green Kent 13 D7
Ham Green Kent 20 E5
Ham Green N Som 15 D11
Ham Green Worcs 27 B7
Ham Street Som 8 A4
Hamble-le-Rice Hants 10 D3
Hambleden Bucks 18 C4
Hambledon Hants 10 C5
Hambledon Sur 18 H6
Hambleton Lancs 49 E3
Hambleton N Yorks 52 F1
Hambridge Som 8 B2
Hambrook S Glos 16 D3
Hambrook W Sus 11 D6
Hameringham Lincs 47 F7
Hamerton Cambs 37 H7
Hametoun Shetland 96 K1
Hamilton S Lanark 68 E6
Hammer W Sus 11 A7
Hammerpot W Sus 11 D9
Hammersmith London 19 D9
Hammerwich Staffs 35 E6
Hammerwood E Sus 12 C3
Hammond Street Herts 19 A10
Hammoon Dorset 9 C7
Hamnavoe Shetland 96 E4
Hamnavoe Shetland 96 E5
Hamnavoe Shetland 96 F6
Hamnavoe Shetland 96 K5
Hampden Park E Sus 12 F5
Hamperden End Essex 30 E2
Hampnett Glos 27 G7
Hampole S Yorks 45 A9
Hampreston Dorset 9 E9
Hampstead London 19 C9
Hampstead Norreys W Berks 18 D2
Hampsthwaite N Yorks 51 D8
Hampton London 19 E8
Hampton Shrops 34 G3
Hampton Worcs 27 D7
Hampton Bishop Hereford 26 E2
Hampton Heath Ches W 43 H7
Hampton in Arden W Mid 35 G8
Hampton Loade Shrops 34 G3
Hampton Lovett Worcs 26 B5
Hampton Lucy Warks 27 C9
Hampton on the Hill Warks 27 B9
Hampton Poyle Oxon 28 G2
Hamrow Norf 38 C5
Hamsey E Sus 12 E3
Hamsey Green London 19 F10
Hamstall Ridware Staffs 35 D7
Hamstead IoW 10 E3
Hamstead W Mid 34 F6
Hamstead Marshall W Berks 17 E11
Hamsterley Durham 58 C2
Hamsterley Durham 63 H7
Hamstreet Kent 13 C9
Hamworthy Poole 9 E8
Hanbury Staffs 35 C7
Hanbury Worcs 26 B6
Hanbury Woodend Staffs 35 C7
Hanby Lincs 36 B6
Hanchurch Staffs 34 A4
Handbridge Ches W 43 F7
Handcross W Sus 12 D1
Handforth Ches E 44 D2
Handley Ches W 43 G7
Handsacre Staffs 35 D6
Handsworth S Yorks 45 D8
Handsworth W Mid 34 F6
Handy Cross Devon 6 D3
Hanford Stoke 34 A4
Hanging Langford Wilts 17 H7
Hangleton W Sus 11 D9
Hanham S Glos 16 D3
Hankelow Ches E 43 H9
Hankerton Wilts 16 B6
Hankham E Sus 12 F5
Hanley Stoke 44 H2
Hanley Castle Worcs 26 D5
Hanley Child Worcs 26 B3
Hanley Swan Worcs 26 D5
Hanley William Worcs 26 B3
Hanlith N Yorks 50 C5
Hanmer Wrex 33 B10
Hannah Lincs 47 E9
Hannington Hants 18 F2
Hannington Northants 28 A5
Hannington Swindon 17 B8
Hannington Wick Swindon 17 B8
Hansel Village S Ayrs 67 C6
Hanslope M Keynes 28 D5
Hanthorpe Lincs 37 C6
Hanwell London 19 C8
Hanwell Oxon 27 D11
Hanwood Shrops 33 E10
Hanworth London 19 D8
Hanworth Norf 39 B7
Happendon S Lanark 69 G7
Happisburgh Norf 39 B9
Happisburgh Common Norf 39 C9
Hapsford Ches W 43 E7
Hapton Lancs 50 F3
Hapton Norf 39 F7
Harberton Devon 5 F8
Harbertonford Devon 5 F8
Harbledown Kent 21 F8
Harborne W Mid 34 G6
Harborough Magna Warks 35 H10
Harbottle Northumb 62 C5
Harbury Warks 27 C10
Harby Leics 36 B3
Harby Notts 46 E2
Harcombe Devon 7 G10
Harden W Mid 34 E6
Harden W Yorks 51 F6
Hardenhuish Wilts 16 D6
Hardgate Aberds 83 C9
Hardham W Sus 11 C9
Hardingham Norf 38 E6
Hardingstone Northants 28 C4
Hardington Som 16 F4
Hardington Mandeville Som 8 C4
Hardington Marsh Som 8 D4
Hardley Hants 10 D3
Hardley Street Norf 39 E9
Hardmead M Keynes 28 D6
Hardrow N Yorks 57 G10
Hardstoft Derbys 45 F8
Hardway Hants 10 D5
Hardway Som 8 A6
Hardwick Bucks 28 G5
Hardwick Cambs 29 C10
Hardwick Norf 38 D2
Hardwick Norf 39 G8
Hardwick Northants 28 B5
Hardwick Notts 45 E10
Hardwick Oxon 27 H10
Hardwick Oxon 28 F2
Hardwick W Mid 35 F6
Hardwicke Glos 26 F6
Hardwicke Glos 26 G4
Hardwicke Hereford 25 D9
Hardy's Green Essex 30 F6
Hare Green Essex 31 F7
Hare Hatch Wokingham 18 D5
Hare Street Herts 29 F10
Hareby Lincs 47 F7
Hareden Lancs 50 D2
Harefield London 19 B7
Harehills W Yorks 51 F9
Harehope Northumb 62 A6
Haresceugh Cumb 57 B8
Harescombe Glos 26 G5
Haresfield Glos 26 G5
Hareshaw N Lanark 69 D7
Hareshaw Head Northumb 62 E4
Harewood W Yorks 51 E9
Harewood End Hereford 26 F2
Harford Carms 24 D3
Harford Devon 5 F7
Hargate Norf 39 F7
Hargatewall Derbys 44 E5
Hargrave Ches W 43 F7
Hargrave Northants 29 A7
Hargrave Suff 30 C4
Harker Cumb 61 G9
Harkland Shetland 96 E6
Harkstead Suff 31 E8
Harlaston Staffs 35 D8
Harlaw Ho. Aberds 83 A9
Harlaxton Lincs 36 B4
Harle Syke Lancs 50 F4
Harlech Gwyn 41 G7
Harlequin Notts 36 B2
Harlescott Shrops 33 D11
Harlesden London 19 C9
Harleston Devon 5 G8
Harleston Norf 39 G8
Harleston Suff 31 C7
Harlestone Northants 28 B4
Harley S Yorks 45 C7
Harley Shrops 34 E1
Harleyholm S Lanark 69 G8
Harlington C Beds 29 E7
Harlington London 19 D7
Harlington S Yorks 45 B8
Harlosh Highld 85 D7
Harlow Essex 29 G11
Harlow Hill N Yorks 51 D8
Harlow Hill Northumb 62 G6
Harlthorpe E Yorks 52 F3
Harlton Cambs 29 C10
Harman's Cross Dorset 9 F8
Harmby N Yorks 58 H2
Harmer Green Herts 29 G9
Harmer Hill Shrops 33 C10
Harmondsworth London 19 D7
Harmston Lincs 46 F3
Harnham Northumb 62 F6
Harnhill Glos 17 A7
Harold Hill London 20 B2
Harold Wood London 20 B2
Haroldston West Pembs 22 E3
Haroldswick Shetland 96 B8
Harome N Yorks 52 A2
Harpenden Herts 29 G8
Harpford Devon 7 G9
Harpham E Yorks 53 C6
Harpley Norf 38 C3
Harpley Worcs 26 B3
Harpole Northants 28 B3
Harpsdale Highld 94 E3
Harpsden Oxon 18 C4
Harpswell Lincs 46 D3
Harpur Hill Derbys 44 E4
Harpurhey Gtr Man 44 B2
Harraby Cumb 56 A6
Harrapool Highld 85 F11
Harrier Shetland 96 J1
Harrietfield Perth 76 E2
Harrietsham Kent 20 F5
Harrington Cumb 56 D1
Harrington Lincs 47 E7
Harrington Northants 36 G3
Harringworth Northants 36 F5
Harris Highld 78 B6
Harrogate N Yorks 51 D9
Harrold Bedford 28 C6
Harrow London 19 C8
Harrow on the Hill London 19 C8
Harrow Street Suff 30 E6
Harrow Weald London 19 B8
Harrowbarrow Corn 4 E4
Harrowden Bedford 29 D7
Harrowgate Hill Darl 58 E3
Harston Cambs 29 C11
Harston Leics 36 B4
Harswell E Yorks 52 E4

Hart Hrtlpl 58 C5
Hart Common Gtr Man 43 B9
Hart Hill Luton 29 F8
Hart Station Hrtlpl 58 C5
Hartburn Northumb 62 E6
Hartburn Stockton 58 E5
Hartest Suff 30 C5
Hartfield E Sus 12 C3
Hartford Cambs 29 A9
Hartford Ches W 43 E9
Hartford End Essex 30 G3
Hartfordbridge Hants 18 F4
Hartforth N Yorks 58 F2
Harthill Ches W 43 G8
Harthill N Lanark 69 D8
Harthill S Yorks 45 D8
Hartington Derbys 44 F5
Hartland Devon 6 D1
Hartlebury Worcs 26 A5
Hartlepool Hrtlpl 58 C6
Hartley Cumb 57 F9
Hartley Kent 13 C6
Hartley Kent 20 E3
Hartley Northumb 63 F9
Hartley Westpall Hants 18 F3
Hartley Wintney Hants 18 F4
Hartlip Kent 20 E5
Hartoft End N Yorks 59 G8
Harton N Yorks 52 C3
Harton Shrops 33 G10
Harton T&W 63 G9
Hartpury Glos 26 F4
Hartshead W Yorks 51 G7
Hartshill Warks 35 F9
Hartshorne Derbys 35 C9
Hartsop Cumb 56 E6
Hartwell Northants 28 C4
Hartwood N Lanark 69 E7
Harvieston Stirling 68 B4
Harvington Worcs 27 D7
Harvington Cross Worcs 27 D7
Harwell Oxon 17 C11
Harwich Essex 31 E9
Harwood Durham 57 C10
Harwood Gtr Man 43 A10
Harwood Dale N Yorks 59 G10
Harworth Notts 45 C10
Hasbury W Mid 34 G5
Hascombe Sur 18 G6
Haselbech Northants 36 H3
Haselbury Plucknett Som 8 C3
Haseley Warks 27 B9
Haselor Warks 27 C8
Hasfield Glos 26 F5
Hasguard Pembs 22 F3
Haskayne Lancs 42 B6
Hasketon Suff 31 C9
Hasland Derbys 45 F7
Haslemere Sur 11 A8
Haslingden Lancs 50 G3
Haslingfield Cambs 29 C11
Haslington Ches E 43 G10
Hassall Ches E 43 G10
Hassall Green Ches E 43 G10
Hassell Street Kent 21 G7
Hassendean Borders 61 A11
Hassingham Norf 39 E9
Hassocks W Sus 12 E1
Hassop Derbys 44 E6
Hastigrow Highld 94 D4
Hastingleigh Kent 13 B9
Hastings E Sus 13 F7
Hastingwood Essex 29 H11
Hastoe Herts 28 H6
Haswell Durham 58 B4
Haswell Plough Durham 58 B4
Hatch C Beds 29 D8
Hatch Hants 18 F3
Hatch Wilts 9 B8
Hatch Beauchamp Som 8 B2
Hatch End London 19 B8
Hatch Green Som 8 C2
Hatchet Gate Hants 10 D2
Hatching Green Herts 29 G8
Hatchmere Ches W 43 E8
Hatcliffe NE Lincs 46 B6
Hatfield Hereford 26 C2
Hatfield Herts 29 H9
Hatfield S Yorks 45 B10
Hatfield Worcs 26 C5
Hatfield Broad Oak Essex 30 G2
Hatfield Garden Village Herts 29 H9
Hatfield Heath Essex 30 G2
Hatfield Hyde Herts 29 G9
Hatfield Peverel Essex 30 G4
Hatfield Woodhouse S Yorks 45 B10
Hatford Oxon 17 B10
Hatherden Hants 17 F10
Hatherleigh Devon 6 F4
Hathern Leics 35 C10
Hatherop Glos 27 H8
Hathersage Derbys 44 D6
Hathershaw Gtr Man 44 B3
Hatherton Ches E 43 H9
Hatherton Staffs 34 D5
Hatley St George Cambs 29 C9
Hatt Corn 4 E4
Hattingley Hants 18 H3
Hatton Aberds 89 E10
Hatton Derbys 35 C8
Hatton Lincs 46 E5
Hatton Shrops 33 F10
Hatton Warks 27 B9
Hatton Warr 43 D8
Hatton Castle Aberds 89 D7
Hatton Heath Ches W 43 F7
Hatton of Fintray Aberds 83 B10
Hattoncrook Aberds 89 F8
Haugh E Ayrs 67 D7
Haugh Gtr Man 44 A3
Haugh Lincs 47 E8
Haugh Head Northumb 71 H9
Haugh of Glass Moray 88 E4
Haugh of Urr Dumfries 55 C11
Haugham Lincs 47 D7
Haughley Suff 31 B7
Haughley Green Suff 31 B7
Haughs of Clinterty Aberdeen 83 B10
Haughton Notts 45 E10
Haughton Shrops 33 C9
Haughton Shrops 34 D1
Haughton Shrops 34 E3
Haughton Shrops 34 F2
Haughton Staffs 34 C4
Haughton Castle Northumb 62 F5
Haughton Green Gtr Man 44 C3
Haughton Moss Ches E 43 G8
Haultwick Herts 29 F10
Haunn Argyll 78 G6
Haunn W Isles 84 G2
Haunton Staffs 35 D8
Hauxley Northumb 63 C8
Hauxton Cambs 29 C11
Havant Hants 10 D6
Haven Hereford 25 C11
Haven Bank Lincs 46 G6
Haven Side E Yorks 53 G7
Havenstreet IoW 10 E4
Havercroft W Yorks 45 A7
Haverfordwest = Hwlffordd Pembs 22 E4
Haverhill Suff 30 D3
Haverigg Cumb 49 B1
Havering-atte-Bower London 20 B2
Haveringland Norf 39 C7
Haversham M Keynes 28 D5
Haverthwaite Cumb 49 A3
Haverton Hill Stockton 58 D5
Hawarden = Penarlâg Flint 42 F6
Hawcoat Cumb 49 B2
Hawen Ceredig 23 B8
Hawes N Yorks 57 H10
Hawes' Green Norf 39 F8
Hawes Side Blackpool 49 F3
Hawford Worcs 26 B5
Hawick Borders 61 B11
Hawk Green Gtr Man 44 D3
Hawkchurch Devon 8 D2
Hawkedon Suff 30 C4
Hawkenbury Kent 12 C4
Hawkenbury Kent 13 B7
Hawkeridge Wilts 16 F5
Hawkerland Devon 7 H9
Hawkes End W Mid 35 G9
Hawkesbury S Glos 16 C4
Hawkesbury Warks 35 G9
Hawkesbury Upton S Glos 16 C4
Hawkhill Northumb 63 B8
Hawkhurst Kent 13 C6
Hawkinge Kent 21 H9
Hawkley Hants 10 B6
Hawkridge Som 7 C7
Hawkshead Cumb 56 G5
Hawkshead Hill Cumb 56 G5
Hawksland S Lanark 69 G7
Hawkswick N Yorks 50 B5
Hawksworth Notts 36 A3
Hawksworth W Yorks 51 E7
Hawksworth W Yorks 51 F8
Hawkwell Essex 20 B5
Hawley Hants 18 F5
Hawley Kent 20 D2
Hawling Glos 27 F7
Hawnby N Yorks 59 H6
Haworth W Yorks 50 F6
Hawstead Suff 30 C5
Hawthorn Durham 58 B5
Hawthorn Rhondda 15 C7
Hawthorn Wilts 16 E5
Hawthorn Hill Brack 18 D5
Hawthorn Hill Lincs 46 G6
Hawthorpe Lincs 36 C6
Hawton Notts 45 G11
Haxby York 52 D2
Haxey N Lincs 45 C11
Hay Green Norf 37 D11
Hay-on-Wye = Y Gelli Gandryll Powys 25 D9
Hay Street Herts 29 F10
Haydock Mers 43 C8
Haydon Dorset 8 C5
Haydon Bridge Northumb 62 G4
Haydon Wick Swindon 17 C8
Haye Corn 4 E4
Hayes London 19 C8
Hayes London 19 E11
Hayfield Derbys 44 D4
Hayfield Fife 69 A11
Hayhill E Ayrs 67 E7
Hayhillock Angus 77 C8
Hayle Corn 2 F4
Haynes C Beds 29 D7
Haynes Church End C Beds 29 D7
Hayscastle Pembs 22 D3
Hayscastle Cross Pembs 22 D4
Hayshead Angus 77 C9
Hayton Aberdeen 83 C11
Hayton Cumb 56 B3
Hayton Cumb 61 H11
Hayton E Yorks 52 E4
Hayton Notts 45 D11
Hayton's Bent Shrops 33 G11
Haytor Vale Devon 5 D8
Haywards Heath W Sus 12 D2
Haywood S Yorks 45 A9
Haywood Oaks Notts 45 G10
Hazel Grove Gtr Man 44 D3
Hazel Street Kent 12 C5
Hazelbank S Lanark 69 F7
Hazelbury Bryan Dorset 8 D6
Hazeley Hants 18 F4
Hazelhurst Gtr Man 44 B3
Hazelslade Staffs 34 D6
Hazelton Glos 27 G7
Hazelton Walls Fife 76 E6
Hazelwood Derbys 45 H7
Hazlemere Bucks 18 B5
Hazlerigg T&W 63 F8
Hazlewood N Yorks 51 D6
Hazon Northumb 63 C7
Heacham Norf 38 B2
Head of Muir Falk 69 B7
Headbourne Worthy Hants 10 A3
Headbrook Hereford 25 C10
Headcorn Kent 13 B7
Headingley W Yorks 51 F8
Headington Oxon 28 H2
Headlam Durham 58 E2
Headless Cross Worcs 27 B7
Headley Hants 18 E2
Headley Hants 18 H5
Headley Sur 19 F9
Headon Notts 45 E11
Heads S Lanark 68 F6
Heads Nook Cumb 61 H10
Heage Derbys 45 G7
Healaugh N Yorks 51 E10
Healaugh N Yorks 58 G1
Heald Green Gtr Man 44 D2
Heale Devon 6 B5
Heale Som 16 G3
Healey Gtr Man 50 H4
Healey N Yorks 51 A7
Healey Northumb 62 H6
Healing NE Lincs 46 A6
Heamoor Corn 2 F3
Heanish Argyll 78 G3
Heanor Derbys 45 H8
Heanton Punchardon Devon 6 C4
Heapham Lincs 46 D2
Hearthstane Borders 69 H10
Heasley Mill Devon 7 C6
Heast Highld 85 G11
Heath Cardiff 15 D7
Heath Derbys 45 F8
Heath and Reach C Beds 28 F6
Heath End Hants 18 E2
Heath End Sur 18 G5
Heath End Warks 27 B9
Heath Hayes Staffs 34 D6
Heath Hill Shrops 34 D3
Heath House Som 15 G10
Heath Town W Mid 34 F5
Heathcote Derbys 44 F5
Heather Leics 35 D9
Heatherfield Highld 85 D9
Heathfield Devon 5 D9
Heathfield E Sus 12 D4
Heathfield Som 7 D10
Heathhall Dumfries 60 F5
Heathrow Airport London 19 D7
Heathstock Devon 8 D1
Heathton Shrops 34 F4
Heatley Warr 43 D10
Heaton Lancs 49 C4
Heaton Staffs 44 F3
Heaton T&W 63 G8
Heaton W Yorks 51 F7
Heaton Moor Gtr Man 44 C2
Heaverham Kent 20 F2
Heaviley Gtr Man 44 D3
Heavitree Devon 7 G8
Hebburn T&W 63 G9
Hebden N Yorks 50 C6
Hebden Bridge W Yorks 50 G5
Hebron Anglesey 40 B6
Hebron Carms 22 D6
Hebron Northumb 63 E7
Heck Dumfries 60 E6
Heckfield Hants 18 E4
Heckfield Green Suff 39 H7
Heckfordbridge Essex 30 F6
Heckington Lincs 37 A7
Heckmondwike W Yorks 51 G8
Heddington Wilts 16 E6
Heddle Orkney 95 G4
Heddon-on-the-Wall Northumb 63 G7
Hedenham Norf 39 F9
Hedge End Hants 10 C3
Hedgerley Bucks 18 C6
Hedging Som 8 B2
Hedley on the Hill Northumb 62 H6
Hednesford Staffs 34 D6
Hedon E Yorks 53 G7
Hedsor Bucks 18 C6
Hedworth T&W 63 G9
Hegdon Hill Hereford 26 C2
Heggerscales Cumb 57 E10
Heglibister Shetland 96 H5
Heighington Darl 58 D3
Heighington Lincs 46 F4
Heights of Brae Highld 87 E8
Heights of Kinlochewe Highld 86 E3
Heilam Highld 92 C7
Heiton Borders 70 G6
Hele Devon 6 B4
Hele Devon 7 F8
Helensburgh Argyll 73 E11
Helford Corn 3 G6
Helford Passage Corn 3 G6
Helhoughton Norf 38 C4
Helions Bumpstead Essex 30 D3
Hellaby S Yorks 45 C9
Helland Corn 4 D1
Hellesdon Norf 39 D8
Hellidon Northants 28 C2
Hellifield N Yorks 50 D4
Hellingly E Sus 12 E4
Hellington Norf 39 E9
Hellister Shetland 96 J5
Helm Northumb 63 D7
Helmdon Northants 28 D2
Helmingham Suff 31 C8
Helmington Row Durham 58 C2
Helmsdale Highld 93 H13
Helmshore Lancs 50 G3
Helmsley N Yorks 52 A2
Helperby N Yorks 51 C10
Helperthorpe N Yorks 52 B5
Helpringham Lincs 37 A7
Helpston Pboro 37 E7
Helsby Ches W 43 E7
Helsey Lincs 47 E9
Helston Corn 2 G5
Helstone Corn 4 C1
Helton Cumb 57 D7
Helwith Bridge N Yorks 50 C4
Hemblington Norf 39 D9
Hemel Hempstead Herts 29 H7
Hemingbrough N Yorks 52 F2
Hemingby Lincs 46 E6
Hemingford Abbots Cambs 29 A9
Hemingford Grey Cambs 29 A9
Hemingstone Suff 31 C8
Hemington Leics 35 C10
Hemington Northants 37 G6
Hemington Som 16 F4
Hemley Suff 31 D9
Hemlington Mbro 58 E6
Hemp Green Suff 31 B10
Hempholme E Yorks 53 D6
Hempnall Norf 39 F8
Hempnall Green Norf 39 F8
Hempriggs House Highld 94 F5
Hempstead Essex 30 E3
Hempstead Medway 20 E4
Hempstead Norf 39 B7
Hempstead Norf 39 C10
Hempsted Glos 26 G5
Hempton Norf 38 C5
Hempton Oxon 27 E11
Hemsby Norf 39 D10
Hemswell Lincs 46 C3
Hemswell Cliff Lincs 46 D3
Hemsworth W Yorks 45 A8
Hemyock Devon 7 E10
Hen-feddau fawr Pembs 23 C7
Henbury Bristol 16 D2
Henbury Ches E 44 E2
Hendon London 19 C9
Hendon T&W 63 H10
Hendre Flint 42 F4
Hendre-ddu Conwy 41 D10
Hendreforgan Rhondda 14 C5
Hendy Carms 23 F10
Heneglwys Anglesey 40 C6
Henfield W Sus 11 C11
Henford Devon 6 G2
Henghurst Kent 13 C8
Hengoed Caerph 15 B7
Hengoed Powys 25 C9
Hengoed Shrops 33 B8
Hengrave Suff 30 B5
Henham Essex 30 F2
Heniarth Powys 33 E7
Henlade Som 8 B1
Henley Shrops 33 H11
Henley Som 8 A3
Henley Suff 31 C8
Henley W Sus 11 B7
Henley-in-Arden Warks 27 B8
Henley-on-Thames Oxon 18 C4
Henley's Down E Sus 12 E6
Henllan Ceredig 23 B8
Henllan Denb 42 F3
Henllan Amgoed Carms 22 D6
Henllys Torf 15 B8
Henlow C Beds 29 E8
Hennock Devon 5 C9
Henny Street Essex 30 E5
Henryd Conwy 41 C9
Henry's Moat Pembs 22 D5
Hensall N Yorks 52 G1
Henshaw Northumb 62 G3
Hensingham Cumb 56 E1
Henstead Suff 39 G10
Henstridge Som 8 C6
Henstridge Ash Som 8 B6
Henstridge Marsh Som 8 B6
Henton Oxon 18 A4
Henton Som 15 G10
Henwood Corn 4 D3
Heogan Shetland 96 J6
Heol-las Swansea 14 B2
Heol Senni Powys 24 F6
Heol-y-Cyw Bridgend 14 C5
Hepburn Northumb 62 A6
Hepple Northumb 62 C5
Hepscott Northumb 63 E8
Heptonstall W Yorks 50 G5
Hepworth Suff 30 A6
Hepworth W Yorks 44 B5
Herbrandston Pembs 22 F3
Hereford Hereford 26 D2
Heriot Borders 70 E2
Hermiston Edin 69 C10
Hermitage Borders 61 D11
Hermitage Dorset 8 D5
Hermitage W Berks 18 D2
Hermitage W Sus 11 D6
Hermon Anglesey 40 D5
Hermon Carms 23 C8
Hermon Carms 24 F3
Hermon Pembs 23 C7
Herne Kent 21 E8
Herne Bay Kent 21 E8
Herner Devon 6 D4
Hernhill Kent 21 E7
Herodsfoot Corn 4 E3
Herongate Essex 20 B3
Heronsford S Ayrs 54 A4
Herriard Hants 18 G3
Herringfleet Suff 39 F10
Herringswell Suff 30 A4
Hersden Kent 21 E9
Hersham Corn 6 F1
Hersham Sur 19 E8
Herstmonceux E Sus 12 E5
Herston Orkney 95 J5
Hertford Herts 29 G10
Hertford Heath Herts 29 G10
Hertingfordbury Herts 29 G10
Hesket Newmarket Cumb 56 C5
Hesketh Bank Lancs 49 G4
Hesketh Lane Lancs 50 E2
Heskin Green Lancs 49 H5
Hesleden Durham 58 C5
Hesleyside Northumb 62 E4
Heslington York 52 D2
Hessay York 51 D11
Hessenford Corn 4 F4
Hessett Suff 30 B6
Hessle E Yorks 52 G6
Hest Bank Lancs 49 C4
Heston London 19 D8
Hestwall Orkney 95 G3
Heswall Mers 42 D5
Hethe Oxon 28 F2
Hethersett Norf 39 E7
Hethersgill Cumb 61 G10
Hethpool Northumb 71 H7
Hett Durham 58 C3
Hetton N Yorks 50 D5
Hetton-le-Hole T&W 58 B4
Hetton Steads Northumb 71 G9
Heugh Northumb 62 F6
Heugh-head Aberds 82 B5
Heveningham Suff 31 A10
Hever Kent 12 B3
Heversham Cumb 49 A4
Hevingham Norf 39 C7
Hewas Water Corn 3 E8
Hewelsfield Glos 16 A2
Hewish N Som 15 E10
Hewish Som 8 D3
Heworth York 52 D2
Hexham Northumb 62 G5
Hextable Kent 20 D2
Hexton Herts 29 E8
Hexworthy Devon 5 D7
Hey Lancs 50 E4
Heybridge Essex 20 B3
Heybridge Essex 30 H5
Heybridge Basin Essex 30 H5
Heybrook Bay Devon 4 G6
Heydon Cambs 29 D11
Heydon Norf 39 C7
Heydour Lincs 36 B6
Heylipol Argyll 78 G2
Heylor Shetland 96 E4
Heysham Lancs 49 C4
Heyshott W Sus 11 C7
Heyside Gtr Man 44 B3
Heytesbury Wilts 16 G6
Heythrop Oxon 27 F10
Heywood Gtr Man 44 A2
Heywood Wilts 16 F5
Hibaldstow N Lincs 46 B3
Hickleton S Yorks 45 B8
Hickling Norf 39 C10
Hickling Notts 36 C2
Hickling Green Norf 39 C10
Hickling Heath Norf 39 C10
Hickstead W Sus 12 D1
Hidcote Boyce Glos 27 D8
High Ackworth W Yorks 51 H10
High Angerton Northumb 62 E6
High Bankhill Cumb 57 B7
High Barnes T&W 63 H9
High Beach Essex 19 B11
High Bentham N Yorks 50 C2
High Bickington Devon 6 D5
High Birkwith N Yorks 50 B3
High Blantyre S Lanark 68 E5
High Bonnybridge Falk 69 C7
High Bradfield S Yorks 44 C6
High Bray Devon 6 C5
High Brooms Kent 12 B4
High Bullen Devon 6 D4
High Buston Northumb 63 C8
High Callerton Northumb 63 F7
High Catton E Yorks 52 D3
High Cogges Oxon 27 H10
High Coniscliffe Darl 58 E3
High Cross Hants 10 B6
High Cross Herts 29 G10
High Easter Essex 30 G3
High Eggborough N Yorks 52 G1
High Ellington N Yorks 51 A7
High Ercall Telford 34 D1
High Etherley Durham 58 D2
High Garrett Essex 30 F4
High Grange Durham 58 C2
High Green Norf 39 E7
High Green S Yorks 45 C7
High Green Worcs 26 D5
High Halden Kent 13 C7
High Halstow Medway 20 D4
High Ham Som 8 A3
High Harrington Cumb 56 D2
High Hatton Shrops 34 C2
High Hawsker N Yorks 59 F10
High Hesket Cumb 57 B6
High Hesleden Durham 58 C5
High Hoyland S Yorks 44 A6
High Hunsley E Yorks 52 F5
High Hurstwood E Sus 12 D3
High Hutton N Yorks 52 C3
High Ireby Cumb 56 C4
High Kelling Norf 39 A7
High Kilburn N Yorks 51 B11
High Lands Durham 58 D2
High Lane Gtr Man 44 D3
High Lane Worcs 26 B3
High Laver Essex 30 H2
High Legh Ches E 43 D10
High Leven Stockton 58 E5
High Littleton Bath 16 F3
High Lorton Cumb 56 D3
High Marishes N Yorks 52 B4
High Marnham Notts 46 E2
High Melton S Yorks 45 B9
High Mickley Northumb 62 G6
High Mindork Dumfries 54 D6
High Newton Cumb 49 A4
High Newton-by-the-Sea Northumb 71 H11
High Nibthwaite Cumb 56 H4
High Offley Staffs 34 C3
High Ongar Essex 20 A2
High Onn Staffs 34 D4
High Roding Essex 30 G3
High Row Cumb 56 C5
High Salvington W Sus 11 D10
High Sellafield Cumb 56 F2
High Shaw N Yorks 57 G10
High Spen T&W 63 H7
High Stoop Durham 58 B2
High Street Corn 3 D8
High Street Kent 12 C6
High Street Suff 30 D5
High Street Suff 31 A11
High Street Suff 31 C11
High Street Green Suff 31 C7
High Throston Hrtlpl 58 C5
High Toynton Lincs 46 F6
High Trewhitt Northumb 62 C6
High Valleyfield Fife 69 B9
High Westwood Durham 58 A2
High Wray Cumb 56 F5
High Wych Herts 29 G11
High Wycombe Bucks 18 B5
Higham Derbys 45 G7
Higham Kent 20 D4
Higham Lancs 50 F4
Higham Suff 30 B4
Higham Suff 31 E7
Higham Dykes Northumb 63 F7
Higham Ferrers Northants 28 B6
Higham Gobion C Beds 29 E8
Higham on the Hill Leics 35 F9
Higham Wood Kent 20 G2
Highampton Devon 6 F3
Highbridge Highld 80 E3
Highbridge Som 15 G9
Highbrook W Sus 12 C2
Highburton W Yorks 44 A5
Highbury Som 16 G3
Highclere Hants 17 E11
Highcliffe Dorset 9 E11
Higher Ansty Dorset 9 D6
Higher Ashton Devon 5 C9
Higher Ballam Lancs 49 F3
Higher Bartle Lancs 49 F5
Higher Boscaswell Corn 2 F2
Higher Burwardsley Ches W 43 G8
Higher Clovelly Devon 6 D2
Higher End Gtr Man 43 B8
Higher Kinnerton Flint 42 F6
Higher Penwortham Lancs 49 G5
Higher Town Scilly 2 C3
Higher Walreddon Devon 4 D5
Higher Walton Lancs 50 G1
Higher Walton Warr 43 D8
Higher Wheelton Lancs 50 G2
Higher Whitley Ches W 43 D9
Higher Wincham Ches W 43 E9
Higher Wych Ches W 33 A10
Highfield E Yorks 52 F3
Highfield Gtr Man 43 B10
Highfield N Ayrs 66 A6
Highfield Oxon 28 F2
Highfield S Yorks 45 D7
Highfield T&W 63 H7
Highfields Cambs 29 C10
Highfields Northumb 71 E8
Highgate London 19 C9
Highlane Ches E 44 F2
Highlane Derbys 45 D8
Highlaws Cumb 56 B3
Highleadon Glos 26 F4
Highleigh W Sus 11 E7
Highley Shrops 34 G3
Highmoor Cross Oxon 18 C4
Highmoor Hill Mon 15 C10
Highnam Glos 26 G4
Highnam Green Glos 26 F4
Highsted Kent 20 E6
Highstreet Green Essex 30 E4
Hightae Dumfries 60 F6
Hightown Ches E 44 F2
Hightown Mers 42 B6
Hightown Green Suff 30 C6
Highway Wilts 17 D7
Highweek Devon 5 D9
Highworth Swindon 17 B9
Hilborough Norf 38 E4
Hilcote Derbys 45 G8
Hilcott Wilts 17 F8
Hilden Park Kent 20 G2
Hildenborough Kent 20 G2
Hildersham Cambs 30 D2
Hilderstone Staffs 34 B5
Hilderthorpe E Yorks 53 C7
Hilfield Dorset 8 D5
Hilgay Norf 38 F2
Hill Pembs 22 F6
Hill S Glos 16 B3
Hill W Mid 35 F7
Hill Brow W Sus 11 B6
Hill Dale Lancs 43 A7
Hill Dyke Lincs 47 H7
Hill End Durham 58 C1
Hill End Fife 76 H3
Hill End N Yorks 51 D6
Hill Head Hants 10 D4
Hill Head Northumb 62 G5
Hill Mountain Pembs 22 F4
Hill of Beath Fife 69 A10
Hill of Fearn Highld 87 D11
Hill of Mountblairy Aberds 89 C6
Hill Ridware Staffs 35 D6
Hill Top Durham 57 D11
Hill Top Hants 10 D3
Hill Top W Mid 34 F5
Hill Top W Yorks 51 H9
Hill View Dorset 9 E8
Hillam N Yorks 51 G11
Hillbeck Cumb 57 E9
Hillborough Kent 21 E9
Hillbrae Aberds 83 A9
Hillbrae Aberds 88 D6
Hillbutts Dorset 9 D8
Hillclifflane Derbys 44 H6
Hillcommon Som 7 D10
Hillend Fife 69 B10
Hillerton Devon 7 G6
Hillesden Bucks 28 F3
Hillesley Glos 16 C4
Hillfarrance Som 7 D10
Hillhead Aberds 88 E5
Hillhead Devon 5 F10
Hillhead S Ayrs 67 E7
Hillhead of Auchentumb Aberds 89 C9
Hillhead of Cocklaw Aberds 89 D10
Hillhouse Borders 70 E4
Hilliclay Highld 94 D3
Hillingdon London 19 C7
Hillington Glasgow 68 D4
Hillington Norf 38 C3
Hillmorton Warks 28 A2
Hillockhead Aberds 82 B6
Hillockhead Aberds 82 C5
Hillside Aberds 83 D11
Hillside Angus 77 A10
Hillside Mers 42 A6
Hillside Orkney 95 J5
Hillside Shetland 96 G6
Hillswick Shetland 96 F4
Hillway IoW 10 F5
Hillwell Shetland 96 M5
Hilmarton Wilts 17 D7
Hilperton Wilts 16 F5
Hilsea Ptsmth 10 D5
Hilston E Yorks 53 F8
Hilton Aberds 89 E9
Hilton Cambs 29 B9
Hilton Cumb 57 D9
Hilton Derbys 35 B8
Hilton Dorset 9 D6
Hilton Durham 58 D2
Hilton Highld 87 C10
Hilton Shrops 34 F3
Hilton Stockton 58 E5
Hilton of Cadboll Highld 87 D11
Himbleton Worcs 26 C6
Himley Staffs 34 F4
Hincaster Cumb 49 A5
Hinckley Leics 35 F10
Hinderclay Suff 38 H6
Hinderton Ches W 42 E6
Hinderwell N Yorks 59 E8
Hindford Shrops 33 B9
Hindhead Sur 18 H5
Hindley Gtr Man 43 B9
Hindley Green Gtr Man 43 B9
Hindlip Worcs 26 C5
Hindolveston Norf 38 C6
Hindon Wilts 9 A8
Hindringham Norf 38 B5
Hingham Norf 38 E6
Hinstock Shrops 34 C2
Hintlesham Suff 31 D7
Hinton Hants 9 E11
Hinton Hereford 25 E10
Hinton Northants 28 C2
Hinton S Glos 16 D4
Hinton Shrops 33 E10
Hinton Ampner Hants 10 B4
Hinton Blewett Bath 16 F2
Hinton Charterhouse Bath 16 F4
Hinton-in-the-Hedges Northants 28 E2
Hinton Martell Dorset 9 D9
Hinton on the Green Worcs 27 D7
Hinton Parva Swindon 17 C9
Hinton St George Som 8 C3
Hinton St Mary Dorset 9 C6
Hinton Waldrist Oxon 17 B10
Hints Shrops 26 A3
Hints Staffs 35 E7
Hinwick Bedford 28 B6
Hinxhill Kent 13 B9
Hinxton Cambs 29 D11
Hinxworth Herts 29 D9
Hipperholme W Yorks 51 G7
Hipswell N Yorks 58 G2
Hirael Gwyn 41 C7
Hiraeth Carms 22 D6
Hirn Aberds 83 C9
Hirnant Powys 33 C6
Hirst N Lanark 69 D7
Hirst Northumb 63 E8
Hirst Courtney N Yorks 52 G2
Hirwaen Denb 42 F4
Hirwaun Rhondda 24 H6
Hiscott Devon 6 D4
Histon Cambs 29 B11
Hitcham Suff 30 C6
Hitchin Herts 29 F8
Hither Green London 19 D10
Hittisleigh Devon 7 G6
Hive E Yorks 52 F4
Hixon Staffs 34 C6
Hoaden Kent 21 F9
Hoaldalbert Mon 25 F10
Hoar Cross Staffs 35 C7
Hoarwithy Hereford 26 F2
Hoath Kent 21 E9
Hobarris Shrops 33 H9
Hobbister Orkney 95 H4
Hobkirk Borders 61 B11
Hobson Durham 63 H7
Hoby Leics 36 D2
Hockering Norf 39 D6
Hockerton Notts 45 G11
Hockley Essex 20 B5
Hockley Heath W Mid 27 A8
Hockliffe C Beds 28 F6
Hockwold cum Wilton Norf 38 G3
Hockworthy Devon 7 E9
Hoddesdon Herts 29 H10
Hoddlesden Blackburn 50 G3
Hoddom Mains Dumfries 61 F7
Hoddomcross Dumfries 61 F7
Hodgeston Pembs 22 G5
Hodley Powys 33 F7
Hodnet Shrops 34 C2
Hodthorpe Derbys 45 E9
Hoe Hants 10 C4
Hoe Norf 38 D5
Hoe Gate Hants 10 C5
Hoff Cumb 57 E8
Hog Patch Sur 18 G5
Hoggard's Green Suff 30 C5
Hoggeston Bucks 28 F5
Hogha Gearraidh W Isles 84 A2
Hoghton Lancs 50 G2
Hognaston Derbys 44 G6
Hogsthorpe Lincs 47 E9
Holbeach Lincs 37 C9
Holbeach Bank Lincs 37 C9
Holbeach Clough Lincs 37 C9
Holbeach Drove Lincs 37 D9
Holbeach Hurn Lincs 37 C9
Holbeach St Johns Lincs 37 D9
Holbeach St Marks Lincs 37 B9
Holbeach St Matthew Lincs 37 B10
Holbeck Notts 45 E9
Holbeck W Yorks 51 F8
Holbeck Woodhouse Notts 45 E9
Holberrow Green Worcs 27 C7
Holbeton Devon 5 F7
Holborn London 19 C10
Holbrook Derbys 35 A9
Holbrook S Yorks 45 D8
Holbrook Suff 31 E8
Holburn Northumb 71 G9
Holbury Hants 10 D3
Holcombe Devon 5 D10
Holcombe Som 16 G3
Holcombe Rogus Devon 7 E9
Holcot Northants 28 B4
Holden Lancs 50 E3
Holdenby Northants 28 B3
Holdenhurst Bmouth 9 E10
Holdgate Shrops 34 G1
Holdingham Lincs 46 H4
Holditch Dorset 8 D2
Hole-in-the-Wall Hereford 26 F3
Holefield Borders 71 G7
Holehouses Ches E 43 E10
Holemoor Devon 6 F3
Holestane Dumfries 60 D4
Holford Som 7 B10
Holgate York 52 D1
Holker Cumb 49 B3
Holkham Norf 38 A4
Hollacombe Devon 6 F2
Holland Orkney 95 C5
Holland Orkney 95 F7
Holland Fen Lincs 46 H6
Holland-on-Sea Essex 31 G9
Hollandstoun Orkney 95 C8
Hollee Dumfries 61 G8
Hollesley Suff 31 D10
Hollicombe Torbay 5 E9
Hollingbourne Kent 20 F5
Hollington Derbys 35 B8
Hollington E Sus 13 E6
Hollington Staffs 35 B6
Hollington Grove Derbys 35 B8
Hollingworth Gtr Man 44 C4
Hollins Gtr Man 44 B2
Hollins Green Warr 43 C9
Hollins Lane Lancs 49 D4
Hollinsclough Staffs 44 F4
Hollinwood Gtr Man 44 B3
Hollinwood Shrops 33 B11
Hollocombe Devon 6 E5
Hollow Meadows S Yorks 44 D6
Holloway Derbys 45 G7
Hollowell Northants 28 A3
Holly End Norf 37 E10
Holly Green Worcs 26 D5
Hollybush Caerph 15 A7
Hollybush E Ayrs 67 E6
Hollybush Worcs 26 E4
Hollym E Yorks 53 G9
Hollywood Worcs 35 H6
Holmbridge W Yorks 44 B5
Holmbury St Mary Sur 19 G8
Holmbush Corn 3 D9
Holmcroft Staffs 34 C5
Holme Cambs 37 G7
Holme Cumb 49 B5
Holme N Yorks 51 A9
Holme Notts 46 G2
Holme W Yorks 44 B5
Holme Chapel Lancs 50 G4
Holme Green N Yorks 52 E1
Holme Hale Norf 38 E4
Holme Lacy Hereford 26 E2
Holme Marsh Hereford 25 C10
Holme next the Sea Norf 38 A3
Holme-on-Spalding-Moor E Yorks 52 F4
Holme on the Wolds E Yorks 52 E5
Holme Pierrepont Notts 36 B2
Holme St Cuthbert Cumb 56 B3
Holme Wood W Yorks 51 F7
Holmer Hereford 26 D2
Holmer Green Bucks 18 B6
Holmes Chapel Ches E 43 F10
Holmesfield Derbys 45 E7
Holmeswood Lancs 49 H4
Holmewood Derbys 45 F8
Holmfirth W Yorks 44 B5
Holmhead Dumfries 60 E3
Holmhead E Ayrs 67 D8
Holmisdale Highld 84 D6
Holmpton E Yorks 53 G9
Holmrook Cumb 56 G2
Holmsgarth Shetland 96 J7
Holmwrangle Cumb 57 B7
Holne Devon 5 E8
Holnest Dorset 8 D5
Holsworthy Devon 6 F2
Holsworthy Beacon Devon 6 F2
Holt Dorset 9 D9
Holt Norf 39 B6
Holt Wilts 16 E5
Holt Worcs 26 B5
Holt Wrex 43 G7
Holt End Hants 18 H3
Holt End Worcs 27 B7
Holt Fleet Worcs 26 B5
Holt Heath Worcs 26 B5
Holt Park W Yorks 51 E8
Holtby York 52 D2
Holton Oxon 28 H3
Holton Som 8 B5
Holton Suff 39 H9
Holton cum Beckering Lincs 46 D5
Holton Heath Dorset 9 E8
Holton le Clay Lincs 46 B6
Holton le Moor Lincs 46 C4
Holton St Mary Suff 31 E7
Holwell Dorset 8 C6
Holwell Herts 29 E8
Holwell Leics 36 C3
Holwell Oxon 27 H9
Holwick Durham 57 D11
Holworth Dorset 9 F6
Holy Cross Worcs 34 H5
Holy Island Northumb 71 F10
Holybourne Hants 18 G4
Holyhead = Caergybi Anglesey 40 B4
Holymoorside Derbys 45 F7
Holyport Windsor 18 D5
Holystone Northumb 62 C5
Holytown N Lanark 68 D6
Holywell Cambs 29 A10
Holywell Corn 3 D6
Holywell Dorset 8 D4
Holywell E Sus 12 G4
Holywell = Treffynnon Flint 42 E4
Holywell Northumb 63 F9
Holywell Green W Yorks 51 H6
Holywell Lake Som 7 D10
Holywell Row Suff 38 H3
Holywood Dumfries 60 E5
Hom Green Hereford 26 F2
Homer Shrops 34 E2
Homersfield Suff 39 G8
Homington Wilts 9 B10
Honey Hill Kent 21 E8
Honey Street Wilts 17 E8
Honey Tye Suff 30 E6
Honeyborough Pembs 22 F4
Honeybourne Worcs 27 D8
Honeychurch Devon 6 F5
Honiley Warks 27 A9
Honing Norf 39 C9
Honingham Norf 39 D7
Honington Lincs 36 A5
Honington Suff 30 A6
Honington Warks 27 D9
Honiton Devon 7 F10
Honley W Yorks 44 A5
Hoo Green Ches E 43 D10
Hoo St Werburgh Medway 20 D4
Hood Green S Yorks 45 B7
Hooe E Sus 12 F5
Hooe Plym 4 F6
Hooe Common E Sus 12 E5
Hook E Yorks 52 G3
Hook Hants 18 F4
Hook London 19 E8
Hook Pembs 22 E4
Hook Wilts 17 C7
Hook Green Kent 12 C5
Hook Green Kent 20 E3
Hook Norton Oxon 27 E10
Hooke Dorset 8 E4
Hookgate Staffs 34 B3
Hookway Devon 7 G7
Hookwood Sur 12 B1
Hoole Ches W 43 F7
Hooley Sur 19 F9
Hoop Mon 26 H2
Hooton Ches W 42 E6
Hooton Levitt S Yorks 45 C9
Hooton Pagnell S Yorks 45 B8
Hooton Roberts S Yorks 45 C8
Hop Pole Lincs 37 D7
Hope Derbys 44 D5
Hope Devon 5 H7
Hope = Yr Hôb Flint 42 G6
Hope Highld 92 C7
Hope Powys 33 E8
Hope Shrops 33 E9
Hope Staffs 44 G5
Hope Bagot Shrops 26 A2
Hope Bowdler Shrops 33 F10
Hope End Green Essex 30 F2
Hope Green Ches E 44 D3
Hope Mansell Hereford 26 G3
Hope under Dinmore Hereford 26 C2
Hopeman Moray 88 B1
Hope's Green Essex 20 C4
Hopesay Shrops 33 G9
Hopley's Green Hereford 25 C10
Hopperton N Yorks 51 D10
Hopstone Shrops 34 F3
Hopton Shrops 33 C9
Hopton Shrops 34 C1
Hopton Staffs 34 C5
Hopton Suff 38 H5
Hopton Cangeford Shrops 33 G11
Hopton Castle Shrops 33 H9
Hopton on Sea Norf 39 E11
Hopton Wafers Shrops 34 H2
Hoptonheath Shrops 33 H9
Hopwas Staffs 35 E7
Hopwood Gtr Man 44 B2
Hopwood Worcs 34 H6
Horam E Sus 12 E4
Horbling Lincs 37 B7
Horbury W Yorks 51 H8
Horcott Glos 17 A8
Horden Durham 58 B5
Horderley Shrops 33 G10
Hordle Hants 10 E1
Hordley Shrops 33 B9
Horeb Carms 23 D10
Horeb Carms 23 F9
Horeb Ceredig 23 B8
Horfield Bristol 16 D3
Horham Suff 31 A9
Horkesley Heath Essex 30 F6
Horkstow N Lincs 52 H5
Horley Oxon 27 D11
Horley Sur 12 B1
Hornblotton Green Som 8 A4
Hornby Lancs 50 C1
Hornby N Yorks 58 F4
Hornby N Yorks 58 G3
Horncastle Lincs 46 F6
Hornchurch London 20 C2
Horncliffe Northumb 71 F8
Horndean Borders 71 F7
Horndean Hants 10 C6
Horndon Devon 4 D6
Horndon on the Hill Thurrock 20 C3
Horne Sur 12 B2
Horniehaugh Angus 77 A7
Horning Norf 39 D9
Horninghold Leics 36 F4
Horninglow Staffs 35 C8
Horningsea Cambs 29 B11
Horningsham Wilts 16 G5
Horningtoft Norf 38 C5
Horns Corner Kent 12 D6
Horns Cross Devon 6 D2
Horns Cross E Sus 13 D7
Hornsby Cumb 57 A7
Hornsea E Yorks 53 E8
Hornsea Bridge E Yorks 53 E8
Hornsey London 19 C10
Hornton Oxon 27 D10
Horrabridge Devon 4 E6
Horringer Suff 30 B5
Horringford IoW 10 F4
Horse Bridge Staffs 44 G3
Horsebridge Devon 4 D5
Horsebridge Hants 10 A2
Horsebrook Staffs 34 D4
Horsehay Telford 34 E2
Horseheath Cambs 30 D3
Horsehouse N Yorks 50 A6
Horsell Sur 19 F7
Horseman's Green Wrex 33 A10
Horseway Cambs 37 G10
Horsey Norf 39 C10
Horsford Norf 39 D7
Horsforth W Yorks 51 F8
Horsham W Sus 11 A10
Horsham Worcs 26 C4
Horsham St Faith Norf 39 D8
Horsington Lincs 46 F5
Horsington Som 8 B6
Horsley Derbys 35 A9
Horsley Glos 16 B5
Horsley Northumb 62 D4
Horsley Northumb 62 G6
Horsley Cross Essex 31 F8
Horsley Woodhouse Derbys 35 A9
Horsleycross Street Essex 31 F8
Horsleyhill Borders 61 B11
Horsleyhope Durham 58 B1
Horsmonden Kent 12 B5
Horspath Oxon 18 A2
Horstead Norf 39 D8
Horsted Keynes W Sus 12 D2
Horton Bucks 28 G6
Horton Dorset 9 D9
Horton Lancs 50 D4
Horton Northants 28 C5
Horton S Glos 16 C4
Horton Shrops 33 C10
Horton Som 8 C2
Horton Staffs 44 G3
Horton Swansea 23 H9

Horton Wilts 17 E7
Horton Windsor 19 D7
Horton-cum-Studley Oxon 28 G2
Horton Green Ches W 43 H7
Horton Heath Hants 10 C3
Horton in Ribblesdale N Yorks 50 B4
Horton Kirby Kent 20 E2
Hortonlane Shrops 33 D10
Horwich Gtr Man 43 A9
Horwich End Derbys 44 D4
Horwood Devon 6 D4
Hose Leics 36 C3
Hoselaw Borders 71 G7
Hoses Cumb 56 G4
Hosh Perth 75 E11
Hosta W Isles 84 A2
Hoswick Shetland 96 L6
Hotham E Yorks 52 F4
Hothfield Kent 20 G6
Hoton Leics 36 C1
Houbie Shetland 96 D8
Houdston S Ayrs 66 G4
Hough Ches E 43 G10
Hough Ches E 44 E2
Hough Green Halton 43 D7
Hough-on-the-Hill Lincs 46 H3
Hougham Lincs 36 A4
Houghton Cambs 29 A9
Houghton Cumb 61 H10
Houghton Hants 10 A2
Houghton Pembs 22 F4
Houghton W Sus 11 C9
Houghton Conquest C Beds 29 D7
Houghton Green E Sus 13 D8
Houghton Green Warr 43 C9
Houghton-le-Side Darl 58 D3
Houghton-Le-Spring T&W 58 B4
Houghton on the Hill Leics 36 E2
Houghton Regis C Beds 29 F7
Houghton St Giles Norf 38 B5
Houlland Shetland 96 F7
Houlland Shetland 96 H5
Houlsyke N Yorks 59 F8
Hound Hants 10 D3
Hound Green Hants 18 F4
Houndslow Borders 70 F5
Houndwood Borders 71 D7
Hounslow London 19 D8
Hounslow Green Essex 30 G3
Housay Shetland 96 F8
House of Daviot Highld 87 G10
House of Glenmuick Aberds 82 D5
Housetter Shetland 96 E5
Houss Shetland 96 K5
Houston Renfs 68 D3
Houstry Highld 94 G3
Houton Orkney 95 H4
Hove Brighton 12 F1
Hoveringham Notts 45 H10
Hoveton Norf 39 D9
Hovingham N Yorks 52 B2
How Cumb 61 H11
How Caple Hereford 26 E3
How End C Beds 29 D7
How Green Kent 19 G11
Howbrook S Yorks 45 C7
Howden Borders 62 A2
Howden E Yorks 52 G3
Howden-le-Wear Durham 58 C2
Howe Highld 94 D5
Howe N Yorks 51 A9
Howe Norf 39 E8
Howe Bridge Gtr Man 43 B9
Howe Green Essex 20 A4
Howe of Teuchar Aberds 89 D7
Howe Street Essex 30 E3
Howe Street Essex 30 G3
Howell Lincs 46 H5
Howey Powys 25 C7
Howgate Midloth 69 E11
Howick Northumb 63 B8
Howle Durham 58 D1
Howle Telford 34 C2
Howlett End Essex 30 E2
Howley Som 8 D1
Hownam Borders 62 B3
Hownam Mains Borders 62 A3
Howpasley Borders 61 C9
Howsham N Lincs 46 B4
Howsham N Yorks 52 C3
Howslack Dumfries 60 C6
Howtel Northumb 71 G7
Howton Hereford 25 F11
Howtown Cumb 56 E6
Howwood Renfs 68 D2
Hoxne Suff 39 H7
Hoy Orkney 95 H3
Hoylake Mers 42 D5
Hoyland S Yorks 45 B7
Hoylandswaine S Yorks 44 B6
Hubberholme N Yorks 50 B5
Hubbert's Bridge Lincs 37 A8
Huby N Yorks 51 E8
Huby N Yorks 52 C1
Hucclecote Glos 26 G5
Hucking Kent 20 F5
Hucknall Notts 45 H9
Huddersfield W Yorks 51 H7
Huddington Worcs 26 C6
Hudswell N Yorks 58 F2
Huggate E Yorks 52 D4
Hugglescote Leics 35 D10
Hugh Town Scilly 2 C3
Hughenden Valley Bucks 18 B5
Hughley Shrops 34 F1
Huish Devon 6 E4
Huish Wilts 17 E8
Huish Champflower Som 7 D9
Huish Episcopi Som 8 B3
Huisinis W Isles 90 F4
Hulcott Bucks 28 G5
Hulland Derbys 44 H6
Hulland Ward Derbys 44 H6
Hullavington Wilts 16 C5
Hullbridge Essex 20 B5
Hulme Gtr Man 44 C2
Hulme End Staffs 44 G5
Hulme Walfield Ches E 44 F2
Hulver Street Suff 39 G10
Hulverstone IoW 10 F2
Humber Hereford 26 C2
Humber Bridge N Lincs 52 G6
Humberston NE Lincs 47 B7
Humbie E Loth 70 D3
Humbleton E Yorks 53 F8
Humbleton Northumb 71 H8
Humby Lincs 36 B6
Hume Borders 70 F6
Humshaugh Northumb 62 F5
Huna Highld 94 C5
Huncoat Lancs 50 F3
Huncote Leics 35 F11
Hundalee Borders 62 B2
Hunderthwaite Durham 57 D11
Hundle Houses Lincs 46 G6
Hundleby Lincs 47 F7
Hundleton Pembs 22 F4
Hundon Suff 30 D4
Hundred Acres Hants 10 C4
Hundred End Lancs 49 G4
Hundred House Powys 25 C8
Hungarton Leics 36 E2
Hungerford Hants 9 C10
Hungerford W Berks 17 E10
Hungerford Newtown W Berks 17 D10
Hungerton Lincs 36 C4
Hungladder Highld 85 A8
Hunmanby N Yorks 53 B6
Hunmanby Moor N Yorks 53 B7
Hunningham Warks 27 B10
Hunny Hill IoW 10 F3
Hunsdon Herts 29 G11
Hunsingore N Yorks 51 D10
Hunslet W Yorks 51 F9
Hunsonby Cumb 57 C7
Hunspow Highld 94 C4
Hunstanton Norf 38 A2
Hunstanworth Durham 57 B11
Hunsterson Ches E 43 H9
Hunston Suff 30 B6
Hunston W Sus 11 D7
Hunstrete Bath 16 E3
Hunt End Worcs 27 B7
Hunter's Quay Argyll 73 F10
Hunthill Lodge Angus 82 F6
Hunting-tower Perth 76 E3
Huntingdon Cambs 29 A9
Huntingfield Suff 31 A10
Huntingford Dorset 9 A7
Huntington E Loth 70 C3
Huntington Hereford 25 C9
Huntington Staffs 34 D5
Huntington York 52 D2
Huntley Glos 26 G4
Huntly Aberds 88 E5
Huntlywood Borders 70 F5
Hunton Kent 20 G4
Hunton N Yorks 58 G2
Hunt's Corner Norf 39 G6
Hunt's Cross Mers 43 D7
Huntsham Devon 7 D9
Huntspill Som 15 G9
Huntworth Som 8 A2
Hunwick Durham 58 C2
Hunworth Norf 39 B6
Hurdsfield Ches E 44 E3
Hurley Warks 35 F8
Hurley Windsor 18 C5
Hurlford E Ayrs 67 C7
Hurliness Orkney 95 K3
Hurn Dorset 9 E10
Hurn's End Lincs 47 H8
Hursley Hants 10 B3
Hurst N Yorks 58 F1
Hurst Som 8 C3
Hurst Wokingham 18 D4
Hurst Green E Sus 12 D6
Hurst Green Lancs 50 F2
Hurst Wickham W Sus 12 E1
Hurstbourne Priors Hants 17 G11
Hurstbourne Tarrant Hants 17 F10
Hurstpierpoint W Sus 12 E1
Hurstwood Lancs 50 F4
Hurtmore Sur 18 G6
Hurworth Place Darl 58 F3
Hury Durham 57 E11
Husabost Highld 84 C7
Husbands Bosworth Leics 36 G2
Husborne Crawley C Beds 28 E6
Husthwaite N Yorks 51 B11
Hutchwns Bridgend 14 D4
Huthwaite Notts 45 G8
Huttoft Lincs 47 E9
Hutton Borders 71 E8
Hutton Cumb 56 D6
Hutton E Yorks 52 D6
Hutton Essex 20 B3
Hutton Lancs 49 G4
Hutton N Som 15 F9
Hutton Buscel N Yorks 52 A5
Hutton Conyers N Yorks 51 B9
Hutton Cranswick E Yorks 52 D6
Hutton End Cumb 56 C6
Hutton Gate Redcar 59 E6
Hutton Henry Durham 58 C5
Hutton-le-Hole N Yorks 59 G8
Hutton Magna Durham 58 E2
Hutton Roof Cumb 50 B1
Hutton Roof Cumb 56 C5
Hutton Rudby N Yorks 58 F5
Hutton Sessay N Yorks 51 B10
Hutton Village Redcar 59 E6
Hutton Wandesley N Yorks 51 D11
Huxley Ches W 43 F8
Huxter Shetland 96 G7
Huxter Shetland 96 H5
Huxton Borders 71 D7
Huyton Mers 43 C7
Hwlffordd = Haverfordwest Pembs 22 E4
Hycemoor Cumb 56 H2
Hyde Glos 16 A5
Hyde Gtr Man 44 C3
Hyde Hants 9 C10
Hyde Heath Bucks 18 A6
Hyde Park S Yorks 45 B9
Hydestile Sur 18 G6
Hylton Castle T&W 63 H9
Hyndford Bridge S Lanark 69 F8
Hynish Argyll 78 H2
Hyssington Powys 33 F9
Hythe Hants 10 D3
Hythe Kent 21 H8
Hythe End Windsor 19 D7
Hythie Aberds 89 C10

I

Ibberton Dorset 9 D6
Ible Derbys 44 G6
Ibsley Hants 9 D10
Ibstock Leics 35 D10
Ibstone Bucks 18 B4
Ibthorpe Hants 17 F10
Ibworth Hants 18 F2
Ichrachan Argyll 74 D3
Ickburgh Norf 38 F4
Ickenham London 19 C7
Ickford Bucks 28 H3
Ickham Kent 21 F9
Ickleford Herts 29 E8
Icklesham E Sus 13 E7
Ickleton Cambs 29 D11
Icklingham Suff 30 A4
Ickwell Green C Beds 29 D8
Icomb Glos 27 F9
Idbury Oxon 27 G9
Iddesleigh Devon 6 F4
Ide Devon 7 G7
Ide Hill Kent 19 F11
Ideford Devon 5 D9
Iden E Sus 13 D8
Iden Green Kent 12 C6
Iden Green Kent 13 C7
Idle W Yorks 51 F7
Idlicote Warks 27 D9
Idmiston Wilts 17 H8
Idole Carms 23 E9
Idridgehay Derbys 44 H6
Idrigill Highld 85 B8
Idstone Oxon 17 C9
Idvies Angus 77 C8
Iffley Oxon 18 A2
Ifield W Sus 19 H9
Ifold W Sus 11 A9
Iford E Sus 12 F3
Ifton Heath Shrops 33 B9
Ightfield Shrops 34 B1
Ightham Kent 20 F2
Iken Suff 31 C11
Ilam Staffs 44 G5
Ilchester Som 8 B4
Ilderton Northumb 62 A6
Ilford London 19 C11
Ilfracombe Devon 6 B4
Ilkeston Derbys 35 A10
Ilketshall St Andrew Suff 39 G9
Ilketshall St Lawrence Suff 39 G9
Ilketshall St Margaret Suff 39 G9
Ilkley W Yorks 51 E7
Illey W Mid 34 G5
Illingworth W Yorks 51 G6
Illogan Corn 2 E5
Illston on the Hill Leics 36 F3
Ilmer Bucks 28 H4
Ilmington Warks 27 D9
Ilminster Som 8 C2
Ilsington Devon 5 D8
Ilston Swansea 23 G10
Ilton N Yorks 51 B7
Ilton Som 8 C2
Imachar N Ayrs 66 B1
Imeraval Argyll 64 D4
Immingham NE Lincs 46 A5
Impington Cambs 29 B11
Ince Ches W 43 E7
Ince Blundell Mers 42 B6
Ince in Makerfield Gtr Man 43 B8
Inch of Arnhall Aberds 83 F8
Inchbare Angus 83 G8
Inchberry Moray 88 C3
Inchbraoch Angus 77 B10
Incheril Highld 86 E3
Inchgrundle Angus 82 F6
Inchina Highld 86 B2
Inchinnan Renfs 68 D3
Inchkinloch Highld 93 E8
Inchlaggan Highld 80 C3
Inchlumpie Highld 87 D8
Inchmore Highld 86 G6
Inchnacardoch Hotel Highld 80 B5
Inchnadamph Highld 92 G5
Inchree Highld 74 A3
Inchture Perth 76 E5
Inchyra Perth 76 E4
Indian Queens Corn 3 D8
Inerval Argyll 64 D4
Ingatestone Essex 20 B3
Ingbirchworth S Yorks 44 B6
Ingestre Staffs 34 C5
Ingham Lincs 46 D3
Ingham Norf 39 C9
Ingham Suff 30 A5
Ingham Corner Norf 39 C9
Ingleborough Norf 37 D10
Ingleby Derbys 35 C9
Ingleby Lincs 46 E2
Ingleby Arncliffe N Yorks 58 F5
Ingleby Barwick Stockton 58 E5
Ingleby Greenhow N Yorks 59 F6
Inglemire Hull 53 F6
Inglesbatch Bath 16 E4
Inglesham Swindon 17 B9
Ingleton Durham 58 D2
Ingleton N Yorks 50 B2
Inglewhite Lancs 49 E5
Ingliston Edin 69 C10
Ingoe Northumb 62 F6
Ingol Lancs 49 F5
Ingoldisthorpe Norf 38 B2
Ingoldmells Lincs 47 F9
Ingoldsby Lincs 36 B6
Ingon Warks 27 C9
Ingram Northumb 62 B6
Ingrow W Yorks 51 F6
Ings Cumb 56 G6
Ingst S Glos 16 C2
Ingworth Norf 39 C7
Inham's End Cambs 37 F8
Inkberrow Worcs 27 C7
Inkpen W Berks 17 E10
Inkstack Highld 94 C4
Inn Cumb 56 F6
Innellan Argyll 73 F10
Innerleithen Borders 70 G2
Innerleven Fife 76 G6
Innermessan Dumfries 54 C3
Innerwick E Loth 70 C6
Innerwick Perth 75 C8
Innis Chonain Argyll 74 E4
Insch Aberds 83 A8
Insh Highld 81 C10
Inshore Highld 92 C6
Inskip Lancs 49 F4
Instoneville S Yorks 45 A9
Instow Devon 6 C3
Intake S Yorks 45 B9
Inver Aberds 82 D4
Inver Highld 87 C11
Inver Perth 76 C3
Inver Mallie Highld 80 E3
Inverailort Highld 79 C10
Inveraldie Angus 77 D7
Inveralligin Highld 85 C13
Inverallochy Aberds 89 B10
Inveran Highld 87 B8
Inveraray Argyll 73 C9
Inverarish Highld 85 E10
Inverarity Angus 77 C7
Inverarnan Stirling 74 F6
Inverasdale Highld 91 J13
Inverbeg Argyll 74 H6
Inverbervie Aberds 83 F10
Inverboyndie Aberds 89 B6
Inverbroom Highld 86 C4
Invercassley Highld 92 J7
Invercauld House Aberds 82 D3
Inverchaolain Argyll 73 F9
Invercharnan Highld 74 C4
Inverchoran Highld 86 F5
Invercreran Argyll 74 C3
Inverdruie Highld 81 B11
Inverebrie Aberds 89 E9
Invereck Argyll 73 E10
Inverernan Ho. Aberds 82 B5
Invereshie House Highld 81 C10
Inveresk E Loth 70 C2
Inverey Aberds 82 E2
Inverfarigaig Highld 81 A7
Invergarry Highld 80 C5
Invergelder Aberds 82 D4
Invergeldie Perth 75 E10
Invergordon Highld 87 E10
Invergowrie Perth 76 D6
Inverguseran Highld 85 H12
Inverhadden Perth 75 B9
Inverharroch Moray 88 E3
Inverherive Stirling 74 E6
Inverie Highld 79 B10
Inverinan Argyll 73 B8
Inverinate Highld 85 F14
Inverkeilor Angus 77 C9
Inverkeithing Fife 69 B10
Inverkeithny Aberds 89 D6
Inverkip Invclyd 73 F11
Inverkirkaig Highld 92 H3
Inverlael Highld 86 C4
Inverlochlarig Stirling 75 F7
Inverlochy Argyll 74 E4
Inverlochy Highld 80 F3
Inverlussa Argyll 72 E5
Invermark Lodge Angus 82 E6
Invermoidart Highld 79 D9
Invermoriston Highld 80 B6
Invernaver Highld 93 C10
Inverneill Argyll 73 E7
Inverness Highld 87 G9
Invernettie Aberds 89 D11
Invernoaden Argyll 73 D10
Inveroran Hotel Argyll 74 C5
Inverpolly Lodge Highld 92 H3
Inverquharity Angus 77 B7
Inverquhomery Aberds 89 D10
Inverroy Highld 80 E4
Inversanda Highld 74 B2
Invershiel Highld 80 B1
Invershin Highld 87 B8
Inversnaid Hotel Stirling 74 G6
Inverugie Aberds 89 D11
Inveruglas Argyll 74 G6
Inveruglass Highld 81 C10
Inverurie Aberds 83 A9
Invervar Perth 75 C9
Inverythan Aberds 89 D7
Inwardleigh Devon 6 G4
Inworth Essex 30 G5
Iochdar W Isles 84 D2
Iping W Sus 11 B7
Ipplepen Devon 5 E9
Ipsden Oxon 18 C3
Ipsley Worcs 27 B7
Ipstones Staffs 44 G4
Ipswich Suff 31 D8
Irby Mers 42 D5
Irby in the Marsh Lincs 47 F8
Irby upon Humber NE Lincs 46 B5
Irchester Northants 28 B6
Ireby Cumb 56 C4
Ireby Lancs 50 B2
Ireland Orkney 95 H4
Ireland Shetland 96 L5
Ireland's Cross Shrops 34 A3
Ireleth Cumb 49 B2
Ireshopeburn Durham 57 C10
Irlam Gtr Man 43 C10
Irnham Lincs 36 C6
Iron Acton S Glos 16 C3
Iron Cross Warks 27 C7
Ironbridge Telford 34 E2
Irongray Dumfries 60 F5
Ironmacannie Dumfries 55 B9
Ironside Aberds 89 C8
Ironville Derbys 45 G8
Irstead Norf 39 C9
Irthington Cumb 61 G10
Irthlingborough Northants 28 A6
Irton N Yorks 52 A6
Irvine N Ayrs 66 C6
Isauld Highld 93 C12
Isbister Orkney 95 F3
Isbister Orkney 95 G4
Isbister Shetland 96 D5
Isbister Shetland 96 G7
Isfield E Sus 12 E3
Isham Northants 28 A5
Isle Abbotts Som 8 B2
Isle Brewers Som 8 B2
Isle of Whithorn Dumfries 55 F7
Isleham Cambs 30 A3
Isleornsay Highld 85 G12
Islesburgh Shetland 96 G5
Islesteps Dumfries 60 F5
Isleworth London 19 D8
Isley Walton Leics 35 C10
Islibhig W Isles 90 E4
Islington London 19 C10
Islip Northants 36 H5
Islip Oxon 28 G2
Istead Rise Kent 20 E3
Isycoed Wrex 43 G7
Itchen Soton 10 C3
Itchen Abbas Hants 10 A4
Itchen Stoke Hants 10 A4
Itchingfield W Sus 11 B10
Itchington S Glos 16 C3
Itteringham Norf 39 B7
Itton Devon 6 G5
Itton Common Mon 15 B10
Ivegill Cumb 56 B6
Iver Bucks 19 C7
Iver Heath Bucks 19 C7
Iveston Durham 58 A2
Ivinghoe Bucks 28 G6
Ivinghoe Aston Bucks 28 G6
Ivington Hereford 25 C11
Ivington Green Hereford 25 C11
Ivy Chimneys Essex 19 A11
Ivy Cross Dorset 9 B7
Ivy Hatch Kent 20 F2
Ivybridge Devon 5 F7
Ivychurch Kent 13 D9
Iwade Kent 20 E6
Iwerne Courtney or Shroton Dorset 9 C7
Iwerne Minster Dorset 9 C7
Ixworth Suff 30 A6
Ixworth Thorpe Suff 30 A6

J

Jack Hill N Yorks 51 D8
Jack in the Green Devon 7 G9
Jacksdale Notts 45 G8
Jackstown Aberds 89 E7
Jacobstow Corn 4 B2
Jacobstowe Devon 6 F4
Jameston Pembs 22 G5
Jamestown Dumfries 61 D9
Jamestown Highld 86 F7
Jamestown W Dunb 68 B2
Jarrow T&W 63 G9
Jarvis Brook E Sus 12 D4
Jasper's Green Essex 30 F4
Java Argyll 79 H10
Jawcraig Falk 69 C7
Jaywick Essex 31 G8
Jealott's Hill Brack 18 D5
Jedburgh Borders 62 A2
Jeffreyston Pembs 22 F5
Jellyhill E Dunb 68 C5
Jemimaville Highld 87 E10
Jersey Farm Herts 29 H8
Jesmond T&W 63 G8
Jevington E Sus 12 F4
Jockey End Herts 29 G7
John o' Groats Highld 94 C5
Johnby Cumb 56 C6
John's Cross E Sus 12 D6
Johnshaven Aberds 83 G9
Johnston Pembs 22 E4
Johnstone Renfs 68 D3
Johnstonebridge Dumfries 60 D6
Johnstown Carms 23 E9
Johnstown Wrex 42 H6
Joppa Edin 70 C2
Joppa S Ayrs 67 E7
Jordans Bucks 18 B6
Jordanthorpe S Yorks 45 D7
Jump S Yorks 45 B7
Jumpers Green Dorset 9 E10
Juniper Green Edin 69 D10
Jurby East IoM 48 C3
Jurby West IoM 48 C3

K

Kaber Cumb 57 E9
Kaimend S Lanark 69 F8
Kaimes Edin 69 D11
Kalemouth Borders 70 H6
Kames Argyll 73 B7
Kames Argyll 73 F8
Kames E Ayrs 68 H5
Kea Corn 3 E7
Keadby N Lincs 46 A2
Keal Cotes Lincs 47 F7
Kearsley Gtr Man 43 B10
Kearstwick Cumb 50 A2
Kearton N Yorks 57 G11
Kearvaig Highld 92 B5
Keasden N Yorks 50 C3
Keckwick Halton 43 D8
Keddington Lincs 47 D7
Kedington Suff 30 D4
Kedleston Derbys 35 A9
Keelby Lincs 46 A5
Keele Staffs 44 H2
Keeley Green Bedford 29 D7
Keeston Pembs 22 E4
Keevil Wilts 16 F6
Kegworth Leics 35 C10
Kehelland Corn 2 E5
Keig Aberds 83 B8
Keighley W Yorks 51 E6
Keil Highld 74 B2
Keilarsbrae Clack 69 A7
Keilhill Aberds 89 C7
Keillmore Argyll 72 E5
Keillor Perth 76 C5
Keillour Perth 76 E2
Keills Argyll 64 B5
Keils Argyll 72 G4
Keinton Mandeville Som 8 A4
Keir Mill Dumfries 60 D4
Keisby Lincs 36 C6
Keiss Highld 94 D5
Keith Moray 88 C4
Keith Inch Aberds 89 D11
Keithock Angus 77 A9
Kelbrook Lancs 50 E5
Kelby Lincs 36 A6
Keld Cumb 57 E7
Keld N Yorks 57 F10
Keldholme N Yorks 59 H8
Kelfield N Lincs 46 B2
Kelfield N Yorks 52 F1
Kelham Notts 45 G11
Kellan Argyll 79 G8
Kellas Angus 77 D7
Kellas Moray 88 C1
Kellaton Devon 5 H9
Kelleth Cumb 57 F8
Kelleythorpe E Yorks 52 D5
Kelling Norf 39 A6
Kellingley N Yorks 51 G11
Kellington N Yorks 52 G1
Kelloe Durham 58 C4
Kelloholm Dumfries 60 B3
Kelly Devon 4 C4
Kelly Bray Corn 4 D4
Kelmarsh Northants 36 H3
Kelmscot Oxon 17 B9
Kelsale Suff 31 B10
Kelsall Ches W 43 F8
Kelsall Hill Ches W 43 F8
Kelshall Herts 29 E10
Kelsick Cumb 56 A3
Kelso Borders 70 G6
Kelstedge Derbys 45 F7
Kelstern Lincs 46 C6
Kelston Bath 16 E4
Keltneyburn Perth 75 C10
Kelton Dumfries 60 F5
Kelty Fife 69 A10
Kelvedon Essex 30 G5
Kelvedon Hatch Essex 20 B2
Kelvin S Lanark 68 E5
Kelvinside Glasgow 68 D4
Kelynack Corn 2 F2
Kemback Fife 77 F7
Kemberton Shrops 34 E3
Kemble Glos 16 B6
Kemerton Worcs 26 E6
Kemeys Commander Mon 15 A9
Kemnay Aberds 83 B9
Kemp Town Brighton 12 F2
Kempley Glos 26 F3
Kemps Green Warks 27 A8
Kempsey Worcs 26 D5
Kempsford Glos 17 B8
Kempshott Hants 18 F3
Kempston Bedford 29 D7
Kempston Hardwick Bedford 29 D7
Kempton Shrops 33 G9
Kemsing Kent 20 F2
Kemsley Kent 20 E6
Kenardington Kent 13 C8
Kenchester Hereford 25 D11
Kencot Oxon 17 A9
Kendal Cumb 57 G7
Kendoon Dumfries 67 H9
Kendray S Yorks 45 B7
Kenfig Bridgend 14 C4
Kenfig Hill Bridgend 14 C4
Kenilworth Warks 27 A9
Kenknock Stirling 75 D7
Kenley London 19 F10
Kenley Shrops 34 E1
Kenmore Highld 85 C12
Kenmore Perth 75 C10
Kenn Devon 5 C10
Kenn N Som 15 E10
Kennacley W Isles 90 H6
Kennacraig Argyll 73 G7
Kennerleigh Devon 7 F7
Kennet Clack 69 A8
Kennethmont Aberds 83 A7
Kennett Cambs 30 B3
Kennford Devon 5 C10
Kenninghall Norf 38 G6
Kenninghall Heath Norf 38 G6
Kennington Kent 13 B9
Kennington Oxon 18 A2
Kennoway Fife 76 G6
Kenny Hill Suff 38 H2
Kennythorpe N Yorks 52 C3
Kenovay Argyll 78 G2
Kensaleyre Highld 85 C9
Kensington London 19 D9
Kensworth C Beds 29 G7
Kensworth Common C Beds 29 G7
Kent Street E Sus 13 E6
Kent Street Kent 20 F3
Kent Street W Sus 11 B11
Kentallen Highld 74 B3
Kentchurch Hereford 25 F11
Kentford Suff 30 B4
Kentisbeare Devon 7 F9
Kentisbury Devon 6 B5
Kentisbury Ford Devon 6 B5
Kentmere Cumb 56 F6
Kenton Devon 5 C10
Kenton Suff 31 B8
Kenton T&W 63 G8
Kenton Bankfoot T&W 63 G8
Kentra Highld 79 E9
Kents Bank Cumb 49 B3
Kent's Green Glos 26 F4
Kent's Oak Hants 10 B2
Kenwick Shrops 33 B10
Kenwyn Corn 3 E7
Keoldale Highld 92 C6
Keppanach Highld 74 A3
Keppoch Highld 85 F14
Keprigan Argyll 65 G7
Kepwick N Yorks 58 G5
Kerchesters Borders 70 G6
Keresley W Mid 35 G9
Kernborough Devon 5 G8
Kerne Bridge Hereford 26 G2
Kerris Corn 2 G3
Kerry Powys 33 G7
Kerrycroy Argyll 73 G10
Kerry's Gate Hereford 25 E10
Kerrysdale Highld 85 A13
Kersall Notts 45 F11
Kersey Suff 31 D7
Kershopefoot Cumb 61 E10
Kersoe Worcs 26 E6
Kerswell Devon 7 F9
Kerswell Green Worcs 26 D5
Kesgrave Suff 31 D9
Kessingland Suff 39 G11
Kessingland Beach Suff 39 G11
Kessington E Dunb 68 C4
Kestle Corn 3 E8
Kestle Mill Corn 3 D7
Keston London 19 E11
Keswick Cumb 56 D4
Keswick Norf 39 B9
Keswick Norf 39 E8
Ketley Telford 34 D2
Ketley Bank Telford 34 D2
Ketsby Lincs 47 E7
Kettering Northants 36 H4
Ketteringham Norf 39 E7
Kettins Perth 76 D5
Kettlebaston Suff 30 C6
Kettlebridge Fife 76 G6
Kettleburgh Suff 31 B9
Kettlehill Fife 76 G6
Kettleholm Dumfries 61 F7
Kettleness N Yorks 59 E9
Kettleshume Ches E 44 E3
Kettlesing Bottom N Yorks 51 D8
Kettlesing Head N Yorks 51 D8
Kettlestone Norf 38 B5
Kettlethorpe Lincs 46 E2
Kettletoft Orkney 95 E7
Kettlewell N Yorks 50 B5
Ketton Rutland 36 E5
Kew London 19 D8
Kew Br. London 19 D8
Kewstoke N Som 15 E9
Kexbrough S Yorks 45 B7
Kexby Lincs 46 D2
Kexby York 52 D3
Key Green Ches E 44 F2
Keyham Leics 36 E2
Keyhaven Hants 10 E2
Keyingham E Yorks 53 G8
Keymer W Sus 12 E2
Keynsham Bath 16 E3
Keysoe Bedford 29 B7
Keysoe Row Bedford 29 B7
Keyston Cambs 36 H6
Keyworth Notts 36 B2
Kibblesworth T&W 63 H8
Kibworth Beauchamp Leics 36 F2
Kibworth Harcourt Leics 36 F2
Kidbrooke London 19 D11
Kiddemore Green Staffs 34 E4
Kidderminster Worcs 34 H4
Kiddington Oxon 27 F11
Kidlington Oxon 27 G11
Kidmore End Oxon 18 D3
Kidsgrove Staffs 44 G2
Kidstones N Yorks 50 A5
Kidwelly = Cydweli Carms 23 F9
Kiel Crofts Argyll 74 D2
Kielder Northumb 62 D2
Kierfiold Ho Orkney 95 G3
Kilbagie Fife 69 B8
Kilbarchan Renfs 68 D3
Kilbeg Highld 85 H11
Kilberry Argyll 72 G6
Kilbirnie N Ayrs 66 A6
Kilbride Argyll 74 E2
Kilbride Argyll 79 J11
Kilbride Highld 85 F10
Kilburn Angus 82 G5
Kilburn Derbys 45 H7
Kilburn London 19 C9
Kilburn N Yorks 51 B11
Kilby Leics 36 F2
Kilchamaig Argyll 73 G7
Kilchattan Argyll 72 D2
Kilchattan Bay Argyll 66 A4
Kilchenzie Argyll 65 F7
Kilcheran Argyll 79 H11
Kilchiaran Argyll 64 B3
Kilchoan Argyll 72 B6
Kilchoan Highld 78 E7
Kilchoman Argyll 64 B3
Kilchrenan Argyll 74 E3
Kilconquhar Fife 77 G7
Kilcot Glos 26 F3
Kilcoy Highld 87 F8
Kilcreggan Argyll 73 E11
Kildale N Yorks 59 F7
Kildalloig Argyll 65 G8
Kildary Highld 87 D10
Kildermorie Lodge Highld 87 D8
Kildonan N Ayrs 66 D3
Kildonan Lodge Highld 93 G12
Kildonnan Highld 78 C7
Kildrummy Aberds 82 B6
Kildwick N Yorks 50 E6
Kilfinan Argyll 73 F8
Kilfinnan Highld 80 D4
Kilgetty Pembs 22 F6
Kilgwrrwg Common Mon 15 B10
Kilham E Yorks 53 C6
Kilham Northumb 71 G7
Kilkenneth Argyll 78 G2
Kilkerran Argyll 65 G8
Kilkhampton Corn 6 E1
Killamarsh Derbys 45 D8
Killay Swansea 14 B2
Killbeg Argyll 79 G9
Killean Argyll 65 D7
Killearn Stirling 68 B4
Killen Highld 87 F9
Killerby Darl 58 E2
Killichonan Perth 75 B8
Killiechonate Highld 80 E4
Killiechronan Argyll 79 G8
Killiecrankie Perth 76 A2
Killiemore House Argyll 78 J7
Killilan Highld 86 H2
Killimster Highld 94 E5
Killin Stirling 75 D8
Killin Lodge Highld 81 C7
Killinallan Argyll 64 A4
Killinghall N Yorks 51 D8
Killington Cumb 57 H8
Killingworth T&W 63 F8
Killmahumaig Argyll 72 D6
Killochyett Borders 70 F3
Killocraw Argyll 65 E7
Killundine Highld 79 G8
Kilmacolm Invclyd 68 D2
Kilmaha Argyll 73 C8
Kilmahog Stirling 75 G9
Kilmalieu Highld 79 F11
Kilmaluag Highld 85 A9
Kilmany Fife 76 E6
Kilmarie Highld 85 G10
Kilmarnock E Ayrs 67 C7
Kilmaron Castle Fife 76 F6
Kilmartin Argyll 73 D7
Kilmaurs E Ayrs 67 B7
Kilmelford Argyll 73 B7
Kilmeny Argyll 64 B4
Kilmersdon Som 16 F3
Kilmeston Hants 10 B4
Kilmichael Argyll 65 F7
Kilmichael Glassary Argyll 73 D7
Kilmichael of Inverlussa Argyll 72 E6
Kilmington Devon 8 E1
Kilmington Wilts 16 H4
Kilmonivaig Highld 80 E3
Kilmorack Highld 86 G7
Kilmore Argyll 79 J11
Kilmore Highld 85 H11
Kilmory Argyll 72 F6
Kilmory Highld 79 D8
Kilmory Highld 85 H8
Kilmory N Ayrs 66 D2
Kilmuir Highld 84 D7
Kilmuir Highld 85 A8
Kilmuir Highld 87 D10
Kilmuir Highld 87 G9
Kilmun Argyll 73 B8
Kilmun Argyll 73 E10
Kiln Pit Hill Northumb 58 A1
Kilncadzow S Lanark 69 F7
Kilndown Kent 12 C6
Kilnhurst S Yorks 45 C8
Kilninian Argyll 78 G6
Kilninver Argyll 79 J11
Kilnsea E Yorks 53 H10
Kilnsey N Yorks 50 C5
Kilnwick E Yorks 52 E5
Kilnwick Percy E Yorks 52 D4
Kiloran Argyll 72 D2
Kilpatrick N Ayrs 66 D2
Kilpeck Hereford 25 E11
Kilphedir Highld 93 H12
Kilpin E Yorks 52 G3
Kilpin Pike E Yorks 52 G3
Kilrenny Fife 77 G8
Kilsby Northants 28 A2
Kilspindie Perth 76 E5
Kilsyth N Lanark 68 C6
Kiltarlity Highld 87 G8
Kilton Notts 45 E9
Kilton Som 7 B10
Kilton Thorpe Redcar 59 E7
Kilvaxter Highld 85 B8
Kilve Som 7 B10
Kilvington Notts 36 A3
Kilwinning N Ayrs 66 B6
Kimber worth S Yorks 45 C8
Kimberley Norf 39 E6
Kimberley Notts 35 A11
Kimble Wick Bucks 28 H5
Kimblesworth Durham 58 B3
Kimbolton Cambs 29 B7
Kimbolton Hereford 26 B2
Kimcote Leics 36 G1
Kimmeridge Dorset 9 G8
Kimmerston Northumb 71 G8
Kimpton Hants 17 G9
Kimpton Herts 29 G8
Kinbrace Highld 93 F11
Kinbuck Stirling 75 G10
Kincaple Fife 77 F7
Kincardine Fife 69 B8
Kincardine Highld 87 C9
Kincardine Bridge Falk 69 B8
Kincardine O'Neil Aberds 83 D7
Kinclaven Perth 76 D4
Kincorth Aberdeen 83 C11
Kincorth Ho. Moray 87 E13
Kincraig Highld 81 C10
Kincraigie Perth 76 C2
Kindallachan Perth 76 C2
Kineton Glos 27 F7
Kineton Warks 27 C10
Kinfauns Perth 76 E4
King Edward Aberds 89 C7
King Sterndale Derbys 44 E4
Kingairloch Highld 79 F11
Kingarth Argyll 73 H9
Kingcoed Mon 25 H11
Kingerby Lincs 46 C4
Kingham Oxon 27 F9
Kingholm Quay Dumfries 60 F5
Kinghorn Fife 69 B11
Kingie Highld 80 C3
Kinglassie Fife 76 H5
Kingoodie Perth 76 E6
King's Acre Hereford 25 D11
King's Bromley Staffs 35 D7
King's Caple Hereford 26 F2
King's Cliffe Northants 36 F6
King's Coughton Warks 27 C7
King's Heath W Mid 35 G6
Kings Hedges Cambs 29 B11
King's Hill Kent 20 F3
Kings Langley Herts 19 A7
King's Lynn Norf 38 C2
King's Meaburn Cumb 57 D8
King's Mills Wrex 42 H6
Kings Muir Borders 69 G11
King's Newnham Warks 35 H10
King's Newton Derbys 35 C9
King's Norton Leics 36 E2
King's Norton W Mid 35 H6
King's Nympton Devon 6 E5
King's Pyon Hereford 25 C11
King's Ripton Cambs 37 H8
King's Somborne Hants 10 A2
King's Stag Dorset 8 C6
King's Stanley Glos 16 A5
King's Sutton Northants 27 E11
King's Thorn Hereford 26 E2
King's Walden Herts 29 F8
Kings Worthy Hants 10 A3
Kingsand Corn 4 F5
Kingsbarns Fife 77 F8
Kingsbridge Devon 5 G8
Kingsbridge Som 7 C8
Kingsburgh Highld 85 C8
Kingsbury London 19 C9
Kingsbury Warks 35 F8
Kingsbury Episcopi Som 8 B3
Kingsclere Hants 18 F2
Kingscote Glos 16 B5
Kingscott Devon 6 E4
Kingscross N Ayrs 66 D3
Kingsdon Som 8 B4
Kingsdown Kent 21 G10
Kingseat Fife 69 A10
Kingsey Bucks 28 H4
Kingsfold W Sus 19 H8
Kingsford E Ayrs 67 B7
Kingsford Worcs 34 G4
Kingsforth N Lincs 52 H6
Kingsgate Kent 21 D10
Kingsheanton Devon 6 C4
Kingshouse Hotel Highld 74 B5
Kingside Hill Cumb 56 A3
Kingskerswell Devon 5 E9
Kingskettle Fife 76 G6
Kingsland Anglesey 40 B4
Kingsland Hereford 25 B11
Kingsley Ches W 43 E8
Kingsley Hants 18 H4
Kingsley Staffs 44 H4
Kingsley Green W Sus 11 A7
Kingsley Holt Staffs 44 H4
Kingsley Park Northants 28 B4
Kingsmuir Angus 77 C7
Kingsmuir Fife 77 G8
Kingsnorth Kent 13 C9
Kingstanding W Mid 35 F6
Kingsteignton Devon 5 D9
Kingsthorpe Northants 28 B4
Kingston Cambs 29 C10
Kingston Devon 5 G7
Kingston Dorset 9 D6
Kingston Dorset 9 G8
Kingston E Loth 70 B4
Kingston Hants 9 D10
Kingston IoW 10 F3
Kingston Kent 21 F8
Kingston Moray 88 B3
Kingston Bagpuize Oxon 17 B11
Kingston Blount Oxon 18 B4
Kingston by Sea W Sus 11 D11
Kingston Deverill Wilts 16 H5
Kingston Gorse W Sus 11 D9
Kingston Lisle Oxon 17 C10
Kingston Maurward Dorset 8 E6
Kingston near Lewes E Sus 12 F2
Kingston on Soar Notts 35 C11
Kingston Russell Dorset 8 E4
Kingston St Mary Som 7 D11
Kingston Seymour N Som 15 E10
Kingston Upon Hull Hull 53 G6
Kingston upon Thames London 19 E8
Kingston Vale London 19 D9
Kingstone Hereford 25 E11
Kingstone Som 8 C2
Kingstone Staffs 35 C6
Kingstown Cumb 61 H9
Kingswear Devon 5 F9
Kingswells Aberdeen 83 C10
Kingswinford W Mid 34 G4
Kingswood Bucks 28 G3
Kingswood Glos 16 B4
Kingswood Hereford 25 C9
Kingswood Kent 20 F5
Kingswood Powys 33 E8
Kingswood S Glos 16 D3
Kingswood Sur 19 F9
Kingswood Warks 27 A8
Kingthorpe Lincs 46 E5
Kington Hereford 25 C9
Kington Worcs 26 C6
Kington Langley Wilts 16 D6
Kington Magna Dorset 9 B6
Kington St Michael Wilts 16 D6
Kingussie Highld 81 C9
Kingweston Som 8 A4
Kininvie Ho. Moray 88 D3
Kinkell Bridge Perth 76 F2
Kinknockie Aberds 89 D10
Kinlet Shrops 34 G3
Kinloch Fife 76 F5
Kinloch Highld 78 B6
Kinloch Highld 85 G11
Kinloch Highld 92 F6
Kinloch Perth 76 C5
Kinloch Perth 76 C4
Kinloch Hourn Highld 80 C1
Kinloch Laggan Highld 81 E7
Kinloch Lodge Highld 93 D8
Kinloch Rannoch Perth 75 B9
Kinlochan Highld 79 E11
Kinlochard Stirling 75 G7
Kinlochbeoraid Highld 79 C11
Kinlochbervie Highld 92 D5
Kinlocheil Highld 80 F1
Kinlochewe Highld 86 E3
Kinlochleven Highld 74 A4
Kinlochmoidart Highld 79 D10
Kinlochmorar Highld 79 B11
Kinlochmore Highld 74 A4
Kinlochspelve Argyll 79 J9
Kinloid Highld 79 C9
Kinloss Moray 87 E13
Kinmel Bay Conwy 42 D2
Kinmuck Aberds 83 B10
Kinmundy Aberds 83 B10
Kinnadie Aberds 89 D9
Kinnaird Perth 76 E5
Kinnaird Castle Angus 77 B9
Kinneff Aberds 83 F10
Kinnelhead Dumfries 60 C6
Kinnell Angus 77 B9
Kinnerley Shrops 33 C9
Kinnersley Hereford 25 D10
Kinnersley Worcs 26 D5
Kinnerton Powys 25 B9
Kinnesswood Perth 76 G4
Kinninvie Durham 58 D1
Kinnordy Angus 76 B6
Kinoulton Notts 36 B2
Kinross Perth 76 G4
Kinrossie Perth 76 D4
Kinsbourne Green Herts 29 G8
Kinsey Heath Ches E 34 A2
Kinsham Hereford 25 B10
Kinsham Worcs 26 E6
Kinsley W Yorks 45 A8
Kinson Bmouth 9 E9
Kintbury W Berks 17 E10
Kintessack Moray 87 E12
Kintillo Perth 76 F4
Kintocher Aberds 83 C7
Kinton Hereford 25 A11
Kinton Shrops 33 D9
Kintore Aberds 83 B9
Kintour Argyll 64 C5
Kintra Argyll 64 D4
Kintra Argyll 78 J6
Kintraw Argyll 73 C7
Kinuachdrachd Argyll 72 D6
Kinveachy Highld 81 B11
Kinver Staffs 34 G4
Kippax W Yorks 51 F10
Kippen Stirling 68 A5
Kippford or Scaur Dumfries 55 D11
Kirbister Orkney 95 F7
Kirbister Orkney 95 H4
Kirbuster Orkney 95 F3
Kirby Bedon Norf 39 E8
Kirby Bellars Leics 36 D3
Kirby Cane Norf 39 F9
Kirby Cross Essex 31 F9
Kirby Grindalythe N Yorks 52 C5
Kirby Hill N Yorks 51 C9
Kirby Hill N Yorks 58 F2
Kirby Knowle N Yorks 58 H5
Kirby-le-Soken Essex 31 F9
Kirby Misperton N Yorks 52 B3
Kirby Muxloe Leics 35 E11
Kirby Row Norf 39 F9
Kirby Sigston N Yorks 58 G5

Kirby Underdale E Yorks 52 D4
Kirby Wiske N Yorks 51 A9
Kirdford W Sus 11 B9
Kirk Highld 94 E4
Kirk Bramwith S Yorks 45 A10
Kirk Deighton N Yorks 51 D9
Kirk Ella E Yorks 52 G6
Kirk Hallam Derbys 35 A10
Kirk Hammerton N Yorks 51 D10
Kirk Ireton Derbys 44 G6
Kirk Langley Derbys 35 B8
Kirk Merrington Durham 58 C3
Kirk Michael IoM 48 C3
Kirk of Shotts N Lanark 69 D7
Kirk Sandall S Yorks 45 B10
Kirk Smeaton N Yorks 51 H11
Kirk Yetholm Borders 71 H7
Kirkabister Shetland 96 K6
Kirkandrews Dumfries 55 E9
Kirkandrews upon Eden Cumb 61 H9
Kirkbampton Cumb 61 H9
Kirkbean Dumfries 60 H5
Kirkbride Cumb 61 H8
Kirkbuddo Angus 77 C8
Kirkburn Borders 69 G11
Kirkburn E Yorks 52 D5
Kirkburton W Yorks 44 A5
Kirkby Lincs 46 C4
Kirkby Mers 43 C7
Kirkby N Yorks 59 F6
Kirkby Fleetham N Yorks 58 G3
Kirkby Green Lincs 46 G4
Kirkby In Ashfield Notts 45 G9
Kirkby-in-Furness Cumb 49 A2
Kirkby la Thorpe Lincs 46 H5
Kirkby Lonsdale Cumb 50 B2
Kirkby Malham N Yorks 50 C4
Kirkby Mallory Leics 35 E10
Kirkby Malzeard N Yorks 51 B8
Kirkby Mills N Yorks 59 H8
Kirkby on Bain Lincs 46 F6
Kirkby Overflow N Yorks 51 E9
Kirkby Stephen Cumb 57 F9
Kirkby Thore Cumb 57 D8
Kirkby Underwood Lincs 37 C6
Kirkby Wharfe N Yorks 51 E11
Kirkbymoorside N Yorks 59 H7
Kirkcaldy Fife 69 A11
Kirkcambeck Cumb 61 G11
Kirkcarswell Dumfries 55 E10
Kirkcolm Dumfries 54 C3
Kirkconnel Dumfries 60 B3
Kirkconnell Dumfries 60 G5
Kirkcowan Dumfries 54 C6
Kirkcudbright Dumfries 55 D9
Kirkdale Mers 42 C6
Kirkfieldbank S Lanark 69 F7
Kirkgunzeon Dumfries 55 C11
Kirkham Lancs 49 F4
Kirkham N Yorks 52 C3
Kirkhamgate W Yorks 51 G8
Kirkharle Northumb 62 E6
Kirkheaton Northumb 62 F6
Kirkheaton W Yorks 51 H7
Kirkhill Angus 77 A9
Kirkhill Highld 87 G8
Kirkhill Midloth 69 D11
Kirkhill Moray 88 E2
Kirkhope Borders 61 A9
Kirkhouse Borders 70 G2
Kirkiboll Highld 93 D8
Kirkibost Highld 85 G10
Kirkinch Angus 76 C6
Kirkinner Dumfries 55 D7
Kirkintilloch E Dunb 68 C5
Kirkland Cumb 56 E2
Kirkland Cumb 57 C8
Kirkland Dumfries 60 B3
Kirkland Dumfries 60 D4
Kirkleatham Redcar 59 D6
Kirklevington Stockton 58 F5
Kirkley Suff 39 F11
Kirklington N Yorks 51 A9
Kirklington Notts 45 G10
Kirklinton Cumb 61 G10
Kirkliston Edin 69 C10
Kirkmaiden Dumfries 54 F4
Kirkmichael Perth 76 B3
Kirkmichael S Ayrs 66 F6
Kirkmuirhill S Lanark 68 F6
Kirknewton Northumb 71 G8
Kirknewton W Loth 69 D10
Kirkney Aberds 88 E5
Kirkoswald Cumb 57 B7
Kirkoswald S Ayrs 66 F5
Kirkpatrick Durham Dumfries 60 F3
Kirkpatrick-Fleming Dumfries 61 F8
Kirksanton Cumb 49 A1
Kirkstall W Yorks 51 F8
Kirkstead Lincs 46 F5
Kirkstile Aberds 88 E5
Kirkstyle Highld 94 C5
Kirkton Aberds 83 A8
Kirkton Aberds 89 D6
Kirkton Angus 77 C7
Kirkton Angus 77 D7
Kirkton Borders 61 B11
Kirkton Dumfries 60 E5
Kirkton Fife 76 E6
Kirkton Highld 85 F13
Kirkton Highld 86 G2
Kirkton Highld 87 B10
Kirkton Highld 87 F10
Kirkton Perth 76 F2
Kirkton S Lanark 60 A5
Kirkton Stirling 75 G8
Kirkton Manor Borders 69 G11
Kirkton of Airlie Angus 76 B6
Kirkton of Auchterhouse Angus 76 D6
Kirkton of Auchterless Aberds 89 D7
Kirkton of Barevan Highld 87 G11
Kirkton of Bourtie Aberds 89 F8
Kirkton of Collace Perth 76 D4
Kirkton of Craig Angus 77 B10
Kirkton of Culsalmond Aberds 89 E6
Kirkton of Durris Aberds 83 D9
Kirkton of Glenbuchat Aberds 82 B5
Kirkton of Glenisla Angus 76 A5
Kirkton of Kingoldrum Angus 76 B6
Kirkton of Largo Fife 77 G7
Kirkton of Lethendy Perth 76 C4
Kirkton of Logie Buchan Aberds 89 F9
Kirkton of Maryculter Aberds 83 D10
Kirkton of Menmuir Angus 77 A8
Kirkton of Monikie Angus 77 D8
Kirkton of Oyne Aberds 83 A8
Kirkton of Rayne Aberds 83 A8
Kirkton of Skene Aberds 83 C10
Kirkton of Tough Aberds 83 B8
Kirktonhill Borders 70 E3
Kirktown Aberds 89 C10
Kirktown of Alvah Aberds 89 B6
Kirktown of Deskford Moray 88 B5
Kirktown of Fetteresso Aberds 83 E10
Kirktown of Mortlach Moray 88 E3
Kirktown of Slains Aberds 89 F10
Kirkurd Borders 69 F10
Kirkwall Orkney 95 G5
Kirkwhelpington Northumb 62 E5
Kirmington N Lincs 46 A5
Kirmond le Mire Lincs 46 C5
Kirn Argyll 73 F10
Kirriemuir Angus 76 B6
Kirstead Green Norf 39 F8
Kirtlebridge Dumfries 61 F8
Kirtleton Dumfries 61 E8
Kirtling Cambs 30 C3
Kirtling Green Cambs 30 C3
Kirtlington Oxon 27 G11
Kirtomy Highld 93 C10
Kirton Lincs 37 B9
Kirton Notts 45 F10
Kirton Suff 31 E9
Kirton End Lincs 37 A8
Kirton Holme Lincs 37 A8
Kirton in Lindsey N Lincs 46 C3
Kislingbury Northants 28 C3
Kites Hardwick Warks 27 B11
Kittisford Som 7 D9
Kittle Swansea 23 H10
Kitt's Green W Mid 35 G7
Kitt's Moss Gtr Man 44 D2
Kittybrewster Aberdeen 83 C11
Kitwood Hants 10 A5
Kivernoll Hereford 25 E11
Kiveton Park S Yorks 45 D8
Knaith Lincs 46 D2
Knaith Park Lincs 46 D2
Knap Corner Dorset 9 B7
Knaphill Sur 18 F6
Knapp Perth 76 D5
Knapp Som 8 B2
Knapthorpe Notts 45 G11
Knapton Norf 39 B9
Knapton York 52 D1
Knapton Green Hereford 25 C11
Knapwell Cambs 29 B10
Knaresborough N Yorks 51 D9
Knarsdale Northumb 57 A8
Knauchland Moray 88 C5
Knaven Aberds 89 D8
Knayton N Yorks 58 H5
Knebworth Herts 29 F9
Knedlington E Yorks 52 G3
Kneesall Notts 45 F11
Kneesworth Cambs 29 D10
Kneeton Notts 45 H11
Knelston Swansea 23 H9
Knenhall Staffs 34 B5
Knettishall Suff 38 G5
Knightacott Devon 6 C5
Knightcote Warks 27 C10
Knightley Dale Staffs 34 C4
Knighton Devon 4 G6
Knighton Leicester 36 E1
Knighton = Tref-y-Clawdd Powys 25 A9
Knighton Staffs 34 A3
Knighton Staffs 34 C3
Knightswood Glasgow 68 D4
Knightwick Worcs 26 C4
Knill Hereford 25 B9
Knipton Leics 36 B4
Knitsley Durham 58 B2
Kniveton Derbys 44 G6
Knock Argyll 79 H8
Knock Cumb 57 D8
Knock Moray 88 C5
Knockally Highld 94 H3
Knockan Highld 92 H5
Knockandhu Moray 82 A4
Knockando Moray 88 D1
Knockando Ho. Moray 88 D2
Knockbain Highld 87 F9
Knockbreck Highld 84 B7
Knockbrex Dumfries 55 E8
Knockdee Highld 94 D3
Knockdolian S Ayrs 66 H4
Knockenkelly N Ayrs 66 D3
Knockentiber E Ayrs 67 C6
Knockespock Ho. Aberds 83 A7
Knockfarrel Highld 87 F8
Knockglass Dumfries 54 D3
Knockholt Kent 19 F11
Knockholt Pound Kent 19 F11
Knockie Lodge Highld 80 B6
Knockin Shrops 33 C9
Knockinlaw E Ayrs 67 C7
Knocklearn Dumfries 60 F3
Knocknaha Argyll 65 G7
Knocknain Dumfries 54 C2
Knockrome Argyll 72 F4
Knocksharry IoM 48 D2
Knodishall Suff 31 B11
Knolls Green Ches E 44 E2
Knolton Wrex 33 B9
Knolton Bryn Wrex 33 B9
Knook Wilts 16 G6
Knossington Leics 36 E4
Knott End-on-Sea Lancs 49 E3
Knotting Bedford 29 B7
Knotting Green Bedford 29 B7
Knottingley W Yorks 51 G11
Knotts Cumb 56 D6
Knotts Lancs 50 D3
Knotty Ash Mers 43 C7
Knotty Green Bucks 18 B6
Knowbury Shrops 26 A2
Knowe Dumfries 54 B6
Knowehead Dumfries 67 G9
Knowes of Elrick Aberds 88 C6
Knowesgate Northumb 62 E5
Knoweton N Lanark 68 E6
Knowhead Aberds 89 C9
Knowl Hill Windsor 18 D5
Knowle Bristol 16 D3
Knowle Devon 6 C3
Knowle Devon 7 F6
Knowle Devon 7 H9
Knowle Shrops 26 A2
Knowle W Mid 35 H7
Knowle Green Lancs 50 F2
Knowle Park W Yorks 51 E6
Knowlton Dorset 9 C9
Knowlton Kent 21 F9
Knowsley Mers 43 C7
Knowstone Devon 7 D7
Knox Bridge Kent 13 B6
Knucklas Powys 25 A9
Knuston Northants 28 B6
Knutsford Ches E 43 E10
Knutton Staffs 44 H2
Knypersley Staffs 44 G2
Kuggar Corn 2 H6
Kyle of Lochalsh Highld 85 F12
Kyleakin Highld 85 F12
Kylerhea Highld 85 F12
Kylesknoydart Highld 79 B11
Kylesku Highld 92 F5
Kylesmorar Highld 79 B11
Kylestrome Highld 92 F5
Kyllachy House Highld 81 A9
Kynaston Shrops 33 C9
Kynnersley Telford 34 D2
Kyre Magna Worcs 26 B3

L

La Fontenelle Guern 11
La Planque Guern 11
Labost W Isles 91 C7
Lacasaidh W Isles 91 E8
Lacasdal W Isles 91 D9
Laceby NE Lincs 46 B6
Lacey Green Bucks 18 B5
Lach Dennis Ches W 43 E10
Lackford Suff 30 A4
Lacock Wilts 16 E6
Ladbroke Warks 27 C11
Laddingford Kent 20 G3
Lade Bank Lincs 47 G7
Ladock Corn 3 D7
Lady Orkney 95 D7
Ladybank Fife 76 F6
Ladykirk Borders 71 F7
Ladysford Aberds 89 B9
Laga Highld 79 E9
Lagalochan Argyll 73 B7
Lagavulin Argyll 64 D5
Lagg Argyll 72 F4
Lagg N Ayrs 66 D2
Laggan Argyll 64 C3
Laggan Highld 79 D10
Laggan Highld 80 D4
Laggan Highld 81 D8
Laggan S Ayrs 54 A5
Lagganulva Argyll 78 G7
Laide Highld 91 H13
Laigh Fenwick E Ayrs 67 B7
Laigh Glengall S Ayrs 66 E6
Laighmuir E Ayrs 67 B7
Laindon Essex 20 C3
Lair Highld 86 G3
Lairg Highld 93 J8
Lairg Lodge Highld 93 J8
Lairg Muir Highld 93 J8
Lairgmore Highld 87 H8
Laisterdyke W Yorks 51 F7
Laithes Cumb 56 C6
Lake IoW 10 F4
Lake Wilts 17 H8
Lakenham Norf 39 E8
Lakenheath Suff 38 G3
Lakesend Norf 37 F11
Lakeside Cumb 56 H5
Laleham Sur 19 E7
Laleston Bridgend 14 D4
Lamarsh Essex 30 E5
Lamas Norf 39 C8
Lambden Borders 70 F6
Lamberhurst Kent 12 C5
Lamberhurst Quarter Kent 12 C5
Lamberton Borders 71 E8
Lambeth London 19 D10
Lambhill Glasgow 68 D4
Lambley Northumb 62 H2
Lambley Notts 45 H10
Lamborough Hill Oxon 17 A11
Lambourn W Berks 17 D10
Lambourne End Essex 19 B11
Lambs Green W Sus 19 H9
Lambston Pembs 22 E4
Lambton T&W 58 A3
Lamerton Devon 4 D5
Lamesley T&W 63 H8
Laminess Orkney 95 E7
Lamington Highld 87 D10
Lamington S Lanark 69 G8
Lamlash N Ayrs 66 C3
Lamloch Dumfries 67 G8
Lamonby Cumb 56 C6
Lamorna Corn 2 G3
Lamorran Corn 3 E7
Lampardbrook Suff 31 B9
Lampeter = Llanbedr Pont Steffan Ceredig 23 B10
Lampeter Velfrey Pembs 22 E6
Lamphey Pembs 22 F5
Lamplugh Cumb 56 D2
Lamport Northants 28 A4
Lamyatt Som 16 H3
Lana Devon 6 G2
Lanark S Lanark 69 F7
Lancaster Lancs 49 C4
Lanchester Durham 58 B2
Lancing W Sus 11 D10
Landbeach Cambs 29 B11
Landcross Devon 6 D3
Landerberry Aberds 83 C9
Landford Wilts 10 C1
Landford Manor Wilts 10 B1
Landimore Swansea 23 G9
Landkey Devon 6 C4
Landore Swansea 14 B2
Landrake Corn 4 E4
Landscove Devon 5 E8
Landshipping Pembs 22 E5
Landshipping Quay Pembs 22 E5
Landulph Corn 4 E5
Landwade Suff 30 B3
Lane Corn 3 C7
Lane End Bucks 18 B5
Lane End Cumb 56 G3
Lane End Dorset 9 E7
Lane End Hants 10 B4
Lane End IoW 10 F5
Lane End Lancs 50 E4
Lane Ends Lancs 50 D3
Lane Ends Lancs 50 F3
Lane Ends N Yorks 50 E5
Lane Head Derbys 44 E5
Lane Head Durham 58 E2
Lane Head Gtr Man 43 C9
Lane Head W Yorks 44 B5
Lane Side Lancs 50 G3
Laneast Corn 4 C3
Laneham Notts 46 E2
Lanehead Durham 57 B10
Lanehead Northumb 62 E3
Lanercost Cumb 61 G11
Laneshaw Bridge Lancs 50 E5
Lanfach Caerph 15 B8
Langar Notts 36 B3
Langbank Renfs 68 C2
Langbar N Yorks 51 D6
Langburnshiels Borders 61 C11
Langcliffe N Yorks 50 C4
Langdale Highld 93 E9
Langdale End N Yorks 59 G10
Langdon Corn 4 C4
Langdon Beck Durham 57 C10
Langdon Hills Essex 20 C3
Langdyke Fife 76 G6
Langenhoe Essex 31 G7
Langford C Beds 29 D8
Langford Devon 7 F9
Langford Essex 30 H5
Langford Notts 46 G2
Langford Oxon 17 A9
Langford Budville Som 7 D10
Langham Essex 31 E7
Langham Norf 38 A6
Langham Rutland 36 D4
Langham Suff 30 B6
Langhaugh Borders 69 G11
Langho Lancs 50 F3
Langholm Dumfries 61 E9
Langleeford Northumb 62 A5
Langley Ches E 44 E3
Langley Hants 10 D3
Langley Herts 29 F9
Langley Kent 20 F5
Langley Northumb 62 G4
Langley Slough 19 D7
Langley W Sus 11 B7
Langley Warks 27 B8
Langley Burrell Wilts 16 D6
Langley Common Derbys 35 B8
Langley Heath Kent 20 F5
Langley Lower Green Essex 29 E11
Langley Marsh Som 7 D9
Langley Park Durham 58 B3
Langley Street Norf 39 E9
Langley Upper Green Essex 29 E11
Langney E Sus 12 F5
Langold Notts 45 D9
Langore Corn 4 C4
Langport Som 8 B3
Langrick Lincs 46 H6
Langridge Bath 16 E4
Langridge Ford Devon 6 D4
Langrigg Cumb 56 B3
Langrish Hants 10 B6
Langsett S Yorks 44 B6
Langshaw Borders 70 G4
Langside Perth 75 F10
Langskaill Orkney 95 D5
Langstone Hants 10 D6
Langstone Newport 15 B9
Langthorne N Yorks 58 G3
Langthorpe N Yorks 51 C9
Langthwaite N Yorks 58 F1
Langtoft E Yorks 52 C6
Langtoft Lincs 37 D7
Langton Durham 58 E2
Langton Lincs 46 F6
Langton Lincs 47 E7
Langton N Yorks 52 C3
Langton by Wragby Lincs 46 E5
Langton Green Kent 12 C4
Langton Green Suff 31 A8
Langton Herring Dorset 8 F5
Langton Matravers Dorset 9 G9
Langtree Devon 6 E3
Langwathby Cumb 57 C7
Langwell Ho. Highld 94 H3
Langwell Lodge Highld 92 J4
Langwith Derbys 45 F9
Langwith Junction Derbys 45 F9
Langworth Lincs 46 E4
Lanivet Corn 3 C9
Lanlivery Corn 4 F1
Lanner Corn 2 F6
Lanreath Corn 4 F2
Lansallos Corn 4 F2
Lansdown Glos 26 F6
Lanteglos Highway Corn 4 F2
Lanton Borders 62 A2
Lanton Northumb 71 G8
Lapford Devon 7 F6
Laphroaig Argyll 64 D4
Lapley Staffs 34 D4
Lapworth Warks 27 A8
Larachbeg Highld 79 G9
Larbert Falk 69 B7
Larden Green Ches E 43 G8
Largie Aberds 88 E6
Largiemore Argyll 73 E8
Largoward Fife 77 G7
Largs N Ayrs 73 H11
Largybeg N Ayrs 66 D3
Largymore N Ayrs 66 D3
Larkfield Invclyd 73 F11
Larkhall S Lanark 68 E6
Larkhill Wilts 17 G8
Larling Norf 38 G5
Larriston Borders 61 D11
Lartington Durham 58 E1
Lary Aberds 82 C5
Lasham Hants 18 G3
Lashenden Kent 13 B7
Lassington Glos 26 F4
Lassodie Fife 69 A10
Lastingham N Yorks 59 G8
Latcham Som 15 G10
Latchford Herts 29 F10
Latchford Warr 43 D9
Latchingdon Essex 20 A5
Latchley Corn 4 D5
Lately Common Warr 43 C9
Lathbury M Keynes 28 D5
Latheron Highld 94 G3
Latheronwheel Highld 94 G3
Latheronwheel Ho. Highld 94 G3
Lathones Fife 77 G7
Latimer Bucks 19 B7
Latteridge S Glos 16 C3
Lattiford Som 8 B5
Latton Wilts 17 B7
Latton Bush Essex 29 H11
Lauchintilly Aberds 83 B9
Lauder Borders 70 F4
Laugharne Carms 23 E8
Laughterton Lincs 46 E2
Laughton E Sus 12 E3
Laughton Leics 36 G2
Laughton Lincs 37 B6
Laughton Lincs 46 C2
Laughton Common S Yorks 45 D9
Laughton en le Morthen S Yorks 45 D9
Launcells Corn 6 F1
Launceston Corn 4 C4
Launton Oxon 28 F3
Laurencekirk Aberds 83 F9
Laurieston Dumfries 55 C9
Laurieston Falk 69 C8
Lavendon M Keynes 28 C6
Lavenham Suff 30 D6
Laverhay Dumfries 61 D7
Laversdale Cumb 61 G10
Laverstock Wilts 9 A10
Laverstoke Hants 17 G11
Laverton Glos 27 E7
Laverton N Yorks 51 B8
Laverton Som 16 F4
Lavister Wrex 42 G6
Law S Lanark 69 E7
Lawers Perth 75 D9
Lawers Perth 75 E10
Lawford Essex 31 E7
Lawhitton Corn 4 C4
Lawkland N Yorks 50 C3
Lawley Telford 34 E2
Lawnhead Staffs 34 C4
Lawrenny Pembs 22 F5
Lawshall Suff 30 C5
Lawton Hereford 25 C11
Laxey IoM 48 D4
Laxfield Suff 31 A9
Laxfirth Shetland 96 H6
Laxfirth Shetland 96 J6
Laxford Bridge Highld 92 E5
Laxo Shetland 96 G6
Laxobigging Shetland 96 F6
Laxton E Yorks 52 G3
Laxton Northants 36 F5
Laxton Notts 45 F11
Laycock W Yorks 50 E6
Layer Breton Essex 30 G6
Layer de la Haye Essex 30 G6
Layer Marney Essex 30 G6
Layham Suff 31 D7
Laylands Green W Berks 17 E10
Laytham E Yorks 52 F3
Layton Blackpool 49 F3
Lazenby Redcar 59 D6
Lazonby Cumb 57 C7
Le Planel Guern 11
Le Skerne Haughton Darl 58 E4
Le Villocq Guern 11
Lea Derbys 45 G7
Lea Hereford 26 F3
Lea Lincs 46 D2
Lea Shrops 33 E10
Lea Shrops 33 G9
Lea Wilts 16 C6
Lea Marston Warks 35 F8
Lea Town Lancs 49 F4
Leabrooks Derbys 45 G8
Leac a Li W Isles 90 H6
Leachkin Highld 87 G9
Leadburn Midloth 69 E11
Leaden Roding Essex 30 G2
Leadenham Lincs 46 G3
Leadgate Cumb 57 B9
Leadgate Durham 58 A2
Leadgate T&W 63 H7
Leadhills S Lanark 60 B4
Leafield Oxon 27 G10
Leagrave Luton 29 F7
Leake N Yorks 58 G5
Leake Commonside Lincs 47 G7
Lealholm N Yorks 59 F8
Lealt Argyll 72 D5
Lealt Highld 85 B10
Leamington Hastings Warks 27 B11
Leamonsley Staffs 35 E7
Leamside Durham 58 B4
Leanaig Highld 87 F8
Leargybreck Argyll 72 F4
Leasgill Cumb 49 A4
Leasingham Lincs 46 H4
Leasingthorne Durham 58 D3
Leasowe Mers 42 C5
Leatherhead Sur 19 F8
Leatherhead Common Sur 19 F8
Leathley N Yorks 51 E8
Leaton Shrops 33 D10
Leaveland Kent 21 F7
Leavening N Yorks 52 C3
Leaves Green London 19 E11
Leazes Durham 63 H7
Lebberston N Yorks 53 A6
Lechlade-on-Thames Glos 17 B9
Leck Lancs 50 B2
Leckford Hants 17 H10
Leckfurin Highld 93 D10
Leckgruinart Argyll 64 B3
Leckhampstead Bucks 28 E4
Leckhampstead W Berks 17 D11
Leckhampstead Thicket W Berks 17 D11
Leckhampton Glos 26 G6
Leckie Highld 86 E3
Leckmelm Highld 86 B4
Leckwith V Glam 15 D7
Leconfield E Yorks 52 E6
Ledaig Argyll 74 D2
Ledburn Bucks 28 F6
Ledbury Hereford 26 E4
Ledcharrie Stirling 75 E8
Ledgemoor Hereford 25 C11
Ledicot Hereford 25 B11
Ledmore Highld 92 H5
Lednagullin Highld 93 C10
Ledsham Ches W 42 E6
Ledsham W Yorks 51 G10
Ledston W Yorks 51 G10
Ledston Luck W Yorks 51 F10
Ledwell Oxon 27 F11
Lee Argyll 78 J7
Lee Devon 6 B3
Lee Hants 10 C2
Lee Lancs 50 D1
Lee Shrops 33 B10
Lee Brockhurst Shrops 33 C11
Lee Clump Bucks 18 A6
Lee Mill Devon 5 F7
Lee Moor Devon 5 E6
Lee-on-the-Solent Hants 10 D4
Leeans Shetland 96 J5
Leebotten Shetland 96 L6
Leebotwood Shrops 33 F10
Leece Cumb 49 C2
Leechpool Pembs 22 E4
Leeds Kent 20 F5
Leeds W Yorks 51 F8
Leedstown Corn 2 F5
Leek Staffs 44 G3
Leek Wootton Warks 27 B9
Leekbrook Staffs 44 G3
Leeming N Yorks 58 H3
Leeming Bar N Yorks 58 G3
Lees Derbys 35 B8
Lees Gtr Man 44 B3
Lees W Yorks 50 F6
Leeswood Flint 42 G5
Legbourne Lincs 47 D7
Legerwood Borders 70 F4
Legsby Lincs 46 D5
Leicester Leicester 36 E1
Leicester Forest East Leics 35 E11
Leigh Dorset 8 D5
Leigh Glos 26 F5
Leigh Gtr Man 43 B9
Leigh Kent 20 G2
Leigh Shrops 33 E9
Leigh Sur 19 G9
Leigh Wilts 17 B7
Leigh Worcs 26 C4
Leigh Beck Essex 20 C5
Leigh Common Som 8 B6
Leigh Delamere Wilts 16 D5
Leigh Green Kent 13 C8
Leigh on Sea Southend 20 C5
Leigh Park Hants 10 D6
Leigh Sinton Worcs 26 C4
Leigh upon Mendip Som 16 G3
Leigh Woods N Som 16 D2
Leighswood W Mid 35 E6
Leighterton Glos 16 B5
Leighton N Yorks 51 B7
Leighton Powys 33 E8
Leighton Shrops 34 E2
Leighton Som 16 G4
Leighton Bromswold Cambs 37 H7
Leighton Buzzard C Beds 28 F6
Leinthall Earls Hereford 25 B11
Leinthall Starkes Hereford 25 B11
Leintwardine Hereford 25 A11
Leire Leics 35 F11
Leirinmore Highld 92 C7
Leiston Suff 31 B11
Leitfie Perth 76 C5
Leith Edin 69 C11
Leitholm Borders 70 F6
Lelant Corn 2 F4
Lelley E Yorks 53 F8
Lem Hill Worcs 26 A4
Lemmington Hall Northumb 63 B7
Lempitlaw Borders 70 G6
Lenchwick Worcs 27 D7
Lendalfoot S Ayrs 66 H4
Lendrick Lodge Stirling 75 G8
Lenham Kent 20 F5
Lenham Heath Kent 20 G6
Lennel Borders 71 F7
Lennoxtown E Dunb 68 C5
Lenton Lincs 36 B6
Lenton Nottingham 36 B1
Lentran Highld 87 G8
Lenwade Norf 39 D6
Leny Ho. Stirling 75 G9
Lenzie E Dunb 68 C5
Leoch Angus 76 D6
Leochel-Cushnie Aberds 83 B7
Leominster Hereford 25 C11
Leonard Stanley Glos 16 A5
Leorin Argyll 64 D4
Lepe Hants 10 E3
Lephin Highld 84 D6
Lephinchapel Argyll 73 D8
Lephinmore Argyll 73 D8
Leppington N Yorks 52 C3
Lepton W Yorks 51 H8
Lerryn Corn 4 F2
Lerwick Shetland 96 J6
Lesbury Northumb 63 B8
Leslie Aberds 83 A7
Leslie Fife 76 G5
Lesmahagow S Lanark 69 G7
Lesnewth Corn 4 B2
Lessendrum Aberds 88 D5
Lessingham Norf 39 C9
Lessonhall Cumb 56 A4
Leswalt Dumfries 54 C3
Letchmore Heath Herts 19 B8
Letchworth Herts 29 E9
Letcombe Bassett Oxon 17 C10
Letcombe Regis Oxon 17 C10
Letham Angus 77 C8
Letham Falk 69 B7
Letham Fife 76 F6
Letham Perth 76 E3
Letham Grange Angus 77 C9
Lethenty Aberds 89 D8
Letheringham Suff 31 C9
Letheringsett Norf 39 B6
Lettaford Devon 5 C8
Lettan Orkney 95 D8
Letterewe Highld 86 D2
Letterfearn Highld 85 F13
Letterfinlay Highld 80 D4
Lettermorar Highld 79 C10
Lettermore Argyll 78 G7
Letters Highld 86 C4
Letterston Pembs 22 D4
Lettoch Highld 82 B2
Lettoch Highld 87 H13
Letton Hereford 25 A10
Letton Hereford 25 D10
Letton Green Norf 38 E5
Letty Green Herts 29 G9
Letwell S Yorks 45 D9
Leuchars Fife 77 E7
Leuchars Ho. Moray 88 B2
Leumrabhagh W Isles 91 F8
Levan Invclyd 73 F11
Levaneap Shetland 96 G6
Levedale Staffs 34 D4
Leven E Yorks 53 E7
Leven Fife 76 G6
Levencorroch N Ayrs 66 D3
Levens Cumb 57 H6
Levens Green Herts 29 F10
Levenshulme Gtr Man 44 C2
Levenwick Shetland 96 L6
Leverburgh = An t-Ob W Isles 90 J5
Leverington Cambs 37 D10
Leverton Lincs 47 H8
Leverton Highgate Lincs 47 H8
Leverton Lucasgate Lincs 47 H8
Leverton Outgate Lincs 47 H8
Levington Suff 31 E9
Levisham N Yorks 59 G9
Levishie Highld 80 B6
Lew Oxon 27 H10
Lewannick Corn 4 C3
Lewdown Devon 4 C5
Lewes E Sus 12 E3
Leweston Pembs 22 D4
Lewisham London 19 D10
Lewiston Highld 81 A7
Lewistown Bridgend 14 C5
Lewknor Oxon 18 B4
Leworthy Devon 6 C5
Leworthy Devon 6 F2
Lewtrenchard Devon 4 C5
Lexden Essex 30 F6
Ley Aberds 83 B7
Ley Corn 4 E2
Leybourne Kent 20 F3
Leyburn N Yorks 58 G2
Leyfields Staffs 35 E8
Leyhill Bucks 18 A6
Leyland Lancs 49 G5
Leylodge Aberds 83 B9
Leymoor W Yorks 51 H7
Leys Aberds 89 C10
Leys Perth 76 D5
Leys Castle Highld 87 G9
Leys of Cossans Angus 76 C6
Leysdown-on-Sea Kent 21 D7
Leysmill Angus 77 C9
Leysters Pole Hereford 26 B2
Leyton London 19 C10
Leytonstone London 19 C10
Lezant Corn 4 D4
Leziate Norf 38 D2
Lhanbryde Moray 88 B2
Liatrie Highld 86 H5
Libanus Powys 24 F6
Libberton S Lanark 69 F8
Liberton Edin 69 D11
Liceasto W Isles 90 H6
Lichfield Staffs 35 E7
Lickey Worcs 34 H5
Lickey End Worcs 26 A6
Lickfold W Sus 11 B8
Liddel Orkney 95 K5
Liddesdale Highld 79 F10
Liddington Swindon 17 C9
Lidgate Suff 30 C4
Lidget S Yorks 45 B10
Lidget Green W Yorks 51 F7
Lidgett Notts 45 F10
Lidlington C Beds 28 E6
Lidstone Oxon 27 F10
Lieurary Highld 94 D2
Liff Angus 76 D6
Lifton Devon 4 C4
Liftondown Devon 4 C4
Lighthorne Warks 27 C10
Lightwater Sur 18 E6
Lightwood Stoke 34 A5
Lightwood Green Ches E 34 A2
Lightwood Green Wrex 33 A9
Lilbourne Northants 36 H1
Lilburn Tower Northumb 62 A6
Lilleshall Telford 34 D3
Lilley Herts 29 F8
Lilley W Berks 17 D11
Lilliesleaf Borders 61 A11
Lillingstone Dayrell Bucks 28 E4
Lillingstone Lovell Bucks 28 D4
Lillington Dorset 8 C5
Lillington Warks 27 B10
Lilliput Poole 9 E9
Lilstock Som 7 B10
Lilyhurst Shrops 34 D3
Limbury Luton 29 F7
Limebrook Hereford 25 B10
Limefield Gtr Man 44 A2
Limekilnburn S Lanark 68 E6
Limekilns Fife 69 B9
Limerigg Falk 69 C7
Limerstone IoW 10 F3
Limington Som 8 B4
Limpenhoe Norf 39 E9
Limpley Stoke Wilts 16 E4
Limpsfield Sur 19 F11
Limpsfield Chart Sur 19 F11
Linby Notts 45 G9
Linchmere W Sus 11 A7
Lincluden Dumfries 60 F5
Lincoln Lincs 46 E3
Lincomb Worcs 26 B5
Lincombe Devon 5 F8
Lindal in Furness Cumb 49 B2
Lindale Cumb 49 A4
Lindean Borders 70 G3
Lindfield W Sus 12 D2
Lindford Hants 18 H5
Lindifferon Fife 76 F6
Lindley W Yorks 51 H7
Lindley Green N Yorks 51 E8
Lindores Fife 76 F5
Lindridge Worcs 26 B3
Lindsell Essex 30 F3
Lindsey Suff 30 D6
Linford Hants 9 D10
Linford Thurrock 20 D3
Lingague IoM 48 E2
Lingards Wood W Yorks 44 A4
Lingbob W Yorks 51 F6
Lingdale Redcar 59 E7
Lingen Hereford 25 B10
Lingfield Sur 12 B2
Lingreabhagh W Isles 90 J5
Lingwood Norf 39 E9
Linicro Highld 85 B8
Linkenholt Hants 17 F10
Linkhill Kent 13 D7
Linkinhorne Corn 4 D4
Linklater Orkney 95 K5
Linksness Orkney 95 H3
Linktown Fife 69 A11
Linley Shrops 33 F9
Linley Green Hereford 26 C3
Linlithgow W Loth 69 C9
Linlithgow Bridge W Loth 69 C8
Linshiels Northumb 62 C4
Linsiadar W Isles 90 D7
Linsidemore Highld 87 B8
Linslade C Beds 28 F6
Linstead Parva Suff 39 H9
Linstock Cumb 61 H10
Linthwaite W Yorks 44 A5
Lintlaw Borders 71 E7
Lintmill Moray 88 B5
Linton Borders 70 H6
Linton Cambs 30 D2
Linton Derbys 35 D8
Linton Hereford 26 F3
Linton Kent 20 G4
Linton N Yorks 50 C5
Linton Northumb 63 D8
Linton W Yorks 51 E9
Linton-on-Ouse N Yorks 51 C10
Linwood Hants 9 D10
Linwood Lincs 46 D5
Linwood Renfs 68 D3
Lionacleit W Isles 84 D2
Lional W Isles 91 A10
Liphook Hants 11 A7
Liscard Mers 42 C6
Liscombe Som 7 C7
Liskeard Corn 4 E3
L'Islet Guern 11
Liss Hants 11 B6
Liss Forest Hants 11 B6
Lissett E Yorks 53 D7
Lissington Lincs 46 D5
Lisvane Cardiff 15 C7
Liswerry Newport 15 C9
Litcham Norf 38 D4
Litchborough Northants 28 C3
Litchfield Hants 17 F11
Litherland Mers 42 C6
Litlington Cambs 29 D10
Litlington E Sus 12 F4
Little Abington Cambs 30 D2
Little Addington Northants 28 A6
Little Alne Warks 27 B8
Little Altcar Mers 42 B6
Little Asby Cumb 57 F8
Little Assynt Highld 92 G4
Little Aston Staffs 35 E6
Little Atherfield IoW 10 F3
Little Ayre Orkney 95 J4
Little-ayre Shetland 96 G5
Little Ayton N Yorks 59 E6
Little Baddow Essex 30 H4
Little Badminton S Glos 16 C5
Little Ballinluig Perth 76 B2
Little Bampton Cumb 61 H8
Little Bardfield Essex 30 E3
Little Barford Bedford 29 C8
Little Barningham Norf 39 B7
Little Barrington Glos 27 G9
Little Barrow Ches W 43 E7
Little Barugh N Yorks 52 B3
Little Bavington Northumb 62 F5
Little Bealings Suff 31 D9
Little Bedwyn Wilts 17 E9
Little Bentley Essex 31 F8
Little Berkhamsted Herts 29 H9
Little Billing Northants 28 B5
Little Birch Hereford 26 E2
Little Blakenham Suff 31 D8
Little Blencow Cumb 56 C6
Little Bollington Ches E 43 D10
Little Bookham Sur 19 F8
Little Bowden Leics 36 G3
Little Bradley Suff 30 C3
Little Brampton Shrops 33 G9
Little Brechin Angus 77 A8
Little Brickhill M Keynes 28 E6
Little Brington Northants 28 B3
Little Bromley Essex 31 F7
Little Broughton Cumb 56 C2
Little Budworth Ches W 43 F8
Little Burstead Essex 20 B3
Little Bytham Lincs 36 D6
Little Carlton Lincs 47 D7
Little Carlton Notts 45 G11
Little Casterton Rutland 36 E6
Little Cawthorpe Lincs 47 D7
Little Chalfont Bucks 18 B6
Little Chart Kent 20 G6
Little Chesterford Essex 30 D2
Little Cheverell Wilts 16 F6
Little Chishill Cambs 29 E11
Little Clacton Essex 31 G8
Little Clifton Cumb 56 D2
Little Colp Aberds 89 D7
Little Comberton Worcs 26 D6
Little Common E Sus 12 F6
Little Compton Warks 27 E9
Little Cornard Suff 30 E5
Little Cowarne Hereford 26 C3
Little Coxwell Oxon 17 B9
Little Crakehall N Yorks 58 G3
Little Cressingham Norf 38 F4
Little Crosby Mers 42 B6
Little Dalby Leics 36 D3
Little Dawley Telford 34 E2
Little Dens Aberds 89 D10
Little Dewchurch Hereford 26 E2
Little Downham Cambs 37 G11
Little Driffield E Yorks 52 D6
Little Dunham Norf 38 D4
Little Dunkeld Perth 76 C3
Little Dunmow Essex 30 F3
Little Easton Essex 30 F3
Little Eaton Derbys 35 A9
Little Eccleston Lancs 49 E4
Little Ellingham Norf 38 F6
Little End Essex 20 A2
Little Eversden Cambs 29 C10
Little Faringdon Oxon 17 A9
Little Fencote N Yorks 58 G3
Little Fenton N Yorks 51 F11
Little Finborough Suff 31 C7
Little Fransham Norf 38 D5
Little Gaddesden Herts 28 G6
Little Gidding Cambs 37 G7
Little Glemham Suff 31 C10
Little Glenshee Perth 76 D2
Little Gransden Cambs 29 C9
Little Green Som 16 G4
Little Grimsby Lincs 47 C7
Little Gruinard Highld 86 C2
Little Habton N Yorks 52 B3
Little Hadham Herts 29 F11
Little Hale Lincs 37 A7
Little Hallingbury Essex 29 G11
Little Hampden Bucks 18 A5
Little Harrowden Northants 28 A5
Little Haseley Oxon 18 A3
Little Hatfield E Yorks 53 E7
Little Hautbois Norf 39 C8
Little Haven Pembs 22 E3
Little Hay Staffs 35 E7
Little Hayfield Derbys 44 D4
Little Haywood Staffs 34 C6
Little Heath W Mid 35 G9
Little Hereford Hereford 26 B2
Little Horkesley Essex 30 E6
Little Horsted E Sus 12 E3
Little Horton W Yorks 51 F7
Little Horwood Bucks 28 E4
Little Houghton Northants 28 C5
Little Houghton S Yorks 45 B8
Little Hucklow Derbys 44 E5
Little Hulton Gtr Man 43 B10
Little Humber E Yorks 53 G7
Little Hungerford W Berks 18 D2
Little Irchester Northants 28 B6
Little Kimble Bucks 28 H5
Little Kineton Warks 27 C10
Little Kingshill Bucks 18 B5
Little Langdale Cumb 56 F5
Little Langford Wilts 17 H7
Little Laver Essex 30 H2
Little Leigh Ches W 43 E9
Little Leighs Essex 30 G4
Little Lever Gtr Man 43 B10
Little London Bucks 28 G3
Little London E Sus 12 E4
Little London Hants 17 G10
Little London Hants 18 F3
Little London Lincs 37 C10
Little London Lincs 37 C8
Little London Norf 39 C7
Little London Powys 32 G6
Little Longstone Derbys 44 E5
Little Lynturk Aberds 83 B7
Little Malvern Worcs 26 D4
Little Maplestead Essex 30 E5
Little Marcle Hereford 26 E3
Little Marlow Bucks 18 C5
Little Marsden Lancs 50 F4
Little Massingham Norf 38 C3
Little Melton Norf 39 E7
Little Mill Mon 15 A9
Little Milton Oxon 18 A3
Little Missenden Bucks 18 B6
Little Musgrave Cumb 57 E9
Little Ness Shrops 33 D10
Little Neston Ches W 42 E5
Little Newcastle Pembs 22 D4
Little Newsham Durham 58 E2
Little Oakley Essex 31 F9
Little Oakley Northants 36 G4
Little Orton Cumb 61 H9

128 Mon–Nor

Monmouth Cap Mon 25 F10
Monnington on Wye Hereford 25 D10
Monreith Dumfries 54 E6
Monreith Mains Dumfries 54 E6
Mont Saint Guern 11
Montacute Som 8 C3
Montcoffer Ho. Aberds 89 B6
Montford Argyll 73 G10
Montford Shrops 33 D10
Montford Bridge Shrops 33 D10
Montgarrie Aberds 83 B7
Montgomery = Trefaldwyn Powys 33 F8
Montrave Fife 76 G6
Montrose Angus 77 B10
Montsale Essex 21 B7
Monxton Hants 17 G10
Monyash Derbys 44 F5
Monymusk Aberds 83 B8
Monzie Perth 75 E11
Monzie Castle Perth 75 E11
Moodiesburn N Lanark 68 C5
Moonzie Fife 76 F6
Moor Allerton W Yorks 51 F8
Moor Crichel Dorset 9 D8
Moor End E Yorks 52 F4
Moor End York 52 D2
Moor Monkton N Yorks 51 D11
Moor of Granary Moray 87 F13
Moor of Ravenstone Dumfries 54 E6
Moor Row Cumb 56 E2
Moor Street Kent 20 E5
Moorby Lincs 46 F6
Moordown Bmouth 9 E9
Moore Halton 43 D8
Moorend Glos 16 A4
Moorends S Yorks 52 H2
Moorgate S Yorks 45 C8
Moorgreen Notts 45 H8
Moorhall Derbys 45 E7
Moorhampton Hereford 25 D10
Moorhead W Yorks 51 F7
Moorhouse Cumb 61 H9
Moorhouse Notts 45 F11
Moorlinch Som 15 H9
Moorsholm Redcar 59 E7
Moorside Gtr Man 44 B3
Moorthorpe W Yorks 45 A8
Moortown Hants 9 D10
Moortown IoW 10 F3
Moortown Lincs 46 C4
Morangie Highld 87 C10
Morar Highld 79 B9
Morborne Cambs 37 F7
Morchard Bishop Devon 7 F6
Morcombelake Dorset 8 E3
Morcott Rutland 36 E5
Morda Shrops 33 C8
Morden Dorset 9 E8
Morden London 19 E9
Mordiford Hereford 26 E2
Mordon Durham 58 D4
More Shrops 33 F9
Morebath Devon 7 D8
Morebattle Borders 62 A3
Morecambe Lancs 49 C4
Morefield Highld 86 B4
Moreleigh Devon 5 F8
Morenish Perth 75 D8
Moresby Cumb 56 D1
Moresby Parks Cumb 56 E1
Morestead Hants 10 B4
Moreton Dorset 9 F7
Moreton Essex 30 H2
Moreton Mers 42 C5
Moreton Oxon 18 A3
Moreton Staffs 34 D3
Moreton Corbet Shrops 34 C1
Moreton-in-Marsh Glos 27 E9
Moreton Jeffries Hereford 26 D3
Moreton Morrell Warks 27 C10
Moreton on Lugg Hereford 26 D2
Moreton Pinkney Northants 28 D2
Moreton Say Shrops 34 B2
Moreton Valence Glos 26 H4
Moretonhampstead Devon 5 C8
Morfa Carms 23 E10
Morfa Carms 23 G10
Morfa Bach Carms 23 E8
Morfa Bychan Gwyn 41 G7
Morfa Dinlle Gwyn 40 E6
Morfa Glas Neath 24 H5
Morfa Nefyn Gwyn 40 F4
Morfydd Denb 42 H4
Morgan's Vale Wilts 9 B10
Moriah Ceredig 32 H2
Morland Cumb 57 D7
Morley Derbys 35 A9
Morley Durham 58 D2
Morley W Yorks 51 G8
Morley Green Ches E 44 D2
Morley St Botolph Norf 39 F6
Morningside Edin 69 C11
Morningside N Lanark 69 E7
Morningthorpe Norf 39 F8
Morpeth Northumb 63 E8
Morphie Aberds 77 A10
Morrey Staffs 35 D7
Morris Green Essex 30 E4
Morriston Swansea 14 B2
Morston Norf 38 A6
Mortehoe Devon 6 B3
Mortimer W Berks 18 E3
Mortimer West End Hants 18 E3
Mortimer's Cross Hereford 25 B11
Mortlake London 19 D9
Morton Cumb 56 A5
Morton Derbys 45 F8
Morton Lincs 37 C6
Morton Lincs 46 C2
Morton Lincs 46 F2
Morton Norf 39 D7
Morton Notts 45 G11
Morton S Glos 16 B3
Morton Shrops 33 C8
Morton Bagot Warks 27 B8
Morton-on-Swale N Yorks 58 G4
Morvah Corn 2 F3
Morval Corn 4 F3
Morvich Highld 80 A1
Morvich Highld 93 J10
Morville Shrops 34 F2
Morville Heath Shrops 34 F2
Morwenstow Corn 6 E1
Mosborough S Yorks 45 D8
Moscow E Ayrs 67 B7
Mosedale Cumb 56 C5
Moseley W Mid 34 F5
Moseley W Mid 35 G6
Moseley Worcs 26 C5
Moss Argyll 78 G2
Moss Highld 79 E9
Moss S Yorks 45 A9
Moss Wrex 42 G6
Moss Bank Mers 43 C8
Moss Edge Lancs 49 E4
Moss End Brack 18 D5
Moss of Barmuckity Moray 88 B2
Moss Pit Staffs 34 C5
Moss-side Highld 87 F11
Moss Side Lancs 49 F3
Mossat Aberds 82 B6
Mossbank Shetland 96 F6
Mossbay Cumb 56 D1
Mossblown S Ayrs 67 D7
Mossbrow Gtr Man 43 D10
Mossburnford Borders 62 B2
Mossdale Dumfries 55 B9
Mossend N Lanark 68 D6
Mosser Cumb 56 D3
Mossfield Highld 87 D9
Mossgiel E Ayrs 67 D7
Mosside Angus 77 B7
Mossley Ches E 44 F2
Mossley Gtr Man 44 B3
Mossley Hill Mers 43 D6
Mosstodloch Moray 88 C3
Mosston Angus 77 C8
Mossy Lea Lancs 43 A8
Mosterton Dorset 8 D3
Moston Gtr Man 44 B2
Moston Shrops 34 C1
Moston Green Ches E 43 F10
Mostyn Flint 42 D4
Mostyn Quay Flint 42 D4
Motcombe Dorset 9 B7
Mothecombe Devon 5 G7
Motherby Cumb 56 D6
Motherwell N Lanark 68 E6
Mottingham London 19 D11
Mottisfont Hants 10 B2
Mottistone IoW 10 F3
Mottram in Longdendale Gtr Man 44 C3
Mottram St Andrew Ches E 44 E2
Mouilpied Guern 11
Mouldsworth Ches W 43 E8
Moulin Perth 76 B2
Moulsecoomb Brighton 12 F2
Moulsford Oxon 18 C2
Moulsoe M Keynes 28 D6
Moulton Ches W 43 F9
Moulton Lincs 37 C9
Moulton N Yorks 58 F3
Moulton Northants 28 B4
Moulton Suff 30 B3
Moulton V Glam 14 D6
Moulton Chapel Lincs 37 D8
Moulton Eaugate Lincs 37 D9
Moulton St Mary Norf 39 E9
Moulton Seas End Lincs 37 C9
Mounie Castle Aberds 83 A9
Mount Corn 3 D6
Mount Corn 4 E2
Mount Highld 87 G12
Mount Bures Essex 30 E6
Mount Canisp Highld 87 D10
Mount Hawke Corn 2 E6
Mount Pleasant Ches E 44 G2
Mount Pleasant Derbys 35 D8
Mount Pleasant Derbys 45 H7
Mount Pleasant Flint 42 E5
Mount Pleasant Hants 10 E1
Mount Pleasant W Yorks 51 G8
Mount Sorrel Wilts 9 B9
Mount Tabor W Yorks 51 G6
Mountain W Yorks 51 F6
Mountain Ash = Aberpennar Rhondda 14 B6
Mountain Cross Borders 69 F10
Mountain Water Pembs 22 D4
Mountbenger Borders 70 H2
Mountfield E Sus 12 D6
Mountgerald Highld 87 E8
Mountjoy Corn 3 C7
Mountnessing Essex 20 B3
Mounton Mon 15 B11
Mountsorrel Leics 36 D1
Mousehole Corn 2 G3
Mousen Northumb 71 G10
Mouswald Dumfries 60 F6
Mow Cop Ches E 44 G2
Mowhaugh Borders 62 A4
Mowsley Leics 36 G2
Moxley W Mid 34 F5
Moy Highld 80 E6
Moy Highld 87 H10
Moy Hall Highld 87 H10
Moy Ho. Moray 87 E13
Moy Lodge Highld 80 E6
Moyles Court Hants 9 D10
Moylgrove Pembs 22 B6
Muasdale Argyll 65 D7
Much Birch Hereford 26 E2
Much Cowarne Hereford 26 D3
Much Dewchurch Hereford 25 E11
Much Hadham Herts 29 G11
Much Hoole Lancs 49 G4
Much Marcle Hereford 26 E3
Much Wenlock Shrops 34 E2
Muchalls Aberds 83 D11
Muchelney Som 8 B3
Muchlarnick Corn 4 F3
Muchrachd Highld 86 H5
Muckernich Highld 87 F8
Mucking Thurrock 20 C3
Muckleford Dorset 8 E5
Mucklestone Staffs 34 B3
Muckleton Shrops 34 C1
Muckletown Aberds 83 A7
Muckley Corner Staffs 35 E6
Muckton Lincs 47 D7
Mudale Highld 93 F8
Muddiford Devon 6 C4
Mudeford Dorset 9 E10
Mudford Som 8 C4
Mudgley Som 15 G10
Mugdock Stirling 68 C4
Mugeary Highld 85 E9
Mugginton Derbys 35 A8
Muggleswick Durham 58 B1
Muie Highld 93 J9
Muir Aberds 82 E2
Muir of Fairburn Highld 86 F7
Muir of Fowlis Aberds 83 B7
Muir of Ord Highld 87 F8
Muir of Pert Angus 77 D7
Muirden Aberds 89 C7
Muirdrum Angus 77 D8
Muirhead Angus 76 D6
Muirhead Fife 76 G5
Muirhead N Lanark 68 D5
Muirhead S Ayrs 66 C6
Muirhouselaw Borders 70 H5
Muirhouses Falk 69 B9
Muirkirk E Ayrs 68 H5
Muirmill Stirling 68 B6
Muirshearlich Highld 80 E3
Muirskie Aberds 83 D10
Muirtack Aberds 89 E9
Muirton Highld 87 E10
Muirton Perth 76 E4
Muirton Perth 76 F2
Muirton Mains Highld 86 F7
Muirton of Ardblair Perth 76 C4
Muirton of Ballochy Angus 77 A9
Muiryfold Aberds 89 C7
Muker N Yorks 57 G11
Mulbarton Norf 39 E7
Mulben Moray 88 C3
Mulindry Argyll 64 C4
Mullardoch House Highld 86 H5
Mullion Corn 2 H5
Mullion Cove Corn 2 H5
Mumby Lincs 47 E9
Munderfield Row Hereford 26 C3
Munderfield Stocks Hereford 26 C3
Mundesley Norf 39 B9
Mundford Norf 38 F4
Mundham Norf 39 F9
Mundon Essex 20 A5
Mundurno Aberdeen 83 B11
Munerigie Highld 80 C4
Muness Shetland 96 C8
Mungasdale Highld 86 B2
Mungrisdale Cumb 56 C5
Munlochy Highld 87 F9
Munsley Hereford 26 D3
Munslow Shrops 33 G11
Murchington Devon 5 C7
Murcott Oxon 28 G2
Murkle Highld 94 D3
Murlaggan Highld 80 D2
Murlaggan Highld 80 E5
Murra Orkney 95 H3
Murrayfield Edin 69 C11
Murrow Cambs 37 E9
Mursley Bucks 28 F5
Murthill Angus 77 B7
Murthly Perth 76 D3
Murton Cumb 57 D9
Murton Durham 58 B4
Murton Northumb 71 F8
Murton York 52 D2
Musbury Devon 8 E1
Muscoates N Yorks 52 A2
Musdale Argyll 74 E2
Musselburgh E Loth 70 C2
Muston Leics 36 B4
Muston N Yorks 53 B6
Mustow Green Worcs 26 A5
Mutehill Dumfries 55 E9
Mutford Suff 39 G10
Muthill Perth 75 F11
Mutterton Devon 7 F9
Muxton Telford 34 D3
Mybster Highld 94 E3
Myddfai Carms 24 F4
Myddle Shrops 33 C10
Mydroilyn Ceredig 23 A9
Myerscough Lancs 49 F4
Mylor Bridge Corn 3 F7
Mynachlog-ddu Pembs 22 C6
Myndtown Shrops 33 G9
Mynydd Bach Ceredig 32 H3
Mynydd-bach Mon 15 B10
Mynydd Bodafon Anglesey 40 B6
Mynydd-isa Flint 42 F5
Mynyddygarreg Carms 23 F9
Mynytho Gwyn 40 G5
Myrebird Aberds 83 D9
Myrelandhorn Highld 94 E4
Myreside Perth 76 E5
Myrtle Hill Carms 24 E4
Mytchett Sur 18 F5
Mytholm W Yorks 50 G5
Mytholmroyd W Yorks 50 G6
Myton-on-Swale N Yorks 51 C10
Mytton Shrops 33 D10

N

Na Gearrannan W Isles 90 C6
Naast Highld 91 J13
Naburn York 52 E1
Nackington Kent 21 F8
Nacton Suff 31 D9
Nafferton E Yorks 53 D6
Nailbridge Glos 26 G3
Nailsbourne Som 7 D11
Nailsea N Som 15 D10
Nailstone Leics 35 E10
Nailsworth Glos 16 B5
Nairn Highld 87 F11
Nalderswood Sur 19 G9
Nancegollan Corn 2 F5
Nancledra Corn 2 F3
Nanhoron Gwyn 40 G4
Nannau Gwyn 32 C3
Nannerch Flint 42 F4
Nanpantan Leics 35 D11
Nanpean Corn 3 D8
Nanstallon Corn 3 C9
Nant-ddu Powys 25 G7
Nant-glas Powys 24 B6
Nant Peris Gwyn 41 E8
Nant Uchaf Denb 42 G3
Nant-y-Bai Carms 24 D4
Nant-y-cafn Neath 24 H5
Nant-y-derry Mon 25 H10
Nant-y-ffin Carms 23 C10
Nant-y-moel Bridgend 14 B5
Nant-y-pandy Conwy 41 C8
Nanternis Ceredig 23 A8
Nantgaredig Carms 23 D9
Nantgarw Rhondda 15 C7
Nantglyn Denb 42 F3
Nantgwyn Powys 32 H5
Nantlle Gwyn 41 E7
Nantmawr Shrops 33 C8
Nantmel Powys 25 B7
Nantmor Gwyn 41 F8
Nantwich Ches E 43 G9
Nantycaws Carms 23 E9
Nantyffyllon Bridgend 14 B4
Nantyglo Bl Gwent 25 G8
Naphill Bucks 18 B5
Nappa N Yorks 50 D4
Napton on the Hill Warks 27 B11
Narberth = Arberth Pembs 22 E6
Narborough Leics 35 F11
Narborough Norf 38 D3
Nasareth Gwyn 40 E6
Naseby Northants 36 H2
Nash Bucks 28 E4
Nash Hereford 25 B10
Nash Newport 15 C9
Nash Shrops 26 A3
Nash Lee Bucks 28 H5
Nassington Northants 37 F6
Nasty Herts 29 F10
Nateby Cumb 57 F9
Nateby Lancs 49 E4
Natland Cumb 57 H7
Naughton Suff 31 D7
Naunton Glos 27 F8
Naunton Worcs 26 E5
Naunton Beauchamp Worcs 26 C6
Navenby Lincs 46 G3
Navestock Heath Essex 20 B2
Navestock Side Essex 20 B2
Navidale Highld 93 H13
Nawton N Yorks 52 A2
Nayland Suff 30 E6
Nazeing Essex 29 H11
Neacroft Hants 9 E10
Neal's Green Warks 35 G9
Neap Shetland 96 H7
Near Sawrey Cumb 56 G5
Neasham Darl 58 E4
Neath = Castell-Nedd Neath 14 B3
Neath Abbey Neath 14 B3
Neatishead Norf 39 C9
Nebo Anglesey 40 A6
Nebo Ceredig 24 B2
Nebo Conwy 41 E10
Nebo Gwyn 40 E6
Necton Norf 38 E4
Nedd Highld 92 F4
Nedderton Northumb 63 E8
Nedging Tye Suff 31 D7
Needham Norf 39 G8
Needham Market Suff 31 C7
Needingworth Cambs 29 A10
Needwood Staffs 35 C7
Neen Savage Shrops 34 H2
Neen Sollars Shrops 26 A3
Neenton Shrops 34 G2
Nefyn Gwyn 40 F5
Neilston E Renf 68 E3
Neinthirion Powys 32 E5
Neithrop Oxon 27 D11
Nelly Andrews Green Powys 33 E8
Nelson Caerph 15 B7
Nelson Lancs 50 F4
Nelson Village Northumb 63 F8
Nemphlar S Lanark 69 F7
Nempnett Thrubwell N Som 15 E11
Nene Terrace Lincs 37 E8
Nenthall Cumb 57 B9
Nenthead Cumb 57 B9
Nenthorn Borders 70 G5
Nerabus Argyll 64 C3
Nercwys Flint 42 F5
Nerston S Lanark 68 E5
Nesbit Northumb 71 G8
Ness Ches W 42 E6
Nesscliffe Shrops 33 D9
Neston Ches W 42 E5
Neston Wilts 16 E5
Nether Alderley Ches E 44 E2
Nether Blainslie Borders 70 F4
Nether Booth Derbys 44 D5
Nether Broughton Leics 36 C2
Nether Burrow Lancs 50 B2
Nether Cerne Dorset 8 E5
Nether Compton Dorset 8 C4
Nether Crimond Aberds 89 F8
Nether Dalgliesh Borders 61 C8
Nether Dallachy Moray 88 B3
Nether Exe Devon 7 F8
Nether Glasslaw Aberds 89 C8
Nether Handwick Angus 76 C6
Nether Haugh S Yorks 45 C8
Nether Heage Derbys 45 G7
Nether Heyford Northants 28 C3
Nether Hindhope Borders 62 B3
Nether Howecleuch S Lanark 60 B6
Nether Kellet Lancs 49 C5
Nether Kinmundy Aberds 89 D10
Nether Langwith Notts 45 E9
Nether Leask Aberds 89 E10
Nether Lenshie Aberds 89 D6
Nether Monynut Borders 70 D6
Nether Padley Derbys 44 E6
Nether Park Aberds 89 C10
Nether Poppleton York 52 D1
Nether Silton N Yorks 58 G5
Nether Stowey Som 7 C10
Nether Urquhart Fife 76 G4
Nether Wallop Hants 17 H10
Nether Wasdale Cumb 56 F3
Nether Whitacre Warks 35 F8
Nether Worton Oxon 27 E11
Netheravon Wilts 17 G8
Netherbrae Aberds 89 C7
Netherbrough Orkney 95 G4
Netherburn S Lanark 69 F7
Netherbury Dorset 8 E3
Netherby Cumb 61 F9
Netherby N Yorks 51 E9
Nethercote Warks 28 B2
Nethercott Devon 6 C3
Netherend Glos 16 A2
Netherfield E Sus 12 E6
Netherhampton Wilts 9 B10
Netherlaw Dumfries 55 E10
Netherley Aberds 83 D10
Netherley Mers 43 D7
Nethermill Dumfries 60 E6
Nethermuir Aberds 89 D9
Netherplace E Renf 68 E4
Netherseal Derbys 35 D8
Netherthird E Ayrs 67 E8
Netherthong W Yorks 44 B5
Netherthorpe S Yorks 45 D9
Netherton Angus 77 B8
Netherton Devon 5 D9
Netherton Hants 17 F10
Netherton Mers 42 B6
Netherton Northumb 62 C5
Netherton Oxon 17 B11
Netherton Perth 76 B4
Netherton Stirling 68 C4
Netherton W Mid 34 G5
Netherton W Yorks 44 A5
Netherton W Yorks 51 H8
Netherton Worcs 26 D6
Nethertown Cumb 56 F1
Nethertown Highld 94 C5
Netherwitton Northumb 63 D7
Netherwood E Ayrs 68 H5
Nethy Bridge Highld 82 A2
Netley Hants 10 D3
Netley Marsh Hants 10 C2
Netteswell Essex 29 G11
Nettlebed Oxon 18 C4
Nettlebridge Som 16 G3
Nettlecombe Dorset 8 E4
Nettleden Herts 29 G7
Nettleham Lincs 46 E4
Nettlestead Kent 20 F3
Nettlestead Green Kent 20 F3
Nettlestone IoW 10 E5
Nettlesworth Durham 58 B3
Nettleton Lincs 46 B5
Nettleton Wilts 16 D5
Neuadd Carms 24 F3
Nevendon Essex 20 B4
Nevern Pembs 22 B5
New Abbey Dumfries 60 G5
New Aberdour Aberds 89 B8
New Addington London 19 E10
New Alresford Hants 10 A4
New Alyth Perth 76 C5
New Arley Warks 35 G8
New Ash Green Kent 20 E3
New Barn Kent 20 E3
New Barnetby N Lincs 46 A4
New Barton Northants 28 B5
New Bewick Northumb 62 A6
New-bigging Angus 76 C5
New Bilton Warks 35 H10
New Bolingbroke Lincs 47 G7
New Boultham Lincs 46 E3
New Bradwell M Keynes 28 D5
New Brancepeth Durham 58 B3
New Bridge Wrex 33 A8
New Brighton Flint 42 F5
New Brighton Mers 42 C6
New Brinsley Notts 45 G8
New Broughton Wrex 42 G6
New Buckenham Norf 39 F6
New Byth Aberds 89 C8
New Catton Norf 39 D8
New Cheriton Hants 10 B4
New Costessey Norf 39 D7
New Cowper Cumb 56 B3
New Cross Ceredig 32 H2
New Cross London 19 D10
New Cumnock E Ayrs 67 E9
New Deer Aberds 89 D8
New Delaval Northumb 63 F8
New Duston Northants 28 B4
New Earswick York 52 D2
New Edlington S Yorks 45 C9
New Elgin Moray 88 B2
New Ellerby E Yorks 53 F7
New Eltham London 19 D11
New End Worcs 27 C7
New Farnley W Yorks 51 F8
New Ferry Mers 42 D6
New Fryston W Yorks 51 G10
New Galloway Dumfries 55 B9
New Gilston Fife 77 G7
New Grimsby Scilly 2 C2
New Hainford Norf 39 D8
New Hartley Northumb 63 F9
New Haw Sur 19 E7
New Hedges Pembs 22 F6
New Herrington T&W 58 A4
New Hinksey Oxon 18 A2
New Holkham Norf 38 B4
New Holland N Lincs 53 G6
New Houghton Derbys 45 F8
New Houghton Norf 38 C3
New Houses N Yorks 50 B4
New Humberstone Leicester 36 E2
New Hutton Cumb 57 G7
New Hythe Kent 20 F4
New Inn Carms 23 C9
New Inn Mon 15 A10
New Inn Pembs 22 C5
New Inn Torf 15 B9
New Invention Shrops 33 H8
New Invention W Mid 34 E5
New Kelso Highld 86 G2
New Kingston Notts 35 C11
New Lanark S Lanark 69 F7
New Lane Lancs 43 A7
New Lane End Warr 43 C9
New Leake Lincs 47 G8
New Leeds Aberds 89 C9
New Longton Lancs 49 G5
New Luce Dumfries 54 C4
New Malden London 19 E9
New Marske Redcar 59 D7
New Marton Shrops 33 B9
New Micklefield W Yorks 51 F10
New Mill Aberds 83 E9
New Mill Herts 28 G6
New Mill W Yorks 44 B5
New Mill Wilts 17 E8
New Mills Ches E 43 D10
New Mills Corn 3 D7
New Mills Derbys 44 D3
New Mills Powys 33 E6
New Milton Hants 9 E11
New Moat Pembs 22 D5
New Ollerton Notts 45 F10
New Oscott W Mid 35 F6
New Park N Yorks 51 D8
New Pitsligo Aberds 89 C8
New Polzeath Corn 3 B8
New Quay = Ceinewydd Ceredig 23 A8
New Rackheath Norf 39 D8
New Radnor Powys 25 B9
New Rent Cumb 56 C6
New Ridley Northumb 62 H6
New Road Side N Yorks 50 E5
New Romney Kent 13 D9
New Rossington S Yorks 45 C10
New Row Ceredig 24 A4
New Row Lancs 50 F2
New Row N Yorks 59 E7
New Sarum Wilts 9 A10
New Silksworth T&W 58 A4
New Stevenston N Lanark 68 E6
New Street Staffs 44 G4
New Street Lane Shrops 34 B2
New Swanage Dorset 9 F9
New Totley S Yorks 45 E7
New Town E Loth 70 C3
New Tredegar = Tredegar Newydd Caerph 15 A7
New Trows S Lanark 69 G7
New Ulva Argyll 72 E6
New Walsoken Cambs 37 E10
New Waltham NE Lincs 46 B6
New Whittington Derbys 45 E7
New Wimpole Cambs 29 D10
New Winton E Loth 70 C3
New Yatt Oxon 27 G10
New York Lincs 46 G6
New York N Yorks 51 C7
Newall W Yorks 51 E7
Newark Orkney 95 D8
Newark Pboro 37 E8
Newark-on-Trent Notts 45 G11
Newarthill N Lanark 68 E6
Newbarns Cumb 49 B2
Newbattle Midloth 70 D2
Newbiggin Cumb 49 C2
Newbiggin Cumb 56 D6
Newbiggin Cumb 56 G2
Newbiggin Cumb 57 B7
Newbiggin Cumb 57 D8
Newbiggin Durham 57 D11
Newbiggin N Yorks 57 G11
Newbiggin N Yorks 57 H11
Newbiggin-by-the-Sea Northumb 63 E9
Newbiggin-on-Lune Cumb 57 F9
Newbigging Angus 77 D7
Newbigging Angus 77 D7
Newbigging S Lanark 69 F9
Newbold Derbys 45 E7
Newbold Leics 35 D10
Newbold on Avon Warks 35 H10
Newbold on Stour Warks 27 D9
Newbold Pacey Warks 27 C9
Newbold Verdon Leics 35 E10
Newborough Anglesey 40 D6
Newborough Pboro 37 E8
Newborough Staffs 35 C7
Newbottle Northants 28 E2
Newbottle T&W 58 A4
Newbourne Suff 31 D9
Newbridge Caerph 15 B8
Newbridge Ceredig 23 A10
Newbridge Corn 2 F3
Newbridge Corn 4 E4
Newbridge Dumfries 60 F5
Newbridge Edin 69 C10
Newbridge Hants 10 C1
Newbridge IoW 10 F3
Newbridge Pembs 22 C4
Newbridge Green Worcs 26 E5
Newbridge-on-Usk Mon 15 B9
Newbridge on Wye Powys 25 C7
Newbrough Northumb 62 G4
Newbuildings Devon 7 F6
Newburgh Aberds 89 C9
Newburgh Aberds 89 F9
Newburgh Borders 61 B9
Newburgh Fife 76 F5
Newburgh Lancs 43 A7
Newburn T&W 63 G7
Newbury W Berks 17 E11
Newbury Park London 19 C11
Newby Cumb 57 D7
Newby Lancs 50 E4
Newby N Yorks 50 B3
Newby N Yorks 58 E6
Newby N Yorks 59 G11
Newby Bridge Cumb 56 H5
Newby East Cumb 61 H10
Newby West Cumb 56 A5
Newby Wiske N Yorks 58 H4
Newcastle Mon 25 G11
Newcastle Shrops 33 G8
Newcastle Emlyn = Castell Newydd Emlyn Carms 23 B8
Newcastle-under-Lyme Staffs 44 H2
Newcastle Upon Tyne T&W 63 G8
Newcastleton or Copshaw Holm Borders 61 E10
Newchapel Pembs 23 C7
Newchapel Powys 32 G5
Newchapel Staffs 44 G2
Newchapel Sur 12 B2
Newchurch Carms 23 D8
Newchurch IoW 10 F4
Newchurch Kent 13 C9
Newchurch Lancs 50 F4
Newchurch Mon 15 B10
Newchurch Powys 25 C9
Newchurch Staffs 35 C7
Newcott Devon 7 F11
Newcraighall Edin 70 C2
Newdigate Sur 19 G8
Newell Green Brack 18 D5
Newenden Kent 13 D7
Newent Glos 26 F4
Newerne Glos 16 A3
Newfield Durham 58 C3
Newfield Highld 87 D10
Newford Scilly 2 C3
Newfound Hants 18 F2
Newgale Pembs 22 D3
Newgate Norf 39 A6
Newgate Street Herts 19 A10
Newhall Ches E 43 H9
Newhall Derbys 35 C8
Newhall House Highld 87 E9
Newhall Point Highld 87 E10
Newham Northumb 71 H10
Newham Hall Northumb 71 H10
Newhaven Derbys 44 G5
Newhaven E Sus 12 F3
Newhaven Edin 69 C11
Newhey Gtr Man 44 A3
Newholm N Yorks 59 E9
Newhouse N Lanark 68 D6
Newick E Sus 12 D3
Newingreen Kent 13 C10
Newington Kent 20 E5
Newington Kent 21 E10
Newington Kent 21 H8
Newington Notts 45 C10
Newington Oxon 18 B3
Newington Shrops 33 G10
Newland Glos 26 H2
Newland Hull 53 F6
Newland N Yorks 52 G2
Newland Worcs 26 D4
Newlandrig Midloth 70 D2
Newlands Borders 61 D11
Newlands Highld 87 G10
Newlands Moray 88 C3
Newlands Northumb 62 H6
Newland's Corner Sur 19 G7
Newlands of Geise Highld 94 D2
Newlands of Tynet Moray 88 B3
Newlands Park Anglesey 40 B4
Newlandsmuir S Lanark 68 E5
Newlot Orkney 95 G6
Newlyn Corn 2 G3
Newmachar Aberds 83 B10
Newmains N Lanark 69 E7
Newmarket Suff 30 B3
Newmarket W Isles 91 D9
Newmill Borders 61 B10
Newmill Corn 2 F3
Newmill Moray 88 C4
Newmill of Inshewan Angus 77 A7
Newmills of Boyne Aberds 88 C5
Newmiln Perth 76 D4
Newmilns E Ayrs 67 C8
Newnham Cambs 29 C11
Newnham Glos 26 G3
Newnham Hants 18 F4
Newnham Herts 29 E9
Newnham Kent 20 F6
Newnham Northants 28 C2
Newnham Bridge Worcs 26 B3
Newpark Fife 77 F7
Newport Devon 6 C4
Newport E Yorks 52 F4
Newport Essex 30 E2
Newport Highld 94 H3
Newport IoW 10 F4
Newport = Casnewydd Newport 15 C9
Newport Norf 39 D11
Newport = Trefdraeth Pembs 22 C5
Newport Telford 34 D3
Newport-on-Tay Fife 77 E7
Newport Pagnell M Keynes 28 D5
Newpound Common W Sus 11 B9
Newquay Corn 3 C7
Newsbank Ches E 44 F2
Newseat Aberds 89 D10
Newseat Aberds 89 E7
Newsham N Yorks 51 A9
Newsham N Yorks 58 E2
Newsham Northumb 63 F9
Newsholme E Yorks 52 G3
Newsholme Lancs 50 D4
Newsome W Yorks 44 A5
Newstead Borders 70 G4
Newstead Northumb 71 H10
Newstead Notts 45 G9
Newthorpe N Yorks 51 F10
Newton Argyll 73 D9
Newton Borders 62 A1
Newton Bridgend 14 D4
Newton Cambs 29 D11
Newton Cambs 37 D10
Newton Cardiff 15 D8
Newton Ches W 43 E8
Newton Ches W 43 F7
Newton Ches W 43 G8
Newton Cumb 49 B2
Newton Derbys 45 G8
Newton Dorset 9 C6
Newton Dumfries 61 D7
Newton Dumfries 61 F8
Newton Gtr Man 44 C3
Newton Hereford 25 E10
Newton Hereford 26 C2
Newton Highld 87 E10
Newton Highld 87 G10
Newton Highld 92 F5
Newton Highld 94 F5
Newton Lancs 49 F4
Newton Lancs 50 B1
Newton Lancs 50 D2
Newton Lincs 36 B6
Newton Moray 88 B1
Newton Norf 38 D4
Newton Northants 36 G4
Newton Northumb 62 G6
Newton Notts 36 A2
Newton Perth 75 D11
Newton S Lanark 68 D5
Newton S Lanark 69 G8
Newton S Yorks 45 B9
Newton Staffs 34 C6
Newton Suff 30 D6
Newton Swansea 14 C2
Newton W Loth 69 C9
Newton Warks 35 H11
Newton Wilts 9 B11
Newton Abbot Devon 5 D9
Newton Arlosh Cumb 61 H7
Newton Aycliffe Durham 58 D3
Newton Bewley Hrtlpl 58 D5
Newton Blossomville M Keynes 28 C6
Newton Bromswold Northants 28 B6
Newton Burgoland Leics 35 E9
Newton by Toft Lincs 46 D4
Newton Ferrers Devon 4 G6
Newton Flotman Norf 39 F8
Newton Hall Northumb 62 G6
Newton Harcourt Leics 36 F2
Newton Heath Gtr Man 44 B2
Newton Ho. Aberds 83 A8
Newton Kyme N Yorks 51 E10
Newton-le-Willows Mers 43 C8
Newton-le-Willows N Yorks 58 H3
Newton Longville Bucks 28 E5
Newton Mearns E Renf 68 E4
Newton Morrell N Yorks 58 F3
Newton Mulgrave N Yorks 59 E8
Newton of Ardtoe Highld 79 D9
Newton of Balcanquhal Perth 76 F4
Newton of Falkland Fife 76 G5
Newton on Ayr S Ayrs 66 D6
Newton on Ouse N Yorks 51 D11
Newton-on-Rawcliffe N Yorks 59 G9
Newton-on-the-Moor Northumb 63 C7
Newton on Trent Lincs 46 E2
Newton Park Argyll 73 G10
Newton Poppleford Devon 7 H9
Newton Purcell Oxon 28 E3
Newton Regis Warks 35 E8
Newton Reigny Cumb 57 C6
Newton St Cyres Devon 7 G7
Newton St Faith Norf 39 D8
Newton St Loe Bath 16 E4
Newton St Petrock Devon 6 E3
Newton Solney Derbys 35 C8
Newton Stacey Hants 17 G11
Newton Stewart Dumfries 55 C7
Newton Tony Wilts 17 G9
Newton Tracey Devon 6 D4
Newton under Roseberry Redcar 59 E6
Newton upon Derwent E Yorks 52 E3
Newton Valence Hants 10 A6
Newtonairds Dumfries 60 E4
Newtongrange Midloth 70 D2
Newtonhill Aberds 83 D11
Newtonhill Highld 87 G8
Newtonmill Angus 77 A9
Newtonmore Highld 81 D9
Newtown Argyll 73 C9
Newtown Ches W 43 E8
Newtown Corn 2 G6
Newtown Cumb 56 B2
Newtown Cumb 61 G11
Newtown Derbys 44 D3
Newtown Devon 7 D6
Newtown Glos 16 A3
Newtown Glos 26 E6
Newtown Hants 10 B2
Newtown Hants 10 C4
Newtown Hants 10 C1
Newtown Hants 10 C5
Newtown Hants 10 D3
Newtown Hants 17 E11
Newtown Hereford 26 D3
Newtown Highld 80 C5
Newtown IoM 48 E3
Newtown IoW 10 E3
Newtown Northumb 62 C6
Newtown Northumb 71 G8
Newtown Northumb 71 H9
Newtown Poole 9 E9
Newtown = Y Drenewydd Powys 33 F7
Newtown Shrops 33 B10
Newtown Staffs 44 F4
Newtown Staffs 44 F3
Newtown Wilts 9 B8
Newtown Linford Leics 35 E11
Newtown St Boswells Borders 70 G4
Newtown Unthank Leics 35 E10
Newtyle Angus 76 C5
Neyland Pembs 22 F4
Niarbyl IoM 48 E2
Nibley S Glos 16 C3
Nibley Green Glos 16 B4
Nibon Shetland 96 F5
Nicholashayne Devon 7 E10
Nicholaston Swansea 23 H10
Nidd N Yorks 51 C9
Nigg Aberdeen 83 C11
Nigg Highld 87 D11
Nigg Ferry Highld 87 E10
Nightcott Som 7 D7
Nilig Denb 42 G3
Nine Ashes Essex 20 A2
Nine Mile Burn Midloth 69 E10
Nine Wells Pembs 22 D2
Ninebanks Northumb 57 A9
Ninfield E Sus 12 E6
Ningwood IoW 10 F2
Nisbet Borders 70 H5
Nisthouse Orkney 95 G4
Nisthouse Shetland 96 G7
Niton IoW 10 G4
Nitshill Glasgow 68 D4
No Man's Heath Ches W 43 H8
No Man's Heath Warks 35 E8
Noak Hill London 20 B2
Noblethorpe S Yorks 44 B6
Nobottle Northants 28 B3
Nocton Lincs 46 F4
Noke Oxon 28 G2
Nolton Pembs 22 E3
Nolton Haven Pembs 22 E3
Nomansland Devon 7 E7
Nomansland Wilts 10 C1
Noneley Shrops 33 C10
Nonikiln Highld 87 D9
Nonington Kent 21 F9
Noonsbrough Shetland 96 H4
Norbreck Blackpool 49 E3
Norbridge Hereford 26 D4
Norbury Ches E 43 H8
Norbury Derbys 35 A7
Norbury Shrops 33 F9
Norbury Staffs 34 C3
Nordelph Norf 38 E1
Norden Gtr Man 44 A2
Norden Heath Dorset 9 F8
Nordley Shrops 34 F2
Norham Northumb 71 F8
Norley Ches W 43 E8
Norleywood Hants 10 E2
Norman Cross Cambs 37 F7
Normanby N Lincs 52 H4
Normanby N Yorks 52 A3
Normanby Redcar 59 E6
Normanby-by-Spital Lincs 46 D4
Normanby by Stow Lincs 46 D2
Normanby le Wold Lincs 46 C5
Normandy Sur 18 F6
Norman's Bay E Sus 12 F5
Norman's Green Devon 7 F9
Normanstone Suff 39 F11
Normanton Derby 35 B9
Normanton Leics 36 A4
Normanton Lincs 46 H3
Normanton Notts 45 G11
Normanton Rutland 36 E5
Normanton W Yorks 51 G9
Normanton le Heath Leics 35 D9
Normanton on Soar Notts 35 C11
Normanton-on-the-Wolds Notts 36 B2
Normanton on Trent Notts 45 F11
Normoss Lancs 49 F3
Norney Sur 18 G6
Norrington Common Wilts 16 E5
Norris Green Mers 43 C6
Norris Hill Leics 35 D9
North Anston S Yorks 45 D9
North Aston Oxon 27 F11
North Baddesley Hants 10 C2
North Ballachulish Highld 74 A3
North Barrow Som 8 B5
North Barsham Norf 38 B5
North Benfleet Essex 20 C4
North Bersted W Sus 11 D8
North Berwick E Loth 70 B4
North Boarhunt Hants 10 C5
North Bovey Devon 5 C8
North Bradley Wilts 16 F5
North Brentor Devon 4 C5
North Brewham Som 16 H4
North Buckland Devon 6 B3
North Burlingham Norf 39 D9
North Cadbury Som 8 B5
North Cairn Dumfries 54 B2
North Carlton Lincs 46 E3
North Carrine Argyll 65 H7
North Cave E Yorks 52 F4
North Cerney Glos 27 H7
North Charford Wilts 9 C10
North Charlton Northumb 63 A7
North Cheriton Som 8 B5
North Cliff E Yorks 53 E8
North Cliffe E Yorks 52 F4
North Clifton Notts 46 E2
North Cockerington Lincs 47 C7
North Coker Som 8 C4
North Collafirth Shetland 96 E5
North Common E Sus 12 D2
North Connel Argyll 74 D2
North Cornelly Bridgend 14 C4
North Cotes Lincs 47 B7
North Cove Suff 39 G10
North Cowton N Yorks 58 F3
North Crawley M Keynes 28 D6
North Cray London 19 D11
North Creake Norf 38 B4
North Curry Som 8 B2
North Dalton E Yorks 52 D5
North Dawn Orkney 95 H5
North Deighton N Yorks 51 D9
North Duffield N Yorks 52 F2
North Elkington Lincs 46 C6
North Elmham Norf 38 C5

Nor–Pen 129

North Elmshall W Yorks 45 A8
North End Bucks 28 F5
North End E Yorks 53 F8
North End Essex 30 G3
North End Hants 17 E11
North End Lincs 37 A8
North End N Som 15 E10
North End Ptsmth 10 D5
North End Som 8 B1
North End W Sus 11 D10
North Erradale Highld 91 J12
North Fambridge Essex 20 B5
North Fearns Highld 85 E10
North Featherstone W Yorks 51 G10
North Ferriby E Yorks 52 G5
North Frodingham E Yorks 53 D7
North Gluss Shetland 96 F5
North Gorley Hants 9 C10
North Green Norf 39 G8
North Green Suff 31 B10
North Greetwell Lincs 46 E4
North Grimston N Yorks 52 C4
North Halley Orkney 95 H6
North Halling Medway 20 E4
North Hayling Hants 10 D6
North Hazelrigg Northumb 71 G9
North Heasley Devon 7 C6
North Heath W Sus 11 B9
North Hill Cambs 37 H10
North Hill Corn 4 D3
North Hinksey Oxon 27 H11
North Holmwood Sur 19 G8
North Howden E Yorks 52 F3
North Huish Devon 5 F8
North Hykeham Lincs 46 F3
North Johnston Pembs 22 E4
North Kelsey Lincs 46 B4
North Kelsey Moor Lincs 46 B4
North Kessock Highld 87 G9
North Killingholme N Lincs 53 H7
North Kilvington N Yorks 58 H5
North Kilworth Leics 36 G2
North Kirkton Aberds 89 C11
North Kiscadale N Ayrs 66 D3
North Kyme Lincs 46 G5
North Lancing W Sus 11 D10
North Lee Bucks 28 H5
North Leigh Oxon 27 G10
North Leverton with Habblesthorpe Notts 45 D11
North Littleton Worcs 27 D7
North Lopham Norf 38 G6
North Luffenham Rutland 36 E5
North Marden W Sus 11 C7
North Marston Bucks 28 F4
North Middleton Midloth 70 E2
North Middleton Northumb 62 A6
North Molton Devon 7 D6
North Moreton Oxon 18 C2
North Mundham W Sus 11 D7
North Muskham Notts 45 G11
North Newbald E Yorks 52 F5
North Newington Oxon 27 E11
North Newnton Wilts 17 F8
North Newton Som 8 A1
North Nibley Glos 16 B4
North Oakley Hants 18 F2
North Ockendon London 20 C2
North Ormesby Mbro 58 D6
North Ormsby Lincs 46 C6
North Otterington N Yorks 58 H4
North Owersby Lincs 46 C4
North Perrott Som 8 D3
North Petherton Som 8 A1
North Petherwin Corn 4 C3
North Pickenham Norf 38 E4
North Piddle Worcs 26 C6
North Poorton Dorset 8 E4
North Port Argyll 74 E3
North Queensferry Fife 69 B10
North Radworthy Devon 7 C6
North Rauceby Lincs 46 H4
North Reston Lincs 47 D7
North Rigton N Yorks 51 E8
North Rode Ches E 44 F2
North Roe Shetland 96 E5
North Runcton Norf 38 D2
North Sandwick Shetland 96 D7
North Scale Cumb 49 C1
North Scarle Lincs 46 F2
North Seaton Northumb 63 E8
North Shian Argyll 74 C2
North Shields T&W 63 G9
North Shoebury Southend 20 C6
North Shore Blackpool 49 F3
North Side Cumb 56 D2
North Side Pboro 37 F8
North Skelton Redcar 59 E7
North Somercotes Lincs 47 C8
North Stainley N Yorks 51 B8
North Stainmore Cumb 57 E10
North Stifford Thurrock 20 C3
North Stoke Bath 16 E4
North Stoke Oxon 18 C3
North Stoke W Sus 11 C9
North Street Hants 10 A5
North Street Kent 21 F7
North Street Medway 20 D5
North Street W Berks 18 D3
North Sunderland Northumb 71 G11
North Tamerton Corn 6 G2
North Tawton Devon 6 F5
North Thoresby Lincs 46 C6
North Tidworth Wilts 17 G9
North Togston Northumb 63 C8
North Tuddenham Norf 38 D6
North Walbottle T&W 63 G7
North Walsham Norf 39 B8
North Waltham Hants 18 G2
North Warnborough Hants 18 F4
North Water Bridge Angus 83 G8
North Watten Highld 94 E4
North Weald Bassett Essex 19 A11
North Wheatley Notts 45 D11
North Whilborough Devon 5 E9
North Wick Bath 16 E2
North Willingham Lincs 46 D5
North Wingfield Derbys 45 F8
North Witham Lincs 36 C5
North Woolwich London 19 D11
North Wootton Dorset 8 C5
North Wootton Norf 38 C2
North Wootton Som 16 G2
North Wraxall Wilts 16 D5
North Wroughton Swindon 17 C8
Northacre Norf 38 F5
Northallerton N Yorks 58 G4
Northam Devon 6 D3
Northam Soton 10 C3
Northampton Northants 28 B4
Northaw Herts 19 A9
Northbeck Lincs 37 A6
Northborough Pboro 37 E7
Northbourne Kent 21 F10
Northbridge Street E Sus 12 D6
Northchapel W Sus 11 B8
Northchurch Herts 28 H6
Northcott Devon 6 G2
Northdown Kent 21 D10
Northdyke Orkney 95 F3
Northend Bath 16 E4
Northend Bucks 18 B4
Northend Warks 27 C10
Northenden Gtr Man 44 C2
Northfield Aberdeen 83 C11
Northfield Borders 71 D8
Northfield E Yorks 52 G6
Northfield W Mid 34 H6
Northfields Lincs 36 E6
Northfleet Kent 20 D3
Northgate Lincs 37 C7
Northhouse Borders 61 C10
Northiam E Sus 13 D7
Northill C Beds 29 D8
Northington Hants 18 H2
Northlands Lincs 47 G7
Northlea Durham 58 A5
Northleach Glos 27 G8
Northleigh Devon 7 G10
Northlew Devon 6 G4
Northmoor Oxon 17 A11
Northmoor Green or Moorland Som 8 A2
Northmuir Angus 76 B6
Northney Hants 10 D6
Northolt London 19 C8
Northop Flint 42 F5
Northop Hall Flint 42 F5
Northorpe Lincs 37 B8
Northorpe Lincs 37 D6
Northorpe Lincs 46 C2
Northover Som 8 B4
Northover Som 15 H10
Northowram W Yorks 51 G7
Northport Dorset 9 F8
Northpunds Shetland 96 L6
Northrepps Norf 39 B8
Northtown Orkney 95 J5
Northway Glos 26 E6
Northwich Ches W 43 E9
Northwick S Glos 16 C2
Northwold Norf 38 F3
Northwood Derbys 44 F6
Northwood IoW 10 E3
Northwood Kent 21 E10
Northwood London 19 B7
Northwood Shrops 33 B10
Northwood Green Glos 26 G4
Norton E Sus 12 F3
Norton Glos 26 F5
Norton Halton 43 D8
Norton Herts 29 E9
Norton IoW 10 F2
Norton Mon 25 G11
Norton Northants 28 B3
Norton Notts 45 E9
Norton Powys 25 B10
Norton S Yorks 51 H11
Norton Shrops 33 G10
Norton Shrops 34 E1
Norton Shrops 34 E3
Norton Stockton 58 D5
Norton Suff 30 B6
Norton W Sus 11 D8
Norton W Sus 11 E7
Norton Wilts 16 C5
Norton Worcs 26 C5
Norton Worcs 27 D7
Norton Bavant Wilts 16 G6
Norton Bridge Staffs 34 B4
Norton Canes Staffs 34 E6
Norton Canon Hereford 25 D10
Norton Corner Norf 39 C6
Norton Disney Lincs 46 G2
Norton East Staffs 34 E6
Norton Ferris Wilts 16 H4
Norton Fitzwarren Som 7 D10
Norton Green IoW 10 F2
Norton Hawkfield Bath 16 E2
Norton Heath Essex 20 A3
Norton in Hales Shrops 34 B3
Norton-in-the-Moors Stoke 44 G2
Norton-Juxta-Twycross Leics 35 E9
Norton-le-Clay N Yorks 51 B10
Norton Lindsey Warks 27 B9
Norton Malreward Bath 16 E3
Norton Mandeville Essex 20 A2
Norton-on-Derwent N Yorks 52 B3
Norton St Philip Som 16 F4
Norton sub Hamdon Som 8 C3
Norton Woodseats S Yorks 45 D7
Norwell Notts 45 F11
Norwell Woodhouse Notts 45 F11
Norwich Norf 39 E8
Norwick Shetland 96 B8
Norwood Derbys 45 D8
Norwood Hill Sur 19 G9
Norwoodside Cambs 37 F10
Noseley Leics 36 F3
Noss Shetland 96 M5
Noss Mayo Devon 4 G6
Nosterfield N Yorks 51 A8
Nostie Highld 85 F13
Notgrove Glos 27 F8
Nottage Bridgend 14 D4
Nottingham Nottingham 36 B1
Nottington Dorset 8 F5
Notton W Yorks 45 A7
Notton Wilts 16 E6
Nounsley Essex 30 G4
Noutard's Green Worcs 26 B4
Novar House Highld 87 E9
Nox Shrops 33 D10
Nuffield Oxon 18 C3
Nun Hills Lancs 50 G4
Nun Monkton N Yorks 51 D11
Nunburnholme E Yorks 52 E4
Nuncargate Notts 45 G9
Nuneaton Warks 35 F9
Nuneham Courtenay Oxon 18 B2
Nunney Som 16 G4
Nunnington N Yorks 52 B2
Nunnykirk Northumb 62 D6
Nunsthorpe NE Lincs 46 B6
Nunthorpe Mbro 59 E6
Nunthorpe York 52 D2
Nunton Wilts 9 B10
Nunwick N Yorks 51 B9
Nupend Glos 26 H4
Nursling Hants 10 C2
Nursted Hants 11 B6
Nutbourne W Sus 11 C9
Nutbourne W Sus 11 D6
Nutfield Sur 19 F10
Nuthall Notts 35 A11
Nuthampstead Herts 29 E11
Nuthurst W Sus 11 B10
Nutley E Sus 12 D3
Nutley Hants 18 G3
Nutwell S Yorks 45 B10
Nybster Highld 94 D5
Nyetimber W Sus 11 E7
Nyewood W Sus 11 B7
Nymet Rowland Devon 6 F6
Nymet Tracey Devon 7 F6
Nympsfield Glos 16 A5
Nynehead Som 7 D10
Nyton W Sus 11 D8

O

Oad Street Kent 20 E5
Oadby Leics 36 E2
Oak Cross Devon 6 G4
Oakamoor Staffs 35 A6
Oakbank W Loth 69 D9
Oakdale Caerph 15 B7
Oake Som 7 D10
Oaken Staffs 34 E4
Oakenclough Lancs 49 E5
Oakengates Telford 34 D3
Oakenholt Flint 42 E5
Oakenshaw Durham 58 C3
Oakenshaw W Yorks 51 G7
Oakerthorpe Derbys 45 G7
Oakes W Yorks 51 H7
Oakfield Torf 15 B9
Oakford Ceredig 23 A9
Oakford Devon 7 D8
Oakfordbridge Devon 7 D8
Oakgrove Ches E 44 F3
Oakham Rutland 36 E4
Oakhanger Hants 18 H4
Oakhill Som 16 G3
Oakhurst Kent 20 F2
Oakington Cambs 29 B11
Oaklands Herts 29 G9
Oaklands Powys 25 C7
Oakle Street Glos 26 G4
Oakley Bedford 29 C7
Oakley Bucks 28 G3
Oakley Fife 69 B9
Oakley Hants 18 F2
Oakley Oxon 18 A4
Oakley Poole 9 E9
Oakley Suff 39 H7
Oakley Green Windsor 18 D6
Oakley Park Powys 32 G5
Oakmere Ches W 43 F8
Oakridge Glos 16 A6
Oakridge Hants 18 F3
Oaks Shrops 33 E10
Oaks Green Derbys 35 B7
Oaksey Wilts 16 B6
Oakthorpe Leics 35 D9
Oakwoodhill Sur 19 H8
Oakworth W Yorks 50 F6
Oape Highld 92 J7
Oare Kent 21 E7
Oare Som 7 B7
Oare W Berks 18 D2
Oare Wilts 17 E8
Oasby Lincs 36 B6
Oathlaw Angus 77 B7
Oatlands N Yorks 51 D9
Oban Argyll 79 J11
Oban Highld 79 C11
Oborne Dorset 8 C5
Obthorpe Lincs 37 D6
Occlestone Green Ches W 43 F9
Occold Suff 31 A8
Ochiltree E Ayrs 67 D8
Ochtermuthill Perth 75 F11
Ochtertyre Perth 75 E11
Ockbrook Derbys 35 B10
Ockham Sur 19 F7
Ockle Highld 79 D8
Ockley Sur 19 H8
Ocle Pychard Hereford 26 D2
Octon E Yorks 52 C6
Octon Cross Roads E Yorks 52 C6
Odcombe Som 8 C4
Odd Down Bath 16 E4
Oddendale Cumb 57 E7
Odder Lincs 46 E3
Oddingley Worcs 26 C6
Oddington Glos 27 F9
Oddington Oxon 28 G2
Odell Bedford 28 C6
Odie Orkney 95 F7
Odiham Hants 18 F4
Odstock Wilts 9 B10
Odstone Leics 35 E9
Offchurch Warks 27 B10
Offenham Worcs 27 D7
Offham E Sus 12 E2
Offham Kent 20 F3
Offham W Sus 11 D9
Offord Cluny Cambs 29 B9
Offord Darcy Cambs 29 B9
Offton Suff 31 D7
Offwell Devon 7 G10
Ogbourne Maizey Wilts 17 D8
Ogbourne St Andrew Wilts 17 D8
Ogbourne St George Wilts 17 D9
Ogil Angus 77 A7
Ogle Northumb 63 F7
Ogmore V Glam 14 D4
Ogmore-by-Sea V Glam 14 D4
Ogmore Vale Bridgend 14 B5
Okeford Fitzpaine Dorset 9 C7
Okehampton Devon 6 G4
Okehampton Camp Devon 6 G4
Okraquoy Shetland 96 K6
Old Northants 28 A4
Old Aberdeen Aberdeen 83 C11
Old Alresford Hants 10 A4
Old Arley Warks 35 F8
Old Basford Nottingham 35 A11
Old Basing Hants 18 F3
Old Bewick Northumb 62 A6
Old Bolingbroke Lincs 47 F7
Old Bramhope W Yorks 51 E8
Old Brampton Derbys 45 E7
Old Bridge of Tilt Perth 81 G10
Old Bridge of Urr Dumfries 55 C10
Old Buckenham Norf 39 F6
Old Burghclere Hants 17 F11
Old Byland N Yorks 59 H6
Old Cassop Durham 58 C4
Old Castleton Borders 61 D11
Old Catton Norf 39 D8
Old Clee NE Lincs 46 B6
Old Cleeve Som 7 B9
Old Clipstone Notts 45 F10
Old Colwyn Conwy 41 C10
Old Coulsdon London 19 F10
Old Crombie Aberds 88 C5
Old Dailly S Ayrs 66 G5
Old Dalby Leics 36 C2
Old Deer Aberds 89 D9
Old Denaby S Yorks 45 C8
Old Edlington S Yorks 45 C9
Old Eldon Durham 58 D3
Old Ellerby E Yorks 53 F7
Old Felixstowe Suff 31 E10
Old Fletton Pboro 37 F7
Old Glossop Derbys 44 C4
Old Goole E Yorks 52 G3
Old Hall Powys 32 G5
Old Heath Essex 31 F7
Old Heathfield E Sus 12 D4
Old Hill W Mid 34 G5
Old Hunstanton Norf 38 A2
Old Hurst Cambs 37 H8
Old Hutton Cumb 57 H7
Old Kea Corn 3 E7
Old Kilpatrick W Dunb 68 C3
Old Kinnernie Aberds 83 C9
Old Knebworth Herts 29 F9
Old Langho Lancs 50 F3
Old Laxey IoM 48 D4
Old Leake Lincs 47 G8
Old Malton N Yorks 52 B3
Old Micklefield W Yorks 51 F10
Old Milton Hants 9 E11
Old Milverton Warks 27 B9
Old Monkland N Lanark 68 D6
Old Netley Hants 10 D3
Old Philpstoun W Loth 69 C9
Old Quarrington Durham 58 C4
Old Radnor Powys 25 C9
Old Rattray Aberds 89 C10
Old Rayne Aberds 83 A8
Old Romney Kent 13 D9
Old Sodbury S Glos 16 C4
Old Somerby Lincs 36 B5
Old Stratford Northants 28 D4
Old Thirsk N Yorks 51 A10
Old Town Cumb 50 A1
Old Town Cumb 57 B6
Old Town Northumb 62 D4
Old Town Scilly 2 C3
Old Trafford Gtr Man 44 C2
Old Tupton Derbys 45 F7
Old Warden C Beds 29 D8
Old Weston Cambs 37 H6
Old Whittington Derbys 45 E7
Old Wick Highld 94 E5
Old Windsor Windsor 18 D6
Old Wives Lees Kent 21 F7
Old Woking Sur 19 F7
Old Woodhall Lincs 46 F6
Oldany Highld 92 F4
Oldberrow Warks 27 B8
Oldborough Devon 7 F6
Oldbury Shrops 34 F3
Oldbury W Mid 34 G5
Oldbury Warks 35 F9
Oldbury-on-Severn S Glos 16 B3
Oldbury on the Hill Glos 16 C5
Oldcastle Bridgend 14 D5
Oldcastle Mon 25 F10
Oldcotes Notts 45 D9
Oldfallow Staffs 34 D5
Oldfield Worcs 26 B5
Oldford Som 16 F4
Oldham Gtr Man 44 B3
Oldhamstocks E Loth 70 C6
Oldland S Glos 16 D3
Oldmeldrum Aberds 89 F8
Oldshore Beg Highld 92 D4
Oldshoremore Highld 92 D5
Oldstead N Yorks 51 A11
Oldtown Aberds 83 A7
Oldtown of Ord Aberds 88 C6
Oldway Swansea 23 H10
Oldways End Devon 7 D7
Oldwhat Aberds 89 C8
Olgrinmore Highld 94 E2
Oliver's Battery Hants 10 B3
Ollaberry Shetland 96 E5
Ollerton Ches E 43 E10
Ollerton Notts 45 F10
Ollerton Shrops 34 C2
Olmarch Ceredig 24 C3
Olney M Keynes 28 C5
Olrig Ho. Highld 94 D3
Olton W Mid 35 G7
Olveston S Glos 16 C3
Olwen Ceredig 23 B10
Ombersley Worcs 26 B5
Ompton Notts 45 F10
Onchan IoM 48 E3
Onecote Staffs 44 G4
Onen Mon 25 G11
Ongar Hill Norf 38 C1
Ongar Street Hereford 25 B10
Onibury Shrops 33 H10
Onich Highld 74 A3
Onllwyn Neath 24 G5
Onneley Staffs 34 A3
Onslow Village Sur 18 G6
Onthank E Ayrs 67 B7
Openwoodgate Derbys 45 H7
Opinan Highld 85 A12
Opinan Highld 91 H13
Orange Lane Borders 70 F6
Orange Row Norf 37 C11
Orasaigh W Isles 91 F8
Orbliston Moray 88 C3
Orbost Highld 84 D7
Orby Lincs 47 F8
Orchard Hill Devon 6 D3
Orchard Portman Som 8 B1
Orcheston Wilts 17 G7
Orcop Hereford 25 F11
Orcop Hill Hereford 25 F11
Ord Highld 85 G11
Ordhead Aberds 83 B8
Ordie Aberds 82 C6
Ordiequish Moray 88 C3
Ordsall Notts 45 E10
Ore E Sus 13 E7
Oreton Shrops 34 G2
Orford Suff 31 D11
Orford Warr 43 C9
Orgreave Staffs 35 D7
Orlestone Kent 13 C8
Orleton Hereford 25 B11
Orleton Worcs 26 B3
Orlingbury Northants 28 A5
Ormesby Redcar 59 E6
Ormesby St Margaret Norf 39 D10
Ormesby St Michael Norf 39 D10
Ormiclate Castle W Isles 84 E2
Ormiscaig Highld 91 H13
Ormiston E Loth 70 D3
Ormsaigbeg Highld 78 E7
Ormsaigmore Highld 78 E7
Ormsary Argyll 72 F6
Ormsgill Cumb 49 B1
Ormskirk Lancs 43 B7
Orpington London 19 E11
Orrell Gtr Man 43 B8
Orrell Mers 42 C6
Orrisdale IoM 48 C3
Orroland Dumfries 55 E10
Orsett Thurrock 20 C3
Orslow Staffs 34 D4
Orston Notts 36 A3
Orthwaite Cumb 56 C4
Ortner Lancs 49 D5
Orton Cumb 57 F8
Orton Northants 36 H4
Orton Longueville Pboro 37 F7
Orton-on-the-Hill Leics 35 E9
Orton Waterville Pboro 37 F7
Orwell Cambs 29 C10
Osbaldeston Lancs 50 F2
Osbaldwick York 52 D2
Osbaston Shrops 33 C9
Osbournby Lincs 37 B6
Oscroft Ches W 43 F8
Ose Highld 85 D8
Osgathorpe Leics 35 D10
Osgodby Lincs 46 C4
Osgodby N Yorks 52 F2
Osgodby N Yorks 53 A6
Oskaig Highld 85 E10
Oskamull Argyll 78 G7
Osmaston Derby 35 B9
Osmaston Derbys 35 A8
Osmington Dorset 8 F6
Osmington Mills Dorset 8 F6
Osmotherley N Yorks 58 G5
Ospisdale Highld 87 C10
Ospringe Kent 21 E7
Ossett W Yorks 51 G8
Ossington Notts 45 F11
Ostend Essex 20 B6
Oswaldkirk N Yorks 52 B2
Oswaldtwistle Lancs 50 G3
Oswestry Shrops 33 C8
Otford Kent 20 F2
Otham Kent 20 F4
Othery Som 8 A2
Otley Suff 31 C9
Otley W Yorks 51 E8
Otter Ferry Argyll 73 E8
Otterbourne Hants 10 B3
Otterburn N Yorks 50 D4
Otterburn Northumb 62 D4
Otterburn Camp Northumb 62 D4
Otterham Corn 4 B2
Otterhampton Som 15 G8
Ottershaw Sur 19 E7
Otterswick Shetland 96 E7
Otterton Devon 7 H9
Ottery St Mary Devon 7 G10
Ottinge Kent 21 G8
Ottringham E Yorks 53 G8
Oughterby Cumb 61 H8
Oughtershaw N Yorks 50 A4
Oughterside Cumb 56 B3
Oughtibridge S Yorks 45 C7
Oughtrington Warr 43 D9
Oulston N Yorks 51 B11
Oulton Cumb 56 A4
Oulton Norf 39 C7
Oulton Staffs 34 B5
Oulton Suff 39 F11
Oulton W Yorks 51 G9
Oulton Broad Suff 39 F11
Oulton Street Norf 39 C7
Oundle Northants 36 G6
Ousby Cumb 57 C8
Ousdale Highld 94 H2
Ousden Suff 30 C4
Ousefleet E Yorks 52 G4
Ouston Durham 58 A3
Ouston Northumb 62 F6
Out Newton E Yorks 53 G9
Out Rawcliffe Lancs 49 E4
Outertown Orkney 95 G3
Outgate Cumb 56 G5
Outhgill Cumb 57 F9
Outlane W Yorks 51 H6
Outwell Norf 37 E11
Outwick Hants 9 C10
Outwood Sur 19 G10
Outwood W Yorks 51 G9
Outwoods Staffs 34 D3
Ovenden W Yorks 51 G6
Ovenscloss Borders 70 G3
Over Cambs 29 A10
Over Ches W 43 F9
Over S Glos 16 C2
Over Compton Dorset 8 C4
Over Green W Mid 35 F7
Over Haddon Derbys 44 F6
Over Hulton Gtr Man 43 B9
Over Kellet Lancs 49 B5
Over Kiddington Oxon 27 F11
Over Knutsford Ches E 43 E10
Over Monnow Mon 26 G2
Over Norton Oxon 27 F10
Over Peover Ches E 43 E10
Over Silton N Yorks 58 G5
Over Stowey Som 7 C10
Over Stratton Som 8 C3
Over Tabley Ches E 43 D10
Over Wallop Hants 17 H9
Over Whitacre Warks 35 F8
Over Worton Oxon 27 F11
Overbister Orkney 95 D7
Overbury Worcs 26 E6
Overcombe Dorset 8 F5
Overgreen Derbys 45 E7
Overleigh Som 15 H10
Overley Green Warks 27 C7
Overpool Ches W 43 E6
Overscaig Hotel Highld 92 G7
Overseal Derbys 35 D8
Oversland Kent 21 F7
Overstone Northants 28 B5
Overstrand Norf 39 A8
Overthorpe Northants 27 D11
Overton Aberdeen 83 B10
Overton Ches W 43 E8
Overton Dumfries 60 G5
Overton Hants 18 G2
Overton Lancs 49 D4
Overton N Yorks 52 D1
Overton Shrops 26 A2
Overton Swansea 23 H9
Overton W Yorks 51 H8
Overton = Owrtyn Wrex 33 A9
Overton Bridge Wrex 33 A9
Overtown N Lanark 69 E7
Oving Bucks 28 F4
Oving W Sus 11 D8
Ovingdean Brighton 12 F2
Ovingham Northumb 62 G6
Ovington Durham 58 E2
Ovington Essex 30 D4
Ovington Hants 10 A4
Ovington Norf 38 E5
Ovington Northumb 62 G6
Ower Hants 10 C2
Owermoigne Dorset 9 F6
Owlbury Shrops 33 F9
Owler Bar Derbys 44 E6
Owlerton S Yorks 45 D7
Owl's Green Suff 31 B9
Owlswick Bucks 28 H4
Owmby Lincs 46 B4
Owmby-by-Spital Lincs 46 D4
Owrtyn = Overton Wrex 33 A9
Owslebury Hants 10 B4
Owston Leics 36 E3
Owston S Yorks 45 A9
Owston Ferry N Lincs 46 B2
Owstwick E Yorks 53 F8
Owthorne E Yorks 53 G9
Owthorpe Notts 36 B2
Oxborough Norf 38 E3
Oxcombe Lincs 47 E7
Oxen Park Cumb 56 H5
Oxenholme Cumb 57 H7
Oxenhope W Yorks 50 F6
Oxenton Glos 26 E6
Oxenwood Wilts 17 F10
Oxford Oxon 28 H2
Oxhey Herts 19 B8
Oxhill Warks 27 D10
Oxley W Mid 34 E5
Oxley Green Essex 30 G6
Oxley's Green E Sus 12 D5
Oxnam Borders 62 B3
Oxshott Sur 19 E8
Oxspring S Yorks 44 B6
Oxted Sur 19 F10
Oxton Borders 70 E3
Oxton Notts 45 G10
Oxwich Swansea 23 H9
Oxwick Norf 38 C5
Oykel Bridge Highld 92 J6
Oyne Aberds 83 A8

P

Pabail Iarach W Isles 91 D10
Pabail Uarach W Isles 91 D10
Pace Gate N Yorks 51 D7
Packington Leics 35 D9
Padanaram Angus 77 B7
Padbury Bucks 28 E4
Paddington London 19 C9
Paddlesworth Kent 21 H8
Paddock Wood Kent 12 B5
Paddockhaugh Moray 88 C2
Paddockhole Dumfries 61 E8
Padfield Derbys 44 C4
Padiham Lancs 50 F3
Padog Conwy 41 E10
Padside N Yorks 51 D7
Padstow Corn 3 B8
Padworth W Berks 18 E3
Page Bank Durham 58 C3
Pagham W Sus 11 E7
Paglesham Churchend Essex 20 B6
Paglesham Eastend Essex 20 B6
Paibeil W Isles 84 B2
Paible W Isles 90 H5
Paignton Torbay 5 E9
Pailton Warks 35 G10
Painscastle Powys 25 D8
Painshawfield Northumb 62 G6
Painsthorpe E Yorks 52 D4
Painswick Glos 26 H5
Pairc Shiaboist W Isles 90 C7
Paisley Renfs 68 D3
Pakefield Suff 39 F11
Pakenham Suff 30 B6
Pale Gwyn 32 B5
Palestine Hants 17 G9
Paley Street Windsor 18 D5
Palfrey W Mid 34 F6
Palgowan Dumfries 54 A6
Palgrave Suff 39 H7
Pallion T&W 63 H9
Palmarsh Kent 13 C10
Palnackie Dumfries 55 D11
Palnure Dumfries 55 C7
Palterton Derbys 45 F8
Pamber End Hants 18 F3
Pamber Green Hants 18 F3
Pamber Heath Hants 18 E3
Pamphill Dorset 9 D8
Pampisford Cambs 29 D11
Pan Orkney 95 J4
Panbride Angus 77 D8
Pancrasweek Devon 6 F1
Pandy Gwyn 32 E2
Pandy Mon 25 F10
Pandy Powys 32 E5
Pandy Wrex 33 B7
Pandy Tudur Conwy 41 D10
Panfield Essex 30 F4
Pangbourne W Berks 18 D3
Pannal N Yorks 51 D9
Panshanger Herts 29 G9
Pant Shrops 33 C8
Pant-glâs Powys 32 F3
Pant-glas Carms 23 D10
Pant-glas Gwyn 40 F6
Pant-glas Shrops 33 B8
Pant-lasau Swansea 14 B2
Pant Mawr Powys 32 G4
Pant-teg Carms 23 D9
Pant-y-Caws Carms 22 D6
Pant-y-dwr Powys 32 H5
Pant-y-ffridd Powys 33 E7
Pant-y-Wacco Flint 42 E4
Pant-yr-awel Bridgend 14 C5
Pantgwyn Carms 23 D10
Pantgwyn Ceredig 23 B7
Panton Lincs 46 E5
Pantperthog Gwyn 32 E3
Pantyffynnon Carms 24 G3
Pantymwyn Flint 42 F4
Panxworth Norf 39 D9
Papcastle Cumb 56 C3
Papigoe Highld 94 E5
Papil Shetland 96 K5
Papley Orkney 95 J5
Papple E Loth 70 C4
Papplewick Notts 45 G9
Papworth Everard Cambs 29 B9
Papworth St Agnes Cambs 29 B9
Par Corn 4 F1
Parbold Lancs 43 A7
Parbrook Som 16 H2
Parbrook W Sus 11 B9
Parc Gwyn 41 G10
Parc-Seymour Newport 15 B10
Parc-y-rhôs Carms 23 B10
Parclyn Ceredig 23 A7
Pardshaw Cumb 56 D2
Parham Suff 31 B10
Park Dumfries 60 D5
Park Corner Oxon 18 C3
Park Corner Windsor 18 C5
Park End Mbro 58 E6
Park End Northumb 62 F4
Park Gate Hants 10 D4
Park Hill N Yorks 51 C9
Park Hill Notts 45 G10
Park Street W Sus 11 A10
Parkend Glos 26 H3
Parkeston Essex 31 E9
Parkgate Ches W 42 E5
Parkgate Dumfries 60 E6
Parkgate Kent 13 C7
Parkgate Sur 19 G9
Parkham Devon 6 D2
Parkham Ash Devon 6 D2
Parkhill Ho. Aberds 83 B10
Parkhouse Mon 15 A10
Parkhouse Green Derbys 45 F8
Parkhurst IoW 10 E3
Parkmill Swansea 23 H10
Parkneuk Aberds 83 F9
Parkstone Poole 9 E9
Parley Cross Dorset 9 E9
Parracombe Devon 6 B5
Parrog Pembs 22 C5
Parsley Hay Derbys 44 F5
Parson Cross S Yorks 45 C7
Parson Drove Cambs 37 E9
Parsonage Green Essex 30 H4
Parsonby Cumb 56 C3
Parson's Heath Essex 31 F7
Partick Glasgow 68 D4
Partington Gtr Man 43 C10
Partney Lincs 47 F8
Parton Cumb 56 D1
Parton Dumfries 55 B9
Parton Glos 26 F5
Partridge Green W Sus 11 C10
Parwich Derbys 44 G5
Passenham Northants 28 E4
Paston Norf 39 B9
Patchacott Devon 6 G3
Patcham Brighton 12 F2
Patching W Sus 11 D9
Patchole Devon 6 B5
Pateley Bridge N Yorks 51 C7
Paternoster Heath Essex 30 G6
Path of Condie Perth 76 F3
Pathe Som 8 A2
Pathhead Aberds 77 A10
Pathhead E Ayrs 67 E9
Pathhead Fife 69 A11
Pathhead Midloth 70 D2
Pathstruie Perth 76 F3
Patna E Ayrs 67 E7
Patney Wilts 17 F7
Patrick IoM 48 D2
Patrick Brompton N Yorks 58 G3
Patrington E Yorks 53 G9
Patrixbourne Kent 21 F8
Patterdale Cumb 56 E5
Pattingham Staffs 34 F4
Pattishall Northants 28 C3
Pattiswick Green Essex 30 F5
Patton Bridge Cumb 57 G7
Paul Corn 2 G3
Paulerspury Northants 28 D4
Paull E Yorks 53 G7
Paulton Bath 16 F3
Pavenham Bedford 28 C6
Pawlett Som 15 G9
Pawston Northumb 71 G7
Paxford Glos 27 E8
Paxton Borders 71 E8
Payhembury Devon 7 F9
Paythorne Lancs 50 D4
Peacehaven E Sus 12 F3
Peak Dale Derbys 44 E4
Peak Forest Derbys 44 E5
Peakirk Pboro 37 E7
Pearsie Angus 76 B6
Pease Pottage W Sus 12 C1
Peasedown St John Bath 16 F4
Peasemore W Berks 17 D11
Peasenhall Suff 31 B10
Peaslake Sur 19 G7
Peasley Cross Mers 43 C8
Peasmarsh E Sus 13 D7
Peaston E Loth 70 D3
Peastonbank E Loth 70 D3
Peat Inn Fife 77 G7
Peathill Aberds 89 B9
Peatling Magna Leics 36 F1
Peatling Parva Leics 36 G1
Peaton Shrops 33 G11
Peats Corner Suff 31 B8
Pebmarsh Essex 30 E5
Pebworth Worcs 27 D8
Pecket Well W Yorks 50 G5
Peckforton Ches E 43 G8
Peckham London 19 D10
Peckleton Leics 35 E10
Pedlinge Kent 13 C10
Pedmore W Mid 34 G5
Pedwell Som 15 H10
Peebles Borders 69 F11
Peel IoM 48 D2
Peel Common Hants 10 D4
Peel Park S Lanark 68 E5
Peening Quarter Kent 13 D7
Pegsdon C Beds 29 E8
Pegswood Northumb 63 E8
Pegwell Kent 21 E10
Peinchorran Highld 85 E10
Peinlich Highld 85 C9
Pelaw T&W 63 G8
Pelcomb Bridge Pembs 22 E4
Pelcomb Cross Pembs 22 E4
Peldon Essex 30 G6
Pellon W Yorks 51 G6
Pelsall W Mid 34 E6
Pelton Durham 58 A3
Pelutho Cumb 56 B3
Pelynt Corn 4 F3
Pemberton Gtr Man 43 B8
Pembrey Carms 23 F9
Pembridge Hereford 25 C10
Pembroke = Penfro Pembs 22 F4
Pembroke Dock = Doc Penfro Pembs 22 F4
Pembury Kent 12 B5
Pen-bont Rhydybeddau Ceredig 32 G2
Pen-clawdd Swansea 23 G10
Pen-ffordd Pembs 22 D5
Pen-groes-oped Mon 25 H10
Pen-llyn Anglesey 40 B5
Pen-lon Anglesey 40 D6
Pen-sarn Gwyn 32 C1
Pen-sarn Gwyn 40 F6
Pen-twyn Mon 26 H2
Pen-y-banc Carms 24 F3
Pen-y-bont Carms 23 D8
Pen-y-bont Gwyn 32 C2
Pen-y-bont Gwyn 32 E3
Pen-y-bont Powys 33 C8
Pen-y-bont ar Ogwr = Bridgend Bridgend 14 D5
Pen-y-bryn Gwyn 32 D2
Pen-y-bryn Pembs 22 B6
Pen-y-cae Powys 24 G5
Pen-y-cae-mawr Mon 15 B10
Pen-y-cefn Flint 42 E4
Pen-y-clawdd Mon 25 H11
Pen-y-coedcae Rhondda 14 C6
Pen-y-fai Bridgend 14 C4
Pen-y-garn Carms 23 C10
Pen-y-garn Ceredig 32 G2
Pen-y-garnedd Anglesey 41 C7
Pen-y-gop Conwy 32 A5
Pen-y-graig Gwyn 40 G3
Pen-y-groes Carms 23 E10
Pen-y-groeslon Gwyn 40 G4
Pen-y-Gwryd Hotel Gwyn 41 E8
Pen-y-stryt Denb 42 G4
Pen-yr-heol Mon 25 G11
Pen-yr-Heolgerrig M Tydf 25 H7
Penallt Mon 26 G2
Penally Pembs 22 G6
Penalt Hereford 26 F2
Penare Corn 3 E8
Penarlâg = Hawarden Flint 42 F6
Penarth V Glam 15 D7
Penbryn Ceredig 23 A7
Pencader Carms 23 C9
Pencaenewydd Gwyn 40 F6
Pencaitland E Loth 70 D3
Pencarnisiog Anglesey 40 C5
Pencarreg Carms 23 B10
Pencelli Powys 25 F7
Pencoed Bridgend 14 C5
Pencombe Hereford 26 C2
Pencoyd Hereford 26 F2
Pencraig Hereford 26 F2
Pencraig Powys 32 C6
Pendeen Corn 2 F2
Penderyn Rhondda 24 H6
Pendine Carms 23 F7
Pendlebury Gtr Man 43 B10
Pendleton Lancs 43 F3
Pendock Worcs 26 E4
Pendoggett Corn 3 B9
Pendomer Som 8 C4
Pendoylan V Glam 14 D6
Pendre Bridgend 14 C5
Penegoes Powys 32 E3
Penfro = Pembroke Pembs 22 F4
Pengam Caerph 15 B7
Penge London 19 D10
Pengenffordd Powys 25 E8
Pengorffwysfa Anglesey 40 A6
Pengover Green Corn 4 E3
Penhale Corn 2 H5
Penhale Corn 3 D8
Penhalvaen Corn 2 F6
Penhill Swindon 17 C8
Penhow Newport 15 B10
Penhurst E Sus 12 E5
Peniarth Gwyn 32 E2
Penicuik Midloth 69 D11
Peniel Carms 23 D9
Peniel Denb 42 F3
Penifiler Highld 85 D9
Peninver Argyll 65 F8
Penisarwaun Gwyn 41 D7
Penistone S Yorks 44 B6
Penjerrick Corn 3 F6
Penketh Warr 43 D8
Penkill S Ayrs 66 G5
Penkridge Staffs 34 D5
Penley Wrex 33 B10
Penllergaer Swansea 14 B2
Penllyn V Glam 14 D5
Penmachno Conwy 41 E9
Penmaen Swansea 23 H10
Penmaenan Conwy 41 C9
Penmaenmawr Conwy 41 C9
Penmaenpool Gwyn 32 D2
Penmark V Glam 14 E6
Penmarth Corn 2 F6
Penmon Anglesey 41 B8
Penmore Mill Argyll 78 F7
Penmorfa Ceredig 23 A8
Penmorfa Gwyn 41 F7
Penmynydd Anglesey 41 C7
Penn Bucks 18 B6
Penn W Mid 34 F4
Penn Street Bucks 18 B6
Pennal Gwyn 32 E3
Pennan Aberds 89 B8
Pennant Ceredig 24 B2
Pennant Denb 32 B6
Pennant Denb 42 G3
Pennant Powys 32 F4
Pennant Melangell Powys 32 C6
Pennar Pembs 22 F4
Pennard Swansea 23 H10
Pennerley Shrops 33 F9
Pennington Cumb 49 B2
Pennington Gtr Man 43 C9
Pennington Hants 10 E2
Penny Bridge Cumb 49 A3
Pennycross Argyll 79 J8
Pennygate Norf 39 C9
Pennygown Argyll 79 G8
Pennymoor Devon 7 E7
Pennywell T&W 63 H9
Penparc Ceredig 23 B7
Penparc Pembs 22 C3
Penparcau Ceredig 32 G1
Penperlleni Mon 15 A9
Penpillick Corn 4 F1
Penpol Corn 3 F7
Penpoll Corn 4 F2
Penpont Dumfries 60 D4
Penpont Powys 24 F6
Penrhôs Mon 25 G11
Penrherber Carms 23 C7
Penrhiw goch Carms 23 E10
Penrhiw-llan Ceredig 23 B8
Penrhiw-pâl Ceredig 23 B8
Penrhiwceiber Rhondda 14 B6
Penrhos Gwyn 40 G5
Penrhos Powys 24 G4
Penrhosfeilw Anglesey 40 B4
Penrhyn Bay Conwy 41 B10
Penrhyn-coch Ceredig 32 G2
Penrhyndeudraeth Gwyn 41 G8
Penrhynside Conwy 41 B10
Penrice Swansea 23 H9
Penrith Cumb 57 C7
Penrose Corn 3 B7
Penruddock Cumb 56 D6
Penryn Corn 3 F6
Pensarn Carms 23 E9
Pensarn Conwy 42 E2
Pensax Worcs 26 B4
Pensby Mers 42 D5
Penselwood Som 9 A6
Pensford Bath 16 E3
Penshaw T&W 58 A4
Penshurst Kent 12 B4
Pensilva Corn 4 E3
Penston E Loth 70 C3
Pentewan Corn 3 E9
Pentir Gwyn 41 D7
Pentire Corn 3 C6
Pentlow Essex 30 D5
Pentney Norf 38 D3
Penton Mewsey Hants 17 G10
Pentraeth Anglesey 41 C7
Pentre Carms 23 E10
Pentre Powys 33 F8
Pentre Powys 33 G6
Pentre Rhondda 14 B5
Pentre Shrops 33 D9
Pentre Wrex 33 A8
Pentre Wrex 33 B8
Pentre-bâch Ceredig 23 B10
Pentre-bach Powys 24 E6
Pentre Berw Anglesey 40 C6
Pentre-bont Conwy 41 E9
Pentre-celyn Denb 42 G4
Pentre-Celyn Powys 32 E4
Pentre-chwyth Swansea 14 B2
Pentre-cwrt Carms 23 C8
Pentre Dolau-Honddu Powys 24 D6
Pentre-dwr Swansea 14 B2
Pentre-galar Pembs 22 C6
Pentre-Gwenlais Carms 24 G3
Pentre Gwynfryn Gwyn 32 C1
Pentre Halkyn Flint 42 E5
Pentre-Isaf Conwy 41 D10
Pentre Llanrhaeadr Denb 42 F3
Pentre-llwyn-llŵyd Powys 24 C6
Pentre-llyn Ceredig 24 A3

Pentre-llyn cymmer Conwy 42 G2
Pentre Meyrick V Glam 14 D5
Pentre-poeth Newport 15 C8
Pentre-rhew Ceredig 24 C3
Pentre-tafarn-y-fedw Conwy 41 D10
Pentre-ty-gwyn Carms 24 E5
Pentrebach M Tydf 14 A6
Pentrebach Swansea 24 H3
Pentrebeirdd Powys 33 D7
Pentrecagal Carms 23 B8
Pentredwr Denb 42 H4
Pentrefelin Carms 23 D10
Pentrefelin Ceredig 24 D3
Pentrefelin Conwy 41 C10
Pentrefelin Gwyn 41 G7
Pentrefoelas Conwy 41 E10
Pentregat Ceredig 23 A8
Pentreheyling Shrops 33 F8
Pentre'r Felin Conwy 41 D10
Pentre'r-felin Powys 24 E6
Pentrich Derbys 45 G7
Pentridge Dorset 9 C9
Pentyrch Cardiff 15 C7
Penuchadre V Glam 14 D4
Penuwch Ceredig 24 B2
Penwithick Corn 3 D9
Penwyllt Powys 24 G5
Penybanc Carms 24 G3
Penybont Powys 25 B8
Penybontfawr Powys 33 C6
Penycae Wrex 42 H5
Penycwm Pembs 22 D3
Penyffordd Flint 42 F6
Penyffridd Gwyn 41 E7
Penygarnedd Powys 33 C7
Penygraig Rhondda 14 B5
Penygroes Gwyn 40 E6
Penygroes Pembs 22 C6
Penyrheol Caerph 15 C7
Penysarn Anglesey 40 A6
Penywaun Rhondda 14 A5
Penzance Corn 2 F3
Peopleton Worcs 26 C6
Peover Heath Ches E 43 E10
Peper Harow Sur 18 G6
Perceton N Ayrs 67 B6
Percie Aberds 83 D7
Percyhorner Aberds 89 B9
Periton Som 7 B8
Perivale London 19 C8
Perkinsville Durham 58 A3
Perlethorpe Notts 45 E10
Perranarworthal Corn 3 F6
Perranporth Corn 3 D6
Perranuthnoe Corn 2 G4
Perranzabuloe Corn 3 D6
Perry Barr W Mid 35 F6
Perry Green Herts 29 G11
Perry Green Wilts 16 C6
Perry Street Kent 20 D3
Perryfoot Derbys 44 D5
Pershall Staffs 34 B4
Pershore Worcs 26 D6
Pert Angus 83 G8
Pertenhall Bedford 29 B7
Perth Perth 76 E4
Perthy Shrops 33 B9
Perton Staffs 34 F4
Pertwood Wilts 16 H5
Peter Tavy Devon 4 D6
Peterborough Pboro 37 F7
Peterburn Highld 91 J12
Peterchurch Hereford 25 E10
Peterculter Aberdeen 83 C10
Peterhead Aberds 89 D11
Peterlee Durham 58 B5
Peter's Green Herts 29 G8
Peters Marland Devon 6 E3
Petersfield Hants 10 B6
Peterston super-Ely V Glam 14 D6
Peterstone Wentlooge Newport 15 C8
Peterstow Hereford 26 F2
Petertown Orkney 95 H4
Petham Kent 21 F8
Petrockstow Devon 6 F4
Pett E Sus 13 E7
Pettaugh Suff 31 C8
Petteridge Kent 12 B5
Pettinain S Lanark 69 F8
Pettistree Suff 31 C9
Petton Devon 7 D9
Petton Shrops 33 C10
Petts Wood London 19 E11
Petty Aberds 89 E7
Pettycur Fife 69 B11
Pettymuick Aberds 89 F9
Petworth W Sus 11 B8
Pevensey E Sus 12 F5
Pevensey Bay E Sus 12 F5
Pewsey Wilts 17 E8
Philham Devon 6 D1
Philiphaugh Borders 70 H3
Phillack Corn 2 F4
Philleigh Corn 3 F7
Philpstoun W Loth 69 C9
Phocle Green Hereford 26 F3
Phoenix Green Hants 18 F4
Pica Cumb 56 D2
Piccotts End Herts 29 H7
Pickering N Yorks 52 A3
Picket Piece Hants 17 G10
Picket Post Hants 9 D10
Pickhill N Yorks 51 A9
Picklescott Shrops 33 F10
Pickletillem Fife 77 E7
Pickmere Ches E 43 E9
Pickney Som 7 D10
Pickstock Telford 34 C3
Pickwell Devon 6 B3
Pickwell Leics 36 D3
Pickworth Lincs 36 B6
Pickworth Rutland 36 D5
Picton Ches W 43 E7
Picton Flint 42 D4
Picton N Yorks 58 F5
Piddinghoe E Sus 12 F3
Piddington Northants 28 C5
Piddington Oxon 28 G3
Piddlehinton Dorset 8 E6
Piddletrenthide Dorset 8 E6
Pidley Cambs 37 H9
Piercebridge Darl 58 E3
Pierowall Orkney 95 D5
Pigdon Northumb 63 E7
Pikehall Derbys 44 G5
Pilgrims Hatch Essex 20 B2
Pilham Lincs 46 C2
Pill N Som 15 D11
Pillaton Corn 4 E4
Pillerton Hersey Warks 27 D10
Pillerton Priors Warks 27 D9
Pilleth Powys 25 B9
Pilley Hants 10 E2
Pilley S Yorks 45 B7
Pilling Lancs 49 E4
Pilling Lane Lancs 49 E3
Pillowell Glos 26 H3
Pillwell Dorset 9 C6
Pilning S Glos 16 C2
Pilsbury Derbys 44 F5
Pilsdon Dorset 8 E3
Pilsgate Pboro 37 E6
Pilsley Derbys 44 E6
Pilsley Derbys 45 F8
Pilton Devon 6 C4
Pilton Northants 36 G6
Pilton Rutland 36 E5
Pilton Som 16 G2
Pilton Green Swansea 23 H9
Pimperne Dorset 9 D8
Pin Mill Suff 31 E9
Pinchbeck Lincs 37 C8
Pinchbeck Bars Lincs 37 C7
Pinchbeck West Lincs 37 C8
Pincheon Green S Yorks 52 H2
Pinehurst Swindon 17 C8
Pinfold Lancs 43 A6
Pinged Carms 23 F9
Pinhoe Devon 7 G8
Pinkneys Green Windsor 18 C5
Pinley W Mid 35 H9
Pinminnoch S Ayrs 66 G4
Pinmore S Ayrs 66 G5
Pinmore Mains S Ayrs 66 G5
Pinner London 19 C8
Pinvin Worcs 26 D6
Pinwherry S Ayrs 66 H4
Pinxton Derbys 45 G8
Pipe and Lyde Hereford 26 D2
Pipe Gate Shrops 34 A3
Piperhill Highld 87 F11
Piper's Pool Corn 4 C3
Pipewell Northants 36 G4
Pippacott Devon 6 C4
Pipton Powys 25 E8
Pirbright Sur 18 F6
Pirnmill N Ayrs 66 B1
Pirton Herts 29 E8
Pirton Worcs 26 D5
Pisgah Ceredig 32 H2
Pisgah Stirling 75 G10
Pishill Oxon 18 C4
Pistyll Gwyn 40 F5
Pitagowan Perth 81 G10
Pitblae Aberds 89 B9
Pitcairngreen Perth 76 E3
Pitcalnie Highld 87 D11
Pitcaple Aberds 83 A9
Pitch Green Bucks 18 A4
Pitch Place Sur 18 F6
Pitchcombe Glos 26 H5
Pitchcott Bucks 28 F4
Pitchford Shrops 33 E11
Pitcombe Som 8 A5
Pitcorthie Fife 77 G8
Pitcox E Loth 70 C5
Pitcur Perth 76 D5
Pitfichie Aberds 83 B8
Pitforthie Aberds 83 F10
Pitgrudy Highld 87 B10
Pitkennedy Angus 77 B8
Pitkevy Fife 76 G5
Pitkierie Fife 77 G8
Pitlessie Fife 76 G6
Pitlochry Perth 76 B2
Pitmachie Aberds 83 A8
Pitmain Highld 81 C9
Pitmedden Aberds 89 F8
Pitminster Som 7 E11
Pitmuies Angus 77 C8
Pitmunie Aberds 83 B8
Pitney Som 8 B3
Pitscottie Fife 77 F7
Pitsea Essex 20 C4
Pitsford Northants 28 B4
Pitsmoor S Yorks 45 D7
Pitstone Bucks 28 G6
Pitstone Green Bucks 28 G6
Pittendreich Moray 88 B1
Pittentrail Highld 93 J10
Pittenweem Fife 77 G8
Pittington Durham 58 B4
Pittodrie Aberds 83 A8
Pitton Wilts 9 A11
Pittswood Kent 20 G3
Pittulie Aberds 89 B9
Pity Me Durham 58 B3
Pityme Corn 3 B8
Pityoulish Highld 81 B11
Pixey Green Suff 39 H8
Pixham Sur 19 F8
Pixley Hereford 26 E3
Place Newton N Yorks 52 B4
Plaidy Aberds 89 C7
Plains N Lanark 68 D6
Plaish Shrops 33 F11
Plaistow W Sus 11 A9
Plaitford Wilts 10 C1
Plank Lane Gtr Man 43 C9
Plas-canol Gwyn 32 D1
Plas Gogerddan Ceredig 32 G2
Plas Llwyngwern Powys 32 E3
Plas Nantyr Wrex 33 B7
Plas-yn-Cefn Denb 42 E3
Plastow Green Hants 18 E2
Platt Kent 20 F3
Platt Bridge Gtr Man 43 B9
Platts Common S Yorks 45 B7
Plawsworth Durham 58 B3
Plaxtol Kent 20 F3
Play Hatch Oxon 18 D4
Playden E Sus 13 D8
Playford Suff 31 D9
Playing Place Corn 3 E7
Playley Green Glos 26 E4
Plealey Shrops 33 E10
Plean Stirling 69 B7
Pleasington Blackburn 50 G2
Pleasley Derbys 45 F9
Pleckgate Blackburn 50 F2
Plenmeller Northumb 62 G3
Pleshey Essex 30 G3
Plockton Highld 85 E13
Plocrapol W Isles 90 H6
Ploughfield Hereford 25 D10
Plowden Shrops 33 G9
Ploxgreen Shrops 33 E9
Pluckley Kent 20 G6
Pluckley Thorne Kent 13 B8
Plumbland Cumb 56 C3
Plumley Ches E 43 E10
Plumpton Cumb 57 C6
Plumpton E Sus 12 E2
Plumpton Green E Sus 12 E2
Plumpton Head Cumb 57 C7
Plumstead London 19 D11
Plumstead Norf 39 B7
Plumtree Notts 36 B2
Plungar Leics 36 B3
Plush Dorset 8 D6
Plwmp Ceredig 23 A8
Plymouth Plym 4 F5
Plympton Plym 4 F6
Plymstock Plym 4 F6
Plymtree Devon 7 F9
Pockley N Yorks 59 H7
Pocklington E Yorks 52 E4
Pode Hole Lincs 37 C8
Podimore Som 8 B4
Podington Bedford 28 B6
Podmore Staffs 34 B3
Point Clear Essex 31 G7
Pointon Lincs 37 B7
Pokesdown Bmouth 9 E10
Pol a Charra W Isles 84 G2
Polbae Dumfries 54 B5
Polbain Highld 92 H2
Polbathic Corn 4 F4
Polbeth W Loth 69 D9
Polchar Highld 81 C10
Pole Elm Worcs 26 D5
Polebrook Northants 37 G6
Polegate E Sus 12 F4
Poles Highld 87 B10
Polesworth Warks 35 E8
Polgigga Corn 2 G2
Polglass Highld 92 J3
Polgooth Corn 3 D8
Poling W Sus 11 D9
Polkerris Corn 4 F1
Polla Highld 92 D6
Pollington E Yorks 52 H2
Polloch Highld 79 E10
Pollok Glasgow 68 D4
Pollokshields Glasgow 68 D4
Polmassick Corn 3 E8
Polmont Falk 69 C8
Polnessan E Ayrs 67 E7
Polnish Highld 79 C10
Polperro Corn 4 F3
Polruan Corn 4 F2
Polsham Som 15 G11
Polstead Suff 30 E6
Poltalloch Argyll 73 D7
Poltimore Devon 7 G8
Polton Midloth 69 D11
Polwarth Borders 70 E6
Polyphant Corn 4 C3
Polzeath Corn 3 B8
Ponders End London 19 B10
Pondersbridge Cambs 37 F8
Pondtail Hants 18 F5
Ponsanooth Corn 3 F6
Ponsworthy Devon 5 D8
Pont Aber Carms 24 F4
Pont Aber-Geirw Gwyn 32 C3
Pont-ar-gothi Carms 23 D10
Pont ar Hydfer Powys 24 F5
Pont-ar-llechau Carms 24 F4
Pont Cwm Pydew Denb 32 B6
Pont Cyfyng Conwy 41 E9
Pont Cysyllte Wrex 33 A8
Pont Dolydd Prysor Gwyn 41 G9
Pont-faen Powys 24 E6
Pont Fronwydd Gwyn 32 C4
Pont-gareg Pembs 22 B6
Pont-Henri Carms 23 F9
Pont-Llogel Powys 32 D6
Pont Pen-y-benglog Gwyn 41 D8
Pont Rhyd-goch Conwy 41 D8
Pont-Rhyd-sarn Gwyn 32 C4
Pont Rhyd-y-cyff Bridgend 14 C4
Pont-rhyd-y-groes Ceredig 24 A4
Pont-rug Gwyn 41 D7
Pont Senni = Sennybridge Powys 24 F6
Pont-siân Ceredig 23 B9
Pont-y-gwaith Rhondda 14 B6
Pont-y-Pŵl = Pontypool Torf 15 A8
Pont-y-pant Conwy 41 E9
Pont y Pennant Gwyn 32 C5
Pont yr Afon-Gam Gwyn 41 F9
Pont-yr-hafod Pembs 22 D4
Pontamman Carms 24 G3
Pontantwn Carms 23 E9
Pontardawe Neath 14 A3
Pontarddulais Swansea 23 F10
Pontarsais Carms 23 D9
Pontblyddyn Flint 42 F5
Pontbren Araeth Carms 24 F3
Pontbren Llwyd Rhondda 24 H6
Pontefract W Yorks 51 G10
Ponteland Northumb 63 F7
Ponterwyd Ceredig 32 G3
Pontesbury Shrops 33 E9
Pontfadog Wrex 33 B8
Pontfaen Pembs 22 C5
Pontgarreg Ceredig 23 A8
Ponthir Torf 15 B9
Ponthirwaun Ceredig 23 B7
Pontllanfraith Caerph 15 B7
Pontlliw Swansea 14 A2
Pontllyfni Gwyn 40 E6
Pontlottyn Caerph 25 H8
Pontneddfechan Powys 24 H6
Pontnewydd Torf 15 B8
Pontrhydfendigaid Ceredig 24 B4
Pontrhydyfen Neath 14 B3
Pontrilas Hereford 25 F10
Pontrobert Powys 33 D7
Ponts Green E Sus 12 E5
Pontshill Hereford 26 F3
Pontsticill M Tydf 25 G7
Pontwgan Conwy 41 C9
Pontyates Carms 23 F9
Pontyberem Carms 23 E10
Pontyclun Rhondda 14 C6
Pontycymer Bridgend 14 B5
Pontyglasier Pembs 22 C6
Pontypool = Pont-y-Pŵl Torf 15 A8
Pontypridd Rhondda 14 C6
Pontywaun Caerph 15 B8
Pooksgreen Hants 10 C2
Pool Corn 2 E5
Pool W Yorks 51 E8
Pool o' Muckhart Clack 76 G3
Pool Quay Powys 33 D8
Poole Poole 9 E9
Poole Keynes Glos 16 B6
Poolend Staffs 44 G3
Poolewe Highld 91 J13
Pooley Bridge Cumb 56 D6
Poolfold Staffs 44 G2
Poolhill Glos 26 F4
Poolsbrook Derbys 45 E8
Pootings Kent 19 G11
Pope Hill Pembs 22 E4
Popeswood Brack 18 E5
Popham Hants 18 G2
Poplar London 19 C10
Popley Hants 18 F3
Porchester Nottingham 36 A1
Porchfield IoW 10 E3
Porin Highld 86 F6
Poringland Norf 39 E8
Porkellis Corn 2 F5
Porlock Som 7 B7
Porlock Weir Som 7 B7
Port Ann Argyll 73 E8
Port Appin Argyll 74 C2
Port Arthur Shetland 96 K5
Port Askaig Argyll 64 B5
Port Bannatyne Argyll 73 G9
Port Carlisle Cumb 61 G8
Port Charlotte Argyll 64 C3
Port Clarence Stockton 58 D5
Port Driseach Argyll 73 F8
Port e Vullen IoM 48 C4
Port Ellen Argyll 64 D4
Port Elphinstone Aberds 83 B9
Port Erin IoM 48 F1
Port Erroll Aberds 89 E10
Port-Eynon Swansea 23 H9
Port Gaverne Corn 3 A9
Port Glasgow Invclyd 68 C2
Port Henderson Highld 85 A12
Port Isaac Corn 3 A8
Port Lamont Argyll 73 F9
Port Lion Pembs 22 F4
Port Logan Dumfries 54 E3
Port Mholair W Isles 91 D10
Port Mor Highld 78 D7
Port Mulgrave N Yorks 59 E8
Port Nan Giùran W Isles 91 D10
Port nan Long W Isles 84 A3
Port Nis W Isles 91 A10
Port of Menteith Stirling 75 G8
Port Quin Corn 3 A8
Port Ramsay Argyll 79 G11
Port St Mary IoM 48 F2
Port Sunlight Mers 42 D6
Port Talbot Neath 14 B3
Port Tennant Swansea 14 B2
Port Wemyss Argyll 64 C2
Port William Dumfries 54 E6
Portachoillan Argyll 72 H6
Portavadie Argyll 73 G8
Portbury N Som 15 D11
Portchester Hants 10 D5
Portclair Highld 80 B6
Portencalzie Dumfries 54 B3
Portencross N Ayrs 66 B4
Portesham Dorset 8 F5
Portessie Moray 88 B4
Portfield Gate Pembs 22 E4
Portgate Devon 4 C5
Portgordon Moray 88 B3
Portgower Highld 93 H13
Porth Corn 3 C7
Porth Rhondda 14 B6
Porth Navas Corn 3 G6
Porth Tywyn = Burry Port Carms 23 F9
Porth-y-waen Shrops 33 C8
Porthaethwy = Menai Bridge Anglesey 41 C7
Porthallow Corn 3 G6
Porthallow Corn 4 F3
Porthcawl Bridgend 14 D4
Porthcothan Corn 3 B7
Porthcurno Corn 2 G2
Porthgain Pembs 22 C3
Porthill Shrops 33 D10
Porthkerry V Glam 14 E6
Porthleven Corn 2 G5
Porthllechog Anglesey 40 A6
Porthmadog Gwyn 41 G7
Porthmeor Corn 2 F3
Portholland Corn 3 E8
Porthoustock Corn 3 G7
Porthpean Corn 3 D9
Porthtowan Corn 2 E5
Porthyrhyd Carms 23 E10
Porthyrhyd Carms 24 E4
Portincaple Argyll 73 D11
Portington E Yorks 52 F3
Portinnisherrich Argyll 73 B8
Portinscale Cumb 56 D4
Portishead N Som 15 D10
Portkil Argyll 73 E11
Portknockie Moray 88 B4
Portlethen Aberds 83 D11
Portling Dumfries 55 D11
Portloe Corn 3 F8
Portmahomack Highld 87 C12
Portmeirion Gwyn 41 G7
Portmellon Corn 3 E9
Portmore Hants 10 E2
Portnacroish Argyll 74 C2
Portnahaven Argyll 64 C2
Portnalong Highld 85 E8
Portnaluchaig Highld 79 C9
Portnancon Highld 92 C7
Portnellan Stirling 75 E7
Portobello Edin 70 C2
Porton Wilts 17 H8
Portpatrick Dumfries 54 D3
Portreath Corn 2 E5
Portree Highld 85 D9
Portscatho Corn 3 F7
Portsea Ptsmth 10 D5
Portskerra Highld 93 C11
Portskewett Mon 15 C11
Portslade Brighton 12 F1
Portslade-by-Sea Brighton 12 F1
Portsmouth Ptsmth 10 D5
Portsmouth W Yorks 50 G5
Portsonachan Argyll 74 E3
Portsoy Aberds 88 B5
Portswood Soton 10 C3
Porttanachy Moray 88 B3
Portuairk Highld 78 E7
Portway Hereford 25 E11
Portway Worcs 27 A7
Portwrinkle Corn 4 F4
Poslingford Suff 30 D4
Postbridge Devon 5 D7
Postcombe Oxon 18 B4
Postling Kent 13 C10
Postwick Norf 39 E8
Potholm Dumfries 61 E9
Potsgrove C Beds 28 F6
Pott Row Norf 38 C3
Pott Shrigley Ches E 44 E3
Potten End Herts 29 H7
Potter Brompton N Yorks 52 B5
Potter Heigham Norf 39 D10
Potter Street Essex 29 H11
Potterhanworth Lincs 46 F4
Potterhanworth Booths Lincs 46 F4
Potterne Wilts 16 F6
Potterne Wick Wilts 17 F7
Potternewton W Yorks 51 F9
Potters Bar Herts 19 A9
Potter's Cross Staffs 34 G4
Potterspury Northants 28 D4
Potterton Aberds 83 B11
Potterton W Yorks 51 F10
Potto N Yorks 58 F5
Potton C Beds 29 D9
Poughill Corn 6 F1
Poughill Devon 7 F7
Poulshot Wilts 16 F6
Poulton Glos 17 A8
Poulton Mers 42 C6
Poulton-le-Fylde Lancs 49 F3
Pound Bank Worcs 26 A4
Pound Green E Sus 12 D4
Pound Green IoW 10 F2
Pound Green Worcs 34 H3
Pound Hill W Sus 12 C1
Poundfield E Sus 12 C4
Poundland S Ayrs 66 H4
Poundon Bucks 28 F3
Poundsgate Devon 5 D8
Poundstock Corn 4 B3
Powburn Northumb 62 B6
Powderham Devon 5 C10
Powerstock Dorset 8 E4
Powfoot Dumfries 61 G7
Powick Worcs 26 C5
Powmill Perth 76 H3
Poxwell Dorset 8 F6
Poyle Slough 19 D7
Poynings W Sus 12 E1
Poyntington Dorset 8 C5
Poynton Ches E 44 D3
Poynton Green Telford 34 D1
Poystreet Green Suff 30 C6
Praa Sands Corn 2 G4
Pratt's Bottom London 19 E11
Praze Corn 2 F4
Praze-an-Beeble Corn 2 F5
Predannack Wollas Corn 2 H5
Prees Shrops 34 B1
Prees Green Shrops 34 B1
Prees Heath Shrops 34 B1
Prees Higher Heath Shrops 34 B1
Prees Lower Heath Shrops 34 B1
Preesall Lancs 49 E3
Preesgweene Shrops 33 B8
Prenderguest Borders 71 E8
Prendwick Northumb 62 B6
Prengwyn Ceredig 23 B9
Prenteg Gwyn 41 F7
Prenton Mers 42 D6
Prescot Mers 43 C7
Prescott Shrops 33 C10
Pressen Northumb 71 G7
Prestatyn Denb 42 D3
Prestbury Ches E 44 E3
Prestbury Glos 26 F6
Presteigne = Llanandras Powys 25 B10
Presthope Shrops 34 F1
Prestleigh Som 16 G3
Preston Borders 70 E6
Preston Brighton 12 F2
Preston Devon 5 D9
Preston Dorset 8 F6
Preston E Loth 70 C4
Preston E Yorks 53 F7
Preston Glos 17 A7
Preston Glos 26 E3
Preston Herts 29 F8
Preston Kent 21 E9
Preston Kent 21 E7
Preston Lancs 49 G5
Preston Northumb 71 H10
Preston Rutland 36 E4
Preston Shrops 33 D11
Preston Wilts 17 D7
Preston Wilts 17 D9
Preston Bagot Warks 27 B8
Preston Bissett Bucks 28 F3
Preston Bowyer Som 7 D10
Preston Brockhurst Shrops 33 C11
Preston Brook Halton 43 D8
Preston Candover Hants 18 G3
Preston Capes Northants 28 C2
Preston Crowmarsh Oxon 18 B3
Preston Gubbals Shrops 33 D10
Preston on Stour Warks 27 C9
Preston on the Hill Halton 43 D8
Preston on Wye Hereford 25 D10
Preston Plucknett Som 8 C4
Preston St Mary Suff 30 C6
Preston-under-Scar N Yorks 58 G1
Preston upon the Weald Moors Telford 34 D2
Preston Wynne Hereford 26 D2
Prestonmill Dumfries 60 H5
Prestonpans E Loth 70 C2
Prestwich Gtr Man 44 B2
Prestwick Northumb 63 F7
Prestwick S Ayrs 67 D6
Prestwood Bucks 18 A5
Price Town Bridgend 14 B5
Prickwillow Cambs 38 G1
Priddy Som 15 F11
Priest Hutton Lancs 49 B5
Priest Weston Shrops 33 F8
Priesthaugh Borders 61 C10
Primethorpe Leics 35 F11
Primrose Green Norf 39 D6
Primrose Valley N Yorks 53 B7
Primrosehill Herts 19 A7
Princes Gate Pembs 22 E6
Princes Risborough Bucks 18 A5
Princethorpe Warks 27 A11
Princetown Caerph 25 G8
Princetown Devon 5 D6
Prion Denb 42 F3
Prior Muir Fife 77 F8
Prior Park Northumb 71 E8
Priors Frome Hereford 26 E2
Priors Hardwick Warks 27 C11
Priors Marston Warks 27 C11
Priorslee Telford 34 D3
Priory Wood Hereford 25 D9
Priston Bath 16 E3
Pristow Green Norf 39 G7
Prittlewell Southend 20 C5
Privett Hants 10 B5
Prixford Devon 6 C4
Probus Corn 3 E7
Proncy Highld 87 B10
Prospect Cumb 56 B3
Prudhoe Northumb 62 G6
Ptarmigan Lodge Stirling 74 G6
Pubil Perth 75 C7
Puckeridge Herts 29 F10
Puckington Som 8 C2
Pucklechurch S Glos 16 D3
Pucknall Hants 10 B2
Puckrup Glos 26 E5
Puddinglake Ches W 43 F10
Puddington Ches W 42 E6
Puddington Devon 7 E7
Puddledock Norf 39 F6
Puddletown Dorset 9 E6
Pudleston Hereford 26 C2
Pudsey W Yorks 51 F8
Pulborough W Sus 11 C9
Puleston Telford 34 C3
Pulford Ches W 43 G6
Pulham Dorset 8 D6
Pulham Market Norf 39 G7
Pulham St Mary Norf 39 G8
Pulloxhill C Beds 29 E7
Pumpherston W Loth 69 D9
Pumsaint Carms 24 D3
Puncheston Pembs 22 D5
Puncknowle Dorset 8 F4
Punnett's Town E Sus 12 D5
Purbrook Hants 10 D5
Purewell Dorset 9 E10
Purfleet Thurrock 20 D2
Puriton Som 15 G9
Purleigh Essex 20 A5
Purley London 19 E10
Purley W Berks 18 D3
Purlogue Shrops 33 H8
Purls Bridge Cambs 37 G10
Purse Caundle Dorset 8 C5
Purslow Shrops 33 G9
Purston Jaglin W Yorks 51 H10
Purton Glos 16 A3
Purton Glos 16 A3
Purton Wilts 17 C7
Purton Stoke Wilts 17 B7
Pury End Northants 28 D4
Pusey Oxon 17 B10
Putley Hereford 26 E3
Putney London 19 D9
Putsborough Devon 6 B3
Puttenham Herts 28 G5
Puttenham Sur 18 G6
Puxton N Som 15 E10
Pwll Carms 23 F9
Pwll-glas Denb 42 G4
Pwll-trap Carms 23 E7
Pwll-y-glaw Neath 14 B3
Pwllcrochan Pembs 22 F4
Pwllgloyw Powys 25 E7
Pwllheli Gwyn 40 G5
Pwllmeyric Mon 15 B11
Pye Corner Newport 15 C9
Pye Green Staffs 34 D5
Pyecombe W Sus 12 E1
Pyewipe NE Lincs 46 A6
Pyle = Y Pîl Bridgend 14 C4
Pyle IoW 10 G3
Pylle Som 16 H3
Pymoor Cambs 37 G10
Pyrford Sur 19 F7
Pyrton Oxon 18 B3
Pytchley Northants 28 A5
Pyworthy Devon 6 F2

Q

Quabbs Shrops 33 G8
Quadring Lincs 37 B8
Quainton Bucks 28 G4
Quarley Hants 17 G9
Quarndon Derbys 35 A9
Quarrier's Homes Invclyd 68 D2
Quarrington Lincs 37 A6
Quarrington Hill Durham 58 C4
Quarry Bank W Mid 34 G5
Quarryford E Loth 70 D4
Quarryhill Highld 87 C10
Quarrywood Moray 88 B1
Quarter S Lanark 68 E6
Quatford Shrops 34 F3
Quatt Shrops 34 G3
Quebec Durham 58 B2
Quedgeley Glos 26 G5
Queen Adelaide Cambs 38 G1
Queen Camel Som 8 B4
Queen Charlton Bath 16 E3
Queen Dart Devon 7 E7
Queen Oak Dorset 9 A6
Queen Street Kent 20 G3
Queen Street Wilts 17 C7
Queenborough Kent 20 D6
Queenhill Worcs 26 E5
Queen's Head Shrops 33 C9
Queen's Park Bedford 29 D7
Queen's Park Northants 28 B4
Queensbury W Yorks 51 F7
Queensferry Edin 69 C10
Queensferry Flint 42 F6
Queenstown Blackpool 49 F3
Queenzieburn N Lanark 68 C5
Quemerford Wilts 17 E7
Quendale Shetland 96 M5
Quendon Essex 30 E2
Queniborough Leics 36 D2
Quenington Glos 17 A8
Quernmore Lancs 49 D5
Quethiock Corn 4 E4
Quholm Orkney 95 G3
Quicks Green W Berks 18 D2
Quidenham Norf 38 G6
Quidhampton Hants 18 F2
Quidhampton Wilts 9 A10
Quilquox Aberds 89 E9
Quina Brook Shrops 33 B11
Quindry Orkney 95 J5
Quinton Northants 28 C4
Quinton W Mid 34 G5
Quintrell Downs Corn 3 C7
Quixhill Staffs 35 A7
Quoditch Devon 6 G3
Quoig Perth 75 E11
Quorndon Leics 36 D1
Quothquan S Lanark 69 G8
Quoyloo Orkney 95 F3
Quoyness Orkney 95 H3
Quoys Shetland 96 B8
Quoys Shetland 96 G6

R

Raasay Ho. Highld 85 E10
Rabbit's Cross Kent 20 G4
Raby Mers 42 E6
Rachan Mill Borders 69 G10
Rachub Gwyn 41 D8
Rackenford Devon 7 E7
Rackham W Sus 11 C9
Rackheath Norf 39 D8
Racks Dumfries 60 F6
Rackwick Orkney 95 D5
Rackwick Orkney 95 J3
Radbourne Derbys 35 B8
Radcliffe Gtr Man 43 B10
Radcliffe Northumb 63 C8
Radcliffe on Trent Notts 36 B2
Radclive Bucks 28 E3
Radcot Oxon 17 B9
Raddery Highld 87 F10
Radernie Fife 77 G7
Radford Semele Warks 27 B10
Radipole Dorset 8 F5
Radlett Herts 19 B8
Radley Oxon 18 B2
Radmanthwaite Notts 45 F9
Radmoor Shrops 34 C2
Radmore Green Ches E 43 G8
Radnage Bucks 18 B4
Radstock Bath 16 F3
Radstone Northants 28 D2
Radway Warks 27 D10
Radway Green Ches E 43 G10
Radwell Bedford 29 C7
Radwell Herts 29 E9
Radwinter Essex 30 E3
Radyr Cardiff 15 C7
Rafford Moray 87 F13
Ragdale Leics 36 D2
Raglan Mon 25 H11
Ragnall Notts 46 E2
Rahane Argyll 73 E11
Rainford Mers 43 B7
Rainford Junction Mers 43 B7
Rainham London 20 C2
Rainham Medway 20 E5
Rainhill Mers 43 C7
Rainhill Stoops Mers 43 C8
Rainow Ches E 44 E3
Rainton N Yorks 51 B9
Rainworth Notts 45 G9
Raisbeck Cumb 57 F8
Raise Cumb 57 B9
Rait Perth 76 E5
Raithby Lincs 47 D7
Raithby Lincs 47 F7
Rake W Sus 11 B7
Rakewood Gtr Man 44 A3
Ram Carms 23 B10
Ram Lane Kent 20 G6
Ramasaig Highld 84 D6
Rame Corn 2 F6
Rame Corn 4 G5
Rameldry Mill Bank Fife 76 G6
Ramnageo Shetland 96 C8
Rampisham Dorset 8 D4
Rampside Cumb 49 C2
Rampton Cambs 29 B11
Rampton Notts 45 E11
Ramsbottom Gtr Man 50 H3
Ramsbury Wilts 17 D9
Ramscraigs Highld 94 H3
Ramsdean Hants 10 B6
Ramsdell Hants 18 F2
Ramsden Oxon 27 G10
Ramsden Bellhouse Essex 20 B4
Ramsden Heath Essex 20 B4
Ramsey Cambs 37 G8
Ramsey Essex 31 E9
Ramsey IoM 48 C4
Ramsey Forty Foot Cambs 37 G9
Ramsey Heights Cambs 37 G8
Ramsey Island Essex 30 H6
Ramsey Mereside Cambs 37 G8
Ramsey St Mary's Cambs 37 G8
Ramseycleuch Borders 61 B8
Ramsgate Kent 21 E10
Ramsgill N Yorks 51 B7
Ramshorn Staffs 44 H4
Ramsnest Common Sur 11 A8
Ranais W Isles 91 E9
Ranby Lincs 46 E6
Ranby Notts 45 D10
Rand Lincs 46 E5
Randwick Glos 26 H5
Ranfurly Renfs 68 D2
Rangag Highld 94 F3
Rangemore Staffs 35 C7
Rangeworthy S Glos 16 C3
Rankinston E Ayrs 67 E7
Ranmoor S Yorks 45 D7
Ranmore Common Sur 19 F8
Rannerdale Cumb 56 E3
Rannoch Station Perth 75 B7
Ranochan Highld 79 C11
Ranskill Notts 45 D10
Ranton Staffs 34 C4
Ranworth Norf 39 D9
Raploch Stirling 68 A6
Rapness Orkney 95 D6
Rascal Moor E Yorks 52 F4
Rascarrel Dumfries 55 E10
Rashiereive Aberds 89 F9
Raskelf N Yorks 51 B10
Rassau Bl Gwent 25 G8
Rastrick W Yorks 51 G7
Ratagan Highld 85 G14
Ratby Leics 35 E11
Ratcliffe Culey Leics 35 F9
Ratcliffe on Soar Leics 35 C10
Ratcliffe on the Wreake Leics 36 D2
Rathen Aberds 89 B10
Rathillet Fife 76 E6
Rathmell N Yorks 50 D4
Ratho Edin 69 C10
Ratho Station Edin 69 C10
Rathven Moray 88 B4
Ratley Warks 27 D10
Ratlinghope Shrops 33 F10
Rattar Highld 94 C4
Ratten Row Lancs 49 E4
Rattery Devon 5 E8
Rattlesden Suff 30 C6
Rattray Perth 76 C4
Raughton Head Cumb 56 B5
Raunds Northants 28 A6
Ravenfield S Yorks 45 C8
Ravenglass Cumb 56 G2
Raveningham Norf 39 F9
Ravenscar N Yorks 59 F10
Ravenscraig Invclyd 73 F11
Ravensdale IoM 48 C3
Ravensden Bedford 29 C7
Ravenseat N Yorks 57 F10
Ravenshead Notts 45 G9
Ravensmoor Ches E 43 G9
Ravensthorpe Northants 28 A3
Ravensthorpe W Yorks 51 G8
Ravenstone Leics 35 D10
Ravenstone M Keynes 28 C5
Ravenstonedale Cumb 57 F9
Ravenstown Cumb 49 B3
Ravenstruther S Lanark 69 F8
Ravensworth N Yorks 58 F2
Raw N Yorks 59 F10
Rawcliffe E Yorks 52 G2
Rawcliffe York 52 D1
Rawcliffe Bridge E Yorks 52 G2
Rawdon W Yorks 51 F8
Rawmarsh S Yorks 45 C8
Rawreth Essex 20 B4
Rawridge Devon 7 F11
Rawtenstall Lancs 50 G4
Raxton Aberds 89 E8
Raydon Suff 31 E7
Raylees Northumb 62 D5
Rayleigh Essex 20 B5
Rayne Essex 30 F4
Rayners Lane London 19 C8
Raynes Park London 19 E9
Reach Cambs 30 B2
Read Lancs 50 F3
Reading Reading 18 D4
Reading Street Kent 13 C8
Reagill Cumb 57 E8
Rearquhar Highld 87 B10
Rearsby Leics 36 D2
Reaster Highld 94 D4
Reawick Shetland 96 J5
Reay Highld 93 C12
Rechullin Highld 85 C13
Reculver Kent 21 E9
Red Dial Cumb 56 B4
Red Hill Worcs 26 C5
Red Houses Jersey 11
Red Lodge Suff 30 A3
Red Rail Hereford 26 F2
Red Rock Gtr Man 43 B8
Red Roses Carms 23 E7
Red Row Northumb 63 D8
Red Street Staffs 44 G2
Red Wharf Bay Anglesey 41 B7
Redberth Pembs 22 F5
Redbourn Herts 29 G8
Redbourne N Lincs 46 C3
Redbrook Mon 26 G2
Redbrook Wrex 33 A11
Redburn Highld 87 E8
Redburn Highld 87 G12
Redburn Northumb 62 G3
Redcar Redcar 59 D7
Redcastle Angus 77 B9
Redcastle Highld 87 G8
Redcliff Bay N Som 15 D10
Redding Falk 69 C8
Reddingmuirhead Falk 69 C8
Reddish Gtr Man 44 C2
Redditch Worcs 27 B7
Rede Suff 30 C5
Redenhall Norf 39 G8
Redesdale Camp Northumb 62 D4
Redesmouth Northumb 62 E4
Redford Aberds 83 F9
Redford Angus 77 C8
Redford Durham 58 C1
Redfordgreen Borders 61 B9
Redgorton Perth 76 E3
Redgrave Suff 38 H6
Redhill Aberds 83 C9
Redhill Aberds 89 E6
Redhill N Som 15 E11
Redhill Sur 19 F9
Redhouse Argyll 73 G7
Redhouses Argyll 64 B4
Redisham Suff 39 G10
Redland Bristol 16 D2
Redland Orkney 95 F4
Redlingfield Suff 31 A8
Redlynch Som 8 A6
Redlynch Wilts 9 B11
Redmarley D'Abitot Glos 26 E4
Redmarshall Stockton 58 D4
Redmile Leics 36 B3
Redmire N Yorks 58 G1
Redmoor Corn 4 E1
Rednal Shrops 33 C9
Redpath Borders 70 G4
Redpoint Highld 85 B12
Redruth Corn 2 E5
Redvales Gtr Man 44 B2
Redwick Newport 15 C10
Redwick S Glos 15 C11
Redworth Darl 58 D3
Reed Herts 29 E10
Reedham Norf 39 E10
Reedness E Yorks 52 G3
Reeds Beck Lincs 46 F6
Reepham Lincs 46 E4
Reepham Norf 39 C6
Reeth N Yorks 58 G1
Regaby IoM 48 C4
Regoul Highld 87 F11
Reiff Highld 92 H2
Reigate Sur 19 F9
Reighton N Yorks 53 B7
Reighton Gap N Yorks 53 B7
Reinigeadal W Isles 90 G7
Reiss Highld 94 E5
Rejerrah Corn 3 D6
Releath Corn 2 F5
Relubbus Corn 2 F4
Relugas Moray 87 G12
Remenham Wokingham 18 C4
Remenham Hill Wokingham 18 C4
Remony Perth 75 C10
Rempstone Notts 36 C1
Rendcomb Glos 27 H7
Rendham Suff 31 B10
Rendlesham Suff 31 C10
Renfrew Renfs 68 D4
Renhold Bedford 29 C7
Renishaw Derbys 45 E8
Rennington Northumb 63 B8
Renton W Dunb 68 C2
Renwick Cumb 57 B7
Repps Norf 39 D10
Repton Derbys 35 C9
Reraig Highld 85 F13
Rescobie Angus 77 B8
Resipole Highld 79 E10
Resolis Highld 87 E9
Resolven Neath 14 A4
Reston Borders 71 D7
Reswallie Angus 77 B8
Retew Corn 3 D8
Retford Notts 45 D11
Rettendon Essex 20 B4
Rettendon Place Essex 20 B4
Revesby Lincs 46 F6
Revesby Bridge Lincs 47 F7
Rew Street IoW 10 E3
Rewe Devon 7 G8
Reydon Suff 39 H10
Reydon Smear Suff 39 H10
Reymerston Norf 38 E6
Reynalton Pembs 22 F5
Reynoldston Swansea 23 G9
Rezare Corn 4 D4
Rhôs Carms 23 C8
Rhôs Neath 14 A3
Rhlŷd-y-foel Conwy 42 E2
Rhaeadr Gwy = Rhayader Powys 24 B6
Rhandirmwyn Carms 24 D4
Rhayader = Rhaeadr Gwy Powys 24 B6
Rhedyn Gwyn 40 G4
Rhemore Highld 79 F8
Rhencullen IoM 48 C3
Rhes-y-cae Flint 42 E4
Rhewl Denb 42 F4
Rhewl Denb 42 H4
Rhian Highld 93 H8
Rhicarn Highld 92 G3
Rhiconich Highld 92 D5
Rhicullen Highld 87 D9
Rhidorroch Ho. Highld 86 B4
Rhifail Highld 93 E10
Rhigos Rhondda 24 H6
Rhilochan Highld 93 J10
Rhiroy Highld 86 C4
Rhisga = Risca Caerph 15 B8
Rhiw Gwyn 40 H4
Rhiwabon = Ruabon Wrex 33 A9
Rhiwbina Cardiff 15 C7
Rhiwbryfdir Gwyn 41 F8
Rhiwderin Newport 15 C8
Rhiwlas Gwyn 32 B5
Rhiwlas Gwyn 41 D7
Rhiwlas Powys 33 B7
Rhodes Gtr Man 44 B2
Rhodes Minnis Kent 21 G8
Rhodesia Notts 45 E9
Rhodiad Pembs 22 D2
Rhondda Rhondda 14 B5
Rhonehouse or Kelton Hill Dumfries 55 D10
Rhoose = Y Rhws V Glam 14 E6
Rhos-fawr Gwyn 40 G5
Rhos-goch Powys 25 D8
Rhos-hill Pembs 22 B6
Rhos-on-Sea Conwy 41 B10
Rhos-y-brithdir Powys 33 C7
Rhos-y-garth Ceredig 24 A3
Rhos-y-gwaliau Gwyn 32 B5
Rhos-y-llan Gwyn 40 G4
Rhos-y-Madoc Wrex 33 A9
Rhos-y-meirch Powys 25 B9
Rhosaman Carms 24 G4
Rhosbeirio Anglesey 40 A5
Rhoscefnhir Anglesey 41 C7
Rhoscolyn Anglesey 40 C4
Rhoscrowther Pembs 22 F4
Rhosesmor Flint 42 F5
Rhosgadfan Gwyn 41 E7
Rhosgoch Anglesey 40 B6
Rhoshirwaun Gwyn 40 H3
Rhoslan Gwyn 40 F6
Rhoslefain Gwyn 32 E1
Rhosllanerchrugog Wrex 42 H5
Rhosmaen Carms 24 F3
Rhosmeirch Anglesey 40 C6
Rhosneigr Anglesey 40 C5
Rhosnesni Wrex 42 G6
Rhosrobin Wrex 42 G6
Rhossili Swansea 23 H9
Rhosson Pembs 22 D2
Rhostryfan Gwyn 40 E6
Rhostyllen Wrex 42 H6
Rhosybol Anglesey 40 B6
Rhu Argyll 73 E11
Rhu Argyll 73 G7
Rhuallt Denb 42 E3

Rhuddall Heath Ches W 43 F8
Rhuddlan Ceredig 23 B9
Rhuddlan Denb 42 E3
Rhue Highld 86 B3
Rhulen Powys 25 D8
Rhunahaorine Argyll 65 D8
Rhuthun = Ruthin Denb 42 G4
Rhyd Gwyn 41 F8
Rhyd Powys 32 E5
Rhyd-Ddu Gwyn 41 E7
Rhyd-moel-ddu Powys 33 H6
Rhyd-Rosser Ceredig 24 B2
Rhyd-uchaf Gwyn 32 B5
Rhyd-wen Gwyn 32 D3
Rhyd-y-clafdy Gwyn 40 G5
Rhyd-y-fro Neath 24 H4
Rhyd-y-gwin Swansea 14 A2
Rhyd-y-meirch Mon 25 H10
Rhyd-y-meudwy Denb 42 G4
Rhyd-y-pandy Swansea 14 A2
Rhyd-y-sarn Gwyn 41 F8
Rhyd-yr-onen Gwyn 32 E2
Rhydaman = Ammanford Carms 24 G3
Rhydargaeau Carms 23 D9
Rhydcymerau Carms 23 C10
Rhydd Worcs 26 D5
Rhydding Neath 14 B3
Rhydfudr Ceredig 24 B2
Rhydlewis Ceredig 23 B8
Rhydlios Gwyn 40 G3
Rhydlydan Conwy 41 E10
Rhydness Powys 25 D8
Rhydowen Ceredig 23 B9
Rhydspence Hereford 25 D9
Rhydtalog Flint 42 G5
Rhydwyn Anglesey 40 B5
Rhydycroesau Powys 33 B8
Rhydyfelin Ceredig 32 H1
Rhydyfelin Rhondda 14 C6
Rhydymain Gwyn 32 C4
Rhydymwyn Flint 42 F5
Rhyl = Y Rhyl Denb 42 D3
Rhymney = Rhymni Caerph 25 H8
Rhymni = Rhymney Caerph 25 H8
Rhynd Fife 77 E7
Rhynd Perth 76 E4
Rhynie Aberds 82 A6
Rhynie Highld 87 D11
Ribbesford Worcs 26 A4
Ribblehead N Yorks 50 B3
Ribbleton Lancs 50 F1
Ribchester Lancs 50 F2
Ribigill Highld 93 D8
Riby Lincs 46 B5
Riby Cross Roads Lincs 46 B5
Riccall N Yorks 52 F2
Riccarton E Ayrs 67 C7
Richards Castle Hereford 25 B11
Richings Park Bucks 19 D7
Richmond London 19 D8
Richmond N Yorks 58 F2
Rickarton Aberds 83 E10
Rickinghall Suff 38 H6
Rickleton T&W 58 A3
Rickling Essex 29 E11
Rickmansworth Herts 19 B7
Riddings Cumb 61 F10
Riddings Derbys 45 G8
Riddlecombe Devon 6 E5
Riddlesden W Yorks 51 E6
Riddrie Glasgow 68 D5
Ridge Dorset 9 F8
Ridge Hants 10 C2
Ridge Wilts 9 A8
Ridge Green Sur 19 G10
Ridge Lane Warks 35 F8
Ridgebourne Powys 25 B7
Ridgehill N Som 15 E11
Ridgeway Cross Hereford 26 D4
Ridgewell Essex 30 D4
Ridgewood E Sus 12 E3
Ridgmont C Beds 28 E6
Riding Mill Northumb 62 G6
Ridleywood Wrex 43 G7
Ridlington Norf 39 B9
Ridlington Rutland 36 E4
Ridsdale Northumb 62 E5
Riechip Perth 76 C3
Riemore Perth 76 C3
Rienachait Highld 92 F3
Rievaulx N Yorks 59 H6
Rift House Hrtlpl 58 C5
Rigg Dumfries 61 G8
Riggend N Lanark 68 C6
Rigsby Lincs 47 E8
Rigside S Lanark 69 G7
Riley Green Lancs 50 G2
Rileyhill Staffs 35 D7
Rilla Mill Corn 4 D3
Rillington N Yorks 52 B4
Rimington Lancs 50 E4
Rimpton Som 8 B5
Rimswell E Yorks 53 G9
Rinaston Pembs 22 D4
Ringasta Shetland 96 M5
Ringford Dumfries 55 D9
Ringinglow S Yorks 44 D6
Ringland Norf 39 D7
Ringles Cross E Sus 12 D3
Ringmer E Sus 12 E3
Ringmore Devon 5 G7
Ringorm Moray 88 D2
Ring's End Cambs 37 E9
Ringsfield Suff 39 G10
Ringsfield Corner Suff 39 G10
Ringshall Herts 28 G6
Ringshall Suff 31 C7
Ringshall Stocks Suff 31 C7
Ringstead Norf 38 A3
Ringstead Northants 36 H5
Ringwood Hants 9 D10
Ringwould Kent 21 G10
Rinmore Aberds 82 B6
Rinnigill Orkney 95 J4
Rinsey Corn 2 G4
Riof W Isles 90 D6
Ripe E Sus 12 E4
Ripley Derbys 45 G7
Ripley Hants 9 E10
Ripley N Yorks 51 C8
Ripley Sur 19 F7
Riplingham E Yorks 52 F5
Ripon N Yorks 51 B9
Rippingale Lincs 37 C6
Ripple Kent 21 G10
Ripple Worcs 26 E5
Ripponden W Yorks 50 H6
Rireavach Highld 86 B3
Risabus Argyll 64 D4
Risbury Hereford 26 C2
Risby Suff 30 B4
Risca = Rhisga Caerph 15 B8
Rise E Yorks 53 E7
Riseden E Sus 12 C5
Risegate Lincs 37 C8
Riseholme Lincs 46 E3
Riseley Bedford 29 B7
Riseley Wokingham 18 E4
Rishangles Suff 31 B8
Rishton Lancs 50 F3
Rishworth W Yorks 50 H6
Rising Bridge Lancs 50 G3
Risley Derbys 35 B10
Risley Warr 43 C9
Risplith N Yorks 51 C8
Rispond Highld 92 C7
Rivar Wilts 17 E10
Rivenhall End Essex 30 G5
River Bank Cambs 30 B2
Riverhead Kent 20 F2
Rivington Lancs 43 A9
Roa Island Cumb 49 C2
Roachill Devon 7 D7
Road Green Norf 39 F8
Roade Northants 28 C4
Roadhead Cumb 61 F11
Roadmeetings S Lanark 69 F7
Roadside Highld 94 D3
Roadside of Catterline Aberds 83 F10
Roadside of Kinneff Aberds 83 F10
Roadwater Som 7 C9
Roag Highld 85 D7
Roath Cardiff 15 D7
Roberton Borders 61 B10
Roberton S Lanark 69 H8
Robertsbridge E Sus 12 D6
Roberttown W Yorks 51 G7
Robeston Cross Pembs 22 F3
Robeston Wathen Pembs 22 E5
Robin Hood W Yorks 51 G9
Robin Hood's Bay N Yorks 59 F10
Roborough Devon 4 E6
Roborough Devon 6 E4
Roby Mers 43 C7
Roby Mill Lancs 43 B8
Rocester Staffs 35 B7
Roch Pembs 22 D3
Roch Gate Pembs 22 D3
Rochdale Gtr Man 44 A2
Roche Corn 3 C8
Rochester Medway 20 E4
Rochester Northumb 62 D4
Rochford Essex 20 B5
Rock Corn 3 B8
Rock Northumb 63 A8
Rock W Sus 11 C10
Rock Worcs 26 A4
Rock Ferry Mers 42 D6
Rockbeare Devon 7 G9
Rockbourne Hants 9 C10
Rockcliffe Cumb 61 G9
Rockcliffe Dumfries 55 D11
Rockfield Highld 87 C12
Rockfield Mon 25 G11
Rockford Hants 9 D10
Rockhampton S Glos 16 B3
Rockingham Northants 36 F4
Rockland All Saints Norf 38 F5
Rockland St Mary Norf 39 E9
Rockland St Peter Norf 38 F5
Rockley Wilts 17 D8
Rockwell End Bucks 18 C4
Rockwell Green Som 7 D10
Rodborough Glos 16 A5
Rodbourne Swindon 17 C8
Rodbourne Wilts 16 C6
Rodbourne Cheney Swindon 17 C8
Rodd Hereford 25 B10
Roddam Northumb 62 A6
Rodden Dorset 8 F5
Rode Som 16 F5
Rode Heath Ches E 44 G2
Rodeheath Ches E 44 F2
Roden Telford 34 D1
Rodhuish Som 7 C9
Rodington Telford 34 D1
Rodley Glos 26 G4
Rodley W Yorks 51 F8
Rodmarton Glos 16 B6
Rodmell E Sus 12 F3
Rodmersham Kent 20 E6
Rodney Stoke Som 15 F10
Rodsley Derbys 35 A8
Rodway Som 15 H8
Rodwell Dorset 8 G5
Roe Green Herts 29 E10
Roecliffe N Yorks 51 C9
Roehampton London 19 D9
Roesound Shetland 96 G5
Roffey W Sus 11 A10
Rogart Highld 93 J10
Rogart Station Highld 93 J10
Rogate W Sus 11 B7
Rogerstone Newport 15 C8
Roghadal W Isles 90 J5
Rogiet Mon 15 C10
Rogue's Alley Cambs 37 E9
Roke Oxon 18 B3
Roker T&W 63 H10
Rollesby Norf 39 D10
Rolleston Leics 36 E3
Rolleston Notts 45 G11
Rolleston-on-Dove Staffs 35 C8
Rolston E Yorks 53 E8
Rolvenden Kent 13 C7
Rolvenden Layne Kent 13 C7
Romaldkirk Durham 57 D11
Romanby N Yorks 58 G4
Romannobridge Borders 69 F10
Romansleigh Devon 7 D6
Romford London 20 C2
Romiley Gtr Man 44 C3
Romsey Hants 10 B2
Romsey Town Cambs 29 C11
Romsley Shrops 34 G3
Romsley Worcs 34 H5
Ronague IoM 48 E2
Rookhope Durham 57 B11
Rookley IoW 10 F4
Rooks Bridge Som 15 F9
Roos E Yorks 53 F8
Roosebeck Cumb 49 C2
Rootham's Green Bedford 29 C8
Rootpark S Lanark 69 E8
Ropley Hants 10 A5
Ropley Dean Hants 10 A5
Ropsley Lincs 36 B5
Rora Aberds 89 C10
Rorandle Aberds 83 B8
Rorrington Shrops 33 E9
Roscroggan Corn 2 E5
Rose Corn 3 D6
Rose Ash Devon 7 D6
Rose Green W Sus 11 E8
Rose Grove Lancs 50 F4
Rose Hill E Sus 12 E3
Rose Hill Lancs 50 F4
Rose Hill Suff 31 D8
Roseacre Kent 20 F4
Roseacre Lancs 49 F4
Rosebank S Lanark 69 F7
Rosebrough Northumb 71 H10
Rosebush Pembs 22 D5
Rosecare Corn 4 B2
Rosedale Abbey N Yorks 59 G8
Roseden Northumb 62 A6
Rosefield Highld 87 F11
Rosehall Highld 92 J7
Rosehaugh Mains Highld 87 F9
Rosehearty Aberds 89 B9
Rosehill Shrops 34 B2
Roseisle Moray 88 B1
Roselands E Sus 12 F5
Rosemarket Pembs 22 F4
Rosemarkie Highld 87 F10
Rosemary Lane Devon 7 E10
Rosemount Perth 76 C4
Rosenannon Corn 3 C8
Rosewell Midloth 69 D11
Roseworth Stockton 58 D5
Roseworthy Corn 2 F5
Rosgill Cumb 57 E7
Roshven Highld 79 D10
Roskhill Highld 85 D7
Roskill House Highld 87 F9
Rosley Cumb 56 B5
Roslin Midloth 69 D11
Rosliston Derbys 35 D8
Rosneath Argyll 73 E11
Ross Dumfries 55 E9
Ross Northumb 71 G10
Ross Perth 75 E10
Ross-on-Wye Hereford 26 F3
Rossett Wrex 42 G6
Rossett Green N Yorks 51 D9
Rossie Ochill Perth 76 F3
Rossie Priory Perth 76 D5
Rossington S Yorks 45 C10
Rosskeen Highld 87 E9
Rossland Renfs 68 C3
Roster Highld 94 G4
Rostherne Ches E 43 D10
Rosthwaite Cumb 56 E4
Roston Derbys 35 A7
Rosyth Fife 69 B10
Rothbury Northumb 62 C6
Rotherby Leics 36 D2
Rotherfield E Sus 12 D4
Rotherfield Greys Oxon 18 C4
Rotherfield Peppard Oxon 18 C4
Rotherham S Yorks 45 C8
Rothersthorpe Northants 28 C4
Rotherwick Hants 18 F4
Rothes Moray 88 D2
Rothesay Argyll 73 G9
Rothiebrisbane Aberds 89 E7
Rothienorman Aberds 89 E7
Rothiesholm Orkney 95 F7
Rothley Leics 36 D1
Rothley Northumb 62 E6
Rothley Shield East Northumb 62 D6
Rothmaise Aberds 89 E6
Rothwell Lincs 46 C5
Rothwell Northants 36 G4
Rothwell W Yorks 51 G9
Rothwell Haigh W Yorks 51 G9
Rotsea E Yorks 53 D6
Rottal Angus 82 G5
Rotten End Suff 31 B10
Rottingdean Brighton 12 F2
Rottington Cumb 56 E1
Roud IoW 10 F4
Rough Close Staffs 34 B5
Rough Common Kent 21 F8
Rougham Norf 38 C4
Rougham Suff 30 B6
Rougham Green Suff 30 B6
Roughburn Highld 80 E5
Roughlee Lancs 50 E4
Roughley W Mid 35 F7
Roughsike Cumb 61 F11
Roughton Lincs 46 F6
Roughton Norf 39 B8
Roughton Shrops 34 F3
Roughton Moor Lincs 46 F6
Roundhay W Yorks 51 F9
Roundstonefoot Dumfries 61 C7
Roundstreet Common W Sus 11 B9
Roundway Wilts 17 E7
Rous Lench Worcs 27 C7
Rousdon Devon 8 E1
Routenburn N Ayrs 73 G10
Routh E Yorks 53 E6
Row Corn 4 D1
Row Cumb 56 H6
Row Heath Essex 31 G8
Rowanburn Dumfries 61 F10
Rowardennan Stirling 74 H6
Rowde Wilts 16 E6
Rowen Conwy 41 C9
Rowfoot Northumb 62 G2
Rowhedge Essex 31 F7
Rowhook W Sus 11 A10
Rowington Warks 27 B9
Rowland Derbys 44 E6
Rowlands Castle Hants 10 C6
Rowlands Gill T&W 63 H7
Rowledge Sur 18 G5
Rowlestone Hereford 25 F10
Rowley E Yorks 52 F5
Rowley Shrops 33 E9
Rowley Hill W Yorks 44 A5
Rowley Regis W Mid 34 G5
Rowly Sur 19 G7
Rowney Green Worcs 27 A7
Rownhams Hants 10 C2
Rowrah Cumb 56 E2
Rowsham Bucks 28 G5
Rowsley Derbys 44 F6
Rowstock Oxon 17 C11
Rowston Lincs 46 G4
Rowton Ches W 43 F7
Rowton Shrops 33 D9
Rowton Telford 34 D2
Roxburgh Borders 70 G6
Roxby N Lincs 52 H5
Roxby N Yorks 59 E8
Roxton Bedford 29 C8
Roxwell Essex 30 H3
Royal Leamington Spa Warks 27 B10
Royal Oak Darl 58 D3
Royal Oak Lancs 43 B7
Royal Tunbridge Wells Kent 12 C4
Royal Wootton Bassett Wilts 17 C7
Roybridge Highld 80 E4
Roydhouse W Yorks 44 A6
Roydon Essex 29 H11
Roydon Norf 38 C3
Roydon Norf 39 G6
Roydon Hamlet Essex 29 H11
Royston Herts 29 D10
Royston S Yorks 45 A7
Royton Gtr Man 44 B3
Rozel Jersey 11
Ruabon = Rhiwabon Wrex 33 A9
Ruaig Argyll 78 G3
Ruan Lanihorne Corn 3 E7
Ruan Minor Corn 2 H6
Ruarach Highld 80 A1
Ruardean Glos 26 G3
Ruardean Woodside Glos 26 G3
Rubery Worcs 34 H5
Ruckcroft Cumb 57 B7
Ruckhall Hereford 25 E11
Ruckinge Kent 13 C9
Ruckland Lincs 47 E7
Ruckley Shrops 33 E11
Rudbaxton Pembs 22 D4
Rudby N Yorks 58 F5
Ruddington Notts 36 B1
Rudford Glos 26 F4
Rudge Shrops 34 F4
Rudge Som 16 F5
Rudgeway S Glos 16 C3
Rudgwick W Sus 11 A9
Rudhall Hereford 26 F3
Rudheath Ches W 43 E9
Rudley Green Essex 20 A5
Rudry Caerph 15 C7
Rudston E Yorks 53 C6
Rudyard Staffs 44 G3
Rufford Lancs 49 H4
Rufforth York 51 D11
Rugby Warks 35 H11
Rugeley Staffs 34 D6
Ruglen S Ayrs 66 F5
Ruilick Highld 87 G8
Ruishton Som 8 B1
Ruisigearraidh W Isles 90 J4
Ruislip London 19 C7
Ruislip Common London 19 C7
Rumbling Bridge Perth 76 H3
Rumburgh Suff 39 G9
Rumford Corn 3 B7
Rumney Cardiff 15 D8
Runcorn Halton 43 D8
Runcton W Sus 11 D7
Runcton Holme Norf 38 E2
Rundlestone Devon 5 D6
Runfold Sur 18 G5
Runhall Norf 39 E6
Runham Norf 39 D10
Runham Norf 39 E11
Runnington Som 7 D10
Runsell Green Essex 30 H4
Runswick Bay N Yorks 59 E9
Runwell Essex 20 B4
Ruscombe Wokingham 18 D4
Rush Green London 20 C2
Rush-head Aberds 89 D8
Rushall Hereford 26 E3
Rushall Norf 39 G7
Rushall W Mid 34 E6
Rushall Wilts 17 F8
Rushbrooke Suff 30 B5
Rushbury Shrops 33 F11
Rushden Herts 29 E10
Rushden Northants 28 B6
Rushenden Kent 20 D6
Rushford Norf 38 G5
Rushlake Green E Sus 12 E5
Rushmere Suff 39 G10
Rushmere St Andrew Suff 31 D9
Rushmoor Sur 18 G5
Rushock Worcs 26 A5
Rusholme Gtr Man 44 C2
Rushton Ches W 43 F8
Rushton Northants 36 G4
Rushton Shrops 34 E2
Rushton Spencer Staffs 44 F3
Rushwick Worcs 26 C5
Rushyford Durham 58 D3
Ruskie Stirling 75 G9
Ruskington Lincs 46 G4
Rusland Cumb 56 H5
Rusper W Sus 19 H9
Ruspidge Glos 26 G3
Russell's Water Oxon 18 C4
Russel's Green Suff 31 A9
Rusthall Kent 12 C4
Rustington W Sus 11 D9
Ruston N Yorks 52 A5
Ruston Parva E Yorks 53 C6
Ruswarp N Yorks 59 F9
Rutherford Borders 70 G5
Rutherglen S Lanark 68 D5
Ruthernbridge Corn 3 C9
Ruthin = Rhuthun Denb 42 G4
Ruthrieston Aberdeen 83 C11
Ruthven Aberds 88 D5
Ruthven Angus 76 C5
Ruthven Highld 81 D9
Ruthven Highld 87 H11
Ruthven House Angus 76 C6
Ruthvoes Corn 3 C8
Ruthwell Dumfries 60 G6
Ruyton-XI-Towns Shrops 33 C9
Ryal Northumb 62 F6
Ryal Fold Blackburn 50 G2
Ryall Dorset 8 E3
Ryarsh Kent 20 F3
Rydal Cumb 56 F5
Ryde IoW 10 E4
Rye E Sus 13 D8
Rye Foreign E Sus 13 D7
Rye Harbour E Sus 13 E8
Rye Park Herts 29 G10
Rye Street Worcs 26 E4
Ryecroft Gate Staffs 44 F3
Ryehill E Yorks 53 G8
Ryhall Rutland 36 D6
Ryhill W Yorks 45 A7
Ryhope T&W 58 A5
Rylstone N Yorks 50 D5
Ryme Intrinseca Dorset 8 C4
Ryther N Yorks 52 F1
Ryton Glos 26 E4
Ryton N Yorks 52 B3
Ryton Shrops 34 E3
Ryton T&W 63 G7
Ryton-on-Dunsmore Warks 27 A10

S

Sabden Lancs 50 F3
Sacombe Herts 29 G10
Sacriston Durham 58 B3
Sadberge Darl 58 E4
Saddell Argyll 65 E8
Saddington Leics 36 F2
Saddle Bow Norf 38 D2
Saddlescombe W Sus 12 E1
Sadgill Cumb 57 F6
Saffron Walden Essex 30 E2
Sageston Pembs 22 F5
Saham Hills Norf 38 E5
Saham Toney Norf 38 E5
Saighdinis W Isles 84 B3
Saighton Ches W 43 F7
St Abbs Borders 71 D8
St Abb's Haven Borders 71 D8
St Agnes Corn 2 D6
St Agnes Scilly 2 D2
St Albans Herts 29 H8
St Allen Corn 3 D7
St Andrews Fife 77 F8
St Andrew's Major V Glam 15 D7
St Anne Ald 11
St Annes Lancs 49 G3
St Ann's Dumfries 60 D6
St Ann's Chapel Corn 4 D5
St Ann's Chapel Devon 5 G7
St Anthony-in-Meneage Corn 3 G6
St Anthony's Hill E Sus 12 F5
St Arvans Mon 15 B11
St Asaph = Llanelwy Denb 42 E3
St Athan V Glam 14 E6
St Aubin Jersey 11
St Austell Corn 3 D9
St Bees Cumb 56 E1
St Blazey Corn 4 F1
St. Boswells Borders 70 G4
St Brelade Jersey 11
St Breock Corn 3 B8
St Breward Corn 4 D1
St Briavels Glos 16 A2
St Bride's Pembs 22 E3
St Brides Major V Glam 14 D4
St Bride's Netherwent Mon 15 C10
St Brides super Ely V Glam 14 D6
St Brides Wentlooge Newport 15 C8
St Budeaux Plym 4 F5
St Buryan Corn 2 G3
St Catherine Bath 16 D4
St Catherine's Argyll 73 C10
St Clears = Sanclêr Carms 23 E7
St Cleer Corn 4 E3
St Clement Corn 3 E7
St Clements Jersey 11
St Clether Corn 4 C3
St Colmac Argyll 73 G9
St Columb Major Corn 3 C8
St Columb Minor Corn 3 C7
St Columb Road Corn 3 D8
St Combs Aberds 89 B10
St Cross South Elmham Suff 39 G8
St Cyrus Aberds 77 A10
St David's Perth 76 E2
St David's = Tyddewi Pembs 22 D2
St Day Corn 2 E6
St Dennis Corn 3 D8
St Devereux Hereford 25 E11
St Dogmaels Pembs 22 B6
St Dogwells Pembs 22 D4
St Dominick Corn 4 E5
St Donat's V Glam 14 E5
St Edith's Wilts 16 E6
St Endellion Corn 3 B8
St Enoder Corn 3 D7
St Erme Corn 3 D7
St Erney Corn 4 F4
St Erth Corn 2 F4
St Ervan Corn 3 B7
St Eval Corn 3 C7
St Ewe Corn 3 E8
St Fagans Cardiff 15 D7
St Fergus Aberds 89 C10
St Fillans Perth 75 E9
St Florence Pembs 22 F5
St Genny's Corn 4 B2
St George Conwy 42 E2
St George's V Glam 14 D6
St Germans Corn 4 F4
St Giles Lincs 46 E3
St Giles in the Wood Devon 6 E4
St Giles on the Heath Devon 6 G2
St Harmon Powys 24 A6
St Helen Auckland Durham 58 D2
St Helena Warks 35 E8
St Helen's E Sus 13 E7
St Helens IoW 10 F5
St Helens Mers 43 C8
St Helier Jersey 11
St Helier London 19 E9
St Hilary Corn 2 F4
St Hilary V Glam 14 D6
Saint Hill W Sus 12 C2
St Illtyd Bl Gwent 15 A8
St Ippollytts Herts 29 F8
St Ishmael's Pembs 22 F3
St Issey Corn 3 B8
St Ive Corn 4 E4
St Ives Cambs 29 A10
St Ives Corn 2 E4
St Ives Dorset 9 D10
St James South Elmham Suff 39 G9
St Jidgey Corn 3 C8
St John Corn 4 F5
St John's IoM 48 D2
St John's Jersey 11
St John's Sur 18 F6
St John's Worcs 26 C5
St John's Chapel Durham 57 C10
St John's Fen End Norf 37 D11
St John's Highway Norf 37 D11
St John's Town of Dalry Dumfries 55 A9
St Judes IoM 48 C3
St Just Corn 2 F2
St Just in Roseland Corn 3 F7
St Katherine's Aberds 89 E7
St Keverne Corn 3 G6
St Kew Corn 3 B9
St Kew Highway Corn 3 B9
St Keyne Corn 4 E3
St Lawrence Corn 3 C9
St Lawrence Essex 20 A6
St Lawrence IoW 10 G4
St Leonard's Bucks 28 H6
St Leonards Dorset 9 D10
St Leonards E Sus 13 F6
Saint Leonards S Lanark 68 E5
St Levan Corn 2 G2
St Lythans V Glam 15 D7
St Mabyn Corn 3 B9
St Madoes Perth 76 E4
St Margaret South Elmham Suff 39 G9
St Margaret's Hereford 25 E10
St Margarets Herts 29 G10
St Margaret's at Cliffe Kent 21 G10
St Margaret's Hope Orkney 95 J5
St Mark's IoM 48 E2
St Martin Corn 4 F3
St Martins Corn 2 G6
St Martin's Jersey 11
St Martins Perth 76 D4
St Martin's Shrops 33 B9
St Mary Bourne Hants 17 F11
St Mary Church V Glam 14 D6
St Mary Cray London 19 E11
St Mary Hill V Glam 14 D5
St Mary Hoo Medway 20 D5
St Mary in the Marsh Kent 13 D9
St Mary's Jersey 11
St Mary's Orkney 95 H5
St Mary's Bay Kent 13 D9
St Maughans Mon 25 G11
St Mawes Corn 3 F7
St Mawgan Corn 3 C7
St Mellion Corn 4 E4
St Mellons Cardiff 15 C8
St Merryn Corn 3 B7
St Mewan Corn 3 D8
St Michael Caerhays Corn 3 E8
St Michael Penkevil Corn 3 E7
St Michael South Elmham Suff 39 G9
St Michael's Kent 13 C7
St Michaels Worcs 26 B2
St Michael's on Wyre Lancs 49 E4
St Minver Corn 3 B8
St Monans Fife 77 G8
St Neot Corn 4 E2
St Neots Cambs 29 B8
St Newlyn East Corn 3 D7
St Nicholas Pembs 22 C3
St Nicholas V Glam 14 D6
St Nicholas at Wade Kent 21 E9
St Ninians Stirling 68 A6
St Osyth Essex 31 G8
St Osyth Heath Essex 31 G8
St Ouens Jersey 11
St Owens Cross Hereford 26 F2
St Paul's Cray London 19 E11
St Paul's Walden Herts 29 F8
St Peter Port Guern 11
St Peter's Jersey 11
St Peter's Kent 21 E10
St Petrox Pembs 22 G4
St Pinnock Corn 4 E3
St Quivox S Ayrs 67 D6
St Ruan Corn 2 H6
St Sampson Guern 11
St Stephen Corn 3 D8
St Stephen's Corn 4 C4
St Stephens Corn 4 F5
St Stephens Herts 29 H8
St Teath Corn 4 C1
St Thomas Devon 7 G8
St Tudy Corn 4 D1
St Twynnells Pembs 22 G4
St Veep Corn 4 F2
St Vigeans Angus 77 C9
St Wenn Corn 3 C8
St Weonards Hereford 25 F11
Saintbury Glos 27 E8
Salcombe Devon 5 H8
Salcombe Regis Devon 7 H10
Salcott Essex 30 G6
Sale Gtr Man 43 C10
Sale Green Worcs 26 C6
Saleby Lincs 47 E8
Salehurst E Sus 12 D6
Salem Carms 24 F3
Salem Ceredig 32 G2
Salen Argyll 79 G8
Salen Highld 79 E9
Salesbury Lancs 50 F2
Salford C Beds 28 E6
Salford Gtr Man 44 C2
Salford Oxon 27 F9
Salford Priors Warks 27 C7
Salfords Sur 19 G9
Salhouse Norf 39 D9
Saline Fife 69 A9
Salisbury Wilts 9 B10
Sallachan Highld 74 A2
Sallachy Highld 86 H2
Sallachy Highld 93 J8
Salle Norf 39 C7
Salmonby Lincs 47 E7
Salmond's Muir Angus 77 D8
Salperton Glos 27 F7
Salph End Bedford 29 C7
Salsburgh N Lanark 69 D7
Salt Staffs 34 C5
Salt End E Yorks 53 G7
Saltaire W Yorks 51 F7
Saltash Corn 4 F5
Saltburn Highld 87 E10
Saltburn-by-the-Sea Redcar 59 D7
Saltby Leics 36 C4
Saltcoats Cumb 56 G2
Saltcoats N Ayrs 66 B5
Saltdean Brighton 12 F2
Salter Lancs 50 C2
Salterforth Lancs 50 E4
Salterswall Ches W 43 F9
Saltfleet Lincs 47 C8
Saltfleetby All Saints Lincs 47 C8
Saltfleetby St Clements Lincs 47 C8
Saltfleetby St Peter Lincs 47 D8
Saltford Bath 16 E3
Salthouse Norf 39 A6
Saltmarshe E Yorks 52 G3
Saltney Flint 43 F6
Salton N Yorks 52 B3
Saltwick Northumb 63 F7
Saltwood Kent 21 H8
Salum Argyll 78 G3
Salvington W Sus 11 D10
Salwarpe Worcs 26 B5
Salwayash Dorset 8 E3
Sambourne Warks 27 B7
Sambrook Telford 34 C3
Samhla W Isles 84 B2
Samlesbury Lancs 50 F1
Samlesbury Bottoms Lancs 50 G2
Sampford Arundel Som 7 E10
Sampford Brett Som 7 B9
Sampford Courtenay Devon 6 F5
Sampford Peverell Devon 7 E9
Sampford Spiney Devon 4 D6
Sampool Bridge Cumb 56 H6
Samuelston E Loth 70 C3
Sanachan Highld 85 D13
Sanaigmore Argyll 64 A3
Sanclêr = St Clears Carms 23 E7
Sancreed Corn 2 G3
Sancton E Yorks 52 F5
Sand Highld 86 B2
Sand Shetland 96 J5
Sand Hole E Yorks 52 F4
Sand Hutton N Yorks 52 D2
Sandaig Highld 85 H12
Sandal Magna W Yorks 51 H9
Sandale Cumb 56 B4
Sandbach Ches E 43 F10
Sandbank Argyll 73 E10
Sandbanks Poole 9 F9
Sandend Aberds 88 B5
Sanderstead London 19 E10
Sandfields Glos 26 F6
Sandford Cumb 57 E9
Sandford Devon 7 F7
Sandford Dorset 9 F8
Sandford IoW 10 F4
Sandford N Som 15 F10
Sandford S Lanark 68 F6
Sandford Shrops 34 B1
Sandford on Thames Oxon 18 A2
Sandford Orcas Dorset 8 B5
Sandford St Martin Oxon 27 F11
Sandfordhill Aberds 89 D11
Sandgate Kent 21 H8
Sandgreen Dumfries 55 D8
Sandhaven Aberds 89 B9
Sandhead Dumfries 54 E3
Sandhills Sur 18 H6
Sandhoe Northumb 62 G5
Sandholme E Yorks 52 F4
Sandholme Lincs 37 B9
Sandhurst Brack 18 E5
Sandhurst Glos 26 F5
Sandhurst Kent 13 D6
Sandhurst Cross Kent 13 D6
Sandhutton N Yorks 51 A9
Sandiacre Derbys 35 B10
Sandilands Lincs 47 D9
Sandilands S Lanark 69 G7
Sandiway Ches W 43 E9
Sandleheath Hants 9 C10
Sandling Kent 20 F4
Sandlow Green Ches E 43 F10
Sandness Shetland 96 H3
Sandon Essex 20 A4
Sandon Herts 29 E10
Sandon Staffs 34 B5
Sandown IoW 10 F4
Sandplace Corn 4 F3
Sandridge Herts 29 G8
Sandridge Wilts 16 E6
Sandringham Norf 38 C2
Sandsend N Yorks 59 E9
Sandside Ho. Highld 93 C12
Sandsound Shetland 96 J5
Sandtoft N Lincs 45 B11
Sandway Kent 20 F5
Sandwell W Mid 34 G6
Sandwich Kent 21 F10
Sandwick Cumb 56 E6
Sandwick Orkney 95 K5
Sandwick Shetland 96 L6
Sandwith Cumb 56 E1
Sandy C Beds 29 D8
Sandy Carms 23 F9
Sandy Bank Lincs 46 G6
Sandy Haven Pembs 22 F3
Sandy Lane Wilts 16 E6
Sandy Lane Wrex 33 A9
Sandycroft Flint 42 F6
Sandyford Dumfries 61 D8
Sandyford Stoke 44 G2
Sandygate IoM 48 C3
Sandyhills Dumfries 55 D11
Sandylands Lancs 49 C4
Sandypark Devon 5 C8
Sandysike Cumb 61 G9
Sangobeg Highld 92 C7
Sangomore Highld 92 C7
Sanna Highld 78 E7
Sanndabhaig W Isles 84 D3
Sanndabhaig W Isles 91 D9
Sannox N Ayrs 66 B3
Sanquhar Dumfries 60 C3
Santon N Lincs 46 A3
Santon Bridge Cumb 56 F3
Santon Downham Suff 38 G4
Sapcote Leics 35 F10
Sapey Common Hereford 26 B4
Sapiston Suff 38 H5
Sapley Cambs 29 A9
Sapperton Glos 16 A6
Sapperton Lincs 36 B6
Saracen's Head Lincs 37 C9
Sarclet Highld 94 F5
Sardis Carms 23 F10
Sarn Bridgend 14 C5
Sarn Powys 33 F8
Sarn Bach Gwyn 40 H5
Sarn Meyllteyrn Gwyn 40 G4
Sarnau Carms 23 E8
Sarnau Ceredig 23 A8
Sarnau Gwyn 32 B5
Sarnau Powys 25 E7
Sarnau Powys 33 D8
Sarnesfield Hereford 25 C10
Saron Carms 23 C8
Saron Carms 24 G3
Saron Denb 42 F3
Saron Gwyn 40 E6
Saron Gwyn 41 D7
Sarratt Herts 19 B7
Sarre Kent 21 E9
Sarsden Oxon 27 F9
Sarsgrum Highld 92 C6
Satley Durham 58 B2
Satron N Yorks 57 G11
Satterleigh Devon 6 D5
Satterthwaite Cumb 56 G5
Satwell Oxon 18 C4
Sauchen Aberds 83 B8
Saucher Perth 76 D4
Sauchie Clack 69 A7
Sauchieburn Aberds 83 G8
Saughall Ches W 42 E6
Saughtree Borders 61 D11
Saul Glos 26 H4
Saundby Notts 45 D11
Saundersfoot Pembs 22 F6
Saunderton Bucks 18 A4
Saunton Devon 6 C3
Sausthorpe Lincs 47 F7
Saval Highld 93 J8
Savary Highld 79 G9
Savile Park W Yorks 51 G6
Sawbridge Warks 28 B2
Sawbridgeworth Herts 29 G11
Sawdon N Yorks 59 H10
Sawley Derbys 35 B10
Sawley Lancs 50 E3
Sawley N Yorks 51 C8
Sawston Cambs 29 D11
Sawtry Cambs 37 G7
Saxby Leics 36 D4
Saxby Lincs 46 D4
Saxby All Saints N Lincs 52 H5
Saxelbye Leics 36 C3
Saxham Street Suff 31 B7
Saxilby Lincs 46 E2
Saxlingham Norf 38 B6
Saxlingham Green Norf 39 F8
Saxlingham Nethergate Norf 39 F8
Saxlingham Thorpe Norf 39 F8
Saxmundham Suff 31 B10
Saxon Street Cambs 30 C3
Saxondale Notts 36 B2
Saxtead Suff 31 B9
Saxtead Green Suff 31 B9
Saxthorpe Norf 39 B7
Saxton N Yorks 51 F10
Sayers Common W Sus 12 E1
Scackleton N Yorks 52 B2
Scadabhagh W Isles 90 H6
Scaftworth Notts 45 C10
Scagglethorpe N Yorks 52 B4
Scaitcliffe Lancs 50 G3
Scalasaig Argyll 72 D2
Scalby E Yorks 52 G4
Scalby N Yorks 59 G11
Scaldwell Northants 28 A4
Scale Houses Cumb 57 B7
Scaleby Cumb 61 G10
Scaleby Hill Cumb 61 G10
Scales Cumb 49 B2
Scales Cumb 56 D5
Scales Lancs 49 F4
Scalford Leics 36 C3
Scaling Redcar 59 E8
Scallastle Argyll 79 H9
Scalloway Shetland 96 K6
Scalpay W Isles 90 H7
Scalpay Ho. Highld 85 F11
Scalpsie Argyll 73 H9
Scamadale Highld 79 B10
Scamblesby Lincs 46 E6
Scamodale Highld 79 D11
Scampston N Yorks 52 B4
Scampton Lincs 46 E3
Scapa Orkney 95 H5
Scapegoat Hill W Yorks 51 H6
Scar Orkney 95 D7
Scarborough N Yorks 59 H11
Scarcliffe Derbys 45 F8
Scarcroft W Yorks 51 E9
Scarcroft Hill W Yorks 51 E9
Scardroy Highld 86 F5
Scarff Shetland 96 E4
Scarfskerry Highld 94 C4
Scargill Durham 58 E1
Scarinish Argyll 78 G3
Scarisbrick Lancs 43 A6
Scarning Norf 38 D5
Scarrington Notts 36 A3
Scartho NE Lincs 46 B6
Scarwell Orkney 95 F3
Scatness Shetland 96 M5
Scatraig Highld 87 H10
Scawby N Lincs 46 B3
Scawsby S Yorks 45 B9
Scawton N Yorks 51 A11
Scayne's Hill W Sus 12 D2
Scethrog Powys 25 F8
Scholar Green Ches E 44 G2
Scholes W Yorks 44 B5
Scholes W Yorks 51 F9
Scholes W Yorks 51 G7
School Green Ches W 43 F9
Scleddau Pembs 22 C4
Sco Ruston Norf 39 C8
Scofton Notts 45 D10
Scole Norf 39 H7
Scolpaig W Isles 84 A2
Scone Perth 76 E4
Sconser Highld 85 E10
Scoonie Fife 77 G7
Scoor Argyll 78 K7
Scopwick Lincs 46 G4
Scoraig Highld 86 B3
Scorborough E Yorks 52 E6
Scorrier Corn 2 E6
Scorton Lancs 49 E5
Scorton N Yorks 58 F3
Scotbheinn W Isles 84 C3
Scotby Cumb 61 H10
Scotch Corner N Yorks 58 F3
Scotforth Lancs 49 D4
Scothern Lincs 46 E4
Scotland Gate Northumb 63 E8
Scotlandwell Perth 76 G4
Scots' Gap Northumb 62 E6
Scotsburn Highld 87 D10
Scotscalder Station Highld 94 E2
Scotscraig Fife 77 E7
Scotston Aberds 83 F9
Scotston Perth 76 C2
Scotstoun Glasgow 68 D4
Scotstown Highld 79 E11
Scotswood T&W 63 G7
Scottas Highld 85 H12
Scotter Lincs 46 B2
Scotterthorpe Lincs 46 B2
Scottlethorpe Lincs 37 C6
Scotton Lincs 46 C2
Scotton N Yorks 51 D9
Scotton N Yorks 58 G2
Scottow Norf 39 C8
Scoughall E Loth 70 B5
Scoulag Argyll 73 H10
Scoulton Norf 38 E5
Scourie Highld 92 E4
Scourie More Highld 92 E4
Scousburgh Shetland 96 M5
Scrabster Highld 94 C2
Scrafield Lincs 47 F7
Scrainwood Northumb 62 C5
Scrane End Lincs 37 A9
Scraptoft Leics 36 E2
Scratby Norf 39 D11
Scrayingham N Yorks 52 C3
Scredington Lincs 37 A6
Scremby Lincs 47 F8
Scremerston Northumb 71 F9
Screveton Notts 36 A3
Scrivelsby Lincs 46 F6
Scriven N Yorks 51 D9
Scrooby Notts 45 C10
Scropton Derbys 35 B7
Scrub Hill Lincs 46 G6
Scruton N Yorks 58 G3
Sculcoates Hull 53 F6
Sculthorpe Norf 38 B4
Scunthorpe N Lincs 46 A2
Scurlage Swansea 23 H9
Sea Palling Norf 39 C10
Seaborough Dorset 8 D3
Seacombe Mers 42 C6
Seacroft Lincs 47 F9
Seacroft W Yorks 51 F9
Seadyke Lincs 37 B9
Seafield S Ayrs 66 D6
Seafield W Loth 69 D9
Seaford E Sus 12 G3
Seaforth Mers 42 C6
Seagrave Leics 36 D2
Seaham Durham 58 B5
Seahouses Northumb 71 G11
Seal Kent 20 F2
Sealand Flint 42 F6
Seale Sur 18 G5
Seamer N Yorks 52 A6
Seamer N Yorks 58 E5
Seamill N Ayrs 66 B5
Searby Lincs 46 B4
Seasalter Kent 21 E7
Seascale Cumb 56 F2
Seathorne Lincs 47 F9
Seathwaite Cumb 56 E4
Seathwaite Cumb 56 G4
Seatoller Cumb 56 E4
Seaton Corn 4 F4
Seaton Cumb 56 C2
Seaton Devon 8 F1
Seaton Durham 58 A4
Seaton E Yorks 53 E7
Seaton Northumb 63 F9
Seaton Rutland 36 F5
Seaton Burn T&W 63 F8
Seaton Carew Hrtlpl 58 D6
Seaton Delaval Northumb 63 F9
Seaton Ross E Yorks 52 E3
Seaton Sluice Northumb 63 F9
Seatown Aberds 88 B5
Seatown Dorset 8 E3
Seave Green N Yorks 59 F6
Seaview IoW 10 E5
Seaville Cumb 56 A3
Seavington St Mary Som 8 C3
Seavington St Michael Som 8 C3
Sebergham Cumb 56 B5
Seckington Warks 35 E8
Second Coast Highld 86 B2
Sedbergh Cumb 57 G8
Sedbury Glos 15 B11
Sedbusk N Yorks 57 G10
Sedgeberrow Worcs 27 E7
Sedgebrook Lincs 36 B4
Sedgefield Durham 58 D4
Sedgeford Norf 38 B3
Sedgehill Wilts 9 B7
Sedgley W Mid 34 F5
Sedgwick Cumb 57 H7
Sedlescombe E Sus 13 E6
Sedlescombe Street E Sus 13 E6
Seend Wilts 16 E6
Seend Cleeve Wilts 16 E6
Seer Green Bucks 18 B6
Seething Norf 39 F9
Sefton Mers 42 B6
Seghill Northumb 63 F8
Seifton Shrops 33 G10
Seighford Staffs 34 C4
Seilebost W Isles 90 H5
Seion Gwyn 41 D7
Seisdon Staffs 34 F4
Seisiadar W Isles 91 D10
Selattyn Shrops 33 B8
Selborne Hants 10 A6
Selby N Yorks 52 F2
Selham W Sus 11 B8
Selhurst London 19 E10
Selkirk Borders 70 H3
Sellack Hereford 26 F2
Sellafirth Shetland 96 D7
Sellibister Orkney 95 D8
Sellindge Kent 13 C9
Sellindge Lees Kent 13 C10
Selling Kent 21 F7
Sells Green Wilts 16 E6
Selly Oak W Mid 34 G6
Selmeston E Sus 12 F4
Selsdon London 19 E10
Selsey W Sus 11 E7
Selsfield Common W Sus 12 C2
Selsted Kent 21 G9
Selston Notts 45 G8
Selworthy Som 7 B8
Semblister Shetland 96 H5
Semer Suff 30 D6
Semington Wilts 16 E5
Semley Wilts 9 B7
Send Sur 19 F7
Send Marsh Sur 19 F7
Senghenydd Caerph 15 B7
Sennen Corn 2 G2
Sennen Cove Corn 2 G2
Sennybridge = Pont Senni Powys 24 F6
Serlby Notts 45 D10
Sessay N Yorks 51 B10
Setchey Norf 38 D2

Setley Hants 10 D2
Setter Shetland 96 E6
Setter Shetland 96 H5
Setter Shetland 96 J7
Settiscarth Orkney 95 G4
Settle N Yorks 50 C4
Settrington N Yorks 52 B4
Seven Kings London 19 C11
Seven Sisters Neath 24 H5
Sevenhampton Glos 27 F7
Sevenoaks Kent 20 F2
Sevenoaks Weald Kent 20 F2
Severn Beach S Glos 15 C11
Severn Stoke Worcs 26 D5
Severnhampton Swindon 17 B9
Sevington Kent 13 B9
Sewards End Essex 30 E2
Sewardstone Essex 19 B10
Sewardstonebury Essex 19 B10
Sewerby E Yorks 53 C7
Seworgan Corn 2 F6
Sewstern Leics 36 C4
Sezincote Glos 27 E8
Sgarasta Mhor W Isles 90 H5
Sgiogarstaigh W Isles 91 A10
Shabbington Bucks 28 H3
Shackerstone Leics 35 E9
Shackleford Sur 18 G6
Shade W Yorks 50 G5
Shadforth Durham 58 B4
Shadingfield Suff 39 G10
Shadoxhurst Kent 13 C8
Shadsworth Blackburn 50 G3
Shadwell Norf 38 G5
Shadwell W Yorks 51 F9
Shaftesbury Dorset 9 B7
Shafton S Yorks 45 A7
Shalbourne Wilts 17 E10
Shalcombe IoW 10 F2
Shalden Hants 18 G3
Shaldon Devon 5 D10
Shalfleet IoW 10 F3
Shalford Essex 30 F4
Shalford Sur 19 G7
Shalford Green Essex 30 F4
Shallowford Devon 6 B6
Shalmsford Street Kent 21 F7
Shalstone Bucks 28 E3
Shamley Green Sur 19 G7
Shandon Argyll 73 E11
Shandwick Highld 87 D11
Shangton Leics 36 F3
Shankhouse Northumb 63 F8
Shanklin IoW 10 F4
Shanquhar Aberds 88 E5
Shanzie Perth 76 B5
Shap Cumb 57 E7
Shapwick Dorset 9 D8
Shapwick Som 15 H10
Shardlow Derbys 35 B10
Shareshill Staffs 34 E5
Sharlston W Yorks 51 H9
Sharlston Common W Yorks 51 H9
Sharnbrook Bedford 28 C6
Sharnford Leics 35 F10
Sharoe Green Lancs 49 F5
Sharow N Yorks 51 B9
Sharp Street Norf 39 C9
Sharpenhoe C Beds 29 E7
Sharperton Northumb 62 C5
Sharpness Glos 16 A3
Sharpthorne W Sus 12 C2
Sharrington Norf 38 B6
Shatterford Worcs 34 G3
Shaugh Prior Devon 4 E6
Shavington Ches E 43 G10
Shaw Gtr Man 44 B3
Shaw W Berks 17 E11
Shaw Wilts 16 E5
Shaw Green Lancs 49 H5
Shaw Mills N Yorks 51 C8
Shawbury Shrops 34 C1
Shawdon Hall Northumb 62 B6
Shawell Leics 35 G11
Shawford Hants 10 B3
Shawforth Lancs 50 G4
Shawhead Dumfries 60 F4
Shawhill Dumfries 61 G8
Shawton S Lanark 68 F5
Shawtonhill S Lanark 68 F5
Shear Cross Wilts 16 G5
Shearington Dumfries 60 G6
Shearsby Leics 36 F2
Shebbear Devon 6 F3
Shebdon Staffs 34 C3
Shebster Highld 93 C13
Sheddens E Renf 68 E4
Shedfield Hants 10 C4
Sheen Staffs 44 F5
Sheepscar W Yorks 51 F9
Sheepscombe Glos 26 G5
Sheepstor Devon 5 E6
Sheepwash Devon 6 F3
Sheepway N Som 15 D10
Sheepy Magna Leics 35 E9
Sheepy Parva Leics 35 E9
Sheering Essex 30 G2
Sheerness Kent 20 D6
Sheet Hants 11 B6
Sheffield S Yorks 45 D7
Sheffield Bottom W Berks 18 E3
Sheffield Green E Sus 12 D3
Shefford C Beds 29 E8
Shefford Woodlands W Berks 17 D10
Sheigra Highld 92 C4
Sheinton Shrops 34 E2
Shelderton Shrops 33 H10
Sheldon Derbys 44 F5
Sheldon Devon 7 F10
Sheldon W Mid 35 G7
Sheldwich Kent 21 F7
Shelf W Yorks 51 G7
Shelfanger Norf 39 G7
Shelfield W Mid 34 E6
Shelfield Warks 27 B8
Shelford Notts 36 A2
Shellacres Northumb 71 F7
Shelley Essex 20 A2
Shelley Suff 31 E7
Shelley W Yorks 44 A6
Shellingford Oxon 17 B10
Shellow Bowells Essex 30 H3
Shelsley Beauchamp Worcs 26 B4
Shelsley Walsh Worcs 26 B4
Shelthorpe Leics 35 D11
Shelton Bedford 29 B7
Shelton Norf 39 F8
Shelton Notts 36 A3
Shelton Shrops 33 D10
Shelton Green Norf 39 F8
Shelve Shrops 33 F9
Shelwick Hereford 26 D2
Shenfield Essex 20 B3
Shenington Oxon 27 D10
Shenley Herts 19 A8
Shenley Brook End M Keynes 28 E5
Shenley Church End M Keynes 28 E5
Shenleybury Herts 19 A8
Shenmore Hereford 25 E10
Shennanton Dumfries 54 C6
Shenstone Staffs 35 E7
Shenstone Worcs 26 A5
Shenton Leics 35 E9
Shenval Highld 80 A6
Shenval Moray 82 A4
Shepeau Stow Lincs 37 D9
Shephall Herts 29 F9
Shepherd's Green Oxon 18 C4
Shepherd's Port Norf 38 B2
Shepherdswell Kent 21 G9
Shepley W Yorks 44 B5
Shepperdine S Glos 16 B3
Shepperton Sur 19 E7
Shepreth Cambs 29 D10
Shepshed Leics 35 D10
Shepton Beauchamp Som 8 C3
Shepton Mallet Som 16 G3
Shepton Montague Som 8 A5
Shepway Kent 20 F4
Sheraton Durham 58 C5
Sherborne Dorset 8 C5
Sherborne Glos 27 G8
Sherborne St John Hants 18 F3
Sherbourne Warks 27 B9
Sherburn Durham 58 B4
Sherburn N Yorks 52 B5
Sherburn Hill Durham 58 B4
Sherburn in Elmet N Yorks 51 F10
Shere Sur 19 G7
Shereford Norf 38 C4
Sherfield English Hants 10 B1
Sherfield on Loddon Hants 18 F3
Sherford Devon 5 G8
Sheriff Hutton N Yorks 52 C2
Sheriffhales Shrops 34 D3
Sheringham Norf 39 A7
Sherington M Keynes 28 D5
Shernal Green Worcs 26 B6
Shernborne Norf 38 B3
Sherrington Wilts 16 H6
Sherston Wilts 16 C5
Sherwood Green Devon 6 D4
Shettleston Glasgow 68 D5
Shevington Gtr Man 43 B8
Shevington Moor Gtr Man 43 A8
Shevington Vale Gtr Man 43 B8
Sheviock Corn 4 F4
Shide IoW 10 F3
Shiel Bridge Highld 80 B1
Shieldaig Highld 85 A13
Shieldaig Highld 85 C13
Shieldhill Dumfries 60 E6
Shieldhill Falk 69 C7
Shieldhill S Lanark 69 F9
Shielfoot Highld 79 E9
Shielhill Angus 77 B7
Shielhill Invclyd 73 F11
Shifford Oxon 17 A10
Shifnal Shrops 34 E3
Shilbottle Northumb 63 C7
Shildon Durham 58 D3
Shillingford Devon 7 D8
Shillingford Oxon 18 B2
Shillingford St George Devon 5 C10
Shillingstone Dorset 9 C7
Shillington C Beds 29 E8
Shillmoor Northumb 62 C4
Shilton Oxon 27 H9
Shilton Warks 35 G10
Shilvington Northumb 63 E7
Shimpling Norf 39 G7
Shimpling Suff 30 C5
Shimpling Street Suff 30 C5
Shincliffe Durham 58 B3
Shiney Row T&W 58 A4
Shinfield Wokingham 18 E4
Shingham Norf 38 E3
Shingle Street Suff 31 D10
Shinner's Bridge Devon 5 E8
Shinness Highld 93 H8
Shipbourne Kent 20 F2
Shipdham Norf 38 E5
Shipham Som 15 F10
Shiphay Torbay 5 E9
Shiplake Oxon 18 D4
Shipley Derbys 35 A10
Shipley Northumb 63 B7
Shipley Shrops 34 F4
Shipley W Sus 11 B10
Shipley W Yorks 51 F7
Shipley Shiels Northumb 62 D3
Shipmeadow Suff 39 G9
Shippea Hill Sta. Cambs 38 G2
Shippon Oxon 17 B11
Shipston-on-Stour Warks 27 D9
Shipton Glos 27 G7
Shipton N Yorks 52 D1
Shipton Shrops 34 F1
Shipton Bellinger Hants 17 G9
Shipton Gorge Dorset 8 E3
Shipton Green W Sus 11 D7
Shipton Moyne Glos 16 C5
Shipton on Cherwell Oxon 27 G11
Shipton Solers Glos 27 G7
Shipton-under-Wychwood Oxon 27 G9
Shiptonthorpe E Yorks 52 E4
Shirburn Oxon 18 B3
Shirdley Hill Lancs 42 A6
Shirebrook Derbys 45 F9
Shiregreen S Yorks 45 C7
Shirehampton Bristol 15 D11
Shiremoor T&W 63 F9
Shirenewton Mon 15 B10
Shireoaks Notts 45 D9
Shirkoak Kent 13 C8
Shirl Heath Hereford 25 C11
Shirland Derbys 45 G7
Shirley Derbys 35 A8
Shirley London 19 E10
Shirley Soton 10 C3
Shirley W Mid 35 H7
Shirrell Heath Hants 10 C4
Shirwell Devon 6 C4
Shirwell Cross Devon 6 C4
Shiskine N Ayrs 66 D2
Shobdon Hereford 25 B11
Shobnall Staffs 35 C8
Shobrooke Devon 7 F7
Shoby Leics 36 D2
Shocklach Ches W 43 H7
Shoeburyness Southend 20 C6
Sholden Kent 21 F10
Sholing Soton 10 C3
Shoot Hill Shrops 33 D10
Shop Corn 3 B7
Shop Corn 6 E1
Shop Corner Suff 31 E9
Shore Mill Highld 87 E10
Shoreditch London 19 C10
Shoreham Kent 20 E2
Shoreham-By-Sea W Sus 11 D11
Shoresdean Northumb 71 F8
Shoreswood Northumb 71 F8
Shoreton Highld 87 E9
Shorncote Glos 17 B7
Shorne Kent 20 D3
Short Heath W Mid 34 E5
Shortacombe Devon 4 C6
Shortgate E Sus 12 E3
Shortlanesend Corn 3 E7
Shortlees E Ayrs 67 C7
Shortstown Bedford 29 D7
Shorwell IoW 10 F3
Shoscombe Bath 16 F4
Shotatton Shrops 33 C9
Shotesham Norf 39 F8
Shotgate Essex 20 B4
Shotley Suff 31 E9
Shotley Bridge Durham 58 A1
Shotley Gate Suff 31 E9
Shotleyfield Northumb 58 A1
Shottenden Kent 21 F7
Shottermill Sur 11 A7
Shottery Warks 27 C8
Shotteswell Warks 27 D11
Shottisham Suff 31 D10
Shottle Derbys 45 H7
Shottlegate Derbys 45 H7
Shotton Durham 58 C5
Shotton Flint 42 F6
Shotton Northumb 71 G7
Shotton Colliery Durham 58 B4
Shotts N Lanark 69 D7
Shotwick Ches W 42 E6
Shouldham Norf 38 E2
Shouldham Thorpe Norf 38 E2
Shoulton Worcs 26 C5
Shover's Green E Sus 12 C5
Shrawardine Shrops 33 D10
Shrawley Worcs 26 B5
Shrewley Common Warks 27 B9
Shrewsbury Shrops 33 D10
Shrewton Wilts 17 G7
Shripney W Sus 11 D8
Shrivenham Oxon 17 C9
Shropham Norf 38 F5
Shrub End Essex 30 F6
Shucknall Hereford 26 D2
Shudy Camps Cambs 30 D3
Shulishadermor Highld 85 D9
Shurdington Glos 26 G6
Shurlock Row Windsor 18 D5
Shurrery Highld 93 D13
Shurrery Lodge Highld 93 D13
Shurton Som 7 B11
Shustoke Warks 35 F8
Shute Devon 7 F7
Shute Devon 8 E1
Shutford Oxon 27 D10
Shuthonger Glos 26 E5
Shutlanger Northants 28 C4
Shuttington Warks 35 E8
Shuttlewood Derbys 45 E8
Siabost bho Dheas W Isles 90 C7
Siabost bho Thuath W Isles 90 C7
Siadar W Isles 91 B8
Siadar Iarach W Isles 91 B8
Siadar Uarach W Isles 91 B8
Sibbaldbie Dumfries 61 E7
Sibbertoft Northants 36 G2
Sibdon Carwood Shrops 33 G10
Sibford Ferris Oxon 27 E10
Sibford Gower Oxon 27 E10
Sible Hedingham Essex 30 E4
Sibsey Lincs 47 G7
Sibson Cambs 37 F6
Sibson Leics 35 E9
Sibthorpe Notts 45 H11
Sibton Suff 31 B10
Sibton Green Suff 31 A10
Sicklesmere Suff 30 B5
Sicklinghall N Yorks 51 E9
Sid Devon 7 H10
Sidbury Devon 7 G10
Sidbury Shrops 34 G2
Sidcot N Som 15 F10
Sidcup London 19 D11
Siddick Cumb 56 C2
Siddington Ches E 44 E2
Siddington Glos 17 B7
Sidemoor Worcs 26 A6
Sidestrand Norf 39 B8
Sidford Devon 7 G10
Sidlesham W Sus 11 E7
Sidley E Sus 12 F6
Sidlow Sur 19 G9
Sidmouth Devon 7 H10
Sigford Devon 5 D8
Sigglesthorne E Yorks 53 E7
Sighthill Edin 69 C10
Sigingstone V Glam 14 D5
Signet Oxon 27 G9
Silchester Hants 18 E3
Sildinis W Isles 91 F7
Sileby Leics 36 D1
Silecroft Cumb 49 A1
Silfield Norf 39 F7
Silian Ceredig 23 A10
Silk Willoughby Lincs 37 A6
Silkstone S Yorks 44 B6
Silkstone Common S Yorks 44 B6
Silloth Cumb 56 A3
Sills Northumb 62 C4
Sillyearn Moray 88 C5
Siloh Carms 24 E4
Silpho N Yorks 59 G10
Silsden W Yorks 50 E6
Silsoe C Beds 29 E7
Silver End Essex 30 G5
Silverburn Midloth 69 D11
Silverdale Lancs 49 B4
Silverdale Staffs 44 H2
Silvergate Norf 39 C7
Silverhill E Sus 13 E6
Silverley's Green Suff 39 H8
Silverstone Northants 28 D3
Silverton Devon 7 F8
Silvington Shrops 34 H2
Silwick Shetland 96 J4
Simmondley Derbys 44 C4
Simonburn Northumb 62 F4
Simonsbath Som 7 C6
Simonstone Lancs 50 F3
Simprim Borders 71 F7
Simpson M Keynes 28 E5
Simpson Cross Pembs 22 E3
Sinclair's Hill Borders 71 E7
Sinclairston E Ayrs 67 E7
Sinderby N Yorks 51 A9
Sinderhope Northumb 57 A10
Sindlesham Wokingham 18 E4
Singdean Borders 61 C11
Singleborough Bucks 28 E4
Singleton Lancs 49 F3
Singleton W Sus 11 C7
Singlewell Kent 20 D3
Sinkhurst Green Kent 13 B7
Sinnahard Aberds 82 B6
Sinnington N Yorks 59 H8
Sinton Green Worcs 26 B5
Sipson London 19 D7
Sirhowy Bl Gwent 25 G8
Sisland Norf 39 F9
Sissinghurst Kent 13 C6
Sisterpath Borders 70 F6
Siston S Glos 16 D3
Sithney Corn 2 G5
Sittingbourne Kent 20 E5
Six Ashes Staffs 34 G3
Six Hills Leics 36 C2
Six Mile Bottom Cambs 30 C2
Sixhills Lincs 46 D5
Sixpenny Handley Dorset 9 C8
Sizewell Suff 31 B11
Skail Highld 93 E10
Skaill Orkney 95 E5
Skaill Orkney 95 G3
Skaill Orkney 95 H6
Skares E Ayrs 67 E8
Skateraw E Loth 70 C6
Skaw Shetland 96 G7
Skeabost Highld 85 D9
Skeabrae Orkney 95 F3
Skeeby N Yorks 58 F3
Skeffington Leics 36 E3
Skeffling E Yorks 53 H9
Skegby Notts 45 F8
Skegness Lincs 47 F9
Skelberry Shetland 96 M5
Skelbo Highld 87 B10
Skelbrooke S Yorks 45 A9
Skeldyke Lincs 37 B9
Skellingthorpe Lincs 46 E3
Skellister Shetland 96 H6
Skellow S Yorks 45 A9
Skelmanthorpe W Yorks 44 A6
Skelmersdale Lancs 43 B7
Skelmonae Aberds 89 E8
Skelmorlie N Ayrs 73 G10
Skelmuir Aberds 89 D9
Skelpick Highld 93 D10
Skelton Cumb 56 C6
Skelton E Yorks 52 G3
Skelton N Yorks 58 F1
Skelton Redcar 59 E7
Skelton York 52 D1
Skelton-on-Ure N Yorks 51 C9
Skelwick Orkney 95 D5
Skelwith Bridge Cumb 56 F5
Skendleby Lincs 47 F8
Skene Ho. Aberds 83 C9
Skenfrith Mon 25 F11
Skerne E Yorks 52 D6
Skeroblingarry Argyll 65 F8
Skerray Highld 93 C9
Skerton Lancs 49 C4
Sketchley Leics 35 F10
Sketty Swansea 14 B2
Skewen Neath 14 B3
Skewsby N Yorks 52 B2
Skeyton Norf 39 C8
Skiag Bridge Highld 92 G5
Skibo Castle Highld 87 C10
Skidbrooke Lincs 47 C8
Skidbrooke North End Lincs 47 C8
Skidby E Yorks 52 F6
Skilgate Som 7 D8
Skillington Lincs 36 C4
Skinburness Cumb 61 H7
Skinflats Falk 69 B8
Skinidin Highld 84 D7
Skinnet Highld 93 C8
Skinningrove Redcar 59 D8
Skipness Argyll 73 H7
Skippool Lancs 49 E3
Skipsea E Yorks 53 D7
Skipsea Brough E Yorks 53 D7
Skipton N Yorks 50 D5
Skipton-on-Swale N Yorks 51 B9
Skipwith N Yorks 52 F2
Skirbeck Lincs 37 A9
Skirbeck Quarter Lincs 37 A9
Skirlaugh E Yorks 53 F7
Skirling Borders 69 G9
Skirmett Bucks 18 C4
Skirpenbeck E Yorks 52 D3
Skirwith Cumb 57 C8
Skirza Highld 94 D5
Skulamus Highld 85 F11
Skullomie Highld 93 C9
Skyborry Green Shrops 25 A9
Skye of Curr Highld 82 A1
Skyreholme N Yorks 51 C6
Slackhall Derbys 44 D4
Slackhead Moray 88 B4
Slad Glos 26 H5
Slade Devon 6 B4
Slade Pembs 22 E4
Slade Green London 20 D2
Slaggyford Northumb 57 A8
Slaidburn Lancs 50 D3
Slaithwaite W Yorks 44 A4
Slaley Northumb 62 H5
Slamannan Falk 69 C7
Slapton Bucks 28 F6
Slapton Devon 5 G9
Slapton Northants 28 D3
Slatepit Dale Derbys 45 F7
Slattocks Gtr Man 44 B2
Slaugham W Sus 12 D1
Slaughterford Wilts 16 D5
Slawston Leics 36 F3
Sleaford Hants 18 H5
Sleaford Lincs 46 H4
Sleagill Cumb 57 E7
Sleapford Telford 34 D2
Sledge Green Worcs 26 E5
Sledmere E Yorks 52 C5
Sleightholme Durham 57 E11
Sleights N Yorks 59 F9
Slepe Dorset 9 E8
Slickly Highld 94 D4
Sliddery N Ayrs 66 D2
Sligachan Hotel Highld 85 F9
Slimbridge Glos 16 A4
Slindon Staffs 34 B4
Slindon W Sus 11 D8
Slinfold W Sus 11 A10
Sling Gwyn 41 D8
Slingsby N Yorks 52 B2
Slioch Aberds 88 E5
Slip End C Beds 29 G7
Slip End Herts 29 E9
Slipton Northants 36 H5
Slitting Mill Staffs 34 D6
Slochd Highld 81 A10
Slockavullin Argyll 73 D7
Sloley Norf 39 C8
Sloothby Lincs 47 E8
Slough Slough 18 D6
Slough Green W Sus 12 D1
Sluggan Highld 81 A10
Slumbay Highld 85 E13
Slyfield Sur 18 F6
Slyne Lancs 49 C4
Smailholm Borders 70 G5
Small Dole W Sus 11 C11
Small Hythe Kent 13 C7
Smallbridge Gtr Man 50 H5
Smallburgh Norf 39 C9
Smallburn Aberds 89 D10
Smallburn E Ayrs 68 H5
Smalley Derbys 35 A10
Smallfield Sur 12 B2
Smallridge Devon 8 D2
Smannell Hants 17 G10
Smardale Cumb 57 F9
Smarden Kent 13 B7
Smarden Bell Kent 13 B7
Smeatharpe Devon 7 E10
Smeeth Kent 13 C9
Smeeton Westerby Leics 36 F2
Smercleit W Isles 84 G2
Smerral Highld 94 G3
Smethwick W Mid 34 G6
Smirisary Highld 79 D9
Smisby Derbys 35 D9
Smith Green Lancs 49 D4
Smithfield Cumb 61 G10
Smithincott Devon 7 E9
Smith's Green Essex 30 F2
Smithstown Highld 85 A12
Smithton Highld 87 G10
Smithy Green Ches E 43 E10
Smockington Leics 35 G10
Smoogro Orkney 95 H4
Smythe's Green Essex 30 G6
Snaigow House Perth 76 C3
Snailbeach Shrops 33 E9
Snailwell Cambs 30 B3
Snainton N Yorks 52 A5
Snaith E Yorks 52 G2
Snape N Yorks 51 A8
Snape Suff 31 C10
Snape Green Lancs 43 A6
Snarestone Leics 35 E9
Snarford Lincs 46 D4
Snargate Kent 13 D8
Snave Kent 13 D9
Snead Powys 33 F9
Snead Common Worcs 26 B4
Sneath Common Norf 39 G7
Sneaton N Yorks 59 F9
Sneatonthorpe N Yorks 59 F10
Snelland Lincs 46 D4
Snelston Derbys 35 A7
Snettisham Norf 38 B2
Sniseabhal W Isles 84 E2
Snitter Northumb 62 C6
Snitterby Lincs 46 C3
Snitterfield Warks 27 C9
Snitton Shrops 34 H1
Snodhill Hereford 25 D10
Snodland Kent 20 E3
Snowden Hill S Yorks 44 B6
Snowdown Kent 21 F9
Snowshill Glos 27 E7
Snydale W Yorks 51 H10
Soar Anglesey 40 C5
Soar Carms 24 F3
Soar Devon 5 H8
Soar-y-Mynydd Ceredig 24 C4
Soberton Hants 10 C5
Soberton Heath Hants 10 C5
Sockbridge Cumb 57 D7
Sockburn Darl 58 F4
Soham Cambs 30 A2
Soham Cotes Cambs 38 H1
Solas W Isles 84 A3
Soldon Cross Devon 6 E2
Soldridge Hants 10 A5
Sole Street Kent 20 E3
Sole Street Kent 21 G7
Solihull W Mid 35 H7
Sollers Dilwyn Hereford 25 C11
Sollers Hope Hereford 26 E3
Sollom Lancs 49 H4
Solva Pembs 22 D2
Somerby Leics 36 D3
Somerby Lincs 46 B4
Somercotes Derbys 45 G8
Somerford Dorset 9 E10
Somerford Keynes Glos 17 B7
Somerley W Sus 11 E7
Somerleyton Suff 39 F10
Somersal Herbert Derbys 35 B7
Somersby Lincs 47 E7
Somersham Cambs 37 H9
Somersham Suff 31 D7
Somerton Oxon 27 F11
Somerton Som 8 B3
Sompting W Sus 11 D10
Sonning Wokingham 18 D4
Sonning Common Oxon 18 C4
Sonning Eye Oxon 18 D4
Sontley Wrex 42 H6
Sopley Hants 9 E10
Sopwell Herts 29 H8
Sopworth Wilts 16 C5
Sorbie Dumfries 55 E7
Sordale Highld 94 D3
Sorisdale Argyll 78 E5
Sorn E Ayrs 68 H4
Sornhill E Ayrs 67 C8
Sortat Highld 94 D4
Sotby Lincs 46 E6
Sots Hole Lincs 46 F5
Sotterley Suff 39 G10
Soudley Shrops 34 C3
Soughton Flint 42 F5
Soulbury Bucks 28 F5
Soulby Cumb 57 E9
Souldern Oxon 28 E2
Souldrop Bedford 28 B6
Sound Ches E 43 H9
Sound Shetland 96 H5
Sound Shetland 96 J6
Sound Heath Ches E 43 H9
Soundwell S Glos 16 D3
Sourhope Borders 62 A4
Sourin Orkney 95 E5
Sourton Devon 6 G4
Soutergate Cumb 49 A2
South Acre Norf 38 D4
South Allington Devon 5 H8
South Alloa Falk 69 A7
South Ambersham W Sus 11 B8
South Anston S Yorks 45 D9
South Ascot Windsor 18 E6
South Ballachulish Highld 74 B3
South Balloch S Ayrs 66 G6
South Bank Redcar 59 D6
South Barrow Som 8 B5
South Beach Gwyn 40 G5
South Benfleet Essex 20 C4
South Bersted W Sus 11 D8
South Brent Devon 5 E7
South Brewham Som 16 H4
South Broomhill Northumb 63 D8
South Burlingham Norf 39 E9
South Cadbury Som 8 B5
South Cairn Dumfries 54 C2
South Carlton Lincs 46 E3
South Cave E Yorks 52 F5
South Cerney Glos 17 B7
South Chard Som 8 D2
South Charlton Northumb 63 A7
South Cheriton Som 8 B5
South Cliffe E Yorks 52 F4
South Clifton Notts 46 E2
South Cockerington Lincs 47 D7
South Cornelly Bridgend 14 C4
South Cove Suff 39 G10
South Creagan Argyll 74 C2
South Creake Norf 38 B4
South Croxton Leics 36 D2
South Croydon London 19 E10
South Dalton E Yorks 52 E5
South Darenth Kent 20 E2
South Duffield N Yorks 52 F2
South Elkington Lincs 46 D6
South Elmsall W Yorks 45 A8
South End Bucks 28 F5
South End Cumb 49 C2
South End N Lincs 53 G7
South Erradale Highld 85 A12
South Fambridge Essex 20 B5
South Fawley W Berks 17 C10
South Ferriby N Lincs 52 G5
South Garth Shetland 96 D7
South Garvan Highld 80 F1
South Glendale W Isles 84 G2
South Godstone Sur 19 G10
South Gorley Hants 9 C10
South Green Essex 20 B3
South Green Kent 20 E5
South-haa Shetland 96 E5
South Ham Hants 18 F3
South Hanningfield Essex 20 B4
South Harting W Sus 11 C6
South Hatfield Herts 29 H9
South Hayling Hants 10 E6
South Hazelrigg Northumb 71 G9
South Heath Bucks 18 A6
South Heighton E Sus 12 F3
South Hetton Durham 58 B4
South Hiendley W Yorks 45 A7
South Hill Corn 4 D4
South Hinksey Oxon 18 A2
South Hole Devon 6 D1
South Holme N Yorks 52 B2
South Holmwood Sur 19 G8
South Hornchurch London 20 C2
South Hykeham Lincs 46 F3
South Hylton T&W 63 H9
South Kelsey Lincs 46 C4
South Kessock Highld 87 G9
South Killingholme N Lincs 53 H7
South Kilvington N Yorks 51 A10
South Kilworth Leics 36 G2
South Kirkby W Yorks 45 A8
South Kirkton Aberds 83 C9
South Kiscadale N Ayrs 66 D3
South Kyme Lincs 46 H5
South Lancing W Sus 11 D10
South Leigh Oxon 27 H10
South Leverton Notts 45 D11
South Littleton Worcs 27 D7
South Lopham Norf 38 G6
South Luffenham Rutland 36 E5
South Malling E Sus 12 E3
South Marston Swindon 17 C8
South Middleton Northumb 62 A5
South Milford N Yorks 51 F10
South Millbrex Aberds 89 D8
South Milton Devon 5 G8
South Mimms Herts 19 A9
South Molton Devon 6 D6
South Moreton Oxon 18 C2
South Mundham W Sus 11 D7
South Muskham Notts 45 G11
South Newbald E Yorks 52 F5
South Newington Oxon 27 E11
South Newton Wilts 9 A9
South Normanton Derbys 45 G8
South Norwood London 19 E10
South Nutfield Sur 19 G10
South Ockendon Thurrock 20 C2
South Ormsby Lincs 47 E7
South Otterington N Yorks 58 H4
South Owersby Lincs 46 C4
South Oxhey Herts 19 B8
South Perrott Dorset 8 D3
South Petherton Som 8 C3
South Petherwin Corn 4 C4
South Pickenham Norf 38 E4
South Pool Devon 5 G8
South Port Argyll 74 E3
South Radworthy Devon 7 C6
South Rauceby Lincs 46 H4
South Raynham Norf 38 C4
South Reston Lincs 47 D8
South Runcton Norf 38 E2
South Scarle Notts 46 F2
South Shian Argyll 74 C2
South Shields T&W 63 G9
South Shore Blackpool 49 F3
South Somercotes Lincs 47 C8
South Stainley N Yorks 51 C9
South Stainmore Cumb 57 E10
South Stifford Thurrock 20 D3
South Stoke Oxon 18 C2
South Stoke W Sus 11 D9
South Street E Sus 12 E2
South Street Kent 21 E8
South Street Kent 21 F7
South Street London 19 F11
South Tawton Devon 6 G5
South Thoresby Lincs 47 E8
South Tidworth Wilts 17 G9
South Town Hants 18 H3
South View Hants 18 F3
South Walsham Norf 39 D9
South Warnborough Hants 18 G4
South Weald Essex 20 B2
South Weston Oxon 18 B4
South Wheatley Corn 4 B3
South Wheatley Notts 45 D11
South Whiteness Shetland 96 J5
South Widcombe Bath 16 F2
South Wigston Leics 36 F1
South Willingham Lincs 46 D5
South Wingfield Derbys 45 G7
South Witham Lincs 36 D5
South Wonston Hants 17 H11
South Woodham Ferrers Essex 20 B5
South Wootton Norf 38 C2
South Wraxall Wilts 16 E5
South Zeal Devon 6 G5
Southall London 19 C8
Southam Glos 26 F6
Southam Warks 27 B11
Southampton Soton 10 C3
Southborough Kent 12 B4
Southbourne Bmouth 9 E10
Southbourne W Sus 11 D6
Southburgh Norf 38 E5
Southburn E Yorks 52 D5
Southchurch Southend 20 C6
Southcott Wilts 17 F8
Southcourt Bucks 28 G5
Southdean Borders 62 C2
Southdene Mers 43 C7
Southease E Sus 12 F3
Southend Argyll 65 H7
Southend W Berks 18 D2
Southend Wilts 17 D8
Southend-on-Sea Southend 20 C5
Southernden Kent 20 G5
Southerndown V Glam 14 D4
Southerness Dumfries 60 H5
Southery Norf 38 F2
Southfield Northumb 63 F8
Southfleet Kent 20 D3
Southgate Ceredig 32 H1
Southgate London 19 B9
Southgate Norf 39 C7
Southgate Swansea 23 H10
Southill C Beds 29 D8
Southleigh Devon 7 G11
Southminster Essex 20 B6
Southmoor Oxon 17 B10
Southoe Cambs 29 B8
Southolt Suff 31 B8
Southorpe Pboro 37 E6
Southowram W Yorks 51 G7
Southport Mers 49 H3
Southpunds Shetland 96 L6
Southrepps Norf 39 B8
Southrey Lincs 46 F5
Southrop Glos 17 A8
Southrope Hants 18 G3
Southsea Ptsmth 10 E5
Southstoke Bath 16 E4
Southtown Norf 39 E11
Southtown Orkney 95 J5
Southwaite Cumb 56 B6
Southwark London 19 D10
Southwater W Sus 11 B10
Southwater Street W Sus 11 B10
Southway Som 15 G11
Southwell Dorset 8 G5
Southwell Notts 45 G10
Southwick Hants 10 D5
Southwick Northants 36 F6
Southwick T&W 63 H9
Southwick W Sus 11 D11
Southwick Wilts 16 F5
Southwold Suff 39 H11
Southwood Norf 39 E9
Southwood Som 8 A4
Soval Lodge W Isles 91 E8
Sowber Gate N Yorks 58 H4
Sowerby N Yorks 51 A10
Sowerby W Yorks 50 G6
Sowerby Bridge W Yorks 51 G6
Sowerby Row Cumb 56 C5
Sowood W Yorks 51 H6
Sowton Devon 7 G8
Soyal Highld 87 B8
Spa Common Norf 39 B8
Spacey Houses N Yorks 51 D9
Spadeadam Farm Cumb 61 F11
Spalding Lincs 37 C8
Spaldington E Yorks 52 F3
Spaldwick Cambs 29 A8
Spalford Notts 46 F2
Spanby Lincs 37 B6
Sparham Norf 39 D6
Spark Bridge Cumb 49 A3
Sparkford Som 8 B5
Sparkhill W Mid 35 G6
Sparkwell Devon 5 F6
Sparrow Green Norf 38 D5
Sparrowpit Derbys 44 D4
Sparsholt Hants 10 A3
Sparsholt Oxon 17 C10
Spartylea Northumb 57 B10
Spaunton N Yorks 59 H8
Spaxton Som 7 C11
Spean Bridge Highld 80 E4
Spear Hill W Sus 11 C10
Speen Bucks 18 B5
Speen W Berks 17 E11
Speeton N Yorks 53 B7
Speke Mers 43 D7
Speldhurst Kent 12 B4
Spellbrook Herts 29 G11
Spelsbury Oxon 27 F10
Spelter Bridgend 14 B4
Spencers Wood Wokingham 18 E4
Spennithorne N Yorks 58 H2
Spennymoor Durham 58 C3
Spetchley Worcs 26 C5
Spetisbury Dorset 9 D8
Spexhall Suff 39 G9
Spey Bay Moray 88 B3
Speybridge Highld 82 A2
Speyview Moray 88 D2
Spilsby Lincs 47 F8
Spindlestone Northumb 71 G10
Spinkhill Derbys 45 E8
Spinningdale Highld 87 C9
Spirthill Wilts 16 D6
Spital Hill S Yorks 45 C10
Spital in the Street Lincs 46 D3
Spithurst E Sus 12 E3
Spittal Dumfries 54 D6
Spittal E Loth 70 C3
Spittal Highld 94 E3
Spittal Northumb 71 E9
Spittal Pembs 22 D4
Spittal Stirling 68 B4
Spittal of Glenmuick Aberds 82 E5
Spittal of Glenshee Perth 82 F3
Spittalfield Perth 76 C4
Spixworth Norf 39 D8
Splayne's Green E Sus 12 D3
Spofforth N Yorks 51 D9
Spon End W Mid 35 H9
Spon Green Flint 42 F5
Spondon Derby 35 B10
Spooner Row Norf 39 F6
Sporle Norf 38 D4
Spott E Loth 70 C5
Spratton Northants 28 A4
Spreakley Sur 18 G5
Spreyton Devon 6 G5
Spridlington Lincs 46 D4
Spring Vale S Yorks 44 B6
Spring Valley IoM 48 E3
Springburn Glasgow 68 D5
Springfield Dumfries 61 G9
Springfield Essex 30 H4
Springfield Fife 76 F6
Springfield Moray 87 F13
Springfield W Mid 35 G6
Springhill Staffs 34 E5
Springholm Dumfries 55 C11
Springkell Dumfries 61 F8
Springside N Ayrs 67 C6
Springthorpe Lincs 46 D2
Springwell T&W 63 H8
Sproatley E Yorks 53 F7
Sproston Green Ches W 43 F10
Sprotbrough S Yorks 45 B9
Sproughton Suff 31 D8
Sprouston Borders 70 G6
Sprowston Norf 39 D8
Sproxton Leics 36 C4
Sproxton N Yorks 52 A2
Spurstow Ches E 43 G8
Spynie Moray 88 B2
Squires Gate Blackpool 49 F3
Srannda W Isles 90 J5
Sronphadruig Lodge Perth 81 F9
Stableford Shrops 34 F3
Stableford Staffs 34 B4
Stacey Bank S Yorks 44 C6
Stackhouse N Yorks 50 C4
Stackpole Pembs 22 G4
Staddiscombe Plym 4 F6
Staddlethorpe E Yorks 52 G4
Stadhampton Oxon 18 B3
Stadhlaigearraidh W Isles 84 E2
Staffield Cumb 57 B7
Staffin Highld 85 B9
Stafford Staffs 34 C5
Stagsden Bedford 28 D6
Stainburn Cumb 56 D2
Stainburn N Yorks 51 E8
Stainby Lincs 36 C5
Staincross S Yorks 45 A7
Staindrop Durham 58 D2
Staines-upon-Thames Sur 19 D7
Stainfield Lincs 37 C6
Stainfield Lincs 46 E5
Stainforth N Yorks 50 C4
Stainforth S Yorks 45 A10
Staining Lancs 49 F3
Stainland W Yorks 51 H6
Stainsacre N Yorks 59 F10
Stainsby Derbys 45 F8
Stainton Cumb 57 D6
Stainton Cumb 57 H7
Stainton Durham 58 E1
Stainton Mbro 58 E5
Stainton N Yorks 58 G2
Stainton S Yorks 45 C9
Stainton by Langworth Lincs 46 E4
Stainton le Vale Lincs 46 C5
Stainton with Adgarley Cumb 49 B2
Staintondale N Yorks 59 G10
Stair Cumb 56 D4
Stair E Ayrs 67 D7
Stairhaven Dumfries 54 D5
Staithes N Yorks 59 E8
Stake Pool Lancs 49 E4
Stakeford Northumb 63 E8
Stalbridge Dorset 8 C6
Stalbridge Weston Dorset 8 C6
Stalham Norf 39 C9
Stalham Green Norf 39 C9
Stalisfield Green Kent 20 F6
Stalling Busk N Yorks 57 H11
Stallingborough NE Lincs 46 A5
Stalmine Lancs 49 E3
Stalybridge Gtr Man 44 C3
Stambourne Essex 30 E4
Stambourne Green Essex 30 E4
Stamford Lincs 36 E6
Stamford Bridge Ches W 43 F7
Stamford Bridge E Yorks 52 D3
Stamfordham Northumb 62 F6
Stanah Cumb 56 E5
Stanborough Herts 29 G9
Stanbridge C Beds 28 F6
Stanbridge Dorset 9 D9
Stanbrook Worcs 26 D5
Stanbury W Yorks 50 F6
Stand Gtr Man 43 B10
Stand N Lanark 68 D6
Standburn Falk 69 C8
Standeford Staffs 34 E5
Standen Kent 13 B7
Standford Hants 11 A7
Standingstone Cumb 56 C2
Standish Gtr Man 43 A8
Standlake Oxon 17 A10
Standon Hants 10 B3
Standon Herts 29 F10
Standon Staffs 34 B4
Stane N Lanark 69 E7
Stanfield Norf 38 C5
Stanford C Beds 29 D8
Stanford Kent 13 C10
Stanford Bishop Hereford 26 C3
Stanford Bridge Worcs 26 B4
Stanford Dingley W Berks 18 D2
Stanford in the Vale Oxon 17 B10
Stanford-le-Hope Thurrock 20 C3
Stanford on Avon Northants 36 H1
Stanford on Soar Notts 35 C11
Stanford on Teme Worcs 26 B4
Stanford Rivers Essex 20 A2
Stanfree Derbys 45 E8
Stanghow Redcar 59 E7
Stanground Pboro 37 F8
Stanhoe Norf 38 B4
Stanhope Borders 69 H10
Stanhope Durham 57 C11
Stanion Northants 36 G5
Stanley Derbys 35 A10
Stanley Durham 58 A2
Stanley Lancs 43 B7
Stanley Perth 76 D4
Stanley Staffs 44 G3
Stanley W Yorks 51 G9
Stanley Common Derbys 35 A10
Stanley Gate Lancs 43 B7
Stanley Hill Hereford 26 D3
Stanlow Ches W 43 E7
Stanmer Brighton 12 F2
Stanmore Hants 10 B3
Stanmore London 19 B8
Stanmore W Berks 17 D11
Stannergate Dundee 77 D7
Stanningley W Yorks 51 F8
Stannington Northumb 63 F8
Stannington S Yorks 45 D7
Stansbatch Hereford 25 B10
Stansfield Suff 30 C4
Stanstead Suff 30 D5
Stanstead Abbotts Herts 29 G10
Stansted Kent 20 E3
Stansted Airport Essex 30 F2
Stansted Mountfitchet Essex 30 F2
Stanton Glos 27 E7
Stanton Mon 25 F10
Stanton Northumb 63 E7
Stanton Staffs 44 H5
Stanton Suff 30 A6
Stanton by Bridge Derbys 35 C9
Stanton-by-Dale Derbys 35 B10
Stanton Drew Bath 16 E2
Stanton Fitzwarren Swindon 17 B8

Thixendale N Yorks 52 C4
Thockrington Northumb 62 F5
Tholomas Drove Cambs 37 E9
Tholthorpe N Yorks 51 C10
Thomas Chapel Pembs 22 F6
Thomas Close Cumb 56 B6
Thomastown Aberds 88 E5
Thompson Norf 38 F5
Thomshill Moray 88 C2
Thong Kent 20 D3
Thongsbridge W Yorks 44 B5
Thoralby N Yorks 58 H1
Thoresway Lincs 46 C5
Thorganby Lincs 46 C6
Thorganby N Yorks 52 E2
Thorgill N Yorks 59 G8
Thorington Suff 31 A11
Thorington Street Suff 31 E7
Thorlby N Yorks 50 D5
Thorley Herts 29 G11
Thorley Street Herts 29 G11
Thorley Street IoW 10 F2
Thormanby N Yorks 51 B10
Thornaby-on-Tees Stockton 58 E5
Thornage Norf 38 B6
Thornborough Bucks 28 E4
Thornborough N Yorks 51 B8
Thornbury Devon 6 F3
Thornbury Hereford 26 C3
Thornbury S Glos 16 B3
Thornbury W Yorks 51 F7
Thornby Northants 36 H2
Thorncliffe Staffs 44 G4
Thorncombe Dorset 8 D2
Thorncombe Dorset 9 D7
Thorncombe Street Sur 19 G7
Thorncote Green C Beds 29 D8
Thorncross IoW 10 F3
Thorndon Suff 31 B8
Thorndon Cross Devon 6 G4
Thorne S Yorks 45 A10
Thorne St Margaret Som 7 D9
Thorner W Yorks 51 E9
Thorney Notts 46 E2
Thorney Pboro 37 E8
Thorney Crofts E Yorks 53 G8
Thorney Green Suff 31 B7
Thorney Hill Hants 9 E10
Thorney Toll Pboro 37 E9
Thornfalcon Som 8 B1
Thornford Dorset 8 C5
Thorngumbald E Yorks 53 G8
Thornham Norf 38 A3
Thornham Magna Suff 31 A8
Thornham Parva Suff 31 A8
Thornhaugh Pboro 37 E6
Thornhill Cardiff 15 C7
Thornhill Cumb 56 F2
Thornhill Derbys 44 D5
Thornhill Dumfries 60 D4
Thornhill Soton 10 C3
Thornhill Stirling 75 H9
Thornhill W Yorks 51 H8
Thornhill Edge W Yorks 51 H8
Thornhill Lees W Yorks 51 H8
Thornholme E Yorks 53 C7
Thornley Durham 58 C4
Thornley Durham 58 C2
Thornliebank E Renf 68 E4
Thorns Suff 30 C4
Thorns Green Ches E 43 D10
Thornsett Derbys 44 D4
Thornthwaite Cumb 56 D4
Thornthwaite N Yorks 51 D7
Thornton Angus 76 C6
Thornton Bucks 28 E4
Thornton E Yorks 52 E3
Thornton Fife 76 H5
Thornton Lancs 49 E3
Thornton Leics 35 E10
Thornton Lincs 46 F6
Thornton Mbro 58 E5
Thornton Mers 42 B6
Thornton Northumb 71 F8
Thornton Pembs 22 F4
Thornton W Yorks 51 F7
Thornton Curtis N Lincs 53 H6
Thornton Heath London 19 E10
Thornton Hough Mers 42 D6
Thornton in Craven N Yorks 50 E5
Thornton-le-Beans N Yorks 58 G4
Thornton-le-Clay N Yorks 52 C2
Thornton-le-Dale N Yorks 52 A4
Thornton le Moor Lincs 46 C4
Thornton-le-Moor N Yorks 58 H4
Thornton-le-Moors Ches W 43 E7
Thornton-le-Street N Yorks 58 H5
Thornton Rust N Yorks 57 H11
Thornton Steward N Yorks 58 H2
Thornton Watlass N Yorks 58 H3
Thorntonhall S Lanark 68 E4
Thorntonloch E Loth 70 C6
Thorntonpark Northumb 71 F8
Thornwood Common Essex 19 A11
Thornydykes Borders 70 F5
Thoroton Notts 36 A3
Thorp Arch W Yorks 51 E10
Thorpe Derbys 44 G5
Thorpe E Yorks 52 E5
Thorpe Lincs 47 D8
Thorpe N Yorks 50 C6
Thorpe Norf 39 F10
Thorpe Notts 45 H11
Thorpe Sur 19 E7
Thorpe Abbotts Norf 39 H7
Thorpe Acre Leics 35 C11
Thorpe Arnold Leics 36 C3
Thorpe Audlin W Yorks 51 H10
Thorpe Bassett N Yorks 52 B4
Thorpe Bay Southend 20 C6
Thorpe by Water Rutland 36 F4
Thorpe Common Suff 31 E9
Thorpe Constantine Staffs 35 E8
Thorpe Culvert Lincs 47 F8
Thorpe End Norf 39 D8
Thorpe Fendykes Lincs 47 F8
Thorpe Green Essex 31 F8
Thorpe Green Suff 30 C6
Thorpe Hesley S Yorks 45 C7
Thorpe in Balne S Yorks 45 A9
Thorpe in the Fallows Lincs 46 D3
Thorpe Langton Leics 36 F3
Thorpe Larches Durham 58 D4
Thorpe-le-Soken Essex 31 F8
Thorpe le Street E Yorks 52 E4
Thorpe Malsor Northants 36 H4
Thorpe Mandeville Northants 28 D2
Thorpe Market Norf 39 B8
Thorpe Marriot Norf 39 D7
Thorpe Morieux Suff 30 C6
Thorpe on the Hill Lincs 46 F3
Thorpe St Andrew Norf 39 E8
Thorpe St Peter Lincs 47 F8
Thorpe Salvin S Yorks 45 D9
Thorpe Satchville Leics 36 D3
Thorpe Thewles Stockton 58 D5
Thorpe Tilney Lincs 46 G5
Thorpe Underwood N Yorks 51 D10
Thorpe Waterville Northants 36 G6
Thorpe Willoughby N Yorks 52 F1
Thorpeness Suff 31 C11
Thorrington Essex 31 F7
Thorverton Devon 7 F8
Thrandeston Suff 39 H7
Thrapston Northants 36 H5
Thrashbush N Lanark 68 D6
Threapland Cumb 56 C3
Threapland N Yorks 50 C5
Threapwood Ches W 43 H7
Threapwood Staffs 34 A6
Three Ashes Hereford 26 F2
Three Bridges W Sus 12 C1
Three Burrows Corn 2 E6
Three Chimneys Kent 13 C7
Three Cocks Powys 25 E8
Three Crosses Swansea 23 G10
Three Cups Corner E Sus 12 D5
Three Holes Norf 37 E11
Three Leg Cross E Sus 12 C5
Three Legged Cross Dorset 9 D9
Three Oaks E Sus 13 E7
Threehammer Common Norf 39 D9
Threekingham Lincs 37 B6
Threemile Cross Wokingham 18 E4
Threemilestone Corn 3 E6
Threemiletown W Loth 69 C9
Threlkeld Cumb 56 D5
Threshfield N Yorks 50 C5
Thrigby Norf 39 D10
Thringarth Durham 57 D11
Thringstone Leics 35 D10
Thrintoft N Yorks 58 G4
Thriplow Cambs 29 D11
Throckenholt Lincs 37 E9
Throcking Herts 29 E10
Throckley T&W 63 G7
Throckmorton Worcs 26 D6
Throphill Northumb 63 E7
Thropton Northumb 62 C6
Throsk Stirling 69 A7
Throwleigh Devon 6 G5
Throwley Kent 20 F6
Thrumpton Notts 35 B11
Thrumster Highld 94 F5
Thrunton Northumb 62 B6
Thrupp Glos 16 A5
Thrupp Oxon 27 G11
Thrushelton Devon 4 C5
Thrussington Leics 36 D2
Thruxton Hants 17 G9
Thruxton Hereford 25 E11
Thrybergh S Yorks 45 C8
Thulston Derbys 35 B10
Thundergay N Ayrs 66 B1
Thundersley Essex 20 C4
Thundridge Herts 29 G10
Thurcaston Leics 36 D1
Thurcroft S Yorks 45 D8
Thurgarton Norf 39 B7
Thurgarton Notts 45 H10
Thurgoland S Yorks 44 B6
Thurlaston Leics 35 F11
Thurlaston Warks 27 A11
Thurlbear Som 8 B1
Thurlby Lincs 37 D7
Thurlby Lincs 46 F3
Thurleigh Bedford 29 C7
Thurlestone Devon 5 G7
Thurloxton Som 8 A1
Thurlstone S Yorks 44 B6
Thurlton Norf 39 F10
Thurlwood Ches E 44 G2
Thurmaston Leics 36 E2
Thurnby Leics 36 E2
Thurne Norf 39 D10
Thurnham Kent 20 F5
Thurnham Lancs 49 D4
Thurning Norf 39 C6
Thurning Northants 37 G6
Thurnscoe S Yorks 45 B8
Thurnscoe East S Yorks 45 B8
Thursby Cumb 56 A5
Thursford Norf 38 B5
Thursley Sur 18 H6
Thurso Highld 94 D3
Thurso East Highld 94 D3
Thurstaston Mers 42 D5
Thurston Suff 30 B6
Thurstonfield Cumb 61 H9
Thurstonland W Yorks 44 A5
Thurton Norf 39 E9
Thurvaston Derbys 35 B8
Thuxton Norf 38 E6
Thwaite N Yorks 57 G10
Thwaite Suff 31 B8
Thwaite St Mary Norf 39 F9
Thwaites W Yorks 51 E6
Thwaites Brow W Yorks 51 E6
Thwing E Yorks 53 B6
Tibbermore Perth 76 E3
Tibberton Glos 26 F4
Tibberton Telford 34 C2
Tibberton Worcs 26 C6
Tibenham Norf 39 G7
Tibshelf Derbys 45 F8
Tibthorpe E Yorks 52 D5
Ticehurst E Sus 12 C5
Tichborne Hants 10 A4
Tickencote Rutland 36 E5
Tickenham N Som 15 D10
Tickhill S Yorks 45 C9
Ticklerton Shrops 33 F10
Ticknall Derbys 35 C9
Tickton E Yorks 53 E6
Tidcombe Wilts 17 F9
Tiddington Oxon 18 A3
Tiddington Warks 27 C9
Tidebrook E Sus 12 D5
Tideford Corn 4 F4
Tideford Cross Corn 4 E4
Tidenham Glos 16 B2
Tideswell Derbys 44 E5
Tidmarsh W Berks 18 D3
Tidmington Warks 27 E9
Tidpit Hants 9 C9
Tidworth Wilts 17 G9
Tiers Cross Pembs 22 E4
Tiffield Northants 28 C3
Tifty Aberds 89 D7
Tigerton Angus 77 A8
Tigh-na-Blair Perth 75 F10
Tighnabruaich Argyll 73 F8
Tighnafiline Highld 91 J13
Tigley Devon 5 E8
Tilbrook Cambs 29 B7
Tilbury Thurrock 20 D3
Tilbury Juxta Clare Essex 30 D4
Tile Cross W Mid 35 G7
Tile Hill W Mid 35 H8
Tilehurst Reading 18 D3
Tilford Sur 18 G5
Tilgate W Sus 12 C1
Tilgate Forest Row W Sus 12 C1
Tillathrowie Aberds 88 E4
Tilley Shrops 33 C11
Tillicoultry Clack 76 H2
Tillingham Essex 20 A6
Tillington Hereford 25 D11
Tillington W Sus 11 B8
Tillington Common Hereford 25 D11
Tillyarblet Angus 83 G7
Tillybirloch Aberds 83 C8
Tillycorthie Aberds 89 F9
Tillydrine Aberds 83 D8
Tillyfour Aberds 83 B7
Tillyfourie Aberds 83 B8
Tillygarmond Aberds 83 D8
Tillygreig Aberds 89 F8
Tillykerrie Aberds 89 F8
Tilmanstone Kent 21 F10
Tilney All Saints Norf 38 D1
Tilney High End Norf 38 D1
Tilney St Lawrence Norf 37 D11
Tilshead Wilts 17 G7
Tilstock Shrops 33 B11
Tilston Ches W 43 G7
Tilstone Fearnall Ches W 43 F8
Tilsworth C Beds 28 F6
Tilton on the Hill Leics 36 E3
Timberland Lincs 46 G5
Timbersbrook Ches E 44 F2
Timberscombe Som 7 B8
Timble N Yorks 51 D7
Timperley Gtr Man 43 D10
Timsbury Bath 16 F3
Timsbury Hants 10 B2
Timsgearraidh W Isles 90 D5
Timworth Green Suff 30 B5
Tincleton Dorset 9 E6
Tindale Cumb 62 H2
Tingewick Bucks 28 E3
Tingley W Yorks 51 G8
Tingrith C Beds 29 E7
Tingwall Orkney 95 F4
Tinhay Devon 4 C4
Tinshill W Yorks 51 F8
Tinsley S Yorks 45 C8
Tintagel Corn 4 C1
Tintern Parva Mon 15 A11
Tintinhull Som 8 C4
Tintwistle Derbys 44 C4
Tinwald Dumfries 60 E6
Tinwell Rutland 36 E6
Tipperty Aberds 89 F9
Tipsend Norf 37 F11
Tipton W Mid 34 F5
Tipton St John Devon 7 G9
Tiptree Essex 30 G5
Tir-y-dail Carms 24 G3
Tirabad Powys 24 D5
Tiraghoil Argyll 78 J6
Tirley Glos 26 F5
Tirphil Caerph 15 A7
Tirril Cumb 57 D7
Tisbury Wilts 9 B8
Tisman's Common W Sus 11 A9
Tissington Derbys 44 G5
Titchberry Devon 6 D1
Titchfield Hants 10 D4
Titchmarsh Northants 36 H6
Titchwell Norf 38 A3
Tithby Notts 36 B2
Titley Hereford 25 B10
Titlington Northumb 63 B7
Titsey Sur 19 F11
Tittensor Staffs 34 B4
Tittleshall Norf 38 C4
Tiverton Ches W 43 F8
Tiverton Devon 7 E8
Tivetshall St Margaret Norf 39 G7
Tivetshall St Mary Norf 39 G7
Tividale W Mid 34 F5
Tivy Dale S Yorks 44 B6
Tixall Staffs 34 C5
Tixover Rutland 36 E5
Toab Orkney 95 H6
Toab Shetland 96 M5
Toadmoor Derbys 45 G7
Tobermory Argyll 79 F8
Toberonochy Argyll 72 C6
Tobha Mor W Isles 84 E2
Tobhtarol W Isles 90 D6
Tobson W Isles 90 D6
Tocher Aberds 89 E6
Tockenham Wilts 17 D7
Tockenham Wick Wilts 17 C7
Tockholes Blackburn 50 G2
Tockington S Glos 16 C3
Tockwith N Yorks 51 D10
Todber Dorset 9 B7
Todding Hereford 33 H10
Toddington C Beds 29 F7
Toddington Glos 27 E7
Todenham Glos 27 E9
Todhills Cumb 61 G9
Todlachie Aberds 83 B8
Todmorden W Yorks 50 G5
Todrig Borders 61 B10
Todwick S Yorks 45 D8
Toft Cambs 29 C10
Toft Lincs 37 D6
Toft Hill Durham 58 D2
Toft Hill Lincs 46 F6
Toft Monks Norf 39 F10
Toft next Newton Lincs 46 D4
Toftrees Norf 38 C4
Tofts Highld 94 D5
Toftwood Norf 38 D5
Togston Northumb 63 C8
Tokavaig Highld 85 G11
Tokers Green Oxon 18 D4
Tolastadh a Chaolais W Isles 90 D6
Tolastadh bho Thuath W Isles 91 C10
Toll Bar S Yorks 45 B9
Toll End W Mid 34 F5
Toll of Birness Aberds 89 E10
Tolland Som 7 C10
Tollard Royal Wilts 9 C8
Tollbar End W Mid 35 H9
Toller Fratrum Dorset 8 E4
Toller Porcorum Dorset 8 E4
Tollerton N Yorks 51 C11
Tollerton Notts 36 B2
Tollesbury Essex 30 G6
Tolleshunt D'Arcy Essex 30 G6
Tolleshunt Major Essex 30 G6
Tolm W Isles 91 D9
Tolpuddle Dorset 9 E6
Tolvah Highld 81 D10
Tolworth London 19 E8
Tomatin Highld 81 A10
Tombreck Highld 87 H9
Tomchrasky Highld 80 B4
Tomdoun Highld 80 C3
Tomich Highld 80 A5
Tomich Highld 87 D9
Tomich House Highld 87 G8
Tomintoul Aberds 82 D3
Tomintoul Moray 82 B3
Tomnaven Moray 88 E4
Tomnavoulin Moray 82 A4
Ton-Pentre Rhondda 14 B5
Tonbridge Kent 20 G2
Tondu Bridgend 14 C4
Tonfanau Gwyn 32 E1
Tong Shrops 34 E3
Tong W Yorks 51 F8
Tong Norton Shrops 34 E3
Tonge Leics 35 C10
Tongham Sur 18 G5
Tongland Dumfries 55 D9
Tongue Highld 93 D8
Tongue End Lincs 37 D7
Tongwynlais Cardiff 15 C7
Tonna Neath 14 B3
Tonwell Herts 29 G10
Tonypandy Rhondda 14 B5
Tonyrefail Rhondda 14 C6
Toot Baldon Oxon 18 A2
Toot Hill Essex 20 A2
Toothill Hants 10 C2
Top of Hebers Gtr Man 44 B2
Topcliffe N Yorks 51 B10
Topcroft Norf 39 F8
Topcroft Street Norf 39 F8
Toppesfield Essex 30 E4
Toppings Gtr Man 43 A10
Topsham Devon 5 C10
Torbay Torbay 5 F10
Torbeg N Ayrs 66 D2
Torboll Farm Highld 87 B10
Torbrex Stirling 68 A6
Torbryan Devon 5 E9
Torcross Devon 5 G9
Tore Highld 87 F9
Torinturk Argyll 73 G7
Torksey Lincs 46 E2
Torlum W Isles 84 C2
Torlundy Highld 80 F3
Tormarton S Glos 16 D4
Tormisdale Argyll 64 C2
Tormitchell S Ayrs 66 G5
Tormore N Ayrs 66 C1
Tornagrain Highld 87 G10
Tornahaish Aberds 82 C4
Tornaveen Aberds 83 C8
Torness Highld 81 A7
Toronto Durham 58 C2
Torpenhow Cumb 56 C4
Torphichen W Loth 69 C8
Torphins Aberds 83 C8
Torpoint Corn 4 F5
Torquay Torbay 5 E10
Torquhan Borders 70 F3
Torran Argyll 73 C7
Torran Highld 85 D10
Torran Highld 87 D10
Torrance E Dunb 68 C5
Torrans Argyll 78 J7
Torranyard N Ayrs 67 B6
Torre Torbay 5 E10
Torridon Highld 86 F2
Torridon Ho. Highld 85 C13
Torrin Highld 85 F10
Torrisdale Highld 93 C9
Torrisdale-Square Argyll 65 E8
Torrish Highld 93 H12
Torrisholme Lancs 49 C4
Torroble Highld 93 J8
Torry Aberdeen 83 C11
Torry Aberds 88 E4
Torryburn Fife 69 B9
Torterston Aberds 89 D10
Torthorwald Dumfries 60 F6
Tortington W Sus 11 D9
Tortworth S Glos 16 B4
Torvaig Highld 85 D9
Torver Cumb 56 G4
Torwood Falk 69 B7
Torworth Notts 45 D10
Tosberry Devon 6 D1
Toscaig Highld 85 E12
Toseland Cambs 29 B9
Tosside N Yorks 50 D3
Tostock Suff 30 B6
Totaig Highld 84 C7
Totaig Highld 85 F13
Tote Highld 85 D9
Totegan Highld 93 C11
Tothill Lincs 47 D8
Totland IoW 10 F2
Totnes Devon 5 E9
Toton Notts 35 B11
Totronald Argyll 78 F4
Totscore Highld 85 B8
Tottenham London 19 B10
Tottenhill Norf 38 D2
Tottenhill Row Norf 38 D2
Totteridge London 19 B9
Totternhoe C Beds 28 F6
Tottington Gtr Man 43 A10
Totton Hants 10 C2
Touchen End Windsor 18 D5
Tournaig Highld 91 J13
Toux Aberds 89 C9
Tovil Kent 20 F4
Tow Law Durham 58 C2
Toward Argyll 73 G10
Towcester Northants 28 D3
Towednack Corn 2 F3
Tower End Norf 38 D2
Towersey Oxon 28 H4
Towie Aberds 82 B6
Towie Aberds 89 B8
Towiemore Moray 88 D3
Town End Cambs 37 F10
Town End Cumb 49 A4
Town Row E Sus 12 C4
Town Yetholm Borders 71 H7
Townend W Dunb 68 C3
Towngate Lincs 37 D7
Townhead Cumb 57 C7
Townhead Dumfries 55 E9
Townhead S Ayrs 66 F5
Townhead S Yorks 44 B5
Townhead of Greenlaw Dumfries 55 C10
Townhill Fife 69 B10
Townsend Bucks 28 H4
Townsend Herts 29 H8
Townshend Corn 2 F4
Towthorpe York 52 D2
Towton N Yorks 51 F10
Towyn Conwy 42 E2
Toxteth Mers 42 D6
Toynton All Saints Lincs 47 F7
Toynton Fen Side Lincs 47 F7
Toynton St Peter Lincs 47 F8
Toy's Hill Kent 19 F11
Trabboch E Ayrs 67 D7
Traboe Corn 2 G6
Tradespark Highld 87 F11
Tradespark Orkney 95 H5
Trafford Park Gtr Man 43 C10
Trallong Powys 24 F6
Tranent E Loth 70 C3
Tranmere Mers 42 D6
Trantlebeg Highld 93 D11
Trantlemore Highld 93 D11
Tranwell Northumb 63 E7
Trapp Carms 24 G3
Traprain E Loth 70 C4
Traquair Borders 70 G2
Trawden Lancs 50 F5
Trawsfynydd Gwyn 41 G9
Tre-Gibbon Rhondda 24 H6
Tre-Taliesin Ceredig 32 F2
Tre-vaughan Carms 23 D8
Tre-wyn Mon 25 F10
Trealaw Rhondda 14 B6
Treales Lancs 49 F4
Trearddur Anglesey 40 C4
Treaslane Highld 85 C8
Trebanog Rhondda 14 B6
Trebanos Neath 14 A3
Trebartha Corn 4 D3
Trebarwith Corn 4 C1
Trebetherick Corn 3 B8
Treborough Som 7 C9
Trebudannon Corn 3 C7
Trebullett Corn 4 D4
Treburley Corn 4 D4
Trebyan Corn 4 E1
Trecastle Powys 24 F5
Trecenydd Caerph 15 C7
Trecwn Pembs 22 C4
Trecynon Rhondda 14 A5
Tredavoe Corn 2 G3
Treddiog Pembs 22 D3
Tredegar Bl Gwent 25 H8
Tredegar Newydd = New Tredegar Caerph 15 A7
Tredington Glos 26 F6
Tredington Warks 27 D9
Tredinnick Corn 3 B8
Tredomen Powys 25 E8
Tredunnock Mon 15 B9
Tredustan Powys 25 E8
Treen Corn 2 G2
Treeton S Yorks 45 D8
Tref-y-Clawdd = Knighton Powys 25 A9
Trefaldwyn = Montgomery Powys 33 F8
Trefasser Pembs 22 C3
Trefdraeth Anglesey 40 C6
Trefdraeth = Newport Pembs 22 C5
Trefecca Powys 25 E8
Trefechan Ceredig 32 G1
Trefeglwys Powys 32 F5
Trefenter Ceredig 24 B3
Treffgarne Pembs 22 D4
Treffynnon = Holywell Flint 42 E4
Treffynnon Pembs 22 D3
Trefgarn Owen Pembs 22 D3
Trefil Bl Gwent 25 G8
Trefilan Ceredig 23 A10
Trefin Pembs 22 C3
Treflach Shrops 33 C8
Trefnanney Powys 33 D8
Trefnant Denb 42 E3
Trefonen Shrops 33 C8
Trefor Anglesey 40 B5
Trefor Gwyn 40 F5
Treforest Rhondda 14 C6
Trefriw Conwy 41 D9
Trefynwy = Monmouth Mon 26 G2
Tregadillett Corn 4 C3
Tregaian Anglesey 40 C6
Tregare Mon 25 G11
Tregaron Ceredig 24 C3
Tregarth Gwyn 41 D8
Tregeare Corn 4 C3
Tregeiriog Wrex 33 B7
Tregele Anglesey 40 A5
Tregidden Corn 3 G6
Treglemais Pembs 22 D3
Tregole Corn 4 B2
Tregonetha Corn 3 C8
Tregony Corn 3 E8
Tregoss Corn 3 C8
Tregoyd Powys 25 E9
Tregroes Ceredig 23 B9
Tregurrian Corn 3 C7
Tregynon Powys 33 F6
Trehafod Rhondda 14 B6
Treharris M Tydf 14 B6
Treherbert Rhondda 14 B5
Trekenner Corn 4 D4
Treknow Corn 4 C1
Trelan Corn 2 H6
Trelash Corn 4 B2
Trelassick Corn 3 D7
Trelawnyd Flint 42 E3
Trelech Carms 23 C7
Treleddyd-fawr Pembs 22 D2
Trelewis M Tydf 15 B7
Treligga Corn 4 C1
Trelights Corn 3 B8
Trelill Corn 3 B9
Trelissick Corn 3 F7
Trellech Mon 26 H2
Trelleck Grange Mon 15 A10
Trelogan Flint 42 D4
Trelystan Powys 33 E8
Tremadog Gwyn 41 F7
Tremail Corn 4 C2
Tremain Ceredig 23 B7
Tremaine Corn 4 C3
Tremar Corn 4 E3
Trematon Corn 4 F4
Tremeirchion Denb 42 E3
Trenance Corn 3 C7
Trenarren Corn 3 E9
Trench Telford 34 D2
Treneglos Corn 4 C3
Trenewan Corn 4 F2
Trent Dorset 8 C4
Trent Vale Stoke 34 A4
Trentham Stoke 34 A4
Trentishoe Devon 6 B5
Treoes V Glam 14 D5
Treorchy = Treorci Rhondda 14 B5
Treorci = Treorchy Rhondda 14 B5
Tre'r-ddôl Ceredig 32 F2
Trerulefoot Corn 4 F4
Tresaith Ceredig 23 A7
Tresawle Corn 3 E7
Trescott Staffs 34 F4
Trescowe Corn 2 F4
Tresham Glos 16 B4
Tresillian Corn 3 E7
Tresinwen Pembs 22 B4
Treskinnick Cross Corn 4 B3
Tresmeer Corn 4 C3
Tresparrett Corn 4 B2
Tresparrett Posts Corn 4 B2
Tressait Perth 75 A11
Tresta Shetland 96 D8
Tresta Shetland 96 H5
Treswell Notts 45 E11
Trethosa Corn 3 D8
Trethurgy Corn 3 D9
Tretio Pembs 22 D2
Tretire Hereford 26 F2
Tretower Powys 25 F8
Treuddyn Flint 42 G5
Trevalga Corn 4 C1
Trevalyn Wrex 43 G6
Trevanson Corn 3 B8
Trevarren Corn 3 C8
Trevarrian Corn 3 C7
Trevarrick Corn 3 E8
Trevaughan Carms 22 E6
Treveighan Corn 4 D1
Trevellas Corn 2 D6
Treverva Corn 3 F6
Trevethin Torf 15 A8
Trevigro Corn 4 E4
Treviscoe Corn 3 D8
Trevone Corn 3 B7
Trewarmett Corn 4 C1
Trewassa Corn 4 C2
Trewellard Corn 2 F2
Trewen Corn 4 C3
Trewennack Corn 2 G5
Trewern Powys 33 D8
Trewethern Corn 3 B9
Trewidland Corn 4 F3
Trewint Corn 4 B2
Trewint Corn 4 C3
Trewithian Corn 3 F7
Trewoofe Corn 2 G3
Trewoon Corn 3 D8
Treworga Corn 3 E7
Treworlas Corn 3 F7
Treyarnon Corn 3 B7
Treyford W Sus 11 C7
Trezaise Corn 3 D8
Triangle W Yorks 50 G6
Trickett's Cross Dorset 9 D9
Triffleton Pembs 22 D4
Trimdon Durham 58 C4
Trimdon Colliery Durham 58 C4
Trimdon Grange Durham 58 C4
Trimingham Norf 39 B8
Trimley Lower Street Suff 31 E9
Trimley St Martin Suff 31 E9
Trimley St Mary Suff 31 E9
Trimpley Worcs 34 H3
Trimsaran Carms 23 F9
Trimstone Devon 6 B3
Trinafour Perth 75 A10
Trinant Caerph 15 A8
Tring Herts 28 G6
Tring Wharf Herts 28 G6
Trinity Angus 77 A9
Trinity Jersey 11
Trisant Ceredig 32 H3
Trislaig Highld 80 F2
Trispen Corn 3 D7
Tritlington Northumb 63 D8
Trochry Perth 76 C2
Trodigal Argyll 65 F7
Troed-rhiwdalar Powys 24 C6
Troedyraur Ceredig 23 B8
Troedyrhiw M Tydf 14 A6
Tromode IoM 48 E3
Trondavoe Shetland 96 F5
Troon Corn 2 F5
Troon S Ayrs 66 C6
Trosaraidh W Isles 84 G2
Trossachs Hotel Stirling 75 G8
Troston Suff 30 A5
Trottiscliffe Kent 20 E3
Trotton W Sus 11 B7
Troutbeck Cumb 56 D5
Troutbeck Cumb 56 F6
Troutbeck Bridge Cumb 56 F6
Trow Green Glos 26 H2
Trowbridge Wilts 16 F5
Trowell Notts 35 B10
Trowle Common Wilts 16 F5
Trowley Bottom Herts 29 G7
Trows Borders 70 G5
Trowse Newton Norf 39 E8
Trudoxhill Som 16 G4
Trull Som 7 D11
Trumaisgearraidh W Isles 84 A3
Trumpan Highld 84 B7
Trumpet Hereford 26 E3
Trumpington Cambs 29 C11
Trunch Norf 39 B8
Trunnah Lancs 49 E3
Truro Corn 3 E7
Trusham Devon 5 C9
Trusley Derbys 35 B8
Trusthorpe Lincs 47 D9
Trysull Staffs 34 F4
Tubney Oxon 17 B11
Tuckenhay Devon 5 F9
Tuckhill Shrops 34 G3
Tuckingmill Corn 2 E5
Tuddenham Suff 30 A4
Tuddenham St Martin Suff 31 D8
Tudeley Kent 20 G3
Tudhoe Durham 58 C3
Tudorville Hereford 26 F2
Tudweiliog Gwyn 40 G4
Tuesley Sur 18 G6
Tuffley Glos 26 G5
Tufton Hants 17 G11
Tufton Pembs 22 D5
Tugby Leics 36 E3
Tugford Shrops 34 G1
Tullibardine Perth 76 F2
Tullibody Clack 75 H11
Tullich Argyll 73 B9
Tullich Highld 81 A8
Tullich Muir Highld 87 D10
Tulliemet Perth 76 B2
Tulloch Aberds 83 F9
Tulloch Aberds 89 E8
Tulloch Perth 76 E3
Tulloch Castle Highld 87 E8
Tullochgorm Argyll 73 D8
Tulloes Angus 77 C8
Tullybannocher Perth 75 E10
Tullybelton Perth 76 D3
Tullyfergus Perth 76 C5
Tullymurdoch Perth 76 B4
Tullynessle Aberds 83 B7
Tumble Carms 23 E10
Tumby Woodside Lincs 46 G6
Tummel Bridge Perth 75 B10
Tunga W Isles 91 D9
Tunstall E Yorks 53 F9
Tunstall Kent 20 E5
Tunstall Lancs 50 B2
Tunstall N Yorks 58 G3
Tunstall Norf 39 E10
Tunstall Stoke 44 G2
Tunstall Suff 31 C10
Tunstall T&W 58 A4
Tunstead Derbys 44 E5
Tunstead Gtr Man 44 B4
Tunstead Norf 39 C8
Tunworth Hants 18 G3
Tupsley Hereford 26 D2
Tupton Derbys 45 F7
Tur Langton Leics 36 F3
Turgis Green Hants 18 F3
Turin Angus 77 B8
Turkdean Glos 27 G8
Turleigh Wilts 16 E5
Turn Lancs 50 H4
Turnastone Hereford 25 E10
Turnberry S Ayrs 66 F5
Turnditch Derbys 44 H6
Turners Hill W Sus 12 C2
Turners Puddle Dorset 9 E7
Turnford Herts 19 A10
Turnhouse Edin 69 C10
Turnworth Dorset 9 D7
Turriff Aberds 89 C7
Turton Bottoms Blackburn 50 H3
Turves Cambs 37 F9
Turvey Bedford 28 C6
Turville Bucks 18 B4
Turville Heath Bucks 18 B4
Turweston Bucks 28 E3
Tushielaw Borders 61 B9
Tutbury Staffs 35 C8
Tutnall Worcs 26 A6
Tutshill Glos 15 B11
Tuttington Norf 39 C8
Tutts Clump W Berks 18 D2
Tuxford Notts 45 E11
Twatt Orkney 95 F3
Twatt Shetland 96 H5
Twechar E Dunb 68 C5
Tweedmouth Northumb 71 E8
Tweedsmuir Borders 60 A6
Twelve Heads Corn 3 E6
Twemlow Green Ches E 43 F10
Twenty Lincs 37 C7
Twerton Bath 16 E4
Twickenham London 19 D8
Twigworth Glos 26 F5
Twineham W Sus 12 E1
Twinhoe Bath 16 F4
Twinstead Essex 30 E5
Twinstead Green Essex 30 E5
Twiss Green Warr 43 C9
Twiston Lancs 50 E4
Twitchen Devon 7 C6
Twitchen Shrops 33 H9
Two Bridges Devon 5 D7
Two Dales Derbys 44 F6
Two Mills Ches W 42 E6
Twycross Leics 35 E9
Twyford Bucks 28 F3
Twyford Derbys 35 C9
Twyford Hants 10 B3
Twyford Leics 36 D3
Twyford Lincs 36 C5
Twyford Norf 38 C6
Twyford Wokingham 18 D4
Twyford Common Hereford 26 E2
Twyn-y-Sheriff Mon 25 H11
Twynholm Dumfries 55 D9
Twyning Glos 26 E5
Twyning Green Glos 26 E6
Twynllanan Carms 24 F4
Twynmynydd Carms 24 G3
Twywell Northants 36 H5
Ty-draw Conwy 41 E10
Ty-hen Carms 23 D8
Ty-hen Gwyn 40 G3
Ty-mawr Anglesey 40 B6
Ty Mawr Carms 23 B10
Ty Mawr Cwm Conwy 42 H2
Ty-nant Conwy 32 A5
Ty-nant Gwyn 32 C5
Ty-uchaf Powys 32 C6
Tyberton Hereford 25 E10
Tyburn W Mid 35 F7
Tycroes Carms 24 G3
Tycrwyn Powys 33 D7
Tydd Gote Lincs 37 D10
Tydd St Giles Cambs 37 D10
Tydd St Mary Lincs 37 D10
Tyddewi = St David's Pembs 22 D2
Tyddyn-mawr Gwyn 41 F7
Tye Green Essex 29 H11
Tye Green Essex 30 E2
Tye Green Essex 30 F4
Tyldesley Gtr Man 43 B9
Tyler Hill Kent 21 E8
Tylers Green Bucks 18 B6
Tylorstown Rhondda 14 B6
Tylwch Powys 32 G5
Tyn-y-celyn Wrex 33 B7
Tyn-y-coed Shrops 33 C8
Tyn-y-fedwen Powys 33 B7
Tyn-y-ffridd Powys 33 B7
Tyn-y-graig Powys 25 C7
Ty'n-y-groes Conwy 41 C9
Ty'n-y-maes Gwyn 41 D8
Tyn-y-pwll Anglesey 40 B6
Ty'n-yr-eithin Ceredig 24 B3
Tyncelyn Ceredig 24 B3
Tyndrum Stirling 74 D6
Tyne Tunnel T&W 63 G9
Tyneham Dorset 9 F7
Tynehead Midloth 70 E2
Tynemouth T&W 63 G9
Tynewydd Rhondda 14 B5
Tyninghame E Loth 70 C5
Tynron Dumfries 60 D4
Tynygongl Anglesey 41 B7
Tynygraig Ceredig 24 B3
Tŷ'r-felin-isaf Conwy 41 D10
Tyrie Aberds 89 B9
Tyringham M Keynes 28 D5
Tythecott Devon 6 E3
Tythegston Bridgend 14 D4
Tytherington Ches E 44 E3
Tytherington S Glos 16 C3
Tytherington Som 16 G4
Tytherington Wilts 16 G6
Tytherleigh Devon 8 D2
Tywardreath Corn 4 F1
Tywyn Conwy 41 C9
Tywyn Gwyn 32 E1

U

Uachdar W Isles 84 C2
Uags Highld 85 E12
Ubbeston Green Suff 31 A10
Ubley Bath 15 F11
Uckerby N Yorks 58 F3
Uckfield E Sus 12 D3
Uckington Glos 26 F6
Uddingston S Lanark 68 D5
Uddington S Lanark 69 G7
Udimore E Sus 13 E7
Udny Green Aberds 89 F8
Udny Station Aberds 89 F9
Udston S Lanark 68 E5
Udstonhead S Lanark 68 F6
Uffcott Wilts 17 D8
Uffculme Devon 7 E9
Uffington Lincs 37 E6
Uffington Oxon 17 C10
Uffington Shrops 33 D11
Ufford Pboro 37 E6
Ufford Suff 31 C9
Ufton Warks 27 B10
Ufton Nervet W Berks 18 E3
Ugadale Argyll 65 F8
Ugborough Devon 5 F7
Uggeshall Suff 39 G10
Ugglebarnby N Yorks 59 F9
Ughill S Yorks 44 C6
Ugley Essex 30 F2
Ugley Green Essex 30 F2
Ugthorpe N Yorks 59 E8
Uidh W Isles 84 J1
Uig Argyll 73 E10
Uig Highld 84 C6
Uig Highld 85 B8
Uigen W Isles 90 D5
Uigshader Highld 85 D9
Uisken Argyll 78 K6
Ulbster Highld 94 F5
Ulceby Lincs 47 E8
Ulceby N Lincs 46 A5
Ulceby Skitter N Lincs 46 A5
Ulcombe Kent 20 G5
Uldale Cumb 56 C4
Uley Glos 16 B4
Ulgham Northumb 63 D8
Ullapool Highld 86 B4
Ullenhall Warks 27 B8
Ullenwood Glos 26 G6
Ulleskelf N Yorks 51 E11
Ullesthorpe Leics 35 G11
Ulley S Yorks 45 D8
Ullingswick Hereford 26 D2
Ullinish Highld 85 E8
Ullock Cumb 56 D2
Ulnes Walton Lancs 49 H5
Ulpha Cumb 56 G3
Ulrome E Yorks 53 D7
Ulsta Shetland 96 E6
Ulva House Argyll 78 H7
Ulverston Cumb 49 B2
Ulwell Dorset 9 F9
Umberleigh Devon 6 D5
Unapool Highld 92 F5
Unasary W Isles 84 F2
Underbarrow Cumb 56 G6
Undercliffe W Yorks 51 F7
Underhoull Shetland 96 C7
Underriver Kent 20 F2
Underwood Notts 45 G8
Undy Mon 15 C10
Unifirth Shetland 96 H4
Union Cottage Aberds 83 D10
Union Mills IoM 48 E3
Union Street E Sus 12 C6
Unstone Derbys 45 E7
Unstone Green Derbys 45 E7
Unthank Cumb 56 C6
Unthank Cumb 57 B8
Unthank End Cumb 56 C6
Up Cerne Dorset 8 D5
Up Exe Devon 7 F8
Up Hatherley Glos 26 F6
Up Holland Lancs 43 B8
Up Marden W Sus 11 C6
Up Nately Hants 18 F3
Up Somborne Hants 10 A2
Up Sydling Dorset 8 D5
Upavon Wilts 17 F8
Upchurch Kent 20 E5
Upcott Hereford 25 C10
Upend Cambs 30 C3
Upgate Norf 39 D7
Uphall W Loth 69 C9
Uphall Station W Loth 69 C9
Upham Devon 7 F7
Upham Hants 10 B4
Uphampton Worcs 26 B5
Uphill N Som 15 F9
Uplawmoor E Renf 67 A7
Upleadon Glos 26 F4
Upleatham Redcar 59 E7
Uplees Kent 20 E6
Uploders Dorset 8 E4
Uplowman Devon 7 E9
Uplyme Devon 8 E2
Upminster London 20 C2
Upnor Medway 20 D4
Upottery Devon 7 F11
Upper Affcot Shrops 33 G10
Upper Ardchronie Highld 87 C9
Upper Arley Worcs 34 G3
Upper Arncott Oxon 28 G3
Upper Astrop Northants 28 E2
Upper Badcall Highld 92 E4
Upper Basildon W Berks 18 D2
Upper Beeding W Sus 11 C10
Upper Benefield Northants 36 G5
Upper Bighouse Highld 93 D11
Upper Boddington Northants 27 C11
Upper Borth Ceredig 32 G2
Upper Boyndlie Aberds 89 B9
Upper Brailes Warks 27 E10
Upper Breakish Highld 85 F11
Upper Breinton Hereford 25 D11
Upper Broadheath Worcs 26 C5
Upper Broughton Notts 36 C2
Upper Bucklebury W Berks 18 E2
Upper Burnhaugh Aberds 83 D10
Upper Caldecote C Beds 29 D8
Upper Catesby Northants 28 C2
Upper Chapel Powys 25 D7
Upper Church Village Rhondda 14 C6
Upper Chute Wilts 17 F9
Upper Clatford Hants 17 G10
Upper Clynnog Gwyn 40 F6
Upper Cumberworth W Yorks 44 B6
Upper Cwm-twrch Powys 24 G4
Upper Cwmbran Torf 15 B8
Upper Dallachy Moray 88 B3
Upper Dean Bedford 29 B7
Upper Denby W Yorks 44 B6
Upper Denton Cumb 62 G2
Upper Derraid Highld 87 H13
Upper Dicker E Sus 12 F4
Upper Dovercourt Essex 31 E9
Upper Druimfin Argyll 79 F8
Upper Dunsforth N Yorks 51 C10
Upper Eathie Highld 87 E10
Upper Elkstone Staffs 44 G4
Upper End Derbys 44 E4
Upper Farringdon Hants 18 H4
Upper Framilode Glos 26 G4
Upper Glenfintaig Highld 80 E4
Upper Gornal W Mid 34 F5
Upper Gravenhurst C Beds 29 E8
Upper Green Mon 25 G10
Upper Green W Berks 17 E10
Upper Grove Common Hereford 26 F2
Upper Hackney Derbys 44 F6
Upper Hale Sur 18 G5
Upper Halistra Highld 84 C7
Upper Halling Medway 20 E3
Upper Hambleton Rutland 36 E5
Upper Hardres Court Kent 21 F8
Upper Hartfield E Sus 12 C3
Upper Haugh S Yorks 45 C8
Upper Heath Shrops 34 G1
Upper Hellesdon Norf 39 D8
Upper Helmsley N Yorks 52 D2
Upper Hergest Hereford 25 C9
Upper Heyford Northants 28 C3
Upper Heyford Oxon 27 F11
Upper Hill Hereford 25 C11
Upper Hopton W Yorks 51 H7
Upper Horsebridge E Sus 12 E4
Upper Hulme Staffs 44 F4
Upper Inglesham Swindon 17 B9
Upper Inverbrough Highld 87 H11
Upper Killay Swansea 23 G10
Upper Knockando Moray 88 D1
Upper Lambourn W Berks 17 C10
Upper Leigh Staffs 34 B6
Upper Lenie Highld 81 A7
Upper Lochton Aberds 83 D8
Upper Longdon Staffs 35 D6
Upper Lybster Highld 94 G4
Upper Lydbrook Glos 26 G3
Upper Maes-coed Hereford 25 E10
Upper Midway Derbys 35 C8
Upper Milovaig Highld 84 D6
Upper Minety Wilts 17 B7
Upper Mitton Worcs 26 A5
Upper North Dean Bucks 18 B5
Upper Obney Perth 76 D3
Upper Ollach Highld 85 E10
Upper Padley Derbys 44 E6
Upper Pollicott Bucks 28 G4
Upper Poppleton York 52 D1

Upper Quinton Warks 27 D8
Upper Ratley Hants 10 B2
Upper Rissington Glos 27 G9
Upper Rochford Worcs 26 B3
Upper Sandaig Highld 85 G12
Upper Sanday Orkney 95 H6
Upper Sapey Hereford 26 B3
Upper Saxondale Notts 36 B2
Upper Seagry Wilts 16 C6
Upper Shelton C Beds 28 D6
Upper Sheringham Norf 39 A7
Upper Skelmorlie N Ayrs 73 G11
Upper Slaughter Glos 27 F8
Upper Soudley Glos 26 G3
Upper Stondon C Beds 29 E8
Upper Stowe Northants 28 C3
Upper Stratton Swindon 17 C8
Upper Street Hants 9 C10
Upper Street Norf 39 D9
Upper Street Norf 39 D9
Upper Street Suff 31 E8
Upper Strensham Worcs 26 E6
Upper Sundon C Beds 29 F7
Upper Swell Glos 27 F8
Upper Tean Staffs 34 B6
Upper Tillyrie Perth 76 G4
Upper Tooting London 19 D9
Upper Tote Highld 85 C10
Upper Town N Som 15 E11
Upper Treverward Shrops 33 H8
Upper Tysoe Warks 27 D10
Upper Upham Wilts 17 D9
Upper Wardington Oxon 27 D11
Upper Weald M Keynes 28 E4
Upper Weedon Northants 28 C3
Upper Wield Hants 18 H3
Upper Winchendon Bucks 28 G4
Upper Witton W Mid 35 F6
Upper Woodend Aberds 83 B8
Upper Woodford Wilts 17 H8
Upper Wootton Hants 18 F2
Upper Wyche Hereford 26 D4
Upperby Cumb 56 A6
Uppermill Gtr Man 44 B3
Uppersound Shetland 96 J6
Upperthong W Yorks 44 B5
Upperthorpe N Lincs 45 B11
Upperton W Sus 11 B8
Uppertown Derbys 45 F7
Uppertown Highld 94 C5
Uppertown Orkney 95 J5
Uppingham Rutland 36 F4
Uppington Shrops 34 E2
Upsall N Yorks 58 H5
Upshire Essex 19 A11
Upstreet Kent 21 E9
Upthorpe Suff 30 A6
Upton Cambs 37 H7
Upton Ches W 43 F7
Upton Corn 6 F1
Upton Dorset 8 F6
Upton Dorset 9 E8
Upton Hants 10 C2
Upton Hants 17 F10
Upton Leics 35 F9
Upton Lincs 46 D2
Upton Mers 42 D5
Upton Norf 39 D9
Upton Northants 28 B4
Upton Notts 45 E11
Upton Notts 45 G11
Upton Oxon 18 C2
Upton Pboro 37 E7
Upton Slough 18 D6
Upton Som 7 D8
Upton W Yorks 45 A8
Upton Bishop Hereford 26 F3
Upton Cheyney S Glos 16 E3
Upton Cressett Shrops 34 F2
Upton Cross Corn 4 D3
Upton Grey Hants 18 G3
Upton Hellions Devon 7 F7
Upton Lovell Wilts 16 G6
Upton Magna Shrops 34 D1
Upton Noble Som 16 H4
Upton Pyne Devon 7 G8
Upton St Leonard's Glos 26 G5
Upton Scudamore Wilts 16 G5
Upton Snodsbury Worcs 26 C6
Upton upon Severn Worcs 26 D5
Upton Warren Worcs 26 B6
Upwaltham W Sus 11 C8
Upware Cambs 30 A2
Upwell Norf 37 E10
Upwey Dorset 8 F5
Upwood Cambs 37 G8
Uradale Shetland 96 K6
Urafirth Shetland 96 F5
Urchfont Wilts 17 F7
Urdimarsh Hereford 26 D2
Ure Shetland 96 F4
Ure Bank N Yorks 51 B9
Urgha W Isles 90 H6
Urishay Common Hereford 25 E10
Urlay Nook Stockton 58 E4
Urmston Gtr Man 43 C10
Urpeth Durham 58 A3
Urquhart Highld 87 F8
Urquhart Moray 88 B2
Urra N Yorks 59 F6
Urray Highld 87 F8
Ushaw Moor Durham 58 B3
Usk = Brynbuga Mon 15 A9
Usselby Lincs 46 C4
Usworth T&W 63 H9
Utkinton Ches W 43 F8
Utley W Yorks 50 E6
Uton Devon 7 G7
Utterby Lincs 47 C7
Uttoxeter Staffs 35 B6
Uwchmynydd Gwyn 40 H3
Uxbridge London 19 C7
Uyeasound Shetland 96 C7
Uzmaston Pembs 22 E4

V

Valley Anglesey 40 C4
Valley Truckle Corn 4 C1
Valleyfield Dumfries 55 D9
Valsgarth Shetland 96 B8
Valtos Highld 85 B10
Van Powys 32 G5
Vange Essex 20 C4
Varteg Torf 25 H9
Vatten Highld 85 D7
Vaul Argyll 78 G3
Vaynor M Tydf 25 G7
Veensgarth Shetland 96 J6
Velindre Powys 25 E8
Vellow Som 7 C9
Veness Orkney 95 F6
Venn Green Devon 6 E2
Venn Ottery Devon 7 G9
Vennington Shrops 33 E9
Venny Tedburn Devon 7 G7
Ventnor IoW 10 G4
Vernham Dean Hants 17 F10
Vernham Street Hants 17 F10
Vernolds Common Shrops 33 G10
Verwood Dorset 9 D9
Veryan Corn 3 F8
Vicarage Devon 7 H11
Vickerstown Cumb 49 C1
Victoria Corn 3 C8
Victoria S Yorks 44 B5
Vidlin Shetland 96 G6
Viewpark N Lanark 68 D6
Vigo Village Kent 20 E3
Vinehall Street E Sus 13 D6
Vine's Cross E Sus 12 E4
Viney Hill Glos 26 H3
Virginia Water Sur 18 E6
Virginstow Devon 6 G2
Vobster Som 16 G4
Voe Shetland 96 E5
Voe Shetland 96 G6
Vowchurch Hereford 25 E10
Voxter Shetland 96 F5
Voy Orkney 95 G3

W

Wackerfield Durham 58 D2
Wacton Norf 39 F7
Wadbister Shetland 96 J6
Wadborough Worcs 26 D6
Waddesdon Bucks 28 G4
Waddingham Lincs 46 C3
Waddington Lancs 50 E3
Waddington Lincs 46 F3
Wadebridge Corn 3 B8
Wadeford Som 8 C2
Wadenhoe Northants 36 G6
Wadesmill Herts 29 G10
Wadhurst E Sus 12 C5
Wadshelf Derbys 45 E7
Wadsley S Yorks 45 C7
Wadsley Bridge S Yorks 45 C7
Wadworth S Yorks 45 C9
Waen Denb 42 F4
Waen Denb 42 F2
Waen Fach Powys 33 D8
Waen Goleugoed Denb 42 E3
Wag Highld 93 G13
Wainfleet All Saints Lincs 47 G8
Wainfleet Bank Lincs 47 G8
Wainfleet St Mary Lincs 47 G9
Wainfleet Tofts Lincs 47 G8
Wainhouse Corner Corn 4 B2
Wainscott Medway 20 D4
Wainstalls W Yorks 50 G6
Waitby Cumb 57 F9
Waithe Lincs 46 B6
Wake Lady Green N Yorks 59 G7
Wakefield W Yorks 51 G9
Wakerley Northants 36 F5
Wakes Colne Essex 30 F5
Walberswick Suff 31 A11
Walberton W Sus 11 D8
Walbottle T&W 63 G7
Walcot Lincs 37 B6
Walcot N Lincs 52 G4
Walcot Shrops 33 G9
Walcot Swindon 17 C8
Walcot Telford 34 D1
Walcot Green Norf 39 G7
Walcote Leics 36 G1
Walcote Warks 27 C8
Walcott Lincs 46 G5
Walcott Norf 39 B9
Walden N Yorks 50 A6
Walden Head N Yorks 50 A5
Walden Stubbs N Yorks 52 H1
Waldersey Cambs 37 E10
Walderslade Medway 20 E4
Walderton W Sus 11 C6
Walditch Dorset 8 E3
Waldley Derbys 35 B7
Waldridge Durham 58 A3
Waldringfield Suff 31 D9
Waldringfield Heath Suff 31 D9
Waldron E Sus 12 E4
Wales S Yorks 45 D8
Walesby Lincs 46 C5
Walesby Notts 45 E10
Walford Hereford 25 A10
Walford Hereford 26 F2
Walford Shrops 33 C10
Walford Heath Shrops 33 D10
Walgherton Ches E 43 H9
Walgrave Northants 28 A5
Walhampton Hants 10 E2
Walk Mill Lancs 50 F4
Walkden Gtr Man 43 B10
Walker T&W 63 G8
Walker Barn Ches E 44 E3
Walker Fold Lancs 50 E2
Walkerburn Borders 70 G2
Walkeringham Notts 45 C11
Walkerith Lincs 45 C11
Walkern Herts 29 F9
Walker's Green Hereford 26 D2
Walkerville N Yorks 58 G3
Walkford Dorset 9 E11
Walkhampton Devon 4 E6
Walkington E Yorks 52 F5
Walkley S Yorks 45 D7
Wall Northumb 62 G5
Wall Staffs 35 E7
Wall Bank Shrops 33 F11
Wall Heath W Mid 34 G4
Wall under Heywood Shrops 33 F11
Wallaceton Dumfries 60 E4
Wallacetown S Ayrs 66 D6
Wallacetown S Ayrs 66 F5
Wallands Park E Sus 12 E3
Wallasey Mers 42 C6
Wallcrouch E Sus 12 C5
Wallingford Oxon 18 C3
Wallington Hants 10 D4
Wallington Herts 29 E9
Wallington London 19 E9
Wallis Pembs 22 D5
Walliswood Sur 19 H8
Walls Shetland 96 J4
Wallsend T&W 63 G8
Wallston V Glam 15 D7
Wallyford E Loth 70 C2
Walmer Kent 21 F10
Walmer Bridge Lancs 49 G4
Walmersley Gtr Man 44 A2
Walmley W Mid 35 F7
Walpole Suff 31 A10
Walpole Cross Keys Norf 37 D11
Walpole Highway Norf 37 D11
Walpole Marsh Norf 37 D10
Walpole St Andrew Norf 37 D11
Walpole St Peter Norf 37 D11
Walsall W Mid 34 F6
Walsall Wood W Mid 34 E6
Walsden W Yorks 50 G5
Walsgrave on Sowe W Mid 35 G9
Walsham le Willows Suff 30 A6
Walshaw Gtr Man 43 A10
Walshford N Yorks 51 D10
Walsoken Cambs 37 D10
Walston S Lanark 69 F9
Walsworth Herts 29 E9
Walters Ash Bucks 18 B5
Walterston V Glam 14 D6
Walterstone Hereford 25 F10
Waltham Kent 21 G8
Waltham NE Lincs 46 B6
Waltham Abbey Essex 19 A10
Waltham Chase Hants 10 C4
Waltham Cross Herts 19 A10
Waltham on the Wolds Leics 36 C4
Waltham St Lawrence Windsor 18 D5
Walthamstow London 19 C10
Walton Cumb 61 G11
Walton Derbys 45 F7
Walton Leics 36 G1
Walton M Keynes 28 E5
Walton Mers 42 C6
Walton Pboro 37 E7
Walton Powys 25 C9
Walton Som 15 H10
Walton Staffs 34 B4
Walton Suff 31 E9
Walton Telford 34 D1
Walton W Yorks 51 E10
Walton W Yorks 51 H9
Walton Warks 27 C9
Walton Cardiff Glos 26 E6
Walton East Pembs 22 D5
Walton-in-Gordano N Som 15 D10
Walton-le-Dale Lancs 50 G1
Walton-on-Thames Sur 19 E8
Walton on the Hill Staffs 34 C5
Walton on the Hill Sur 19 F9
Walton-on-the-Naze Essex 31 F9
Walton on the Wolds Leics 36 D1
Walton-on-Trent Derbys 35 D8
Walton West Pembs 22 E3
Walwen Flint 42 E5
Walwick Northumb 62 F5
Walworth Darl 58 E3
Walworth Gate Darl 58 D3
Walwyn's Castle Pembs 22 E3
Wambrook Som 8 D1
Wanborough Sur 18 G6
Wanborough Swindon 17 C9
Wandsworth London 19 D9
Wangford Suff 39 H10
Wanlockhead Dumfries 60 B4
Wansford E Yorks 53 D6
Wansford Pboro 37 F6
Wanstead London 19 C11
Wanstrow Som 16 G4
Wanswell Glos 16 A3
Wantage Oxon 17 C10
Wapley S Glos 16 D4
Wappenbury Warks 27 B10
Wappenham Northants 28 D3
Warbleton E Sus 12 E5
Warblington Hants 10 D6
Warborough Oxon 18 B2
Warboys Cambs 37 G9
Warbreck Blackpool 49 F3
Warbstow Corn 4 B3
Warburton Gtr Man 43 D10
Warcop Cumb 57 E9
Ward End W Mid 35 G7
Ward Green Suff 31 B7
Warden Kent 21 D7
Warden Northumb 62 G5
Wardhill Orkney 95 F7
Wardington Oxon 27 D11
Wardlaw Borders 61 B8
Wardle Ches E 43 G9
Wardle Gtr Man 50 H5
Wardley Rutland 36 E4
Wardlow Derbys 44 E5
Wardy Hill Cambs 37 G10
Ware Herts 29 G10
Ware Kent 21 E9
Wareham Dorset 9 F8
Warehorne Kent 13 C8
Waren Mill Northumb 71 G10
Warenford Northumb 71 H10
Warenton Northumb 71 G10
Wareside Herts 29 G10
Waresley Cambs 29 C9
Waresley Worcs 26 A5
Warfield Brack 18 D5
Warfleet Devon 5 F9
Wargrave Wokingham 18 D4
Warham Norf 38 A5
Warhill Gtr Man 44 C3
Wark Northumb 62 F4
Wark Northumb 71 G7
Warkleigh Devon 6 D5
Warkton Northants 36 H4
Warkworth Northants 27 D11
Warkworth Northumb 63 C8
Warlaby N Yorks 58 G4
Warland W Yorks 50 G5
Warleggan Corn 4 E2
Warlingham Sur 19 F10
Warmfield W Yorks 51 G9
Warmingham Ches E 43 F10
Warmington Northants 37 F6
Warmington Warks 27 D11
Warminster Wilts 16 G5
Warmlake Kent 20 F5
Warmley S Glos 16 D3
Warmley Tower S Glos 16 D3
Warmonds Hill Northants 28 B6
Warmsworth S Yorks 45 B9
Warmwell Dorset 9 F6
Warndon Worcs 26 C5
Warnford Hants 10 B5
Warnham W Sus 11 A10
Warninglid W Sus 11 B11
Warren Ches E 44 E2
Warren Pembs 22 G4
Warren Heath Suff 31 D9
Warren Row Windsor 18 C5
Warren Street Kent 20 F6
Warrington M Keynes 28 C5
Warrington Warr 43 D9
Warsash Hants 10 D3
Warslow Staffs 44 G4
Warter E Yorks 52 D4
Warthermarske N Yorks 51 B8
Warthill N Yorks 52 D2
Wartling E Sus 12 F5
Wartnaby Leics 36 C3
Warton Lancs 49 B4
Warton Lancs 49 G4
Warton Northumb 62 C6
Warton Warks 35 E8
Warwick Warks 27 B9
Warwick Bridge Cumb 61 H10
Warwick on Eden Cumb 61 H10
Wasbister Orkney 95 E4
Wasdale Head Cumb 56 F3
Wash Common W Berks 17 E11
Washaway Corn 3 C9
Washbourne Devon 5 F8
Washfield Devon 7 E8
Washfold N Yorks 58 F1
Washford Som 7 B9
Washford Pyne Devon 7 E7
Washingborough Lincs 46 E4
Washington T&W 63 H9
Washington W Sus 11 C10
Wasing W Berks 18 E2
Waskerley Durham 58 B1
Wasperton Warks 27 C9
Wasps Nest Lincs 46 F4
Wass N Yorks 52 B1
Watchet Som 7 B9
Watchfield Oxon 17 B9
Watchfield Som 15 G9
Watchgate Cumb 57 G7
Watchhill Cumb 56 B3
Watcombe Torbay 5 E10
Watendlath Cumb 56 E4
Water Devon 5 C8
Water Lancs 50 G4
Water End E Yorks 52 F3
Water End Herts 19 A9
Water End Herts 29 G7
Water Newton Cambs 37 F7
Water Orton Warks 35 F7
Water Stratford Bucks 28 E3
Water Yeat Cumb 56 H4
Waterbeach Cambs 29 B11
Waterbeck Dumfries 61 F8
Waterden Norf 38 B4
Waterfall Staffs 44 G4
Waterfoot E Renf 68 E4
Waterfoot Lancs 50 G4
Waterford Hants 10 E2
Waterford Herts 29 G10
Waterhead Cumb 56 F5
Waterhead Dumfries 61 D7
Waterheads Borders 69 E11
Waterhouses Durham 58 B2
Waterhouses Staffs 44 G4
Wateringbury Kent 20 F3
Waterloo Gtr Man 44 B3
Waterloo Highld 85 F11
Waterloo Mers 42 C6
Waterloo N Lanark 69 E7
Waterloo Norf 39 D8
Waterloo Perth 76 D3
Waterloo Poole 9 E9
Waterloo Shrops 33 B10
Waterloo Port Gwyn 40 D6
Waterlooville Hants 10 D5
Watermeetings S Lanark 60 B5
Watermillock Cumb 56 D6
Waterperry Oxon 28 H3
Waterrow Som 7 D9
Water's Nook Gtr Man 43 B9
Waters Upton Telford 34 D2
Watersfield W Sus 11 C9
Waterside Aberds 89 F10
Waterside Blackburn 50 G3
Waterside Cumb 56 B4
Waterside E Ayrs 67 B7
Waterside E Ayrs 67 F7
Waterside E Dunb 68 C5
Waterside E Renf 68 E4
Waterstock Oxon 28 H3
Waterston Pembs 22 F4
Watford Herts 19 B8
Watford Northants 28 B3
Watford Gap Staffs 35 E7
Wath N Yorks 51 B9
Wath N Yorks 51 C7
Wath N Yorks 52 B2
Wath Brow Cumb 56 E2
Wath upon Dearne S Yorks 45 B8
Watlington Norf 38 D2
Watlington Oxon 18 B3
Watnall Notts 45 H9
Watten Highld 94 E4
Wattisfield Suff 31 A7
Wattisham Suff 31 C7
Wattlesborough Heath Shrops 33 D9
Watton E Yorks 52 D6
Watton Norf 38 E5
Watton at Stone Herts 29 G10
Wattston N Lanark 68 C6
Wattstown Rhondda 14 B6
Wauchan Highld 80 E1
Waulkmill Lodge Orkney 95 H4
Waun Powys 32 E4
Waun-y-clyn Carms 23 F9
Waunarlwydd Swansea 14 B2
Wauncluda Carms 24 E3
Waunfawr Gwyn 41 E7
Waungron Swansea 23 F10
Waunlwyd Bl Gwent 25 H8
Wavendon M Keynes 28 E6
Waverbridge Cumb 56 B4
Waverton Ches W 43 F7
Waverton Cumb 56 B4
Wavertree Mers 43 D6
Wawne E Yorks 53 F6
Waxham Norf 39 C10
Waxholme E Yorks 53 G9
Way Kent 21 E10
Way Village Devon 7 E7
Wayfield Medway 20 E4
Wayford Som 8 D3
Waymills Shrops 34 A1
Wayne Green Mon 25 G11
Wdig = Goodwick Pembs 22 C4
Weachyburn Aberds 89 C6
Weald Oxon 17 A10
Wealdstone London 19 C8
Weardley W Yorks 51 E8
Weare Som 15 F10
Weare Giffard Devon 6 D3
Wearhead Durham 57 C10
Weasdale Cumb 57 F8
Weasenham All Saints Norf 38 C4
Weasenham St Peter Norf 38 C4
Weatherhill Sur 12 B2
Weaverham Ches W 43 E9
Weaverthorpe N Yorks 52 B5
Webheath Worcs 27 B7
Wedderlairs Aberds 89 E8
Wedderlie Borders 70 E5
Weddington Warks 35 F9
Wedhampton Wilts 17 F7
Wedmore Som 15 G10
Wednesbury W Mid 34 F5
Wednesfield W Mid 34 E5
Weedon Bucks 28 G5
Weedon Bec Northants 28 C3
Weedon Lois Northants 28 D3
Weeford Staffs 35 E7
Week Devon 7 E6
Week St Mary Corn 4 B3
Weeke Hants 10 A3
Weekley Northants 36 G4
Weel E Yorks 53 F6
Weeley Essex 31 F8
Weeley Heath Essex 31 F8
Weem Perth 75 C11
Weeping Cross Staffs 34 C5
Weethley Gate Warks 27 C7
Weeting Norf 38 G3
Weeton E Yorks 53 G9
Weeton Lancs 49 F3
Weeton N Yorks 51 E8
Weetwood Hall Northumb 71 H9
Weir Lancs 50 G4
Weir Quay Devon 4 E5
Welborne Norf 39 E6
Welbourn Lincs 46 G3
Welburn N Yorks 52 A2
Welburn N Yorks 52 C3
Welbury N Yorks 58 F4
Welby Lincs 36 B5
Welches Dam Cambs 37 G10
Welcombe Devon 6 E1
Weld Bank Lancs 50 H1
Weldon Northumb 63 D7
Welford Northants 36 G2
Welford W Berks 17 D11
Welford-on-Avon Warks 27 C8
Welham Leics 36 F3
Welham Notts 45 D11
Welham Green Herts 29 H9
Well Hants 18 G4
Well Lincs 47 E8
Well N Yorks 51 A8
Well End Bucks 18 C5
Well Heads W Yorks 51 F6
Well Hill Kent 19 E11
Well Town Devon 7 F8
Welland Worcs 26 D4
Wellbank Angus 77 D7
Welldale Dumfries 61 G7
Wellesbourne Warks 27 C9
Welling London 19 D11
Wellingborough Northants 28 B5
Wellingham Norf 38 C4
Wellingore Lincs 46 G3
Wellington Cumb 56 F2
Wellington Hereford 25 D11
Wellington Som 7 D10
Wellington Telford 34 D2
Wellington Heath Hereford 26 D4
Wellington Hill W Yorks 51 F9
Wellow Bath 16 F4
Wellow IoW 10 F2
Wellow Notts 45 F10
Wellpond Green Herts 29 F11
Wells Som 15 G11
Wells Green Ches E 43 G9
Wells-Next-The-Sea Norf 38 A5
Wellsborough Leics 35 E9
Wellswood Torbay 5 E10
Wellwood Fife 69 B9
Welney Norf 37 F11
Welsh Bicknor Hereford 26 G2
Welsh End Shrops 33 B11
Welsh Frankton Shrops 33 B9
Welsh Hook Pembs 22 D4
Welsh Newton Hereford 25 G11
Welsh St Donats V Glam 14 D6
Welshampton Shrops 33 B10
Welshpool = Y Trallwng Powys 33 E8
Welton Cumb 56 B5
Welton E Yorks 52 G5
Welton Lincs 46 E4
Welton Northants 28 B2
Welton Hill Lincs 46 D4
Welton le Marsh Lincs 47 F8
Welton le Wold Lincs 46 D6
Welwick E Yorks 53 G9
Welwyn Herts 29 G9
Welwyn Garden City Herts 29 G9
Wem Shrops 33 C11
Wembdon Som 15 H8
Wembley London 19 C8
Wembury Devon 4 G6
Wembworthy Devon 6 F5
Wemyss Bay Invclyd 73 G10
Wenallt Ceredig 24 A3
Wenallt Gwyn 32 A5
Wendens Ambo Essex 30 E2
Wendlebury Oxon 28 G2
Wendling Norf 38 D5
Wendover Bucks 28 H5
Wendron Corn 2 F5
Wendy Cambs 29 D10
Wenfordbridge Corn 4 D1
Wenhaston Suff 39 H10
Wennington Cambs 37 H8
Wennington Lancs 50 B2
Wennington London 20 C2
Wensley Derbys 44 F6
Wensley N Yorks 58 H1
Wentbridge W Yorks 51 H10
Wentnor Shrops 33 F9
Wentworth Cambs 37 H10
Wentworth S Yorks 45 C7
Wenvoe V Glam 15 D7
Weobley Hereford 25 C11
Weobley Marsh Hereford 25 C11
Wereham Norf 38 E2
Wergs W Mid 34 E4
Wern Powys 32 D5
Wern Powys 33 D8
Wernffrwd Swansea 23 G10
Wernyrheolydd Mon 25 G10
Werrington Corn 4 C4
Werrington Pboro 37 E7
Werrington Staffs 44 H3
Wervin Ches W 43 E7
Wesham Lancs 49 F4
Wessington Derbys 45 G7
West Acre Norf 38 D3
West Adderbury Oxon 27 E11
West Allerdean Northumb 71 F8
West Alvington Devon 5 G8
West Amesbury Wilts 17 G8
West Anstey Devon 7 D7
West Ashby Lincs 46 E6
West Ashling W Sus 11 D7
West Ashton Wilts 16 F5
West Auckland Durham 58 D2
West Ayton N Yorks 52 A5
West Bagborough Som 7 C10
West Barkwith Lincs 46 D5
West Barnby N Yorks 59 E9
West Barns E Loth 70 C5
West Barsham Norf 38 B5
West Bay Dorset 8 E3
West Beckham Norf 39 B7
West Bedfont Sur 19 D7
West Benhar N Lanark 69 D7
West Bergholt Essex 30 F6
West Bexington Dorset 8 F4
West Bilney Norf 38 D3
West Blatchington Brighton 12 F1
West Bowling W Yorks 51 F7
West Bradford Lancs 50 E3
West Bradley Som 16 H2
West Bretton W Yorks 44 A6
West Bridgford Notts 36 B1
West Bromwich W Mid 34 F6
West Buckland Devon 6 C5
West Buckland Som 7 D10
West Burrafirth Shetland 96 H4
West Burton N Yorks 58 H1
West Burton W Sus 11 C8
West Butterwick N Lincs 46 B2
West Byfleet Sur 19 E7
West Caister Norf 39 D11
West Calder W Loth 69 D9
West Camel Som 8 B4
West Challow Oxon 17 C10
West Chelborough Dorset 8 D4
West Chevington Northumb 63 D8
West Chiltington W Sus 11 C9
West Chiltington Common W Sus 11 C9
West Chinnock Som 8 C3
West Chisenbury Wilts 17 F8
West Clandon Sur 19 F7
West Cliffe Kent 21 G10
West Clyne Highld 93 J11
West Clyth Highld 94 G4
West Coker Som 8 C4
West Compton Dorset 8 E4
West Compton Som 16 G2
West Cowick E Yorks 52 G2
West Cranmore Som 16 G3
West Cross Swansea 14 C2
West Cullery Aberds 83 C9
West Curry Corn 6 G1
West Curthwaite Cumb 56 B5
West Darlochan Argyll 65 F7
West Dean W Sus 11 C7
West Dean Wilts 10 B1
West Deeping Lincs 37 E7
West Derby Mers 43 C6
West Dereham Norf 38 E2
West Didsbury Gtr Man 44 C2
West Ditchburn Northumb 63 A7
West Down Devon 6 B4
West Drayton London 19 D7
West Drayton Notts 45 E11
West Ella E Yorks 52 G6
West End Bedford 28 C6
West End E Yorks 52 F5
West End E Yorks 53 F7
West End Hants 10 C3
West End Lancs 50 G3
West End N Som 15 E10
West End N Yorks 51 D7
West End Norf 38 E5
West End Norf 39 D11
West End Oxon 17 A11
West End S Lanark 69 F8
West End S Yorks 45 B10
West End Suff 39 G10
West End Sur 18 E6
West End W Sus 11 C11
West End Wilts 9 B8
West End Wilts 16 D6
West End Green Hants 18 E3
West Farleigh Kent 20 F4
West Felton Shrops 33 C9
West Fenton E Loth 70 B3
West Ferry Dundee 77 D7
West Firle E Sus 12 F3
West Ginge Oxon 17 C11
West Grafton Wilts 17 E9
West Green Hants 18 F4
West Greenskares Aberds 89 B7
West Grimstead Wilts 9 B11
West Grinstead W Sus 11 B10
West Haddlesey N Yorks 52 G1
West Haddon Northants 28 A3
West Hagbourne Oxon 18 C2
West Hagley Worcs 34 G5
West Hall Cumb 61 G11
West Hallam Derbys 35 A10
West Halton N Lincs 52 G5
West Ham London 19 C11
West Handley Derbys 45 E7
West Hanney Oxon 17 B11
West Hanningfield Essex 20 B4
West Hardwick W Yorks 51 H10
West Harnham Wilts 9 B10
West Harptree Bath 16 F2
West Hatch Som 8 B1
West Head Norf 38 E1
West Heath Ches E 44 F2
West Heath Hants 18 F2
West Heath Hants 18 F5
West Helmsdale Highld 93 H13
West Hendred Oxon 17 C11
West Heslerton N Yorks 52 B5
West Hill Devon 7 G9
West Hill E Yorks 53 C7
West Hill N Som 15 D10
West Hoathly W Sus 12 C2
West Holme Dorset 9 F7
West Horndon Essex 20 C3
West Horrington Som 16 G2
West Horsley Sur 19 F7
West Horton Northumb 71 G9
West Hougham Kent 21 G9
West Houlland Shetland 96 H4
West-houses Derbys 45 G8
West Huntington York 52 D2
West Hythe Kent 13 C10
West Ilsley W Berks 17 C11
West Itchenor W Sus 11 D6
West Keal Lincs 47 F7
West Kennett Wilts 17 E8
West Kilbride N Ayrs 66 B5
West Kingsdown Kent 20 E2
West Kington Wilts 16 D5
West Kinharrachie Aberds 89 E9
West Kirby Mers 42 D5
West Knapton N Yorks 52 B4
West Knighton Dorset 8 F6
West Knoyle Wilts 9 A7
West Kyloe Northumb 71 F9
West Lambrook Som 8 C3
West Langdon Kent 21 G10
West Langwell Highld 93 J9
West Lavington W Sus 11 B7
West Lavington Wilts 17 F7
West Layton N Yorks 58 F2
West Lea Durham 58 B5
West Leake Notts 35 C11
West Learmouth Northumb 71 G7
West Leigh Devon 6 F5
West Lexham Norf 38 D4
West Lilling N Yorks 52 C2
West Linton Borders 69 E10
West Liss Hants 11 B6
West Littleton S Glos 16 D4
West Looe Corn 4 F3
West Luccombe Som 7 B7
West Lulworth Dorset 9 F7
West Lutton N Yorks 52 C5
West Lydford Som 8 A4
West Lyng Som 8 B2
West Lynn Norf 38 C2
West Malling Kent 20 F3
West Malvern Worcs 26 D4
West Marden W Sus 11 C6
West Marina E Sus 13 F6
West Markham Notts 45 E11
West Marsh NE Lincs 46 A6
West Marton N Yorks 50 D4
West Meon Hants 10 B5
West Mersea Essex 31 G7
West Milton Dorset 8 E4
West Minster Kent 20 D6
West Molesey Sur 19 E8
West Monkton Som 8 B1
West Moors Dorset 9 D9
West Morriston Borders 70 F5
West Muir Angus 77 A8
West Ness N Yorks 52 B2
West Newham Northumb 62 F6
West Newton E Yorks 53 F7
West Newton Norf 38 C2
West Norwood London 19 D10
West Ogwell Devon 5 D9
West Orchard Dorset 9 C7
West Overton Wilts 17 E8
West Park Hrtlpl 58 C5
West Parley Dorset 9 E9
West Peckham Kent 20 F3
West Pelton Durham 58 A3
West Pennard Som 15 H11
West Pentire Corn 3 C6
West Perry Cambs 29 B8
West Putford Devon 6 E2
West Quantoxhead Som 7 B10
West Rainton Durham 58 B4
West Rasen Lincs 46 D4
West Raynham Norf 38 C4
West Retford Notts 45 D10
West Rounton N Yorks 58 F5
West Row Suff 38 H2
West Rudham Norf 38 C4
West Runton Norf 39 A7
West Saltoun E Loth 70 D3
West Sandwick Shetland 96 E6
West Scrafton N Yorks 51 A6
West Sleekburn Northumb 63 E8
West Somerton Norf 39 D10
West Stafford Dorset 8 F6
West Stockwith Notts 45 C11
West Stoke W Sus 11 D7
West Stonesdale N Yorks 57 F10
West Stoughton Som 15 G10
West Stour Dorset 9 B6
West Stourmouth Kent 21 E9
West Stow Suff 30 A5
West Stowell Wilts 17 E8
West Strathan Highld 93 C8
West Stratton Hants 18 G2
West Street Kent 20 F6
West Tanfield N Yorks 51 B8
West Taphouse Corn 4 E2
West Tarbert Argyll 73 G7
West Thirston Northumb 63 D7
West Thorney W Sus 11 D6
West Thurrock Thurrock 20 D2
West Tilbury Thurrock 20 D3
West Tisted Hants 10 B5
West Tofts Norf 38 F4
West Tofts Perth 76 D4
West Torrington Lincs 46 D5
West Town Hants 10 E6
West Town N Som 15 E10
West Tytherley Hants 10 B1
West Tytherton Wilts 16 D6
West Walton Norf 37 D10
West Walton Highway Norf 37 D10
West Wellow Hants 10 C1
West Wemyss Fife 70 A2
West Wick N Som 15 E9
West Wickham Cambs 30 D3
West Wickham London 19 E10
West Williamston Pembs 22 F5
West Willoughby Lincs 36 A5
West Winch Norf 38 D2
West Winterslow Wilts 9 A11
West Wittering W Sus 11 E6
West Witton N Yorks 58 H1
West Woodburn Northumb 62 E4
West Woodhay W Berks 17 E10
West Woodlands Som 16 G4
West Worldham Hants 18 H4
West Worlington Devon 7 E6
West Worthing W Sus 11 D10
West Wratting Cambs 30 C3
West Wycombe Bucks 18 B5
West Wylam Northumb 63 G7
West Yell Shetland 96 E6
Westacott Devon 6 C4
Westbere Kent 21 E8
Westborough Lincs 36 A4
Westbourne Bmouth 9 E9
Westbourne Suff 31 D8
Westbourne W Sus 11 D6
Westbrook W Berks 17 D11
Westbury Bucks 28 E3
Westbury Shrops 33 E9
Westbury Wilts 16 F5
Westbury Leigh Wilts 16 F5
Westbury-on-Severn Glos 26 G4
Westbury on Trym Bristol 16 D2
Westbury-sub-Mendip Som 15 G11
Westby Lancs 49 F3
Westcliff-on-Sea Southend 20 C5
Westcombe Som 16 H3
Westcote Glos 27 F9
Westcott Bucks 28 G4
Westcott Devon 7 F9
Westcott Sur 19 G8
Westcott Barton Oxon 27 F11
Westdean E Sus 12 G4
Westdene Brighton 12 F1
Wester Aberchalder Highld 81 A7
Wester Balgedie Perth 76 G4
Wester Culbeuchly Aberds 89 B6
Wester Dechmont W Loth 69 D9
Wester Denoon Angus 76 C6
Wester Fintray Aberds 83 B10
Wester Gruinards Highld 87 B8
Wester Lealty Highld 87 D9
Wester Milton Highld 87 F12
Wester Newburn Fife 77 G7
Wester Quarff Shetland 96 K6
Wester Skeld Shetland 96 J4
Westerdale Highld 94 E3
Westerdale N Yorks 59 F7
Westerfield Shetland 96 H5
Westerfield Suff 31 D8
Westergate W Sus 11 D8
Westerham Kent 19 F11
Westerhope T&W 63 G7
Westerleigh S Glos 16 D4
Westerton Angus 77 B9
Westerton Durham 58 C3
Westerton W Sus 11 D7
Westerwick Shetland 96 J4
Westfield Cumb 56 D1
Westfield E Sus 13 E7
Westfield Hereford 26 D4
Westfield Highld 94 D2
Westfield N Lanark 68 C6
Westfield Norf 38 E5
Westfield W Loth 69 C8
Westfields Dorset 8 D6
Westfields of Rattray Perth 76 C4
Westgate Durham 57 C11
Westgate N Lincs 45 B11
Westgate Norf 38 A4
Westgate Norf 38 A5
Westgate on Sea Kent 21 D10
Westhall Aberds 83 A8
Westhall Suff 39 G10
Westham Dorset 8 G5
Westham E Sus 12 F5
Westham Som 15 G10
Westhampnett W Sus 11 D7
Westhay Som 15 G10
Westhead Lancs 43 B7
Westhide Hereford 26 D2
Westhill Aberds 83 C10
Westhill Highld 87 G10
Westhope Hereford 25 C11
Westhope Shrops 33 G10
Westhorpe Lincs 37 B8
Westhorpe Suff 31 B7
Westhoughton Gtr Man 43 B9
Westhouse N Yorks 50 B2
Westhumble Sur 19 F8
Westing Shetland 96 C7
Westlake Devon 5 F7
Westleigh Devon 6 D3
Westleigh Devon 7 E9
Westleigh Gtr Man 43 B9
Westleton Suff 31 B11
Westley Shrops 33 E9
Westley Suff 30 B5
Westley Waterless Cambs 30 C3
Westlington Bucks 28 G4
Westlinton Cumb 61 G9
Westmarsh Kent 21 E9
Westmeston E Sus 12 E2
Westmill Herts 29 F10
Westminster London 19 D10
Westmuir Angus 76 B6
Westness Orkney 95 F4
Westnewton Cumb 56 B3
Westnewton Northumb 71 G8
Westoe T&W 63 G9
Weston Bath 16 E4
Weston Ches E 43 G10
Weston Devon 7 H10
Weston Dorset 8 G5
Weston Halton 43 D8
Weston Hants 10 B6
Weston Herts 29 E9
Weston Lincs 37 C8
Weston N Yorks 51 E7
Weston Northants 28 D2
Weston Notts 45 F11
Weston Shrops 34 C1
Weston Shrops 34 F1
Weston Staffs 34 C5
Weston W Berks 17 D10
Weston Beggard Hereford 26 D2
Weston by Welland Northants 36 F3
Weston Colville Cambs 30 C3
Weston Coyney Stoke 34 A5
Weston Favell Northants 28 B4
Weston Green Cambs 30 C3
Weston Green Norf 39 D7
Weston Heath Shrops 34 D3
Weston Hills Lincs 37 C8
Weston-in-Gordano N Som 15 D10
Weston Jones Staffs 34 C3
Weston Longville Norf 39 D7
Weston Lullingfields Shrops 33 C10
Weston-on-the-Green Oxon 28 G2
Weston-on-Trent Derbys 35 C10
Weston Patrick Hants 18 G3
Weston Rhyn Shrops 33 B8
Weston-Sub-Edge Glos 27 D8
Weston-super-Mare N Som 15 E9
Weston Turville Bucks 28 G5
Weston under Lizard Staffs 34 D4
Weston under Penyard Hereford 26 F3
Weston under Wetherley Warks 27 B10
Weston Underwood Derbys 35 A8
Weston Underwood M Keynes 28 C5
Westonbirt Glos 16 C5
Westoncommon Shrops 33 C10
Westoning C Beds 29 E7
Westonzoyland Som 8 A2
Westow N Yorks 52 C3
Westport Argyll 65 F7
Westport Som 8 C2
Westrigg W Loth 69 D8
Westruther Borders 70 F5
Westry Cambs 37 F9
Westville Notts 45 H9
Westward Cumb 56 B4
Westward Ho! Devon 6 D3
Westwell Kent 20 G6
Westwell Oxon 27 H9
Westwell Leacon Kent 20 G6
Westwick Cambs 29 B11
Westwick Durham 58 E1
Westwick Norf 39 C8
Westwood Devon 7 G9
Westwood Wilts 16 F5
Westwoodside N Lincs 45 C11
Wetheral Cumb 56 A6
Wetherby W Yorks 51 E10
Wetherden Suff 31 B7
Wetheringsett Suff 31 B8
Wethersfield Essex 30 E4
Wethersta Shetland 96 G5